Lesbians,

Gay Men,

and the Law

Lesbians, Gay Men, and the Law

Edited by William B. Rubenstein

The New Press, New York

Published in the United States by The New Press, New York
Distributed by W.W. Norton & Company, Inc.
500 Fifth Avenue, New York, NY 10110

LIBRARY OF CONGRESS CATALOGING-IN-PUBLICATION

Lesbians, gay men, and the law / [edited by] William B. Rubenstein. — 1st ed.
p.   cm — (The New Press law in context series)
Includes bibliographical references and index.
ISBN 1-56584-027-5 (hc) : — ISBN 1-56584-037-2 (pb) :
1. Homosexuality — Law and legislation — United States — Cases. 2. Lesbians — Civil rights —
United States — Cases. 3. Gay men — Civil rights — United States — Cases. 4. Homosexuality —
United States. 5. Lesbians — United States. 6. Gay men — United States.
I. Rubenstein, William B.   II. Series.

KF4754.5.A7L48 1993
342.73'087— dc20
[347.30287]
92-53735
CIP

First Edition

Book design by Acme Art

Established in 1990 as a major alternative to the large, commercial publishing houses, The New Press is
intended to be the first full-scale nonprofit American book publisher outside of the university presses. The
Press is operated editorially in the public interest, rather than for private gain; it is committed to publishing
in innovative ways works of educational, cultural, and community value, which despite their intellectual
merits might not normally be "commercially" viable. The New Press's editorial offices are located at The
City University of New York.

Printed in the United States of America.

ACKNOWLEDGMENTS

Thanks to the following for permission to print or reprint the works listed: (*continues on page 569*)

SEXUAL BEHAVIOR IN THE HUMAN MALE, by Alfred Kinsey, Wardell B. Pomeroy, Clyde E. Martin. Copyright © 1948 by W. B. Saunders Company. Reprinted by permission of the Kinsey Institute for Research in Sex, Gender, and Reproduction, Inc.

SEXUAL BEHAVIOR IN THE HUMAN FEMALE, by Alfred C. Kinsey, Wardell B. Pomeroy, Clyde E. Martin, Paul H. Gebhard. Copyright © 1953 by W. B. Saunders Company. Reprinted by permission of the Kinsey Institute for Research in Sex, Gender, and Reproduction, Inc.

Born or Bred?, by David Gelman, from NEWSWEEK, February 2, 1992. Copyright © 1992 by Newsweek, Inc. All rights reserved. Reprinted by permission.

Revolutions, Universals and Sexual Categories, by John Boswell. Reprinted from HIDDEN FROM HISTORY: RECLAIMING THE GAY LESBIAN PAST (Duberman et al., eds.), copyright © 1989 by Martin Bauml Duberman, Martha Vicinus, George Chauncey, Jr., by permission of John Boswell/Francis Goldin.

Capitalism and Gay Identity, by John D'Emilio. Reprinted from POWERS OF DESIRE: THE POLITICS OF SEXUALITY (Snitow et al., eds.), copyright © 1983 by Ann Snitow, Christine Stansell, and Sharon Thompson, by permission of Monthly Review Foundation.

Compulsory Heterosexuality and the Lesbian Existence, by Adrienne Rich. Reprinted from POWERS OF DESIRE: THE POLITICS OF SEXUALITY (Snitow et al., eds.) copyright © 1983 by Ann Snitow, Christine Stansell, and Sharon Thompson, by permission of Monthly Review Foundation.

"Go the Way Your Blood Beats" : An Interview with James Baldwin, by Richard Goldstein. Copyright © 1984 by Richard Goldstein. Reprinted from JAMES BALDWIN: THE LEGACY (Troupe, ed.), copyright © 1989 by Quincy Troupe, by permission of Richard Goldstein.

Selections from GAY/LESBIAN ALMANAC, by Jonathan Ned Katz, copyright © 1983 by Jonathan Ned Katz. Reprinted by permission of Jonathan Ned Katz.

Selections from GAY AMERICAN HISTORY, by Jonathan Ned Katz, copyright © 1976 by Jonathan Ned Katz. Reprinted by permission of Jonathan Ned Katz.

Homosexuality, by J. F. Harvey, from THE NEW CATHOLIC ENCYCLOPEDIA. Copyright © 1967 by Catholic University of America. Reprinted by permission of Catholic University of America.

HOMOSEXUALITY AND AMERICAN PSYCHIATRY: THE POLITICS OF DIAGNOSIS, by Ronald Bayer. Copyright © 1987 by Princeton University Press. Reprinted by permission of Princeton University Press.

Summary of Contents

Detailed Table of Contents

ACKNOWLEDGMENTS

So many people contributed in so many different ways to the preparation of this casebook that it is difficult to know how to acknowledge adequately all of their various efforts. Needless to say, the list will be incomplete, though not for any lack of appreciation on my part.

This volume is based on the cases and materials I used for a course I taught at the Harvard Law School in 1991, 1992, and 1993, called "Sexual Orientation and the Law." As I prepared these materials, I learned a great deal from studying the materials of many who have taught this or similar courses at other schools, including (in no particular order) Tom Stoddard, Jon Davidson, Matt Coles and Nan Hunter. I was assisted in the mechanical preparation of my course materials by Mark Bednar (1991) and Brian Hanna (1992).

Working from my course materials, during the spring of 1992 a group of Harvard Law School students undertook the initial additional research and writing to convert my materials into a casebook. Bruce Deming was responsible for what are now Chapters One and Six; Chad Johnson for Chapters Two and Four; Patrick Cheng for Chapter Three; and Trent Norris for Chapter Five. Michele Anglade and Michelle Benecke also offered overall insight and advice. While each of these student's contributions was invaluable, I am especially indebted to Bruce Deming and Trent Norris; their work was truly extraordinary.

Despite their herculean efforts, the book still needed substantial work. I was fortunate to have working with me at the ACLU's Lesbian and Gay Rights Project during the summer of 1992 three law students — Tanya Herrera, William Hohengarten, and Karin Schwartz — who devoted countless hours to helping me fine-tune the text. The Lesbian and Gay Rights Project's staff assistants, Nancy Tenney and Michael Perelman, contributed their talents during the summer as well. Michael Perelman deserves further considerable gratitude for undertaking the laborious task of securing the permissions that allowed us to reprint other's people work in this volume. He did so with assistance from Raymond Heigemeir.

Once this book was in galley form, Patrick Cheng, Chris Stoll, and Trent Norris volunteered to ensure its accuracy and its adherence to the *Blue Book: A Uniform System of Citation*. Finally, Steven Homer, another of my students at Harvard, should be sainted for initially preparing the Table of Contents and Table of Cases that accompanies this volume.

While this explains how this book came to be, it does not begin to recognize the human and intellectual influences that helped shaped my vision of what this book should be about. Those fall, roughly, into three sets of people. Before acknowledging their assistance, though, I would like to express my gratitude to André Schiffrin, who had the courage to undertake publication of these materials in this form at a time when commercial publishers were unwilling to do so.

First, two of my teachers at the Harvard Law School contributed substantially to my understanding of the law and to the preparation of this casebook. Professor Gerald Frug made me want to teach law and greatly helped enable me to do so. Perhaps most important, though, in more ways than I can begin to acknowledge, he has helped me love the law and appreciate its importance as an instrument of social change. Professor Martha Minow's influence on this work is everywhere. As a student in her Family Law course in 1985, I first learned that law school course materials could include nonlegal documents and, in fact, could be made much more meaningful by their inclusion. In the intervening years, she has consistently provided unparalleled encouragement and support for my legal, teaching, and scholarly endeavors. Throughout the process of completing this work, she — often singlehandedly —

provided the reassurance that inspired me to go forward. Without her encouragement this work would not exist.

A second source of strength has been my family. My partner Steve Bromer has lived with this project for nearly four years with unwavering dedication to helping me complete it. Had he not provided stability, comfort, support, good humor, and ridiculous amounts of love and patience, you would not be reading this work. My parents have also been unusually supportive of all of the choices I have made in my life, and their love has been unwavering.

I am especially indebted to my grandfather, Joseph Gellman (1901-1992), for encouraging those aspects of my life that led me to undertake the legal work that I do and to publish this sort of book. He made me appreciate books long before I could even read, and he made reading such a delightful part of life itself that it is difficult to imagine books not being a central part of that experience. The primary pleasure he derived from reading was *talking* about what he had read to others, and talking to my grandfather about books was an enchanting experience. My grandfather also instilled in me the importance of fighting for social change, and I attribute to his influence what has become the central focus of my entire life. His death this past winter has deprived me — and many others — of a passionate conversationalist with whom to share our reading, and an advocate of social action with whom to share our accomplishments. Some of the magic that is the experience of life itself is irrevocably lost in his absence — but certainly will never be forgotten.

Finally, this book is dedicated to those who have been my central source of support and community for the past six years — my colleagues in the fight for equal rights for lesbians and gay men, particularly my colleagues at the American Civil Liberties Union. They have both shown me how to do this work and have provided the day-to-day companionship that makes it all worthwhile. I am particularly grateful in this regard to the incomparable Ruth Harlow, and to Nan Hunter, Matt Coles, and Chai Feldblum.

EDITOR'S NOTE

This volume is a collection of legal cases and materials from other fields, including fiction, psychology, sociology, oral history, and journalism. In compiling this book, I have edited the various texts: text deleted within a paragraph is indicated by ellipses (. . .), and the omission of entire paragraphs is indicated by three square bullets (■ ■ ■). As is the practice with legal casebooks, citations and footnotes in the cases and readings are often deleted without any indication; however, those footnotes that have been retained are numbered as they were in the original. Thus, a case as presented here might have three footnotes in it, numbered 1, 4, and 18; this is not an error but, rather, it reflects the notes' numbering in the original text.

All citations in my text and in the Notes sections that accompany the readings follow the style set forth in *Bluebook: A Uniform System of Citation* (15th ed., 1991). However, all citations within cases and readings were left exactly as they appear in the original. Similarly, reprinted cases and materials are copied verbatim from the original text, even where that text had, for instance, grammatical errors.

I hope that this volume will be reissued in further editions; if so, I shall attempt to keep it current and correct. I therefore welcome corrections, comments, criticisms, and updates. Please address all correspondence to me care of The New Press, 450 West 41st Street, New York, New York, 10036.

TABLE OF CASES

Principal cases in italics; cases cited in editor's text and notes in roman.

INTRODUCTION

The struggle for equality by lesbians and gay men has moved to the center of American life at the outset of the 1990s, and during the coming decade lesbian and gay issues will form a greater part of the American political scene and public consciousness than during any other era in American history. With Bill Clinton's election and his first presidential directives a heated debate has erupted regarding the presence of lesbians and gay men in the U.S. military. Nearly every religious organization in the country is struggling with questions ranging from gay marriage to the ordination of openly gay ministers. And at no time in American history have gay people been more visible: with lesbians and gay men battling in Congress, in the streets, and in courtrooms for civil rights, well-known figures publicly discussing their sexual orientation, and gay characters on prime-time television shows, few Americans can continue to claim that they do not come into contact with gay people.

At the same time, lesbians and gay men face stiffer opposition than ever before. A well-organized and well-funded religious right has pledged that "gay rights will be the 'abortion' issue of the 1990s" — the message being that its adherents will vehemently challenge advances by gay people. And more and more lesbians and gay men are attacked every year simply for being gay: antigay violence rose 31 percent between 1990 and 1991 in five major cities (Boston, Chicago, Minneapolis/St. Paul, New York, and San Francisco), with more than 1800 incidents of antigay/lesbian violence reported in these cities alone.

The law is a primary arena in which the struggle for gay rights has been, and will continue to be, played out. Throughout American history, sexual relations have been a concern of the secular legal system, as well as an issue of religious morality and medical "science"; American society has long maintained laws that directly dictate what combinations of individuals may have sex with one another and in what manner. For example, sex outside of marriage was traditionally proscribed by most states, as was sex between people of different races. It was not until the late 1960s that the United States Supreme Court struck down as unconstitutional laws that criminalized interracial marriages. In addition to these direct prohibitions, the state has long maintained various mechanisms to channel sexual relations indirectly. For example, government jobs could be denied to individuals whose sexual practices were not approved by the state.

For lesbians and gay men, state regulation of sexuality has been particularly harsh. State sodomy laws have criminalized one way in which gay people express their love for one another. Discrimination against lesbians and gay men exists in employment and housing, and gay people are often denied access to programs and public places solely because of their sexual orientation. No state has recognized lesbian and gay relationships, and sexual orientation has often been used to deny gay people custody of, or visitation with, their own children. Lesbians and gay men have been legally barred from adopting children or becoming foster parents.

Not only has the law typically failed to redress discrimination against gay people but such discrimination is often sanctioned by the government itself. The federal government, for example, has openly denied lesbians and gay men the opportunity to serve their country in the military, effectively denied employment to gay people in the FBI, CIA, and other security-related positions, and placed burdens on gay applicants for security clearances.

Alongside this stark picture of the barriers faced by lesbians and gay men lives another image, however. This portrait is of a constantly growing movement to eradicate these barriers, of lesbians and gay men and their advocates who, in the past forty years, have made enormous strides in abolishing some of the barriers to equal participation by gay people in American society.

This book represents an effort to understand the legal situation of lesbians and gay men. It provides both a snapshot of the current state of lesbian and gay rights and a moving picture of the strides of the gay rights movement. After an introductory chapter that considers how sexual orientation is understood in our society, the book is arranged according to the real-life situations of lesbians and gay men. Chapter Two looks at the state's regulation of lesbian and gay sexuality. Chapter Three considers the process of "coming out" for lesbians and gay men, and examines in particular how society erects barriers to impede assertions of lesbian/gay identity. Chapter Four considers how lesbians and gay men negotiate their presence in the workplace, how open they can be about their sexuality in different fields of employment, and what barriers they face to equality in this primary arena of American life. Chapters Five and Six consider issues of lesbian and gay family law, including, respectively, lesbian and gay relationships and lesbian and gay parenting.

Several areas of the law — sodomy law reform, discrimination, and family law — are particularly highlighted in this book. These subjects represent the central areas of the struggle for lesbian/gay equality, and they provide a unique opportunity to understand both the nature of that struggle and the work that still needs to be accomplished.

SODOMY LAW

In modern American society, sodomy laws have served as a legal basis for the regulation of lesbian and gay sexuality and of lesbians and gay life generally. Discrimination against lesbians and gay men is often predicated on the existence of laws prohibiting lesbian/gay sex, and thus sodomy laws are understood as criminalizing not merely homosexual acts but lesbians and gay men themselves. Sodomy laws were not always understood in this way. Historically, sodomy laws were drafted in order to proscribe sexual behavior that did not lead to procreation, including oral and anal sex between people of the same or opposite genders.

In 1961 every state in the United States had a sodomy law. While most of these laws outlawed heterosexual as well as homosexual sodomy, every one of them criminalized the manner in which gay men and lesbians express love for one another — even if the acts took place between consenting adults in the privacy of their home.

Today fewer than half the states have sodomy laws. Nearly all of the 26 states that no longer have sodomy laws abolished their law through legislative action rather than through a court decision declaring it unconstitutional. In particular, many state legislatures in the past 30 years have modernized their entire system of criminal law by adopting a version of the "Model Penal Code," a document drafted in the late 1950s by an influential institute of lawyers and law professors to modernize state criminal codes. The Model Penal Code proposed decriminalizing private, consensual, adult sexual behavior, including homosexual sex. As state legislatures adopted the Code throughout the 1960s and 1970s, they did away with their sodomy laws. In several states, though, the legislatures were so appalled to be without a prohibition on homosexual sodomy that they added new laws barring *only* homosexual sodomy.

The other major locus for sodomy law reform has been the courts. However, despite much effort and a number of highly publicized legal challenges, only a few states, sodomy laws have been declared unconstitutional by the highest court in that state. Most important, in 1986 the United States Supreme Court rejected a constitutional challenge to Georgia's sodomy law in the *Bowers v. Hardwick* case. Michael Hardwick was arrested for having sex with another man in his own bedroom. Although the state did not criminally prosecute him for this act, Hardwick brought a civil suit challenging the sodomy law as violating his constitutional rights. He was joined in this effort by a heterosexual couple who complained that they feared that the Georgia law — which applied to *all* oral and anal intercourse — could be enforced against them as well. By a 5-4 vote, the Supreme Court ruled against Hardwick. Despite the Georgia law's ban on all oral and anal intercourse, the Court focused only on *homosexual* sodomy: it held that the "right to privacy" recognized under the federal constitution did not encompass a right to engage in homosexual sodomy and, therefore, that states are free to criminalize such conduct.

The *Hardwick* decision was a major blow to the movement for lesbian and gay rights in the United States. It means that despite the progress made in the past few decades, late in the twentieth century, in nearly half the states in the United States of America, it is still illegal for lesbians and gay men to express love to one another. To lesbians and gay men, this means, as Larry Kramer has written, "We are denied the right to love. Can you imagine being denied the right to love?" Worse still, the U.S. Supreme Court has condoned this oppression, ruling in the *Hardwick* case that our love for one another has no place in American constitutional jurisprudence.

Despite its harsh outcome, the *Hardwick* decision has not retarded the movement for gay rights; in fact, some argue that the decision activated many in the lesbian/gay community and solidified support for this fight among many nongay people. Notwithstanding *Hardwick*, for example, the effort to eradicate sodomy laws has continued, based on challenges brought in state courts under *state* constitutional theories. Since *Hardwick*, sodomy laws have been declared unconstitutional by lower courts in Michigan and Texas, and by the highest court in Kentucky. Nor has *Hardwick* impaired gains in other areas.

Chapter Two places these developments in an historical context and traces the development of the law in this area. It considers questions such as:

What constitutional theories have antisodomy law litigants relied on, and how have these arguments been received in the courts?

What was the Supreme Court's ruling in the *Hardwick* case? How has it been criticized?

What are avenues for sodomy law reform after *Hardwick*?

DISCRIMINATION

Although the argument for the repeal of sodomy statutes has been based on an argument of "privacy," privacy has been only one of the goals of the lesbian/gay rights movement. Beyond wanting to be left alone by the government regarding the most intimate decisions, lesbians and gay men also want to be able to "come out" — to be open about our sexual orientation — without fearing discrimination or worse. By contrast to sodomy's argument for privacy, the argument for civil rights protections for lesbians and gay men is one of "publicness."

In 1971 there was not a single law, ordinance, or policy prohibiting discrimination against lesbians and gay men. No one had ever heard of, nor had any public or private entity ever adopted, a policy that prohibited discrimination on the basis of sexual orientation.

Today, seven states, the District of Columbia, and more than 100 municipalities ban discrimination against lesbians and gay men. These laws generally ban discrimination on the basis of sexual orientation in employment, housing, and places of public accommodation. In 1981 Wisconsin became the first state to pass a lesbian/gay rights law on a statewide level, but for the next nine years no state followed. Since 1990, however, six states have done so — Massachusetts, Hawaii, Connecticut, New Jersey, Vermont, and California. (Interestingly, these laws are sometimes passed *before* the state repeals its sodomy law. Wisconsin passed its gay rights law in 1981 but did not repeal its sodomy law until 1983. Massachusetts enacted a gay rights law in 1990 even though it still has a sodomy law.)

Notwithstanding these advances, in 43 states it remains perfectly legal for a private-sector employer to deny employment or refuse to serve or to rent to lesbians and gay men based solely on their sexual orientation — unless one happens to be in a municipality that has a gay rights ordinance. In 1991 a restaurant chain, Cracker Barrel, fired all of its lesbian and gay employees, announcing that it was a "family" restaurant where such employees were not welcome. Although Cracker Barrel operates in many states throughout the country, its actions were in no case subject to a locale that protected against discrimination on this basis.

Not only do 43 states and the federal government permit this discrimination, though; even worse, in many places government itself sanctions the prejudice. Governmental actions are policed by the constitution, and in some instances the constitution has furnished protections to lesbians and gay men. For instance, courts have ruled that the government generally cannot simply fire lesbians and gay men without first articulating some nexus between the worker's sexual orientation and his or her ability to do the job; this "nexus" requirement is also a part of the federal civil service regulations protecting federal employees. At the same time, though, the federal government has successfully prohibited lesbians and gay men from serving their country in the armed forces, banned lesbians and gay men from working for the FBI and CIA, and created extra burdens for lesbians and gay men who apply for security clearance. State and local governments are often no better: often, they openly ban lesbians and gay men from holding jobs ranging from teaching to police work. Despite the nexus requirement and other constitutional standards, courts have with near and unique uniformity ruled that such government line-drawing that discriminates against gay people does not offend the constitution. The courts have condoned the military's bias against lesbians and gay men as well as that of the FBI, CIA, Foreign Service, Defense Department Security Clearance office, and many school boards and police departments. The constitution has been little more than a promise to lesbians and gay men.

Thus, in most areas of the United States lesbians and gay men are not protected from the reach of the criminal law in their homes, and they are left, in effect, legally naked if they chose to come out publicly. With such minimal legal protection — and often confronted by employers who frown upon them — gay people must negotiate how open to be about their sexual orientation in the workplace:

Can a lesbian discuss her relationship with her coworkers?

Can a gay teacher march in a gay pride parade?

Will lesbians and gay men who advocate for workplace benefits for their partners be fired from their jobs?

Can the law help lesbians and gay men in these efforts?

These and related issues are discussed in Chapter Four.

FAMILY RIGHTS

Lesbians and gay men form relationships with one another in much the same way heterosexuals do. Unlike heterosexual unions, however, lesbian and gay relationships are not recognized by law. In seeking protection for relationships, lesbians and gay men are looking both to guarantee the privacy and autonomy society provides to heterosexual couples — particularly to marriages — and to gain the public recognition and economic responsibilities and benefits that go with marital status.

In 1981 no public or private entity in the United States recognized lesbian/gay relationships. Indeed, until the early 1980s few advocates within the lesbian and gay rights movement prioritized family issues. The exception was the many lesbian and gay parents — especially the former — who were losing their rights to their natural children in custody and visitation battles with their former (heterosexual) spouses. In the 1980s the concept of "domestic partnership" was invented as a basis for the recognition of lesbian and gay relationships.

Today dozens of municipalities and many more private institutions recognize lesbian and gay relationships through "domestic partnership" programs, according different types of benefits to these newly acknowledged unions. Additionally, the highest court in the state of New York recognized gay couples as "family" in a 1989 decision. Similar developments have permeated parenting law, as well, with state courts less and less considering a parent's sexual orientation as a pertinent factor in custody and visitation decisions. Moreover, courts in about half a dozen states have recognized "second-parent adoptions," permitting a lesbian/gay coparent to adopt his or her partner's biological children.

Among many developments, two central events of the 1980s for lesbian and gay men helped spur this family rights movement — AIDS and the Sharon Kowalski case. AIDS has made the lack of a legal relationship crushingly apparent to lesbian and gay couples: for instance, a gay man whose partner is dying may have difficulty inquiring about his condition or visiting him in the hospital because the men have no legal relationship to one another. Once the lover dies, his surviving partner will not automatically share in his estate, nor enjoy the tax benefits of so doing, and may indeed lose control of property the couple purchased together. He may also face eviction from his home. The survivor, moreover, could well face legal challenges from his partner's biological family regarding a will or even the disposition of his lover's remains.

The situation of Sharon Kowalski and Karen Thompson has similarly focused attention within the lesbian and gay community on family rights. Kowalski and Thompson lived together as partners for four years when, in 1983, Kowalski was in a tragic car accident, leaving her physically and mentally disabled. After the accident — for more than nine years — Thompson had to fight with Kowalski's biological family for the right to be Kowalski's legal guardian. The plight of the couple received a great deal of attention within the lesbian/gay community and highlighted the consequences of the legal system's failure to recognize our relationships.

Because of AIDS, because of Sharon Kowalski, and because of many similar though less publicized cases, lesbian and gay couples have become increasingly sophisticated about preparing legal documents to secure their relationships to one another. But for many, such second-class attempts to make a relationship resemble a marriage do not go far enough. A number of gay couples around the country have filed challenges to their states' marriage statutes; statutes have also been introduced in state legislatures that would change the definition of marriage to include gay couples. Other activists strongly believe that marriage is not the answer, based on their belief that lesbian and gay couples should not appropriate the mechanisms of oppression — particularly of the oppression of women — in order to secure legal recognition of our relationships. These activists have focused their attentions more on the domestic partnership movement.

Despite significant gains over the past decade, lesbian/gay couples' legal situation remains abysmal. Not one state recognizes lesbian and gay relationships by permitting gay people to marry one another — not one. Lesbians and gay men continue to be deprived of custody of, or visitation with, their own children solely because of their sexual orientation. In some states, lesbians and gay men are explicitly legally barred from adopting children or becoming foster parents; in others, they are prohibited in practice from doing so. Even as they develop new family structures with one another and with the assistance of emerging technological advances, lesbians and gay men still have no legal protection for the families they form. We remain a strange anomaly to the area of family law, challenging the very structure of an edifice constructed upon the model of a mother, father, and 2.4 children.

Chapters Five and Six take up the issues of lesbian and gay relationships and lesbian and gay parents, respectively. They look at issues across a range of topics:

How have the courts reacted to arguments that prohibitions on gay marriage are unconstitutional? Can we expect social change on this issue in the courts in the near future?

What other legal strategies have lesbians and gay men employed to gain recognition of their relationships?

How have courts treated lesbian and gay parents?

How must the legal system adapt to the growing phenomenon of gay parenting? Will it?

STRUGGLE

A final theme of this book is that of struggle. In considering the law as it relates to each of the areas that most affect lesbian and gay life, this work attempts to capture the essence of the struggle for lesbian and gay rights. Those battling for rights have been brave men and women who have risked their comfort, their livelihood, their families, and in some cases their lives for justice. Chapter Three outlines the challenges that lesbians and gay men have confronted in coming out and in organizing politically to lay the groundwork for full citizenship.

That chapter considers how lesbians and gay men have been denied the right to form social and political organizations, to meet with one another in bars and restaurants, to march for equal rights, and to speak publicly about our issues. The organizing legal theme of this chapter is the First Amendment to the United States Constitution, which has, with varying degrees of success, safeguarded lesbian and gay political organization throughout the battles described in these pages. Thus, an early portion of this book, Chapter Three, examines cases involving questions such as:

> Can a public high school prohibit a gay male student from bringing another man to his high school prom?

> Can a state university refuse to recognize and grant benefits to a lesbian/gay student group?

> Can the state legitimately prohibit lesbian and gay political organizations from meeting?

> Can a state silence gay-positive messages? What about antigay slurs?

If a goal of this book is to depict the fight for lesbian and gay rights, the purpose of Chapter Three is to depict the extent to which lesbians and gay men have been forced to fight for the right to fight for their rights.

This struggle will continue to be just that in the 1990s. New efforts to deprive lesbians and gay men of legal protections are keeping pace with the enactment of those protections. In late 1992, for example, the voters in the state of Colorado amended that state's constitution to prohibit the enactment of laws that would ban discrimination against lesbians and gay men. Similarly, voters in Tampa, Florida, repealed that municipality's recently enacted gay rights law.

It is my hope that this book will be a resource in the struggle for equal rights for lesbian and gay Americans. It is designed to be used in law school classrooms as a basic text to help educate law students about the legal situation of lesbians and gay men in the United States. It has also been written to be read by nonlawyers — by anyone interested in these increasingly important issues. I have tried to contextualize the legal cases discussed here with works of fiction, psychology, sociology, oral history, and journalism. This stems from my belief that the law is in no way a domain separate and apart from society itself but, rather, is always already part of and a constituent force in the construction of society. The law represents a unique promise to members of our society and, at the same time, can reflect the basest desires and most repulsive instincts of human beings. Despite this tension, the struggle for legal rights for lesbians and gay men is, for good reason, at the heart of our revolution — because the law holds out the hope that our society is capable of treating *all* of its citizens, including lesbians and gay men, with the dignity and respect that each deserves.

ONE

Basic Documents

I. SEXUALITY

◆

SEXUAL BEHAVIOR IN THE HUMAN MALE
Alfred Kinsey, et al.

HOMOSEXUAL OUTLET

In the total male population, single and married, between adolescence and old age, twenty-four percent of the total outlet is derived from solitary sources (masturbation and nocturnal emissions), 69.4 percent is derived from heterosexual sources (petting and coitus), and 6.3 percent of the total number of orgasms is derived from homosexual contacts. It is not more than 0.3 percent of the outlet which is derived from relations with animals of other species.

Homosexual contacts account, therefore, for a rather small but still significant portion of the total outlet of the human male. The significance of the homosexual is, furthermore, much greater than the frequencies of outlet may indicate, because a considerable portion of the population, perhaps the major portion of the male population, has at least some homosexual experience between adolescence and old age. In addition, about sixty percent of the pre-adolescent boys engage in homosexual activities, and there is an additional group of adult males who avoid overt contacts but who are quite aware of their potentialities for reacting to other males.

The social significance of the homosexual is considerably emphasized by the fact that both Jewish and Christian churches have considered this aspect of human sexuality to be abnormal and immoral. Social custom and our Anglo-American law are sometimes very severe in penalizing one who is discovered to have had homosexual relations. In consequence, many persons who have had

ALFRED KINSEY, WARDELL POMEROY & CLYDE MARTIN, *Homosexual Outlet, in* SEXUAL BEHAVIOR IN THE HUMAN MALE 610 (1948).

such experience are psychically disturbed, and not a few of them have been in open conflict with the social organization.

It is, therefore, peculiarly difficult to secure factual data concerning the nature and the extent of the homosexual in Western European or American cultures, and even more difficult to find strictly objective presentations of such data as are available. Most of the literature on the homosexual represents either a polemic against the heinous abnormality of such activity, or a biased argument in defense of an individual's right to choose his patterns of sexual behavior.

Until the extent of any type of human behavior is adequately known, it is difficult to assess its significance, either to the individuals who are involved or to society as a whole; and until the extent of the homosexual is known, it is practically impossible to understand its biologic or social origins. It is one thing if we are dealing with a type of activity that is unusual, without precedent among other animals, and restricted to peculiar types of individuals within the human population. It is another thing if the phenomenon proves to be a fundamental part, not only of human sexuality, but of mammalian patterns as a whole. The present chapter is, therefore, wholly confined to an analysis of the data which we now have on the incidence and the frequencies of homosexual activity in the white male population in this country. Analyses of the factors which affect the development of both heterosexual and homosexual patterns of behavior will be presented in a subsequent volume in this series.

■ ■ ■

DEFINITION

For nearly a century the term homosexual in connection with human behavior has been applied to sexual relations, either overt or psychic, between individuals of the same sex. Derived from the Greek root *homo* rather than from the Latin word for man, the term emphasizes the *sameness* of the two individuals who are involved in a sexual relation. The word is, of course, patterned after and intended to represent the antithesis of the word heterosexual, which applies to a relation between individuals of different sexes.

The term homosexual has had an endless list of synonyms in the technical vocabularies and a still greater list in the vernaculars. The terms homogenic love, contrasexuality, homo-eroticism, similisexualism, uranism and others have been used in English. The terms sexual inversion, intersexuality, transsexuality, the third sex, psychosexual hermaphroditism, and others have been applied not merely to designate the nature of the partner involved in the sexual relation, but to emphasize the general opinion that individuals engaging in homosexual activity are neither male nor female, but persons of mixed sex. These latter terms are, however, most unfortunate, for they provide an interpretation in anticipation of any sufficient demonstration of the fact; and consequently they prejudice investigations of the nature and origin of homosexual activity.

The term lesbian, referring to such female homosexual relations as were immortalized in the poetry of Sappho of the Greek isle of Lesbos, has gained considerable usage within recent years, particularly in some of the larger Eastern cities where the existence of female homosexuality is more generally recognized by the public at large. Although there can be no objection to designating relations between females by a special term, it should be recognized that such activities are quite the equivalent of sexual relations between males.

It is unfortunate that the students of animal behavior have applied the term homosexual to a totally different sort of phenomenon among the lower mammals. In most of the literature on animal behavior it is applied on the basis of the general conspectus of the behavior pattern of the animal, its aggressiveness in seeking the sexual contact, its postures during coitus, its position relative to the other animal in the sex relation, and the conformance or disconformance of that behavior to the usual positions and activities of the animal during heterosexual coitus.

In most mammals the behavior of the female in a heterosexual performance usually involves the acceptance of the male which is trying to make intromission. The female at such a moment is less aggressive than the male, even passive in her acceptance of the male's approaches, and subordinate in position to him during actual coitus. This means that the female usually lies beneath the male or in front of him during copulation, either submitting from the very beginning of the sexual relation or (as in the cats, ferret, mink, and some other animals) being forced into submission by the assault of the male. In the case of the mink, the female is far from being passive during the initial stages of the contact, and the courting performances involve as strenuous fighting as the most extreme non-sexual circumstances could produce. There is no sexual relation, however, until the female has been sufficiently subdued to allow the male to effect coitus. In the case of the rat, the female which is in heat as the result of the hormones which her ovaries secrete near the time of ovulation, is more readily induced to crouch on the floor, arch her back (in lordosis) so her body is raised posteriorly, and pass into a nervous state which is characterized by a general rigidity of most of the body, but by a constant and rapid trembling of the ears and by peculiar hopping movements. This is the behavior which is characteristic of the female in a heterosexual contact, and this is what the students of animals describe as typically feminine behavior.

Throughout the mammals it is the male which more often (but not always) pursues the female for a sexual contact. In species where there is a struggle before the female submits to coitus, the male must be physically dominant and capable of controlling the female. In the ultimate act it is the male which more often mounts in back of the female and makes the active pelvic thrusts

which effect intromission. This is the behavior that students of the lower mammals commonly refer to as typically masculine behavior.

But among many species of mammals and, indeed, probably among all of them, it not infrequently happens that males and females assume other than their usual positions in a sexual contact. This may be dependent upon individual differences in the physiology or anatomy of certain individuals, on differences in hormones, on environmental circumstances, or on some previous experience which has conditioned the animal in its behavior.

In a certain number of cases the assumption of the attitudes and positions of the opposite sex, among these lower mammals, seems to depend upon nothing more than the accident of the position in which the individual finds itself. The same male rat that has mounted a female in typical heterosexual coitus only a few moments before, may crouch on the floor, arch its back, and rear its posterior when it is approached by another rat from the rear. The same female which rises from the floor where she has been crouching in front of a copulating male may bump into another rat as she runs around the cage, rear on her haunches in front of the decumbent partner, and go through all of the motions that a male ordinarily goes through in heterosexual copulation. She may move her pelvis in thrusts which are quite like those of the male. She may strike her genital area against the genital area of the rat in front, quite as she would if she had a penis to effect entrance. And, what is most astounding, she may double up her body as she pulls back from the genital thrusts and manipulate her own genitalia with her mouth, exactly as the male rat ordinarily manipulates his penis between the thrusts that he makes when he is engaged in the masculine role in the usual type of heterosexual relation.

The assumption by a male animal of a female position in a sexual relation, or the assumption by a female of a position which is more typical of the male in a heterosexual relation, is what the students of animal behavior have referred to as homosexuality. This, of course, has nothing whatsoever to do with the use of the term among the students of human behavior, and one must be exceedingly careful how one transfers the conclusions based on these animal studies.

In studies of human behavior, the term *inversion* is applied to sexual situations in which males play female roles and females play male roles in sex relations. Most of the data on "homosexuality" in the animal studies actually refer to inversion. Inversion, of course, may occur in either heterosexual or homosexual relations, although there has been a widespread opinion, even among students of human psychology, and among some persons whose experience has been largely homosexual, that inversion is an invariable accompaniment of homosexuality. However, this generalization is not warranted. A more elaborate presentation of our data would show that there are a great many males who remain as masculine, and a great many females who remain as feminine, in their attitudes and their approaches in homosexual relations, as the males or females who have nothing but heterosexual relations. Inversion and homosexuality are two distinct and not always correlated types of behavior.

More recently some of the students of animal behavior have used the term *bisexual* to apply to individuals which assume sometimes male and sometimes female roles during sexual activities. This, however, is not a happy correction of the terminology, because the term bisexual has a long-standing meaning in biology which is totally different from the meaning intended here. Moreover, in regard to human behavior, the term bisexual has already been misapplied to persons who include both heterosexual and homosexual activities in their current histories. (See the discussion on "Bisexuality" in a later section in this chapter.) The student of animal behavior is observing an

inversion of behavior patterns, and this is a phenomenon apart from either homosexuality or bisexuality, as those terms have ordinarily been used.

The inappropriate use of the term homosexual in the literature on animal behavior has led to unfortunate misinterpretations of the data. Thus, for instance, several investigators have shown that the injection of gonadal hormones may modify the frequency with which an animal shows an inversion of behavior of the sort described above. Among many clinicians this work has been taken to mean that the sex hormones control the heterosexuality or homosexuality of an individual's behavior. This, of course, is a totally unwarranted interpretation. The animal work merely shows that there may be an inversion of female and male roles as a result of hormonal injections. It points to a relationship between the amount of hormone and the aggressiveness of an individual in approaching other animals for sexual relations. The injection of male hormones quite generally increases the frequency and intensity of an animal's reactions, but there is no evidence that it affects its choice of a partner in a sexual relation . . . The males who most often assume the female type of behavior are the ones who "invariably prove to be the most vigorous copulators," when they assume the more usual masculine role in coitus. There is clinical experience with the human male which similarly shows that the intensity of his sexual activity is increased when male hormones are administered, while his choice of a partner (*i.e.*, his heterosexuality or his homosexuality) is not modified.

If the term homosexual is restricted as it should be, the homosexuality or heterosexuality of any activity becomes apparent by determining the sexes of the two individuals involved in the relationship. For instance, mouth-genital contacts between males and females are certainly heterosexual, even though some persons may think of them as homosexual. And although one may hear of a male "who has sex relations with his wife in a homosexual way," there is no logic in such a use of the term, and analyses of the behavior and of the motivations of the behavior in such cases do not show them necessarily related to any homosexual experience.

On the other hand, the homosexuality of certain relationships between individuals of the same sex may be denied by some persons, because the situation does not fulfill other criteria that they think should be attached to the definition. Mutual masturbation between two males may be dismissed, even by certain clinicians, as not homosexual, because oral or anal relations or particular levels of psychic response are required, according to their concept of homosexuality. There are persons who insist that the active male in an anal relation is essentially heterosexual in his behavior, and that the passive male in the same relation is the only one who is homosexual. These, however, are misapplications of terms, which are often unfortunate because they obscure the interpretations of the situation which the clinician is supposed to help by his analysis.

These misinterpretations are often encouraged by the very persons who are having homosexual experience. Some males who are being regularly fellated by other males without, however, ever performing fellatio themselves, may insist that they are exclusively heterosexual and that they have never been involved in a truly homosexual relation. Their consciences are cleared and they may avoid trouble with society and with the police by perpetrating the additional fiction that they are incapable of responding to a relation with a male unless they fantasy themselves in contact with a female. Even clinicians have allowed themselves to be diverted by such pretensions. The actual histories, however, show few if any cases of sexual relations between males which could be considered anything but homosexual.

Many individuals who have had considerable homosexual experience, construct a

hierarchy on the basis of which they insist that anyone who has not had as much homosexual experience as they have had, or who is less exclusively aroused by homosexual stimuli, is "not really homosexual." It is amazing to observe how many psychologists and psychiatrists have accepted this sort of propaganda, and have come to believe that homosexual males and females are discretely different from persons who merely have homosexual experience, or who react sometimes to homosexual stimuli. Sometimes such an interpretation allows for only two kinds of males and two kinds of females, namely, those who are heterosexual and those who are homosexual. But as subsequent data in this chapter will show, there is only about half of the male population whose sexual behavior is exclusively heterosexual, and there are only a few percent who are exclusively homosexual. Any restriction of the term homosexuality to individuals who are exclusively so demands, logically, that the term heterosexual be applied only to those individuals who are exclusively heterosexual; and this makes no allowance for the nearly half of the population which has had sexual contacts with, or reacted psychically to, individuals of their own as well as of the opposite sex. Actually, of course, one must learn to recognize every combination of heterosexuality and homosexuality in the histories of various individuals.

It would encourage clearer thinking on these matters if persons were not characterized as heterosexual or homosexual, but as individuals who have had certain amounts of heterosexual experience and certain amounts of homosexual experience. Instead of using these terms as substantives which stand for persons, or even as adjectives to describe persons, they may better be used to describe the nature of the overt sexual relations, or of the stimuli to which an individual erotically responds.

■ ■ ■

THE HETEROSEXUAL-HOMOSEXUAL BALANCE

Concerning patterns of sexual behavior, a great deal of the thinking done by scientists and laymen alike stems from the assumption that there are persons who are "heterosexual" and persons who are "homosexual," that these two types represent antitheses in the sexual world, and that there is only an insignificant class of "bisexuals" who occupy an intermediate position between the other groups. It is implied that every individual is innately — inherently — either heterosexual or homosexual. It is further implied that from the time of birth one is fated to be one thing or the other, and that there is little chance for one to change his pattern in the course of a lifetime.

It is quite generally believed that one's preference for a sexual partner of one or the other sex is correlated with various physical and mental qualities, and with the total personality which makes a homosexual male or female physically, psychically, and perhaps spiritually distinct from a heterosexual individual. It is generally thought that these qualities make a homosexual person obvious and recognizable to any one who has a sufficient understanding of such matters. Even psychiatrists discuss "the homosexual personality" and many of them believe that preferences for sexual partners of a particular sex are merely secondary manifestations of something that lies much deeper in the totality of that intangible which they call the personality.

It is commonly believed, for instance, that homosexual males are rarely robust physically, are uncoordinated or delicate in their movements, or perhaps graceful enough but not strong and vigorous in their physical expression. Fine skins, high-pitched voices, obvious hand movements, a feminine carriage of the hips, and peculiarities of walking gaits are supposed accompaniments of a preference for a male as a sexual partner. It is commonly believed that the homosexual male is artistically sensitive, emotionally unbalanced, temperamental to the point of being unpredictable, difficult to get along with, and undependable in meeting specific obligations. In physical characters there have been attempts to show that the homosexual male has a considerable crop of hair and less often becomes bald, has teeth which are more like those of the female, a broader pelvis, larger genitalia, and a tendency toward being fat, and that he lacks a linea alba. The homosexual male is supposed to be less interested in athletics, more often interested in music and the arts, more often engaged in such occupations as bookkeeping, dress design, window display, hairdressing, acting, radio work, nursing, religious service, and social work. The converse to all of these is supposed to represent the typical heterosexual male. Many a clinician attaches considerable weight to these things in diagnosing the basic heterosexuality or homosexuality of his patients. The characterizations are so distinct that they seem to leave little room for doubt that homosexual and heterosexual represent two very distinct types of males.

The Terman-Miles scale for determining the degree of masculinity or femininity of an individual is largely based upon these preconceptions. Some other psychology scales have utilized very much the same principles. While these scales have made it more apparent that there may be gradations between exclusively heterosexual and exclusively homosexual individuals, or between the extremes of masculinity and the extremes of femininity, the implication is always present that an individual's choice of a sexual partner is closely related to the masculinity or femininity of his personality.

It should be pointed out that scientific judgments on this point have been based on little more than the same sorts of impressions which the general public has had concerning homosexual persons. But before any sufficient study can be made of such possible correlations between patterns of sexual behavior and other qualities in the individual, it is necessary to understand the incidences and frequencies of the homosexual in the population as a whole, and the relation of the homosexual activity to the rest of the sexual pattern in each individual's history.

The histories which have been available in the present study make it apparent that the heterosexuality or homosexuality of many individuals is not an all-or-none proposition. It is true that there are persons in the population whose histories are exclusively heterosexual, both in regard to their overt experience and in regard to their psychic reactions. And there are individuals in the population whose histories are exclusively homosexual, both in experience and in psychic reactions. But the record also shows that there is a considerable portion of the population whose members have combined, within their individual histories, both homosexual and heterosexual experience and/or psychic responses. There are some whose heterosexual experiences predominate, there are some whose homosexual experiences predominate, there are some who have had quite equal amounts of both types of experience.

Some of the males who are involved in one type of relation at one period in their lives, may have only the other type of relation at some later period. There may be considerable fluctuation of patterns from time to time. Some males may be involved in both heterosexual and homosexual activities within the same period of time. For instance, there are some who engage in both heterosexual and homosexual activities in the same year, or in the same month or week, or even in the same day. There are not a few individuals who engage in group activities in which they may make simultaneous contact with partners of both sexes.

Males do not represent two discrete populations, heterosexual and homosexual. The world is not to be divided into sheep and goats. Not all things are black nor all things white. It is a fundamental of taxonomy that nature rarely deals with discrete categories. Only the human mind invents categories and tries to force facts into separated pigeon-holes. The living world is a continuum in each and every one of its aspects. The sooner we learn this concerning human sexual behavior the sooner we shall reach a sound understanding of the realities of sex.

While emphasizing the continuity of the gradations between exclusively heterosexual and exclusively homosexual histories, it has seemed desirable to develop some sort of classification which could be based on the relative amounts of heterosexual and of homosexual experience or response in each history. An individual may be assigned a position on this scale, for each age period in his life, in accordance with the following definitions of the various points on the scale:

0. Individuals are rated as **0**'s if they make no physical contact which result in erotic arousal or orgasm, and make no psychic responses to individuals of their own sex. Their socio-sexual contacts and responses are exclusively with individuals of the opposite sex.

1. Individuals are rated as **1**'s if they have only incidental homosexual contacts which have involved physical or psychic response, or incidental psychic responses without physical contact. The great preponderance of their socio-sexual experience and reactions is directed toward individuals of the opposite sex. Such homosexual experiences as these individuals have may occur only a single time or two, or at least infrequently in comparison to the amount of their heterosexual experience. Their homosexual experiences never involve as specific psychic reactions as they make to heterosexual stimuli. Sometimes the homosexual activities in which they engage may be inspired by curiosity, or may be more or less forced upon them by other individuals, perhaps when they are asleep or when they are drunk, or under some other peculiar circumstance.

2. Individuals are rated as **2**'s if they have more than incidental homosexual experience, and/or if they respond rather definitely to homosexual stimuli. Their heterosexual experiences and/or reactions still surpass their homosexual experiences and/or reactions. These individuals may have only a small amount of homosexual experience or they may have a considerable amount of it, but in every case it is surpassed by the amount of heterosexual experience that they have within the same period of time. They usually recognize their quite specific arousal by homosexual stimuli, but their responses to the opposite sex are still stronger. A few of these individuals may even have all of their overt experience in the homosexual, but their psychic reactions to persons of the opposite sex indicate that they are still predominantly heterosexual. This latter situation is most often found among younger males who have not yet ventured to have actual intercourse with girls, while their orientation is definitely heterosexual. On the other hand, there are some males who should be rated as 2's because of their strong reactions to individuals of their own sex, even though they have never had overt relations with them.

3. Individuals who are rated **3**'s stand midway on the heterosexual-homosexual scale. They are about equally homosexual and heterosexual in their overt experience and/or their psychic reactions. In general, they accept and equally enjoy both types of contacts, and have no strong preferences for one or the other. Some persons are rated 3's, even though they may have a larger amount of experience of one sort, because they respond psychically to partners of both sexes, and it is only a matter of circumstance that brings them into more frequent contact with one of the sexes. Such a situation is not unusual among single males, for male contacts are often more available to

them than female contacts. Married males, on the other hand, find it simpler to secure a sexual outlet through intercourse with their wives, even though some of them may be as interested in males as they are in females.

4. Individuals are rated as **4**'s if they have more overt activity and/or psychic reactions in the homosexual, while still maintaining a fair amount of heterosexual activity and/or responding rather definitely to heterosexual stimuli.

5. Individuals are rated as **5**'s if they are almost entirely homosexual in their overt activities and/or reactions. They do have incidental experience with the opposite sex and sometimes react psychically to individuals of the opposite sex.

6. Individuals are rated as **6**'s if they are exclusively homosexual, both in regard to their overt experience and in regard to their psychic reactions.

It will be observed that this is a seven-point scale, with 0 and 6 as the extreme points, and with 3 as the midpoint in the classification. On opposite sides of the midpoint the following relations hold:

0 is the opposite of 6
1 is the opposite of 5
2 is the opposite of 4

It will be observed that the rating which an individual receives has a dual basis. It takes into account his overt sexual experience and/or his psychosexual reactions. In the majority of instances the two aspects of the history parallel, but sometimes they are not in accord. In the latter case, the rating of an individual must be based upon an evaluation of the relative importance of the overt and the psychic in his history.

In each classification there are persons who have had no experience or a minimum of overt sexual experience, but in the same classification there may also be persons who have had hundreds of sexual contacts. In every case, however, all of the individuals in each classification show the same balance between the heterosexual and homosexual elements in their histories. The position of an individual on this scale is always based upon the relation of the heterosexual to the homosexual in his history, rather than upon the actual amount of overt experience or psychic reaction.

Finally, it should be emphasized again that the reality is a continuum, with individuals in the population occupying not only the seven categories which are recognized here, but every gradation between each of the categories, as well. Nevertheless, it does no great injustice to the fact to group the population as indicated above.

From all of this, it should be evident that one is not warranted in recognizing merely two types of individuals, heterosexual and homosexual, and that the characterization of the homosexual as a third sex fails to describe any actuality.

It is imperative that one understand the relative amounts of the heterosexual and homosexual in an individual's history if one is to make any significant analysis of him. Army and Navy officials and administrators in schools, prisons, and other institutions should be more concerned with the degree of heterosexuality or homosexuality in an individual than they are with the question of whether he has ever had an experience of either sort. It is obvious that the clinician must determine the balance that exists between the heterosexual and homosexual experience and reactions of his patient, before he can begin to help him. Even courts of law might well consider the totality of the individual's history, before passing judgment on the particular instance that has brought him into the hands of the law.

Everywhere in our society there is a tendency to consider an individual "homosexual" if he is known to have had a single experience with another individual of his own sex. Under the law an individual may receive the same penalty for a single homosexual experience that he would for a continuous record of experiences. In penal and mental institutions a male is likely to be rated "homosexual" if he is discovered to have a single contact with another male. In society at large, a male who has worked out a highly successful marital adjustment is likely to be rated "homosexual" if the community learns about a single contact that he has had with another male. All such misjudgments are the product of the tendency to categorize sexual activities under only two heads, and of a failure to recognize the endless gradations that actually exist.

From all of this, it becomes obvious that any question as to the number of persons in the world who are homosexual and the number who are heterosexual is unanswerable. It is only possible to record the number of those who belong to each of the positions on such a heterosexual-homosexual scale as is given above. Summarizing our data on the incidence of overt homosexual experience in the white male population, and the distribution of various degrees of heterosexual-homosexual balance in that population, the following generalizations may be made:

37 percent of the total male population has **at least some overt homosexual experience** to the point of orgasm between adolescence and old age. This accounts for nearly 2 males out of every 5 that one may meet.

50 percent of the males **who remain single until age 35** have had overt homosexual experience to the point of orgasm, since the onset of adolescence.

58 percent of the males who belong to the group that goes into **high school** but not beyond, **50 percent of the grade school level**, and **47 percent of the college level** have had homosexual experience to the point of orgasm if they remain single to the age of 35.

63 percent of all males **never have overt** homosexual experience to the point of orgasm after the onset of adolescence.

50 percent of all males (approximately) **have neither overt nor psychic experience** in the homosexual after the onset of adolescence.

13 percent of all males (approximately) **react erotically** to other males **without having overt** homosexual contacts after the onset of adolescence.

30 percent of all males **have at least incidental homosexual experience** or reactions (*i.e.*, rate 1 to 6) over at least a three-year period between the ages of 16 and 55. This accounts for one male out of every three in the population who is past the early years of adolescence.

25 percent of the male population **has more than incidental homosexual experience** or reactions (*i.e.*, rates 2–6) for at least three years between the ages of 16 and 55. In terms of averages, one male out of approximately every four has had or will have such distinct and continued homosexual experience.

18 percent of the males have at least **as much of the homosexual as the heterosexual** in their histories (*i.e.*, rate 3–6) for at least three years between the ages of 16 and 55. This is more than one in six of the white male population.

13 percent of the population **has more of the homosexual than the heterosexual** (*i.e.*, rates 4–6) for at least three years between the ages of 16 and 55. This is one in eight of the white male population.

10 percent of the males are **more or less exclusively homosexual** (*i.e.*, rate 5 or 6) for at least three years between the ages of 16 and 55. This is one male in ten in the white male population.

8 percent of the males are **exclusively homosexual** (*i.e.*, rate a 6) for at least three years between the ages of 16 and 55. This is one male in every 13.

4 percent of the white males are **exclusively homosexual throughout their lives**, after the onset of adolescence.

None of those who have previously attempted to estimate the incidence of the homosexual have made any clear-cut definition of the degree of homosexuality which they were including in their statistics. As a matter of fact, it seems fairly certain that none of them had any clear-cut conception of what they intended, other than their assurance that they were including only those "who were really homosexual." For that reason it is useless to compare the 2 or 3 percent figure of Havelock Ellis, or the 2 to 5 percent figure of Hirschfeld, or the 0.1 percent figure of the Army induction centers with any of the data given above. The persons who are identified as "homosexuals" in much of the legal and social practice have rated anything between 1 and 6 on the above scale. On the other hand, there are some persons who would not rate an individual as "really homosexual" if he were anything less than a 5 or 6. Nevertheless, it should be emphasized again that there are persons who rate 2's or 3's who, in terms of the number of contacts they have made, may have had more homosexual experience than many persons who rate 6, and the clinician, the social worker, court officials, and society in general are not infrequently concerned with persons who rate no more than 2's or 3's. Many who rate only 1 or 2 are much disturbed over their homosexual experience, and they are frequently among those who go to clinicians for help.

Finally, it should be emphasized that the social significance of an individual's history may or may not have any relation to his rating on the above scale. An older male who has never before had homosexual contact, may force a sexual relation with a small boy; and although he rates only a 1, he may so outrage the community that the full force of the law may be stirred up against him. On the contrary, most persons who rate 1's have histories which do not disturb anybody. At the other end of the scale, some of the exclusively homosexual males may so confine their overt contacts that no social problems are raised, while others who also rate 6 are active wolves who are in continual trouble because of their open affronts to social conventions.

BISEXUALITY

Since only 50 percent of the population is exclusively heterosexual throughout its adult life, and since only 4 percent of the population is exclusively homosexual throughout its life, it appears that nearly half (46 percent) of the population engages in both heterosexual and homosexual activities, or reacts to persons of both sexes, in the course of their adult lives. The term bisexual has been applied to at least some portion of this group. Unfortunately, the term as it has been used has never been strictly delimited, and consequently it is impossible to know whether it refers to all individuals who rate anything from 1 to 5, or whether it is being limited to some smaller number of categories, perhaps centering around group 3. If the latter is intended, it should be emphasized that the 1's, 2's, 4's, and 5's have not yet been accounted for, and they constitute a considerable portion of the population.

In any event, such a scheme provides only a three-point scale (heterosexual, bisexual, and homosexual), and such a limited scale does not adequately describe the continuum which is the reality in nature. A seven-point scale comes nearer to showing the many gradations that actually exist.

As previously pointed out, it is rather unfortunate that the word bisexual should have been chosen to describe this intermediate group. The term is used as a substantive, designating individuals — persons; and the root meaning of the word and the way in which it is usually used imply that these persons have both masculine qualities and feminine qualities within their single bodies. We have objected to the use of the terms heterosexual and homosexual when used as nouns which stand for individuals. It is similarly untenable to imply that these "bisexual" persons have an anatomy or an endocrine system or other sorts of physiologic or psychologic capacities which make them partly male and partly female, or of the two sexes simultaneously.

The term bisexual has been used in biology for structures or individuals or aggregates of individuals that include the anatomy or functions of both sexes. There are unisexual species which are exclusively female and reproduce parthenogenetically (from eggs that are not fertilized). In contrast, there are bisexual species which include both males and females and which commonly reproduce through fertilization of the eggs produced by the females. Among plants and animals which have an alternation of generations, there are unisexual or parthenogenetic generations in which there are only females, and bisexual generations in which there are both males and females. In regard to the embryonic structures from which the gonads of some of the vertebrates develop, the term bisexual is applied because these embryonic structures have the potentialities of both sexes and may develop later into either ovaries or testes. Hermaphroditic animals, like earthworms, some snails, and a rare human, may be referred to as bisexual, because they have both ovaries and testes in their single bodies. These are the customary usages for the term bisexual in biology.

On the other hand, as applied to human sexual behavior, the term indicates that there are individuals who choose to have sexual relations with both males and females; and until it is demonstrated, as it certainly is not at the present time, that such a catholicity of taste in a sexual relation is dependent upon the individual containing within his anatomy both male and female structures, or male and female physiologic capacities, it is unfortunate to call such individuals bisexual. Because of its wide currency, the term will undoubtedly continue in use among students of human behavior and in the public in general. It should, however, be used with the understanding that it is patterned on the words heterosexual and homosexual and, like them, refers to the sex of the partner, and proves nothing about the constitution of the person who is labelled bisexual.

■ ■ ■

♦

SEXUAL BEHAVIOR IN THE HUMAN FEMALE
Alfred Kinsey, et al.

The classification of sexual behavior as masturbatory, heterosexual, or homosexual is based upon the nature of the stimulus which initiates the behavior. The present chapter, dealing with the homosexual behavior of the females in our sample, records the sexual responses which they had made to other females, and the overt contacts which they had had with other females in the course of their sexual histories.

The term homosexual comes from the Greek prefix *homo*, referring to the sameness of the individuals involved, and not from the Latin word *homo* which means man. It contrasts with the term heterosexual which refers to responses or contacts between individuals of different (*hetero*) sexes.

While the term homosexual is quite regularly applied by clinicians and by the public at large to relations between males, there is a growing tendency to refer to sexual relationships between females as *lesbian* or *sapphic*. Both of these terms reflect the homosexual history of Sappho who lived on the isle of Lesbos in ancient Greece. While there is some advantage in having a terminology which distinguishes homosexual relations which occur between females from those which occur between males, there is a distinct disadvantage in using a terminology which suggests that there are fundamental differences between the homosexual responses and activities of females and of males.

PHYSIOLOGIC AND PSYCHOLOGIC BASES

It cannot be too frequently emphasized that the behavior of any animal must depend upon the nature of the stimulus which it meets, its anatomic and physiologic capacities, and its background of previous experience. Unless it has been conditioned by previous experience, an animal should respond identically to identical stimuli, whether they emanate from some part of its own body, from another individual of the same sex, or from an individual of the opposite sex.

ALFRED KINSEY, WARDELL POMEROY, CLYDE MARTIN & PAUL GEBHARD, *Homosexual Responses and Contacts*, in SEXUAL BEHAVIOR IN THE HUMAN FEMALE 446 (1953).

The classification of sexual behavior as masturbatory, heterosexual, or homosexual is, therefore, unfortunate if it suggests that three different types of responses are involved, or suggests that only different types of persons seek out or accept each kind of sexual activity. There is nothing known in the anatomy or physiology of sexual response and orgasm which distinguishes masturbatory, heterosexual, or homosexual reactions. The terms are of value only because they describe the source of the sexual stimulation, and they should not be taken as descriptions of the individuals who respond to the various stimuli. It would clarify our thinking if the terms could be dropped completely out of our vocabulary, for then sociosexual behavior could be described as activity between a female and a male, or between two females, or between two males, and this would constitute a more objective record of the fact. For the present, however, we shall have to use the term homosexual in something of its standard meaning, except that we shall use it primarily to describe sexual *relationships*, and shall prefer not to use it to describe the *individuals* who were involved in those relationships.

The inherent physiologic capacity of an animal to respond to any sufficient stimulus seems, then, the basic explanation of the fact that some individuals respond to stimuli originating in other individuals of their own sex — and it appears to indicate that every individual could so respond if the opportunity [were] offered and one were not conditioned against making such responses. There is no need of hypothesizing peculiar hormonal factors that make certain individuals especially liable to engage in homosexual activity, and we know of no data which prove the existence of such hormonal factors. There are no sufficient data to show that specific hereditary factors are involved. Theories of childhood attachments to one or the other parent, theories of fixation at some infantile level of sexual development, interpretations of homosexuality as neurotic or psychopathic behavior or moral degeneracy, and other philosophic interpretations are not supported by scientific research, and are contrary to the specific data on our series of female and male histories. The data indicate that the factors leading to homosexual behavior are (1) the basic physiologic capacity of every mammal to respond to any sufficient stimulus; (2) the accident which leads an individual into his or her first sexual experience with a person of the same sex; (3) the conditioning effects of such experience; and (4) the indirect but powerful conditioning which the opinions of other persons and the social codes may have on an individual's decision to accept or reject this type of sexual contact.

■ ■ ■

PERCENTAGE WITH EACH RATING

It should again be pointed out, as we did in our volume on the male, that it is impossible to determine the number of persons who are "homosexual" or "heterosexual." It is only possible to determine how many persons belong, at any particular time, to each of the classifications on a heterosexual-homosexual scale. . . . The heterosexual-homosexual ratings are based on psychologic responses and overt experience, while the accumulative and active incidences previously shown are based solely on overt contacts.

The following generalizations may be made concerning the experience of the females in the sample, up to the time at which they contributed their histories to the present study.

Something between 11 and 20 percent of the unmarried females and 8 to 10 percent of the married females in the sample were making at least incidental homosexual responses, or making incidental or more specific homosexual contacts — *i.e.*, rated 1 to 6 — in each of the years between twenty and thirty-five years of age. Among the previously married females, 14 to 17 percent were in that category.

Something between 6 and 14 percent of the unmarried females, and 2 to 3 percent of the married females, were making more than incidental responses, and/or making more than incidental homosexual contacts — *i.e.*, rated 2 to 6 — in each of the years between twenty and thirty-five years of age. Among the previously married females, 8 to 10 percent were in that category.

Between 4 and 11 percent of the unmarried females in the sample, and 1 to 2 percent of the married females, had made homosexual responses, and/or had homosexual experience, at least as frequently as they had made heterosexual responses and/or had heterosexual experience — *i.e.*, rated 3 to 6 — in each of the years between twenty and thirty-five years of age. Among the previously married females, 5 to 7 percent were in that category.

Between 3 and 8 percent of the unmarried females in the sample, and something under 1 per cent of the married females, had made homosexual responses and/or had homosexual experience more often than they had responded heterosexually and/or had heterosexual experience — *i.e.*, rated 4 to 6 — in each of the years between twenty and thirty-five years of age. Among the previously married females, 4 to 7 percent were in that category.

Between 2 and 6 percent of the unmarried females in the sample, but less than 1 percent of the married females, had been more or less exclusively homosexual in their responses and/or overt experience — *i.e.*, rated 5 or 6 — in each of the years between twenty and thirty-five years of age. Among the previously married females, 1 to 6 percent were in that category.

Between 1 and 3 percent of the unmarried females in the sample, but less than three in a thousand of the married females, had been exclusively homosexual in their psychologic responses and/or overt experience — *i.e.*, rated 6 — in each of the years between twenty and thirty-five years of age. Among the previously married females, 1 to 3 percent were in that category.

Between 14 and 19 percent of the unmarried females in the sample, and 1 to 3 percent of the married females, had not made any socio-sexual responses (either heterosexual or homosexual) — *i.e.*, rated X — in each of the years between twenty and thirty-five years of age. Among the previously married females, 5 to 8 percent were in that category.

EXTENT OF FEMALE VS. MALE HOMOSEXUALITY

The incidences and frequencies of homosexual responses and contacts, and consequently the incidences of the homosexual ratings, were much lower among the females in our sample than they were among the males on whom we have previously reported. Among the females, the accumulative incidences of homosexual responses had ultimately reached 28 percent; they had reached 50 percent in the males. The accumulative tendencies of overt contacts to the point of orgasm among the females had reached 13 percent; among the males they had reached 37 percent. This means that homosexual responses had occurred in about half as many females as males, and contacts which had proceeded to orgasm had occurred in about a third as many females as males. Moreover, compared with the males, there were only about a half to a third as many of the females who were, in any age period, primarily or exclusively homosexual.

A much smaller proportion of the females had continued their homosexual activities for as many years as most of the males in the sample.

A much larger proportion (71 percent) of the females who had had any homosexual contact had restricted their homosexual activities to a single partner or two; only 51 percent of the males who had had homosexual experience had so restricted their contacts. Many of the males had been highly promiscuous, sometimes finding scores or hundreds of sexual partners.

There is a widespread opinion which is held both by clinicians and the public at large, that homosexual responses and completed contacts occur among more females than males. This opinion is not borne out by our data, and it is not supported by previous studies which have been based on specific data. This opinion may have originated in the fact that females are more openly affectionate than males in our culture. Women may hold hands in public, put arms about each other, publicly fondle and kiss each other, and openly express their admiration and affection for other females without being accused of homosexual interests, as men would be if they made such an open display of their interests in other men. Males, interpreting what they observe in terms of male psychology, are inclined to believe that the female behavior reflects emotional interests that must develop sooner or later into overt sexual relationships. Nevertheless, our data indicate that a high proportion of this show of affection on the part of the female does not reflect any psychosexual interest, and rarely leads to overt homosexual activity.

Not a few heterosexual males are erotically aroused in contemplating the possibilities of two females in a homosexual relation; and the opinion that females are involved in such relationships more frequently than males may represent wishful thinking on the part of such heterosexual males. Psychoanalysts may also see in it an attempt among males to justify or deny their own homosexual interests.

The considerable amount of discussion and bantering which goes on among males in regard to their own sexual activities, the interest which many males show in their own genitalia and in the genitalia of other males, the amount of exhibitionistic display which so many males put on in locker rooms, in shower rooms, at swimming pools, and at informal swimming holes, the male's interest in photographs and drawings of genitalia and sexual action, in erotic fiction which describes male as well as female sexual prowess, and in toilet wall inscriptions portraying male genitalia and male genital functions, may reflect homosexual interests which are only infrequently found in female histories. The institutions which have developed around male homosexual interests include cafes, taverns, nightclubs, public baths, gymnasia, swimming pools, physical culture and more specifically homosexual magazines, and organized homosexual discussion groups; they rarely have any counterpart among females. Many of these male institutions, such as the homosexually oriented baths and gymnasia, are of ancient historic origin, but there do not seem to have been such institutions for females at any time in history. The street and institutionalized homosexual prostitution which is everywhere available for males, in all parts of the world, is rarely available for females, anywhere in the world. All of these differences between female and male homosexuality depend on basic psychosexual differences between the two sexes.

■ ■ ■

♦

BORN OR BRED?

Newsweek

Until the age of 28, Doug Barnett[1] was a practicing heterosexual. He was vaguely attracted to men, but with nurturing parents, a lively interest in sports and appropriate relations with women, he had little reason to question his proclivities. Then an astonish-

---

1. Not his real name.

David Gelman, *Born Or Bred?*, NEWSWEEK, February 24, 1992, at 46.

ing thing happened: his identical twin brother "came out" to him, revealing he was gay. Barnett, who believed sexual orientation is genetic, was bewildered. He recalls thinking, "If this is inherited and we're identical twins — what's going on here?" To find out, he thought he should try sex with men. When he did, he says, "The bells went off, for the first time. Those homosexual encounters were more fulfilling." A year later both twins told their parents they were gay.

Simon LeVay knew he was homosexual by the time he was 12. Growing up bookish, in England, he fit the "sissy boy" profile limned by psychologists: an aversion to rough sports, a strong attachment to his mother, a hostile relationship with his father. It was, LeVay acknowledges, the perfect Freudian recipe for homosexuality — only he was convinced Freud had cause and effect backward: hostile fathers didn't make some gay; fathers turned hostile because the sons were "unmasculine" to begin with.

Last year, LeVay, now a neuro-scientist at the Salk Institute in La Jolla, California, got a chance to examine his hunch up close. What he found is still reverberating among scientists and may have a profound impact on how the rest of us think about homosexuality. Scanning the brains of 41 cadavers, including 19 homosexual males, LeVay determined that a tiny area believed to control sexual activity was less than half the size in the gay men than in the heterosexuals. It was perhaps the first direct evidence of what some gays have long contended — that whether or not they choose to be different, they are born different.

Doug Barnett, meanwhile, got an opportunity to make his own contribution to the case. Two years ago he was recruited for an ambitious study of homosexuality in twins, undertaken by psychologist Michael Bailey, of Northwestern University, and psychiatrist Richard Pillard, of the Boston University School of Medicine. Published last December, only months after LeVay's work, the results showed that if one identical twin is gay, the other is almost three times more likely to be gay than if the twins are fraternal — suggesting that something in the identical twins' shared genetic makeup affected their sexual orientation.

In both studies, the implications are potentially huge. For decades, scientists and the public at large have debated whether homosexuals are born or made — whether their sexual orientation is the result of a genetic roll of the dice or a combination of formative factors in their upbringing. If it turns out, indeed, that homosexuals are born that way, it could undercut the animosity gays have had to contend with for centuries. "It would reduce being gay to something like being left-handed, which is in fact all that it is," says gay San Francisco journalist and author Randy Shilts.

But instead of resolving the debate, the studies may well have intensified it. Some scientists profess not to be surprised at all by LeVay's finding of brain differences. "Of course it [sexual orientation] is in the brain," says Johns Hopkins University psychologist John Money, sometimes called the dean of American sexologists. "The real question is, When did it get there? Was it prenatal, neonatal, during childhood, puberty? That we do not know."

Others are sharply critical of the Bailey-Pillard study. Instead of proving the genetics argument, they think it only confirms the obvious: that twins are apt to have the same sort of shaping influences. "In order for such a study to be at all meaningful, you'd have to look at twins raised apart," says Anne Fausto Stirling, a developmental biologist at Brown University in Providence, Rhode Island, "It's such badly interpreted genetics."

In the gay community itself, many welcome the indication that gayness begins in the chromosomes. Theoretically, it could gain them the civil-rights protections accorded any "natural" minority, in which the legal linchpin is the question of an "immutable" characteristic. Moreover, it could lift the burden of self-blame from their parents. "A genetic component in sexual orientation says, 'This is not a fault, and it's not your fault'," says Pillard.

Yet the intimation that an actual gene for gayness might be found causes some foreboding. If there is a single, identifiable cause, how long before some nerdy genius finds a "cure"? Many scientists say it's naive to think a single gene could account for so complex a behavior as homosexuality. Yet at least three research projects, one of them at the National Institutes of Health, are believed to be searching for a "gay gene" or group of genes. LeVay, for one, thinks a small number of sex genes may be isolated, perhaps within five years: "And that's going to blow society's mind."

For some people, it is not too great a leap from there to Nazi-style eugenics. In the nightmare scenario, once a gay fetus is detected *in utero*, it is aborted, or a genetic switch is "flipped" to ensure its heterosexuality. The gay population simply fades away. Would mothers permit such tampering? Even parents who've come to terms with their child's homosexuality might. "No parent would choose to have a child born with any factor that would make life difficult for him or her," says Laurie Coburn, program director of the Federation of Parents and Friends of Lesbians and Gays (ParentsFLAG).

On this subject, feelings are seldom restrained. But cooler voices can be heard, mainly those of lesbians. Many of them say their choice of lesbianism was as much a feminist statement as a sexual one, so the fuss over origins doesn't interest them. "It's mostly fascinating to heteros," says one gay activist. On the whole, lesbians are warier of the research, and their conspicuous absence from most studies angers them. "It's part of the society's intrinsic sexism," says Penny Perkins, public-education coordinator for Lambda Legal Defense and Education Fund, which works to promote lesbian and gay men's rights. Frances Stevens, editor-in-chief of Deneuve, a lesbian news magazine, admits her personal history supports biological causes; although she came from a whole-

some "Brady Bunch" family, she knew she was gay "from day one." But she is skeptical of the studies, she says. "My response was: If the gay guy's [hypothalamus] is smaller, what's it like for dykes? Is it the same size as a straight male's?" That's something researchers still have to find out.

Gay men have their own reasons to be irate: as they see it, looking for a "cause" of homosexuality implies it is deviant and heterosexuality is the norm. When John De Cecco, professor of psychology at San Francisco State University and editor of the *Journal of Homosexuality*, began one of his classes recently by suggesting students discuss the causes of homosexuality, someone called out, "Who cares?" and the class burst into applause.

All the same, homosexuals must care deeply about how the straight world perceives them. History has taught them that the consequences of those perceptions can be deadly. Over the centuries they have been tolerated or reviled, enfranchised or oppressed. According to John Boswell's 1980 book, *Christianity, Social Tolerance and Homosexuality*, things didn't turn truly nasty until the 13th century, when the church, on the heels of a diatribe from Saint Thomas Aquinas, began to view gays as not only unnatural but dangerous.

In our own century of *sex et lux,* beginning with Sigmund Freud, psychiatrists ascribed male homosexuality to unconscious conflicts and fixations that have their roots in early childhood. (Freud was always foggier on female sexuality.) But that view was officially dropped in 1973, when more stringent diagnostic standards — and the lobbying of gay activists — persuaded the American Psychiatric Association to expunge homosexuality from the list of emotional disorders. The decision was bitterly disputed; 37 percent of APA members voted against it in a 1974 referendum. But younger psychiatrists now are taught that rather than trying to "cure" homosexuals, they should help them feel more comfortable about themselves.

LeVay resolved to look for sex differences in the brain after the slow, wrenching death from AIDS of his companion of twenty-one years. He'd been impressed by a study done by a UCLA graduate student, Laura Allen, working with biologist Robert Gorski, showing that a portion of the hypothalamus in the brains of males was more than twice as large as that of women. LeVay's report, published in the journal *Science* on August 30, 1991, was based on his own yearlong study of the hypothalamus in 41 cadavers, including 19 self-avowed homosexual men, 16 heterosexual men and 6 heterosexual women. All the homosexuals had died of AIDS, as had seven of the heterosexuals — including one of the women. What emerged with almost startling clarity was that, with some exceptions, the cluster of neurons known as INAH 3 (the third interstitial nucleus of the anterior hypothalamus, which LeVay calls "the business end as far as sex goes") was more than twice as large in the heterosexual males as in the homosexuals, whose INAH 3 was around the same size as in the women. In the sensation that greeted the report, its cautious wording was all but ignored. "What I reported was a difference in the brain structure of the hypothalamus," says LeVay. "We can't say on the basis of that what makes people gay or straight. But it opens the door to find the answer to that question."

One of the major criticisms of the study was that AIDS could have affected the brain structure of the homosexual subjects. LeVay has been able to field that one by pointing out that he found no pathology suggesting such damage either in gay or straight men who died of the disease. Later, in fact, he examined the brain of a homosexual who died of lung cancer, and again found INAH 3 much smaller.

The trickier question is whether things might work the other way around: could sexual orientation affect brain structure? Kenneth Klivington, as assistant to the president of the Salk Institute, points to a body of evidence showing that the brain's neural networks reconfigure themselves in response to certain experiences. One fascinating NIH study found that in people reading Braille after becoming blind, the area of the brain controlling the reading finger grew larger. There are also intriguing conundrums in animal brains. In male songbirds, for example, the brain area associated with mating is not only larger than in the female but varies according to the season.

Says Klivington: "From the study of animals, we know that circulating sex hormones in the mother can have a profound effect on the organization of the brain of the fetus. Once the individual is born, the story gets more complex because of the interplay between the brain and experience. It's a feedback loop: the brain influences behavior, behavior shapes experience, experience affects the organization of the brain, and so forth."

LeVay knows he is somewhat vulnerable on that score. Because his subjects were all dead, he knew "regrettably little" about their sexual histories, besides their declared or presumed orientation. "That's a distinct shortcoming of my study," he concedes. Did the gay men play the passive or aggressive roles in sex? Were some bisexual, another variable, and could that have affected their neuron clusters? To find answers, LeVay plans next to study living subjects with the new MRI (magnetic resonance imaging) technology. But he remains convinced that biology is destiny. "If there are environmental influences," he says, "they operate very early in life, at the fetal or early infancy stage, when the brain is still putting itself together. I'm very much skeptical of the idea that sexual orientation is a cultural thing."

The Bailey-Pillard twin study had its own shortcomings. The numbers alone were impressive. The researchers found that of 56 identical twins, 52 percent were both gay, as against 22 percent of fraternal twins, who have somewhat weaker genetic bonds. (Of the adoptive, nongenetically related brothers in the study, only 11 percent were both gay.)

The suggestion of a shared genetic destiny is strong, but many critics have wondered: what about the discordant twins — those where only one was homosexual? Many in the study were not only discordant, but dramatically different.

Most sexuality studies use the Kinsey scale, which rates orientation on a seven-point spectrum from strictly heterosexual to exclusively homosexual. The study found that most of the discordant identical twins were at opposite ends of the Kinsey spectrum. How could two individuals with identical genetic traits and upbringing wind up with totally different sexual orientation? Richard Green, a noted UCLA researcher of homosexuality, says he believes research should focus on that finding, which he deems "astounding." Although Pillard and Bailey are certain that biology plays the dominant role, Bailey acknowledges: "There must be something in the environment to yield the discordant twins."

What that might be is uncertain. None of the usual domineering-mother, distant-father theories has been conclusively shown to determine sexuality. Meanwhile the case for biology has grown stronger. "If you look at all societies," says Frederick Whitam, who has researched homosexuality in cultures as diverse as the United States, Central America and the Philippines, " homosexuality occurs at the same rates with the same kinds of behavior. That suggests something biological going on. The biological evidence has been growing for twenty or more years."

"Something in the environment," "something biological" — the truth is, the nature/nurture argument is no longer as polarized as it once was. Scientists are beginning to realize there is a complex interplay between the two, still to be explored. June Reinisch, director of the Kinsey Institute, prefers to think we are only "flavored, not programmed." Genetics, she says, only give us "a range of outcomes."

Should it really matter to gays what makes them gay? Whitam says it does matter. In a 1989 study of attitudes toward gays in four different societies, those who believed homosexuals "were born that way" represented a minority but were also the least homophobic. Observes Whitam: "There is a tendency for people, when told that homosexuality is biological, to heave a sign of relief. It relieves the families and homosexuals of guilt. It also means that society doesn't have to worry about things like gay teachers."

For the most part, gays remain doubtful that even the strongest evidence of biological origins will cut much ice with confirmed homophobes. Many find the assumption naive. "Our organization considers the studies useless," says Dr. Howard Grossman, a gay doctor who heads New York Physicians for Human Rights. "It's just like the military — you can show them a thousand studies that show gay soldiers aren't a security risk and they still don't care."

The doctor's pessimism is not unwarranted. Jacquelyn Holt Park, author of a moving novel about the sorrows of growing up lesbian in the sexually benighted 1940s and '50s, is just back from a 9,000-mile book tour where she was astonished to find how little has changed. "There are talk shows," says Park, "where fundamentalists and the like still say [homosexuality] is an abomination, it's vile. They said, 'You're not black, blacks can't change their color, but you can change.' I guess these new studies might address some of those feelings."

Even within the enlightened ranks of the American Psychoanalytic Association there is still some reluctance to let homosexual analysts practice. As arrested cases themselves, the argument goes, they are ill-equipped to deal with developmental problems. The belief that homosexuality can and should be "cured" persists in some quarters of the profession.

Others are exasperated by that view. Richard Isay, chairperson of the APA's Committee on Gay, Lesbian and Bisexual Issues, is convinced analysis can be more damaging than beneficial to gays. "I still see many gay men who come to me after they've been in analysis where the therapist has been trying to change their orientation," he says. "That's extremely harmful to the self-esteem of a gay man." Isay thinks the approach, instead, should be to try to clear away "roadblocks" that may interfere with a gay's ability to function.

Perhaps the most voluble spokesman for the "fix it" school is Charles Socarides, a New York City analyst who claims a flourishing practice in turning troubled homosexuals into "happy, fulfilled heterosexuals." To Socarides, the only biological evidence is "that we're anatomically made to go in male-female pairs." Thus he reconstructs patients' lives to learn why they can't mate with opposite-sex partners. There can be many reasons, he says: "abdicating fathers, difficult wives, marital disruptions." From there, he "opens up the path" to hetero happiness, for which, he says, one gratified customer cabled him recently: "The eagle has landed."

Some psychiatrists still see the removal of homosexuality from the official list of emotional disorders as a mistake. (Instead, it was innocuously identified as "sexual orientation disturbance.") "Psychology and psychiatry have essentially abandoned a whole population of people who feel dissatisfied with their feelings of homosexuality," says psychologist Joseph Nicolosi, author of *Reparative Therapy of Male Homosexuality* (Jason Aronson: New York, 1991). In graduate school, says Nicolosi, he found the stance was that if a client came in complaining about his gayness, the therapist's job was to teach him to accept it. "It was like the old joke of the patient who tells the doctor his arm hurts when he bends it and the doctor advises him not to bend it."

Nicolosi tries to do more than that for his patients, most of them men in their 20s and 30s who are unhappy with their homosexuality. As director of the Thomas Aquinas Psychology Clinic in Encino, California, he tries to bolster his patients' sense of male identity, which he sees as crucial to their orientation. The biological evidence is inconclusive, Nicolosi says; there is much more proof for familial causes of homosexuality. "Research has shown repeatedly that a poor relationship with a distant, aloof father and an overpossessive, domineering mother could cause homosexuality in males," he says.

In fact, some of that research, dating back to the 1950s, has been discredited because of faulty techniques, among other problems. Nicolosi is at any rate modest in his own claims. No cures as such, but "a diminishment of homosexual feelings" to the point where some patients can marry and have families. How long is treatment? "Probably a lifetime process," he says.

With the debate over origins still going strong, comes one more exhibit in evidence. Recently, Bailey and Pillard divulged just a tidbit from their not-yet-published study of lesbian twins. Finding enough females for the study took twice as long as their earlier project, says Bailey, but apparently it was worth the effort. "If there are genes for homosexuality, they're not gender blind," he says. Lesbians in the study had more lesbian sisters than they did gay brothers.

Nature? Nurture? Perhaps the most appropriate answer comes from Evelyn Hooker, who showed in an important 1950s study that it is impossible to distinguish heterosexuals from homosexuals on psychological tests. Hooker takes the long view of the search for origins. "Why do we want to know the cause?" she asks. "It's a mistake to hope that we will be able to modify or change homosexuality . . . If we understand its nature and accept it as a given, then we come much closer to the kind of attitudes which will make it possible for homosexuals to lead a decent life in society." The psychiatric profession heeded Hooker when it stopped calling homosexuality an illness. At eighty-four, her voice has grown fainter, but the rest of us could do worse than listen to her now.

II. IDENTITY

♦

REVOLUTIONS, UNIVERSALS, AND SEXUAL CATEGORIES
John Boswell

Do categories exist because humans recognize real distinctions in the world around them, or are categories arbitrary conventions, simply names for things that have categorical force because humans agree to use them in certain ways? The two traditional sides in this controversy, which is called "the problem of universals," are "realists" and "nominalists." Realists consider categories to be the footprints of reality ("universals"): They exist because humans perceive a real order in the universe and name it. The order is present without human observation, according to realists; the human contribution is simply the naming and describing of it. Most scientists operate — tacitly — in a realist mode, on the assumption that they are discovering, not inventing, the relationships within the physical world. The scientific method is, in fact, predicated on realist attitudes. On the other hand, the philosophical structure of the modern West is closer to nominalism: the belief that categories are only the names (Latin: *nomina*) of things agreed upon by humans, and that the "order" people see is their creation rather than their perception. Most modern philosophy and language theory is essentially nominalist, and even the more theoretical sciences are nominalist to some degree: In biology, for example, taxonomists disagree strongly about whether they are discovering (realists) or inventing (nominalists) distinctions among phyla, genera, species, etc. (When, for example, a biologist announces that bats, being mammals, are "more closely related to" humans than to birds, is he expressing some real relationship, present in nature and detected by humans, or is he employing an arbitrary convention, something that helps humans organize and sort information but that bears no "truth" or significance beyond this utility?)

This seemingly arcane struggle now underlies an epistemological controversy raging among those studying the history of gay people. The "universals" in this case are categories of sexual preference or orientation (the difference is crucial). Nominalists ("social constructionists" in the current debate) in the matter aver that categories of sexual preference and behavior are created by humans and human societies. Whatever reality they have is the consequence of the power they exert in those societies and the socialization processes that make them seem real to persons influenced by them. People consider themselves "homosexual" or "heterosexual" because they are induced to believe that humans are either "homosexual" or "heterosexual." Left to their own devices, without such processes or socialization, people would simply be sexual. The category "heterosexuality," in other words, does not

John Boswell, *Revolutions, Universals, And Sexual Categories*, in HIDDEN FROM HISTORY: RECLAIMING THE GAY AND LESBIAN PAST 17 (Martin Duberman, et al. eds., 1989).

so much describe a pattern of behavior inherent in human beings as it creates and establishes it.

Realists ("essentialists") hold that this is not the case. Humans are, they insist, differentiated sexually. Many categories might be devised to characterize human sexual taxonomy, some more or less apt than others, but the accuracy of human perceptions does not affect reality. The heterosexual/homosexual dichotomy exists in speech and thought because it exists in reality: It was not invented by sexual taxonomists, but observed by them.

Neither of these positions is usually held absolutely: Most nominalists would be willing to admit that some aspects of sexuality are present, and might be distinguished, without direction from society. And most realists are happy to admit that the same real phenomenon might be described by various systems of categorization, some more accurate and helpful than others. One might suppose that "moderate nominalists" and "moderate realists" could therefore engage in a useful dialogue on those areas where they agree and, by careful analysis of their differences, promote discussion and understanding of these issues.

Political ramifications hinder this. Realism has historically been viewed by the nominalist camp as conservative, if not reactionary, in its implicit recognition of the value and/or immutability of the status quo; and nominalism has generally been regarded by realists as an obscurantist radical ideology designed more to undercut and subvert human values than to clarify them. Precisely these political overtones can be seen to operate today in scholarly debate over issues of sexuality. The efforts of sociobiology to demonstrate an evolutionary etiology of homosexuality have been vehemently denounced by many who regard the enterprise as reactionary realism, an effort to persuade people that social categories are fixed and unchangeable, while on the other side, psychiatric "cures" of homosexuality are bitterly resented by many as the cynical folly of

nominalist pseudoscience: Convince someone he shouldn't want to be a homosexual, persuade him to think of himself as a "heterosexual," and — presto! — he is a heterosexual. The category is the person.

Whether or not there are "homosexual" and "heterosexual" persons, as opposed to persons called "homosexual" or "heterosexual" by society, is obviously a matter of substantial import to the gay community, since it brings into question the nature and even the existence of such a community. It is, moreover, of substantial epistemological urgency to nearly all of society, and the gravity and extent of this can be seen in the case of the problems it creates for history and historians.

The history of minorities poses ferocious difficulties: censorship and distortion, absence or destruction of records, the difficulty of writing about essentially personal and private aspects of human feelings and behavior, problems of definition, political dangers attendant on choosing certain subjects, etc. But if the nominalists are correct and the realists wrong, the problems in regard to the history of gay people are of an entirely different order: If the categories "homosexual/heterosexual" and "gay/straight" are the inventions of particular societies rather than real aspects of the human psyche, there is no gay history. If "homosexuality" exists only when and where people are persuaded to believe in it, "homosexual" persons will have a "history" only in those particular societies and cultures.

In its most extreme form, this nominalist view has argued that only early modern and contemporary industrial societies have produced "homosexuality," and it is futile and misguided to look for "homosexuality" in earlier human history.

> What we call "homosexuality" (in the sense of the distinguishing traits of "homosexuals"), for example, was not considered a unified set of acts, much less a set of qualities defining particular persons, in pre-capitalist societies .

. . Heterosexuals and homosexuals are involved in social "roles" and attitudes which pertain to a particular society, modern capitalism.[2]

If this position is sustained, it will permanently alter, for better or worse, the nature and extent of minority history.

Clearly it has much to recommend it. No characteristics interact with the society around them uniformly through time. Perceptions of, reactions to, and social response regarding blackness, blindness, left-handedness, Jewishness, or any other distinguishing (or distinguished) aspect of persons or peoples must necessarily vary as widely as the social circumstance in which they occur, and for this reason alone it could be reasonably argued that being Jewish, black, blind, left-handed, etc., is essentially different from one age and place to another. In some cultures, for example, Jews are categorized chiefly as an ethnic minority; in others they are not or are not perceived to be ethnically distinct from the peoples around them, and are distinguished solely by their religious beliefs. Similarly, in some societies anyone darker than average is considered "black"; in others, a complex and highly technical system of racial categorization classes some persons as black even when they are lighter in color than many "whites." In both cases, moreover, the differences in attitudes held by the majority must affect profoundly the self-perception of the minority itself, and its patterns of life and behavior are in all probability notably different from those of "black" or "Jewish" people in other circumstances.

There can be no question that if minority history is to merit respect it must carefully weigh such fundamental subtleties of context: Merely cataloguing references to "Jews" or to "Blacks" may distort more than it reveals of human history if due attention is not paid to the meaning, in their historical

setting, of such words and the concepts to which they apply. Do such reservations, on the other hand, uphold the claim that categories such as "Jew," "black," or "gay" are not diachronic and can not, even with apposite qualification, be applied to ages and times other than those in which the terms themselves were used in precisely their modern sense? Extreme realists, without posing the question, have assumed the answer was no; extreme nominalists seem to be saying yes.

The question can not be addressed intelligently without first noting three points. First, the positions are not in fact as clearly separable as this schema implies. It could be well argued, for example, that Padgug, Weeks, et al., are in fact extreme *realists* in assuming that *modern* homosexuality is not simply one of a series of conventions designated under the same rubric, but is instead a "real" phenomenon that has no "real" antecedent in human history. Demonstrate to us the "reality" of this homosexuality, their opponents might legitimately demand, and prove to us that it has a unity and cohesiveness that justifies your considering it a single, unparalleled entity rather than a loose congeries of behaviors. Modern scientific literature increasingly assumes that what is at issue is not "homosexuality" but "homosexualities"; if these disparate patterns of sexuality can be grouped together under a single heading in the present, why make such a fuss about a diachronic grouping?

Second, adherents of both schools fall prey to anachronism. Nearly all of the most prominent nominalists are historians of the modern U.S., modern Britain, or modern Europe, and it is difficult to eschew the suspicion that they are concentrating their search where the light is best rather than where the answers are to be found, and formulating a theoretical position to justify their approach. On the other hand, nominalist objections are

2.   Robert A. Padgug, *Sexual Matters: On Conceptualizing Sexuality in History, in* HIDDEN FROM HISTORY: RECLAIMING THE GAY AND LESBIAN PAST 54, 59 (Martin Duberman et al. eds., 1989).

in part a response to an extreme realist position that has been predicated on the unquestioned, unproven, and overwhelmingly unlikely assumption that exactly the same categories and patterns of sexuality have always existed, pure and unchanged by the systems of thought and behavior in which they were enmeshed.

Third, both extremes appear to be paralyzed by words. The nominalists are determined that the same word can not apply to a wide range of meaning and still be used productively in scholarly discourse: In order to have a meaning, "gay," for example, must be applied only as the speaker would apply it, with all the precise ramifications he associates with it. This insistence follows understandably from the implicit assumption that the speaker is generating the category himself, or in concert with certain contemporaries, rather than receiving it from a human experience of great longevity and adjusting it to fit his own understanding. Realist extremists, conversely, assume that lexical equivalence betokens experiential equality, and that the occurrence of a word that "means" "homosexual" demonstrates the existence of "homosexuality," as the modern realist understands it, at the time the text was composed.

It is my aim to circumvent these difficulties as far as possible in the following remarks, and my hope that in so doing I may reduce the rhetorical struggle over "universals" in these matters and promote thereby more useful dialogue among the partisans. Let it be agreed at the outset that something can be discussed, by modern historians or ancient writers, without being named or defined. (Ten people in a room might argue endlessly about proper definitions of "blue" and "red," but could probably agree instantly whether a given object was one or the other [or a combination of both].) "Gravity" offers a useful historical example. A nominalist position would be that gravity did not exist before Newton invented it, and a nominalist historian might be able to mount a convincing case that there is no mention of gravity in any texts before Newton. "Nonsense," realists would object. "The Latin *gravitas*, which is common in Roman literature, describes the very properties of matter Newton called 'gravity.' Of course gravity existed before Newton discovered it."

Both, of course, are wrong. Lack of attention to something in historical sources can in no wise be taken as evidence of its nonexistence, and discovery can not be equated with creation or invention. But *gravitas* does not mean "gravity"; it means "heaviness," and the two are not at all the same thing. Noting that objects have heaviness is entirely different from understanding the nature and operations of gravity. For adherents of these two positions to understand each other each would have to abandon specific nomenclature, and agree instead on questions to be asked of the sources. If the proper questions were addressed, the nominalist could easily be persuaded that the sources prove that gravity existed before Newton, in the sense that the operations of the force now designated gravity are well chronicled in nearly all ancient literature. And the realist could be persuaded that despite this fact the nature of gravity was not clearly articulated — whether or not it was apprehended — before Newton.

The problem is rendered more difficult in the present case by the fact that the equivalent of gravity has not yet been discovered: There is still no essential agreement in the scientific community about the nature of human sexuality. Whether humans are "homosexual" or "heterosexual" or "bisexual" by birth, by training, by choice, or at all is still an open question. Neither realists nor nominalists can, therefore, establish any clear correlation — positive or negative — between modern sexuality and its ancient counterparts. But it is still possible to discuss whether modern conceptualizations of sexuality are novel and completely socially relative, or correspond to constants of human epistemology which can be documented in the past.

POSTSCRIPT

This essay was written five years ago, and several of the points it raises now require clarification or revision. I would no longer characterize the constructionist-essentialist controversy as a "debate" in any strict sense: One of its ironies is that no one involved in it actually identifies him- or herself as an "essentialist," although constructionists (of whom, in contrast, there are many) sometimes so label other writers. Even when applied by its opponents the label seems to fit extremely few contemporary scholars. This fact is revealing, and provides a basis for understanding the controversy more accurately not as a dialogue between two schools of thought, but as a revisionist (and largely one-sided) critique of assumptions believed to underlie traditional historiography. This understanding is not unrelated to my nominalist/realist analogy: One might describe constructionism (with some oversimplification) as a nominalist rejection of a tendency to "realism" in the traditional historiography of sexuality. The latter treated "homosexuality" as a diachronic, empirical entity (not quite a "universal," but "real" apart from social structures bearing on it); constructionists regard it as a culturally dependent phenomenon or, as some would have it, not a "real" phenomenon at all. It is not, nonetheless, a debate, since no current historians consciously defend an essentialist point of view.

Second, although it is probably still accurate to say that "most" constructionists are historians of the nineteenth and twentieth centuries, a number of classicists have now added their perspective to constructionist theory. This has broadened and deepened the discussion, although, strikingly, few if any historians of periods between Periclean Athens and the late nineteenth century articulate constructionist views.

Third, my own position, perhaps never well understood, has changed. In my book *Christianity, Social Tolerance and Homosexuality* I defined "gay persons" as those "conscious of erotic inclination toward their own gender as a distinguishing characteristic." It was the supposition of the book that such persons have been widely and identifiably present in Western society at least since Greco-Roman times, and this prompted many constructionists to label the work "essentialist." I would now define "gay persons" more simply as those whose erotic interest is predominantly directed toward their own gender (i.e., regardless of how conscious they are of this as a distinguishing characteristic). This is the sense in which, I believe, it is used by most American speakers, and although experts in a field may well wish to employ specialized language, when communicating with the public it seems to me counterproductive to use common words in senses different from or opposed to their ordinary meanings.

In this sense, I would still argue that there have been "gay persons" in most Western societies. It is not clear to me that this is an "essentialist" position. Even if societies formulate or create "sexualities" that are highly particular in some ways, it might happen that different societies would construct similar ones, as they often construct political or class structures similar enough to be subsumed under the same rubric (democracy, oligarchy, proletariat, aristocracy, etc. — all of which are both particular and general).

Most constructionist arguments assume that essentialist positions necessarily entail a further supposition: that society does not create erotic feelings, but only acts on them. Some other force — genes, psychological forces, etc. — creates "sexuality," which is essentially independent of culture. This was not a working hypothesis of *Christianity, Social Tolerance and Homosexuality*. I was and remain agnostic about the origins and etiology of human sexuality.

♦

CAPITALISM AND GAY IDENTITY
John D'Emilio

■ ■ ■

. . . . When the gay liberation movement began at the end of the 1960s, gay men and lesbians had no history that we could use to fashion our goals and strategy. In the ensuing years, in building a movement without a knowledge of our history, we instead invented a mythology. This mythical history drew on personal experience, which we read backward in time. For instance, most lesbians and gay men in the 1960s first discovered their homosexual desires in isolation, unaware of others, and without resources for naming and understanding what they felt. From this experience, we constructed a myth of silence, invisibility, and isolation as the essential characteristics of gay life in the past as well as the present. Moreover, because we faced so many oppressive laws, public policies, and cultural beliefs, we projected this into an image of the abysmal past: until gay liberation, lesbians and gay men were always the victims of systematic, undifferentiated, terrible oppression.

These myths have limited our political perspective. They have contributed, for instance, to an overreliance on a strategy of coming out — if every gay man and lesbian in America came out, gay oppression would end — and have allowed us to ignore the institutionalized ways in which homophobia and heterosexism are reproduced. They have encouraged, at times, an incapacitating despair, especially at moments like the present: How can we unravel a gay oppression so pervasive and unchanging?

There is another historical myth that enjoys nearly universal acceptance in the gay movement, the myth of the "eternal homosexual." The argument runs something like this: gay men and lesbians always were and always will be. We are everywhere; not just now, but throughout history, in all societies and all periods. This myth served a positive political function in the first years of gay liberation. In the early 1970s, when we battled an ideology that either denied our existence or defined us as psychopathic individuals or freaks of nature, it was empowering to assert that "we are everywhere." But in recent years it has confined us as surely as the most homophobic medical theories, and locked our movement in place.

Here I wish to challenge this myth. I want to argue that gay men and lesbians have *not* always existed. Instead, they are a product of history, and have come into existence in a specific historical era. Their emergence is associated with the relations of capitalism; it has been the historical development of capitalism — more specifically, its free labor system — that has allowed large numbers of men and women in the late twentieth century to call themselves gay, to see themselves as part of a community of similar men and women, and to organize politically on the basis of that identity. . . .

■ ■ ■

The expansion of capital and the spread of wage labor have effected a profound transformation in the structure and functions of the nuclear family, the ideology of family life, and the meaning of heterosexual rela-

John D'Emilio, *Capitalism And Gay Identity, in* Powers Of Desire: The Politics of Sexuality 100 (Ann Snitow et al. eds., 1983).

tions. It is these changes in the family that are most directly linked to the appearance of a collective gay life.

The white colonists in seventeenth-century New England established villages structured around a household economy, composed of family units that were basically self-sufficient, independent, and patriarchal. Men, women, and children farmed land owned by the male head of household. Although there was a division of labor between men and women, the family was truly an independent unit of production: the survival of each member depended on the co-operation of all. The home was a workplace where women processed raw farm products into food for daily consumption, where they made clothing, soap, and candles, and where husbands wives, and children worked together to produce the goods they consumed.

By the nineteenth century, this system of household production was in decline. In the Northeast, as merchant capitalists invested the money accumulated through trade in the production of goods, wage labor became more common. Men and women were drawn out of the largely self-sufficient household economy of the colonial era into a capitalist system of free labor. For women in the nineteenth century, working for wages rarely lasted beyond marriage; for men, it became a permanent condition.

The family was thus no longer an independent unit of production. But although no longer independent, the family was still interdependent. Because capitalism had not expanded very far, because it had not yet taken over — or socialized — the production of consumer goods, women still performed necessary productive labor in the home. Many families no longer produced grain, but wives still baked into bread the flour they bought with their husbands' wages; or, when they purchased yarn or cloth, they still made clothing for their families. By the mid-1800s, capitalism had destroyed the economic self-sufficiency of many families, but not the mutual dependence of the members.

This transition away from the household family-based economy to a fully developed capitalist free labor economy occurred very slowly, over almost two centuries. As late as 1920, 50 percent of the U.S. population lived in communities of fewer than 2,500 people. The vast majority of blacks in the early twentieth century lived outside the free labor economy, in a system of share-cropping and tenancy that rested on the family. Not only did independent farming as a way of life still exist for millions of Americans, but even in towns and small cities women continued to grow and process food, make clothing, and engage in other kinds of domestic production.

But for those people who felt the brunt of these changes, the family took on new significance as an affective unit, an institution that produced not only goods but emotional satisfaction and happiness. By the 1920s among the white middle class, the ideology surrounding the family described it as the means through which men and women formed satisfying, mutually enhancing relationships and created an environment that nurtured children. The family became the setting for a "personal life," sharply distinguished from the public world of work and production.

The meaning of heterosexual relations also changed. In colonial New England, the birthrate averaged over seven children per woman of childbearing age. Men and women needed the labor of children. Producing offspring was as necessary for survival as producing grain. Sex was harnessed to procreation. The Puritans did not celebrate *hetero*sexuality but rather marriage; they condemned *all* sexual expression outside the marriage bond and did not differentiate sharply between sodomy and heterosexual fornication.

By the 1970s, however, the birthrate had dropped to under two. With the exception of the post-World War II baby boom, the decline has been continuous for two centuries, paralleling the spread of capitalist relations of production. It occurred even when access to contraceptive devices and abortion was systematically curtailed. The decline has included every segment of the population — urban and rural families, blacks and whites, ethnics and WASPs, the middle class and the working class.

As wage labor spread and production became socialized, then, it became possible to release sexuality from the "imperative" to procreate. Ideologically, heterosexual expression came to be a means of establishing intimacy, promoting happiness, and experiencing pleasure. In divesting the household of its economic independence and fostering the separation of sexuality from procreation, capitalism has created conditions that allow some men and women to organize a personal life around their erotic/emotional attraction to their own sex. It has made possible the formation of urban communities of lesbians and gay men and, more recently, of a politics based on a sexual identity.

Evidence from colonial New England court records and church sermons indicates that male and female homosexual behavior existed in the seventeenth century. Homosexual *behavior*, however, is different from homosexual *identity*. There was, quite simply, no "social space" in the colonial system of production that allowed men and women to be gay. Survival was structured around participation in a nuclear family. There were certain homosexual acts — sodomy among men, "lewdness" among women — in which individuals engaged, but family was so pervasive that colonial society lacked even the category of homosexual or lesbian to describe a person. It is quite possible that some men and women experienced a stronger attraction to their own sex than to the opposite sex — in fact, some colonial court cases refer to men who persisted in their "unnatural" attractions — but one could not fashion out of that preference a way of life. Colonial Massachusetts even had laws prohibiting unmarried adults from living outside family units.

By the second half of the nineteenth century, this situation was noticeably changing as the capitalist system of free labor took hold. Only when *individuals* began to make their living through wage labor, instead of as parts of an interdependent family unit, was it possible for homosexual desire to coalesce into a personal identity — an identity based on the ability to remain outside the heterosexual family and to construct a personal life based on attraction to one's own sex. By the end of the century, a class of men and women existed who recognized their erotic interest in their own sex, saw it as a trait that set them apart from the majority, and sought others like themselves. These early gay lives came from a wide social spectrum: civil servants and business executives, department store clerks and college professors, factory operatives, ministers, lawyers, cooks, domestics, hoboes, and the idle rich: men and women, black and white, immigrant and native born.

In this period, gay men and lesbians began to invent ways of meeting each other and sustaining a group life. Already, in the early twentieth century, large cities contained male homosexual bars. Gay men staked out cruising areas, such as Riverside Drive in New York City and Lafayette Park in Washington. In St. Louis and the nation's capital, annual drag balls brought together large numbers of black gay men. Public bathhouses and YMCAs became gathering spots for male homosexuals. Lesbians formed literary societies and private social clubs. Some working-class women "passed" as men to obtain better paying jobs and lived with other women — lesbian couples who appeared to the world as husband and wife. Among the faculties of women's colleges, in the settlement houses, and in the professional associations and clubs that women formed one could find lifelong intimate relationships supported by a web of lesbian friends. By the 1920s and 1930s, large cities such as New

York and Chicago contained lesbian bars. These patterns of living could evolve because capitalism allowed individuals to survive beyond the confines of the family.

Simultaneously, ideological definitions of homosexual behavior changed. Doctors developed theories about homosexual*ity*, describing it as a condition, something that was inherent in a person, a part of his or her "nature." These theories did not represent scientific breakthroughs, elucidations of previously undiscovered areas of knowledge; rather, they were an ideological response to a new way of organizing one's personal life. The popularization of the medical model, in turn, affected the consciousness of the women and men who experienced homosexual desire, so that they came to define themselves through their erotic life.

These new forms of gay identity and patterns of group life also reflected the differentiation of people according to gender, race, and class that is so pervasive in capitalist societies. Among whites, for instance, gay men have traditionally been more visible than lesbians. This partly stems from the division between the public male sphere and the private female sphere. Streets, parks, and bars, especially at night, were "male space." Yet the greater visibility of white gay men also reflected their larger numbers. The Kinsey studies of the 1940s and 1950s found significantly more men than women with predominantly homosexual histories, a situation caused, I would argue, by the fact that capitalism had drawn far more men than women into the labor force, and at higher wages. Men could more easily construct a personal life independent of attachments to the opposite sex, whereas women were more likely to remain economically dependent on men. Kinsey also found a strong positive correlation between years of schooling and lesbian activity. College-educated white women, far more able than their working-class sisters to support themselves, could survive more easily without intimate relationships with men.

Among working-class immigrants in the early twentieth century, closely knit kin networks and an ethic of family solidarity placed constraints on individual autonomy that made gayness a difficult option to pursue. In contrast, for reasons not altogether clear, urban black communities appeared relatively tolerant of homosexuality. The popularity in the 1920s and 1930s of songs with lesbian and gay male themes — "B. D. Woman," "Prove It on Me," "Sissy Man," "Fairey Blues" — suggests an openness about homosexual expression at odds with the mores of whites. Among men in the rural West in the 1940s, Kinsey found extensive incidence of homosexual behavior, but, in contrast with the men in large cities, little consciousness of gay identity. Thus even as capitalism exerted a homogenizing influence by gradually transforming more individuals into wage laborers and separating them from traditional communities, different groups of people were also affected in different ways.

The decisions of particular men and women to act on their erotic/emotional preference for the same sex, along with the new consciousness that this preference made them different, led to the formation of an urban subculture of gay men and lesbians. Yet at least through the 1930s this subculture remained rudimentary, unstable, and difficult to find. How, then, did the complex, well-developed gay community emerge that existed by the time the gay liberation movement exploded? The answer is to be found during World War II, a time when the cumulative changes of several decades coalesced into a qualitatively new shape.

The war severely disrupted traditional patterns of gender relations and sexuality, and temporarily created a new erotic situation conducive to homosexual expression. It plucked millions of young men and women, whose sexual identities were just forming, out of their homes, out of towns and small cities, out of the heterosexual environment of the family, and dropped them into sex-segregated situations — as GIs, as WACs and WAVEs, in same-sex rooming houses for women workers who relocated to seek employment. The war freed millions of men and women from the settings where heterosexuality was normally imposed. For men and women already gay, it provided an opportunity to meet people like themselves. Others could become gay because of the temporary freedom to explore sexuality that the war provided.

■ ■ ■

The gay men and women of the 1940s were pioneers. Their decisions to act on their desires formed the underpinnings of an urban subculture of gay men and lesbians. Throughout the 1950s and 1960s, the gay subculture grew and stabilized so that people coming out then could more easily find other gay women and men than in the past. Newspapers and magazines published articles describing gay male life. Literally hundreds of novels with lesbian themes were published. Psychoanalysts complained about the new ease with which their gay male patients found sexual partners. And the gay subculture was not just to be found in the largest cities. Lesbian and gay male bars existed in places like Worcester, Massachusetts, and Buffalo, New York; in Columbia, South Carolina, and Des Moines, Iowa. Gay life in the 1950s and 1960s became a nationwide phenomenon. By the time of the Stonewall Riots in New York City in 1969 — the event that ignited the gay liberation movement — our situation was hardly one of silence, invisibility, and isolation. A massive, grass-roots liberation movement could form almost overnight precisely because communities of lesbians and gay men existed.

Although gay community was a precondition for a mass movement, the oppression of lesbians and gay men was the force that propelled the movement into existence. As the subculture expanded and grew more visible in the post-World War II era, oppression by the state intensified, becoming more systematic and inclusive. The Right scapegoated "sexual perverts" during the McCarthy era. Eisenhower imposed a total ban on the employment of gay women and men by the federal government and government contractors. Purges of lesbians and homosexuals from the military rose sharply. The FBI instituted widespread surveillance of gay meeting places and of lesbian and gay organizations, such as the Daughters of Bilitis and the Mattachine Society. The Post Office placed tracers on the correspondence of gay men and passed evidence of homosexual activity on to employers. Urban vice squads invaded private homes, made sweeps of lesbian and gay male bars, entrapped gay men in public places, and fomented local witch hunts. The danger involved in being gay rose even as the possibilities of being gay were enhanced. Gay liberation was a response to this contradiction.

■ ■ ■

. . . . [A]s I argued earlier, capitalism has gradually undermined the material basis of the nuclear family by taking away the economic functions that cemented the ties between family members. As more adults have been drawn into the free labor system, and as capital has expanded its sphere until it produces as commodities most goods and services we need for our survival, the forces that propelled men and women into families and kept them there have weakened. [At the same time,] the ideology of capitalist society has enshrined the family as the source of love, affection, and emotional security, the place where our need for stable, intimate human relationships is satisfied.

This elevation of the nuclear family to preeminence in the sphere of personal life is not accidental. Every society needs structures for reproduction and childrearing, but the possibilities are not limited to the nuclear family. Yet the privatized family fits well with capitalist relations of production. Capitalism has socialized production while maintaining that the products of socialized labor belong to the owners of private property. In many ways, childrearing has also been progressively socialized over the last two centuries, with schools, the media, peer groups, and employers taking over functions that once belonged to parents. Nevertheless, capitalist society maintains that reproduction and childrearing are private tasks, that children "belong" to parents, who exercise the rights of ownership. Ideologically, capitalism drives people into heterosexual families, each generation comes of age having internalized a heterosexist model of intimacy and personal relationships. Materially, capitalism weakens the bonds that once kept families together so that their members experience a growing instability in the place they have come to expect happiness and emotional security. Thus, while capitalism has knocked the material foundation away from family life, lesbians, gay men, and heterosexual feminists have become the scapegoats for the social instability of the system.

■ ■ ■

I have argued that lesbian and gay identity and communities are historically created, the result of a process of capitalist development that has spanned many generations. A corollary of this argument is that we are *not* a fixed social minority composed for all time of a certain percentage of the population. *There are more of us* than one hundred years ago, more of us than forty years ago. And there may very well be more gay men and lesbians in the future. Claims made by gays and nongays that sexual orientation is fixed at an early age, that large numbers of visible gay men and lesbians in society, the media, and the

schools will have no influence on the sexual identity of the young, are wrong. Capitalism has created the material conditions for homosexual desire to express itself as a central component of some individuals' lives; now, our political movements are changing consciousness, creating the ideological conditions that make it easier for people to make that choice.

■ ■ ■

I have also argued that capitalism has led to the separation of sexuality from procreation. Human sexual desire need no longer be harnessed to reproductive imperatives, to procreation; its expression has increasingly entered the realm of choice. Lesbians and homosexuals most clearly embody the potential of this split, since our gay relationships stand entirely outside a procreative framework. The acceptance of our erotic choices ultimately depends on the degree to which society is willing to affirm sexual expression as a form of play, positive and life-enhancing. Our movement may have begun as the struggle of a "minority," but what we should now be trying to "liberate" is an aspect of the personal lives of all people — sexual expression.

Finally, I have suggested that the relationship between capitalism and the family is fundamentally contradictory. On the one hand, capitalism continually weakens the material foundation of family life, making it possible for individuals to live outside the family, and for a lesbian and gay male identity to develop. On the other, it needs to push men and women into families, at least long enough to reproduce the next generation of workers. The elevation of the family to ideological preeminence guarantees that capitalist society will reproduce not just children, but heterosexism and homophobia. In the most profound sense, capitalism is the problem.

■ ■ ■

♦

COMPULSORY HETEROSEXUALITY
AND LESBIAN EXISTENCE
Adrienne Rich

■ ■ ■

Biologically men have only one innate orientation — a sexual one that draws them to women — while women have two innate orientations, sexual toward men and reproductive toward their young.[1]

I was a woman terribly vulnerable, critical, using femaleness as a sort of standard or yardstick to measure and discard men. Yes — something like that. I was an Anna who invited defeat from men without ever being conscious of it. (But I am conscious of it. And being conscious of it means I shall leave it all behind me and become — but what?) I was stuck fast in an emotion common to women of our time, that can turn them bitter, or Lesbian, or solitary. Yes, that Anna during that time was . . .

[Another blank line across the page:][2]

I

The bias of compulsory heterosexuality through which lesbian experience is perceived on a scale ranging from deviant to abhorrent, or simply rendered invisible, could be illustrated from many other texts than the two just preceding. The assumption made by Rossi, that women are "innately sexually oriented" toward men, or by Lessing, that the lesbian choice is simply an acting-out of bitterness toward men, are by no means theirs alone; they are widely current in literature and in the social sciences.

I am concerned here with two other matters as well: first, how and why women's choice of women as passionate comrades, life partners, co-workers, lovers, tribe, has been crushed, invalidated, forced into hiding and disguise; and second, the virtual or total neglect of lesbian existence in a wide range of writings, including feminist scholarship. Obviously there is a connection here I believe that much feminist theory and criticism is stranded on this shoal.

My organizing impulse is the belief that it is not enough for feminist thought that specifically lesbian texts exist. Any theory or cultural/political creation that treats lesbian

---

1. Alice Rossi, "Children and Work in the Lives of Women," paper delivered at the University of Arizona, Tucson, February, 1976.

2. Doris Lessing, *The Golden Notebook* (1962; New York: Bantam Books, 1977), p. 480.

Adrienne Rich, *Compulsory Heterosexuality and Lesbian Existence, in* POWERS OF DESIRE: THE POLITICS OF SEXUALITY 177 (Ann Snitow et al. eds., 1983).

existence as a marginal or less "natural" phenomenon, as mere "sexual preference," or as the mirror image of either heterosexual or male homosexual relations is profoundly weakened thereby, whatever its other contributions. Feminist theory can no longer afford merely to voice a toleration of "lesbianism" as an "alternative life style," or make token allusion to lesbians. A feminist critique of compulsory heterosexual orientation for women is long overdue. In this exploratory paper, I shall try to show why.

■ ■ ■

II

If women are the earliest sources of emotional caring and physical nurture for both female and male children, it would seem logical, from a feminist perspective at least, to pose the following questions: whether the search for love and tenderness in both sexes does not originally lead toward women; *why in fact women would ever redirect that search*; why species-survival, the means of impregnation, and emotional/erotic relationships should ever have become so rigidly identified with each other; and why such violent strictures should be found necessary to enforce women's total emotional, erotic loyalty and subservience to men. I doubt that enough feminist scholars and theorists have taken the pains to acknowledge the societal forces that wrench women's emotional and erotic energies away from themselves and other women and from woman-identified values. These forces, as I shall try to show, range from literal physical enslavement to the disguising and distorting of possible options.

I do not, myself, assume that mothering-by-women is a "sufficient cause" of lesbian existence. But the issue of mothering-by-women has been much in the air of late, usually accompanied by the view that increased parenting by men would minimize

antagonism between the sexes and equalize the sexual imbalance of power of males over females. These discussions are carried on without reference to compulsory heterosexuality as a phenomenon let alone as an idealogy. I do not wish to psychologize here, but rather to identify sources of male power. I believe large numbers of men could, in fact, undertake child care on a large scale without radically altering the balance of male power in a male-identified society.

■ ■ ■

III

I have chosen to use the terms *lesbian existence* and *lesbian continuum* because the word *lesbianism* has a clinical and limiting ring. *Lesbian existence* suggests both the fact of the historical presence of lesbians and our continuing creation of the meaning of that existence. I mean the term *lesbian continuum* to include a range — through each woman's life and throughout history — of woman-identified experience; not simply the fact that a woman has had or consciously desired genital sexual experience with another woman. If we expand it to embrace many more forms of primary intensity between and among women, including the sharing of a rich inner life, the bonding against male tyranny, the giving and receiving of practical and political support; if we can also hear in it such associations as *marriage resistance* and the "haggard" behavior identified by Mary Daly (obsolete meanings: "intractable," "willful," "wanton," and "unchaste" . . . "a woman reluctant to yield to wooing")[45] — we begin to grasp breadths of female history and psychology that have lain out of reach as a consequence of limited, mostly clinical, definitions of "lesbianism."

Lesbian existence comprises both the breaking of a taboo and the rejection of a compulsory way of life. It is also a direct or indirect attack on male right of access to

---

45. Mary Daly, *Gyn/Ecology: The Meta-Ethics of Radical Feminism* (Boston: Beacon Press, 1978), p. 15.

women. But it is more than these, although we may first begin to perceive it as a form of nay-saying to patriarchy, an act of resistance. It has of course included role-playing, self-hatred, breakdown, alcoholism, suicide, and intrawoman violence; we romanticize at our peril what it means to love and act against the grain, and under heavy penalties; and lesbian existence has been lived (unlike, say, Jewish or Catholic existence) without access to any knowledge of a tradition, a continuity, a social underpinning. The destruction of records and memorabilia and letters documenting the realities of lesbian existence must be taken very seriously as a means of keeping heterosexuality compulsory for women, since what has been kept from our knowledge is joy, sensuality, courage, and community, as well as guilt, self-betrayal, and pain.

Lesbians have historically been deprived of a political existence through "inclusion" as female versions of male homosexuality. To equate lesbian existence with male homosexuality because each is stigmatized is to deny and erase female reality once again. To separate those women stigmatized as "homosexual" or "gay" from the complex continuum of female resistance to enslavement, and attach them to a male pattern, is to falsify our history. Part of the history of lesbian existence is, obviously, to be found where lesbians, lacking a coherent female community, have shared a kind of social life and common cause with homosexual men. But this has to be seen against the differences: women's lack of economic and cultural privilege relative to men; qualitative differences in female and male relationships, for example, the prevalence of anonymous sex and the justification of pederasty among male homosexuals, the pronounced ageism in male homosexual standards of sexual attractiveness, and so forth. In defining and describing lesbian existence I would hope to move toward a dis-

sociation of lesbian from male homosexual values and allegiances. I perceive the lesbian experience as being, like motherhood, a profoundly *female* experience, with particular oppressions, meanings, and potentialities we cannot comprehend as long as we simply bracket it with other sexually stigmatized existences. Just as the term *parenting* serves to conceal the particular and significant reality of being a parent who is actually a mother, the term *gay* serves the purpose of blurring the very outlines we need to discern, which are of crucial value for feminism and for the freedom of women as a group.

As the term lesbian has been held to limiting, clinical associations in its patriarchal definition, female friendship and comradeship have been set apart from the erotic, thus limiting the erotic itself. But as we deepen and broaden the range of what we define as lesbian existence, as we delineate a lesbian continuum, we begin to discover the erotic in female terms: as that which is unconfined to any single part of the body or solely to the body itself, as an energy not only diffuse but, as Audre Lorde has described it, omnipresent in "the sharing of joy, whether physical, emotional, psychic," and in the sharing of work; as the empowering joy which "makes us less willing to accept powerlessness, or those other supplied states of being which are not native to me, such as resignation, despair, self-effacement, depression, self-denial."[47] In another context, writing of women and work, I quoted the autobiographical passage in which the poet H.D. described how her friend Bryher supported her in persisting with the visionary experience that was to shape her mature work:

> I knew that this experience, this writing-on-the-wall before me, could not be shared with anyone except the girl who stood so bravely there beside me.

---

47. Audre Lorde, *Uses of the Erotic: The Erotic as Power*, Out & Out Books Pamphlet No. 3 (New York: Out & Out Books [476 2d Street, Brooklyn, New York 11215], 1979).

This girl had said without hesitation, "Go on." It was she really who had the detachment and integrity of the Pythoness of Delphi. But it was I, battered and dissociated . . . who was seeing the pictures, and who was reading the writing or granted the inner vision. Or perhaps, in some sense, we were "seeing" it together, for without her, admittedly, I could not have gone on.[48]

If we consider the possibility that all women — from the infant suckling her mother's breast, to the grown woman experiencing orgasmic sensations while suckling her own child, perhaps recalling her mother's milk-smell in her own; to two women, like Virginia Woolf's Chloe and Olivia, who share a laboratory; to the woman dying at ninety, touched and handled by women — exist on a lesbian continuum, we can see ourselves as moving in and out of this continuum, whether we identify ourselves as lesbian or not. It allows us to connect aspects of woman-identification as diverse as the impudent, intimate girl-friendships of eight- or nine-year-olds and the banding together of those women of the twelfth and fifteenth centuries known as Beguines who "shared houses, rented to one another, bequeathed houses to their room-mates . . . in cheap subdivided houses in the artisans' area of town," who "practiced Christian virtue on their own, dressing and living simply and not associating with men," who earned their livings as spinners, bakers, nurses, or ran schools for young girls, and who managed — until the Church forced them to disperse — to live independent both of marriage and of conventional restrictions. It allows us to connect these women with the more celebrated "Lesbians" of the women's school around Sappho of the seventh century B.C.; with the secret sororities and economic networks reported among African women; and with the Chinese marriage resistance sisterhoods — communities of women who refused marriage, or who if married often refused to consummate their marriages and soon left their husbands — the only women in China who were not footbound and who, Agnes Smedley tells us, welcomed the births of daughters and organized successful women's strikes in the silk mills. It allows us to connect and compare disparate instances of marriage resistance; for example, the type of autonomy claimed by Emily Dickinson, a nineteenth-century white woman genius, with the strategies available to Zora Neale Hurston, a twentieth-century black woman genius. Dickinson never married, had tenuous intellectual friendships with men, lived self-convented in her genteel father's house, and wrote a lifetime of passionate letters to her sister-in-law Sue Gilbert and a smaller group of such letters to her friend Kate Scott Anthon. Hurston married twice but soon left each husband, scrambled her way from Florida to Harlem to Columbia University to Haiti and finally back to Florida, moved in and out of white patronage and poverty, professional success and failure; her survival relationships were all with women, beginning with her mother. Both of these women in their vastly different circumstances were marriage resisters, committed to their own work and selfhood, and were later characterized as "apolitical." Both were drawn to men of intellectual quality; for both of them women provided the ongoing fascination and sustenance of life.

If we think of heterosexuality as the "natural" emotional and sensual inclination for women, lives such as these are seen as deviant, as pathological, or as emotionally and sensually deprived. Or, in more recent and permissive jargon, they are banalized as "life-styles." And the work of such women — whether merely the daily work of individual or collective survival and resistance, or the work of the writer, the activist, the reformer, the anthropologist, or the artist —

---

48. Adrienne Rich, "Conditions for Work: The Common World of Women," in *On Lies, Secrets, and Silence*, p. 209; H.D., *Tribute to Freud* (Oxford: Carcanet Press, 1971), pp. 50-54.

the work of self-creation — is undervalued, or seen as the bitter fruit of "penis envy," or the sublimation of repressed eroticism, or the meaningless rant of a "manhater." But when we turn the lens of vision and consider the degree to which, and the methods whereby, heterosexual "preference" has actually been imposed on women, not only can we understand differently the meaning of individual lives and work, but we can begin to recognize a central fact of women's history: that women have always resisted male tyranny. A feminism of action, often, though not always, without a theory, has constantly reemerged in every culture and in every period. We can then begin to study women's struggle against powerlessness, women's radical rebellion, not just in male-defined "concrete revolutionary situations" but in all the situations male ideologies have not perceived as revolutionary: for example, the refusal of some women to produce children, aided at great risk by other women; the refusal to produce a higher standard of living and leisure for men (. . . both are part of women's unacknowledged, unpaid, and un-unionized economic contribution); that female antiphallic sexuality which, as Andrea Dworkin notes, has been "legendary," which, defined as "frigidity" and "puritanism," has actually been a form of subversion of male power — "an ineffectual rebellion, but . . . rebellion nonetheless."[53] We can no longer have patience with Dinnerstein's view that women have simply collaborated with men in the "sexual arrangements" of history; we begin to observe behavior, both in history and in individual biography, that has hitherto been invisible or misnamed; behavior that often constitutes, given the limits of the counterforce exerted in a given time and place, radical rebellion. And we can connect these rebellions and the necessity for them with the physical passion of woman for woman that is central to lesbian existence: the erotic sensuality that has

been, precisely, the most violently erased fact of female experience.

Heterosexuality has been both forcibly and subliminally imposed on women, yet everywhere women have resisted it, often at the cost of physical torture, imprisonment, psychosurgery, social ostracism, and extreme poverty. "Compulsory heterosexuality" was named as one of the "crimes against women" by the Brussels Tribunal on Crimes Against Women in 1976. Two pieces of testimony, from women from two very different cultures, suggest the degree to which persecution of lesbians is a global practice here and now. A report from Norway relates:

A lesbian in Oslo was in a heterosexual marriage that didn't work, so she started taking tranquilizers and ended up at the health sanatorium for treatment and rehabilitation. . . . The moment she said in family group therapy that she believed she was a lesbian, the doctor told her she was not. He knew from "looking into her eyes," he said. She had the eyes of a woman who wanted sexual intercourse with her husband. So she was subjected to so-called "couch therapy." She was put into a comfortably heated room, naked, on a bed, and for an hour her husband was to . . . try to excite her sexually. . . The idea was that the touching was always to end with sexual intercourse. She felt stronger and stronger aversion. She threw up and sometimes ran out of the room to avoid this "treatment." The more strongly she asserted that she was a lesbian, the more violent the forced heterosexual intercourse became. This treatment went on for about six months. She escaped from the hospital, but she was brought back. Again she escaped. She has not been there since. In the end she realized that she had

---

53. Andrea Dworkin, *Pornography: Men Possessing Women* (New York: G. P. Putnam Sons, 1981).

been subjected to forcible rape for six months.

(This, surely, is an example of female sexual slavery according to Barry's definition.) And from Mozambique:

> I am condemned to a life of exile because I will not deny that I am a lesbian, that my primary commitments are, and will always be to other women. In the new Mozambique, lesbianism is considered a left-over from colonialism and decadent Western civilization. Lesbians are sent to rehabilitation camps to learn through self-criticism the correct line about themselves. . . . If I am forced to denounce my own love for women, if I therefore denounce myself, I could go back to Mozambique and join forces in the exciting and hard struggles of rebuilding a nation, including the struggle for the emancipation of Mozambiquan women. As it is I either risk the rehabilitation camps, or remain in exile.

Nor can it be assumed that women like those in Carroll Smith-Rosenberg's study, who married, stayed married, yet dwelt in a profoundly female emotional and passional world, "preferred" or "chose" heterosexuality. Women have married because it was necessary, in order to survive economically, in order to have children who would not suffer economic deprivation or social ostracism, in order to remain respectable, in order to do what was expected of women because coming out of "abnormal" childhoods they wanted to feel "normal," and because heterosexual romance has been represented as the great female adventure, duty, and fulfillment. We may faithfully or ambivalently

have obeyed the institution, but our feelings — and our sensuality — have not been tamed or contained within it. There is no statistical documentation of the numbers of lesbians who have remained in heterosexual marriages for most of their lives. But in a letter to the early lesbian publication *Ladder*, the playwright Lorraine Hansberry had this to say:

> I suspect that the problem of the married woman who would prefer emotional-physical relationships with other women is proportionally much higher than a similar statistic for men. (A statistic surely no one will ever really have.) This because the estate of woman being what it is, how could we ever begin to guess the numbers of women who are not prepared to risk a life alien to what they have been taught all their lives to believe was their "natural" destiny — AND — their only expectation for ECONOMIC security. It seems to be that this is why the question has an immensity that it does not have for male homosexuals. . . . A woman of strength and honesty may, if she chooses, sever her marriage and marry a new male mate and society will be upset that the divorce rate is rising so — but there are few places in the United States, in any event, where she will be anything remotely akin to an "outcast." Obviously this is *not* true for a woman who would end her marriage to take up life with another woman." [55]

This *double-life* — this apparent acquiescence to an institution founded on male interest and prerogative — has been characteristic of female experience: in motherhood, and in many kinds of heterosexual behavior,

---

55. I am indebted to Jonathan Katz's *Gay American History* for bringing to my attention Hansberry's letters to *Ladder* and to Barbara Grier for supplying me with copies of relevant pages from *Ladder*, quoted here by permission of Barbara Grier. See also the reprinted series of *Ladder*, ed. Jonathan Katz et al. (New York: Arno Press); and Deirdre Carmody, "Letters by Eleanor Roosevelt Detail Friendship with Lorena Hickok," *New York Times*, 21 October 1979.

including the rituals of courtship; the pretense of asexuality by the nineteenth-century wife; the simulation of orgasm by the prostitute, the courtesan, the twentieth-century "sexually liberated" woman.

■ ■ ■

IV

Woman-identification is a source of energy, a potential springhead of female power, violently curtailed and wasted under the institution of heterosexuality. The denial of reality and visibility to women's passion for women, women's choice of women as allies, life companions, and community; the forcing of such relationships into dissimulation and their disintegration under intense pressure, have meant an incalculable loss to the power of all women *to change the social relations of the sexes, to liberate ourselves and each other*. The lie of compulsory female heterosexuality today afflicts not just feminist scholarship, but every profession, every reference work, every curriculum, every organizing attempt, every relationship or conversation over which it hovers. It creates, specifically, a profound falseness, hypocrisy, and hysteria in the heterosexual dialogue, for every heterosexual relationship is lived in the queasy strobelight of that lie. However we choose to identify ourselves, however we find ourselves labeled, it flickers across and distorts our lives.

The lie keeps numberless women psychologically trapped, trying to fit mind, spirit, and sexuality into a prescribed script because they cannot look beyond the parameters of the acceptable. It pulls on the energy of such women even as it drains the energy of "closeted" lesbians — the energy exhausted in the double-life. The lesbian trapped in the "closet," the woman imprisoned in prescriptive ideas of the "normal," share the pain of blocked options, broken connections, lost access to self-definition freely and powerfully assumed.

The lie is many-layered. In Western tradition, one layer — the romantic — asserts that women are inevitably, even if rashly and tragically, drawn to men, that even when that attraction is suicidal (e.g., *Tristan und Isolde,* Kate Chopin's *The Awakening*) it is still an organic imperative. In the tradition of the social sciences it asserts that primary love between the sexes is "normal," that women *need* men as social and economic protectors, for adult sexuality, and for psychological completion; that the heterosexually constituted family is the basic social unit; that women who do not attach their primary intensity to men must be, in functional terms, condemned to an even more devastating outsiderhood than their outsiderhood as women. Small wonder that lesbians are reported to be a more hidden population than male homosexuals. The black lesbian/feminist critic, Lorraine Bethel, writing on Zora Neale Hurston, remarks that for a black woman — already twice an outsider — to choose to assume still another "hated identity" is problematic indeed. Yet the lesbian continuum has been a lifeline for black women both in Africa and the United States.

> Black women have a long tradition of bonding together . . . in a Black/women's community that has been a source of vital survival information, psychic and emotional support for us. We have a distinct Black women-identified folk culture based on our experiences as Black women in this society; symbols, language and modes of expression that are specific to the realities of our lives. . . . Because Black women were rarely among those Blacks and females who gained access to literary and other acknowledged forms of artistic expression, this Black female bonding and Black woman-identification has often been hidden and unrecorded except in the individual lives of Black women through our own memories of our particular Black female tradition.

Another layer of the lie is the frequently encountered implication that women turn to women out of hatred for men. Profound skepticism, caution, and righteous paranoia about men may indeed be part of any healthy woman's response to the woman-hatred embedded in male-dominated culture, to the forms assumed by "normal" male sexuality, and to *the failure even of "sensitive" or "political" men to perceive or find these troubling.* Yet woman-hatred is so embedded in culture, so "normal" does it seem, so profoundly is it neglected as a social phenomenon, that many women, even feminists and lesbians, fail to identify it until it takes, in their own lives, some permanently unmistakable and shattering form. Lesbian existence is also represented as mere refuge from male abuses, rather than as an electric and empowering charge between women. I find it interesting that one of the most frequently quoted literary passages on lesbian relationship is that in which Colette's Renee, in *The Vagabond,* describes "the melancholy and touching image of two weak creatures who have perhaps found shelter in each other's arms, there to sleep and weep, safe from man who is often cruel, and there to taste *better than any pleasure, the bitter happiness of feeling themselves akin, frail and forgotten* [emphasis added]. Colette is often considered a lesbian writer; her popular reputation has, I think, much to do with the fact that she writes about lesbian existence as if for a male audience; her earliest "lesbian" novels, the Claudine series, were written under compulsion for her husband and published under both their names. At all events, except for her writings on her mother, Colette is a far less reliable source on lesbian than, I would think, Charlotte Brontë, who understood that while women may, indeed must, be one another's allies, mentors, and comforters in the female struggle for survival, there is quite extraneous delight in each other's company and attraction to each others' minds and character, which proceeds from a recognition of each others' strengths.

By the same token, we can say that there is a *nascent* feminist political content in the act of choosing a woman lover or life partner in the face of institutionalized heterosexuality. But for lesbian existence to realize this political content in an ultimately liberating form, the erotic choice must deepen and expand into conscious woman-identification — into lesbian/feminism.

The work that lies ahead, of unearthing and describing what I call here lesbian existence, is potentially liberating for all women. It is work that must assuredly move beyond the limits of white and middle-class Western women's studies to examine women's lives, work, and groupings within every racial, ethnic, and political structure. There are differences, moreover, between lesbian existence and the lesbian continuum — differences we can discern even in the movement of our own lives. The lesbian continuum, I suggest, needs delineation in light of the double-life of women, not only women self-described as heterosexual but also of self-described lesbians. We need a far more exhaustive account of the forms the double-life has assumed. Historians need to ask at every point how heterosexuality as institution has been organized and maintained through the female wage scale, the enforcement of middle-class women's "leisure," the glamorization of so-called sexual liberation, the withholding of education from women, the imagery of "high art" and popular culture, the mystification of the "personal" sphere, and much else. We need an economics that comprehends the institution of heterosexuality, with its doubled workload for women and its sexual divisions of labor, as the most idealized of economic relations.

The question inevitably will arise: Are we then to condemn all heterosexual relationships, including those that are least oppressive? I believe this question, though often heartfelt, is the wrong question here. We have been stalled in a maze of false dichotomies that prevents our apprehending the institution as a whole: "good" versus "bad" marriages; "marriage for love" versus arranged marriage; "liberated" sex versus prostitution; heterosexual intercourse versus rape; Liebeschmerz versus humiliation and dependency. Within the institution exist, of course, qualitative differences of experience; but the absence of choice remains the great unacknowledged reality, and in the absence of choice, women will remain dependent on the chance or luck of particular relationships and will have no collective power to determine the meaning and place of sexuality in their lives. As we address the institution itself, moreover, we begin to perceive a history of female resistance that has never fully understood itself because it has been so fragmented, miscalled, erased. It will require a courageous grasp of the politics and economics, as well as the cultural propaganda, of heterosexuality to carry us beyond individual cases or diversified group situations into the complex kind of overview needed to undo the power men everywhere wield over women, power that has become a model for every other form of exploitation and illegitimate control.

◆

"GO THE WAY YOUR BLOOD BEATS": AN INTERVIEW WITH JAMES BALDWIN
Richard Goldstein

In the early 1980s I read a long interview with James Baldwin in *The New York Times Book Review*, which didn't include a whisper about its subject's sexuality. Since I belong to the generation of gay men for whom Baldwin's fiction was an early vector of self-discovery, I decided to broach the subject for myself. So I tracked Baldwin down and badgered him with politics and personal charm until he agreed to meet me at the Riviera Cafe in the Village, an old hangout for him. When I arrived, Baldwin was sitting at an outside table, watching the exotica with that faintly distracted look Europeans cultivate. I proceeded to "orient" him for the interview that would follow, only to discover that he knew very little about the state of American gay life today: What's a "clone," he wanted to know, and how is AIDS transmitted? What transpired over the next few days was one of the most powerful experiences of my professional life — an insight into the paradoxical nature of gay culture from a man who traced much of his acuity and pain to the nexus of racism and homophobia. But what I remember most about that afternoon is the sight of Baldwin, gnomelike and far from serene, surrounded by passersby who recognize him, and just wanted to say, as I did, how full of him our lives will always be.

GOLDSTEIN: Do you feel like a stranger in gay America?

BALDWIN: Well, first of all I feel like a stranger in America from almost every conceivable angle except, oddly enough, as a black person. The word "gay" has always rubbed me the wrong way. I never understood exactly what is meant by it. I don't want to sound distant or patronizing because I don't really feel that. I simply feel it's a world that has very little to do with me, with where I did my growing up. I was never at home in it. Even in my early years in the

Richard Goldstein, *"Go The Way Your Blood Beats": An Interview With James Baldwin, in* JAMES BALDWIN: THE LEGACY 173 (Quincy Troupe ed., 1989).

Village, what I saw of that world absolutely frightened me, bewildered me. I didn't understand the necessity of all the role playing. And in a way I still don't.

GOLDSTEIN: You never thought of yourself as being gay?

BALDWIN: No, I didn't have a word for it. The only one I had was "homosexual" and that didn't quite cover whatever it was I was beginning to feel. Even when I began to realize things about myself, began to suspect who I was and what I was likely to become, it was still very personal, absolutely personal. It was really a matter between me and God. I would have to live the life he made me to live. I told him quite a long, long time ago there would be two of us at the Mercy Seat. He would not be asking all the questions.

GOLDSTEIN: When did you first begin to think of yourself in those terms?

BALDWIN: It hit me with great force while I was in the pulpit. I must have been fourteen. I was still a virgin. I had no idea what you were supposed to do about it. I didn't really understand any of what I felt except I knew I loved one boy, for example. But it was private. And by the time I left home, when I was seventeen or eighteen and still a virgin, it was like everything else in my life, a problem which I would have to resolve myself. You know, it never occurred to me to join a club. I must say I felt very, very much alone. But I was alone on so many levels and this was one more aspect of it.

GOLDSTEIN: So when we talk about gay life, which is so group-oriented, so tribal . . .

BALDWIN: And I am not that kind of person at all.

GOLDSTEIN: . . . do you feel baffled by it?

BALDWIN: I feel remote from it. It's a phenomenon that came along much after I was formed. In some sense, I couldn't have afforded it. You see, I am not a member of anything. I joined the Church when I was very, very young, and haven't joined anything since, expect for a brief stint in the Socialist Party. I'm a maverick, you know. But that doesn't mean I don't feel very strongly for my brothers and sisters.

GOLDSTEIN: Do you have a special feeling of responsibility toward gay people?

BALDWIN: Toward that phenomenon we call gay, yeah. I feel special responsibility because I would have to be a kind of witness to it, you know.

GOLDSTEIN: You're one of the architects of it by the act of writing about it publicly and elevating it into the realm of literature.

BALDWIN: I made a public announcement that we're private, if you see what I mean.

GOLDSTEIN: When I consider what a risk it must have been to write about homosexuality when you did . . .

BALDWIN: You're talking about *Giovanni's Room*. Yeah, that was rough. But I had to do it to clarify something for myself.

GOLDSTEIN: What was that?

BALDWIN: Where I was in the world. I mean, what I'm made of. Anyway, *Giovanni's Room* is not really about homosexuality. It's the vehicle through which the book moves. *Go Tell It on the Mountain*, for example, is not about a church and *Giovanni* is not really about homosexuality. It's about what happens to you if you're afraid to love anybody. Which is much more interesting than the question of homosexuality.

GOLDSTEIN: But you didn't mask the sexuality.

BALDWIN: No.

GOLDSTEIN: And that decision alone must have been enormously risky.

BALDWIN: Yeah. The alternative was worse.

GOLDSTEIN: What would that have been?

BALDWIN: If I hadn't written that book I would probably have had to stop writing altogether.

GOLDSTEIN: It was that serious.

BALDWIN: It *is* that serious. The question of human affection, of integrity, in my case, the question of trying to become a writer, are all linked with the question of sexuality. Sexuality is only a part of it. I don't know even if it's the most important part. But it's indispensable.

GOLDSTEIN: Did people advise you not to write the book so candidly?

BALDWIN: I didn't ask anybody. When I turned the book in, I was told I shouldn't have written it. I was told to bear in mind that I was a young Negro writer with a certain audience, and I wasn't supposed to alienate that audience. And if I published the book, it would wreck my career. They wouldn't publish the book, they said, as a favor to me. So I took the book to England and I sold it there before I sold it here.

GOLDSTEIN: Do you think your unresolved sexuality motivated you, at the start, to write?

BALDWIN: Yeah. Well, everything was unresolved. The sexual thing was only one of the things. It was for a while the most tormenting thing and it could have been the most dangerous.

GOLDSTEIN: How so?

BALDWIN: Well, because it frightened me so much.

GOLDSTEIN: I don't think straight people realize how frightening it is to finally admit to yourself that this is going to be you forever.

BALDWIN: It's very frightening. But the so-called straight person is no safer than I am really. Loving anybody and being loved by anybody is a tremendous danger, a tremendous responsibility. Loving of children, raising of children. The terrors homosexuals go through in this society would not be so great if the society did not go through so many terrors which it doesn't want to admit. The discovery of one's sexual preference doesn't have to be a trauma. It's a trauma because it's such a traumatized society.

GOLDSTEIN: Have you got any sense of what causes people to hate homosexuals?

BALDWIN: Terror, I suppose. Terror of the flesh. After all, we're supposed to mortify the flesh, a doctrine which has led to untold horrors. This is a very biblical culture; people believe the wages of sin is death. In fact, the wages of sin *is* death, but not the way the moral guardians of this time and place understand it.

GOLDSTEIN: Is there a particularly American component of homophobia?

BALDWIN: I think Americans are terrified of feeling anything. And homophobia is simply an extreme example of the American terror that's concerned with growing up. I never met a people more infantile in my life.

GOLDSTEIN: You sound like Leslie Fiedler.

BALDWIN: I hope not. [Laughter]

GOLDSTEIN: Are you as apocalyptic about the prospects for sexual reconciliation as you are about racial reconciliation?

BALDWIN: Well, they join. The sexual question and the racial question have always been entwined, you know. If Americans can mature on the level of racism, then they have to mature on the level of sexuality.

GOLDSTEIN: I think we would agree there's a retrenchment going on in race relations. Do you sense that happening also in sex relations?

BALDWIN: Yeah. There's what we would have to call a backlash which, I'm afraid, is just beginning.

GOLDSTEIN: I suspect most gay people have fantasies about genocide.

BALDWIN: Well, it's not a fantasy exactly since the society makes its will toward you very, very clear. Especially the police, for example, or truck drivers. I know from my own experience that the macho men — truck drivers, cops, football players — these people are far more complex than they want to realize. That's why I call them infantile. They have needs which, for them, are literally inexpressible. They don't dare look into the mirror. And that is why they need faggots. They've created faggots in order to act out a sexual fantasy on the body of another man and not take any responsibility for it. Do you see what I mean? I think it's very important for the male homosexual to realize that he is a sexual target for other men, and that is why he is despised, and why he is called a faggot. He is called a faggot because other males need him.

GOLDSTEIN: Why do you think homophobia falls so often on the right of the political spectrum?

BALDWIN: It's a way of controlling people. Nobody *really* cares who goes to bed with whom, finally. I mean, the State doesn't really care, the Church doesn't really care. They care that you should be frightened of what you do. As long as you feel guilty about it, the State can rule you. It's a way of exerting control over the universe, by terrifying people.

GOLDSTEIN: Why don't black ministers need to share in this rhetoric?

BALDWIN: Perhaps because they're more grown-up than most white ministers.

GOLDSTEIN: Did you ever hear antigay rhetoric in church?

BALDWIN: Not in the church I grew up in. I'm sure that's still true. Everyone is a child of God, according to us.

GOLDSTEIN: Didn't people ever call you "faggot" uptown?

BALDWIN: Of course. But there's a difference in the way it's used. It's got less venom, at least in my experience. I don't know of anyone who has ever denied his brother or his sister because they were gay. No doubt it happens. It must happen. But in the generality, a black person has got quite a lot to get through the day without getting entangled in all the American fantasies.

GOLDSTEIN: Do black gay people have the same sense of being separate as white gay people do? I mean, I feel distinct from other white people.

BALDWIN: Well, I think that is because you are penalized, as it were, unjustly; you're placed outside a certain safety to which you were born. A black gay person who is a sexual conundrum to society is already, long before the question of sexuality comes into it, menaced and marked because he's black or she's black. The sexual question comes after the question of color; it's simply one more aspect of the danger in which all black people live. I think white gay people feel cheated because they were born, in principle, into a society in which they were supposed to be safe. The anomaly of their sexuality puts them in danger, unexpectedly. Their reaction seems to me in direct proportion to the sense of feeling cheated of the advantages which accrue to white people in a white society. There's an element, it has always seemed to me, of bewilderment and complaint. Now that may sound very harsh, but the gay world as such is no more prepared to accept black people than anywhere else in society. It's a very hermetically sealed world with very unattractive features, including racism.

GOLDSTEIN: Are you optimistic about the possibilities of blacks and gays forging a political coalition? Do you see any special basis for empathy between us?

BALDWIN: Yeah. Of course.

GOLDSTEIN: What would that be?

BALDWIN: Well, the basis would be shared suffering, shared perceptions, shared hopes.

GOLDSTEIN: What perceptions do we share?

BALDWIN: I supposed one would be the perception that love is where you find it. If you see what I mean.

GOLDSTEIN: [Laughter] Or where you lose it, for that matter.

BALDWIN: Uhm-hmm.

GOLDSTEIN: But are gay people sensitized by the perceptions we share with blacks?

BALDWIN: Not in my experience, no.

GOLDSTEIN: So I guess you're not very hopeful about that kind of coalition as something that could make a difference in urban politics.

BALDWIN: It's simply that the whole question has entered my mind another way. I know a great many white people, men and women, straight and gay, whatever, who are unlike the majority of their countrymen. On what basis we could form a coalition is still an open question. The idea of basing it on sexual preference strikes me as somewhat dubious, strikes me as being less than a firm foundation. It seems to me that a coalition has to be based on the grounds of human dignity. Anyway, what connects us, speaking about the private life, is mainly unspoken.

GOLDSTEIN: I sometimes think gay people look to black people as healing them . . .

BALDWIN: Not only gay people.

GOLDSTEIN: . . . healing their alienation.

BALDWIN: That has to be done, first of all, by the person and then you will find your company.

GOLDSTEIN: When I heard Jesse Jackson speak before a gay audience, I wanted him to say there wasn't any sin, that I was forgiven.

BALDWIN: Is that a question for you still? That question of sin?

GOLDSTEIN: I think it must be, on some level, even though I am not a believer.

BALDWIN: How peculiar. I didn't realize you thought of it as sin. Do many gay people feel that?

GOLDSTEIN: I don't know. [Laughter] I guess I'm throwing something at you, which is the idea that gays look to blacks as conferring a kind of acceptance by embracing them in a coalition. I find it unavoidable to think in those terms. When I fantasize about a black mayor or a black president, I think of it as being better for gay people.

BALDWIN: Well, don't be romantic about gay people. Though I can see what you mean.

GOLDSTEIN: Do you think black people have heightened capacity for tolerance, even acceptance, in its truest sense?

BALDWIN: Well, there is a capacity in black people for experience, simply. And that capacity makes other things possible. It dictates the depth of one's acceptance of other people. The capacity for experience is what burns out fear. Because the homophobia we're talking about really is a kind of fear. It's a terror of flesh. It's really a terror of being able to be touched.

GOLDSTEIN: Do you think about having children?

BALDWIN: Not any more. It's one thing I really regret, maybe the only regret I have. But I couldn't have managed it then. Now it's too late.

GOLDSTEIN: But you're not disturbed by the idea of gay men being parents.

BALDWIN: Look, men have been sleeping with men for thousands of years — and raising tribes. This is a Western sickness, it really is. It's an artificial division. Men will

be sleeping with each other when the trumpet sounds. It's only this infantile culture which has made such a big deal of it.

GOLDSTEIN: So you think of homosexuality as universal?

BALDWIN: Of course. There's nothing in me that is not in everybody else, and nothing in everybody else that is not in me. We're trapped in language, of course. But homosexual is not a noun. At least not in my book.

GOLDSTEIN: What part of speech would it be?

BALDWIN: Perhaps a verb. You see, I can only talk about my own life. I loved a few people and they loved me. It had nothing to do with these labels. Of course, the world has all kinds of words for us. But that's the world's problem.

GOLDSTEIN: Is it problematic for you, the idea of having sex only with other people who are identified as gay?

BALDWIN: Well, you see, my life has not been like that at all. The people who were my lovers were never, well, the word gay wouldn't have meant anything to them.

GOLDSTEIN: That means that they moved in the straight world.

BALDWIN: They moved in the world.

GOLDSTEIN: Do you think of the gay world as being a false refuge?

BALDWIN: I think perhaps it imposes a limitation which is unnecessary. It seems to me simply a man is a man, a woman is a woman, and who they go to bed with is nobody's business but theirs. I suppose what I am really saying is that one's sexual preference is a private matter. I resent the interference of the State, or the Church, or any institution in my only journey to whatever it is we are journeying toward. But it has been made a public question by the institutions of this country. I can see how the gay world comes about in response to that. And to contradict myself, I suppose, or more precisely, I hope that it is easier for the transgressor to become reconciled with himself or herself than it was for many people in my generation — and it was difficult for me. It is difficult to be despised, in short. And if the so-called gay movement can cause men and women, boys and girls, to come to some kind of terms with themselves more speedily and with less pain, then that's a very great advance. I'm not sure it can be done on that level. My own point of view, speaking out of black America, when I had to try to answer that stigma, that species of social curse, it seemed a great mistake to answer in the language of the oppressor. As long as I react as a "nigger," as long as I protest my case on evidence or assumptions held by others, I'm simply reinforcing those assumptions. As long as I complain about being oppressed, the oppressor is in consolation of knowing that I know my place, so to speak.

GOLDSTEIN: You will always come forward and make the statement that you're homosexual. You will never hide it, or deny it. And yet you refuse to make a life out of it?

BALDWIN: Yeah. That sums it up pretty well.

GOLDSTEIN: That strikes me as a balance some of us might want to look to, in a climate where it's possible.

BALDWIN: One has to make that climate for oneself.

GOLDSTEIN: Do you have fantasies about the future?

BALDWIN: I have good fantasies and bad fantasies.

GOLDSTEIN: What are some of the good ones?

BALDWIN: Oh, that I am working toward the New Jerusalem. That's true, I'm not joking. I won't live to see it but I do believe in it. I think we're going to be better than we are.

GOLDSTEIN: What do you think gay people will be like then?

BALDWIN: No one will have to call themselves gay. Maybe that's at the bottom of my impatience with the term. It answers a false argument, a false accusation.

GOLDSTEIN: Which is what?

BALDWIN: Which is that you have no right to be here, that you have to prove your right to be here. I'm saying I have nothing to prove. The world also belongs to me.

GOLDSTEIN: What advice would you give a gay man who's about to come out?

BALDWIN: Coming out means to publicly say?

GOLDSTEIN: I guess I'm imposing these terms on you.

BALDWIN: Yeah, they're not my terms. But what advice can you possibly give? Best advice I ever got was an old friend of mine, a black friend, who said you have to go the way your blood beats. If you don't live the only life you have, you won't live some other life, you won't live any life at all. That's the only advice you can give anybody. And it's not advice, it's an observation.

♦

QUEERS READ THIS

Anonymous Queers

Being queer is not about a right to privacy; it is about the freedom to be public, to just be who we are. It means everyday fighting oppression; homophobia, racism, misogyny, the bigotry of religious hypocrites and our own self-hatred. (We have been carefully taught to hate ourselves.) And now of course it means fighting a virus as well, and all those homo-haters who are using AIDS to wipe us off the face of the earth.

Being queer means leading a different sort of life. It's not about the mainstream,

ANONYMOUS QUEERS, QUEERS READ THIS (1990) (newspaper distributed at the New York City gay pride parade, June 1990).

profit margins, patriotism, patriarchy or being assimilated. It's not about executive directors, privilege and elitism. It's about being on the margins, defining ourselves; it's about gender-fuck and secrets, what's beneath the belt and deep inside the heart; it's about the night. Being queer is "grass roots" because we know that everyone of us, every body, every cunt, every heart and ass and dick is a world of pleasure waiting to be explored. Everyone of us is a world of infinite possibility.

We are an army because we have to be. We are an army because we are so powerful. (We have so much to fight for; we are the most precious of endangered species.) And we are an army of lovers because it is we who know what love is. Desire and lust, too. We invented them. We come out of the closet, face the rejection of society, face firing squads, just to love each other! Every time we fuck, we win.

We must fight for ourselves (no one else is going to do it) and if in that process we bring greater freedom to the world at large then great. (We've given so much to that world: democracy, all the arts, the concepts of love, philosophy and the soul, to name just a few gifts from our ancient Greek Dykes, Fags.) Let's make every space a lesbian and gay space. Every street a part of our sexual geography. A city of yearning and then total satisfaction. A city and a country where we can be safe and free and more. We must look at our lives and see what's best in them, see what is queer and what is straight and let that straight chaff fall away! Remember there is so, so little time. And I want to be a lover of each and every one of you. Next year, we march naked.

■ ■ ■

I hate straight people who think they have anything intelligent to say about "outing." I hate straight people who think stories about themselves are "universal" but stories about us are only about homosexuality. I hate straight recording artists who make their careers off of queer people, then attack us, then act hurt when we get angry and then deny having wronged us rather than apologize for it. I hate straight people who say, "I don't see why you feel the need to wear those buttons and t-shirts. I don't go around telling the whole world I'm straight."

I hate that in twelve years of public education I was never taught about queer people. I hate that I grew up thinking I was the only queer in the world, and I hate even more that most queer kids still grow up the same way. I hate that I was tormented by other kids for being a faggot, but more that I was taught to feel ashamed for being the object of their cruelty, taught to feel it was my fault. I hate that the Supreme Court of this country says it's okay to criminalize me because of how I make love. I hate that so many straight people are so concerned about my goddamned sex life. I hate that so many twisted straight people become parents, while I have to fight like hell to be *allowed* to be a father. I hate straights.

■ ■ ■

I wear my pink triangle everywhere. I do not lower my voice in public when talking about lesbian love or sex. I always tell people I'm a lesbian. I don't wait to be asked about my "boyfriend." I don't say it's "no one's business."

I don't do this for straight people. Most of them don't know what the pink triangle even means. Most of them couldn't care less that my girlfriend and I are totally in love or having a fight on the street. Most of them don't notice us no matter what we do. I do what I do to reach other lesbians. I do what I do because I don't want lesbians to assume I'm a straight girl. I am out all the time, everywhere, because I WANT TO REACH YOU. Maybe you'll notice me, maybe we'll start talking, maybe we'll exchange numbers, maybe we'll become friends. Maybe we won't say a word but our eyes will meet and I will imagine you naked, sweating, open-mouthed, your back arched as I am fucking you. And we'll be happy to show we aren't the only ones in the world. We'll be happy because we found each other, without saying a word, maybe just for a moment.

But no.

You won't wear a pink triangle on that linen lapel. You won't meet my eyes if I flirt with you on the street. You avoid me on the job because I'm "too" out. You chastise me in bars because I'm "too political." You ignore me in public because I bring "too much" attention to "my" lesbianism. But then you want me to be your lover, you want me to be your friend, you want me to love you, support you, fight for "OUR" right to exist.

■ ■ ■

Queer!

Ah, do we really have to use that word? It's trouble. Every gay person has his or her own take on it. For some it means strange and eccentric and kind of mysterious. That's okay, we like that. But some gay girls and boys don't. They think they're more normal than strange. And for others "queer" conjures up those awful memories of adolescent suffering. Queer. It's forcibly bittersweet and quaint at best — weakening and painful at worst. Couldn't we just use "gay" instead. It's a much brighter word. And isn't it synonymous with "happy"? When will you militants grow up and get over the novelty of being different?

WHY QUEER

Well, yes, "gay" is great. It has its place. But when a lot of lesbians and gay men wake up in the morning we feel angry and disgusted, not gay. So we've chosen to call ourselves queer. Using "queer" is a way of reminding us how we are perceived by the rest of the world. It's a way of telling ourselves we don't have to be witty and charming people who keep our lives discreet and marginalized in the straight world. We use queer as gay men loving lesbians and lesbians loving being queer. Queer, unlike GAY, doesn't mean MALE.

And when spoken to other gays and lesbians it's a way of suggesting we close ranks, and forget (temporarily) our individual differences because we face a more insidious common enemy. Yeah, QUEER can be a rough word but it is also a sly and ironic weapon we can steal from the homophobe's hands and use against him.

■ ■ ■

III. SIN

◆

PLYMOUTH COLONY SODOMY STATUTES AND CASES

1636, NOVEMBER 15
Plymouth: "Sodomy" Law

In the earliest codification of laws in colonial America, Plymouth, founded sixteen years earlier, included eight offenses punishable by death:

> Treason or rebellion against the person of the King, State, or Common Wealth, either of England or these Colonies:

Plymouth Colony Sodomy Statutes and Cases, *in* JONATHAN NED KATZ, GAY/LESBIAN ALMANAC 74-122 (1983).

Willfull Murder.

Solemn compaction or conversing with the devil by way of witchcraft, conjuration or the like.

Willfull and purposed burning of ships houses.

Sodomy, rapes, buggery.

Adultery to be punished.

This Plymouth law was next revised in 1671.

1637, AUGUST 6
Plymouth: John Allexander
and Thomas Roberts

"Lewd behavior and unclean carriage"

The Plymouth court found Allexander and Roberts guilty of "often spending their seed one upon the other." The Plymouth crime of "sodomy" was not mentioned in connection with the case, for "sodomy," then, required "penetration," not mere emission, even if this emission was mutual, and "often." The class difference of the parties was also suggested; Allexander, presented as the instigator, was apparently a free man, Roberts an indentured servant. Whether this intermingling of social orders, as well as of seed, lent gravity to the crime in the eyes of the judges was not disclosed. The record states:

> John Allexander & Thomas Roberts were both examined and found guilty of lewd behavior and unclean carriage one with another, by often spending their seed one upon another, which was proved both by witness & their own confession; the said Allexander [was] found to have been formerly notoriously guilty that way, and seeking to allure others thereunto. The said John Allexander was therefore censured [sentenced] by the Court to be severely whipped, and burnt in the shoulder with a hot iron, and to be perpetually banished [from] the government [territory] of New Plymouth, and if he be at any time found within the same, to be

whipped out again by the appointment [order] of the next justice, etc., and so as oft as he shall be found within this government. Which penalty was accordingly inflicted.

> Thomas Roberts was censured to be severley whipped, and to return to his master, Mr. Atwood, and serve out his time with him, but to be disabled hereby to enjoy any lands within this government, except he manifest better desert

The last five qualifying words were added, as an afterthought, in the margin.

On October 2, 1637, Thomas Roberts was one of four men charged by the Plymouth Court with "disorderly living, & therefore to be required to give an account how they live."

Four years later, on January 5, 1642, a "Thomas Roberts," possibly the same individual cited above, was mentioned in the Plymouth Court records:

> Thomas Roberts, of Duxborrow, is ordered by the Court that he shall lodge no more with George Morrey, a diseased person, and betwixt this and the next Court of Assistants provide himself of lodging; and then make report to the Court how it may be probable he may live without being chargeable.

■ ■ ■

1642, MARCH 1
Plymouth: Edward Michell
and Edward Preston

"Lewd & sodomitical practices"

The Plymouth court cited Edward Michell and Edward Preston for "lewd & sodomitical practices tending to sodomy" with each other. Conviction under the Plymouth sodomy law of 1636 meant death, but these guilty parties were only whipped. The court, then, made a major distinction between "sodomy" proper, punished by death, and "sodomitical" (or sodomy-like) practices —

those "tending toward sodomy" — punished by a whipping. The record states:

> Edward Michell, for his lewd & sodomitical practices tending to sodomy with Edward Preston, and other lewd carriages with Lydia Hatch, is censured to be presently whipped at Plymouth, at the public place, and once more at Barnestable, in convenient time, in the presence of Mr. Freeman and the committees of the said town.
>
> Edward Preston, for his lewd practices tending to sodomy with Edward Michell, and pressing John Keene thereunto (if he would have yielded), is also censured [sentenced] to be forthwith whipped at Plymouth, and once more at Barnestable (when Edward Michell is whipped), in the presence of Mr. Freeman & the committees of the same town.
>
> John Keene, because he resisted the temptation, & used means to discover it, is appointed to stand by whilst Michell and Preston are whipped, though in some thing he was faulty.

The same court proceeding also cited

> Lydia Hatch, for suffering Edward Michell to attempt to abuse her body by uncleanness, & did not discover [report] it, & [for] lying in the same bed with her brother, Jonathan, is censured to be publicly whipped; was accordingly done.

■ ■ ■

1642
William Bradford:

"Things Fearful to Name"

In his history of the Plymouth Colony (unpublished in his lifetime), Bradford commented on an outbreak in 1642 of sodomy, bestiality, fornication, adultery, and rape. After discussing the Humfry case, Bradford marveled that "wickedness did grow and break forth" in New England, a land where wickedness was so much spoken against, investigated, and severely punished, "as in no place more." Even "moderate and good men" had censured New Englanders for their "severity in punishments." But all the orations against wickedness, and the strict punishments accorded it, "could not suppress the breaking out," that year and others, of various "notorious sins . . . . especially drunkenness and uncleanness." Bradford referred not only to "incontinency" between married persons, but to "that which is worse" — even "sodomy and buggery (things fearful to name)" had "broke forth in this land oftener than once."

Bradford suggested that such crimes might originate in "our corrupt natures, which are so hardly bridled, subdued and mortified." A more specific reason for such outbreaks might be that "the Devil" was more spiteful against New England churches because they tried harder than others to "cast a blemish and stain" upon New Englanders for their virtues; Bradford would rather think that than believe that "Satan" had "more power in these heathen lands" than in more thoroughly Christian nations.

Bradford also suggested that in New England "wickedness being more stopped by strict laws," and so closely looked into, was like "waters when their streams are . . . dammed up." When such dams broke, the waters previously held back "flow with more violence and make more noise and disturbance than when they are suffered to run quietly in their own channels." Bradford thus speculated that the strict suppression of sin caused it to break out in especially violent forms, that repression caused violent sexual expressions — a suggestion surprising to find in the words of an early Puritan.

Bradford did not think the discovery of wickedness in New England indicated the presence of more sin there than elsewhere. He did think that evils were more likely to be made public in New England by strict magistrates and by churches which "look narrowly to their members." In other places, with larger populations, "many horrible evils" were never discovered, whereas in relatively little populated New England, they were "brought into the light," and "made conspicuous to all."

Bradford described the case of Thomas Granger, a teen-ager executed in September 1642, for buggery with "a mare, a cow, two goats, five sheep, two calves and a turkey." Granger, and an individual who "had made some sodomitical attempts upon another," * were questioned about "how they came first to the knowledge and practice of such wickedness." The sodomitical individual "confessed he had long used it [the practice] in Old England." Granger "said he was taught it [bestiality] by another that had heard of such things from some in England when he was there, and they kept cattle together." This indicated, Bradford said, "how one wicked person may infect the many." He therefore advised masters to take great care about "what servants they bring into their families."

It might be asked, said Bradford, how "so many wicked persons and profane people should so quickly come over into this land and mix themselves among us" — "us" being those "religious men that began the work," who "came for religion's sake."

Bradford answered that wherever the Lord sowed good seed the "envious man" will try to sow bad. Second, in the American wilderness "much labor and service," much "building and planting" was necessary, and "many untoward servants . . . were thus brought over, both men and womenkind"; these eventually founded their own families and multiplied (presumably increasing the numbers of "untoward" children). Third, and "a main reason," said Bradford, "some began to make a trade" of shipping passengers to America; these traders, to "advance their profit," did not care whom they transported as long as their passengers "had money to pay them." And "by this means the country

became pestered with many unworthy persons."

Finally, a "mixed multitude" came into the American wilderness, some being sent with the "hope that they would be made better," others so that they would be "kept from shame at home." Such persons "would necessarily follow their dissolute courses" in the New World. Thus, Bradford concluded, in the twenty years since the first truly pious settlers had arrived, the colonial population had perhaps grown "the worser."

■ ■ ■

1649, MARCH 6
Plymouth: Sara Norman
and Mary Hammon

"Lewd Behavior . . . upon a bed"

Plymouth Colony records included the accusation against two women, Sara Norman and Mary Hammon (or Hammond):

> We present [charge] the wife of Hugh Norman, and Mary Hammon, both of Yarmouth, for lewd behavior each with [the] other upon a bed. . . .

Recent research by J.R. Roberts in the Plymouth manuscript records provides background information on Norman and Hammon. At the time of the above charges Mary Hammon was fifteen years old, and recently married. Sara Norman's age is unknown, but she was apparently somewhat older, as she had been married in 1639. About the time of the court's first charge, 1649, Hugh Norman, Sara's husband, deserted his wife and children.

A marginal note in the Plymouth court record of March 6, 1649, reported that Mary Hammon was "cleared with admonition" — perhaps because of her youth. Sara Norman's case was evidently held over for later judgment.

A year after the first charge, on March 6, 1650, Sara Norman was cited again in the

---

* Probably Edward Michell or Edward Preston; see 1642, March 1.

Plymouth court records, this time accused of "unclean practices" with a male, Teage Joanes. This charge was subsequently dropped, when her accuser pleaded guilty of perjury.

On October 2, 1650, the records report the outcome of the original charge against Sara Norman. The court punished her with a warning, and asked her to acknowledge publicly her "unchaste behavior" with Mary Hammon. This punishment, though publicly humiliating, was lenient compared to the death penalty imposed for male-male "sodomy."

Patriarchal custom was evident in the fact that court records in this case referred to the "wife of Hugh Norman"; although Sara Norman was publicly charged with a serious crime, her whole name was used only once in the documents.

The court record of 1650 said:

> Whereas the wife of Hugh Norman, of Yarmouth, hath stood presented [in] divers Courts for misdemeanor and lewd behavior with Mary Hammon upon a bed, with divers lascivious speeches by her also spoken, but she could not appear by reason of some hindrances unto this Court, the said Court have therefore sentenced her, the said wife of Hugh Norman, for her wild behavior in the aforesaid particulars, to make a public acknowledgement, so far as conveniently may be, of her unchaste behavior, and have also warned her to take heed of such carriages for the future, lest her former carriage come in remembrance against her to make her punishment the greater.

1649, OCTOBER 29
Plymouth: Richard Berry
and Teage Joanes

"Sodomy" Charge

The Plymouth Court records reported a "sodomy" charge by Richard Berry against Teage Joanes. After hearing "what can be said in the case for present" the court held the case over for a further hearing at the next session, five months away, taking money bonds to insure that the accuser, the accused, and their witnesses would then appear.

On March 6, 1650, the Plymouth court records reported the outcome of Richard Berry's charge:

> Whereas . . . Richard Berry accused Teage Joanes of sodomy, & other unclean practices also with Sara, the wife of Hugh Norman, & for that cause the said parties were both bound over to answer to this Court, & accordingly appeared: the said Richard Berry acknowledged before the Court that he did wrong the aforesaid Teage Joanes in both the aforesaid particulars, & had born false witness against him upon oath; and for the same the said Richard Berry was sentenced to be whipped at the post, which accordingly was performed.

False witness for the purpose of taking a man's life was not yet a capital crime under Plymouth law or Berry might have received a death sentence.

Three years after the above hearing, on June 9, 1653, the Plymouth Colony court records reported:

> An order was . . . passed from the Court requiring that Teage Joanes and Richard Berry, and others with them, be caused to part their uncivil living together, as they will answer for it.

Six years later, or October 6, 1659, a "Richard Beare" (probably the same "Richard Berry"), of Marshfield, was cited in the Plymouth Colony court records as

> being a grossly scandalous person, debauched, having been formerly convicted of filthy, obscene practices, and for the same by the Court sentenced.

The records stated that "Beare," who had fallen afoul of the law, was summoned by the court to receive personally the sentence of "disfranchisement" from Plymouth, but he had not appeared. The court ordered that Beare "be disfranchised of his freedom" in the colony (banished and deprived of rights).

■ ■ ■

1671, JUNE 6
Plymouth: "Sodomy" law

The General Court of Plymouth added several capital crimes to those specified in 1636. The new laws also qualified the "sodomy" statute, making persons under fourteen and the party to forcible sodomy exempt from death. The further qualification, that "all other sodomitical filthiness" shall be punished according to its nature, may have meant that anal penetration was necessary for the death penalty, and that other types of non-penetrative, "sodomitical" (sodomy-like) acts, such as mutual or public masturbation, were not to be punished so severely.

The sixteen crimes punishable by death in the Plymouth law of 1671 were listed as (1) "Idolatry," (2) "Blasphemy," (3) "Treason," (4) "Conspiring against the Jurisdiction" (attempted invasion, insurrection, or rebellion), (5) "Willful murder," (6) "Sudden Murder in Passion," (7) "Murder by Guile or Poisoning," (8) "Witchcraft," (9) "Bestiality," (10) "Sodomy," (11) "Falsewitness," (12) "Man-stealing," (13) "Cursing or Smiting Father or Mother," (14) "The Rebellious Son," (15) "Rape," (16) "Willful burning of Houses, Ships, etc."

The provision, whose margin referred to "sodomy," reads:

> If any Man lyeth with Mankind, as he lyeth with a Woman, both of them have committed Abomination; they both shall surely be put to Death, unless the one party were forced, or be under fourteen years of Age: And all other Sodomitical filthiness, shall be surely punished according to the nature of it.

This Plymouth law was revised when Plymouth was united with Massachusetts, in 1697.

■ ■ ■

1697, MAY 26
Massachusetts: "Buggery" law

After the Massachusetts Bay and the Plymouth colonies were joined as the Massachusetts Colony, a revision of the old Massachusetts Bay law, of 1672, made a terminological change in the new sodomy statute. The crime was now called "buggery" with men or beast; it was still "detestable and abominable" but it was now also "contrary to the very Light of Nature" (hinting that "Nature" was playing a new, prominent role in legal philosophy). Unlike most earlier laws in which sodomy was distinguished from bestiality, the term "buggery" here applied to both kinds of contacts. And both still remained capital crimes.

This Massachusetts "buggery" law, requiring death for the human participants and, in the case of bestiality, the execution and burning of the beast, was one of a series of provisions which also included acts against murder, rape, and "Atheism and Blasphemie" (the latter punished by "boring through the tongue with a red hot iron").

"An Act for the Punishment of Buggery" read:

> For avoiding of the detestable and abominable Sin of Buggery with Mankind or Beast, which is contrary to the very Light of Nature; Be it Enacted and Declared . . . That the same Offence be adjudged Felony . . . And that every Man, being duly convicted of lying with Mankind, as he lieth with a Woman; and every Man or Woman that shall have carnal Copulation with any Beast or Brute Creature, the Offender and Offenders, in either of the

Cases before mentioned, shall suffer the Pains of Death, and the Beast shall be slain and burnt.

This law remained in force until its revision in 1785. A law of 1805 abolished the death penalty for "Sodomy and Bestiality."

◆

HOMOSEXUALITY
The New Catholic Encyclopedia

HOMOSEXUALITY

The terms homosexual and invert describe anyone who is erotically attracted to a notable degree toward persons of his or her own sex and who engages, or is psychologically disposed to engage, in sexual activity prompted by this attraction. In popular thought no distinction is drawn between act and habit, or between a psychological predisposition and its voluntary expression, or between male and female homosexuals. Actually the comparatively few studies made of female homosexuals (Lesbians) reveal traits similar to those of male homosexuals. What is said here about the homosexual applies to both sexes, unless stated otherwise.

Erotic attraction toward the same sex is persistent and enduring. Absence of erotic attraction to the other sex and an aversion for physical relationships with persons of the opposite sex are generally found in homosexuals, but these must not be confused with delay in development of heterosexual interests, or with the low sexual drive of some heterosexuals. The homosexual's aversion from physical relationships with the opposite sex does not preclude cordial friendship.

Contrary to the popular notion that the homosexual has deliberately chosen abnormal over normal sexual activities, almost invariably he discovers his condition during adolescence, and feels overwhelmingly anxious and guilty. It is necessary to distinguish between psychologically conditioned but involuntary homosexuality, and the deliberate formation (if indeed it ever occurs) and the gratification of such impulses. The homosexual is very rarely an abnormally lustful person seeking pleasure in the willful perversion of the sexual instinct. There is no evidence that his sexual drive, in itself, is more intense than that of heterosexuals; consequently, he can control it with the grace of God despite many internal struggles. In almost all cases, the homosexual is emotionally disturbed, fears physical intimacy with the other sex, and is tormented by various obsessive-compulsive drives and depression, which includes the risk of suicide. He is rarely an alcoholic or a threat to immature children.

■ ■ ■

MORALITY OF HOMOSEXUALITY

In considering the morality of homosexuality, three aspects of the matter must be distinguished: (1) responsibility for the homosexual condition, (2) the objective morality of the homosexual act, and (3) the

J. F. Harvey, *Homosexuality, in* VII THE NEW CATHOLIC ENCYCLOPEDIA 116 (1967).

subjective responsibility of the homosexual for particular acts.

Responsibility. Contrary to popular opinion, a person does not become a homosexual because he wants to be one. By the time an individual discovers his homosexual tendencies it is usually too late to do more than learn how to control them. Even in instances where the individual is warned that repeated acts may confirm his homosexual tendency, it is most likely that the proclivity existed before he indulged in deviant practices. In the practical order, therefore, it can generally be assumed that an individual is not responsible for being homosexual. The condition develops gradually over many years as a result of complex influences not under the control of the potential homosexual. He cannot reasonably be expected to foresee the outcome of these influences, or to alter their course.

Objective Morality. The homosexual act by its essence excludes all possibility of transmission of life; such an act cannot fulfill the procreative purpose of the sexual faculty and is, therefore, an inordinate use of that faculty. Since it runs contrary to a very important goal of human nature, it is a grave transgression of the divine will. It is also a deviation from the normal attraction of man for woman, which leads to the foundation of the basic stable unit of society, the family.

Those who hold that it is "natural" for homosexuals to express mutual love by overt acts put themselves in a position in which it is difficult to avoid logically the condoning of any form of sexual irresponsibility. As soon as one separates completely the procreative function of the reproductive organs and of the marital act from their personal and individual values, there remains no principle "by which any mutual act of two people, married or unmarried, of opposite sexes, or of the same sex, can be condemned as immoral, if they simply state that this is the way they choose to express their mutual love.

While there are several passages in Holy Scripture where homosexual connotations are at least doubtful, there are six references that refer to homosexual acts, five referring to males and females. In all cases the practice is condemned in general terms. The first two references are in Lv 18.22 and 20.13, with the latter ordering the death penalty. In the New Testament, three passages refer to male homosexuality: Rom 1:27, 1 Cor 6.9-10, and 1 Tm 1.9-10. Romans 1.26 can be understood as referring to acts between women: "For this cause God has given them up to shameful lusts: for their women have exchanged natural intercourse for what is against nature . . ." This verse is made clearer by the comparison in the following verse, "and in the same way men too, having given up natural intercourse with women, have burned in their lusts toward one another, men with men practicing that well known shamelessness and receiving in their own persons the fitting punishment of their perversity."

The Sodom and Gomorrah account (Gn 19.4-11), from which the sin of sodomy derives its name, is controverted, although in past ages it was assumed to be the *locus classicus* of the divine condemnation of homosexual acts as among the most heinous of sins. Unfortunately, the "traditional" interpretation has given the impression that homosexuals are moral monsters for whom God has selected special punishments. St. Paul, however, mentions other sins that exclude those who are guilty of them from the kingdom of God (1 Cor 6.10; Rom 1.28-32; and Gal 5.19-21).

Subjective Responsibility. Without discounting the objective gravity of a homosexual act, considerations concerning subjective aspects must also be presented to obtain a complete view of the problem as it may exist in particular cases. It is important to distinguish between a tendency toward homosexuality (expressed by dreams, day dreaming, and indeliberate urges) and deliberate consent to these experiences. Only truly free consent involves moral guilt; many homosexuals simply do not know whether they have given consent to the desires incessantly besieging them. Their unhappiness suggests that they have not. At times they are conscious of guilt, but more often than not they seem to act under compulsion, at least in the interior realm of erotic fantasy and desire.

Compulsion is attended by a narrowing of consciousness with respect either to a fascination for some object or to obedience to an impulse regarded as intolerable unless accepted. Included within the term in a broader sense is the conviction, born of bitter failure to control it, that the urge is irresistible. There may be subsequent acceptance of the same idea as the result of indoctrination, for example, by unreliable homosexual literature, or by harsh and vengeful religious writings.

Usually, compulsive fantasy leads to compulsive masturbation. The individual generally has more control over temptations to sin with others than over the ingrained habit of self-abuse. In these circumstances the homosexual is bound to seek help either to live with the compulsion without giving voluntary consent to its movements or rid himself of it by therapy. It may seem contradictory to say that the sexual drive of the homosexual is no stronger than that of the heterosexual and then to speak of compulsive tendencies in the homosexual. However, the source of the compulsion is not in the strength of the sexual drive itself, but in disorders within the whole person that find most ready expression in sexual fantasy or act.

As long as he is willing to follow the counsel of an experienced confessor or a psychiatrist, or both, to mitigate his disorder, and as long as he resists spontaneous carnal desires, he is not accountable for possession of homosexual drives; but if he temporizes with this interior disorder by fostering habits of indiscreet reading, fails to control his senses, cultivates dangerous friendships, and frequents homosexual haunts, he is guilty of placing himself unnecessarily in the proximate occasion of sin.

At times, especially after a long period of self-control, urges to sin become almost irresistible; and, consequently, erotic fantasy, or voyeurism, or a subsequent homosexual act seem irresistible. Since individuals vary in their ability to control apparently compulsive tendencies, only therapists and spiritual counselors, familiar with the invert's background, can form reliable judgments concerning his ability to avoid consent to these drives. Even they are not sure at times. In most instances the counselor's judgment should incline toward compassionate leniency, but he must impress upon the invert his basic obligation to seek help to lead an ordered life of service to God and to his neighbor.

From pastoral experience it is noted that in many cases of the almost irresistible urge discussed above the individual could have stopped the whole process of mounting passion at an early stage, but he did not do so. He knows he ought to stop, he can, but he does not do so. Later he is not able to control the fantasy or the masturbation. Unless he were not able to control temptation from the beginning, he is responsible *in causa* for the effects of the occasion of sin. It is necessary that the homosexual be rigorously honest with himself in evaluating occasions of sin, for promiscuity is just as insidious to him as to the heterosexual. Since there is the possibility that the urge was irresistible from the beginning, the priest should judge the matter leniently.

PASTORAL GUIDANCE

The pastoral approach to the adolescent with apparent homosexual tendencies differs from the guidance given to an adult homosexual. In some instances it may be uncertain whether an adolescent is homosexual, and diagnosis cannot be made before the mid-20s. The counselor should seek a full account of the youth's background and inner motivations, which can be done only after the confidence of the youth has been won. Whatever the youth reveals should be received without condemnation. Only a passing inversion may be discovered, such as a homosexual act performed in a moment of passion, occasioned by curiosity. In this instance, advice to the apparent homosexual will be concerned principally with the avoidance of the proximate occasions of sin.

Very often, despite insufficient evidence of homosexuality, other characteristics, such as depression or anxiety, suggest psychiatric treatment. Referral should be made to a psychiatrist with whom the priest is willing to cooperate, but it should be made clear to the youth that such treatment will be in addition to, and not a substitute for, continual spiritual guidance. Frequently, the apparent homosexual, although involved in an exclusive friendship with a member of his own sex, does not commit repeated acts of homosexuality. In this critical situation the priest may be able to encourage the youth to form several adequate friendships with others as compensation for giving up an exclusive friendship. But whether or not the priest discovers the youth to be an apparent or a real homosexual, he must exercise caution in revealing his insights to the youth. It is not unknown for adolescents who were told that they were homosexual to commit suicide. Some have chosen suicide because they realized that others, particularly their parents, knew of their condition. Other inverts have left the Church because of harsh treatments.

The priest must reeducate the homosexual youth on the nature of love. All true love is a going-out of oneself, a self-giving; but, all unconsciously, homosexual love is bent back upon the self in a closed circle, a sterile love of self, disguised in apparent love for another. What seems like ideal love to the homosexual must be shown to be narcissism. Furthermore, he needs a vocation of service to God and to men that the priest can help him to find. He is no accident in the blueprint of Divine Providence, although it is not clear to him or to anyone why God has allowed him to be inflicted with this disorder against which he has waged battle, oftentimes almost to the point of despair.

The youth may have realized an almost total incapacity to resist the tendency to homosexuality, although he did not will it to be. Unable to understand, much less to cope with this inward movement, he is filled with confusion, guilt, and bitterness. Perception of this condition restrains the priest from undue severity and challenges him to provide the youth with solid hope. He should make the youth feel that he can discuss his problems without fear of censure or rejection.

It should be stressed that a homosexual is just as pleasing to God as a heterosexual, as long as he makes a sincere effort to control his deviant bent with the help of grace. Although the individual may feel certain that his inversion is so deep that he cannot redirect his tendencies, he must accept them and seek to fulfill some purpose in the world.

All the positive directives that the priest gives to the adolescent homosexual may be applied to the adult homosexual. He must be impressed with the divine purpose of suffering in every life. He must make out a plan of life under the guidance of his confessor or director, who will suggest the ways in which the homosexual can render chaste service to the Church and to the world. Such a plan will involve a radical rethinking of an inadequate philosophy of life, a deep determination to redirect the will to supernatural values, and a gradual formation of systematic practices designed to help the invert in leading a virtuous life. This plan must be specific enough to include certain ascetical activities every day, yet pliable enough to allow for the exigencies of daily life. Included in this plan would be some form of meditation for at least 20 minutes a day, Mass and Communion as often as possible during the week, daily examination of conscience, a carefully chosen confessor, and habitual involvement in works of charity.

That the proposed plan of life excludes marriage surprises no one familiar with the dynamics of homosexuality. Considering the poor prognosis of redirection of the deviate's sexual drive into normal channels (according to current research), it would be imprudent to counsel matrimony for any homosexual.

Pastoral experience reveals that the priest can inspire the invert to undertake apostle work for the Church as a means of spiritual adjustment and fulfillment. Like other unmarried individuals, the invert must sacrifice completely any indulgence in sexual pleasure. He can find the vocation willed by God for him in spite of sexual neurosis, just as others have redeemed an empty past by engagement in the lay apostle.

On the negative but practical side, the priest should spell out, especially for the adolescent, specific ways of avoiding the various sources of strong temptations to homosexual acts. The invert should be urged to shun situations wherein immunity from adult observation is combined with a high degree of physical exposure; he should dress discreetly, never compromise himself, and confine himself to normal and respectable social circles. Similar counsel should be given to adolescent girls who suffer similar problems.

The best way to assist the homosexual to achieve self-control is not in listing things to be done or to be avoided, but in a direct appeal to his heart. The goal in a plan of life is to teach the invert both to love God and to realize God's love for him. All the details of that plan must become expressions of love. Beginning with charity, one increases in love by constant acts of charity. This is no belittlement of the powers of reason and faith, which function better when motivated by love. Love of God must become the driving motive in the life of the homosexual who, otherwise, will grow lonely for the kind of fellowship found in homosexual haunts — in which he had been formerly enslaved, to which he is still attracted, and in place of which a stronger love must be found.

IV. SICKNESS

♦

TREATMENT

Jonathan Ned Katz

INTRODUCTION

. . . Lesbians and Gay men have long been subjected to a varied, often horrifying list of "cures" at the hands of psychiatric-psychological professionals, treatments usually aimed at asexualization or heterosexual reorientation. This treatment has almost invariably involved a negative value judgment concerning the inherent character of homo-

JONATHAN NED KATZ, GAY AMERICAN HISTORY 197-205 (1976).

sexuality. The treatment of Lesbians and Gay men by psychiatrists and psychologists constitutes one of the more lethal forms of homosexual oppression.

Among the treatments are surgical measures: castration, hysterectomy, and vasectomy. In the 1800s, surgical removal of the ovaries and of the clitoris are discussed as a "cure" for various forms of female "erotomania," including, it seems, Lesbianism. Lobotomy was performed as late as 1951. A variety of drug therapies have been employed, including the administration of hormones, LSD, sexual stimulants, and sexual depressants. Hypnosis, used on Gay people in America as early as 1899, was still being used to treat such "deviant behavior" in 1967. Other documented "cures" are shock treatment, both electric and chemical; aversion therapy, employing nausea-inducing drugs, electric shock, and/or negative verbal suggestion; and a type of behavior called "sensitization," intended to increase heterosexual arousal, making ingenious use of pornographic photos. Often homosexuals have been the subjects of Freudian psychoanalysis and other varieties of individual and group psychotherapy. Some practitioners (a Catholic one is quoted) have treated homosexuals by urging an effort of the will directed toward the goal of sexual abstinence. Primal therapists, vegetotherapists, and the leaders of each new psychological fad have had their say about treating homosexuals. Even musical analysis has reportedly assisted a doctor in such a "cure." Astrologers, Scientologists, Aesthetic Realists, and other quack philosophers have followed the medical profession's lead with their own suggestions for treatment.

■ ■ ■

The treatment of homosexuality by medical practitioners is of relatively recent origin, and is closely tied to the conceptualization of homosexuality as a medical-psychological phenomenon, a "mental illness." This conceptualization is itself a fairly recent invention: European discussion of homosexuality as a medical phenomenon dates to the early 1800s. Before that time, ecclesiastical authorities conceived of homosexuality as essentially a theological-moral phenomenon, a sin. Next, legislative bodies declared it a legal matter, a crime. The historical change in the conception of homosexuality from sin to crime to sickness is intimately associated with the rise to power of a class of petit bourgeois medical professionals, a group of individual medical entrepreneurs, whose stock in trade is their alleged "expert" understanding of homosexuality, a special-interest group whose façade of scientific objectivity covers their own emotional, economic, and career investments in their status as such authorities. At its time of origin, the medical practitioners' concept of homosexuality as a sickness may have been a liberal and humane advance over the conception and punishment of homosexuality as a crime. In 1976, psychiatrists and psychologists are among the major idealogues of homosexual oppression.

Research is now starting to trace the exact historical process by which these medical businessmen (for they are mostly males) acquired the power to define the character of homosexuals — and to trace that political movement by which Gay people are beginning to redefine themselves, struggling for power over that society which affects their lives. Today, Gay liberationists are challenging the long-accepted, medically derived notion that homosexuality is essentially a psychological phenomenon — any more than it is a political, economic, or historical one. They are disputing that view by which the complex human phenomena of homosexual behavior, emotion, lifestyle, culture, and history are reduced to mere psychology. Neither homosexuality nor heterosexuality, they argue, is encompassed by the psychological. Calling for the reconceptualization of homosexuality in broad, humanistic, and social terms, Gay people are today beginning the work of reconceptualizing themselves.

■ ■ ■

The medical treatment literature documents a history of horrors, one of which has been the way Gay people themselves were made the agents of their own violation and destruction. Treatment has been perpetrated, sometimes, upon acquiescent victims. The very act of entering treatment for one's homosexuality involved a negative evaluation of one's own, often basic, feelings. There is clearly a link between socially induced feelings of guilt and worthlessness, and the self-punishing behavior of some homosexuals reported in these documents. Numbers of these histories concern guilt-ridden, self-hating homosexuals, who have so internalized society's condemnation that they seek out cruel forms of treatment as punishment; they play what can only be termed a masochistic game, in which the doctor is assigned, and accepts, a truly sadistic (as well as remunerative) role. There is surely a link between self-punishment as an internally motivated individual act and punishment as an external legal sanction, between castration as an early form of legal punishment (as proposed by Thomas Jefferson, and enacted into law in Pennsylvania) and castration as an early form of medical treatment.

A connection between the legal and medical establishments is also evident when doctors prominent in the business of treating homosexuals are simultaneously employed by the penal system. Justice is literally on their side when these agents of the medico-legal establishment seek to "rehabilitate" homosexuals who have come into active conflict with the law. This law derives from religious concepts, and Judeo-Christian morality is frequently found in these medical texts, propagated in secularized, pseudoscientific terms, even though such strictures supposedly have no place in a society theoretically based on separation of church and state.

The question of doctors' responsibility is not answered satisfactorily by reference to patients' alleged voluntary and informed consent to treatment and their desire to "go straight". For despite the current popularity of a simplistic libertarian ideology, we are not always in touch with, and do not always know, our own deepest feelings and best interests. In ways Gay people themselves have not fully realized, we do not yet always know our own minds, we are not always immediately able to affirm our own deepest desires. In this respect the present author's own history is like that of many:

> I entered analysis, voluntarily I thought, with the idea that my "problem" was my homosexuality, and my goal a heterosexual "cure," although even then I was wise enough to know I never wanted to be "adjusted" to a society which was itself desperately in need of radical change. Paradoxically, my experience in therapy turned out to be an extremely good one, helping me to know and affirm positive parts of myself, among them my homosexuality. By accident I had found a therapist who helped people to find and be themselves, who did *not* view my "problem" as I did myself. But it was only with the development of the Gay liberation movement, and my own involvement in it, that it came to me, in a rather brief and mind-spinning few months, that I, too, was a member of an oppressed group. Only then, after perhaps ten years of therapy, and only as a result of this organized movement of Gay people, did I understand that I had earlier been socially pressured into feeling myself a psychological freak, in need of treatment. In entering therapy, my goal had, in truth, not been voluntarily chosen at all.

Therapists who do not help their homosexual patients to fully explore the possibility of homosexuality as a legitimate option have not helped to expand those individuals' freedom.

The treatment documents demonstrate that the conflict between Gay people and the psychiatric-psychological profession is of long standing; it did not begin with the recent Gay liberation movement. Dr. Edmund Bergler's lecture before the New York Psychoanalytic Society in 1942 provides evidence of those antihomosexual views which have led many Gay people to despise psychiatrists and psychologists — a conflict of whose origin Bergler is blithely unaware. Bergler's report indicates no sensitivity on his part to the fact that the "ill-repute enjoyed by our therapy among homosexuals" might be due to those therapists' negative evaluation of homosexuals as "sick" (Bergler's term). Bergler has no awareness that recurring conflicts with his homosexual patients (reported by himself) just might have something to do with his own attitudes toward "perverts" and "perversion" (his terms). His characterization of homosexuals as "injustice" collectors, who provoke trouble upon themselves to justify self-pity, must have struck some homosexuals as a provocative way of blaming the victim — even before the rise of the Gay liberation movement. The great irritation Gay liberationists will no doubt feel while reading Bergler's account today is simply a more conscious, less ambivalent form of that same dislike experienced (according to his own report) by many of Bergler's patients. Even in pre-Gay liberation days some homosexuals must have resented, however ambivalently, Bergler's positive evaluation of their pain — based on his belief that a certain high level of guilt indicated a good prognosis for heterosexual reorientation. In Bergler's report, it is indeed odd to find a man supposedly concerned with the alleviation of mental suffering so positively gleeful about the guilt feelings of homosexuals. If, as Bergler points out, many Gay people in treatment with him displayed masochistic tendencies, then he was undoubtedly the sadist in those partnerships. Bergler's provocative comments do raise serious questions abut masochism as a form of socially conditioned Gay self-oppression, and about the often sadistic treatment of Gay people by psychiatrists and psychologists.

Bergler's antihomosexual views are typical of many other doctors, few of whom show any sign of seriously questioning their own motives, feelings, and fundamental assumptions in treating homosexuals. Their basic system of values has remained quite simple and unchanged through the years. America's psychological establishment has quite simplemindedly propagated the absolute virtues of heterosexuality, marriage, monogamy, parenthood, and the most traditional, narrow definitions of femininity, masculinity, and of male and female roles. The doctors' reports are characterized by a complacent, middle-class sensibility, a smug philistinism. This moralizing is most evident in the earliest documents quoted — those from the end of the nineteenth century and the start of the twentieth. At that time, doctors un-self-consciously invoked morality — God, country, family — in describing their treatment of homosexuals. More recent documents usually replace such overt moralizing with quieter, often unspoken, hidden evaluations, expressive of a technocratic consciousness focused on getting a job done, a new heterosexual created. Doctors have increasingly turned to technical language and jargon to disguise and suppress their own emotions and underlying values. Although secularization has transformed the rhetoric, mystification remains.

The focus here is on treatment — actual medical practice — rather than on either of the two other major areas of medical discourse on homosexuality: its alleged nature, its supposed cause. These character assessments and etiological discussions have often been of a highly abstract, theoretical, and speculative character, disassociated from any social reality. The literature on treatment, on the other hand, conveys what was actually done to, and even experienced by, Lesbians and Gay men. The diverse theories of the alleged character and cause of homosexuality, and their relation to particular forms of treatment, do need to be studied in social-historical perspective — an important task for the future. Here, the doctors' causative theories may often be inferred from the type of treatment they prescribe. Aversion therapy, for instance, rests upon the tenets of behavioral psychology holding that homosexuality is a learned response, capable of being unlearned. This concept is only distantly related to the more complex notion of those psychoanalysts who regard sexual orientation as the outcome of early experience, especially within the family, by which social norms and role models come to influence the undefined psyche of a child. Opposed to both these views are various physiological theories of causation, now generally regarded as outmoded, according to which homosexuality is either treatable by biological means, such as hormones, or is an unalterable, hereditary trail. It is now becoming clear that the causation of homosexuality cannot be understood apart from the causation of sexual orientation of every variety (including heterosexuality, bestiality, and object fetishism) — if the subject is to be studied at all. Past interest in the subject was almost always motivated and obscured by either pro- or anti-homosexual views: the cause of homosexuality is inborn, it was argued, therefore homosexuals should be free of legal harassment or medical treatment; or homosexuality is a "bad thing," which understanding might make alterable. Contemporary Gay liberationists emphasize that study of the cause and cure of heterosexuals' seeming obsessive antihomosexuality should have higher priority.

Except for their vested interest in incomprehension, it should not be too difficult for even the most obtuse psychiatrists to understand that to characterize homosexuals as products of arrested emotional development, or to propagate any such all-encompassing negative judgment, is to perpetuate an oppression that has caused Gay people much mental anguish. By the suffering they have caused, the damage they have done, psychiatric-psychological professionals have revealed their own moral character. There is a special obscenity about bigotry in the guise of "help," antihomosexual pronouncements in the name of "mental health," or similar prejudice from religious authorities in the name of morality. The early Puritans were at least open about their hate; homosexuals were "abominations," to be punished by death. Simple. Clear. Contemporary puritans are less candid. Today, Gay liberationists are doing what they can to delegitimize those "experts" who have done their best to delegitimize them. The psychiatric-psychological profession's collective responsibility for causing homosexuals years of pain invalidates its claim to speak as a humane and moral authority on the subject of homosexuals' "mental health." It might begin to rehabilitate itself by publicly recognizing its own role in Gay oppression and by using its very real power to call for the immediate, universal repeal of all laws criminalizing sexual activity between consenting persons, as well as for civil rights legislation to protect individuals discriminated against on the basis of sexual or affectional orientation.

Not all the medical treatment literature conveys quite so much in quite so little space as the following British report, dating to 1964, of aversion treatment:

> Aversion therapy was conducted with a male homosexual who had a heart condition. The particular form of aversion therapy involved creation of nausea, by means of an emetic, accompanied by talking about his homosexuality. The second part of the therapy involved recovery from the nausea and talking about pleasant ideas and heterosexual fantasies, which was sometimes aided by lysergic acid. In this case, the patient died as a result of a heart attack brought on by the use of the emetic.

♦

HOMOSEXUALITY AND AMERICAN PSYCHIATRY: THE POLITICS OF DIAGNOSIS
Ronald Bayer

EARLY SCIENTIFIC THEORIES OF HOMOSEXUALITY

In the early decades of the nineteenth century, what medical discussion of homosexuality did take place clearly bore the mark of the more powerful religious tradition. Though it was acknowledged that in some instances such behavior could be the result of insanity, in most instances it was considered freely willed and therefore a vice. Sir Alexander Morison wrote in his "Outlines on Lectures on Mental Disease," prepared in 1825, that

> Monomania with Unnatural Propensity is a variety of partial insanity, the principal feature of which is an irresistible propensity to the crime against nature. This offense is so generally abhorred, that in treatises upon law it is termed 'peccatum illud horribile inter Christianas non nominandum'. . . . Being of so detestable a character it is a consolation to know that it is sometimes the consequence of insanity: it is, however, a melancholy truth that the offense has been committed in Christian countries by persons in full possession of their reason and capable of controlling their actions.

Only in the last half of the century did homosexuality become the subject of concerted scientific investigation. Those who sought to explain the "propensity to the crime against nature" were divided between those who saw it as an acquired char-

acteristic and those who viewed it as inborn. Despite its greater compatibility with the tradition of assigning culpability to the individual homosexual, however, the acquired school did not dominate scientific inquiry during this period, but rather had to share its influence with that which focused on the importance of heredity.

Carl Westphal, a professor of psychiatry in Berlin, is credited with placing the study of homosexuality on a clinical, scientific footing by publishing a case history of a female homosexual in 1869. Terming her condition "contrary sexual feeling," he concluded that her abnormality was congenital rather than acquired. In the next years he went on to study more than two hundred such cases, developing a classification of the variety of behaviors associated with homosexuality. In France, Jean Martin Charcot, the director of the Salpêtrière, also concluded that homosexuality was inherited after he failed to effect a cure through hypnosis. For his fellow countryman Paul Moreau, homosexuality was the outgrowth of both an inherited "constitutional weakness" and environmental forces. Given an inborn predisposition to perversion, a "hereditary taint," factors ranging from poverty and climate to masturbation could precipitate the manifestation of homosexuality. In a state midway between reason and madness, those afflicted were in constant danger of becoming insane and thus required the protection of the asylum. Most important of the late nineteenth-century students of sexual deviance was Richard von Krafft-Ebbing, whose monumental *Psychopathia Sexualis* had an enormous impact on informed opinion about

RONALD BAYER, HOMOSEXUALITY AND AMERICAN PSYCHIATRY: THE POLITICS OF DIAGNOSIS 18–40 (1981), homosexuality. Considering any form of nonprocreative sexuality a perversion with potentially disastrous personal and social consequences, he attempted, like others in this period, to explain the existence of homosexuality in terms of both environmental and inherited factors. Each of his case studies sought to document a history of family pathology — insanity, epilepsy, hysteria, convulsions, alcoholism, and physical disorders — in those who developed, as a result of their life experiences, some form of sexual pathology.

The tendency to view homosexuality as inherited was linked by many investigators to a more general interest in the extent to which various forms of degeneracy represented an atavistic reappearance of primitive tendencies. Some believed that not only did homosexuals deviate from civilized sexual standards, but they were likely to engage in uncontrolled primitive and animal-like behavior as well. These views were most notable expressed by Cesar Lombroso, the late nineteenth-century Italian criminologist, who argued that homosexuals were at a lower stage of human development than heterosexuals. Though the human race had evolved over eons, leaving behind its own primitive behavior, each child was required to recapitulate the process in the course of its own development. Those with defective heredity failed to complete that process and remained at a less civilized point in the evolutionary course. Since, in Lombroso's view, homosexuals could not be held responsible for their own failure, no justification existed for their punishment. Social defense, however, required that they be restricted to asylums because of the danger they posed.

Not only did many of those who assumed that homosexuality represented a profound deviation from the normal pattern of human sexuality turn to hereditary factors in order to explain its roots; so too did those who had begun to challenge the dominant view. Karl Ulrichs, one of the most prolific nineteenth-century defenders of homosexuals, had asserted, beginning in the 1860s, that homosexuality was a hereditary anomaly: While the genitals of homosexuals developed along expected lines, their brains did not, and so it was possible for a female soul to be lodged in a male's body. These views anticipated those of Havelock Ellis, whose work *Sexual Inversion* sought to demonstrate that homosexuality was inborn, *and therefore* natural. Finally, Magnus Hirschfeld, the great advocate of homosexual rights in Germany, held that homosexuality was not pathological but rather the result of inborn characteristics determined by glandular secretions.

Thus scientific formulations were relied upon by those with the most fundamentally divergent standpoints. Newly discovered facts did little to frame the understanding of homosexuality; rather, it was the perspective on homosexuality that determined the meaning of those facts.

PSYCHOANALYSIS AND HOMOSEXUALITY: FREUD

For Freud, as for most of those who undertook the scientific study of sexuality in the last years of the nineteenth century and the first years of the twentieth century, there was no question but that heterosexuality represented the normal end of psychosexual development. Despite the complex and uncertain process of maturation, "one of the tasks implicit in object choice is that it should find its way to the opposite sex." Here Freud saw no conflict between the demands of convention and nature's course.

In his first effort to account for what he termed sexual inversion, Freud set himself in sharp opposition to those scientists who claimed that homosexuality was an indication of degeneracy. In his *Three Essays on the Theory of Sexuality* he asserted that such a diagnosis could be justified only if homosexuals typically exhibited a number of serious deviations from normal behavior and if their capacity for survival and "efficient functioning" was severely impaired. Since Freud believed that homosexuality was found in men and women who exhibited no other deviations, whose efficiency was unimpaired, and who were "indeed distinguished by specially high intellectual development and ethical culture," it made little sense to him to employ the classification "degenerate" for inverts.

This perspective distinguished him from many of his earliest followers as well as from later psychoanalytic clinicians who would see in homosexuality a profound disturbance affecting every aspect of social functioning. He rejected the suggestion on the part of some of his collaborators, including Ernest Jones, that homosexuals be barred from membership in psychoanalytic societies. "In effect we cannot exclude such persons without other sufficient reasons, as we cannot agree with their legal prosecution. We feel that a decision in such cases should depend upon a thorough examination of the other qualities of the candidate." To a similar suggestion by the Berlin psychoanalytic society he responded that while barring homosexuals from psychoanalytic work might serve as something of a "guideline," it was necessary to avoid a rigid posture since there were many types of homosexuality as well as quite diverse psychological mechanisms that could account for its existence.

Unlike those who saw homosexuality as a thing apart from normal sexuality, Freud characterized it as a natural feature of human psychosexual existence, a component of the libidinal drives of all men and women. All children experienced a homosexual phase in their psychosexual development, passing through it on the route to heterosexuality. Even in those who advanced successfully beyond the earlier phase of development, however, homosexual tendencies remained. "The homosexual tendencies are not ... done away with or brought to a stop." They were rather "deflected" from their original target and served other ends. For Freud the social instincts such as friendship, camaraderie, and "the general love for mankind" all derived their strength, their erotic component, from the unconscious homosexual impulses of those who had achieved the capacity for heterosexual relations.

The capacity for both homosexual and heterosexual love was linked by Freud to what he believed was an instinctual, constitutional bisexuality. Activity, passivity, the desire to introduce a part of one's body into that of another or to have a part of another's body introduced into oneself, and finally, masculinity and femininity, were all reflections of bisexuality. At times the active, masculine drives dominated, at others the feminine, passive drives did. In no case was a person utterly without both sets of drives. Just as with homosexual impulses, the repressed was not obliterated. Even in adults who had traversed the course to heterosexuality, masculine and feminine impulses coexisted.

Given the bisexual endowments of human beings, how did Freud account for the existence of exclusive homosexuality in the adult male?* Rather than propose an elaborated theory, Freud set forth a number of explanations for the perversion of the normal course of psychosexual development. The classical mechanisms discovered during his psychoan-

---

* Since it is not my purpose to present a full account of the various psychoanalytic theories of homosexuality, but rather to note the ways in which the issue was approached, I have decided for purposes of brevity to restrict this discussion almost exclusively to male homosexuality, leaving aside the question of the etiology of lesbianism. It should be noted that in part because of the greater clinical exposure on the part of psychoanalysts to homosexual men, women have received less attention in the literature. This tendency has, of course, also been explained in terms of the minimization of female sexuality. Nevertheless, the issue was not ignored, as is made clear by Freud's lengthy case history, "The Psychogenesis of a Case of Homosexuality in a Woman" (1920) in *Sexuality and the Psychology of Love*. See also Fenichel, *Psychoanalytic Theory*, pp. 338–44.

alytic work stressed a number of possibilities, any one of which might determine a homosexual outcome. Regardless of the specific factors involved, however, all of them started from the assumption that exclusive homosexuality represented an arrest of the developmental process, an instinctual fixation at a stage short of normal heterosexuality.

Among Freud's first formulations on the etiology of homosexuality was one that focused on the male child's attachment to his own genitals as a source of pleasure. Like all boys, those who are destined to become homosexual find in the penis a source of enormous pleasure. But, Freud believed, there existed in future homosexuals an "excessive" inborn interest in their own genitals during the autoerotic phase of psychosexual development. "Indeed it is the high esteem felt by the homosexual for the male organ which decides his fate." Like other boys, those with such a fixation initially select woman, their mothers and sometimes their sisters, as objects of sexual desire. But that attraction ends when they discover that the female has no penis. Since these boys cannot give up the male organ they may turn to men for sexual pleasure. For Freud those who became homosexual for this reason had failed to traverse the course between autoeroticism and the more mature stage of object love. "They . . . remained at a point of fixation between the two."

Later, Freud asserted that homosexuality was linked to the profound frustration experienced during the oedipal phase by those boys who had developed especially intense attachments to their mothers. Denied the sexual gratification for which they yearned, these boys regressed to an earlier stage of development, and identified with the woman they could not have. They then sought as sexual partners young men who resembled themselves and loved them in the way they would have had their mothers love them.

In those cases where an intense attachment to the mother was combined with a fixation upon the erotic pleasures of the anus, the dy-

namics were somewhat different. In these instances, a desire to receive sexual gratification from the mother was transformed into a wish to enjoy sex in the way she did. "With this as a point of departure, the father becomes the object of love, and the individual strives to submit to him as the mother does, in a passive-receptive manner."

While Freud saw the child's attachment to the mother as pivotal in most cases, he was careful to note instances in which the father and other male figures played a central role in the etiology of homosexuality. In some cases the absence of the mother could determine the homosexual outcome. Deprived of the presence of a woman, the young boy might develop a deep attachment to his father or another older male and as a result seek in his later sexual partners someone reminiscent of the primary object of his love. Alternatively, fear of the anger aroused in his father by the son's oedipal strivings could account for homosexuality. Terrified at the prospect of his father's retaliatory rage, the young boy could be forced to withdraw from his intense attachment to his mother. Having chosen to "retire in favor" of the more powerful male in this instance, such a boy would then leave the field of women entirely. Thereafter only a homosexual attachment to men could provide sexual gratification without anxiety about castration. Finally, a later speculation of Freud's suggested yet another formulation involving a powerful male in the etiology of homosexuality. Here an older male sibling was crucial. In such cases, jealousy derived from intense competition for the mother's attention generated murderous impulses in the younger boy. Partially because of training, but more importantly because the boy recognized his own relative weakness, he was forced to repress those wishes. Transformed in the process, they would then express themselves as homosexual love for the formerly hated brother.

Running throughout Freud's efforts to identify the roots of homosexuality was a complex series of combinations of inherited, "constitutional" factors and environmental or "accidental" influences. He strove to find a middle ground in the debate between those who asserted that either biology or conditioning forces were exclusively responsible for a homosexual outcome. Although acknowledging in both his case histories and his theoretical work the presence of accidental determinants in many instances of homosexuality, he could not accept an exclusive reliance upon environment. The fact that not everyone subjected to similar influences became homosexual suggested an important role for biological forces. Confronted by an extraordinary richness of detail in his case studies, Freud remarked that he had uncovered a "continual mingling and blending" of what in theory "we should try to separate into a pair of opposites — namely inherited and acquired factors."

As a theoretician Freud was committed to the proposition that all psychic phenomena were determined by antecedent forces beyond the conscious control of individuals. It was this determinism as well as his own more generous attitude toward the basic instinctual drives of human beings that made him so unalterably opposed to the rigid, condemnatory stance of his society toward homosexuals. That same determinism made his work anathema to those whose world-view demanded that individuals be held to account for their willful violations of civilized sexual standards. But despite his determinism, Freud acknowledged difficulty in assigning importance and predictive force to the various innate and environmental factors he had isolated in the analysis of homosexuals. These etiological elements were only known "qualitatively and not in their relative strength." Thus the anomalous situation had emerged in which "it is always possible by analysis to recognize causation with certainty, whereas a prediction of it by synthesis is impossible." Unable to predict homosexuality, psychoanalysis could nevertheless unequivocally assert that in those cases where it had developed could there have been no other outcome.

Always critical of those whom he termed "therapeutic enthusiasts," Freud was especially pessimistic about the prospects for the psychoanalytic cure of homosexuality: "One must remember that normal sexuality also depends upon a restriction in the choice of object; in general to undertake to convert a fully developed homosexual into a heterosexual is not much more promising than to do the reverse, only that for good practical reasons the latter is never attempted." At the basis of this profound limitation on his own technique was his belief that the cure of homosexuals involved the conversion of one "variety of genital organization of sexuality into the other" rather than the resolution of a neurotic conflict. Unlike the neuroses, which were a source of pain and discomfort, homosexuality was a source of pleasure. "Perversions are the negative of neuroses." To treat a homosexual successfully would necessitate convincing him that if he gave up his current source of erotic pleasure he could again "find the pleasure he had renounced." Aware of how difficult it was for neurotics to change, Freud was unable to strike a positive therapeutic stance here. Only where the homosexual fixation was relatively weak, or where there remained "considerable rudiments and vestiges of a heterosexual choice of object" was the prognosis more favorable.

Freud's therapeutic pessimism as well as his acknowledgment that many homosexuals, though arrested in their development, could derive pleasure from both love and work provides the context in which his compassionate and now famous "Letter to an American Mother" of 1935 must be read.

Dear Mrs. . . .

I gather from your letter that your son is a homosexual. I am most impressed by the fact that you do not mention this term yourself in your information about him. May I question you, why you avoid it? Homosexuality is assuredly no advantage, but it is nothing to be ashamed of, no vice, no degradation, it cannot be classified as an illness; we consider it to be a variation of the sexual function produced by a certain arrest of sexual development. Many highly respectable individuals of ancient and modern times have been homosexuals, several of the greatest men among them (Plato, Michelangelo, Leonardo da Vinci, etc.). It is a great injustice to persecute homosexuality as a crime, and cruelty too. If you do not believe me, read the books of Havelock Ellis.

By asking me if I can help, you mean, I suppose, if I can abolish homosexuality and make normal heterosexuality take its place. The answer is, in a general way, we cannot promise to achieve it. In a certain number of cases we succeed in developing the blighted germs of heterosexual tendencies which are present in every homosexual, in the majority of cases it is no more possible. It is a question of the quality and the age of the individual. The result of treatment cannot be predicted.

What analysis can do for your son runs in a different line. If he is unhappy, neurotic, torn by conflicts, inhibited in his social life, analysis may bring him harmony, peace of mind, full efficiency whether he remains a homosexual or gets changed.

Sincerely yours with kind wishes,
Freud

PSYCHOANALYSIS AND HOMOSEXUALITY: RADO, BIEBER, AND SOCARIDES

Though some analysts were more sanguine, Freud's pessimism regarding the possibility of the therapeutic reversal of homosexuality dominated psychoanalytic thinking for almost forty years. Here, at any rate, the psychoanalytic movement did not differ dramatically from the congenital school, which held that homosexuality was an irreversible anomaly. A marked shift took place in the 1940s, influenced in large measure by the work of Sandor Rado and his adaptational school of psychoanalysis. Rejecting the core Freudian concept of bisexuality, Rado and his followers were able to rethink the roots of homosexuality, and adopt a more optimistic therapeutic posture.

■ ■ ■

PSYCHIATRY AND THE "DISEASE" OF HOMOSEXUALITY

Although the theories elaborated by Bieber and Socarides gained considerable prominence in the 1960s and early 1970s, other psychoanalytic formulations retained adherents during this period, and were a guide to both theoretical developments and therapeutic intervention. Such diversity was not simply the result of the creative efforts of clinicians to explain the presence of the homosexual symptom in the very different patients with whom they worked; it represented profoundly divergent theoretical orientations. Freudians and neo-Freudians, those inspired by the libido theory and those who followed Rado, proponents of the pre-oedipal and oedipal etiological formulations all agreed, however, on one point. Homosexuality was a pathological condition. When the dominance of psychoanalytic theory in American psychiatry began to wane in the 1960s, other schools of thought incorporated, without much difficulty, the view that homosexuality was an abnormality. For behaviorists, for example, homosexuality was simply transformed from a perversion of the normal pattern of psychosexual development into the "maladaptive consequence" of "inappropriate learning."

The virtual unanimity regarding the pathological status of homosexuality was underscored in a striking context by Karl Menninger in his 1963 introduction to the American edition of the British Wolfenden Report. That report, which had gained international attention by calling for the decriminalization of homosexual activity between consenting adults, had rejected the classification of homosexuality as a disease. Applauding its criminal law recommendation, Menninger ignored the latter point, writing:

> From the standpoint of the psychiatrist . . . homosexuality . . . constitutes evidence of immature sexuality and either arrested psychological development or regression. Whatever it be called by the pubic, there is no question in the minds of psychiatrists regarding the abnormality of such behavior.

Although the psychiatric consensus on homosexuality was still undisturbed in 1963, it had already come under serious political challenge from homosexual activists and their ideological allies.

The situation had been very different in 1952 when the American Psychiatric Association issued its first official listing of mental disorders. At that time voices of dissent were beginning to surface but had little political force. The *Diagnostic and Statistical Manual, Mental Disorders (DSM-I)* had evolved from the efforts of a working group brought together under the aegis of the United States Public Health Service to design a nosological scheme adequate to the needs of modern psychiatry. The listing of psychiatric disorders contained in the American Medical Association's *Standard Classified Nomenclature of Disease* had proved inadequate. Designed primarily for the classification of chronic mental patients, it lacked the scope required by clinicians engaged in psychiatric practice. More important, it was considered outmoded by the increasing numbers of psychodynamically oriented psychiatrists emerging from training centers dominated by psychoanalytic

theory. *DSM-I* thus represented a major effort on the part of American psychiatry to establish the boundaries of its work.

In the new nomenclature homosexuality and the other sexual deviations were included among the sociopathic personality disturbances. These disorders were characterized by the absence of subjectively experienced distress or anxiety despite the presence of profound pathology. Thus it was possible to include homosexuality in the nosology despite the apparent lack of discomfort or dis-ease on the part of some homosexuals. It was the pattern of behavior that established the pathology. Explicitly acknowledging the centrality of dominant social values in defining such conditions, *DSM-1* asserted that individuals so diagnosed were "ill primarily in terms of society and of conformity with the prevailing cultural milieu."

This first classificatory scheme remained unchanged until 1968 when a revised nomenclature was issued. In the revised *Diagnostic and Statistical Manual of Psychiatric Disorders (DSM-II)* homosexuality was removed from the category of sociopathic personality disturbances and listed together with the other sexual deviations — fetishism, pedophilia, transvestitism, exhibitionism, voyeurism, sadism and masochism — among the "other non-psychotic mental disorders." Despite the existence of a very well-developed homophile movement at the time *DSM-II* was issued, homosexual activists appear to have been unconcerned with its publication. Two years later the classification of homosexuality in the *Manual* was to become the central focus of the Gay Liberation movement's attack on psychiatry.

In 1973, as the result of three years of challenge on the part of gay activists and their allies within the American Psychiatric Association, homosexuality was deleted from the nomenclature. That decision marked the culmination of two decades of struggle that had shattered the fundamental moral and professional consensus on homosexuality.

BOUTILIER v. IMMIGRATION AND NATURALIZATION SERVICE

387 U.S. 118 (1967)

MR. JUSTICE CLARK delivered the opinion of the Court.

The petitioner, an alien, has been ordered deported to Canada as one who upon entry into this country was a homosexual and therefore "afflicted with psychopathic personality" and excludable under § 212(a)(4) of the Immigration and Nationality Act of 1952, 8 USC § 1182(a)(4). Petitioner's appeal from the finding of the Special Inquiry Officer was dismissed by the Board of Immigration Appeals, without opinion, and his petition for review in the Court of Appeals was dismissed, with one judge dissenting. It held that the term "psychopathic personality," as used by the Congress in § 212(a)(4), was a term of art intended to exclude homosexuals from entry into the United States. It further found that the term was not void for vagueness and was, therefore, not repugnant to the Fifth Amendment's Due Process Clause. We . . . now affirm.

I

Petitioner, a Canadian national, was first admitted to this country on June 22, 1955, at the age of 21. His last entry was in 1959, at which time he was returning from a short trip to Canada. His mother and stepfather and three of his brothers and sisters live in the United States. In 1963 he applied for citizenship and submitted to the Naturalization Examiner an affidavit in which he admitted that he was arrested in New York in October 1959, on a charge of sodomy, which was later reduced to simple assault and thereafter dismissed on default of the complainant. In 1964, petitioner, at the request of the Government, submitted another affidavit which revealed the full history of his sexual deviate behavior. It stated that his first homosexual

experience occurred when he was 14 years of age, some seven years before his entry into the United States. Petitioner was evidently a passive participant in this encounter. His next episode was at age 16 and occurred in a public park in Halifax, Nova Scotia. Petitioner was the active participant in this affair. During the next five years immediately preceding his first entry into the United States petitioner had homosexual relations on an average of three or four times a year. He also stated that prior to his entry he had engaged in heterosexual relations on three or four occasions. During the eight and one-half years immediately subsequent to his entry, and up to the time of his second statement, petitioner continued to have homosexual relations on an average of three or four times a year. Since 1959 petitioner had shared an apartment with a man with whom he had had homosexual relations.

The 1964 affidavit was submitted to the Public Health Service for its opinion as to whether petitioner was excludable for any reason at the time of his entry. The Public Health Service issued a certificate in 1964 stating that in the opinion of the subscribing physicians petitioner "was afflicted with a class A condition, namely, psychopathic personality, sexual deviate" at the time of his admission. Deportation proceedings were then instituted. "No serious question," the Special Inquiry Officer found, "has been raised either by the respondent [petitioner here], his counsel or the psychiatrists [employed by petitioner] who have submitted reports on the respondent as to his sexual deviation." Indeed, the officer found that both of petitioner's psychiatrists "concede that the respondent has been a homosexual for a number of years but conclude that by reason of such sexual deviation the respondent is not a psychopathic personality."

Finding against petitioner on the facts, the issue before the officer was reduced to the purely legal question of whether the term "psychopathic personality" included homosexuals and if it suffered illegality because of vagueness.

II

The legislative history of the Act indicates beyond a shadow of a doubt that the Congress intended the phrase "psychopathic personality" to include homosexuals such as petitioner.

Prior to the 1952 Act the immigration law excluded "persons of constitutional psychopathic inferiority." Beginning in 1950, a subcommittee of the Senate Committee on the Judiciary conducted a comprehensive study of the immigration laws and in its report found "that the purpose of the provision against 'persons with constitutional psychopathic inferiority' will be more adequately served by changing that term to 'persons afflicted with psychopathic personality,' and that the classes of mentally defectives should be enlarged to include homosexuals and other sex perverts." The resulting legislation . . . used the new phrase "psychopathic personality." The bill, however, contained an additional clause providing for the exclusion of aliens "who are homosexuals or sex perverts." As the legislation progressed, however, it omitted the latter clause "who are homosexuals or sex perverts" and used only the phrase "psychopathic personality." The omission is explained by the Judiciary Committee Report on the bill:

> The provisio[n] of S716 [one of the earlier bills not enacted] which specifically excluded homosexuals and sex perverts as a separate excludable class does not appear in the instant bill. The Public Health Service has advised that the provision for the exclusion of aliens afflicted with psychopathic personality or a mental defect which appears in the instant bill is sufficiently broad to provide for the exclusion of homosexuals and sex perverts. *This change of nomenclature is not to be construed in any way as modifying the intent to exclude all aliens who are sexual deviates.*

Likewise, a House bill, HR 5678, adopted the position of the Public Health Service that the phrase "psychopathic personality" excluded from entry homosexuals and sex perverts. The report that accompanied the bill shows clearly that the House Judiciary Committee adopted the recommendation of the Public Health Service that "psychopathic personality" should be used in the Act as a phrase that would exclude from admission homosexuals and sex perverts. It quoted at length, and specifically adopted, the Public Health Service report which recommended that the term "psychopathic personality" be used to "specify such types of pathologic behavior as homosexuality or sexual perversion." We, therefore, conclude that the Congress used the phrase "psychopathic personality" not in the clinical sense, but to effectuate its purpose to exclude from entry all homosexuals and other sex perverts.

Petitioner stresses that only persons *afflicted* with psychopathic personality are excludable. This, he says, is "a condition, physical or psychiatric, which may be manifested in different ways, including sexual behavior." Petitioner's contention must fall by his own admissions. For over six years prior to his entry petitioner admittedly followed a continued course of homosexual conduct. The Public Health Service doctors found and certified that at the time of his entry petitioner "was afflicted with a class A condition, namely, psychopathic personality, sexual deviate . . . ." It was stipulated that if these doctors were to appear in the case they would testify to this effect and that "no useful purpose would be served by submitting this additional psychiatric material [furnished by petitioner's doctors] to the United States Public Health Service . . . ." The Government clearly established that petitioner was a homosexual at entry. Having substantial support in the record, we do not now disturb that finding, especially since petitioner admitted being a homosexual at the time of his entry. The existence of this condition over a continuous and uninterrupted period prior to and at the time of petitioner's entry clearly supports the ultimate finding upon which the order of deportation was based.

III

Petitioner says, even so, the section as construed is constitutionally defective because it did not adequately warn him that his sexual affliction at the time of entry could lead to his deportation. It is true that this Court has held the "void for vagueness" doctrine applicable to civil as well as criminal actions. However, this is where "the exaction of obedience to a rule or standard . . . was so vague and indefinite as really to be no rule or standard at all. . . ." In short, the exaction must strip a participant of his rights to come within the principle of the cases. But the "exaction" of § 212(a)(4) never applied to petitioner's conduct after entry. The section imposes neither regulation of nor sanction for conduct. In this situation, therefore, no necessity exists for guidance so that one may avoid the applicability of the law. The petitioner is not being deported for conduct engaged in after his entry into the United States, but rather for characteristics he possessed *at the time of* his entry. Here, when petitioner first presented himself at our border for entrance, he was already afflicted with homosexuality. The pattern was cut, and under it he was not admissible.

The constitutional requirement of fair warning has no applicability to standards such as are laid down in § 212(a)(4) for admission of aliens to the United States. It has long been held that the Congress has plenary power to make rules for the admission of aliens and to exclude those who possess those characteristics which Congress has forbidden. Here Congress commanded that homosexuals not be allowed to enter. The petitioner was found to have that characteristic and was ordered deported. The basis of the deportation order was his affliction for a long period of time *prior to entry*, i.e., six and one-half years before his entry. It may be, as some claim, that "psychopathic personality" is a medically ambiguous term, including several separate and distinct afflictions. But the test here is what the Congress intended, not what differing psychiatrists may think. It was not laying down a clinical test, but an exclusionary standard which it declared to be inclusive of those having homosexual and perverted characteristics. It can hardly be disputed that the legislative history of § 212(a)(4) clearly shows that Congress so intended.

But petitioner says that he had no warning and that no interpretation of the section had come down at the time of his 1955 entry. Therefore, he argues, he was unaware of the fact that homosexual conduct engaged in after entry could lead to his deportation. We do not believe that petitioner's post-entry conduct is the basis for his deportation order. At the time of his first entry he had continuously been afflicted with homosexuality for over six years. To us the statute is clear. It fixes "the time of entry" as the crucial date and the record shows that the findings of the Public Health Service doctors and the Special Inquiry Officer all were based on that date. We find no indication that the post-entry evidence was of any consequence in the ultimate decision of the doctors, the hearing officer or the court. Indeed, the proof was uncontradicted as to petitioner's characteristic at the time of entry and this brought him within the excludable class. A standard applicable solely to time of entry could hardly be vague as to post-entry conduct.

■ ■ ■

Affirmed.

MR. JUSTICE BRENNAN dissents for the reasons stated by Judge Moore of the Court of Appeals, 363 F.2d 488, 496-499.

MR. JUSTICE DOUGLAS, with whom MR. JUSTICE FORTAS concurs, dissenting.

The term "psychopathic personality" is a treacherous one like "communist" or in an earlier day "Bolshevik." A label of this kind when freely used may mean only an unpopular person. It is much too vague by constitutional standards for the imposition of penalties or punishment.

Cleckley defines "psychopathic personality" as one who has the following characteristics:

> (1) Superficial charm and good "intelligence." (2) Absence of delusions and other signs of irrational "thinking." (3) Absence of "nervousness" or psychoneurotic manifestations. (4) Unreliability. (5) Untruthfulness and insincerity. (6) Lack of remorse or shame. (7) Inadequately motivated antisocial behavior. (8) Poor judgment and failure to learn by experience. (9) Pathologic egocentricity and incapacity for love. (10) General poverty in major affective reactions. (11) Specific loss of insight. (12) Unresponsiveness in general interpersonal relations. (13) Fantastic and uninviting behavior with drink and sometimes without. (14) Suicide rarely carried out. (15) Sex life impersonal, trivial and poorly integrated. (16) Failure to follow any life plan. Cleckley, THE MASK OF SANITY 238-255 (1941).

The word "psychopath" according to some means "a sick mind." Guttmacher & Weihofen, PSYCHIATRY AND THE LAW 86 (1952):

In the light of present knowledge, most of the individuals called psychopathic personalities should probably be considered as suffering from neurotic character disorders. They are, for the most part, unhappy persons, harassed by tension and anxiety, who are struggling against unconscious conflicts which were created during the very early years of childhood. The nature and even the existence of these conflicts which drive them restlessly on are unknown to them. When the anxiety rises to a certain pitch, they seek relief through some antisocial act. The frequency with which this pattern recurs in the individual is dependent in part upon the intensity of the unconscious conflict, upon the tolerance for anxiety, and upon chance environmental situations which may heighten or decrease it. One of the chief diagnostic criteria of this type of neurotically determined delinquency is the repetitiveness of the pattern. The usual explanation, as for example, that the recidivistic check-writer has just 'got in the habit of writing bad checks' is meaningless. *Id.*, at 88–89.

Many experts think that it is a meaningless designation. "Not yet is there any common agreement . . . as to classification or... etiology." Noyes, MODERN CLINICAL PSYCHIATRY 410 (3d ed. 1948). "The only conclusion that seems warrantable is that, at some time or other and by some reputable authority, the term psychopathic personality has been used to designate every conceivable type of abnormal character." Curran & Mallinson, *Psychopathic Personality*, 90 J. MENTAL SCI. 266, 278. It is much too treacherously vague a term to allow the high penalty of deportation to turn on it.

When it comes to sex, the problem is complex. Those "who fail to reach sexual maturity (hetero-sexuality), and who remain at a narcissistic or homosexual stage" are the products "of heredity, of glandular dysfunction, [or] of environmental circumstances." Henderson, *Psychopathic Constitution and Criminal Behaviour*, in MENTAL ABNORMALITY AND CRIME 105, 114 (Radzinowicz & Turner ed. 1949).

The homosexual is one, who by some freak, is the product of an arrested development:

> All people have originally bisexual tendencies which are more or less developed and which in the course of time normally deviate either in the direction of male or female. This may indicate that a trace of homosexuality, no matter how weak it may be, exists in every human being. It is present in the adolescent stage, where there is a considerable amount of undifferentiated sexuality. Abrahamsen, CRIME AND THE HUMAN MIND 117 (1944).

Many homosexuals become involved in violations of laws; many do not. Kinsey reported:

> It is not possible to insist that any departure from the sexual mores, or any participation in socially taboo activities, always, or even usually, involves a neurosis or psychosis, for the case histories abundantly demonstrate that most individuals who engage in taboo activities make satisfactory social adjustments. There are, in actuality, few adult males who are particularly disturbed over their sexual histories. Psychiatrists, clinical psychologists, and others who deal with cases of maladjustment, sometimes come to feel that most people find difficulty in adjusting their sexual lives; but a clinic is no place to secure incidence figures. The incidence of tuberculosis in a tuberculosis sanitarium is no measure of the incidence of tuberculosis in the population as a whole; and the incidence of disturbance over sexual activities, among the persons who come to a clinic, is no measure of the frequency of similar disturbances outside of clinics. The impression that such 'sexual irregularities' as 'excessive' masturbation, pre-marital intercourse, responsibility for a pre-marital pregnancy, extra-marital intercourse, mouth-genital contacts, homosexual activity, or animal intercourse, always produce psychoses and abnormal personalities is based upon the fact that the persons who do go to professional sources for advice are upset by these things.

> It is unwarranted to believe that particular types of sexual behavior are always expressions of psychoses or neuroses. In actuality, they are more often expressions of what is biologically basic in mammalian and anthropoid behavior, and of a deliberate disregard for social convention. Many of the socially and intellectually most significant persons in our histories, successful scientists, educators, physicians, clergymen, business men, and persons of high position in governmental affairs, have socially taboo items in their sexual histories, and among them they have accepted nearly the whole range of so-called sexual abnormalities. Among the socially most successful and personally best adjusted persons who have contributed to the present study, there are some whose rates of outlet are as high as those in any case labelled nymphomania or satyriasis in the literature, or recognized as such in the clinic. Kinsey, SEXUAL BEHAVIOR IN THE HUMAN MALE, (1948) pp. 201–202.

It is common knowledge that in this century homosexuals have risen high in our own public service — both in Congress and in the Executive Branch — and have served with distinction. It is therefore not credible that Congress wanted to deport everyone and anyone who was a sexual deviate, no matter how blameless his social conduct had been nor how creative his work nor how valuable his contribution to society. I agree with Judge Moore, dissenting below, that the legislative history should not be read as imputing to Congress a purpose to classify under the heading "psychopathic personality" every person who had ever had a homosexual experience:

> Professor Kinsey estimated that 'at least 37 percent' of the American male population has at least one homosexual experience, defined in terms of physical contact to the point of orgasm, between the beginning of adolescence and old age. Earlier estimates had ranged from one percent to 100 percent. The sponsors of Britain's current reform bill on homosexuality have indicated that one male in 25 is a homosexual in Britain. To label a group so large 'excludable aliens' would be tantamount to saying that Sappho, Leonardo da Vinci, Michelangelo, Andre Gide, and perhaps even Shakespeare, were they to come to life again, would be deemed unfit to visit our shores.[3] Indeed, so broad a definition might well comprise more than a few members of legislative bodies. 363 F.2d 488, 497-498.

The Public Health Service, from whom Congress borrowed the term "psychopathic personality" admits that the term is "vague and indefinite."

If we are to hold, as the Court apparently does, that any acts of homosexuality suffice to deport the alien, whether or not they are part of a fabric of antisocial behavior, then we face a serious question of due process. By that construction a person is judged by a standard that is almost incapable of definition. I have already quoted from clinical experts to show what a wide range the term "psychopathic personality" has. Another expert[4] classifies such a person under three headings:

> *Acting*: (1) inability to withstand tedium, (2) lack of a sense of responsibility, (3) a tendency to "blow up" under pressure, (4) maladjustment to law and order, and (5) recidivism.
>
> *Feeling*: they tend to (1) be emotionally deficient, narcissistic, callous, inconsiderate, and unremorseful, generally projecting blame on others, (2) have hair-trigger emotions, exaggerated display of emotion, and be irritable and impulsive, (3) be amoral (socially and sexually) and (4) worry, but do nothing about it.
> *Thinking*: they display (1) defective judgment, living for the present rather than for the future, and (2) inability to profit from experience, i. e., they are able to realize the consequences intelligently, but not to evaluate them.

We held in *Jordan v. De George*, 341 U.S. 223, that the crime of a conspiracy to defraud the United States of taxes involved

---

3. Sigmund Freud wrote in 1935:

> "Homosexuality is assuredly no advantage, but it is nothing to be ashamed of, no vice, no degradation, it cannot be classified as an illness; we consider it to be a variation of the sexual function produced by a certain arrest of sexual development. Many highly respectable individuals of ancient and modern times have been homosexuals, several of the greatest men among them (Plato, Michelangelo, Leonardo da Vinci, etc.). It is a great injustice to persecute homosexuality as a crime, and cruelty too. If you do not believe me, read the books of Havelock Ellis." Ruitenbeek, *The Problem of Homosexuality in Modern Society* 1 (1963).

4. Caldwell, *Constitutional Psychopathic State (Psychopathic Personality) Studies of Soldiers in the U.S. Army*, 3 J. Crim. Psychopathology, 171-172 (1941).

"moral turpitude" and made the person subject to deportation. That, however, was a term that has "deep roots in the law." But the grabbag — "psychopathic personality" — has no "deep roots" whatsoever. Caprice of judgment is almost certain under this broad definition. Anyone can be caught who is unpopular, who is off-beat, who is nonconformist.

Deportation is the equivalent to banishment or exile. Though technically not criminal, it practically may be. The penalty is so severe that we have extended to the resident alien the protection of due process. Even apart from deportation cases, we look with suspicion at those delegations of power so broad as to allow the administrative staff the power to formulate the fundamental policy. . . . We deal here also with an aspect of "liberty" and the requirements of due process. They demand that the standard be sufficiently clear as to forewarn those who may otherwise be entrapped and to provide full opportunity to conform. "Psychopathic personality" is so broad and vague as to be hardly more than an epithet. The Court seeks to avoid this question by saying that the standard being applied relates only to what petitioner had done prior to his entry, not to his postentry conduct. *But at least half of the questioning of this petitioner related to his postentry conduct.*

Moreover, the issue of deportability under § 212 (a) of the Immigration and Nationality Act of 1952 turns on whether petitioner is "afflicted with psychopathic personality." On this I think he is entitled to a hearing to satisfy both the statute and the requirement of due process.

One psychiatrist reported:

On psychiatric examination of Mr. Boutilier, there was no indication of delusional trend or hallucinatory phenomena. He is not psychotic. From his own account, he has a psychosexual problem but is beginning treatment for this disorder. Diagnostically, I would consider him as having a Character

Neurosis, believe that the prognosis in therapy is reasonably good and do not think he represents any risk of decompensation into a dependent psychotic reaction nor any potential for frank criminal activity.

Another submitted a long report ending as follows:

The patient's present difficulties obviously weigh very heavily upon him. He feels as if he has made his life in this country and is deeply disturbed at the prospect of being cut off from the life he has created for himself. He talks frankly about himself. What emerged out of the interview was not a picture of a psychopath but that of a dependent, immature young man with a conscience, an awareness of the feelings of others and a sense of personal honesty. His sexual structure still appears fluid and immature so that he moves from homosexual to heterosexual interests as well as abstinence with almost equal facility. His homosexual orientation seems secondary to a very constricted, dependent personality pattern rather than occurring in the context of a psychopathic personality. My own feeling is that his own need to fit in and be accepted is so great that it far surpasses his need for sex in any form.

I do not believe that Mr. Boutilier is a psychopath.

In light of these statements, I cannot say that it has been determined that petitioner was "afflicted" in the statutory sense either at the time of entry or at present. "Afflicted" means possessed or dominated by. Occasional acts would not seem sufficient. "Afflicted" means a way of life, an accustomed pattern of conduct. Whatever disagreement there is as to the meaning of "psychopathic personality," it has generally been understood to refer to a consistent, lifelong pattern of behavior conflicting with social norms without accompanying guilt. Nothing of that character was shown to exist at the time of entry. The fact that he presently has a problem, as one psychiatrist said, does not mean that he is or was necessarily "afflicted" with homosexuality. His conduct is, of course, evidence material to the issue. But the informed judgment of experts is needed to make the required finding. We cruelly mutilate the Act when we hold otherwise. For we make the word of the bureaucrat supreme, when it was the expertise of the doctors and psychiatrists on which Congress wanted the administrative action to be dependent.

TWO

The Regulation of Lesbian and
Gay Sexuality

Can you imagine being denied the right to love?
— Larry Kramer[*]

Aprimary means for society's regulation of sexuality, especially lesbian and gay sexuality, has been the criminal law. Various forms of sexual relationships have been proscribed throughout history and many remain illegal today. These include masturbation (sex with one's self), prostitution (sex for money), fornication (sex between unmarried persons), adultery (sex by a married person with someone other than his or her spouse), bestiality (sex with an animal), incest (sex between persons closely related to one another), rape and molestation (sex without consent or with a person, such as a minor, who is said to lack the capacity to consent), and sodomy (defined in various ways, as discussed below). Society has also directly regulated sexuality through penal restrictions on the use of contraception and abortion.

This chapter focuses on sodomy laws. This focus on sodomy laws is chosen — and is the *first* substantive law chapter in this book — because in modern American society, sodomy laws are used to provide a legal basis for regulation of lesbian and gay sexuality, and of lesbian and gay life generally. Each of the subsequent chapters in this book presents cases in which discrimination against lesbians and gay men — in the workplace, regarding their relationships, and regarding custody and visitation rights to their children — is justified by the existence of laws prohibiting certain sexual practices.

Sodomy laws were not always understood in this way. The first section of this chapter examines historical understandings of sodomy laws. The second examines the modern American attempt to eradicate sodomy laws through legislative repeal and through litigation. The third section examines the Supreme Court decision, *Bowers v. Hardwick*,[1] and the final section looks at sodomy law after *Hardwick*.

---

1. 478 U.S. 186 (1986).

*LARRY KRAMER, *Whose Constitution Is It, Anyway?*, in REPORTS FROM THE HOLOCAUST: THE MAKING OF AN AIDS ACTIVIST 178 (1987).

I. WHAT ARE SODOMY LAWS?

A. Background

MODEL PENAL CODE § 213.2 CMT. 1

(1962, Comments Revised 1980)

The phrase "deviate sexual intercourse" as used by the Model Code covers a number of situations that were treated differently in older law. Chiefly it refers to "sodomy," a generic term that in its broadest import includes anal intercourse with a male or female and copulation with an animal. The term "sodomy" is also used in an older and narrower sense to describe only anal intercourse between males, and it is from this usage in the context of male homosexual relations that sodomy derives the name "crime against nature." In ancient times, sodomy was not a crime but was subject to punishment by the ecclesiastical authorities. Early statutes, however, made sodomy a secular offense, so that it was received by the American colonies as a common law felony.

The original English enactments proscribed only anal intercourse between males, and this limitation had several peculiar consequences under derivative statutes. For one thing, the exclusion of oral sex effectively excepted female homosexuality from the realm of the criminal law, even though copulation between males was punished as a very grave offense. Moreover, different kinds of sexual activity between males became subject to dramatically disparate sanctions. Anal intercourse might be punished by a maximum term of twenty years in prison while oral intercourse between the same persons was not reached by the early sodomy laws and would therefore be subject only to the comparatively minor sanctions authorized for such crimes as lewd and lascivious behavior.

By the time the Model Penal Code was drafted, however, most states no longer ob-

served the early limitation of sodomy to anal copulation. The pattern at that time was to punish fellatio (oral stimulation of the penis) and cunninilingus (oral stimulation of the vulva or clitoris) as well as anal intercourse and bestiality (copulation between human and animal). This expansion of coverage was accomplished by express statutory language, by judicial interpretation of such traditional phrases as "crime against nature," and in at least one state by enactment of a separate provision against oral copulation. Sexual intercourse with a corpse was also included in this category in some formulations. The Model Code deals with this last category of behavior in Section 250.10.

At the time the Model Code was under consideration, all jurisdictions maintained some criminal prohibition against deviate sexual intercourse as that term is used here. Such provisions generally applied to consensual as well as non-consensual behavior, and many statutes even reached departures from standard sexual practice between husband and wife. Where both actors were willing participants, each was guilty of the offense, though children under the age of fourteen were traditionally excepted from liability. Penetration was required, as distinct from mere touching, but emission was not. This rule was effected in some jurisdictions by express provision and in others by judicial analogy to the law of rape. Whether the offense was know as sodomy or by some other name, it usually carried penalties of extreme severity. A number of states enacted sexual psychopath laws that permitted long or indefinite sentences until "cure." Aside from such provisions, maximum imprisonment for sodomy ranged from three years to life, with ten years the most for common authorized maximum (seventeen states) and twenty years the next most frequent (nine states). Older statutes still in force ranged from five years to life, with ten and twenty years the most commonly specified maximum terms for the aggravated form of the offense. Several older statutes fixed minimum sentences, while others established a range of years. A handful of older statutes specified aggravated penalties for deviate sexual intercourse with a child. Most older laws did not differentiate the sanctions for consensual and nonconsensual conduct, so that voluntary sexual relations between adults was ostensibly an offense of the same grade as homosexual rape. Not surprisingly, such statutes were enforced against consenting adults only rarely and against husband and wife virtually never.

B. Sample Statutes — 1992

GA. CODE ANN. § 16-6-2 (1992)

§ 16-6-2. Sodomy; aggravated sodomy

(a) A person commits the offense of sodomy when he performs or submits to any sexual act involving the sex organs of one person and the mouth or anus of another. A person commits the offense of aggravated sodomy when he commits sodomy with force and against the will of the other person.

(b) A person convicted of the offense of sodomy shall be punished by imprisonment for not less than one nor more than 20 years. A person convicted of the offense of aggravated sodomy shall be punished by imprisonment for life or by imprisonment for not less than one nor more than 20 years.

TEX. PENAL CODE ANN. § 21.06 (1992)

§ 21.01. Definitions

In this chapter:

(1) "Deviate sexual intercourse" means:

(A) any contact between any part of the genitals of one person and the mouth or anus of another person; or

(B) the penetration of the genitals or the anus of another person with an object.

§ 21.06. Homosexual Conduct

(a) A person commits an offense if he engages in deviate sexual intercourse with another individual of the same sex.

(b) An offense under this section is a Class C misdemeanor.

OKLA. STAT. TIT. 21 § 886 (1992)

§ 886. Crime against nature

Every person who is guilty of the detestable and abominable crime against nature, committed with mankind or with a beast, is punishable by imprisonment in the penitentiary not exceeding ten (10) years.

Note

1. In addition to Georgia, Oklahoma, and Texas the following states still have sodomy laws:
    Alabama (ALA. CODE, § 13A-6-65(a)(3) (1982)); Arizona (ARIZ. REV. STAT. ANN., §§ 13-1411 to 13-1412, (Supp. 1988)); Arkansas (ARK. STAT. ANN., § 5-14-122 (1987)); Florida (FLA. STAT., §800.02 (1987)); Idaho (IDAHO CODE, § 18-6605 (1987)); Kansas (KAN. STAT. ANN., § 21-3505 (Supp. 1987)); Louisiana (LA. REV. STAT. ANN., § 14:89 (1986)); Maryland (MD. CODE ANN., art. 27, §§ 553-554 (1987)); Michigan (MICH. COMP. LAWS, §§ 750.158, 750-338-.338(b) (1979)); Minnesota (MINN. STAT. § 609.293 (1988)); Mississippi (MISS. CODE ANN. § 97-29-59 (1972)); Missouri (MO. REV. STAT., § 566.090); Montana (MONT. CODE ANN., §§ 45-2-101, 45-5-505 (1987)); Nevada (NEV. REV. STAT., § 201.190 (1987)); North Carolina (N.C. GEN. STAT., § 14-177 (1986)); Rhode Island (R.I. GEN. LAWS, § 11-10-1 (1986)); South Carolina (S.C. CODE ANN., § 16-15-120 (1985)); Tennessee (TENN. CODE ANN., § 39-2-612 (1982)); Utah (UTAH CODE ANN., § 76-5-403 (Supp. 1988)); Virginia (VA. CODE ANN., § 18-2-361 (1988)).

    The Massachusetts sodomy law, MASS. GEN. L. ch. 272, § 34 (1986), was arguably invalidated when a companion statute criminalizing "lewd and lascivious acts" was found unconstitutional as applied to private, consensual acts. *See Commonwealth v. Balthazar*, 318 N.E.2d 478, 481 (Mass. 1974); *see also* EDITORS OF THE HARVARD LAW REVIEW, SEXUAL ORIENTATION AND THE LAW 9 n.2 (1990).

    The District of Columbia also has a sodomy law. *See* D.C. CODE ANN. § 22-3502 (1981).

2. *Specificity.* The lack of specificity of sodomy laws has lead to various, largely unsuccessful, challenges to the laws. *See Wainwright v. Stone*, 414 U.S. 21 (1973) (per curiam) (finding that the Florida "abomidable and detestable crime against nature statute" is not unconstitutionally vague); *Rose v. Locke*, 423 U.S. 48 (1975) (per curiam) (finding that the Tennessee crime against nature statute is not unconstitutionally vague). *But see Balthazar v. Superior Court*, 573 F.2d 698 (1st Cir. 1978) (finding that the Massachusetts unnatural and lascivious acts statute is vague for acts of fellatio and oral/anal contact).

C. The Regulation of *Lesbian* Sexuality

♦

CRIMES OF LESBIAN SEX
Ruthann Robson

About half the jurisdictions in the United States have statutes that criminalize lesbian sexual expressions, and virtually every state has had a statute as recently as 1968 that would imprison someone for lesbian sexual expression. Many of us tend to dismiss such

RUTHANN ROBSON, *Crimes of Lesbian Sex, in* LESBIAN (OUT)LAW 47 (1992).

statutes as not really applicable to us: the statutes are anachronisms; the statutes are law in states that are conservative; the statutes are meant to apply to acts other than what we do; the statutes are directed at other sorts of lesbians. Rarely do we know what these statues actually say. Yet these statues are the legal text of lesbian sexuality. Enacted and codified, interpreted and applied, these statutes are the legislative pronouncements and judicial interpretations.

The statutes are generally referred to as sodomy statutes and usually discussed in terms of gay male sexuality. Centering lesbian concerns, I instead refer to the statutes as the lesbian sex statutes. This does not mean, however, that I concede the statues always or only apply to lesbian sexuality. The statutes, individually, and collectively, are idiosyncratic in their application to various expressions of lesbian sexuality.

The existing lesbian sex statutes employ what I consider to be three different strategies to describe that which they criminalize: oral/anal, natural, and gender specificity. These strategies may overlap within a given statute, or a state may have a statutory scheme that utilizes more than one.

What I am calling the oral/anal strategy usually prohibits any sexual contact between the sex organs (described also as genitals) of one person, and the mouth or anus or another. These statutes are anatomically specific to a certain extent, but they also target what is generally considered sodomy — sexual contact between a man's penis and an anus, or sexual contact between a man's penis and a mouth, also called fellatio. A few states broaden this strategy by also including objects, fingers, and body parts as prohibited penetrators of sexual organs.

The second strategy relies on so-called natural understanding for its meaning. Statutes criminalize the "the crime against nature," or the "abominable and detestable crime against nature," or reversing the adjectives, "the detestable and abominable crime against nature"

or the "infamous crime against nature." This strategy, standing alone, is amazingly insufficient to advise anyone of any acts that are within the prohibition. Nevertheless, many courts — including the United States Supreme Court — have upheld such statutes from constitutional vagueness attacks by reasoning that our common understanding includes knowledge of what such statutes prohibit, or that even if common knowledge is not so definite, judges interpreting the statute can rely on established legal understandings.[1] The failure to name what is prohibited, reminiscent of the tactics of the sixteenth-century jurist Germain Colladon and the 1920s members of British Parliament is inherent in statutes that rely on natural understandings. If one wanted to learn specifics about lesbian sexuality, or about any type of sexuality, the natural strategy statutes would definitely not be the place to go.

The third strategy relies on gender specificity for meaning. Often, although not always, gender specificity targets persons of the same sex, and often, although again not always, this strategy is combined with either the oral/anal or the natural strategies. Interestingly, the specificity of gender is also usually coupled with a prohibition against sexual contact with animals. Statutes within this strategy can be some of the broadest in terms of criminalizing lesbian sexual expressions, especially if such statutes criminalize sexual contact between person of the same sex.

There are not many reported cases — cases which have been through an appeal process and are printed in official state reporters— in which any of these statutes have been applied to consensual activity, and even fewer of those cases involve adult women. There are a few cases, however, and in one a 1968 Michigan appellate court upheld the conviction and prison sentence of one and one-half to five years in the Detroit House of Corrections based on facts it described as follows:

Defendant [Julie Livermore] visited Mrs. Carolyn French at the pubic camping

1. See Rose v. Locke, 423 U.S. 48 (1975).

grounds at Sunrise Lake in Osceola County, Michigan. Mrs. French had been tent-camping with her 4 children at Sunrise Lake for several days.

About 9 p.m. that same evening, defendant and Mrs. French were observed by complainant Jerry Branch and others, to be in close bodily contact with each other, which continued for approximately one hour. The defendant and Mrs. French then entered the latter's tent.

Later, on receiving a complaint, Troopers. . .of the Michigan State Police, proceeded to the Sunrise Lake camping ground. They arrived there about midnight, talked to the complainant and others and then stood within 15 feet of the French tent. Obscene language and conversation indicative of sexual conduct occurring between two female persons was overheard by the troopers for about ten minutes. From the information received from complainant, the obscene language and conversation, and noises overheard, the troopers took action in the belief that a felony had been committed or was being committed at that time. They approached the tent, identified themselves and requested admittance; there was no reply; the troopers unzipped the outer flap, and aided by a flashlight observed a cot located directly in front of the doorway on which defendant and Mrs. French were lying, partially covered by a blanket; the two females were advised that they were

under arrest and after taking several flash pictures the troopers permitted them to dress in private. [2]

No matter the wording of any particular statute, each statute has the capacity to be interpreted to include two women "lying, partially covered by a blanket" who have been overheard engaged in "obscene language and conversation indicative of sexual conduct." This case indicates the horrific potential that all the statutes possess.

The case is also typical in its lack of specificity. A lesbian sex statute may explicitly exempt the state from a requirement that it specify the acts alleged to be criminal.[3] Judicial opinions often decline to relate the actual acts that constitute the crime.[4] When described at all, lesbian sexuality is described in clinical terms or with reference to male sexuality, or simply as unnatural, deviant, or sexual. The few factual descriptions are not provided by lesbians, but by lawyers and judges interpreting lesbian sexual activity. Similarly, I think it is a fairly safe assumption, given the continuing infrequency of women legislators, that none of the lesbian sex statutes was authored by a lesbian. Lesbians are at the margins of the legal text of our own sexuality. One way to center lesbians is to engage in a specific and contextualized analysis of the legal interpretations of some common lesbian sexual activities as described from a lesbian point of view.

The main character, and sometimes narrator, of Judith McDaniel's recent novel *Just Say Yes* is the twenty-six-year-old lesbian, Lindsey.[5] She is waitressing in Province-

2. People v. Livermore, 9 Mich. App. 47, 155 N.W. 2d 711, 712 (Mich. Ct. App. 1968).

3. For example, the District of Columbia statute entitled Sodomy provides in part that any indictment for such offenses "it shall not be necessary to set forth the particular unnatural or perverted sexual practice with the commission of which the defendant may be charged, nor to set forth the manner in which said unnatural or perverted sexual practice was committed."

4. As one judge states, "the sordid unnatural acts testified to by this witness are such that little could be gained by setting them forth in this opinion." Warner v. State, 489 P.2d 526 (Cr. Ct. App. Okl. 1971) (case involved "oral sodomy" betwen two women and between a woman and a man).

5. All italicized passages are excerpted and slightly edited from JUDITH McDANIEL, JUST SAY YES (Ithaca, New York: Firebrand Books, 1990). The passages appear on pages 15, 36, 124–5, 67–8, and 172.

town for the summer, wondering about her life, and experiencing sexual encounters. The following five passages and their legal analyses reveal how our sexual practices violate — and fail to violate — the various laws in various states in idiosyncratic ways.

1.

Ra's hands spread the lips of her cunt wide and her voice invited Lindsey to stroke the clitoris, move slowly up to the shell-pink little button hiding under the fleshy hood. . . Letting her one hand follow Ra's rhythm, Lindsey began to stroke lightly with her other, up the belly first, then to the bottom cup of one breast, then the other. . . . Suddenly Ra's knees jerked, and Lindsey felt the orgasm starting under her fingers. She rubbed Ra's clitoris until she was sure she'd gone over the edge, then let her fingers burrow into Ra's wet center and catch at the waves of orgasm pulsing down her abdomen.

Whether Lindsey and Ra are guilty of criminal conduct depends, in part, upon which strategy a state uses in its lesbian sex statute(s). However, in all states that might criminalize this encounter — as well as any other lesbian encounter — if one partly is guilty, then both are guilty, assuming consent. The state can choose to prosecute only one person, which will assist the state in proving its case if the other person cooperates. Consent will not be a defense.

In states that employ only the oral/anal strategy, the sexual encounter between Lindsey and Ra is not within the statute. Thus in Alabama, Kentucky, Georgia, and Utah, Lindsey has not committed any crime. Whether Lindsey's acts violate statutes dedicated to the natural strategy depends on whether the courts in the particular state have chosen to interpret the statute narrowly (to prohibit only oral/anal sexual activity) or broadly (to "cover the entire field of unnatural acts," as a Nevada court expressed it).

In Idaho, committed to a broad interpretation by prior case law, if a court found Lindsey's acts within the statute, the mandatory minimum sentence would be five years; since no maximum sentence is listed, it could legally be life imprisonment.

Lindsey's acts are most likely to violate the statutes that target not acts, but actors — persons of the same gender. In Louisiana, for example, the "use of genital organ of one of the offenders" is sufficient to constitute the crime if both parties are of the same sex. And in Missouri, "any sexual act involving the genitals of one person and the mouth, tongue, hand, or anus of another preson" is a crime if the parties are of the same sex. In Arkansas, the statute combines anatomical specificity with gender specificity to criminalize penetration of the vagina or anus by any body member of a person of the same sex. Lindsey's fingers surely qualify as body members, but how does their "burrowing" translate into the legally required penetration? Arkansas' penetration requirement is not unique, and statutes that resort to any of the three strategies often include a penetration requirement either in the statute itself or in judicial interpretations of the statute. But even if *burrow* means legal penetration, Lindsey might not be a criminal in Texas, where the recently enacted statute criminalizes deviate sexual intercourse defined as activities between persons of the same sex in which "the penetration of the genitals or the anus of another person with an object" occurs. In Texas, then, if Lindsey had burrowed with a dildo, she would violate the statute, but the question remains as to whether her fingers qualify as an object. While our everyday understanding of the word object might be limited to the inanimate, a Texas court could decide to give effect to the intention of the legislature. Confronted with Lindsey and Ra, a court might attempt to decide whether Texas legislators intended to include fingers as objects, or whether criminalizing Lindsey and Ra's activities had been their intention.

2.

Ra knelt, and Lindsey felt her shoulders between her knees, her tongue probing as her fingers parted the lips of Lindsey's vagina. Ra sucked and nibbled, swallowed from Lindsey's smooth wetness, then moved her tongue hard against Lindsey's clitoris, pushing, circling, then pushing again until an orgasm pulsed out of Lindsey's toes, pushing up to her thighs, swelling her cunt, and throbbing finally into her uterus.

In states that rely upon the oral/anal strategy in their lesbian sex statutes, Ra's tongue on Lindsey's clitoris is a crime. Lindsey and Ra could be jailed for twenty years in Georgia, five years in Virginia, one year in Alabama and Kentucky, and six months in Utah. The absence of anal sex will not help Lindsey and Ra, unless they are in the California prison system, which only criminalizes anal penetration by a penis by inmates, and possibly if they are in South Carolina, which only criminalizes the undefined act of "buggery."[6]

One of the more interesting states in which to consider the placement of Ra's tongue is Kansas. Kansas criminalizes what it calls sodomy between persons of the same sex, but the statute explicitly defines sodomy as "oral-anal copulation, including oral-genital stimulation between the tongue of a male and the genital area of a female." The "including" in the Kansas statute, added by a 1990 amendment, is an excluding of female tongues. At least this is the interpretation of authoritative comments to the statutes, as well as the state's highest court. In Kansas, Ra and Lindsey do not violate the proscription of oral sex.

The Kansas situation is not historically unique. A 1939 Georgia court held that lesbian cunnilingus was not a crime under the statute that prohibited the "carnal knowledge and connection against the order of nature, by man with man, or in the same unnatural manner with woman." The court concluded that "man" was the exclusive actor, and held the unspecified acts between two women were excluded even though they were "just as loathsome."[7] The Georgia legislature subsequently amended the statue to rely on the oral/anal strategy and eliminate any gender references.

Courts in other states, however, have found lesbian cunnilingus clearly illegal. Under Louisiana's prior crime against nature statute (since amended to reflect the oral/anal strategy), the women who participated in "oral copulation by and between both of the accused" had their convictions of thirty months in prison affirmed.[8] In Oklahoma, under a crime against nature statute still in effect, in a case involving interracial lesbian (and heterosexual) acts, the court had no difficulty accepting the proposition that the statute's reference to "mankind" included both male and female and that "copulation *per os* between two females" was criminal.[9] Yet because Oklahoma's statutory scheme also includes a requirement of "penetration, however slight" an appellate court — despite its expressed disagreement with the penetration requirement — reversed the conviction of a woman who admitted performing cunnilingus on another female because the prosecutor "made no effort to introduce any evidence, either direct or circumstantial, proving the essential element of penetration." [10] What penetration means — and what it is that must be penetrated — is unclear. Is Ra's tongue against Lindsey's clitoris penetration?

---

6. *Buggery* is often interchangeably with *sodomy*, but according to Black's Law Dictionary, even when so used it does not necessarily include fellatio.

7. Thompson v. Aldredge, 200 S.E. 799 (1939).

8. State v. Young, 193 So. 2d 243 (La. 1967).

9. Warner v. State, 489 P.2d 526 (Cr. Ct. App. Okl. 1971).

10. Saylers v. State, 755 P.2d 97 (Cr. Ct. App. Okl. 1988).

3.

They didn't undress, and there seemed to be little urgency in their movements at first, just a gentle rocking of bodies entwined, interlocked in the right way. Sindar had slipped her hard, round thigh between Lindsey's legs, brought it right up against the rough seam of her pants crotch, and began to move up and down, up and down. Mesmerized, Lindsey lay quietly at first, one hand holding Sindar's shoulder as she rocked, the other resting on the back of her head, feeling the tightly braided dreads, pressing Sindar's mouth tight into her own. . . . Together they rocked, feeling the tension build, the wetness seep through the cloth. . . . Lindsey felt Sindar's orgasm begin when her rhythm changed, became more urgent, forceful, and her faster thrusts brought Lindsey over the edge too, let her gasp with relief as she felt the orgasm ripple up her thighs and into her belly.

The clinical term for Lindsey and Sindar's lovemaking is *tribadism,* and as an activity that does not include oral/anal contact with sexual organs, or any penetration, it is criminalized only by the most broadly worded statutes that would also criminalize Lindsey's previously discussed interactions with Ra. Among the broadest of these statues are ones that clearly target same-sex activities. For example, Montana's criminalization of "deviate sexual intercourse" includes "any touching of the sexual or other intimate parts of another[of the same sex] for the purposes of arousing or gratifying the sexual desire of either party." If the touchings between Lindsey and Sindar are intended to sexually arouse or gratify either of them, they are guilty in Montana and could be sentenced to ten years. Michigan's statute prohibiting gross indecency between women — the statute under which Julie Livermore was convicted because her activities at the campground with Carolyn French — is also sufficiently broad to allow a conviction of Lindsey and Sindar, as well as many lesbians at the annual Michigan Women's Music Festival.

4.

Carol was leading the way now, walking toward the end of the pier. . . . Suddenly, Carol did what she had been doing all week in the freedom of this new environment — she threw her natural caution into the breeze blowing off the ocean and put her arms around Lindsey. Lindsey's lips were waiting. . . . They kissed slowly at first, lips exploring the contours of a face, tasting the skin, breathing in the scent of a new person. Once again her bare thighs were touching Carol's. She began to explore the velvet-smooth skin under Carol's blouse. . . . Her fingers traced the length of Carol's spine, up from the waist to the back of her neck, beneath the shorts to her tailbone, to her firm ass.

"Oh, my." Carol moved away from the kiss and took a deep breath.

Carol and Lindsey are kissing and touching on a public pier, and although each of the previous three scenes also took place in public in Judith McDaniel's novel, I analyzed them as if they occurred behind the proverbial drapes-drawn, locked-door bedroom. We need to reconsider privacy. In the context of lesbian sex statutes, lesbian sex in public — or in any place with a window or other indication that might be interpreted to be less than absolutely private — is subject to being criminalized as indecent exposure, public lewdness, or open and gross lewdness.

Every state in the United Sates has some sort of statute that prohibits public lesbian sexual expressions. Many of these statutes are aimed at "flashers," and thus target exposure of the genitals in public in a manner likely to be observed. So limited, the statutes would not criminalize Lindsey and Carol's activities on the pier, although Lindsey's prior acts with Ra on that same pier would be criminalized. However, even relatively benign statutes enacted in states that do not have specific lesbian sex statutes contain words that could be interpreted to criminalize Lindsey and Carol. New Jersey prohibits any "flagrantly lewd and offensive act." New York prohibits any "lewd act." New Mexico criminalizes exposure of the breasts. And in Vermont, "open and gross lewdness and lascivious behavior" is a crime that can provoke a five-year prison sentence.

5.

I was learning real quick that arguing with a lawyer can take a lot of time and preparation. I let it drop for then because we were climbing those narrow steps again, Carol ahead, me behind. I put both hands under her ass as she climbed. "I don't know about legal definitions," I told her, "but I'd be glad to show you in person what I think a lesbian is."

That Lindsey's new lover is an attorney with the public defender's office might be convenient should Lindsey be arrested for the crime of solicitation to violate a lesbian sex statute. Soliciting a person to commit a crime is an independent offense in many jurisdictions. Solicitation is often used to prosecute what the state considers prostitution, but there need not be a mention of money if the act solicited is lesbian sex. In the District of Columbia, for example, it is illegal "for any person to invite, entice, persuade, or address for the purpose of inviting, enticing, or persuading" any person for an "immoral or lewd purpose." The D.C. courts have expressly limited "immoral and lewd" to acts encompassed by their sodomy statute, which uses the oral/anal strategy to criminalize lesbian sex. The courts have rejected free speech challenges to this criminal solicitation statute and have also held that the solicitation need not occur in a public place. So, depending on whether or not Lindsey thinks oral sex would demonstrate "what a lesbian is," she could be subject to a $300 fine. And

for her second offense, perhaps inviting Carol over the next day with a similar promise, Lindsey is subject to another $300 fine and ten days in jail. And for every invitation, enticement, or persuasion thereafter Lindsey is subject to an additional $300 fine and ninety days in jail.

As the crimes of Lindsey, Carol, Sindar, and Ra demonstrate, lesbian sexual expressions and various lesbian sex statutes have a rather idiosyncratic relationship. Cunnilingus between women is not criminal in Kansas, but should the tongue stray toward the anus and any "penetration, however slight" occur, then it is a crime with a sentence of six months in prison. A finger inside a lesbian lover is illegal in Missouri; a dildo is legal. But not in Texas, where dildo use will be a criminal act and fingers, unless they are objects, are legal. Such disparities are partially explained by the commitment to male sexuality embedded in the statutes. While the statutes seek to criminalize lesbian sex — I cannot think of any applicable statute that actually intends to exclude lesbianism from sexual deviancy — the attempted criminalization occurs within a frame of reference that centers male sexuality.

There are several lesbian theorist, most notably Marilyn Frye, arguing that sex is a term not applicable to lesbians. Frye's view is supported by the haphazard manner in which the lesbian sex statutes, considered as a whole, apply to lesbians. When we consider statutes or interpretations that require penetration, for example, it does not mean that lesbians have a uniform disdain or appreciation for penetration — whatever penetration means — but that penetration is not definitional of lesbian sex. Whatever our personal preferences, I think most of us would describe both Lindsey's interactions with Ra and with Sindar as "sex," and most of us would not consider one encounter as "less sex" than any other from Lindsey's point of view. The lesbian sex statutes and their judicial constructions centralize male sexuality, however, not lesbian sexuality.

While I am certainly not advocating that all statutes be broadened to include all lesbian relating, the statutes and their interpretations do constitute the legal text of our sexuality, and we need to think about the absences and rationales in that text. The refusal to explicitly state the acts criminalized is a violence The absence is violent not only because if one wished to comply with the law (as the law assumes), one would need to avoid a wide spectrum of activities, but also because the only references to our sexuality within the legal text are constructed around profound absences. The rationales in the text are also violent. Although it is a relief in some ways to know that in Kansas my tongue on another lesbians' clitoris is legal, this relief is tempered by its rationale: my tongue is somehow less sexual because it shares a body with a clitoris instead of a penis. There is a random violence inherent in determinations of my criminal culpability based upon how deep my tongue penetrates, whether I use my tongue or my fingers, my fingers or an object, whether I eroticize a lover's clitoris, her anus, or her mouth, whether we are clothed or inside or in what state we happen to find ourselves. There is also a violence in the legal text of our sexuality that would describe any activities within our lovemaking as "deviate," as "perverted," as "unnatural," or even with reference to words like *intercourse* or *copulation*.

The violence of the lesbian sex statutes is the violence of propaganda, the propaganda of non-lesbiansism. Because the statutes are rarely enforced — a rarity that insulates them from being challenged or attracting interest — we are tempted to think of the lesbian sex statutes as ineffectual attempts at brainwashing. Yet as propaganda they are effective, not because they prevent us from engaging in lesbian activity, but because they perpetuate violence upon our lesbian survival. They negatively affect our daily survival as support for legal determinations that tolerate discrimination against us, that remove our children from us as threats that regulate our choices about being open with our sexuality.

The rules of the law that are the lesbian sex statutes domesticate us. They are the supporting legal text for any feelings any of us might have that our sexuality is wrong. These laws domesticate us with their paradoxical message: our sexuality is not worthy of inclusion within any legal text; our sexuality is worthy only of being criminalized. It is a violence that may seem intangible, but it is ultimately supported by very tangible people like police, prosecutors, judges, and prison guards. When we appeal to the law as lesbians, we appeal to a legal text that has historically criminalized us and continues to do so.

II. THE MOVEMENT TO ERADICATE SODOMY LAWS

As of 1961, all fifty states in the United States still had some sort of sodomy law on their books.[1] Today, fewer than half the states do.[2] The eradication of sodomy laws throughout the United States has come mainly through legislative repeal, particularly with states'

1. *Survey of the Law: Survey of the Constitutional Right to Privacy in the Context of Homosexual Activity*, 40 U. MIAMI L. REV. 521, 526 n.23 (1986), citing, Note, *The Constitutionality of Sodomy Statutes*," 45 FORDHAM L. REV. 553, 554–57 (1977).

2. *See supra* at 80.

adoption of the Model Penal Code. This movement is considered in Part A below. Some state courts have declared sodomy laws to be unconstitutional. These cases are considered in Part B below.

A. Legislative Repeal

The American Law Institute (ALI), an influential body of American legal scholars and practicing lawyers, drafts "model" laws for different areas of legal practice. In the mid-1950s, the ALI drafted a "Model Penal Code" to update and unify American criminal law. A critical development in that code was the de-criminalization of sexual behavior, including homosexual conduct, between consenting adults in private.

MODEL PENAL CODE § 213.2 CMT. 2

(1962, Comments Revised 1980)

DEVIATE SEXUAL INTERCOURSE BETWEEN CONSENTING ADULTS

Section 231.2 of the Model Code makes a fundamental departure from prior law in excepting from criminal sanctions deviate sexual intercourse between consenting adults. This policy applies to the various styles of sexual intimacy between man and wife and to sexual relations between unmarried persons, regardless of gender. Of course, the exclusion from liability does not extend to sexual relations with a person who is underage or otherwise incapable of giving meaningful consent. Such conduct is proscribed in terms by this section. Additionally, the exclusion does not reach open display, which is covered by Section 251.1 of the Model Code, nor does the exclusion reach prostitution, which constitutes an offense under 251.2, nor public solicitation, which is proscribed by Section 251.3. But under the Model Code deviate sexual intercourse is not criminal where both participants consent, where each is of sufficient age and mental capacity to render consent effective, and where they conduct their relations in private and create no public nuisance.

Decriminalization of consensual sodomy reaches three situations commonly covered by pre-Model Code statutes. First, it excludes the prospect of penal sanctions for untraditional sexual practices between husband and wife. This is the weakest case for continuing criminal penalties. So-called deviate sexual intercourse between spouses may contravene an ethical or religious notion that there is nothing approaching societal consensus on this point. Both the popular literature and available empirical data reveal that such practices are anything but uncommon. Moreover, current scientific thinking confirms that so-called deviate sexual intercourse may be part of a healthy and normal marital relationship. While it is difficult to see that non-standard sexual intimacy between spouses occasions any harm of which the state properly might take cognizance, it is easy to identify criminal sanctions for such conduct as inconsistent with the social goal of protecting the marital relationship against outside interference. Indeed, it seems likely that the newly enunciated constitutional right of marital privacy extends to all forms of consensual sexual activity between husband and wife. It is probable, therefore, that imposition of criminal punishment for such behavior is not only unwise, but is also constitutionally impermissible. The Model Code position on this point has proved decidedly influential. Many modern revision efforts and proposed codes have excluded criminal sanctions for any form of sexual intimacy between husband and wife.

The second situation excluded from coverage is consensual sodomy between male and female outside the marital relationship. This is distinguished from the first case only in that sexual intimacy out of wedlock is not affirmatively sanctioned by law. Acceptance of the proposition that the state has no good reason to try to suppress non-standard sexual practices between married persons puts this second situation in its proper perspective. Criminal punishment of so-called deviate sexual intercourse between a man and a woman who are not married to one another presents the same issues of social policy that are raised by laws against genital copulation by such persons. The wrong, if one exists, arises from the fact of sexual intimacy out of wedlock and not from the kind of conduct with which gratification is achieved. In other words, application of sodomy statues in this context really involves only a variant of adultery or fornication. The Model Code includes no penal provision against adultery or fornication, for reasons which are explained in some detail in the Note on Adultery and Fornication following the commentary to Section 213.6. The point here is only to emphasize that there is no reason to distinguish among styles of sexual intimacy for the purpose of imposing criminal sanctions on relations out of wedlock. Whatever policy governs traditional heterosexual intercourse between unmarried persons should also extend to other forms of sexual gratification by those same persons.

The third and most controversial case of consensual sodomy is homosexual relations. Here articulation of a legitimate state interest in suppression of such conduct is arguably more plausible. Because ordinary genital copulation is not possible between persons of the same gender, homosexual relations typically involve some sort of deviate sexual intercourse as that term is defined in Section 213. The popular aversion to such conduct arises not so much from the physical characteristics of sexuality as from the fact of sexual gratification with a person of one's own gender. This type of sexual preference constitutes a far more dramatic contravention of societal norms and prevailing moral attitudes than is involved in either of the first two situations discussed above. Continued criminal punishment of homosexual relations may be advocated on the ground that such conduct threatens the moral fabric of society by undermining the viability of the family or on the supposition that permitting such behavior between consenting adults leads inevitably to the corruption of youth. Arguments of the former sort of raise the broad issue of the proper relation of the criminal law to community morality — a matter that is discussed more fully below. The view that activity between consenting adults should be proscribed in order to protect young persons flounders on the absence of either empirical data or reasoned analysis to suggest that one leads to the other. Perhaps more important than either of these factors is the simple truth that homosexuality excites widespread and often violent emotional hostility. Its manifestation in sexual conduct is viewed by many persons with a deep antipathy. The origin of this reaction is as much aesthetic as moral, and its force is not diminished by the difficulty of specifying exactly what harm is occasioned thereby. The conviction that homosexual conduct is "bad" quickly translates into the conclusion that it therefore should be punished, and there is a corresponding fear that removing criminal sanctions would amount to implied endorsement of a kind of behavior that majoritarian sentiment finds abhorrent.

While these concerns may be dispositive to some, the Model Code takes the view that private homosexual conduct between consenting adults should not be punished as a crime. In part, this conclusion stems from uncertainty about the morality of such conduct. Without delving into the question of the causes of homosexuality, one can identify at least three ways of looking at the phenomenon. First, of course, it may be regarded as a sin. Most orthodox theologies take this position, through there are increasing challenges to this view even from sources within organized religion.

Second, homosexuality may be viewed as a disease. There are two lines of thought in the disease model of homosexuality. Some theorists have posited that homosexuality is a pathological condition, the result of abnormal genetic or hormonal influence. To date, however, studies designed to show a biological basis have been inconclusive at best. Modern authorities have abandoned the position that homosexuality is an inherited genetic trait. On the other hand, many scientists today have adopted a psychological theory of homosexuality, thus viewing it as an emotional or mental disorder. The common theory is that the homosexual's emotional disturbance is caused by childhood environment. Even if this view is correct, however, homosexuality is subject to no known cure, save perhaps as psychiatry or behavior modification may attempt restructuring of the individual personality. For purposes of the criminal law, the real significance of viewing homosexuality as an illness lies not in the realms of medicine and science, but rather in the normative implications conveyed by labeling the homosexual as "sick." On the other hand, the disease model conceded that homosexual behavior is deviate, abnormal, unwelcome, and unattractive. It postulates that homosexuality should not be encour-

aged and that a "cure" would be desirable if one could be found. On the other hand, describing homosexuality as a kind of illness avoids imputation of moral failing to the individual so afflicted. In other words, the individual who find himself sexually attracted to persons of his own gender is not blameworthy in the sense with which the criminal law is concerned.

The third view of homosexuality is that it is neither a sin nor an abnormality but only a difference. The notion here is that homosexual conduct is simply a matter of personal preference and is devoid of any normative content whatever. This is the position of the gay rights movement, and it may be gaining support in the community at large.

No doubt this statement of three distinct points of view is simplistic. They are not cleanly different as described above but exist in an infinite variety of gradations and emphases. To the extent, however, that these positions may be taken as paradigms of broadly differing attitudes toward the subject, they suggest an important point. Only one of the three conception — i.e. the view that homosexual conduct is a sin — provides an appropriate starting point for imposition of penal sanctions. No principle is more broadly accepted than that the criminal law, involving as it does both punishment and condemnation should be concerned with conduct that is morally reprehensible or culpable. To the extent that it seems inappropriate to regard homosexual relations as blameworthy — that is, as representative of moral failing by the actor — the essential premise for assigning criminal punishment is vitiated. Of course, many in the community view homosexual conduct as morally reprehensible, but it is equally clear that many do not. Given the absence of harm to the secular interests of the community occasioned by atypical sexuality between consenting adults, the problematical nature of the underlying ethical issue should suggest the need for caution in continuing criminal proscription of this kind of behavior.

The foregoing reasoning is supportive of the Model Code position on consensual sodomy, but not essential to its acceptance. Even if one starts from the proposition that homosexual conduct is a moral default for which the actor may justifiably be condemned, there are still sufficient reasons to withhold penal sanctions. The criminal law cannot encompass all behavior that the average citizen may regard as immoral or deviate. In every field of activity the ethical precepts of the community set standards higher than the law can expediently enforce. Verbal cruelty, lying, racial and religious biases in private relationships, and the kiss that betrays a marriage are but a few examples of reprehensible conduct that no sensible legislator would make into a crime. Some of the reasons why the penal law must stop well short of encompassing all immoral conduct are eminently practical. Economic resources are finite. The amount of money that may be spent on law enforcement is limited by the wealth of the community and by the competing demands of other social interests. It seems sensible, therefore, that the criminal justice system should concentrate on repressing murder, robbery, rape, theft, and other crimes that directly threaten security of person and property. Authorization of penalties for consensual sodomy suggests not only that such conduct is wrongful, but also that it is sufficiently important to warrant diversion of resources from other areas. Furthermore, any genuine effort to enforce such prohibitions will be extremely costly and difficult. Private sexual behavior between consenting adults has no victim. There is no one who can be counted on to complain to the police or to provide evidence against suspected offenders. The resulting difficulty of identifying and convicting violators usually leads police to forego any attempt to enforce laws against consensual sodomy except in the rare case that happens to come to their attention. Cases that do surface commonly involve violence, corruption of minors, public solicitation, or some other aggravating factor that would continue to be punished under the Model Code. To the extent, however, that laws against deviate sexual behavior are enforced against private conduct between consenting adults, the result is episodic and capricious selection of an infinitesimal fraction of offenders for severe punishment. This invitation to arbitrary enforcement not only offends notions of fairness and horizontal equity, but it also creates unwarranted opportunity for private blackmail and official extortion. There is also the point that the methods available to the police for enforcing such laws involve tactics which are often unseemly and which, by their very nature, stretch the limits of constitutionality. Moreover, these costs may be incurred without gaining any corresponding benefit, for there is every reason to believe that continued criminal proscription of private sexual relations would prove largely ineffective to deter or inhibit such conduct.

To these practical concerns must be added a broader objection to criminal punishment of atypical behavior between consenting adults. Any exercise of the coercive power of the state against individual citizens diminishes freedom. Nowhere is this curtailment of liberty more pronounced than where the state, acting through the penal law, punishes by incarceration. No doubt such action is necessary to prevent injury to other individuals, to guard them in the secure possession of their property, and to further the interest of all citizens in the unobstructed workings of their government. Less clearly, criminal penalties may also be appropriate in some instances where the actor's behavior does not threaten directly to impair any of these interests. The usual justification for laws against such conduct is that, even though it does not injure any identifiable victim, it contributes to moral deterioration of society. One need not endorse wholesale repeal of all "victimless" crimes in order to recognize that legislating penal sanctions solely to maintain widely held concepts of morality and aesthetics is a costly enterprise. It sacrifices personal liberty, not because the actor's conduct results in harm to another citizen but only because it is inconsistent with the majoritarian notion of acceptable behavior. In the words of the Wolfenden Report, the decisive factor favoring decriminalization of laws against private homosexual relations between consenting adults is "the importance which society and the law ought to give individual freedom of choice and action in matters of private morality."

These considerations moved the Reporters of the Model Code to recommend no criminal penalties for consensual sexual relations conducted in private. The Advisory Committee unanimously agreed, but the Council of the American Law Institute by a divided vote endorsed continued coverage of this subject. Some members of the Council, including most notably Judge John H. Parker of the United States Court of Appeals for the Fourth Circuit, argued that deviate sexual practices were either symptom or cause of moral decay and should be repressed by law. Other Council members agreed with this conclusion but on quite different grounds. They thought that the Reporters' recommendation was rationally correct, but feared that failure to make a concession to violent emotional hostility among legislators and the public at large might jeopardize acceptance of the Model Code as a whole. Finally, a minority of the Council followed the lead of Judge Learned Hand of the United States Court of Appeals for the Second Circuit in supporting decriminalization. Despite this adverse action by the Council, the Institute approved the Reporters' recommendation at its 1955 meeting, and the Council subsequently acquiesced.

As of that date, the Model Code exclusion of criminal penalties for consensual sodomy was without precedent in this country. Many Europeans [countries] had excepted private sexual behavior from their penal laws, and Great Britain has since followed suit by enacting the recommendations of the Wolfenden Commission in 1967. In 1961, Illinois became the first American jurisdiction to adopt the Model Code position. A number of other states have taken this step in recent revisions, and decriminalization of consensual sodomy is also a feature of several recently drafted proposals. The impact of the Model Code is, however, more pervasive than this summary suggests, for even though many states still punish consensual sodomy, most modern revision efforts effect a substantial reduction in the gravity of sanctions authorized for such behavior. Thus, consensual sodomy, which traditionally constituted a serious felony, is only a misdemeanor in at least seven states and is so classified under at least two proposed codes. As a practical matter, moreover, many law enforcement agencies decline to enforce applicable statutes unless there exists some aggravating factor such as use of force or corruption of minors.

Notes

1. In 1961, Illinois became the first state to repeal its sodomy law; it did so by adopting the Model Penal Code. No state followed for ten years, until Connecticut did so in 1971. Subseqently, 19 states have repealed their sodomy laws.
2. In the late 1970s, the repeal effort slowed and was eventually replaced by a process of "specification," which Nan Hunter describes as follows:

   The last repeal of a sodomy law occurred in Wisconsin in 1983. Starting in the 1970s, however, a counter-trend began, in which specification replaced repeal. Since 1973, eight states have amended their laws to specify that oral or anal sex is prohibited only between persons of the same sex and not between opposite sex partners.[30] In one state, Oklahoma, a state appellate court ruled on constitutional grounds that the sodomy statute's gender neutral prohibition could not be enforced against opposite-sex partners.[31] Even in the majority of the states that retain gender neutral language, the ancillary effects of the sodomy prohibition are directed against lesbian and gay citizens.

It is intriguing to speculate about why state legislatures stopped repealing sodomy statutes and began to single out homosexual acts as crimes. The specification trend coincided with the emergence of the contemporary versions of both the lesbian and gay rights movement and a renewed movement for religious fundamentalism in American politics. In 1973, the year that specification amendments began, two critical events occurred: The American Psychiatric Association removed homosexuality from its list of mental diseases and the United States Civil Service Commission forbade personnel supervisors from finding a person unsuitable for a federal government job based solely on homosexuality. By 1985, anti-discrimination laws had been adopted by the District of Columbia, San Francisco, Minneapolis, Seattle, Detroit and several smaller cities. Anti-equality forces mobilized during the 1970s also, securing repeal of a civial rights law in Dade County, Florida, and conducting two electoral campaigns to enact laws mandating the firing of state schools systems employees who advocated homosexuality — one unsuccessfully (California) and the other successfully (Oklahoma). For states revising their criminal codes, the specification of homosexual acts as a crime marked both the greater visibility of homosexuality in a positive sense and the tremendous social anxiety which that visibility generated.

See Nan D. Hunter, *Life After* Hardwick, 27 HARV. C.R. - C.L.L. REV. 531, 538-39 (1992).

---

30. ARK. CODE § 5-14-122 (1987); KAN. CRIM. CODE. ANN. § 21-3505 (Vernon 1992); KY. REV. STAT. ANN., § 510.100 (Michie 1990); MO. REV. STAT. 566.090 (1986); MONT. CODE § 45-5-505 (1991); NEV. REV. STAT. ANN. § 201.190 (Michie 1986); TENN. CODE ANN. § 39-13-510 (West 1991); and TEX. PENAL CODE TEX., § 21.06 (West 1989). . . .The amendments that constitute this specification trend were enacted in 1973 (Montana and Texas); 1974 (Kentucky); 1977 (Arkansas, Missouri and Nevada); 1983 (Kansas); and 1989 (Tennessee).

31. Oklahoma v. Post, 715 P.2d 1105 (Okla. Crim. App. 1986), *cert. denied*, 479 U.S. 890 (1986).

B. Constitutional Litigation

While some states have repealed their sodomy laws, in other states sodomy laws have been declared unconstitutional by the courts. Cases challenging the constitutionality of sodomy laws have arisen in the context of defenses to criminal charges and as civil "test" cases. They have been litigated in state and federal courts. Before reading these cases, it is important to examine the jurisprudential basis of the constitutional argument ("the right to privacy") that arises in them.

Even if the state is granted the authority to regulate private, non-harmful behavior in the first instance, a second question that arises in American jurisprudence concerns whether the Constitution overrides the state's authority, prohibiting certain types of restrictions. Majoritarian rule is checked in American law by the U.S. Constitution. The Constitution's Bill of Rights places certain subjects off limits as protected individual liberties. The First Amendment, for instance, prohibits states from making laws establishing religion or limiting freedom of speech. In the area of the regulation of sexuality, legislative majoritarianism has been checked by judicial recognition of a "right to privacy." The contours of this right were first recognized in a 1965 U.S. Supreme Court decision, *Griswold v. Connecticut*,[1] striking down a Connecticut law that prohibited married couples from using contraceptive devices. The right to privacy has developed in the last thirty years in a series of related cases, as described below:

> The Court first announced the new privacy doctrine . . . in *Griswold v. Connecticut*. In *Griswold* the Court invalidated statutes prohibiting the use and distribution of contraceptive devices. Eschewing an approach explicitly grounded in Lochnerian substantive due process, the Court stated that a "right to privacy" could be discerned in the "penumbras" of the first, third, fourth, fifth, and ninth amendments.[47] This right included the freedom of married couples to decide for themselves what to do in the "privacy" of their bedrooms.
>
> Two years later, in *Loving v. Virginia*, the Court struck down a law criminalizing interracial marriage. The Court ruled that states could not interfere in that manner with an individual's choice of whom to marry.[50] On similar grounds, the Court also invalidated laws restricting the ability of poor persons to marry or to divorce.[51]
>
> Although it remained possible after *Loving* to understand the new privacy doctrine as limited (for some unelaborated reason) to marital decisions, in *Eisenstadt v. Baird* the Court extended its *Griswold* holding to protect the distribution of contraceptives to unmarried persons as well. "If the right to privacy means anything," the Court stated, "it is the right of the *individual*, married or single, to be free from unwarranted governmental intrusion into matters so fundamentally affecting a person as the decision whether to bear or beget a child."[53]
>
> The next year, the Court took a further step from the confines of marriage and delivered its most controversial opinion since *Brown v. Board of Education*. Justice Blackmun, with only two Justices dissenting, wrote in *Roe v. Wade* that the right to privacy was "broad enough to encompass a woman's decision whether or not to terminate her pregnancy." Subsequent cases have reaffirmed *Roe* in the context of state efforts to "regulate" abortions, but the Court's support of *Roe* appears to be rapidly diminishing.[57]
>
> The right to privacy was further expanded in the 1977 case of *Moore v. City of East Cleveland*, in which the Court struck down a zoning ordinance that limited occupancy of dwelling units to members of a nuclear family — the "nominal head of a household," his

---

1. 381 U.S. 479 (1965).

47. . . .The *Griswold* Court used the ideal of "privacy" both in its more intelligible, informational sense — an interest in keeping certain matters out of public view — and in its relatively more obscure, substantive sense — an interest in making one's own decisions about certain "private" matters. . . .

50. Although the Court relied in part on the holding that the statute violated the equal protection clause, the opinion rested on a privacy rationale as well.

51. *See* Zablocki v. Redhail, 434 U.S. 374 (1978); Boddie v. Connecticut, 401 U.S. 371 (1971).

53. . . . [S]*ee also* Carey v. Population Servs. Int'l, 431 U.S. 678 (1977) (holding unconstitutional a state statute strictly limiting distribution and advertisement of contraceptive devices); Skinner v. Oklahoma, 316 U.S. 535 (1942) (holding, on equal protection grounds, that a statute authorizing forced sterilization of certain convicted felons was unconstitutional).

57. *See, e.g.*, Thornburgh v. American College of Obstetricians & Gynecologists, 476 U.S. 747 (1986) (5-4 decision); City of Akron v. Akron Center for Reproductive Health, 462 U.S. 416 (1983); Planned Parenthood v. Danforth, 428 U.S. 52 (1976). The word "regulate" appears with quotation marks because these cases often seem to involve state attempts to discourage or prevent — rather than regulate — abortions. . . .

or her spouse, and their parents and children. Although there was no majority opinion, the four-Justice plurality expressly relied on the *Griswold* line of cases, as well as *Meyer* and *Pierce*, emphasizing the "'private realm of family life which the state cannot enter.'"

Jed Rubenfeld, *The Right of Privacy*, 102 HARV. L. REV. 737, 744-746 (1989).

The right to privacy generally, and these cases in particular, lay the jurisprudential ground for challenges to state sodomy laws.

DOE v. COMMONWEALTH'S ATTORNEY

403 F. Supp. 1199 (E.D. Va.1975), *aff'd*, 425 U.S. 901 (1976)

BRYAN, Senior Circuit Judge

Virginia's statute making sodomy a crime is unconstitutional, each of the male plaintiffs aver, when it is applied to his active and regular homosexual relations with another *adult male, consensually* and *in private*. They assert that local State officers threaten them with prosecution for violation of this law, that such enforcement would deny them their Fifth and Fourteenth Amendments' assurance of due process, the First Amendment's protection of their rights of freedom of expression, the First and Ninth Amendments' guarantee of privacy, and the Eighth Amendment's forbiddance of cruel and unusual punishments. . . .

So far as relevant, the Code of Virginia, 1950, as amended, provides:

"§ 18.1-212. Crimes against nature. — If any person shall carnally know in any manner any brute animal, or carnally know any male or female person by the anus or by or with the mouth, or voluntarily submit to such carnal knowledge, he or she shall be guilty of a felony and shall be confined in the penitentiary not less than one year nor more than three years."

Our decision is that on its face and in the circumstances here it is not unconstitutional. No judgment is made upon the wisdom or policy of the statute. It is simply that we cannot say that the statute offends the Bill of Rights or any other of the Amendments and the wisdom or policy is a matter for the State's resolve.

I.

Precedents cited to us as *contra* rest exclusively on the precept that the Constitution condemns State legislation that trespasses upon the privacy of the incidents of marriage, upon the sanctity of the home, or upon the nurture of family life. This and only this concern has been the justification for nullification of State regulation in this area. Review of plaintiffs' authorities will reveal these as the principles underlying the referenced decisions.

In *Griswold v. Connecticut*, 381 U.S. 479 (1965), plaintiffs' chief reliance, the Court has most recently announced its views on the question here. Striking down a State statute forbidding the use of contraceptives, the ruling was put on the right of marital privacy — held to be one of the specific guarantees of the Bill of Rights — and was also put on the sanctity of the home and family. Its thesis is epitomized by the author of the opinion, Mr. Justice Douglas, in his conclusion:

> We deal with a right of privacy older than the Bill of Rights — older than our political parties, older than our school system. Marriage is a coming together for better or for worse, hopefully enduring and intimate to the degree of being sacred. It is an association that promotes a way of life, not causes; a harmony in living, not political faiths; a bilateral loyalty, not commercial or social projects. Yet it is an association for as noble a purpose as any involved in our prior decisions.

That *Griswold* is premised on the right of privacy and that homosexual intimacy is denunciable by the State is unequivocally demonstrated by Mr. Justice Goldberg in his concurrence, in his adoption of Mr. Justice Harlan's dissenting statement in *Poe v. Ullman*, 367 U.S. 497, 553 (1961):

> Adultery, *homosexuality* and the like are sexual intimacies *which the State forbids* . . . but the intimacy of husband and wife is necessarily an essential and accepted feature of the institution of marriage, an institution which the State not only must allow, but which always and in every age it has fostered and protected. *It is one thing when the State exerts its power either to forbid extramarital sexuality* . . . or to say who may marry, but it is quite another when, having acknowledged a marriage and the intimacies inherent in it, it undertakes to regulate by means of the criminal law the details of that intimacy.

Equally forceful is the succeeding paragraph of Justice Harlan:

> In sum, even though the State has determined that the use of contraceptives is as iniquitous as any act of extra-marital sexual immorality, the intrusion of the whole machinery of the criminal law into the very heart of marital privacy, requiring husband and wife to render account before a criminal tribunal of their uses of that intimacy is surely *a very different thing indeed from punishing those who establish intimacies which the law has always forbidden and which can have no claim to social protection.*

Justice Harlan's words are nonetheless commanding merely because they were written in dissent. To begin with, as heretofore observed, they are authentically approved in *Griswold*. Moreover, he was not differing with the majority there on the merits of the substantive case but only as to the procedural reason of its dismissal. At all events, the Justice's exegesis is that of a jurist of widely acknowledged superior stature and weighty whatever its context.

With his standing, what he had further to say in *Poe v. Ullman, supra*, is worthy of high regard. On the plaintiffs' effort presently to shield the practice of homosexuality from State incrimination by according it immunity when committed in private as against public exercise, the Justice said this:

> Indeed to attempt a line between public behavior and that which is purely consensual or solitary would be to withdraw from community concern a range of subjects with which every society in civilized times has found it necessary to deal. The laws regarding marriage which provide both when the sexual powers may be used and the legal and societal context in which children are born and brought up, as well as *laws forbidding adultery, fornication and homosexual practices which express the negative of the proposition*, confining sexuality to lawful marriage, form a pattern so deeply pressed into the substance of our social life that any Constitutional doctrine in this area must build upon that basis.

Again:

Thus, I would not suggest that *adultery, homosexuality, fornication and incest are immune* from criminal enquiry, *however privately practiced.* So much has been explicitly recognized in acknowledging the State's rightful concern for its people's moral welfare. . . . But not to discriminate between what is involved in this case and either the traditional offenses against good morals or crimes which, though they may be committed anywhere, *happen to have been committed or concealed in the home*, would entirely misconceive the argument that is being made.

Many states have long had, and still have, statutes and decisional law criminalizing conduct depicted in the Virginia legislation . . . .

II.

With no authoritative judicial bar to the proscription of homosexuality — since it is obviously no portion of marriage, home or family life — the next question is whether there is any ground for barring Virginia from branding it as criminal. If a State determines that punishment therefor, even when committed in the home, is appropriate in the promotion of morality and decency, it is not for the courts to say that the State is not free to do so. In short, it is an inquiry addressable only to the State's Legislature.

Furthermore, if the State has the burden of proving that it has a legitimate interest in the subject of the statute or that the statute is rationally supportable, Virginia has completely fulfilled this obligation. Fundamentally, the State action is simply directed to the suppression of crime, whether committed in public or

in private. Both instances . . . are within the reach of the police power.

Moreover, to sustain its action, the State is not required to show that moral delinquency actually results from homosexuality. It is enough for upholding the legislation to establish that the conduct is likely to end in a contribution to moral delinquency. Plainly, it would indeed be impracticable to prove the actuality of such a consequence, and the law is not so exacting.

If such a prospect or expectation was in the mind of the General Assembly of Virginia, the prophecy proved only too true in the occurrences narrated in *Lovisi v. Slayton*, 363 F.Supp. 620 (E.D. Va. 1973, now on appeal in the Fourth Circuit). The graphic outline by the District Judge there describes just such a sexual orgy as the statute was evidently intended to punish. The Lovisis, a married couple, advertised their wish "to meet people" and in response a man came to Virginia to meet the Lovisis on several occasions. In one instance the three of them participated in acts of fellatio. Photographs of the conduct were taken by a set camera and the acts were witnessed by the wife's daughters, aged 11 and 13. The pictures were carried by them to school.

Although a questionable law is not removed from question by the lapse of any prescriptive period, the longevity of the Virginia statute does testify to the State's interest and its legitimacy. It is not an upstart notion; it has ancestry going back to Judaic and Christian law.[2] The immediate parentage may be readily traced to the Code of Virginia of 1792.[3] All the while the law has been kept alive, as evidenced by periodic amendments, the last in the 1968 Acts of the General Assembly of Virginia, c. 427.

In sum, we believe that the sodomy statute, so long in force in Virginia, has a rational basis

---

2. Leviticus 18:22: "Thou shalt not lie with mankind, as with womankind: it is abomination." Again, 20:13: "If a man also lie with mankind, as he lieth with a woman, both of them have committed an abomination: they shall surely be put to death; their blood shall be upon them." . . .

3. "Sodomy" was used in the earlier laws interchangeably with buggery and other "unnatural sex acts". Davis, *Criminal Law*, (1838) p. 133.

of State interest demonstrably legitimate and mirrored in the cited decisional law of the Supreme Court. Indeed, the Court has treated as free of infirmity a State law with a background similar to the Virginia enactment in suit. *Wainwright v. Stone*, 414 U.S. 21 (1973).

The prayers for a declaratory judgment and an injunction invalidating the sodomy statute will be denied.

MERHIGE, District Judge (dissenting)

. . . In my view, in the absence of any legitimate interest or rational basis to support the statute's application we must, without regard to our own proclivities and reluctance to judicially bar the state proscription of homosexuality, hold the statute as it applies to the plaintiffs to be violative of their rights under the Due Process Clause of the Fourteenth Amendment to the Constitution of the United States. The Supreme Court decision in *Griswold v. Connecticut*, 381 U.S. 479, 499 (1965), is, as the majority points out, premised on the right of privacy, but I fear my brothers have misapplied its precedential value through an apparent over-adherence to its factual circumstances.

The Supreme Court has consistently held that the due process clause of the Fourteenth Amendment protects the right of individuals to make personal choices, unfettered by arbitrary and purposeless restraints, in the private matters of marriage and procreation. *Roe v. Wade*, 410 U.S. 113, 153, 169 (1973); *accord Doe v. Bolton*, 410 U.S. 179 (1973). See also *Griswold v. Connecticut, supra*, 381 U.S. 479, 498 (Harlan, J., concurring). I view those cases as standing for the principle that every individual has a right to be free from unwarranted governmental intrusion into one's decisions on private matters of intimate concern. A mature individual's choice of an adult sexual partner, in the privacy of his or her own home, would appear to me to be a decision of the utmost private and intimate concern. Private consensual sex acts between adults are matters, absent evidence

that they are harmful, in which the state has no legitimate interest.

To say, as the majority does, that the right of privacy, which every citizen has, is limited to matters of marital, home or family life is unwarranted under the law. Such a contention places a distinction in marital-nonmarital matters which is inconsistent with current Supreme Court opinions and is unsupportable.

In my view, the reliance of the majority on Mr. Justice Harlan's dissenting statement in *Poe v. Ullman*, 367 U.S. 497, 553 (1961), is misplaced. An analysis of the cases indicates that in 1965 when *Griswold*, which invalidated a statute prohibiting the use of contraceptives by married couples, was decided, at least three of the Court, relying primarily on Mr. Justice Harlan's dissent in *Poe v. Ullman*, and Mr. Justice Harlan himself, would not have been willing to attach the right of privacy to homosexual conduct. In my view, *Griswold* applied the right of privacy to its particular factual situation. That the right of privacy is not limited to the facts of *Griswold* is demonstrated by later Supreme Court decisions. After *Griswold*, by virtue of *Eisenstadt v. Baird*, 405 U.S. 430 (1972), the legal viability of a marital-nonmarital distinction in private sexual acts if not eliminated, was at the very least seriously impaired. In *Eisenstadt, supra*, the Court declined to restrict the right of privacy in sexual matters to married couples:

> Yet the marital couple is not an independent entity with a mind and heart of its own, but an association of two individuals each with a separate intellectual and emotional makeup. If the right of privacy means anything, it is the right of the *individual*, married or single, to be free from unwarranted governmental intrusion into matters so fundamentally affecting a person as the decision whether to bear or beget a child. 405 U.S. at 453.

In significantly diminishing the importance of the marital-nonmarital distinction, the Court to a great extent vitiated any implication that the state can, as suggested by Mr. Justice Harlan in *Poe v. Ullman*, forbid extra-marital sexuality, and such implications are no longer fully accurate.

> It is one thing when the State exerts its power either to forbid extra-marital sexuality altogether, or to say who may marry, but it is quite another when, having acknowledged a marriage and the intimacies inherent in it, it undertakes to regulate by means of the criminal law the details of that intimacy. 367 U.S. at 553 (Harlan, J., dissenting).

Griswold, supra, in its context, applied the right of privacy in sexual matters to the marital relationship. *Eisenstadt, supra*, however, clearly demonstrates that the right to privacy in sexual relationships is not limited to the marital relationship. Both *Roe, supra*, and *Eisenstadt, supra*, cogently demonstrate that intimate personal decisions or private matters of substantial importance to the well-being of the individuals involved are protected by the Due Process Clause. The right to select consenting adult sexual partners must be considered within this category. The exercise of that right, whether heterosexual or homosexual, should not be proscribed by state regulation absent compelling justification.

This approach does not unqualifiedly sanction personal whim. If the activity in question involves more than one participant, as in the instant case, each must be capable of consenting, and each must in fact consent to the conduct for the right of privacy to attach. For example, if one of the participants in homosexual contact is a minor, or force is used to coerce one of the participants to yield, the right will not attach. Similarly, the right of privacy cannot be extended to protect conduct that takes place in publicly frequented areas. However, if the right of privacy does apply to specific courses of conduct, legitimate state restriction on personal autonomy may be justified only under the compelling state interest test. See *Roe v. Wade, supra*, 410 U.S. 113, 215-18 (Douglas, J., concurring).

Plaintiffs are adults seeking protection from the effects of the statute under attack in order to engage in homosexual relations in private. Viewing the issue as we are bound to, as Mr. Justice Blackmun stated in *Roe v. Wade, supra*, at 116, "by constitutional measurement, free of emotion and predilection," it is my view that they are entitled to be protected in their right to privacy by the due process clause.

The defendants, represented by the highest legal officer of the state, made no tender of any evidence which even impliedly demonstrated that homosexuality causes society any significant harm. No effort was made by the defendants to estabish either a rational basis or a compelling state interest so as to justify the proscription of § 8.1-212 of the Code of Virginia, presently under attack.[4] To suggest, as defendants do, that the prohibition of homosexual conduct will in some manner encourage new heterosexual marriages and prevent the dissolution of existing ones is unworthy of judicial response. In any event, what we know as men is not forgotten as judges — it is difficult to envision any substantial number of heterosexual marriages being in danger of dissolution because of the private sexual activites of homosexuals.

On the basis of this record one can only conclude that the sole basis of the proscription of homosexuality was what the majority refers to as the promotion of morality and decency. As salutary a legislative goal as this may be, I can find no authority for intrusion by the state into the private dwelling of a citizen. *Stanley v. Georgia*, 394 U.S. 557 (1969) teaches us that socially condemned activity, excepting that of demonstrable ex-

---

4. See, Note, The Constitutionality of Laws Forbidding Private Homosexual Conduct, 72 Mich.L.Rev. 1613 (1975), for discussion on the lack of empirical data on adverse effect of homosexuals on the social system.

ternal effect, is and was intended by the Constitution to be beyond the scope of state regulation when conducted within the privacy of the home. "The Constitution extends special safeguards to the privacy of the home, ..." *United States v. Orito*, 413 U.S. 139 (1975). Whether the guarantee of personal privacy springs from the First, Fourth, Fifth, Ninth, the penumbra of the Bill of Rights, or, as I believe, in the concept of liberty guaranteed by the first section of the Fourteenth Amendment, the Supreme Court has made it clear that fundamental rights of such an intimate facet of an individual's life as sex, absent circumstances warranting intrusion by the state, are to be respected. My brothers, I respectfully suggest, have by today's ruling misinterpreted the issue — the issue centers not around morality or decency, but the constitutional right of privacy.

I respectfully note my dissent.

Note

The *Doe* case was appealed to the U.S. Supreme Court. Typically, cases are taken to the highest court through the filing of a "writ of certiorari." In such a case, the Court has discretion to review the lower court's determination; its refusal to do so, or "denial of certiorari" has no precedential value, that is, it is not a Supreme Court decision on the merits of the case (*see* ROBERT STERN ET AL., SUPREME COURT PRACTICE § 5.7 (6th ed. 1986)). The *Doe* case, however, arose under a now-outdated procedure by which challenges to the constitutionality of state statutes were heard by a three-judge district court and then *appealed* directly to the Supreme Court. In such instances, the Court had to either take the case, summarily affirm the result below, or summarily reverse the result below.

In *Doe v. Commonwealth's Attorney*, the Court summarily affirmed the decision printed above. *See Doe v. Commonwealth's Attorney*, 425 U.S. 901 (1976). Justices William Brennan, Thurgood Marshall, and John Paul Stevens voted to have the Court hear the case. The Court rendered its decision without a separate written opinion, and thus it is not know on what basis the Supreme Coourt agreed with the lower court's result. Nonetheless, until the Supreme Court directly confronted the question of the constitutionality of sodomy laws in *Bowers v. Hardwick*, the summary affirmance in *Doe v. Commonwealth's Attorney* was the Court's primary pronouncement on the issue. Accordingly, there was considerable academic commentary about the meaning of the summary affirmance. *See*, *e.g.*, Elisa Fuller, Hardwick v. Bowers: *An Attempt to Pull the Meaning of* Doe v. Commonwealth's Attorney *Out of the Closet*, 39 U. MIAMI L. REV. 973 (1985). Tom Gerety, *Redefining Privacy*, 12 HARV. C.R.-C.L. L. REV. 223, 279-80 (1977) (the precedential value of *Doe* is severely lessened by its status as summarily affirmed by the Court rather than affirmed on the merits).

Notwithstanding *Doe*, a federal district court in Texas struck down that state's sodomy law as violating the federal Constitution in 1982. *See Baker v. Wade*, 553 F. Supp. 1121 (N.D. Tex. 1982). Relying on *Doe v. Commonwealth's Attorney*, the U.S. Court of Appeals for the Fifth Circuit reversed the *Baker* decision in a summary decision:

In *Doe v. Commonwealth's Attorney*, 425 U.S. 901 (1976), the Supreme Court summarily affirmed the judgment of a three-judge district court upholding the constitutionality of a Virginia sodomy statute similar to the Texas statute which is attacked in the present suit. We consider the decision of the Court in *Doe* to be binding upon us . . . . We should follow that controlling authority until the Supreme Court itself has issued an unequivocal statement that *Doe* no longer controls. We refuse to speculate, on the basis of the writings cited to us by the appellee, about what the Court might do today on this issue.

Baker v. Wade, 769 F.2d 289, 292 (5th Cir. 1985)(en banc).

Although it was reversed, the district court decision in *Baker*, a portion of which follows, is particularly interesting for its discussion of the plaintiff and his life.

BAKER v. WADE

553 F. Supp. 1121 (N.D. Tex. 1982), *rev'd,* 769 F. 2d 289 (5th Cir. 1985)(en banc), *cert. denied,* 478 U.S. 1022 (1986)

BUCHMEYER, DISTRICT JUDGE.

This is a suit by a homosexual, Donald F. Baker, attacking the constitutionality of § 21.06 ("Homosexual Conduct") of the Texas Penal Code. Section 21.06 (and the related definitions in §§ 1.05 and 21.01) provide:

"A person commits an offense if he [or she] engages in deviate sexual intercourse with another individual of the same sex.

" 'Deviate sexual intercourse' means any contact between any part of the genitals of one person and the mouth or anus of another person."

A violation of this statute is a "Class C misdemeanor," punishable only by "a fine not to exceed $200." *Tex. Penal Code Ann.*, § 12.23 (Vernon 1974).

■ ■ ■

The complaint seeks a declaration that § 21.06 (Homosexual Conduct) of the Texas Penal Code is unconstitutional because it violates (i) the plaintiff's fundamental right to privacy, (ii) the equal protection clause of the fourteenth amendment, and (iii) the establishment of religion clause of the first amendment.

THE STATUTE

Texas has had three sodomy statutes . . . .

The first was enacted in 1860. It prohibited "the abominable and detestable crime against nature" (punishable by 5-15 years imprisonment). However, this statute did not condemn oral sex, but only anal sex and beastiality. Thus, for a period of 83 years, oral sodomy was not illegal in Texas — whether committed by man and wife, by unmarried male and female, or by homosexuals.

The second statute was Article 524, *Texas Penal Code Ann.*, adopted in 1943. It prohibited "carnal copulation" with human or beast (punishable by 2-15 years imprisonment), and condemned *all* oral and anal sex and beastiality. Thus, for the next 31 years, it was a felony for *anyone* in Texas — married couples, single males and females, male homosexuals or lesbians — to engage in oral or anal sodomy, even in private with another consenting adult.

The third statute, § 21.06, was passed in 1974 as part of the first comprehensive reform of the state's criminal laws since the initial penal code had been enacted in 1856. It prohibited only homosexual sodomy. All prohibitions against oral or anal sex between consenting adults of opposite sex, whether married or not, were rescinded (as were criminal laws against fornication and adultry). Thus, for the past 8 years in Texas, only homosexuals have been prohibited from engaging in private, consensual sodomy (although punishment was drastically reduced by § 21.06, with no imprisonment and a maximum fine of $200). At least three sessions of the Texas legislature have rejected attempts to repeal § 21.06, and this is the first *direct* constitutional attack upon it.

There are practical difficulties in prosecuting persons under § 21.06 for private homosexual conduct. If the acts are between two people in private, there may be no witness to testify at trial. Moreover, "the consenting parties to acts of sodomy are equally guilty and their testimony as witnesses for the state would require corroboration."

However, homosexuals have in fact been prosecuted under the Texas sodomy statutes. And, the parties in this case stipulated in the final pretrial order that the plaintiff is "an admitted practicing homosexual"; that he has not been arrested or prosecuted for a violation of § 21.06; but that cases involving violations of this statute "have been prosecuted by various assistant city attorneys and assistant district attorneys" in Dallas; and

that both defendants "would prosecute the plaintiff and other homosexuals under § 21.06 if a provable violation of the law came to their attention."

THE FACTS

■ ■ ■

The Plaintiff

Donald F. Baker, 35, is a former Dallas school teacher who received his master's degree in education from Southern Methodist University in 1980. He has never been arrested or convicted of any criminal offense. He is an active and devout Christian. And, he is a good citizen, having served as precinct chairman and as a delegate to two state Democratic Party conventions.

But Donald Baker is a homosexual. He has never had sex with a woman, or even been sexually aroused by a female. He does engage in private sexual acts with other adult males, but is not capable of doing so with females. Therefore, *Donald Baker is also a criminal* under § 21.06 of the Texas Penal Code.

Baker was a very sincere, very credible witness.[7] While his parents listened in the courtroom, Baker gave the following testimony about his adolescent ignorance of his homosexuality, his disgust and self-loathing upon recognition of it, his isolation and suffering, his suicidal tendencies, and his eventual change from a "homosexual" into a "gay."[8]

Baker was born on April 24, 1947, into a very stable and religious family in Dallas.

---

7. Although people tend to stereotype homosexuals, just as they do corporate executives and truck drivers, "contrary to the frequently held notion that all homosexuals are alike, they are in fact very heterogeneous." National Institute of Mental Health Task Force on Homosexuality, p. 2 (Oct. 1969) ("Task Force on Homosexuality"). During trial, Donald Baker dressed conservatively, was very articulate, and had the appearance that most people might expect of a school teacher or bank executive.

8. According to Baker, a "homosexual" is one who has an emotional, erotic attachment to one of the same sex — while a "gay" is one "who is proud of being a homosexual." *See Cyr v. Walls*, 439 F.Supp. 697, 699 n.2.

His grandfather had been an Assembly of God minister, and Baker was very active in this church. He was a leader in various youth activities, including the church choir and the boy scouts. During his junior high school years, when Baker was 13 or 14, he started to become aware that he was somehow "different." Although he dated some girls because of peer pressure, he found this awkward. He began realizing that he had strong feelings for his male friends, but could not understand his frustration and loneliness. He knew that "queers were bad," and had no idea that he might be homosexual.

In 1965 Baker graduated from high school and attended East Texas State University. There, he became even more aware that he was "different." He did "some study" of the "general area of homosexuality," and learned it was illegal. He grew very disappointed in himself, and simply could not understand why he was having feelings that were "wrong" and "criminal" and "sinful."

After two years at East Texas (1965-67), Baker transferred to the University of Texas at Austin. There, he continued his church activities and worked at a campus bookstore. He had never engaged in any homosexual conduct and still did not know he was homosexual. Then, in November of 1967 — when Donald Baker was 20 — he had his first homosexual "experience."

On that day, Baker took a break from work at the bookstore to watch a football game on television in the student union. The room was crowded and Baker soon became aware of a man standing next to him. After a while, Baker looked up, and the man — blond, early twenties, medium height — was staring at Baker, with a look that was "erotic." Baker felt intense anxiety and attraction. He followed the man to the restroom, but nothing happened. Baker refused the man's advances, and returned to work, where he broke into sobs.

Baker was overwhelmed with fear and with disgust. He knew his desires for sexual contact with the man were wrong, and were contrary to his family and religious values. Baker felt he was a "dirty, nasty thing." He left work, and went to sing in the church choir, but broke down there, too. He tried to talk to his minister, but could not bring himself to tell the minister what was really wrong.

After that day, Baker cut himself off from the world. He refused to open the door to his room or answer the phone for over two weeks. Baker was afraid he had a "disease" and might contaminate others. He was sure that "God hated him" and that "society hated him" and that "his family hated him." In May of 1968, Baker joined the Navy because "he needed to run away from what he was."

Baker had not engaged in any homosexual conduct while in college, nor would he do so while he was in the Navy. He served in the Navy for four years (1968-72), with an excellent record. During this time, Baker continued to attend church and agonized about "what he was." He knew that if he was homosexual, then "he wouldn't have a job, his family would reject him, and he would burn in hell." Baker prayed for deliverance.

In January of 1972, Baker was honorably discharged. He came home to Dallas, but had a "terrible fear," and left after only two weeks to live with friends in Massachusetts. During the next two years, Baker felt isolated and rejected — his suffering and disgust continued — and he seriously considered suicide. Baker still had not engaged in any homosexual conduct. In 1974, he enrolled at the State University of New York in Cortland, continuing his studies in elementary and secondary school education (graduating cum laude in 1975).

One day Baker decided to attend a meeting of a gay organization at Cornell University in Ithaca, thirty miles away. He was nervous, and walked around the Cornell campus for about an hour. Finally, he sneaked into the building, and stood hidden on a balcony where he could see the meeting down below. It was the first time Donald

Baker had ever seen other human beings that he knew were homosexual, too, but who were not ashamed of that fact.

At age 27, Donald Baker was starting "to come out of the closet." He became acquainted with other "gays," and "learned that that they were not monsters." During the next year, he studied history, sociology and psychology; he re-examined the Bible and satisfied himself that he could be a devout Christian as well as a homosexual; and he gradually "came to terms with the fact that he was homosexual," although he was still discreet in telling others.

In 1975, Baker returned to Dallas and "came out" to his family, admitting to them that he was homosexual. He obtained a job with the Dallas Independent School District, and taught there for four years (1975-79) as a language arts and social studies teacher in grades 4-6. His private life as a homosexual did not adversely affect his job performance or his abilities as a teacher.[9] Indeed, Baker was recognized by DISD as an excellent teacher.[10] And, when Baker left DISD in 1979 to return to Southern Methodist University to work on his master's degree, the School District recommended him for the teaching fellowship which he was awarded.

Before completing his master's degree, Baker became actively involved in gay rights organizations. In 1979, he became vice-president of the Dallas Gay Political Caucus and, in November of that year, this suit was filed. In 1980, the name of the organization was changed, and Baker became President of the Dallas Gay Alliance. He is also active on state and national levels.

Baker also testified that he will continue to engage in private homosexual conduct in violation of § 21.06, but has no intention of doing so in public . . . that he does not desire or need psychiatric treatment . . . that § 21.06 does have serious effects upon homosexuals because it makes them criminals . . . that this "stigma" encourages police harassment of homosexuals and results in discrimination against homosexuals by employers, apartment owners, domestic relations courts (in child custody matters), and others.

The Plaintiff's Experts

The two principal expert witnesses[12] presented by the plaintiff were Dr. Judd Marmor, a psychiatrist, and Dr. William Simon, a sociologist. Both had studied and written extensively in the area of homosexuality and they are experts in this field. Their qualifications were impeccable and their testimony established the following facts:

---

9. During the period he taught at DISD, Baker did engage in sexual conduct with other males in private at his home. However, he was never sexually attracted to any students and never had any sexual contact with them. He did not advocate homosexuality to the students. Instead, he lived in fear and anxiety of being "discovered" — because the DISD superintendent had stated publicly that he would fire any homosexual teachers. A school board member testified that Baker would have been fired if there had even been a suspicion that he had violated § 21.06.

10. Baker's evaluations included these comments: "Mr. Baker is an asset to our school. He has done a good job for us this year. Potential of being an excellent teacher" (1976) . . . "An excellent teacher. He is well liked by students, parents, and co-teachers" (1977) . . . "He has done a good job. He is becoming an excellent teacher, a hard and dedicated worker" (1978).

12. Through another expert, Dr. Victor Furnish, a theologian and professor of the New Testament at S.M.U., the plaintiff introduced a number of resolutions by church bodies condemning the repression of homosexuality and urging repeal of statutes like § 21.06. Dr. Furnish testified that, in his expert opinion, the Bible does not condemn *consensual* homosexual conduct. He noted that there is no reference to homosexuality in the Ten Commandments; that Christ made no statements about homosexuality; and that homosexuality was not a "prominent biblical concern," since it is the subject of only a few passages. Dr. Furnish interpreted the story of Sodom as an "intended gang rape" of the strangers (the two angels in Lot's house), and thus a condemnation of violence and force, not consensual homosexual conduct. He gave a similar interpretation to the two passages in Leviticus — *Leviticus* 18:22: "Thou shalt not lie with mankind, as with womankind: it is abomination." *Leviticus* 20:13: "If a man also lie with mankind, as he lieth with a woman,

Section 21.06 makes "criminals" of a substantial number of individuals in Texas. At least five percent of American males are "exclusive" or obligatory homosexuals[13] — who have no heterosexual experiences and who have no desire to change. This means that there are at least 500,000 exclusive homosexual males in Texas. In addition, some two-three percent of the females in Texas (or, approximately 130,000 – 200,000) are exclusive lesbians.[14]

These "exclusive homosexuals" did not choose to be homosexuals. Obligatory homosexuality is not a matter of choice: it is fixed at an early age — before one even begins to participate in sexual activities — and only a small minority can be changed or "cured," if at all. Although there are different theories about the "cause" of homosexuality, the overwhelming majority of experts agree that individuals become homosexuals because of biological or genetic factors, or environmental conditioning, or a combination of these and other causes — and that sexual orientation would be difficult and painful, if not impossible, to reverse by psychiatric treatment.

Indeed, homosexuality is not a "disease" and it is not, in and of itself, a mental disorder.[15] Although society — and courts — may still grapple with this question, in 1973 the American Psychiatric Association removed homosexuality from its list of psychic disorders, resolving that "homosexuality *per se* implies no impairment in judgment, stability, reliability or general social or vocational capabilities" and that "*in the reasoned judgment of most American psychiatrists today, homosexuality per se does not constitute any form of mental disease.*" In 1970, 1973 and 1975, respectively, the American Anthropological Association, the American Bar Association,[16] and the American Psychological As-

---

both of them have committed an abomination: they shall surely be put to death; their blood shall be upon them" — and also noted that neither the Bible nor these passages "say anything about female homosexuality." However, Dr. Furnish conceded that other biblical scholars may disagree with his opinions and that, in fact, many religions do condemn homosexuality.

13. Under the "Kinsey scale," — which begins with category 0 (exclusively heterosexual) — category 6 is "exclusively homosexual" (no heterosexual experiences, obligatory) and category 5 is "more or less exclusively homosexual" (only incidental heterosexual experiences, with no desire to change, obligatory). The figures given in this opinion are for categories 5 and 6, combined, since these are considered "exclusive homosexuals." However, among the 95% of American males who are not "exclusive homosexuals," 15-20% do engage in some homosexual activities. For example, individuals whose heterosexual preference is predominant may, under certain circumstances (such as imprisonment), become involved in homosexual behavior. *See* Task Force on Homosexuality, p. 2 (Dr. Judd Marmor was a member of this Task Force and helped write the report).

14. These numbers may be even higher. According to the magazine article introduced as Defendant Wade's Exhibit 1, the revolutionary Kinsey survey — which revealed a surprising level of homosexual behavior not previously known and which has been confirmed by later studies — estimated that ten percent of the American men, and approximately three-five percent of the women, were exclusively homosexual. This would mean that there may be over 650,000 exclusive homosexual males and as many as 200-300,000 exclusive homosexual females in Texas. Kinsey also estimated that fifty percent of all American males have had homosexual experiences. Ennis, "What Do These Rugged Texas He-Men Have in Common?," Texas Monthly (June 1980), pp. 107-113, 209-226. The plaintiff testified that the statements made about him in this article were basically correct.

15. Dr. Marmor testified that homosexuality was not "contagious" or infectious; that, although there was "some disagreement," almost all American psychiatrists feel that "homosexuality per se does not constitute any form of mental disorder"; and that there is no respected medical literature to the contrary.

16. The American Law Institute in its Model Penal Code recommended that criminal statutes covering sexual conduct "be recast in such a way as to remove legal penalties against acts in private among consenting adults." *See* Task Force on Homosexuality, p. 6.

sociation adopted similar resolutions. And, in 1975, even the American Medical Association resolved:

"That the American Medical Association support in principle repeal of laws which classify as criminal any form of non-commercial sexual conduct between consenting adults in private, saving only those portions of the law which protect minors, public decorum, or the mentally incompetent."

Each of these resolutions urged the repeal of statutes which, like § 21.06, prohibit only private sexual conduct by consenting adults. If this were done — i.e., if there was a "decriminalization" of homosexual acts in private by consenting adults — this would not result in an increase in homosexuality. In some countries (e.g., England, France, Holland, Finland), homosexual conduct has been decriminalized for years, and there is no greater incidence of homosexuality in those countries than in the United States. Moreover, there have been no adverse side effects in the twenty-one states that have now decriminalized consensual sodomy between adults in private.

There is no basis to assume that criminal laws (like § 21.06) reduce the number of homosexuals. Persons do not choose homosexuality, and only a small percentage of exclusive homosexuals can be cured or changed. Criminal sanctions do not deter homosexual sodomy — because "sex, next to hunger and thirst, is the most powerful drive that human beings experience," and it is unrealistic to think that such laws will force total abstinence. Moreover, homosexuality has never been stamped out by criminal laws; it has been common in almost every type of society, at all economic levels, and among all ethnic and cultural groups.

In addition, the existence of these criminal laws, even if they are not enforced (like § 21.06), does result in stigma, emotional stress and other adverse effects. The anxieties caused to homosexuals — fear of arrest, loss of jobs, discovery, etc. — can cause severe mental health problems. Homosexuals, as criminals, are often alienated from society and institutions, particularly law enforcement officals. They do suffer discrimination in housing, employment and other areas.

Neither Dr. Marmor nor Dr. Simon could find any legitimate state interest to justify statutes like § 21.06. Although "homophobia" — an exaggerated fear of homosexuals — may exist among many heterosexuals, there is no rational basis for this. The vast majority of sex crimes committed by adults upon children are heterosexual, not homosexual.[18] Homosexuals do not have a criminal propensity simply because they are homosexuals, any more than heterosexuals do. Homosexuals are not ill or mentally diseased. And, homosexuality in society does not adversely affect the growth and development of children.[19]

Accordingly, both of the plaintiff's experts felt there was no rational basis and no state interest that would justify § 21.06. The Court credits the testimony and the opinions of Dr. Marmor and Dr. Simon, particularly since they were uncontradicted — except, as next discussed, by part of the testimony of the defendants' "expert."

---

18. *See* Responding to Child Sexual Abuse: A Report to the 67th Session of the Texas Legislature (Sam Houston State Univ., Criminal Justice Center 1980).

19. Dr. Marmor was cross-examined about a statement he made in the book *Sexual Inversion* that "Psychiatric intervention is prophylactically indicated for children or adolescents who seem to be failing to make appropriate gender role identifications." He explained that sexual preference is fixed at an early age (probably before age 6), and that "highly effeminate children" — who are vilified by their peers and badly traumatized "in a society that regards homosexuality as an undesirable behavioral deviation" — may benefit from psychiatric treatment. His explanation was credible, and his testimony as a whole clearly established that the normal growth and development of children was not fostered by laws which make homosexual conduct illegal.

The Defendants' Witnesses

The defendants presented Dr. James Grigson, a psychiatrist primarily engaged in what he termed "legal psychiatry,"[20] as an expert witness. It was his opinion "that the members of society, including the homosexual individuals, do benefit from the law [against homosexual conduct] which we have here in the state of Texas." He did not explain how "members of society" benefited from § 21.06, but testified specifically that it was helpful to children and to homosexuals because:

(i) As to *children*, § 21.06 "primarily reinforces their own super-ego or conscience" and thus fosters their "growth and development" by reinforcing "the culture of society's norm pattern or expected pattern of behavior."

(ii) As to *homosexuals*, "if sodomy was decriminalized, it would be harmful to the homosexual, because it would result in a lessening in terms of those individuals going ahead and seeking help and resolving their problems."

Dr. Grigson also testified that, in his opinion, homosexuals "are less stable and have more pathological emotional mental illnesses than the general population as a whole" — and that "homosexuality is an illness and a disease and that certainly homosexual behavior is deviant behavior."[21]

This court completely discounts Dr. Grigson's testimony and his opinions.[22] These opinions were not based upon any independent research or supported by "any respected medical or psychiatric literature." Indeed, Dr. Grigson had personally treated only forty-fifty homosexuals in his nineteen-year practice (although he had seen "a far larger number" just for the purpose of doing evaluations on them)[23] — and he could not name any other psychiatrist who shared his opinion "that homosexuality or private homosexual conduct between consenting adults ought to be criminalized."

Moreover, Dr. Grigson's opinions were directly contrary to those of the plaintiff's experts[24] — whose qualifications as experts in the field of homosexuality were outstanding and whose testimony was very

20. Dr. Grigson explained that "legal psychiatry" revolves around "determination of competency, sanity, likelihood of making probation of defendants, occasional civil cases involving psychiatric questions, occasional probate cases involving competency of an individual to make a will." He spends about 20% of his time testifying on behalf of the District Attorney's office in criminal cases, and appeared in over 100 criminal cases in *each* of the past four years (1977-80), an average of three times per week. Dr. Grigson also teaches psychiatry part-time at Southwestern Medical School in Dallas.

21. Accordingly [sic] to Dr. Grigson, this is true of *all* homosexuals, not just exclusive or obligatory homosexuals; "regardless of whether they want [heterosexual relationships] or don't want them, they're still, if they are homosexual, suffering from an illness."

22. In making this determination, this Court has — in addition to the matters discussed above — considered all of the circumstances under which the witness testified, including his relationship to the District Attorney's office (see note 12) and the extent to which he was supported or contradicted by other credible evidence. No weight was given to the fact that Dr. Grigson had been reprimanded by the American Psychiatric Association on a collateral matter. *See Estelle v. Smith*, 451 U.S. 454 (1981). There was nothing to show that Dr. Grigson was not a competent psychiatrist; however, he was not a credible witness concerning homosexuality and laws condemning homosexual conduct.

23. Dr. Grigson was tendered as an expert because of his experience in diagnosis and treatment "of sexual disorders or conditions relating to sexual problems," including the diagnosis or treatment "of individuals who had problems relating to homosexuality."

24. Dr. Grigson, again without any support, (i) disagreed with the plaintiff's experts that "sexual preference is fixed at a very early age," and thought that many individuals changed their sexual preferences "around puberty" or even "in later life," and (ii) disagreed that homosexuality "is a condition that is virtually unchangeable, at least in approximately 70% of the homosexual population."

credible — and to positions adopted by various medical and psychiatric associations. For example, Dr. Grigson disagreed with the American Psychiatric Association resolution that "homosexuality per se does not constitute any form of mental disease" — and with the American Medical Association resolution supporting "repeal of laws which classify as criminal any form of non-commercial sexual conduct between consenting adults in private." And, even standing alone, Dr. Grigson's "opinions" were flawed, in-consistent, and directly contrary to other credible evidence accepted by this Court:

(i) As to *children*, Dr. Grigson conceded that their "normal growth and behavioral patterns" are reinforced by their "parents, school, religion and churches" — but did not even attempt an explanation as to why criminal sanctions against homosexuality would also be needed to reinforce children's "super-ego or conscience." Moreover, it is a fact under the evidence in this record (*Fed.R.Civ.P.*52) that "sexual preference is fixed at a very early age," probably before the age of six, and that people do not "choose" to become homosexuals. Thus, there is no basis for Dr. Grigson's opinion — which is contrary to the medical literature and the opinions of "most American psychiatrists today" — that children might become homosexuals or develop homosexual tendencies unless homosexual conduct is illegal and punished by a $200 fine.[25]

(ii) As to *homosexuals*, the idea that criminal sanctions will cause such anxieties in homosexuals that they will seek psychiatric treatment and be "cured" is not only preposterous[26] — it, too, is contrary to the facts established by the credible evidence in this record (*Fed.R. Civ.P.*52): persons do not choose to be homosexuals; most "exclusive homosexuals" do not want to be changed and do not seek any treatment; the "cure rate" for all homosexuals will, at best, be only thirty percent;[27] and criminal laws simply do not reduce the number of homosexuals in society.

In contrast to Dr. Grigson, neither of the two defendants — District Attorney Henry Wade and City Attorney Lee Holt — could even attempt to explain how §21.06 furthers the state's interests in protecting decency, the welfare of society, procreation, morality, or any other interest. Wade testified (by deposition):

"... Can you explain to me how this law furthers the state interest of *decency*, if any, by prohibiting private homosexual conduct but permitting private heterosexual conduct that constitutes deviate sexual conduct, as defined by the statute?
"**A.** No.
"**Q.** You also indicate... that one of the purposes of this law is to further the *welfare of society*. And what I'd like to know is what kind of societal welfare is

---

25. Dr. Grigson did testify that it "could be extremely harmful in terms of their sexual identification" for children to observe "homosexuals behaving in a sexual way." However, this could be prohibited — if it is not already — by specific, limited statutes dealing with sexual abuse and children. *See* Tex. Penal Code Ann. §§ 21.09-21.11 (Vernon 1974).

26. Even the most severe criminal penalties — including death in some countries — have not ended homosexuality. The maximum penalty for homosexual conduct under § 21.06 is only a $200.00 fine — and Dr. Grigson did think "there would be more people who would be seeking treatment if the penalties were greater."

27. The Task Report on Homosexuality, p. 5, indicates that "the current literature suggests that perhaps *one-fifth* of those exclusively homosexual individuals who present themselves for treatment are enabled to achieve some heterosexual interests and competence if they are motivated to do so."

furthered by a law that intrudes into the bedroom of consenting sexual adults?

"**A.** I don't know of any. There may be some.

"**Q.** And I take it since you don't know of any, you don't know how it's furthered by the statute?

"**A.** No.

"**Q.** Do you know how this statute furthers the *welfare of society* by prohibiting homosexual sodomy but permitting heterosexual sodomy?

"**A.** No.

"...

"**Q.** And can you explain to me how this statute furthers the state interest, if any, in *procreation* by permitting heterosexual sodomy, but prohibiting homosexual sodomy?

"**A.** I didn't even know it permitted either one.

"**Q.** What it does on its face, for your information, is prohibits private deviate sexual intercourse between persons of the same sex, but by its very language and also by your answers to discovery, you've admitted that it does not prohibit private deviate sexual intercourse by members of a different sex.

"**A.** I don't think procreation is involved in either one of them; is it?

"...

"**Q.** How does this law further *morality* of society by prohibiting private homosexual sodomy but permitting private heterosexual sodomy?

"**A.** I don't really know."

City Attorney Holt also testified (by deposition) that he had no knowledge of any way in which "private consenting homosexual conduct frustrates procreation" or protects the "morals" of society.

But both Wade and Holt felt the legislature "must" have had some public interest in mind or they would not have passed § 21.06. District Attorney Wade testified:

"**Q.** In your candid opinion with thirty years experience as a prosecutor, public prosecutor in Dallas County, do you know of any public interest, *any public interest*, period, furthered by this statute?

"**A.** Well, I think the legislature wouldn't have passed it if there wasn't a public interest in it.

"...

"**Q.** You also indicate in your answers that one legally, or one state interest that is furthered by the statute is one of 'morals.' What state interest, if any, is there in the morality of private sexual conduct that you know of?

"**A.** The only thing I know, the legislature, after hearings, passed a law against it. I assume they had some public interest in it or they wouldn't have passed it."

Similarly, City Attorney Holt testified that the "legitimate interest" would have "to be for others to say because I think it has to be determined from the intent of the legislature and those to whom they looked for advice in passing these laws."

However, no legislative history is available to assist the Court in determining the intent of the legislature in passing §21.06 — i.e., why the penalties against oral and anal sodomy between males and females were repealed, but those against private and consensual homosexual conduct were retained. Contrary to the testimony of defendants Wade and Holt, there is no evidence (indeed, even no indication) that any of the interests advanced to support §21.06 — "morality, decency, health, welfare, safety, and procreation" — were considered by the legislature when this statute was passed as part of the general revision of the Penal Code.

The same interests were advanced by the state to justify the predecessor sodomy statute, Article 524, which condemned *all* sodomy — whether by married couples, single males and females, or homosexuals.[28] If these interests (morality, decency, etc.) no

---

28. And, these same state interests (morality, decency, etc.) were the justification for the first Texas sodomy statute — even though it prohibited only anal sodomy and did not condemn oral sex by homosexuals or heterosexuals.

longer justified the prohibition against heterosexual sodomy in 1974 when §26.01 was enacted, how did they continue to justify the condemnation of private homosexual conduct? And, if they did, were they so weakened that they no longer warranted a punishment of imprisonment (2-15 years), but only a fine of $200 or less?

In fact, the legislature did not even condemn *all* homosexual conduct by §21.06. That statute, as passed in 1974, prohibited only contact between the genitals of one person and the mouth or anus of another of the same sex. It did not prohibit homosexuals from kissing or sexually stimulating their partner with hands and fingers. Nor did § 21.06 condemn the use of an artificial device, such as a vibrator or dildo (until an amendment in 1981 which also prohibited "the penetration of the genitals or the anus of another person with an object"). Because of these — and other puzzling inconsistencies in the Penal Code[29] — it seems likely that political considerations motivated the legislature in passing §21.06.[30]

THE LAW

...

The "right of privacy" protects certain fundamental personal liberties from undue interference by government. *Carey v.*

Population Services, 431 U.S. 678 (1977); *Roe v. Wade*, 410 U.S. 113 (1973); *Eisenstadt v. Baird*, 405 U.S. 438 (1972); *Stanley v. Georgia*, 394 U.S. 557 (1969); *Griswold v. Connecticut*, 381 U.S. 479 (1965). Although Supreme Court opinions have found various constitutional provisions to be the source of this right of privacy — the First Amendment's freedoms of association and of speech; the due process and equal protection clauses of the Fourteenth Amendment; the Fourth and the Ninth Amendments; the "penumbras" of specific guarantees of the Bill of Rights — its existence is now "an established part of our constitutional jurisprudence.

It is clear that the right of privacy protects individual decisions concerning marriage, procreation, contraception, abortion, and family relationships — and that any government regulation upon such fundamental rights "may be justified only by a compelling state interest and must be narrowly drawn to express only the legitimate state interests at stake." However, the "outer limits" of the right of privacy have not been established. *Carey v. Population Services*, 431 U.S. at 684. Development of this area of the law has proceeded on almost a case-by-case basis, and there are still other fundamental personal liberties — besides those involved in past Supreme Court decisions — that are protected by the right of privacy.

Does the right of privacy extend to private sexual behavior between consenting

---

29. Beastiality is prohibited only if it occurs in public; thus, under the Texas Penal Code, one may engage in private sexual acts with "an animal or fowl," § 21.07 (Public Lewdness) — but may not engage in private oral or anal sex with a consenting adult of the same sex, § 21.06 (Homosexual Conduct). And for seven years after 1974, a 17-year-old boy could have been prosecuted as a felon "for fondling a 16-year-old girl at her invitation in private, but not for engaging in sexual intercourse with her" — because it is a defense to statutory rape if the defendant is "not more than two years older than the victim," § 21.10, but there was no such defense to "indecency with a child," § 21.11, until this section was amended in 1981. Tex. Penal Code Ann. § 21.11 (Practice Commentary).

30. [I]t has been suggested that members of the Texas House of Representatives "decided to support § 21.06, as proposed, fearing a backlash against the entire Penal Code [revision] should [private homosexual conduct] be decriminalized." Similarly, in *New York* v. *Onofre*, 415 N.E.2d 936 (1980), *cert. denied*, 451 U.S. 987 (1981), the court emphasized "the statement contained in the memorandum prepared by the chairman of the Temporary Commission: "It would appear that the Legislature's decision to restore the consensual sodomy offense was, as with adultery, based largely upon the premises that *deletion thereof might ostensibly by construed as legislative approval of deviate conduct.*"

adults? In particular: Can a husband and wife be subjected to criminal prosecution for engaging in oral or anal sex in the privacy of their own home? Can a state law constitutionally prohibit unmarried males and females from engaging in oral or anal sodomy or, indeed, any extramarital sexual relations? Can a homosexual be prosecuted for sexual conduct with another adult homosexual, consensually and in private?

The Supreme Court has not answered these questions in any opinion. Indeed, it has refused to do so on several occasions, including these three cases: *Buchanan v. Batchelor*, 308 F.Supp. 729 (N.D. Tex. 1970), rev'd on other grounds sub nom, *Wade v. Buchanan*, 401 U.S. 989 (1971); *Doe v. Commonwealth's Attorney*, 403 F.Supp. 1199 (E.D. Va. 1975), *summary affirmance without opinion*, 425 U.S. 901 (1976); and *New York v. Onofre*, 415 N.E.2d 936 (N.Y. 1980), *cert. denied*, 451 U.S. 987 (1981).

[The court then discussed these three cases.]

■ ■ ■

Private Homosexual Conduct
Is Protected

This Court agrees with the analysis of the right of privacy by the dissenting opinion of Judge Merhige in *Doe v. Commonwealth's Attorney*, 403 F.Supp. 1199, and by the majority opinion in *New York v. Onofre*, 415 N.E.2d 936.

Every individual has the right to be free from undue interference by the state in important and intimate personal matters. Decisions concerning a person's sexual needs or desires are "in a field that by definition concerns the most intimate of human activities and relationships." *Carey*, 431 U.S. at 685. The right of two individuals to choose what type of sexual conduct they will enjoy in private is just as personal, just as important, just as sensitive — indeed, even more so — than the decision by the same couple to engage in sex using a contraceptive to prevent unwanted pregnancy. *Carey*, 431 U.S. at 685, 687. "If the right of privacy means anything, it is the right of the *individual*, married or single, to be free of unwarranted government intrusion into matters fundamentally affecting a person" as the decision to engage in private sexual conduct with another consenting adult. *Eisenstadt*, 405 U.S. at 453.

This is true whether it is a husband and wife choosing to engage in oral or anal sex in the privacy of their bedroom — or whether it is an unmarried male and female privately engaging in extramarital sexual relations of their own choice.[51] And, it is equally true as to a homosexual choosing to engage in sodomy in private with a consenting adult of the same sex.[52] The right of privacy, therefore, does extend to private sexual conduct between consenting adults (whether heterosexual or homosexual) — and any regulation of this fundamental right must be justified by a compelling state interest.

The right of privacy is not, as defendants contend, "limited to only two aspects of sexual behavior" — marital intimacy (by virtue of *Griswold v. Connecticut*) and procreative choice (by reason of *Eisenstadt v. Baird*). Indeed, *Eisenstadt* makes it clear that the right of privacy in sexual matters is not limited to married couples:

> If under *Griswold* the distribution of contraceptives to married persons can-

---

51. Although these issues are not directly presented in this case, it seems obvious that the right of privacy would not extend to private homosexual conduct if it did not extend to private heterosexual conduct.

52. From the testimony of the plaintiff, Donald F. Baker, about his life — the reluctant, painful recognition of his homosexuality; his disgust and self-loathing and fear; his isolation and suffering; and the eventual reconciliation of his "exclusive homosexuality" with his devout religious beliefs and family values — it is evident that Baker's resulting decisions concerning his sexual needs and desires are of the most personal, intimate and important concern (just as they are for heterosexuals).

not be prohibited, a ban on distribution to unmarried persons would be equally impermissible. It is true that in *Griswold* the right of privacy in question inhered in the marital relationship. Yet the marriage couple is not an independent entity with a mind and heart of its own, but an association of two individuals each with a separate intellectual and emotional makeup. If the right of privacy means anything, it is the right of the *individual*, married or single, to be free from unwarranted governmental intrusion into matters so fundamentally affecting a person as the decision whether to bear or beget a child. *See Stanley v. Georgia*, 394 U.S. 557 (1969) . . ." (405 U.S. at 453).

Moreover, in *Stanley v. Georgia*, 394 U.S. 557 (1969), the right of privacy involved neither "marital intimacy" or "procreative choice." There, the defendant possessed films and printed material which were pornographic. As discussed in *New York v. Onofre*:

> . . . In *Stanley* the court found violative of the individual's right to be free from governmental interference in making important, protected decisions a statute which made criminal the possession of obscene matter within the privacy of the defendant's home. Although the material itself was entitled to no protection against government proscription (*Roth v. United States*, 354 U.S. 476), the defendant's choice to seek sexual gratification by viewing it and the effectuation of that choice within the bastion of his home, removed from the public eye, was held to be blanketed by the constitutional right of privacy." (415 N.E.2d at 939).

See *Doe v. Commonwealth's Attorney*, 403 F.Supp. at 1204-05 (Merhige, J., dissenting).

Under the *Stanley* and *Eisenstadt* extensions of the right of privacy, the plaintiff could possess and enjoy *in private* pornographic material — movies, videotapes, magazines, books, etc. — which graphically depicts sexual activities by homosexuals. It seems ludicrous to attempt to draw some constitutional distinction, as defendants do, between his right to "seek sexual gratification by viewing" such obscene material, and his right to seek sexual gratification with a consenting adult partner in private.

The right of privacy does extend to private, voluntary, intimate relationships — between husband and wife, between unmarried males and females, between homosexuals. Accordingly, homosexual conduct in private between consenting adults is protected by a fundamental right of privacy. Any state restriction upon that right must be justified by some compelling state interest.

No State Interest

The right of privacy is not absolute. But any regulation of this fundamental right "may be justified only by a compelling state interest and must be narrowly drawn to express only the legitimate state interests at stake."

Obviously, the state has a compelling interest in regulating some types of sexual conduct — rape, indecent acts in public, sex offenses involving minors, etc. *New York v. Onofre*, 415 N.E. 2d at 941; *Doe v. Commonwealth's Attorney*, 403 F.Supp. at 1204 (Merhige, J., dissenting). But does the state have any interest in regulating private sexual conduct between consenting adults — or in criminally prosecuting homosexuals for private, consensual sodomy?

Basically, the defendants claim that the state's interests justifying the ban on homosexual conduct by § 21.06 are (**i**) morality and decency, (**ii**) public health, (**iii**) welfare and safety, and (**iv**) procreation. However, the evidence presented at trial *did not* support any of these claims. Instead, it established that the state has no "compelling interest" to justify § 21.06 — and that, indeed, this statute is not even "rationally related" to any "legitimate state interest."

The defendants did not produce a single witness, or any other evidence, to support the alleged state interests of "morality and decency, welfare and safety, and procreation." They did present one witness who testified about the state's supposed interest in "public health" furthered by § 21.06. This was Dr. James Grigson — who was not an expert in the field of homosexuality — but who testified that criminal sanctions against homosexual conduct would promote the health of (i) children, by fostering their growth and development, and (ii) homosexuals, by forcing them to seek psychiatric treatment and be "cured." These opinions are not based upon any independent research; they are contrary to the medical and psychiatric literature, to the opinions of most American psychiatrists today, and to the very credible evidence given by plaintiff's experts. For these, and the other reasons discussed above, this Court completely discounts Dr. Grigson's testimony and opinions.

In addition to the lack of any expert testimony supporting the claimed state interests, both District Attorney Wade and City Attorney Holt were unable to explain how § 21.06 futhered the supposed interests of morality or decency, the welfare of society, procreation, or any other interest. Nor was there any evidence that the Texas legislature had even considered these alleged interests when it passed § 21.06 as part of the general revision of the Penal Code in 1974. Therefore, *under the record in this case, the defendants have nothing to rely upon but the assertion of general platitudes* (morality, decency, etc.). This is totally inadequate to justify § 21.06, as shown by *Commonwealth's Attorney*:

> "The defendants, represented by the highest legal officer of the state, made no tender of any evidence which even impliedly demonstrated that homosexuality causes society any significant harm. No effort was made by the defendants to establish either a rational basis or a compelling state interest so as to justify the proscription of § 8.1-212 of the Code of Virginia, presently under attack.
>
> " . . .
>
> "On the basis of this record one can only conclude that the sole basis of the proscription of homosexuality was what the majority refers to as the promotion of morality and decency. As salutary a legislative goal as this may be, I can find no authority for intrusion by the state into the private dwelling of a citizen. *Stanley v. Georgia*, 394 U.S. 557. . . . The Supreme Court has made it clear that fundamental rights of such an intimate facet of an individual's life as sex, absent circumstances warranting intrusion by the state, are to be respected. My brothers, I respectfully suggest, have by today's ruling misinterpreted the issue — the issue centers not around morality or decency, but the constitutional right of privacy." (403 F.Supp. at 1205) (Merhige, J., dissenting).

Moreover, the plaintiff's evidence establishes that there is no compelling state interest served by § 21.06 — and that, indeed, this statute's condemnation of homosexual conduct is not even rationally related to a legitimate state interest. In particular, this evidence (including the testimony of the experts, Dr. Marmor and Dr. Simon) established the following:

> Homosexuals are not ill or mentally diseased. They are not criminals. They have no propensity for crimes, those involving sexual offenses or otherwise, any more than heterosexuals. But over 700,000 individuals are "criminals" in Texas today because of § 21.06.
>
> Homosexuality is not a matter of choice. It is fixed at a very early age. Only a small percentage of homosexuals can be changed or "cured" by psychiatric treatment. The numbers of homosexuals in society are not reduced

by criminal laws like § 21.06, nor would they be increased if such laws did not exist.

Homosexuality is not communicable. The absence of § 21.06 would not lead to increased crime or violence or other threats to public health or safety. This statute does not further the "growth and development" of children and it harms, rather than helps, the mental health of homosexuals. There is simply no rational connection between the acts proscribed by § 21.06 and the claimed interests of morality, decency, health, welfare, safety, and procreation.

Therefore, § 21.06 is not justified by any "compelling state interest." Moreover, its prohibition against private homosexual conduct between consenting adults is not even rationally related to any legitimate state interest. Accordingly, § 21.06 is unconstitutional because it violates the plaintiff's fundamental right of privacy.

Equal Protection

Section 21.06 does not prohibit sodomy between consenting adults of the opposite sex; only oral or anal sex between consenting adults of the same sex is illegal. Thus, *on its face*, § 21.06 discriminates against homosexuals by making acts criminal when committed by them, but not by heterosexuals. This violates the plaintiff's right to equal protection of the law unless the discrimination between heterosexuals and homosexuals bears "some rational relationship to legitimate state purposes." *San Antonio School District v. Rodriquez*, 411 U.S. 1, 40 (1973).

As discussed in the preceding section, the evidence in this case established that none of the interests claimed by defendants (morality and decency, public health, welfare and safety, and procreation) were furthered by § 21.06 — and that this statute is not "rationally related" to any "legitimate state interest." Indeed, the defendant Wade

conceded this; he testified that he knew of no rational basis for the discrimination in § 21.06 between homosexual sodomy and heterosexual sodomy:

> "**Q.** Doesn't the statute, § 21.06, doesn't it permit private sodomy by heterosexuals but not homosexuals?
> "**A.** I wouldn't even know that, but I'm taking your word for it.
> "**Q.** Assume it does.
> "**A.** Yeah.
> "**Q.** What rational basis is there for that classification, if you know of any?
> "**A.** I don't know of any."

Therefore, § 21.06 is invalid because it violates the plaintiff's right to equal protection. *New York v. Onofre*, 415 N.E.2d 936, held that a statute which prohibited sodomy between unmarried persons (whether heterosexual or homosexual), but not between married couples, was unconstitutional:

> "*As to The Denial of defendants' right to equal protection.* Section 130.38 of the Penal Law on its face discriminates between married and unmarried persons, making criminal when done by the latter what is innocent when done by the former. With that distinction drawn, we look to see whether there is, as a minimum, 'some ground of difference that rationally explains the different treatment accorded married and unmarried persons' under the statute. . . . In our view, none has been demonstrated or identified by the People. . . . The statute therefore must fall as violative of the right to equal protection enjoyed by persons not married to each other." (415 N.E.2d at 942).

■ ■ ■

Public Distaste

The defendants claim that "it is undisputed that homosexual sodomy, far from being a proud and cherished tradition, is a practice which has been abhorred in Western civilization and has long inspired an almost universal phobic response." Similar statements are found in some of the cases involving Texas sodomy statutes.

These are overstatements. In several countries today, homosexuality is not criminal; and it has been decriminalized, without adverse effects, in some twenty-one states in this country.[59] But even if there is widespread public distaste, this would not be any "legitimate state interest" to rationalize a denial of equal protection — nor would it be a "compelling state interest" to justify a denial of the right of privacy. *See United States v. Moreno*, 413 U.S. 528, 534-35 (1973). As discussed in *New York v. Onofre*:

> "... it has been deemed irrelevant by the United States Supreme Court that the purchase and use of contraceptives by unmarried persons would arouse moral indignation among broad segments of our community or that the viewing of pornographic materials even within the privacy of one's home would not evoke general approbation (*Eisenstadt v. Baird, Stanley v. Georgia*). We are not unmindful of the sensibilities of many persons who are deeply persuaded that consensual sodomy is evil and should be prohibited. That is not the issue before us. . . . The community and its members are entirely free to employ theological teaching, moral suasion, parental advice, psychological and psychiatric counseling and other noncoercive means to condemn the practice of consensual sodomy. The narrow question before us is whether the Federal Constitution permits the use of the criminal law for that purpose." (415 N.E.2d at 940 n. 3).

Indeed, the Supreme Court has emphasized that cases involving controversial sexual issues must be resolved "by constitutional measurement, free of emotion and free of predilection" because the Constitution is made for people of fundamental differing views, and "the accident" of our finding certain opinions "novel and even shocking ought not to conclude our judgment upon the question" of constitutionality. *Roe v. Wade*, 410 U.S. at 116-17, quoting the "now-vindicated dissent" of Justice Holmes in *Lochner v. New York*, 198 U.S. 45, 76 (1905).

■ ■ ■

Establishment of Religion

The plaintiff's claim that § 21.06 violated the establishment clause of the first amendment was a second-line attack upon this statute. The evidence did not establish any such constitutional violation.

To the contrary, the testimony of the plaintiff's expert in religion (Dr. Furnish) was that private consensual homosexual conduct was not condemned by the bible, although he conceded other scholars disagreed with his opinions (*see* note 15). The plaintiff claims that, despite this disagreement among biblical scholars, "it is clear that Biblical law has been advanced as a reason for the enactment of this and similar laws." However, as discussed above, it is impossible to ascribe *any* intent to the legislature in its enactment of § 21.06.

Therefore, § 21.06 does not violate the establishment clause because there was no proof that "the principal or primary effect of this statute was to advance or inhibit religion." *Harris v. McRae*, 448 U.S. 297, 318-20 (1980).

---

59. Dr. Judd Marmor, the plaintiff's expert, also testified that "Ford and Beach did a study of seventy-six societies and found in almost two-thirds of them, homophobia [an exaggerated fear of homosexuals among heterosexuals] did not exist, and some form of homosexuality was permitted. One-third of the societies they studied did have the similar kind of restrictive attitudes toward overt homosexual behavior that ours does."

■ ■ ■

CONCLUSION

Homosexuality is an emotional and controversial issue in our society. It causes fear and disgust among many people. This may well result in condemnation of this decision — but, if so, the critics should at least have a clear understanding that this decision has little effect upon the general public.

At issue is a statute which is not enforced by criminal prosecutions; and, even if it were, the only punishment is a fine of $200 of less. But this statute, § 21.06, makes criminals out of more than 700,000 individuals in Texas who are homosexuals, although they did not choose to be, and who engage in private sexual conduct with other consenting adults. This is prohibited by the constitutional right of privacy (as well as equal protection of the law) — because, if it were not, the state would have the same power to intrude into the private lives and bedrooms of heterosexuals, and regulate the intimate sexual relationships of married couples and single males and females.

Of course, this decision does not mean that the Constitution shields *all* types of homosexual conduct or that it "unqualifiedly sanctions personal whim." *Doe v. Commonwealth's Attorney*, 403 F.Supp. at 1204-05 (Merhige, J., dissenting). There is no constitutional protection if force is used, or if a minor is involved, or if the sexual conduct takes place in public, and this is true whether heterosexuals or homosexuals are involved.

Homosexuals, like heterosexuals, are still subject to prosecution — just as they have been for years, *under Texas Penal Code provisions not involved in this case* — for (i) rape and sexual abuse by force, §§ 21.02 and 21.04, (ii) sexual offenses involving children, §§ 21.09-21.11, and (iii) sexual conduct or indecent exposure in a public place, §§ 21.07 and 21.08.

Nor does this decision mean that all consensual activities in private are constitutionally protected, or that an individual has an absolute right to do whatever he pleases in his own home. Obviously, the right of privacy does not apply to private conduct harmful to the individual participants or to society, such as the use of harmful drugs. See *New York v. Onofre*, 415 N.E.2d at 941-42.

But, for the reasons discussed above, the right of privacy does extend to private sexual conduct between consenting adults — whether husband and wife, unmarried males and females, or homosexuals — and the right of equal protection condemns a state statute which (like § 21.06) prohibits homosexual sodomy, but not heterosexual sodomy, without any rational basis.

D*oe* and *Baker* were cases brought to challenge directly the constitutionality of the sodomy laws. Sodomy law challenges also arise in criminal cases, as a defense to criminal charges, and sometimes in employment cases — where employment decisions against lesbians and gay men are predicated on the existence of the sodomy laws. In *Dronenburg v. Zech*, which follows, the plaintiff raised a challenge to the military's sodomy law in contesting his discharge from the Navy. The case provided a forum for Judge Robert Bork to criticize the Supreme Court's development of the Constitutional right to privacy, and the decision was later a factor in the U.S. Senate's rejection of Judge Bork's nomination to the U.S. Supreme Court. The decision also laid a jurisprudential framework for the Supreme Court's decision in the *Bowers v. Hardwick* case two years later.

DRONENBURG v. ZECH

741 F.2d 1388 (D.C. Cir. 1984)

BORK, CIRCUIT JUDGE.

■ ■ ■

I.

On April 21, 1981, the United States Navy discharged James L. Dronenburg for homosexual conduct. For the previous nine years he had served in the Navy as a Korean linguist and cryptographer with a top-security clearance. During that time he maintained an unblemished service record and earned many citations praising his job performance. At the time of his discharge Dronenburg, then a 27-year-old petty officer, was enrolled as a student in the Defense Language Institute in Monterey, California.

The Navy's investigation of Dronenburg begin eight months prior to the discharge, in August 1980, when a 19-year-old seaman recruit and student of the Language Institute made sworn statements implicating Dronenburg in repeated homosexual acts. The appellant, after initially denying these allegations, subsequently admitted that he was a homosexual and that he had repeatedly engaged in homosexual conduct in a barracks on the Navy base. On September 18, 1980, the Navy gave Dronenburg formal notice that it was considering administratively discharging him for misconduct due to homosexual acts, a violation of SEC/NAV Instruction 1900.9C (Jan. 20, 1978); Joint Appendix ("J.A.") at 216, which provided in pertinent part, that

> [a]ny member [of the Navy] who solicits, attempts or engages in homosexual acts shall normally be separated from the naval service. The presence of such a member in a military environment seriously impairs combat readiness, efficiency, security and morale.[1]

On January 20 and 22, 1981, at a hearing before a Navy Administrative Discharge Board (Board) Dronenburg testified at length in his own behalf, with counsel representing him. He again acknowledged engaging in homosexual acts in a navy barracks.

The Board voted unanimously to recommend Dronenburg's discharge for misconduct due to homosexual acts. Two members of the Board voted that the discharge be characterized as a general one, while the third member voted that the discharge be an honorable one. The Secretary of the navy,

---

1. Discharge for homosexual conduct was not invariably mandatory. Instruction 1900.9C ¶ 6b (Jan. 20, 1978) provides that:

> A member who has solicited, attempted, or engaged in a homosexual act on a single occasion and who does not profess or demonstrate proclivity to repeat such an act may be considered for retention in the light of all relevant circumstances. Retention is to be permitted only if the aforesaid conduct is not likely to present any adverse impact either upon the member's continued performance of military duties or upon the readiness, efficiency, or morale of the unit to which the member is assigned either at the time of the conduct or at the time of processing according to the alternatives set forth herein.

J.A. at 218. Moreover, the Secretary of the Navy retained the power to keep a person in service despite homosexual conduct on an ad hoc basis for reasons of military necessity.

These regulations have since been replaced by SEC/NAV Instruction 1900.9D (Mar. 12, 1981) which implements a Department of Defense Directive. J.A. at 219. The policy of 1900.9C, under which appellant was discharged, is continued in effect by 1900.9D.

reviewing this case at appellant's request, reaffirmed the discharge but ordered that it be characterized as honorable. On April 20, 1981, the appellant filed suit in district court challenging the Navy's policy mandating discharge of all homosexuals. This district court granted summary judgment for the Navy.

■ ■ ■

III.

Appellant advances two constitutional arguments, a right of privacy and a right to equal protection of the laws. Resolution of the second argument is to some extent dependent upon that of the first. Whether the appellant's asserted constitutional right to privacy is based upon fundamental human rights, substantive due process, the Ninth Amendment or emanations from the Bill of Rights, if no such right exists, then appellant's right to equal protection is not infringed unless the Navy's policy is not rationally related to a permissible end. *Kelley v. Johnson*, 425 U.S. 238, 247-49 (1976). We think neither right has been violated by the Navy.

A.

According to appellant, *Griswold v. Connecticut*, 381 U.S. 479 (1965), and the cases that came after it, such as *Loving v. Virginia*, 388 U.S. 1 (1967); *Eisenstadt v. Baird*, 405 U.S. 438 (1972); *Roe v. Wade*, 410 U.S. 113 (1973); and *Carey v. Population Services International*, 431 U.S. 678 (1977), have "developed a right of privacy of constitutional dimension." Appellant finds in these cases "a thread of principle: that the government should not interfere with an individual's freedom to control intimate personal decisions regarding his or her own body" except by the least restrictive means available and in the presence of a compelling

state interest. Given this principle, he urges, private consensual homosexual activity must be held to fall within the zone of constitutionally protected privacy.

Whatever thread of principle may be discerned in the right-of-privacy cases, we do not think it is the one discerned by appellant. Certainly the Supreme Court has never defined the right so broadly as to encompass homosexual conduct. Various opinions have expressly disclaimed any such sweep, *see, e.g., Poe v. Ullman*, 367 U.S. 497, 553 (1961) (Harlan, J., dissenting from a decision that the controversy was not yet justiciable and expressing views on the merits later substantially adopted in *Griswold*). More to the point, the Court in *Doe v. Commonwealth's Attorney for Richmond*, 425 U.S. 901 (1976), summarily affirmed a district court judgment, 403 F. Supp. 1199 (E.D. Va. 1975), upholding a Virginia statute making it a criminal offense to engage in private consensual homosexual conduct. The district court in *Doe* had found that the right to privacy did not extend to private homosexual conduct because the latter bears no relation to marriage, procreation, or family life. The Supreme Court's summary disposition of a case constitutes a vote on the merits; as such, it is binding on lower federal courts. *See Hicks v. Miranda*, 422 U.S. 332, 343-45 (1975). If a statute proscribing homosexual conduct in a civilian context is sustainable, then such a regulation is certainly sustainable in a military context. That the military has needs for discipline and good order justifying restrictions that go beyond the needs of civilian society has repeatedly been made clear by the Supreme Court. *See, e.g., Greer v. Spock*, 424 U.S. 828 (1976); *Parker v. Levy*, 417 U.S. 733 (1974).

It is urged upon us, however, that *Doe v. Commonwealth's Attorney* cannot be taken as an authoritative decision by the Supreme Court. The case should be viewed, it is said, as an affirmance based not on the constitutionality of the statute but rather upon plaintiffs' lack of standing. Plaintiffs were homosexuals who had not been threatened with prosecution under the statute. Indeed, those plaintiffs may have lacked standing, but the majority of the three-judge district court placed its decision squarely on the constitutionality of the statute, and the Supreme Court's summary affirmance gives no indication that the Court proceeded upon any other rationale. It would have been easy enough to affirm summarily giving a lack of standing as the reason. Under these circumstances, we doubt that a court of appeals ought to distinguish a Supreme Court precedent on the speculation that the Court might possibly have had something else in mind.

But even should we agree the *Doe v. Commonwealth's Attorney* is somewhat ambiguous precedent, we would not extend the right of privacy created by the Supreme Court to cover appellant's conduct here. An examination of the cases cited by appellant shows that they contain little guidance for lower courts. The right of privacy first achieved constitutional stature in *Griswold v. Connecticut*, 381 U.S. 479 (1965). The *Griswold* Court began by noting that "specific guarantees in the Bill of Rights have penumbras, formed by emanations from those guarantees that help give them life and substance," 381 U.S. at 484. The cases cited in support of that unexceptional proposition demonstrated, for example, that a state could not force disclosure of the NAACP's membership lists because of the chilling effect upon the members' First Amendment rights of assembly and political advocacy. The "penumbra" was no more than a perception that it is sometimes necessary to protect actions or associations not guaranteed by the Constitution in order to protect an activity that is. The penumbral right has no life of its own as a right independent of its relationship to a First Amendment freedom. Where that relationship does not exist, the penumbral right evaporates. The Court referred to the First Amendment's penumbra as a protection of "privacy," noted that other amendments created "zones of privacy," and concluded that there was a general right of privacy that lay outside the "zones" or "pe-

numbras" of particular amendments, *Id*. It was not explained how areas not lying within any "penumbra" or "zone of privacy" became part of a more general "right of privacy," but clearly that is what the Court intended. The right of a husband and wife to use contraceptives, which the challenged Connecticut statute prohibited, was held to be guaranteed by this general right, though not by any individual amendment, penumbra, or zone. The *Griswold* opinion stressed the sanctity of marriage. It did not indicate what other activities might be protected by the new right of privacy and did not provide any guidance for reasoning about future claims laid under the right.

Loving v. Virginia, 388 U.S. 1 (1967), struck down a state anti-miscegenation statute because it constituted an invidious racial classification violative of the equal protection clause of the Fourteenth Amendment and because it deprived appellants of liberty without due process of law in violation of the same amendment. The equal protection ruling followed from prior cases and the historical purpose of the clause. It is not entirely clear whether the due process analysis broke new ground. The Court spoke of a right of marriage but emphasized heavily the racial discrimination worked by this statute, a point central to the equal protection holding. In its brief analysis of the due process holding, the Court said only:

> The freedom to marry has long been recognized as one of the vital personal rights essential to the orderly pursuit of happiness by free men.
>
> Marriage is one of the "basic civil rights of man," fundamental to our very existence and survival. *Skinner v. Oklahoma*, 316 U.S. 535, 541 (1942). *See also Maynard v. Hill*, 125 U.S. 190 (1888). To deny this fundamental freedom on so unsupportable a basis as the racial classifications embodied in these statutes, classifications so directly subversive to the principle of equality at the heart of the Fourteenth Amend-

ment, is surely to deprive all the State's citizens of liberty without due process of law. The Fourteenth Amendment requires that the freedom of choice to marry not be restricted by invidious racial discrimination. Under our Constitution, the freedom to marry, or not marry, a person of another race resides with the individual and cannot be infringed by the State.

388 U.S. at 11-12. There is in this passage no mode of analysis that suggests an answer to the present case, certainly none that favors appellant.

Eisenstadt v. Baird, 405 U.S. 438 (1972), invalidated under the equal protection clause of the Fourteenth Amendment a Massachusetts law prohibiting the distribution of contraceptives. The law in question provided that married persons could obtain contraceptives to prevent pregnancy on prescription only, single persons could not obtain contraceptives at all in order to prevent pregnancy, and married and single persons could obtain contraceptives from anyone to prevent the spread of disease, *Id.*, at 442. The Court reasoned that there was no difference that rationally explains the different treatment accorded married and unmarried persons" under the statute. *Id.*, at 447. The Court demonstrated that the purpose of the statute could not rationally be to deter fornication or to safeguard health. The opinion then came to the aspect presumably of most interest here: could the statute be sustained simply as a prohibition on contraception? The Court explicitly declined to decide whether such a law would conflict with "fundamental human rights" and offered instead this line of reasoning:

If under *Griswold* the distribution of contraceptives to married persons cannot be prohibited, a ban on distribution to unmarried persons would be equally impermissible. It is true that in *Griswold* the right of privacy in question inhered in the marital relationship. Yet the marital couple is not an independent entity with a mind and heart of its own, but an association of two individuals each with a separate intellectual and emotional makeup. If the right of privacy means anything, it is the right of the *individual*, married or single, to be free from unwarranted governmental intrusion into matters so fundamentally affecting a person as the decision whether to bear or beget a child.

Id., at 453 (emphasis in original). In order to apply *Eisenstadt* to a future case not involving the same personal decision, a court would have to know whether the challenged governmental regulation was "unwarranted" and whether the regulation was of a matter "so fundamentally affecting a person as the decision whether to bear or beget a child." *Eisenstadt* itself does not provide any criteria by which either of those decisions can be made.

Roe v. Wade, 410 U.S. 113 (1973), severely limited the states' power to regulate abortions in the name of the right of privacy. The pivotal legal discussion was as follows:

The Constitution does not explicitly mention any right of privacy. In a line of decisions, however, going back perhaps as far as *Union Pacific R. Co. v. Botsford*, 141 U.S. 250, 251 (1891), the Court has recognized that a right of personal privacy, or a guarantee of certain areas or zones of privacy, does exist under the Constitution. In varying contexts, the Court or individual Justices have, indeed, found at least the roots of that right in the First Amendment, *Stanley v. Georgia*, 394 U.S. 557, 564 (1969); in the Fourth and Fifth Amendments, *Terry v. Ohio*, 392 U.S. 1, 8-9 (1968), *Katz v. United States*, 389 U.S. 347, 350 (1967), *Boyd v. United States*, 116 U.S. 616 (1886), *see Olmstead v. United States*, 277 U.S. 438, 478 (1928) (Brandeis, J., dissenting); in the penumbras of the Bill of

Rights, *Griswold v. Connecticut*, 381 U.S. at 484-485; in the Ninth Amendment, *id.*, at 486 (Goldberg J., concurring); or in the concept of liberty guaranteed by the first section of the Fourteenth Amendment, *see Meyer v. Nebraska*, 262 U.S. 390, 399 (1923). These decisions make it clear that only personal rights that can be deemed "fundamental" or "implicit in the concept of ordered liberty," *Palko v. Connecticut*, 302 U.S. 319, 325 (1937), are included in this guarantee of personal privacy. They also make it clear that the right has some extension to activities relating to marriage, *Loving v. Virginia*, 388 U.S. 1, 12 (1967); procreation, *Skinner v. Oklahoma*, 316 U.S. 535, 541-542 (1942); contraception, *Eisenstadt v. Baird*, 405 U.S. at 453-454; *id.*, at 460, 463-465 (White, J., concurring in result); family relationships, *Prince v. Massachusetts*, 321 U.S. 158, 166 (1944); and childrearing and education, *Pierce v. Society* of Sisters, 268 U.S. 510 (1925), *Meyer v. Nebraska, supra.*

This right of privacy, whether it be founded in the Fourteenth Amendment's concept of personal liberty and restrictions upon state action, as we feel it is, or, as the District Court determined, in the Ninth Amendment's reservation of rights to the people, is broad enough to encompass a woman's decision whether or not to terminate her pregnancy. The detriment that the State would impose upon the pregnant woman by denying this choice altogether is apparent. Specific and direct harm medically diagnosable even in early pregnancy may be involved. Maternity, or additional offspring, may force upon the woman a distressful life and future. Psychological harm may be imminent. Mental and physical health may be taxed by child care. There is also the distress, for all concerned, associated with the

unwanted child, and there is the problem of bringing a child into a family already unable, psychologically and otherwise, to care for it. In other cases, as in this one, the additional difficulties and continuing stigma of unwed motherhood may be involved. All these are factors the woman and her responsible physician necessarily will consider in consultation.

410 U.S. at 152-53. The Court nevertheless refused to accept the argument that the right to abort is absolute.

The Court's decisions recognizing a right of privacy also acknowledge that some state regulation in areas protected by that right is appropriate. As noted above, a State may properly assert important interests in safeguarding health, in maintaining medical standards, and in protecting potential life. At some point in pregnancy, these respective interests become sufficiently compelling to sustain regulation of the factors that govern the abortion decision. *The privacy right involved, therefore, cannot be said to be absolute. In fact, it is not clear to us that the claim asserted by some amici that one has an unlimited right to do with one's body as one pleases bears a close relationship to the right of privacy previously articulated in the Court's decisions.* The Court has refused to recognize an unlimited right of this kind in the past. *Jacobson v. Massachusetts*, 197 U.S. 11 (1905) (vaccination); *Buck v. Bell*, 274 U.S. 200 (1927) (sterilization).

Id., at 153-54 (emphasis added). Thus, though the Court gave an illustrative list of privacy rights, it also denied that the right was as broad as the right to do as one pleases with one's body. Aside from listing prior holdings, the Court provided no explanatory principle that informs a lower court how to reason about what is and what is not encompassed by the right of privacy.

Carey v. Population Services International, 431 U.S. 678 (1977), held unconstitutional yet another regulation of access to contraceptives on grounds of privacy. The New York statute required that distribution of contraceptives to persons over sixteen be only by a licensed pharmacist. That provision was held unconstitutional because no compelling state interest was perceived that the could overcome "the teaching of Griswold ... that the Constitution protects individual decisions in matters of childbearing from unjustified intrusion by the State." *Id.* at 687. A compelling state interest was required "not because there is an independent fundamental 'right of access to contraceptives,' but because such access is essential to exercise of the constitutionally protected right of decision in matters of childbearing that is the underlying foundation of the holdings in *Griswold, Eisenstadt v. Baird*, and *Roe v. Wade*." *Id.* at 688-89. Limiting distribution to licensed pharmacists significantly burdened that right. *Id.* at 689.

These cases, and the suggestion that we apply them to protect homosexual conduct in the Navy, pose a peculiar jurisprudential problem. When the Supreme Court decides cases under a specific provision or amendment to the Constitution it explicates the meaning and suggests the contours of a value already stated in the document or implied by the Constitution's structure and history. The lower court judge finds in the Supreme Court's reasoning about those legal materials, as well as in the materials themselves, guidance for applying the provision or amendment to a new situation. But when the Court creates new rights, as some Justices who have engaged in the process state that they have done, *see, e.g., Doe v. Bolton*, 410 U.S. 179, 221-22 (1973) (White, J., dissenting); *Roe v. Wade*, 410 U.S. 113, 167-68 (1973) (Stewart, J., concurring), lower courts have none of these materials available and can look only to what the Supreme Court has stated to be the principle involved.

In this group of cases, and in those cited in the quoted language from the Court's opinions, we do not find any principle articulated even approaching in breadth that which appellant seeks to have us adopt. The Court has listed as illustrative of the right or privacy such matters as activities relating to marriage, procreation, contraception, family relationships, and child rearing and education. It need hardly be said that none of these covers a right to homosexual conduct.

The question then becomes whether there is a more general principle that explains these cases and is capable of extrapolation to new claims not previously decided by the Supreme Court. It is true that the principle appellant advances would explain all of these cases, but then so would many other, less sweeping principles. The most the Court has said on that topic is that only rights that are "fundamental" or "implicit in the concept of ordered liberty" are included in the right of privacy. These formulations are not particularly helpful to us, however, because they are less prescriptions of a mode of reasoning than they are conclusions about particular rights enunciated. We would find it impossible to conclude that a right to homosexual conduct is "fundamental" or "implicit in the concept of ordered liberty" unless any and all private sexual behavior falls within those categories, a conclusion we are unwilling to draw.

In dealing with a topic like this, in which we are asked to protect from regulation a form of behavior never before protected, and indeed traditionally condemned, we do well to bear in mind the concerns expressed by Justice White, dissenting in *Moore v. City of East Cleveland*, 431 U.S. 494, 544 (1977):

> That the Court has ample precedent for the creation of new constitutional rights should not lead it to repeat the process at will. The Judiciary, including this Court, is the most vulnerable and comes nearest to illegitimacy when it deals with judge-made constitutional law having little or no cognizable roots

in the language or even the design of the Constitution. Realizing that the present construction of the due process clause represents a major judicial gloss on its terms, as well as on the anticipation of the Framers, and that much of the underpinning for the broad, substantive application of the clause disappeared in the conflict between the executive and the judiciary in the 1930s and 1940s, the Court should be extremely reluctant to breathe still further substantive content into the due process clause so as to strike down legislation adopted by a state or city to promote its welfare. Whenever the judiciary does so, it unavoidably preempts for itself another part of the governance of the country without express constitutional authority.

Whatever its application to the Supreme Court, we think this admonition should be taken very seriously by inferior federal courts. No doubt there is "ample precedent for the creation of new constitutional rights," but, as Justice White said, the creation of such rights "comes nearest to illegitimacy" when judges make "law having little or no cognizable roots in the language or even the design of the Constitution." If it is in any degree doubtful that the Supreme Court should freely create new constitutional rights,[5] we think it certain that lower courts should not do so. We have no guidance from the Constitution or, as we have shown with respect to the case at hand, from articulated

Supreme Court principle. If courts of appeals should, in such circumstances, begin to create new rights freely, the volume of decisions would mean that many would evade Supreme Court review, a great body of judge-made law would grow up, and we would have "pre-empt[ed] for [ourselves] another part of the governance of the country without express constitutional authority." If the revolution in sexual mores that appellant proclaims is in fact ever to arrive, we think it must arrive through the moral choices of the people and their elected representatives, not through the judicial ukase of this court.

Turning from the decided cases, which we do not think provide even an ambiguous warrant for the constitutional right he seeks, appellant offers arguments based upon a constitutional theory. Though that theory is obviously untenable, it is so often heard that it is worth stating briefly why we reject it.

Appellant denies that morality can ever be the basis for legislation or, more specifically, for a naval regulation, and asserts two reasons why that is so. The first argument is: "if the military can defend its blanket exclusion of homosexuals on the ground that they are offensive to the majority or to the military's view of what is socially acceptable, then no rights are safe from encroachment and no minority is protected against discrimination." Passing the inaccurate characterization of the Navy's position here, it deserves to be said that this argument is completely frivolous. The Constitution has provisions that create specific rights. These protect, among others, racial, ethnic, and

---

5. It may be only candid to say at this point that the author of this opinion, when in academic life, expressed the view that no court should create new constitutional rights; that is, rights must be fairly derived by standard modes of legal interpretation from the text, structure, and history of the Constitution. Or, as it has been aptly put, "the work of the political branches is to be invalidated only in accord with an inference whose starting point, whose underlying premise, is fairly discoverable in the Constitution. That the complete inference will not be found there — because the situation is not likely to have been foreseen — is generally common ground." J. Ely, *Democracy and Distrust* 2 (1980). These views are, however, completely irrelevant to the function of a circuit judge. The Supreme Court has decided that it may create new constitutional rights and, as judges of constitutionally inferior courts, we are bound absolutely by that determination. The only questions open for us are whether the Supreme Court has created a right which, fairly defined, covers the case before us or whether the Supreme Court has specified a mode of analysis, a methodology, which, honestly applied, reaches the case we must now decide.

religious minorities. If a court refuses to create a new constitutional right to protect homosexual conduct, the court does not thereby destroy established constitutional rights that are solidly based in constitutional text and history.

Appellant goes further, however, and contends that the existence of moral disapproval for certain types of behavior is the very fact that disables government from regulating it. He says that as a matter of general constitutional principle, "it is difficult to understand how an adult's selection of a partner to share sexual intimacy is not immune from burden by the state as an element of constitutionally protected privacy. That the particular choice of partner may be repugnant to the majority argues for its vigilant protection — not its vulnerability to sanction." This theory that majority morality and majority choice is always made presumptively invalid by the Constitution attacks the very predicate of democratic government. When the Constitution does not speak to the contrary, the choices of those put in authority by the electoral process, or those who are accountable to such persons, come before us not as suspect because majoritarian but as conclusively valid for that very reason. We stress, because the possibility of being misunderstood is so great, that this deference to democratic choice does not apply where the Constitution removes the choice from majorities. Appellant's theory would, in fact, destroy the basis for much of the most valued legislation our society has. It would, for example, render legislation about civil rights, worker safety, the preservation of the environment, and much more, unconstitutional. In each of these areas, legislative majorities have made moral choices contrary to the desires of minorities. It is to be doubted that very many laws exist whose ultimate justifi-

cation does not rest upon the society's morality.[6] For these reasons, appellant's argument will not withstand examination.

We conclude, therefore, that we can find no constitutional right to engage in homosexual conduct and that, as judges, we have no warrant to create one. We need ask, therefore, only whether the Navy's policy is rationally related to a permissible end. *See Kelley v. Johnson*, 425 U.S. 238, 247-49 (1976). We have said that legislation may implement morality. So viewed, this regulation bears a rational relationship to a permissible end. It may be argued, however, that a naval regulation, unlike the act of a legislature, must be rationally related not to morality for its own sake but to some further end which the Navy is entitled to pursue because of the Navy's assigned function. We need not decide that question because, if such a connection is required, this regulation is plainly a rational means of advancing a legitimate, indeed a crucial, interest common to all our armed forces. To ask the question is to answer it. The effects of homosexual conduct within a naval or military unit are almost certain to be harmful to morale and discipline. The Navy is not required to produce social science data or the results of controlled experiments to prove what common sense and common experience demonstrate. This very case illustrates dangers of the sort the Navy is entitled to consider: a 27-year-old petty officer had repeated sexual relations with a 19-year-old seaman recruit. The latter then chose to break off the relationship. Episodes of this sort are certain to be deleterious to morale and discipline, to call into question the even-handedness of superiors' dealings with lower ranks, to make personal dealings uncomfortable where the relationship is sexually ambiguous, to generate dislike and

---

6. At oral argument, appellant's counsel was pressed by the court concerning his proposition that the naval regulations may not permissibly be founded in moral judgments. Asked whether moral abhorrence could never be a basis for a regulation, counsel replied that it could not. Asked then about the propriety of prohibiting bestiality, counsel replied that that could be prohibited but on the ground of cruelty to animals. The objection to cruelty to animals is, of course, an objection on grounds of morality.

disapproval among many who find homosexuality morally offensive, and, it must be
said, given the powers of military superiors
over their inferiors, to enhance the possibility of homosexual seduction.

The Navy's policy requiring discharge of
those who engage in homosexual conduct
serves legitimate state interests which include the maintenance of "discipline, good
order and morale[,] . . . mutual trust and
confidence among service members, . . .
insur[ing] the integrity of the system of rank
and command, . . . recruit[ing] and re-

tain[ing] members of the naval service . . .
and . . . prevent[ing] breaches of security."
We believe that the policy requiring discharge for homosexual conduct is a rational
means of achieving these legitimate interests. *See Beller v. Middendorf*, 632 F.2d 788,
812 (9th Cir.), *cert. denied*, 452 U.S. 905
(1980). The unique needs of the military, "a
specialized society separate from civilian society," *Parker v. Levy*, 417 U.S. 733, 743
(1974), justify the Navy's determination
that homosexual conduct impairs its capacity to carry out its mission.

III. *BOWERS v. HARDWICK*

A. Background

In 1986, the United States Supreme Court ruled in *Bowers v. Hardwick*[1] that the constitutional right to privacy did not protect lesbian and gay sexual conduct; thus, the Court affirmed
the constitutionality of state statutes criminalizing homosexual behavior. The incident
discussed in the case arose when an Atlanta police officer entered Michael Hardwick's
bedroom while Hardwick was engaged in oral sex with another man. As the following
reading reveals, however, the police officer's presence in Michael Hardwick's bedroom was
actually linked to the officer's earlier public identification of Hardwick as a gay man.

♦

INTERVIEW WITH MICHAEL HARDWICK
Peter Irons

I was born in Miami in 1954 and raised in
Miami. My mother is a very wonderful and

intelligent and sensitive woman. My father
was a very intelligent and crafty-type man.

PETER IRONS, *What Are you Doing in My Bedroom?, in* THE COURAGE OF THEIR CONVICTIONS 392 (1988).

---

1.   478 U.S. 186 (1986).

He was a fireman and worked during the Cuban missile crisis with fallout shelters and radiation. My parents divorced when I was twelve years old and I lived with my mom until I was seventeen. I went to high school here and it was pretty normal. Just like high school anywhere.

I have two sisters and a brother that are all older than me. My older sister is forty and she is a lesbian. She has a daughter who is sixteen and she's been a strong influence on me all my life. I have an older brother who is straight and married and has children.

I wanted to be a landscape architect, and I went to school in botany and horticulture at Florida State University in Gainesville. I spent three years up there, pretty much as a spiritual recluse. I was seriously considering becoming a Buddhist monk, and I was into a very spiritual frame, as far as Karma and all of that. My family was all Catholic, so they were rather disturbed about this. They were actually relieved when I told them I was coming out instead. Their attitude was, Thank God!

From Gainesville I went up to Atlanta and met this man that I fell in love with. When I met this guy it seemed like a perfectly normal thing and that was that. Things didn't work out between me and this man in Atlanta. He had a lover, which I didn't know, so I left and went to Knoxville, Tennessee. I went there because I had a girlfriend I had originally gone up to see in Atlanta who was also gay, and she and her girlfriend were moving to Knoxville. They were telling me, You've got to do something; you're a mess. So they brought me up there and nursed me back to mental health. I was totally devastated for about six months. All I did was listen to Billy Holliday and have The Blues. When I got my balance I went to Gatlinburg, up in the Smoky Mountains, and I really loved it up there. It was good for me inside, soul-searching and putting things back into perspective. I really liked the place.

Then I left and went back down to Miami and told my mother and sister I was gay, and they were very supportive. I was twenty-one years old at the time. And I've been out since

then. My mother was very accepting. She has become very independent for the first time in her life. She's now living all by herself on fourteen acres of land up in Gainesville, and she's loving it. She's been great all along.

I started working in Miami, and I opened a business called Growth Concept Environmental Design. Because I had bartended in a private gay restaurant, very elité, I knew all these top designers. So when I opened by business I immediately had an excellent clientele. I worked for about a year and a half and I finally decided I needed more time by myself. I had questions that I really hadn't worked out. So I sold my business to my junior partner and I moved back to Gatlinburg because I was so taken with the Smoky Mountains. I opened a health-food store and I hiked about forty miles a week. I was there for two years and I lost my ass in the health-food store, but at the same time I gained a lot of knowledge of myself and became a friend to myself, which is what I was really seeking to do.

This girlfriend that had pulled me out four years earlier was living in Atlanta, so I went down there to visit her, which is how this whole case started. I had been working for about a year, in a gay bar that was getting ready to open up a discotheque. I was there one night until seven o'clock in the morning, helping them put in insulation. When I left, I went up to the bar and they gave me a beer. I was kind of debating whether I wanted to leave, because I was pretty exhausted, or stay and finish the beer. I decided to leave, and I opened the door and threw the beer bottle into this trash can by the front door of the bar. I wasn't really in the mood for the beer.

Just as I did that I saw a cop drive by. I walked about a block, and he turned around and came back and asked me where the beer was. I told him I had thrown it in the trash can in front of the bar. He insisted I had thrown the beer bottle right as he pulled up. He made me get in the car and asked what I was doing. I told him that I worked there, which immediately identified me as a homosexual, because he knew it was a homosexual bar. He was enjoying *his* position as opposed to *my* position.

After about twenty minutes of bickering he drove me back so I could show him where the beer bottle was. There was no way of getting out of the back of a cop car. I told him it was in the trash can and he said he couldn't see it from the car. I said, "Fine, just give me a ticket for drinking in public." He was just busting my chops because he knew I was gay.

Anyway, the ticket had a court date on the top and a date in the center and they didn't coincide; they were one day apart. Tuesday was the court date, and the officer had written Wednesday on top of the ticket. So Tuesday, two hours after my court date, he was at my house with a warrant for my arrest. This was Officer Torick. This was unheard of, because it takes forty-eight hours to process a warrant. What I didn't realize, and didn't find out until later, was that he had personally processed a warrant for the first time in ten years. So I think there is reason to believe that he had it out for me.

I wasn't there when he came with the warrant. I got home that afternoon and my roommate said there was a cop here with a warrant. I said, That's impossible; my court date isn't until tomorrow. I went and got my ticket and realized the court date was Tuesday, not Wednesday. I asked my roommate if he'd seen the warrant and he said he hadn't. So I went down to the county clerk and showed him the discrepancy on the ticket. He brought it before the judge, and he fined me $50. I told the county clerk the cop had already been at my house with a warrant and he said that was impossible. He wrote me a receipt just in case I had any problems with it further down the road. That was that, and I thought I had taken care of it and everything was finished, and I didn't give it much thought.

Three weeks went by, and my mom had come up to visit me. I came home one morning after work at 6:30 and there were three guys standing in front of my house. I cannot say for *sure* that they had anything to do with this, but they were very straight, middle thirties, civilian clothes. I got out of the car, turned around, and they said "Michael" and I said yes, and they proceeded to beat the hell out of me. Tore all the cartilage out of my nose, kicked me in the face, cracked about six of my ribs. I passed out. I don't know how long I was unconscious. When I came to, all I could think of was, God, I don't want my *mom* to see me like this!

I managed to crawl up the stairs into the house, into the back bedroom. What I didn't realize was that I'd left a trail of blood all the way back. My mom woke up, found this trail of blood, found me passed out, and just freaked out. I assured her that everything was okay, that it was like a fluke accident, these guys were drunk or whatever. They weren't drunk, they weren't ruffians, and they knew who I was. I convinced her everything was okay and she left to go visit a friend in Pennsylvania.

I had a friend come in a few days later who was from out of town, in Atlanta to apply for a government job. He waited for me to get off work. That night at work, another friend of mine had gotten really drunk, and I took his car keys, put him in a cab, and sent him to my house, so he was passed out on the couch in the living room. He did not hear me and my friend come in. I retired with my friend. He had left the front door open, and Officer Torick came into my house about 8:30 in the morning. He had a warrant that had not been valid for three weeks and that he didn't bother to call in and check on. Officer Torick came in and woke up the guy who was passed out on my couch, who didn't know I was there and had a friend with me.

Officer Torick then came to my bedroom. The door was cracked, and the door opened up and I looked up and there was nobody there. I just blew it off as the wind and went back to what I was involved in, which was mutual oral sex. About thirty-five seconds went by and I heard another noise and I looked up, and this officer is standing in my bedroom. He identified himself when he realized I had seen him. He said, "My name is Officer Torick. Michael Hardwick, you are under arrest." I said, "For what? What are you doing in my bedroom?" He said, "I have a warrant for your arrest." I told him the warrant isn't any good. He said, "It doesn't matter, because I [am] acting under good faith."

I asked Torick if he would leave the room so we could get dressed and he said, "There's no reason for that, because I have already seen you in your most intimate aspect." He stood there and watched us get dressed, and then he brought us over to a substation. We waited in the car for about twenty-five minutes, handcuffed to the back floor. Then he brought us in and made sure everyone in the holding cells and guard and people who were processing us knew I was in there for "cock-sucking" and that I should be able to get what I was looking for. The guards were having *real* good time with that.

There was somebody there to get me out of jail within an hour, but it took them twelve hours to get me out. In the meantime, after they processed me and kept me in a holding cell for about four hours, they brought me up to the third floor, where there [were] convicted criminals. I had no business being up there. They again told all the people in the cells what I was in there for. It was not a pleasant experience. My friend was freaking out, and when I got out of jail I came back within an hour and got him out. He decided because of his government position he could not go on with the case.

I was contacted about three days later by a man named Clint Sumrall who was working in and out of the ACLU. For the last five years, he would go to the courts every day and find sodomy cases and try to get a test case. By this time, my mom had come back into town and found out what had happened. We had a typical mother conversation — she was saying, I *knew* I shouldn't have left! So she went with me to meet with Sumrall and this team of ten lawyers. I asked them what was the worst that could happen, what was the best that could happen? They explained

to me that the judge could make an example out of me and give me twenty years in jail. My mom was saying, Do you realize I'll be *dead* before I see you again? So they said, Just think about it for two or three days.

I realized that if there was anything I could do, even it if was just laying the foundation to change this horrendous law, that I would feel pretty bad about myself if I just walked away from it. One thing that influenced me was that they'd been trying for five years to get a perfect case. Most of the arrests that are made for sodomy in Atlanta are of people who are having sex outside in public; or an adult and a minor; or two consenting adults, but their families don't know they are gay; or they went through seven years of college to teach and they'd be jeopardizing their teaching position. There's a lot of different reasons why people would not want to go on with it. I was fortunate enough to have a supportive family who knew I was gay. I'm a bartender, so I can always work in a gay bar. And I was arrested in my own house. So I was a perfect test case.

I immediately met with these ten lawyers and decided on two of them to represent me. I chose John Sweet and Louis Levenson. They told me I had to get prosecuted and have a conviction from the Superior Court in order to get into the federal courts and be a test case. There was also a small amount of marijuana in my room, so there was a misdemeanor charge and a felony. So I had to go into the municipal courts before the Superior Court.

So here I go, marching into municipal court with two of the best hot-shot lawyers in Georgia on a possession-of-marijuana misdemeanor. Officer Torick got up there and said he had been let into my house; he didn't realize it had been twenty-one days since the warrant, and he was acting under good faith. The only question my lawyers asked him was why he stood there for thirty-five seconds before he identified himself. He answered that the lights were low in the room and he wasn't sure what was going on. The judge kind of chuckled and asked my attorneys how I pled, and they said 'Guilty' with no argument. We didn't want them to get suspicious as to what we were up to.

The transcripts went up to the Superior Court level, and when the prosecutors saw who was representing me, and saw that I pled guilty on the marijuana charge, they got suspicious. They sensed that something was coming and they didn't want to get involved in it. So they refused to set a court date for me, which would have meant that I would have four years of the case pending. Once the time had run out, I would not be able to start a federal suit. At that point it was very touchy. I'd been meeting with my lawyers about once a week for two or three hours while they were preparing me for testimony. So we met, and they said, "You can let things ride, but what we really need to do — and we're taking a *very* large chance — is to push it." So I agreed to do that, and we insisted that the district attorney prosecute me, because I did not want this pending over me. They wrote back a letter saying they had no intentions of further prosecution, which was in itself a judgment from the Superior Court.

At that point, Kathy Wilde came into the case as my lawyer, working with the ACLU, and I ended up getting very, very close to her. She was the perfect lawyer to work with me and we saw eye-to-eye on everything. We started at the federal level, and we filed a complaint that I was suing the police commissioner of Atlanta and state attorney, Michael Bowers. There was also a John and Mary Doe who joined my case. They came in through Kathy as co-plaintiffs, stating that the reason they were pursuing this was because the officer coming into my house had had a chilling effect on their own personal relationship. They did not want to be identified. So we went to the federal court, and Judge Hall saw that this was going to be a major thing. So he immediately dismissed the case and said that I did not have a case.

My lawyers had assured me that was okay. Then we went to the court of appeals. They decided two-to-one in my favor.‡

I didn't realize when I went into all of this that I was going to be suing the police commissioner, nor did I realize that while in the federal courts I had to continue to live in a city where the KKK was rather strong. The case lasted about five years, and in that time I moved and got an apartment in someone else's name — my phone bills, electric bills, everything was in someone else's name. I was still working as a bartender, plus I had opened up a floral shop with a friend of mine, but all in his name again, because I didn't want them to have any way of tracing me, especially after the beating. I lived very incognito for the rest of the five years.

After the appeals court decided in my favor, the state brought it into the Supreme Court. At that time I wanted to get out of the city. I'd been living there in fear for three years and I just wanted to leave the city, but my lawyers said it might hurt the case in the Supreme Court, and there was only six months to go. I stuck it out for about five more months and moved down to Miami about a month before the case was argued before the Supreme Court.

Then I went to the Supreme Court and was there for the hearing. No one knew who I was. At that point, I had not done any interviews or speaking in public. This issue was privacy, and I wanted to keep it a private issue. My lawyer had informed me from the very beginning that it would be better to keep a low profile because we did not want the personal aspects of the case to come into it, which I agreed with. They thought that if there was a lot of personal publicity it would affect the decision of the Supreme Court.

It was an education to be there. I had forty-two lawyers working on my case, plus Laurence Tribe of Harvard Law School arguing the case for me. I had met with all of

‡ *Hardwick v. Bowers*, 760 F.2d 1202 (11th Cir. 1985).

them early that morning for breakfast, and we were kind of psyching each other up. I was going to be sitting with one of the people who wrote the *amicus* brief for Lambda, which does gay legal defense in New York, and they once again assured me that no one knew who I was. So I sat in the Supreme Court as a completely anonymous person. The whole omnipresence of the room, the procedure of the judges coming in, is sort of overpowering. I expected the room to be huge, but it wasn't; it was a very small room. You could see the judges' faces and their expressions no matter where you sat.

The guy from the state came up first and argued for about five minutes and he was an idiot. He kept going on about how the state *did* have a justified government interest in continuing to enforce the law because it prevented adultery and retarded children and bestiality, and that if they changed the law all of those things would be legal. He made absolutely no sense. I think it was Justice Burger who asked why, if they had my head on a silver platter, if they had such a justified government interest in enforcing this law, did they refuse to prosecute me. At which point, his answer was that he wasn't at liberty to discuss that. The nine Justices and the whole place cracked up and he pretty much ended his argument.

Then Laurence Tribe got up and articulately argued for about forty-five minutes. He was incredible. I've never seen any person more in control of his senses than he was. When he got done, everyone was very much pre-victory. They were *sure* I would win. About forty of us went to lunch around the corner, and everything seemed very positive and optimistic, and I flew back to Miami to work. Then came the waiting period. That was the worst phase for me, because we never knew when the decision was coming. I would be on pins and needles, and every time the phone rang I'd be jumping. They made it the last decision of the year, of course. They waited until just

after all of the Gay Pride parades around the country.

I was at work when I heard about the decision. I cater a complimentary buffet for about a hundred people a day, so I go into work about four or five hours before anyone else gets there to do all my prep work. On this particular morning I could not sleep, and I got to work about nine o'clock. A friend of mine had been watching cable news and had seen it and knew where to find me and came over. When I opened the door he was crying and saying that he was sorry, and I didn't know what the hell he was talking about. Finally I calmed him down and he told me what had happened: that I had lost by a five-to-four vote.

I was totally stunned. My friend took off and I was there for about four hours by myself and that's when it really sunk in. I just cried — not so much because I had failed but because to me it was frightening to think that in the year of 1986 our Supreme Court, next to God, could make a decision that was more suitable to the mentality of the Spanish Inquisition. It was frightening and it stunned me. I was scared. I had been fighting this case for five years and everyone had seemed so confident that I was really *not* expecting this decision the way that they handed it down.

So I called Kathy Wilde and I called Laurence Tribe. I think he was more devastated than I was. Nobody expected it. I was calling for some kind of reaffirming that everything was going to be okay and that something could be done. But they said, That's it! There's nothing we can do. I learned later that I originally *had* five votes in my favor on the Supreme Court. Justice Powell came out a week later and said to the press that he had originally decided in my favor. I *still* don't understand why Powell changed his mind in my case. What a half-assed decision!

At that time, everyone thought I was still in Atlanta. And I thought this was okay, I'll just get through this personally. People who knew what I was doing kept coming into the bar and saying, I'm sorry. And I'd say that I'd rather not talk about it. I figured the best place for me would be behind the bar, because it would make me pull myself out of it.

About eight o'clock that night, in comes this woman from Channel 11 news, with a man behind her with a camera on his shoulder. This is in a gay club. I was stunned. All of a sudden it sunk in that they could find me. I asked her how she knew where I was and she said she was very resourceful. She wanted to do an interview, and I immediately left the bar and went upstairs. I was shaking. She got pissed off because she couldn't do an interview with me, and on the eleven o'clock news she's talking about MichaelHardwick, and the whole time she has the camera focused on the bar I work at.

About two days went by where I was just kind of stunned. There wasn't anything I could do to change the way I [felt], and I'm normally a very positive person. It wasn't that I was negative. I was just nonresponsive to anything. Then all of a sudden I started getting pissed off, angry. Kathy called me two days later and she said that *Newsweek* magazine just came out with a national poll that said fifty-seven percent of the people were opposed to the decision. And she said, By the way, Phil Donahue called and wants to know if you'll do his show. She was very clever, letting me know the nation was behind me, and then hitting me with the Donahue show. Up until then, they had all advised me to keep it private. But she said, "This is one approach you can take: you can come out and let people know this was not a homosexual decision, as they tried to put it out, but that it affects everyone as individuals, as consenting adults. And the only way you're going to get that across to them is to use this opportunity."

That was the first time I'd ever spoken publicly. Donahue called and said he was putting me on with Jerry Falwell, and I said I wouldn't do the show — it wasn't a religious issue. So he called back and said, "We got rid of Falwell, but you'll have to do the whole show by yourself." "Okay." So I flew up there and did that, and that was probably the hardest thing I've ever done in my life. But it went very well, and everyone who saw the program said I was a good spokesman. That started something I had never anticipated. I did a lot of talk shows after that, a lot of newspaper interviews.

They told me after Donahue that in a month I'd be old news, but this has been the most hectic year of my life. Just about the time the whole thing died out, we started on the two-hundredth birthday of the Constitution. I did a special with Bill Moyers on PBS, and one with Peter Jennings. And I've been speaking at a lot of rallies.

■ ■ ■

Because of my personal perspective in life, I have a tendency to dwell on the positive instead of the negative. I feel very fortunate I was given the opportunity to do it. Speaking and coming out nationally was a very healthy experience for me, because it made me develop a confidence I never would have had if I had gone along with my individual life. It also gave me a sense of importance, because right now there is a very strong need for the gay community to pull together, and also for the heterosexual community to pull together, against something that's affecting both of us. I feel that no matter what happens, I gave it my best shot. I will continue to give it my best shot.

B. Supreme Court

BOWERS v. HARDWICK

478 U.S. 186 (1986)

JUSTICE WHITE delivered the opinion of the Court.

In August 1982, respondent Hardwick (hereafter respondent) was charged with violating the Georgia statute criminalizing sodomy[1] by committing that act with another adult male in the bedroom of respondent's home. After a preliminary hearing, the District Attorney decided not to present the matter to the grand jury unless further evidence developed.

Respondent then brought suit in the Federal District Court, challenging the constitutionality of the statute insofar as it criminalized consensual sodomy.[2] He asserted that he was a practicing homosexual, that the Georgia sodomy statute, as administered by the defendants, placed him in imminent danger of arrest, and that the statute for several reasons violates the Federal Constitution. The District Court granted the defendants' motion to dismiss for failure to state a claim, relying on *Doe v. Commonwealth's Attorney for the City of Richmond*, 403 F.Supp. 1199 (ED Va. 1975), which this Court summarily affirmed, 425 U.S. 901 (1976).

A divided panel of the Court of Appeals for the Eleventh Circuit reversed. 760 F.2d 1202 (1985). The court first held that, because *Doe* was distinguishable and in any event had been undermined by later decisions, our summary affirmance in that case did not require affirmance of the District Court. Relying on our decisions in *Griswold v. Connecticut*, 381 U.S. 479 (1965); *Eisenstadt v. Baird*, 405 U.S. 438 (1972); *Stanley v. Georgia*, 394 U.S. 557 (1969); and *Roe v. Wade*, 410 U.S. 113 (1973), the court went on to hold that the Georgia statute violated respondent's fundamental rights because his homosexual activity is a private and intimate association that is beyond the reach of state regulation by reason of the Ninth Amendment and the due process

---

1. Georgia Code Ann., § 16-6-2 (1984) provides, in pertinent part, as follows:

    "(a) A person commits the offense of sodomy when he performs or submits to any sexual act involving the sex organs of one person and the mouth or anus of another. . . .

    "(b) A person convicted of the offense of sodomy shall be punished by imprisonment for not less than one nor more than 20 years. . . ."

2. John and Mary Doe were also plaintiffs in the action. They alleged that they wished to engage in sexual activity proscribed by § 16-6-2 in the privacy of their home, and that they had been "chilled and deterred" from engaging in such activity by both the existence of the statute and Hardwick's arrest. The District Court held, however, that because they had neither sustained, nor were in immediate danger of sustaining, any direct injury from the enforcement of the statute, they did not have proper standing to maintain the action. The Court of Appeals affirmed the District Court's judgment dismissing the Does' claim for lack of standing, 760 F.2d 1202, 1206–1207 (11th Cir. 1985), and the Does do not challenge that holding in this Court.

    The only claim properly before the Court, therefore, is Hardwick's challenge to the Georgia statute as applied to consensual homosexual sodomy. We express no opinion on the constitutionality of the Georgia statute as applied to other acts of sodomy.

clause of the Fourteenth Amendment. The case was remanded for trial, at which, to prevail, the State would have to prove that the statute is supported by a compelling interest and is the most narrowly drawn means of achieving that end.

Because other Courts of Appeals have arrived at judgments contrary to that of the Eleventh Circuit in this case,[3] we granted the Attorney General's petition for certiorari questioning the holding that the sodomy statute violates the fundamental rights of homosexuals. We agree with petitioner that the Court of Appeals erred, and hence reverse its judgment.[4]

This case does not require a judgment on whether laws against sodomy between consenting adults in general, or between homosexuals in particular, are wise or desirable. It raises no question about the right or propriety of state legislative decisions to repeal their laws that criminalize homosexual sodomy, or of state-court decisions invalidating those laws on state constitutional grounds. The issue presented is whether the Federal Constitution confers a fundamental right upon homosexuals to engage in sodomy and hence invalidates the laws of the many States that still make such conduct illegal and have done so for a very long time. The case also calls for some judgment about the limits of the Court's role in carrying out its constitutional mandate.

We first register our disagreement with the Court of Appeals and with respondent that the Court's prior cases have construed the Constitution to confer a right of privacy that extends to homosexual sodomy and for all intents and purposes have decided this case. The reach of this line of cases was sketched in *Carey v. Population Services International*, 431 U.S. 678, 685 (1977). *Pierce v. Society of Sisters*, 268 U.S. 510

(1925), and *Meyer v. Nebraska*, 262 U.S. 390 (1923), were described as dealing with child rearing and education; *Prince v. Massachusetts*, 321 U.S. 158 (1944), with family relationships; *Skinner v. Oklahoma ex rel. Williamson*, 316 U.S. 535 (1942), with procreation; *Loving v. Virginia*, 388 U.S. 1 (1967), with marriage; *Griswold v. Connecticut, supra*, and *Eisenstadt v. Baird, supra*, with contraception; and *Roe v. Wade*, 410 U.S. 113 (1973), with abortion. The latter three cases were interpreted as construing the due process clause of the Fourteenth Amendment to confer a fundamental individual right to decide whether or not to beget or bear a child. *Carey v. Population Services International, supra*, at 688-689.

Accepting the decisions in these cases and the above description of them, we think it evident that none of the rights announced in those cases bears any resemblance to the claimed constitutional right of homosexuals to engage in acts of sodomy that is asserted in this case. No connection between family, marriage, or procreation on the one hand and homosexual activity on the other has been demonstrated, either by the Court of Appeals or by respondent. Moreover, any claim that these cases nevertheless stand for the proposition that any kind of private sexual conduct between consenting adults is constitutionally insulated from state proscription is unsupportable. Indeed, the Court's opinion in *Carey* twice asserted that the privacy right, which the *Griswold* line of cases found to be one of the protections provided by the due process clause, did not reach so far.

Precedent aside, however, respondent would have us announce, as the Court of Appeals did, a fundamental right to engage in homosexual sodomy. This we are quite unwilling to do. It is true that despite the language of the due process clauses of the

---

3. See *Baker v. Wade*, 769 F.2d 289, rehearing denied, 774 F.2d 1285 (5th Cir. 1985) (en banc); *Dronenburg v. Zech*, 741 F.2d 1388 (D.C. Cir. 1984), rehearing denied, 746 F.2d 1579 (1984).

4. Petitioner also submits that the Court of Appeals erred in holding that the District Court was not obligated to follow our summary affirmance in *Doe*. We need not resolve this dispute, for we prefer to give plenary consideration to the merits of this case rather than rely on our earlier action in *Doe*.

Fifth and Fourteenth Amendments, which appears to focus only on the processes by which life, liberty, or property is taken, the cases are legion in which those clauses have been interpreted to have substantive content, subsuming rights that to a great extent are immune from federal or state regulation or proscription. Among such cases are those recognizing rights that have little or no textual support in the constitutional language. *Meyer*, *Prince*, and *Pierce* fall in this category, as do the privacy cases from *Griswold* to *Carey*.

Striving to assure itself and the public that announcing rights not readily identifiable in the Constitution's text involves much more than the imposition of the Justices' own choice of values on the States and the Federal Government, the Court has sought to identify the nature of the rights qualifying for heightened judicial protection. In *Palko v. Connecticut*, 302 U.S. 319, 325, 326 (1937), it was said that this category includes those fundamental liberties that are "implicit in the concept of ordered liberty," such that "neither liberty nor justice would exist if [they] were sacrificed." A different description of fundamental liberties appeared in *Moore v. East Cleveland*, 431 U.S. 494, 503 (1977) (opinion of Powell, J.), where they are characterized as those liberties that are "deeply rooted in this Nation's history and tradition." *Id.*, at 503 (Powell, J.). *See also Griswold v. Connecticut*, 381 U.S., at 506.

It is obvious to us that neither of these formulations would extend a fundamental right to homosexuals to engage in acts of consensual sodomy. Proscriptions against that conduct have ancient roots. *See generally*, "Survey on the Constitutional Right to Privacy in the Context of Homosexual Activity, 40 *U. Miami L. Rev.* 521, 525 (1986). Sodomy was a criminal offense at common law and was forbidden by the laws of the original thirteen states when they ratified the Bill of Rights. In 1868, when the Fourteenth Amendment was ratified, all but five of the thirty-seven States in the Union had criminal sodomy laws. In fact, until 1961,[7] all fifty States outlawed sodomy, and today, twenty-four states and the District of Columbia continue to provide criminal penalties for sodomy performed in private and between consenting adults. *See* Survey, U. Miami L. Rev., *supra*, at 524, n. 9. Against this background, to claim that a right to engage in such conduct is "deeply rooted in this nation's history and tradition" or "implicit in the concept of ordered liberty" is, at best, facetious.

Nor are we inclined to take a more expansive view of our authority to discover new fundamental rights imbedded in the due process clause. The Court is most vulnerable and comes nearest to illegitimacy when it deals with judge-made constitutional law having little or no cognizable roots in the language or design of the Constitution. That this is so was painfully demonstrated by the face-off between the Executive and the Court in the 1930s, which resulted in the repudiation of much of the substantive gloss that the Court had placed on the Due Process Clauses of the Fifth and Fourteenth Amendments. There should be, therefore, great resistance to expand the substantive reach of those Clauses, particularly if it requires redefining the category of rights deemed to be fundamental. Otherwise, the Judiciary necessarily takes to itself further authority to govern the country without express constitutional authority. The claimed right pressed on us today falls far short of overcoming this resistance.

Respondent, however, asserts that the result should be different where the homosexual conduct occurs in the privacy of the home. He relies on *Stanley v. Georgia*, 394

---

7. In 1961, Illinois adopted the American Law Institute's Model Penal Code, which decriminalized adult, consensual, private, sexual conduct. Criminal Code of 1961, §§ 11–2, 11–3, 1961 Ill. Laws, pp. 1985, 2006 (codified as amended at Ill. Rev. Stat., ch. 38, paras. 11–2, 11–3 (1983) (repealed 1984)). See American Law Institute, "Model Penal Code," § 213.2 (Proposed Official Draft 1962).

U.S. 557 (1969), where the Court held that the First Amendment prevents conviction for possessing and reading obscene material in the privacy of one's home: "If the First Amendment means anything, it means that a State has no business telling a man, sitting alone in his house, what books he may read or what films he may watch." *Id.*, at 565.

Stanley did protect conduct that would not have been protected outside the home, and it partially prevented the enforcement of state obscenity laws; but the decision was firmly grounded in the First Amendment. The right pressed upon us here has no similar support in the text of the Constitution, and it does not qualify for recognition under the prevailing principles for construing the Fourteenth Amendment. Its limits are also difficult to discern. Plainly enough, otherwise illegal conduct is not always immunized whenever it occurs in the home. Victimless crimes, such as the possession and use of illegal drugs, do not escape the law where they are committed at home. *Stanley* itself recognized that its holding offered no protection for the possession in the home of drugs, firearms, or stolen goods. *Id.*, at 568, n. 11. And if respondent's submission is limited to the voluntary sexual conduct between consenting adults, it would be difficult, except by fiat, to limit the claimed right to homosexual conduct while leaving exposed to prosecution adultery, incest, and other sexual crimes even though they are committed in the home. We are unwilling to start down that road.

Even if the conduct at issue here is not a fundamental right, respondent asserts that there must be a rational basis for the law and that there is none in this case other than the presumed belief of a majority of the electorate in Georgia that homosexual sodomy is immoral and unacceptable. This is said to be an inadequate rationale to support the law. The law, however, is constantly based on notions of morality, and if all laws represent-

ing essentially moral choices are to be invalidated under the Due Process Clause, the courts will be very busy indeed. Even respondent makes no such claim, but insists that majority sentiments about the morality of homosexuality should be declared inadequate. We do not agree, and are unpersuaded that the sodomy laws of some 25 States should be invalidated on this basis.[8]

Accordingly, the judgment of the Court of Appeals is

Reversed.

CHIEF JUSTICE BURGER, concurring.

I join the Court's opinion, but I write separately to underscore my view that in constitutional terms there is no such thing as a fundamental right to commit homosexual sodomy.

As the Court notes, the proscriptions against sodomy have very "ancient roots." Decisions of individuals relating to homosexual conduct have been subject to state intervention throughout the history of Western civilization. Condemnation of those practices is firmly rooted in Judeao-Christian moral and ethical standards. Homosexual sodomy was a capital crime under Roman law. See Code Theod. 9.7.6; Code Just. 9.9.31. See also D. Bailey, Homosexuality and the Western Christian Tradition, 70-81 (1975). During the English Reformation when powers of the ecclesiastical courts were transferred to the King's Courts, the first English statute criminalizing sodomy was passed. 25 Hen. VIII, ch. 6. Blackstone described "the infamous *crime against nature*" as an offense of "deeper malignity" than rape, a heinous act "the very mention of which is a disgrace to human nature," and "a crime not fit to be named." 4 W. Blackstone, Commentaries *215. The common law of England, including its prohibition of sodomy, became the received law of Georgia

---

8. Respondent does not defend the judgment below based on the Ninth Amendment, the Equal Protection Clause, or the Eighth Amendment.

and the other Colonies. In 1816 the Georgia Legislature passed the statute at issue here, and that statute has been continuously in force in one form or another since that time. To hold that the act of homosexual sodomy is somehow protected as a fundamental right would be to cast aside millennia of moral teaching.

This is essentially not a question of personal "preferences" but rather of the legislative authority of the State. I find nothing in the Constitution depriving a State of the power to enact the statute challenged here.

JUSTICE POWELL, concurring.

I join the opinion of the Court. I agree with the Court that there is no fundamental right — i. e., no substantive right under the due process clause — such as that claimed by respondent Hardwick, and found to exist by the Court of Appeals. This is not to suggest, however, that respondent may not be protected by the Eighth Amendment of the Constitution. The Georgia statute at issue in this case, Ga. Code Ann., § 16-6-2 (1984), authorizes a court to imprison a person for up to 20 years for a single private, consensual act of sodomy. In my view, a prison sentence for such conduct — certainly a sentence of long duration — would create a serious Eighth Amendment issue. Under the Georgia statute a single act of sodomy, even in the private setting of a home, is a felony comparable in terms of the possible sentence imposed to serious felonies such as aggravated battery, § 16-5-24, first-degree arson, § 16-7-60, and robbery, § 16-8-40.[1]

In this case, however, respondent has not been tried, much less convicted and sentenced.[2] Moreover, respondent has not raised the Eighth Amendment issue below. For these reasons this constitutional argument is not before us.

JUSTICE BLACKMAN, with whom JUSTICE BRENNAN, JUSTICE MARSHALL, and JUSTICE STEVENS join, dissenting.

This case is no more about "a fundamental right to engage in homosexual sodomy," as the Court purports to declare, than *Stanley v. Georgia*, 394 U.S. 557 (1969), was about a fundamental right to watch obscene movies, or *Katz v. United States*, 389 U.S. 347 (1967), was about a fundamental right to place interstate

---

1. Among those States that continue to make sodomy a crime, Georgia authorizes one of the longest possible sentences. See Ala. Code § 13A-6-65(a)(3) (1982) (1-year maximum); Ariz. Rev. Stat. Ann. §§ 13-1411, 13-1412 (West Supp. 1985) (30 days); Ark. Stat. Ann. § 41-1813 (1977) (1-year maximum); D. C. Code § 22-3502 (1981) (10-year maximum); Fla. Stat. § 800.02 (1985) (60-day maximum); Ga. Code Ann. § 16-6-2 (1984) (1 to 20 years); Idaho Code § 18-6605 (1979) (5-year minimum); Kan. Stat. Ann. § 21-3505 (Supp. 1985) (6-month maximum); Ky. Rev. Stat. § 510.100 (1985) (90 days to 12 months); La. Rev. Stat. Ann. § 14:89 (West 1986) (5-year maximum); Md. Ann. Code, Art. 27, §§ 553–554 (1982) (10-year maximum); Mich. Comp. Laws § 750.158 (1968) (15-year maximum); Minn. Stat. § 609.293 (1984) (1-year maximum); Miss. Code Ann. § 97-29-59 (1973) (10-year maximum); Mo. Rev. Stat. § 566.090 (Supp. 1984) (1-year maximum); Mont. Code Ann. § 45-5-505 (1985) (10-year maximum); Nev. Rev. Stat. § 201.190 (1985) (6-year maximum); N. C. Gen. Stat. § 14–177 (1981) (10-year maximum); Okla. Stat., Tit. 21, § 886 (1981) (10-year maximum); R. I. Gen. Laws § 11-10-1 (1981) (7 to 20 years); S. C. Code § 16-15-120 (1985) (5-year maximum); Tenn. Code Ann. § 39-2-612 (1982) (5 to 15 years); Tex. Penal Code Ann. § 21.06 (1974) ($ 200 maximum fine); Utah Code Ann. § 76-5-403 (1978) (6-month maximum); Va. Code § 18.2-361 (1982) (5-year maximum).

2. It was conceded at oral argument that, prior to the complaint against respondent Hardwick, there had been no reported decision involving prosecution for private homosexual sodomy under this statute for several decades. See *Thompson v. Aldredge*, 200 S. E. 799 (Ga. 1939). Moreover, the State has declined to present the criminal charge against Hardwick to a grand jury, and this is a suit for declaratory judgment brought by respondents challenging the validity of the statute. The history of nonenforcement suggests the moribund character today of laws criminalizing this type of private, consensual conduct. Some 26 States have repealed similar statutes. But the constitutional validity of the Georgia statute was put in issue by respondents, and for the reasons stated by the Court, I cannot say that conduct condemned for hundreds of years has now become a fundamental right.

bets from a telephone booth. Rather, this case is about "the most comprehensive of rights and the right most valued by civilized men," namely, "the right to be let alone." *Olmstead v. United States*, 277 U.S. 438, 478 (1928) (Brandeis, J., dissenting).

The statute at issue, Ga. Code Ann. § 16-6-2 (1984), denies individuals the right to decide for themselves whether to engage in particular forms of private, consensual sexual activity. The Court concludes that § 16-6-2 is valid essentially because "the laws of . . . many States . . . still make such conduct illegal and have done so for a very long time." But the fact that the moral judgments expressed by statutes like § 16-6-2 may be "'natural and familiar . . . ought not to conclude our judgment upon the question whether statutes embodying them conflict with the Constitution of the United States.'" *Roe v. Wade*, 410 U.S. 113, 117 (1973), quoting *Lochner v. New York*, 198 U.S. 45, 76 (1905) (Holmes, J., dissenting). Like Justice Holmes, I believe that "[it] is revolting to have no better reason for a rule of law than that so it was laid down in the time of Henry IV. It is still more revolting if the grounds upon which it was laid down have vanished long since, and the rule simply persists from blind imitation of the past." Holmes, "The Path of the Law," 10 Harv. L. Rev. 457, 469 (1897). I believe we must analyze respondent Hardwick's claim in the light of the values that underlie the constitutional right to privacy. If that right means anything, it means that, before Georgia can prosecute its citizens for making choices about the most intimate aspects of their lives, it must do more than assert that the choice they have made is an "'abominable crime not fit to be named among Christians.'" *Herring v. State*, 46 S. E. 876, 882 (Ga. 1904).

In its haste to reverse the Court of Appeals and hold that the Constitution does not "[confer] a fundamental right upon homosexuals to engage in sodomy," the Court relegates the actual statute being challenged to a footnote and ignores the procedural posture of the case before it. A fair reading of the statute and of the complaint clearly reveals that the majority has distorted the question this case presents.

First, the Court's almost obsessive focus on homosexual activity is particularly hard to justify in light of the broad language Georgia has used. Unlike the Court, the Georgia Legislature has not proceeded on the assumption that homosexuals are so different from other citizens that their lives may be controlled in a way that would not be tolerated if it limited the choices of those other citizens. Rather, Georgia has provided that "[a] person commits the offense of sodomy when he performs or submits to any sexual act involving the sex organs of one person and the mouth or anus of another." Ga. Code Ann. § 16-6-2(a) (1984). The sex or status of the persons who engage in the act is irrelevant as a matter of state law. In fact, to the extent I can discern a legislative purpose for Georgia's 1968 enactment of § 16-6-2, that purpose seems to have been to broaden the coverage of the law to reach heterosexual as well as homosexual activity.[1] I therefore see no basis for the Court's decision to treat this case as an "as applied" challenge to § 16-6-2, or for Georgia's attempt, both in its brief and at oral argument, to defend § 16-6-2 solely on the grounds that it prohibits homosexual activity. Michael Hardwick's standing may rest in significant part on Georgia's apparent willingness to enforce against homosexuals

---

1. Until 1968, Georgia defined sodomy as "the carnal knowledge and connection against the order of nature, by man with man, or in the same unnatural manner with woman." Ga. Crim. Code § 26–5901 (1933). In *Thompson v. Aldredge*, 200 S. E. 799 (Ga. 1939), the Georgia Supreme Court held that § 26–5901 did not prohibit lesbian activity. And in *Riley v. Garrett*, 133 S. E. 2d 367 (Ga. 1963), the Georgia Supreme Court held that § 26–5901 did not prohibit heterosexual cunnilingus. Georgia passed the act-specific statute currently in force "perhaps in response to the restrictive court decisions such as *Riley*," Note, The Crimes Against Nature, 16 J. Pub. L. 159, 167, n. 47 (1967).

a law it seems not to have any desire to enforce against heterosexuals. But his claim that § 16-6-2 involves an unconstitutional intrusion into his privacy and his right of intimate association does not depend in any way on his sexual orientation.

Second, I disagree with the Court's refusal to consider whether § 16-6-2 runs afoul of the Eighth or Ninth Amendments or the equal protection clause of the Fourteenth Amendment. Respondent's complaint expressly invoked the Ninth Amendment, and he relied heavily before this Court on *Griswold v. Connecticut*, 381 U.S. 479, 484 (1965), which identifies that Amendment as one of the specific constitutional provisions giving "life and substance" to our understanding of privacy. More importantly, the procedural posture of the case requires that we affirm the Court of Appeals' judgment if there is *any* ground on which respondent may be entitled to relief. This case is before us on petitioner's motion to dismiss for failure to state a claim, Fed. Rule Civ. Proc. 12(b)(6). It is a well-settled principle of law that "a complaint should not be dismissed merely because a plaintiff's allegations do not support the particular legal theory he advances, for the court is under a duty to examine the complaint to determine if the allegations provide for relief on any possible theory." Thus, even if respondent did not advance claims based on the Eighth or Ninth Amendments, or on the equal protection clause, his complaint should not be dismissed if any of those provisions could entitle him to relief. I need not reach either the Eighth Amendment or the equal protection clause issues because I believe that Hardwick has stated a cognizable claim that § 16-6-2 interferes with constitutionally protected interests in privacy and freedom of intimate association. But neither the Eighth Amendment nor the equal protection clause is so clearly irrelevant that a claim resting on either provision should be peremptorily dismissed.[2] The Court's cramped reading of the issue before it makes

2. In *Robinson v. California*, 370 U.S. 660 (1962), the Court held that the Eighth Amendment barred convicting a defendant due to his "status" as a narcotics addict, since that condition was "apparently an illness which may be contracted innocently or involuntarily." *Id.*, at 667. In *Powell v. Texas*, 392 U.S. 514 (1968), where the Court refused to extend *Robinson* to punishment of public drunkenness by a chronic alcoholic, one of the factors relied on by Justice Marshall, in writing the plurality opinion, was that Texas had not "attempted to regulate appellant's behavior in the privacy of his own home." *Id.*, at 532. Justice White wrote separately:

"Analysis of this difficult case is not advanced by preoccupation with the label 'condition.' In *Robinson* the Court dealt with "a statute which makes the "status" of narcotic addiction a criminal offense. . . .' 370 U.S., at 666. By precluding criminal conviction for such a 'status' the Court was dealing with a condition brought about by acts remote in time from the application of the criminal sanctions contemplated, a condition which was relatively permanent in duration, and a condition of great magnitude and significance in terms of human behavior and values. . . . If it were necessary to distinguish between 'acts' and 'conditions' for purposes of the Eighth Amendment, I would adhere to the concept of 'condition' implicit in the opinion in *Robinson*. . . . The proper subject of inquiry is whether volitional acts brought about the 'condition' and whether those acts are sufficiently proximate to the 'condition' for it to be permissible to impose penal sanctions on the 'condition.'"

Despite historical views of homosexuality, it is no longer viewed by mental health professionals as a "disease" or disorder. See Brief for American Psychological Association and American Public Health Association as *Amici Curiae* 8–11. But, obviously, neither is it simply a matter of deliberate personal election. Homosexual orientation may well form part of the very fiber of an individual's personality. Consequently, under Justice White's analysis in *Powell*, the Eighth Amendment may pose a constitutional barrier to sending an individual to prison for acting on that attraction regardless of the circumstances. An individual's ability to make constitutionally protected "decisions concerning sexual relations," *Carey v. Population Services International*, 431 U.S. 678, 711 (1977) (Powell, J., concurring in part and concurring in judgment), is rendered empty indeed if he or she is given no real choice but a life without any physical intimacy.

for a short opinion, but it does little to make for a persuasive one.

II.

"Our cases long have recognized that the Constitution embodies a promise that a certain private sphere of individual liberty will be kept largely beyond the reach of government." *Thornburgh v. American College of Obstetricians & Gynecologists*, 476 U.S. 747, 772 (1986). In construing the right to privacy, the Court has proceeded along two somewhat distinct, albeit complementary, lines. First, it has recognized a privacy interest with reference to certain *decisions* that are properly for the individual to make. E. g., *Roe v. Wade*, 410 U.S. 113 (1973); *Pierce v. Society of Sisters*, 268 U.S. 510 (1925). Second, it has recognized a privacy interest with reference to certain *places* without regard for the particular activities in which the individuals who occupy them are engaged. E. g., *United States v. Karo*, 468 U.S. 705 (1984); *Payton v. New York*, 445 U.S. 573 (1980); *Rios v. United States*, 364 U.S. 253 (1960). The case before us implicates both the decisional and the spatial aspects of the right to privacy.

A.

The Court concludes today that none of our prior cases dealing with various decisions that individuals are entitled to make free of governmental interference "bears any resemblance to the claimed constitutional right of homosexuals to engage in acts of sodomy that is asserted in this case." While it is true that these cases may be characterized by their connection to protection of the family, see *Roberts v. United States Jaycees*, 468 U.S. 609, 619 (1984), the Court's conclusion that they extend no further than this boundary ignores the warning in *Moore v. East Cleveland*, 431 U.S. 494, 501 (1977) (plurality opinion), against "[closing] our eyes to the basic reasons why certain rights associated with the family have been accorded shelter under the Fourteenth Amendment's due process clause." We protect those rights not because they contribute, in some direct and material way, to the general public welfare, but because they form so central a part of an individual's life. "[The] concept of privacy embodies the 'moral fact that a person belongs to himself and not others nor to society as a whole.'" *Thornburgh v. American College of Obstetricians & Gynecologists*, 476 U.S., at 777, n. 5 (Stevens, J., concurring), quoting Fried, Correspondence, 6 Phil. & Pub. Affairs, 288–289 (1977). And so we protect the decision whether to marry precisely because marriage "is an association that promotes a way of life, not causes; a harmony in living, not political faiths; a bilateral loyalty, not commercial or social projects." *Griswold v. Connecticut*, 381 U.S., at 486. We protect the decision whether to have a child because parenthood alters so dramatically an individual's self-definition, not because of demographic considerations or the Bible's command to be fruitful and multiply. Cf. *Thornburgh v. American College of Obstetricians & Gynecologists*, *supra*, at 777, n. 6 (Stevens, J., concurring).

With respect to the equal protection clause's applicability to § 16-6-2, I note that Georgia's exclusive stress before this Court on its interest in prosecuting homosexual activity despite the gender-neutral terms of the statute may raise serious questions of discriminatory enforcement, questions that cannot be disposed of before this Court on a motion to dismiss. See *Yick Wo v. Hopkins*, 118 U.S. 356, 373–374 (1886). The legislature having decided that the sex of the participants is irrelevant to the legality of the acts, I do not see why the state can defend § 16-6-2 on the ground that individuals singled out for prosecution are of the same sex as their partners. Thus, under the circumstances of this case, a claim under the equal protection clause may well be available without having to reach the more controversial question whether homosexuals are a suspect class. See, *e. g.*, *Rowland v. Mad River Local School District*, 470 U.S. 1009 (1985) (Brennan, J., dissenting from denial of certiorari); Note, The Constitutional Status of Sexual Orientation: Homosexuality as a Suspect Classification, 98 Harv. L. Rev. 1285 (1985).

And we protect the family because it contributes so powerfully to the happiness of individuals, not because of a preference for stereotypical households. Cf. *Moore v. East Cleveland*, 431 U.S., at 500-506 (plurality opinion). The Court recognized in Roberts, 468 U.S., at 619, that the "ability independently to define one's identity that is central to any concept of liberty" cannot truly be exercised in a vacuum; we all depend on the "emotional enrichment from close ties with others." *Ibid.*

Only the most willful blindness could obscure the fact that sexual intimacy is "a sensitive, key relationship of human existence, central to family life, community welfare, and the development of human personality," *Paris Adult Theatre I v. Slaton*, 413 U.S. 49, 63 (1973); *see also Carey v. Population Services International*, 431 U.S. 678, 685 (1977). The fact that individuals define themselves in a significant way through their intimate sexual relationships with others suggests, in a nation as diverse as ours, that there may be many "right" ways of conducting those relationships, and that much of the richness of a relationship will come from the freedom an individual has to *choose* the form and nature of these intensely personal bonds. *See* Karst, The Freedom of Intimate Association, 89 Yale L. J. 624, 637 (1980); cf. *Eisenstadt v. Baird*, 405 U.S. 438, 453 (1972); *Roe v. Wade*, 410 U.S., at 153.

In a variety of circumstances we have recognized that a necessary corollary of giving individuals freedom to choose how to conduct their lives is acceptance of the fact that different individuals will make different choices. For example, in holding that the clearly important state interest in public education should give way to a competing claim by the Amish to the effect that extended formal schooling threatened their way of life, the Court declared: "There can be no assumption that today's majority is "right" and the Amish and others like them are "wrong." A way of life that is odd or even erratic but interferes with no rights or interests of others is not to be condemned because it is different." *Wisconsin v. Yoder*, 406 U.S. 205, 223-224 (1972). The Court claims that its decision today merely refuses to recognize a fundamental right to engage in homosexual sodomy; what the Court really has refused to recognize is the fundamental interest all individuals have in controlling the nature of their intimate associations with others.

B.

The behavior for which Hardwick faces prosecution occurred in his own home, a place to which the Fourth Amendment attaches special significance. The Court's treatment of this aspect of the case is symptomatic of its overall refusal to consider the broad principles that have informed our treatment of privacy in specific cases. Just as the right to privacy is more than the mere aggregation of a number of entitlements to engage in specific behavior, so too, protecting the physical integrity of the home is more than merely a means of protecting specific activities that often take place there. Even when our understanding of the contours of the right to privacy depends on "reference to a 'place,'" *Katz v. United States*, 389 U.S., at 361 (Harlan, J., concurring), "the essence of a Fourth Amendment violation is 'not the breaking of [a person's] doors, and the rummaging of his drawers,' but rather is 'the invasion of his indefeasible right of personal security, personal liberty and private property.'" *California v. Ciraolo*, 476 U.S. 207, 226 (1986) (Powell, J., dissenting), quoting *Boyd v. United States*, 116 U.S. 616, 630 (1886).

The Court's interpretation of the pivotal case of *Stanley v. Georgia*, 394 U.S. 557 (1969), is entirely unconvincing. *Stanley* held that Georgia's undoubted power to punish the public distribution of constitutionally unprotected, obscene material did not permit the State to punish the private possession of such material. According to the majority here, *Stanley* relied entirely on the First Amendment, and thus, it is claimed, sheds no light on cases not involving printed materials. But that is not what *Stanley* said. Rather, the *Stanley* Court anchored its holding in the Fourth Amendment's special protection for the individual in his home:

" 'The makers of our Constitution undertook to secure conditions favorable to the pursuit of happiness. They recognized the significance of man's spiritual nature, of his feelings and of his intellect. They knew that only a part of the pain, pleasure and satisfactions of life are to be found in material things. They sought to protect Americans in their beliefs, their thoughts, their emotions and their sensations.'

"These are the rights that appellant is asserting in the case before us. He is asserting the right to read or observe what he pleases — the right to satisfy his intellectual and emotional needs in the privacy of his own home." 394 U.S., at 564-565, quoting, *Olmstead v. United States*, 277 U.S., at 478 (Brandeis, J., dissenting).

The central place that *Stanley* gives Justice Brandeis' dissent in *Olmstead*, a case raising no First Amendment claim, shows that *Stanley* rested as much on the Court's understanding of the Fourth Amendment as it did on the First. Indeed, in *Paris Adult Theatre I v. Slaton*, 413 U.S. 49 (1973), the Court suggested that reliance on the Fourth Amendment not only supported the Court's outcome in *Stanley* but actually was *necessary* to it: "If obscene material unprotected by the First Amendment in itself carried with it a 'penumbra' of constitutionally protected privacy, this Court would not have found it necessary to decide *Stanley* on the narrow

basis of the 'privacy of the home,' which was hardly more than a reaffirmation that 'a man's home is his castle.'" 413 U.S., at 66. "The right of the people to be secure in their . . . houses," expressly guaranteed by the Fourth Amendment, is perhaps the most "textual" of the various constitutional provisions that inform our understanding of the right to privacy, and thus I cannot agree with the Court's statement that "[the] right pressed upon us here has no . . . support in the text of the Constitution." Indeed, the right of an individual to conduct intimate relationships in the intimacy of his or her own home seems to me to be the heart of the Constitution's protection of privacy.

III

The Court's failure to comprehend the magnitude of the liberty interests at stake in this case leads it to slight the question whether petitioner, on behalf of the State, has justified Georgia's infringement on these interests. I believe that neither of the two general justifications for § 16-6-2 that petitioner has advanced warrants dismissing respondent's challenge for failure to state a claim.

First, petitioner asserts that the acts made criminal by the statute may have serious adverse consequences for "the general public health and welfare," such as spreading communicable diseases or fostering other criminal activity. Inasmuch as this case was dismissed by the District Court on the pleadings, it is not surprising that the record before us is barren of any evidence to support petitioner's claim.[3]

---

3. Even if a court faced with a challenge to § 16-6-2 were to apply simple rational-basis scrutiny to the statute, Georgia would be required to show an actual connection between the forbidden acts and the ill-effects it seeks to prevent. The connection between the acts prohibited by § 16-6-2 and the harms identified by petitioner in his brief before this Court is a subject of hot dispute, hardly amenable to dismissal under Federal Rule of Civil Procedure 12(b)(6). Compare, *e. g.*, Brief for Petitioner 36–37 and Brief for David Robinson, Jr., as *Amicus Curiae* 23–28, on the one hand, with *People v. Onofre*, 415 N. E. 2d 936, 941 (N.Y. 1980); Brief for the Attorney General of the State of New York, joined by the Attorney General of the State of California, as *Amici Curiae* 11–14; and Brief for the American Psychological Association and American Public Health Association as *Amici Curiae* 19–27, on the other.

In light of the state of the record, I see no justification for the Court's attempt to equate the private, consensual sexual activity at issue here with the "possession in the home of drugs, firearms, or stolen goods," to which *Stanley* refused to extend its protection. 394 U.S., at 568, n. 11. None of the behavior so mentioned in *Stanley* can properly be viewed as "[victimless]:" drugs and weapons are inherently dangerous, see, *e. g.*, *McLaughlin v. United States*, 476 U.S. 16 (1986), and for property to be "stolen," someone must have been wrongfully deprived of it. Nothing in the record before the Court provides any justification for finding the activity forbidden by § 16-6-2 to be physically dangerous, either to the persons engaged in it or to others.[4]

The core of petitioner's defense of § 16-6-2, however, is that respondent and others who engage in the conduct prohibited by § 16-6-2 interfere with Georgia's exercise of the " 'right of the Nation and of the States to maintain a decent society,' " *Paris Adult Theatre I v. Slaton*, 413 U.S., at 59-60, quoting *Jacobellis v. Ohio*, 378 U.S. 184, 199 (1964) (Warren, C. J., dissenting). Essentially, petitioner argues, and the Court agrees, that the fact that the acts described in § 16-6-2 "for hundreds of years, if not thousands, have been uniformly condemned as immoral" is a sufficient reason to permit a State to ban them today.

I cannot agree that either the length of time a majority has held its convictions or the passions with which it defends them can withdraw legislation from this Court's scrutiny. See, *e. g.*, *Roe v. Wade*, 410 U.S. 113 (1973); *Loving v. Virginia*, 388 U.S. 1 (1967); *Brown v. Board of Education*, 347 U.S. 483 (1954).[5] As Justice Jackson wrote so eloquently for the Court in *West Virginia Board of Education v. Barnette*, 319 U.S. 624, 641-642 (1943), "we apply the limitations of the Constitution with no fear that

---

4. Although I do not think it necessary to decide today issues that are not even remotely before us, it does seem to me that a court could find simple, analytically sound distinctions between certain private, consensual sexual conduct, on the one hand, and adultery and incest (the only two vaguely specific "sexual crimes" to which the majority points), on the other. For example, marriage, in addition to its spiritual aspects, is a civil contract that entitles the contracting parties to a variety of governmentally provided benefits. A state might define the contractual commitment necessary to become eligible for these benefits to include a commitment of fidelity and then punish individuals for breaching that contract. Moreover, a state might conclude that adultery is likely to injure third persons, in particular, spouses and children of persons who engage in extramarital affairs. With respect to incest, a court might well agree with respondent that the nature of familial relationships renders true consent to incestuous activity sufficiently problematical that a blanket prohibition of such activity is warranted. Notably, the Court makes no effort to explain why it has chosen to group private, consensual homosexual activity with adultery and incest rather than with private, consensual heterosexual activity by unmarried persons or, indeed, with oral or anal sex within marriage.

5. The parallel between *Loving* and this case is almost uncanny. There, too, the State relied on a religious justification for its law. Compare 388 U.S., at 3 (quoting trial court's statement that "Almighty God created the races white, black, yellow, malay and red, and he placed them on separate continents. . . . The fact that he separated the races shows that he did not intend for the races to mix"), with Brief for Petitioner 20–21 (relying on the Old and New Testaments and the writings of St. Thomas Aquinas to show that "traditional Judeo-Christian values proscribe such conduct"). There, too, defenders of the challenged statute relied heavily on the fact that when the Fourteenth Amendment was ratified, most of the States had similar prohibitions. Compare Brief for Appellee in *Loving v. Virginia*, O. T. 1966, No. 395, pp. 28–29, with [majority opinion]. There, too, at the time the case came before the Court, many of the states still had criminal statutes concerning the conduct at issue. Compare 388 U.S., at 6, n. 5 (noting that sixteen states still outlawed interracial marriage), with [majority opinion] (noting that twenty-four states and the District of Columbia have sodomy statutes). Yet the Court held, not only that the invidious racism of Virginia's law violated the equal protection clause, see 388 U.S., at 7–12, but also that the law deprived the Lovings of due process by denying them the "freedom of choice to marry" that had "long been recognized as one of the vital personal rights essential to the orderly pursuit of happiness by free men." *Id.*, at 12.

freedom to be intellectually and spiritually diverse or even contrary will disintegrate the social organization. . . . [Freedom] to differ is not limited to things that do not matter much. That would be a mere shadow of freedom. The test of its substance is the right to differ as to things that touch the heart of the existing order." See also Karst, 89 Yale L. J., at 627. It is precisely because the issue raised by this case touches the heart of what makes individuals what they are that we should be especially sensitive to the rights of those whose choices upset the majority.

The assertion that "traditional Judeo-Christian values proscribe" the conduct involved cannot provide an adequate justification for § 16-6-2. That certain, but by no means all, religious groups condemn the behavior at issue gives the State no license to impose their judgments on the entire citizenry. The legitimacy of secular legislation depends instead on whether the State can advance some justification for its law beyond its conformity to religious doctrine. See, e. g., McGowan v. Maryland, 366 U.S. 420, 429-453 (1961); Stone v. Graham, 449 U.S. 39 (1980). Thus, far from buttressing his case, petitioner's invocation of Leviticus, Romans, St. Thomas Aquinas, and sodomy's heretical status during the Middle Ages undermines his suggestion that § 16-6-2 represents a legitimate use of secular coercive power.[6] A State can no more punish private behavior because of religious intolerance than it can punish such behavior because of racial animus. "The Constitution cannot control such prejudices, but neither can it tolerate them. Private biases may be outside the reach of the law, but the law cannot, directly

or indirectly, give them effect." Palmore v. Sidoti, 466 U.S. 429, 433 (1984). No matter how uncomfortable a certain group may make the majority of this Court, we have held that "[mere] public intolerance or animosity cannot constitutionally justify the deprivation of a person's physical liberty." O'Connor v. Donaldson, 422 U.S. 563, 575 (1975). See also Cleburne v. Cleburne Living Center, Inc., 473 U.S. 432 (1985); United States Dept. of Agriculture v. Moreno, 413 U.S. 528, 534 (1973).

Nor can § 16-6-2 be justified as a "morally neutral" exercise of Georgia's power to "protect the public environment," Paris Adult Theatre I, 413 U.S. at 68-69. Certainly, some private behavior can affect the fabric of society as a whole. Reasonable people may differ about whether particular sexual acts are moral or immoral, but "we have ample evidence for believing that people will not abandon morality, will not think any better of murder, cruelty and dishonesty, merely because some private sexual practice which they abominate is not punished by the law." H. L. A. Hart, "Immorality and Treason," reprinted in The Law As Literature 220, 225 (L. Blom-Cooper ed. 1961). Petitioner and the Court fail to see the difference between laws that protect public sensibilities and those that enforce private morality. Statutes banning public sexual activity are entirely consistent with protecting the individual's liberty interest in decisions concerning sexual relations: the same recognition that those decisions are intensely private which justifies protecting them from governmental interference can justify protecting individuals from unwilling exposure to the

---

6. The theological nature of the origin of Anglo-American anti-sodomy statutes is patent. It was not until 1533 that sodomy was made a secular offense in England. 25 Hen. VIII, ch. 6. Until that time, the offense was, in Sir James Stephen's words, "merely ecclesiastical." 2 J. Stephen, A History of the Criminal Law of England, 429–430 (1883). Pollock and Maitland similarly observed that "[the] crime against nature . . . was so closely connected with heresy that the vulgar had but one name for both." 2 F. Pollock & F. Maitland, The History of English Law 554, (1895). The transfer of jurisdiction over prosecutions for sodomy to the secular courts seems primarily due to the alteration of ecclesiastical jurisdiction attendant on England's break with the Roman Catholic Church, rather than to any new understanding of the sovereign's interest in preventing or punishing the behavior involved. Cf. 6 E. Coke, Institutes, ch. 10 (4th ed. 1797).

sexual activities of others. But the mere fact that intimate behavior may be punished when it takes place in public cannot dictate how States can regulate intimate behavior that occurs in intimate places. See *Paris Adult Theatre I*, 413 U.S. at 66, n. 13 ("marital intercourse on a street corner or a theater stage" can be forbidden despite the constitutional protection identified in *Griswold v. Connecticut*, 381 U.S. 479 (1965).[7]

This case involves no real interference with the rights of others, for the mere knowledge that other individuals do not adhere to one's value system cannot be a legally cognizable interest, cf. *Diamond v. Charles*, 476 U.S. 54, 65-66 (1986), let alone an interest that can justify invading the houses, hearts, and minds of citizens who choose to live their lives differently.

IV

It took but three years for the Court to see the error in its analysis in *Minersville School District v. Gobitis*, 310 U.S. 586 (1940), and to recognize that the threat to national cohe-

sion posed by a refusal to salute the flag was vastly outweighed by the threat to those same values posed by compelling such a salute. See *West Virginia Board of Education v. Barnette*, 319 U.S. 624 (1943). I can only hope that here, too, the Court soon will reconsider its analysis and conclude that depriving individuals of the right to choose for themselves how to conduct their intimate relationships poses a far greater threat to the values most deeply rooted in our Nation's history than tolerance of nonconformity could ever do. Because I think the Court today betrays those values, I dissent.

JUSTICE STEVENS, with whom JUSTICE BRENNAN and JUSTICE MARSHALL join, dissenting.

Like the statute that is challenged in this case,[1] the rationale of the Court's opinion applies equally to the prohibited conduct regardless of whether the parties who engage in it are married or unmarried, or are of the same or different sexes.[2] Sodomy was condemned as an odious and sinful type of behavior during the formative period of the common law.[3] That condemnation was equally damning for heterosexual and homo-

---

7. At oral argument a suggestion appeared that, while the Fourth Amendment's special protection of the home might prevent the State from enforcing § 16-6-2 against individuals who engage in consensual sexual activity there, that protection would not make the statute invalid. The suggestion misses the point entirely. If the law is not invalid, then the police *can* invade the home to enforce it, provided, of course, that they obtain a determination of probable cause from a neutral magistrate. One of the reasons for the Court's holding in *Griswold v. Connecticut*, 381 U.S. 479 (1965), was precisely the possibility, and repugnancy, of permitting searches to obtain evidence regarding the use of contraceptives. *Id.*, at 485–486. Permitting the kinds of searches that might be necessary to obtain evidence of the sexual activity banned by § 16-6-2 seems no less intrusive, or repugnant. Cf. *Winston v. Lee*, 470 U.S. 753 (1985); *Mary Beth G. v. City of Chicago*, 723 F.2d 1263, 1274 (7th Cir. 1983).

1. See Ga. Code Ann. § 16-6-2(a) (1984) ("A person commits the offense of sodomy when he performs or submits to any sexual act involving the sex organs of one person and the mouth or anus of another").

2. The Court states that the "issue presented is whether the Federal Constitution confers a fundamental right upon homosexuals to engage in sodomy and hence invalidates the laws of the many States that still make such conduct illegal and have done so for a very long time." In reality, however, it is the indiscriminate prohibition of sodomy, heterosexual as well as homosexual, that has been present "for a very long time." See nn. 3, 4, and 5, *infra*. Moreover, the reasoning the Court employs would provide the same support for the statute as it is written as it does for the statute as it is narrowly construed by the Court.

3. See, *e. g.*, 1 W. Hawkins, Pleas of the Crown 9 (6th ed. 1787) ("All unnatural carnal copulations, whether with man or beast, seem to come under the notion of sodomy, which was felony by the ancient common law, and punished, according to some authors, with burning; according to others, . . . with burying alive"); 4 W. Blackstone, Commentaries

sexual sodomy.[4] Moreover, it provided no special exemption for married couples.[5] The license to cohabit and to produce legitimate offspring simply did not include any permission to engage in sexual conduct that was considered a "crime against nature."

The history of the Georgia statute before us clearly reveals this traditional prohibition of heterosexual, as well as homosexual, sodomy.[6] Indeed, at one point in the twentieth century, Georgia's law was construed to permit certain sexual conduct between homosexual women even though such conduct was prohibited between heterosexuals.[7] The history of the statutes cited by the majority as proof for the proposition that sodomy is not constitutionally protected, similarly reveals a prohibition on heterosexual, as well as homosexual, sodomy.[8]

Because the Georgia statute expresses the traditional view that sodomy is an immoral kind of conduct regardless of the identity of the persons who engage in it, I believe that a proper analysis of its constitutionality requires consideration of two questions: First, may a State totally prohibit the described conduct by means of a neutral law applying without exception to all persons subject to its jurisdiction? If not, may the State save the statute by announcing that it will only enforce the law against homosexuals? The two questions merit separate discussion.

I

Our prior cases make two propositions abundantly clear. First, the fact that the governing majority in a State has traditionally viewed a particular practice as immoral is not a sufficient reason for upholding a law prohibiting the practice; neither history nor tradition could save a law prohibiting miscegenation from constitutional attack.[9] Second, individual decisions by married persons, concerning the intimacies of their physical relationship, even when not intended to produce offspring, are a form of "liberty" protected by the due process clause

---

*215 (discussing "the infamous *crime against nature*, committed either with man or beast; a crime which ought to be strictly and impartially proved, and then as strictly and impartially punished").

4. See 1 E. East, Pleas of the Crown, 480 (1803) ("This offence, concerning which the least notice is the best, consists in a carnal knowledge committed against the order of nature by man with man, or in the same unnatural manner with woman, or by man or woman in any manner with beast"); J. Hawley & M. McGregor, The Criminal Law 287 (3d ed. 1899) ("Sodomy is the carnal knowledge against the order of nature by two persons with each other, or of a human being with a beast. . . . The offense may be committed between a man and a woman, or between two male persons, or between a man or a woman and a beast").

5. See J. May, The Law of Crimes § 203 (2d ed. 1893) ("Sodomy, otherwise called buggery, bestiality, and the *crime against nature*, is the unnatural copulation of two persons with each other, or of a human being with a beast. . . . It may be committed by a man with a man, by a man with a beast, or by a woman with a beast, or by a man with a woman — his wife, in which case, if she consent, she is an accomplice").

6. The predecessor of the current Georgia statute provided: "Sodomy is the carnal knowledge and connection against the order of nature, by man with man, or in the same unnatural manner with woman." Ga. Code, Tit. 1, Pt. 4, § 4251 (1861).

   This prohibition of heterosexual sodomy was not purely hortatory. See, *e. g.*, *Comer v. State*, 94 S. E. 314 (Ga. App. 1917) (affirming prosecution for consensual heterosexual sodomy).

7. See *Thompson v. Aldredge*, 200 S. E. 799 (Ga. 1939).

8. A review of the statutes cited by the majority discloses that, in 1791, in 1868, and today, the vast majority of sodomy statutes do not differentiate between homosexual and heterosexual sodomy.

9. See *Loving v. Virginia*, 388 U.S. 1 (1967). Interestingly, miscegenation was once treated as a crime similar to sodomy. See Hawley & McGregor, The Criminal Law, at 287 (discussing crime of sodomy); *id.*, at 288 (discussing crime of miscegenation).

of the Fourteenth Amendment. *Griswold v. Connecticut*, 381 U.S. 479 (1965). Moreover, this protection extends to intimate choices by unmarried as well as married persons. *Carey v. Population Services International*, 431 U.S. 678 (1977); *Eisenstadt v. Baird*, 405 U.S. 438 (1972).

In consideration of claims of this kind, the Court has emphasized the individual interest in privacy, but its decisions have actually been animated by an even more fundamental concern. As I wrote some years ago:

"These cases do not deal with the individual's interest in protection from unwarranted public attention, comment, or exploitation. They deal, rather, with the individual's right to make certain unusually important decisions that will affect his own, or his family's, destiny. The Court has referred to such decisions as implicating 'basic values,' as being 'fundamental,' and as being dignified by history and tradition. The character of the Court's language in these cases brings to mind the origins of the American heritage of freedom — the abiding interest in individual liberty that makes certain state intrusions on the citizen's right to decide how he will live his own life intolerable. Guided by history, our tradition of respect for the dignity of individual choice in matters of conscience and the restraints implicit in the federal system, federal judges have accepted the responsibility for recognition and protection of these rights in appropriate cases." *Fitzgerald v. Porter Memorial Hospital*, 523 F.2d 716, 719-720 (7th Cir. 1975) (footnotes omitted), *cert. denied*, 425 U.S. 916 (1976).

Society has every right to encourage its individual members to follow particular traditions in expressing affection for one another and in gratifying their personal desires. It, of course, may prohibit an individual from imposing his will on another to satisfy his own selfish interests. It also may prevent an individual from interfering with, or violating, a legally sanctioned and protected relationship, such as marriage. And it may explain the relative advantages and disadvantages of different forms of intimate expression. But when individual married couples are isolated from observation by others, the way in which they voluntarily choose to conduct their intimate relations is a matter for them — not the State — to decide.[10] The essential "liberty" that animated the development of the law in cases like *Griswold*, *Eisenstadt*, and *Carey* surely embraces the right to engage in nonreproductive, sexual conduct that others may consider offensive or immoral.

Paradoxical as it may seem, our prior cases thus establish that a State may not prohibit sodomy within "the sacred precincts of marital bedrooms," *Griswold*, 381 U.S., at 485, or, indeed, between unmarried heterosexual adults. *Eisenstadt*, 405 U.S., at 453. In all events, it is perfectly clear that the State of Georgia may not totally prohibit the conduct proscribed by § 16-6-2 of the Georgia Criminal Code.

II

If the Georgia statute cannot be enforced as it is written — if the conduct it seeks to prohibit is a protected form of liberty for the vast majority of Georgia's citizens — the State

---

10. Indeed, the Georgia Attorney General concedes that Georgia's statute would be unconstitutional if applied to a married couple. See Tr. of Oral Arg. 8 (stating that application of the statute to a married couple "would be unconstitutional" because of the "right of marital privacy as identified by the Court in *Griswold*"). Significantly, Georgia passed the current statute three years after the Court's decision in *Griswold*.

must assume the burden of justifying a selective application of its law. Either the persons to whom Georgia seeks to apply its statute do not have the same interest in "liberty" that others have, or there must be a reason why the State may be permitted to apply a generally applicable law to certain persons that it does not apply to others.

The first possibility is plainly unacceptable. Although the meaning of the principle that "all men are created equal" is not always clear, it surely must mean that every free citizen has the same interest in "liberty" that the members of the majority share. From the standpoint of the individual, the homosexual and the heterosexual have the same interest in deciding how he will live his own life, and, more narrowly, how he will conduct himself in his personal and voluntary associations with his companions. State intrusion into the private conduct of either is equally burdensome.

The second possibility is similarly unacceptable. A policy of selective application must be supported by a neutral and legitimate interest — something more substantial than a habitual dislike for, or ignorance about, the disfavored group. Neither the State nor the Court has identified any such interest in this case. The Court has posited as a justification for the Georgia statute "the presumed belief of a majority of the electorate in Georgia that homosexual sodomy is immoral and unacceptable." But the Georgia electorate has expressed no such belief — instead, its representatives enacted a law that presumably reflects the belief that *all sodomy* is immoral and unacceptable. Unless the Court is prepared to conclude that such a law

is constitutional, it may not rely on the work product of the Georgia legislature to support its holding. For the Georgia statute does not single out homosexuals as a separate class meriting special disfavored treatment.

Nor, indeed, does the Georgia prosecutor even believe that all homosexuals who violate this statute should be punished. This conclusion is evident from the fact that the respondent in this very case has formally acknowledged in his complaint and in court that he has engaged, and intends to continue to engage, in the prohibited conduct, yet the State has elected not to process criminal charges against him. As Justice Powell points out, moreover, Georgia's prohibition on private, consensual sodomy has not been enforced for decades.[11] The record of non-enforcement, in this case and in the last several decades, belies the Attorney General's representations about the importance of the State's selective application of its generally applicable law.[12]

Both the Georgia statute and the Georgia prosecutor thus completely fail to provide the Court with any support for the conclusion that homosexual sodomy, *simpliciter*, is considered unacceptable conduct in that State, and that the burden of justifying a selective application of the generally applicable law has been met.

III

The Court orders the dismissal of respondent's complaint even though the State's statute prohibits all sodomy; even

---

11. [citing to Justice Powell's concurrence]. See also Tr. of Oral Arg. 4–5 (argument of Georgia Attorney General) (noting, in response to question about prosecution "where the activity took place in a private residence," the "last case I can recall was back in the 1930s or 40s").

12. It is, of course, possible to argue that a statute has a purely symbolic role. Cf. *Carey v. Population Services International*, 431 U.S. 678, 715, n. 3 (1977) (Stevens, J., concurring in part and concurring in judgment) ("The fact that the State admittedly has never brought a prosecution under the statute . . . is consistent with appellants' position that the purpose of the statute is merely symbolic"). Since the Georgia Attorney General does not even defend the statute as written, however, see n. 10, *supra*, the State cannot possibly rest on the notion that the statute may be defended for its symbolic message.

though that prohibition is concededly unconstitutional with respect to heterosexuals; and even though the State's *post hoc*
explanations for selective application are
belied by the State's own actions. At the
very least, I think it clear at this early stage

of the litigation that respondent has alleged
a constitutional claim sufficient to withstand a motion to dismiss.[13]

I respectfully dissent.

Notes

1. The *Hardwick* case was decided by a 5-4 vote, with Justice Powell providing the critical fifth
   vote for the majority. Several days after the decision was issued, the *Washington Post* ran a
   story shedding light on Justice Powell's vote:

   > The most controversial Supreme Court ruling this year, the 5-to-4 decision upholding a
   > Georgia law criminalizing certain homosexual acts, was initially decided the other way
   > until Justice Lewis F. Powell Jr. changed his mind, according to informed sources.
   >
   > The case, *Bowers v. Hardwick* — which gay rights groups call their Dred Scott decision
   > — was argued on Monday, March 31, and the Justices met in secret conference several
   > days later to discuss it.
   >
   > Four Justices, led by Harry A. Blackmun, voted to say that a constitutional right to
   > privacy protects homosexuals and that the state would have to show important reasons to
   > outlaw sodomy among consenting adults.
   >
   > Though Powell did not agree with the reasoning, he voiced sufficient distaste for the
   > anti-sodomy law that he agreed to provide the crucial fifth vote for an overall decision
   > striking the Georgia statute.
   >
   > Four other Justices, led by Byron R. White, said the Constitution does not grant
   > homosexuals a right to such conduct, even in their homes.
   >
   > Powell's vote was tentative. All votes in conference are preliminary and can be changed
   > at any time up to the formal announcement of the decision by the court.
   >
   > With a fifth vote, Blackmun could have written a majority opinion that would have
   > had the effect of overturning antisodomy laws in 24 states and the District of Columbia.
   >
   > Within several days of the conference, however, Powell sent a brief memo to his fellow
   > justices saying that he was switching his vote and would, given the "posture" of this case,
   > join White and the others to uphold the Georgia law.
   >
   > Sources were unable to pinpoint why Powell changed his mind. They said a critical
   > factor was that Michael Hardwick, a gay Atlanta bartender, had not been prosecuted.
   > Instead, Hardwick, through a civil lawsuit, was asking the court to declare the law
   > unconstitutional.

---

13. Indeed, at this stage, it appears that the statute indiscriminately authorizes a policy of selective prosecution that is
    neither limited to the class of homosexual persons nor embraces all persons in that class, but rather applies to those
    who may be arbitrarily selected by the prosecutor for reasons that are not revealed either in the record of this case or
    in the text of the statute. If that is true, although the text of the statute is clear enough, its true meaning may be "so
    intolerably vague that evenhanded enforcement of the law is a virtual impossibility." *Marks v. United States*, 430 U.S.
    188, 198 (1977) (Stevens, J., concurring in part and dissenting in part).

Powell stayed with White, despite a strident dissent circulated by a furious Blackmun, and joined the majority opinion issued June 30. . . .

When the court announced its ruling in the Georgia case, Powell issued a one-paragraph concurring opinion explaining why he was joining White. He strongly hinted that he would not vote to uphold such laws in future cases if lawyers argued that excessive prison terms for homosexual acts violated the constitutional prohibition against cruel and unusual punishment. . . .

Powell, sources said, dislikes anti-sodomy laws, feeling that they are useless, never enforced and unenforceable. . . . The sources said Powell would vote to repeal antisodomy laws if he were a legislator. There have been proscriptions against sodomy from the first days of recorded history. The court virtually would have to cast these aside under Blackmun's theory, Powell felt.

In addition, Powell has long had trouble with the notion that the court could substitute its views of morality for those of elected officials. He was reluctant to have the Court recognize more special rights not spelled out in the Constitution, the sources said.

Powell's switch came before Blackmun had circulated his opinion to the other Justices for review. White also had not circulated a dissent. Powell, sources said, simply changed his mind.

Al Kamen, *Powell Changed Vote in Sodomy Case*, WASH. POST, July 13, 1986, at A1.

2. Several years later, during a speech at New York University, Justice Powell lamented his decision in the case:

Retired Supreme Court justice Lewis F. Powell Jr. told a group of law students last week that he regrets his 1986 vote upholding a Georgia statute that made homosexual sodomy a criminal offense. . . . . "I think I probably made a mistake in that one," Powell told a group of New York University law students, according to a story prepared for Monday's edition of the National Law Journal.

In an interview yesterday, Powell confirmed that he made the brief remarks when asked whether there was "any decision I made I had doubts about in retrospect." . . . Powell said yesterday that the case was a "close call" and that his vote was based on the fact that the statute had not been enforced for several decades. "That case was not a major case, and one of the reasons I voted the way I did was the case was a frivolous case" brought "just to see what the Court would do" on the subject, he said.

"So far as I'm concerned it's just a part of my past and not very important," he said. "I don't suppose I've devoted half an hour" to thinking about the decision since it was made.

Ruth Marcus, *Powell Regrets Backing Sodomy Law*, WASH. POST, Oct. 26, 1990, at A3. *See also* Allan Ides, Bowers v. Hardwick: *The Enigmatic Fifth Vote and the Reasonableness of Moral Certitude*, 49 WASH. & LEE L.R. 93 (1992).

3. There has been a considerable amount of academic commentary about the *Hardwick* decision, little of it favorable. *See, e.g.,* CHARLES FRIED, ORDER AND LAW: ARGUING THE REAGAN REVOLUTION 81-84 (1991) (arguing that *Hardwick* is wrongly decided); STEPHEN MACEDO, THE NEW RIGHT AND THE CONSTITUTION 70-71 (1987) (arguing that "original intent" in Justice White's majority opinion in *Hardwick* is a typical, "essentialist" avoidance of the "hard moral judgments required by the words actually adopted and written into law"); Anne B. Goldstein, *History, Homosexuality, and Political Values: Searching for the Hidden Determinants of* Bowers v. Hardwick, 97 YALE L.J. 1073 (1988); Thomas Stoddard, Bowers v. Hardwick: *Precedent by Personal Predilection*, 54 U. CHI. L. R. 648 (1987); Yvonne Tharpes, Comment, Bowers v. Hardwick *and the Legitimization of Homophobia in America*, 30 HOWARD L. J.

537 (1987); Mitchell Lloyd Brooks, Case Note, *Making the Best of an Unfortunate Decision*, 63 N.Y.U. LAW REV. 154 (1988).

4. While most of the commentary have focused on the Court's poor reasoning, some has challenged the framing of the case itself. The following is an excerpt from a provocative article by the philosopher Michael Sandel, *Moral Argument and Liberal Toleration: Abortion and Homosexuality*, 77 CAL. L. REV. 521 (1989) (citations omitted):

> The dissenters' argument for toleration in *Bowers v. Hardwick* illustrates the difficulties with the version of liberalism that ties toleration to autonomy rights alone. In refusing to extend the right of privacy to homosexuals, the majority in *Bowers* declared that none of the rights announced in earlier privacy cases resembled the rights homosexuals were seeking: "No connection between family, marriage, or procreation on the one hand and homosexual activity on the other has been demonstrated. . . ." Any reply to the Court's position would have to show some connection between the practices already subject to privacy protection and the homosexual practices not yet protected. What then is the resemblance between heterosexual intimacies on the one hand, and homosexual intimacies on the other, such that both are entitled to a constitutional right of privacy?
>
> This question might be answered in at least two different ways — one voluntarist, the other substantive. The first argues from the autonomy the practices reflect, whereas the second appeals to the human goods the practices realize. The voluntarist answer holds that people should be free to choose their intimate associations for themselves, regardless of the virtue or popularity of the practices they choose so long as they do not harm others. In this view, homosexual relationships resemble the heterosexual relationships the Court has already protected in that all reflect the choices of autonomous selves.
>
> By contrast, the substantive answer claims that much that is valuable in conventional marriage is also present in homosexual unions. In this view, the connection between heterosexual and homosexual relations is not that both result from individual choice but that both realize important human goods. Rather than rely on autonomy alone, this second line of reply articulates the virtues homosexual intimacy may share with heterosexual intimacy, along with any distinctive virtues of its own. It defends homosexual privacy the way *Griswold* defended marital privacy, by arguing that, like marriage, homosexual union may also be "intimate to the degree of being sacred . . . a harmony in living . . . a bilateral loyalty," an association for a "noble . . . purpose."
>
> Of these two possible replies, the dissenters in *Bowers* relied wholly on the first. Rather than protect homosexual intimacies for the human goods they share with intimacies the Court already protects, Justice Blackmun cast the Court's earlier cases in individualist terms, and found their reading applied equally to homosexuality because "much of the richness of a relationship will come from the freedom an individual has to choose the form and nature of these intensely personal bonds." At issue was not homosexuality as such but respect for the fact that "different individuals will make different choices" in deciding how to conduct their lives.
>
> Justice Stevens, in a separate dissent, also avoided referring to the values of homosexual intimacy may share with heterosexual love. Instead, he wrote broadly of "'the individual's right to make certain unusually important decisions'" and "'respect for the dignity of individual choice,'" rejecting the notion that such liberty belongs to heterosexuals alone. "From the standpoint of the individual, the homosexual and the heterosexual have the same interest in deciding how he will live his own life, and, more narrowly, how he will conduct himself in his personal and voluntary associations with his companions."

■ ■ ■

The case for toleration that brackets the morality of homosexuality has a powerful appeal. In the face of deep disagreement about values, it seems to ask the least of the contending parties. It offers social peace and respect for rights without the need for moral conversion. Those who view sodomy as sin need not be persuaded to change their minds, only to tolerate those who practice it in private. By insisting only that each respect the freedom of others to live the lives they choose, this toleration promises a basis for political agreement that does not await shared conceptions of morality.

Despite its promise, however, the neutral case for toleration is subject to two related difficulties. First, as a practical matter, it is by no means clear that social cooperation can be secured on the strength of autonomy rights alone, absent some measure of agreement on the moral permissibility of the practices at issue. It may not be accidental that the first practices subject to the right of privacy were accorded constitutional protection in cases that spoke of the sanctity of marriage and procreation. Only later did the Court abstract privacy rights from these practices and protect them without reference to the human goods they were once thought to make possible. This suggests that the voluntarist justification of privacy rights is dependent — politically as well as philosophically — on some measure of agreement that the practices protected are morally permissible.

A second difficulty with the voluntarist case for toleration concerns the quality of respect it secures. As the New York case [*People v. Onofre*] suggests, the analogy with *Stanley* tolerates homosexuality at the price of demeaning it; it puts homosexual intimacy on a par with obscenity — a base thing that should nonetheless be tolerated so long as it takes place in private. If *Stanley* rather than *Griswold* is the relevant analogy, the interest at stake is bound to be reduced, as the New York court reduced it, to "sexual gratification." (The only intimate relationship at stake in *Stanley* was between a man and his pornography.)

The majority in *Bowers* exploited this assumption by ridiculing the notion of a "fundamental right to engage in homosexual sodomy." The obvious reply is that *Bowers* is no more about a right to homosexual sodomy than *Griswold* was about a right to heterosexual intercourse. But by refusing to articulate the human goods that homosexual intimacy may share with heterosexual unions, the voluntarist case for toleration forfeits the analogy with *Griswold* and makes the ridicule difficult to refute.

The problem with the neutral case for toleration is the opposite side of its appeal; it leaves wholly unchallenged the adverse views of homosexuality itself. Unless those views can be plausibly addressed, even a court ruling in their favor is unlikely to win for homosexuals more than a thin and fragile toleration. A fuller respect would require, if not admiration, at least some appreciation of the lives homosexuals live. Such appreciation, however, is unlikely to be cultivated by a legal and political discourse conducted in terms of autonomy rights alone.

5. The lesbian and gay community in the United States reacted with outrage to the *Hardwick* decision. Demonstrations were staged throughout the United States, *see Hundreds Protest Supreme Court Sodomy Ruling,* N.Y. TIMES, Aug. 12, 1986, at A20, including a massive protest at the Supreme Court held during the 1987 March on Washington. This action, during which 600 individuals were arrested, was the largest civil disobedience ever at the Supreme Court. *See* Douglas Jehl, *600 Gay Rights Activists Arrested in Capitol Protest,* L.A. TIMES, Oct. 14, 1987, at 1.

The following excerpt expresses some of the anger that the decision evoked.

◆

CLOSE TO THE KNIVES

David Wojnarowicz

A number of months ago I read in the newspaper that there was a Supreme Court ruling which states that homosexuals in America have no constitutional rights against the government's invasion of their privacy. The paper stated that homosexuality is traditionaly condemned in America and only people who are heterosexual or married or who have families can expect these constitutional rights. There were no editorials. Nothing. Just flat cold type in the morning paper informing people of this. In most areas of the u.s.a. it is possible to murder a man and when one is brought to trial one has only to say that the victim was a queer and that he tried to touch you and the courts will set you free. When I read the newspaper article I felt something stirring in my hand; I felt a sensation like seeing oneself from miles above the earth or like looking at one's reflection in a mirror through the wrong end of a telescope. Realizing that I have nothing left to lose in my actions I let my hands become weapons, my teeth become weapons, every bone and muscle and fiber and ounce of blood become weapons, and I feel prepared for the rest of my life.

In my dreams I crawl across freshly clipped front lawns, past statues and dogs and cars containing your guardians. I enter your houses through the smallest cracks in the bricks that keep you feeling comfortable and safe. I cross your living rooms and go up your staircases and into your bedrooms where you lie sleeping. I wake you up and tell you a story about when I was ten years old and walking around Times Square looking for the weight of some man to lie across me and to replace the nonexistent hugs and kisses from my mom and dad, I got picked up by some guy who took me to a remote area of the waterfront in his car and proceeded to beat the shit out of me because he was so afraid of the impulses of heat stirring in his belly. I would have strangled him but my hands were too small to fit around his neck. I will wake you up and welcome you to your bad dream.

IV. AFTER *HARDWICK*

A. State Court Challenges

1. Within days of the *Hardwick* decision, the Missouri Supreme Court upheld the constitutionality of Missouri's sodomy law, rejecting a challenge based on the federal and state constitution. *Missouri v. Walsh*, 713 S.W.2d 508 (Mo. 1986).

DAVID WOJNAROWICZ, CLOSE TO THE KNIVES 80–81 (1991).

2. Since the *Hardwick* decision, the attempt to seek judicial repeal of state sodomy laws has shifted to the state court system, where advocates have argued that sodomy laws violate *state* constitutions. This effort was foreshadowed by a 1980 New York Court of Appeals decision striking down New York's sodomy law as violative of the federal and New York State constitutions, *People v. Onofre*, 51 N.Y.2d 476 (1980), *cert. denied*, 451 U.S. 987 (1981), and by the growing body of academic commentary calling for the utilization of state constitutions. *See, e.g.*, Juli A. Morris, *Challenging Sodomy Statutes: State Constitutional Protections for Sexual Privacy*, 66 IND. L.J. 609 (1991); Nan Feyler, *The Use of the State Constitutional Right to Privacy to Defeat State Sodomy Laws*, 14 N.Y.U. REV. L. & SOC. CHANGE 973 (1986); Jeff Rosen, *Salvaging Privacy: State Constitutions are Safest Refuge for Individual Rights*, LOS ANGELES DAILY J., July 12, 1991, at 6.

   Since *Hardwick*, state courts in Michigan, Kentucky, and Texas have struck down their state's sodomy law as violative of the state's constitution. The Michigan case was a decision by a state trial court judge, see *County Judge Strikes Down Michigan Sodomy Law*, U.P.I., July 10, 1990, that was not appealed by the state.

   In September of 1992, the Kentucky Supreme Court struck down that state's sodomy laws as violating the state constitution's right to privacy and equal protection. *Commonwealth v. Wasson*, 1992 Ky. LEXIS 140 (Sept. 24, 1992).

   In *State v. Morales*, 826 S.W.2d 201 (Tex. App. 1992), an intermediate state court struck down the Texas sodomy law. *Morales* was heard by the state's highest court in January 1993.

3. In a Minnesota case widely watched as a challenge to the constitutionality of that state's sodomy law, the state's highest court avoided consideration of the straightforward constitutional question by framing the facts of the case that they involved "commercial sex." *See State v. Gray*, 413 N.W.2d 107 (Minn. 1987) (en banc).

4. Sodomy law challenges have also arisen in criminal prosecutions of individuals for *forcible* sodomy. In some of these cases, the defense is that the act complained of happened, but was consensual, not forcible. If a jury cannot convict the defendant of forcible sodomy — because of the disputed testimony about whether the victim consented — the jury will sometimes convict the defendant of the lesser included offense of consensual sodomy. Defendants so convicted then have raised constitutional objections to their confinement for consensual sodomy. *See, e.g., Post v. State*, 715 P.2d 1105 (Okl. Crim. App. 1986); *Schochet v. State*, 580 A.2d 176 (Md. 1990); *Fry v. Patseavouras*, 1992 U.S. App. LEXIS 21048 (4th Cir. 1992). These cases involved heterosexual sodomy. In the *Post* case, the Oklahoma Supreme Court struck down the defendant's conviction for consensual heterosexual sodomy, ruling that it violated the federal constitutional right to privacy. The case was decided the same year as the *Hardwick* case, but the Supreme Court declined the opportunity to review it. *Oklahoma v. Post*, 479 U.S. 890 (1986). In the *Schochet* case, Maryland's highest court ruled that in enacting the state's sodomy law, the legislature did not intend for it to cover consensual heterosexual sodomy. In the *Fry* case, the U.S. Court of Appeals for the Fourth Circuit ruled that the rationale of the *Hardwick* case applied to sodomy committed by unmarried heterosexuals.

B. Lesbian/Gay Life After *Hardwick*

1. The existence of sodomy laws means that lesbians and gay men continue to risk arrest simply by expressing their love for one another, even if the expression takes place in private, between consenting adults. Sodomy laws are rarely directly enforced, though occasionally, individuals

are arrested for consensual sex in private. *See, e.g., United States v. Baum*, 30 M.J. 626 (N.-M.C.C.M.R. 1990) (military prosecution for violation of sodomy law, 10 U.S.C. § 925, by engaging in oral sex, among other less serious offenses).

2. More often, individuals, particularly gay men, are arrested for engaging in sex acts in quasi-public places. *See, e.g., Carter v. State*, 500 S.W.2d 368 (Ark. 1973) (conviction for fellatio in car upheld, along with relevant sodomy statute and defendant's eight-year sentence); *Canfield v. State*, 506 F.2d 987 (Okl. Crim. App. 1973) (upholding conviction and fifteen-year sentence upheld for act of oral sodomy in parked car).

    The existence and constitutionality of sodomy laws are somewhat irrelevant to these arrests as the police often use other statutes as a means of harassing and abusing lesbians and gay men. Loitering, lewd and lascivious behavior, indecent exposure, and other laws and ordinances give law enforcement officials semi-legitimate power to harass gay people. *See, e.g., People v. Superior Court*, 758 P.2d 1046 (Cal. 1988) (upholding "loitering with a lewd purpose" statute that is often used against gay people, declaring that the statute is not unduly vague or disproportionately applied to gay people); *Elmore v. Atlantic Zayre, Inc.*, 341 S.E.2d 905 (Ga. App. 1986) (a civil wrongful arrest and violation of privacy suit declaring that arrest based on "peeking through a crack in the bathroom ceiling" was not unreasonable regardless of whether sodomy was committed). *See generally* JOHN D'EMILIO, SEXUAL POLITICS, SEXUAL COMMUNITIES 146 n.50 (1983). Courts rarely are sympathetic to the constitutional aspects of these arrests. *But see D.C. M.S. v. City of St. Louis*, 795 F.2d 652 (8th Cir. 1986) (ruling that ordinances — against cross-dressing and "lewd and indecent conduct" — upon which two men were arrested were unconstitutionally vague, not providing fair notice).

3. The existence of sodomy laws indirectly affects the lives of lesbians and gay men every day. As will be apparent throughout this book, sodomy laws are frequently used as the basis for constraining — or denying — lesbian and gay legal rights. The Court's ruling in *Hardwick* sustaining the constitutionality of these laws has also been read to undermine other constitutionally based claims made by lesbians and gay men, particularly claims under the equal protection clause. *See, infra*, at Chapter Four, *Lesbians and Gay Men in the Workplace*.

THREE

The Regulation of Lesbian and Gay Identity:
Coming Out — Speaking Out — Joining In

Free expression plays a central role in the lives of lesbians and gay men because virtually all the milestones of lesbian and gay life — coming out, meeting other gay people, finding a lover, participating in a gay rights rally — depend upon the public identification of oneself as homosexual. This is so because, unlike many other minority groups, lesbians and gay men are not visually identifiable. Therefore, gay people simply do not "exist" in the eyes of the public unless they identify themselves by "coming out." Until lesbians and gay men can identify themselves without fear of harassment or imprisonment, however, many will not be able to fulfill a central aspect of their personhood.

Free expression also enables lesbians and gay men to create their own groups, communities, and cultures. If gay people could not identify themselves openly they would never be able to meet with other lesbians and gay men to form meaningful friendships, sexual relationships, support groups, lobbying groups, educational groups, or legal-aid organizations.

This chapter explores these events in the lives of lesbians and gay men. Part I considers lesbian and gay high school students and their quest to come out. Part II extends the focus to college and university students. Part III focuses on adult lesbian and gay associations, ranging from lesbian and gay political groups to lesbian and gay bars. Part IV considers the regulation of speech about lesbian and gay issues. Part V looks at the legal regulation of "outing." And the Chapter concludes with several readings about the current state of the lesbian/gay community.

The organizing legal principle of this chapter is the First Amendment to the United States Constitution. Historically, federal and state government officials have attempted to silence lesbians and gay men by firing public employees who admit that they are gay, by banning the formation of lesbian and gay student organizations, by denying legal recognition to organizations and establishments that primarily serve lesbians and gay men (through refusals to incorporate, to grant tax-exemption, or to license), by forbidding gay people to assemble and to rally for political change, and by censoring homoerotic publications, pornography, speech, and artwork.

The First Amendment of the U.S. Constitution is meant to protect lesbians and gay men from this kind of undue governmental interference. Thus, as this chapter examines the "coming out" process for lesbians and gay men, it simultaneously traces the government's attempts to regulate lesbian and gay speech and the resulting effort to ensure legal protection.

I. HIGH SCHOOL

A. Lesbian and Gay Adolescence

Adolescence is a time when most young people first consider their own sexuality, and hence their own sexual orientation. For those who believe they are lesbians or gay men, this can be a very perilous time. The following pieces provide some context to this struggle.

♦

GAY YOUTH AND THE RIGHT TO EDUCATION
Donna Dennis and Ruth Harlow

[T]oday education has become the *sine qua non* of useful existence.
—California Supreme Court in *Serrano v. Priest*[5]

I. THE SCHOOLS' OBSTRUCTION OF GAY STUDENTS' PUBLIC EDUCATION

Public school administrators and teachers prevent gay students from learning in many devastating ways. They harass, misinform, and unfairly punish gay students; almost always, they refuse to protect gay youth from peer violence. In many schools, the discriminatory atmosphere forces gay students to concentrate on survival rather than education and destroys gay teenagers' self-esteem during a crucial developmental period.[7]

Teacher attacks on gay students directly obstruct learning. Because teachers most often harass gay students to punish deviations from traditional sex roles, effeminate boys or girls with "masculine" traits inspire the cruelest and most frequent abuse. Recently a high school gym teacher ridiculed for months a sixteen-year-old boy, known to be gay, and finally compelled him to attend girls' gym class. Although the student complained to his principal, no remedial action was taken. The boy consequently dropped out of school.

Teachers also use harassment to show gay students and their classmates that gay persons are not welcome members of the community. In the District of Columbia, for example, several teachers repeatedly taunted an openly gay fifteen-year-old, calling him "faggot" and "fruit," knowing that he was also being harassed and beaten by fellow students. When he complained to other

---

5. Serrano v. Priest, 487 P.2d 1241, 1257 (Cal. 1971).

7. One 18-year-old writes, "High school to me was a terrifying and intimidating place for a young gay male." Testimony by Young Adults and Teachers, transcribed by Philadelphia Lesbian and Gay Task Force (1985) (available from Philadelphia Lesbian and Gay Task Force). A 24-year-old woman says,

Donna Dennis & Ruth Harlow, *Gay Youth And The Right To Education*, 4 YALE LAW & POLICY REVIEW 446 (1986).

teachers and the principal, they blamed the gay student for his mistreatment and recommended that he leave school. In Rhode Island, a high school principal expressed relief in his opening-day speech to the student body that the one openly gay student in the school would not be returning for his senior year. The principal neglected to mention that the boy quit school because teachers and students taunted him when he "came out" the previous year.[11]

Other high school authorities respond to gay students as if they were emotionally or mentally handicapped. Although gay students are often isolated, confused, and in need of advice, few schools permit constructive counseling that advises gay teenagers how to contend with taunting and violence and provides them with accurate information about their sexual orientation. Instead, administrators and teachers often label gay students "ill" and send them to counselors for a cure. Last year officials at a New York high school transferred a fifteen-year-old girl to a school for the mentally retarded simply because she had written a love note to her female teacher.

School administrators also act in more subtle ways to deprive gay teenagers of pub-lic education's benefits. In some high schools, guidance counselors inform gay students that homosexuals cannot become professionals and must settle for less challenging occupations. School-board committees choose sex education textbooks that depict male homosexuals as depraved child molesters. School boards subject books that display tolerance toward homosexuality or are relevant to the experience of gay adolescents to an especially stringent process of review, making it impossible for these books to reach school libraries or classrooms.

For gay teenagers, the failure of school officials to provide protection from peer harassment and violence stands out as the predominant feature of the discriminatory public school environment. When schools condone attacks on gay students, they endanger the students' safety and obstruct their ability to learn. Peer violence against gay youth is often severe. In the District of Columbia, for instance, gay students attend school aware that some gay students have been hospitalized after beatings by other students. Fear of such assaults leads many gay teenagers to drop out of school. In Philadelphia a gay teenager, illiterate, was finally

---

[L]esbianism was totally invalidated by the institution in the following ways:

1. Gay teachers invisible — closeted, did not feel safe to "come out."

2. Curriculum completely heterosexist.....

3. Heterosexual assumptions by teachers, and administrators, in the classroom and all other settings. No validation whatsoever for the lesbian/gay student.

4. Frequent instances of teachers or administrators demonstrating through "jokes," stories, examples or innuendos their anti-gay bias.

5. Harassment or intimidation by other students was *encouraged* by all of these official sanctions for homophobia....

I feel very strongly that I was cheated out of educational and social supports thru the public school system because of its institutionalized homophobia, and suffered mental and emotional trauma with no recourse.

Testimony by Young Adults and Teachers, transcribed by Philadelphia Lesbian and Gay Task Force (1984) (emphasis in original). Students in San Francisco relate similar problems with the schools. *See* Minutes of Coordination Council, San Francisco Delinquency Prevention Commission (Apr. 3, 1986).

11. *See* A. FRICKE, REFLECTIONS OF A ROCK LOBSTER 55–56 (1981). Teachers often convey animosity toward gay persons through "jokes" or sarcastic remarks. For example, in an eighth-grade sex education class, the teacher responded to a student's remark by saying, "Yeah, you let some faggot try to stick his thing up my butt, I'll break his nose and then cut his joint off." The class broke out in laughter; the gay boy in the class joined in "to hide my embarrassment and disgust with myself." Testimony by Young Adults and Teachers, Transcribed by Philadelphia Lesbian and Gay Task Force (1984).

driven out of high school by violent assaults from fellow students. Before he left school, beatings and verbal abuse in corridors and classrooms went unaddressed by teachers who witnessed the incidents.

School officials breach their duty to provide for the welfare of all students when they fail to safeguard gay students from verbal or physical harassment. The responsibility of administrators to provide a safe environment derives from the schools' power to compel attendance, and from the schools' position *in loco parentis* during the day. School authorities have tremendous, almost exclusive, control over the children legally entrusted to their care. If school administrators refuse to take action against overt homophobia — the harassment of gay pupils — these officials are inflicting cognizable injury through their inaction.

Moreover, education codes in most states make interference with another student's ability to function in school the most serious offense a student can commit. By choosing not to punish students who participate in gay-baiting or gay-bashing,[23] school officials selec-

tively enforce vital disciplinary rules.[24] Gay students and, where they exist, advocates for gay youth frequently inform school authorities about the occurrence of harassment, only to see officials do nothing. Adding to injury, school officials sometimes punish the gay student who resists peer violence. In a Rhode Island school, the vice-principal refused to protect an openly gay student who asked him for help in stopping threats and assaults he received in gym class. When the student skipped class to avoid the abuse, the vice-principal disciplined him. Knowing that the student's classmates abused him for being gay, the principal nonetheless punished him with an in-house suspension — the practical effect of which was three school days of being spit at and baited by the other students on suspension.

Although homophobia most blatantly affects students who are known to gay, it also inflicts injury on those students who conceal their homosexual orientation. Some teenagers hide their sexual orientation to avoid direct harassment; others do so because they have been taught to hate themselves for being gay.[29] The prejudiced atmosphere of

---

23. "Gay-baiting," verbal assaults on gay persons, and "gay-bashing," physical assaults, have become sport to groups of male teenagers, in schools as well as outside them. "[N]ame calling, taunting, hatred and violence" are "carried out by groups of fourteen- to nineteen-year-olds, and such violence is escalating sharply."

24. The steps schools take that result in injuries to gay youth should be distinguished from random instances of school officials harming, or allowing other students to harm, teenagers entrusted to the schools' care. Harassment and violence against gay students form a consistent, enduring pattern of injury to members of one minority group. Schools are aware of this pattern and have the power to change it. In addition, the experience of gay students in high schools differs from that of children who are teased because they have unusual personal characteristics (*e.g.*, they are short, or red-haired) in two respects: First, teachers and administrators do not participate in the teasing of, for example, red-haired children, nor do they condone outbursts of violence against them, or at least not on a systematic basis. Second, children who possess an unusual characteristic such as red hair are not discriminated against on account of that characteristic when they become adults. The acceptance of prejudice (and, more patently, the encouragement of prejudice) against sexual or racial minority children is more serious because it reflects and reinforces the discrimination that these individuals will face as adults.

29. As Martin states,

> Accepting homosexuality as normal would be optimal since it would make it possible for the adolescent to reach that fusion of sexuality and emotionality described as gay identity. However, acceptance, if it is ever attained, usually occurs only after much struggle and pain. For most, hiding and attempts to change are the strategies used to cope with their stigmatized status. Society does all in its power to reinforce these two strategies and thus prevents self-acceptance.

Martin, *Learning to Hide: The Socialization of the Gay Adolescent*, 10 ANNALS OF AM. SOC'Y FOR ADOLESCENT PSYCHAITRY 52, 57 (1982).

many public schools leads hidden gay students to develop feelings of isolation and despair, which, together with the fear of discovery, restrict their access to the benefits of public education.

Homophobic attitudes and actions occur in varying degrees within public schools. Some schools may demonstrate fairly enlightened attitudes toward the gay students in their midst.

Surveys of gay youth and interviews with gay youth advocates, however, reveal that the teaching, curriculum, and administration of many schools reflect persistent homophobia. In these schools, the institutions — not isolated students or school employees — are responsible for the pervasive discrimination against gay students, and the institutions should act to correct the problem.

♦

CAT
Julie Carter

It is three days after my twelfth birthday and my mother is sitting beside me on the edge of my bed. She is holding a box of sanitary napkins and a little booklet that reads "What Every Young Girl Should Know" and telling me for the third straight year that I am to read the book and keep the pads hidden from the sight of Daddy and Leroy. I am hardly listening. I am sneaking furtive glances out the window and patiently waiting for her to finish so I can meet the boys out on the lot for our softball game.

My mother is saying, "Look, you've thrown your pretty dress on the floor." She is bending down to pick it up. It is a white flared dress with large yellow flowers. Daddy bought it for my birthday. I am remembering the party, the coconut cake with the twelve ballerinas holding twelve pink candles. Momma had straightened my hair but refused to wave it tight to my head so it would look like a process, the way I usually wear it. Instead she has fluffed up the curls like she does my sister Dee Dee's hair. Momma is serving punch in a white apron

or just standing around with her hands in the pockets. When she catches my eye she motions with her head for me to go over and talk with the other girls who are standing in a cluster around the record player. I smile nervously back at her, but remain where I am. My friends are all acting strange. Leroy, my brother and very best friend, has been stuck up under Diedra Young all evening and Raymond and Zip-Zip are out on the back steps giggling with Peggy and Sharon. Jeffrey teases me about my knobby black knees under my new dress until I threaten to punch him in the mouth. I wander out to the kitchen to play with Fluffy, our cat, until Momma misses me and comes to drag me back to the party.

Now, sitting on my bed with Momma, she is saying she will have to get me a training bra. I self-consciously reach up and touch my breasts then jerk my hands down again. I hate them. I'm always hurting them when I bump into things and now when I fight I not only have to protect my face and head I have to worry about getting hit in the breast too.

Julie Carter, *Cat, in* HOME GIRLS: A BLACK FEMINIST ANTHOLOGY 159 (Barbara Smith ed. 1983).

"Momma, can I go now? I gotta pitch today," I say. Momma puts her arm around my shoulder and pulls me close to her. "Sugar, you've got to stop playing with those boys all the time; why don't you go play with Sheila, that nice young girl who's staying with the Jenkins?"

"But I don't know her."

"Well, you can get to know her. She's a nice girl and she doesn't know anybody. You can introduce her to the rest of the girls."

"But Dee Dee know them better than I do."

"Yeah, sugar, but Sheila doesn't have any girlfriends and you don't either, so you could be friends with each other."

I pull away from her. "I got friends," I say. I'm getting annoyed with the conversation, I want to go out and play. I get up and walk over to the window and stand there with my back to her.

"O.K.," Momma says finally, "but I've invited the Jenkins over for lunch Sunday and if you want to be friends with Sheila fine, if not..." She shrugs her shoulders.

"You gonna make Dee Dee be there, too?"

"Yup."

"Can we invite Zip-Zip and Jeffrey?"

She hesitates a moment. "...Maybe next time."

"O.K., can I go now?" I am inching toward the door.

"All right, scoot." She pats me on the butt as I pass her. I am running down the steps, jumping over the last two. Dee Dee, who has been listening at the door, says, "Can I go with you, Cat?"

"No."

"Why not?"

"'Cause you can't."

I reach the vacant lot where we play ball. There is no game today. The boys are busy gathering ammunition—dirt clods, rocks, bottles for the fight with the white boys from across the tracks.

Dee Dee whines to Leroy: "Leroy, I wanna go."

"You can't," Leroy says.

"How come?"

"'Cause you're too young."

"I'm just as old as Jeffrey!"

"You can't go," Leroy says, "...besides you're a girl."

"Cat's a girl," she says indignantly.

We all ignore her. We are gathering sticks and rocks and throwing them into an empty milk crate.

"How come I can't go? Huh? How come?" Nobody answers her. We are all walking across the lot. Raymond and Leroy are carrying the ammunition; Dee Dee is standing where we left her, yelling, "I'm gonna tell Momma what you're up to! I'm gonna tell you going cross the tracks to fight with those white boys." Then, after a moment or two: "...And Cat's got Kotex in her dresser drawer!" My neck burns but I keep walking.

I am sixteen years old and sitting in Sheila's dining room. We are playing checkers and I am losing and not minding at all. Her cousin Bob comes in. He is stationed in Georgia and on leave from the army. He says hi to Sheila, ignores me completely and walks through to the back with his green duffel bag in his left hand. His voice drifts in from the kitchen, "Where'd the little bulldagger come from?" Sheila springs back from the table so fast her chair overturns. She yells in the kitchen doorway, "You shut your nasty mouth, Bob Jenkins!" The next day we are supposed to make cookies for her aunt's birthday but she calls to suggest we do it over my house instead. I do not go back over Sheila's again unless Dee Dee is with me, or there is no one home.

We are in Fairmount Park within some semi-enclosed shrubbery. Sheila and I are lying on our backs on an old army blanket. We look like Siamese twins joined together at the head. The sky is blue above us and I am chewing on the straw that came with my coke.

"Cat, tell me again how you used to almost be late for school all the time 'cause you used to be waiting for me to come out of my house so we could walk to school together," Sheila says.

"I've told you three thousand times already."

"Well, tell me again, I like to hear it."

"If you hadn't been peeping from behind the curtains yourself and waiting for *me* to come out we'd both have gotten to school on time."

She laughs softly then turns over on her stomach.

"I want a kiss," she says.

I lean up on my elbow, check around to make sure nobody's peeping through the bushes then turn and press my lips to hers. After a few seconds she pulls away. "Man, Cat, I never felt this way about anybody before."

"Me neither." I reach over and touch her hand. We kiss again, briefly, our lips just touching. Then we turn and lie as we were before but continue holding hands.

"Cat?"

"Yeah?"

"I think I'm in love."

"Me too."

She squeezes my hand. I squeeze hers back.

"What would you do if Bob came by and saw us now?"

Sheila asks.

"What would you do?"

"I don't know. I'd just say hi, I guess."

"Then I would too," I say.

The sun has moved and is now shining directly over us. I cover my eyes with my arm.

"Bob would say we're both bulldaggers," Sheila says after a while.

"Yeah, I guess he would," I say.

"We aren't bulldaggers, are we, Cat?"

"No, bulldaggers want to be men and we don't want to be men, right?"

"Right, we just love each other and there's nothing wrong with loving someone."

"Yeah and nobody can choose who you fall in love with."

"Right."

Sheila and I are in her bedroom; her uncle is standing over the bed shouting, "What the hell's going on here?" He is home from work early. Sheila and I scramble for the sheet and clutch it across our bodies. I am waiting for her uncle to leave so I can get up and dressed, but he just stands there staring, thunder in his face. Finally I release my end of the sheet and scramble to the foot of the bed. Sheila's stockings are entwined in my blouse. I cram panties into my pocket and pull blue jeans over naked, ashen legs. I am trembling. Her uncle's eyes follow me around the room like harsh spotlights.

Later at my house, Momma, Daddy and I are in the dining room. Leroy and Dee Dee are in their rooms, the doors are shut tight; they've been ordered not to open them. My mother sits on the couch wringing her hands. I sit stiffly forward on the edge of a straight backed chair. My head down. My teeth clenched. My father stomps back and forth across the floor, his hands first behind him, holding each other at the butt, then gesturing out in front of him. He is asking, "What's this I hear about you being in bed with the Jenkins girl?" I sit still on the edge of my chair, looking straight ahead.

"I'm talking to you, Catherine!" His voice is booming to the rafters, I'm sure the neighbors hear. It is dark outside and a slight breeze puffs out the window curtains. I am holding a spool of thread that had been on the table. I am squeezing it in my hands, the round edges intrude into my palms. I continue to squeeze.

"You hear me talking to you, girl?" He is standing directly over me now, his voice reverberates in my ear. I squeeze the spool of thread and stare at a spider-shaped crack in the wall above the light switch. There is an itch on my left leg, below my knee. I do not scratch. Dogs bark in the backyards and one of the Williams kids is getting a spanking. I hear the strap fall, a child wailing, and an angry female voice.

My father is saying, "Look, you'd better say something, you brazen heifer!" He jerks my head around to face him. I yank it back to stare at the crack in the wall.

"You're lucky Tom Jenkins didn't have you arrested—forcing yourself on that girl like that..."

"What? What? What force? Sheila didn't say I forced her to do anything!"

"If you didn't force her, then what happened?"

"Sheila didn't say that! She didn't say it! Mr. Jenkins must have said it!" I am on my feet and trembling, and screaming at the top of my lungs.

"Then what did happen?" my father screams back at me. I sit back down in the chair and again stare at the crack in the wall over the light switch. Trying to concentrate on it, blot out my father's voice. I cannot. I get up and run to the chair where my mother sits. I am pulling on her arm. "Momma, Sheila didn't say that, did she? She didn't say I forced her?"

Momma sits there biting on her bottom lip and wringing her hands. She does not look at me. She lays her hand on my head and does not speak. My father grabs my arm and yanks me away. I am enveloped in his sour breath as he shouts, "Look, I'm a man of God and don't you dare doubt my word!" I yank my arm from his grip and run toward the steps, toward the safety of my bedroom.

"I haven't dismissed you!" I hear my father's footsteps behind me. He grabs me by my tee shirt and swings me around. I lose my footing and fall at the bottom of the steps.

"Arthur, Arthur!" My mother is running behind us. My father's knee is in my chest; he is yelling in a hoarse angry voice, "Catherine Johnson, I have one more thing to say to you, then we needn't discuss it anymore, but you listen carefully because I mean every word I say: There will be no bulldaggers in my house, do you understand me? THERE

WILL BE NO BULLDAGGERS IN MY HOUSE!"

I am sitting beside Sheila on a bench in Fairmount Park; we are within walking distance of the spot where we used to meet with our lunch on Daddy's old army blanket. The grass is completely green except for one long crooked brown streak where the boys trampled a short cut to the basketball court. The leaves are green too, save for one or two brown and yellow ones beneath the bench at our feet. Sheila's head is bent.

"I'm sorry," she is saying. She is picking minute pieces of lint from a black skirt. "I'm really sorry but you don't know how my uncle is when he gets mad." I am silent. I am watching three boys play basketball on the court about twenty yards away. A tall white kid leaps up and dunks the ball.

"I just didn't know what else to do," Sheila continues. "I was scared and Uncle Jim kept saying, 'She made you do it, didn't she? She made you do it, didn't she?' And before I knew it, I'd said 'yes'." A short black kid knocks the ball out of bounds and a fat boy in a green sweat shirt darts out to retrieve it.

"Cathy?" Her hand is on my forearm and I turn to look her full in the face. "I'm sorry, Cat, I just didn't know what else to do." I turn again toward the basketball court. The tall white boy is holding the ball under his arm and shaking the hand of a short kid. The fat boy in the green sweat shirt is pulling a navy blue poncho on over his head.

"Cathy, please?" Sheila is saying. I turn to look her full in the face. "It's all right, Sheila, it's all right." It is getting windy. The basketball court empties and Sheila asks if I'll meet her at our spot next Saturday. I lie and say yes. She checks to make sure no one's looking, pecks me on the cheek, then gets up to leave. I sit watching the empty basketball court for a long time, then I get up and take the long way home.

◆

GAY AND LESBIAN YOUTH SUICIDE
Paul Gibson

SUMMARY

Gay and lesbian youth belong to two groups at high risk of suicide: youth and homosexuals. A majority of suicide attempts by homosexuals occur during their youth, and gay youth are 2 to 3 times more likely to attempt suicide than other young people. They may comprise up to thirty percent of completed youth suicides annually. The earlier youth are aware of their orientation and identify themselves as gay, the greater the conflicts they have. Gay youth face problems in accepting themselves due to internalization of a negative self image and the lack of accurate information about homosexuality during adolescence. Gay youth face extreme physical and verbal abuse, rejection and isolation from family and peers. They often feel totally alone and socially withdrawn out of fear of adverse consequences. As a result of these pressures, lesbian and gay youth are more vulnerable than other youth to psychosocial problems including substance abuse, chronic depression, school failure, early relationship conflicts, being forced to leave their families, and having to survive on their own prematurely. Each of these problems presents a risk factor for suicidal feelings and behavior among gay, lesbian, bisexual and transsexual youth.

The root of the problem of gay youth suicide is a society that discriminates against and stigmatizes homosexuals while failing to recognize that a substantial number of its youth has a gay or lesbian orientation. Legislation should guarantee homosexuals equal rights in our society. We need to make a conscious effort to promote a positive image of homosexuals at all levels of society that provides gay youth with a diversity of lesbian and gay male adult role models. We each need to take personal responsibility for revising homophobic attitudes and conduct. Families should be educated about the development and positive nature of homosexuality. They must be able to accept their child as gay or lesbian. Schools need to include information about homosexuality in their curriculum and protect gay youth from abuse by peers to ensure they receive an equal education. Helping professionals need to accept and support a homosexual orietation in youth. Social services need to be developed that are sensitive to and reflective of the needs of gay and lesbian youth.

INTRODUCTION

Problems Facing Gay Youth

Lesbian and gay youth are the most invisible and outcast group of young people with whom you will come into contact. If open about who they are, they may feel some sense of security within themselves but face tremendous external conflicts with family and peers. If closed about who they are, they may be able to "pass" as "straight" in their communities while facing a tremendous internal struggle to understand and accept themselves. Many gay youth choose to

Paul Gibson, *Gay and Lesbian Youth Suicide*, in U.S. Department Of Health And Human Services Youth Suicide Report 110 (1989).

maintain a façade and hide their true feelings and identity, leading a double-life, rather than confront situations too painful for them. They live in constant fear of being found out and recognized as gay. The reasons for their silence are good ones.

Gay youth are the only group of adolescents that face total rejection from their family unit with the prospect of no ongoing support. Many families are unable to reconcile their child's sexual identity with moral and religious values. Huckleberry House in San Francisco, a runaway shelter for adolescents, found that gay and lesbian youth reported a higher incidence of verbal and physical abuse from parents and siblings than other youth. They were more often forced to leave their homes as "push-aways" or "throw-aways" rather than running away on their own. In a study of young gay males, Remafedi found that half had experienced negative parental response to their sexual orientation with twenty-six percent forced to leave home because of conflicts over their sexual identity.

Openly gay and lesbian youth or those "suspected" of being so can expect harassment and abuse in junior high and high schools. The National Gay Task Force, in a nationwide survey, found that forty-five percent of gay males and nearly twenty percent of lesbians had experienced verbal or physical assault in secondary schools. The shame of ridicule and fear of attack makes school a fearful place to go resulting in frequent absences and sometimes academic failure. Remafedi reports twenty-eight percent of his subjects were forced to drop out because of conflicts about their sexual orientation. Gay youth are the only group of adolescents with no peer group to identify with or receive support from. Many report extreme isolation and the loss of close friends.

Gay youth also face discrimination in contacts with the juvenile justice system and foster and group home placements. Many families and group homes refuse to accept or keep an adolescent if they know he or she is gay. A report by the San Francisco Juvenile Justice Commission found that gay youth stay in detention longer than other youth awaiting placement because of a lack of appropriate program resources. Many programs are unable to address the concerns or affirm the identity of a gay adolescent. They can be subjected to verbal, physical, and even sexual abuse with little recourse. Even sympathetic staff often don't know how to relate to a gay youth or support them in conflicts with other residents. They frequently become isolated, ignored by youth and staff who feel uncomfortable with them. They are easy targets for being blamed and scapegoated as the "source" of the problem in efforts to force them to leave.

The result of this rejection and abuse in all areas of their lives is devastating for lesbian and gay youth and perhaps the most serious problems they face are emotional ones. When you have been told that you are sick, bad, and wrong for being who you are, you begin to believe it. Gay youth have frequently internalized a negative image of themselves. Those who hide their identity are surrounded by homophobic attitudes and remarks, often by unknowing family members and peers, that have a profound impact on them. Hank Wilson, founder of the Gay and Lesbian Teachers Coalition in San Francisco, believes these youth constitute a large group who are silently scapegoated, especially vulnerable to being stigmatized, and who develop poor self-esteem. Gay youth become fearful and withdrawn. More than other adolescents, they feel totally alone often suffering from chronic depression, despairing of life that will always be as painful and hard as the present one.

In response to these overwhelming pressures, gay youth will often use two coping mechanisms which only tend to make their situation worse: substance use and professional help. Lesbian and gay male youth belong to two groups at high risk for substance abuse: homosexuals and adolescents. Rofes found, in a review of the literature, that:

> Lesbians and gay men are at much higher risk than the heterosexual population for alcohol abuse. Approximately thirty percent of both the lesbian and gay male populations have problems with alcoholism.

Substance use often begins in early adolescence when youth first experience conflicts around their sexual orientation. It initially serves the functional purposes of (1) reducing the pain and anxiety of external conflicts and (2) reducing the internal inhibitions of homosexual feelings and behavior. Prolonged substance abuse, however, only contributes to the youth's problems and magnifies suicidal feelings.

Several studies have found that a majority of gay youth received professional help for conflicts usually related to their sexual identity. These interventions often worsen condidtions for these youth because the therapist or socialworker is unwilling to acknowledge or support an adolescent's homosexual identity. Many gay and lesbian youth are still encouraged to "change" their identities while being forced into therapy and mental hospitals under the guise of "treatment."

Those who seek help while hiding their identity often find the source of their conflicts is never resolved because the therapist is unable to approach the subject. This silence is taken as further repudiation of an "illness" that dare not speak its name.

A suicide attempt can be a final cry for help by gay youth in their home community. If the response is hostile or indifferent, they prepare to leave. Alone and frightened, they go to large cities — hoping to find families and friends to replace the ones that did not want them or could not accept them. The English group "The Bronski Beat" describes

the plight of the gay adolescent in their song "Smalltown Boy":

> Pushed around and kicked around,
>   always the lonely boy
> You were the one they talked about
> Around town as they put you down
> But as hard as they would try
>   just to make you cry
> You would never cry to them
>   — just to your soul
> Runaway, turnaway, runaway,
>   turnaway, runaway.

Gay male, lesbian, bisexual, and transsexual youth comprise as many as twenty-five percent of all youth living on the streets in this country. Here, they enter a further outcast status that presents serious dangers and an even greater risk of suicide. Without an adequate education or vocational training, many are forced to become involved in prostitution in order to survive. They face physical and sexual assaults on a daily basis and constant exposure to sexually transmitted diseases including AIDS. They often become involved with a small and unstable element of the gay community that offers them little hope for a better life. Their relationships are transitory and untrustworthy. For many street youth, their struggle for survival becomes the fulfillment of a "suicide script" which sees them engaging in increasingly self-destructive behaviors including unsafe sexual activity and intravenous drug use. Overwhelmed by the complexities of street life and feeling they have reached the "wrong end of the rainbow" a suicide attempt may result.

While it has become easier in recent years to be a gay male or lesbian adult it may be harder than ever to be a gay youth. With all of the conflicts they face in accepting themselves, coming out to families and peers, establishing themselves prematurely in independent living and, for young gay males, confronting the haunting specter of AIDS, there is a growing danger that their lives are becoming a tragic nightmare with living only a small part of dying.

Notes

1. For a further discussion of the problems of gay youth, see Mary Tabor, *For High School Seniors, Nightmare Is Almost Over*, N. Y. TIMES, June 14, 1992, § 1, at 41.
2. The conclusions of the government's youth suicide study proved controversial. Under pressure from conservative legislators, the Reagan/Bush administrations attempted to censor the results of the study. The following article, Susan Okie, *Sullivan Cold-Shoulders Suicide Report: Section Urging Acceptance of Gays Draws Heat From Conservatives*, WASH. POST, Jan. 13, 1990, at A5, describes these developments:

    > In a move that has angered some gay rights organizations, Secretary of Health and Human Services Louis W. Sullivan has sought to distance the Bush administration from a controversial HHS report on youth suicide because [the report] says homosexuality is natural and urges steps to end discrimination against homosexuals.
    >
    > Published a year ago, the four-volume report examines possible reasons for the tripling of the suicide rate among Americans ages fifteen to twenty-four in the last thirty years.
    >
    > Noting that homosexuals in this age group are about three times as likely as heterosexuals to try to kill themselves, the report concluded that homosexuality was one of the risk factors for youth suicide.
    >
    > It called for efforts to eliminate discrimination against homosexual teenagers and young adults, greater awareness of their needs on the part of mental health counselors, and additional research.
    >
    > The report infuriated conservative Rep. William E. Dannemeyer (R-Calif.), who wrote to Sullivan, to former assistant secretary of health James O. Mason, and President Bush calling on them to publicly denounce the portions dealing with homosexuality. Dannemeyer is a longtime crusader against any form of tolerance of homosexuals.
    >
    > Charging that the report failed to affirm "traditional family values," Dannemeyer quoted passages from a position paper in the report written by Paul Gibson, a San Francisco socialworker, urging that parents, churches and society accept homosexuality as natural and healthy.
    >
    > In a reply to Dannemeyer last October, Sullivan said, "I neither endorse nor approve the report from the Task Force on Youth Suicide." Noting that the report was written in the Reagan administration, Sullivan said he was examining its recommendations. He added that the views expressed by Gibson "do not in any way represent my personal beliefs or the policy of this department."

    ■ ■ ■

    > "We are taking the recommendations of the task force to heart," a spokesman said. "The report is available. I am not aware of any effort not to distribute it."
    >
    > But Dannemeyer spokesman Paul Mero provided a copy of a letter from Sullivan to Dannemeyer dated January 3 in which Sullivan said that "the department printed 2,000 copies of the report and has no plans to reprint. The distribution by the department of the complete report was, therefore, limited."
    >
    > Mero said Dannemeyer objected not only to the Gibson paper, but also to several of the report's recommendations. For example, it recommends that schools and youth organizations end discrimination on the basis of such characteristics as sexual orientation and that they "enlist adult group leaders who reflect the population of youth served."
    >
    > Mero said such recommendations encouraged the view, also expressed in the Gibson paper, that homosexuality is normal for some people.

"The underlying premise is . . . that the reason they [homosexuals] are committing suicide isn't that they're troubled, but that society is persecuting them," Mero said. "We think that's a myth. It's something that we disagree wholeheartedly with."

Psychiatrists formally removed homosexuality from the profession's official list of mental disorders more than a decade ago, but they generally agree that homosexuals are at increased risk of depression and suicide. The report cites a 1978 study that found eighteen percent of male homosexuals and twenty-three percent of lesbians had attempted suicide.

"I think suicide is the result of a depressive or psychotic illness," said Harold Eist, a child and adolescent psychiatrist who teaches at Howard University Medical School. "Regardless of sexual orientation, people can get these illnesses. If they're additionally stressed because of homophobia or whatever, that might contribute . . . to their feeling hopeless and despondent."

"It's not a matter to be taken lightly," he said. "It shouldn't become a political football."

B. Litigating the Rights of Lesbian and Gay High School Students

FRICKE v. LYNCH

491 F. Supp. 381 (D.R.I. 1980)

PETTINE, Chief Judge

Most of the time, a young man's choice of a date for the senior prom is of no great interest to anyone other than the student, his companion, and, perhaps, a few of their classmates. But in Aaron Fricke's case, the school authorities actively disapprove of his choice, the other students are upset, the community is abuzz, and out-of-state newspapers consider the matter newsworthy. All this fuss arises because Aaron Fricke's intended escort is another young man. Claiming that the school's refusal to allow him to bring a male escort violates his First and Fourteenth Amendment rights, Fricke seeks a preliminary injunction ordering the school officials to allow him to attend with a male escort.

Two days of testimony have revealed the following facts. The senior reception at

Cumberland High School is a formal dinner-dance sponsored and run by the senior class. It is held shortly before graduation but is not a part of the graduation ceremonies. This year the students have decided to hold the dance at the Pleasant Valley Country Club in Sutton, Massachusetts on Friday, May 30. All seniors except those on suspension are eligible to attend the dance; no one is required to go. All students who attend must bring an escort, although their dates need not be seniors or even Cumberland High School students. Each student is asked the name of his date at the time he buys the tickets.

The principal testified that school dances are chaperoned by him, two assistant principals, and one or two class advisers. They are sometimes joined by other teachers who volunteer to help chaperone; such teachers are not paid. Often these teachers will drop in for part of the dance. Additionally, police officers are on duty at the dance. Usually two officers attend; last year three plainclothes officers were at the junior prom.

The seeds of the present conflict were planted a year ago when Paul Guilbert, then a junior at Cumberland High School, sought permission to bring a male escort to the junior prom. The principal, Richard Lynch (the defendant here), denied the request, fearing that student reaction could lead to a disruption at the dance and possibly to physical harm to Guilbert. The request and its denial were widely publicized and led to widespread community and student reaction adverse to Paul. Some students taunted and spit at him, and once someone slapped him; in response, principal Lynch arranged an escort system, in which Lynch or an assistant principal accompanied Paul as he went from one class to the next. No other incidents or violence occurred. Paul did not attend the prom. At that time Aaron Fricke (plaintiff here) was a friend of Paul's and supported his position regarding the dance.

This year, during or after an assembly in April in which senior class events were discussed, Aaron Fricke, a senior at Cumberland High School, decided that he wanted to attend the senior reception with a male companion. Aaron considers himself a homosexual, and has never dated girls, although he does socialize with female friends. He has never taken a girl to a school dance. Until this April, he had not "come out of the closet" by publicly acknowledging his sexual orientation.

Aaron asked principal Lynch for permission to bring a male escort, which Lynch denied. A week later (during vacation), Aaron asked Paul Guilbert—who now lives in New York—to be his escort (if allowed), and Paul accepted. Aaron met again with Lynch, at which time they discussed Aaron's commitment to homosexuality; Aaron indicated that although it was possible he might someday be bisexual, at the present he is exclusively homosexual and could not conscientiously date girls. Lynch gave Aaron written reasons for his action;[2] his prime concern was the fear that a disruption would occur and Aaron or, especially, Paul would be hurt. He indicated in court that he would allow Aaron to bring a male escort if there were no threat of violence.

After Aaron filed suit in this Court, an event reported by the Rhode Island and Boston papers, a student shoved and, the next day, punched Aaron. The unprovoked, surprise assault necessitated five stitches under Aaron's right eye. The assailant was sus-

---

2. Principal Lynch sent the following letter to Aaron's home and handed it to him in person:

   I am denying your request for the following reasons:

   1. The real and present threat of physical harm to you, your male escort and to others;

   2. The adverse effect among your classmates, other students, the school and the town of Cumberland, which is certain to follow approval of such a request for overt homosexual interaction (male or female) at a class function;

   3. Since the dance is being held out of state and this is a function of the students of Cumberland High School, the school department is powerless to insure protection in Sutton, Massachusetts. That protection would be required of property as well as persons and would expose all concerned to liability for harm which might occur;

   4. It is long-standing school policy that no unescorted student, male or female, is permitted to attend. To enforce this rule, a student must identify his or her escort before the committee will sell the ticket.

   I suspect that other objections will be raised by your fellow students, the Cumberland School Department, parents and other citizens, which will heighten the potential for harm.

pended for nine days. After this, Aaron was given a special parking space closer to the school doors and has been provided with an escort (principal or assistant principal) between classes. No further incidents have occurred.

■ ■ ■

Aaron contends that the school's action violates his First Amendment right of association, his First Amendment right to free speech, and his Fourteenth Amendment right to equal protection of the laws. (The equal protection claim is a "hybrid" one — that he has been treated differently than others because of the content of his communication.)[3]

The starting point in my analysis of Aaron's First Amendment free speech claim must be, of course, to determine whether the action he proposes to take has a "communicative content sufficient to bring it within the ambit of the First Amendment." *Gay Students Organization v. Bonner*, 509 F.2d 652 (1st Cir. 1974) (hereinafter *Bonner*). . . . [T]he "speech pure"/"speech plus" demarcation is problematic, both in logic and in practice. This normally difficult task is made somewhat easier here, however, by the precedent set in *Bonner*, *supra*. In that case, the University of New Hampshire prohibited the Gay Students' Organization (GSO) from holding dances and other social events. The First Circuit explicitly rejected the idea that traditional First Amendment rights of expression were not involved. The Court found that not only did discussion and exchange of ideas take place at informal social functions, but also that:

> beyond the specific communications at
> such events is the basic "message"

GSO seeks to convey — that homosexuals exist, that they feel repressed by existing laws and attitudes, that they wish to emerge from their isolation, and that public understanding of their attitudes and problems is desirable for society.

Here too the proposed activity has significant expressive content. Aaron testified that he wants to go because he feels he has a right to attend and participate just like all the other students and that it would be dishonest to his own sexual identity to take a girl to the dance. He went on to acknowledge that he feels his attendance would have a certain political element and would be a statement for equal rights and human rights. Admittedly, his explanation of his "message" was hesitant and not nearly as articulate as Judge Coffin's restatement of the GSO's message, cited above. Nevertheless, I believe Aaron's testimony that he is sincerely — although perhaps not irrevocably — committed to a homosexual orientation and that attending the dance with another young man would be a political statement. While mere communicative intent may not always transform conduct into speech, *United States v. O'Brien*, 391 U.S. 367, 376 (1968), *Bonner* makes clear that this exact type of conduct as a vehicle for transmitting this very message can be considered protected speech.

Accordingly, the school's action must be judged by the standards articulated in *United States v. O'Brien*, 391 U.S. 367 (1968), and applied in *Bonner*: (1) was the regulation within the constitutional power of the government; (2) did it further an important or substantial governmental interest; (3) was the governmental interest unrelated to the suppression of free expression; and (4) was

---

3. The plaintiff has not advanced the plausible arguments that homosexuals constitute a suspect class, *see* L. Tribe, *American Constitutional Law* (1978) at 944-45 n. 17, or that one has a constitutional right to be a homosexual, *see*, *e.g.*, *Acanfora v. Board of Education*, 359 F.Supp. 843 (D. Md. 1973), *aff'd on other grounds*, 491 F.2d 498 (4th Cir. 1974). The first amendment aspect of the case makes it unnecessary for me to reach these issues, although they may very well be applicable to this kind of case.

the incidental restriction on alleged first amendment freedoms no greater than essential to the furtherance of that interest?

I need not dwell on the first two *O'Brien* requirements: the school unquestionably has an important interest in student safety and has the power to regulate students' conduct to ensure safety. As to the suppression of free expression, Lynch's testimony indicated that his personal views on homosexuality did not affect his decision, and that but for the threat of violence he would let the two young men go together. Thus the government's interest here is not in squelching a particular message because it objects to its content as such. On the other hand, the school's interest is in suppressing certain speech activity because of the reaction its message may engender. Surely this is still suppression of free expression.

It is also clear that the school's action fails to meet the last criterion set out in *O'Brien*, the requirement that the government employ the "least restrictive alternative" before curtailing speech. The plaintiff argues, and I agree, that the school can take appropriate security measures to control the risk of harm. Lynch testified that he did not know if adequate security could be provided, and that he would still need to sit down and make the necessary arrangements. In fact he has not made any effort to determine the need for and logistics of additional security. Although Lynch did not say that any additional security measures would be adequate, from the testimony I find that significant measures could be taken and would — in all probability — critically reduce the likelihood of any disturbance. As Lynch's own testimony indicates, police officers and teachers will be present at the dance, and have been quite successful in the past in controlling whatever problems arise, including unauthorized drinking. Despite the ever-present possibility of violence at sports events, adequate discipline has been maintained. From Lynch's testimony, I have every rea-

son to believe that additional school or law enforcement personnel could be used to "shore up security" and would be effective. It should also be noted that Lynch testified that if he considered it impossible to provide adequate security he would move to cancel the dance. The Court appreciates that controlling high school students is no easy task. It is, of course, impossible to guarantee that no harm will occur, no matter what measures are taken. But only one student so far has attempted to harm Aaron, and no evidence was introduced of other threats. The measures taken already, especially the escort system, have been highly effective in preventing any further problems at school. Appropriate security measures coupled with a firm, clearly communicated attitude by the administration that any disturbance will not be tolerated appear to be a realistic, and less restrictive, alternative to prohibiting Aaron from attending the dance with the date of his choice.

The analysis so far has been along traditional First Amendment lines, making no real allowance for the fact that this case arises in a high school setting. The most difficult problem this controversy presents is how this setting should affect the result. *Tinker v. Des Moines Independent Community School District*, 393 U.S. 503 (1969), makes clear that high school students do not "shed their constitutional rights to freedom of speech or expression at the schoolhouse gate."

■ ■ ■

Tinker did, however, indicate that there are limits on first amendment rights within the school:

> A student's rights, therefore, do not embrace merely the classroom hours. When he is in the cafeteria, or on the playing field, or on the campus during

the authorized hours, he may express his opinions, even on controversial subjects like the conflict in Vietnam, if he does so without "materially and substantially interfer[ing] with the requirements of appropriate discipline in the operation of the school" and without colliding with the rights of others. *But conduct by the student, in class or out of it, which for any reason—whether it stems from time, place or type of behavior-materially disrupts classwork or involves substantial disorder or invasion of the rights of others is, of course, not immunized by the constitutional guarantee of freedom of speech.*

It seems to me that here, not unlike in *Tinker*, the school administrators were acting on "an undifferentiated fear or apprehension of disturbance." True, Aaron was punched and then security measures were taken, but since that incident he has not been threatened with violence nor has he been attacked. There has been no disruption at the school; classes have not been cancelled, suspended, or interrupted. In short, while the defendants have perhaps shown more of a basis for fear of harm than in *Tinker*, they have failed to make a "showing" that Aaron's conduct would "materially and substantially interfere" with school discipline. However, even if the Court assumes that there is justifiable fear and that Aaron's peaceful speech leads, or may lead, to a violent reaction from others, the question remains: may the school prohibit the speech, or must it protect the speaker?

It is certainly clear that outside of the classroom the fear — however justified — or a violent reaction is not sufficient reason to restrain such speech in advance, and an actual hostile reaction is rarely an adequate basis for curtailing free speech. Thus, the question here is whether the interest in school discipline and order, recognized in *Tinker*, requires a different approach.

After considerable thought and research, I have concluded that even a legitimate interest in school discipline does not outweigh a student's right to peacefully express his views in an appropriate time, place, and manner.[5] To rule otherwise

---

5. The second reason relied upon by the *Bonner* court in finding the GSO social events to be speech-related was the interpretation placed upon those events by the community. There the university prohibited the gay social events because the community considered them "shocking and offensive," "a spectacle, an abomination," an "affront" to townspeople, "grandstanding," inflammatory, "undermin[ing]" the university within the state," and distasteful. The first circuit concluded that "[we] do not see how these statements can be interpreted to avoid the conclusion that the regulation imposed was based in large measure, if not exclusively, on the content of the GSO's expression." *Bonner* at 661. I quite agree that these statements of community outrage indicate that the *content*, i.e. the homosexual-ness, of the GSO's activities led to the strong reaction and the prohibition, not the fact that they were dances. With all due respect, however, I am puzzled by how this reaction proves the *expressive* nature of these activities. Community outrage per se does not transform conduct into speech, or even indicate that it is speech; communities have reacted with outrage similar to that of the citizens of New Hampshire to such non-expressive activities as Hester Prynne's adultery, the dumping of chemicals into Love Canal, and the Son of Sam murders. It is hard in *Bonner* to separate the community's opposition to the GSO's acts from its opposition to its message (if the acts had a message); surely they opposed both. Same-sex dancing may have an expressive element, but it is also action, and potentially objectionable as such.

Insofar as *Bonner* directs me to consider community reaction in assessing expressive content, I conclude that the community disapproves of the content of Aaron's message and that the vehemence of their opposition to his intended escort is based in part on this disapproval of what he is trying to communicate. The school here professes to be unconcerned with the content of the plaintiff's message, but their concern with townspeople's reaction is, indirectly, content-related.

would completely subvert free speech in the schools by granting other students a "heckler's veto," allowing them to decide — through prohibited and violent methods — what speech will be heard. The first amendment does not tolerate mob rule by unruly school children. This conclusion is bolstered by the fact that any disturbance here, however great, would not interfrere with the main business of school—education. No classes or school work would be affected; at the very worst an optional social event, conducted by the students for their own enjoyment, would be marred. In such a context, the school does have an obligation to take reasonable measures to protect and foster free speech, not to stand helpless before unauthorized student violence.

■ ■ ■

The present case is so difficult because the court is keenly sensitive to the testimony regarding the concerns of a possible disturbance, and of physical harm to Aaron or Paul. However, I am convinced that meaningful security measures are possible, and the first amendment requires that such steps be taken to protect — rather than to stifle — free expression. Some may feel that Aaron's attendance at the reception and the message he will thereby convey is trivial compared to other social debates, but to engage in this kind of a weighing in process is to make the content-based evaluation forbidden by the First Amendment.

As to the other concern raised by *Tinker*, some people might say that Aaron Fricke's

conduct would infringe the rights of the other students, and is thus unprotected by *Tinker*. This view is misguided, however. Aaron's conduct is quiet and peaceful; it demands no response from others and — in a crowd of some five hundred people — can be easily ignored. Any disturbance that might interfere with the rights of others would be caused by those students who resort to violence, not by Aaron and his companion, who do not want a fight.

Because the free speech claim is dispositive, I find it unnecessary to reach the plaintiff's right of association argument or to deal at length with his equal protection claim.[6] I find that the plaintiff has established a probability of success on the merits and has shown irreparable harm; accordingly his request for a preliminary injunction is hereby granted.

As a final note, I would add that the social problems presented by homosexuality are emotionally charged; community norms are in flux, and the psychiatric profession itself is divided in its attitude toward homosexuality. This Court's role, of course, is not to mandate social norms or impose its own view of acceptable behavior. It is instead, to interpret and apply the Constitution as best it can. The Constitution is not self-explanatory, and answers to knotty problems are inevitably inexact. All that an individual judge can do is to apply the legal precedents as accurately and as honestly as he can, uninfluenced by personal predilections or the fear of community reaction, hoping each time to disprove the legal maxim that "hard cases make bad law."

6. This case can also be profitably analyzed under the Equal Protection Clause of the fourteenth amendment. In preventing Aaron Fricke from attending the senior reception, the school has afforded disparate treatment to a certain class of students—those wishing to attend the reception with companions of the same sex. Ordinarily, a government classification need only bear a rational relationship to a legitimate public purpose; . . . [however] [w]here, as here, government classification impinges on a first amendment right, the government is held to a higher level of scrutiny. *Chicago Police Department v. Mosley*, 408 U.S. 92 (1972). I find that principal Lynch's reason for prohibiting Aaron's attendance at the reception — the potential for disruption — is not sufficiently compelling to justify a classification that would abridge first amendment rights.

◆

ONE LIFE, ONE PROM

Aaron Fricke

The simple, obvious thing would have been to go to the senior prom with a girl. But that would have been a lie — a lie to myself, to the girl, and to all the other students.

What I *wanted* to do was to take a male date. But as Paul Guilbert had shown the year before when he had attempted to take another man to the prom, such honesty is not always easy. There was an important difference between Paul's case and mine, though. Paul had not been able to fight for his rights because he was seventeen at the time. I was now eighteen and legally able to make my own decisions. If I wanted to go to the prom with a male escort and the school tried to stop me, I could take the case to court.

But should I do that? This would require a lot of thought if I was to make a decision without being selfish, uncaring, or irrational.

If I went to the prom with another guy, what would be the benefits? For myself, it would mean participating in an important social event and doing so with a clear conscience and a sense of wholeness. But how would it affect the rest of the people involved?

I believed that those who had themselves faced discrimination or prejudice would immediately understand what I was doing and its implications for human rights. There would be others who may never have had direct experiences with prejudice but who would recognize my right to the date of my choice. These people may have been misled to believe that homosexuality is wrong, but they could still understand that my rights were being denied.

At the opposite end of the spectrum were the homophobics who might react violently. But the example I set would be perfect for everyone. We would be just one more happy couple. Our happiness together would be something kids could relate to. I would be showing that my dignity and value as a human being was not affected by my sexual preference.

I concluded that taking a guy to the prom would be a strong positive statement about the existence of gay people. Any opposition to my case (and I anticipated a good bit) would show the negative side of society — not of homosexuality.

To attend the prom with a girl would not be unenjoyable, but it would be dishonest to my true feelings. Besides, most kids now knew I was gay. If I went with a female, I would probably have received more taunts than from going with a male. By going with a male I would win some respect from the more mature students, and I would keep my self-esteem.

I tried not to worry about the possibility of violence. Certainly I would face opposition. It was inevitable given the rampant prejudice against homosexuals today. But the threat of violence was not enough to change my mind, since I encountered that every day to some degree. Perhaps such threats would diminish in the future as people saw more homosexuals participating openly in everyday life.

My biggest concern was for my parents. Although the entire student body and administration of Cumberland High School knew or assumed I was gay, my family had remained blissfully blind to this reality. The news could be heartbreaking to them. Plus, it might get them ostracized by the neighbors, banned from town social gatherings...from church...from Tupperware parties! Was I willing to take this risk? No! As much as I believed in my rights, I valued my relationship with my parents too much to have it abruptly severed. After all, for years I had hidden my sexuality for fear of

Aaron Fricke, *One Life, One Prom*, in THE CHRISTOPHER STREET READER 21 (Michael Denneny et al, eds.,1983).

losing my parents' love. As a child it had been *the* most important thing to me. Now, as a man, it was just as important as before. I wanted to go to my prom, but it was not as important as eighteen years of love.

I decided to tell my parents of my homo-sexuality first, then ask them how they would feel about my going to the prom. If it seemed like too much for them to accept, I would forget the prom and just be happy that I no longer had to be secretive with my parents. But if they rejected me merely because I was gay, then I would still pursue my rights, even at the prom, realizing that my parents were good people but were horribly misled.

Until now, I had never spoken to them about my homosexuality. Like many adolescents I had drifted away from my parents lately. Now I had an impetus to improve my communication with them. I decided to approach my parents separately; a thousand times I rehearsed what I would say.

It began, "Ever since I was a kid..." and ended, " I hope you love me enough not to reject me." But when the moment of truth came, I felt more self-confident and said, "I don't know if you've had any suspicions, but I'm gay."

Long pause. My mother replied, "I'm so glad you were finally able to be honest with me." She had long suspected. My father had not; when I told him he broke down and cried. Yet they both loved me uncondition-ally. When I explained why I wanted to go to the prom, they were supportive. I was my own man, they each said, and I would have to make my own decisions.

It felt great to be able to talk to my parents about this. Their reaction was en-couraging, and I decided to go ahead. I would invite Paul Guilbert to the prom.

Anne Guillet wrote me a note in environ-mental science class when I asked for her advice about the prom. She wrote:

Dear Aaron,

Last year, Paul's attempt to bring a guy to the prom was seen by most people,

in fact I think by all, as a grab at publicity. That was because no one knew Paul, he just showed up out of a clear blue sky (and raised a ruckus). Since you've been in Cumberland much longer and have more close friends, people won't suspect you of such ill motives so easily, but this is what they will think:

1. Paul made you do it.
2. You're crazy.
3. You believe in gay rights.

In that order. Now *I* know you did it for reason 3, but you should think about how other people are going to react and I think you should make an effort to explain what you believe. I respect any decision you make, as long as you really think about it carefully.

Love,
Anne

I took her advice and painstakingly wrote a letter to the school newspaper, explaining why I decided to go to the prom with a male date. The letter said that I hoped no one would be hurt by what I was doing, that a victory in court would be a victory for every Cumberland High student because it would be a blow against prejudice. The next issue of the school paper had space for all sorts of trivia, but my letter never appeared.

Later in April, the school theater group took its annual bus trip to New York City. Our teacher, Miss Frappier, was an excep-tionally warm and friendly person, and we were a tight-knit bunch — one of those rare groups of thespians whose members had no pent-up distrust or jealousy toward each other. On the bus Miss Frappier gave out the spring awards; I received one of them for an outstanding performance in "A Thurber Carnival."

In New York we went to the Gug-genheim Museum and to the Broadway pro-duction of "They're Playing Our Song"; then when the group returned to Rhode Island, I stayed in New York to spend time with Paul, who had moved there from Cumberland.

Paul seemed to be getting happier in the city. Our friendship had not faded, although Paul and I had not seen each other in months. We took a long walk through the Village, bringing each other up to date on what we'd been doing, and enjoying the feeling of the trees in bloom and spring in the air.

By evening I had settled any doubts I still had about who I wanted to invite to the prom. And so, with sweaty palms and butterflies in my stomach, I finally asked Paul: "I was wondering, um, do you have a date for the Cumberland High prom this year?"

Paul began laughing. "I'd love to attend the senior prom with you," he finally said. My feeling of happiness lasted all the way back to Rhode Island.

In Cumberland, prom tickets were on sale. Rather than go through the motion of trying to buy tickets in the cafeteria, where they would want the name of my date and would refuse to sell me the tickets anyway, I went right to the main office and asked Mrs. Dunbarton to tell Mr. Lynch, the principal, that I wanted to speak with him. She courteously took my name, leaned over the intercom, and buzzed Mr Lynch. I couldn't hear much of what she said, but my imagination filled in the silence: "Oh, Mr. Lynch, that little faggot is here to see you."

Mr. Lynch soon appeared and, on my insistence, granted me the privacy of his office to speak to him. His office was familiar to me by now. I'd sat in it the year before when Mr. Lynch gave me that in-house suspension for cutting gym. But this time things were different.

Without mentioning Paul by name, I explained that I wanted to take a male escort to the prom. Mr. Lynch listened politely, then did exactly what I had assumed he would do.

He said no.

[Aaron Fricke brought suit in federal district court. The court's opinion granting him a preliminary injunction is reproduced *supra*, at 167.]

When we arrived at the prom site on the night of May 30, 1980, we were greeted with a glare of television lights. Flash bulbs were popping and everybody was talking and trying to ask questions as we walked toward the building. The reporters broke down the velvet ropes that were supposed to hold them back. I was too full of anticipation and excitement to think of anything to say. So a second before walking in the door, in a grand gesture of looniness, camp, and high drama, I turned to the reporters, waved, and stuck out my tongue.

Once inside, Mr. Lynch quickly ushered Paul and me away from the door so that the reporters would be unable to see us. We were shown to an empty table, which neither of us enjoyed because there were no kids to talk to. My ninth-grade Spanish teacher, Mrs. Noelte, eventually sat with us.

Dinner was soon served. It was chicken cordon something or other and consisted of mushed chicken encased in oil. My piece looked like a monster from the film *Alien*. The salad looked better, but when I bit into the cherry tomato, it splattered right onto my pants. I did my best to ignore the stain, but it kept showing up in the pictures people took.

After dinner was cleared away, many students began coming by to offer us a few good words. There was more good feeling than I would ever have anticipated. One after another, students came by and expressed their happiness that we could share the prom with each other.

I wandered over to a big picture window and stared out. Several reporters were talking outside on the lawn. For a moment I thought of all the people who would have enjoyed going to their proms with the date of their choice, but were denied that right; of all the people in the past who wanted to live respectably with the person they loved but could not; of all the men and women who had been hurt or killed because they were gay; and of the rich history of lesbians and homosexual men that had so long been ignored. Gradually we were triumphing over ignorance. One day we would be free.

The dance music came on. Kelleen Driskell came over and asked me to dance the first song with her. I was happy to accept. I'd known Kelleen in elementary shool, but I had drifted away from her, as from so many other people, during my fat years. We fast-danced for that song and just through our physical movements together, without exchanging words, it felt as if we were re-establishing a communication.

After the dance I had to use the bathroom. Throughout the evening, Paul and I would see all kinds of defense mechanisms from the other guys whenever we went to the bathroom. Some of them made a beeline for the door as soon as we walked in. Others stayed, their desire to escape temporarily overcome by their curiosity about how gay people go to the bathroom.

When I got back to the dance floor, Paul asked me if I wanted to slowdance. I did. The next song was Bob Seger's "We've Got the Night," and we stepped out onto the dance floor.

The crowd receded. As I laid my head on Paul's shoulder, I saw a few students start to stare at us. I closed my eyes and listened to the music, my thoughts wandering over the events of that evening. When the song ended, I opened my eyes. A large crowd of students had formed a ring around us. Probably most of them had never before seen two happy men embracing in a slow dance. For a moment I was uncomfortable. Then I heard the sound that I knew so well as a B-52's fan. One of my favorite songs was coming up: "Rock Lobster."

Paul and I began dancing free-style. Everyone else was still staring at us, but by the end of the first stanza, several couples had also begun dancing. The song had a contagious enthusiasm to it, and with each bar, more dancers came onto the floor.

More students were coming onto the floor to dance. I doubt that any two people were dancing with the same movements: the dancing was an expression of our individuality, and no one felt bad about being different. Everyone was free to be themselves.

A quarter of the way into the song, thirty people were on the dance floor. "Down,

Down, Down," commanded the lyrics. Everyone on the dance floor sank to their knees and crouched on the ground. I lifted my head slightly to look around. Dozens of intertwining bodies crouched on their knees as if praying. We were all one; we shared a unity of pure love. And those who did not want to share it sat on the sidelines.

"Red snappers snappin'
Clamshells clappin'"

Everyone jumped to their feet again and resumed dancing. Many more kids had joined us and there must have been sixty or eighty people on the dance floor now.

As Paul and I danced, we had gradually drifted from our original space on the floor. "Down, Down, Down," cried the B-52's again, and we all went down. The feeling of unity among us permeated the air again. There were at least a hundred people on the dance floor. The tempo became more frenetic and everyone danced faster.

"Let's Rock!!!" bellowed from the speakers, and to my surprise, when I looked up, I saw that Paul had disappeared. I looked around; several other guys were dancing with each other, and girls were dancing with girls. Everybody was rockin', everybody was fruggin'. Who cared why? Maybe they were doing it to mock me and Paul, maybe they were doing it because they wanted to, maybe one was an excuse for the other....I didn't know and I didn't care. It was fun. Everyone was together. I danced with girls, I danced with guys, I danced with the entire group.

Then the music stopped. "Rock Lobster" has an abrupt ending, and no one was quite ready for it to stop. I had been having so much fun that I lost track of time; I had also lost track of Paul and had to look around the room for him.

I could see that everyone felt a sense of disorientation. For six minutes and forty-nine seconds, the students on the dance floor had forgotten about their defenses, forgotten about their shells. We just had fun.

■ ■ ■

My last day at Cumberland High School ended on a particularly sad note. As I walked off the football field after commencement, now escorted by several uniformed policemen, two children approached me before I stepped into my car. "Faggot!" one said. "You queer," said the other. I had never felt so defenseless. They were only about ten years old, and I felt no hostility toward them. But I pity the society that sits back and encourages children to feel bitterness and hatred toward anything.

Note

In 1992, a female high school student in Massachusetts was denied the right to go to the prom with another women *unless* she stated she was a lesbian. *See* Victoria Benning, *Prom Fight; In Dedham, Students Decry Noncouples Policy*, BOSTON GLOBE, May 14, 1992, at 29. In Michigan, gay teenagers organized a "gay" prom. *See Gays Create a "Fantasy" — Their Prom*, CHICAGO TRIBUNE, May 24, 1992, at 24.

II. COLLEGE

College is a time many lesbians and gay men struggle with the decision to "come out." Often, those who do come out, or those who are engaged in this struggle, seek the company of others. Thus, lesbian and gay student groups are a common gathering place on college campuses throughout the United States. Lesbian and gay organizations serve as a place to meet new friends and to rally for political reform. Nevertheless, many state university officials have refused to recognize, to fund, and to give equal facility access to lesbian and gay student organizations. The case that follows exemplifies some of the arguments that are raised in the context of lesbian and student organizations that seek legal recognition by state university officials.

A. Litigating the Rights of Lesbian and Gay College Students

GAY LIB v. UNIVERSITY OF MISSOURI

558 F.2d 848 (8th Cir. 1977), *cert. denied sub nom.*
Ratchford v. Gay Lib, 434 U.S. 1080 (1978)

LAY, Circuit Judge.

The issue before us is whether officials of a state university may lawfully withhold formal recognition of a student organization, comprised largely of homosexuals, whose basic purpose is to provide a forum for discussion about homosexuality. . . . [The district court, 416 F.Supp. 1350 (W.D. Mo. 1976), ruled] that recognition of Gay Lib would probably result in the commission of felonious acts of sodomy in violation of Missouri law.[3] . . .

On appeal, plaintiffs contend: (1) that the district court erred in holding that plaintiffs' First Amendment rights were not impermissibly infringed; and (2) that the action of the defendants deprived plaintiffs of equal protection of the law. We reverse.

Factual Background.

Formal recognition of a student organization by the University of Missouri entitles the group to use campus facilities for meetings and to apply for financial support from student activities funds. Written University policies with respect to recognition of campus groups provide that:

> Groups are recognized on the basis of their own statements as to name, aims, nature and program.
>
> Recognition of an organization by the Committee does not constitute

approval or endorsement of the organization's aims and activities.

■ ■ ■

Gay Lib began its efforts to gain formal recognition in early 1971. In accordance with established University procedures, the group submitted a petition for recognition to the Missouri Students Association (MSA).

■ ■ ■

Both the MSA Rules Committee and the Senate approved Gay Lib's petition. The matter was then referred to the Committee on Student Organizations, Government and Activities (SOGA), which was comprised of students and faculty. While the matter was pending before SOGA, Gay Lib submitted a revised, more detailed statement of purposes.[4]

In December, 1971, SOGA voted to recommend recognition of Gay Lib. The recommendation, however, was vetoed by Edwin Hutchins, then Dean of Student Affairs. Hutchins based his veto on "a concern for the impact of recognition on the general

---

3. Mo. Ann. Stat. § 563.230 (Vernon) provides:

> Every person who shall be convicted of the detestable and abominable crime against nature, committed with mankind or with beast, with the sexual organs or with the mouth, shall be punished by imprisonment in the penitentiary not less than two years.

4. The revised statement provided:

> 1. Gay Lib intends to create a forum for the study of the sexual statutes of this state and especially of the sodomy law now in effect. Through study of the intent of the law and of its psychological and sociological implications, it will be possible to more fully understand what the full meaning is of being gay. Through knowledge of the law, it becomes possible to create an atmosphere within which the present statute may be revised or eliminated through an educational and candid look at all ramifications of such laws and their rationale. Changes of other such laws outside of Missouri and in nations such as Great Britain will provide a fuller context.
>
> 2. Gay Lib seeks to promote meaningful communication between all members of the University community, whether homosexual or heterosexual. With candor and compassion on both sides, much of the fear of the unknown can be eliminated and scars of past repression may be healed. This communication is specifically intended to be two-way in nature. The gay world has just as much to learn from the straight world as they have to offer it. We seek to develop an atmosphere in which people are themselves first and sexual entities second.
>
> 3. Gay Lib wants to provide information to the vast majority of those who really don't know what homosexuality or bisexual behavior is. Too much of the same prejudice is now directed at gay people just as it is directed at ethnic minorities.
>
> 4. Gay Lib does not seek to proselytize, convert, or recruit. On the other hand, people who have already established a pattern of homosexuality when they enter college must adjust to this fact.

relationship of the University to the public at large."

Gay Lib appealed the nonrecognition decision to successive levels of the University heirarchy, ending with the President of the University. Each level sustained Hutchins' ruling. Thereafter, Gay Lib appealed the decision to the University's Board of Curators. The Board consolidated the appeal with a related matter arising out of the University of Missouri at Kansas City, and appointed a hearing officer, Cullen Coil, a Jefferson City attorney and former Commissioner of the Missouri Supreme Court, to develop the facts. At the hearings substantial lay and expert testimony was adduced. Following the hearings, Coil recommended that the University deny formal recognition to the organization.[7] Subsequently, the Board denied Gay Lib's appeal, adopting the following resolution:

Be it hereby resolved that the Board of Curators of the University of Missouri concurs with and hereby adopts the Hearing Officer's Recommended Findings of Fact made by the Honor-

able Cullen Coil and further makes the following specific findings of fact:

1. The Gay Lib movement as exemplified by the Gay Lib Organization at UMC and the Gay People's Union at UMKC is premised upon homosexuality being normal behavior, contrary to the further findings herein.

2. A homosexual is one who seeks to satisfy his or her sexual desires by practicing some or all of the following: fellatio, cunnilingus, masturbation, anal eroticism and perhaps in other ways.

3. Homosexuality is a compulsive type of behavior.

4. There are potential or latent homosexuals, i.e. persons who come into adolescence or young adulthood unaware that they have homosexual tendencies, but who have fears of sexual relations with a member of the opposite sex.

5. What happens to a latent or potential homosexual from the standpoint of his environment can cause him to become or not to become a homosexual.

---

5. Gay Lib hopes to help the gay community to rid itself of its subconscious burden of guilt. Society imprints this self-image on homosexuals and makes adjustment with the straight world more difficult.

6. Gay Lib hopes to function as a channel for those who find difficulty in sexual adjustment. While we do not pretend to have psychiatric expertise, we can reach people who do not trust normal channels for such help and enable them to contact professional help as required.

7. As an educational group, Gay Lib does not advocate any violation of state statutes. We serve as a forum for understanding and knowledge where this is now lacking.

7. Coil found that formal recognition of Gay Lib would:

(1) give a formal status to and tend to reinforce the personal identities of the homosexual members of those organizations and will perpetuate and expand an abnormal way of life, unless contrary to their intention as stated in their written purposes, the homosexual members make a concerted effort to seek treatment, recognize homosexuality as abnormal and attempt to cease their homosexual practices;

(2) tend to cause latent or potential homosexuals who become members to become overt homosexuals;

(3) tend to expand homosexual behavior which will cause increased violations of section 563.230 of the Revised Statutes of Missouri;

(4) be undesirable insofar as homosexuals will counsel other homosexuals, i.e., the sick and abnormal counseling others who are similarly ill and abnormal; and

(5) constitute an implied approval by the University of the abnormal homosexual life-style as a normal way of life and would be so understood by many students and other members of the public, even though, and despite the fact that, the University's regulations for student organizations provide that recognition of an organization by the University does not constitute approval or endorsement of the organization's aims or activities.

6. That homosexuality is an illness and should and can be treated as such and is clearly abnormal behavior.

7. Certain homosexual practices violate provisions of Section 563.230 of the Revised Statutes of Missouri.

8. That formal recognition by the University of either or both the proposed Gay Lib and Gay People's Union will: (The Board of Curators here adopted verbatim Mr. Coil's above-cited conclusions as to the effect of formal recognition.)

Plaintiffs filed this civil rights action to compel the University to formally recognize Gay Lib, alleging that nonrecognition infringed their First Amendment freedom of association and denied them equal protection . . . . The district court... received depositions of three medical doctors taken by the parties. No other evidence was presented.

First Amendment.

Although the district court denied plaintiffs relief, Judge Hunter, recognizing *Healy v. James*, 408 U.S. 169 (1972), stated:

> [T]he University, acting here as an instrumentality of the State, has no right to restrict speech or association "simply because it finds the views expressed to be abhorrent."

416 F. Supp. at 1370, quoting *Healy, supra* at 187.

Since the Supreme Court's decision in *Healy*, the First and Fourth Circuits have sustained the rights of groups similar to Gay Lib to sponsor social functions involving the use of university facilities, *Gay Students Org. of Univ. of New Hampshire v. Bonner*, 509 F.2d 652 (1st Cir. 1974); and to register as a student organization. *Gay Alliance of Students v. Matthews*, 544 F.2d 162 (4th Cir. 1976). The analytical discussion offered by these two courts strongly supports recognition of Gay Lib here.[9]

Notwithstanding these decisions, defendants assert that the record in this case contains expert medical testimony which provides a legal justification for withholding formal recognition from Gay Lib. They argue, and the district court found, that recognition of Gay Lib would likely result in imminent violations of Missouri sodomy laws.

The district court placed reliance on the testimony of two psychiatrists, Dr. Harold Voth and Dr. Charles Socarides. Dr. Voth testified that formal recognition would tend to "perpetuate" or "expand" homosexual behavior. However, on cross-examination, Dr. Voth further testified that his conclusion was "an inference," and "[t]here is no way in the world for me or anyone else to know." Dr. Socarides stated that he believed "that wherever you have a convocation of homosexuals, that you are going to have increased homosexual activities which, of course includes sodomy." He concluded that "any gathering would certainly promote such sexual contact."

---

9. As Judge Winter of the Fourth Circuit observes:

> If the University is attempting to prevent homosexuals from meeting one another to discuss their common problems and possible solutions to those problems, then its purpose is clearly inimical to basic First Amendment values. Individuals of whatever sexual persuasion have the fundamental right to meet, discuss current problems, and to advocate changes in the status quo, so long as there is no "incitement to imminent lawless action."
>
> If, on the other hand, VCU's concern is with a possible rise in the incidence of actual homosexual conduct between students, then a different problem is presented. We have little doubt that the University could constitutionally regulate such conduct. Additionally, it may regulate any conduct (homosexual or otherwise) which "materially and substantially disrupt[s] the work and discipline of the school." But denial of registration is overkill.
>
> "[T]he critical line for First Amendment purposes must be drawn between advocacy, which is entitled to full protection, and action, which is not." There is no evidence that GAS is an organization devoted to

Also relevant to the district court's determination was the medical opinion proffered by defendants' experts that homosexual behavior is compulsive. However, as demonstrated by the substantial body of professional medical opinion conflicting with defendants' case, it must be acknowledged that there is no scientific certitude to the opinions offered.

The district court noted testimony from Dr. Robert Kolodny, a medical doctor with some training in psychiatry. Dr. Kolodny testified that he believed recognition would not have "any discernible effect upon the sexual behavior of the student population." He based his conclusion on his clinical knowledge of human sexual behavior and "from actual knowledge of what, in fact has occurred on several campuses where homosexual groups have been allowed to acquire office space, hold social functions, and sponsor university activities."

Defendants urge that their experts are more worthy of belief because of their outstanding professional credentials. We need not pause here since defendants' evidence turns solely on Dr. Voth's conclusory "inference" and Dr. Socarides' "belief," for which no historical or empirical basis is disclosed.

Even accepting the opinions of defendants' experts at face value, we find it insufficient to justify a governmental prior restraint on the right of a group of students to associate for the purposes avowed in their statement and revised statement of purposes. While it is difficult to articulate generalized standards as to the quantum and quality of proof necessary to justify the abridgment of First Amendment rights, the many Supreme Court cases dealing with prior restraints and other First Amendment issues make clear that the restriction of First Amendment rights in the present context may be justified only by a far greater showing of a likelihood of imminent lawless action than that presented here.

Mr. Justice Harlan, in delivering the opinion of the Supreme Court in *NAACP v. Alabama*, 357 U.S. 449 (1958), emphasized the importance of freedom to engage in association:

> Effective advocacy of both public and private points of view, particularly controversial ones, is undeniably enhanced by group association, as this Court has more than once recognized by remarking upon the close nexus between the freedoms of speech and assembly. It is beyond debate that freedom to engage in association for the advancement of beliefs and ideas

carrying out illegal, specifically proscribed sexual practices. While Virginia law proscribes the practice of certain forms of homosexuality, Va.Code § 18.2-361, Virginia law does not make it a crime to *be* a homosexual. Indeed, a statute criminalizing such status and prescribing punishment therefor would be invalid.

It follows that even if affording GAS registration does increase the opportunity for homosexual contacts, that fact is insufficient to overcome the associational rights of members of GAS. Given the right to exclude individuals who are convicted of practicing proscribed forms of homosexuality, or whose homosexual conduct, although not proscribed, materially and substantially disrupts the work and discipline at VCU, the suppression of associational rights because the opportunity for homosexual contacts is increased constitutes prohibited overbreadth.

Gay Alliance of Students v. Matthews, 544 F.2d 162, 166 (4th Cir. 1976).

Chief Judge Coffin similarly wrote for the First Circuit:

Another interest asserted by appelants is that in preventing illegal activity, which may include "deviate" sex acts, "lascivious carriage", and breach of the peace. . . . Mere "undifferentiated fear or apprehension" of illegal conduct, *Tinker v. Des Moines Indep. Community School Dist.*, 393 U.S. at 508, is not enough to overcome First Amendment rights and speculation that individuals might at some time engage in illegal activity is insufficient to justify regulation by the state.

Gay Students Org. of Univ. of New Hampshire v. Bonner, 509 F.2d 652, 661-63 (1st Cir. 1974).

is an inseparable aspect of the "liberty" assured by the due process clause of the Fourteenth Amendment, which embraces freedom of speech. [Citations omitted.] Of course, it is immaterial whether the beliefs sought to be advanced by association pertain to political, economic, religious or cultural matters, and state action which may have the effect of curtailing the freedom to associate is subject to the closest scrutiny.

357 U.S. at 460-61.

In the present case, none of the purposes or aims of Gay Lib, at least in this record, evidences advocacy of present violations of state law[16] or of university rules or regulations, and the district court made no finding of such advocacy. The district court further made no finding that Gay Lib would "infringe reasonable campus rules, interrupt classes, or substantially interfere with the opportunity of other students to obtain an education." *Healy v. James, supra*, at 189. So far as the avowed purposes and aims of this association are concerned, in the words of the Fourth Circuit:

[I]t is, at most, a "pro-homosexual" political organization advocating a liberalization of legal restrictions against the practice of homosexuality and one seeking, by the educational and informational process, to generate understanding and acceptance of individuals whose sexual orientation is wholly or partly homosexual.

Gay Alliance of Students v. Matthews, supra, at 164.

It is difficult to singularly ascribe evil connotations to the group simply because they are homosexuals. An interesting fact is that not all members of the group are homosexuals.[17] Furthermore, this approach blurs the constitutional line between mere advocacy and advocacy directed to inciting or producing imminent lawless action. Finally, such an approach smacks of penalizing persons for their status rather than their conduct, which is constitutionally impermissible. *See Robinson v. California*, 370 U.S. 660 (1962).

We, of course, acknowledge the statement in *Tinker v. Des Moines Indep. Community School Dist.*, 393 U.S. 503, 506 (1969), repeated in *Healy v. James, supra* at

---

16. Surely, it is no longer a valid argument to suggest that an organization cannot be formed to peaceably advocate repeal of certain criminal laws. *See Street v. New York*, 394 U.S. 576, 591 (1969).

     Chief Judge Markey of the Court of Customs and Patent Appeals, sitting by designation, concurred in Judge Winter's analysis in *Gay Alliance of Students v. Matthews, supra*, and cogently added:

     Consistent with the present decision, associations advocating any idea, any change in the law or policy of the general society, are as fully entitled to registration as is the plaintiff. Thus, associations devoted to peaceful advocacy of decriminalization or social acceptance of sadism, euthanasia, masochism, murder, genocide, segregation, master-race theories, gambling, voodoo, and the abolishment of all higher education, to list a few, must be granted registration, upon proper application and indicated compliance with reasonable regulations, if VCU continues to "register" associations.

     It is of no moment, in First Amendment jurisprudence, that ideas advocated by an association may to some or most of us be abhorrent, even sickening. The stifling of advocacy is even more abhorrent, even more sickening. It rings the death knell of a free society. Once used to stifle "the thought that we hate," in Holmes' phrase, it can stifle ideas we love. It signals a lack of faith in people, in its supposition that they are unable to choose in the marketplace of ideas.

     544 F.2d at 167-68.

17. Would defendants allow a group of heterosexual students to meet to discuss the problems of homosexuals and the repeal of the sodomy laws? Presumably so, since there would be no basis to "infer" that the compulsive behavior of the students would incite violations of the law. However, assuming this to be so, it is obvious that equal protection principles become more sharply focused.

180, that the factual circumstances must be evaluated in light of the "special characteristics" of the school environment. In this sense, it is clear that a university has residual power "to assure that the traditional academic atmosphere is safeguarded," and to promulgate reasonable rules and regulations. *Healy, supra* at 194 n.24. It may be, as Mr. Justice Rehnquist observed in his concurring opinion in *Healy*, that the "school administrator may impose upon . . . students reasonable regulations that would be impermissible if imposed by the government upon all citizens." 408 U.S. at 203. We note, however, that the interest asserted by defendants in justification for the abridgement of plaintiffs' First Amendment rights is not peculiar to the academic environment. Moreover, it is also axiomatic that the First Amendment must flourish as much in the academic setting as anywhere else. *See Papish v. University of Missouri Curators*, 410 U.S. 667, 671 (1973); *Shelton v. Tucker*, 364 U.S. 479, 487 (1960). To invoke censorship in an academic environment is hardly the recognition of a healty democratic society.

■ ■ ■

CONCLUSION

We hold that the defendants' refusal to recognize Gay Lib as a campus organization denied plaintiffs their First Amendment rights. The judgment of the district court is reversed and the cause remanded for the entry of appropriate injunctive relief and an award of attorneys' fees.

WEBSTER, Circuit Judge, concurring.

■ ■ ■

I have no doubt that the ancient halls of higher learning at Columbia will survive even the most offensive verbal assaults upon traditional moral values; solutions to tough problems are not found in repression of ideas. I am equally certain that the university possesses the power

and the right to deal with individuals and organizations, "recognized" or not, that violate either its lawful regulations or the laws of the state. There will be time for that if appellees' dire predictions should somehow prove to be correct. The nature of our government demands that we abide that time.

REGAN, District Judge, dissenting.

I respectfully dissent.

■ ■ ■

I do not read *Healy* as mandating that in *every* case involving non-recognition of a campus group a showing of the certitude of imminent overt lawless or disruptive activity must be made. Rather, the issue is whether, under the circumstances, *justification* of the appropriateness of denial of recognition has sufficiently been shown.

The credible testimony of highly qualified psychiatrists persuasively demonstrates to me, as it did to the District Court, that homosexual behavior is compulsive and that homosexuality is an illness and clearly abnormal. In view of the expert testimony which in my view is neither "skimpy [nor] speculative," defendants were warranted in concluding that formal recognition of Gay Lib would tend to expand homosexual behavior and activity on campus and likely result in felonious acts of sodomy proscribed by Missouri law. As the District Court stated: "The legitimate interest of the University as a state institution includes the right to refuse the requested recognition and its concomitants where the result predictably is to bring on the commission of crimes against the sodomy statutes of the State of Missouri."

■ ■ ■

Moreover, state university officials have a responsibility not only to taxpayers but to *all* students on campus, and that responsibility encompasses a right to protect latent or potential homosexuals from becoming overt homosexual students. In carrying out these responsibilities, they were aware that unlike recognition of political associations, whether of the right, center or left, an organization dedicated to the furtherance and advancement of homosexuality would, in any realistic sense, certainly so to impressionistic students, imply approval not only of the organization per se but of homo-sexuality and the normality of such conduct, and thus adversely affect potential homosexual students. In my opinion, the University was entitled to protect itself and the other students on campus, in this small way, against abnormality, illness and compulsive conduct of the kind here described in the evidence.

■ ■ ■

Following denial of a petition for rehearing *en banc*, the University of Missouri filed a petition for *certiorari* with the Supreme Court which refused to hear the case. Justices Rehnquist and Blackmun, however, filed the following dissent from the Court's denial of *certiorari*.

RATCHFORD v. GAY LIB

434 U.S. 1080 (1978)

MR. JUSTICE REHNQUIST, with whom MR. JUSTICE BLACKMUN joins, dissenting [from the denial of certiorari].

There is a natural tendency on the part of any conscientious court to avoid embroiling itself in a controversial area of social policy unless absolutely required to do so. I therefore completely understand, if I do not agree with, the Court's decision to deny certiorari in this case. In quick summary, the University of Missouri, exercising the traditional authority granted to it by the State to regulate what student organizations will have access to campus facilities, denied recognition to respondent Gay Lib. The denial stemmed from a finding by a University-appointed hearing officer that formal University recognition would "tend to expand homosexual behavior which will cause increased violations of [the State's sodomy statute]." Respondents, choosing to remove the dispute from its traditional University setting to the federal courts, sued in the United States District Court for the Western District of Missouri, claiming that the denial infringed their constitutional rights to free speech and freedom of association. The District Court held that the University had not violated respondents' constitutional rights. Respondents, continuing to pursue a judicial solution to their problem, persuaded two judges of a three-judge panel of the Court of Appeals for the Eighth Circuit to reverse the District Court. A petition for rehearing en banc was denied by an equally divided court. The University now seeks certiorari here to review that decision.

Courts by nature are passive institutions and may decide only those issues raised by litigants in lawsuits before them. The obverse side of that passivity is the requirement that they *do* dispose of those lawsuits that are before them and entitled to attention. The

District Court and the Court of Appeals were doubtless as chary as we are of being thrust into the middle of this controversy but were nonetheless obligated to decide the case. Unlike the District Court and the Court of Appeals, Congress has accorded to us through the Judiciary Act of 1925, 28 U.S.C. § 1254, the discretion to decline to hear a case such as this on the merits without explaining our reasons for doing so. But the existence of such discretion does not imply that it should be used as a sort of judicial storm cellar to which we may flee to escape from controversial or sensitive cases. Our Rules provide that one of the considerations governing review on certiorari is whether a Court of Appeals "has decided an important question of federal law which has not been, but should be, settled by this [C]ourt; or has decided a federal question in a way in conflict with applicable decisions of this [C]ourt." Rule 19(1)(b). In my opinion the panel decision of the Court of Appeals meets both of these tests, and I would therefore grant certiorari and hear the case on the merits.

The sharp split amongst the judges who considered this case below demonstrates that our past precedents do not conclusively address the issues central to this dispute. In the same manner that we expect considered and deliberate treatment of cases by these courts, we have a concomitant responsibility to aid them where confusion or uncertainty in the law prevails. By refusing to grant certiorari in this case, we ignore our function and responsibility in the framework of the federal court system and place added burdens on other courts in that system.

Writ large, the issue posed in this case is the extent to which a self-governing democracy, having made certain acts criminal, may prevent or discourage individuals from engaging in speech or conduct which encourages others to violate those laws. The Court of Appeals holds that a state university violates the First and Fourteenth Amendments when it refuses to recognize an organization whose activities both a University factfinder and the District Court found were likely to incite violations of an admittedly valid criminal statute. Neither the Court of Appeals nor respondents contend that the testimony of the expert psychologists at these hearings was insufficient to support such a finding. They appear to take instead the position that such a finding is not governed by the normal "clearly erroneous" test established in Fed. Rule Civ. Proc. 52(a). This unusual conclusion, in itself, would seem to me to be sufficient to warrant a grant of certiorari.

But lurking behind this procedural question is one which surely goes to the heart of the inevitable clash between the authority of a State to prevent the subversion of the lawful rules of conduct which it has enacted pursuant to its police power and the right of individuals under the First and Fourteenth Amendments who disagree with various of those rules to urge that they be changed through democratic processes. The University in this case did not ban the discussion in the classroom, or out of it, of the wisdom of repealing sodomy statutes. The State did not proscribe membership in organizations devoted to advancing "gay liberation." The University merely refused to recognize an organization whose activities were found to be likely to incite a violation of a valid state criminal statute. While respondents disavow any intent to advocate present violations of state law, the organization intends to engage in far more than political discussion. Among respondent Gay Lib's asserted purposes are the following:

> "3. Gay Lib wants to provide information to the vast majority of those who really don't know what homosexuality or bisexual behavior really is. Too much of the same prejudice is now directed at gay people just as it is directed at ethnic minorities.
> "4. Gay lib [sic] does not seek to proselytize, convert, or recruit. On the other hand, people who have already established a pattern of homosexuality when they enter college must adjust to this fact.

"5. Gay Lib hopes to help the gay community to rid itself of its subconscious burden of guilt. Society imprints this self-image on homosexuals and makes adjustment with the straight world more difficult."

Expert psychological testimony below established the fact that the meeting together of individuals who consider themselves homosexual in an officially recognized university organization can have a distinctly different effect from the mere advocacy of repeal of the State's sodomy statute. As the University has recognized, this danger may be particularly acute in the university setting where many students are still coping with the sexual problems which accompany late adolescence and early adulthood.

The University's view of respondents' activities and respondents' own view of them are diametrically opposed. From the point of view of the latter, the question is little different from whether university recognition of a college Democratic club in fairness also requires recognition of a college Republican club. From the point of view of the University, however, the question is more akin to whether those suffering from measles have a constitutional right, in violation of quarantine regulations, to associate together and with others who do not presently have measles, in order to urge repeal of a state law providing that measle sufferers be quarantined. The very act of assemblage under these circumstances undercuts a significant interest of the State which a plea for the repeal of the law would nowise do. Where between these two polar characterizations of the issue the truth lies is not as important as whether a federal appellate court is free to reject the University's characterization, particularly when it is supported by the findings of the District Court.

. . . [T]he question is not whether Gay Lib as an organization will abide by university regulations. Nor is it really whether Gay Lib will persuasively advocate violations of the sodomy statute. Instead, the question is whether a university can deny recognition to an organization the activities of which expert psychologists testify will in and of themselves lead directly to violations of a concededly valid state criminal law.

As our cases establish from *Schenck v. United States*, 249 U.S. 47 (1919), in which Mr. Justice Holmes, speaking for a unanimous Court, held that the Government has a right to criminally punish words which are "used in such circumstances and are of such a nature as to create a clear and present danger that they will bring about the substantive evils that Congress has a right to prevent," to *Brandenburg v. Ohio*, 395 U.S. 444 (1969), some speech that has a propensity to induce action prohibited by the criminal laws may itself be prohibited. A fortiori, speech and conduct combined which have that effect may surely be placed off limits of a university campus without doing violence to the First or Fourteenth Amendments.

Healy was decided by the lower courts in what may fairly be described as a factual vacuum. There this Court stated that a student organization need not be recognized if such recognition is likely to incite criminal violations, but did not have to consider how that standard would be applied to a particular factual situation. No attempt had been made by the University to demonstrate that imminent lawless action was likely as a result of the speech in question, nor was there any hint that any such effort was likely to have been successful. Here, such a demonstration was undertaken, and the District Court sitting as a finder of fact concluded that petitioners had made out their case. The Court of Appeals' panel opinion, for me at least, sheds no light on why this conclusion of the District Court could be rejected. By denying certiorari, we must leave university officials in complete confusion as to how, if ever, they may meet the standard that we laid out in *Healy*.

The mathematically even division of the Court of Appeals on the petition for rehearing en banc gives some indication of the divergence of judicial views which may be expected from conscientious judges on difficult constitutional questions such as this. Our views may be no less divergent, and no less persuasive to one another, than were the views of the eight judges of the Court of Appeals. But believing as I do that we cannot under our Rules properly leave this important question of law in its present state, I would grant the petition for certiorari.

Notes

1. There have been numerous attempts such as that by the University of Missouri to deny recognition and/or funding to gay student groups. In every instance in which the issue has been litigated, the gay group's rights have ultimately been protected. *See, e.g., Gay and Lesbian Students Ass'n v. Gohn,* 850 F.2d 361 (8th Cir. 1988); *Gay Student Servs. v. Texas A & M Univ.,* 737 F.2d 1317 (5th Cir. 1984), *cert. denied,* 471 U.S. 1001 (1985); *Gay Alliance of Students v. Matthews,* 544 F.2d 162 (4th Cir. 1976); *Gay Students Org. of the Univ. of N.H. v. Bonner,* 509 F.2d 652 (1st Cir. 1974); *Student Coalition for Gay Rights v. Austin Peay Univ.,* 477 F. Supp. 1267 (M.D. Tenn. 1979); *Wood v. Davison,* 351 F. Supp. 543 (N.D. Ga. 1972). *See, generally,* Jean F. Rydstrom, Annotation, *Validity, Under First Amendment and 42 U.S.C.S. § 1983, of Public College or University's Refusal to Grant Formal Recognition to, or Prevent Meetings of, Student Homosexual Organizations on Campus,* 50 A.L.R. FED. 516 (1991).

2. One gay student group case arose at a private Catholic school, Georgetown University, in the District of Columbia. The gay student group filed suit under the local D.C. human rights act which prohibits discrimination in public and private educational institutions on the basis of sexual orientation. Georgetown interposed a First Amendment defense, arguing that forcing recognition of the gay student group would violate its rights of free exercise of religion. The District of Columbia's highest court, the D.C. Court of Appeals, issued a compromise decision. It chose not to interpret the local human rights law as requiring that Georgetown University "endorse" the gay student group, agreeing that this would violate the school's First Amendment rights. It did interpret the law, however, as requiring Georgetown to grant equal benefits to the group; with regard to the granting of benefits, the court held that the District's compelling interest in eradicating discrimination on the basis of sexual orientation outweighed the University's first amendment religious rights. *See Gay Rights Coalition of Georgetown Univ. Law Center v. Georgetown Univ.,* 536 A.2d 1 (D.C. App. 1987).

    Following the *Georgetown* decision, Congress initially attempted to force the District of Columbia City Council to amend its human rights law to exempt religiously-affiliated educational institutions from having to comply with the gay rights provisions of the law. Nation's Capital Religious Liberty and Freedom Act, Pub. L. No 100-462, § 145, 102 Stat. 2269 (1988) (adopting the Armstrong Amendment). The federal appellate court in the District of Columbia, however, ruled that forcing the Council to adopt such an amendment violated the First Amendment speech rights of the city councillors. *Clarke v. United States,* 886 F.2d 404 (D.C. Cir. 1989), *reh'g denied,* 898 F.2d 161, *vacated on other grounds,* 915 F.2d 699 (1990). In response, Congress went ahead the next year and, with its plenary authority over the District of Columbia, amended the human rights law directly to exempt Georgetown and other religiously-affiliated institutions from the gay rights law. District of Columbia Appropriations Act of 1990, Pub. L. No. 101-168, § 141, 103 Stat. 1267, 1284 (1989).

In the meantime, Georgetown University announced its intention to abide by the initial court result, regardless of the later Congressional intervention, and signed a consent decree to that effect. *See* Lawrence Feinberg, *GU to Treat Homosexuals Equally*, WASH. POST, November 11, 1988, at D5.

3. In *Department of Educ. v. Lewis*, 416 So.2d 455 (Fla. 1982), the Florida Supreme Court struck down a law that read as follows:

> No funds appropriated herein shall be used to finance any state-supported public or private postsecondary educational institution that charters or gives official recognition or knowingly gives assistance to or provides meeting facilities for any group or organization that recommends or advocates sexual relations between persons not married to each other.
>
> Sexual relations means contact with sexual organs of one person by the body of another person for sexual gratification.
>
> Any postsecondary educational institution found in violation of this provision shall have all state funds withheld until that institution is again in compliance with the law.
>
> No state financial aid shall be given to students enrolled at any postsecondary educational institution located in Florida which is in violation of this provision.

The court ruled that this restriction violated the First Amendment, as well as other provisions of the Florida state constitution. *Id.*

A similar law was enacted in Alabama in 1992. Ala. H. 454 (enacted Apr. 16, 1992).

B. Lesbian and Gay College Life Today

The following article by John D'Emilio assesses the current state of gay life on universities campuses throughout the United States.

◆

THE CAMPUS ENVIRONMENT FOR GAY AND LESBIAN LIFE

John D'Emilio

The theme of this issue of *Academe* confirms the profound influence of feminism on contemporary life. Just over twenty years ago, a new generation of feminists coined the phrase "the personal is political." Although the slogan has carried different meanings for those who use it, one implication has been to challenge our notions of private and public. Feminists have argued, and rightly so, that defining women's sphere and women's con-

John D'Emilio, *The Campus Environment For Gay And Lesbian Life*, in ACADEME, Jan/Feb. 1990, at 16.

cerns as "private" has effectively excluded women from full and equal participation in the "public realm." As more and more women in the 1970s and 1980s fought for entry into academic life, higher education institutions increasingly have had to deal with a host of issues that were once safely tucked away in the private domain.

Colleges and universities in the pre-feminist era addressed privacy only in the breach, particularly with respect to matters of sexual identity. Consider the following examples:

- In 1959, at a small *midwestern* college, a student told her faculty adviser that one of her friends was a homosexual. The adviser informed a dean, who called in the student in question and pressured him into naming others. Within twenty-four hours, three students had been expelled; a week later, one of them hung himself.

- About the same time, a faculty member at a Big Ten school was arrested in mid-semester on a morals charge (at that time, *all* homosexual expression was subject to criminal penalties). The police alerted the administration, and the professor was summarily told to leave the campus. He never appeared before his classes again.

- At an elite college in the Northeast, male students in the 1960s were in the habit of training a telescope on the windows of the women's dormitories. In one instance, they spied two female students erotically engaged. The women — not the men — were disciplined.

- At a women's college in New England, where accusations of lesbianism were periodically leveled against roommates in the 1960s, the standard solution was to separate the accused by housing them in different dorms.

I could list many more such examples. They came to me not through research but through the gay and lesbian academic grapevine. Stories like these are the substance of an oral tradition by which gay academics who came of age before the 1970s warned one another of the dangers they faced and socialized their younger peers into necessary habits of caution and discretion.

The point, I trust, is clear. For gay men and lesbians, the past is a history of privacy invaded, of an academy that enforced, maintained, and reproduced a particular moral order — a moral order aggressively antagonistic toward homosexual expression.

Since 1969, when the Stonewall Riots in New York City ushered in the gay liberation movement, activists across the country have challenged that order. We have formed organizations by the thousands, lobbied legislatures, initiated public education campaigns, engaged in civil disobedience, and promoted self-help efforts. We have attempted to emancipate gays and lesbians from the laws, policies, scientific theories, and cultural attitudes that have consigned us to an inferior position in society.

When one considers that the political climate for most of the last twenty years has been conservative, and that this new conservatism has taken shape largely through an appeal to "traditional" notions of family, sexuality, and gender roles, the successes of the gay movement appear rather impressive. Half the states have repealed their sodomy laws. Many of the nation's largest cities have enacted some form of gay civil rights ordinance, and a number of states are seriously debating the issue. The American Psychiatric Association has removed homosexuality from its list of mental disorders. Several religious denominations are revising their positions on the morality of homsexual relationships. And lesbian and gay organizations around the country are better financed and more stable now than at any point in their past.

Those of us associated with institutions of higher education have contributed to this movement and have benefited from it as well. Because the birth of gay liberation was so closely tied to the social movements of the 1960s, student groups have been part of the gay political and social landscape from the beginning. Currently, more than four hundred of these groups exist, in community colleges and research universities, in public institutions and private ones. Braving the ostracism and harassment that visibility sometimes brings, these young women and men have often had to battle for recognition and funding. In the process, their struggles have created a substantial body of judicial opinion that protects gay student groups as an expression of First Amendment rights of speech and assembly.

Faculty members, too, have organized. Initially forming separate organizations, such as the Gay Academic Union, they have increasingly turned to their professional associations as venues for action. Most social science and humanities disciplines now have lesbian and gay caucuses that publish newsletters, review current literature, and sponsor well-attended sessions at annual meetings. A vibrant new scholarship has emerged in the last decade that is substantial enough to spark a movement for gay studies programs in institutions as diverse as San Francisco City College, Yale University, and the City University of New York.

If one's reference point is university life a generation ago, one can say that things *are* getting better for gay faculty, students, administrators, and staff. Grit, courage, and determination have opened up some space in which it is possible to live, breathe, and work openly. Our situation no longer appears uniformly grim.

Nevertheless, being openly gay on campus still goes against the grain. Despite the changes in American society in the last two decades, gay people are still swimming in a largely oppressive sea. Most campuses do not have gay student groups. Most gay faculty members and administrators have not come out. Even on campuses that have proven responsive to gay and lesbian concerns, progress has often come through the work of a mere handful of individuals who have chosen to be visible. And, although I do not have statistics to measure this precisely, I know that there are still many, many campuses in the United States where no lesbian or gay man feels safe enough to come out. From a gay vantage point, something is still wrong in the academy.

Oppression in its many forms is still alive, and the university is not immune to it. Indeed, as the gay population has become a better organized and stronger force in the 1980s, we have also become easier to target. In recent years, harassment, violence, and other hate-motivated acts against lesbians and gay men have surfaced with alarming frequency on campuses across the country. Institutions such as the University of Kansas and the University of Chicago, to name just two, have witnessed campaigns of terror against their gay members. At Pennsylvania State University, a report on tolerance found that bias-motivated incidents most frequently targeted gay people.

Unlike many other groups — women and African-Americans, for instance — in which one's identity is clear for the world to see, most gay men and lesbians have the option to remain invisible. I cannot fault individuals who choose that path: the costs of visibility often can be high. Yet the fear that compels most gay people to remain hidden exacts a price of its own. It leads us to doubt our own self-worth and dignity. It encourages us to remain isolated and detached from our colleagues and peers, as too much familiarity can lead to exposure. And it often results in habitual patterns of mistrust and defensiveness because anyone, potentially, may cause our downfall. Hence, speaking about gay oppression involves not only addressing injustice in the abstract but also acknowledging the emotional toll it levies on particular individuals and the institutions of which they are a part.

For reasons that I cannot quite fathom, I still expect the academy to embrace higher standards of civility, decency, and justice than the society around it. Having been granted the extraordinary privilege of thinking critically as a way of life, we should be astute enough to recognize when a group of people is being systematically mistreated. We have the intelligence to devise solutions to problems that appear in our community. I expect us also to have the courage to lead rather than to follow.

Although gay oppression has deep roots in American society, the actions that would combat it effectively on campuses are not especially difficult to devise and formulate. What sort of policies would make a difference? What would a gay-positive institution look like?

One set of policies would place institutions of higher education firmly on the side of equal treatment. Gay faculty, administrators, staff, and students need to know that their school is committed to fairness, to treating us on the basis of our abilities. At a minimum that would mean:

A nondiscrimination policy, formally enacted, openly announced, and in print wherever the institution *proclaims its policy* with regard to race, gender, and religion. Such a policy would apply to hiring, promotion, tenure, admissions, and financial aid. Because of the history of discrimination in this country, it is not enough for an administration to claim that it subscribes to the principle of fairness for everyone. Sexual orientation, sexual preference, sexual identity, or whatever term one chooses to adopt, needs to be explicitly acknowledged.

Spousal benefits for the partners of gay men and lesbians, at every level of institutional life and for every service that is normally provided to husbands and wives. These benefits include health insurance, library privileges, access to the gym and other recreational facilities, listings in school directories if spouses are customarily listed, and access to married students' housing for gay and lesbian couples.

An approach to gay student groups that is identical to that for all other groups with regard to recognition procedures, funding, and access to facilities. Administrators who place obstructions in the way of these groups are doing a costly disservice to their institutions since courts have uniformly sustained the rights of gay students to organize.

Subscribing to the above policies would simply place lesbians and gays in a *de jure* position of parity. Implementing these measures would go a long way toward alleviating the fears that we live with, integrating us fully into the life of the campus, and letting us know that we are valued and "welcomed."

The university's responsibility toward its gay members goes well beyond these elementary procedures of fairness, however. Administrators will need to take an activist stance to counteract the misinformation about gays and lesbains that many members of the university community have, the cultural prejudices that are still endemic in the United States, and the growing problem of hate-motivated incidents. The following areas need attention:

1. One of the prime locations where harassment occurs is in residence halls. Dormitory directors and their assistants need to be sensitized about gay issues and trained in how to respond quickly and firmly to instances of oppressive behavior and harassment. In an age when heterosexual undergraduates routinely hold hands, walk arm-in-arm, and engage in other simple displays of affection, lesbian and gay students need to know that they will not have their rooms ransacked, or their physical safety endangered, for doing the same. They also need reassurance that campus activism on gay issues will not come back to haunt them when they return to their dorms each night.

2. Student affairs programming is an important tool in fostering toleration, understanding, and enthusiasm for differences in culture and identity. Resources should be made available to sponsor special gay awareness week events, as well as to integrate gay films, public lectures, and other events and activities into the regular programming.

3. Late adolescence is an especially stressful time for gay men and lesbians. These may be the years when they become sexually active, form their first relationships, and grapple with issues of identity. School counseling services need personnel who are sensitive to these issues and who can foster self-acceptance and self-esteem rather than reinforce self-hatred.

4. Because the issues and situations affecting lesbians and gay men range widely across the structure of large- and medium-size campuses, hiring an "ombudsperson" for gay and lesbian concerns makes good institutional sense. Someone who can think expansively about these issues, provide a resource where needed, and intervene decisively in emergencies can move a whole campus forward.

5. When hate-motivated incidents occur — and the evidence of the last few years suggests that they happen with greater frequency than we care to admit — the *highest* officers of the university need to exercise their *full* authority in condemning the attacks and correcting the underlying problems which encourage such incidents. Bias-motivated incidents are awful, but they also offer a unique opportunity for raising consciousness and for shifting the climate of opinion on a campus.

6. An institution that prohibits discrimination against gays ought not to countenance the presence on campus of institutions and organizations that engage in such discrimination. The government intelligence agencies and the military are the most egregious perpetrators of anti-gay bias. Recent actions by the military against its gay and lesbian personnel amount to a form of terrorism. Military recruiters and ROTC programs ought to be banned from American campuses until the armed forces change their policies.

7. Last, but not least, is the issue of research. The 1980s have witnessed an efflorescence of scholarship on gay and lesbian issues in several disciplines. Yet many topics go begging for researchers because faculty members know that prejudiced department heads and tenure committess will label such work trivial and insignificant. Gay scholarship, opening as it does a new window on human experience, must be encouraged.

On sunny mornings, I am optimistic that the 1990s will see a dramatic improvement in the quality of life for gay men and lesbians in higher education: the body of scholarship is growing and pressure for gay studies programs will mount; academics in many disciplines have created stable and permanent caucuses which will strengthen our networks; regional associations of gay student groups are forming to reinforce those groups already established on individual campuses. In addition, the National Gay and Lesbian Task Force in Washington, D.C., recently initiated a campus-organizing project so that gay men and lesbians on each campus no longer have to reinvent the wheel.

Of equal importance, perhaps, some administrators are moving beyond the most elementary issues of visibility and recognition. They are addressing the key areas of equal treatment and deep- rooted prejudice. Such a stance — on every campus — is long overdue.

III. SOCIAL/POLITICAL ASSOCIATIONS AND THE STATE

A. Background

◆

AN UNDERGROUND BAR
Judy Grahn

*In the closeted world of the late 1950s, when you brought me out, Von,
we worried a great deal that you might lose your teaching credentials
if we were seen as lesbians. We made up stories for people we were
sisters-in-law. And we were frightened all the time. Yet still we found
our world exciting and wouldn't have stopped being gay for anything.
We loved being able to love each other and to explore areas of human
behavior that didn't seem to be open to other young women we knew.
We were part of a secret network of lesbians who knew each other,
who were busy learning the stances and attitudes of gayness, and who
met for parties or to play cards. There was yet another part of the gay
underground culture that I would get to know in the next couple of
years: the gay bar. This was to be the only public expression of Gay
culture that I would find in a closeted world.*

During the late fifties and early sixties, my Von, when virtually everyone was in the closet, including you as you finished college after tearfully sending me on my way out into the world to become a "real writer," the only place I found to locate a gathering of gay people was a downtown big-city bar....

I can see now it was a necessary part of my initiation; going to my first gay bar certainly felt as terrifying, mystifying, and life-altering as any ritual procedure could have felt.

The bar was on a sleazy street of pawnshops, clubs featuring women dancers pushing watered-down drinks on a quota system between dances, tattoo parlors, rundown hotels, and hamburger counters staying open till just past bar-closing time to serve coffee and sobering-up food to customers too drunk to walk to a bus stop. A nearby bus stand for service personnel dropped off loads of sailors and soldiers with weekend passes and just enough money to get drunk and do a little carousing. MPs patrolled the block as often as did the city police.

Judy Grahn, *An Underground Bar, in* ANOTHER MOTHER TONGUE 28–33 (1984).

The street had a permanently dislocated look, unwashed and untended, a look of transience and worn-out baggage. Our fresh young faces, not yet wary, cynical, or bitter, were a startling contrast to the environment. Dim, multicolored neon lights added to the dinginess and aura of danger. Brassy whores in tight, bright mini-skirts were trailed down the street by knots of self-conscious sailors and singular, decrepit winos.

Nothing distinguished the Rendezvous Bar from any of the others except that its reputation among queers was that it was "ours." Why we should have wanted it is anybody's guess. Perhaps we took what dregs were available. All the world at that time was divided very severely into male and female, with no one crossing the line easily; there was no androgyny. Women did not wear pants on the street; men did not make graceful gestures, let alone carry purses or wear make-up. In those days homosexuality was so closely guarded and so heavily punished that it might as well have been illegal just to gather in a bar together. Only heavy payoffs, I have heard, kept any of the bars open for business to a gay clientele. Quite a contrast to the snazzy, clean, well-lit, beautiful, and often gay-owned bars of today....But the sleazy Rendezvous was where we bottom-of-the-world overt gay people could go and be "ourselves."

I went there one night with another lesbian I had met in the service; I remember the fear I felt on the bus ride downtown. The bus passed through a dark tunnel and the driver had a black curtain wrapped around his seat. I felt I was on a journey to hell and had to laugh at my young self for undertaking such a perilous journey. There would be no turning back for me once I had entered such a place; I knew very distinctly that I had "crossed over."

From the minute I entered the doors of the Rendezvous, past the gay bouncer (who looked exactly like Li'l Abner in the comics), and gaped in thrilled shock at the self-assured, proud lesbians in pants and the men in make-up and sculptured, displayed, eerily beautiful faces, I saw myself as part of a group that included some very peculiar characters and characteristics. I ceased then to be a nice white Protestant girl with a tomboy nature who had once had a secret and very loving lesbian relationship with another nice girl who was attending college to become a teacher. That definition no longer applied, as I stepped into my first Gay bar to become a full-fledged dyke, a more-than-a-lesbian.

Imitating the women I found at the Rendezvous, I dressed for the dyke part each evening before riding the bus to my new world. I combed my hair back from my face, having cut it as short as I could and still hold my job. Using men's hairdressing I slicked it into a duck tail; with peroxide I streaked a blond swath into the front and arranged a curl to fall down the center of my forehead. Next came boys' trousers and either a black turtleneck sweater or a boys' white shirt with a T-shirt underneath. Black clothing was the color of choice. Cigarettes tucked in the front pocket, boys' black loafers, and a comb completed the outfit. No makeup of any kind, certainly no purse. A jacket, if it were pouring rain or freezing cold. The boys' heavy black loafers that I had invaded a men's shoe store to buy were a special point of pride; they had taken real courage to get.

No one in the bar used a last name in front of the others, and I suspect that all first names were assumed: We had names we took for ourselves as dykes or fairies in that particular setting, just as we had a special slang laguage. I took the name Sonny.

For all our boyish clothes and mannerisms (known as being "butch") we women did not pass as men or boys. We dykes did not want to be taken for men and were insulted and ashamed (I certainly was, anyhow) when someone said we were "trying to be men" or when a clerk called me "Sir." In fact, on those rare occassions when a woman came in who was passing in society as a man, word about this went around the tables and we studied her secretly and gossiped about her. For our point was not to be men; our point was to be butch and get away with it.

We always kept something back: a high-pitched voice, a slant of the head, or a limpness of hand gestures, something that was clearly labeled female. I believe our statement was "Here is another way of being a woman," not "Here is a woman trying to be taken for a man."

The fairies also held something back that prevented them from passing over into the female gender; no matter how many sequins or feathers she wore, a drag queen was a gay queen, not a man-passing-as-a-woman. Proper bar etiquette required that the drag queens be called "she." They referred to each other as "sister" (by which they meant friends with whom one did not have sex). "Mary" was another term for male homosexuals, and so was "Nellie" (used as an adjective). We dykes were sometimes spoken of as "he," but this was relatively rare compared to the use of female pronouns to indicate the queens.

A hawk-eyed, bent-over old crone with a heavy European accent and not a trace of warmth or goodwill owned the bar, cheating us nightly on the beer and refusing to supply toilet paper or other niceties. She glared at all of us equally with apparent rank contempt when we stood at the bar to order our beers. Her standard method of letting us know it was closing time was to shine a blazing searchlight into our beer-sodden faces until we got the message, stumbling out into the starkly unwelcoming streets.

The bar had considerable dangers. Sailors lurked in the alleys outside, waiting to prove their "manhood" on our bodies; more than once they beat someone I knew — dike or faggot — on her or his way home. A brick crashed through the front window one night, scattering glass splinters over the dance floor where, fortunately, none of us were clenched together swaying to early sixties "Moon River" melodies, thrilled to death (in my case at least) to be holding a member of the same sex in her arms, to be two women publicly dancing.

One night a furious femme wearing a tight dress and carrying a purse attacked one of the dykes at another table — a woman dressed like myself in sedate dark colors and men's clothing, slicked-back hair. The femme stormed up behind the dyke, who was probably her girlfriend, beating her on the head with the sharp peg of her high-heeled shoe. It was my first understanding that women fight each other.

Another night two policemen came up to the table where I sat with my friend from the service. They shined a flashlight into our eyes and commanded us to stand up or else be arrested. Then they demanded that we say our real names, first and last, several times, as loud as we could. Sweat poured down my ribs as I obeyed. After they left, my friend and I sat with our heads lowered, too ashamed of our weakness to look around or even to look each other in the face. We had no internal defense from the self-loathing our helplessness inspired and no analysis that would help us perceive oppression as oppression and not as a personal taint of character. Only the queens with their raucous sly tongues helped us get over these kinds of incidents. They called the policemen "Alice Blue Gowns," insulting them behind their backs. "Alice Blue Gown tried to sit on *my* nightstick but I said No! You dirty boy! I know you're menthtrating!" one plump faggot in a cashmere sweater would begin and soon we would be laughing and feeling strong again.

The dykes had a special way of talking, with a minimum of inflection, a flat matter-of-fact, everything-is-under-control effect. It was considered more dykish to be planted solidly in one place than to flit, to use tightly controlled gestures rather than anything grandiose.

The dykes and femmes of the bar provided a kind of low-key, solid background of being; the queens (often with a sailor or two in tow) took the foreground, talking in loud voices, using flamboyant costumes and body language to create a starry effect. Sometimes they came in full drag, with wigs and makeup, and at other times just with a big fluffy sweater for a costume but always with the particular broad gestures, lilting voice, and special queen talk. Or shrieking. The special language of a queen, or even an ordinary garden-variety faggot, is so distinct I find I can distinguish it even in a crowd of men in a restaurant or on the street, far from any gay scene. It's a full or modified lisp coupled with dramatic inflection and, as used in full-drag queen-style, it accompanies a running monologue of commentary, jokes, puns and "gay talk," most of it sexual but with a great deal of social and political content. Bruce Rodger's dictionary of gay slang, *Gay Talk* (originally called *The Queen's Vernacular*), has more than 12,000 entries. This slang talk is used most particularly by gay men, especially the fairy queens, and less so by the bar dykes.

I noticed some differences between my experience as a single woman in that gay bar and my experiences in other kinds of bars, where, of course, I did not dress in an extreme dyke fashion. In the gay bar I could sit and drink and not be surrounded by men demanding my attention. I could ask someone to dance. I could lead when we danced, or I could find someone who like to lead and let her do it. I could dance with either men or women. I could sing along with the lyrics and not be embarrassed to be using the "wrong" gender. I could sit with a serious face and not have smiles and pleasantries demanded of me. I noticed also great differences in gay coupling; for the most part, lovers who were going together for any length of time were of similar size; one did not tower over the other. In the playing they did together in company, there was not the same stress on conquering-male, conquered-female that I saw in straight bars, where the pairing was different, with different purposes and a different social structure to support it.

◆

AIDS STORIES
John Weir

Last year I ran a writers' group for people with AIDS. We met on Monday nights for about nine months in the kitchen of the Gay Men's Health Crisis, in Manhattan. Twelve men were in the group, though never more than six of them came at once. I met the first of them two years ago, near Thanksgiving; they started dying the following February. One of them is still alive. For a while, they went about one a month. I would get phone calls and friends would say, "Oh, by the way, you remember so and so," and I would know that he had died.

The boys in my group died in hospitals, or in their apartments, or they went back to their parents. One guy killed himself after leaving a message on his phone machine. Hank. He was writing a novel about a species of underground beings who are terribly lonely but have this remarkable immunity to disease. Hank and Francisco became lovers after meeting in the group. Francisco was my age, twenty-six. He was from Puerto Rico. He had long, long fingernails and shiny black hair. Hank was forty, and rugged-looking. He had been everywhere, had taught

John Weir, *AIDS Stories*, Harper's Magazine, Sept. 1987, at 22.

writing at a prep school in Pennsylvania, had worked on an oil rig off the coast of Texas.

Francisco used to drag himself all the way across town to our meetings, from Bellevue, where he went once a week to get all kinds of debilitating treatments — spinal taps and bronchoscopies and twenty-four-hour injections. The first time he shuffled into the kitchen, I thought he looked like Ratso Rizzo in *Midnight Cowboy*, only younger, and much more resigned. We went out to dinner after the workshop and he had a slice of cheesecake and chocolate milk. Gradually, he and Hank became lovers. Francisco had meningitis, among other things, and he was always sick. Hank was pretty healthy. After a while they went away and got married — they had rings — and stopped coming to the group.

The last time I saw Francisco was just before he died, at Bellevue, a place you should not have to walk into, much less die in. It's the Grand Central Station of hospitals: cavernous, full of people, dirty, scary. It's nineteenth-century. It's Olivia De Havilland in *The Snake Pit*. Francisco was hooked up to a machine that made him breathe, and he was swaddled in white. The bandages ended just above his nipples; he might have been wearing a strapless gown.

His mother stood next to his bed and cried. I tried to talk to her but she didn't speak English. When she went away I touched Francisco's forehead. I said, "I'm sorry." I saw Hank later that night and he said that Francisco had died about ten minutes after I left the room.

A week later I called Hank and got his suicide message, which I have written down somewhere. I had to call his number about a dozen times to get it all down. Took a handful of downers, he said, and swam for England. Melodramatic queen. He was not that sick and I'm still angry that he did it.

We wrote a lot of things in the workshop. Hank read portions of his novel, and we wrote letters — "A Letter to Nancy Reagan," "An Open Letter to the Universe,"

"A Letter to a Friend I Will Not See Before I Die." Benny Stein wrote poetry. He looked like Marlon Brando, from the Bronx. He walked into his first group meeting with a pillow, sat down, and started discussing his rectal tumors. Everything he said, everything he wrote about, turned out to be about his tumors, or his pain, or death. Poor Thomas Benjamin would leave the room every time Benny started talking. Thomas didn't want to know that he was dying.

But Benny's poems: they would be beautiful poems about raindrops falling through the atmosphere and straight down through the ocean to the ocean floor, and then into the core of the earth, and we would say, "Well, Benny, that was lovely, what was that about," and he would say, "It's about what it's like to shit when you have rectal tumors."

I loved Benny very much; I think I had a crush on him. I like his style. He did a performance piece for me one night, in his apartment. He was staying in the apartment of a friend of a friend of a friend. He did this ballet number for me, putting on and taking off his robe, crawling on and off the bed, answering the phone, apologizing for himself, discussing his illness, his vitamins, his doctors, his insurance. I thought he was Delmore Schwartz, updated and gay — brilliant and paranoiac and dying all the time.

The first thing he ever talked about in the group was having to experience his own death, and he terrified everyone; the second thing he said was how wonderful it felt at seventeen to get fucked on the downtown IRT, speeding on Methedrine. He said it right to my face and laughed; in a group of dying men who must have had a lot to say about sex, he was the only one who ever talked about dying, or having sex.

Gustavo talked about reincarnation. He was from Argentina, and he wore round glasses that made him look like T.S. Eliot, or Ernie Kovacs impersonating T.S. Eliot. One of his eyes watered constantly from chemotherapy. I always thought that he was crying, and I hugged him a lot, and touched him a lot. He was Benny's age, thirty-five. He spoke fluent Italian, and read philosophy.

The day I meet him, he said, "Ah, but I do not think I reincarnate again." I said, "Why not?" And he said, "The more you have this pain, the more thoroughly it cleanses you, and when you are clean, you are through, you reach Nirvana. I have so much pain this lifetime. I think I must be clean."

Eventually he dropped out of the group, and a few months later he died. I went to his memorial service. Benny dropped out of the group, too. He went into the hospital, but I never visited him. The last time I saw him he was walking with a cane up Hudson Street. It was July, and it was hot. He was stooped and very thin. He said, "I had a body once," and thumped his chest. He died in the fall.

The last session of the writers' group was in July of 1985, and one man came. He was the only one left. The rest were dead, or about to be. We stared at each other across the table and talked about other things, terrified to say what both of us were thinking. Just us two.

The last memorial service I attended for a member of the group was Gerald's. He died the day of the last workshop. He had been in the group from the beginning, even before I started running it. He was an intern in radiology at a hospital on the East Side when he was diagnosed. For about a year he looked perfectly healthy. Then he came back early from a vacation in Atlanta and went straight into the hospital. His lesions multiplied and he went on chemotherapy. When I first met him, Gerald was a dandy — fastidiously dressed, charming, affable. He wore wonderful argyle socks and a big ring with his initials on it; he flirted with everyone. But he fell apart very quickly. He lost a lot of weight and his hair fell out. A month after he was admitted to the hospital, he died. He was twenty-eight.

His memorial service was at the Gay Synagogue in the Village. Gerald had a big, supportive family. They all knew he was gay. The service was in Hebrew. His father got up to read his part. Gerald's father was the kind of Jewish man that Bernard Malamud wrote about — barely assimilated, still with the rough edges, the accent, the conspicuousness of an immigrant. He was a butcher in the Bronx.

He started reading, but then he let go of the text, and tipped his head back, and clasped his palms together, and roared. He wailed and shouted and roared in a language that I couldn't understand, but I knew exactly what he meant, I knew exactly what he meant, I think I knew exactly what he meant.

Clearly, this goes on and on. Terry, who walked into the group for the first time and handed around an X-ray of his skull; Joe, who went to Italy in khaki shorts even though he had lesions all over his legs, and educated an entire Italian village about AIDS; Greg, who is still alive, oh, and so on. This is all very impressionistic. I don't know how to organize it. I do know that AIDS has given me what little wisdom I think I possess; it is the difference between my childhood and the rest of my life, the line dividing everything in two. It is also still going on; it's hard to see out of it, into the rest of life. I have six friends who have been diagnosed since last May.

Almost none of the coverage of AIDS seems accurate to me; nothing gets even close to my experience, and the experience of my friends. Television is whitewashed, pretending that AIDS is a family concern. My experience has been that families are rarely anywhere around; gay men, yes, gay women, longime straight best friends, current lovers and ex-lovers, volunteers, but not much family. I cannot talk about myself without getting around to AIDS. It has profoundly affected my sense of New York City, of friendship, of death (which I had never thought about before), of gayness, of sex; really, of just about everything.

B. Government Regulation of Lesbian
and Gay Organizations

Many organizations exist to serve the social, political, and legal needs of lesbians and gay men. To take advantage of special tax provisions, limited liability, and official state recognition available to nonprofit corporations, these organizations have often sought incorporation.

STATE ex rel. GRANT v. BROWN

313 N.E.2d 847 (Ohio 1974), *cert. denied sub nom.*
Duggan v. Brown, 420 U.S. 916 (1975).

PER CURIAM.

On August 9, 1972, relators tendered articles of incorporation for a nonprofit corporation to respondent, Secretary of State. He refused to accept those articles because:

> ". . . this office finds that acceptance of the proposed articles of incorporation for Greater Cincinnati Gay Society, Inc. appear to be contrary to public policy since homosexuality as a 'valid life style' has been and is currently defined by statute as a criminal act."

On August 24, 1972, a complaint was filed in this court asking for a writ of mandamus to require the Secretary of State to accept, approve, file and record those articles of incorporation.

Respondent filed a motion to dismiss, arguing that relator was improperly denominated in the complaint as a corporation; that its avowed purpose was, on its face, contrary to public policy; and that it might be advocating furtherance of its objectives by means other than legal.

This court overruled the motion to dismiss, and allowed relator to amend its complaint by changing the name of relator.

In the amended complaint, relators argue that "there is no statute whatsoever which prohibits the state of being a homosexual or promoting homosexuality as a valid life style." They argue further that nowhere in the articles of incorporation can a purpose to engage in, or urge others to engage in, criminal acts be found. Finally, relators argue that R. C. Chapter 2907 of the new Criminal Code, effective January 1, 1974, dealing with sexual offenses, shows no specific animus against the activities of homosexuals so that promoting homosexual conduct cannot be said to be contrary to public policy in Ohio. The subject, as a whole, invites more extensive discussion, but we forbear.

The Secretary of State refused to accept the articles of incorporation pursuant to R.C. 1702.07(A), which, in pertinent part, provides:

> "When articles of incorporation and other certificates relating to the corporation are filed with the secretary of state, he shall, *if he finds that they comply* with the provisions of Sections 1702.01 to 1702.58, inclusive, of the Revised Code, endorse thereon his approval . . . ."

The Secretary of State found that the articles of incorporation, as tendered, did not comply with R.C. 1702.03, which provides:

"A corporation may be formed for any purpose or purposes for which natural persons *lawfully* may associate themselves . . . ."

It is the opinion of this court that the statutes (R.C. 1702.01 to 1702.58) give the Secretary of State discretion in determining which articles of incorporation he will accept.

Although homosexual acts between consenting adults are no longer statutory offenses since the new Criminal Code came into effect, there is still reason for denying the writ. We agree with the Secretary of State that the promotion of homosexuality as a valid life style is contrary to the public policy of the state.

Writ denied.

STERN, J. dissenting.

As I read the majority opinion, it is henceforth unlawful in this state for any group of persons to attempt, in any fashion, to persuade the public that homosexuality represents a valid, alternative life style.[1] Because I believe this position to have no basis in law, I dissent.

The majority is factually inaccurate in stating that respondent's decision was based upon public policy grounds. In his final brief, filed on November 5, 1973, in this court, the Secretary of State explained:

"Respondent did state, when giving a reason for not accepting and filing relator's articles of incorporation, that they appear to be contrary to public policy. *This does not mean, however, that the Secretary of State is attempting to dictate what is contrary to public policy. The use of that term was merely another way of saying that relator's purpose clause could logically be interpreted as encouraging the commission of unlawful acts (as established by the Legislature).*"

Specifically, according to respondent, he is concerned with relators' potential violations of R.C. 2905.44, which prohibited sodomy, and R.C. 2905.30, which prohibited the solicitation of acts of sex perversion.

It is clear, at least to me, that as of January 1, 1974, when Amended Substitute House Bill 511 became effective, respondent's objections to relators' articles of incorporation are moot.[2] Sodomy, and solicitation of acts of sex perversion, are no longer crimes in this state. The General Assembly has seen fit to decriminalize all private sexual activity between consenting adults, and it is wholly unreasonable and improper to infer from the general language of relators' purpose clause any intent to violate any provision in the Criminal Code.

What is most disturbing about the majority opinion, however, is that it confers broad discretionary power upon the Secretary of State, and at least implies that the office of the Secretary of State is a vehicle for formulating and implementing state public policy.

---

1. The last sentence of the majority opinion states: "We agree with the Secretary of State that the promotion of homosexuality as a valid life style is contrary to the public policy of the state." The purpose clause tendered by relators, however, reads, in part: "To promote *acceptance* of homosexuality as a valid life style . . ." A fair reading of relators' enunciated purpose indicates that they hope to foster community acceptance of *themselves*, as individuals, and not that they seek to convert the community to homosexuality, as suggested by the majority.

2. It is interesting to note that, even prior to January 1, 1974, all the attorneys involved in this litigation were of the opinion that relators' articles of incorporation should be accepted for filing. The ultimate responsibility, however, rests with the Secretary of State who has consistently maintained his position that "the articles of incorporation for Greater Cincinnati Gay Society, Inc. will only be filed if I am ordered to do so by the Supreme Court of Ohio."

Both of these notions are in direct conflict with the long-standing law . . . .

■ ■ ■

. . . As I have stated, the large body of law elsewhere, and the specific case law in this state, views the role of the Secretary of State as being largely ministerial. However, even if one were to accept the conclusion of the majority, several problems arise.

The Secretary of State, in discharging his duties pursuant to R.C. Chapter 1702, cannot be viewed as the original spokesman or interpreter of state public policy. Neither his office, nor his assigned responsibilities permit him this initiative. If the Secretary of State is to act upon policy considerations at all, those considerations must stem from discernible and particularized pronouncements by the people, through their constitutions, legislators, or judicial officers.

Since the majority has declared relators' avowed purpose to be against public policy, one must assume that their decision is based upon considerations to be found in our constitutions, our statutes, or our judicial pronouncements. The Ohio Constitution displays no preference for sexual life style. Both the Ohio Constitution (Section 11, Article I) and the United States Constitution (First Amendment) do contain, however, a bias in favor of permitting people to speak their minds and promote their causes in a peaceful manner.

The recent amendments to R.C. Title 29, which decriminalize all private sexual activity between consenting adults, indicate an express public policy to tolerate the existence of different sexual life styles in this state. Insofar as the Criminal Code in Ohio is now concerned, no distinction is drawn between heterosexual and homosexual activities.

Past judicial pronouncements of this court also fail to support the majority's public policy pronouncement. In fact, nowhere in the recorded decisions of the Ohio Supreme Court has any justice ever used the term "homosexual" or "homosexuality,"[3] let alone discuss the policy implications of such a life style. Thus, the cryptic comment that "the subject, as a whole, invites more extensive discussion, but we forbear," leaves this reader without a hint of the underlying rationale that has prompted the majority decision.

Under the law of this state, as I perceive it, this court is duty-bound to allow respondents the opportunity to associate for the purpose of fostering acceptance of their freely chosen life style. The writ of mandamus should be allowed.

■ ■ ■

Notes

1. For a critique of the type of discretion granted to the state in cases similar to *State ex rel. Grant v. Brown*, see Henry Hansmann, *Reforming Nonprofit Corporation Law*, 129 U. PA. L. REV. 497, 526 & n.70 (1981).
2. In 1972 the highest court in New York ordered a lower court to allow the incorporation of a lesbian and gay legal organization, Lambda Legal Defense and Education Fund. *See In Re Thom*, 33 N.Y.2d 609 (1973). The lower court had denied Lambda's application to become a recognized public interest organization. *See In Re Thom* 337 N.Y.S.2d. 588 (App. Div. 1972).

---

3. Computerized research, using LEXIS, discloses this fact.

3. The same year it decided *In Re Thom*, the New York Court of Appeals ordered the New York Secretary of State to incorporate the Gay Activists Alliance, a nonprofit organization. *In Re Gay Activists Alliance v. Lomenzo*, 293 N.E.2d 255 (N.Y. 1973). The court held that the Secretary of State's denial of incorporation on "public policy" grounds was arbitrary and that incorporation could not be denied if the formal filing requirements were met and if the organization's purposes were lawful. It also affirmed the lower court's ruling that the word "gay" was permissible and that there was no criterion of appropriateness for corporate names.

4. In a related context pertaining to the use of corporate names, the United States Supreme Court upheld an injunction against the use of the word "Olympic" for the Gay Olympic Games, an international athletic event sponsored by a gay nonprofit organization, on grounds that such use violated the Amateur Sports Act of 1978, 36 U.S.C. §§ 371 – 396 (1988), which allows the United States Olympic Committee to prohibit certain commercial and promotional uses of the word "Olympic." *See San Francisco Arts & Athletics, Inc. v. United States Olympic Comm.*, 483 U.S. 522 (1987). Earlier, when the case was denied a rehearing *en banc* on the Ninth Circuit, circuit judge Alex Kozinski wrote a scathing dissent and noted that the enjoined action "lies at the very heart of the First Amendment. . . ." *See International Olympic Comm. v. San Francisco Arts & Athletics, Inc.*, 789 F.2d 1319, 1325 (9th Cir 1986) (Kozinski, J., dissenting from the denial of rehearing *en banc*).

5. The difficulty that some nonprofit gay organizations have experienced when seeking tax-exempt status under state and federal law parallels the obstacles faced historically by groups simply seeking incorporation. In *Big Mama Rag, Inc. v. United States*, 621 F.2d 1030, 1034 (D.C. Cir. 1980), the Court of Appeals for the District of Columbian Circuit struck down as unconstitutionally vague a treasury department regulation that was relied on to deny federal tax-exempt status to a feminist magazine that addressed lesbian issues. *See also* Rev. Rul. 78-305, 1978-2 C.B. 172, IRB LEXIS 167 (1978) (providing that nonprofit organizations that educate about homosexuality qualify for tax-exempt status).

C. Government Regulation of Lesbian and Gay Meeting Places

Bars have traditionally been an important place where lesbians and gay men have socialized and met with other lesbians and gay men. According to one gay historian, "bars were the first institutions in the United States that contradicted . . . stigmas and gave gay Americans a sense of pride in themselves and their sexuality. As such, gay bars . . . are an integral part of gay political history . . . . In a nation which has for generations mobilized its institutions toward making gay people invisible, illegal, isolated, ignorant and silent, the creation of gay . . . bars were daring, political acts, the first stages in creating the roots of America's national movement for civil rights for gay people."[1] In fact, the modern era of the movement for lesbian and gay rights is said to have begun with a riot in 1969 at the Stonewall Bar in Greenwich Village, New York, when gays fought back during a police raid of the bar.

---

1. Declaration of Allan Berube in Support of Memorandum of Points and Authorities in Support of Ex Parte Application for Leave to Intervene, *State ex rel. Agnost v. Owen*, No. 830–321, at 4 (Cal. App. Dep't Super. Ct. filed Nov. 7, 1984).

ONE ELEVEN WINES & LIQUORS, INC.
v.
DIVISION OF ALCOHOLIC BEVERAGE CONTROL

235 A.2d 12 (N.J. 1967)

JACOBS, J.

The Division of Alcoholic Beverage Control disciplined the appellants for permitting apparent homosexuals to congregate at their licensed premises. It suspended the licenses of One Eleven Wines & Liquors, Inc. and Val's Bar, Inc. and revoked the license of Murphy's Tavern, Inc. On One Eleven's appeal to the Appellate Division the suspension of its license was sustained . . . . We granted certification on the licensee's application. . . .

The disastrous experiences of national prohibition led to the adoption of the Twenty-First Amendment and to the return of liquor control to the states in 1933. When our Legislature during that year first created the Department of Alcoholic Beverage Control, it vested broad regulatory powers in a state commissioner who immediately set about to ensure that abuses which had originally contributed so heavily in bringing about national prohibition, would not be permitted to recur. He adopted stringent regulations which he rigidly enforced and which the courts supported with great liberality. He concerned himself not alone with matters of lawfulness but also with matters of public sensitivity for he firmly believed that the effectiveness of the new mode of control would turn on the extent of the public's acceptance of the manner in which licensed establishments were conducted. Here again the courts sustained his pertinent regulatory actions with broad sweep.

Among the commissioner's early regulations were Rules 4 and 5 which were adopted in 1934. Rule 4 provided that no licensee shall allow in the licensed premises "any known criminals, gangsters, racke-

teers, pick-pockets, swindlers, confidence men, prostitutes, female impersonators, or other persons of ill repute." And Rule 5 provided that no licensee shall allow "any disturbances, brawls, or unnecessary noises" or allow the place of business to be conducted "in such manner as to become a nuisance." In 1936 Rule 5 was revised to include an express prohibition of "lewdness" and "immoral activities," and in 1950 it was again revised to include an express prohibition of "foul, filthy, indecent or obscene language or conduct."

During the years prior to 1954 the department instituted proceedings under Rule 4 on the basis of evidence that apparent homosexuals had been permitted to congregate at the licensed premises. Apparently the department considered that the effeminate manifestations of the patrons brought them within the prohibition of "female impersonators" although that term relates more properly to transvestites who are, for the most part said to be non-homosexuals. *In Re M. Potter, Inc.*, A.B.C. Bulletin 474, Item 1 (August 7, 1941) the investigators had observed a group of male patrons, "whose voices, gestures and actions were effeminate," dancing and kissing among themselves. Although there was an express finding that "no actual acts of immorality" were committed at the licensed premises, the license was nonetheless suspended. In the course of his formal opinion, the acting commissioner said that the mere "presence of female impersonators in and upon licensed premises presents a definite social problem"; and in line with the then widespread intolerance and limited public understanding of the subject, he made reference to "the deep-rooted personal contempt felt by a normal red-blooded man" and to the notion that "the mere thought of such perverts is repugnant to the normal person."

Since 1954 and despite increasing public tolerance and understanding, departmental proceedings aimed at the congregation of apparent homosexuals have continued apace but have been brought under Rule 5 rather than Rule 4. They have not been based on any specific and individualized charges of lewd or immoral conduct but rather on general charges that by permitting the apparent homosexuals to congregate, the licensees had allowed their places of business to be conducted in such manner "as to become a nuisance" within the contemplation of Rule 5. *In Re Polka Club, Inc.*, A.B.C. Bulletin 1045, Item 6 (December 27, 1954), the then director, in suspending a license on a charge of violation of Rule 5, said that he would not permit licensed premises to become "havens for deviates." *In Re Kaczka and Trobiano*, A.B.C. Bulletin 1063, Item 1 (April 21, 1955) the licensee introduced expert testimony that homosexuality is not contagious and that seeing groups of homosexuals would not affect normal people but the license was nonetheless suspended. As illustrated in many of his rulings, including, *In Re Louise G. Mack*, A.B.C. Bulletin 1088, Item 2 (November 2, 1955), the director entertained the view that since exposure to homosexuals might be harmful to "*some* members of the public" the congregating of homosexuals must be prohibited as a "threat to the safety and morals of the public." *See Paddock Bar, Inc. v. Alcoholic Beverage Control* Division, 134 A.2d 779 (N.J. App. Div. 1957).

In the very cases before us the Division of Alcoholic Beverage Control made it clear that it has not in anywise moderated its long standing position that permitting the congregation of apparent homosexuals, without more, is violative of Rule 5. The evidence against Murphy's Tavern disclosed many individual acts which could have been the basis of specified and individualized charges of lewd or immoral conduct at the licensed premises. But no such charges were preferred and when, during the course of cross-examination, one of the division's investigators was asked whether he had observed any lewdness at Murphy's Tavern, the prosecuting attorney pointed out that the division had not alleged "any immoral activity or lewdness itself" but had simply alleged that the licensee had "permitted the licensed place of business to become a nuisance" in that it had allowed "these persons to come in and congregate upon the premises."

In the One Eleven proceeding there was no charge and no substantial evidence that lewd or immoral conduct was permitted at the licensed premises. There was a charge and sufficient evidence that the licensee had permitted apparent homosexuals to congregate there. Investigators had visited the premises on several occasions and had observed the patrons; the testimony included the following partial account of their behavior:

> They were conversing and some of them in a lisping tone of voice, and during certain parts of their conversations they used limp-wrist movements to each other. One man would stick his tongue out at another and they would laugh and they would giggle. They were very, very chummy and close. When they drank their drinks, they extended their pinkies in a very dainty manner. They took short sips from their straws; took them quite a long time to finish their drink. . . .
>
> They were very, very endearing to one another, very very delicate to each other. . . .
>
> They looked in each other's eyes when they conversed. They spoke in low tones like an effeminate male. When walking, getting up from the stools, they very politely excused each other, hold on to the arm and swish and sway down to the other end of the bar and come back. . . .

Their actions and mannerisms and demeanor appeared to me to be males impersonating females, they appeared to be homosexuals commonly known as queers, fags, fruits, and other names.

Similarly in the proceeding against Val's Bar there was no charge nor any substantial evidence at the hearing before the director that lewd or immoral conduct was permitted at the licensed premises. Investigators had visited the premises on several occasions and testified in detail as to the behavioral characteristics which led them to the permissible conclusion that the patrons were apparent homosexuals. The investigators acknowledged that for the most part the patrons were "normally dressed" and showed "very good behavior." Dr. Wardell B. Pomeroy, called as an expert witness by the licensee, testified that, although it could not be said from mere observation that any given individual was a homosexual, he would be of the opinion that tavern patrons with the characteristics described by the investigators were apparent homosexuals.

Dr. Pomeroy was associated with the Kinsey Institute for twenty years and was the co-author of several books dealing with sexual behavior and offenses. He referred to the Kinsey studies which contained startling indications that 13% of the males in the country were "more homosexual than heterosexual" and that 37% had "at least one homosexual experience to the point of orgasm in the course of their life." He also referred to indications that 55% of the population was neutral on the subject of homosexuality and there is now "a more acceptance attitude" than there was twenty years ago. See Mosk, "Forward to the Consenting Adult Homosexuals and the Law," 13 U.C.L.A. L. Rev. 644, 645 (1966). In response to an inquiry by the division's hearer, Dr. Pomeroy voiced the opinion that no adverse social effects would result from permitting homosexuals to congregate in licensed establishments. He noted that non-homosexuals would not be harmed by being in the same premises with homosexuals, and that any who found their mere presence to be offensive would presumably leave. He expressed the view that permitting their congregation in taverns would tend to eliminate clandestine associations in unregulated and unsupervised places of public nature. See Cory and Le Roy, The Homosexual and His Society 119, 121 (1963); see also Schur, Crimes Without Victims 86, 87 (1965) where Dr. Schur dealt with the so-called "gay" bars operating in our neighboring states and elsewhere:

"Although such establishments are sometimes condemned as breeding grounds of homosexuality, the charge is not convincing. Most of the people who go there (apart from tourists and some 'straight' friends) already are involved in the homosexual life. Anyone who wanders in and who is offended by what he sees is perfectly free to leave. The authors of a recent 'view from within' emphasize that although an increase in homosexuality may increase the demand for homosexual bars, the bars can scarcely be said to produce homosexuals. Indeed, as these writers go on to suggest, the bars serve to keep homosexuals 'in their place' — out of more public places and, to a certain extent, beyond the public view."

The views expressed by Doctors Pomeroy and Schur find significant legal support in various judicial holdings, notably those of the California Supreme Court. In Stoumen v. Reilly, 234 P.2d 969 (Cal. 1951) the license was suspended because the licensee had permitted "persons of known homosexual tendencies" to patronize and meet at the licensed premises. Under Section 58 of the California Alcoholic Beverage Control Act, it was unlawful to permit the licensed premises to be conducted as a disorderly house or as a place "to which people resort for purposes which are injurious to the public morals, health, convenience or safety." The court, in setting aside the suspension, held that mere patronage "without proof of the commission of illegal or immoral acts on the premises, or resort thereto for such purposes" was not sufficient to show a violation of Section 58. Elsewhere in its opinion it stressed that in order to establish "good cause" for suspension of the license, something more must be shown than that many of the patrons were homosexuals and used the premises "as a meeting place." 234 P.2d at p. 971.

After the *Stoumen* case was decided, the California Legislature enacted the provision in Section 24200, subdivision (e) of the Business and Professions Code under which licensed premises were prohibited from being used as resorts for "sexual perverts." In *Vallerga v. Dept. of Alcoholic Beverage Control*, 347 P.2d 909 (Cal. 1959) a license was revoked because the licensee had permitted his premises to become a resort for homosexuals. The revocation was set aside by the California Supreme Court which held that the legislative provision was unconstitutional under *Stoumen*. The court also considered the contention that, apart from the provision declared unconstitutional, the revocation could be sustained on the ground that continuance of the license would be "contrary to public welfare and morals" within the lower court holdings in *Nickola v. Munro*, 328 P.2d 271 (Cal. 1958) and *Kershaw v. Department of Alcoholic Beverage Control*, 318 P.2d 494 (Cal. 1957); in this connection it said:

> "In the Nickola case the court held generally that seeking sexual gratification in a public tavern with another of the same sex would offend the moral sense of the general public. The court stated, 328 P.2d at page 276: 'There are many things that can be done in the privacy of the home which may not be illegal, but if done in a public tavern are directly offensive to public morals and decency, and

demonstrate that the participants are sex perverts. The continuance of the license under such circumstances "would be contrary to public welfare or morals" as provided in our Constitution. . . . Further than that we do not have to go.' Conduct which may fall short of aggressive and uninhibited participation in fulfilling the sexual urges of homosexuals, reported in some instances, may nevertheless offend good morals and decency by displays in public which do no more than manifest such urges. This is not to say that homosexuals might properly be held to a higher degree of moral conduct than are heterosexuals. But any public display which manifests sexual desires, whether they be heterosexual or homosexual in nature may, and historically have been, suppressed and regulated in a moral society." (347 P.2d, at p. 912.)

The court in *Vallerga* was of the opinion that the record before it contained sufficient evidence of overtly offensive acts within the licensed premises upon which specific and individualized charges of conduct "contrary to public welfare or morals" could have been preferred against the licensee. But no such charges had been preferred and the only charge preferred, namely, permitting the premises to become a resort for homosexuals in violation of subdivision (e), was the one held by the court to be constitutionally infirm. The court's setting aside of the revocation was presumably without prejudice to the right to proceed against the licensee on specific and individualized charges and proof of overt acts within the licensed premises offensive to "good morals and decency." *See* 347 P.2d, at pp. 913-914.

While the New York cases contain obscurities, many of them seem to take an approach comparable to that taken by the California Supreme Court. Thus in *People v. Arenella*, 139 N.Y.S. 2d 186 (N.Y.C. Mag.Ct.1954) the court, in dealing with a criminal charge that a licensee had allowed his premises to become disorderly, differentiated cases deemed disorderly where the premises were frequented by homosexuals in "open and notorious manner, for the purpose of soliciting others to commit lewd and indecent acts" from others, not deemed disorderly, where the evidence established nothing more than that homosexuals patronized the premises without engaging in prohibited acts therein. 139 N.Y.S.2d, at p. 189. Similarly in *Kerma Restaurant Corporation v. State Liquor Authority*, 278 N.Y.S.2d 951 (App. Div. 1966) the court, while sustaining the revocation of a license on the basis of solicitation and other overtly offensive acts within the licensed premises, acknowledged that the "mere congregation of homosexuals, where there is no breach of the peace, does not make the premises disorderly" within the meaning of New York's Alcoholic Beverage Control Law.

In *Re Revocation of Licence of Clock Bar, Inc.*, 85 Dauph. 125 (Pa. 1966) the court sustained a suspension grounded on evidence of improper solicitations by homosexuals at the licensed premises. However, in the course of its opinion it pointed out there was "no law which forbids homosexuals from being patrons of licensed premises," that the mere, though open, congregation of homosexuals at the licensed premises would not sustain a charge that the licensee maintained "a disorderly house," and that homosexuals at licensed premises become objectionable only "when they make a nuisance of themselves" by improper solicitation or other overtly offensive conduct. 85 Dauph. at 131.

Though in our culture homosexuals are indeed unfortunates, their status does not make them criminals or outlaws. *Cf. Robinson v. State of California*, 370 U.S. 660 (1962). So long as their public behavior violates no legal proscriptions they have the undoubted right to congregate in public. And so long as their public behavior conforms with currently acceptable standards of decency and morality, they may, at least in the present context, be viewed as having the equal right to congregate within licensed establishments such as taverns, restaurants and the like. In sustaining the suspension of One Eleven's license, the Appellate Division took the position that it was not concerned with the rights of the patrons since technically the legal issue before it was the validity of Rule 5 under which the license was suspended. But the asserted rights of the homosexuals to assemble in and patronize licensed establishments are intertwined with the asserted rights of licensed establishments to serve them. Surely in these circumstances, the licensees are properly to be viewed as having standing to seek vindication of the various rights involved in order that the Court's ultimate determination may soundly rest on the complete mosaic. *Cf. Griswold v. State of Connecticut*, 381 U.S. 479, 481 (1965); *NAACP v. State of Alabama*, 357 U.S. 449, 458 (1958); *Barrows v. Jackson*, 346 U.S. 249, 255 (1953); *Pierce v. Society of Sisters*, 268 U.S. 510, 535 (1925).

The Division of Alcoholic Beverage Control . . . contends that the mere congregation of apparent homosexuals in taverns is contrary to the public welfare and may therefore reasonably be prohibited under its wide police powers. It points to the fact that the very term "apparent homosexuals" contemplates effeminate behavioral characteristics, such as those described earlier in this opinion, but apparently it concedes, as it must in the light of the times, that such behavioral characteristics without more, would not constitute overt conduct offensive to current standards of morality and decency. It expresses various fears which we have carefully considered but which lack significant support in the records before us or in the available materials on the subject.

Thus the division suggests that the presence of apparent homosexuals in so-called "gay" bars may serve to harm the occasional non-homosexual patrons who happen to stray there but it produces nothing to rebut the expert testimony or the published writings to the contrary. *See Cory and LeRoy, supra* at p. 121; *Schur, supra* at p. 87. It further suggests that offensive conduct by apparent homosexuals within the licensed premises "may lead to violence" against them by non-homosexuals but this ignores the licensee's comprehensive capacity and responsibility, at the peril of its license, for precluding offensive conduct and for conducting its establishment in lawful and orderly fashion. Finally, it points out that it has consistently tried "to increase public respect and confidence in the liquor industry" and suggests that permitting the congregation of apparent homosexuals, even though carefully supervised, will impair such public respect and confidence. But here again it furnishes nothing affirmative in support of its position which appears to disregard the burgeoning movement toward greater tolerance and deeper understanding of the subject. *See Mosk, supra*, 13 U.C.L.A. L.Rev. at p. 645; Model Penal Code § 207.5, Comment (Tent. Draft No. 4, 1955).

When in the 1930s the Department of Alcoholic Beverage Control first took its severe position, it acted on the assumption that the mere congregation of apparent homosexuals had to be outlawed to achieve effective control. It, of course, had no experience to support the assumption but it took the prohibitory course as the safer one for the then fledgling system. At the time, the interests of the patrons in question were given little consideration and were in any event overwhelmed by the then highly felt transitional need for sweeping restraint. Now, in the 1960s, the transitional need as such is long past and it is entirely appropriate that full sweep be given to current understandings and concepts. Under them it seems clear that, so long as the division can deal effectively with the matter through lesser regulations which do not impair the rights of well-behaved apparent homosex-

uals to patronize and meet in licensed premises, it should do so. Such narrower course would be consonant with the settled and just principle that restrictions adopted in the exercise of police powers must be reasonable and not go beyond the public need.

It must be borne in mind that the division has produced nothing to support any need for continuance of its flat prohibition. Nor has it produced anything to indicate that it could not readily prepare and enforce a fair and sensible regulation which, while permitting apparent homosexuals to assemble in and patronize licensed establishments, prohibits overtly indecent conduct and public displays of sexual desires manifestly offensive to currently acceptable standards of propriety. Such a regulation might well be adopted forthwith to the end that future proceedings would rightly be based on specific charges of improper conduct at the licensed premises rather than, as here, upon general charges of mere congregation which we deem to be unreasonable and legally unsupportable. In the meantime, the discipline imposed in the three cases before us must be set aside, without prejudice, however, to any new charges which the division may prefer against the licensees, or any of them, clearly describing the individual acts alleged to be violative of the provisions in Rule 5 aimed at lewd and immoral conduct within the licensed premises.

Reversed.

PROCTOR, J. (concurring)

Since the charges against the three taverns did not specify any particular offensive acts by the patrons, I concur with the majority opinion. However, I wish to emphasize that, although well-behaved homosexuals cannot be forbidden to patronize taverns, they may not engage in any conduct which would be offensive to public decency. In the record before us it appears that there was evidence of conduct (men kissing each other on the lips, etc.) which would form the basis for disciplinary action at least against One Eleven and Murphy's had they properly been charged. A tavern should not provide an arena for the behavior disclosed by this record. I appreciate that the majority opinion does not say that such conduct will be tolerated, but nonetheless I am expressing my positive view that it should not be.

Notes

1. As they did in the *One Eleven Wines* case, state actors have frequently tried to prevent lesbians and gay men from meeting in bars by revoking liquor licenses from establishments that serve primarily homosexuals. Many courts have upheld these actions. *See Kotteman v. Grevemberg*, 96 So. 2d 601, 603 (La. 1957) (upholding the revocation of a beer permit of a "notorious . . . place in which perverts and sex deviates congregated"); *In Re Kifisia Foods, Inc. v. New York State Liquor Auth.*, 281 N.Y.S.2d 611 (N.Y. App. Div. 1967) (per curiam) (upholding the Authority's revocation of a license when policemen testified about homosexual solicitation); *In Re Freedman Liquor License Case*, 235 A.2d 624, 625 (Pa. Super. Ct. 1967) (upholding the suspension of a license on the basis of unspecified "revolting" testimony about homosexuals).

    Although no liquor licensing case has directly addressed First Amendment issues, *but cf. Francisco Enter., Inc. v. Kirby*, 482 F.2d 481 (9th Cir. 1973) (precluding the [First Amendment] review of a complaint against a liquor board on res judicata grounds), *cert. denied*, 415 U.S. 916 (1974), *some* courts have held that states may not revoke liquor licenses simply because homosexuals frequent the establishment. *See, e.g., Vallerga v. Department of Alcoholic Beverage Control*, 347 P.2d 909 (Cal. 1959) (striking down revocation under state law of a license based on the presence of gay people *per se*, but acknowledging the revocation might have been sustained if it had instead been based on public displays of homosexual "urges").

2. Some state liquor boards have also tried to prevent lesbians and gay men from congregating by forcing organizations to disclose their membership lists before granting a liquor license. At least one court has upheld the right of a liquor board to require such disclosure. *See Freeman v. Hittle*, 747 F.2d 1299 (9th Cir. 1984).

3. In *Cyr v. Walls*, 439 F.Supp. 697 (N.D. Tex. 1977), it was alleged that the Fort Worth (Texas) Police Department harassed attendees at the 1974 Texas Gay Conference. Challenging the police practices as violations of their constitutional rights, the gay plaintiffs claimed that the police "circled the church repeatedly, recorded the license plate numbers of numerous parked automobiles, and stopped some of the participants leaving the meeting for questioning and driver's license checks. . . the license numbers and names recorded were later released for publication to Forth Worth newspaper reporters." *Id.* The court refused to grant defendants' motion to dismiss this case, affirming that plaintiffs had stated a claim upon which relief could be granted for the violation of their constitutional rights.

4. In the early 1980s, in response to the AIDS crisis, public authorities in New York City closed that city's bathhouses, another popular meeting spot for gay men. The courts rejected claims similar to those raised in *One Eleven* and *Cyr*, and concluded that the state interest in health and safety outweighed the right of association. *See City of New York v. New St. Mark's Baths*, 497 N.Y.S.2d 979 (N.Y. Sup. Ct. 1986), *aff'd*, 505 N.Y.S.2d 1015 (N.Y. App. Div. 1986), *appeal dismissed*, 512 N.E.2d 555 (N.Y. 1987).

5. For a general discussion of this topic, see M.J. Greene, Annotation, *The Sale of Liquor to Homosexuals* or *Permitting Their Congregation at Licensed Premises as Grounds for Suspension or Revocation of Liquor License*, 27 A.L.R. 3D 1254 (1991).

D. Government Regulation of Lesbian and Gay Assembly

GAY VETERANS ASSOCIATION v. THE AMERICAN LEGION

621 F. Supp. 1510 (S.D.N.Y. 1985)

MOTLEY, CH. J.

■ ■ ■

Congress decided in 1919 to designate November 11 as a national holiday, Veterans Day, to honor those individuals who have served in the Armed Forces of the United States, placing their lives and welfare at risk in the defense of this country. 5 U.S.C. section 6103(a). In addition, New York State and New York City have recognized Veterans Day as an official holiday. Section 12 of the New York General City Law provides that the City may expend monies to observe Veterans Day in cooperation with veterans' organizations.

Since 1923, the American Legion has held a Veterans Day parade in Manhattan. The parade now commences at 9 A.M. at 39th Street and Fifth Avenue, and finishes at the Eternal Light Monument which commemorates the American Expeditionary Forces in France during World War I. This monument is located at 24th Street. A ceremony consisting of speeches, wreath and flag laying, and a moment of silent prayer immediately follow the parade at the monument.

In addition to the American Legion's parade, several other organizations have ceremonies in New York City on Veterans Day. On November 10, the Federation of World War Veterans of France holds a rally in Riverside Park to commemorate World War II victories and to honor World War I and II Veterans. On November 11, the Vietnam Veterans of America will hold a memorial service in Abingdon Square Park. In Queens, Post 422 of the American Legion will hold a ceremony in Daniel Beard Park. The United

Veterans' Committee will hold a parade and ceremony in Memorial Park in the Bronx. The United War Veterans Memorial and Executive Committee will hold a ceremony in Pelham Bay Park. The American Legion's parade is the only parade in Manhattan, the hub of New York City. The City of New York does not provide funding for any of these events, including the American Legion's parade. The City, in fact, presently has no official City celebration of Veterans Day other than giving its employees the day off from work.

Each year the American Legion procures a permit from the City of New York for the parade as required . . . . The defendant New York City Police Department reserves the permit for the American Legion since it is an annual event. Chief Gerard J. Kerins, a defendant in this action, stated that permits are reserved for traditional parades. A traditional parade is one for which a parade permit has been issued to the same group or organization for two or more years. He testified that by utilizing this method of issuing permits, the City is able to estimate in advance the police manpower it will require to govern the parade. It also provides the City with a means to determine who should receive a permit when two parties with conflicting goals seek a parade permit for the same route.

In 1984, the Gay Veterans sought permission of the American Legion to participate in the Veterans Day Parade. Receiving no response from the American Legion, plaintiffs complained to the Mayor. Lee Hudson, assistant to Herbert P. Rickman, Special Assistant to the Mayor, arranged a meeting between representatives of the

American Legion and the Gay Veterans. The Legion advised the Gay Veterans that parade participants were members of the American Legion.

The official parade program for the 1984 American Legion Parade, however, indicates that several veteran groups not affiliated with the American Legion participated in the American Legion parade. In addition, the program also provides that the parade is conducted by the American Legion "under the auspices of the City of New York." Philip Kaplan, Master of Ceremonies and past Post Commander of the New York County American Legion, testified that the parade was not held under the auspices of New York City, and that although this phrase had been included on other programs for many years, it was an error. He testified that the American Legion received no financial support from the City and paid all of its costs in sponsoring the parade.

On January 2, 1985, the Gay Veterans filed two applications with the New York Police Department for a parade permit. The first application requested permission to march down Fifth Avenue from 39th Street to the Eternal Light Monument on November 11, 1985 at 10:00 A.M. This is the same time and place that the American Legion holds its annual parade down Fifth Avenue. The request was disapproved by Chief Kerins on the grounds that this was a new parade for Fifth Avenue and that there is "a traditional Veterans Day Parade held on November 11, 1985."

Plaintiffs' second application sought a permit for a parade to start at Jeanette Park on Water Street and to finish at the Eternal Light Monument on 24th Street. The permit was disapproved because the parade would result in a "complete disruption of traffic in the financial district during a work day" and manpower requirements for the parade at the time, date and location would be excessive. Chief Kerins testified that many businesses are open on Veterans Day and that plaintiffs' request for a parade three and one-half miles long would be excessively disruptive to busi-

ness. Chief Kerins recommended disapproval of the parade because it would deplete already scarce personnel resources and further disrupt traffic. He testified that the Police Department would prefer one Veterans Day parade but that two parades would be manageable if they were held on parallel routes or if one parade was held following the other. Plaintiffs never sought a permit for another parade route, although the City defendants have agreed to issue them a permit for another location in Manhattan.

On July 23, 1985, defendant Reginald B. Allen, Jr., Parade Chairman of the New York County American Legion, filed an application requesting a permit for the organization's Veterans Day Parade. The request was granted. On August 21, the Gay Veterans wrote to defendant Anthony F. Tuccillo, Adjutant of the American Legion, requesting to be included in the 1985 parade. The letter also provided that the gay Veterans "insist on being allowed to carry our banner, which clearly identifies us as gay veterans." By letter dated September 25, 1985, defendant Tuccillo "categorically denied" plaintiffs request to participate in the parade carrying the Banner.

On September 28, 1985, plaintiffs wrote to Mayor Koch, requesting that the City revoke the permit issued to the American Legion on the ground that it discriminated against the Gay Veterans. The Mayor has refused to revoke the permit. By letter dated October 9, 1985, however, Mayor Koch wrote to defendant Tuccillo, expressing his "sincere hope that [the American Legion] reconsider [its] position in this matter." The Mayor stated:

> I have always believed that those who served our country honorably and were so discharged from the service have a right and almost an obligation to display their pride on Veterans Day. All those who served and sacrificed in defense of the nation deserve to be honored — regardless of their religious beliefs, ethnic background or sexual

orientation. All veterans should be entitled to march on November 11 regardless of their particular organizational affiliation.

The American Legion apparently did not respond to the Mayor's impassioned plea for equality of recognition and acceptance of all who died or risked their lives for us all.

Plaintiffs then commenced this action against defendants New York County American Legion, Reginald B. Allen, Jr. and Anthony F. Tuccillo ["American Legion defendant"], and the City of New York, Mayor Koch, New York City Police Department, Benjamin Ward, Commissioner of the New York City Police Department, Robert J. Johnson, Jr., Gerard J. Kerins, Tosano J. Simonetti, J. Johnson, Henry A. Harrison, and John Doe, officers of the New York City Police Department ["City Defendants"].

DISCUSSION

■ ■ ■

*American Legion's Motion
to Dismiss*

Defendant American Legion — New York County, Reginald B. Allen, Jr. and Anthony F. Tuccillo, have moved to dismiss the action because, they assert, plaintiffs are not veterans. According to the American Legion defendants, plaintiffs only want to participate in the parade "to showcase their life style and have others recognize it." Relying on the certificate of incorporation of plaintiff, Gay Veterans Association, Inc., the American Legion defendants allege the organization is merely a social club.[1] Since the certificate of incorporation does not indicate that the Gay Veterans have organized for patriotic reasons, or does not limit membership to only veterans, American Legion defendants contend that preliminary relief must be denied and the action dismissed.

Evidence presented at the evidentary hearing, however, established that membership in the Gay Veterans is limited to veterans and those currently serving in the Armed Forces of the United States. Prior to approval of any application for membership in the Gay Veterans Association, a prospective member must show his or her Form DD-214 or other document indicating attachment to or separation from a branch of the Armed Forces. In addition, plaintiff Robert Walden, Secretary of the organization, testified that among the activities undertaken by the association are visiting gay veterans in Veterans Administration hospitals, assisting its members in receiving benefits due to them from the Veterans Administration, assisting gay males and lesbians currently serving in the Armed Services, and participating in patriotic events, such as the Vietnam Veterans Parade held in New York City in May, 1985, and a Memorial Day wreath laying ceremony at the Tomb of the Unknown Solider in Arlington National Cemetery on Memorial Day. The evidence clearly establishes that plaintiff, Gay Veterans Association, Inc., is a veterans organization, dedicated to assisting its members and honoring those who have served in the Armed Forces of this country. Accordingly, American Legions'

---

1. The Certificate of Incorporation of the Gay Veterans Association, Inc., sets forth the purposes of the organization as follows:

   To promote friendship among its members; to inculcate in them a high sense of loyalty to each other; to stimulate their intellectual advancement, and to hold meetings and social gatherings for the better realization of such purposes.

   To do any other act or other thing incidental to or connected with the foregoing purposes or in advancement thereof, but not for the pecuniary profit or financial gain of its members, directors, or officers except as permitted under Article 5 of the Not-For-Profit Corporation Law.

defendants motion to dismiss the complaint on the ground that plaintiff is not a bona fide veterans' organization is denied.

Preliminary Injunction

Plaintiffs, in order to obtain a preliminary injunction, must demonstrate irreparable harm and either a likelihood of success on the merit or substantial questions going to the merits to make them fair ground for litigation, coupled with a balance of hardship tilting in their favor.

"'The loss of First Amendment freedoms, for even minimal periods of time, unquestionably constitutes irreparable injury.'" *Olivieri v. Ward.* 766 F.2d 690, 695 (2d Cir.1985) (Kearse, J., dissenting). In the absence of preliminary relief, plaintiffs would be denied the opportunity to march in the American Legion's Veterans Day parade on November 11, 1985. Such injury would be irreparable. Therefore, the issues before the court are whether plaintiffs can demonstrate a likelihood of success on the merits of their First Amendment claim, or at least serious questions on the merits and a balance of hardships tilting in their favor.

■ ■ ■

The Ninth Circuit noted that "suspect" or "quasi-suspect" classifications have not been given to gay males or lesbians. In addition, Congress has rejected attempts to pass legislation providing this group with special protection. *Id.* Accordingly, pursuant to the current state of the law, it appears plaintiffs will not prevail on their claims under sections 1985(3). Since section 1986 refers to the class of persons protected by section 1985, it also is apparent that plaintiffs will not prevail on their section 1986 cause of action. Consequently, there is an absence of any serious questions on the merits in regards to these claims.

Plaintiffs' cause of action predicated on 42 U.S.C. section 1983, alleges that the American Legion defendants and City defendants conspired together to deprive plaintiffs of their constitutional right to freedom of expression and equal access to a public forum. To prevail on their 1983 claim, plaintiffs must establish (1) that defendants subjected plaintiffs to a deprivation of a federally protected right; (2) that the defendants acted "under color of law", and (3) that plaintiffs are protected "persons" within the meaning of the statute. It is undisputed that plaintiffs are "persons" under section 1983. It also is undisputed that the defendant City officials acted under color of state law. It is further undisputed that the Mayor urged the American Legion to permit plaintiffs' members to march in the parade identifying themselves by their banner. It is likewise uncontested that the Mayor offered and still offers to sit down with plaintiffs and work out an alternative route for plaintiffs' parade on the same day. Furthermore, plaintiffs were permitted to march during the one City sponsored ticker-tape parade held in honor of veterans, the Vietnam Veterans Parade in May. There is consequently insufficient evidence to support plaintiffs' conspiracy theory.

It is undisputed that the American Legion will not permit plaintiff to march in the parade carrying their banner indicating that its members are gay veterans, while other organizations which participate in the parade are permitted to carry banners or flags with their names on it. There is, however, insufficient evidence of action "under color of law." The City of New York provides no funding to the American Legion or its Veterans Day parade. The parade is not the only event of the day or an official event. It is just one of many ceremonies held throughout New York City to commemorate Veterans Day.

The City did deny plaintiffs' request for a parade permit for a parade down Fifth Avenue on the ground that at that date, time and hour, the American Legion traditionally held its parade. The First Amendment requires that a policy concerning the issuance of parade permits be (1) content neutral, (2) narrowly tailored to serve significant government interests, and (3) leave open ample alternative channels for communication. *Clark v. Community for Creative Non-Violence*, 486 U.S. 288 (1984).

The City's decision to deny the Gay Veterans the permit for a parade down Fifth Avenue, however, was not because of any discriminatory animus, or an attempt to deprive plaintiffs of their First Amendment rights, but because, as a matter of administrative policy, it reserves certain routes, dates, times and places for what have become annual events. For instance, a parade permit is reserved for the New York County Board of the Ancient Order of Hiberians for the St. Patricks Day Parade on March 17. A permit will be issued for no other parade on Fifth Avenue other than the Gay Pride Parade on the last day of June. Fifth Avenue is reserved on Labor Day for the parade of the New York City Central Labor Council AFL-CIO. Any group is eligible for priority after it has held two parades. Thus, the evidence indicates that the permit issued to the American Legion was pursuant to a content-neutral standard.

Furthermore, the evidence indicates that the tradition system serves a significant government interests in New York. It allows the police to determine their man-power needs in advance. In addition, according to Chief Kerins, if permits were issued on a first come, first served basis as suggested by plaintiffs, friction could develop between the many ethnic groups who have parades in the City, as they raced to the precinct window to file for the best parade route. Moreover, this system serves the constitutional rights of the spectators who desire to witness the huge annual parades.

The Police Department's decision to deny the request for a permit for a parade commencing up Water Street was reasonable. While Veterans Day is a public holiday, many businesses are open, including retail stores. A parade three and one-half miles long through the City's financial district and

business areas would cause a significant disruption of traffic. Since there are other alternative routes available to the plaintiffs in the City, the denial of the permit did not constitute a violation of the First Amendment.

It is not disputed that the mere issuance of a permit does not constitute state action. Although the American Legion is given a priority as to the issuance of a permit for a Fifth Avenue parade on the morning of November 11, 1985, other groups also are given a priority. As indicated previously, a permit is reserved for the Gay Pride Parade on the last Sunday in June in order to allow the Gay community the opportunity to express its views. Since society's interests in order dictate that all groups seeking to parade cannot do so at the same time or place, the granting of a preference as to a particular time and site is not enough to convert the acts of the American Legion into state action.

Plaintiffs argue that the American Legion parade is a public forum because its purpose is to celebrate a public holiday, Veterans Day, in a public street. This, however, does not turn a private parade into a public forum. Under New York law, the sponsorship of parades to celebrate Veterans Day is not an exclusively public function. The evidence at the hearing also indicates that even traditionally it was not an exclusive governmental function. While the City, pursuant to the New York General City Law, may spend money for Veterans Day observances, it is not required to and does not do so.

Plaintiffs rely on *North Shore Right to Life v. Manhassett American Legion*, 452 F.Supp. 834 (E.D.N.Y.1978), in which Chief Judge Weinstein held that the refusal of the American Legion to allow a controversial organization to march in the local Memorial Day parade constituted state action in violation of the group's civil rights. In that case, the Town of North Hempstead had granted the American Legion permission to conduct a parade on Memorial Day for many years. This parade, however, was in a small town and the entire community participated in the parade. It was not only a Memorial Day parade, it was the town's annual parade. This is not true of American Legion's Veterans Day parade in New York City. Ample alternative channels for communication exist for plaintiffs as demonstrated by the fact that other veterans' organizations hold ceremonies commemorating the holiday throughout the City.

In addition, Chief Judge Weinstein relied on *Evans v. Newton*, 382 U.S. 296 (1966), where the Supreme Court held:

> Conduct that is formally 'private' may become so entwined with governmental character as to become subject to the constitutional limitations placed upon state action. . . . [W]hen private individuals or groups are endowed by the State with powers or functions governmental in nature, they become agencies or instrumentalities of the State and subject to its constitutional limitations.

Id. at 299.

Since Chief Judge Weinstein's decision, however, the Supreme Court has provided further guidelines in determining whether the actions of a private group constitute state action. In *Rendell-Baker v. Kohn*, 457 U.S. 830, 842 (1982), the Court ruled that in de-termining whether a private actor is performing a public function the court must consider "whether the function performed has been 'traditionally the exclusive prerogative of the state.'" The mere performance of a public function does not make the acts of a private entity state action.

In this case, the sponsorship of parades to celebrate public holidays, even Veterans Day, has not been traditionally an exclusively governmental function. Accordingly, based on the evidence and law, this court must find for the purposes of the preliminary injunction motion, that the American Legion was not acting under color of law when it refused plaintiffs' request.

This court finds that plaintiffs have failed to prove a likelihood of success on the merits. Additionally there appears to be no serious questions going to the merits. Even if serious questions going to the merits were to exist, it cannot be said that the balance of hardships tips decidedly in plaintiffs' favor; for in the absence of a showing of state action, the First Amendment rights of the American Legion defendants must also be considered.

Plaintiffs' motion for a preliminary injunction is denied. The American Legion defendants' motion to dismiss the complaint is denied.

Notes

1. The refusal to allow lesbian and gay groups to march in the St. Patrick's Day parade gave rise to litigation in Boston and New York City in 1992; the issues in these cases parallel those in the *Gay Veterans* case. In Boston, the Irish-American Gay, Lesbian and Bisexual Group of Boston ("GLIB") successfully challenged its exclusion from the parade in state court on the grounds that the organization of the parade constituted state action. *See* Don Aucoin, *Judge Lets Gays March in Parade; South Boston Group Won't Appeal*, BOSTON GLOBE, March 12, 1992, Metro, at 1 (quoting the decision by Judge Hilber B. Zobel of the Suffolk County Superior Court on March 11, 1992). The Boston parade is entitled the "City of Boston Evacuation Day/St. Patrick's Day Parade" (in partial commemoration of the expulsion of the British from the city in 1776), is subsidized by the city, and city employees help organize the event. Thus, unlike in the *Gay Veterans* case, state action was present in the planning of the parade and the exclusion of the gay group therefore violated its First Amendment rights.

    In New York, both a state administrative law judge and a federal district court rejected separate attempts to compel the Ancient Order of Hibernians ("AOH") to accept the Irish Lesbian and Gay

Organization ("ILGO") into New York's St. Patrick's Day Parade. The ALJ ruled that the St. Patrick's Day parade was a "place of public accommodation" as that term is defined in the city law, and that the AOH had discriminated against ILGO; she nonetheless denied the injunction on the grounds that AOH's constitutional rights of freedom of speech and expressive association (and apparently of freedom of religion) precluded such relief. *See New York City Comm'n on Human Rights v. Ancient Order of Hibernians, Inc.*, No. MPA-0362 (N.Y. City Comm'n Hum. Rts., Mar. 13, 1992).

The federal court did not reach the constitutional issues presented by the ILGO case, ruling instead that independent of the likelihood of success on the merits, the balance of hardships tipped in favor of the Hibernians and was dispositive. *See Irish Lesbian and Gay Org. v. New York State Bd. of Ancient Order of Hibernians*, 788 F.Supp. 172 (S.D.N.Y. 1992).

2. In *Olivieri v. Ward*, 637 F. Supp. 851 (S.D.N.Y. 1986), a federal district court enjoined the New York City police department from blocking off the sidewalk in front of St. Patrick's Cathedral, the center of the Roman Catholic Archdiocese of New York, during the city's annual Gay Pride Parade, holding that the restriction during the city's annual Gay Pride Parade violated the content-neutral and narrowly-tailored prongs of the time, manner, and place restrictions test.

IV. CENSORSHIP

In addition to the pure political activism described in Part III above, many lesbians and gay men choose to express themselves and lobby for change through publications or speech. The readings in this part are designed to provide a broader sense of the implications of silencing lesbian and gay voices.

MISSISSIPPI GAY ALLIANCE v. GOUDELOCK

536 F.2d 1073 (5th Cir. 1976), *cert denied,* 430 U.S. 982 (1977)

COLEMAN, Circuit Judge.

This is not the ordinarily encountered First Amendment case in which a university student newspaper seeks to set aside an order directing it not to publish something which it wishes to publish.

To the contrary, it is a case in which a nebulous group, the Mississippi Gay Alliance, representing itself to be an association "basically comprised of homosexuals", seeks judicial compulsion against a student newspaper requiring publication of an advertisement which that paper does not want to publish.

The District Court refused to command publication. We affirm.

On August 16, 1973, a female, the self-styled chairwoman of the Mississippi Gay Alliance, presented a proposed paid advertisement to *The Reflector*, the student newspaper at Mississippi State University.

The proposed advertisement read as follows:

"Gay Center — open 6:00 to 9:00 Monday, Wednesday and Friday nights.

"We offer — counseling, *legal aid,* and a library of homosexual literature.

"Write to — The Mississippi Gay Alliance
P.O. Box 1328
Mississippi State University,
MS 39762."

The editor of the student newspaper refused to accept the tendered paid advertisement.

On February 8, 1974, the same person presented an announcement to be printed in the "briefs" section of *The Reflector*. This, too, was rejected. The content of that announcement does not appear in the record.

Whereupon, suit was filed against the editor and others, alleging that the refusal to print the paid advertisement and announcement deprived the Gay Alliance of its First Amendment rights and praying that the defendants be ordered to print the rejected material. The suit also sought an order requiring defendants to print future advertisements and announcements tendered by the Gay Alliance. Actual and punitive damages were also demanded.

The parties agreed to stipulations, which might be summarized as follows:

1. The named plaintiffs are not MSU students nor is the MGA a recognized student organization.

2. No member of the MGA was enrolled as an MSU student.

[This second stipulation was, at plaintiff's request, modified by court order in December 1974, after the district court's ruling was issued. The new stipulation apparently says that some members of the MGA were MSU students. This modification did not affect the ruling of the district court].

3. The MSU student body elected Bill Goudelock as editor of *The Reflector.*

4. Funds supporting *The Reflector* are derived at least in part from a non-waivable fee charged to students at MSU.

5. [University officials] Giles, Meyer, and Dudley did not give Goudelock any instructions not to accept the proffered material.

■ ■ ■

. . . [T]he District Court found, on the complaint and the stipulated facts, that there was no *indication* that any University official or faculty member had anything to do with the rejection of the advertisement or the announcement; that there was a complete lack of control over the student newspaper on the part of University officials.

The Court concluded that the rejection of the advertisement "does not constitute state action in any sense of the term."

■ ■ ■

While it is true that the student newspaper is supported, in part, by activity fees collected by the University, the students elect the editor. The complaint did not allege and the stipulations did not assert that University officials supervise or control what is to be published or not published in the newspaper.

As a matter of fact, in the context of the matter before us, this Court has held that the University authorities could not have ordered the newspaper not to publish the Gay

Alliance advertisement, had it chosen to do so, *see Bazaar v. Fortune*, 476 F.2d 570 (5th Cir. 1973), *affirmed as modified*, 489 F.2d 225 (*en banc*).

In *Miami Herald Publishing Company v. Tornillo*, 418 U.S. 241 (1974), the Supreme Court flatly declared:

> "The choice of material to go into a newspaper . . . constitute[s] the exercise of editorial control and judgment. It has yet to be demonstrated how governmental regulation of this crucial process can be exercised consistent with First Amendment guarantees of a free press as they have evolved to this time."

Since there is not the slightest whisper that the University authorities had anything to do with the rejection of this material offered by this off-campus cell of homosexuals, since such officials could not lawfully have done so, and since the record really suggests nothing but discretion exercised by an editor chosen by the student body, we think the First Amendment interdicts judicial interference with the editorial decision.

There are special reasons for holding that there was no abuse of discretion by the editor of *The Reflector*.

Hutchinson's Mississippi Code of 1848 included the following provision:

> "Unnatural Intercourse; Punishment.
> "Every person who shall be convicted of the detestable and abominable crime against nature, committed with man-

kind or a beast, shall be punished by imprisonment in the penitentiary for a term of not more than ten years."[1]

The exact language of this provision has been retained in the Code revisions of 1857, 1871, 1880, 1892, 1906, 1917, 1930, 1942, and 1972.[2]

The Mississippi statute condemns any intercourse which is unnatural, detestable and abominable, including acts committed per anus or per os. This is not surprising. The very title of the statute shows it to have been directed against "Unnatural Intercourse."

The statute is not unconstitutional, *State v. Mays*, 329 So.2d 65 (Miss.1976).

The editor of *The Reflector* had a right to take the position that the newspaper would not be involved, even peripherally, with this off-campus homosexually related activity.[4]

The judgment of the District Court is AFFIRMED.

GOLDBERG, Circuit Judge, dissenting.

I respectfully dissent.

I understand the trial court and the majority of this panel to hold that the lack of direct involvement by university officials and the free expression rights of student editors combine to preclude any possible right of access to the *Reflector* on the part of the MGA. I disagree with that holding and, on the allegations, would find a narrowly circumscribed right of access which might extend to the MGA in this case.

The majority opinion here can be read as also deciding, in an alternative holding, that

---

1. Chapter 64, Art. 12, Title 7(20).

2. The current statute is Section 97-29-59, Mississippi Code of 1972. For mention of the significance to be attached to the ancient origin of a similar statute in Virginia, *see Doe v. Commonwealth*, 403 F.Supp. 1199, 1202, 1203 (E.D.Va., 1975), Affirmed, 425 U.S. 901 (1976).

4. One may not be prosecuted for being a homosexual, but he may be prosecuted for the commission of homosexual acts. Taking into consideration the laws of Mississippi on the subject, speaking as only one member of the panel, Judge Coleman is of the opinion that no newspaper in the State may be required to advertise solicitations for homosexual contacts, any more than a paper could be expected to advertise solicitations for contacts with prostitutes. The advertisement tendered by the Gay Alliance offered legal aid. Such an offer is open to various interpretations, one of which is that criminal activity is contemplated, necessitating the aid of counsel.

the advertisement tendered by the MGA was undeserving of any First Amendment protection which might otherwise exist, because the ad might have "involved" the newspaper "with. . . off-campus homosexually-related activity." This latter holding, if indeed it is that, is clearly and absolutely wrong.

■ ■ ■

II. PROTECTED SPEECH

As I have indicated, the majority's discussion of "special reasons" justifying the student editor's refusal to accept this ad can be read as an implicit holding that the MGA ad was "unprotected" speech for first amendment purposes. Such a holding obviously would be fallacious. If other local groups had a right of access to the *Reflector*, that right could not be denied the MGA in respect to the advertisement at issue here. The ad directly solicits nothing approaching criminal activity, and the publication of the ad would not involve the *Reflector*, "even peripherally," in the proscribed activities discussed in the majority opinion.

The advertisement simply sought to notify persons who were homosexuals, who were interested in the subject of homosexuality or who had problems relating to homosexuality that certain services were available to them at a "gay center." No statute, in Mississippi or in any relevant jurisdiction, makes criminal the status of being a homosexual. Indeed, no statute could do that and survive constitutional challenge. *See Robinson v. California*, 370 U.S. 660 (1962). On the face of it, none of the services listed in the advertisement could conceivably be characterized as illegal. The suggestion of

Judge Coleman that the criminal taint in the ad is demonstrated by the offer of "legal aid" implies a presumption of illegality whenever lawyers are involved - surely the level of respect for the profession has not reached this nadir.

Thus, the exception whereby statements which propose illegal transactions are rendered valueless for First Amendment purposes cannot be applied to this advertisement. Neither could the advertisement even arguably be characterized as "unprotected" speech on any other ground. It is not "directed to inciting or producing imminent lawless action."[7] The ad could occasion no substantial disruption of classroom activity, nor could it be construed as an "intolerable" invasion of a "substantial" privacy interest. No basis exists for suggesting that the ad is libelous, obscene or "fighting words." In short, nothing in the record contradicts the following statement of the trial court:

> It is certainly true that this ad tendered by Anne DeBary appears quite innocuous on its face. It certainly would not be such matter that might be regarded as obscene, or, in the eyes of many people, offensive.

The ad carried an informative statement with regard to a matter of social concern, and, as seen, its contents trigger none of the recognized exceptions to freedom of speech.

Thus, this is not an "unnatural intercourse" case, and there exist no "special reasons" related to the content of the ad which would justify its discriminatory rejection in the face of a general right of nondiscriminatory access. I turn, then, to the difficult first amendment questions actually presented in this case.

---

7. *Brandenburg v. Ohio*, 395 U.S. 444, 447 (1969) (per curiam):

> [The] constitutional guarantees of free speech and free press do not permit a State to forbid or proscribe advocacy of the use of force or of law violation except where such advocacy is directed to inciting or producing imminent lawless action and is likely to incite or produce such action.

III. A CONSTITUTIONAL RIGHT
OF ACCESS

■ ■ ■

A. *Equal Access: State Newspapers As Public Forums*

There is authority for the proposition that the first amendment's guarantee of free speech carries with it some requirement that the state provide "minimum access" — that is, that the state accommodate speakers' attempts to obtain access to listeners. Freedom of association, as well as freedom of speech, supports such a requirement in some situations.[15]

Whatever the scope of the minimum access requirements of free speech, a narrower doctrine is well established in Supreme Court precedent — when the state has provided a public forum through which speakers might have access to listeners, the state cannot discriminate among potential speakers on the basis of the content of their message.[16] The notion that there must be equality of access to public forums is compelled not only by speech and associational rights, but also by the full force of the equal protection clause.

■ ■ ■

The state, of course, has considerable discretion in reasonably regulating the time, place and manner in which speech may be made from various public forums. What the state cannot do is to provide a forum through which some members of the public are able effectively to communicate their message to a certain audience while other members of the public are prohibited from utilizing the forum because of the content of their proposed messages.

I take it to be quite clear, for example, that a city, having established a "speaker's corner" in a public park from which almost anyone might speak about almost anything, could not constitutionally prohibit speeches dealing nonobscenely with the topic of homosexuality.

Taking the hypothetical a step closer to the instant case, we might posit a newspaper paid for and published by the state — call it the "Open Forum" — in which all citizens are invited to express their views on any issue, subject only to reasonable space limitations and a small fee to help offset printing costs. Could the "Open Forum" refuse to print a tendered statement on the ground that it expressed a political view contrary to that of the Governor, or on no stated ground at all? Surely not. Conceivably, the state could place many noncontent oriented restrictions on the form of the messages, but the state could not refuse tendered statements otherwise similar in form to those regularly accepted solely because the proffered ads were disagreeable in content.

■ ■ ■

---

15. There is right of the listener to protected speech that, in this case, coincides with the associational rights of some students. MGA asserts that some of its members are MSU students, and the amended stipulation apparently supports this. There may be other MSU students who are interested in attending MGA meetings or using MGA facilities. These and other readers of the *Reflector* have been denied information that may have been necessary or important to the full exercise of their first amendment rights freely to associate with others. It is not sufficient to suggest that other means of communicating the existence of their organization or the time and place of their meetings remain with the MGA, for the *Reflector* may be the cheapest, easiest, and most effective means of communicating with a specific audience. Particularly on a matter as personal as sexual preference, the reader may wish to preserve his or her anonymity, and his or her receipt of a widely distributed school paper may serve this need better than, say, attendance at an MGA speech on campus.

    The guarantee to those interested in homosexuality of the right freely to associate with one another would be a hollow promise indeed unless they are also assured of equal, nondiscriminatory access to information relevant to their concerns. . . .

16. *See Police Dept. of Chicago v. Mosley*, 408 U.S. 92 (1972).

A "state" newspaper could not constitutionally refuse advertisements advocating one side of a public issue while accepting advertisements advocating the other side. No less offensive to the First and Fourteenth Amendments should be a case in which advertisements dealing with public issues are generally accepted, but advertisements on certain public issues are selectively and arbitrarily excluded.

Were the *Reflector* clearly a paper run by and for the state, then, the allegations of the MGA (unaltered by the stipulated facts) that the paper regularly accepted paid and unpaid messages and announcements from other local groups would be sufficient to raise a genuine issue of material fact. If the allegations were true, the state would have denied the MGA equal access to a public forum.

On the other hand, if the *Reflector* were purely a private newspaper, there presumably would exist no such right of access. The editor of a private newspaper is constitutionally protected in a decision not to publish a political reply advertisement, even in the face of a state right to reply statute. *See Miami Herald Publishing Co. v. Tornillo*, 418 U.S. 241 (1974). Clearly, then, a federal court would have no power, under statutes requiring "state action," to prohibit a non-state newspaper from exercising selective content discrimination in its publication of advertisements.

The first question thus becomes whether the *Reflector* can be characterized as the state. Even if, under traditional analysis, "state action" is found, the court must proceed to the further question of whether the newspaper is, at least in part, a public forum. That question will require a review of special considerations relating to student newspapers, and a balancing of competing First Amendment interests.

B. State Action

■ ■ ■

The absence of affirmative involvement by university officials in the decision to refuse the MGA ad should not end the state action inquiry. . . . State action, of course, is not so simple. A number of factors must be examined to determine if the action challenged as detrimental to individual rights should be considered to be state action for Fourteenth Amendment purposes. . . . [T]he ultimate question is whether the facts establish "significant state involvement" in what otherwise may appear to be private activity.

To my mind, the allegations of the MGA, if shown to be true, would establish that actions taken by the *Reflector*, as it deals with and appears to members of the public, should be considered to be state action. The complaint in this action set forth the following allegation:

> The *Reflector* is the official newspaper of MSU, a state supported and controlled institution of higher learning. The major portion of the *Reflector*'s financing comes from the Student Activity Fund which is collected by MSU and disbursed to the *Reflector*. The *Reflector* is printed on MSU facilities and it is an organ of MSU.

The stipulations included the fact that funds supporting *The Reflector* were derived from a non-waivable fee charged to students at MSU.

The *Reflector*'s funding is thus derived from what is in effect a tax charged by the state to the students. The allegations suggest that the imprimatur of the state is clearly stamped on the paper. In these circumstances, I have little doubt that this court would review a decision by the students to exclude blacks from participation on the newspaper staff as a decision imbued with state action. To my mind, the pure "state action" question should be the same in the First Amendment context.

Having concluded, on the issue of "state action," that appellants are deserving of at least a remand, I turn to what I consider the most significant question in this case: does the Constitution permit student editors of an official publication at a state university to pursue a general policy of accepting from local groups advertisements dealing with matters of public interest, but at the same time to exclude, because of its content, a certain advertisement profered by a similarly situated group?

C. A Right to Edit

Clearly, student editors of a campus newspaper are protected by their own first amendment rights. . . . [T]hese rights include in some contexts the right to refuse to print as well as the right to print.

■ ■ ■

> When a college paper receives a subsidy from the state, there are strong arguments for insisting that its columns be open to the expression of contrary views and that its publication enhance, not inhibit, free speech.

[*Joyner v. Whitting*], 477 F.2d 456, 462 (4th Cir. 1973).

In my opinion, however, a requirement of wide-open access to the pages of a student newspaper would sweep much too broadly. To the extent that the right of student editors to free expression is to be protected, that right must include the right to edit. With limited space for news and editorial columns, and with attribution on the masthead as "editors," students operating a student paper must necessarily exercise some discretion in choosing what to publish and what not to publish. This is most clear, perhaps, when the materials to be edited are generated solely by the student staff, but the "right to edit" (based in part on the necessity for editing) would logically extend to articles or columns submitted by outside sources.

. . . The question thus becomes one of competing first amendment interests, and the search must be for a reconciliation between the interests, on the one hand, of student autonomy in control over the contents of the newspaper, and, on the other, of nondiscriminatory public access to a communication forum sponsored by the state.

D. A Reconciliation of Competing Interests

I think that the two interests discussed above can be accommodated through a doctrine which permits student editors of state newspapers unfettered discretion over what might be termed the "editorial product" of the newspaper, yet requires that when the newspaper devotes space to unedited advertisements or announcements from individuals outside the newspaper staff, access to such space must be made available to other similarly situated individuals on a nondiscriminatory basis.

I use "editorial product" to comprehend the news and editorial columns of the paper, and other sections that by tradition and popular perception would be subject to editorial input from the operators of a newspaper. Guest columns and letters to the editor, although closer to the borderline because of the authorship, probably would be included in this "editorial product" notion.

As to the sections of the newspaper which would be subject to the requirement of nondiscriminatory access, I take the two sections of the *Reflector* at issue in this suit to be paradigmatic. According to the allegations of the MGA, the sections of the *Reflector* to which access was sought were regularly available to local organizations for announcements and messages of social, political and informative natures. Also, the student editors apparently do not purport to exercise editorial responsibility over the issues raised by or the content of these paid advertisements and unpaid announcements. No one would be likely to confuse statements appearing in them as officially endorsed by the students or the school. Were there any problems in this regard, clear disclaimers as to the source of the messages easily could be added.

I want to emphasize that the right of equal access I would invoke could, for the purposes of this case, be carefully circumscribed. For example, the newspaper could perhaps provide access only to students or other members of the university community and not be guilty of content discrimination. Perhaps access could even be restricted to local community businesses and groups. The possibility of various source restrictions need not be reached in this case, however. The allegations of the plaintiffs suggest that other local groups, similarly situated to the MGA, were allowed access to the advertising and "briefs" sections of the paper. If that is true, impermissible content discrimination will have been shown — the "state" cannot accept advertisements from some local groups and refuse those from others because of their content.

Conceivably, other limitations on the envisioned right of equal access could arise in response to logistics and cost. A state newspaper which had provided a public forum for the publication of any message from anyone could in one week receive thousands of proposed messages on the same subject. It may not be feasible to print them all. A word-per-message limitation might be useful, but situations still might exist in which there were simply too many similar messages to print. If the "public forum" is to remain that, some content neutral means of selection would become necessary — e.g., requiring payment of a reasonable fee, printing the first however many submissions, or selecting statements at random. Again, we need not reach these questions to decide this case. There is no indication that any other advertisements, or announcements in the "briefs" section, had ever been refused by the newspaper, or that any consideration of space limitations was relevant in the decision to exclude the MGA ad.

I mention these possible limitations on the right of equal access to a state student newspaper to illustrate how narrowly a decision in the instant case could be written, and how careful a court should be in delineating the scope of such a right. These factors are closely related, of course, to the notion that time, place and manner restrictions are permissible "provided that they are justified without reference to the content of the regulated speech, that they serve a significant governmental interest, and that in so doing they leave open ample alternative channels for communication of the information." *Virginia State Bd. of Pharmacy v. Virginia Citizens Consumer Council*, 425 U.S.748 (1976). The best way for the regulating agency to demonstrate that its restrictions are not based on content is through the formulation of specific rules governing what will and will not be published. When no rules guide the decision to exclude a controversial message from what otherwise appears to be a public forum, the courts are properly very skeptical of any proffered justification for the exclusion.

ALASKA GAY COALITION v. SULLIVAN

578 P.2d 951 (Alaska 1978)

BURKE, J.

■ ■ ■

The 1976-77 *Anchorage Blue Book* is a paperback guide to services and organizations in the greater Anchorage area published by the municipality of Anchorage. Although the publication primarily serves as a guide to public services and resources, it also contains information about many private organizations. The book's purpose is to provide Anchorage residents with a single source of information regarding public services, local government, recreational opportunities and crisis assistance. The cost of printing and publishing the guide was initially borne by the Municipality, with such costs to be recouped by sale of the booklet through commercial outlets. An earlier version of the guide, called simply *The Blue Book*, had been published in 1975 under the auspices of the former Greater Anchorage Area Borough.

Preparation of the 1976-77 *Anchorage Blue Book* (hereinafter referred to as the *Blue Book*) was handled jointly by the Municipality and the Anchorage Action Council, a federally-funded community organization, then directed by Lanie Fleischer. Most of the updated information for the *Blue Book* was gathered in February and March of 1976, primarily by Cheryl Jerabek, a VISTA volunteer with the Action Council. Ms. Jerabek contacted all of the groups which had been included in the earlier version of the *Blue Book* as well as many which had not previously been listed. Within the latter category was the Alaska Gay Coalition, which submitted a brief written description of the group's purposes and services. Appellee Bruce Staser, who until mid-April was Public information officer for the municipality, assisted Ms. Jerabek by soliciting updated information from all of the departments and divisions of the municipality. Mr. Staser also wrote and edited portions of the *Blue Book* relating to municipal services.

When all of the information had been compiled, a rough draft of the *Blue Book* was prepared by the graphics department of the Municipality. This draft included, in a section entitled "Women," the following entry submitted by the Gay Coalition:

Alaska Gay Coalition

P. O. Box 2488

Purpose: To develop, secure and maintain the civil liberties, rights and dignity of all homosexual and lesbian individuals, to represent the interest and goals of lesbians and homosexuals

in Alaska; to educate the overall community about those goals and interests.

Services: Referral to related organizations; speakers available in the area of gay rights issues; public education; provide social and political personal support. Meetings every two weeks on Friday evenings. Programs developing as well as special meetings when necessary.

Fees: None.

Four copies of this first draft were distributed to Lanie Fleischer, Carolyn Gay, who had succeeded Bruce Staser as Public information officer for the municipality, Paul Palmer, graphics and publications manager for the municipality, and George Sullivan, mayor of the municipality. Fleischer and Gay were generally considered the co-editors of the publication although the Mayor had final editorial control.

Upon receiving his copy of the first draft, Mayor Sullivan made a number of substantive and structural revisions in the draft, particularly in the section titled "Women." He changed the title of this section to "Men's and Women's Organizations" and suggested the inclusion of several organizations which were not listed, such as the Lions and Kiwanis. As a space-saving measure, and in order to include additional organizations such as the ones he had suggested, the mayor also directed that all of the verbiage describing the various groups' purposes and services be deleted, with the listings to consist only of names and telephone numbers. He further suggested that certain of the women's groups be deleted if necessary. At this time the mayor also ordered that the reference to the Alaska Gay Coalition be deleted in its entirety.

Following the mayor's revisions, as well as other extensive revisions and some deletions by Fleischer, Gay and Palmer, a second draft of the *Blue Book* was prepared. This draft contained no reference to the Alaska Gay Coalition. After further revising, the second draft was sent to be printed.

On July 21, 1976, the Gay Coalition filed a complaint against Mayor Sullivan, Bruce Staser and the Municipality of Anchorage, and at the same time sought a temporary restraining order from the superior court restraining appellees from distributing copies of the *Blue Book*. The superior court granted the requested temporary order on July 29, 1976.

Trial of the action was conducted on August 26-27, 1976. The Coalition argued that appellees' action (1) violated its right to equal protection under the Fourteenth Amendment of the United States Constitution and art. I, sec. 1 of the Alaska Constitution, (2) denied both the Coalition and the public's right to freedom of speech and association, and (3) deprived the Coalition of procedural and substantive due process. In an oral opinion the superior court found against the Coalition on all issues, denying its request for damages, injunctive and declaratory relief. This appeal followed.

The controlling and most significant issue in this case is whether the mayor's action in deleting the Gay Coalition from the *Blue Book* denied that group its right to freedom of speech and association under the First Amendment to the United States Constitution and art. I, sec. 5 of the Alaska Constitution. Appellant contends that the *Blue Book* is a public forum and therefore the municipality could not give some individuals access to that forum but exclude others based solely on the nature of their beliefs. Appellees deny that the *Blue Book* is a public forum. In the alternative, they maintain that the Coalition's failure to show that harm resulted from deletion of its entry is fatal to its claim.

The public forum doctrine as it relates to this case can be briefly stated as follows: Once there exists a government-controlled forum for the dissemination of information and expression of ideas, the government cannot deny equal access to that forum based on content alone. This equality of access is compelled by both the First Amendment and the equal protection clause.

Necessarily, then, under the equal protection clause, not to mention the First Amendment itself, government may not grant the use of a forum to people whose views it finds acceptable, but deny use to those wishing to express less favored or more controversial views. And it may not select which issues are worth discussing or debating in public facilities. There is an "equality of status in the field of ideas," and government must afford all points of view an equal opportunity to be heard. Once a forum is opened up to assembly or speaking by some groups, government may not prohibit others from assembling or speaking on the basis of what they intend to say. Selective exclusions from a public forum may not be based on content alone, and may not be justified by reference to content alone.

Police Department v. Mosley, 408 U.S. 92, 96 (1972). Although the government may not restrict access to a public forum based on content alone, it may, however, place reasonable restrictions on the "time, place and manner" of the exercise of expressive rights. *Id.* at 98. In other words, while the government may reasonably regulate expressive activity, it may not censor such activity.

In the instant case, there is no question that the Gay Coalition was deleted from the *Blue Book* solely on the basis of the personal beliefs of its members. At trial, the mayor gave several reasons for the deletion. First, he believed that the Coalition was primarily a political and lobbying group and that as such it did not belong in the publication, just as political organizations such as the Democrats and Republicans did not belong there. He felt that the group's political nature was inconsistent with the non-political focus of the booklet. Second, the mayor admitted to a personal aversion to homosexuality. Finally, he testified that he felt that state statutes against sodomy and incest made it improper for a government publication to include reference to a group such as the Coalition.

The trial court found that the major reason for the mayor's action was the political focus of the Coalition. In our view, this finding was clearly erroneous. Numerous other political and lobbying groups were included in the *Blue Book* yet the mayor did not find it necessary to delete any of them except appellant. Among these groups were the National Association for the Advancement of Colored People, the American Civil Liberties Union, the Sierra Club, and the Anchorage Tenants Union, to name but a few. Clearly there was no firm policy of excluding all political groups as intimated by the mayor. It is apparent that the Gay Coalition was deleted from the *Blue Book* solely because it was a homosexual organization and not because the group's political focus was otherwise inconsistent with the type of organizations included in the publication. The only question we need resolve, therefore, is whether the *Blue Book* is a public forum to which appellant had a right of equal access.

In the majority of cases dealing specifically with the public forum issue, the question has been whether a particular place, rather than a publication, was a public forum. Public streets, sidewalks and parks were early designated public forums. Courts since then have found a wide variety of places to be public forums including municipal auditoriums, a public school auditorium, city-owned airports, a statehouse rotunda, public utility poles where use was specifically permitted by ordinance, and a state-owned bus terminal. In addition, limited public forums have been found when the state sponsors a one-time event and provides members of the public with an opportunity for expression. Thus, in *Toward a Gayer Bicentennial Committee v. R.I. Bicentennial Foundation*, 417 F.Supp 632 (D. R.I.1976), the court found that when the state opened the Old Statehouse for bicentennial activities, it had created a public forum during that period.

While most cases have dealt with geographical public forums, there is authority for the proposition that a publication may be considered a public forum to which equal access must be afforded. In *Radical Lawyers Caucus v. Pool*, 324 F.Supp 268 (W.D.Tex.1970), the court held that the *Texas Bar Journal*, conceded to be an agency of the state, could not constitutionally refuse the plaintiff's political advertisement when it regularly accepted commercial advertising and where there was evidence that political ads had been accepted in the past. Similarly, in *Lee v. Board of Regents of State Colleges*, 441 F.2d 1257 (7th Cir. 1971), it was held that a state campus newspaper, which was open to commercial and some political and service advertisements, could not constitutionally reject other political advertisements solely because of their content. While neither of these cases specifically designated the publications as public forums, implicit in them was a finding that such a forum existed since the requirement of equal access is predicated on the existence of a public forum. *See also Mississippi Gay Alliance v. Goudelock*, 536, F.2d 1073, 1080 (5th Cir. 1976) (dissenting opinion).

While examination of the public forum cases to date provides no clear precedent upon which we can rest our decision in this case, we have little trouble in designating the *Blue Book* a public forum. There is no question that the publication is "public," as it was prepared and published by the Municipality. Thus we are not concerned with the problem of the public's right to access to private forums of a quasi-public nature. Nor are we faced here with the situation where exercise of First Amendment rights may interfere with the purpose and normal use of a public facility. The *Blue Book* was clearly an appropriate place for the communication of the type of information submitted by the Gay Coalition. Even more than parks, airport terminals and the like, the very purpose of the booklet was communication. The publication was intended to provide a vehicle for the dissemination of information regarding public and private services and organizations in the Anchorage area. The groups listed represented a variety of viewpoints and interests and the *Blue Book* served as a means by which members of the community could discover the existence of others with similar views and interests. In short, the *Blue Book* was designed for and dedicated to expressive and associational use and therefore, once it was opened for such use, the government could not deny appellant access to it based solely on the content of its beliefs.

Appellees contend, however, that the *Blue Book* does not constitute a public forum for two reasons. First, they argue that the *Blue Book* is simply an informational booklet, the tenor of which is "bland, nonadvocative and carefully winnowed of any partisan flavor." They maintain that since it does not provide a vehicle for the interchange of partisan views, ideas and opinions, the *Blue Book* does not "partake of the essential attribute of a public forum." . . . They argue that an examination of public forum cases reveals that such forums were found only in those situations where there was a partisan exchange of views and opinions.

We find this argument unpersuasive.... [T]he First Amendment protects all forms of speech, both bland and partisan. It enables the soapbox orator to give a speech in the park free from unreasonable govenment intrusion, the newspaper to criticize official action at even the highest levels without fear of reprisal, and the pharmacist to advertise that he will sell " 'the X prescription drug at the Y price.' " *Virginia State Board of Pharmacy v. Virginia Citizens Consumer Council*, 425 U.S. 748, 761 (1976). The informational speech at issue here is as significant under our constitutional scheme as more political or partisan speech. In our view, there is but a short step between the dissemination of information such as that contained in the *Blue Book* and the exchange of views and ideas. The dissemination of information is often an invitation to discussion, and as such, it is a necessary and important part of the discussion process itself. Were we to draw the line that appellees suggest, we would be in effect thwarting the very process of communi-

cation which the First Amendment is designed to protect. Moreoever, as the United States Supreme Court has stated, "[E]ven if the First Amendment were thought to be primarily an instrument to enlighten public decision-making in a democracy, we could not say that the free flow of information does not serve that goal." *Virginia State Board of Pharmacy, supra* at 765.

Appellees' argument is flawed in another respect as well. Public forums are not designated such because they are designed to provide a vehicle for partisan expression; rather, they are so called because they are appropriate arenas for people to exercise their constitutional rights of expression and association. In many instances, forums are not designed to provide a vehicle for expression at all, obvious examples being streets and bus terminals, yet they are considered public forums because they are appropriate places for speech activity. In other cases, it is the fact that government has opened a forum for speech activity in general that is determinative of rights of access rather than use of the forum as a vehicle for the exchange of partisan viewpoints. . . .

■ ■ ■

Appellees have advanced one other argument in support of their position that there has been no abridgement of appellant's First Amendment rights in this case. Stated briefly, they contend that the Coalition's failure to show that actual harm resulted from deletion of its entry in the *Blue Book* is fatal to its First Amendment claim. As a corollary to this, they maintain that the availability of alternative means of communication is a factor bearing on the absence of concrete injury to appellant's First Amendment interests.

Appellees' contention is without merit. It is axiomatic that freedom of speech and the correlative freedom of association are fundamental rights which lie at the foundation of our system of government. . .

. . . [T]he First Amendment is designed to ensure that individuals are able to speak (and associate) free from unnecessary government restraint. Inherent in its mandate is the notion that it is the *suppression* of speech *in itself* which is the evil to be avoided for such suppression necessarily impairs the right to speak freely. Any further showing of adverse consequences flowing therefrom is unnecessary. Moreover, contrary to appellees' suggestion, the availability of alternative means of communication does not mitigate the harm resulting from government restraint of speech. As the Supreme Court has stated, "[O]ne is not to have the exercise of his liberty of expression in appropriate places abridged on the plea that it may be exercised in some other place." *Schneider v. Irvington*, 308 U.S. 147, 163 (1939).

■ ■ ■

One final point raised by appellees merits discussion. Appellees have emphasized that because of space limitations it was possible to list in the *Blue Book* only a fraction of the organizations existing in the Anchorage area and they imply that this fact in some way justifies exclusion of the Gay Coalition. We

are not persuaded by this argument for in finding the *Blue Book* to be a public forum we have not ignored this factor. When the municipality decided to publish a limited informational guide to public and private local resources, it did not thereby assume the obligation of providing space to every possible group in Anchorage seeking a listing. Had the municipality deleted groups at random or used criteria not related to the nature of particular organizations, constitutional violations may not have resulted. In deleting the Alaska Gay Coaltion from the *Blue Book*, however, appellees denied that group access to a public forum *based solely on the nature of its beliefs*. In so doing, they violated appellant's constitutional rights to freedom of speech and association and equal protection under the law.

It is our understanding that copies of the 1976-77 *Anchorage Blue Book* are still available for sale to the public. In accordance with our opinion in this case, we hold that further distribution of the publication in its present form constitutes a continuing violation of appellant's constitutional rights. The case is remanded to the superior court with instructions to forthwith order that appellees and their agents be immediately enjoined from further distribution of the 1976-77 *Anchorage Blue Book*.

Notes

1. In a case similar to *Gouldelock*, an appellate court in Wisconsin rejected a claim that lesbian/gay advertisers denied space in the classified advertising section of a private newspaper. *See Hatheway v. Gannett Satellite Info. Network, Inc.*, 459 N.W.2d 873 (Wisc. App. 1990). The court ruled that the newspaper's advertising section was not a place of public accommodation, as defined by state law, and thus was not subject to the state's non-discrimination provisions.
2. In *Loving v. Bellsouth Advertising & Publishing Corp.*, 339 S.E.2d 372 (Ga. Ct. App. 1985), the court held that the local Yellow Pages publisher was a private enterprise, and therefore under no legal obligation to accept advertising from a gay bookstore. Nonetheless, combinations of grass-roots campaigns and legal pressure have convinced Yellow Pages publishers

in other parts of the country to accept gay and lesbian advertising and listings. *See* Anthony Perry, *Alarm Company Backs Up Its Bark With a Dog That Doesn't Bite — or Eat*, L.A. TIMES, Nov. 22, 1989, at B1 (reporting that Pacific Bell directory in San Diego would list gay and lesbian organizations); Constance Hays, *Listing Is Won In Yellow Pages By Gay Groups*, N. Y. TIMES, Jan. 18, 1989, at B1 (reporting that NYNEX would list gay and lesbian organizations in The New England Yellow Pages).

3. In a case not unlike the *Alaska* case, a federal district court in Rhode Island prevented the Rhode Island Bicentennial Foundation from excluding a lesbian and gay group from a calendar of bicentennial events (as well as from utilizing the Old State House), reasoning that the Foundation could not use a subjective standard of tastefulness and suitability. *See Toward a Gayer Bicentennial Comm. v. Rhode Island Bicentennial Found.*, 417 F. Supp. 632 (D.R.I. 1976). And in *Gay Activists Alliance v. Washington Metropolitan Area Transit Auth.*, 5 MED. L. REP. (BNA) 1404 (D.D.C. 1979), the federal district court required the District of Columbia's transit authority to allow a gay group to advertise because the Authority allowed other politically and socially controversial groups to advertise.

4. Courts have consistently excluded homosexual and heterosexual *obscenity* from First Amendment protection. The United States Supreme Court has defined works of obscenity as materials that " 'taken as a whole' appeal to the prurient interest in sex, which portray sexual conduct in a patently offensive way, and which, taken as a whole, do not have serious literary, artistic, political or scientific value." *Miller v. California*, 413 U.S. 15, 24 (1973). However, the Supreme Court has upheld the right of an individual to possess obscene materials in the home, *see Stanley v. Georgia*, 394 U.S. 557 (1969), but not such materials that depict children, *New York v. Ferber*, 458 U.S. 747 (1982).

    The Seventh Circuit invalidated an Indianapolis anti-pornography statute that would have banned, among other things, gay pornography. The Indianapolis ordinance was based on Catharine MacKinnon and Andrea Dworkin's model anti-pornography ordinance, *see* Catharine MacKinnon and Andrea Dworkin, *Proposed Los Angeles County Anti-Pornography Civil Rights Law*, in WILLIAM LOCKHART ET AL., CONSTITUTIONAL LAW 778, 779 (7th ed. 1991). In an opinion later affirmed by the U.S. Supreme Court, Circuit Judge Frank Easterbrook held that the ordinance, because it was not content-neutral, impermissibly infringed on protected speech. *See American Booksellers Ass'n, Inc. v. Hudnut*, 771 F.2d 323 (7th Cir. 1985), *aff'd*, 475 U.S. 1001 (1986).

5. Courts have generally not protected the gay telephone sex services that were largely created as a safer-sex response to the AIDS crisis. In 1990, Congress enacted an amendment to the Communications Act of 1934 devised by Republican Senator Jesse Helms of North Carolina to limit the availability of telephone sex by blocking access to all "dial-a-porn" services with "indecent" (including homoerotic) speech to those who do not register for such access. *See* 47 U.S.C.A. § 223(b), (c) (West Supp. 1990). Although a New York federal district court judge issued a preliminary injunction against application of the Helms amendment in part because it was too vague, the Second Circuit later reversed that decision. *See American Info. Enters., Inc. v. Thornburgh*, 742 F. Supp. 1255 (S.D.N.Y. 1990), *rev'd sub nom. Dial Info. Servs. Corp. v. Thornburgh*, 938 F.2d 1535 (2d Cir. 1991), *cert. denied sub nom. Dial Information Servs. Corp. v. Barr*, 112 S. Ct. 966 (1992). The constitutionality of the Helms provision remains unresolved.

    In a related context, a California federal district court held in a suit by a dial-a-porn service against Pacific Bell (an AT&T subsidiary) that Pacific Bell's withholding of billing and collection services from providers of the service — sanctioned by section 2884.2(a) of the California Public Utilities Code, *see* CAL. PUB. UTIL. CODE, § 2884.2 (a) (West Supp. 1991) (forcing dial-a-porn services to contract independently with telephone carriers for billing and collection services) — constituted state action. *See Westpac Audiotext, Inc. v. Wilks*, 756 F. Supp. 1267 (N.D. Cal. 1991).

6. The National Endowment for the Arts (NEA) has been under severe attack by both conservatives and liberals for its interpretation of congressional funding provisions that denied grants to certain non-obscene materials. In 1990, Congress amended the NEA's governing statute, adding a provision requiring that "general standards of decency and repect for the diverse beliefs and values of the American public" be considered during funding determinations. *See* 20 U.S.C. § 954(d). Four artists, who purportedly worked with homoerotic subject matter and whose applications for NEA grants had been denied, sued the NEA and challenged the "decency" clause of 20 U.S.C. § 954 (d)(1) on constitutional grounds. On June 9, 1992, a United States District Court agreed with the artists, holding that the "decency" clause was void for vagueness under the Fifth Amendment and overbroad under the First Amendment. *Finley v. Nat'l Endowment for the Arts*, No. CV 90-5236 AWT (C.D. Cal. June 9, 1992).

7. Another gay artist has sued the American Family Association (AFA) for reproducing parts of his artwork in a pamphlet designed to raise money in AFA's campaign against NEA funding of homosexual art. *See Wojnarowicz v. American Family Ass'n*, 745 F. Supp. 130 (S.D.N.Y. 1990). The court — citing the New York Artist's Authorship Rights Act, N.Y. ARTS & CULT. AFF. LAW § 14.03 (McKinney's Supp. 1990), which prohibits the unauthorized and false attribution of altered artwork to an artist — held for the plaintiff and ordered injunctive and corrective relief (mailed clarifications by the AFA to previous recipients of the pamphlet). *See also Wojnarowicz v. American Family Ass'n*, 772 F. Supp. 201, 202 (S.D.N.Y. 1991) (warning the AFA, which continued to mail out the pamphlet at issue, to "exercise extreme diligence and caution to prevent future violations of this Court Order").

V. "OUTING"

SIPPLE v. CHRONICLE PUBLISHING CO.

201 Cal. Rptr. 665 (Ct. App. 1984)

CALDECOTT, J.

On September 22, 1975, Sara Jane Moore attempted to assassinate President Gerald R. Ford while the latter was visiting San Francisco, California. Plaintiff Oliver W. Sipple (hereafter appellant or Sipple) who was in the crowd at Union Square, San Francisco, grabbed or struck Moore's arm as the latter was about to fire the gun and shoot at the President. Although no one can be certain whether or not Sipple actually saved the

President's life, the assassination attempt did not succeed and Sipple was considered a hero for his selfless action and was subject to significant publicity throughout the nation following the assassination attempt.

Among the many articles concerning the event was a column written by Herb Caen and published by the *San Francisco Chronicle* on September 24, 1975. The article read in part as follows: "One of the heroes of the day, Oliver 'Bill' Sipple, the ex-Marine who grabbed Sara Jane Moore's arm just as her gun was fired and thereby may have saved the President's life, was the center of midnight attention at the Red Lantern, a Golden Gate Ave. bar he favors. The Rev. Ray Broshears, head of Helping Hands, and Gay Politico, Harvey Milk, who claim to be among Sipple's close friends, describe themselves as 'proud — maybe this will help break the stereotype'. Sipple is among the workers in Milk's campaign for Supervisor."

Thereafter, the *Los Angeles Times* and numerous out-of-state newspapers published articles which, referring to the primary source (i.e., the story published in the *San Francisco Chronicle*), mentioned both the heroic act shown by Sipple and the fact that he was a prominent member of the San Francisco gay community. Some of those articles speculated that President Ford's failure to promptly thank Sipple for his heroic act was a result of Sipple's sexual orientation.

Finding the articles offensive to his private life, on September 30, 1975, Sipple filed an action against the California defendants, the Chronicle Publishing Company, Charles de Young Thieriot, the publisher of the *Chronicle*, Herb Caen, a columnist for the *Chronicle*, the Times Mirror Company, the owner and publisher of the *Los Angeles Times*, and Otis Chandler (hereafter together respondents) and numerous out-of-state newspapers. The complaint was predicated upon the theory of invasion of privacy and alleged in essence that defendants without authorization and consent

published private facts about plaintiff's life by disclosing that plaintiff was homosexual in his personal and private sexual orientation; that said publications were highly offensive to plaintiff inasmuch as his parents, brothers and sisters learned for the first time of his homosexual orientation; and that as a consequence of disclosure of private facts about his life plaintiff was abandoned by his family, exposed to contempt and ridicule causing him great mental anguish, embarrassment and humiliation. Plaintiff finally alleged that defendants' conduct amounted to malice and oppression calling for both compensatory and punitive damages.

[The trial court granted summary judgment to the defendants].

■ ■ ■

Appellant's principal contention on appeal is that . . . the individual elements of the invasion of privacy (i.e., public disclosure of private facts; the offensiveness of the public disclosure; and the newsworthiness of the publication as an exception to tort liability) constituted a factual determination which could not be resolved or adjudicated by way of summary procedure.

Before discussing appellant's contentions on the merit, as an initial matter we set out the legal principles governing the case. It is well settled that there are three elements of a cause of action predicated on tortious invasion of privacy. First, the disclosure of the private facts must be a *public disclosure*. Second, the facts disclosed must be *private facts*, and not public ones. Third, the matter made public must be one which would be *offensive* and objectionable to a reasonable person of ordinary sensibilities. It is likewise recognized, however, that due to the supreme mandate of the constitutional protection of freedom of the press even a tortious invasion of one's privacy is exempt from liability if the publication of private facts is truthful and newsworthy. The latter proposition finds support primarily in Restatement Second of Torts section 652D which provides that "One who gives publicity to a matter concerning the private life of another is subject to liability to the other for invasion of his privacy, if the matter publicized is of a kind that (a) would be highly offensive to a reasonable person, and (b) is not of legitimate concern to the public."

In interpreting the cited section, the cases and authorities emphasize that the privilege to publicize newsworthy matters incorporated in section 652D is not only immunity accorded by the common law, but also one of constitutional dimension based upon the First Amendment of the United States Constitution. As tersely stated in comment d to section 652D: "When the subject-matter of the publicity is of legitimate public concern, there is no invasion of privacy.

> This has now become a rule not just of common law of torts, but of the Federal Constitution as well." (Accord *Cox Broadcasting Corp. v. Cohn*, 420 U.S. 469 (1975); *Time, Inc. v. Hill*, 385 U.S. 374, 383 (1967).

As an additional preliminary matter, it also bears emphasis that a motion for summary judgment in First Amendment cases is an approved procedure because unnecessarily protracted litigation would have a chilling effect upon the exercise of First Amendment rights and because speedy resolution of cases involving free speech is desirable. While the crucial test as to whether to grant a motion for summary judgment remains the same in free speech cases (i.e., whether there is a triable issue of fact presented in the case), the courts impose more stringent burdens on one who opposes the motion and require a showing of high probability that the plaintiff will ultimately prevail in the case. In the absence of such showing the courts are inclined to grant the motion and do not permit the case to proceed beyond the summary judgment stage.

When viewed in light of the aforegoing principles, the summary judgment in this case must be upheld on two grounds. First, as appears from the record properly considered for the purposes of summary judgment, the facts disclosed by the articles were not private facts within the meaning of the law. Second, the record likewise reveals on its face that the publications in dispute were newsworthy and thus constituted a protective shield from liability based upon invasion of privacy.

A. THE FACTS PUBLISHED WERE NOT PRIVATE

As pointed out earlier, a crucial ingredient of the tort premised upon invasion of one's privacy is a public disclosure of *private facts*, that is, the unwarranted publication of intimate details of one's private life which are outside the realm of legitimate public interest. In elaborating on the notion, the cases explain that there can be no privacy with respect to a matter which is already public or which has previously become part of the "public domain". Moreover, it is equally underlined that there is no liability when the defendant merely gives further publicity to information about the plaintiff which is already public or when the further publicity relates to matters which the plaintiff leaves open to the public eye.

The case at bench falls within the aforestated rules. The undisputed facts reveal that prior to the publication of the newspaper articles in question appellant's homosexual orientation and participation in gay community activities had been known by hundreds of people in a variety of cities, including New York, Dallas, Houston, San Diego, Los Angeles and San Francisco. Thus, appellant's deposition shows that prior to the assassination attempt appellant spent a lot of time in "Tenderloin" and "Castro," the well-known gay sections of San Francisco; that he frequented gay bars and other homosexual gatherings in both San Francisco and other cities; that he marched in gay parades on several occasions; that he supported the campaign of Mike Caringi for the election of "Emperor"; that he participated in the coronation of the "Emperor" and sat at Caringi's table on that occasion; that his friendship with Harvey Milk, another prominent gay, was well-known and publicized in gay newspapers; and that his homosexual association and name had been reported in gay magazines (such as *Data Boy*, *Pacific Coast Times*, *Male Express*, etc.) several times before the publications in question. In fact, appellant quite candidly conceded that he did not make a secret of his being a homosexual and that if anyone would ask, he would frankly admit that he was gay. In short, since appellant's sexual orientation was already in public domain and since the articles in question did no more than to give further publicity to matters which appellant left open to the eye of the public, a vital element of the tort was missing rendering it vulnerable to summary disposal.

Although the conclusion reached above applies with equal force to all respondents, we cannot help observing that respondents Times Mirror and its editor are exempt from liability on the additional ground that the *Los Angeles Times* only republished the *Chronicle* article which implied that appellant was gay. It is, of course, axiomatic that no right of privacy attaches to a matter of general interest that has already been publicly released in a periodical or in a newspaper of local or regional circulation.

B. THE PUBLICATION WAS NEWSWORTHY

But even aside from the aforegoing considerations, the summary judgment dismissing the action against respondents was justified on the additional, independent basis that the publication contained in the articles in dispute was newsworthy.

As referred to above, our courts have recognized a broad privilege cloaking the truthful publication of all newsworthy matters. Thus, our Supreme Court [has] stated that a truthful publication is protected if (1) it is newsworthy and (2) it does not reveal facts so offensive as to shock the community notions of decency. While it has been said that the general criteria for determining newsworthiness are (a) the social value of the facts published; (b) the depth of the article's intrusion into ostensibly private affairs; and (c) the extent to which the individual voluntarily acceded to a position of public notoriety, the cases and authorities further explain that the paramount test of newsworthiness is whether the matter is of legitimate public interest which in turn must be determined according to the community mores. "'In determining what is a matter of legitimate public interest, account must be taken of the customs and conventions of the community; and in the last analysis what is proper becomes a matter of the community mores. *The line is to be drawn when the publicity ceases to be the giving of information to which the public is entitled, and becomes a morbid and sensational prying into private lives for its own sake*, with which a reasonable member of the public, with decent standards, would say that he had no concern.'"

In the case at bench the publication of appellant's homosexual orientation which had already been widely known by many people in a number of communities was not so offensive even at the time of the publication as to shock the community notions of decency. Moreover, and perhaps even more to the point, the record shows that the publications were not motivated by a morbid and sensational prying into appellant's private life but rather were prompted by legitimate political considerations, i.e., to dispel the false public opinion that gays were timid, weak and unheroic figures and to raise the equally important political question whether the President of the United States entertained a discriminatory attitude or bias against a minority group such as homosexuals. Thus appellant's case squarely falls within the language of *Kapellas* in which the California Supreme Court emphasized that "when, [as here] the legitimate public interest in the published information is substantial, a much greater intrusion into an individual's private life will be sanctioned, especially if the individual willingly entered into the public sphere." *Kapellas v. Kofman*, 1 Cal.3d 20, 36 (Cal. 1969).

Appellant's contention that by saving the President's life he did not intend to enter into the limelight and become a public figure can be easily answered. In elaborating on involuntary public figures, Restatement Second of Torts section 652D, comment f, sets out in part as follows: "There are other individuals who have not sought publicity or consented to it, but through their own conduct or otherwise have become a legitimate subject of public interest. They have, in other words, becomes 'news.' . . . These persons are regarded as properly subject to the public interest, and publishers are permitted to satisfy the curiosity of the public as to its heroes, leaders, villains and victims, and those who are closely associated with them. As in the case of the voluntary public figure, the authorized publicity is not limited to the event that itself arouses the public interest, and to some reasonable extent includes publicity given to facts about the individual that would otherwise be purely private."

In summary, appellant's assertion notwithstanding, the trial court could determine as a matter of law that the facts contained in the articles were not private facts within the purview of the law and also that the publications relative to the appellant were newsworthy. Since the record thus fails to present any triable issue of fact, the trial court was justified (if not mandated) in granting summary judgment and dismissing the case against respondents by way of summary procedure.

The purported appeal from the order denying a motion for new trial is dismissed as the order is not an appealable order.

The judgment is affirmed.

Notes

1. For an interesting discussion of the clash between privacy interests and First Amendment interests, see generally Jon E. Grant, Note, *"Outing" and Freedom of the Press: Sexual Orientation's Challenge to the Supreme Court's Categorical Jurisprudence*, 77 CORNELL L. REV. 103 (1991).
2. The gay and lesbian community has not reached consensus on the moral and strategic implications of outing. Many gays criticize outing as a "totalitarian thinking," and argue that it is hypocritical to publicly expose people's sexual orientation on the one hand, and to advocate for privacy rights on the other. *See, e.g.*, C. Carr, *Why Outing Must Stop*, VILLAGE VOICE, March 18, 1991, at 37. Others advocate "outing" as a method of educating the public about the diversity of the community, and criticize the media (primarily gossip columnists) as journalistically dishonest for suppressing the truth about celebrities' sexual orientations, and for consciously printing falsehoods. *See* Gabrial Rotello, *Tactical Considerations*, OUTWEEK, May 16, 1990, at 52 (writing that "the 'right to privacy' has now become merely a quest for a right to secrecy, a right to hide one's homosexuality from a hostile world").

VI. LESBIAN AND GAY IDENTITY
IN THE 1990's

♦

IN SEARCH OF GAY AMERICA
Neil Miller

Toward the end of my travels, I returned to Brown University, in Providence, Rhode Island, the college I had graduated from more than twenty years before. When I was at Brown, there was no gay student organization. But this time, as I walked across the College Green and looked up at the brick student union building, there, plainly visible in a third-floor window, was a large pink triangle. It was a signal that the office of the Lesbian and Gay Student Alliance was open. Change can seem so simple once it finally occurs — a sign in a window. I wondered how different my life would have been if there had been that pink triangle in the window when I was at Brown.

As I looked back on all I had experienced and the people I had met over the previous year and a half, I saw gay life as a continuum. At one end was a greater sense of openness, the acceptance and self-acceptance, that fuller, richer life that comfortably combined sexuality with the rest of one's identity. The continuum was personal, political, cultural. Individuals and groups of people were at different points along its progression. Some were just beginning to grasp at a gay identity, to develop a sense of community, like the Latina lesbians in San Antonio and the Native Americans in Minneapolis. Others were so far along that they seemed to be creating an autonomous culture all their own, as in San Francisco. Still others were stalled along the way or hadn't even begun the journey — the gay men in Selma, Alabama, so deeply in the closet that they were "back behind several racks of clothes"; the guys in Morgantown, West Virginia, who lived to get drunk on the weekend; the gay married men having furtive, guilt-ridden sex at X-rated bookstores in North Dakota.

But overall, I perceived a momentum — the ability of at least some gays and lesbians to lead relatively open lives in small towns, the organizations springing up in mid-size cities, the gay churches and synagogues and sports leagues, the lesbian "baby boom," the militant AIDS activism. As the Knoxville gay-pride motto went, "Nothin' can stop us now." Even AIDS, despite its toll, was accelerating the movement toward community-building, toward politicization, toward those hundreds of thousands marching past the White House on Columbus Day weekend.

A major factor in that momentum was the growning interaction between lesbians and gay men, replacing the divisions of the past. Once again, that varied from place to place. During Gay Pride Week in Knoxville, visiting activist Sue Hyde rose to speak and found the male and female members of Knoxville's Ten Percent sitting on opposite

NEIL MILLER, IN SEARCH OF GAY AMERICA: WOMEN AND MEN IN A TIME OF CHANGE 303–09 (1989).

sides of the room. At least they were in the same organization. In New York City, on the other hand, the novelist Sarah Schulman could boast that, based on her experience in AIDS activism, the relationship between lesbians and gay men had been transformed. "We've gone co-ed!" she said. There were other indications of a newly found unity: the beginnings of a confluence of sexual attitudes between men and women; the college women I met who listened to British gay male punk groups instead of women's music and informed me they had "a gay male identity." In smaller places — Bunceton, Bismarck, Fargo — separation between men and women had never been an option. There, the numbers were so few that they had to band together. In general, the separatism of the past was fading; the men and the women were finally realizing they were part of the same community.

There was almost always the personal struggle, the agony and joy of self-discovery, the sense of coming through. I was struck again and again by the tremendous changes in the lives of so many of the people I met as they came to grips with issues of identity and sexuality. A Denver psychotherapist named Britt Alkire, who had gone from being a schoolteacher, to marriage, to divorce, to the military, to coming out, to becoming a psychotherapist and lesbian activist, saw this as central to the gay experience. "There is a requirement for gay people to be more inventive or flounder forever. We are thrown on our own resources," she said. "I think gay people have this assignment in life to invent ourselves and our own relationships. We are in the definition business — to energetically and creatively invent new institutions, relationships, ways of being with eah other in the world. That is how I give menaing to gay life."

I noted, too, a general attempt at healing the wounds of the past — of gays and lesbians trying to overcome the effects of years of believing all the negative things society had told them about themselves. The rise of gay spirituality — from churches and synagogues to alternative approaches like women's spirituality — was a sign of this. Another indication was the proliferation of gay twelve-step groups, modeled on Alcoholic's Anonymous. In the listings section of the monthly San Francisco newspaper *Coming Up!*, I counted a total of thirty-five gay and lesbian self-help groups, ranging from gay AA and Children of Alcoholics groups to those for survivors of incest and abuse. Even in isolated Rapid City, South Dakota, where there was virtually no organized gay and lesbian life, a woman I met was planning to start a group for addicted gay people. This development was in part a response to AIDS; many men were concerned that the use of alcohol and drugs undermined the immune system and could encourage unsafe sex. But it also reflected a growing sense of pride and self-acceptance that translated to an effort to build a healthier community, both physically and mentally.

Everywhere, I found people reevaluating what was important in their lives. Sometimes, this was part of the resolution of issues of self-acceptance. Thus, after much struggle, Jan the West Virginia coal miner, had decided to leave the mines because her increasingly strong self-image as a lesbian made it impossible to continue to work in an environment where she felt she had no recourse but to hide her sexual orientation. For men, AIDS was often a major factor in this re-examination, in ways that went beyond simply changing sexual practices. So Frank, the computer entrepreneur in Boston who had lost his two best friends to AIDS, was putting a new value on a committed relationship, reconsidering whether professional success was providing sufficient meaning for him, and generally asking the question, "How should a man live?" In Los Angeles, I encountered a forty- year-old vice president at a major studio who was quitting his job to search for other sources of satisfaction, a decision precipitated in part because so many of his friends had been diagnosed with AIDS. This premature mid-life crisis was a phenomenon I saw repeated among gay men across the country.

There were changes I had hoped to discover but never did. I didn't find many indications of a new kind of gay male culture emerging out of the AIDS crisis. I had speculated that with the decline of recreational sex as a main focus of life for many gay men, we would begin to create a culture similar to that of lesbians — one centered around music, theatre, and the arts in general. Perhaps this would evolve gradually; the rise of gay sports leagues (even a gay and lesbian version of the Olympics, called the Gay Games) was one sign of a search for alternatives to the social patterns of the past. But this kind of cultural change was clearly a slow process. And despite the pronouncements of the movement, I didn't see the gay community coming to grips with the issues of racism and social class. The divisions between black, white, Latino, and Asian and between middle- and working-class remained deep, reflecting those of America in general.

I found no single vision of the gay future. Instead, I saw various gay and lesbian communities taking different paths, adopting their own strategies as they attempted to create an atmosphere of openness and a sense of security. How they went about it depended on numerical strength, on the quality of leadership, on particular local factors. There was the approach of conservative, mid-size Knoxville, where the gay and lesbian group eschewed the visibility of a march down Gay Street and instead was trying to prove itself through neighborly participation in arts festivals and city beautification programs. There was the model of Key West, where a gay community strong in numbers and in economic power argued that no civil rights protections and (in the view of some) no gay institutions were needed, that assimilation and "amalgamation" were the best ways to win a place in the sun.

In Los Angeles, the gay students at UCLA had formed a gay fraternity and a lesbian sorority — with rushing, pledging, and all the trappings of the Greek letter societies. Although frats and sororities had traditionally been symbols of elitism and homophobia, the students were determined to do things differently — stressing community service, "not beer parties and MRS degrees," as one sorority sister put it. It was still another strategy, one that was particularly inventive and risky — taking an institution that had been oppressive to gays and lesbians in the past and molding it to one's own needs and vision.

Finally, there was the model of some of the larger cities, notably San Francisco, with a sense of gays and lesbians as a people in their own right, with distinct family structures, religious, social, and cultural institutions. In New York City, Richard Burns, executive director of the city's Lesbian and Gay Community Center, saw a similar development. "We are beginning to develop a sense of responsibility for our gay youth and our gay elders," he said. "In the future, you will increasingly see us develop our own social-service agencies, our programs to take care of those portions of our community who are in crisis. We are realizing that we can develop an identity as a people and we can take care of our own."

To my mind, that big-city approach was probably the most promising, but it required a critical mass of gay people; in many respects, it didn't apply to smaller communities, to parts of the country less congenial to gays and lesbians. In the end, most likely, each gay community would continue to find its own solutions, some not even thought of yet.

But there were other, more ominous prospects that could not be discounted. It was still quite possible that the progress and the increasing options gays and lesbians were beginning to enjoy would eventually be overwhelmed by the magnitude of the AIDS epidemic. A man in New York City related that almost all his closest friends had succumbed to AIDS. "I feel like the bomb has already hit," he said. "I went to Seattle for a few days and was amazed that life was still going on." That was another line that extended into the future, a continuum that dramatized how deeply individuals and gay communities had been affected by the AIDS crisis. Everyone fell somewhere along it. The epidemic and its relentless progression was part of the gay present and the gay future, as well, side by side with the gains, the increasing openness. How would the gay community, a fragile community still, cope with the estimated quarter of a million gay men who would be diagnosed with AIDS by 1993? No one had an answer.

Hand in hand with AIDS came the threat of repression, the growing power of the anti-gay religious right. At this writing, the federal and state governments had by and large resisted efforts to apply more coercive social policies — mass testing, quarantine, and the like — to the AIDS epidemic. Yet, reports of delegates to the 1988 Republican National Convention in New Orleans physically attacking gay protesters, shouting "AIDS is not a disease — it's the cure!" vividly illustrated the extent of homophobia that the epidemic had brought to the surface. Sari (Bootsie) Abelson, a fifty-six-year-old lesbian from Birmingham, Alabama, who had gone through two marriages, shock treatments, even institutionalization, before she could make peace with her sexuality, had said to me, "The world is fully capable of bringing on the homosexuals the same thing we allowed to happen to the Jews of the world. I see us acting the same way that my grandparents and my aunts and uncles did in Europe, who told themselves, 'They are not going to bother me.' And they bothered them. They bothered them in a big way. I fully believe it can happen again."

I preferred to take a more optimistic view—that gays and lesbians were creating a power base that would make such a scenario unlikely. But the gay community had serious weaknesses as an interest group. One was an inability to overcome the hostility of the dominant elements of the Republican party. In 1988, ninety-eight openly gay people were delegates to the Democratic National Convention in Atlanta; the following month, at the Republican National Convention, not a single openly gay or lesbian delegate was to be found. Gay Republican activist Bruce Decker had told me that openly gay people were "as welcome as a turd in a punchbowl" in the Grand Old Party. Yet, some degree of influence on both parties, from the inside and outside, was crucial. The same went for other institutions and environments usually viewed as uncongenial to gays, from churches to union halls to police forces. Gays and lesbians had to neutralize (if not win over) hostile segments of society by establishing some kind of presence. That was a major challenge. For that reason, I believed that Rose Mary Denham, the Methodist minister who stood up to her church, was hero; that was why I admired openly gay people who stayed on in small towns; that was why Bob Almstead, the first openly gay cop in Washington, D.C., was hero, too.

And that was why I admired David Hernandez. A twenty-five year old sophomore at UCLA who came from a working-class Chicano family, David was one of the founders of the gay fraternity at his school. He worked part-time at a warehouse with two hundred other men, many of whom were members of minority groups. All were members of the Teamsters, as he was. The day after a photgraph of the gay fraternity brothers appeared in the daily newspaper, David went to work. "Gigantic guys," as he described them, whom he had worked with day after day, were staring at him or coming up and asking, with a mixture of incredulity and menace, "Was that you in the paper?" or "You're gay? *You're* gay?" or "Aren't you afraid of AIDS?" Many others, including his boss, refused even to look in David's direction. David was terrified. "Those were the most difficult hours of my life," he said. "My head, my stomach were spinning. I kept saying to myself, 'I wish I could take it back.' Here was this mob of Teamsters. I didn't know if someone would drop a box on me or run over me with a machine. Your fears go wild."

Still others who had never talked to him before greeted him in a friendly way as he walked past. Within a few days, the storm had passed; the other men went back to treating him as they always had, as the smart college kid who wouldn't wind up spending the rest of his life in the warehouse, as they most likely would. "If you can come out in that atmosphere, you can come out any-where," David said.

Taking risks is the key to continued momentum. If collective action is essential to gay progress, so are individual acts of courage such as David's. Perhaps, in the end, sexual pluralism is something society will never accept. Perhaps demoralization and repression represent the scenario of the gay future, after all. But I believe otherwise. I have seen too many changes in a very short time, met too many people who have taken tremendous risks by becoming open about their sexuality and who will never return to the constricted lives of the past. For them, for all of us, there is simply no going back.

◆

UNDOCUMENTED ALIENS IN THE QUEER NATION
Charles Fernandez

This month I celebrate the seventh anniversay of the first time I had sex with another man. That encounter occurred during my first year in college. Although it initiated my life as a sexually active being, it certainly didn't dispel all of my conflicts. At the same time, I was also escaping my Cuban family and my Puerto Rican upbringing in order to come to terms with my sexuality. I continued to struggle for years over the issue of sexuality with my friends, boyfriends, and therapist.

When I became active in gay politics and facilitated a workshop on heterosexism and homophobia for the first time, I felt I had come to terms with a fundamental truth about myself. That semester I also happened to be enrolled in a course on "Philosophy and Feminism," in which the instructor asked that we write a paper integrating theory and personal experience. In this assignment I wrote, "Along with the earth-shaking joy of finally being able to communicate to myself and others came the anger of realizing that I had been silent and silenced for so long. I had previously assumed that all of us spoke from our experience and our feelings — in short, as ourselves — but

having only recently discovered a voice that finally felt genuine, I realized that I had taken too much for granted. Our society proscribes far too many voices, molding them into an obedient chorus."

I went on, "Reading *This Bridge Called My Back* and *Home Girls*, my understanding went beyond the intellectual level to a deeper, emotional level, even if I could not fully identify with the experiences of those writers. I could not share their experiences of being oppressed because they were women, lesbians, and racial and ethnic minorities, but I could share with them the experiences of simply being oppressed, of being denied because of who we were, of being silenced."

When the professor returned the paper to me, she asked why I didn't identify with Cherrie Moraga and Gloria Anzaldúa in our common ethnicity. At the time I wondered what the hell she meant by that.

I threw myself fully into lesbian and gay organizing on campus, and after college I deepened my commitment by seeking a job in the movement. But by then, I was finally beginning to focus my attention on that other

Charles Fernandez, *Undocumented Aliens In The Queer Nation*, in OUT/LOOK, Spring 1991, at 20.

part of my constructed self, my ethnicity, which had long been neglected and misunderstood. I began by writitng my senior paper on sexual politics in the Cuban Revolution. When I moved to New York I actively sought out the Latino/a gay and lesbian community. Now fully immersed in the politics of ethnic and racial identity, I had another profoundly alienating realization: the lesbian and gay movement that had up to now absorbed my attention and energies privileged a white, middle class, and often male subject that stood in opposition to heterosexual categories.

The movement's subject and protagonist, in all his white, middle-class, and male (homo)geneity, was clearly reflected in the general public's image of the typical homosexual, in the lesbian and gay media's depiction of their target audience, in the movement's agenda and strategies, in the academy's methodology and theorizing, and in the lesbian and gay community's own self-understanding.

In retrospect, I realize that I initially had focused on my sexual identity because it was most in question at the time. My ethnicity didn't seem to require my attention — it was a simple fact with no significant ramifications. As an assimilated, light-skinned man with a very slight accent, I had the dubious and deluded luxury of bieng incorporated in the homogenizing whole.

And while friends, fellow activists, and mentors encouraged and sustained me in these efforts, I never felt encouraged to explore those differences that might break the mold into which I was so neatly forcing myself. A friend from those days recently told me that back then I had no race politics. That's not entirely correct: I did have a sense of race politics, even if rudimentary and inarticulate. What I lacked, however, was a sense of myself as a racialized subject within the context of a politics of race.

A gay person defines herself or himself exclusively in opposition to the category of heterosexual. Both personal and communal identity are constituted by this opposition.

The struggle against homophobia and heterosexism becomes, then, the primary agenda for a movement towards liberation. It is a movement that cannot afford to waste energy fighting against other oppressions — no matter how worthy the causes. Perhaps the best articulation of this position is Richard Mohr's *Gays/Justice* where he argues that coalition politics — engaging substantively in common struggle against sexism, racism, or classism — is fundamentally a drain on the lesbian and gay movement. The struggles of "other" groups, he says, are not "our" struggles. That some gay people might be obliged to struggle against racism, or against sexism, or against class oppression is for Mohr, and many movement leaders today, of no major concern.

These are not only the views of the arch-conservative gay men and lesbians among us. I've heard avowed leftist sex radicals assert that linking the struggle against heterosexism with other struggles represents a homophobic attempt to legitimate the former by means of the latter. Ironically, this ostensibly more progressive political argument shares Mohr's exclusionary conclusion.

These views effectively shut out those among us whose personal and political ideologies are defined by more than simple opposition to heterosexuality. Writing about feminism, Norma Alarcón has argued that "The inclusion of other analytical categories such as race and class becomes impossible for a subject whose consciousness refuses to acknowledge that 'one becomes a woman' in ways that are much more complex than in a simple opposition to men. In cultures in which 'asymmetric race and class relations are a central organizing principle of society,' one may also 'become a woman' in opposition to other women." Similarly, by building an identity exclusively around one's sexuality and developing a political agenda that either excludes or subordinates other forms of oppression, the lesbian and gay movement has narrowly defined its primary subject.

We are rendered invisible even as our differences are touted as examples of the colorful diversity of our gay and lesbian community. As Alarcón writes, "Anglo feminist readers of *This Bridge Called My Back* tend to appropriate it, cite it as an instance of difference between women, and proceed to negate that difference by subsuming women of color into the unitary category of woman/women."

I was unable to identify racially with the writers of *This Bridge* because I was intent on defining myself as queer. This is a matter of great personal pain. It reflects a profound failing, and an indictment of the movement.

The agenda of the early gay liberation movement was meant to transform society and, in the process, liberate a safe social space for lesbians and gay men. But "social space," which was originally meant as a metaphor for the freedom to live openly gay lives, became concretized in the gay ghettoes of our major cities. That quest for social space has now been taken a step further with the rise of queer nationalism. One may well wonder if all of this won't result in a call for a queer homeland anytime soon.

In the "melting pot" that is our Queer Nation, all difference becomes subsumed under the homogenizing "gay and lesbian community," and important political and philosophical differences get dismissed. The rise of queer nationalism leads some of us to wonder if we are to become second-class citizens, three-fifths human, or recognized subjects within it. The historical precedent offers little comfort.

The strange advent of queer nationalism may perhaps be attributed to the lesbian and gay community's even stranger tendency to view itself as something akin to an ethnic minority. Oppressed by a hostile majority from whom it sought assurances of certain rights and privileges, the movement, perhaps predictably, attempts to fashion itself in the image of other groups who had struggled for their own liberation.

In this regard, Steven Epstein argues that the lesbian and gay movement's self-identification as an ethnic minority coincided with a revival of European-American ethnicity during the 1970s. But the lesbian and gay community doesn't compare itself to white ethnic communities, like Greeks, Italians, or Poles. Instead, the movement measures its gains, setbacks and obstacles against those of the "other" minority groups battling for political power in our society: African Americans, Latinos, Asian Americans, and Native Americans. But there are fundamental differences between the experience and reality of white ethnic communities and that of communities of color in this country; the effects of hundreds of years of extinction, slavery, colonization, imperialism, and racial hatred. In this context, it's troubling to witness a white-dominated movement compare its gains and grievances to those of communities of color.

While it is undeniable that racial minorities have endured centuries of brutalizing racism, one could also argue that those who engage in homosexual behavior have certainly fared no better. It is, however, difficult to navigate this assertion without becoming beached on the barren rocks of ranked oppressions. Nevertheless, one cannot help but appreciate the irony of white-led movement with limited racial consciousness turning around and appropriating ethnicity and the stigma of race as legitimating tools.

Who ultimately benefits when the gay and lesbian community embraces an ethnic self-understanding? How does this movement determine political discourse and strategy, or the possibilities of radical political change? What impact does this self-understanding have on the possibility for forming coalitions with communities of color, or engaging substantively with them in the struggle for lesbian and gay liberation? These are some of the questions I have asked myself as I juggle the seemingly irreducible demands of structuring my political commitments. One possible explanation of who benefits may lie in the fact that fractious disenfranchised groups competing in the marketplace of rights, representation, and privileges pose no great danger to the political and social system that oppresses us all.

While identity politics has politicized new arenas of human experience, taken to the extreme it has resulted in a fragmentation of subjects. It has dead-ended in an over-emphasis on identity and personal development rather than liberation, justice, and solidarity. It may be unreasonable for me to hope to find myself as a Latino in the lesbian and gay movement. But it is not unreasonable to de-mand that that movement include my concerns if it expects my continued support and participation. One may hope that a more integrated analysis of what it means to be "gay" or "lesbian" in this country will help spawn a movement that recognizes multiple subjects and the necessity to move toward liberations across a greater spectrum of struggles.

FOUR

Lesbians and Gay Men
in the Workplace

I. INTRODUCTION

A. Background

Lesbians and gay men confront enormous barriers of discrimination, both explicit and subtle, in the workplace. Some companies refuse to hire or fire individuals who they believe, or suspect, are gay. Those lesbians and gay men who do have jobs often must hide their identity. According to one commentator, gay people begin to "underidentify with their jobs . . . [feeling] no security . . . [and consequently are prevented from] giving it a proper degree of commitment, a proper link to self . . ."[1] Or gay people become workaholics to "show themselves [they are] productive enough, worthy enough, good enough, [to] overcome the invisible stigma that lurks within them waiting to suppurate."[2] On-the-job discrimination also has a concrete component: lesbians and gay men usually do not receive the employment benefits for their life partners that married persons receive for their spouses. As a result, lesbian and gay employees do not get "equal pay for equal work."

The following readings provide background information about the challenges facing lesbians and gay men in the workplace.

---

1. RICHARD D. MOHR, GAYS/JUSTICE: A STUDY OF ETHICS, SOCIETY, AND LAW 149 (1988).

2. *Id.*

◆

EMPLOYMENT DISCRIMINATION IN NEW YORK CITY: A SURVEY OF GAY MEN AND WOMEN
National Gay Task Force

INTRODUCTION

Gay rights activists and organizations have long maintained that gay and lesbian employees face widespread discrimination in their jobs. Their claim has been that sexual orientation often is the primary reason why an otherwise qualified individual is not hired for a job, is not promoted, is fired, or suffers general harassment in the workplace. While these arguments seem plausible, there has been a lack of hard and systematically collected data to back them up. Those who oppose or question the value of legislation that would protect gay employees from discrimination have seized upon this lack of data and used it to support *their* view that these problems are not pressing. What little data has been available has not been conclusive and has typically taken the form of personal statements by individuals concerning specific cases of discrimination. There have been few efforts to scientifically gather information on this issue from a broader spectrum of the gay population and to quantify that data in a meaningful way.

In order to provide a more substantial framework for discussion of this issue, the National Gay Task Force conducted a survey of gay and lesbian employees in New York in 1980 by means of a standardized questionnaire. Funding for the project was provided under CETA Title VI, administered by the Department of Labor of the City of New York, and was augmented by an additional grant from the Fund for Human Dignity, Inc.

The main purposes of this research were, first, to document and analyze instances of employment discrimination prompted by the employee's sexual orientation and, second, to explore the attitudes of gay employees about how their sexual orientation colored their job performance and working conditions. The principal question that the survey was designed to answer was: "Do gay men and women experience a denial of opportunities for fair employment based on their sexual orientation?" It was the aim of the survey to ascertain whether the respondents had encountered such discrimination and, if they had, what form it had taken and how they had dealt with it. The data was then analyzed to determine possible *patterns* of employment discrimination that called for legislative redress.

METHOD

This survey, like all responsible investigations concerning the gay community, does not claim the same universal applicability that is possible in other areas of the social sciences. The reasons for this limitation stem from the difficulties inherent in sampling the gay population — obstacles that have long been recognized by researchers. The problem is that many gay people — still perceiving or experiencing stigmatization by society — continue to conceal their sexual

NATIONAL GAY TASK FORCE, EMPLOYMENT DISCRIMINATION IN NEW YORK CITY: A SURVEY OF GAY MEN AND WOMEN (1980).

orientation and thus are inaccessible to survey research.

For that reason, the procedures followed in the analysis of our data have been modeled on the methods used by other researchers to study data derived from samples of an "unknown" population, a population which cannot be characterized in its entirety. The consequence is that when our findings are applied to the general population, they will tend toward the extreme of cautiousness — that is, the findings will probably tend to *under-report* the extent of the problems discussed.

During a two month period in 1980, 1,500 survey questionnaires were distributed to members of the National Gay Task Force and to other gay organizations in New York City area. Respondents had to either live or work in New York City to be accepted for study. Applicants were not required to provide their name. The survey questionnaire did not ask respondents to specify their sexual orientation, but it was assumed that all respondents were gay men or lesbians; the thrust of the questions was clearly based on that assumption and the distribution of the questionnaires was designed to reach a gay population only.

We conducted our research with the assumption that the sexual orientation of gay employees does affect their attitudes toward their jobs and that those attitudes are relatively the same whether or not the employee had been confronted by anti-gay discrimination. Because of this, we encouraged recipients of the questionnaire to participate even if they did not feel they had been a victim of discrimination. We also assumed that many gay employees form attitudes about their jobs not only on the basis of actual discrimination that they might have encountered, but also on the basis of a perceived potential for such discrimination. That is we assumed that a perception of the possibility for discrimination is an influential factor in shaping the attitudes of gay people toward their jobs.

One of the central aims of this study was to determine how the *anticipation* of discrimination colored gay employees' attitudes about their jobs, about their level of job security, and about their expectations for advancement or future employment opportunities. While choices and pressures as subtle and personal as these may be less subject to objective quantification than, for example, the effects of blatant dismissal from a job, the survey analysis still attempts to take into account their impact on the employment circumstances of gay people.

FINDINGS

386 completed questionnaires were received. The profile of the respondents was largely male (85%), white (90%), and highly educated (90% had at least some college education). Most occupations were either in the professional/technical or administrative categories. Most respondents lived or worked in Manhattan, though the other four borough of the City were represented in the sample. These results do not, of course, suggest that the gay community at large reflects this profile.

The questionnaire first sought to determine to what extent respondents were openly gay at their workplaces, i.e., how many of their co-workers respondents thought were aware of their sexual orientation. The survey found that about 85% of the respondents worked in situation where at least some people knew they were gay, either because they had told their co-workers or because they felt it was generally assumed. Only about 15% felt that no one was aware of their sexual orientation.

Anticipated Discrimination The questionnaire then asked the following hypothetical question:

"If it were known or assumed at work that you were lesbian or gay, how much of a problem would this be for you?"

The responses:

- 10%— A major problem
- 20%— A problem
- 31%— A minor problem
- 32%— Not a problem
- 5% — Not a problem — in fact a benefit

Thus, about 61% of the sample stated their belief that it would be a problem — to varying degrees — if it were to become known that they were gay.

Next, in an attempt to determine what they thought those problems would be, we asked respondents to rate the likelihood ("very likely," "likely," "unlikely") that various situations could arise if it were known or assumed at work that they were lesbian or gay:

- 39% said it was very likely or likely that they would have difficulty getting a promotion or transfer.
- 32% percent said it would be unlikely that they would have the same level of job security as a heterosexual.
- 13% said it would be very likely or likely that they would barred from practicing their trade or profession.
- 23% said it would be very likely or likely that they lose customers or clients.

In terms of their personal concerns:

- 26% said it would be unlikely that they would be treated as an equal among heterosexuals.
- 46% said it would be unlikely that they would be respected for their sexual orientation.
- 5% said it would be very likely or likely that they would fear for their physical safety.

Actual Discrimination   The next section of the questionnaire was intended to determine the actual incidence of discrimination based on sexual orientation. 21% responded positively to the following question:

"While working in New York City , do you feel that you have been discrimi-nated against in any of employment because of your sexual orientation?"

■ ■ ■

The remaining questions were aimed specifically at this 21% who had been victims of discrimination and the percentage listed below should be understood as percentages of that 21%.

People can perceive discrimination at various points in the employment process — e.g., hiring, advancement, raises, etc. In order to determine more accurately the nature of the discriminating reported, respondents were asked to specify the area(s) in which employment discrimination had occurred:

- 30% Hiring
- 23% Promotion
- 43% Harassment by superiors, co-workers or supervisors
- 25% Termination
- 12% Work performance evaluation

These results show substantial discrimination reported in all aspects of employment. A subsequent question found that most discrimination came from superiors, rather than from co-workers or subordinates.

When asked if the respondent had any supporting documents, statements of proof, or witnesses to the discriminatory incident, 24% said they did have such supporting evidence, and 76% said they did not. This is important, as it demonstrates that most people reporting discrimination are unable to document their claim. Any means of resolving conflicts — grievance procedures, lawsuits, complaints to company officials — require some ability to prove that the discriminating took place and that it was based solely on the individual's sexual orientation.

Sometimes discrimination may be obvious: An employer may say, "We don't want fags working here!" But usually it is not so overt. Most employers realize that open discrimination of this sort — even without legal sanctions — is unacceptable. It is even less

likely that an employer would provide written documentation that sexual orientation
was the basis for the discriminatory activity.
This problem in documenting discrimination
is even more difficult when the discrimination takes place at the hiring stage, rather
than being directed against existing employees: Employers are not normally bound to
give any explanations to a non-employee.

The fact that such a large proportion of our
sample had no supporting evidence indicates
the difficulty gay people have when they feel
they have been discriminated against. It also
may explain why, in some of the cities that
have enacted laws protecting gay employees,
fewer people have brought discrimination
complaints than had been expected. It is also
an indication of how easy it is for employers to
discriminate — no "paper trail" is left. Finally,
it also may suggest a large measure of skepticism that no fair redress can be achieved —
because, without recourse to legal protections
such as would be provided by passage of gay
rights legislation, many gay people may feel
that it is pointless to compile documentation.

In the current situation where most gay
people have no legal protections against
anti-gay employment discrimination, we
were interested in learning what people did
when they perceived themselves to be the
victims of discrimination. At least some
New York City municipal workers are covered under a 1978 Executive Order barring
discrimination against gay people. Further,
there are some avenues to resolving conflicts
that do not involve legal protections, such as
talking with those causing the difficulty. Respondents therefore were asked what they
did following the incident:

- 40% Took no action
- 23% Talked with the person causing the
  difficulty
- 24% Talked with co-workers not involved in the incident
- 24% Complained to superiors
- 26% Quit
- 15% Were fired
- 6% Consulted an attorney

When confronted with conflict there are
two general options — an active response
where the individual takes action of some
sort, and a passive response where the individual merely responds to external actions
or does nothing. Of those who took some
action, many of these actions were passive.
Among the options mentioned were the following: "changed employment agencies,"
requested a transfer," "resigned or quit."
The action was designed not to fight the
discrimination directly, but rather to remove the individual from the situation.

There may be several reasons for this
lack of action. Of course, most people have
few options open to them in a legal sense.
and many gay people, when faced with
discrimination, prefer to drop the matter so
as not to draw more attention to themselves
and risk further retribution. Often the last
thing that someone in this situation would
want would be the publicity of a lawsuit or
grievance procedure. That a sizeable group
— 26% — reported that they resigned or
quit when faced with discrimination further
indicates the reticence that many gay people feel in fighting back against discrimination.

We also were interested in the further
consequences of the discrimination, recognizing that these consequences may follow
the employee beyond the actual incident.
Respondents reported that, after the incident
occurred, they encountered further difficulties in:

- 26% Getting favorable job references
- 20% Relating to co-workers or supervisors at work
- 23% Finding another job
- 11% Protecting their privacy
- 21% Other
- 36% None of the above

Clearly, a significant group reported subsequent problems in their work lives as a result
of the discrimination. Our research did not
enquire about the further difficulties encountered in the personal, non-business lives of

victims of discrimination, but other research has shown the toll that discrimination takes on the self-esteem and overall level of personal security of its victims.

■ ■ ■

♦

DANCER FROM THE DANCE
Andrew Holleran

In the years before Malone arrived in New York City he had done all those things a young man was supposed to do — a young man from a very good family, that is, a family that had always had in every generation since it transplanted itself in Ohio from a rural town in Germany, a doctor or two, a judge, and a professor. This Germanic family of his father's worked hard, prospered, and gradually scattered all over the globe, even though they retained a certain love for the small town in Ohio in which they had grown up. As a child Malone had been allowed to read the round robin family letter they circulated among themselves: The news was usually about the vegetables they had planted, the weather, the seasons, and those events another family might have considered primary were mentioned almost as an afterthought — Sally was going to Korea to serve in the medical corps, Andrew was going round the world on the ship "Hope," Martha had discovered she had TB while examining her own sputum in the lab one afternoon, Joe was drinking. Pete had been promoted to treasurer of Sears International, Harry had died. "We had a good year for the squash, though the rutabagas didn't come up nearly so fast as we expected. You know how Lawrence loves his squash. It looks like the corn may be a bit late, too..." and on and on and on. Malone loved to read these letters as a child; they seemed so friendly and so calm to him, how peaceful to care only about the weather and the fruit. And as he grew older he came to see how modest they were, too, finding the fate of their vegetables of more interest than the fate of those human plants who were growing, in the background, to even greater glory than the squash — for the family letter, if it sounded like a garden club newsletter, also resembled to Malone's mind those glossy annual reports that corporations his father held stock in sent him every spring: listing debts and assets, profits, and future plans of investment. That was the family on his father's side: dispassionate, sensible, hardworking, and generous with one another.

His father had married a city girl, however — from a big witty Irish family in the suburbs of Chicago — and she had found these Germans sometimes too dispassionate for her tastes. She left Chicago with her new husband, left her friends, her skating parties, rides down Michigan Boulevard, and resorts in Wisconsin, and moved to a small town in southern Indiana; and it was there Malone spent the first few years of his life, chasing rabbits, hunting in the woods, spoiled by his paternal grandmother until his parents went abroad to work for an international engineering firm. It was the golden age of the American corporation, it was the flush of victory

ANDREW HOLLERAN, DANCER FROM THE DANCE 58–78 (1978).

following World War II, and the family participated in this, too.

The family taught Malone to be a polite fellow, self-reliant, hardworking, and to believe in God. He took piano lessons on Saturday morning and he scrubbed the patio each morning before he went to school. Above the side-board in the dining room of their bungalow hung a painting of a woman knitting in a grove of fruit trees while her children played about in her skirts. "That is how my family should be," his father said one day. After lunch his father took a nap — a custom of the tropics — and Malone sat by the telephone on the porch, reading his ancient history, and guarding his father's sleep. His father rose and returned to his air-conditioned office at one o'clock, and when he returned at five o'clock in the blue, windy, twilight, Malone rushed to embrace him on the porch, and pressed his face against the crisp, white shirt that bore, somehow, the odor of air conditioning. His mother, who had often just arisen, having read murder mysteries through the night, had a drink with his father on the porch while Malone sat out back with the maids, who adored him for his curly golden hair.

The events of his childhood were perfectly ordinary, if there is ever such a thing: He wept when his dog got lost, and wept when it was found. On Sunday mornings his mother wore short gloves to church and he held her hand walking up the aisle. He collected coral in his bedroom. A variety of varicolored maids came and went, and he attached his heart to them, in the washhouse behind their bungalow as they plaited their hair and he sat reading his books beside the washtubs fragrant with the blue astringency of bleach. He loved the odor of bleach and the breeze that blew down the hot, empty, baking street and carried the fragrance of the whole island, its thorn trees and cactus; he loved the warm cement, the empty, sunny sky, the maids' laughter. And he gradually over the years forgot those houses that had not only attics, dry and magical, but damp and vivid basements stored with preserves

and tools and old toys; he forgot the snows and turning seasons, and became a habitué of the Equator, whose soul loves light and the pleasures of the senses.

For there is no more sensual place on earth. On Saturdays he went to the blazing white movie house in whose dark womb he watched Errol Flynn jumping onto burning decks to rescue Olivia de Havilland, and when he came outside into the dazzling sunlight, there were the cocoa palms, the lapis lazuli waters of the film itself. At night the trade winds moaned in the louvers as he lay in bed; a dog barked far away under the huge moon, the almond trees creaked in the breeze; and Malone dreamed the usual dreams of a boy his age—of cowboys, and Superman, and pirates — but with this difference: that outside, under the date palms, by the lagoons, was the setting for those dreams, as real as the shoes lying beside his bed on the floor. When he was twelve he gave up the dream of being a pirate, and replaced it with being a saint. He began coming home after school in the afternoons, and the catechism class that followed it, not to play ball, but to sequester himself in his room, kneeling, to pray to a statue of the Sacred Heart of Jesus and hope Christ would manifest Himself. His family said nothing as he prayed a Grace over his soup which lasted so long that by the time he lifted the first spoonful of cold liquid to his lips, they were eating dessert.

His beautiful mother went to parties at night in perfume and necklaces; took Malone to mass in the village and made him light candles for his aunts and uncles in America; drank some evenings, and insisted he sit with her in the cavernous lighted livingroom of their bungalow as she talked about the snow and Christmases in Chicago. Then she would rise and dance to the Victrola — dance about the room, with or without him, as the moths beat against the screens. "Whatever you do," she said, "never lose your sense of humor. And dance! I hope for God's sake you can dance!" And Malone got up and danced for her. Afterward he dreamed of sleighs and snowy nights, of his mother always loving him, of his being the best dancer, of mittens and blankets, and falling snow. On the hottest nights, as the trade winds blew through the bungalow, he dreamed of snow; on the endless afternoons, of being a saint; but he was always dreaming.

Malone had one of those sweet, receptive natures that take impressions like hot wax: Years later, when he had been sent away, he would remember the oil-black shadows the date palms cast on the patio floor in the moonlight; or his mother dancing in that lighted room; the distressed moan of the wind against the shut louvers; the sunburned faces of the Dutch sailors who came out after showering to sit on the veranda of their hotel next to the church he attended with his mother; the cologne she wore to church and tendrils of her hair curled behind her ears, damp from the shower; the sunlight slanting across tiles; the shine of granite rocks baking in the sun; the wind in the sea grape trees. But the impressions he took from that lighted bungalow, like the hot days and dreams of northern snow, were contradictory. His mother bequeathed him a loving heart, his father a certain German coldness that surprised him later in life in the midst of his most emotional episodes, like a cadaver suddenly sitting up in its coffin, when he suddenly saw he was cold, too. This duality of his cerebral father and tempestuous mother — of northern snows and tropic nights, of the sailors serenading the girls walking down the street in the hot sunlight and Christ dying on the cross within the darkness of the church — was like some gigantic fault that lies dormant in the earth until that single day when years of pressure cause it to slip. His being homosexual was only one aspect of this. He did not think his childhood any different from other he heard of which produced heterosexuals out of the same, if not worse, tensions — and he finally concluded, years later after the most earnest search for the cause of this inconvenience, that a witch had passed a wand over him as he lay sleeping in Ceylon.

The Bible says, a man divided is unstable in all ways. The child did not know this. The child was dutiful and well-brought up, and resolved things by bringing home the first Friday of each month (like the mass devoted to the Sacred Heart of Jesus) a report card that pleased both mother and father. These different people both wanted him to do well in school. This he did. His geography teacher, the Portuguese gardener, his classmates: Everyone loved him for excelling. "Get a degree in law and finance," his father told him one day, "and you'll always be in demand." At the age of fifteen he was shipped off to America like an island pineapple of special quality to be enrolled in a boarding school in Vermont; and thus, with everything unresolved, confused, inchoate, in a young man who thought life's greatest challenge would be in passing a trigonometry examination, he waved good-bye to the man and woman whose own lives, he would later feel, held the key to his. As their figures grew smaller on the dock in Surabanda between the palms and whitewashed houses, the maid weeping beside them, he moved even father from a mystery that growing up only obscured, by adding further layers of politeness to a relationship already formal. "Get a degree in law and finance," was all he could think of as his father's white shirt was lost in the specks of color that made up that paradisiacal island.

In New England he found snow — but it was the snow of loneliness, for now he missed his family and felt the first shock that occurs when a heart is sundered from its objects of affection. He studied diligently and postponed his happiness to some future time: a habit he would not abandon for years. Though he was never as great a baseball player as his father had been in his youth, apparently, he was elected captain of his soccer team. He loved the vivid falls — the wildness in the air that singes the soul — and made a few good friends. He was what is so important to Americans: popular. He graduated in a shower of gold. He was ambitious and went to Yale, and from Yale he entered law school, and from law school he enrolled an the University of Stockholm for graduate work in shipping and banking law. He joined a large firm in New York on his return and was immediately assigned a crumb of that enormous banquet that would feed lawyers for decades to come: the Penn Central case. He was considered for a post as a White House fellow. He was then a handsome young man in a dark suit with a vest and tie from J. Press in New Haven, wearing glasses to read, and you might have seen him on the shuttle to Washington, reading a novel of Henry James, or on a summer dusk in Georgetown, lingering outside a bookshop to examine the volume on French cathedrals in the window, before going off to the train station to get the Metroliner back to New York. There are various ways to keep the world at arm's length, and success is one of them: Malone was irreproachable, and something of a snob.

For something had happened to Malone since he'd been sent to America to go to school. During those snowy New England winters, besides learning to rise at five to study calculus and trudge two miles through the drifts for breakfast down the road, he had suppressed some tremendous element in himself that took form in a prudish virginity. While his life was impeccable on the surface, he felt he was behind glass: moving through the world in a separate compartment, touching no one else. This was painful. He walked in one night to find his proctor standing nude from the shower in the middle of his room: He was unstrung. He wrote letters to girls in Ceylon, but they were just that: letters. He listened to stories of boys from Connecticut who had made love their first night home of vacation, to girls in Chevrolets; he listened to stories about the town whore, and he leafed through the copies of *Playboy* that everyone keeps; and he was utterly untouched. This dissociation between his feelings and the feelings of all his friends baffled Malone. He simply suppressed it all, and studied harder, and dreamed of Ceylon. In New Haven he learned to ignore the tie his

roommate hung on the doorknob of his room whenever he had a girl in bed with him, but ties remained for him the symbol of the rich erotic life that other men enjoyed. He himself was still a virgin when he took a room in a large house in the Maryland suburbs in 1972. The house belonged to the widow of an ambassador who had been a friend of his grandmother's when they were girls; and he rented a similar one in Brookfield, Connecticut, since his work was in two cities. Like most of his classmates he loathed cities. His married friends lived in North Salem and he visited them on Sundays. He found it touching and curious that they wanted his company; for he assumed, never having been in love, that they would find another person intrusive. It was important to him that they were happily married and when they got divorced a year later, he was stunned. He felt his presence, somehow, had been a jinx. He had other married friends in the suburbs but seeing them made him feel more solitary.

He began to study wines. He joined the Sierra Club. Every time he planned to join them for a hike, he cancelled at the last moment—ashamed of his loneliness. He was very proud. He hated being a bachelor. He was at the same time devoted to his family. He called his parents once a month. He sent gifts to his niece and nephew at Christmas. He gave them each a hundred-dollar bond on their birthdays. He began to jog. He ran alone down country lanes in autumns whose beauty left him pained. He ate sensibly, avoided cholesterol, and took brewer's yeast with his morning orange juice. He was a member of his class. The world tortured him: its ugliness, venality, vulgarity. Sundays he spent the afternoon reading the *Times*. When he came to New York City on business, he saw its steaming towers downriver with the eyes of most of his classmates: an asphalt slag heap baking under a brown shroud of pollution. He was the kind of person who telephoned Citizens for Clean Air if he saw black smoke issuing from a building smokestack on Manhattan longer than the legal limit of ten minutes. He considered wearing a mask when be bicycled to his office from the Yale Club, but thought it would look silly. Bus fumes infuriated him. Architecture he anxiously judged. Its mediocrity, the absence of beautiful avenues, lovely squares, pained him. He lay awake nights replanning the city. He joined the Committee to Reforest Fifth Avenue, thinking it could all be saved with trees, but eventually he despaired that this would ever happen and dropped away from their fund-raisers and dinner dances.

He felt impotent, he felt doomed. He despaired of politics; the world, like the city, seemed an unmanageable mess, filled with squawking, venal babies — a vast kindergarten of infantile delinquents who had to be supervised. He got lost on freeways late at night in the amber glare of the Jersey refineries, and he felt sure he was in hell. His wines, cross-country running, excursions to the theatre left him as miserable as the moments of indecision in health food stores, when he felt his life had come to a complete halt over the choice of two brands of vitamins. One night going home on the train to Connecticut he found himself in the air-conditioned car staring at a page of *The New Yorker* on his lap. His mind stopped. The page gleamed with a high, cold gloss in the fluorescent light: He stared at its shining surface, the pale gray pinstripe of his dark pants leg. Eventually his stop appeared. He got off in a somnambulistic daze. No one met him at the station. He felt he should call someone for help — but who?

I saw Malone earlier that night, at a party at Hirschl & Adler, the gallery on East Sixty-seventh Street. It was a preview of an exhibit of portraits by John Singleton Copley. It was crowded with corporate lawyers like himself, their wives, and the older men whose tuxedos had been their father's and grandfather's: They continued to exist as a class, impervious to the disintegration of the city. Malone fitted right in and except for golden handsomeness, I would never have picked him out — but I did, as I walked through their midst with the tray of cookies

and champagne. He talked even then in that animated, electrifying way, but it seemed out of place there, out of proportion even to the surroundings. The smile, so dazzling, seemed brittle — almost like a shriek when viewed from a certain angle. But then a smile is often a shriek: a soul screaming at you. Malone left early to get the train back to his room in the country — and I saw him say good-night, in his affectionate way, to friends and then disappear in a Chesterfield and a scarf from Sulka's, to hail a cab. . . . a very handsome man I should never see again, since those people were seen in New York only by one another; they lived otherwise an invisible existence.

He moved furthermore to Washington for a while and lived an even more monastic existence, going home after a long day with the Penn Central accountants to the house of the widow in the Maryland suburbs. The widow always had about her the faint odor of cold cream. She sat in a wheelchair on the veranda and when Malone came home in the evenings, he sat with her sometimes drinking tea. She talked about her husband as Malone watched the light in the garden change, she talked about the loveliness of Saigon in the twenties. She talked of the beaches they had found on little islands in the Seychelles, as the dusk gathered in the deep garden shaded by towering oaks, embalmed with the scent of gardenias and crape myrtle. He felt as if he were a character in Henry James; he began to suspect he was to be that man to whom nothing whatsoever was to happen. "When you find the right girl," she said to him putting her hand on his affectionately, "you must take her to Sadrudabad in April and see the flamboyant trees in bloom. There is nothing so wonderful as seeing the wonders of this earth with someone you love!"

It was a phrase that might have appeared in an article in the *Reader's Digest*, but Malone believed it completely. He was depressed by the thought that he should never do this. But he was a disciplined fellow and he rose the next morning, obedient soul, and went to work as usual, and played squash at one with a fellow associate who had recently been married because, as he told Malone, he thought everyone should be married by the time they're thirty. Even his favorite game now struck him with melancholy, for his partner, an old friend from school, was always saying, "Anne this," and "Anne that," and "Anne and I are going to drive to Salzburg this summer," and he felt even gloomier when he came off the court. He stopped visiting married friends. Married friends, he decided one evening after returning from a visit, depress me.

The gloom he felt then was nothing, however, compared to the terrifying loneliness that assaulted him on Sunday evening around eight o'clock; for then he had spent the whole day by himself, or driving around shopping for antiques with a fellow bachelor, and as he sat in his room looking down into the beautiful garden — the widow having already gone to bed, slathered in cold cream whose scent clung to the air of the hallway — he felt himself so utterly alone, he could not imagine anyone being sadder. Tears came to his eyes as he sat there. This day, Sunday, was his favorite of the week; this day, Sunday, a family always spent together in the evening as they came home from their various errands for a cold supper and a perusal of the Sunday paper; this day, Sunday, the softest, most human, tenderest time, found him sitting upright at his little desk by the window, hearing around his ears the beating of wings — the invisible birds assaulting him, beating the air about him with their accusing presence. He was alone, like Prometheus chained to his rock. Tomorrow the rush of men, all working for a living, would drown him; but now, at this moment, in this soft green twilight, this soft green Sunday evening, when the heart of the world seemed to lie beating in the palm of his hand, he sat in that huge house upstairs terrified that he would never live.

He resolved to do anything to avoid solitude at this particular moment — which he regarded with the same fear an insomniac

does the hour he must go to bed. He began seeing a girl he had been introduced to by a fellow in his firm at a concert of Bach cantatas, a graduate student at the American University whose father was an undersecretary of state for the Far East. She would come up the drive in her little white sports car on Sunday afternoon, tooting the horn, and the widow smiled at what she was sure was romance — but the romance consisted of discussions of Henry Adams's *Mont-Saint-Michel and Chartres* — and when he said good-bye to her, and her little white Triumph disappeared down the drive in the shadow of the big oak trees, he felt more depressed than he did when he spent the evening alone; depressed with all the genteel talk on stained glass, the ache of too many smiles with too little feeling, the kisses they did not say goodnight with, and the seduction that had not occurred in his room upstairs beneath the eaves. What is wrong with me, he wondered.

And then Michael Floria came to work for the widow after school. Malone had given up by this time his swim after work, his browsing through the bookstores in Georgetown, the chamber music concerts he had taken the girl to, as a ridiculous pretense, all of it. He drove straight home in the evenings now to work in the widow's yard and wipe out the strains of a day of intellectual effort with the cold comfort of the dark earth that clung to his hands as they scooped it up to make room for a new plant. She had brought back with her from the highlands of Asia, and the Vale of Kashmir, and these he began transplanting in wintertime. Seeing his interest the widow hired a local high school student whose father was an agronomist with the Department of Agriculture to help Malone. He was friendly, dark-eyed Italian-American who swam for his school and was applying to several colleges. As they knelt in the old flower beds, turning over the soil and patting it down around the newly transplanted tea plants, Malone gave him what helpful advice he could. He was very happy then: the cold black soil around his hands, the light glinting on the dark magnolia leaves above them, and the dark beauty of this young man beside him. "He's a great help!" Malone told the widow happily. "A really nice kid."

He thought of the deep flush of hysteria that comes at that age when you start to laugh. He loved to make Michael laugh. He laughed so hard sometimes he fell over onto the ground and lay, laughing, like someone wounded, between the rows of tea roses and frangipani trees from Kashmir, on a late winter afternoon. But it was not he who was wounded. It was Malone. But like the man who looks down to see what is sticky on his foot, and finds he has been bleeding, Malone was not to know till sometime later.

His own work kept Malone busy and one night he came home from a long day of writing loan agreements and heard the widow tell him it was Michael's last day there. He had taken a job in Colorado for the summer and would be off to college at Beloit in the fall. Malone could not understand the emotion that suddenly drained the blood from his limbs. He walked down from the house in his suit and tie from J. Press, carrying his briefcase full of his rough drafts, as if to appear nonchalant, and found Michael standing with a bag of powdered insecticide, carefully spooning it into a five-gallon jug. It was then that he felt his own wounds. It was very definite, as if he had been stabbed. "The very best of luck," Malone smiled as he shook his hand, hoping only that Mike could not see through the gray cloth of his suit the vibration created by the fact that Malone's knees had suddenly started to shake violently. He did not trust his voice either so he turned away.

This physical betrayal astonished him, and he went back upstairs to his room under a cloud of blackest anger. He kicked the waste basket, slammed the drawers shut, cursed out loud as he undressed. It was of course completely wrong, the completely inconvenient sort of love; it was the one thing he — who had succeeded at everything else, who had been so virtuous, such a

model — could not allow. It was as if he had finally admitted to himself that he had cancer. He saw in that instant a life he could not conceive of opening before him, a hopeless abyss. Either way he was doomed: He did what was wrong, and condemned himself, or he did what was right, and remained a ghost. He could see himself in twenty years in a house like this in the suburbs, twenty-eight rooms and no one in them. It made him furious that he, who had led so disciplined, so correct a life, was reduced now to helplessness and hot tears over this perfectly oblivious senior going off to Beloit College on the swimming team.

He stood up from his bed and looked out the window at the gardener laboring in the azaleas. He felt in one instant the vast indifference of nature — the perfect chaos, the haphazard character of the universe — as he stared through the window at his friend; for it was obvious that he, bent over the plants, was thinking of the proper composition of the liquids poison he was mixing to kill the red spiders that had attacked the camellia bushes, and he, Malone, was going through an unendurable tragedy at the same time.

A sensible man would have laughed at Malone; would have called him melodramatic, sentimental; would have told him to get on with life, and stop thinking he had been cast into outer darkness — nonsense! But Malone was not this sensible man. Some love more for love than others. And he experienced a death that night, as he lay upstairs in the widow's house, on that vast floor of empty rooms in whose hallway outside his own the odor of cold cream, the sound of a television program being watched downstairs, hovered. At the moment when the organism usually fructifies Malone perished, like the marigolds that had shriveled up the week before in their pots for no earthly reason they could see.

His entire love had progressed, like the growing and dying of a plant, from indifference to love to extinction, and not one embrace, not one kiss, not one word had been exchanged between him and his beloved. He heard the widow talking to him down below, he heard the door slam as she withdrew into the kitchen, and he heard the gate open and close by which the boy let himself into the adjacent field and began his walk home, while he lay there staring at the ceiling like the effigy on an Etruscan tomb.

That night he got up out of bed and put on his maroon polo shirt, which everyone said he looked so handsome in, and went downstairs and drove off in his car, where he did not know. He just drove. He drove around that wilderness of gas stations and fast-food franchises that surrounds Washington as once the armies of the Confederacy had, drove around in that crimson glow of doughnut shops and new-car showrooms, in which all things, cars, faces, bodies, gleam with an otherworldly light, and he kept driving — never admitting what he was about — until he came to Dupont Circle and there he stopped and got out under the green trees and met a man and went into the park and blew him.

All this occurred in a state both trancelike and sharply conscious; as if another being had momentarily occupied the physical shell that was Malone.

When he got home, and emerged from this dream-play, like a man who has just murdered someone and returns to his apartment and sits down to a bowl of soup, Malone took a shower that lasted over an hour and washed his mouth out with soap. He sat up the rest of the night writing in his journal. He wrote a poem. He wrote of the fact that for the first time he had used his mouth for something other than those two blameless functions — speech and the ingestion of food — and that now he had profaned it utterly. Those lips, that throat, which were stained with milk, apples, bread and life-giving things, had been soiled beyond redemption now. For Malone believed in some undefined but literal sense that the body was the temple of the Holy Ghost: the pure vessel. He sat and watched the garden outside emerge from the darkness. It was his first miserable, yet

strangely vivid, dawn of that sort and he watched it silently in a white, rigid state of self-condemnation before which any judgment of God would have paled.

A year went by as if that night never occurred. Malone was chaste. The widow died the following spring, and Malone moved into town and took an apartment in the northwest section on the city; and he lived a quiet life. He played squash with the associate who had married because he felt one should be at thirty. He visited museums and gazed at his favorite Watteau, and drove to sites of Civil War battles in the surrounding hills. But his interest in history now seemed to him an interest in death, and the cold skin of his face as he stood on a tawny hill staring at the bare trees against the page blue sky no longer exhilarated his soul but made him feel condemned against his will to the company of nature. His mind began to stray over the intricacies of loan repayments and he could no longer plow through the papers on his desk with his usual celerity. In the middle of the day, he fell into that abyss he carried within him now, the knowledge that he could not live alone forever, or without love. This fact changed his attitude toward his work. It seemed little more than a mercenary exchange for dining out, tennis lessons, and a week in summer at the French cathedrals. The bourgeois arrangement of the world, his own parasitical relationship with a vast, impersonal economy by which he drew off his living, repelled him strangely. He read Heine's remark, "Fame isn't worth a milkmaid's kiss," and thought: Neither is money, nor comfort, nor prestige.

On his most miserable nights he would go out to a public park in Washington and simply sit watching these compatriots of his — these citizens of hell, he thought gloomily, this *paseo* of the damned — till birds began to sing around him and he hurried home at dawn, like a man who stands on a beach a long time at the water's edge and then decides not to swim that evening after all. The water is colder than he thought, the sky forbidding; he loses heart. He sat at his desk and, like a penitent in the confessional, pored over the journal his love for the gardener had impelled him to begin. The brief paragraphs therein did not even contain the young man's name, but referred to him as X (so appalled was Malone by his own emotions). Malone had been raised by a lady both Irish and Catholic, in a good bourgeois home in which careless table manners were a sin, much less this storm in his heart.

"My only hope," he wrote in his hardbound ledger, resembling the account books of store clerks in the early part of this century, "is with those men circling the fountain. They are my fate and if I wish to have Life, it must be with *them*. What is most remarkable, I have no choice. I who have never been constrained by poverty, disease, accident, am now constrained by this. God's joke. His little joke. To keep us human. To humble the proud. And I have been so proud."

It seemed sentimental to think of it as the cross he must bear in life, but if it wasn't that, what was it? The sound of a late-night show drifted down the hall from the television of the woman who lived next door to him, and its very laughter, cold and eerie and distant, made his heart beat faster; for he himself was dying. He wrote again: "You are doomed to a life that will repeat itself again and again, as do all lives — for lives are static things, readings of already written papers — but whereas some men are fortunate to repeat a good pattern, others have the opposite luck — and you can surely see by now that your life is doomed to this same humiliation, endlessly repeated.

"Imagine a pleasure in which the moment of satisfaction is simultaneous with the moment of destruction: to kiss is to poison; lifting to your lips this face after which you have ached, dreamed, longed for, the face shatters, every time." And with one final stroke he scrawled across the page: "IF THE EYE OFFENDS THEE, PLUCK IT OUT."

But how was he to? The great fault in his character was slipping after all these years, was giving way as he went about the empty

rituals of his life in the succeeding weeks. His life was a sham. He hated the law; its Pharisaical quibbling over the division of property seemed another aspect of death-in-life. He wasn't even good at it. He had achieved everything only through the most dogged hard work. He hadn't one of those minds that dealt with contract disputes and the Byzantine innuendos of the tax code, like one of those mechanical devices that slice up a vegetable in twelve seconds. He was more than ever certain that he had a vague romantic destiny. Little wonder that when he looked at strangers on the street now, his unquiet yearning for rescue went out to them. No one came to his aid — till late one night on a visit to New York City he was working in an office on Wall Street, high in a fluorescent cell, on a promissory note for the Republic of Zaire, when a messenger boy came in with a batch of Telexes from his boss in London. Malone, who felt at that moment like a rat gnawing his leg off to get free of a trap, looked up at him. How could he know that his desires, his loneliness, were written on his face as clear as characters on a printed page? For that was his charm, that his feelings were always in his eyes and face. He could hide nothing. The messenger boy, a young Puerto Rican from the Bronx in maroon pants and tennis sneakers, put the Telexes down on the desk and then let his hand fall on Malone's back. The hand drew a circle on his back, and then strayed around to his chest and stomach; and Malone turned to look at him. They kissed. It was the kiss of life. He felt a wild gladness in his heart. Someone entered the outer office, the boy, left, and Malone sat there with an expression on his face such as the Blessed Virgin wears in the paintings of the Annunciation.

In the summer New York is a tropical city — in all seasons, for that matter — and when Malone left the office late that night the streets were thronged with faces that glistened beneath the streetlights. Every street his taxi passed seemed to hold a terrible promise. He went to the Yale Club and

continued on page 259

Work & Career: the Results

*I*N ISSUE #1 (Spring 1988), the subject of the Queery was "Work and Career." More than 500 of you responded and valiant volunteers Beth Miller and Chris Idzik of Jamaica Plain Massachussetts, analyzed the data.

We were delighted to learn what the survey told us about our readers. You are not only surviving, but thriving, within a wide range of work environments and career situations.

Most of you have managed to land in workplaces that are gay tolerant and/or gay owned; most of you are out to the people you work with. A significant percentage of you don't suspect your sexual orientation of blocking your career paths. Acceptance does not extend to complete equality, though—very few work places extend health insurance to your partners.

Almost half of you bring your same-sex sweeties to office soirées.

Over one-third of you have felt comfortable enough (or overwhelmed by lust? Or desperate enough for a little on-the-job intrigue?) to engage in a little whoopie by the water cooler.

Suprisingly, there was not much difference between the different age groups—as many people in their forties were out at their workplaces as those in their twenties.

Here are the details of your responses to some of the questions:

THE RESPONDENTS

SEX
Men	42%
Women	58%

AGE
under 30	32%
30 to 39	42%
40 to 49	19%
over 50	7%

INCOME
	Men	Women
< $10,000	4%	10%
$10-14,000	9%	12%
$15-19,000	12%	12%
$20-24,000	16%	18%
$25-29,000	11%	16%
$30-34,000	15%	10%
$35-39,000	8%	8%
$40,000 +	26%	13%

TYPE OF WORK
	Men	Women
Professional	52%	56%
Office	15%	15%
Managerial	14%	10%
Technical	9%	7%
Manual	1%	6%
Other	9%	6%

WORK & SOCIAL FUNCTIONS
If you have a lover, and there's a party at work, you:
- bring your lover 46%
- go alone 30%
- plead a headache 10%
- bring a date of the opposite sex 3%
- find another solution 13%

HOMOPHOBIA AT WORK
Where you work is:
- gay-tolerant 46%
- gay-hostile 20%
- gay-sensitive 18%
- gay-owned 11%
- blind to gays 2%

At work, you are out to:
	Men	Women
some co-workers	58%	61%
all co-workers	34%	22%
no one	8%	17%

OCCUPATIONAL ROMANCE
Have you ever had sex with a co-worker?
	Men	Women
Yes	24%	37%
No	76%	63%

IMPACT ON CAREERS
Has your sexual preference stood in the way of your career advancement?
	Men	Women
yes	21%	16%
no	38%	43%
don't know	41%	41%

Some of the specific ways you said being gay has affected your vocational choices include:
- avoiding jobs requiring security clearances
- worrying about harassment when you teach or work with children
- making it a priority to work on AIDS or with PWAs.

BEST ASPECT OF YOUR JOBS
Creativity and flexibility were some of the positive points mentioned, along with:
- independence   • co-workers
- teaching   • challenges
- interaction with people
- being out to co-workers
- rewarding work

WORST ASPECT OF YOUR JOBS
Rampant heterosexism and not being out was mentioned, but just as much as:
- stress   • office politics
- "too straight"   • gossip
- too much work • boredom
- the boss   • dead end
- lack of control • AIDS burnout

Work & Career: The Results, OUT/LOOK, Fall 1988, at 94.

Advertisement, VARIETY, Mar. 18, 1988, at 41, *reprinted in* Ryan, *Homophobia In Hollywood*, THE ADVOCATE, March 26, 1991, at 37.

wrote a long letter to his parents explaining his unhappiness with the law, and the next day he resigned from Coudert Brothers in order to "pursue a career in journalism." What he wished to pursue was a career in love. One night he had got lost on the subway and had come up in Sheridan Square, which was filled, that summer evening, with young men staring at each other, talking boisterous throngs. Malone headed there now to find a room nearby. It was the middle of August. He did not wish to be the man to whom nothing was ever to happen. He vanished meanwhile from his former friends and family as if he had gone to Bali, or died in a traffic accident. He was completely free now to pursue with the same passion for success he had brought to squash matches and the law, the one thing that had eluded him utterly till now: love.

For love, he felt as he watched the Puerto Rican boys unloading soda pop for the Gem Spa on his new corner, love was all in life that mattered; without it, there was no point in having lived at all. And so that last Sunday evening of August 1973 found him sitting on his stoop like a monk who comes finally to the shrine of Santiago de Compostela—devoted not to Christ, in whom he no longer believed, but love.

B. American Employment Law

In focusing on the working lives of lesbians and gay men, this chapter explores the landscape of employment discrimination law in the United States. Such an examination is an immense and complex task. Employment discrimination protections can be adopted by all three branches of the government — legislative (through statutes), executive (through rules, regulations, and executive orders), and judicial (through judicial decisions) — and by all levels of government — federal, state, and local. Moreover, employers, and therefore jobs themselves, are highly differentiated: military, civil service, public and private education, quasi-public utilities, government contractors, large and small corporations, partnerships, and other private employers. Employment discrimination law is also inconsistent, not only between jurisdictions and job types, but also on its own terms. The terrain is constantly shifting — particularly with the changing nature of the American judiciary and with the changing nature of American industry — and is thus difficult to capture in a study such as this.

This chapter attempts to organize the vast subject of employment discrimination by dividing it into two parts — one explores the "public" workplace (government employment), the other the "private" workplace (corporate America and other non-governmental jobs). The chapter is divided in this manner because American labor law is divided in this manner. As described more fully below, the law governing non-governmental employers traditionally permits such employers to hire and fire employees "at [the employer's] will." By contrast, generally speaking, government employees have greater protections, including civil service protections and the protections of the constitution of the United States.[1]

---

1. *See generally*, CHARLES A. SULLIVAN, MICHAEL J. ZIMMER & RICHARD F. RICHARDS, EMPLOYMENT DISCRIMINATION 353-56, 383-434 (2d ed. 1988); *id.* at 103-04 (Supp. 1990).

C. Lesbians/Gay Men and the Equal Protection Clause

A central doctrinal issue which emerges in this chapter concerns the applicability of the Constitution's equal protection clause to government-based employment decisions. While constitutional equal protection doctrine applies to all government actions that make distinctions on the basis of sexual orientation, many of the precedent-setting lawsuits have arisen in the employment context and therefore are discussed in this chapter.

What the equal protection clause is designed to police is group-based discrimination by the government. If a group is excluded from a government program or government employment — for instance, if schools will not hire black teachers because of their race — the equal protection clause is implicated. The U.S. Supreme Court has, in the past thirty years, developed an elaborate jurisprudential scheme for enforcing the equal protection clause. According to the type of discrimination being considered, the Court has articulated three levels of review for equal protection cases: strict, intermediate, and what is called "rational basis" review.

The Court has determined that some classifications made by the government — classifications based on race, religion, or national origin — are "suspect" and require "strict" judicial scrutiny to ensure that they are not illegitimate attempts to discriminate on these bases. In these cases, the judge's task is to ensure that the government's classification is "*necessary* to promote a *compelling* governmental interest."[2] It is usually very difficult for the government to justify a classification under this strict standard.

At the opposite end of the spectrum are governmental distinctions that are considered ordinary, like those based on people's living arrangements. The government must justify these types of distinctions by showing only that "the classification itself is rationally related to a legitimate governmental interest."[3] This standard the government can almost always meet.

A third, intermediate category, has also developed — here classifications, such as those based on sex, are sometimes thought to be based on legitimate differences between the sexes, but are often in fact discriminatory. Thus, courts are instructed to employ a medium level of scrutiny to ensure that such classifications "serve important governmental objectives and [are] substantially related to achievement of those objectives."[4]

This schema has been severely criticized, both by some members of the Court itself,[5] and by academic commentators.[6] One of the primary criticisms of this method of jurisprudence is that the level of scrutiny a court employs often determines whether a plaintiff prevails.[7] Thus, much of the fight in equal protection cases concerns the level of scrutiny applicable to the case. The Supreme Court has articulated a series of principles that determine whether a classification should trigger strict, or "heightened," judicial scrutiny. These include whether there has been a history of discrimination against the group at issue, whether the discrimination is unrelated to the individual group members's abilities, and whether the members of the group are poorly represented in the political processes such that those processes could not be expected to correct the harm at issue.[8] Some courts have also said

---

2. *Dunn* v. *Blumstein*, 405 U.S. 330, 342 (1972) (quoting, *Shapiro* v. *Thompson*, 394 U.S. 618, 634 (1969)).

3. *United States Dep't of Agric.* v. *Moreno*, 413 U.S. 528, 533 (1973).

4. *Craig* v. *Boren*, 429 U.S. 190, 197 (1976).

5. *See, e.g., San Antonio Indep. Sch. Dist.* v. *Rodriguez*, 411 U.S. 1, 98-99 (1973) (Marshall, J., dissenting).

6. *See, e.g.,* Gerald Gunther, *The Supreme Court 1971 — Foreword. In Search of Evolving Doctrine in a Changing Court: A Model for a Newer Equal Protection,* 86 HARV. L. REV. 1, 17-18 (1972).

7. *See id.* at 8.

8. *Frontiero* v. *Richardson*, 411 U.S. 677, 684-88 (1973).

that the trait that defines the class must be "immutable" for the group to be deserving of heightened judicial scrutiny.[9]

A number of cases in this chapter concern the level of scrutiny that courts should use in considering equal protection challenges to discrimination on the basis of sexual orientation, and thus the level of protection that will be afforded to lesbians and gay men under the equal protection clause. Thus, the *Rowland v. Mad River* case, *infra* at 305, was the occasion for the first U.S. Supreme Court decision — a dissent by Justice Brennan written in 1985 — articulating the argument for heightened judicial scrutiny of classifications based on sexual orientation.[10] Perry Watkins's challenge to his discharge from the military, *infra* at 342, resulted in the first federal appellate court decision finding heightened judicial scrutiny of classifications based on sexual orientation, although this decision was subsequently vacated and the case was decided on other grounds.[11] Several federal district court employment decisions — including *High Tech Gays v. Defense Industrial Security Clearance Office*,[12] and *Jantz v. Muci*[13] — have also provided important articulations of this argument, although both were reversed on appeal.

Thus, a critical aspect of constitutional protection for lesbians and gay men is playing itself out in modern American jurisprudence in cases involving employment rights.

D. How Gay Is Too Gay?

In addition to the critical doctrinal issue of the standard of scrutiny for equal protection challenges, the employment discrimination cases reflect an important dilemma for lesbians and gay men — namely, how "open" can gay people be in the workplace. As articulated more fully below, an emerging standard in the public workplace is that homosexuality *per se* is not grounds for dismissal; however, a lesbian or gay employee can be legally dismissed if their employment disrupts the functioning of the workplace. In effect, this type of standard gives the employer — and co-workers — a "heckler's veto" over expressions of lesbian and gay sexuality with which they are uncomfortable. Compare, for instance, the *Norton* case, *infra* at 279, with the *Singer* case which follows it. A close examination of the distinctions between acceptable and unacceptable lesbian and gay employees in these cases provides a broader understanding of how society polices sexual orientation.

■ ■ ■

With these themes in mind, the chapter now turns to a consideration of the legal documents themselves, first in the private employment setting and then in the governmental employment setting.

---

9. *See id* at 686.

10. *See Rowland* v. *Mad River Local Sch. Dist.*, 470 U.S. 1009, 1014-17 (1985) (Brennan, J., dissenting from denial of certiorari).

11. *See Watkins* v. *United States Army*, 847 F.2d 1329 (9th Cir. 1989), *vacated*, 875 F.2d 699 (9th Cir. 1989) (en banc).

12. 668 F. Supp. 1361 (N.D. Cal. 1987), *rev'd*, 895 F.2d 563 (9th Cir. 1990).

13. 759 F.Supp. 1543 (D. Kan. 1991), *rev'd*, 976 F. 2d 623 (10th Cir. 1992).

II. PRIVATE EMPLOYMENT

The traditional concept governing relations between workers and employers in America has historically been "employment at will." "Employment at will," meant that employment was solely within the discretion of, or "at the will of," the employer. An employee could be hired or fired for good reason, bad reason, or no reason at all.[1]

Throughout the last fifty years, the employment-at-will concept has been altered by expanding notions of rights for employees and thus restrictions on the unfettered discretion of employers. Some of these restrictions are statutory protections, created by Congress and state legislatures. The most important is Title VII of the Civil Rights Act of 1964,[2] which is a federal law prohibiting discrimination in almost all employment in the United States on the basis of race, color, religion, sex, or national origin. Congress has further extended private employment protections to bar discrimination on the basis of age, *see* Age Discrimination in Employment Act,[3] and disability, *see* Americans with Disabilities Act.[4] Most states also have laws that prohibit employment discrimination based on race, sex, national origin, alienage, religion, and handicap.

In addition to these statutory protections, collective bargaining agreements negotiated between labor and management have provided job protection, and protection against discrimination, for many American workers throughout the twentieth century. Finally, there is a growing body of law holding that promises made by employers — such as promises to not discriminate on certain bases — are enforceable and thus creating workplace protections based on tort and contract law.

Unfortunately, few of these protections have provided much assistance to lesbians and gay men in the private workplace.[5] There is no federal law prohibiting discrimination on the basis of sexual orientation, although one has been pending in Congress since Bella Abzug first introduced it in 1974.[6] Lesbian and gay plaintiffs have attempted to seek protection from the existing federal employment laws, without success. On a state level, only six states currently have laws that ban such discrimination, and five of these laws have been enacted since 1990. These statutory developments are described in Part A below.

Part B surveys non-statutory protections for workers, including employer policies and collective bargaining agreements.

---

1. *See generally* CHARLES A. SULLIVAN, MICHAEL J. ZIMMER & RICHARD F. RICHARDS, EMPLOYMENT DISCRIMINATION 4 (2d ed. 1988).

2. 42 U.S.C. §§ 2000e–2000e–17 (1988).

3. 29 U.S.C. §§ 621–634 (1988).

4. 42 U.S.C.A. §§ 12101–12213 (West Supp. 1992).

5. *See generally* James Douglas, *I Sit and Look Out: Employment Discrimination Against Homosexuals and the New Law of Unjust Dismissal,* 33 WASH. U. J. URB. & CONTEMP. L. 73 (1988); Gail Heatherly, *Gay and Lesbian Rights: Employment Discrimination,* 4 ANN. SURV. AM. L. 901 (1986).

6. *See* Civil Rights Amendment Act of 1991, H.R. 1430, 102d Cong., 1st Sess. (1991); S. 574, 102 Cong., 1st Sess. (1991).

A. Statutory/Constitutional Protections

DESANTIS v. PACIFIC TELEPHONE & TELEGRAPH CO.

608 F.2d 327 (9th Cir. 1979)

Choy, Circuit Judge:

Male and female homosexuals brought three separate federal district court actions claiming that their employers or former employers discriminated against them in employment decisions because of their homosexuality. They alleged that such discrimination violated Title VII of the Civil Rights Act of 1964, 42 U.S.C. § 2000e, and 42 U.S.C. § 1985(3). The district courts dismissed the complaints as failing to state claims under either statute . . . We affirm.

I. STATEMENT OF THE CASE

A. *Strailey* v. *Happy Times Nursery School, Inc.*

Appellant Strailey, a male, was fired by the Happy Times Nursery School after two years' service as a teacher. He alleged that he was fired because he wore a small gold ear-loop to school prior to the commencement of the school year. . . .

B. *DeSantis* v. *Pacific Telephone & Telegraph Co.*

DeSantis, Boyle, and Simard, all males, claimed that Pacific Telephone & Telegraph Co. (PT&T) impermissibly discriminated against them because of their homosexuality. DeSantis alleged that he was not hired when a PT&T supervisor concluded that he was a homosexual. According to appellants' brief, "BOYLE was continually harrassed by his co-workers and had to quit to preserve his health after only three months because his supervisors did nothing to alleviate this condition." Finally, "SIMARD was forced to quit under similar conditions after almost four years of employment with PT&T, but he was harrassed by his supervisors [as well].... In addition, his personnel file has been marked as not eligible for rehire, and his applications for employment were rejected by PT&T in 1974 and 1976." Appellants DeSantis, Boyle, and Simard also alleged that PT&T officials have publicly stated that they would not hire homosexuals.

C. *Lundin* v. *Pacific Telephone & Telegraph*

Lundin and Buckley, both females, were operators with PT&T. They filed suit in federal court alleging that PT&T discriminated against them because of their known lesbian relationship and eventually fired them. They also alleged that they endured numerous insults by PT&T employees because of their relationship. Finally, Lundin alleged that the union that represented her as a PT&T operator failed adequately to represent her interests and failed adequately to present her grievance regarding her treatment. . . .

II. TITLE VII CLAIM

Appellants argue first that the district courts erred in holding that Title VII does not prohibit discrimination on the basis of sexual preference. They claim that in prohibiting certain employment discrimination on the basis of "sex," Congress meant to include discrimination on the basis of sexual orientation. They add that in a trial they could establish that discrimination against homosexuals disproportionately affects men and that this disproportionate impact and correlation between discrimination on the basis of sexual preference and discrimination on the basis of "sex" requires that sexual preference be considered a subcategory of the "sex" category of Title VII. *See* 42 U.S.C. § 2000e-2.

A. Congressional Intent in Prohibiting "Sex" Discrimination

In *Holloway v. Arthur Andersen & Co.*, 566 F.2d 659 (9th Cir. 1977), plaintiff argued that her employer had discriminated against her because she was undergoing a sex transformation and that this discrimination violated Title VII's prohibition on sex discrimination. This court rejected that claim, writing:

> The cases interpreting Title VII sex discrimination provisions agree that they were intended to place women on an equal footing with men.
>
> Giving the statute its plain meaning, this court concludes that Congress had only the traditional notions of "sex" in mind. Later legislative activity makes this narrow definition even more evident. Several bills have been introduced to amend the Civil Rights Act to prohibit discrimination against "sexual preference." None have [sic] been enacted into law.
>
> Congress has not shown any intent other than to restrict the term "sex" to its traditional meaning. Therefore, this court will not expand Title VII's application in the absence of Congressional

mandate. The manifest purpose of Title VII's prohibition against sex discrimination in employment is to ensure that men and women are treated equally, absent a bona fide relationship between the qualifications for the job and the person's sex.

Id. at 662-63.

Following *Holloway,* we conclude that Title VII's prohibition of "sex" discrimination applies only to discrimination on the basis of gender and should not be judicially extended to include sexual preference such as homosexuality.[3]

B. Disproportionate Impact

Appellants argue that recent decisions dealing with disproportionate impact require that discrimination against homosexuals fall within the purview of Title VII. They contend that these recent decisions, like *Griggs v. Duke Power Co.*, 401 U.S. 424 (1971), establish that any employment criterion that affects one sex more than the other violates Title VII. . . . They claim that in a trial they could prove that discrimination against homosexuals disproportionately affects men both because of the greater incidence of homesexuality in the male population and because of the greater likelihood of an employer's discovering male homosexuals compared to female homosexuals.

Assuming that appellants can otherwise satisfy the requirement of *Griggs*, we do not believe that *Griggs* can be applied to extend Title VII protection to homosexuals. In finding that the disproportionate impact of educational tests on blacks violated Title VII, the Supreme Court in *Griggs* sought to effectuate a major congressional purpose in enacting Title VII: protection of blacks from employment discrimination. For as the Su-

---

3. Based on a similar reading of the legislative history and the principle that "words used in statutes are to be given their ordinary meaning," the EEOC has concluded "that when Congress used the word sex in Title VII it was referring to a person's gender" and not to "sexual practices." EEOC Dec. No. 76-75, [1976] *Emp. Prac. Guide (CCH)* P6495, at 4266. . . .

preme Court noted in *Philbrook v. Goldgett*, 421 U.S. 707 (1975), in construing a statute, "[our] objective... is to ascertain the congressional intent and give effect to the legislative will." *Id.* at 713.

The *Holloway* court noted that in passing Title VII Congress did not intend to protect sexual orientation and has repeatedly refused to extend such protection. Appellants now ask us to employ the disproportionate impact decisions as an artifice to "bootstrap" Title VII protection for homosexuals under the guise of protecting men generally.

This we are not free to do. Adoption of this bootstrap device would frustrate congressional objectives as explicated in *Holloway*, not effectuate congressional goals as in *Griggs*. It would achieve by judicial "construction" what Congress did not do and has consistently refused to do on many occasions. It would violate the rule that our duty in construing a statute is to "ascertain... and give effect to the legislative will." *Philbrook*, 421 U.S. at 713. We conclude that the *Griggs* disproportionate impact theory may not be applied to extend Title VII protection to homosexuals.

C. Differences in Employment Criteria

Appellants next contend that recent decisions have held that an employer generally may not use different employment criteria for men and women. They claim that if a male employee prefers males as sexual partners, he will be treated differently from a female who prefers male partners. They conclude that the employer thus uses different employment criteria for men and women . . . .

We must again reject appellants' efforts to "bootstrap" Title VII protection for homosexuals. While we do not express approval of an employment policy that differentiates according to sexual preference, we note that whether dealing with men or women the employer is using the same criterion: It will not hire or promote a person who prefers sexual partners of the same sex. Thus this policy does not involve different decisional criteria for the sexes.

D. Interference With Association

Appellants argue that the EEOC has held that discrimination against an employee because of the race of the employee's friends may constitute discrimination based on race in violation of Title VII. They contend that analogously discrimination because of the sex of the employees' sexual partner should constitute discrimination based on sex.

Appellants, however, have not alleged that appellees have policies of discriminating against employees because of the gender of their friends. That is, they do not claim that the appellees will terminate anyone with a male (or female) friend. They claim instead that the appellees discriminate against employees who have a certain type of relationship — i.e., homosexual relationship — with certain friends. As noted earlier, that relationship is not protected by Title VII. *See* part IIA *supra*. Thus, assuming that it would violate Title VII for an employer to discriminate against employees because of the gender of their friends, appellants' claims do not fall within this purported rule.

E. Effeminacy

Appellant Strailey contends that he was terminated by the Happy Times Nursery School because that school felt that it was inappropriate for a male teacher to wear an earring to school. He claims that the school's reliance on a stereotype — that a male should have a virile rather than an effeminate appearance — violates Title VII.

In *Holloway* this court noted that Congress intended Title VII's ban on sex discrimination in employment to prevent discrimination because of gender, not because of sexual orientation or preference. Recently the Fifth Circuit similarly read the legislative history of Title VII and concluded that Title VII thus does not protect against discrimination because of effeminacy. *Smith v. Liberty Mutual Insurance*

Co., 569 F.2d at 326-27. We agree and hold that discrimination because of effeminacy, like discrimination because of homosexuality or transsexualism does not fall within the purview of Title VII.

III. § 1985(3) CLAIM

The district courts dismissed the male appellants' claims under 42 U.S.C. § 1985(3). The district court also refused to allow the women appellants to amend their complaint to state a claim under § 1985(3). We affirm.

Section 1985(3) provides in relevant part:

> If two or more persons... conspire or go in disguise on the highway or on the premises of another, for the purpose of depriving, either directly or indirectly, any person or class of persons of the equal protection of the laws, or of equal privileges and immunities under the laws... in any case of conspiracy set forth in this section, if one or more persons engaged therein do, or cause to be done, any act in furtherance of the object of such conspiracy, whereby another is injured in his person or property, or deprived of having and exercising any right or privilege of a citizen of the United States, the party so injured or deprived may have an action for the recovery of damages occasioned by such injury or deprivation, against any one or more of the conspirators.

Appellants argue that the concerted actions of various agents of their employers and others, to effectuate the discriminatory policy of the employers constituted a conspiracy in violation of § 1985(3). They conclude that regardless of this court's holding as to Title VII, they can assert a viable § 1985(3) claim.

The forerunner of § 1985(3) was enacted as part of the Ku Klux Klan Act of 1871. It was intended to provide special federal assistance to southern blacks and their allies in protecting their rights under the Fourteenth Amendment and other reconstruction legislation against the Ku Klux Klan and others organized to thwart reconstruction efforts.

A century later the Supreme Court held that § 1985(3) applied only when there is "some racial, or perhaps otherwise class-based, invidiously discriminatory animus behind the conspirators' action." *Griffin v. Breckenridge*, 403 U.S. 88, 102 (1971). Because *Griffin* dealt with allegations by blacks of a conspiracy to deprive them of their civil rights, the Supreme Court did not decide "whether a conspiracy motivated by invidiously discriminatory intent other than racial bias would be actionable" under § 1985(3). *Id.* at 102 n.9.

In *Life Insurance Co. of North America v. Reichardt*, 591 F.2d 499 (9th Cir. 1979), this court held that plaintiffs alleging a conspiracy to deprive women of equal rights could invoke § 1985(3). 591 F.2d at 502. Appellants here claim that since *Reichardt* moved beyond the narrow historical perspective of 1871, homosexuals (and all groups) can now claim the special protection of § 1985(3).

We disagree. While § 1985(3) has been liberated from the now anachronistic historical circumstances of reconstruction America, we may not uproot § 1985(3) from the principle underlying its adoption: the Governmental determination that some groups require and warrant special federal assistance in protecting their civil rights. This underlying principle must continue to determine the coverage of § 1985(3).

In contradistinction to southern blacks of 1871, the blacks of *Griffin*, and the women of *Reichardt*, it cannot be said that homosexuals have been afforded special federal assistance in protecting their civil rights. The courts have not designated homosexuals a "suspect" or "quasi-suspect" classification so as to require more exacting scrutiny of classifications involving homosexuals. *Cf. Doe v. Commonwealth's Attorney*, 403

F.Supp. 1199, 1202 (E.D.Va. 1975) (three judge court) (constitutionality of Virginia sodomy law upheld against due process and other challenges under legitimate interest and rational relationship tests), *aff'd mem.*, 425 U.S. 901 (1976). And as noted in part II *supra*, Congress did not — and has consistently refused to — include homosexuals as a group within the special protection of Title VII. *See* 42 U.S.C. § 2000e-2.

We conclude that homosexuals are not a "class" within the meaning of § 1985(3). The district courts therefore properly rejected appellants' § 1985(3) claims.

AFFIRMED.

SNEED, J., (concurring and dissenting):

I respectfully dissent from subpart B which holds that male homosexuals have not stated a Title VII claim under the disproportionate impact theories of *Griggs v. Duke Power Co.*, 401 U.S. 424 (1971). My position is not foreclosed by our holding, with which I agree, that Title VII does not afford protection to homosexuals, male or female. The male appellants' complaint, as I understand it, is based on the contention that the use of homosexuality as a disqualification for employment, which for *Griggs'* purposes must be treated as a facially neutral criterion,

impacts disproportionately on males because of the greater visibility of male homosexuals and a higher incidence of homosexuality among males than females.

To establish such a claim will be difficult because the male appellants must prove that as a result of the appellee's practices there exists discrimination against males *qua* males. That is, to establish a prima facie case under *Griggs* it will not be sufficient to show that appellees have employed a disproportionately large number of female *homosexuals* and a disproportionately small number of male *homosexuals*. Rather it will be necessary to establish that the use of homosexuality as a bar to employment disproportionately impacts on *males*, a class that enjoys Title VII protection. Such a showing perhaps could be made were male homosexuals a very large proportion of the total applicable male population.

My point of difference with the majority is merely that the male appellants in their *Griggs* claim are not using that case "as an artifice to 'bootstrap' Title VII protection for homosexuals under the guise of protecting men generally." Their claim, if established properly, would in fact protect males generally. I would permit them to try to make their case and not dismiss it on the pleadings.

■ ■ ■

Notes

1. For commentary on the *DeSantis* decision, see Douglas Warner, *Homophobia, 'Manifest Homosexuals' and Political Activity: A New Approach to Gay Rights and the 'Issue' of Homosexuality*, 11 GOLDEN GATE U. L. REV. 635 (1981); Betsy Rieke, Case Note, *Title VII and Private Sector Employment Discrimination against Homosexuals*, 22 ARIZ. L. REV. 94 (1980); Donna Wise, Case Note, *Challenging Sexual Preference Discrimination in Private Employment*, 41 OHIO ST. L. J. 501 (1980). A more general discussion can be found in Wayne Chew, *Title VII Rights of Homosexuals*, 10 GOLDEN GATE U. L. REV. 53 (1980).

2. All courts that have considered this question have concurred with the *DeSantis* decision. *See Smith v. Liberty Mut. Ins. Co.*, 395 F. Supp. 1098 (N.D. Ga. 1975), *aff'd*, 569 F.2d 325 (5th Cir. 1978)(finding that sexual or affectional orientation discrimination is not sex discrimination); *cf. Holloway v. Arthur Andersen & Co.*, 566 F.2d 659 (9th Cir. 1977) (holding that

Title VII does not apply to transsexuals); *Voyles v. Ralph K. Davies Med. Ctr.*, 403 F. Supp. 456 (N.D. Cal. 1975) (holding that Title VII does not apply to transsexuals).

3. In *Dorr v. First Kentucky Nat. Corp.* 796 F.2d 179 (6th Cir. 1986), plaintiff invoked Title VII's provisions prohibiting discrimination because of religion, 42 U.S.C. § 2000e-2(a)(1), to avoid a gay-related employment dismissal. Plaintiff, a bank employee, informed his employer of his involvement with Integrity, a nationwide organization ministering to gay Episcopalians and of his public position with that organization. The bank demanded he retire as president of Integrity or else resign his job. He quit the bank and brought suit. The district court dismissed his case, but a panel of the Sixth Circuit reversed and remanded. However, this decision was vacated by the Sixth Circuit sitting en banc. *See Dorr v. First Kentucky Nat. Corp.*, 42 Fair Empl. Prac. Cas. (BNA) 64 (6th Cir. 1986) (en banc).

4. Some lesbians and gay men have attempted, without success, to argue that discrimination based on sexual orientation discriminates on the basis of a handicap. *See, e.g., Blackwell v United States Dep't of the Treasury,* 830 F.2d 1183 (D.C. Cir. 1987). This approach requires a statement that homosexuality is, or is perceived to be, a physical or mental impairment. *See, e.g.,* 29 U.S.C. § 706(7)(A)(1988).

   In enacting the Americans with Disabilities Act in 1990, 42 U.S.C.A. §§ 12101-12213 (Supp. 1992), Congress specifically exempted this type of claim from the law's coverage:

   (a) Homosexuality and Bisexuality. For purposes of the definition of "disability" in section 3(2) [42 U.S.C. § 12102(2)], homosexuality and bisexuality are not impairments and as such are not disabilities under this Act.

   (b) Certain conditions. Under this Act, the term "disability" shall not include —
   (1) transvestism, transsexualism, pedophilia, exhibitionism, voyeurism, gender identity disorders not resulting from physical impairments, or other sexual behavior disorders; (2) compulsive gambling, kleptomania, or pyromania; or (3) psychoactive substance use disorders resulting from current illegal use of drugs.

   Id. at § 12211. However, "if a gay man or lesbian has HIV disease [or any other disability] and is discriminated against because of HIV disease, that person is protected in exactly the same way as anyone else with the disease." Chai Feldbulm, *Workplace Issues: HIV and Discrimination, in* AIDS AGENDA: EMERGING ISSUES IN CIVIL RIGHTS 271, 278 (Nan D. Hunter & William B. Rubenstein eds. 1992).

◆

MASSACHUSETTS GAY RIGHTS LAW

Ch. 151B, SECTION 3(6): The term "sexual orientation" shall mean having an orientation for or being identified as having an orientation for heterosexuality, bisexuality, or homosexuality.

SECTION 4(1): [It shall be an unlawful practice f]or an employer, by himself or his agent, because of the race, color. religious creed, national origin, sex, sexual orientation, which shall not include persons whose sexual orientation involves minor children

MASSACHUSETTS GEN. L., ch. 151B, §§ 3-5; ch. 272, §§ 92A, 98 (1990).

as the sex object, or ancestry of any individual to refuse to hire or employ or to bar or to discharge from employment such individual or to discriminate against such individual in compensation or in terms, conditions or privileges of employment, unless based upon a bona fide occupational qualification.

SECTION 4(2): [It shall be an unlawful practice f]or a labor organization, because of the race, color, religious creed, national origin, sex, sexual orientation, which shall not include persons whose sexual orientation involves minor children as the sex object, age or ancestry of any individual, or because of the handicap of any person alleging to be a qualified handicapped person, to exclude from full membership rights or to expel from its membership such individual or to discriminate in any way against any of its members or against any employer or any individual employed by an employer unless based upon a bona fide occupational qualification.

SECTION 4(6): [It shall be an unlawful practice f]or the owner, lessee, sublessee, licensed real estate broker, assignee or managing agent of publicly assisted or multiple dwelling or contiguously located housing accommodations or other person having the right to ownership or possession or right to rent or lease, or sell or negotiate for the sale of such accommodations, or any agent or employee of such a person, or any organization of unit owners in a condominium or housing cooperative: (a) to refuse to rent or lease or sell or negotiate for sale or otherwise to deny to or withhold from any person of group of persons such accommodations because of the race, religious creed, color, national origin, sex, sexual orientation, which shall not include persons whose sexual orientation involves minor children as the sex object, age ancestry, or marital status of such person or persons or because such person is a veteran or member of the armed forces, or because such a person is blind, or hearing impaired...(c) to cause to be made any written or oral inquiry or record concerning the race, religious creed, color, national origin, sex, sexual orientation, which shall not include persons whose sexual orientation involves minor children as the sex object, age, ancestry or marital status of the person seeking to rent or lease or buy any such accommodation, or concerning the fact that such person is a veteran or a member of the armed forces or because such person is blind or hearing impaired.

■ ■ ■

SECTION 4(8): [It shall be an unlawful practice f]or the owner, lessee, sublessee, or managing agent of, or other person having the right of ownership or possession of or the right to sell, rent or lease commercial space: (1) To refuse to sell, rent or lease or otherwise deny to or withhold from any person or group of persons such commercial space because of race, color, religious creed, national origin, sex, sexual orientation, which shall not include persons whose sexual orientation involves minor children as the sex object, age, ancestry or marital status of such person or person.

■ ■ ■

Ch. 272 SECTION § 98: Whoever makes any distinction, discrimination or restriction on account of race, color, religious creed, national origin, sex, sexual orientation, which shall not include persons whose sexual orientation involves minor children as the sex object, deafness, blindness or any physical or mental disability or ancestry relative to the admission of any person to, or his treatment in any place of public accommodation, resort, or amusement . . . or whoever aids or incites such distinction, discrimination, or restriction, shall be punished by fine of not more than twenty-five hundred dollars or by imprisonment for not more than one year, or both, and shall be liable to any person aggrieved thereby for such damages as are enumerated [elsewhere in the statues]; provided , however, that such civil forfeiture shall be of an amount not less than three hundred dollars; but such person so aggrieved shall not recover against more than one person by reason of any one act of distinction, discrimination or restriction. All persons shall have the right to the full and equal accommodations, advantages, facilities and privileges of any place of public accommodation, resort or amusement subject only to the conditions and limitations established by law and applicable to all persons. This right is recognized and declared to be a civil right.

Notes

1. The first ordinances protecting against discrimination on the basis of sexual orientation were adopted in the early 1970s. Since then, nearly 100 municipalities, seven states and the District of Columbia have adopted such laws. *See* EDITORS OF THE HARVARD LAW REVIEW, Sexual Orientation and the Law 158 n. 51 (1990). Wisconsin was the first state to adopt a gay rights law in 1983, *see* WIS. STAT. ANN. § 101.22 (West 1988 & Supp. 1991) and no other state followed until 1990. Since 1990, Massachusetts, MASS. GEN. LAWS ANN. ch. 272 § 98 (West 1990); ch. 151B, § 4 (West Supp. 1992); Hawaii, HAWAII REV. STAT. §§ 368-1, 489-1, et seq. (Supp. 1991); Connecticut, 1991 CONN. ACTS 91-58 (Reg. Sess.); New Jersey, 1991 N.J. SESS. LAW SERV. ch. 519 (West); Vermont (1992); and California (1992) have adopted employment protections for lesbians and gay men.

2. Legislative enactment of these protections — and particularly the political compromises that are contained in the laws — has given rise to academic commentary. *See* Peter Cicchino, Bruce Deming & Katherine Nicholson, *Sex, Lies, and Civil Rights: A Critical History of the Massachusetts Gay Civil Rights Bill*, 26 HARV. C.R.-C.L. L. REV. 549, 612 (1991); *see also* Joyce Cain, *Massachusetts' 1989 Sexual Orientation Nondiscrimination Statute*, 1 LAW & SEXUALITY 285 (1991); Lorena Dumas, *The Sexual Orientation Clause of the District of Columbia's Human Rights Act*, 1 LAW & SEXUALITY 267 (1991).

3. In addition to these seven states, the following counties and municipalities have adopted gay rights protections: Tucson, **Arizona**; Berkeley, Cathedral City, Cupertino, Davis, Laguna Beach, Long Beach, Los Angeles, Mountain View, Oakland, Sacramento, San Diego, San Francisco, San Jose, Santa Barbara, Santa Cruz, Santa Monica, and West Hollywood, **California**; Aspen, Boulder, and Denver, **Colorado**; Hartford, New Haven, and Stamford, **Connecticut**; **Washington, D.C.**; Hillsborough County, Palm Beach County, and Tampa, **Florida**; Atlanta, **Georgia**; Honolulu, **Hawaii**; Champaign, Chicago, Evanston (housing only), and Urbana, **Illinois**; Iowa City, **Iowa**; New Orleans, **Louisiana**; Baltimore, Montgomery County, Prince Georges County, and Rockville, **Maryland**; Boston, Cambridge, and Malden, **Massachusetts**; Ann Arbor, Detroit, East Lansing, Flint, Ingham County (executive order), Lansing, and Saginaw, **Michigan**; Hennepin County (executive order), Minneapolis, and St. Paul, **Minnesota**; Kansas City, Missouri (executive order); Alfred, Brighton, Buffalo (executive order), East Hampton, Ithaca, New York City, Rochester, Suffolk County, Syracuse, Tompkins County, and Troy, **New York**; Chapel Hill, Durham, and Raleigh, **North Carolina**; Columbus, Cuyahoga County (government employees), and Yellow Springs, **Ohio**; Eugene and Portland, **Oregon**; Harrisburg, Philadelphia, and Pittsburgh, **Pennsylvania**; Minnehaha County, **South Dakota** (government employees); Austin, **Texas**; Alexandria and Arlington County, **Virginia**; Clallam County, King County, Olympia, Pullman, Seattle, and Tacoma, **Washington**; Dane County, Madison, and Milwaukee, **Wisconsin**. *See* NAN HUNTER ET AL., THE RIGHTS OF LESBIANS AND GAY MEN 204-208 (3d ed. 1992).

B. Constitutional Provisions

Constitutions are generally designed to restrict government actions and therefore constitutional provisions usually do not apply to non-governmental employers. Nevertheless, some state constitutions — notably, California's — do prohibit discrimination by private and quasi-private employers. In California, these provisions have been read to apply to discrimination by private employers on the basis of sexual orientation.

GAY LAW STUDENTS ASSOCIATION v.
PACIFIC TELEPHONE AND TELEGRAPH COMPANY

595 P.2d 592 (Cal. 1979)

TOBRINER, J.

■ ■ ■

The complaint alleges that "PT&T has maintained and enforced a policy of employment discrimination against homosexuals," and that "PT&T has, since at least 1971, had an articulated policy of excluding homosexuals from employment opportunities with its organization." Plaintiffs adduced detailed allegations to support this charge, including the allegation that "Plaintiff Desantis was refused permission to even apply for employment with Defendant PT&T when Defendant Silverman [the PT&T job interviewer] learned of his homosexual orientation." Exhibits attached to the complaint additionally support plaintiffs' further charge that PT&T follows a policy of discrimination against "manifest" homosexuals.

Plaintiffs explain the economic impact of PT&T's alleged discriminatory policy: "PT&T employs over 93,000 people. . . . Many of PT&T's jobs require skills useful only in telephone companies, and not in the electrical or electronics fields generally. Thus persons having acquired such skills from PT&T or other telephone companies will be effectively denied employment in California if they are known or thought to be

homosexual, as will PT&T employees who cannot obtain advancement within PT&T because of their homosexuality or who are fired in whole or in part for this reason."

In addition to declaratory relief, plaintiffs seek a permanent injunction barring PT&T from continuing to refuse to employ or promote persons because of their sexual orientation. Plaintiffs further ask the court to order PT&T to pay monetary damages to compensate the victims of such discrimination for loss of wages or salaries.

■ ■ ■

. . . The [trial] court . . . entered judgment for defendants on all causes of action. Plaintiffs appeal from that judgment.

2. PLAINTIFFS' ALLEGATIONS OF ARBITRARY EMPLOYMENT DISCRIMINATION AGAINST HOMOSEXUALS STATE A CAUSE OF ACTION AGAINST PT&T.

■ ■ ■

(a) *Article I, Section 7 subdivision (a) of the California Constitution bars a public utility from engaging in arbitrary employment discrimination.*

Plaintiffs contend that PT&T's alleged discriminatory employment practices violate the equal protection guarantee of the California Constitution by arbitrarily denying qualified homosexuals employment opportunities afforded other individuals. In analyzing this constitutional contention, we begin from the premise that both the state and federal equal protection clauses clearly prohibit *the state or any governmental entity* from arbitrarily discriminating against any class of individuals in employment decisions. Moreover, past decisions of this court establish that this general constitutional principle applies to homosexuals as well as to all other members of our polity; under California law, the state may not exclude homosexuals as a class from employment opportunities without a showing that an individual's homosexuality renders him unfit for the job from which he has been excluded. *See, e.g., Morrison v. Board of Education*, 461 P.2d 375 (Cal. 1969). Courts in other jurisdictions have reached similar conclusions. *See, e.g., Norton v. Macy*, 417 F.2d 1161 (D.C. Cir. 1969); *Society for Individual Rights, Inc. v. Hampton*, 63 F.R.D. 399 (N.D. Cal. 1973); *Saal v. Middendorf*, 427 F.Supp. 192, 199-203 (N.D. Cal. 1977); *Martinez v. Brown*, 449 F.Supp. 207, 211-213 (N.D. Cal. 1978); *In Re Kimball*, 301 N.E.2d 436 (N.Y. 1973).

In the instant case, of course, the practice of excluding homosexuals from employment has allegedly been adopted not by the state itself but by PT&T, a public utility to whom the state has granted a monopoly over a significant segment of the telephonic communications industry in California. The constitutional question presented in this regard is whether the protection afforded individuals by the state equal protection clause encompasses protection against the discriminatory treatment alleged in the present complaint.

Article I, section 7, subdivision (a) of the California Constitution provides simply that: "*A person may not be* deprived of life, liberty or property without due process of law or *denied equal protection of the laws.*" (Italics added.) Unlike the due process and equal protection clauses of the Fourteenth Amendment, which by their explicit language operate as restrictions on the actions of states, the California constitutional provision contains no such explicit "state action" requirement.

■ ■ ■

In the instant case, the question with which we are presented is a narrow but important one: Is the California constitutional equal protection guarantee violated when a privately owned public utility, which enjoys a state-protected monopoly or quasi-monopoly, utilizes its authority arbitrarily to exclude a class of individuals from employment opportunities? As we explain, we conclude that arbitrary exclusion of qualified individuals from employment opportunities by a state-protected public utility does, indeed, violate the state constitutional rights of the victims of such discrimination.

In California a public utility is in many respects more akin to a governmental entity than to a purely private employer. In this state, the breadth and depth of governmental regulation of a public utility's business practices inextricably ties the state to a public utility's conduct, both in the public's perception and in the utility's day-to-day activities. Moreover, the nature of the California regulatory scheme demonstrates that the state generally expects a public utility to conduct its affairs more like a governmental entity than like a private corporation. Both the prices which a utility charges for its products or services and the standards which govern its facilities and services are established by the state; in addition, the state determines the system and form of the accounts and records which a public utility maintains and it exercises special scrutiny over a utility's issuance of stocks and bonds. Finally, the state had endowed many public utilities, like PT&T, with considerable powers generally enjoyed only by governmental entities, most notably the power of eminent domain. Under these circumstances, we believe that the state cannot avoid responsibility for a utility's systematic business practices and that a public utility may not properly claim prerogatives of "private autonomy" that may possibly attach to a purely private business enterprise.

Moreover, we believe that PT&T's present claim — that it enjoys the power arbitrarily to exclude classes of individuals from its numerous employment opportunities without regard to constitutional constraints — is particularly untenable. Protection against the arbitrary foreclosing of employment opportunities lies close to the heart of the protection against "second-class citizenship" which the equal protection clause was intended to guarantee. An individual's freedom of opportunity to work and earn a living has long been recognized as one of the fundamental and most cherished liberties enjoyed by members of our society and, as one jurist has aptly noted, "discrimination in employment is one of the most deplorable forms of discrimination known to our society, for it deals not with just an individual's sharing in the 'outer benefits' of being an American citizen, but rather the ability to provide decently for [oneself and] one's family in a job or profession for which he qualifies and chooses." *Culpepper v. Reynolds Metal Company*, 421 F.2d 888, 891 (5th Cir. 1970).

For a number of reasons arbitrary discrimination in employment particularly flouts constitutional principles when it is practiced by a state-protected public utility. First, from the point of view of the individual seeking employment, both the injurious effect of arbitrary exclusion and the risk of such exclusion loom significantly larger in the case of a monopolistic or quasi-monopolistic public utility than in the case of an ordinary employer. An individual who is arbitrarily rejected by a single private employer is generally free to seek a job with that employer's competitors; if he is a qualified applicant, he may well have a good chance of gaining a position in his chosen field of employment because of a private employer's desire to gain an advantage over its competitors and because of the employer's reluctance to permit its competitors to gain such an advantage. Arbitrary rejection from employment by a public utility with a state-protected monopoly such as PT&T, however, frequently leaves an individul no comparable option; since PT&T is the only company authorized to perform many telephone communications services in much of the state, an individual whose occupation falls within PT&T's realm may have no alternative employer to whom he can turn. Moreover, because PT&T has no competition to fear, it does not face the inherent, if limited, check which the free market system places on employment discrimination. Thus, from the standpoint of the individual employee, the potential for employment discrimination by a public utility is high, and the effect of such discrimination when it occurs is devastating.

Second, unlike discrimination by a private employer, employment discrimination by a public utility can be particularly pernicious because, in light of the utility's position, the general public cannot avoid giving indirect support to such discriminatory practices. In the case of the ordinary private employer, members of the public who disapprove of the employer's employment discrimination can avoid supporting such a practice and attempt to eliminate it simply by refusing to purchase the employer's product or service. In the case of a public utility such as PT&T, by contrast, the necessitous service of the utility, not available through other enterprises, means that the general public lacks any choice but indirectly to support the utility's discriminatory practices.

Finally, employment discrimination by a public utility is particularly incompatible with the values underlying our constitutional equal protection guarantee because a public utility's monopolistic or quasi-monopolistic authority over employment opportunities derives directly from its exclusive franchise provided by the state. For example, PT&T's monopoly over nearly 80 percent of the market for telephone service in California — and thus over tens of thousands of jobs — is guaranteed and safeguarded by the state Public Utilities Commission, which possesses the power to refuse to issue certificates of public convenience and necessity to permit potential competition to enter these areas and which establishes rates for telephone service that guarantee PT&T a reasonable rate of return. Thus, to a significant degree, the state has itself immunized PT&T from many of the checks of free market competition and has placed the utility in a position from which it can wield enormous power over an individual's employment opportunities. Under these circumstances, PT&T can point to no legitimate countervailing interest in "privacy" or "personal autonomy" which could reasonably justify exempting its discriminatory employment practices from constitutional constraints.

Accordingly, we conclude that in this state a public utility bears a constitutional obligation to avoid arbitrary employment discrimination.

■ ■ ■

We emphasize that our holding in this regard in no way abridges a public utility's right to prefer the best qualified persons in reaching its hiring or promotion decisions. The equal protection clause prohibits only arbitrary discrimination on grounds unrelated to a worker's qualifications. Thus, while we hold that the California Constitution precludes a public utility's management from automatically excluding all homosexuals from consideration for employment positions — or, by the same token, from excluding any classification of persons because of personal whims or prejudices or any other arbitrary reason — we stress that the constitutional

provision does not deny a public utility's management the authority to exercise legitimate judgment in employment decisions.

In the instant case, of course, plaintiffs have alleged that PT&T has adopted an arbitrarily discriminatory employment policy against homosexuals. In light of the foregoing analysis, we conclude that plaintiffs' complaint states a cause of action against PT&T under article I section 7, subdivision (a) of the California Constitution.

■ ■ ■

3. PLAINTIFFS' COMPLAINT ADDITIONALLY STATES A CAUSE OF ACTION AGAINST PT&T FOR INTERFERING WITH PLAINTIFFS' POLITICAL FREEDOM IN VIOLATION OF LABOR CODE SECTIONS 1101 AND 1102.

Over 60 years ago the California Legislature, recognizing that employers could misuse their economic power to interfere with the political activities of their employees, enacted Labor Code sections 1101 and 1102 to protect the employees' rights. Labor Code section 1101 provides that "No employer shall make, adopt, or enforce any rule, regulation, or policy: (a) Forbidding or preventing employees from engaging or participating in politics . . . . (b) Controlling or directing, or tending to control or direct the political activities of affiliations of employees." Similarly, section 1102 states that "No employer shall coerce or influence or attempt to coerce or influence his employees through or by means of threat of discharge or loss of employment to adopt or follow or refrain from adopting or following any particular course or line of political action or political activity." These sections serve to protect "the fundamental right of employees in general to engage in political activity without interference by employers."

These statutes cannot be narrowly confined to partisan activity. As explained in

Mallard v. Boring, 182 Cal.App.2d 390, 395 (1960): "The term 'political activity' connotes the espousal of a candidate *or a cause*, and some degree of action to promote the acceptance thereof by other persons." The Supreme Court has recognized the political character of activities such as participation in litigation (*N.A.A.C.P. v. Button*, 371 U.S. 415, 429 (1963), the wearing of symbolic armbands (*Tinker v. Des Moines School Dist.*, 393 U.S. 503 (1969), and the association with others for the advancement of beliefs and ideas, *N.A.A.C.P. v. Alabama* 357 U.S. 449 (1958).

Measured by these standards, the struggle of the homosexual community for equal rights, particularly in the field of employment, must be recognized as a political activity. Indeed the subject of the rights of homosexuals incites heated political debate today, and the "gay liberation movement" encourages its homosexual members to attempt to convince other members of society that homosexuals should be accorded the same fundamental rights as heterosexuals. The aims of the struggle for homosexual rights, and the tactics employed, bear a close analogy to the continuing struggle for civil rights waged by blacks, women, and other minorities. *See, e.g., Gay Students Org. of Univ. of New Hampshire v. Bonner*, 509 F.2d 652, 657 (1st Cir. 1974); *Acanfora v. Board of Education of Montgomery County*, 491 F.2d 498 (4th Cir. 1974), cert. den., 419 U.S. 836; *Aumiller v. University of Delaware*, 434 F.Supp. 1273, 1292-1302 (D.Del. 1977).

A principal barrier to homosexual equality is the common feeling that homosexuality is an affliction which the homosexual worker must conceal from his employer and his fellow workers. Consequently one important aspect of the struggle for equal rights is to induce homosexual individuals to "come out of the closet," acknowledge their sexual preferences, and to associate with others in working for equal rights.

In light of this factor in the movement for homosexual rights, the allegations of the plaintiffs' complaint assume a special significance. Plaintiffs allege that PT&T discriminates against "manifest" homosexuals and against persons who make "an issue of their homosexuality." The complaint asserts also that PT&T will not hire anyone referred to them by plaintiff Society for Individual Rights, an organization active in promoting the rights of homosexuals to equal employment opportunities. These allegations can reasonably be construed as charging that PT&T discriminates in particular against persons who identify themselves as homosexual, who defend homosexuality, or who are identified with activist homosexual organizations. So construed, the allegations charge that PT&T has adopted a "policy ... tending to control or direct the political activities or affiliations of employees" in violation of section 1101, and has "attempt[ed] to coerce or influence ... employees ... to ... refrain from adopting [a] particular course or line of political ... activity" in violation of section 1102.

In *Lockheed Aircraft Corp. v. Superior Court*, 171 P.2d 21 (Cal. 1946), our court established the principle that an employee who has been discriminated against in violation of sections 1101 or 1102 may maintain a cause of action against his employer to recover damages sustained as a result of the employer's unlawful conduct. (See also Lab. Code, § 1105.) Thus, since the allegations of the complaint do allege that PT&T has engaged in conduct which violates these statutory provisions, the complaint also states a cause of action against PT&T on this ground.

■ ■ ■

5. CONCLUSION.

If this court were to accede to PT&T's sought sanction for its alleged arbitrary discriminatory practices, we would approve of a rule that would extend beyond the subject of employment discrimination against homosexuals. We would necessarily empower any public utility to engage in an infinity of arbitrary employment practices. To cite only a few examples, the utility could refuse to employ a person because he read books prohibited by the utility, visited countries disapproved by the utility, or simply exhibited irrelevant characteristics of personal appearance or background disliked by the utility. Such possible arbitrary discrimination, casting upon the community the shadow of totalitarianism, becomes crucial when asserted by an institution that exerts the vast powers of a monopoly sanctioned by government itself. We do not believe a public utility can assert such prerogatives in a free society dedicated to the protection of individual rights.

The judgment in favor of PT&T is reversed. . .

■ ■ ■

Notes

1. For further consideration of the *Gay Law Students* case see Patricia Cullison, Case Note, *Constitutional Law — Equal Protection — Employment Discrimination Against Homosexuals by a State Regulated Public Utility, a Private Employer, Constitutes State Action and Is Prohibited by the Equal Protection Clause of the California Constitution*, 2 WHITTIER L. REV. 575 (1980); Lee Ann Johnson, Case Note, *Constitutional and Statutory Restraints on Employment Discrimination against Homosexuals by Public Utilities*, 68 CAL. L. REV. 680 (1980). For a more general discussion, see Mark Vandervelden, *Gay Rights at Work*, 4 CAL. LAW. 46 (1984).

C. Non-Discrimination Policies

In recent years, more and more private employers are realizing that gay people constitute a large segment of the talented and objectively desirable job pool. Law firms in most metropolitan areas, for example, have responded to pressure from law schools and students and have adopted non-discrimination policies affecting recruitment, hiring, and promotion of gay lawyers.[1] Even when gay people break through discrimination barriers and are employed in suitable positions, however, more subtle forms of discrimination appear. While most public and private employers provide health insurance and other benefits to spouses and traditional family members of their employees, gay people and their families seldom enjoy equal treatment.

---

1. *See, e.g.*, Jana Eisinger, *Firms Step Up Hiring of Gay and Lesbian Lawyers*, N. Y. TIMES, Feb. 7, 1992, at B6.

JOACHIM v. AT & T INFORMATION SYSTEMS

793 F.2d 113 (5th Cir. 1986)

PER CURIAM:

In this Texas diversity case, Steven Joachim appeals an adverse summary judgment dismissing his demand for damages for an alleged violation of an implied contract of employment. The issue on appeal is whether defendant's employee handbook created contractual rights which removed Joachim's employment from under the Texas employment-at-will provision. The district court answered this inquiry in the negative. We affirm.

Joachim was employed by AT & T as an associate account executive in San Antonio for one year beginning in February 1983. At the end of that period Joachim had not, in the judgment of his immediate supervisor, completed the requirements needed for certification as an account executive. As a consequence, Joachim was conditionally certified, placed on probation, and a sales quota was set for the ensuing ninety days. At the end of that period, Joachim had achieved only one-third of his assigned quota and his employment was terminated. Joachim maintains that he was subjected to job discrimination, including termination, because of his sexual preference — he is a homosexual. AT & T's personnel handbook, which summarizes company policies, provides that sexual preference will not be used as a basis for job discrimination or termination.

Following his dismissal, Joachim filed the instant suit. The sole question presented to the trial court and to this court on appeal is whether the employee handbook impliedly imposed contractual obligations on AT & T.

In finding and concluding that the handbook did not create any contractual relationship altering Joachim's at-will employment status, the district court primarily relied on *Reynolds Mfg. Co. v. Mendoza*, 644 S.W.2d 536 (Tex.App.— Corpus Christi 1982, *no writ*) as dispositive of Joachim's claims. The Texas Court of Appeals there noted, id. at 538:

> It is well-settled in Texas that, absent any existing contractual limitations, when an employment contract provides for an indefinite term of service, either party may put an end to it at will, with or without cause.

The Texas appellate court went on to hold that absent an express reciprocal agreement dealing with procedures for discharge, employee handbooks "constituted no more than general guidelines," *id.* at 539, and did not create a contractual right in the employees.

That identical situation exists in the case after his year of training.... He had no basis for challenging his discharge unless the employee handbook gave him a contractual right and imposed a concomitant obligation on A T & T.

The holding and rationale of *Reynolds* belie Joachim's argument. Joachim urges that *Reynolds* is not binding on a federal court sitting in diversity, *see Erie R. Co. v. Tompkins*, 304 U.S. 64 (1938), maintaining that *Reynolds* would not be followed by the Texas courts, in light of jurisprudential developments in other states. Joachim cites no Texas cases rejecting *Reynolds*; indeed, he cannot since there is none. The sparse post-*Reynolds* authorities support the conclusion of the district judge, schooled and skilled in the law of Texas. *See Totman v. Control Data Corp.*, 707 S.W.2d 739 (Tex.App.—Ft. Worth 1986, no writ); *Vallone v. Agip Petroleum Co.*, Inc., 705 S.W.2d 757 (Tex.App.— Houston [1st Dist.] 1986, writ ref'd N.R.E.). The district judge appropriately declined to predict a turnabout by the Texas courts and, correctly applied settled Texas precedents.

The judgment of the district court is AFFIRMED.

Notes

1. In *Joachim*, "the court based its decision on Texas precedent that required an 'express reciprocal agreement' for a modification of the employment-at-will doctrine. One year later, however, the Fifth Circuit found that statements in employee manuals can constitute express written contracts under Texas law." EDITORS OF THE HARVARD LAW REVIEW, SEXUAL ORIENTATION AND THE LAW 68 n.156 (1990) (citing *Aiello v. United Air Lines, Inc.*, 818 F.2d 1196, 1198-99 (5th Cir. 1987)).

2. Most employers (private and public) provide spouse-related benefits to their mid- and high-level employees. These benefits often make up a large proportion of the total compensation that employers pay out for their employees. These benefits typically include life insurance for the employee; health insurance coverage for the employee, spouse, and family dependents; and leave for the employee should the employee's family member, spouse, or a relative of the spouse fall ill or die. The extent to which employers have been willing to extend such benefits to the partners of lesbian and gay employees is considered as an aspect of lesbian and gay relationship law, *infra* at Chapter 5, *Legal Recognition of Lesbian and Gay Relationships*.

III. PUBLIC EMPLOYMENT

Many of the statutes discussed above that protect employees in the private sector from discrimination based on race, sex, national origin, religion, disability, and age also apply to employees of the public sector. For example, government employees are covered by Title VII, the Age Discrimination in Employment Act, and the Rehabilitation Act of 1973.[1]

What distinguishes public employment is that government employees, unlike their counterparts in the private sector, are protected not only by statutes and policies, but by civil services rules and constitutional law, as well. While government employees are said not to have a *right* to a government job, they nonetheless cannot be fired for reasons that would violate their constitutional rights.[2] Thus, for instance, government employees cannot be fired for expressing their political views, unless these views interfere with the function-

---

1. *See* CHARLES SULLIVAN, MICHAEL ZIMMER, RICHARD RICHARDS, EMPLOYMENT DISCRIMINATION 353-56, 383-434 (2d ed. 1988); *id.* at 103-04 (Supp. 1990). *See generally* JAMES JONES, JR., WILLIAM MURPHY & ROBERT BOLTON, CASES AND MATERIALS ON DISCRIMINATION IN EMPLOYMENT 461-464 (5th ed. 1987).

2. *See, e.g., Perry* v. *Sindermann*, 408 U.S. 593, 597 (1972).

ing of their workplace.[3] Similarly, the constitution prohibits the government from refusing to hire black employees, or from discriminating in the terms and conditions of employment on the basis of sex, for example.

Discrimination against lesbians and gay men in the public workforce was not often addressed before the 1960s. Since then, a general rule has emerged in the case law that if an individual's homosexual orientation does not directly affect the efficient functioning of the civil service or its public reputation, discrimination is prohibited.[4] The federal government has adopted a personnel policy codifying this decision.[5] Of course, this standard is highly ambiguous — what does it mean for a person's employment to disrupt the functioning of the workplace? In surveying the cases that have responded to this question, several sets of issues emerge. One factor in these cases concerns the particular workplace that is at issue in each case; thus this section is divided into different types of workplaces. A second set of issues concerns the particular facts presented by the plaintiff(s) in each case. In this sense, the cases tend to police how "open" public employees can be about their sexual orientation.

A. General Civil Service

NORTON v. MACY

417 F.2d 1161 (D.C. Cir. 1969)

BAZELON, Chief Judge:

■ ■ ■

I

Appellant's dismissal grew out of his arrest for a traffic violation. In the early morning of October 22, 1963, he was driving his car in the vicinity of Lafayette Square. He pulled over to the curb, picked up one Madison Monroe Procter, drove him once around the Square, and dropped him off at the starting point. The two men then drove off in separate cars. Two Morals Squad officers, having observed this sequence of events, gave chase, traveling at speeds of up to 45 miles per hour. In the parking lot of appellant's Southwest Washington apartment building, Procter told the police that appellant had felt his leg during their brief circuit of Lafayette Square and had then invited him to appellant's apartment for a drink. The officers arrested both men and took them "to the Morals Office to issue a traffic violation notice."

---

3. *See, e.g., Rankin* v. *McPherson,* 483 U.S. 378 (1987); *Connick* v. *Myers,* 461 U.S. 138 (1983); *Pickering* v. *Board of Educ.,* 391 U.S. 563 (1968).

4. *See Norton* v. *Macy,* 417 F.2d 1161 (D.C. Cir. 1969).

5. *See* 5 U.S.C. § 2302(b)(10)(1988) ("Any employee who has authority to take, recommend, or approve any personnel action, shall not, with respect to such authority . . . discriminate for or against any employee or applicant for employment on the basis of conduct which does not adversely affect the performance of the employee or applicant or the performance of others; except that nothing in this paragraph shall prohibit an agency from taking into account in determining suitability or fitness any conviction . . . for any crime . . .").

Pending issuance of the traffic summons, the police interrogated appellant and Procter for two hours concerning their activities that evening and their sexual histories. Meanwhile, pursuant to an arrangement, the head of the Morals Squad telephoned NASA Security Chief Fugler, who arrived on the scene at 3:00 a.m. in time to hear the last of the interrogation. Fugler was then shown the officers' confidential arrest record and was permitted to monitor incognito a twenty-minute interrogation of appellant held especially for his benefit. Throughout, appellant steadfastly denied that he had made a homosexual advance to Procter.

At last, appellant was given his traffic summons. Fugler then identified himself to appellant and invited him down to NASA for a talk. There, in a second floor office of the deserted "Tempo L" building, Fugler and a colleague interrogated him until after 6:00 a.m. During this interrogation, appellant allegedly conceded that he had engaged in mutual masturbation with other males in high school and college, that he sometimes experienced homosexual desires while drinking, that on rare occasions he had undergone a temporary blackout after drinking, and that on two such occasions he suspected he might have engaged in some sort of homosexual activity. He also said that he had experienced a blackout when he met Procter, recalling only that he had invited the man up for a drink.

Subsequently, in his formal reply to a notice of proposed dismissal, appellant specifically denied that he was a homosexual, that he had made an indecent advance to Procter, and that he had knowingly engaged in any homosexual activity during his adult life. Procter, however, confirmed in a written statement the story he gave the police at the time of his arrest and stated that "it would take an idiot not to be able to figure that he [appellant] wanted to have sex act on me."

Procter said he had never seen appellant before that night.

NASA concluded that appellant did in fact make a homosexual advance on October 22, and that this act amounted to "immoral, indecent, and disgraceful conduct." It also determined that on the basis of his own admissions to Fugler, even as subsequently clarified, appellant possesses "traits of character and personality which render [him] . . . unsuitable for further Government employment." A Civil Service Appeals Examiner and the Board of Appeals and Review upheld these conclusions. In appellant's action for reinstatement, the District Court granted appellee's motion for summary judgment.

II

Congress has provided that protected civil servants shall not be dismissed except "for such cause as will promote the efficiency of the service." The Civil Service Commission's regulations provide that an appointee may be removed, *inter alia*, for "infamous . . ., immoral, or notoriously disgraceful conduct" . . . and for "any . . . other disqualification which makes the individual unfit for the service." We think — and appellant does not strenuously deny — that the evidence was sufficient to sustain the charge that, consciously or not, he made a homosexual advance to Procter. Accordingly, the question presented is whether such an advance, or appellant's personality traits as disclosed by the record, are "such cause" for removal as the statute requires.

The Fifth Circuit Court of Appeals recently refused to consider a substantive attack on a dismissal for private homosexual conduct, apparently believing that it had no authority to review on the merits a Civil Service determination of unfitness.[5] The

---

5. *Anonymous v. Macy*, 398 F.2d 317 (5th Cir. 1968). The Court said only:

> Counsel for appellant . . . argue at great length, and with considerable ability, that homosexual acts constitute private acts upon the part of such employees, that they do not affect the efficiency of the service, and should not be the basis of discharge. That contention is not accepted by this Court. . . .

courts have, it is true, consistently recognized that the Commission enjoys a wide discretion in determining what reasons may justify removal of a federal employee; but it is also clear that this discretion is not unlimited. The Government's obligation to accord due process sets at least minimal substantive limits on its prerogative to dismiss its employees: it forbids all dismissals which are arbitrary and capricious. These constitutional limits may be greater where, as here, the dismissal imposes a "badge of infamy," disqualifying the victim from any further Federal employment, damaging his prospects for private employ, and fixing upon him the stigma of an official defamation of character. The due process clause may also cut deeper into the Government's discretion where a dismissal involves an intrusion upon that ill-defined area of privacy which is increasingly if indistinctly recognized as a foundation of several specific constitutional protections. Whatever their precise scope, these due process limitations apply even to those whose employment status is unprotected by statute. And statutes such as the Veterans' Preference Act were plainly designed to confer some additional job security not enjoyed by unprotected federal employees. As we recently observed in a closely related context,

> The requirement that there be "cause" for discharge imposes higher duties on the Government-as-employer than merely abstaining from violation of constitutional rights, a requirement that gives no substantive content to the statute.[12]

Accordingly, this court has previously examined the merits of a dismissal involving a statutorily protected employee charged with off-duty homosexual conduct.[13] In other cases, we have recognized that, besides complying with statutory procedural requirements, the employer agency must demonstrate some "rational basis" for its conclusion that a discharge "will promote the efficiency of the service." "The ultimate criterion [is] whether the employer acted reasonably." . . .

■ ■ ■

III

Preliminarily, we must reject appellee's contention that once the label "immoral" is plausibly attached to an employee's off-duty conduct, our inquiry into the presence of adequate rational cause for removal is at an end. A pronouncement of "immorality" tends to discourage careful analysis because it unavoidably connotes a violation of divine, Olympian, or otherwise universal standards of rectitude. However, the Civil Service Commission has neither the expertise nor the requisite anointment to make or enforce absolute moral judgments, and we do not understand that it purports to do so. Its jurisdiction is at least confined to the things which are Caesar's, and its avowed standard of "immorality" is no more than "the prevailing mores of our society."[18]

---

12. *Carter* v. *United States*, 407 F.2d 1238, 1244 (1968).

13. *Dew* v. *Halaby*, [317 F.2d 582 (1963), *cert. granted*, 376 U.S. 904, *cert. dismissed by agreement of the parties*, 379 U.S. 951 (1964).]

18. Letter from John W. Macy, Jr., Chairman, United States Civil Service Commission, to The Mattachine Society of Washington, Feb. 25, 1966, p. 3. In his brief, appellee says:

> There can be little doubt the Commission could properly determine that Norton's conduct was "immoral." Homosexual conduct is commonly considered as "immoral" under the prevailing mores of our society, as the Commission observed in a 1966 policy statement [i.e., the letter from Chairman Macy, *supra*] issued subsequent to its decision here.

So construed, "immorality" covers a multitude of sins. Indeed, it may be doubted whether there are in the entire Civil Service many persons so saintly as never to have done any act which is disapproved by the "prevailing mores of our society." Analytical philosophers would distinguish between acts conventionally regarded as morally wrong and acts which are disapproved merely as indecent, repulsive, or unesthetic; but if the Commission makes such a distinction, it is of no benefit to employees, who may assertedly be dismissed for "indecent and disgraceful" conduct as well as for "immorality."

We are not prepared to say that the Commission could not reasonably find appellant's homosexual advance to be "immoral," "indecent," or "notoriously disgraceful" under dominant conventional norms. But the notion that it could be an appropriate function of the federal bureaucracy to enforce the majority's conventional codes of conduct in the private lives of its employees is at war with elementary concepts of liberty, privacy, and diversity. And whatever we may think of the Government's qualifications to act *in loco parentis* in this way, the statute precludes it from discharging protected employees except for a reason related to the efficiency of the service. Accordingly, a finding that an employee has done something immoral or indecent could support a dismissal without further inquiry only if all immoral or indecent acts of an employee have some ascertainable deleterious effect on the efficiency of the service. The range of conduct which might be said to affront prevailing mores is so broad and varied that we can hardly arrive at any such conclusion without reference to specific conduct. Thus, we think the sufficiency of the charges against appellant must be evaluated in terms of the effects on the service of what in particular he has done or has been shown to be likely to do.

IV

In *Dew v. Halaby*, we upheld over strong dissent the dismissal of an air traffic controller predicated in part on homosexual acts he had committed some years before. That case does not control the present controversy, since it rested on the special demands of a position entailing continuing responsibility for many lives[21] and on the fact that the appellant was a "new employee with something to hide," not an established employee who had been subjected to a mid-career investigation. Moreover, the Supreme Court granted certiorari in *Dew*. The writ was dismissed by agreement of the parties when the FAA administrator rescinded his adverse action against the appellant, reinstated him, and granted him back pay. If these official actions may not be deemed a confession of error, the history of the case at least casts considerable doubt on the authority of what was, in any event, a narrow holding.

The homosexual conduct of an employee might bear on the efficiency of the

---

21. The court said it could not

> ignore the nature of appellant's duties. He was acting as an airport traffic controller. His duties were to regulate the flow of air traffic, issue clearances for the take-off and landing of planes, and maintain the proper separation of planes on the ground and in the air. His job thus gave him control over safeguarding the lives of passengers, crews, and persons on the ground. That such a position requires skill, alertness, and above all responsibility requires no demonstration. . . . We lack the background and experience to say, contrary to the agency's judgment, that efficiency will not be promoted by removing one from such a post as was held by appellant, when his questioned "conduct or capacity" in the past did not demonstrate qualities of character, stability, and responsibility.

317 F.2d at 587-88.

service in a number of ways. Because of the potential for blackmail, it might jeopardize the security of classified communications. As we acknowledged in *Dew v. Halaby*, it may in some circumstances be evidence of an unstable personality unsuited for certain kinds of work. If an employee makes offensive overtures while on the job, or if his conduct is notorious, the reactions of other employees and of the public with whom he comes in contact in the performance of his official functions may be taken into account. Whether or not such potential consequences would justify removal, they are at least broadly relevant to "the efficiency of the service."

The peculiar feature of appellant's dismissal, however, is that it rests on none of these possible effects on the service. The NASA official who fired him, Mr. Garbarini, testified that appellant was a "competent employee" doing "very good" work. In fact, Garbarini was "not worried" about any possible effect on appellant's performance, and went so far as to inquire of personnel officers "if there was any way around this kind of problem for the man . . . ." He "considered whether or not we had real security problems here to worry about" and concluded "there was not enough of that to influence me." Appellant's duties apparently did not bring him into contact with the public, and his fellow employees were unaware of his "immorality." Nonetheless, Garbarini's advisers told him that dismissal for any homosexual conduct was a "*custom* within the agency," and he decided to follow the custom because continued employment of appellant might "turn out to be embarrassing to the agency" in that "if an incident like this occurred again, it could become a public scandal on the agency."

V

Thus, appellee is now obliged to rely solely on this possibility of embarrassment to the agency to justify appellant's dismissal. The assertion of such a nebulous "cause" poses perplexing problems for a review proceeding which must accord broad discretion to the Commission. We do not doubt that NASA blushes whenever one of its own is caught *in flagrante delictu*; but if the possibility of such transitory institutional discomfiture must be uncritically accepted as a cause for discharge which will "promote the efficiency of the service," we might as well abandon all pretense that the statute provides any substantive security for its supposed beneficiaries. A claim of possible embarrassment might, of course, be a vague way of referring to some specific potential interference with an agency's performance; but it might also be a smokescreen hiding personal antipathies or moral judgments which are excluded by statute as grounds for dismissal. A reviewing court must at least be able to discern some reasonably foreseeable, specific connection between an employee's potentially embarrassing conduct and the efficiency of the service. Once the connection is established, then it is for the agency and the Commission to decide whether it outweighs the loss to the service of a particular competent employee.

In the instant case appellee has shown us no such specific connection. Indeed, on the record appellant is at most an extremely infrequent offender,[26] who neither openly flaunts nor carelessly displays his unorthodox sexual conduct in public.[27] Thus, even the potential for the embarrassment the

---

26. Apart from the incident after which he was arrested, appellant said he suspected he might have engaged in homosexual activity on three occasions since his graduation from college.

27. There is no evidence that he was ever engaged in any offensive conduct in public. His private conduct came to light only through police investigative tactics of at least questionable legality.

agency fears is minimal. We think the un-particularized and unsubstantiated conclusion that such possible embarrassment threatens the quality of the agency's performance is an arbitrary ground for dismissal.[28]

■ ■ ■

Lest there be any doubt, we emphasize that we do not hold that homosexual conduct may never be cause for dismissal of a protected federal employee. Nor do we even conclude that potential embarrassment from an employee's private conduct may in no circumstances affect the efficiency of the service. What we do say is that, if the statute is to have any force, an agency cannot support a dismissal as promoting the efficiency of the service merely by turning its head and crying "shame."

Since we conclude that appellant's discharge cannot be sustained on the grounds relied on by the Commission, the judgment of the District Court must be

Reversed.

TAMM, J. (dissenting):

■ ■ ■

. . . I would affirm. To do otherwise would implicate me in the setting of precedent for the proposition that offduty homosexual conduct, coupled with a capacity for "blackingout" while intoxicated, bears no real relationship to the functioning of an efficient service within a government agency. Homosexuals, sadly enough, do not leave their emotions at Lafayette Square and regardless of their spiritual destinies they still present targets for public reproach and private extortion. I believe this record supports the finding that this individual presents more than a potential risk in this regard and that his termination will serve the efficiency of the service. Despite the billows of puffery that continue to float out of recent opinions on this subject, I believe that the theory that homosexual conduct is not in any way related to the efficiency and effectiveness of governmental business is not an evil theory — just a very unrealistic one.

■ ■ ■

---

28. We note that the Civil Service Commission of the City of New York has recently determined that homosexual conduct is not an automatic bar to employment by the City. Rather, the Commission says:

> Policy dictates that with reference to a homosexual applicant the commission would be required to determine the personal qualities reasonably considered indispensable to the duties of the position, and then to reasonably determine whether the applicant's condition is inconsistent with the possession of these qualities to the extent of rendering him unfit to assume the duties of the position.

New York Times, May 9, 1969, pp. 1, 23.

The most widely accepted study of American sexual practices estimates that "at least thirty-seven percent" of the American male population have at least one homosexual experience during their lifetime. Kinsey, Pomeroy & Martin, *Sexual Behavior in the Human Male* 623 (1948). If this is so, a policy of excluding all persons who have engaged in homosexual conduct from government employ would disqualify for public service over one-third of the male population. This result would be both inherently absurd and devastating to the public service. The public service is protected from the consequences of any such policy by its inability to identify most of the offending males. But we must assume that the Government carries many such potentially embarrassing employees on its roles without noticeable impact on the efficiency of the service.

SINGER v. UNITED STATES CIVIL SERVICE COM'N.

530 F.2d 247 (9th Cir. 1976), *vacated,* 429 U.S. 1034 (1977)

JAMESON, District Judge, sitting by designation:

■ ■ ■

FACTUAL BACKGROUND

On August 2, 1971, Singer was hired by the Seattle Office of the Equal Employment Opportunity Commission (EEOC) as a clerk typist. Pursuant to 5 C.F.R. § 315.801 *et seq.*, he was employed for one year on probationary status, subject to termination if "his work performance or conduct during this period (failed) to demonstrate his fitness or his qualifications for continued employment." At the time he was hired Singer informed the Director of EEOC that he was a homesexual.

On May 12, 1972, an investigator for the Civil Service Commission sent a letter to Singer inviting him "to appear voluntarily for an interview to comment upon, explain or rebut adverse information which has come to the attention of the Commission" as a result of its investigation to determine Singer's "suitability for employment in the competitive Federal service." The interview was set for May 19. Singer appeared at the appointed time with his counsel. Singer was advised that the investigation by the Commission disclosed that "you are homosexual. You openly profess that you are homosexual and you have received wide-spread publicity in this respect in at least two states." Specific acts were noted, which may be summarized as follows:

1. During Singer's previous employment with a San Francisco mortgage firm Singer had "flaunted" his homosexuality by kissing and embracing a male in front of the elevator in the building where he was employed and kissing a male in the company cafeteria;

2. *The San Francisco Chronicle* wrote an article on Singer in November of 1970 in which he stated his name and occupation and views on "closet queens";

3. At the Seattle EEOC office Singer openly admitted being "gay" and indicated by his dress and demeanor that he intended to continue homosexual activity as a "way of life";

4. On September 20, 1971, Singer and another man applied to the King County Auditor for a marriage license, which was eventually refused by the King County Superior Court;[2]

5. As a result of the attempt to obtain the marriage license Singer was the subject of extensive television, newspaper and magazine publicity;

6. Articles published in the Seattle papers of September 21, 1971 included Singer's identification as a typist employed by EEOC and quoted Singer as saying, in part, that he and the man he sought to marry were "two human beings who happen to be in love and want to get married for various reasons";

---

2. The order was appealed. In *Singer* v. *Hara*, 11 Wash. App. 247, 522 P.2d 1187 (1974), the Court of Appeals of Washington affirmed the Superior Court and held that the Washington statutory prohibition against same-sex marriages did not violate any constitutional right. A petition for review was denied by the Supreme Court of Washington.

7. Singer was active as an "organizer, leader and member of the Board of Directors of the Seattle Gay Alliance, Inc."; his name accompanied by (his) "place of employment appeared as one of the individuals involved in the planning and conducting of a symposium presented by the Seattle Gay Community"; he appeared in a radio "talk show" and displayed homosexual advertisements on the windows of his automobile;

8. Singer sent a letter to the Civil Service Commission about a planned symposium on employment discrimination stating in part, "I work for the E.E.O.C., and am openly Gay . . ."

Singer was offered an opportunity to comment "regarding these matters". He did not do so. On May 22 his counsel by letter requested a citation to the Civil Service regulations under which the investigation was proceeding and any regulation related to his alleged unsuitability for employment. In a response dated May 23 the Commission stated that its authority was found in Rule 5, Section 5.2 of the Civil Service Rules and Regulations; and that the "suitability standards in Section 731.201 of the Commission's regulations" cite as disqualifying factors: "Criminal, infamous, dishonest, immoral, or notoriously disgraceful conduct".

Singer and his counsel were given a further opportunity to appear on Wednesday, May 24, to make a statement or give further information. Instead an affidavit was presented dated May 26, in which Singer stated that (1) he had read the investigative report; (2) the identification of his employment as a typist for the EEOC (6 above) was done by the newspaper without his "specific authorization"; (3) the use of his place of employment with respect to the symposium (7 above) was "not specifically authorized" by him and "was done without (his) knowledge or consent"; and (4) he saw nothing in the report "which in any way indicates that my conduct has been in violation of regulations pertaining to federal employees".

By letter dated June 26, 1972 the Chief of the Investigations Division of the Seattle office of the Civil Service Commission notified Singer that by reason of his "immoral and notoriously disgraceful conduct" he was disqualified under Section 731.201(b) of the Civil Service Regulations (5 CFR § 731.201(b)) and that his agency had been directed to separate him from the service.[3]

Singer appealed the decision. Following the submission of briefs, the Hearing Examiner, on September 14, 1972 upheld the decision of the Chief of the Investigations Division. In advising Singer that instructions for his removal were being renewed, the Examiner reviewed the virtually unrefuted charges against Singer and continued in part:

"In reaching a decision on your appeal, careful consideration has been given to the written representations and evidence submitted in your behalf by Attorney Christopher E. Young on

---

3. The reasons for the Commission's conclusion were set forth in the letter as follows:

"The information developed by the investigation, taken with your reply, indicate that you have flaunted and broadcast your homosexual activities and have sought and obtained publicity in various media in pursuit of this goal.... Your activities in these matters are those of an advocate for a socially repugnant concept.

"... In determining that your employment will not promote the efficiency of the service, the Commission has considered such pertinent factors as the potential disruption of service efficiency because of the possible revulsion of other employees to homosexual conduct and/or their apprehension of homosexual advances and solicitations; the hazard that the prestige and authority of a Government position will be used to foster homosexual activity, particularly among youth; the possible use of Government funds and authority in furtherance of conduct offensive to the mores and law of our society; and the possible embarrassment to, and loss of public confidence in, your agency and the Federal civil service."

September 7, 1972, in lieu of an opportunity for personal appearance afforded to you on that date. In pertinent part, these representations contend that your supervisor and co-workers have experienced no complaint with your performance or conduct on the job,[4] and that your removal will not promote the efficiency of the service. The appellate representations otherwise disagree with the Commission's determination that homosexual conduct is immoral in nature and does not meet requirements of suitability for the Federal service, contending that such actions based on an individual's personal sexuality and sexual activities are violative of constitutional rights of privacy and free speech.

"However, there is more to the 'efficiency of the service' than the proper performance of assigned duties. The immoral and notoriously disgraceful conduct which is established by the evidence in your case, in our view, does have a direct and material bearing upon your fitness for Federal employment. Activities of the type you have engaged in, which has not been limited to activity conducted in private, are such that general public knowledge thereof would reflect discredit upon the Federal government as your employer, impeding the efficiency of the service by lessening general public confidence in the fitness of the government to conduct the public business with which it is entrusted. The federal government, like any employer, may be judged by the character and conduct of the persons in its employ, and it will promote the efficiency of the service to remove from its employ any individual whose determental influence will detract from that efficiency."

Singer appealed to the United States Civil Service Commission, Board of Appeals and Review. In a decision and order dated December 1, 1972 the Board affirmed the decision of the Regional Office dated September 14, 1972 saying in part:

"There is evidence in the file which indicated that appellant's actions establish that he has engaged in immoral and notoriously disgraceful conduct, openly and publicly flaunting his homosexual way of life and indicating further continuance of such activities. Activities of the type he has engaged in are such that general public knowledge thereof reflects discredit upon the Federal Government as his employer, impeding the efficiency of the service by lessening general public confidence in the fitness of the Government to conduct the public business with which it is entrusted."

On December 29, 1972 Singer filed this action on behalf of himself and other persons similarly situated, seeking injunctive and declaratory relief. The complaint was later amended to include a prayer for damages and an order restoring Singer to his Civil Service position. Summary judgment of dismissal with prejudice was entered on March 29, 1974.

■ ■ ■

DISMISSAL FOR HOMOSEXUAL ACTIVITES

. . . we turn to those cases which have considered homosexual activities as a basis for dismissal of Civil Service employees. The leading case is *Norton v. Macy.*

■ ■ ■

---

4. In an evaluation report, Singer had been rated by his supervisor as "superior" or "very good" in various categories of job performance. A letter from his co-workers expressed the opinion that Singer had been a competent employee and that their experience with him had been "educational and positive".

Norton v. Macy was construed by another panel of the Court of Appeals for the District of Columbia, in *Gayer v. Schlessinger*, 490 F.2d 740 (1973) . . . The court concluded regarding *Norton*, "Thus the court said in part that a rational connection between an employee's homosexual conduct and the efficiency of the service may exist" justifying agency personnel action. . . . The court in *Gayer* concluded that, "As in other decisions of importance the bearing of particular conduct must be left to a rational appraisal based on relevant facts"; that the determination of the government agency should be "explained in such manner that a reviewing court may be able to discern whether there is a rational connection between the facts relied upon and the conclusions reached"; that some deference must be accorded the decision of the agency; and that the "degree of this deference must be the result of a nice but not easily definable weighing of the ingredients of which the particular case is comprised".

In *Society for Individual Rights, Inc. v. Hampton*, 63 F.R.D. 399 (N.D. Cal. 1973), an organization of homosexual persons and a discharged employee brought an action to "challenge the United States Civil Service Commission's policy as stated in Federal Personnel Manual Supplement (Int.) 731-71, of excluding from government employment all persons who have engaged in or solicited others to engage in homosexual acts".[12] The court found that the decision of the Board of Appeals and Review was "based solely upon the fact that plaintiff is presently a homosexual person and the Commission's view that the employment of such persons will bring the government service into 'public contempt'". Following *Norton v. Macy*, the court held that the "Commission can discharge a person for immoral behavior only if that behavior actually impairs the efficiency

of the service", and that the Commission had not met, or even tried to meet, this standard. The court accordingly ordered reinstatement of the discharged employee and that the Commission "forthwith cease excluding or discharging from government service any homosexual person whom the Commission would deem unfit for government employment solely because the employment of such a person in the government service might bring that service into the type of public contempt which might reduce the government's ability to perform the public business with the essential respect and confidence of the citizens which it serves".

The court recognized, however, that "granting this relief will not interfere with the power of the Commission to dismiss a person for homosexual conduct in those circumstances where more is involved than the Commission's unparticularized and unsubstantiated conclusion that possible embarrassment about an employee's homosexual conduct threatens the quality of the government's performance. Thus, although the overbroad rule stated in Federal Personnel Manual Supplement (Int.) cannot be enforced, the Commission is free to consider what particular circumstances might justify dismissing an employee for charges relating to homosexual conduct."

CHANGES IN CIVIL SERVICE REGULATIONS AND PERSONNEL MANUAL

At oral argument counsel called attention to changes in the Personnel Manual following *Society for Individual Rights v. Hampton*, which were set forth in a bulletin issued

---

12. The manual read in pertinent part:

"*Homosexuality and Sexual Perversion* —

Persons about whom there is evidence that they have engaged in or solicited others to engage in homosexual or sexually perverted acts with them, without evidence of rehabilitation, are not suitable for Federal employment."

December 21, 1973,[14] and also to amendments to the Civil Service Regulations relating to Suitability Disqualification, which became effective July 2, 1975[15] following rule-making proceedings initiated on December 3, 1973. The bulletin issued on December 21, 1973 was not made a part of the record in this case, and it does not appear that it was called to the attention of the district court. The new regulations were adopted subsequent to the entry of judgment and during the pendency of this appeal. Our decision in this case is based on the record before the district court and the regulations and guidelines in effect when appellant's contract was terminated.

REASON FOR TERMINATION
OF EMPLOYMENT

We conclude from a review of the record in its entirety that appellant's employment was not terminated because of his status as a homosexual or because of any private acts of sexual preference. The statements of the Commission's investigation division, hearing examiner, and Board of Appeals make it clear that the discharge was the result of appellant's "openly and publicly flaunting his homosexual way of life and indicating further continuance of such activities", while identifying himself as a member of a federal agency. The Commission found that these activities were such that "general public knowledge thereof reflects discredit upon the Federal Government as his employer, impeding the efficiency of the service by lessening public confidence in the fitness of the Government to conduct the public business with which it was entrusted."

This case is factually distinguishable from *Norton v. Macy* and the other cases discussed *supra*, involving private sexual acts and considering situations where there was no showing that the discharge would "promote the efficiency of the service". It is apparent from their statements that the Commission and its officials appreciated the requirement of *Norton v. Macy*, decided three years earlier, that discharge of a homosexual must be justified by a finding that his conduct affected the efficiency of the service. As noted *supra*, *Norton v. Macy* rec-

---

14. The bulletin called attention to the opinion in *Hampton,* noting that it was a class action and applicable to all federal employees. The Commission, therefore, instructed those "engaged in suitability evaluation" as follows:

    "Accordingly, you may not find a person unsuitable for Federal employment merely because that person is a homosexual or has engaged in homosexual acts, nor may such exclusion be based on a conclusion that a homosexual person might bring the public service into public contempt. You are, however, permitted to dismiss a person or find him or her unsuitable for Federal employment where the evidence establishes that such person's homosexual conduct affects job fitness - excluding from such consideration, however, unsubstantiated conclusions concerning possible embarrassment to the Federal service."

15. 5 C.F.R. Part 73, relating to Suitability Disqualification, was substantially amended. In the provision listing reasons for disqualification, the word "immoral" was deleted, Section 731.202(b), as amended reading in part: "(2) Criminal, dishonest, infamous or notoriously disgraceful conduct". The "Suitability Guidelines for Federal Employment" was revised to conform to the new regulations. The amended guidelines for determining "Infamous or Notoriously Disgraceful Conduct" reads in part:

    "Individual sexual conduct will be considered under the guides discussed above. Court decisions require that persons not be disqualified from Federal employment solely on the basis of homosexual conduct. The Commission and agencies have been enjoined not to find a person unsuitable for Federal employment solely because that person is homosexual or has engaged in homosexual acts. Based upon these court decisions and outstanding injunction, while a person may not be found unsuitable based on unsubstantiated conclusions concerning possible embarrassment to the Federal service, a person may be dismissed or found unsuitable for Federal employment where the evidence establishes that such person's sexual conduct affects job fitness."

ognized that notorious conduct and open flaunting and careless display of unorthodox sexual conduct in public might be relevant to the efficiency of the service. The Commission set forth in detail the specified conduct upon which it relied in determining appellant's unsuitability for continued employment in the competitive Federal service. We are able to discern "a rational connection between the facts relied upon and the conclusions drawn" and agree with the district court that there was substantial evidence to support the findings and conclusions of the Civil Service Commission.

FIRST AMENDMENT RIGHTS

With respect to appellant's contention that his First Amendment rights have been violated, appellant relies on two cases which deserve comment. The first of these cases, *Gay Students Org. of University of New Hampshire v. Bonner*, 509 F.2d 651 (1 Cir. 1974), did not involve public employment, but rather the validity of a regulation prohibiting a homosexual organization from holding social activities on the campus. The court concluded that "The GSO's efforts to organize the homosexual minority, 'educate' the public as to its plight, and obtain for it better treatment from individuals and from the government . . . represent but another example of the associational activity unequivocally singled out for protection in the very 'core' of association cases decided by the Supreme Court". In holding that "conduct may have a communicative content sufficient to bring it within the ambit of the First Amendment", the Court also recognized that "Communicative conduct is subject to regulation as to 'time, place and manner' in the furtherance of a substantial governmental interest, so long as the restrictions imposed are only so broad as required in order to further the interest and are unrelated to the content and subject matter of the message communicated."

In *Acanfora v. Board of Education of Montgomery County*, 491 F.2d 498 (4 Cir. 1974), the Board had transferred Acanfora to a nonteaching position when they found that he was a homosexual. The Board's action was upheld on the ground that Acanfora had deliberately withheld from his application information relating to his homosexuality. In holding, however, that Acanfora's public statements on homosexuality were protected by the First Amendment, the court recognized the balancing test set forth in *Pickering v. Board of Education, supra*, and continued:

"At the invitation of the Public Broadcasting System, Acanfora appeared with his parents on a program designed to help parents and homosexual children cope with the problems that confront them. Acanfora also consented to other television, radio, and press interviews. The transcripts of the television programs, which the district court found to be typical of all the interviews, disclose that he spoke about the difficulties homosexuals encounter, and, while he did not advocate homosexuality, he sought community acceptance. He also stressed that he had not, and would not, discuss his sexuality with the students.

"In short, the record discloses that press, radio, and television commentators considered homosexuality in general, and Acanfora's plight in particular, to be a matter of public interest about which reasonable people could differ, and Acanfora responded to their inquiries in a rational manner. There is no evidence that the interviews disrupted the school, substantially impaired his capacity as a teacher, or gave the school officials reasonable grounds to forecast that these results would flow from what he said. We hold, therefore, that Acanfora's public statements were protected by the first amendment and that they do not justify either the action taken by the school system or the dismissal of his suit."

Bonner and *Acanfora* are factually distinguishable. Neither involved the open and public flaunting or advocacy of homosexual conduct. Applying the balancing test of *Pickering v. Board of Education*, the Commission could properly conclude that under the facts of this case, the interest of the Government as an employer "in promoting the efficiency of the public service" outweighed the interest of its employee in exercising his First Amendment Rights through publicly flaunting and broadcasting his homosexual activities.

Affirmed.

Notes

1. The Ninth Circuit's decision in *Singer* was vacated by the Supreme Court at the request of the United States government following the change in administrations (with President Carter's election in 1976) and the adoption of new civil service regulations.

2. The *Singer* case notes that one of the facts that led to Singer's dismissal was his attempted marriage to another man. This case, *Singer v. Hara*, 522 P.2d 1187 (Wash. App. 1974), is discussed at pp. 410-417, *infra*. Other lesbian and gay employees who have attempted to marry have lost their jobs on this basis. *See* Chapter 5, *infra*, discussing, *inter alia*, *McConnell v. Anderson*, 451 F.2d 193 (8th Cir. 1971); *Shahar v. Bowers*, 58 Fair Empl. Prac. Cas. (BNA) 668 (N.D. Ga. 1992).

3. As noted above, reading *Singer* and *Norton* together raise the issue of how "open" a gay employee can afford to be. Unlike Norton, Singer's openness about his homosexuality cost him his job. The court's adoption of a "flaunting" standard has been used against other lesbian and gay employees. *See, e.g., McConnell v. Anderson*, 451 F.2d 193 (8th Cir. 1971). *But see Aumiller v. University of Delaware.*, 434 F. Supp. 1273 (D. Del. 1977) (public statements about homosexuality did not disrupt workplace and thus plaintiff's employment safeguarded by First Amendment).

4. The *Norton* case also suggests that the nature of the workplace is key to consideration of the rights of the gay employee. Consider, for instance, the court's acceptance of the D.C. Circuit's decision in *Dew v. Hallaby*, 317 F.2d 582 (D.C. Cir. 1963), *cert. granted*, 376 U.S. 904, *cert. dismissed by agreement of the parties*, 379 U.S. 951 (1964). What aspects of an air traffic controller job make lesbians and gay men unfit for such positions? Consider also the different job categories discussed below.

5. In *Swift v. United States of America*, 649 F. Supp. 596 (D.D.C. 1986), the federal District Court denied the government's motion to dismiss an equal protection claim brought by a gay stenographer at the White House who was relieved of his duties after his sexual orientation was discovered.

6. As noted above, public protections for civil servants have been extended to employees of private utilities company on the theory that the company is sufficiently public for the purposes of employment discrimination because the company serves the general public and has public grants of monopoly. In *Gay Law Students Ass'n v. Pacific Telephone & Telegraph Co.*, 595 P.2d 592 (Cal. 1979), the Supreme Court of California ruled that a private utility with a public monopoly must abide by California's employment discrimination rules for public employers.

7. Public employer benefit programs that do not cover partners of lesbian and gay employees have been challenged in court by gay employees under several theories — for example, that they violate statutes prohibiting discrimination on the basis of sexual orientation and/or marital status; and/or that they violate the equal protection clause. The results have been mixed. In *Hinman v. Department of Personnel Administration*, 167 Cal. App. 3d 516, 213 Cal. Rptr. 410 (1985), the court upheld the denial of dental benefits to partners of gay state employees against two main

charges: (1) that it violated the California Constitution's guarantee of equal protection both by not considering gay partners "spouses" or "family members" and by discriminating on the basis of marital status; and (2) that it violated the Governor's Executive Order prohibiting discrimination on the basis of sexual orientation in state employment.

A similar decision was rendered in *Phillips v. Wisconsin Personnel Commission*, 482 N.W.2d 121 (Wisc. Ct. App. 1992), in which the court upheld the denial of family health coverage to the lesbian lover of a state employee. The court stated: "[T]he rule applies equally to hetero- and homosexual employees and thus does not discriminate against the latter group. Nor does the rule treat one gender differently than the other. . . . It is keyed to marriage and . . . it does not illegally discriminate by doing so."

Nevertheless, an appellate court in New York recently upheld a lower court decision denying the city's motion to dismiss in a case challenging the failure of the city to provide health insurance benefits to the partners of lesbian and gay teachers. *Gay Teachers Association v. Board of Education of New York*, 585 N.Y.S. 2d 1016 (App. Div., 1st Dept. 1992). These cases are discussed *infra* at Chapter 5.

B. Teachers

The issue of lesbian and gay school teachers has given rise to a terrific amount of public concern, legislation, and litigation. These cases add an extra dimension to a standard civil service case — namely, the relationship of lesbians and gay men to children. Two related issues arise in this context: first, a mythical concern that there is some connection between sexual orientation and child molestation and second, a concern about whether gay people are good "role models" for children.

A section from Sherwood Anderson's classic work, *Winesburg, Ohio*, illuminates some of the myths about gay school teachers.

◆

WINESBURG, OHIO
Sherwood Anderson

Upon the half decayed veranda of a small frame house that stood near the edge of a ravine near the town of Winesburg, Ohio, a fat little old man walked nervously up and down. Across a long field that had been seeded for clover but that had produced only a dense crop of yellow mustard weeds, he could see the public highway along which went a wagon filled with berry pickers returning from the fields. The berry pickers,

SHERWOOD ANDERSON, WINESBURG, OHIO 27-34 (1919).

youths and maidens, laughed and shouted boisterously. A boy clad in a blue shirt leaped from the wagon and attempted to drag after him one of the maidens, who screamed and protested shrilly. The feet of the boy in the road kicked up a cloud of dust that floated across the face of the departing sun. Over the long field came a thin girlish voice. "Oh, you Wing Biddlebaum, comb your hair, it is falling into your eyes," commanded the voice to the man, who was bald and whose nervous little hands fiddled about the bare white forehead as though arranging a mass of tangled locks.

Wing Biddlebaum, forever frightened and beset by a ghostly band of doubts, did not think of himself as in any way a part of the life of the town where he had lived for twenty years. Among all the people of Winesburg but one had come close to him. With George Willard, son of Tom Willard, the proprietor of the New Willard House, he had formed something like a friendship. George Willard was the reporter on the *Winesburg Eagle* and sometimes in the evenings he walked out along the highway to Wing Biddlebaum's house. Now as the old man walked up and down on the veranda, his hands moving nervously about, he was hoping that George Willard would come and spend the evening with him. After the wagon containing the berry pickers had passed, he went across the field through the tall mustard weeds and climbing a rail fence peered anxiously along the road to the town. For a moment he stood thus, rubbing his hands together and looking up and down the road, and then, fear overcoming him, ran back to walk again upon the porch on his own house.

In the presence of George Willard, Wing Biddlebaum who for twenty years had been the town mystery, lost something of his timidity, and his shadowy personality, submerged in a sea of doubts, came forth to look at the world. With the young reporter at his side, he ventured in the light of day into Main Street or strode up and down on the rickety front porch of his own house, talking excitedly. The voice that had been low and

trembling become shrill and loud. The bent figure straightened. With a kind of wriggle, like a fish returned to the brook by the fisherman, Biddlebaum the silent began to talk, striving to put into words the ideas that had been accumulated by his mind during long years of silence.

Wing Biddlebaum talked much with his hands. The slender expressive fingers, forever active, forever striving to conceal themselves in his pockets or behind his back, came forth and became the piston rods of his machinery of expression.

The story of Wing Biddlebaum is a story of hands. Their restless activity, like unto the beating of the wings of an imprisoned bird, had given him his name. Some obscure poet of the town had thought of it. The hands alarmed their owner. He wanted to keep them hidden away and looked with amazement at the quiet inexpressive hands of other men who worked beside him in the fields, or passed, driving sleepy teams on country roads.

When he talked to George Willard, Wing Biddlebaum closed his fists and beat with them upon a table or on the walls of his house. The action made him more comfortable. If the desire to talk came to him when the two were walking in the fields, he sought out a stump or the top board of a fence and with his hands pounding busily talked with renewed ease.

The story of Wing Biddlebaum's hands is worth a book in itself. Sympathetically set forth it would tap many strange, beautiful qualities in obscure men. It is a job for a poet. In Winesburg the hands had attracted attention merely because of their activity. With them Wing Biddlebaum had picked as high as a hundred and forty quarts of strawberries in a day. They became his distinguishing feature, the source of his fame. Also they made more grotesque an already grotesque and elusive individuality. Winesburg was proud of the hands of Wing Biddlebaum in the same spirit in which it was proud of Banker White's new stone house and Wesley Moyer's bay stallion,

Tony Tip, that had won the two-fifteen trot at the fall races in Cleveland.

As for George Willard, he had many times wanted to ask about hands. At times an almost overwhelming curiosity had taken hold of him. He felt that there must be a reason for their strange activity and their inclination to keep hidden away and only a growing respect for Wing Biddlebaum kept him from blurting out the questions that were often in his mind.

Once he had been on the point of asking. The two were walking in the fields on a summer afternoon and had stopped to sit upon a grassy bank. All afternoon Wing Biddlebaum had talked as one inspired. By a fence he had stopped and beating like a giant woodpecker upon the top board had shouted at George Willard, condemning his tendency to be too much influenced by the people about him. "You are destroying yourself," he cried. "You have the inclination to be alone and to dream and you are afraid of dreams. You want to be like others in town here. You hear them talk and try to imitate them."

On the grassy bank Wing Biddlebaum had tried again to drive his point home. His voice became soft and reminiscent, and with a sigh of contentment he launched into a long rambling talk, speaking as one lost in a dream.

Out of the dream Wing Biddlebaum made a picture for George Willard. In the picture men lived again in a kind of pastoral golden age. Across a green open country came clean-limbed young men, some afoot, some mounted upon horses. In crowds the young men came to gather about the feet of an old man who sat beneath a tree in a tiny garden and who talked to them.

Wing Biddlebaum become wholly inspired. For once he forgot the hands. Slowly they stole forth and lay upon George Willard's shoulders. Something new and bold came into the voice that talked. "You must try to forget all you have learned," said the old man. "You must begin to dream. From this time on you must shut your ears to the roaring of the voices."

Pausing in his speech, Wing Biddlebaum looked long and earnestly at George Willard. His eyes glowed. Again he raised the hands to caress the boy and then a look of horror swept over his face.

With convulsive movement of his body, Wing Biddlebaum sprang to his feet and thrust his hands deep into his trousers pockets. Tears came to his eyes. "I must be getting along home. I can talk no more with you," he said nervously.

Without looking back, the old man had hurried down the hillside and across a meadow, leaving George Willard perplexed and frightened upon the grassy slope. With a shiver of dread the boy arose and went along the road toward town. "I'll not ask him about his hands," he thought, touched by the memory of the terror he had seen in the man's eyes. "There's something wrong, but I don't want to know what it is. His hands have something to do with his fear of me and of everyone."

And George Willard was right. Let us look briefly into the story of the hands. Perhaps our talking of them will arouse the poet who will tell the hidden wonder story of the influence for which the hands were but fluttering pennants of promise.

In his youth Wing Biddlebaum had been a school teacher in a town in Pennsylvania. He was not then known as Wing Biddlebaum, but went by the less euphonic name of Adolph Myers. As Adolph Myers he was much loved by the boys of his school.

Adolph Myers was meant by nature to be a teacher of youth. He was one of those rare, little-understood men who rule by a power so gentle that it passes as a lovable weakness. In their feeling for the boys under their charge such men are not unlike the finer sort of women in their love of men.

And yet that is but crudely stated. It needs the poet there. With the boys of his school, Adolph Myers had walked in the evening or had sat talking until dusk upon the schoolhouse steps lost in a kind of dream. Here and there went his hands, caressing the shoulders of the boys, playing about the tousled heads. As he talked his voice became soft and musical. There was a caress in that also. In a way the voice and the hands, the stroking of the shoulders and the touching of the hair were a part of the school master's effort to carry a dream into the young minds. By the caress that was in his fingers he expressed himself. He was one of those men in whom the force that creates life is diffused, not centralized. Under the caress of his hands doubt and disbelief went out of the minds of the boys and they began also to dream.

And then the tragedy. A half-witted boy of the school became enamored of the young master. In his bed at night he imagined unspeakable things and in the morning went forth to tell his dreams as facts. Strange, hideous accusations fell from his loose-hung lips. Through the Pennsylvania town went a shiver. Hidden, shadowy doubts that had been in men's minds concerning Adolph Myers were galvanized into beliefs.

The tragedy did not linger. Trembling lads were jerked out of bed and questioned. "He put his arms about me," said one. "His fingers were always playing in my hair," said another.

One afternoon a man of the town, Henry Bradford, who kept a saloon, came to the schoolhouse door. Calling Adolph Myers into the school yard he began to beat him with his fists. As his hard knuckles beat down into the frightened face of the schoolmaster, his wrath became more and more terrible. Screaming with dismay, the children ran here and there like disturbed insects. "I'll teach you to put your hands on my boy, you beast," roared the saloon keeper, who, tired of beating the master, had begun to kick him about the yard.

Adolph Myers was driven from the Pennsylvania town in the night. With lanterns in their hands a dozen men came to the door of the house where he lived alone and commanded that he dress and come forth. It was raining and one of the men had a rope in his hands. They had intended to hang the schoolmaster, but something in his figure, so small, white, and pitiful, touched their hearts and they let him escape. As he ran away into the darkness they repented of their weakness and ran after him, swearing and throwing sticks and great balls of soft mud at the figure that screamed and ran faster and faster into the darkness.

For twenty years Adolph Myers had lived alone in Winesburg. He was but forty but looked sixty-five. The name of Biddlebaum he got from a box of goods seen at a freight station as he hurried through an eastern Ohio town. He had an aunt in Winesburg, a black-toothed old woman who raised chickens and with her he lived until she died. He had been ill for a year after the experience in Pennsylvania, and after his recovery worked as a day laborer in the fields, going timidly about and striving to conceal his hands. Although he did not understand what had happened he felt that the hands must be to blame. Again and again the fathers of the boys had talked of the hands. "Keep your hands to yourself," the saloon keeper had roared, dancing with fury in the schoolhouse yard.

Upon the veranda of his house by the ravine, Wing Biddlebaum continued to walk up and down until the sun had disappeared and the road beyond the field was lost in the grey shadows. Going into his house he cut slices of bread and spread honey upon them. When the rumble of the evening train that took away the express cars loaded with the day's harvest of berries had passed and restored the silence of the summer night, he went again to walk upon the veranda. In the darkness he could not see the hands and they became quiet. Although he still hungered for the presence of the boy, who was the medium through which he expressed his love of man, the hunger became again a part of his loneliness and his waiting. Lighting a lamp, Wing Biddlebaum washed the few dishes soiled by his simple meal and, setting up a folding cot by he screen door that led to the porch, prepared to undress for the night. A few stray white bread crumbs lay on the cleanly washed floor by the table; putting the lamp upon a low stool he began to pick up the crumbs, carrying them to his mouth one by one with unbelievable rapidity. In the dense blotch of light beneath the table, the kneeling figure looked like a priest engaged in some service of his church. The nervous expressive fingers, flashing in and out of the light, might well have been mistaken for the fingers of the devotee going swiftly through decade after decade of his rosary.

The following cases illustrate different aspects of the way in which these issues often play out.

GAYLORD v. TACOMA SCHOOL DISTRICT NO. 10

559 P.2d 1340 (Wash. 1977), *cert. denied,* 434 U.S. 879 (1977)

HOROWITZ, J.

■ ■ ■

Defendant school district discharged Gaylord — who held a teacher's certificate — from his teaching position at the Wilson High School in Tacoma on the ground of "immorality" because he was a known homosexual. . . .

We need consider only the assignments of error which raise two basic issues: (1) whether substantial evidence supports the trial court's conclusion plaintiff-appellant Gaylord was guilty of immorality; (2) whether substantial evidence supports the findings, that as a known homosexual, Gaylord's fitness as a teacher was impaired to the injury of the Wilson High School, justifying his discharge by the defendant school district's board of directors. The relevant findings of the trial court may be summarized as follows.

Gaylord knew of his homosexuality for 20 years prior to his trial, actively sought homosexual company for the past several years, and participated in homosexual acts. He knew his status as a homosexual, if known, would jeopardize his employment, damage his reputation, and hurt his parents.

Gaylord's school superior first became aware of his sexual status on October 24, 1972, when a former Wilson High student told the school's vice-principal he thought Gaylord was a homosexual. The vice-principal confronted Gaylord at his home that same day with a written copy of the student's statement. Gaylord admitted he was a homosexual and attempted unsuccessfully to have the vice-principal drop the matter.

On November 21, 1972, Gaylord was notified the board of directors of the Tacoma School Board had found probable cause for his discharge due to his status as a publicly known homosexual. This status was contrary to school district policy No. 4119(5), which provides for discharge of school employees for "immorality." After hearing, the defendant board of directors discharged Gaylord effective December 21, 1972.

The court found an admission of homosexuality connotes illegal as well as immoral acts, because "sexual gratification with a member of one's own sex is implicit in the term 'homosexual.'" These acts were proscribed by RCW 9.79.120 (lewdness) and RCW 9.79.100 (sodomy).

After Gaylord's homosexual status became publicly known, it would and did impair his teaching efficiency. A teacher's efficiency is determined by his relationship with his students, their parents, the school administration, and fellow teachers. If Gaylord had not been discharged after he became known as a homosexual, the result would be fear, confusion, suspicion, parental concern, and pressure on the administration by students, parents, and other teachers.

The court concluded "appellant was properly discharged by respondent upon a charge of immorality upon his admission and disclosure that he was a homosexual" and that relief sought should be denied.

Was Gaylord guilty of immorality?

Our concern here is with the meaning of immorality in the sense intended by school board policy No. 4119(5). . . .

"Immorality" as used in policy No. 4119(5) does not stand alone. RCW 28A.67.110 makes it the duty of all teachers to "endeavor to impress on the minds of their pupils the principles of morality, truth, justice, temperance, humanity and patriotism . . ." RCW 28A.70.140 requires an applicant for a teacher's certificate be "a person of good moral character." RCW 28A.70.160 makes "immorality" a ground for revoking a teacher's certificate. Other grounds include the commission of "crime against the law of the state." The moral conduct of a teacher is relevant to a consideration of that person's fitness or ability to function adequately as a teacher of the students he is expected to teach — in this case high school students.

"Immorality" as a ground of teacher discharge would be unconstitutionally vague if not coupled with resulting actual or prospective adverse performance as a teacher. The basic statute permitting discharge for "sufficient cause" (RCW 28A.58.100(1)) has been construed to require the cause must adversely affect the teacher's performance before it can be invoked as a ground for discharge.

It follows the term "immorality" is not to be construed in its abstract sense apart from its effect upon teaching efficiency or fitness to teach. In its abstract sense the term is not

and perhaps cannot be comprehensively defined although it can be illustrated.

When, as in the case here, the term "immorality" has not been defined in policy No. 4119(5), it would seem reasonable to give the term its ordinary, common, everyday meaning as we would when construing an undefined term in a statute.

Was homosexuality immoral within the meaning of policy No. 4119(5)? We must first examine what the much dicussed term "homosexuality" means. In J. Walinder, *Transsexualism* 3 (1967), the author approves the following statement:

> The crucial characteristic of the homosexual is the desire for a physical sex relation with a person of his own sex. The eonist is repelled by the physical aspect of a homosexual relationship. (2) Homosexuals do not want to change their sex and identity. This is the fundamental anomaly in eonism.

D. West, in *Homosexuality* 10-11 (1967), the author explains:

> Homosexuality simply means the experience of being erotically attracted to a member of the same sex, and men or women who habitually experience strong feelings of this kind are called homosexuals. Those who act upon such feelings by participating in mutual sexual fondling or other forms of sexual stimulation with a partner of the same sex are known as 'overt' or practicing homosexuals. Those whose erotic feelings for the opposite sex are absent altogether, or slight in comparison to their homosexual feelings, are called exclusive or obligatory homosexuals. This is the type doctors usually have in mind when they refer without further qualification to 'homosexuals', or when they speak of 'true' homosexuals or "inverts", or when they consider the condition more or less permanent and unchangeable. Indeed, it is this exclusive, obligatory

type of homosexual who presents the chief problem for contemporary society, and who is the main concern of this book. The thought of intimate contacts with their own sex disgusts many normal persons, but many of these exclusive homosexuals, especially male homosexuals, are even more appalled by the prospect of relations with the opposite sex.

In characterizing homosexuality as immoral, the *New Catholic Encyclopedia*, for example, defines the term homosexual as:

[A]nyone who is erotically attracted to a notable degree toward persons of his or her own sex and who engages, or is psychologically disposed to engage, in sexual activity prompted by this attraction.
. . . . .
Once friendship between persons of the same sex leads to physical expression, a homosexual act has occurred ... The danger remains that the individual will yield to desire for the overt act.

7 *New Catholic Encyclopedia* 116 (1967).

Other observations and definitions of homosexuality are in substance similar to those above quoted. *See* H. English & A. English, *A Comprehensive Dictionary of Psychological and Psychoanalytical Terms* (1958); H. Eysenk & W. Wurzburg, *Encyclopedia of Psychology* 66-67 (1958); 1 R. Goldenson, *The Encyclopedia of Human Behavior* 553-59 (1970); *Blackison's New Gould Medical Dictionary* 471 (1st ed. 1949); *Dorland's Illustrated Medical Dictionary* 686 (24th ed. 1965); *Psychiatric Dictionary* 348-51 (4th ed. 1970); *Steadman's Medical Dictionary* 584 (22d ed. 1972). *See generally The Encyclopedia Americana* 629 (1963); 16 *Encyclopedia Britannica* 603 (1974); 14 *International Encyclopedia of the Social Sciences* 222 (1968).

There appears to be general agreement, so far as it goes, with Webster's definition of homosexual: " 'one whose sexual inclina-

tion is toward those of the individual's own sex rather than the opposite sex.' " . . .

The medical and psychological and psychiatric literature on the subject of homosexuality distinguishes between the overt homosexual and the passive or latent homosexual. An overt homosexual has homosexual inclinations consciously experienced and expressed in actual homosexual behavior as opposed to latent. A latent homosexual is one who has "an erotic inclination toward members of the same sex, not consciously experienced or expressed in overt action; opposite of overt." *Steadman's Medical Dictionary*, *supra* at 584. However, it has been pointed out that "actually, individual homosexuals do not necessarily maintain an active or passive attitude exclusively in a given relationship, inasmuch as they alternate in the male and female roles." 3 A. Deutsch & H. Fishman, *The Encyclopedia of Mental Health* 747 (1963).

Moreover, homosexual experience of an overt nature varies among homosexuals, from males who are more or less exclusively homosexual to males that are only occasionally so. *See* A. Kinsey, W. Pomeroy & C. Martin, *Sexual Behavior in the Human Male* 650-51 (1948). *See generally* C. Socarides, *The Overt Homosexual* (1968); 3 *American Handbook of Psychiatry* (2d ed. 1974).

In the instant case Gaylord "admitted his status as a homosexual," and "from appellant's own testimony it is unquestioned that homosexual acts were participated in by him, although there was no evidence of any overt act having been committed."

These findings concerning Gaylord's homosexuality are based both on his admission and on other evidence . . . . [H]is admission of homosexuality is supported by evidence that Gaylord was and had been a homosexual for 20 years. He also testified that in the 2-year period before his discharge, he actively sought out the company of other male homosexuals and participated actively as a member of the Dorian Society (a society of homosexuals). He responded to a blind advertisement in the society's paper for homosexual company. He concealed his homosexuality from his parents until compelled to reveal it by the present dispute.

If Gaylord meant something other than homosexual in the usual sense, he failed to explain what he meant by his admission of homosexuality or being a homosexual and did not avoid any adverse inference, although he had adequate opportunity at trial to do so. He clearly had a right to explain that he was not an overt homosexual and did not engage in the conduct the court ascribed to him which the court found immoral and illegal. . . . There was uncontroverted evidence plaintiff was a competent and intelligent teacher so the court could reasonably assume Gaylord knew what homosexuality could mean. It was not a word to be thoughtlessly or lightly used. Gaylord's precaution for 20 years to keep his status of being a homosexual secret from his parents is eloquent evidence of his knowledge of the serious consequences attendant upon an undefined admission of homosexuality.

He testified that in June 1970 he realized that if he was "ever going to have [homosexual] friends . . . that I needed, that I was going to have to make more efforts of my own to find these people because I wasn't going to stumble across them by accident as I expected." It was about that time he joined the Dorian Society. He testified he "felt very comfortable with the people there." Eventually he began to attend a good many of their functions. On one occasion a high school boy conferred with the plaintiff about homosexuality and learned that plaintiff was "heavily involved" for a period of a month with a person whose advertisement he had answered. It would have been a simple matter for Gaylord to have explained the physical side, if any, of his relationship but he did not do so.

Our next inquiry is whether homosexuality as commonly understood is considered immoral. Homosexuality is widely condemned as immoral and was so condemned as immoral during biblical times. A. Kinsey, W. Pomeroy & C. Martin, *Sexual Behavior*

in the Human Male 483 (1948); S. Weinberg & C. Williams, *Male Homosexuals* 17–18, 252, 256 (1974); D. West, *supra* at 96–101; 8 *Encyclopaedia Judaica* (1971) col. 961; 7 *New Catholic Encyclopedia* 116–19 (1967); 3 A. Deutsch & H. Fishman, *The Encyclopedia of Mental Health* 763 (1963).

A sociologist testified in the instant case: "A majority of people and adults in this country react negatively to homosexuality." A psychiatrist testified "I would say in our present culture and certainly, in the last few hundred years in Western Europe and in America this [homosexuality] has been a frightening idea . . ."

The court found "sexual gratification with a member of one's own sex is implicit in the term 'homosexual.'" This finding would not necessarily apply to latent homosexuals, however, the court in effect found from the evidence and reasonable inferences therefrom, it applied to Gaylord. These acts — sodomy and lewdness - were crimes during the period of Gaylord's employment and at the time of his discharge. RCW 9.79.100 and RCW 9.79.120.

Volitional choice is an essential element of morality. One who has a disease, for example, cannot be held morally responsible for his condition. Homosexuality is not a disease, however. Gaylord's witness, a psychiatrist, testified on cross-examination that homosexuality except in a case of hormonal or congenital defect (not shown to be present here) is not inborn. Most homosexuals have a "psychological or acquired orientation." Only recently the Board of the American Psychiatric Association has stated: "homosexuality . . . by itself does not necessarily constitute a psychiatric disorder." The Board explained that the new diagnostic category of Sexual Orientation Disturbance applies to:

> individuals whose sexual interests are directed primarily towards people of the same sex and who are either disturbed by, in conflict with, or wish to change their sexual orientation. . . .

[this] distinguished from homosexuality, which by itself does not necessarily constitute a psychiatric disorder.

A.P.A. Rules Homosexuality Not Necessarily a Disorder, 9 *Psychiatric News* (Jan. 1974), at 1.

Nevertheless it is a disorder for those who wish to change their homosexuality which is acquired after birth. In the instant case plaintiff desired no change and has sought no psychiatric help because he feels comfortable with his homosexuality. He has made a voluntary choice for which he must be held morally responsible. L. Hatterer, *Changing Homosexuality in the Male, Treatment for Men Troubled by Homosexuality* 58, 445 app. 1 (1970).

The remaining question on this point is whether the repeal of the sodomy statute (RCW 9.79.100), while this case was pending, deprives sodomy of its immoral character. In the first place the repeal did not go into effect until July 1, 1976, sometime after Gaylord's discharge. Sodomy between consenting adults is no longer a crime. RCW 9A.88; RCW 9A.98.010; RCW 9A.88.100. *See also* RCW 9A.88.010 and .020. Generally the fact that sodomy is not a crime no more relieves the conduct of its immoral status than would consent to the crime of incest.

The next question is whether the plaintiff's performance as a teacher was sufficiently impaired by his known homosexuality to be the basis for discharge. The court found that Gaylord, prior to his discharge on December 21, 1972, had been a teacher at the Wilson High School in the Tacoma School District No. 10 for over 12 years, and had received favorable evaluations of his teaching throughout this time. The court further found that "while plaintiff's status as a homosexual [was] unknown to others in the school," his teaching efficiency was not affected nor did his status injure the school. When, however, it became publicly known that Gaylord was a homosexual "the knowledge thereof would and did impair his effi-

ciency as a teacher with resulting injury to the school had he not been discharged."

The court further found:

A teacher's efficiency is determined by his relationship with students, their parents, fellow teachers and school administrators. In all of these areas the continued employment of appellant after he became known as a homosexual would result, had he not been discharged, in confusion, suspicion, fear, expressed parental concern and pressure upon the administration from students, parents and fellow teachers, all of which would impair appellant's efficiency as a teacher and injure the school.

Gaylord assigns error contending there is no substantial evidence to support either. We do not agree.

First, he argues his homosexuality became known at the school only after the school made it known and that he should not be responsible therefor so as to justify his discharge as a homosexual. The difficulty with this argument is twofold. First, by seeking out homosexual company he took the risk his homosexuality would be discovered. It was he who granted an interview to the boy who talked to him about his homosexual problems. The boy had been referred to Gaylord for that purpose by the homosexual friend to whom Gaylord had responded favorably in answering his advertisement in the paper of the Dorian Society. As a result of that interview the boy came away with the impression plaintiff was a homosexual and later told the assistant high school principal about the matter. The latter in turn conferred with plaintiff for the purpose of verifying the charge that had been made. It was the vice-principal's duty to report the information to his superiors because it involved the performance capabilities of Gaylord. The school cannot be charged with making plaintiff's condition known so as to defeat the school board's duty to protect the school and the students against the impairment of the learning process in all aspects involved.

Second, there is evidence that at least one student expressly objected to Gaylord teaching at the high school because of his homosexuality. Three fellow teachers testified against Gaylord remaining on the teaching staff, testifying it was objectionable to them both as teachers and parents. The vice-principal and the principal, as well as the retired superintendent of instruction, testified his presence on the faculty would create problems. There is conflicting evidence on the issue of impairment but the court had the power to accept the testimony it did on which to base complained of findings. The testimony of the school teachers and administrative personnel constituted substantial evidence sufficient to support the findings as to the impairment of the teacher's efficiency.

It is important to remember that Gaylord's homosexual conduct must be considered in the context of his position of teaching high school students. Such students could treat the retention of the high school teacher by the school board as indicating adult approval of his homosexuality. It would be unreasonable to assume as a matter of law a teacher's ability to perform as a teacher required to teach principles of morality (RCW 28A.67.110) is not impaired and creates no danger of encouraging expression of approval and of imitation. Likewise to say that school directors must wait for prior specific overt expression of homosexual conduct before they act to prevent harm from one who chooses to remain "erotically attracted to a notable degree towards persons of his own sex and is psychologically, if not actually disposed to engage in sexual activity prompted by this attraction" is to ask the school directors to take an unacceptable risk in discharging their fiduciary responsibility of managing the affairs of the school district.

We do not deal here with homosexuality which does not impair or cannot reasonably be said to impair his ability to perform the duties of an occupation in which the homo-sexual engages and which does not impair the effectiveness of the institution which employs him. . . .

Affirmed.

DOLLIVER, J. (dissenting)

The appellant, Mr. Gaylord, had been a teacher at Wilson High School for over 12 years at the time of his discharge. In college, he had been an outstanding scholar; he graduated Phi Beta Kappa from the University of Washington and was selected "Outstanding Senior" in the political science department. He later received a masters degree in librarianship. As a teacher, the evaluations made of Mr. Gaylord were consistently favorable. The most recent evaluation of his teaching performance stated that "Mr. Gaylord continues his high standards and thorough teaching performance. He is both a teacher and student in his field."

Despite this outstanding record, the trial court found that Mr. Gaylord should be discharged for "immorality." To uphold this dismissal, we must find substantial evidence supporting the finding that Mr. Gaylord was discharged for "sufficient cause," as required by RCW 28A.58.100. "Sufficient cause" has been defined as "*conduct which would affect the teacher's efficiency.*" *Gaylord v. Tacoma School Dist. 10*, 535 P.2d 804 (Wash. 1975). This must be proven by the school district by a preponderance of the evidence. RCW 28A.58.450. For all the scholarly research done by the majority here, the most basic point has been missed; the respondent school board did not meet its burden of proof.

The majority upheld the trial court's finding that an admission of a homosexual status connotes illegal as well as immoral acts which are proscribed by RCW 9.79.100 (sodomy) and RCW 9.79.120 (lewdness). RCW 9.79.100 provides:

> Every person who shall carnally know
> in any manner any animal or bird; or
> who shall carnally know any male or

female person by the anus or with the mouth or tongue; or who shall voluntarily submit to such carnal knowledge; or who shall attempt sexual intercourse with a dead body, shall be guilty of sodomy and shall be punished as follows: . . .

RCW 9.79.120 provides:

Every person who shall lewdly and viciously cohabit with another not the husband or wife of such person, and every person who shall be guilty of open or gross lewdness, or make any open and indecent or obscene exposure of his person, or of the person of another, shall be guilty of a gross misdemeanor.

There is not a shred of evidence in the record that Mr. Gaylord participated in any of the acts stated above. . . [W]e are presented here with a record showing no illegal or immoral conduct; we have only an admission of a homosexual status and Gaylord's testimony that he sought male companionship.

Undoubtedly there are individuals with a homosexual identity as there are individuals with a heterosexual identity, who are not sexually active. Mr. Gaylord, for all we know, may be one of these individuals. Certainly in this country we should be beyond drawing severe and farreaching inferences from the admission of a status — a status which may be no more than a state of mind. Furthermore, there are homosexual activities involving a physical relationship which are not prohibited by statute.

The trial court made a most puzzling finding that, "From appellant's own testimony it is unquestioned that homosexual acts were participated in by him, although there was no evidence of any overt acts having been committed." The trial court essentially found that, as an admitted homosexual, unless Mr. Gaylord denied doing a particular immoral or illegal act, he can be assumed to

have done the act. The court has placed upon the appellant the burden to negate what it asserts are the implications that may be drawn from his testimony although he never was accused of participating in acts of sodomy or lewdness.

We must require here, as we have in the past, proof of conduct to justify a dismissal. The only conceivable testimony on conduct was the comment of the student that Gaylord and another male were "deeply involved" for about a month. This hardly qualifies as testimony either as to "immorality," sodomy, or lewdness. Finding no conduct, I am unwilling to take the leap in logic accepted by the majority that admission of a status or identity implies the commission of certain illegal or immoral acts.

In *McConnell v. Anderson*, [316 F.Supp. 809, 814 (D.Minn. 1970)], the court said:

An homosexual is after all a human being, and a citizen of the United States despite the fact that he finds his sex gratification in what most consider to be an unconventional manner. He is as much entitled to the protection and benefits of the laws and due process fair treatment as are others, at least as to public employment in the absence of proof and not mere surmise that he has committed or will commit criminal acts or that his employment efficiency is impaired by his homosexuality. Further, the decided cases draw a distinction between homosexuality, *i.e.*, sexual propensity for persons of one's own sex and the commission of homosexual criminal acts. Homosexuality is said to be a broad term involving all types of deviant sexual conduct with one of the same sex, but not necessarily criminal acts of sodomy.

Surely the majority has adopted a novel approach. Mr. Gaylord was never at any time accused of performing any "homosexual acts." Yet because of his declared status, he must assume the burden of proving he did not commit certain illegal or immoral acts which have at no time been referred to or mentioned, much less described, by the school board. Presumably under this reasoning, an unmarried male who declares himself to be heterosexual will be held to have engaged in "illegal or immoral acts." The opportunities for industrious school districts seem unlimited.

The majority goes to great lengths to differentiate between an overt and a latent homosexual. Authority is cited that overt homosexuality is "consciously experienced and expressed in actual homosexual behavior." Yet there is no evidence in the record of any actual behavior or acts, and the findings of the trial court specifically state "there was no evidence of any overt acts having been committed." The real problem faced by the majority is that the term "homosexual" is not mentioned once in the Revised Code of Washington. There is no law in this state against being a homosexual. All that is banned (prior to July 1, 1976) are certain acts, none of which Mr. Gaylord was alleged to have committed and none of which can it be either assumed or inferred he committed simply because of his status as a homosexual.

The second glaring error in this proceeding is the respondent's failure to establish that Mr. Gaylord's performance as a teacher was impaired by his homosexuality. As pointed out by the trial court in its findings, the evidence is quite clear that, having been a homosexual for the entire time he taught at Wilson High School, the fact of Mr. Gaylord's homosexuality did not impair his performance as a teacher. In other words, homosexuality per se does not preclude competence. *Acanfora v. Board of Educ. of Montgomery County*, 359 F.Supp. 843 (D.Md. 1973).

The evidence before the court is uncontroverted — Mr. Gaylord carefully kept his private life quite separate from the school. Compare *Acanfora v. Board of Educ. of Montgomery County, supra*. He made no sexual advances toward his professional contemporaries or his students. There is absolutely no evidence that Mr. Gaylord failed in any way to perform the duties listed in RCW 28A.67.110. In over 12 years of teaching at the same school, his best friends on the teaching staff were unaware of his homosexuality until the time of his discharge. Gaylord did not use his classroom as a forum for discussing homosexuality. Given the discretion with which Gaylord conducted his private life, it appears that public knowledge of Gaylord's homosexuality occurred, as the trial court found, at the time of his dismissal.

At the trial, a variety of witnesses speculated on the effect that Gaylord's homosexuality might have on his effectiveness in the classroom. The speculation varied considerably. Certainly there were witnesses who testified that Gaylord's effectiveness would be damaged. There were also those who testified to the contrary. As a result, the trial court found that "the continued employment of appellant after he became known as a homosexual would result, had he not been discharged, in confusion, suspicion, fear, expressed parental concern and pressure upon the administration." The question this court must ask is whether a finding of detrimental effect can be made on the basis of conjecture alone.

■ ■ ■

Historically, the private lives of teachers have been controlled by the school districts in many ways. There was a time when a teacher could be fired for a marriage, a divorce, or for the use of liquor or tobacco. Although the practice of firing teachers for these reasons has ceased, there are undoubtedly those who could speculate that any of these practices would have a detrimental effect on a teacher's classroom efficiency as well as cause adverse community reaction. I find such speculation to be an unacceptable method for justifying the dismissal of a teacher who has a flawless record of excellence in his classroom performance.

What if Mr. Gaylord's status was as a black, a Roman Catholic, or a young heterosexual single person, instead of a male homosexual? Would his dismissal be handled in such manner? Mere speculation coupled with status alone is not enough. Finding No. 10 of the trial court reads as follows:

> A teacher's efficiency is determined by his relationship with students, their parents, fellow teachers and school administrators. In all of these areas the continued employment of appellant after he became known as a homosexual would result, had he not been discharged, in confusion, suspicion, fear, expressed parental concern and pressure upon the administration from students, parents and fellow teachers, all of which would impair appellant's efficiency as a teacher and injure the school.

In this finding, substitute the words "black" or "female" for "homosexual" and the defect of the majority approach is brought into sharp focus.

The basic unfairness of this situation was well expressed by Mr. Gaylord when he testified:

> I quite frankly find it rather galling to have sat through the school board hearing and once again through this trial and hear administrators say that I'm a good teacher, I've been a very good teacher, and yet to be without a job, particularly when I see other people who still hold their jobs who haven't read a book or turned out a new lesson plan or come up with anything creative in years.

" 'The right to practice one's profession is sufficiently precious to surround it with a panoply of legal protection.' " *Morrison v. State Bd. of Educ.*, 461 P.2d 375 (Cal. 1969), quoting *Yakov v. Board of Medical Examiners*, 435 P.2d 553 (Cal. 1968). To base a dismissal on the proof of a status with no showing of conduct and no showing of an actual detrimental effect on teaching efficiency violates the constitutional due process rights to which Mr. Gaylord is entitled.

I dissent.

■ ■ ■

Notes

1. The *Gaylord* decision typifies the classic immorality argument used against gay people generally and gay teachers specifically. Other courts have rejected arguments that homosexuality is per se an immoral, disqualifying trait for public school teachers. *See Morrison v. State Bd. of Educ.*, 461 P.2d 375 (Cal. 1969). *See also Aumiller v. University of Delaware*, 434 F. Supp. 1273 (D. Del. 1977) (finding that public statements about homosexuality did not disrupt workplace and thus plaintiff's employment was safeguarded by First Amendment).

2. Other courts have attempted to justify their decisions on grounds other than homosexuality. For instance, in *Acanfora v. Board of Educ.*, 491 F.2d 498 (4th Cir. 1974), the Fourth Circuit agreed with the plaintiff that his transfer based on his speech about homosexuality would have violated the Constitution, but the court upheld his transfer because he omitted his membership in a gay organization from his teaching application.

In *Rowland v. Mad River Local School District*, the school district did not renew plaintiff's contract to continue her work as a high school guidance counselor after she informed co-workers that she was bisexual. The plaintiff sued and a jury awarded her damages, finding a violation of her constitutional rights under the First Amendment and the Fourteenth Amendment's equal protection clause. The U.S. Court of Appeals for the Sixth Circuit reversed, rewriting the facts of the case to find that the plaintiff was actually dismissed for violating the confidentiality of her students. The court asserted that the breach of confidence rationale in no way relates to plaintiff's sexual orientation and, thus, the equal protection and free speech issues need not be addressed.

Although certiorari was denied by the Supreme Court, Justice Brennan wrote a powerful opinion dissenting from the denial of certiorari. His dissent is the first explication by a Supreme Court Justice of why classifications based on sexual orientation are suspect and should be carefully scrutinized by the courts.

ROWLAND v. MAD RIVER LOCAL SCHOOL DISTRICT

470 U.S. 1009 (1985)

JUSTICE BRENNAN, with whom JUSTICE MARSHALL joins, dissenting from the denial of certiorari.

... Because determination of the appropriate constitutional analysis to apply in such a case continues to puzzle lower courts and because this Court has never addressed the issues presented, I would grant certiorari and set this case for oral argument.

■ ■ ■

II

... Petitioner did not lose her job because she disrupted the school environment or failed to perform her job. She was discharged merely because she is bisexual and revealed this fact to acquaintances at her workplace. These facts are rendered completely unambiguous by the jury's findings. Yet after a jury and the trial court who heard and evaluated the evidence rendered verdicts for petitioner, the court below reversed based on a crabbed reading of our precedents and unexplained disregard of the jury and judge's factual findings. Because they are so patently erroneous, these maneuvers suggest only a desire to evade the central question: may a State dismiss a public employee based on her bisexual status alone? I respectfully dissent from the Court's decision not to give its plenary attention to this issue.

A

That petitioner was discharged for her non-disruptive mention of her sexual preferences raises a substantial claim under the First Amendment. "For at least 15 years, it has been settled that a State cannot condition public employment on a basis that infringes the employee's constitutionally protected interest in freedom of expression." [*Connick v. Myers*, 461 U.S. 138, 142 (1983).] Nevertheless, *Connick* held that if "employee expression cannot be fairly considered as relating to any matter of political, social, or other concern to the community," disciplinary measures taken in response to such expression cannot be challenged under the First Amendment "absent the most unusual circumstances." The court below ruled that *Connick* requires the conclusion that a bisexual public employee constitutionally may be dismissed for "talking about it." This conclusion does not result inevitably from *Connick*, and may be questioned on at least two grounds: first, because petitioner's speech did indeed "touch upon" a matter of public concern, and second, because speech even if characterized as private is entitled to constitutional protection when it does not in any way interfere with the employer's business.

Connick recognized that some issues are "inherently of public concern," citing "racial discrimination" as one example. I think it impossible not to note that a similar public debate is currently ongoing regarding the rights of homosexuals. The fact of petitioner's bisexuality, once spoken, necessarily and ineluctably involved her in that debate. Speech that "touches upon" this explosive issue is no less deserving of constitutional attention than speech relating to more widely condemned forms of discrimination.

Connick's reference to "matters of public concern" does not suggest a strict rule that an employee's first statement related to a volatile issue of public concern must go unprotected, simply because it is the first statement in the public debate. Such a rule would reduce public employees to second-class speakers, for they would be prohibited from speaking until and unless others first bring an issue to public attention. It is the *topic* of the speech at issue, and not whether a debate on that topic is yet ongoing, that *Connick* directed federal courts to examine.

Moreover, even if petitioner's speech did not so obviously touch upon a matter of public concern, there remains a substantial constitutional question, reserved in *Connick*, whether it lies "totally beyond the protection of the First Amendment" given its nondisruptive character. The recognized goal of the *Pickering-Connick* rationale is to seek a "balance" between the interest of public employees in speaking freely and that of public employers in operating their workplaces without disruption. As the jury below found, however, the latter interest simply is not implicated in this case. In such circumstances, *Connick* does not require that the former interest still receive no constitutional protection. *Connick*, and, indeed, all our precedents in this area, addressed discipline taken against employees for statements that arguably had some disruptive effect in the workplace. This case, however, involves no critical statements, but rather an entirely harmless mention of a fact about petitioner that apparently triggered certain prejudices held by her supervisors. The Court carefully noted in *Connick* that it did "not deem it either appropriate or feasible to attempt to lay down a general standard against which all such statements may be judged." This case poses the open question whether nondisruptive speech ever can constitutionally serve as the basis for termination under the First Amendment.

B

Apart from the First Amendment, we have held that "[a] State cannot exclude a person from . . . any . . . occupation . . . for reasons that contravene the Due Process or Equal Protection Clause of the Fourteenth Amendment." And in applying the Equal Protection Clause, "we have treated as presumptively invidious those classifications that disadvantage a 'suspect class,' or that impinge upon the exercise of a 'fundamental right.'" *Plyler v. Doe*, 457 U.S. 202, 216-217 (1982) (footnote omitted); *see also id.*, at 245 (Burger, C.J., dissenting) ("The Equal Protection Clause protects against arbitrary and irrational classifications, and against invidious discrimination stemming from prejudice and hostility"). Under this rubric, discrimination against homosexuals or bisexuals based solely on their sexual preference raises significant constitutional questions under both prongs of our settled equal protection analysis.

First, homosexuals constitute a significant and insular minority of this country's population.[7] Because of the immediate and severe opprobrium often manifested against homosexuals once so identified publicly, members of this group are particularly powerless to pursue their rights openly in the political arena. Moreover, homosexuals have historically been the object of pernicious and sustained hostility, and it is fair to say that discrimination against homosexuals is "likely . . . to reflect deep-seated prejudice rather than . . . rationality." State action taken against members of such groups based simply on their status as members of the group traditionally has been subjected to strict, or at least heightened, scrutiny by this Court.

Second, discrimination based on sexual preference has been found by may courts to infringe various fundamental constitutional rights, such as the rights to privacy or freedom of expression. Infringement of such rights found to be "explicitly or implicitly guaranteed by the Constitution," *San Antonio Independent School District v. Rodriguez*, 411 U.S. 1, 33-34 (1973), likewise requires the State to demonstrate some compelling interest to survive strict judicial scrutiny. *Plyler, supra,* at 217. I have previously noted that a multitude of our precedents supports the view that public employees maintain, no less than all other citizens, a fundamental constitutional right to make "private choices involving family life and personal autonomy." Whether constitutional rights are infringed in sexual preference cases, and whether some compelling state interest can be advanced to permit their infringement, are important questions that this Court has never addressed, and which have left the lower courts in some disarray.

Finally, even if adverse state action based on homosexual *conduct* were held valid under application of traditional equal protection principles, such approval would not answer the question, posed here, whether the mere nondisruptive *expression* of homosexual preference can pass muster even under a minimal rationality standard as the basis for discharge from public employment. This record plainly demonstrates that petitioner did not proselytize regarding her bisexuality, but rather that it became known simply in the course of her normal workday conversations.[11] The School District agreed to submit the issue of disruption to the jury, and the jury found that knowledge

---

7. [H]omosexuals may constitute from 8-15% of the average population. . . . Marmor, Homosexual Behavior: A Modern Reappraisal (1980)). . . . [N]onheterosexual preference, like minority race status, "evoke[s] deeply felt prejudices and fears on the part of many people."

11. Petitioner's first mention of her bisexuality at school apparently came in response to friendly but repeated questions from her secretary as to why petitioner seemed in a particularly "good mood" one day. When petitioner eventually responded that she was in love with a woman, the secretary apparently was upset by the unexpected answer, and reported it to petitioner's Principal. On another occasion, petitioner was confronted by an angry mother who wanted to know why petitioner was counseling her to accept her son's expressed homosexuality when such conduct was "against the Bible." Petitioner did not inform the mother of her own preferences, but did inform her Vice Principal, because she was "uneasy" that if the mother complained her own "job would be at stake." Finally, petitioner mentioned her bisexuality to some of her fellow teachers, first simply in the course of her friendships with them and later to enlist their support when it became clear that she would be disciplined for her bisexuality.

This evidence indicates that petitioner's "speech" perhaps is better evaluated as no more than a natural consequence of her sexual orientation, in the same way that co-workers generally know whom their fellow employees are dating or to whom they are married. Under this view, petitioner's First Amendment and equal protection claims may be seen to converge, because it is realistically impossible to separate her spoken statements from her status. The suggestion below that it was error not to separate the claims precisely for the jury's benefit, and reliance on that suggestion to avoid discussion of the merits of petitioner's claim, again simply exposes the Court of Appeals' reluctance to confront forthrightly the difficult issues posed by petitioner's case. The jury's role was to find the facts, which it did in detail. It is the court's proper role to analyze, not avoid, those facts in light of the applicable legal principles.

of petitioner's nonheterosexual status did not interfere with the school's operation "in any way." I have serious doubt in light of that finding whether the result below can be upheld under any standard of equal protection review.

III

The issues in this case are clearly presented. By reversing the jury's verdict, the Court of Appeals necessarily held that adverse state action taken against a public employee based solely on his or her expressed sexual preference is constitutional. Nothing in our precedents requires that result; indeed, we have never addressed the topic. Because petitioner's case raises serious and unsettled constitutional questions relating to this issue of national importance, an issue that cannot any longer be ignored, I respectfully dissent from the decision to deny this petition for a writ of certiorari.

In the early 1980s, the state of Oklahoma passed a statute aimed at denying teaching positions to lesbians, gay men, and other teachers supportive of gay issues.

NATIONAL GAY TASK FORCE v. BOARD OF EDUCATION OF OKLAHOMA CITY

729 F.2d 1270 (10th Cir. 1984), *aff'd by an equally divided Court,* 470 U.S. 903 (1985)

LOGAN, Circuit Judge.

The National Gay Task Force (NGTF), whose membership includes teachers in the Oklahoma public school system, filed this action in the district court challenging the facial constitutional validity of Okla. Stat. tit. 70, § 6-103.15. The district court held that the statute was constitutionally valid. On appeal NGTF contends that the statute violates plaintiff's members' rights to privacy and equal protection, that it is void for vagueness, that it violates the Establishment Clause, and, finally, that it is overbroad.

The challenged statute, Okla. Stat. tit. 70, § 6-103.15, provides:

"A. As used in this section:

1. "Public homosexual activity" means the commission of an act defined in Section 886 of Title 21 of the Oklahoma Statutes, if such act is:

   a. committed with a person of the same sex, and

   b. indiscreet and not practiced in private;

2. "Public homosexual conduct" means advocating, soliciting, imposing, encouraging or promoting public or private homosexual activity in a manner that creates a

substantial risk that such conduct will come to the attention of school children or school employees; and

3. "Teacher" means a person as defined in Section 1-116 of Title 70 of the Oklahoma Statutes.

B. In addition to any ground set forth in Section 6-103 of Title 70 of the Oklahoma Statutes, a teacher, student teacher or a teacher's aide may be refused employment, or reemployment, dismissed, or suspended after a finding that the teacher or teachers' aide has:

1. Engaged in public homosexual conduct or activity; and

2. Has been rendered unfit, because of such conduct or activity, to hold a position as a teacher, student teacher or teachers' aide.

C. The following factors shall be considered in making the determination whether the teacher, student teacher or teachers' aide has been rendered unfit for his position:

1. The likelihood that the activity or conduct may adversely affect students or school employees;

2. The proximity in time or place the activity or conduct to the teacher's, student teacher's or teachers' aide's official duties;

3. Any extenuating or aggravating circumstances; and

4. Whether the conduct or activity is of a repeated or continuing nature which tends to encourage or dispose school children toward similar conduct or activity."

The trial court held that the statute reaches protected speech but upheld the constitutionality of the statute by reading a "material and substantial disruption" test into it. We disagree. The statute proscribes protected speech and is thus facially overbroad, and we cannot read into the statute a "material and substantial disruption" test. Therefore, we reverse the judgment of the trial court.

I

We see no constitutional problem in the statute's permitting a teacher to be fired for engaging in "public homosexual activity." Section 6-103.15 defines "public homosexual activity" as the commission of an act defined in Okla. Stat. tit. 21, § 886, that is committed with a person of the same sex and is indiscreet and not practiced in private. In support of their argument that this provision violates their members' right of privacy, plaintiff cites *Baker v. Wade*, 553 F. Supp. 1121 (N.D. Tex. 1982), and *New York v. Onofre*, 415 N.E.2d 936 (N.Y. 1980), *cert. denied*, 451 U.S. 987 (1981). Both of those cases held that the constitution protects consensual, noncommercial sexual acts in private between adults. *Baker* and *Onofre* are inapplicable to the instant case. Section 6-103.15 does not punish acts performed in private. Thus, the right of privacy, whatever its scope in regard to homosexual acts, is not implicated.

The trial court correctly rejected plaintiff's contention that the Oklahoma statute is vague in regard to "public homosexual activity." . . . The Oklahoma cases construing the "crime against nature" statute have clearly defined the acts that the statute proscribes.[1]

---

1. Section 886 provides: "Every person who is guilty of the detestable and abominable crime against nature, committed with mankind or with a beast, is punishable by imprisonment in the penitentiary not exceeding ten (10) years." The Oklahoma Court of Criminal Appeals has held that § 886 proscribes oral and anal copulation. In *Wainwright v. Stone*, 414 U.S. 21 (1973), the Court held that an almost identical Florida statute was not unconstitutionally vague because the Florida courts had specified that the statute applied to oral and anal copulation. . . .

Plaintiff also argues that the statute violates its members' right to equal protection of the law. We cannot find that a classification based on the choice of sexual partners is suspect, especially since only four members of the Supreme Court have viewed gender as a suspect classification. *Frontiero v. Richardson*, 411 U.S. 677 (1973). *See also Baker v. Wade*, 553 F. Supp. 1121, 1144 n.58. Thus something less than a strict scrutiny test should be applied here. Surely a school may fire a teacher for engaging in an indiscreet public act of oral or anal intercourse. *See Amback v. Norwick*, 441 U.S. 68, 80 (1979). We also agree that the district court correctly rejected the Establishment Clause claim. *See Harris v. McCrae*, 448 U.S. 297 (1980).

II

The part of § 6-103.15 that allows punishment of teachers for "public homosexual conduct" does present constitutional problems. To be sure, this is a facial challenge, and facial challenges based on First Amendment overbreadth are "strong medicine" and should be used "sparingly and only as a last resort." *Broadrick v. Oklahoma*, 413 U.S. 601, 613 (1973). Nonetheless, invalidation is an appropriate remedy in the instant case because this portion of § 6-103.15 is overbroad, is "not readily subject to a narrowing construction by the state courts," and "its deterrent effect on legitimate expression is both real and substantial." *Erznoznik v. City of Jacksonville*, 422 U.S. 205, 216 (1975). Also, we must be especially willing to invalidate a statute for facial overbreadth when, as here, the statute regulates "pure speech." *New York v. Ferber*, 458 U.S. 747, 772-773 (1982); *Broadrick*, 413 U.S. at 615.

Section 6-103.15 allows punishment of teachers for "public homosexual conduct," which is defined as "advocating, soliciting, imposing, encouraging or promoting public or private homosexual activity in a manner that creates a substantial risk that such con-

duct will come to the attention of school children or school employees." Okla. Stat. tit. 70, § 6-103.15(A)(2). The First Amemdnent protects "advocacy" even of illegal conduct except when "advocacy" is "directed to inciting or producing imminent lawless action and is likely to incite or produce such action." *Brandenburg v. Ohio*, 395 U.S. 444, 447 (1969). The First Amendment does not permit someone to be punished for advocating illegal conduct at some indefinite future time.

"Encouraging" and "promoting," like "advocating," do not necessarily imply incitement to imminent action. A teacher who went before the Oklahoma legislature or appeared on television to urge the repeal of the Oklahoma anti-sodomy statute would be "advocating," "promoting," and "encouraging" homosexual sodomy and creating a substantial risk that his or her speech would come to the attention of school children or school employees if he or she said, "I think it is psychologically damaging for people with homsexual desires to suppress those desires. They should act on those desires and should be legally free to do so." Such statements, which are aimed at legal and social change, are at the core of First Amendment protections. As in *Erznoznik*, the statute by its plain terms is not easily susceptible of a narrowing construction. The Oklahoma legislature chose the word "advocacy" despite the Supreme Court's interpretation of that word in *Bradenburg*. Finally, the deterrent effect of § 6-103.15 is both real and substantial. It applies to all teachers, substitute teachers, and teachers aides in Oklahoma. To protect their jobs they must restrict their expression. *See Erznoznik*, 422 U.S. at 217. Thus, the § 6-103.15 proscription of advocating, encouraging, or promoting homosexual activity is unconstitutionally overbroad.

We recognize that a state has interests in regulation the speech of teachers that differ from its interests in regulating the speech of the general citizenry. *Pickering v. Board of Education*, 391 U.S. 563, 568 (1968). But a state's interests outweigh a teacher's interests only when the expression results in a material or substantial interference or disruption in the normal activities of the school. *See Tinker v. Des Moines Independent Community School District*, 393 U.S. 503 (1969). This Court has held that a teacher's First Amendment rights may be restricted only if "the employer shows that some restriction is necessary to prevent the disruption of official functions or to insure effective performance by the employee." *Childers v. Independent School District No. 1*, 676 F.2d 1338, 1341 (10th Cir. 1982). Defendant has made no such showing.

The statute declares that a teacher may be fired under § 6-103.15 only if there is a finding of "unfitness" and lists factors that are to be considered in determining "unfitness": whether the activity or conduct is likely to adversely affect students or school employees; whether the activity or conduct is close in time or place to the teacher's, student teacher's or teachers aide's official duties; whether any extenuating or aggravating circumstances exist; and whether the conduct or activity is of a repeated or continuing nature which tends to encourage or dispose school children toward similar conduct or activity. An adverse effect on students or other employees is the only factor among those listed in § 6-103.15 that is even related to a material and substantial disruption. And although a material and substantial disruption is an adverse effect, many adverse effects are not material and substantial disruptions. The statute does not require that the teacher's public utterance occur in the classroom. Any public statement that would come to the attention of school children, their parents, or school employees that might lead someone to object to the teacher's social and political views would seem to justify a finding that the statement "may adversely affect" students or school employees. The statute does not specify the weight to be given to any of the factors listed. An adverse effect is apparently not even a prerequisite to a finding of unfitness. A statute is saved from a challenge to its overbreadth only if it is "readily subject" to a narrowing construc-

tion. It is not within this Court's power to construe and narrow state statutes. *Grayned v. City of Rockford*, 408 U.S. 104, 110 (1972). The unfitness requirement does not save § 6-103.15 from its unconstitutional overbreadth.

III

. . . We reverse the judgment of the district court, holding that the statute, insofar as it punishes "homosexual conduct," as that phrase is defined in the statute to include "advocating . . . encouraging or promoting public or private homosexual activity" is unconstitutional. We also hold that the unconstitutional portion is severable from the part of the statute that proscribes "homosexual activity," and we find that portion constitutional.

BARRETT, Circuit Judge, dissenting:

■ ■ ■

The majority, unlike the district court, holds that portion of the statute which allows "punishment" for teachers for advocating "public homosexual conduct" to be overbroad because it is "not readily subject to a narrowing construction by the state courts" and "its deterrent effect on legitimate expression is both real and substantial." I disagree. Sodomy is *malum in se*, i.e., immoral and corruptible in its nature without regard to the fact of its being noticed or punished by the law of the state. It is not *malum prohibitum*, i.e., wrong *only* because it is forbidden by law and not involving moral turpitude. It is on this principle that I must part with the majority's holding that the "public homosexual conduct" portion of the Oklahoma statute is overbroad.

Any teacher who advocates, solicits, encourages or promotes the practice of *sodomy* "in a manner that creates a substantial risk that such conduct will come to the attention of school children or school employees" is in fact and in truth *inciting* school children to participate in the abominable and detestable crime against nature. Such advocacy by school teachers, regardless of the situs where made, creates a substantial risk of being conveyed to school children. In my view, it does not merit any constitutional protection. There is no need to demonstrate that such conduct would bring about a material or substantial interference or disruption in the normal activities of the school. A teacher advocating the practice of sodomy to school children is without First Amendment protection. This statute furthers an important and substantial government interest, as determined by the Oklahoma legislature, unrelated to the suppression of free speech. The incidental restriction on alleged First Amendment freedom is no greater than is essential to the furtherance of that interest.

. . . Political expression and association is at the very heart of the First Amendment. The advocacy of a practice as universally condemned as the crime of sodomy hardly qualifies as such. There is no need to establish that such advocacy will interfere, substantially or otherwise, in normal school activities. It is sufficient that such advocacy is advanced in a manner that creates a substantial risk that such conduct will encourage school children to commit the abominable crime against nature. . . .

The Oklahoma legislature has declared that the advocacy by teachers of homosexual acts to school children is a matter of statewide concern. The Oklahoma statute does not condemn or in anywise affect teachers, homosexual or otherwise, except to the extent of the non-advocacy restraint aimed at the protection of school children. It does not deny them any

rights as human beings. To equate such "restraint" on First Amendment speech with the *Tinker* armband display and to require proof that advocacy of the act of sodomy will substantially interfere or disrupt normal school activities is a bow to permissiveness. To the same extent, the advocacy of violence, sabotage and terrorism as a means of effecting political reform held in *Brandenburg v. Ohio*, 395 U.S. 444 (1969) to be protected speech unless demonstrated as directed to and likely to incite or produce such action *did not* involve advocacy of a crime *malum in se* to school children by a school teacher.

■ ■ ■

. . . I submit that in the context of the Oklahoma public school system, the advocacy of sodomy by a teacher in a manner "that creates a substantial risk" it will come to the attention of school children deserves no First Amendment protection.

There is nothing abstract about a teacher advocating to school children the commission of the criminal act proscribed by section 886. The expression proscribed by § 6-103.15 is the advocacy of the commission of the very act held to be a criminal act in *Canfield*. Thus, the deterred speech or conduct concerns "advocating," "promoting" and "encouraging" school children to commit the crime of sodomy. In the context of the public school system involving the teacher-student relationship, it cannot be said that the advocacy of such action is mere advocacy of an abstract doctrine or belief. To hold otherwise ignores the difference between children and adults.

I would affirm.

Notes

1. Without issuing a written opinion, the Supreme Court per curiam affirmed by an equally divided Court the Tenth Circuit's decision in *National Gay Task Force*; Justice Powell did not participate. 470 U.S. 903 (1985).

2. A 1991 teacher's case provided another occasion for a federal court opinion finding height-
    ened scrutiny for discrimination based on sexual orientation. *See Jantz v. Muci*, 759 F. Supp.
    1543 (D. Kan. 1991). *Jantz* was reversed by the Tenth Circuit Court of Appeals on Oct. 9,
    1992. *See Jantz v. Muci*, 976 F.2d 623 (10th Cir. 1992).

C. Security Clearances, FBI, CIA, Police

Security risk has often been cited as a rationale for denying employment to gay people in
intelligence and military fields — lesbians and gay men are closeted and frightened about
others discovering their sexual orientation, it is argued, and thus foreign operatives could
readily prey on such fear, manipulating closeted homosexuals to reveal government secrets.
The following excerpt from Jonathan Ned Katz's *Gay American History* gives some
historical perspective to this argument.

1. BACKGROUND

♦

1950-55: WITCH-HUNT; THE UNITED STATES GOVERNMENT VERSUS HOMOSEXUALS
Jonathan Katz

A sampling of news stories from the years 1950 to 1955 conveys the mood created by the antihomosexual, anti-Communist witch-hunts occurring during that period and continuing for some time after. In the early 1950s, the fledgling homosexual emancipation organization, the Mattachine Society, was just getting started in Los Angeles, with a number of left-wing homosexuals prominent in the leadership. To understand the earliest years of the Mattachine movement it is essential to know about the simultaneous witch-hunting of "perverts" and "subversives" then taking place.

■ ■ ■

In July, Max Lerner began a series of articles on homosexuality in his daily column in the *New York Post*. The first, dated July 11, titled "The Tortured Problem... The Making of Homosexuals," focuses on various psycho-

JONATHAN N. KATZ, *1950-55: Witch-Hunt; The United States Government Versus Homosexuals*, in GAY AMERICAN
HISTORY 139–155 (1976).

logical theories of the causation and character or homosexuality, briefly raising, without answering it, "the question of why homosexuality gives our society so much concern."

On July 17, Lerner's *Post* column, titled "The Senator and the Purge," includes a revealing interview with anti-homosexual crusader Senator Kenneth Wherry:

In a long interview, Senator Kenneth Wherry (R. Nebr.) talked to me about his crusade to harry every last "pervert" from the Federal government services... Now in his second term, he has been a power in the Senate as Republican whip and now as floor leader. A man with a hearty manner in the traditional fashion of American politics, a bit pouchy, with glassed and graying hair, he looks like any small town lawyer or businessman. Sometimes his answers to my questions became harangues so violent as to make me think he would explode, until I saw that they left him unshaken and friendly as ever. Despite years of hard work and political tension, life seems to have left no writing of any kind on his face. It is the face of a man for whom there are no social complexities, no psychological subtleties, few private tragedies.

I asked Senator Wherry whether the problem of homosexuals in the government was primarily a moral or a security issue. He answered that it was both, but security was uppermost in his mind. I asked whether he made a connection between homosexuals and Communists."

"You can't hardly separate homosexuals from subversives," the Senator told me. "Mind you, I don't say every homosexual is a subversive, and I don't say every subversive is a homosexual. But a man of low morality is a menace in the government, whatever he is, and they are all tied up together."

"You don't mean to say, Senator, " I asked, "that there are no homosexuals who might be Democrats or even Republicans?"

"I don't say that by any means," he answered. "But this whole thing is tied together."

I asked whether he would be content to get the homosexuals out of the "sensitive posts" leaving alone those that have nothing to do with military security. There might be "associations," he said, between men in the sensitive and the minor posts. "There should be no people of that type working in any position in the government."

I asked whether the Senator knew the Kinsey findings about the extent of homosexuality in the male population. He had heard of them. "In the light of these figures, Senator," I asked him, "are you aware of the task which the purge of all homosexuals from government jobs opens up?"

"Take this straight," he answered, pounding his desk for emphasis. "I don't agree with the figures. I've read them all, but I don't agree with them. But regardless of the figures, I'll take the full responsibility for cleaning all of them out of the government."

I asked on what he based his view that homosexuals represent an unusual security risk. I cited a group of American psychiatrists who hold that a heterosexual with promiscuous morals may also be a security risk, that some men might be reckless gamblers or confirmed alcoholics and get themselves entangled or blackmailed.

The Senator's answer was firm: "You can stretch the security risk further if you want to," he said, "but right now I want to start with the homosexuals. When we get through with them, then we'll see what comes next."

This brought me to the question of definitions " You must have a clear idea, Senator," I said, "of what a homosexual is. It is a problem that has been troubling the psychiatrists and statisticians. Can you tell me what your idea is?"

"Quite simple," answered the Senator. "A homosexual is a diseased man, an abnormal man."

I persisted. "Do you mean one who has made a habit of homosexuality? Would you include someone who, perhaps in his teens, had some homosexual relations and has never had them since? Would you include those who are capable of both kinds of relation, some who may even be raising families?"

"You can handle it without requiring a definition," the Senator answered. "I'm convinced in my own mind that any homosexual is a bad risk."

"But how about those who get pushed out of their jobs when they are only in minor posts, when no security risk is involved, and when they are forced to resign for something they may have done years ago?"

"They resign voluntarily, don't they?" asked the Senator. "That's an admission of their guilt. That's all I need. My feeling is that there will be very few people hurt."

I cited a case in the State Department of a man who had once served in an American embassy and had allowed himself as a young man to be used by the ambassador. He is now in his forties, and his case is troubling the security officials.

"It might have happened," answered Senator Wherry, "but I'm not going to define what a homosexual is. I say not many will be hurt. The Army and Navy have used their rule of thumb on this. The military has done a good job."

"But not a complete job," I pointed out, "if we follow the Kinsey figures. They show that thirty percent of the men between twenty and twenty-four — the age group most represented in the armed services — have had some homosexual experience. Would you have all of them purged?"

"I repeat," answered Senator Wherry, "we should weed out all of them — wherever they are on the government payroll. . . ."

"I raised a question about the encroachments on privacy. "Get this straight," answered Senator Wherry, "no one believes in freedom of speech more than I do. I don't like anyone snooping around. But I don't like Kinsey snooping around either."

I asked him what he meant by Kinsey's snooping around. He said, "That's how he got the figures, isn't it?" I said that the Kinsey interviews were voluntary and asked whether he had ever had a chance to study Kinsey's book or his methods.

"Well," he answered, "all I know is that Kinsey has never contacted me. Has he contacted you?"

I said I'd had a friendly talk with Dr. Kinsey, and I offered to get the Senator in touch with him.

"But look, Lerner," Senator Wherry continued, breaking the cobwebs of our discussion, "we're both Americans, aren't we? I say, let's get these fellows out of the government."

"We have to know what fellows, we're talking about, Senator," I answered. "That's just what is bothering many of us. What homosexuals are bad risks? How do you treat the others? Can they be helped? Would you, Senator, bring doctors and psychiatrists into the picture and make them part of the machinery for dealing with this problem?"

"No," he answered, "I don't think doctors are needed. We can handle this by rule of thumb."

The next day, July 18, Lerner's column, titled "Lieutenant Blick of the Vice Squad," presents an amazing exposé.

In an age of experts Lieutenant Roy E. Blick, of the District of Columbia Police Department, rates as a very important man in Washington. He is head of the

Vice Squad, one of whose tasks is to deal with homosexuals. "Go see Blick," I was repeatedly told as I tried to track down the security story about homosexuals. "He has the facts and figures." So I did.

Lieutenant Blick is a tough cop. When I came into his office he was in the midst of a phone conversation about homosexuals which would have been wonderful detail for a documentary except that no one would dare put it on the screen. Burly, graying and just ungrammatical enough to match a Hollywood pattern for police lieutenants, Blick has been on the Vice Squad nineteen years, and he has a pride in his job. He has four detectives on his squad who do nothing but check on homosexuals.

He seemed worried about our interview. He didn't like being caught, he said, "between the Democrats and the Republicans." He was referring to his star-witness testimony before the Hill-Wherry subcommittee, in which he had given his classic estimate of five thousand homosexuals in Washington.

"I had no idea," Lieutenant Blick told me, "that I was getting into a political football." When I asked what made him think the homosexual inquiry was just politics, he said darkly, "Something I heard this morning," but wouldn't elaborate.

The committee summons to him had come as a surprise. I asked how it could have been, since Senator Wherry had talked privately with him before he had sprung him dramatically on the committee.

"Yes, the Senator came down here," he admitted, "and talked about these cases with me. But I didn't know what the committee wanted me for. I came there without a note. The figures I gave them were guesses, my own guesses, not official figures."

"We would all like to know," I said, "On what basis you reached your guesses."

Blick seemed to grow more restless at this point. He squirmed and twisted, thrust his hands up in a helpless gesture.

"We have these police records," he finally said. "You take the list. Well, every one of these fellows has friends. You multiply the list by a certain percentage-say three percent or four percent."

"Do you mean," I asked, "that your police list is only three or four percent of the total, and you multiply it by twenty-five or thirty?"

A faltering "Yes."

"If your final estimate was five thousand, does that mean your police list was less than two hundred?"

"No," he answered doubtfully. Then he added, "I mean five percent."

"You mean then that you multiply your list by twenty?"

Again a "Yes," then a "No." Finally, "I multiply my list by five."

You mean you started with a list of one thousand and multiplied by five to get five thousand?"

Blick shifted his gaze around the room. Again the upward thrust of the hands, as if to say "How did a good cop ever get into this sort of situation?" But he didn't answer my question.

I made a fresh start. "You have a list of the men you arrested?" He did.

You also have a larger list, including men you never arrested?" After hesitation-yes, he had a larger list as well.

"Did the fellows you arrested give the names of others?"

"Yes, he answered, this time with eagerness, every one of these fellows has five or six friends. Take Smith. We bring him in. We say to him, "Who are your friends?" He says, "I have none." I say, "Oh, come on, Smith. We know you fellows go around in gangs. We know you go to rug parties. Who are your friends?" Then he tells us — Jones, Robinson."

"So you put Jones and Robinson down on your list?" I asked.

"Yes, we put them down."

"And that's how you complied your list?" Yes, it was.

"But you said a while ago that you took the count of the men you arrested, and multiplied by five."

"Yes, I did"

"Well, which do you do? Multiply by five, or add all the friends you find out about?"

"I do both."

"How much of each?"

Blick finally broke into a smile of relief. "Well, it's sixty-forty. Sixty percent of it I put the friends down on the list, and forty percent of it I multiply by five."

This adventure in higher mathematics had exhausted both of us. I thought back grimly to the reverent way Senators and security officers used Blick's estimate of five thousand homosexuals in Washington, with 3,750 in the government, and I reflected that this was how a statistic got to be born.

"Do you think five thousand are too many?" Blick asked me.

I thought of the Kinsey figures. "If you mean just any kind of homosexual, and use it loosely," I answered, "I suspect you are conservative."

He clutched eagerly at my answer. "That's what I keep saying," he went on, "I'm conservative in my figures. I'm conservative about everything, Mr. Lerner."

I asked how he got his figure for the number of homosexuals working for the government.

"Oh," he said, I took the five thousand for Washington. And I figured that three out of four of them worked for the government."

We spent a long time talking about what types he counted as homosexuals for the purpose of his figures, but the problem of definition proved even more exhausting to both of us than that of statistics. Lieutenant Blick was a cop, not a logician, or a mathematician....

Lieutenant Blick glows at Senator Wherry's recommendation that the District Vice Squad be strengthened with a greater appropriation. He also wishes he had a Lesbian squad.

On December 15, 1950, the Senate Committee on Expenditures in the Executive Departments issues an interim report on "Employment of Homosexuals and Other Sex Perverts in Government," a major document of the 1950s anti-homosexual witch-hunt era. On December 16, the *New York Times* headlines a page 3 story on the report.

FEDERAL VIGILANCE ON PERVERTS ASKED
Senate Group Says They Must Be Kept Out of Government Because of Security Risk

A Senate investigating group labeled sexual perverts today as dangerous security risks and demanded strict and careful screening to keep them off the Government payroll. It said that many Federal agencies had not taken "adequate steps to get these people out of Government."...

Stressing the risk that the Government takes in employing a sex deviate or keeping one on the payroll, the subcommittee said:

"The lack of emotional stability which is found in most sex perverts, and the weakness of their moral fiber, makes them susceptible to the blandishments of foreign espionage agents."

Called Prey to Blackmailers'

The report also noted that perverts were "easy prey to be blackmailed." It said that Communist and Nazi agents had sought to get secret government data from Federal employees "by threatening to expose their abnormal sex activities."

The subcommittee criticized the State Department particularly for "mishandling" ninety-one cases of homosexualism among its employees. It said that many of the employees were allowed to resign "for personal reasons," and that no steps were taken to bar them from other Government jobs.

Tightening Laws Urged

The committee said that it was unable to determine accurately how many perverts now held Federal jobs. It

added, however, that since January 1, 1947, a total of 4,954 cases had been processed, including 4,380 in the military services and 574 on Federal civilian payrolls...

In addition to strict enforcement of Civil Service rules about firing perverts, the subcommittee recommended tightening of the District of Columbia laws on sexual perversion, closer liaison between the Federal agencies and the police and a thorough inquiry by all divisions of the government into all reasonable complaints of perverted sexual activity.

■ ■ ■

Note

This excerpt may seem antiquated, but as the following cases make clear, the security industry in this country still relies to some extent on these types of arguments. Nonetheless, the Defense Department has demonstrated some change in tone in recent years, particularly as controversy swirled in 1991 around the news that an Assistant Secretary of Defense was gay. *See* Lynne Duke, *Military's Last Social Taboo: 13,307 Discharged Since '82 for Homosexuality*, WASH. POST, Aug. 19, 1991, at A1. Following this revelation, the Secretary of Defense commented that the security risk argument was an "old chestnut," although he defended the Defense Department's ban on gays in the military. *See Court Reinstates Lesbian's Lawsuit Against Army*, N.Y. TIMES, Aug. 20, 1991, at A22. The following cases examine the security risk argument in the context of employment by the CIA, FBI, and Defense Department contractors.

2. CIA

One of the few gay cases ever heard by the United States Supreme Court involved security issues, although by the time the case reached the Court, this was not the critical issue in the case. The case, *Webster v. Doe*,[1] involved a gay man who was fired by the CIA after he came out. He challenged his discharge on the grounds that it violated federal regulations, and the due process and equal protection components of the Federal Constitution. A federal district

---

1. 486 U.S. 592 (1988).

court ruled in his favor,[4] but the decision was reversed by a divided D.C. Circuit.[5] Both parties appealed to the Supreme Court.

In the Supreme Court, the Reagan administration's Justice Department argued that CIA hiring and firing decisions were completely insulated from judicial review, whether that review was based on regulation, statute, or the Constitution. The Supreme Court rejected this argument. Although finding that the CIA's decisions could not be reviewed for procedural error under the federal Administrative Procedure Act,[6] the Court did find that the CIA was bound by the Federal Constitution in its employment decisions.[7]

From the perspective of lesbian/gay rights, the critical holding in the case came in a footnote. In addition to arguing that the CIA was immune from the Constitution, the United States had argued that discrimination on the basis of sexual orientation did not offend the Constitution. In a footnote pertaining to this argument, the Court wrote:

> Petitioner asserts, *see* Brief for Petitioner 27-28, n. 23, that respondent fails to present a colorable constitutional claim when he asserts that there is a general CIA policy against employing homosexuals. Petitioner relies on our decision in *Bowers v. Hardwick*, 478 U.S. 186 (1986), to support this view. This question was not presented in the petition for certiorari, and we decline to consider it at this stage of the litigation.[8]

Thus, the *Webster* Court took no position on the ultimate issue equal of protection of lesbians and gay men under the Constitution, in the context of security clearances or any other issue. Doe eventually lost his case.[9]

A later case challenging discrimination by the CIA was settled by the agency after the U.S. Court of Appeals for the Ninth Circuit affirmed the District Court's denial of the agency's motion to dismiss.[10] Pursuant to the settlement, the CIA re-employed the plaintiff.[11]

3. FBI

PADULA v. WEBSTER

822 F.2d 97 (D.C. Cir. 1987)

SILBERMAN, J.

Appellant Margaret A. Padula alleges that the Federal Bureau of Investigation ("FBI" or "Bureau") refused to employ her as a special agent because of her homosexuality, in violation of both Bureau policy and the equal protection guarantee of the Constitu-

---

4. *See Doe* v. *Casey*, 601 F. Supp. 581 (D.D.C. 1985).

5. *See Doe* v. *Casey*, 796 F.2d 1508 (D.C. Cir. 1986).

6. *See Webster*, 486 U.S. at 601.

7. *See id.* at 603-04.

8. *Id.* at 604 n.8.

9. *See Doe* v. *Webster*, 769 F. Supp. 1 (D.D.C. 1991), *aff'd in part and rev'd in part, Doe v. Gates*, 60 Empl. Prac. Dec. (CCH) ¶ 41949 (D.C. Cir. 1993).

10. *See Dubbs* v. *CIA*, 866 F.2d 1114 (9th Cir. 1989).

11. *See Dubbs* v. *CIA*, 769 F.Supp. 1113 (N.D. Cal. 1990).

tion. Ruling on a motion for summary judgment, the district court rejected both these challenges, concluding that the hiring decision was committed to the FBI's discretion by law and did not infringe upon appellant's constitutional rights. We affirm.

I

The FBI's policy towards employing homosexuals has been in some flux. Eight years ago, the Bureau formally represented to this court that it "has always had an absolute policy of dismissing proven or admitted homosexuals form its employ." *Ashton v. Civiletti*, 613 F.2d 923, 926 (D.C. Cir. 1979). Two months later, FBI Director Webster issued a somewhat different formulation of the Bureau's position toward homosexuality:

> Now we treat it as a factor, and I must say in candor, it's a significant factor. It's a troublesome thing; I hope that the particular case will be handled with fairness and justice and I hope that at some point we will have a better understanding of the problem and the policy that should be addressed to it.

Id. at 927 n.5.

Several law schools, concerned with possible discrimination toward their homosexual students during the job recruitment season, requested clarification of the FBI's policy. John Mintz, an Assistant Director of the FBI and the the FBI's Legal Counsel, assumed responsibility for answering these queries. On July 21, 1980, he wrote to Professor Marina Angel of the Temple University School of Law that:

> The FBI's focus in personnel matters has been and continues to be on conduct rather than status or preference and we carefully consider the facts in each case to determine whether the conduct may affect the employment. At the same time, we recognize individual privacy rights of applicants and employees.

In other letters to law school officials, Mintz stated that "individual sexual orientation, whether homosexual or heterosexual, may involve secret conduct that is relevant to employment in the FBI in that it increases employee susceptibility to compromise or breach of trust." He added, however, that "we are confident that the FBI has not engaged in improper discrimination regarding sexual orientation." Mintz also assured one law school dean that administrative action is taken not "simply because of . . . sexual orientation" but homosexual conduct is a significant factor is such decisions. When pressed for clarification, Mintz conceded that

> in fairness . . . based upon experience, I can offer no specific encouragement that a homosexual applicant will be found who satisfies all of the requirements . . . In any event, each case is reviewed independently for an objective determination of suitability.

In the summer of 1982, Padula applied for a position as a special agent with the FBI. On the basis of a written examination and an interview, the FBI ranked her 39th out of 303 qualified female applicants and 297th out of 1273 male and female applicants. Following these screening tests, the FBI concluded a routine background check. In addition to revealing favorable information about the applicant's abilities and character, the background investigation disclosed that appellant is a practicing homosexual. At a follow-up interview, Padula confirmed that she is a homosexual — explaining that although she does not flaunt her sexual orientation, she is unembarrassed and open about it and it is a fact well known to her family, friends and co-workers.

On October 19, 1983, the Bureau notified Padula that it was unable to offer her a position; her subsequent attempt to obtain reconsideration of the decision was denied. It was explained to her that her application had been evaluated in the same manner as all others, but had been rejected due to intense competition. Seventeen months later, Padula filed suit in the United States District Court for the District of Columbia. She alleged the FBI's decision not to hire her was based solely on the fact that she was a homosexual and that this decision violated the Bureau's "stated policy" not to discriminate on the basis of an applicant's sexual orientation. She also charges that the decision violated her constitutional rights to privacy, equal protection and due process under the first, fourth, fifth and ninth amendments to the Constitution.

In a memorandum opinion and order issued on November 15, 1985, the district court granted the FBI's motion for summary judgment. . . .

On appeal, we address two issues: first, whether the appointment decisions of the FBI are subject to judicial review in the absence of reliance upon constitutionally impermissible factors, and second, whether the alleged classification of homosexual applicants violated the equal protection mandate of the Constitution.[1]

II

The Administrative Procedure Act ("APA") establishes a general presumption of reviewability: a person "suffering a legal wrong because of agency action . . . is entitled to judicial review thereof." 5 U.S.C. § 701(a) (1982). But, the Act recognizes the two situations where this presumption does not hold: where a statute precludes judicial review, 5 U.S.C. § 701(a)(1), or where agency action is committed to agency discretion by law, 5 U.S.C. § 701(a)(2). The FBI contends that its hiring decisions are shielded from review by both of these exceptions. We

agree that the challenged hiring decision is sheltered from APA review by the second exception and therefore do not reach the statutory preclusion issue.[2]

Under the "committed to agency discretion by law" exception to the presumption of reviewability, even if Congress has not affirmatively barred review, review will not be had "if no judicially manageable standards are available for judging how and when an agency should exercise its discretion." *Heckler v. Chaney*, 470 U.S. 821 (1985). Judicially manageable standards may be found in formal and informal policy statements and regulations as well as in statutes, but if a court examines all these possible sources and concludes that there is, in fact, "no law to apply," judicial review will be precluded. *Citizens to Preserve Overton Park, Inc. v. Volpe*, 401 U.S. 402 (1971) (quoting S. Rep. No. 752, 79th Cong., 1st Sess. 26 (1945)).

Padula concedes that the Bureau's employment practices have been traditionally unreviewable — Congress has consistently exempted the FBI from statutory schemes governing the civil service — and that there is no meaningful statutory standard against which to judge the FBI's exercise of discretion. She argues, however, that the FBI limited its own discretion by adopting a binding policy regarding the hiring of homosexuals — a policy that purportedly barred the Bureau from refusing to hire an employee on the basis of homosexuality unless the particular applicant's sexual conduct would adversely affect his or her employment responsibilities. Padula maintains that this policy, which was disclosed in various public statements and letters issued from the Bureau, provides us with "law to apply," thus making the FBI's refusal to her reviewable.

It is well settled that an agency, even one that enjoys broad discretion, must adhere to voluntarily adopted, binding policies that

---

1. We do not address Padula's initial assertion that her constitutional rights to privacy and due process were violated since she does not argue this on appeal.

2. The FBI does not argue that our review of appellant's constitutional claim is precluded, by statute or otherwise.

limit its discretion. In determining whether an agency's statements constitute "binding norms," we traditionally look to the present effect of the agency's pronouncements. Statements that are merely prospective, imposing no rights or obligations on the respective parties, will not be treated as binding norms. We also examine whether the agency's statements leave the agency free to exercise its discretion. Pronouncements that impose no significant restraints on the agency's discretion are not regarded as binding norms. As a general rule, an agency pronouncement is transformed into a binding norm if so intended by the agency, and agency intent, in turn, is "ascertained by an examination of the statement's language, the context, and any available extrinsic evidence."

Although the FBI has no published regulation governing what factors may be utilized in selecting a special agent, internal guidelines and rules not formally promulgated have occasionally been held to bind agency conduct. The more than a dozen FBI letters to law schools involved here might well be sufficient to establish a binding policy if they in fact limited the Bureau's discretion. But they do not.

Padula claims that the language of the FBI's various statements and letters makes it clear that the FBI has a policy not to discriminate on the basis of sexual preference, a policy under which only particular sexual conduct that is shown directly to increase employee susceptibility to compromise or breach of trust is a bar to employment. Thus, she maintains that the FBI's binding policy made sexual preference in and of itself irrelevant to the selection process. We read no such message in the FBI's statements. At best for appellant, the pronouncements reaffirm the Bureau's tradi-

tional pledge "not to improperly discriminate against any applicant, " and to direct a "focus in personnel matters . . . on conduct rather than status or preference." Quite explicitly, though, the FBI states that: "[i]ndividual sexual orientation may involve conduct that is relevant to employment in the FBI in that it increases employee susceptibility to compromise or breach of trust." Contrary to Padula's assertion that the FBI has made sexual preference irrelevant to the selection process, these statements indicate that the Bureau does indeed look to an applicant's sexual orientation, for it might "involve conduct that is relevant to employment."

Appellant points out that many of these statements were made in the context of a campaign to enable the FBI to recruit at graduate schools that prohibited recruiting by employers that discriminated on the basis of sexual preference. Be that as it may, we still can find no indication that the FBI renounced homosexuality as a basis for reaching employment decisions.[4] Indeed, the FBI was very careful — if a bit clever — not to tie its hands in any way. For example, instead of executing a statement of nondiscrimination at Syracuse University, the Bureau simply reiterated its policy "not to improperly discriminate against any applicant." When forced to clarify the practical effect of its policy, however, Assistant Director Mintz candidly admitted that homosexual applicants were unlikely to be hired:

> in fairness . . . based upon experience, I can offer no specific encouragement that a homosexual applicant will be found who satisfies all the requirements. . . . In any event, each case is reviewed independently for an objective determination of suitability.

---

4. Padula also relies on statements by FBI field agents, who told her that:

> while *sexual preference is not a basis for hiring decisions*, the FBI does not want to have agents subjected
>
> to blackmail or extortion based upon any practice in which they may engage. [emphasis added by the court].

This statement simply transmits the same message as the Bureau's more formal letters. Sexual preference per se is not a basis for hiring decisions, but sexual conduct is relevant.

Despite the context, then, the FBI's statements cannot be construed, even in the most critical light, as cabining the FBI's traditional hiring discretion in the way appellant suggests. Arguably, the FBI has committed itself not to consider the sexual orientation of an applicant who can show he does not engage in sex, but it clearly has done no more. Appellant's nonconstitutional claim is therefore nonreviewable.

III

We turn to the Constitutional claim for even where agency action is "committed to agency discretion by law," review is still available to determine if the Constitution has been violated. Padula alleges that the FBI refused to hire her solely because of her homosexuality and that this action denied her the equal protection of the law guaranteed by the fourteenth amendment. She urges us to recognize homosexuality as a suspect or quasi-suspect classification. A suspect classification is subjected to strict scrutiny and will be sustained only if "suitably tailored to serve a compelling state interest." *City of Cleburne v. Cleburne Living Center*, 473 U.S. 432 (1985), whereas under heightened scrutiny given to quasi-suspect class, the challenged classification must be "substantially related to a legitimate state interest." *Mills v. Habuetzel*, 456 U.S. 91, 99 (1982).

We perceive ostensible disagreement between the parties as to the description of the class in question. The government insists the FBI's hiring policy focuses only on homosexual conduct, not homosexual status. By that, we understand the government to be saying that it would not consider relevant for employment purposes homosexual orientation that did *not* result in homosexual conduct. Plaintiff rejects that distinction, suggesting that "homosexual status is accorded to people who engage in homosexual conduct, and people who engage in homo-

sexual conduct are accorded homosexual status." But whether or not homosexual status attaches to someone who does not—for whatever reason—engage in homosexual conduct, appellant does not claim those circumstances apply to her. The parties' definitional disagreement is therefore irrelevant to this case. The issue presented us is only whether homosexuals, when defined as persons who engage in homosexual conduct, constitute a suspect or quasi-suspect classification and accordingly whether the FBI's hiring decision is subject to strict or heightened scrutiny.

The Supreme Court has used several explicit criteria to identify suspect and quasi-suspect classification. In *San Antonio School Dist. v. Rodriguez*, 411 U.S. 1 (1973), the Court stated that a suspect class is one "saddled with such disabilities, or rejected to such a history of purposeful unequal treatment, or relegated to such a position of political powerlessness as to command extraordinary protection for the majoritarian political process." *Id.* at 28. The immutability of the group's identifying trait is also a factor to be considered. *See Frontiero v. Richardson*, 411 U.S. 677, 686 (1973). However, the Supreme Court has recognized only three classifications as suspect: race, *Loving v. Virgina*, 388 U.S. 1 (1967), alienage, *Graham v. Richardson*, 403 U.S. 365, 372 (1971); *but see*, *Ambach v. Norwich*, 441 U.S. 68, 72-75 (1979), and national origin, *Korematsu v. United States*, 323 U.S. 214, 216 (1944); and two others as quasi-suspect: gender, *Mississippi University for Women v. Hogan*, 458 U.S. 718 (1982), and illegitimacy, *Lalli v. Lalli*, 439 U.S. 259, 265 (1978). Appellant, asserting that homosexuals meet all the requisite criteria, would have us add homosexuality to that list. Appellees, on the other hand contend that two recent cases, *Bowers v. Hardwick*, 478 U.S. 186 (1986) and *Dronenburg v. Zech*, 741 F.2d 1388 (D.C. Cir. 1984), are insurmountable barriers to appellant's claim. We agree.

In *Dronenburg*, a naval petty officer claimed violation of his constitutional rights to privacy and to equal protection of the laws because he was discharged from the Navy for engaging in homosexual conduct. A panel of this court rejected the claim, holding that "we can find no constitutional right to engage in homosexual conduct and, . . as judges, we have no warrant to create one." *Id.* at 1397. Although the court's opinion focused primarily on whether the constitutional right to privacy protected homosexual conduct, the court reasoned that if the right to privacy did not provide protection "then appellant's right to equal protection is not infringed unless the Navy's policy is not rationally related to a permissible end." *Id.* at 1391. The unique needs of the military, the court concluded, justified discharged for homosexual conduct.

Dronenburg anticipated by two years the Supreme Court's decision in *Hardwick*, in which the Court upheld a Georgia law criminalizing sodomy against a challenge that it violated the due process clause. In *Hardwick*, the Court explained that the right to privacy as defined in its previous decisions inheres only in family relationships, marriage and procreation and does not extend more broadly to all kinds of private sexual conduct between consenting adults. Putting the privacy precedent aside, the Court further concluded that a right to engage in consensual sodomy is not constitutionally protected as a fundamental right since it is neither "implicit in the concept of ordered liberty," nor "deeply rooted in this Nation's history and tradition." Accordingly, the Court's review of the Georgia statute inquired only whether a rational basis for the law existed. And the Court determined that the presumed belief of the Georgia electorate that sodomy is immoral provide an adequate rationale for criminalizing such conduct.

Padula argues that both *Dronenburg* and *Hardwick* are inapposite because they addressed only the scope of the privacy right, not what level of scrutiny is appropriate under equal protection analysis. But as we have noted, *Dronenburg* did involve an equal protection claim. Although the court did not explicitly consider whether homosexuals should be treated as a suspect class,

it seemed to regard that question settled by its conclusion that the Constitution does not afford a privacy right to engage in homosexual conduct. In *Hardwick*, to be sure, plaintiffs did not rely on the equal protection clause, but after the Court rejected an extension of the right to privacy, it responded to plaintiff's alternate argument that the Georgia law should be struck down as without rational basis (under the due process clause) since it was predicated merely on the moral judgment of a majority of the Georgia electorate. The Court summarily rejected that position, refusing to declare the Georgian majoritarian view "inadequate" to meet a rational basis test. We therefore think the court's reasoning in *Hardwick* and *Dronenburg* forecloses appellant's efforts to gain suspect class status for practicing homosexuals. It would be quite anomalous, on its face, to declare status defined by conduct that states may constitutionally criminalize as deserving of strict scrutiny under the equal protection clause. More importantly, in all those cases in which the Supreme Court has accorded suspect or quasi-suspect status to a class, the Court's holding was predicated on an unarticulated, but necessarily implicit, notion that it is plainly unjustifiable (in accordance with standards not altogether clear to us) to discriminate invidiously against the particular class. *E.g. compare Frontiero v. Richardson*, 411 U.S. 677, 686-87 (1973) (statutory distinctions between the sexes often invidiously relegate women to inferior positions); *with Massachusetts Board of Retirement v. Murgia*, 427 U.S. 307, 313 (1976) (aged have not been subject to invidious discrimination justifying extra protection from the political process). If the Court was unwilling to object to state laws that criminalize the behavior that defines the class, it is hardly open to a lower court to conclude that state sponsored discrimination against the class is individous. After all, there can hardly be more palpable discrimination against a class than making the conduct that defines the class criminal. *Accord Baker v. Wade*, 769 F.2d 289, 292 (5th Cir.

1985); *Rich v. Secretary of the Army*, 735 F.2d 1220, 1229 (10th Cir. 1984).

That does not mean, however, that any kind of negative state action against homosexuals would be constitutionally authorized. Laws or government practices must still, if challenged, pass the rational basis test of the equal protection clause. A governmental agency that discriminates against homosexuals must justify that discrimination in terms of some government purpose. Appellant did not specifically argue that the FBI's practices challenged here failed that lesser examination — perhaps because the Supreme Court in *Hardwick* rejected a similar rational basis argument under the due process clause. But assuming the argument is implicit in their equal protection challenge, we think it was squarely rejected in *Dronenburg*. In *Dronenburg*, the court held that it was rational for the Navy to conclude that homosexual conduct was detrimental to the maintenance of morale and discipline. The court observed that homosexuality "generate[s] dislike and disapproval among many.

. . who find it morally offensive," and, moreover, is criminalized in many states.

The FBI, as the Bureau points out, is a national law enforcement agency whose agents must be able to work in all states of the nation. To have agents who engage in conduct criminalized in roughly one-half of the states would undermine the law enforcement credibility of the Bureau. Perhaps more important, FBI agents perform counterintelligence duties that involve highly classified matters relating to national security. It is not irrational for the Bureau to conclude the at the criminalization of homosexual conduct coupled with the general public opprobrium toward homosexuality exposes many homosexuals, even "open" homosexuals, to the risk of possible blackmail to protect their partners, if not themselves. We therefore conclude the Bureau's specialized functions, like the Navy's in *Dronenburg*, rationally justify consideration of homosexual conduct that could adversely affect that agency's responsibilities. The judgment of the district court is hereby

Affirmed.

Notes

1. A preliminary decision in a recent federal court case has cast doubt upon the *Padula* precedent. In *Buttino v. FBI*, 59 Empl. Prac. Dec. (CCH) ¶ 41725 (N.D. Cal. 1992), Buttino alleges that he was fired after more than twenty-years with the FBI after the agency discovered that he was gay. Buttino filed suit arguing, inter alia, that his discharge violated his rights under the equal protection clause. The court rejected the FBI's motion for summary judgment on this claim, stating that it could not conclude that such discrimination, if it did occur, was rational. *Id. See also Buttino v. FBI*, 801 F. Supp. 298 (N.D. Cal. 1992) (denying motion for reconsideration).

2. One of the first cases finding protections for lesbian and gay federal employees involved a mail sorter at the FBI. *See Ashton v. Civiletti*, 613 F.2d 923 (D.C. Cir. 1979). The D.C. Circuit held that Ashton had been deprived of his due process rights to a job in which he had a "property" interest when he was dismissed without a hearing. The importance of the *Ashton* precedent has been undermined by later Supreme Court cases restricting the notion that federal employees have a "property" right in their employment. *See, e.g., Regents of the Univ. of Mich. v. Ewing*, 474 U.S. 214, 224 (1985); *Cleveland Bd. of Educ. v. Loudermill*, 470 U.S. 532, 538 (1985). Moreover, all that was won in *Ashton* — which was quite important at the time — was a right to a hearing, not a right to retain the job.

4. DEFENSE DEPARTMENT SECURITY CLEARANCES

The case that follows concerns employees of companies that do work for the Defense Department. Often employees at such defense contractors need security clearances for the work they are doing with the government. The Defense Department's Industrial Security Clearance Office (or DISCO) is the branch of the government responsible for these decisions. DISCO adopted regulations that subject lesbian and gay employees to heightened security clearance checks. While many gay employees are able to secure clearances, the extra steps they have to take delay their applications and often cost them their jobs.

A group of gay employees working in the Silicon Valley in California called "High Tech Gays" filed suit in 1984 against DISCO challenging this system. In an important 1987 decision, the federal district court declared the agency's process of using special checks on gay employees to be unconstitutional.[1] In so doing, the court employed heightened judicial scrutiny, finding that classifications based on sexual orientation were constitutionally suspect. The Ninth Circuit reversed.

HIGH TECH GAYS v. DEFENSE INDUS. SEC. CLEARANCE OFFICE

895 F.2d 563 (9th Cir. 1990)

BRUNETTI, Circuit Judge:

■ ■ ■

I

■ ■ ■

B

The plaintiffs brought this action in district court claiming:

that DISCO's policy and practice of refusing to grant industrial security clearances to gay persons because of their sexual orientation, private practice thereof with consenting adults, and related social and political activities, including membership in gay organizations, and of subjecting them to unjustifiable and time-consuming in-vestigations because of their sexual orientation and related matters violates their Constitutional rights to freedom of speech and association and to equal protection and due process of law.

The suit proceeded as a class action in the district court with three individually named plaintiffs: Timothy Dooling, Joel Crawford and Robert Weston.

Plaintiff Dooling is a homosexual who applied for a Secret industrial clearance on May 2, 1983. On March 22, 1984, DISCO issued a memorandum recommending that Dooling be considered ineligible for a security clearance and forwarded the case to DISCR [the Directorate for Industrial Security Clearance Review]. DISCR eventually granted Dooling a Secret clearance in May 1984.

---

1. *High Tech Gays* v. *Defense Indus. Sec. Clearance Office*, 668 F.Supp. 1361 (N.D.Cal. 1987).

Plaintiff Crawford is a homosexual who applied for Secret clearance in December 1981. After DISCO recommended that Crawford be considered ineligible for a Secret clearance, DISCR denied Crawford's application for a Secret clearance based on evidence of past drug abuse.

Plaintiff Weston, a homosexual, has a Secret clearance and in 1984 submitted an application for Top Secret clearance as required for his job at Lockheed Missiles & Space Co. Lockheed never forwarded his application to the DoD [Department of Defense] because his application revealed he belonged to a gay organization.

The plaintiffs sought an order: declaring unconstitutional and enjoining the DISCO policy of refusing to grant Secret clearances to gay people who have participated in homosexual activity within the past fifteen years and requiring that applications of gay people be forwarded to DISCR for adjudication; declaring unconstitutional and enjoining the DIS [Defense Investigative Service] practice of subjecting gay applicants to in-depth and time-consuming investigations (required by DIS Manual for Personnel Security Investigations); declaring unconstitutional the five reasons DISCO used to recommend denial of plaintiff Dooling's clearance; and declaring unconstitutional DISCR's processing of plaintiff Crawford's application subsequent to the filing of this lawsuit.

The plaintiffs and the DoD each moved for summary judgment and upon considering the cross-motions, the district court denied the DoD's motion for summary judgment and granted the plaintiffs' motion.

The DoD then filed a motion for reconsideration and a motion for a stay pending appeal. The motion for reconsideration was based on new evidence from several sources indicating that hostile intelligence agencies target persons who are especially vulnerable, and that among others, persons who are homosexuals are considered vulnerable by these agencies. The district court denied the motion for reconsideration but granted the DoD's motion for a stay pending appeal. The DoD contends that its motion should have been granted and asks that we reverse the district court's grant of the plaintiffs' motion.

■ ■ ■

III

Equal Protection

"The equal protection clause of the Fourteenth Amendment commands that no State shall deny to any person within its jurisdiction the equal protection of the laws, which is essentially a direction that all persons similarly situated should be treated alike." *City of Cleburne v. Cleburne Living Center*, 473 U.S. 432, 439 (1985) (quotation omitted).

■ ■ ■

It is . . . clear that there is an equal protection component of the Due Process Clause of the Fifth Amendment which applies to the federal government. *See Bolling v. Sharpe*, 347 U.S. 497 (1954).

■ ■ ■

It is well established that there are three standards we may apply in reviewing the plaintiffs' equal protection challenge to the DoD Security Clearance Regulations: strict scrutiny, heightened scrutiny, and rational basis review. *See Cleburne*, 473 U.S. at 440-41. The plaintiffs assert that homosexuality should be added to the list of suspect or quasi-suspect classifications requiring strict or heightened scrutiny. We disagree and hold that the district court erred in applying heightened scrutiny to the regulations at issue and that the proper standard is rational basis review. *Accord Ben-Shalom v. Marsh*, 881 F.2d 454, 464 (7th Cir. 1989); *Woodward v. United States*, 871 F.2d 1068, 1076 (Fed.Cir. 1989); *Padula v. Webster*, 822 F.2d 97, 103 (D.C.Cir. 1987).

The Supreme Court has ruled that homosexual activity is not a fundamental right protected by substantive due process and that the proper standard of review under the Fifth Amendment is rational basis review. *Bowers v. Hardwick*, 478 U.S. 186, 194-96 (1986). The Court explained that the right to privacy inheres only in family relationships, marriage and procreation, and does not extend to all private sexual conduct between consenting adults. The Court specifically characterized "fundamental liberties" under the Constitution "as those liberties that are deeply rooted in this Nation's history and tradition." *Id.* at 192 (quotation omitted). In holding that the Constitution does not confer a fundamental right upon homosexuals to engage in consensual sodomy, the Court stated:

> There should be, therefore, great resistance to expand the substantive reach of [the Due Process Clauses of the Fifth and Fourteenth Amendments], particularly if it requires redefining the category of rights deemed to be fundamental. Otherwise, the judiciary necessarily takes to itself further authority to govern the country without express constitutional authority.

Id. at 195.

There has been a repudiation of much of the substantive gloss that the Court has placed on the due process clauses of the Fifth and Fourteenth Amendments. *See id.* at 194-95. If for federal analysis we must reach equal protection of the Fourteenth Amendment by the due process clause of the Fifth Amendment, *see Bolling*, 347 U.S. at 499, and if there is no fundamental right to engage in homosexual sodomy under the due process clause of the Fifth Amendment, *see Hardwick*, 478 U.S. at 194, it would be incongruous to expand the reach of equal protection to find a fundamental right of homosexual conduct under the equal protection component of the due process clause of the Fifth Amendment. *See Bolling*, 347 U.S. at 500.

Other circuits are in accord and have held that although the Court in *Hardwick* analyzed the constitutionality of the sodomy statute on a due process rather than equal protection basis, by the *Hardwick* majority holding that the Constitution confers no fundamental right upon homosexuals to engage in sodomy, and because homosexual conduct can thus be criminalized, homosexuals cannot constitute a suspect or quasi-suspect class entitled to greater than rational basis review for equal protection purposes. *See Ben-Shalom*, 881 F.2d at 464-65; *Woodward*, 871 F.2d at 1076; *Padula*, 882 F.2d at 103.

■ ■ ■

There is further support for our holding that homosexuals are not a suspect or quasi-suspect class as specifically applied to the plaintiffs' challenge to the DoD Security Clearance Regulations.

> The general rule is that legislation is presumed to be valid and will be sustained if the classification drawn by the statute is rationally related to a legitimate [governmental] interest. . . .
> The general rule gives way, however, when a statute classifies by race, alienage, or national origin. . . . [B]ecause such discrimination is unlikely to be soon rectified by legislative means, these laws are subjected to strict scrutiny. . . .
> [C]lassifications based on gender also call for heightened standard of review [as do classifications based on] illegitimacy.

Cleburne, 473 U.S. at 440-41 (quotation omitted).

It is apparent that while the Supreme Court has identified that legislative classifications based on race, alienage, or national origin are subject to strict scrutiny and that classifications based upon gender or illegitimacy call for a heightened standard, the Court has never held homosexuality to a heightened standard of review.

To be a "suspect" or "quasi-suspect" class, homosexuals must (1) have suffered a history of discrimination; (2) exhibit obvious, immutable, or distinguishing characteristics that define them as a discrete group; and (3) show that they are a minority or politically powerless, or alternatively show that the statutory classification at issue burdens a fundamental right. *Bowen v. Gilliard*, 483 U.S. 587, 602-03 (1986) (due to a lack of these characteristics, the statutory classifications of the Federal Aid to Families with Dependent Children Program were subject to only a rational basis review) (citing *Lyng v. Castillo*, 477 U.S. 635, 638 (1986) (due to a lack of these characteristics, the statutory classifications of the Federal Food Stamp Program were subject to only a rational basis review)).

While we do agree that homosexuals have suffered a history of discrimination, we do not believe that they meet the other criteria. Homosexuality is not an immutable characteristic; it is behavioral and hence is fundamentally different from traits such as race, gender, or alienage, which define already existing suspect and quasi-suspect classes. *Accord Woodward*, 871 F.2d at 1076. The behavior or conduct of such already recognized classes is irrelevant to their identification. *Id.*

Moreover, legislatures have addressed and continue to address the discrimination suffered by homosexuals on account of their sexual orientation through the passage of anti-discrimination legislation.[10] Thus, homosexuals are not without political power; they have the ability to and do "attract the attention of the lawmakers," as evidenced by such legislation. *See Cleburne*, 473 U.S. at 445. *Accord Ben-Shalom*, 881 F.2d at 466. Lastly, as previously noted, homosexual conduct is not a fundamental right. *Hardwick*, 478 U.S. at 194.

Our review compels us to agree with the other circuits that have ruled on this issue and to hold that homosexuals do not constitute a suspect or quasi-suspect class entitled to greater than rational basis scrutiny under the equal protection component of the Due Process Clause of the Fifth Amendment.

Because the district court erred in granting the plaintiffs' motion for summary judgment by applying heightened scrutiny in its equal protection analysis, we now review the plaintiffs' and defendants' cross-motions for summary judgment applying rational basis scrutiny.[11]

IV.

CROSS-MOTIONS FOR SUMMARY JUDGMENT

A.

■ ■ ■

The DoD contends that the district court improperly granted the plaintiffs' motion for summary judgment. We agree. The

---

10. For example: Wisconsin has a comprehensive statute barring employment discrimination on the basis of sexual orientation, *Wis.Stat.Ann.*, §§ 111.31-.395 (West 1988); California has barred violence against persons or property based on sexual orientation, *Cal.Civ. Code*, § 51.7 (West 1984); and Michigan has barred the denial of care in health facilities on the basis of sexual orientation), *Mich. Comp.Laws Ann.*, § 333.20201(2)(a) (West 1984). Executive Orders in other states prohibit such discrimination. *See e.g.*, *N.Y.Comp.Codes R. & Regs.*, titl. 4, § 28 (1983) (barring discrimination in state employment or in the provision of state services and benefits on the basis of sexual orientation). Many cities and counties have also enacted anti-discrimination regulations, including New York, Los Angeles, Chicago, Washington D.C., Atlanta, Boston, Philadelphia, Seattle, and San Francisco. Developments in the Law, *Sexual Orientation and the Law*, 102 Harv.L.Rev. 1509, 1667-68, n. 49-51 (citations omitted).

11. We recognize that the denial of DoD's motion for summary judgment is not a final decision of the district court and thus, under normal circumstances, would not be appealable. However, because we have jurisdiction to decide DoD's appeal from the granting of plaintiffs' motion for summary judgment, we exercise our discretion to decide their claim of error in the denial of their summary judgment motion as well.

plaintiffs' affidavits and evidence fail to make a sufficient showing that the DoD does not have a rational basis for its expanded security investigation of homosexuals or that there is a genuine issue of material fact for trial. Nor have the plaintiffs offered "any significant probative evidence tending to support [their] complaint." *Anderson* [v. *Liberty Lobby*], 477 U.S. [242] at 256 [(1986)] (quotation omitted).

The plaintiffs first point to the inability of the DoD to find any evidence tending to show that homosexual applicants for clearances have "succumbed to blackmail," "failed to safeguard classified information," or that as a class are a "worse security risk" than heterosexual applicants.

Under a rational basis review as promulgated by the Supreme Court in *Cleburne*, the DoD is not required to conclusively establish that homosexuals have transmitted classified information for its policy of subjecting homosexual applicants to expanded investigations to be constitutional. The DoD need only show a rational basis for its policy and that its policy is rationally related to the legitimate governmental interest of protecting classified material for it to be constitutional. *Cleburne*, 473 U.S. at 440.

Next, the plaintiffs suggest that other "governmental evidence" conclusively demonstrates that homosexuals do not pose a security risk. Relying on the April 1985 hearings before the Senate Permanent Subcommittee on Investigations, the plaintiffs point out that of forty espionage cases, only two involved homosexuals, neither of which involved a blackmail attempt.

The report the plaintiffs refer to consists of unclassified summaries of a limited number of espionage cases involving individuals who have been convicted of compromising United States classified information. *Federal Government Security Programs, 1985: Hearings Before the Permanent Subcomm. on Investigations of the Senate Comm. on Governmental Affairs*, 99th Cong., 1st Sess. 99-166 (1985) (DIA report). Although these case studies involve actual circumstances

where DoD and DoD-related classified information was compromised, the report is not a study of all the significant espionage cases involving homosexuals. Moreover, one of the reported cases points out that homosexuals are targeted by the KGB:

> [He] was a homosexual and this fact interested the KGB handlers since the homosexual frequently is shunted by society and made to feel like a social outcast. Such a personality may seek to retaliate against a society that has placed him in this unenviable position. [He] was such a person and one of his first assignments on behalf of Soviet Intelligence was to spot other homosexuals in the American Community.

Id. at 916.

The plaintiffs' next contention is that their "factual study," illustrating that only two of the nineteen homosexual applicants for security clearance subjected to the expanded investigations were denied security clearances, conclusively establishes that homosexuals who limit their sexual activity to consenting adults in private are a good security risk. This contention is meritless. The plaintiffs' "factual study" of nineteen applications is not a large enough sample of homosexual applicants for security clearances to be able to draw such a broad conclusion. Even if the plaintiffs' contention had merit, it would take an expanded investigation of all homosexual applicants to determine which ones limit their sexual activities to consenting adults.

The plaintiffs' last contention is that the DoD "is more concerned with punishing homosexual clearance applicants than with treating them rationally regarding blackmail." In support, the plaintiffs rely on the deposition of Richard Olinger, former Manager of the Government Security Department at Lockheed Missiles and Space Company, in which Mr. Olinger responded to questions about the subject matter of two conferences he attended during his tenure with Lockheed. According to the plaintiffs, since homosexuality was not discussed at these two conferences on industrial security programs, the DoD has no "real" concern about homosexuals as security risks.

The plaintiffs' conclusion is without merit. A review of the deposition reveals that one of the conferences attended by Mr. Olinger concerned a specific espionage case and the other conference involved a discussion of statistical matters on processing security clearances. Given the limited agenda of these two conferences, it is apparent that the security risk of homosexuals would not be discussed.

We are convinced the DoD has met its burden of persuasion . . . by demonstrating that its investigatory policies and procedures for homosexuals are rationally related to permissible ends, and that the plaintiffs have failed to submit affirmative evidence to negate DoD's evidence. The DoD's justification for their policy of subjecting homosexual applicants to expanded investigations involves a two-step analyses: First, the DoD sought to establish that counterintelligence agencies target homosexuals; and, second, because homosexuals are targeted, the DoD subjects a homosexual applicant to an expanded investigation to determine if the applicant is susceptible to coercion or blackmail or otherwise vulnerable to counterintelligence efforts.

To establish that homosexuals are targeted by counterintelligence agencies, the DoD presented the following evidence. John Donnelly, Assistant Deputy Under Secretary of Defense for Counterintelligence and Security, who is directly responsible for ensuring that the Department's personnel security program remains responsive to the threats posed by hostile intelligence agencies, concluded that the recruitment of individuals by hostile intelligence agencies often involves the "exploitation of what those agencies consider to be human weaknesses, indiscretions and vices," and that with great consistency sexuality is considered a "potentially exploit-

able vulnerability." He states that hostile intelligence agencies attempt to segregate those with alcohol or drug problems, financial problems, a known disregard for security, and/or those who can be exploited sexually; and that although blackmail may sometimes be used after the person is already compromised, "generally the initial efforts of exploitation centers around enticing the targeted individual with money, sexual favors, treatment for alcoholism, etc." While he notes that this does not mean that hostile intelligence agencies always seek out homosexuals as targets, they usually spot individuals with the desired access and then assess them in order to determine the most effective approach.

Major Francis R. Short, USMC, Judge Advocate in the United States Marine Corps, who served as assistant trial counsel in the court-martial of Sergeant Clayton J. Lonetree, a marine convicted of espionage, stated that at the trial of Sergeant Lonetree, the court accepted Mr. John Barron of Annandale, Virginia, as an expert in the field of the methods and operations of the Soviet Intelligence Service (the KGB), and that Mr. Barron testified as to KGB recruitment of homosexuals.

Mr. Barron's testimony addressed the area of homosexuality on two occasions. While discussing the characteristics the KGB looks for in identifying potential targets for recruitment, he testified:

> [T]he KGB will attempt to identify those who are ideologically sympathetic, experiencing career difficulties, unsuccessful in social relationships, *or experiencing problems with* narcotics, alcohol, *homosexuality,* or marital difficulties . . . no one trait may be sufficient, and . . . *the KGB is encouraged when these traits are found in combination.*

Barron also specifically cited an example of just such an entrapment operation, in which the KGB entrapped a Canadian ambassador to the Soviet Union through the exploitation of a homosexual relationship. The DoD also relies on Barron's book, *KGB: The Secret Work of Soviet Secret Agents* (1974), which states that "the KGB is not primarily interested in homosexuals because of their presumed susceptibility to blackmail. In its judgment, homosexuality often is accompanied by personality disorders that make the victim potentially unstable and vulnerable to adroit manipulation." *Id.* at 280.

The DoD also presented extracts of sworn statements of Sergeant Lonetree, provided by Lonetree to Special Agents of the Naval Investigative Service, relating one meeting with his Soviet control Sasha (later identified as Aleksei Yefimou, an officer of the KGB), where Sasha specifically inquired as to homosexuals:

> During a meeting with Sasha *he asked me to tell him who were the homosexuals*, drunks and people who were exploitable who worked in the embassy as civilians. *He also asked for other Marines ... who might be queers*, dopers or drunks.

On at least one other occasion, "Sasha also wanted to know what marines had problems with alcohol or drugs *or those who were homosexual*."

Finally, the DoD relies on both plaintiff Dooling's admission that on one occasion someone attempted to blackmail him because of his sexual orientation, and Richard E. Fay, who described the 1979 Madsen espionage case involving the compromise of classified information by a homosexual.

B.

The DoD has determined what groups are targeted by hostile intelligence efforts. If an applicant falls within a targeted group — like homosexuals — the DoD subjects the applicant to an expanded investigation. The ex-

panded investigation determines whether the applicant is susceptible to coercion or otherwise vulnerable to hostile intelligence efforts. *See Padula*, 822 F.2d at 104 ("criminalization of homosexual conduct coupled with the general public opprobrium toward homosexuality, [subjects] even 'open' homosexuals, to the risk of possible blackmail to protect their partners, if not themselves"); and *McKeand v. Laird*, 490 F.2d 1262 (9th Cir. 1973) (examiner found that McKeand feared disclosure of his homosexuality, thus a target for coercion).

Special deference must be given by the court to the Executive Branch when adjudicating matters involving their decisions on protecting classified information:

> Predictive judgment of this kind must be made by those with the necessary expertise. . . . [T]he protection of classified information must be committed to the broad discretion of the agency responsible, and this must include broad discretion to determine who may have access to it. . . . [C]ourts traditionally have been reluctant to intrude upon the authority of the Executive in military and national security affairs.

Department of Navy v. Egan, 484 U.S. 518 (1988).

No one has the "right" to a security clearance. *Id.* at 824. We recognize that "[t]he attempt to define not only the individual's future actions, but those of outside and unknown influences renders the 'grant or denial of security clearance . . . an inexact science at best.'" *Id.* at 825 (quoting *Adams v. Laird*, 420 F.2d 230, 239 (D.C. Cir. 1969), *cert. denied*, 397 U.S. 1039 (1970)). Inexact science or not the DoD has articulated a rational relationship between their policy of subjecting homosexual applicants to expanded investigations and its compelling interest in national security.[13] *Id.*

---

13. The DoD advances other justifications for its policy: a homosexual may be emotionally unstable and homosexual conduct may be criminal. Because we conclude that the targeting of homosexuals by hostile intelligence agencies is a legitimate if not compelling justification for the expanded investigations, we need not address these additional justifications.

at 825 ("an agency head who must bear the responsibility for the protection of classified information committed to his custody should have the final say in deciding whether to repose his trust in an employee who has access to such information").

Since the DoD has met its initial burden of production, by negating an essential element of the plaintiffs' claim, the burden of production shifted to the plaintiffs to "produce evidentiary materials that demonstrate the existence of a 'genuine issue' for trial." *Celotex*, 477 U.S. at 331 (Brennan, J., dissenting). Thus, it was up to the plaintiffs to meet the issue that the expanded investigations were not, in fact, rationally related to national security concerns.

We conclude that the plaintiffs' affidavits do not raise genuine issues as to any fact material to the alleged constitutional violation, but merely raise an issue as to the alleged irrationality of the KGB's opinion on homosexual behavior. The plaintiffs' evidence is not material to the DoD's basis for expanded investigations of homosexual applicants — that homosexuals are targeted by counterintelligence agencies. *See Anderson*, 477 U.S. at 248 (only disputes over the outcome of the suit under the governing law will properly preclude entry of summary judgment).

For example, the plaintiffs rely on a resolution of the American Psychological Association which states that homosexuality "implies no impairment in judgment, stability, reliability or general social or vocational capabilities." Resolution of American Psychological Association (January 1975). According to the plaintiffs, the "KGB's obsolete opinions on homosexual behavior"

should be rejected in favor of adopting the position of the American Psychological Association. However, the counterintelligence agencies' reasons for targeting homosexuals — even if based on continuing ignorance or prejudice — are irrelevant. If hostile intelligence efforts are directed at homosexuals, the DoD must be assured that because of the targeting, the individual will not compromise national secrets.

The Preliminary Joint Staff Study on Protection of National Secrets (October 25, 1985) relied upon by the plaintiffs also fails to raise a genuine issue for trial. The paper outlines an alternative approach to the current national security procedures and does not discuss the current operations of hostile intelligence efforts.

Accordingly, the district court erred in denying the DoD's motion for summary judgment.

■ ■ ■

VI.

CONCLUSION

We reverse the part of the district court's order granting summary judgment to the plaintiffs, vacate the part denying summary judgment to the DoD, and remand to the District Court for the entry of summary judgment in favor of the DoD, and for reversal of the district court's award of attorneys' fees to the plaintiffs.

Reversed in Part, Vacated in Part, and Remanded.

Note

In *Swift v. United States*, 649 F. Supp. 596 (D.D.C. 1986), the federal district court denied the government's motion to dismiss an equal protection claim brought by a gay stenographer at the White House who was relieved of his duties after his sexual orientation was discovered.

5. POLICE

In *Childers v. Dallas Police Department*,[1] the plaintiff was denied a job as a police officer because of his sexual orientation and sexual conduct. The plaintiff challenged the police department's decision on the grounds that the denial violated his rights under the First Amendment, equal protection and due process clauses. The district court, in applying a "balancing test" adopted by the Supreme Court in *Pickering v. Board of Education*[2] asserted that the First Amendment is not absolute and that considerations of the plaintiff's probable violation of the Texas sodomy law, as well as concerns about plaintiff's objectivity in dealing with violations of the sodomy law and related evidence at the police station storage area, justified the discrimination against him.[3] The district court also denied plaintiff's due process claim, ruling that plaintiff had no protected interest requiring due process protections.[4]

The ruling in *Childers* has been undermined by a subsequent, more modern, decision involving a lesbian denied employment with the Dallas police department. In this case, a state court in Texas declared the state's sodomy law unconstitutional and thus enjoined the police department from discriminating against lesbian and gay employees on the basis that they violate that statute. This decision was affirmed on appeal.[5]

Similarly, a Florida court ordered a county sheriff to rehire a bisexual deputy, ruling that the man's forced resignation violated his right to privacy under the Florida state constitution.[6]

---

1. 513 F. Supp. 134 (N.D. Tex. 1981).

2. 391 U.S. 563 (1968).

3. *Childers*, 513 F. Supp. at 140-42.

4. *Id.* at 143.

5. *See Dallas v. England,* 1993 Tex. App. LEXIS 451 (Feb. 10, 1993).

6. *See Deputy Sheriff Ordered Reinstated Based on Right-to-Privacy Protections,* 30 Gov't Employee Relations, Report (BNA) 893 (June 22, 1992).

D. The Military

1. BACKGROUND

The United States military is one of the last governmental employers in the United States that explicitly discriminates against lesbians and gay men. The military's policy is not a law, but rather a regulation of the Department of Defense. The regulation[1] states:

A. BASIS.

1. Homosexuality is incompatible with military service. The presence in the military environment of persons who engage in homosexual conduct or who, by their statements, demonstrate a propensity to engage in homosexual conduct, seriously impairs

---

1. 32 C.F.R. pt. 41, app. A (1992).

the accomplishment of the military mission. The presence of such members adversely affects the ability of the military services to maintain discipline, good order, and morale; to foster mutual trust and confidence among service-members; to ensure the integrity of the system of rank and command; to facilitate assignment and worldwide deployment of service members who frequently must live and work under close conditions affording minimal privacy; to recruit and retain members of the military services; to maintain the public acceptability of military service; and to prevent breaches of security.

2. As used in this section:

   (a) Homosexual means a person, regardless of sex, who engages in, desires to engage in, or intends to engage in homosexual acts;

   (b) Bisexual means a person who engages in, desires to engage in, or intends to engage in homosexual and heterosexual acts; and

   (c) A homosexual act means bodily contact, actively undertaken or passively permitted, between members of the same sex for the purpose of satisfying sexual desires.

3. The basis for separation may include preservice, prior service, or current service conduct or statements. A member shall be separated under this section if one or more of the following approved findings is made:

   (a) The member has engaged in, attempted to engage in, or solicited another to engage in a homosexual act or acts unless there are approved further findings that:

      (1) Such conduct is a departure from the member's usual and customary behavior;

      (2) Such conduct under all the circumstances is unlikely to recur;

      (3) Such conduct was not accomplished by use of force, coercion, or intimidation by the member during a period of military service;

      (4) Under the particular circumstances of the case, the member's continued presence in the Service is consistent with the interest of the Service in proper discipline, good order, and morale; and

      (5) The member does not desire to engage in or intend to engage in homosexual acts.

   (b) The member has stated that he or she is a homosexual or bisexual unless there is a further finding that the member is not a homosexual or bisexual.

   (c) The member has married or attempted to marry a person known to be of the same biological sex (as evidenced by the external anatomy of the persons involved) unless there are further findings that the member is not a homosexual or bisexual and that the purpose of the marriage or attempt was the avoidance or termination of military service.

B. CHARACTERIZATION OR DESCRIPTION. Characterization of service or description of separation shall be in accordance with the guidance in section 3. of Part B. When the sole basis for separation is homosexuality, a characterization Under Other Than Honorable Conditions may be issued only if such a characterization is warranted under section 3. of Part B and there is a finding that during the current term of service the member attempted, solicited, or committed a homosexual act in the following circumstances:

1. By using force, coercion, or intimidation;

2. With a person under 16 years of age;

3. With a subordinate in circumstances that violate customary military superior-subordinate relationships;

4. Openly in public view;

5. For compensation;

6. Aboard a military vessel or aircraft; or

7. In another location subject to military control under aggravating circumstances noted in the finding that have an adverse impact on discipline, good order, or morale comparable to the impact of such activity aboard a vessel or aircraft.

The current military policy dates to the Second World War. Prior to that time, the military court-martialled and discharged soldiers caught having homosexual sexual encounters, but did not consider the idea of discharging individuals based on their sexual orientation alone.[2] At the beginning of World War II, the military began screening for homosexuality and refusing entry — or discharging — those found to be or suspected of being lesbians and gay men.[3] The military has enforced this policy with varying degrees of harshness over the ensuing half century. This enforcement is often dependent on the political stance of the current Presidential administration and the military's need for bodies.[4] Throughout the 1980s, the regulations were strongly enforced, resulting in more than 1,500 separations — or firings — each year among the three branches of the service. Generally, lesbians and gay men "separated" for homosexuality receive honorable discharges, in the absence of aggravating circumstances.[5]

A bill that would reverse the military's policy was introduced in Congress in 1992,[6] but has been given little serious consideration to date. By contrast, litigation challenging the military's policy has spanned several generations and resulted in numerous district and circuit court decisions.[7]

For a critical and comprehensive analysis of the military's exclusion of gay people, see ALLAN BÉRUBÉ, COMING OUT UNDER FIRE: THE HISTORY OF GAY MEN AND WOMEN IN WORLD WAR TWO (1990). Other discussions include Vicki Quade, *Gays in the Military: Finally Being All That You Can Be*, 18 HUM. RTS. 26 (1991); Conrad Harper & Jane Booth, *End Military Intolerance*, NATIONAL L.J., June 10, 1991, at 17.

---

2. *See generally* ALLAN BÉRUBÉ, COMING OUT UNDER FIRE: THE HISTORY OF GAY MEN AND WOMEN IN WORLD WAR TWO (1990).

3. *Id.*

4. *See* Michelle Benecke & Kirsten Dodge, *Military Women in Nontraditional Job Fields: Casaulties of the Armed Forces' War on Homosexuals*, 13 HARV. WOMEN'S L.J. 215 (1990).

5. *See* 32 C.F.R. pt. 41, app. A (1992).

6. *See* Stephen Power, *Bill Would Ban U.S. Military Exclusions of Gays*, BOSTON GLOBE, May 20, 1992, at 3.

7. *See* William Rubenstein, *Challenging the Military's Antilesbian and Antigay Policy*, 1 LAW & SEXUALITY 239 (1991).

2. EARLY LITIGATION: BASIC DUE PROCESS

CLACKUM v. UNITED STATES

296 F.2d 226 (Ct. of Claims 1960)

MADDEN, J.

The plaintiff was separated from the United States Air Force on January 22, 1952, with a discharge "under conditions other than honorable." She asserts that the purported discharge was invalid, and sues for her pay from the date of the purported discharge. The following "Statement of Facts Alleged", contained in the following four paragraphs, is copied from the Government's brief.

"On February 2, 1951, plaintiff was a reservist in the United States Air Force (WAF — Women in the Air Force) and was ordered to active duty as an airman. She was stationed thereafter at Barksdale Air Force Base, Louisiana, in the grade of corporal, with duty in Headquarters and Headquarters Squadron, 301st Air Base Group.

"On April 18, 1951, plaintiff, among others, was called before her commanding officer and a representative of the O.S.I. (Office of Special Intelligence) and interrogated on matters of homosexuality concerning which plaintiff alleges she had no knowledge. Thereafter, until January 1952, plaintiff was repeatedly interviewed by an officer of the O.S.I. concerning homosexual activities and informed that she was under investigation. She was never informed of any charges against her by the Air Force, although in October 1951 she was informed that some action was contemplated against her. Also in October 1951, plaintiff was called before her commanding officer and was given an

opportunity to resign under A.F.R. 35-66, (5b)(1). Upon being offered the opportunity to resign, plaintiff refused to resign and demanded in writing that she be tried by court-martial. The purpose of this demand was to require the Air Force to confront her with the basis of the accusations against her and to afford her an opportunity to present evidence in her own behalf.

"Although charges were preferred against plaintiff under the Uniform Code of Military Justice, the charges were not referred for investigation under the provisions of the Code, they were not brought to her attention, and she had no knowledge of them until after her discharge. After plaintiff was given an opportunity to resign and refused, she was given a psychiatric examination but was not informed of the report of the psychiatrist. No sworn evidence against plaintiff was taken or received by the O.S.I. or by the Air Force, and prior to her discharge plaintiff was not confronted with the nature of the evidence against her. Plaintiff was demoted to the grade of private on January 22, 1952, and on that same day was discharged from the service under conditions other than honorable under A.F.R. 35-66 dated January 12, 1951.

"Plaintiff brought suit in this Court on June 8, 1956. . . .

Some of the effects upon a soldier of a discharge "under conditions other than honorable" are briefly stated in Air Force Regulations (A.F.R.) 35-66, dated January 12, 1951, 5(b)(1), which says that the person so discharged may be deprived of many rights as a veteran under both Federal and state legislation, and may expect to encounter substantial prejudice in civilian life in situations where the type of service rendered in any branch of the armed forces or the character of discharge received therefrom may have a bearing.

One's reaction to the foregoing narrative is "What's going on here?"

A woman soldier is interrogated about homosexual matters and is orally told that some action is contemplated against her. She is called before her commanding officer and is offered an opportunity to resign. She indignantly denies the implied charges involved in the situation and demands in writing that she be tried by a court-martial so that she can learn what the charges are, face her accusers, and present evidence in her own behalf. Although charges were preferred against her, they were not referred for investigation as the statutes governing courts-martial require, and neither the charges nor the evidence upon which they were based were ever made known to the soldier until after her discharge. She was summarily given a discharge "under conditions other than honorable", her reputation as a decent woman was officially destroyed, her rights to her accrued pay and accrued leave, and to the numerous and valuable benefits conferred by the nation and many of the states upon former soldiers were forfeited.

Air Force Regulations 35-66(5b) related to the handling of homosexual charges against enlisted personnel. They provided for a resignation agreeing to accept an undesirable discharge with all its damaging consequences. If the soldier refused to so resign, the regulations provided that a trial by general court-martial would be considered. If the evidence in the case indicated that conviction by a general court-martial was unlikely, then the Secretary of the Air Force was, by the regulations, authorized to "direct discharge and administratively determine whether an undesirable, general, or honorable type of discharge certificate will be furnished."

A dishonorable discharge is, for a soldier, one of the most severe penalties which may be imposed by a court-martial. Elaborate provisions for review of court-martial sentences within the military hierarchy, and potentially by the Court of Military Appeals, are included in our military laws. Yet the Air Force regulations discussed above provide that if the evidence at hand is so unsubstantial that a conviction by a court-martial would be unlikely, the executive offices of the Air Force may themselves convict the soldier and impose the penalty. It is as if a prosecuting attorney were authorized, in a case where he concluded that he didn't have enough evidence to obtain a conviction in court, to himself impose the fine or imprisonment which he thought the accused person deserved.

The Government defends this remarkable arrangement, and its operation in the instant case, on the ground that it is necessary in the interest of an efficient military establishment for our national defense. We see nothing in this argument. The plaintiff being a member of the Air Force Reserve, on active duty, the Air Force had the undoubted right to discharge her whenever it pleased, for any reason or for no reason, and by so doing preserve the Air Force from even the slightest suspicon of harboring undesirable characters. But it is unthinkable that it should have the raw power, without respect for even the most elementary notions of due process of law, to load her down with penalties. It is late in the day to argue that everything that the executives of the armed forces do in connection with the discharge of soldiers is beyond the reach of judicial scrutiny.

After her discharge, the plaintiff appealed to the Air Force Discharge Review Board. Such an appeal is provided for in the Air Force Regulations. Her appeal and that of another female non-commissioned officer were heard together. They were represented by counsel. They had access to a brief which had been written by an investigator, and which summarized conversations which he had had with various persons. The plaintiff and the other appellant testified at length, directing their testimony to the incidents mentioned in the conversations summarized in the investigator's brief. Their testimony was, of course, entirely favorable to themselves. Some members of the Board asked some questions of the appellants. None of the answers to these questions tended to show that the appellants were guilty. Testimonials of good character from Air Force superiors, civilian employers, clergymen and other acquaintances were placed in evidence.

No witnesses other than the two appellants testified. None of the persons mentioned in the investigator's brief as having made statements derogatory to the appellants were called to testify.

The appellant's counsel made an able argument on their behalf. Among other things, he pointed out the absurdity of the following oracular item in the investigator's brief:

"Psychiatric evaluation of appl. (appellant) 21 Nov. 51 reflected a diagnosis of sexual deviate manifested by homosexuality latent.,"

in view of the plaintiff's uncontradicted testimony that the only psychiatric interview to which she was subjected lasted from 20 to 30 minutes.

The hearing was closed and the Discharge Review Board made the following

"FINDINGS

After consideration of the evidence of record, including the 201 file in the case, the board finds:

"a. That the discharge of the applicants under the provisions of AFR 35-66 (discharge of homosexuals) was in accord with the regulations in force at the time.

"b. That the character of the discharges was amply supported by the evidence of record.

"c. That no additional evidence of sufficient weight and credibility as to warrant reversal of the prior action in these cases has been adduced before the Air Force Discharge Review Board.

CONCLUSIONS

"The Board recommends that no change be made in the type of discharge certificates presently in effect."

The "evidence of record" upon which the Board based its finding of guilt was obviously not the evidence received at the hearing. All of the evidence received at the hearing tended to prove the plaintiff's innocence. The "evidence of record" was a dossier of affidavits of persons, some of whom were not even mentioned in the investigator's brief which was made avilable to the plaintiff at the time of her hearing before the Discharge Review Board, although the statements made in their affidavits, if believed, were extremely damaging to the plaintiff. None of the affidavits was seen by the plaintiff or her counsel until July 24, 1959, long after the plaintiff's case was pending in this court.

The "evidence of record" also contained the confidential reports of the Office of Special Investigations which were forwarded to the Air Force Personnel Counsel and the Secretary of the Air Force, and which have never been made available to the plaintiff or her counsel.

The so-called "hearing" before the Air Force Discharge Board was not a hearing at all, in the usual sense of that word. It was a meaningless formality, to comply with the regulations. The "evidence" upon which the case was going to be decided, and obviously was decided, was not present at the hearing, unless the undisclosed dossier which contained it was in the drawer of the table at which the Board sat. The appellant and her counsel were futilely tilting at shadows. However vulnerable the secret evidence may have been, there was no possible way to attack it.

The plaintiff was, after the proceeding before the Discharge Review Board, as before, a soldier dishonorably discharged, officially branded by the Government as an indecent woman, deprived of valuable rights and benefits which are given to other ex-soldiers. And all this without any semblance of an opportunity to know what the evidence against her was, or to face her accusers in a trial or hearing.

■ ■ ■

. . . the defendant's motion to dismiss the plaintiff's petition is, under our Rule 16(b), treated as a motion for summary judgment. The motion is denied.

It is so ordered.

---

3. LITIGATION THROUGH THE 1970S: THE NEXUS TEST

Throughout the 1970s, discharged lesbian and gay soldiers fought to change the military's policy. These cases culminated in dual district court decisions on the East and West coasts — *Matlovich v. Secretary of the Air Force*,[1] and *Saal v. Middendorf*,[2] — in the late 1970s calling for rudiments of due process in the military's policy. The effects of these victories, however, was short-lived:

> . . . *Saal* argued that a policy which presumes the unfitness to serve in the military of every person engaged in homosexual activity is unconstitutional. Substantive due process requires that an individual's fitness to serve be evaluated in light of all relevant factors, free of a policy of mandatory exclusion. The district court held that the government must demonstrate a "nexus" between the person's homosexuality and unsuitability for service.
>
> Another potential landmark case which exerted great pressure for change on the policy of excluding homosexuals from the military was the well publicized case of *Matlovich v. Secretary of the Air Force*. Sgt Leonard Matlovich was a highly decorated Vietnam veteran with a distinguished service record. He decided to announce publicly his sexual preference and was discharged. After many years of litigation, a federal judge ordered the Air Force to reinstate him based on inconsistencies in the Air Force's explanation of the application of the regulations which allowed for the retention of some homosexual personnel. The case was ultimately resolved with an out-of-court settlement in which Matlovich was paid a sum of money and he agreed not to go back to active duty.
>
> There is no way to evaluate exactly the effect these cases had on the Department of Defense, but in 1978 a discernible softening of policy was apparent. On Jan. 20, 1978, the secretary of the Navy issued a memo to the Chief of Naval Personnel and to the Commandant of the Marine Corps specifying that the character of the discharge for

---

1. 591 F.2d 852 (D.C. Cir. 1978).

2. 427 F. Supp. 192 (N.D. Cal. 1977), *rev'd sub nom. Beller* v. *Middendorf*, 632 F.2d 788 (9th Cir. 1980), *cert. denied*, 452 U.S. 905 (1981).

homosexuality be determined by the overall service record. The underlying philosophy remained the same—homosexuality is incompatible with military service—but the policy permitted lesbians and gay males to leave the service with honorable discharges if their service records warranted it. The easy availability of honorable discharges had a tremendous impact not only on active duty personnel but on large numbers of lesbian and gay veterans who had been discharged with less than honorable discharges from past years.

Unfortunately, the limited grounds upon which *Matlovich* was decided, accompanied by the out of court settlement, severely undercut the precedential value of the case; and *Saal* was overruled on appeal. The Ninth Circuit held that the Navy regulations mandating discharge of homosexuals were reasonable and not unconstitutional.

The reversal of *Saal* signaled a new tightening of policy directly resulting in the issuance of DoD Dir. 1332.14 in 1981. This Department of Defense directive, entitled "Enlisted Administrative Separations," was revised and reissued in 1982. It has been adopted, with slight variation, by each branch of the service.[3]

The regulations adopted in 1981 following the reversal of *Saal* and the election of Ronald Reagan were still in effect at the beginning of 1993.

4. LITIGATING THE RIGHT TO PRIVACY IN THE EMPLOYMENT CONTEXT

Many of the early cases challenging the military's policy relied on the argument that discrimination on the basis of sexual orientation violated the constitutional right to privacy.[4] The decisions in these cases rejected the argument that homosexual sodomy was protected by the federal Constitution, thus foreshadowing the Supreme Court's decision in *Bowers v. Hardwick*.[5] Indeed, Judge Bork's decision in *Dronenburg*, *supra* at Chapter 2, provided the basis for Justice White's majority opinion in *Hardwick*.

5. POST-*HARDWICK* LITIGATION

After the Supreme Court's decision in *Bowers v. Hardwick*,[6] the argument that the right to privacy prohibited government employment decisions based on sexual conduct was foreclosed. Accordingly, subsequent litigation challenging the military's policy has focused on cases in which lesbians and gay men have been discharged not for specific homosexual

---

3. NATIONAL LAWYERS GUILD, SEXUAL ORIENTATION AND THE LAW §6.02[2], at 6-5 to 6-6 (Roberta Achtenberg ed., 1991).

4. *See, e.g., Rich* v. *Secretary of the Army*, 735 F.2d 1220 (10th Cir. 1984); *Dronenburg* v. *Zech*, 741 F.2d 1388 (D.C. Cir. 1984).

5. 478 U.S. 186 (1986).

6. *Id.*

conduct but solely on the basis of their sexual orientation itself. Such discharges have been challenged under both the First Amendment and the Constitution's equal protection clause. The three primary cases to date are *Ben-Shalom v. Marsh*,[7] *Watkins v. United States Army*,[8] and *Pruitt v. Cheney*.[9]

In *Ben-Shalom*, the U.S. Court of Appeals for the Seventh Circuit ruled that discharging a lesbian for stating her sexual orientation did not violate the First Amendment, that *Hardwick* foreclosed heightened judicial scrutiny for discrimination based on sexual orientation, and that the military's policy was rationally related to a legitimate governmental interest. The Supreme Court denied certiorari.

In the following case, *Watkins v. United States Army*, a three-judge panel of the U.S. Court of Appeals for the Ninth Circuit held that the Army regulation violated the equal protection clause. This marked the first federal circuit court decision finding heightened scrutiny for lesbians and gay men. Although it was later vacated (see *infra* at at 367), the decision is especially important because it eloquently presents the two sides to the argument about the continuing validity of gay equal protection claims after the *Hardwick* decision.

---

7.   881 F.2d 454 (7th Cir. 1989), *cert. denied sub nom. Ben-Shalom v. Stone*, 494 U.S. 1004 (1990); *see also Woodward v. United States*, 871 F.2d 1068 (Fed. Cir. 1989), *cert. denied*, 110 S. Ct. 1295 (1990).

8.   847 F.2d 1329 (9th Cir. 1989), *vacated*, 875 F.2d 699 (9th Cir. 1989) (en banc), *cert. denied*, 111 S. Ct. 384 (1990).

9.   943 F.2d 989 (9th Cir. 1991), *amended*, 963 F. 2d 1160 (9th Cir. 1992), *cert. denied sub. nom. Cheney v. Pruitt*, 113 S. Ct. 655 (1992).

WATKINS *v. UNITED STATES ARMY*

837 F.2d 1428 (9th Cir. 1988) *amended,* 847 F.2d 1329,
different results reached on reh'g, 875 F.2d 699 (9th Cir. 1989) (en banc),
cert. denied, 111 S. Ct. 384 (1990)

NORRIS, Circuit Judge

In August 1967, at the age of 19, Perry Watkins enlisted in the United States Army. In filling out the Army's pre-induction medical form, he candidly marked "yes" in response to a question whether he had homosexual tendencies. The Army nonetheless considered Watkins "qualified for admission" and inducted him into its ranks.

Watkins served fourteen years in the Army, and became, in the words of his commanding officer, "one of our most respected and trusted soldiers."

Even though Watkins' homosexuality was always common knowledge, *Watkins v. United States Army*, 551 F. Supp. 212, 216 (W.D. Wash. 1982), the Army has never claimed that his sexual orientation or behavior interfered in any way with military functions.[1]

---

1.   In this opinion we use the term "sexual orientation" to refer to the orientation of an individual's sexual preference, not to his actual sexual conduct. Individuals whose sexual orientation creates in them a desire for sexual relationships with persons of the opposite sex have a heterosexual orientation. Individuals whose sexual orientation creates in them a desire for sexual relationships with persons of the same sex have a homosexual orientation.

In contrast, we use the terms "homosexual conduct" and "homosexual acts" to refer to sexual activity between two members of the same sex whether their orientations are homosexual, heterosexual, or bisexual, and we use the

To the contrary, an Army review board found "there is no evidence suggesting that his behavior has had either a degrading effect upon unit performance, morale or discipline, or upon his own job performance."

In 1981 the Army promulgated new regulations which mandated the disqualification of all homosexuals from the Army without regard to the length or quality of their military service. Pursuant to these new regulations, the Army notified Watkins that he would be discharged and denied reenlistment because of his homosexuality. In this federal court action, Watkins challenges the Army's actions and new regulations on various statutory and constitutional grounds.

I

During Watkins' initial three-year tour of duty, he served in the United States and Korea as a chaplain's assistant, personnel specialist, and company clerk. Even before this tour began, Watkins indicated on his pre-induction medical history form that he had "homosexual tendencies." A year later, in 1968, Watkins signed an affidavit stating that he had been gay from the age of 13 and that, since his enlistment, had engaged in sodomy with two other servicemen, a crime under military law. The Army, which received this affidavit as part of a criminal investigation into Watkins' sexual conduct, dropped the investigation for lack of evidence after the two servicemen whom Watkins had named as his sexual partners denied any sexual involvement with him. Despite repeated investigations of Watkins' sexual behavior after 1968, his 1968 affidavit is the only evidence before this court of Watkins' actual sexual conduct.

When his first enlistment expired in 1970, Watkins received an honorable discharge. In 1971 he reenlisted for a second three-year term, at which time the Army judged him to be "eligible for reentry on active duty." In 1972 the Army again investigated Watkins for allegedly committing sodomy and again terminated the investigation for insufficient evidence. In 1974 the Army accepted Watkins' application for a six-year reenlistment.

In 1975 the Army convened a board of officers to determine whether Watkins should be discharged because of his homosexual tendencies. On this occasion his commanding officer, Captain Bast, testified that Watkins was "the best clerk I have known," that he did "a fantastic job — excellent," and that Watkins' homosexuality did not affect the company. A sergeant testified that Watkins' homosexuality was well-known but caused no problems and generated no complaints from other soldiers. The four officers on the board unanimously found that "Watkins is suitable for retention in the military service" and stated, "In view of the findings, the Board recommends that SP5 Perry J. Watkins be retained in the military service because there is no evidence suggesting that his behavior has had either a degrading effect upon unit performance, morale or discipline, or upon his own job performance. SP5 Watkins is suited for duty in administrative positions and progression through Specialist rating."

In November 1977, the United States Army Artillery Group (the USAAG) granted Watkins a security clearance for information classified as "Secret." His application for a position in the Nuclear Surety Personnel Reliability Program (the PRP), however, was initially rejected because his records — specifically, his own admissions — showed that he had homosexual tendencies. After this

---

terms "heterosexual conduct" and "heterosexual acts" to refer to sexual activity between two members of the opposite sex whether their orientations are homosexual, heterosexual, or bisexual.

Throughout this opinion, the terms "gay" and "homosexual" will be used synonymously to denote persons of homosexual orientation.

initial rejection, Watkins' commanding officer in the USAAG, Captain Pastain, requested that Watkins be requalified for the
position. Captain Pastain stated, "From daily
personal contacts I can attest to the outstanding professional attitude, integrity, and suitability for assignment within the PRP, of SP5
Watkins. In the 6-1/2 months he has been
assigned to this unit SP5 Watkins has had no
problems what-so-ever in dealing with other
assigned members. He has, in fact, become
one of our most respected and trusted soldiers, both by his superiors and his subordinates." An examining Army physician
concluded that Watkins' homosexuality appeared to cause no problem in his work, and
the decision to deny Watkins a position in the
Nuclear Surety Personnel Reliability Program was reversed.

Watkins worked under a security clearance without incident until he again stated,
in an interview on March 15, 1979, that he
was homosexual. This prompted yet another
Army investigation which, in July 1980,
culminated in the revocation of Watkins'
security clearance. As Watkins' notification
of revocation makes clear, the Army based
this revocation on Watkins' 1979 admission
of homosexuality, on medical records containing Watkins' 1968 affidavit stating that
he had engaged in homosexual conduct, and
on his history of performing (with the permission of his commanding officer) as a
female impersonator in various revues. The
Army did not rely on any evidence of homosexual conduct other than Watkins' 1968
affidavit.

In October 1979, the Army accepted
Watkins' application for another three-year
reenlistment.

In 1981 the Army promulgated Army
Regulation, (AR) 635-200, chpt. 15, which
mandated the discharge of all homosexuals
regardless of merit. Pursuant to this regulation, a new Army board convened to consider discharging Watkins. Although this
board explicitly rejected the evidence before
it that Watkins had engaged in homosexual
conduct after 1968,[2] the board recommended that Watkins be separated from the
service "because he has stated that he is a
homosexual."

Major General Elton, the discharge authority overseeing the board, approved this
finding and recommendation and directed
that Watkins be discharged. In addition,
Major General Elton, on. his own initiative,
made an additional finding that Watkins had
engaged in homosexual acts with other soldiers. The district court ruled both that Major
General Elton lacked the regulatory authority to make supplemental findings, *Watkins
v. United States Army*, 541 F. Supp. 249, 259
(W.D. Wash. 1982), and that the evidence
presented at the discharge hearing could not
support a specific finding that Watkins had
engaged in any homosexual conduct after
1968. The Army has not contested either of
these rulings and, on appeal, cites only
Watkins' 1968 affidavit as evidence of homosexual conduct.

In May 1982, after the Army board voted
in favor of Watkins' discharge, but before
the discharge actually issued, the district

---

2. During these discharge proceedings the Army tried to prove that Watkins had engaged in homosexual conduct by
   introducing the testimony of one soldier that a black staff sergeant had "squeezed his leg" and the testimony of another
   soldier that Watkins had "asked him if he'd like to move into [Watkins'] apartment" and that Watkins used to "stare
   at" him. *Watkins* v. *United States Army*, 541 F. Supp. 249, 257 (W.D. Wash. 1982). The first soldier, however, was
   unable to identify Watkins in a line-up as the black sergeant who had squeezed his leg (there were thousands of black
   sergeants at the base). The second soldier testified that he was not sure Watkins had been making a pass at him, that
   he was prejudiced against blacks and against homosexuals, that he had once had a bad experience with a homosexual,
   and that he had once been disciplined by a board of which Watkins was a member. The Army board concluded that
   this evidence did not support a finding that Watkins had engaged in homosexual acts with these two soldiers, and the
   district court ruled that any finding to the contrary would have been arbitrary and unsupported by the evidence.

court enjoined the Army from discharging Watkins on the basis of his statements admitting his homosexuality. The district court reasoned that the discharge proceedings were barred by the Army's regulation against double jeopardy, AR 635-200, para. 1-19b, because they essentially repeated the discharge proceedings of 1975.[4]

During oral argument before the district court, counsel for the Army declared that if the Army were enjoined from discharging Watkins, it would deny Watkins reenlistment, pursuant to AR 601-280, para. 2-21(c), when his current tour of duty expired in October 1982. This reenlistment regulation, which was promulgated in 1981 along with the discharge regulation AR 635-200, chpt. 15, makes homosexuality a nonwaivable disqualification for reenlistment. The district court nonetheless enjoined Watkins' discharge, and the Army fulfilled its promise by rejecting Watkins' reenlistment application "[b]ecause of self admitted homosexuality as well as homosexual acts."[6]

On October 5, 1982, the district court enjoined the Army from refusing to reenlist Watkins because of his admitted homosexuality, holding that the Army was equitably estopped from relying on AR 601-280, para. 2-21(c). *Watkins v. United States Army* 551 F. Supp. 212, 223 (W.D. Wash. 1982).[7] The Army reenlisted Watkins for a six-year term on November 1, 1982, with the proviso that the reenlistment would be voided if the district court's injunction were not upheld on appeal.

While the Army's appeal of the district court injunction was pending, the Army rated Watkins' performance and professionalism. He received 85 out of 85 possible points. His ratings included perfect scores for "Earns respect," "Integrity," "Loyalty," "Moral Courage," "Self-discipline," "Military Appearance," "Demonstrates Initiative," "Performs under pressure," "Attains results," "Displays sound judgment," "Communicates effectively," "Develops subordinates," "Demonstrates technical skills," and "Physical fitness." His military evaluators unanimously recommended that he be promoted ahead of his peers. The Army's written evaluation of Watkins' performance and potential stated:

> SSG Watkins is without exception, one of the finest Personnel Action Center Supervisors I have encountered. Through his diligent efforts, the Battalion Personnel Action Center achieved

---

4. The district court held that the evidence could not support a finding that Watkins engaged in homosexual conduct subsequent to the 1975 discharge proceedings and that the Army's double jeopardy provision barred the Army from basing Watkins' discharge on statements that merely reiterated what Watkins had stated in the 1975 discharge proceedings — that he was homosexual. *See* 541 F. Supp. at 257-58.

6. Again, we emphasize that Watkins' 1968 affidavit stating that he engaged in homosexual acts is the only evidence before this court that provides support for Captain Scott's finding of homosexual conduct. That the Army had no new evidence of homosexual conduct is evident from the Army's interrogation of Watkins at the time that he applied for reenlistment. During extraordinarily aggressive questioning aimed at eliciting a new confession of homosexual conduct from Watkins, the Army's interrogating officer admitted that he had no new basis for suspecting that Watkins had engaged in additional homosexual acts.

    Captain Scott, who made the above findings, also found that Watkins had refused to answer questions concerning his homosexuality and homosexual acts, but the district court ruled that this finding was totally unsupported by the evidence. The Army has not contested this ruling of the district court and does not argue on appeal that Watkins refused to answer questions.

7. This case does not involve an asserted right to reenlist or a claim that courts can exercise general review of the Army's reenlistment decisions. Watkins does not seek a judicial determination on the merits of his reenlistment application. He merely seeks a judicial determination that the Army must consider his reenlistment application on its merits without regard to his homosexuality.

a near perfect processing rate for SIPDERS transactions. During this training period, SSG Watkins has been totally reliable and a wealth of knowledge. He requires no supervision, and with his "can do" attitude, always exceeds the requirements and demands placed upon him. I would gladly welcome another opportunity to serve with him, and firmly believe that he will be an asset to any unit to which he is assigned.

SSG Watkins should be selected to attend ANCOC and placed in a Platoon Sergeant position.

■ ■ ■

SSG Watkins' duty performance has been outstanding in every regard. His section continues to set the standard within the Brigade for submission of accurate, timely personnel and financial transactions. Keeping abreast of ever-changing personnel regulations and directives, SSG Watkins has provided sound advice to the commander as well as to the soldiers within the command. His suggestion to separate S-1 and Personnel Action Center functions and to colocate the Personnel Action Center with the Company Orderly Rooms was adopted and immediately resulted in improved service by both offices. SSG Watkins' positive influence has been felt throughout the Battalion and will be sorely missed.

SSG Watkins' potential is unlimited. He has consistently demonstrated the capacity to manage numerous complex responsibilities concurrently. He is qualified for promotion now and should be selected for attendance at ANCOES at the earliest opportunity.

On appeal, we reversed the district court's injunction. We reasoned that the equity powers of the federal courts could not be exercised to order military officials to violate their own regulations absent a determination that the regulations were repugnant to the Constitution or to the military's statutory authority. *Watkins v. United States Army*, 721 F.2d 687, 690-91 (9th Cir. 1983) [hereinafter *Watkins I*]. On remand, the district court held that the Army's regulations were not repugnant to the Constitution or to statutory authority and accordingly denied Watkins' motion for summary judgment and granted summary judgment in favor of the Army. Watkins appealed, invoking our jurisdiction under 28 U.S.C. § 1291.

Watkins argues on this appeal that the Army's actions in discharging him and denying him reenlistment violate the First Amendment and constitute due process entrapment in violation of the Fifth Amendment. He also argues that the Army's discharge and reenlistment regulations are arbitrary and capricious under the Administrative Procedure Act, 5 U.S.C. 706(2)(A), and deny him equal protection of the laws in violation of the Fifth Amendment. Notably, Watkins recognizes that the Supreme Court's decision in *Bowers v. Hardwick*, 478 U.S. 186 (1986), forecloses this court from deciding that the Army's regulations violate substantive due process.

■ ■ ■

[After rejecting Watkins' other claims, the court considers his equal protection challenge.]

We are left, then, with Watkins' claim that the Army's regulations deny him equal protection of the laws in violation of the Fifth Amendment. Specifically, Watkins argues that the Army's regulations constitute an invidious discrimination based on sexual orientation. To address this claim we must engage in a three-stage inquiry. First, we must decide whether the regulations in fact discriminate on the basis of sexual orientation. Second, we must decide which level of judicial scrutiny applies by asking whether discrimination based on sexual orientation burdens a suspect or quasi-suspect class, which would make it subject, respectively, to strict or intermediate scrutiny. *See City of Cleburne v. Cleburne Living Center*, 473 U.S. 432, 439-41 (1985). If the discrimination burdens no such class, it is subject to ordinary rationality review. Finally, we must decide whether the challenged regulations survive the applicable level of scrutiny by deciding whether, under strict scrutiny, the legal classification is necessary to serve a compelling governmental interest; whether, under intermediate scrutiny, the classification is substantially related to an important governmental interest; or whether, under rationality review, the classification is rationally related to a legitimate governmental interest.

III

We now turn to the threshold question raised by Watkins' equal protection claim: Do the Army's regulations discriminate based on sexual orientation?

■ ■ ■

We conclude that these regulations, on their face, discriminate against homosexuals on the basis of their sexual orientation. Under the regulations any homosexual act or statement of homosexuality gives rise to a presumption of homosexual orientation, and anyone who fails to rebut that presumption is conclusively barred from Army service. In other words, the regulations target homosexual orientation itself. The homosexual acts and statements are merely relevant, and rebuttable, indicators of that orientation.

Under the Army's regulations, "homosexuality," not sexual conduct, is the operative trait for disqualification. For example, the regulations ban homosexuals who have done nothing more than acknowledge their homosexual orientation even in the absence of evidence that the persons ever engaged in any form of sexual conduct. The

reenlistment regulation disqualifies any "admitted homosexual" — a status that can be proved by "[a]ny official, private, or public profession of homosexuality" even if "there is no evidence that they have engaged in homosexual acts either before or during military service." Since the regulations define a "homosexual" as "a person, regardless of sex, who *desires* bodily contact between persons of the same sex, actively undertaken or passively permitted, with the intent to obtain or give sexual gratification," a person can be deemed homosexual under the regulations without ever engaging in a homosexual act. Thus, no matter what statements a person has made, the ultimate evidentiary issue is whether he or she has a homosexual orientation. Under the reenlistment regulation, persons are disqualified from reenlisting only if, based on any "profession of homosexuality" they have made, they are found to have a homosexual orientation. Similarly, under the discharge regulation a soldier must be discharged if "[t]he soldier has stated that he or she is a homosexual or bisexual, *unless* there is a further finding that the soldier is not a homosexual or bisexual." In short, the regulations do not penalize all statements of sexual desire, or even only statements of homosexual desire; they penalize only homosexuals who declare their homosexual orientation.

True, a "person who has committed homosexual acts" is also presumptively "included" under the reenlistment regulation as a person excludable for "homosexuality." But it is clear that this provision is merely designed to round out the possible evidentiary grounds for inferring a homosexual orientation. The regulations define "homosexual acts" to encompass any "bodily contact between persons of the same sex, actively undertaken or passively permitted, with the intent of obtaining or giving sexual satisfaction, or any proposal, solicitation, or attempt to perform such an act." Thus, the regulations barring homosexuals from the Army cover any form of bodily contact between persons of the same sex that gives sexual satisfaction — from oral and anal intercourse to holding hands, kissing, caressing and any number of other sexual acts. Indeed, in this case the Army tried to prove at Watkins' discharge proceedings that he had committed a homosexual act described as squeezing the knee of a male soldier, but failed to prove it was Watkins who did the alleged knee-squeezing. Moreover, even non-sexual conduct can trigger a presumption of homosexuality: The regulations provide for the discharge of soldiers who have "married or attempted to marry a person known to be of the same sex ... *unless* there are further findings that the soldier is not a homosexual or bisexual." With all the acts and statements that can serve as presumptive evidence of homosexuality under the regulations, it is hard to think of any grounds for inferring homosexual orientation that are *not* included.[12] The fact remains, however, that homosexual orientation, not homosexual conduct, is plainly the object of the Army's regulations.

Moreover, under the regulations a person is not automatically disqualified from Army service just because he or she committed a homosexual act. Persons may still qualify for the Army despite their homosexual conduct if they prove to the satisfaction of Army officials that their *orientation* is heterosexual rather than homosexual. To illustrate, the discharge regulation provides that a soldier who engages in homosexual acts can escape discharge if he can show that the conduct was "a departure from the soldier's usual and customary behavior" that "is unlikely to recur because it is shown, for example, that the act occurred because of immaturity, intoxication, coercion, or a desire to avoid military service" *and* that the "soldier does not desire to engage in or intend to engage in homosexual acts." The regulation expressly states, "The intent of this policy is to permit retention *only* of *nonhomosexual* soldiers who, because of extenuating circumstances engaged in, attempted to engage in, or solicited a homosexual act." Similarly, the Army's ban on reenlisting persons who have committed homosexual acts does not apply to "[p]ersons who have been involved in homosexual acts in an apparently isolated episode, stemming solely from immaturity, curiousity [sic], or intoxication, and in the absence of other evidence that the person is a homosexual." If a straight soldier and a gay soldier of the same sex engage in homosexual acts because they are drunk, immature or curious, the straight soldier may remain in the Army while the gay soldier is automatically terminated. In short, the regulations do not penalize soldiers for engaging in homosexual acts; they penalize soldiers who have engaged in homosexual acts only when the Army decides that those soldiers are actually gay.

---

12. In stark contrast to the breadth and focus of the regulations, the only statute Congress has enacted regulating the private consensual sexual activity of military personnel covers only sodomy, not other forms of sexual conduct , and covers sodomy whether engaged in by homosexuals or heterosexuals. 10 U.S.C. § 925 (1982) provides:

   (a)   Any person subject to this chapter who engages in unnatural carnal copulation with another person of the same or opposite sex or with an animal is guilty of sodomy. Penetration, however slight, is sufficient to complete the offense.

   (b)   Any person found guilty of sodomy shall be punished as a court-martial may direct.

   Although the statute does not define "sodomy" or "unnatural carnal copulation," the statute does require proof of "penetration," which apparently limits sodomy to oral and anal copulation. *See United States* v. *Harris*, 8 M.J. 52, 53-59 (C.M.A. 1979). Moreover, the statute explicitly regulates sodomy without regard to sexual orientation by making sodomy illegal whether engaged in by persons of "the same or opposite sex." 10 U.S.C. § 925.

   The Army has never made a finding that Watkins ever engaged in an act of sodomy in violation of section 925. Indeed, the Army twice investigated Watkins for allegedly committing sodomy in violation of section 925 and had to drop both investigations because of "insufficient evidence." While the lack of evidence that Watkins committed sodomy prevents him from being convicted under the statute, it is immaterial under the Army regulations because they presume homosexual orientation from evidence of *any* form of homosexual bodily contact that gives sexual satisfaction.

In sum, the discrimination against homosexual orientation under these regulations is about as complete as one could imagine.[14] The regulations make any act or statement that might conceivably indicate a homosexual orientation evidence of homosexuality; that evidence is in turn weighed against any evidence of a heterosexual orientation. It is thus clear in answer to our threshold equal protection inquiry that the regulations directly burden the class consisting of persons of homosexual orientation.[15]

IV

Before reaching the question of the level of scrutiny applicable to discrimination based on sexual orientation and the question whether the Army's regulations survive the applicable level of scrutiny, we first address the Army's argument that we are foreclosed by existing Supreme Court and Ninth Circuit precedent from holding that the Army's regulations deny Watkins equal protection of the laws because they discriminate on the basis of homosexual orientation. The Army first argues that the Supreme Court's decision in *Bowers v. Hardwick*, 478 U.S. 186 (1986), forecloses Watkins' equal protection challenge to its regulations. In *Hardwick*, the Court rejected a claim by a homosexual that a Georgia statute criminalizing sodomy deprived him of his liberty without due process of law in violation of the Fourteenth Amendment. More specifically, the Court held that the constitutionally protected right to privacy — recognized in cases such as *Griswold v. Connecticut*, 381 U.S. 429 (1965), and *Eisenstadt v. Baird*, 405 U.S 438 (1972) — does not extend to acts of consensual homosexual sodomy.[16] The Court's holding was limited to this due process question. The parties did not argue and the Court explicitly did not decide the question whether the Georgia sodomy statute might violate the equal protection clause. *See* 478 U.S. at 196 & n.8.

The Army nonetheless argues that it would be "incongruous" to hold that its regulations deprive gays of equal protection of the laws when *Hardwick* holds that there is no constitutionally protected privacy right to engage in homosexual sodomy. We disagree. First, while *Hardwick* does indeed hold that the due process clause provides no substantive privacy protection for acts of private homosexual sodomy, nothing in *Hardwick* suggests that the state may penalize gays for their sexual orientation. *Robinson v. California*, 370 U.S. 660 (1962) (holding that state violated due process by criminalizing the status of narcotics addiction, even though the state could criminalize

---

14. We cannot agree with the premise of Judge Reinhardt's dissent that the Army disqualified Watkins from service because of his homosexual *conduct* as opposed to his homosexual *orientation*. First, the regulations encompass all possible evidentiary grounds for inferring homosexual orientation and merely include homosexual acts as one possible, but by no means necessary, ground for drawing that inference. Second, the specific regulations allow some soldiers to remain in the Army despite homosexual conduct if they can prove that they in fact have a non-homosexual orientation.

    We also note that homosexual orientation encompasses a range of emotions, desires, and needs wholly separate from sexual conduct and involves an element of individual self-definition in addition to sexual conduct. We cannot agree with the dissent's view that the class comprised of persons who consider themselves homosexual is virtually identical to the class of persons who engage in homosexual conduct, and sodomy in particular.

15. Of course, in their attempt to identify soldiers of homosexual orientation, the regulations discriminate in their treatment of homosexual and heterosexual *conduct*. While homosexual acts subject the participants to discharge proceedings by triggering the regulatory presumption of "homosexuality," the identical acts when engaged in by members of the opposite sex do not subject the participants to any such proceedings.

16. Under the Court's analysis, because the Constitution's protection of the right to privacy does not extend to homosexual sodomy, a judgment by the state that sodomy is immoral provides a sufficiently rational basis for sodomy laws to satisfy the requirements of substantive due process.

the use of the narcotics — conduct in which narcotics addicts by definition are prone to engage).

Second, although *Hardwick* held that the due process clause does not prevent states from criminalizing acts of homosexual sodomy, nothing in *Hardwick* actually holds that the state may make invidious distinctions when regulating sexual conduct. Unlike the Army's regulations, the Georgia sodomy statute at issue in *Hardwick* was neutral on its face, making anal and oral intercourse a criminal offense whether engaged in by partners of the same or opposite sex. *See id.* 106 S. Ct. at 2842 n.1. In deciding a due process challenge to the Georgia statute as applied to homosexual sodomy,[19] the *Hardwick* Court simply did not address either the question whether heterosexual sodomy also falls outside the scope of the right to privacy or the separate question whether homosexual but not heterosexual sodomy may be criminalized without violating the equal protection clause. We cannot read *Hardwick* as standing for the proposition that government may outlaw sodomy only when committed by a disfavored class of persons. Surely, for example, *Hardwick* cannot be read as a license for the government to outlaw sodomy only when committed by blacks. If government insists on regulating private sexual conduct between consenting adults, it must, at a minimum, do so evenhandedly — prohibiting all persons from engaging in the proscribed sexual acts rather than placing the burden of sexual restraint solely on a disfavored minority.[20]

The Army also argues that *Hardwick*'s concern "about the limits of the Court's role in carrying out its constitutional mandate," should prevent courts from holding that

---

19. The district court had dismissed two heterosexual plaintiffs for lack of standing, and they did not appeal. *Hardwick*, 478 U.S. at 188 n.2.

20. Judge Reinhardt argues in dissent that our opinion reads *Hardwick* as "implicitly permitting the regulation of homosexual conduct" thereby "increas[ing] — exponentially — the damage to the right to privacy caused by *Hardwick*." First, we do not read *Hardwick* as reversing or even undermining any of the cases establishing and defining the right to privacy. We simply read *Hardwick* as refusing to *extend* the constitutionally protected right to privacy to acts of homosexual sodomy. Second, we do not read *Hardwick* as passing judgment one way or the other on whether the constitutionally protected right to privacy extends to heterosexual sodomy. We do note, however, that the Court's reasoning in *Hardwick* rests in major part on its determination that at one time all 50 states outlawed sodomy and that 24 states and the District of Columbia continue to outlaw sodomy. "Against this background," Justice White reasoned, it would be "at best facetious" to claim that "a right to engage in such conduct is 'deeply rooted in our history and tradition' or 'implicit in the concept of ordered liberty.'" In making this point the Court drew no distinction between homosexual and heterosexual sodomy, nor do 19 of the 25 jurisdictions that still outlaw sodomy. *See* Survey on the Constitutional Right to Privacy in the Context of Homosexual Activity, 40 U. Miami L. Rev. 521-26 (1986).

The dissent's interpretation of *Hardwick* — that it authorizes the state to single out homosexual conduct for criminal sanction *because* that conduct is committed by homosexuals — is wide of the mark. *Hardwick* explicitly focused on the question whether the right to privacy extends constitutional protection to the commission of homosexual sodomy. In essence, the dissent shifts *Hardwick*'s focus away from substantive due process and the right to privacy toward the right of homosexuals to enjoy equal treatment under the laws. Such an expansively anti-homosexual reading of *Hardwick* is unsupported and unfair both to homosexuals and the Supreme Court.

We also cannot agree with the dissent's assertion that the equal protection clause is entirely "procedural in nature" and that, therefore, our equal protection analysis is coherent "[o]nly if heterosexual sodomy is not protected by the right to privacy." However the Supreme Court defines the right to privacy — whether that definition includes a right to engage in heterosexual sodomy, homosexual sodomy, neither, or both — the equal protection clause imposes an independent obligation on government not to draw invidious distinctions among its citizens. *See, e.g., Lehr* v. *Robertson*, 463 U.S. 248, 265 (1983)("The concept of equal justice under law requires the State to govern impartially"). We do not read *Hardwick* as in any way eroding that principle.

equal protection doctrine protects homosexuals from discrimination. To be sure, the Court in *Hardwick* justified its refusal to further extend the scope of the right to privacy largely by pointing to the problems allegedly created when judges recognize constitutional "rights not readily identifiable in the Constitution's text" and "having little or no cognizable roots in the language or design of the Constitution." The Court stressed its concern that such rights might be perceived as involving "the imposition of the Justices' own choice of values on the States and the Federal Government" and that this antidemocratic perception might undermine the legitimacy of the Court. Finally, the Court expressed the more specific concern about potential difficulties in defining the contours of the right to privacy.

While it is not our role to question *Hardwick*'s concerns about substantive due process and specifically the right to privacy, these concerns have little relevance to equal protection doctrine. The right to equal protection of the laws has a clear basis in the text of the Constitution. This principle of equal treatment, when imposed against majoritarian rule, arises from the Constitution itself, not from judicial fiat. Moreover, equal protection doctrine does not prevent the majority from enacting laws based on its substantive value choices. Equal protection simply requires that the majority apply its values evenhandedly. Indeed, equal protection doctrine plays an important role in perfecting, rather than frustrating, the democratic process. The constitutional requirement of evenhandedness advances the political legitimacy of majority rule by safeguarding minorities from majoritarian oppression. The requirement of evenhandedness also facilitates a representation of minorities in government that advances the operation of representative democracy. Finally, the practical difficulties of defining the requirements imposed by equal protection, while not insignificant, do not involve the judiciary in the same degree of value-based line-drawing that the Supreme Court

in *Hardwick* found so troublesome in defining the contours of substantive due process. In sum, the driving force behind *Hardwick* is the Court's ongoing concern with the expansion of rights under substantive due process, not an unbounded antipathy toward a disfavored group.

■ ■ ■

In sum, we conclude that no federal appellate court has decided the critical issue raised by Watkins' claim: whether persons of homosexual orientation constitute a suspect class under equal protection doctrine. To be sure, *Hardwick, Beller* [*v. Middendorf*, 632 F.2d 788 (9th Cir. 1980)] and *Hatheway* [*v. Secretary of Army*, 641 F.2d 1376 (9th Cir.), *cert. denied.* 454 U.S. 864 (1981)] foreclose Watkins from making either a due process or equal protection claim that the Army's regulations impinge on an asserted fundamental right to engage in homosexual sodomy. But Watkins makes no such claim. Rather, he claims only that the Army regulations discriminate against him because of his membership in a disfavored group, homosexuals. This claim is not barred by precedent.

V

We now address the merits of Watkins' claim that we must subject the Army's regulations to strict scrutiny because homosexuals constitute a suspect class under equal protection jurisprudence. The Supreme Court has identified several factors that guide our suspect class inquiry.

The first factor the Supreme Court generally considers is whether the group at issue has suffered a history of purposeful discrimination. *See, e.g., Cleburne*, 473 U.S. at 441; *Massachusetts Bd. of Retirement v. Murgia*, 427 U.S. 307, 313 (1976); *Rodriguez*, 411 U.S. at 28; *Frontiero*, 411 U.S. at 684-85 (plurality). As the Army concedes, it is indisputable that "homosexuals have historically been the object of pernicious and sustained hostility." *Rowland v. Mad River Local School Dist.*, 470 U.S. 1009, 1014 (1985) (Brennan, J., dissenting from denial of cert.). More recently, Judge Henderson echoed the same harsh truth: "Lesbians and gays have been the object of some of the deepest prejudice and hatred in American society." *High Tech Gays v. Defense Industrial Security Clearance Office*, 668 F.Supp. 1361 (N.D. Cal. 1987) (invalidating Defense Department practice of subjecting gay security clearance applicants to more exacting scrutiny than heterosexual applicants). Homosexuals have been the frequent victims of violence and have been excluded from jobs, schools, housing, churches, and even families. *See generally* Note, *An Argument for the Application of Equal Protection Heightened Scrutiny to Classifications Based on Homosexuality*, 57 S. Cal. L. Rev. 797, 824-25 (1984) (documenting the history of discrimination). In any case, the discrimination faced by homosexuals in our society is plainly no less pernicious or intense than the discrimination faced by other groups already treated as suspect classes, such as aliens or people of a particular national origin.

The second factor that the Supreme Court considers in suspect class analysis is difficult to capsulize and may in fact represent a cluster of factors grouped around a central idea — whether the discrimination embodies a gross unfairness that is sufficiently inconsistent with the ideals of equal protection to term it invidious. Considering this additional factor makes sense. After all, discrimination exists against some groups because the animus is warranted — no one could seriously argue that burglars form a suspect class. *See* Tribe, *The Puzzling Persistence of Process-Based Constitutional Theories*, 89 Yale L.J. 1063, 1075 (1980); Note, *supra*, at 814-815 & nn. 115-116. In giving content to this concept of gross unfairness, the Court has considered (1) whether the disadvantaged class is defined

by a trait that "frequently bears no relation to ability to perform or contribute to society," *Frontiero*, 411 U.S. at 686 (plurality); (2) whether the class has been saddled with unique disabilities because of prejudice or inaccurate stereotypes; and (3) whether the trait defining the class is immutable. *See Cleburne*, 473 U.S. at 440-44; *Plyler*, 457 U.S. at 216 n.14, 219 n.19, 220, 223; *Murgia*, 427 U.S. at 313; *Frontiero*, 411 U.S. at 685-687 (plurality). We consider these questions in turn.

Sexual orientation plainly has no relevance to a person's "ability to perform or contribute to society." Indeed, the Army makes no claim that homosexuality impairs a person's ability to perform military duties. Sergeant Watkins' exemplary record of military service stands as a testament to quite the opposite. Moreover, as the Army itself concluded, there is not a scintilla of evidence that Watkins' avowed homosexuality "had either a degrading effect upon unit performance, morale or discipline, or upon his own job performance."

This irrelevance of sexual orientation to the quality of a person's contribution to society also suggests that classifications based on sexual orientation reflect prejudice and inaccurate stereotypes — the second indicia of a classification's gross unfairness. *See Cleburne*, 473 U.S. at 440-441. We agree with Justice Brennan that "discrimination against homosexuals is, likely . . . to reflect deep-seated prejudice rather than . . . rationality.'" *Rowland*, 470 U.S. at 1014 (Brennan, J., dissenting from denial of cert.) (quoting *Plyler*, 457 U.S. at 216 n.14). The Army does not dispute the hard fact that homosexuals face enormous prejudice. Nor could it, for the Army justifies its regulations in part by asserting that straight soldiers despise and lack respect for homosexuals and that popular prejudice against homosexuals is so pervasive that their presence in the Army will discourage enlistment and tarnish the Army's public image. Instead, the Army suggests that the public opprobrium directed towards gays does not constitute prejudice in the pejorative sense of the word, but rather represents appropriate public disapproval of persons who engage in immoral behavior. The Army equates homosexuals with sodomists and justifies its regulations as simply reflecting a rational bias against a class of persons who engage in criminal acts of sodomy. In essence, the Army argues that homosexuals, like burglars, cannot form a suspect class because they are criminals.

The Army's argument, essentially adopted by the dissent, rests on two false premises. First, the class burdened by the regulations is defined by the sexual *orientation* of its members, not by their sexual conduct. To our knowledge, homosexual orientation itself has never been criminalized in this country. Moreover, any attempt to criminalize the status of an individual's sexual orientation would present grave constitutional problems. *See generally Robinson v. California*, 370 U.S. 660 (1962).

Second, little of the homosexual *conduct* covered by the regulations is criminal. The regulations reach many forms of homosexual conduct other than sodomy such as kissing, hand-holding, caressing, and hand-genital contact. Yet, sodomy is the only consensual adult sexual conduct that Congress has criminalized, 10 U.S.C. § 925. Indeed, the Army points to no law, Federal or state, which criminalizes any form of private consensual homosexual behavior other than sodomy. The Army's argument that its regulations legitimately discriminate solely against criminals might be relevant if the class at issue were limited to sodomists. But the class banned from Army service is not composed of sodomists, or even of homosexual sodomists; the class is composed of persons of homosexual orientation whether or not they have engaged in sodomy. As the record in this case makes clear, the Army has no proof that Watkins has ever engaged in any act of sodomy — homosexual or heterosexual. Nonetheless, the regulations mandated his discharge and the denial of his reenlistment application.

Finally, we turn to immutability as an indicator of gross unfairness. The Supreme Court has never held that only classes with immutable traits can be deemed suspect. *Cf., e.g., Cleburne*, 473 U.S. at 442 n.10 (casting doubt on immutability theory); *id.* at 440-441 (stating the defining characteristics of suspect classes without mentioning immutability); *Murgia*, 427 U.S. at 313 (same); *Rodriguez*, 411 U.S. at 28 (same). We nonetheless consider immutability because the Supreme Court has often focused on immutability, *see, e.g., Plyler*, 457 U.S. at 220; *Frontiero*, 411 U.S. at 686 (plurality), and has sometimes described the recognized suspect classes as having immutable traits, *see, e.g., Parham v. Hughes*, 441 U.S. 347, 351 (1979) (plurality opinion) (describing race, national origin, alienage, illegitimacy, and gender as immutable).

Although the Supreme Court considers immutability relevant, it is clear that by "immutability" the Court has never meant strict immutability in the sense that members of the class must be physically unable to change or mask the trait defining their class. People can have operations to change their sex. Aliens can ordinarily become naturalized citizens. The status of illegitimate children can be changed. People can frequently hide their national origin by changing their customs, their names, or their associations. Lighter skinned blacks can sometimes "pass" for white, as can Latinos for Anglos, and some people can even change their racial appearance with pigment injections. *See* J. Griffin, Black Like Me (1977). At a minimum, then, the Supreme Court is willing to treat a trait as effectively immutable if changing it would involve great difficulty, such as requiring a major physical change or a traumatic change of identity. Reading the case law in a more capacious manner, "immutability" may describe those traits that are so central to a person's identity that it would be abhorrent for government to penalize a person for refusing to change them, regardless of how easy that change might be physically. Racial discrimination, for example, would not suddenly become constitutional if medical science developed an easy, cheap, and painless method of changing one's skin pigment. *See* Tribe, *supra*, at 1073-74 n.52. *See generally* Note, *The Constitutional Status of Sexual Orientation: Homosexuality As a Suspect Classification*, 98 Harv. L. Rev. 1285, 1303 (arguing that the ability to change a trait is not as important as whether the trait is a "determinative feature of personality").

Under either formulation, we have no trouble concluding that sexual orientation is immutable for the purposes of equal protection doctrine. Although the causes of homosexuality are not fully understood, scientific research indicates that we have little control over our sexual orientation and that, once acquired, our sexual orientation is largely impervious to change. *See* Note, *supra*, 57 S. Cal. L. Rev. at 817-821 (collecting sources). Scientific proof aside, it seems appropriate to ask whether heterosexuals feel capable of changing *their* sexual orientation. Would heterosexuals living in a city that passed an ordinance banning those who engaged in or desired to engage in sex with persons of the *opposite* sex find it easy not only to abstain from heterosexual activity but also to shift the object of their sexual desires to persons of the same sex? It may be that some heterosexuals and homosexuals can change their sexual orientation through extensive therapy, neurosurgery or shock treatment. But the possibility of such a difficult and traumatic change does not make sexual orientation "mutable" for equal protection purposes. To express the same idea under the alternative formulation, we conclude that allowing the government to penalize the failure to change such a central aspect of individual and group identity would be abhorrent to the values animating the constitutional ideal of equal protection of the laws.

The final factor the Supreme Court considers in suspect class analysis is whether the group burdened by official discrimination lacks the political power necessary to obtain redress from the political branches of government. *See, e.g., Cleburne*, 473 U.S. at 441; *Plyler*, 457 U.S. at 216 n.14; *Rodriguez*, 411 U.S. at 28. Courts understandably have been more reluctant to extend heightened protection under equal protection doctrine to groups fully capable of securing their rights through the political process. In evaluating whether a class is politically underrepresented, the Supreme Court has focused on whether the class is a "discrete and insular minority." *See, e.g., Murgia*, 427 U.S. at 313; *see generally United States v. Carolene Products*, 304 U.S. 144, 152-53 n.4 (1938).

The Court has held, for example, that old age does not define a discrete and insular group because "it marks a stage that each of us will reach if we live out our normal span." *Murgia*, 427 U.S. at 313-14. By contrast, most of us are not likely to identify ourselves as homosexual at any time in our lives. Thus, many of us, including many elected officials, are likely to have difficulty understanding or empathizing with homosexuals. Most people have little exposure to gays, both because they rarely encounter gays[27] and because the gays they do encounter may feel compelled to conceal their sexual orientation. In fact, the social, economic, and political pressures to conceal one's homosexuality commonly deter many gays from openly advocating pro-homosexual legislation, thus intensifying their inability to make effective use of the political process. "Because of the immediate and severe opprobrium often manifested against homosexuals once so identified publicly, members of this group are particularly powerless to pursue their rights openly in the political arena." *Rowland*, 470 U.S. at 1014

---

27. Because homosexuals are a minority and are frequently excluded from jobs, schools, churches, and heterosexual social circles, heterosexuals generally have relatively few opportunities to meet homosexuals and overcome any prejudices against homosexuality.

(Brennan, J., dissenting from denial of cert.).[28]

Even when gays overcome this prejudice enough to participate openly in politics, the general animus towards homosexuality may render this participation wholly ineffective. Elected officials sensitive to public prejudice may refuse to support legislation that even appears to condone homosexuality. Indeed, the Army itself argues that its regulations are justified by the need to "maintain the public acceptability of military service," because "toleration of homosexual conduct . . . might be understood as tacit approval" and "the existence of homosexual units might well be a source of ridicule and notoriety." These barriers to political power are underscored by the underrepresentation of avowed homosexuals in the decisionmaking bodies of government and the inability of homosexuals to prevent legislation hostile to their group interests.[29] *See Frontiero*, 411 U.S. at 686 & n.17 (plurality) (underrepresentation of women in government caused in part by history of discrimination); *Cleburne*, 473 U.S. at 445 (reasoning that the existence of legislation responsive to the needs of the mentally disabled belied the claim that they were politically powerless).

In sum, our analysis of the relevant factors in determining whether a given group should be considered a suspect class for the purposes of equal protection doctrine ineluctably leads us to the conclusion that homosexuals constitute such a suspect class. We find not only that our analysis of each of the relevant factors supports our conclusion, but also that the principles underlying equal protection doctrine — the principles that gave rise to these factors in the first place — compel us to conclude that homosexuals constitute a suspect class.

VI

Having concluded that homosexuals constitute a suspect class, we must subject the Army's regulations facially discriminating against homosexuals to strict scrutiny. Consequently, we may uphold the regulations only if "*necessary* to promote a *compelling governmental interest.*'" *Dunn v. Blumstein*, 405 U.S. 330, 342 (1972) (quoting *Shapiro*, 394 U.S. at 634); *see also University of Calif. Regents v. Bakke*, 438 U.S. 265, 357 (1978) (Opinion of Brennan, White, Marshall & Blackmun, JJ.). The requirement of necessity means that no less restrictive alternative is available to promote the compelling governmental interest.

We recognize that even under strict scrutiny, our review of military regulations must be more deferential than comparable review of laws governing civilians. *See Goldman v. Weinberger*, 475 U.S. 503 (1986). While the Supreme Court does not "purport to apply a different equal protection test because of the military context, [it does] stress the deference due congressional choices among alter-

---

28. *See also Adolph Coors Co.* v. *Wallace*, 570 F. Supp. 202, 209 n.24 (N.D. Cal. 1983) ("Homosexuals attempting to form associations to represent their political and social beliefs, free from fatal reprisals for their sexual orientation" constitute discrete and insular minority meriting special protection under *U.S.* v. *Carolene Products Co.*, 304 U.S. 144, 152-53 n.4 (1938) (Williams, J.)).

29. The Army claims that homosexuals cannot be politically powerless because two states, Wisconsin and California, have passed statutes prohibiting discrimination against homosexuals. Two state statutes do not overcome the long and extensive history of laws discriminating against homosexuals in all fifty states. Moreover, at the national level — the relevant political level for seeking protection from military discrimination — homosexuals have been wholly unsuccessful in getting legislation passed that protects them from discrimination. The Army also argues that the repeal of sodomy statutes by many states proves that homosexuals are not politically powerless. However, sodomy statutes restrict the sexual freedom of heterosexuals as well as homosexuals. The repeal of sodomy statutes may thus reflect the liberalization of attitudes about heterosexual behavior more than it reflects the political power of homosexuals.

natives in exercising the congressional authority to raise and support armies and make rules for their governance." *Rostker v. Goldberg*, 453 U.S. 57, 71 (1981) (citing *Schlesinger v. Ballard*, 419 U.S. 498 (1975)). We question whether this special deference is appropriate in Watkins' case given that Congress has chosen not to regulate homosexuality or any form of sexual conduct engaged in by military personnel save for one exception — Congress has chosen to criminalize sodomy by military personnel whether committed "with another person *of the same or opposite sex.*" 10 U.S.C. § 925 (emphasis added). Hence, if anything, section 925 reflects an absence of congressional intent to discriminate on the basis of sexual orientation.

In any case, even granting special deference to the policy choices of the military, we must reject many of the Army's asserted justifications because they illegitimately cater to private biases. For example, the Army argues that it has a valid interest in maintaining morale and discipline by avoiding hostilities and "'tensions between known homosexuals and other members [of the armed services] who despise/detest homosexuality.'"[30] The Army also expresses its "'doubts concerning a homosexual officer's ability to command the respect and trust of the personnel he or she commands'" because many lower-ranked heterosexual soldiers despise and detest homosexuality. Finally, the Army argues that the presence of gays in its ranks "might well be a source of ridicule and notoriety, harmful to the Army's recruitment efforts" and to its public image.[31]

These concerns strike a familiar chord. For much of our history, the military's fear of racial tension kept black soldiers separated from whites. As recently as World War II both the Army chief of staff and the Secretary of the Navy justified racial segregation in the ranks as necessary to maintain efficiency, discipline, and morale. *See* G. Ware, William Hastie: Grace Under Pressure 99, 134 (1984).[32] Today, it is unthinkable that the judiciary would defer to the Army's prior "professional" judgment that

---

30. A somewhat different rationale conceivably could also underlie certain cryptic statements the Army makes about its concerns regarding "close conditions affording minimal privacy," "'potential for difficulties arising out of possible close confinement,'" and "the intimacy of barrack's life." Conceivably, the Army could be concerned in part that the presence of gays in the ranks will create *sexual* tensions — as distinguished from tensions arising from prejudice — because of the practical necessity of housing gays with personnel of the same sex. The Army, however, never articulates this concern. Thus it gives no indication that it regards this concern as compelling or that it believes that weeding *all* homosexuals out of the military — even soldiers as exemplary as Sergeant Watkins — is necessary to advance a compelling military interest in reducing sexual tensions. Indeed, at points in its argument the Army implies that it is concerned about the close confinement of soldiers only insofar as such confinement might exacerbate hostilities and tensions assertedly created by the prejudice some heterosexuals have against homosexuals. Even if the Army had raised the argument that excluding homosexuals from barracks reduces sexual tension and had shown that reducing sexual tension serves a compelling interest, nothing in the record even suggests that a per se rule banning all homosexuals from the Army would be the least restrictive method of advancing this interest.

31. *Goldman* and *Rostker* do not, as the dissent suggests, require us to be so deferential to the military that even under strict scrutiny we cannot overturn the "'considered professional judgment' of the Army as to what kind of persons should be barred from enlisting to insure a disciplined fighting force." This cannot be the law. If the military decided to exclude blacks from its ranks because their presence allegedly undermined morale, the judiciary would be helpless to strike down the action. *Goldman* and *Rostker* require judicial deference, not the abdication of our Article III duty to hold the other branches of government, even the military, accountable to the Constitution.

32. It took an Executive Order in 1945 by President Truman, issued against the advice of almost every admiral and general, to integrate our armed forces. M. Miller, *Plain Speaking: An Oral Biography of Harry S. Truman* 79 (1983). It is also interesting to note that during World War II the Army deliberately minimized any publicity about the existence of black soldiers because it feared that such publicity would tarnish the Army's public image. *See* G. Ware, *supra*, at 100.

black and white soldiers had to be segregated to avoid interracial tensions. Indeed, the Supreme Court has decisively rejected the notion that private prejudice against minorities can ever justify official discrimination, even when those private prejudices create real and legitimate problems. *See Palmore v. Sidoti*, 466 U.S. 429 (1984).

In *Palmore*, a state granted custody of a child to her father because her white mother had remarried a black man. The state rested its decision on the best interests of the child, reasoning that, despite improvements in race relations, the social reality was that the child would likely suffer social stigmatization if she had parents of different races. A unanimous Court, in an opinion by Chief Justice Burger, conceded the importance of the state's interest in the welfare of the child, but nonetheless reversed with the following reasoning:

"It would ignore reality to suggest that racial and ethnic prejudices do not exist or that all manifestations of those prejudices have been eliminated. . . . The question, however, is whether the reality of private biases and the possible injury they might inflict are permissible considerations for removal of an infant child from the custody of its natural mother. We have little difficulty concluding that they are not. The Constitution cannot control such prejudices but neither can it tolerate them. Private biases may be outside the reach of the law, but the law cannot, directly or indirectly, give them effect."

Thus, *Palmore* forecloses the Army from justifying its ban on homosexuals on the ground that private prejudice against homosexuals would somehow undermine the strength of our armed forces if homosexuals were permitted to serve. *See also Cleburne*, 473 U.S. at 448 (even under rationality review of discrimination against group that is neither suspect nor quasi-suspect, catering to private prejudice is not a cognizable state interest).

The Army's defense of its regulations, however, goes beyond its professed fear of prejudice in the ranks. Apparently, the Army believes that its regulations rooting out persons with certain sexual tendencies are not merely a response to prejudice, but are also grounded in legitimate moral norms. In other words, the Army believes that its ban against homosexuals simply codifies society's moral consensus that homosexuality is evil. Yet, even accepting *arguendo* this proposition that anti-homosexual animus is grounded in morality (as opposed to prejudice masking as morality), equal protection doctrine does not permit notions of majoritarian morality to serve as compelling justification for laws that discriminate against suspect classes.

A similar principle animates *Loving v. Virginia*, 388 U.S. 1 (1967), in which the Supreme Court struck down a Virginia statute outlawing marriages between whites and blacks. Although the Virginia legislature may have adopted this law in the sincere belief that miscegenation — the mixing of racial blood lines — was evil, this moral judgment could not justify the statute's discrimination on the basis of race. Like the Army's regulations proscribing sexual acts only when committed by homosexual couples, the Virginia statute proscribed marriage only when undertaken by mixed-race couples. In both cases, the government did not prohibit certain conduct, it prohibited certain conduct selectively — only when engaged in by certain classes of people. Although courts may sometimes have to accept society's moral condemnation as a justification even when the morally condemned activity causes no harm to interests outside notions of morality, our deference to majoritarian notions of morality must be tempered by equal protection principles which require that those notions be applied evenhandedly. Laws that limit the acceptable focus of one's sexual desires to members of the opposite sex, like laws that limit one's choice of spouse (or sexual partner) to members of the same race, cannot withstand constitutional scrutiny absent a compelling governmental justification. This requirement would be reduced to a nullity if the government's assertion of moral objections only to interracial couples or only to homosexual couples could itself serve as a tautological basis for the challenged classification.

The Army's remaining justifications for discriminating against homosexuals may not be illegitimate, but they bear little relation to the regulations at issue. For example, the Army argues that military discipline might be undermined if emotional relationships developed between homosexuals of different military rank. Although this concern might be a compelling and legitimate military interest, the Army's regulations are poorly tailored to advance that interest. No one would suggest that heterosexuals are any less likely to develop emotional attachments within military ranks than homosexuals. Yet the Army's regulations do not address the problem of emotional attachments between male and female personnel, which presumably place similar stress on military discipline. Surely, the Army's interest in preventing emotional relationships that could erode military discipline would be advanced much more directly by a ban on all sexual contact between members of the same unit, whether between persons of the same or opposite sex. *Cf. Cleburne*, 473 U.S. at 449-50 (rejecting certain asserted justifications under *rationality* review where the justification would extend to other groups but the challenged classification did not). Here the Army regulations disqualify all homosexuals whether or not they have developed any emotional or sexual liaisons with other soldiers.

Also bearing little relation to the regulations is the Army's professed concern with breaches of security. Certainly the Army has a compelling interest in excluding persons who may be susceptible to blackmail. It is evident, however, that homosexuality poses a special risk of blackmail only if a homosexual is secretive about his or her sexual orientation. The Army regulations do nothing to lessen this problem. Quite the opposite, the regulations ban homosexuals only after they have declared their homosexuality or have engaged in known homosexual acts. The Army's concern about security risks among gays could be addressed in a more sensible and less restrictive manner by adopting a regulation banning only those gays who had lied about or failed to admit their sexual orientation.[34] In that way, the Army would *encourage*, rather than discourage, declarations of homosexuality, thereby reducing the number of closet homosexuals who might indeed pose a security risk.[35]

CONCLUSION

We hold that the Army's regulations violate the constitutional guarantee of equal protection of the laws because they discriminate against persons of homosexual orientation, a suspect class, and because the regulations are not necessary to promote a legitimate compelling governmental interest. We thus reverse the district court's rulings denying Watkins' motion for summary judgment and granting summary judgment in favor of the Army, and remand with instructions to enter a declaratory judgment that the Army Regulations are constitutionally void on their face, and

---

34. Watkins has forthrightly reported his homosexuality since his induction in 1967, and his homosexuality was always a matter of common knowledge. There is no suggestion in the record before us that Watkins ever feared public disclosure of his homosexualty.

35. Moreover, even if banning homosexuals could lessen security risks, there appears to be no reason for treating homosexuality as a nonwaivable disqualification from military service while treating other more serious potential sources of blackmail as waivable disqualifications.

to enter an injunction requiring the Army to consider Watkins' reenlistment application without regard to his sexual orientation. The district court shall also consider any unresolved claims of Watkins' such as whether the Army acted unlawfully in revoking his security clearance.

REVERSED AND REMANDED.

REINHARDT, J., dissenting

With great reluctance, I have concluded that I am unable to concur in the majority opinion. Like the majority, I believe that homosexuals have been unfairly treated both historically and in the United States today. Were I free to apply my own view of the meaning of the Constitution and in that light to pass upon the validity of the Army's regulations, I too would conclude that the Army may not refuse to enlist homosexuals. I am bound, however, as a circuit judge to apply the Constitution as it has been interpreted by the Supreme Court and our own circuit, whether or not I agree with those interpretations. Because of this requirement, I am sometimes compelled to reach a result I believe to be contrary to the proper interpretation of Constitutional principles. This is, regrettably, one of those times.

I

In this case we consider the constitutionality of a regulation which bars homosexuals from enlisting in the Army. Sergeant Perry Watkins challenges that regulation under the equal protection clause. The majority holds that homosexuals are a suspect class, and that the regulation cannot survive strict scrutiny. Because I am compelled by recent Supreme Court and Ninth Circuit precedent to conclude first, that homosexuals are not a suspect class and second, that the regulation survives both rational and intermediate level scrutiny, I must dissent.

Bowers v. Hardwick, 478 U.S. 186 (1986), is the landmark case involving homosexual conduct. In *Hardwick*, the Supreme Court decided that homosexual sodomy is not protected by the right to privacy, and thus that the states are free to criminalize that conduct. Because *Hardwick* did not challenge the Georgia sodomy statute under the equal protection clause, and neither party presented that issue in its briefs or at oral argument, the Court limited its holding to due process and properly refrained from reaching any direct conclusion regarding an equal protection challenge to the statute.[2] However, the fact that *Hardwick* does not address the equal protection question directly does not mean that the case is not of substantial significance to such an inquiry.

An important part of the function of circuit court judges is to interpret the Supreme Court's opinions. In doing so, we must attempt to understand the principles underlying those opinions, so that we may determine how past decisions affect subsequent cases. With respect to *Hardwick*, the majority balks at performing this task. Instead, it states: "the *Hardwick* Court simply did not address either the question whether heterosexual sodomy also falls outside the scope of the right to privacy or the separate question whether homosexual but not heterosexual sodomy

---

2. *Cf.* L. Tribe, *American Constitutional Law* § 15-21, at 1431 n.7 (2nd ed. 1988) [hereinafter, *Constitutional Law*]:

The *Hardwick* majority's notation that no equal protection issue was before the Court should not be taken to mean that the Justices would have been interested in resolving it if it had been. For the Court denied *certiorari* that same term in *Baker v. Wade*, 769 F.2d 289 (5th Cir. 1985) (en banc), *rehearing en banc denied*, 774 F.2d 1285 (5th Cir. 1985), *cert. denied*, 106 S. Ct. 3337 (1986), which involved a Texas law ... that targeted only homosexual acts.

In his treatise, Professor Tribe notes, in the interest of full disclosure, that he served as Hardwick's counsel before the Supreme Court.

may be criminalized without violating the equal protection clause." The duty to interpret Supreme Court precedent cannot be so easily avoided. Logic and reason are among the tools available to judges who wish to determine the meaning of cases.

The answer to the meaning of *Hardwick* is not difficult to find. There are only two choices: either *Hardwick* is about "sodomy", and heterosexual sodomy is as constitutionally unprotected as homosexual sodomy, or it is about "homosexuality", and there are some acts which are protected if done by heterosexuals but not if done by homosexuals. In applying the opinion to future cases our first effort must be to decide which of the two propositions *Hardwick* stands for. Although the majority refuses to acknowledge that it is making a choice, there can be no doubt that it does so. The sentence after the text quoted above reads: "We cannot read *Hardwick* as standing for the proposition that government may outlaw sodomy only when committed by a disfavored class of persons." By expressly rejecting the "homosexuality" option, the majority implicitly but necessarily selects the "sodomy" alternative. I do not believe that *Hardwick* can reasonably be so construed.

In my opinion, *Hardwick must* be read as standing precisely for the proposition the majority rejects. To put it simply, I believe that after *Hardwick* the government may outlaw homosexual sodomy even though it fails to regulate the private sexual conduct of heterosexuals. In *Hardwick* the Court took great care to make clear that it was saying only that homosexual sodomy is not constitutionally protected, and not that all sexual acts — both heterosexual and homosexual — that fall within the definition of sodomy can be prohibited.

The Georgia statute at issue in *Hardwick* on its face barred all acts of sodomy. The Court could simply have upheld the statute without even mentioning the word "homosexual". Instead it carefully crafted its opinion to proscribe and condemn only homosexual sodomy. While it can be argued

that the Court was faced with only a homosexual sodomy case, under the majority's theory the fact that the particular act of sodomy was homosexual in nature is of no significance. According to the majority, the race and sexual preference of the defendant are equally irrelevant. The majority says: "Surely, for example, *Hardwick* cannot be read as a license to outlaw sodomy only when committed by blacks." Surely not. And surely, had *Hardwick* been black rather than a homosexual, the Court would not, throughout its opinion, have written about "black sodomy" or black sodomists. It would simply have written about sodomy. Here, however, from the Court's standpoint the crucial fact was that *Hardwick* was a homosexual. For that reason, throughout its opinion the Court wrote about "homosexual sodomy".

It is significant that whatever one may think of the soundness of *Hardwick*'s assumptions or conclusions, the decision came as no surprise to those familiar with the rulings of the lower federal courts on the subject of homosexual rights. Well before *Hardwick*, this court, along with most other federal courts, had concluded that the Supreme Court had determined that the right to privacy was inapplicable to homosexual conduct. As we said in *Beller v. Middendorf*, 632 F.2d 788, 809-10 (9th Cir. 1980), "Most federal courts ... have understood the holding [in *Doe v*. Commonwealth's Attorney, 425 U.S. 901 (1976)] to be that homosexual conduct does not enjoy special constitutional protection under the due process clause."

The anti-homosexual thrust of *Hardwick*, and the Court's willingness to condone anti-homosexual animus in the actions of the government, are clear. A prominent constitutional scholar makes this point succinctly. Professor Laurence Tribe, after strongly criticizing the Court's holding and reasoning in *Hardwick*, states that the "'good news' about the Court's decision" is that it was so clearly based on prejudice against homosexuals that it "may therefore pose less of a threat to other privacy precedents than would otherwise be the case." *Constitutional*

Law, supra, § 15-21, at 1430. Justice Blackmun characterized the decision as being "obsessively focus[ed] on homosexual activity", and "proceed[ing] on the assumption that homosexuals are so different from other citizens that their lives may be controlled in a way that would not be tolerated if it limited the choices of ... other citizens. *Hardwick*, 478 U.S. at 200 (Blackmun, J., dissenting). Indeed, it is hard to find any basis in the Court's opinion for interpreting it the way the majority chooses: the Court says explicitly that the statute is justified by "majority sentiments about homosexuality", not by "majority sentiments about sodomy".

My colleagues' interpretation of *Hardwick* is not only unsound, it also unnecessarily and incorrectly increases — exponentially — the damage to the right to privacy caused by *Hardwick*. While in *Hardwick* the Court made it clear that homosexual conduct is not protected by the right to privacy, the Court has never held that the government has the authority to regulate the private heterosexual acts of consenting adults. *See Griswold v. Connecticut*, 381 U.S. 479 (1965); *Eisenstadt v. Baird*, 405 U.S. 438 (1972); *Carey v. Population Services International*, 431 U.S. 678 (1977); *see also Hardwick*, 478 U.S. at 216-18 (Stevens, J., dissenting). To the contrary, it has expressly stated that "intimate relationships" (though apparently only of the heterosexual variety) are constitutionally protected. See *Board of Directors of Rotary International*

v. Rotary Club, 107 S. Ct. 1940, 1945 (1987). Reading *Hardwick* as implicitly permitting the regulation of heterosexual conduct, as the majority's analysis forces it to do, constitutes a serious retreat in the privacy area.[5] If the majority's interpretation of *Hardwick* were correct, states could, for example, criminalize the act of oral sex when engaged in by heterosexuals, including married couples, and in fact would be required to do so if they wished to criminalize homosexual sodomy. Moreover, states would be required to enforce these statutes equally, against heterosexuals and homosexuals alike, a practice not heretofore common in our society. I view the Constitution differently than the majority apparently does: I believe the Constitution protects most, if not all, private heterosexual acts between consenting adults.

The majority opinion undermines the right to privacy in another way. In its eagerness to promote its equal protection analysis and to bolster its characterization of *Hardwick* as an anti-privacy decision, it terms equal protection more objective and more democratic than substantive due process, which it describes as "value-based linedrawing" arising not from the Constitution itself but from "judicial fiat". It is not necessary to denigrate the right to privacy in order to appreciate the importance of the equal protection clause. The majority's attack on substantive due process is unreasoned and unjustified. As the Supreme Court has made clear on numerous occasions, the right to

---

5. The majority's disingenuous statement that it reads *Hardwick* neither one way nor the other on this point, is simply neither logical nor credible. Only if heterosexual sodomy is *not* protected by the right to privacy could the majority's equal protection argument conceivably have any validity. If the right to privacy does apply in the case of heterosexuals who, for example, engage in oral sex, then the equal protection clause obviously does not require equal treatment of homosexual and heterosexual sexual conduct. The clause is procedural in nature and cannot afford substantive rights to a particular group when the Constitution does not otherwise provide them. To put it differently, if one group's sexual conduct is protected by the right to privacy and the other's is not, it is the Constitution itself that distinguishes between the treatment the two groups constitutionally receive. We cannot, then, use the equal protection clause to say that the two groups must be treated identically with respect to that conduct. Since the Court has already held that homosexuals are not protected by the privacy provisions of the Constitution when they commit sodomy, the right to equal treatment exists only if heterosexuals are similarly unprotected. Thus the majority's argument that equal protection applies is *necessarily* premised on the view that heterosexual sodomy, including oral sex between married couples, is not protected by the right to privacy and may be criminalized.

privacy is a fundamental part of our Constitutional protections, originating in the First, Third, Fourth, Fifth, and Ninth Amendments, and of course the due process clause of the Fourteenth Amendment. *See, e.g., Griswold v. Connecticut*, 381 U.S. at 484-85. The protections guaranteed by the right to privacy are no less central to the Constitution than those guaranteed by the equal protection clause. *See generally* Note, "Process, Privacy, and the Supreme Court," 28 *B.C. L. Rev.* 691 (1987). Also, notwithstanding the views of Dean Ely, most commentators agree that equal protection analysis is no more objective and no less difficult to apply than substantive due process analysis. *See, e.g.*, Tribe, "The Puzzling Persistence of Process-Based Constitutional Theory," 89 *Yale L.J.* 1063 (1980); Westen, "The Empty Idea of Equality," 95 *Harv. L. Rev.* 537 (1982). Unlike the majority, I believe we should afford both these fundamental constitutional protections full and equal dignity.

II

The majority opinion concludes that under the criteria established by equal protection case law, homosexuals must be treated as a suspect class. Were it not for *Hardwick* (and other cases discussed *infra*), I would agree, for in my opinion the group meets all the applicable criteria. *See, e.g.*, Note, "The Constitutional Status of Sexual Orientation: Homosexuality As a Suspect Classification," 98 *Harv. L. Rev.* 1285 (1985). However, after *Hardwick*, we are no longer free to reach that conclusion.[8]

The majority opinion treats as a suspect class a group of persons whose defining characteristic is their desire, predisposition, or propensity to engage in conduct that the Supreme Court has held to be constitutionally unprotected, an act that the states can — and approximately half the states have — criminalized. Homosexuals are different from groups previously afforded protection under the equal protection clause in that homosexuals are defined by their conduct — or, at the least, by their desire to engage in certain conduct. With other groups, such as blacks or women, there is no connection between particular conduct and the definition of the group. When conduct that plays a central role in defining a group may be prohibited by the state, it cannot be asserted with any legitimacy that the group is specially protected by the Constitution.[11]

Sodomy is an act basic to homosexuality. In the relevant state statutes, sodomy is usually defined broadly to include "any sexual act involving the sex organs of one person and the mouth or anus of another." The practices covered by this definition are, not surprisingly, the most common sexual practices of homosexuals. Specifically, oral sex is the

---

8. *See Constitutional Law, supra*, § 16-33, at 1616 n.47:

> The fact that the Court in *Bowers v. Hardwick*, 106 S. Ct. 2841 (1986), went out of its way to create a line between heterosexuals and homosexuals, where there was none in the challenged sodomy statute, merely to preserve prosecution of homosexuals under the law from constitutional infirmity, indicates how unlikely it is that homosexuality will be deemed quasi-suspect in the near future. *But compare Brown v. Board of Education*, 347 U.S. 483 (1954), *with Plessy v. Ferguson*, 163 U.S. 537 (1896).

> I note that Professor Tribe's pessimistic forecast relates to intermediate scrutiny and not the even stricter standard that the majority today holds applicable.

11. Thus, it is not even necessary to decide whether the majority's view of *Hardwick* — that it is based on a condemnation of sodomy rather than of homosexuality — is correct. Whatever the explanation for the Court's willingness to allow sodomy to be criminalized — whether its decision is based on its views as to the morality of homosexuality or on its disapproval of sodomy, including the heterosexual variety — that willingness is inconsistent with affording special constitutional protection to homosexuals — a group whose primary form of sexual activity, the Court tells us, may be declared criminal.

primary form of homosexual activity. *See* A. Bell & M. Weinberg, *Homosexualities* 106-11, 327-30 (1978). When the Supreme Court declares that an act that is done by a vast majority of a group's members and is fundamental to their very nature can be criminalized and further states that the basis for such criminalization is "the presumed belief of a majority of the electorate . . . that [the practice] is immoral and unacceptable," I do not think that we are free, whatever our personal views, to describe discriminatory treatment of the group as based on "unreasoning prejudice". Rather we are obligated to accept the Supreme Court's conclusion that what the majority of this panel calls "unreasoning prejudice" is instead a permissible societal moral judgment.

I have already explained the principal reasons why the majority's interpretation of *Hardwick* as covering heterosexual sodomy is not only incorrect but also damaging to constitutional principles. I must now add that the majority errs for another important reason. The majority states that the equal protection clause requires the government (if it wishes to criminalize homosexual sodomy) to prohibit all persons from engaging in "the proscribed sexual acts". This analysis affords equal treatment only in the most superficial meaning of the term. Government actions, neutral on their face, can sometimes have distinctly unequal effects, and carry implicit statements of inequality. *See* L. Tribe, *Constitutional Choices* 238-45 (1985). Laws against sodomy do not affect homosexuals and heterosexuals equally. Homosexuals are more heavily burdened by such legislation, even if we ignore the governmental tendency to prosecute general sodomy statutes selectively against them. Oral sex, a

form of sodomy, is the primary form of sexual activity among homosexuals; however, sexual intercourse is the primary form of sexual activity among heterosexuals.[13] If homosexuals were in fact a suspect class, a statute criminalizing both heterosexual sodomy and homosexual sodomy would still not survive equal protection analysis. For the prohibition to be equal, the government would have to prohibit sexual intercourse — conduct as basic to heterosexuals as sodomy is to homosexuals.[14] This, obviously, the government would not and could not do. Therefore, if equal protection rules apply (i.e. if homosexuals are a suspect class), a ban on homosexual sodomy could not stand no matter how the statute was drawn. *Hardwick* makes it plain that the contrary is true.

Finally, the "protection" of homosexual rights provided by the majority opinion is hollow indeed. The majority unwittingly denigrates the equal protection clause as well as the right to privacy. Until now, a "suspect class" has been a group whose members were afforded special solicitude. That is patently not the case with respect to homosexuals. Many states deny that group the right to engage in their most fundamental form of sexual activity. A "life without any physical intimacy", is hardly the life contemplated for our citizens by the Declaration of Independence ("the pursuit of happiness") or, one would have thought, by the Constitution. While *Hardwick* may not wholly preclude the possibility of lawful physical intimacy for homosexuals, it drastically limits that right. To proclaim that under these circumstances homosexuals are afforded special protection by the Constitution would be hypocritical at best.

---

13. Oral sex, though practiced by a substantial majority of heterosexuals, is not the primary sexual activity for that group. *See* W. Masters, V. Johnson & R. Kolodny, *Human Sexuality* 388-92, 418-22 (2nd ed. 1985).

14. Statutes which are neutral on their face survive equal protection scrutiny unless they are the product of discriminatory intent. However, as the Supreme Court has noted, "when a neutral law has a disparate impact upon a group that has historically been the victim of discrimination, an unconstitutional purpose may still be at work. . . . Certainly, when the adverse consequences of a law upon an identifiable group are . . . inevitable . . . a strong inference that the adverse effects were desired can reasonably be drawn." *Personnel Administrator of Massachusetts* v. *Feeney*, 442 U.S. 256, 273, 279 n.25 (1979).

Before concluding my discussion of *Hardwick*, I wish to record my own view of the opinion. I have delayed doing so until I have applied the case as I believe we have a duty to apply it. Now, I must add that as I understand our Constitution, a state simply has no business treating any group of persons as the State of Georgia and other states with sodomy statutes treat homosexuals. In my opinion, invidious discrimination against a group of persons with immutable characteristics can never be justified on the grounds of society's moral disapproval. No lesson regarding the meaning of our Constitution could be more important for us as a nation to learn. I believe that the Supreme Court egregiously misinterpreted the Constitution in *Hardwick*. In my view, *Hardwick* improperly condones official bias and prejudice against homosexuals, and authorizes the criminalization of conduct that is an essential part of the intimate sexual life of our many homosexual citizens, a group that has historically been the victim of unfair and irrational treatment. I believe that history will view *Hardwick* much as it views *Plessy v. Ferguson*, 163 U.S. 537 (1896). And I am confident that, in the long run, *Hardwick*, like *Plessy*, will be overruled by a wiser and more enlightened Court.

The decision in *Hardwick* has not affected my firm belief that the Constitution, properly interpreted, does afford homosexuals the same protections it affords other groups that are historic victims of invidious discrimination. Nevertheless, for the reasons I have already stated, it is my obligation to follow *Hardwick* as long as it has precedential force — and for now it does.

■ ■ ■

IV

Because we are not free to hold that homosexuals are a suspect class, we can not apply strict scrutiny to the Army's regulations. At the most the regulations must pass intermediate scrutiny — and in *Hatheway* we decided that the military's singling out of homosexual conduct for special adverse treatment survives that level of review: applying intermediate level scrutiny we concluded that prosecutions by the military on the basis of sexual preference bear "a substantial relationship to an important government interest." We then upheld the Army's discriminatory treatment of *Hatheway*. We are bound by *Hatheway* to conclude that military "[c]lassifications which are based solely on sexual preference" survive an intermediate level of review.

Courts must give special deference when adjudicating matters involving the military. *Goldman v. Weinberger*, 106 S. Ct. 1310 (1986); *Rostker v. Goldberg*, 453 U.S. U.S. 57 (1981). In the context of a first amendment challenge, the Supreme Court has recently stated: "Our review of military regulations . . . is far more deferential than constitutional review of similar laws or regulations designed for civilian society." *Goldman v. Weinberger*, 106 S. Ct. at 1313. In *Beller v. Middendorf*, Judge, now Justice, Kennedy writing for our court said: "constitutional rights must be viewed in light of the special circumstances of the armed forces". 632 F.2d at 810-11.

In rejecting the Army's justifications for the regulation, the majority fails to give proper deference to the Army's determinations. Its failure to do so may result in part from its unwillingness to recognize the moral judgments regarding homosexuality approved in *Hardwick*, and deemed permissible, at least for the purpose of military regulations, by Judge Kennedy in *Beller*, 632 F.2d at 811-12. Although I see no merit in the Army's ideas about homosexuals, its beliefs about the consequences of allowing homosexuals to serve in the Army, and its pandering to negative stereotypes of homosexuals, we are not permitted to substitute our views for the Army's "considered professional judgment" as to what kind of persons should be barred from enlisting in order to ensure a disciplined fighting force.[17]

After analyzing the various explanations offered by the Army, the majority dismisses the purposes of the regulations as illegitimate or irrational. Again, the majority takes a position that is not open to us. For not only have our cases told us we must defer to the military judgment in matters of this kind, they have upheld the very reasoning the majority now rejects. The justifications advanced by the Army involving negative views about homosexuals and homosexuality have been accepted by earlier decisions of this court as both legitimate and important. *Beller*, 632 F.2d at 811-812; *see Hatheway*, 641 F.2d at 1381-82. We are not free to reconsider those prior conclusions unless or until our court as a whole agrees to do so en banc.

It is true that, as the majority says on several occasions, the Army could not treat blacks as it treats homosexuals and could not base its regulations on negative judgments regarding blacks. No matter how appealing the analogy may be, we are not free to draw it here. *Beller* and *Hatheway* both approve discriminatory treatment against homosexuals, by the military, based on moral judgments regarding homosexuality. As the majority points out, similar biases against blacks could not form the basis for state

action against that group. *Palmore v. Sidoti*, 466 U.S. 429 (1984). Thus, cases regarding blacks are simply irrelevant.[18]

V

The majority attempts to overcome the problems posed by *Hardwick* (and, to some extent, by *Hatheway*) by distinguishing between the class of persons who engage in homosexual acts and the slightly broader class of persons who have a homosexual orientation. Relying on this distinction, the majority also argues that the Army regulation is about status, not conduct. It is unclear whether the majority is arguing that homosexuals are a suspect class simply because they are a class defined by status rather that conduct, or whether it is arguing that the equal protection question is unaffected by *Hardwick* because that case involves conduct rather than orientation. In either event, I do not believe we can escape the conclusions that "homosexuals", however defined, cannot qualify as a suspect class.

Even if we define the class as those who have a "homosexual orientation", its members will consist principally of active, practicing homosexuals.[19] That the class may also include a small number of persons who

---

17. To the claim in *Goldman* v. *Weinberger* that the military's regulation as applied was irrational and without empirical support, the Court stated:

> But whether or not expert witnesses may feel that religious exceptions to AFR 35-10 are desirable is quite beside the point. The desirability of dress regulations in the military is decided by the appropriate military officers, and they are under no constitutional mandate to abandon their considered professional judgment.

106 S. Ct. at 1314.

18. I am not suggesting, by any means, that all discriminatory statutes affecting homosexuals are valid. We are here dealing only with *military* regulations. Other governmental action, including state statutes, would still be subject to examination under a number of constitutional principles, including the equal protection clause. As far as that clause is concerned, for purposes of this case it is necessary for me to conclude only that strict scrutiny is not the proper standard.

19. The majority appears to be unwilling to acknowledge this point. However, the fact that homosexuals (or persons of "homosexual orientation") engage in or seek to engage in homosexual conduct is as unremarkable as the fact that "heterosexuals" (or persons of "heterosexual orientation") engage in or seek to engage in heterosexual conduct. To pretend that homosexuality or heterosexuality is unrelated to sexual conduct borders on the absurd. What distinguishes the class of homosexuals from the class of heterosexuals is not some vague "range of emotions", but the nature of the member's sexual proclivities or interests.

are or wish to be celibate is irrelevant for purposes of determining whether the group as a whole constitutes a suspect class. I simply see no way to say that homosexuals defined broadly (by status) are a suspect class, but that the same group, if more narrowly defined (by conduct) is not. Whether the group is defined by status or by conduct, is composition is essentially the same. In short, "homosexuals" are either a suspect class or they aren't. The answer cannot depend on the niceties of the class definition.[20]

What the majority may be arguing is that a regulation targeted at "orientation" is too broad to survive rationality review. However, if the majority is making this argument, there are a number of difficult questions it must answer first. For example, under the majority's status/conduct distinction, Watkins could be excluded from the Army based on regulations slightly more narrowly drawn so as to target only the class of persons who have engaged in homosexual conduct. If Watkins' actions fall within that narrower category (and they do), and Watkins is therefore a member of a class of persons that is not constitutionally protected, does he have standing to challenge the constitutionality of these regulations? If he does, would the correct remedy be simply to strike the few words that make the regulations too broad, rather than invalidating all of the regulations?[22] The majority simply does not discuss these and other similarly troublesome questions.

Moreover, I disagree with the majority's status/conduct distinction, as applied to this case, for another reason. I view the case before us as a conduct case. In my opinion, the facts regarding Watkins clearly demonstrate disqualifying acts and the regulations before us may properly be viewed as conduct regulations. First, Watkins has admitted to engaging in homosexual conduct with other servicemen while in the Army. Those admissions form an integral part of the reasons for the Army's refusal to permit him to reenlist. Second, the regulations must be construed in light of the Army's stated policy regarding homosexuality:

> Homosexuality is incompatible with military service. The presence in the military environment of persons who engage in homosexual conduct or who, by their statements, demonstrate a propensity to engage in homosexual conduct, seriously impairs the accomplishment of the military mission.

Army Regulation 635-200 para. 15-2.[23] Read in this light, the regulations constitute an attempt to exclude those who engage in or will engage in homosexual acts. The majority makes much of the fact that the regulation allows a soldier an opportunity to prove that a homosexual act he has engaged in was aberrational. Contrary to the majority, I do not think that this proves that the regulation is about orientation rather than conduct. The regulation's exception relates to conduct: it allows the Army to distinguish between soliders who are likely to engage in homosexual conduct in the future (practicing homosexuals) and those who are not likely to do so (heterosexuals who engage in an isolated homosexual act due to intoxication

20. Nowhere in equal protection jurisprudence can there be found a protected class that is merely a slightly broader form of an unprotected class. In the end, the majority's distinction between status and conduct comes to nought. For if homosexuals were truly a suspect class, an Army regulation based on conduct would be as unconstitutional as one based on status.

22. For example, the underlined words could be removed from the regulation's definition of "homosexual": "Homosexual means a person, regardless of sex, who engages in, *desires to engage in*, or intends to engage in homosexual acts." Army Regulation 635-200 para. 15-2(a) (emphasis added).

23. The statement of policy is from the section "Separation for Homosexuality". However, there is no reason to believe that it would not be equally applicable to the section which states that homosexuality is a nonwaivable disqualification for reenlistment. Both sections use the same definition of "homosexual".

or some similar reason). I consider the inclusion of this exception in the regulation to constitute a rational exercise of discretion — a legitimate attempt to predict future conduct on the basis of past conduct. However, I see little purpose in analyzing the Army's regulations in detail here. Suffice it to say that I disagree with the majority's characterization of them. In my opinion, the regulations are targeted at conduct — past, present, and future, but conduct nonetheless.

In the end the majority's status/conduct distinction does not advance its cause. With or without that part of its analysis, the majority's effort ultimately comes a cropper on *Hardwick, Hatheway, Beller, Goldman* and *Rostker*.

CONCLUSION

As the majority points out, Sgt. Watkins has every reason to feel aggrieved. His homosexuality has been well known for many years. During that entire period, his army service has been exemplary. Those who have worked with him, including his supervisors, are anxious to see him continue with his military career. Yet, under the Supreme Court's (and our own circuit's) interpretation of the Constitution, the Army is free to terminate that career solely because he is a homosexual. There are only three entities which have the authority to afford Sgt. Watkins the relief which I, like the majority, believe a proper interpretation of the Constitution would require. First, the Supreme Court could undo the damage to the Constitution wrought by *Hardwick*; it could overrule that precedent directly or implicitly. Second, the Army could voluntarily abandon its unfair and discriminatory regulation (or, I would assume, the Department of Defense could direct it to do so). Third, the Congress could enact appropriate legislation prohibiting the armed services from excluding homosexuals. I recognize that from a practical standpoint the existence of these forums may offer Sgt. Watkins little solace. Nevertheless, I do not believe that a panel of the Ninth Circuit may, consistent with its duty to apply precedent properly, afford him the relief he seeks.

For the above reasons, I must reluctantly dissent.

Note

1. An en banc panel of the Ninth Circuit reversed this broad holding but held for Watkins on narrower grounds — it ruled that he could not be denied reenlistment on a theory of equitable estoppel, i.e., the Army knew of Watkins' homosexuality for years and permitted reenlistment on several occasions, producing an expectation that Watkins could make a career of his military service. *Watkins v. United States Army*, 875 F.2d 699, 709 (9th Cir. 1989) (en banc). Judge Norris, who wrote for the panel in the first appeal, filed a similar opinion as his concurrence in *Watkins III*. *See id.* at 711 (Norris, J., concurring in judgment).

It is interesting to contrast the Ninth Circuit's decision — which depends on the fact that the Army never was able to prove that Watkins engaged in homosexual conduct — with the following description of his military career by Watkins himself.

◆

INTERVIEW WITH PERRY WATKINS

Mary Ann Humphrey

I was raised by my mother, my grandmother, two aunts, and a sister. Because of that, I never had a problem with the pressures of a male role model, of having to do the male-type things like football, basketball, and all that. So if I wanted to play jacks, play with dolls and things, nobody ever complained. And I was great! I mean, I used to give those girls hell in my neighborhood. They'd hate to see me coming with the jump rope, because they *knew* they were going to catch hell. I played with the girls, but my sexual feelings were for boys.

Junior high and high school was great, especially after I learned that you don't have to tell anyone you're gay in order to have sex. Let someone else do it for you, and you'll have all you can handle for the rest of your life. I guess I believed that after I met this kid one night who was about sixteen or seventeen. I had a weakness for blond hair and blue eyes. And I was quite bold in those days. The kid was close to five nine or ten, and I was maybe five two, if five feet. It was really funny I walked by him on the street, turned around, and said, "Would you like a blow job?" The guy looked at me and said, "What did you say?" I said, " Are you hard of hearing, or what? You know, do you want a blow job?" He said, "Yeah, well... okay. Sure." So we went into this alley, and I did my thing with him.

This fellow happened to be a very good friend of a guy that was in my class. And he told him about this. He immediately spread it all around the school next day. From that point, I never had to ask anyone else anything. They would all come to me. There was never any violence. Which was really inter-

esting to me. It spread around school, and everybody started asking me, "Are you really a cocksucker?" "Yes," I thought, "Why the hell should I lie about it?" They wouldn't have much to do with me in school, but they were wonderful after school. Which was just fine with me. They'd do the most wonderful things to make sure I didn't get into trouble, get hit or beat up. All the boys wanted blow jobs and that was all. Quite honestly, it was purely a sexual thing — they knew it and I knew it, no problem. It was just wham, bam, thank you, ma'am. That was it. Ah, how I remember those days!

After high school I had planned, initially, to remain in Europe for three years and go to school. My father was a career military man, and he had been assigned to a base in Germany. I was studying and teaching dance. My plans were to enter the theater for professional training. I was going to remain in Europe after my father came back, because I would have been twenty-one, so it would have been fine. Well, the best laid plans of mice and men... I got drafted the next year. However, the bottom line was that I knew I was gay, and knew the Army had a policy against gays being in the military, so I wasn't concerned about them taking me. I wasn't aware of what the regulation actually said. I had never read the regulation. I just knew, that's all. Even though my father was a career military man, he never used the word *homosexual — please!* My father has never even discussed my case with me. No. No, no. If knowledge about homosexuality came from conversations with anyone, it would probably have been from other dependent kids that may have mentioned it to me.

MARY ANN HUMPHREY, *Perry Watkins*, *in* MY COUNTRY, MY RIGHT TO SERVE 248 (1988).

I received my little draft notice, went down to the induction center, and checked the "Yes" box for "homosexual tendencies." Which I find amusing now. One of the arguments the Army made in court was that I didn't say I was homosexual. But of course, when they sent me to the psychiatrist immediately afterward — after checking the box — I specifically stated that I was gay. I specifically said to them, "No, I don't mind going into the military. If you want to take me like I am, that's fine with me." The Army's big argument was "Well, you're going to be taking showers with all these young men." Shit, I've been taking showers with naked men since I was twelve years old. Was there something new that I wasn't aware of, maybe a new military weapon or the like? *Please!*

Once at the center, we were all sitting in the room in our underwear, and this doctor looked at my form, looked at me, and said, "Well, what is this?" I thought, "Okay," I said, "What is what?" He said, "Well, what is this? You checked this box." I said, "What does the box say?" He said "Homosexual tendencies." I thought, "Isn't *this* cute?" "Are we embarrassed, or what?" But he continued, "Well, what does this mean?" I said, "Don't you *know*? I mean you're the doctor, aren't you?"

He left the room for a while, came back in, and told me to get dressed. They put me in an ambulance and set me to the hospital for a psychiatric evaluation with a lieutenant colonel. I went in and filled out my little forms once again, and on the back it stated: "Why are you here?" I didn't write anything on the back, which was my first mistake. So this colonel brought it out, threw it in my face, and told me I didn't fill the form out right. So I put down that I'd expressed homosexual tendencies on my Form 88. *Then* he yelled my name exceptionally loud. And I politely informed him, you know, "You don't yell at me like that because I'm not in your goddamn Army." I knew this man had no right to yell at me. Trust me, he did not

scare me in the least, and I was not happy after being embarrassed, anyway.

You know, it's interesting when you're born black and you've been discriminated against all your life, or you've had to deal with it all your life. You can look at people and know this is not going to be easy. I looked at this man and I knew —"You're *going* into the Army. You're going into the Army! This man was pinched. You have upset him." And sure as shit, I had. Now it was his turn to ask the same questions as before. He sat down and said, "Why did you check this box, 'Yes?' Don't you want to go in the Army? Do you have a problem with going to Vietnam?" "No, I don't mind going to Vietnam." Well then, why did you check the box 'Yes?'" It's getting pretty stale for me about this time. I'm also getting slightly irritated because I'm thinking, "Are you deaf? Or what is your problem?" I thought, "No, no, no, no. Let's not be rude." I said, "No, I don't have any objections about going into the Army." Then he said. "What do you do?" Now that one blew me away. I said, "*Excuse me*?" "What do you do?" I looked at him and said, "Do you mean to tell me you are the psychiatrist here and you don't know what a little homosexual does?"

He didn't find it amusing at all. *I* thought it was rather clever. He said, "I want to know." So I told him I liked to suck dick, I liked to get fucked. You know, common, everyday things. Then he said. "Are you active or passive?" I had never heard those terms before. Everyone I was sexually active with, basically, were people my own age who probably also knew nothing about gay communities as such. And you're talking 1968, so I said, "What does that mean?" He explained to me what it meant, and I said, "Well I guess I'm both." I mean, I hadn't really decided whether I was — and still haven't. "Oh well, okay, tonight I get to be on top? Oh well, fine. How nice! No problem. You want to change places in the middle? No problem. No problem. We can do that, too."

After that line of questioning he made talk about things that *I* liked to do. He made me state what I liked to do. I thought, "This is the kind of strange." Then out of left field he looked at me and said, "Do you ever date women?" Now, this is the man who just asked me if I liked to suck dick. Or made me say I liked to suck dick. But yet, he's not going to ask me if I ever *fucked* a woman. He's going to ask me, "Do you ever *date* women?" Obviously, this is a loaded question. Everybody dates women, I mean, I had to obviously take *something* to my senior prom!

The final upshot was that he made the determination that I was suitable for military service. Even though he had also made the determination that I *was* homosexual. Which is in contradiction to the regulation, because the regulation requires that the determination be that the person is *not* gay. That's the only way a person can then be inducted with this on their record. Confused, no matter, I was inducted anyway. It was at the point I realized being in the military was going to be really fun. *Real* fun I thought. "Oh, this could be very amusing."

I'm surprised how well I performed through basic. After all, I wasn't the most macho guy there — quite the contrary. But I even got an accelerated promotion out of basic training, and only got attacked once by some guy in my barracks along the way. This man was determined he was going to fuck me, and I was determined he wasn't. I could kick myself today for being so determined — damn it! I decided I needed to develop a kind of attitude. I was determined that if I was going to be in this man's Army, then they were either going to treat me with the proper respect that I felt I deserved, or they could let me go home.

I never approached anybody for sex. It just simply wasn't necessary. I'd walk in and say, "I'm gay. Leave me the hell alone." All these people would just start traipsing to my door. You know, knocking at my door at all hours of the night. I also figured,

basically, if I never asked anyone, they couldn't say I asked them. They were certainly not going to tell my commanding officer *they* asked *me*. When I was at Fort Dix, I actually got very fed up with all of it and said, "The hell with this I want out." So I went to my commanding officer and said, "I want out of the Army. I'm gay and I want out. I had told the original dip-shit doctor I was gay and I didn't want to come in this son-of-a-bitch to begin with, so let me out of here." Would you believe I went to my commander and actually requested a discharge because I was gay and he said no? There was another person who went to his commander and told him the same damn thing and they let him go home. Of course, he was white. Which I think also had something to do with it — he was white and I was black. It was really funny, because they sent me to CID to fill out this paperwork. I refused to give them names of anyone I'd ever had sex with, because I didn't think that was their business. A month later they came back and said, "Well, we can't let you go because we can't prove you have ever done anything."

Then I went from there to Fort Hamilton, New York. I was going to be a chaplain's assistant. I got a phone call from the chaplain. He called me into his office. He was commandant of the school, a lieutenant colonel. "I've got a statement here from your records saying you're gay. I can't allow you to finish this course." I said, "Excuse me? Then you can allow me to go home, right? I mean, if you're going to put me out of the school because I'm gay, you obviously can put me out of the Army *because* I'm gay."

He sent me to more psychiatrists and psychologists for more evaluation. It was beginning to sound very familiar at this point. One man was such a nelly twit. I mean, I took one look at him and thought, "My God, and I thought *I* was a dizzy queen!" "Are you Private Watkins?" I don't know if he was trying to be funny or just trying to get me to jump up and grab him, but I thought, "Oh, this is rich, it's the blind leading the blind. Yes, girlfriend, I'm Perry Watkins." Well, I was evaluated, and one month later, I got told, "Sorry Charlie, you're not going anyplace. We *still* can't prove you're gay." So in my next bout with CID, they wanted names, and I decided to go for their request in earnest. "Okay, fine. You want names, I'll give you names!" I gave the names of one person I'd had sex with who was in the military and one who was not. I couldn't believe it — both people denied it! Three months later, they called me back in and said, " Since we can't prove any of this happened, you still have to stay in the Army."

Now, pay attention! This is the *third* time I've tried to prove what I had originally stated on my medical form that day I came into the Army. It has all become so ludicrous by now that I didn't really give a shit anymore. I was tired of playing games and I wasn't going to sit around and be abused. So I thought, "Fuck you and the horse you rode in on, Junior!" Since I was being forced to stay in, even though I was obviously and openly gay, I decided to join the gay bar scene. I liked going to the back room bars. They had back rooms where there was actually sexual activity taking place. Orgy rooms. Like, the Mine Shaft in New York, for example, was probably the most notorious sleaze bar. I mean, they had slings, and chains, and everything. It's definitely an S&M bar. That's basically what I really enjoyed. Still do.

When I started going out to the bars, I began having a bit more personal problems, but many of my problems due to my orientation weren't always from whites; I also ran into a lot of conflict from other blacks who wanted to set a double standard by publicly saying that I was an embarrassment because I was black and gay. That I was embarrassing to the race. When they'd get me alone, they'd want to hop in the sack and let me suck their dicks. I thought, "Well now, this isn't going to work at all."

I can remember situations that were truly ironic. There was this one guy, an ex-marine, who was now in the Army. Every day at lunch, he would come over to my office, take me down to his room, and want me to give him a blow job. Everybody in the whole company knew about it. But on the other hand, he was considered straight. He used to go downtown every night and fuck anything that walked. One day I walked into the mess hall, and he asked me to sit near him. This other guy sitting there was a typical asshole. He looked at the ex-marine and said, "I want to know something. I know you let him suck your dick every day, but why?" And without even looking up from his plate, he said, "Well, I like a good blow job, and the women downtown don't know how to suck dick worth a damn. But this man happens to suck mine better than anyone I have ever found in the world. I've been around the world several times and I ain't found nobody yet that can hold a candle to Perry's technique." I didn't hear much from that asshole again. And he was right, I did give good head!

Over the years, I traveled to many places. I did two tours in Korea. During my first tour, I was in combat zone and pulled duty at the DMZ with live ammunition. People were being shot at, wounded, and killed. Believe me, when I heard shots, I ducked. People asked me, you know, "Were you getting shot at?" I don't know if they were shooting at me. I didn't look, I didn't see anything. Here I was, you know, I ducked when I heard shots. Part of that assignment involved foxhole duty. It was fun in an adventurous sort of way. We didn't do much of anything in the foxhole. Normally, we just talked. I can't say I didn't have sex, but geez, I mean, you know, come on, you have to talk beforehand! If they asked nicely, I would submit to their advances.

In fact, once we did call in for a communication check. This poor man was breathing so hard, they said, "What are you guys doing?" Then the first sergeant decided that

I could not be out there pulling duty anymore. You know, while I was there, I realized that the Soviet AK-47 had the strangest sound. You will never forget it if you hear one. And another thing, people don't seem to think of this area as a combat zone, but it is. In a lot of ways it's even more dangerous than Vietnam was, because you never knew what was going to happen. It was easier to be lulled into a false sense of security because there wasn't an actual conflict going on, as it was in Nam.

I came back from there, and got out of the service for a year with an honorable discharge, and performed drag for a year. Then I went back in the service and started *performing drag in the service*. That's when I was sent to Korea for a second time. And at my new unit they were getting ready for Organization Day. We had three guys in our unit — I'll never forget them — Tickle, Pickle and Keyhole. The one setting it up asked Pickle if he'd play the banjo and he said yes. I volunteered that I had worked as a female impersonator for a year. So they asked me if I would do the show in drag. After the show, there was an article written about me in the *Army Times*, which was carried in all the posts and installations worldwide. I got a call from a fellow who became my agent and booked me into recreation centers, Officers' Clubs, and NCO Clubs all over Germany. I even entered a beauty pageant as a joke, during Oktoberfest, with eleven other girls — and *won*. Yes, girlfriend, this queen had the balls to take the top award, and did so. Nobody knew until I took off my costume. "Simone" was a very popular entertainer! So I was doing it all at the time, and doing it quite well, if I do say so. When I returned to the States, I was stationed at Fort Hood, and was asked to do my act there as well. In fact, I even performed drag at our formal NCO ball. All this time, *I was being paid to do it*. It was authorized, if you will.

You know, I've had a strange military career throughout. I've seen combat, been candid about my gayness and even in the public view in drag. I also requested not once but three times that I wanted out of the Army — the first time at Fort Dix, the second at Fort Hamilton, and the third time at Fort Belvoir. Now, the fourth time, the Army *itself* finally decided to remove me. They had actually given me a Chapter 13 proceeding in 1975, during my second tour of duty in Korea. They ran a background check for my position of mail clerk. When they ran through the computer, they found all three of these statements that I had made requesting discharge. The statement that I had made naming people was also found. The information was given to my CO who said, "Now I have to process you for discharge." "Fuck it. That's okay, fine. Do that, you son-of-a-bitch" was my response. This was also the year after Leonard Matlovich's case.

They had a board of four officers. But do you believe they decided there was *no reason* for me to be discharged? My actions were not detrimental to the military, unit morale, or mission accomplishment. Once again, they decided I should remain! However, interestingly enough, the board didn't find me guilty of two things I was accused of previously, and only recommended that I be discharged because I still stated that I was gay. The court said this decision was totally stupid and definitely in contradiction to their regulation and definitely double jeopardy. The Army did not appeal that decision. Then they turned around in October of '82 and said, "Now we're going to deny you *reenlistment* because you say you're gay."

The reenlistment regulation specifically states you cannot deny someone reenlistment for something they cannot be administratively discharged for. The Army blatantly violated their own regulation. So I went through a lot of harassment during my last enlistment before being put out. For example, these same people went into court and said, "We can't promote this man because we have to consider his sexual orientation. You know how people are going to look at that." I wasn't given awards and decorations, because I was gay and they had to consider their "image" when they did things like that. It's absolutely stupid. But I went through it for several years. They were not going to do this to me. I was going out proud.

The whole thing was affecting me a lot. It really did. However, it didn't affect me that much while I was in. I think I was so egotistical and vain that it gave me a great deal of pleasure to be able to deal with the situation as well as I did. When it really, really began to affect me was after I got out. Trying to find a job. I got to the point that I began to feel like maybe I didn't deserve a decent job. Maybe I really was worthless. That attitude seemed to prevail for a long while. They took away my pride, my self-esteem, all of it....But I could still laugh. Even now, when I realize what I've been through, some of it is very humorous. Yet some of it is very sad.

You know, after you've put in fifteen years, an honorable discharge doesn't mean a damn thing. The first thing outsiders do is look at it and say, "Well, why didn't you stay in for twenty?" But. . .I'm not ashamed of the fact that I'm gay. You know, what the hell. If I were a personnel officer hiring someone for a company, I would be leery of a person who refused to answer that kind of question. It made me mad, so I took the Army to court.

I'm not an activist. I'm not a militant person. Even though I'm obviously very stubborn and obviously very determined that I'm going to take this thing as far as it has to go to win, and do my best to do get it done, I'm not an activist, as such. I would have gone out at twenty years ever so quietly, but when someone lies to me, falsifies documents in my records file, and lies about my capabilities as a solider, it just didn't set well with me. I decided, "This is stupid. Now you're attacking me directly and per-

sonally. I didn't lie to you when I came into this damn Army." That's what really pissed me off.

There were times when I felt a tremendous sense of anger, but I don't feel that anger as much anymore. Now I try not to think about negative things. I was taking a lot out on myself. I didn't realize how self-destructive I had become. Emotionally, I wasn't there. You know, the self-pity and the feeling sorry for yourself can really get to you. It's a lot like the feelings you go through when someone dies. You know, the depression. I didn't realize I was doing all of that until after I honestly started coming back from it. When you finally understand what's happening, it's like, "Whoa! I need to stop this bullshit. I need to turn this around." I'll never let that happen again. If anything, I've improved a lot. I know that I'm something, whether I'm black or gay, and will always be something and will always be worth something. If I can be objective about this, it would appear that it is based on both black and gay issues. . .both are ongoing and continuous.

It doesn't matter what kind of laws we have. People have asked me, "How have you managed to tolerate all that discrimination you had to deal with in the military?" My immediate answer to them was "Hell, I grew up black. Give me a break. I mean to be discriminated against because I was gay was a joke." I mean, "Oh, you don't like me because I'm gay? Excuse me, I'm sorry, but *you've* got a problem." And discrimination is a very individual thing. If people are going to discriminate, they're going to find a way — regardless of what laws are in place. I do believe, however, specifically concerning the military, that if I had not been black, my situation would not have happened as it did. A couple of examples jump quickly to mind. I knew one E-7 who was boarded for incest with his twelve-year-old son. Do you know what the Army told him? "Oh, if you have that kind of problem, you need to take care of it at home. We don't need to get involved in your *private life."* I'm still trying to figure out why my private life was not okay, but his was, or at least it didn't affect his job in the military. Like what he did to his own son was not a crime, and what I did with consenting adults was. Incest — no problem! And another example: Every *white* person I knew from Tacoma who was gay and had checked that box "Yes" did not have to go into the service. They were called in and asked, "What does this mean?" They said, "It means I'm gay. I like to suck dick." "Fine. You can go." Very interesting, don't you think?

Through it all, there were some things that I do hold near and dear. I still feel the military benefited me with an education, travel, and allowed me to learn a great deal about people. I had wonderful experiences meeting people, making friends, and growing up in general. I feel, quite personally, they should reinstate the draft. I think a two-year commitment to your country is very little to ask for what America gives. Everybody should go. You don't necessarily have to go into the military; you can teach, work in a hospital, do construction work — something. Learning to live and survive by yourself is one of the most beneficial things that could ever happen to a young adult.

I have few regrets about my overall fifteen years of experience. You can always learn from bad experiences as well as good ones. Everything can't be good in your life. You've got to learn to survive and exist and coexist in the world with other people, like them or not. And I'm a survivor, if nothing else. That I found out on my own. The message seems to be that as long as we continue to hide in the closet, we'll have to put up with this shit. Those high-ranking military members, ones that I met personally, need to stand up and be counted. As I see it, it must start at the top.

It's sad that we need to demand that. Unfortunately, if we don't, because of the way the laws are written, we're shooting ourselves in the foot. So let me reiterate that *as long as we continue to stay in the closet*, we give them credibility. Eliminate the regulation requiring people to admit whether they're gay or not, and then there will be no need to ask anymore. There are enough regulations dealing with moral conduct and professionalism already in place; we don't need any more. Unless it's a problem, then there isn't anything that should be done about it. The Army can always go to court, just like in my case, and say, "He's only one person. Why do we have to change all of our regulations to suit just one person?" It will only change when the courts have to stop and take a serious look and say, "What are you doing? Why are you doing this, and why do we have these *thousands* and *thousands* of cases?" So, if suddenly the Army or any of the armed forces were talking about fifty thousand people, instead of just one or two, if there were suddenly fifty thousand cases in the courts, people might say, "You know, maybe we *ought* to change that regulation." At this point, we seem to be spending millions of the taxpayers' money to carry out the requirements of this needless regulation.

I contend that if that *gay general* I met in Korea can succeed, it is obvious that he has not been limited by his gayness. However, in order to survive, he has had to maintain a very secretive and highly protected private lifestyle, but my point here is, why the hell should he or anyone else who is gay have to go to such extensive measures? Straight soldiers get a chance to prove whether they're good or not, and they're judged on their performance. Gay soldiers aren't. Whether you're good or not, if you're gay you're gone. No other reason necessary. And there is absolutely no basis in fact for any of the military's opposition to gays in the armed force. When is this ruse going to be exposed as pure bullshit? I hope in my lifetime!

6. CURRENT LITIGATION

In *Pruitt v. Cheney*,[1] the U.S. Court of Appeals for the Ninth Circuit reversed the dismissal of a challenge to the military's policy. The plaintiff was a captain in the Army Reserve until an article about her life as a lesbian and pastor was published in the *Los Angeles Times* in 1983. Following publication of the article, the Army dismissed her. Plaintiff filed suit alleging that her discharge violated her First Amendment rights and her right to privacy. The District Court dismissed the case.[2] In reversing, the Ninth Circuit ruled that the Army's actions did not violate Pruitt's First Amendment rights, but, importantly, it refused to grant the government's motion to dismiss Pruitt's equal protection challenge to the military's regulations. The court ruled that the military would have to demonstrate a rationale for its policy — beyond mere prejudice — upon remand to the District Court. The government's petition for certiorari to the United States Supreme Court was denied.[3]

Like Miriam Ben-Shalom, Perry Watkins, and Dusty Pruitt, Joe Steffan was discharged from the military — in this case from the Naval Academy — based solely on his sexual orientation, not on any sexual conduct. He challenged his discharge in a case filed in federal district court in Washington, D.C., in 1988. The federal district court granted summary judgment to the military, ruling that the policy was rationally related to a legitimate governmental interest.[4] The court added a new rationale for the policy, not even argued by the military — AIDS. The case has been appealed to the D.C. Circuit.

---

1. 963 F. 2d 1160 (9th Cir. 1992).
2. *Pruitt v. Weinberger*, 659 F. Supp. 625 (C.D. Cal. 1987).
3. *Cheney v. Pruitt*, 113 S. Ct. 655 (1992).
4. *Steffan v. Cheney*, 780 F. Supp. 1 (D.D.C. 1991).

FIVE

Legal Recognition of Lesbian and Gay Relationships

I. INTRODUCTION

A. Overview

Until quite recently, no jurisdiction in the United States legally recognized same-sex relationships; in fact, many still criminalize same-sex sexual acts. The general lack of legal recognition for same-sex relationships takes a heavy toll on lesbians and gay men. In the broadest sense, it explicitly denies — and even condemns — the legitimacy of important and intimate relationships through which gay people define themselves. Therefore, the search for legal recognition of same-sex relationships is in part a search for "affirmation by the state," through which lesbians and gay men can become "upstanding citizens, building blocks of society, and pillars of the community."[1] The absence of legal recognition also has practical repercussions for lesbian and gay couples. Because lesbians and gay men are almost always treated as legally "single" — at best "roommates" — for the purposes of taxes, immigration, tort law, criminal law, government benefits, and housing restrictions, gay couples are denied access to the mechanisms by which society encourages and grants benefits to heterosexual family relationships.

In the last decade, courts, city governments, and private organizations have begun to recognize unmarried relationships in limited contexts, awarding to lesbian and gay couples — as well as to those male-female couples who choose not to marry — a few of the benefits that states, the federal government, and private employers provide to married couples.

---

1. Harlon Dalton, *Reflections on the Lesbian and Gay Marriage Debate*, 1 LAW & SEXUALITY 1, 7 (1991).

This chapter maps out the search for legal recognition of lesbian and gay relationships. The first part explores marriage: it considers the special constitutional status of marriage; chronicles the variety of efforts — so far unsuccessful — to achieve legal recognition of same-sex marriages in the United States; and examines the debate within the gay community concerning the propriety and priority of efforts to legalize same-sex marriages in light of the shortcomings of the marriage model and the pressing need for resources to fight other gay rights battles. Recognizing that many lesbians and gay men do form couples regardless of the inability to marry, the second unit in this chapter analyzes various other methods — notably domestic partnership ordinances, adoption, guardianship, expanded definitions of "family," and legal instruments — by which same-sex couples have achieved limited legal recognition.

B. Readings

◆

TAR BEACH
Audre Lorde

Gerri was young and Black and lived in Queens and had a powder-blue Ford that she nicknamed Bluefish. With her carefully waved hair and button-down shirts and grey-flannel slacks, she looked just this side of square, without being square at all, once you got to know her.

By Gerri's invitation and frequently by her wheels, Muriel and I had gone to parties on weekends in Brooklyn and Queens at different women's houses.

One of the women I had met at one of these parties was Kitty.

When I saw Kitty again one night years later in the Swing Rendezvous or the Pony Stable or the Page Three — that tour of second-string, gay-girl bars that I had taken to making alone that sad lonely spring of 1957 — it was easy to recall the St. Alban's smell of green Queens' summer night and plastic couch-covers and liquor and hair oil and women's bodies at the party where we had first met.

In that brick-faced frame house in Queens, the downstairs pine-paneled recreation room was alive and pulsing with loud music, good food, and beautiful black women in all different combinations of dress.

There were whip-cord summer suits with starch-shiny shirt collars open at the neck as a concession to the high summer heat, and white gabardine slacks with pleated fronts or slim ivy-league styling for the very slender. There were wheat-colored edge Cowden jeans, the fashion favorite that summer, with knife-edge creases, and even then, one or two back-buckled gray pants

Audre Lorde, *Tar Beach, in* HOME GIRLS: A BLACK FEMINIST ANTHOLOGY 145 (1983) (Barbara Smith ed., 1983).

over well-chalked buckskin shoes. There were garrison belts galore, broad black leather belts with shiny thin buckles that originated in army-navy surplus stores, and oxford-styled shirts of the new, iron-free dacron, with its stiff, see-through crispness. These shirts, short-sleeved and man-tailored, were tucked neatly into belted pants or tight, skinny straight skirts. Only the one or two jersey knit shirts were allowed to fall freely outside.

Bermuda shorts, and their shorter cousins, Jamaicas, were already making their appearance on the dyke-chic scene, the rules of which were every bit as cutthroat as the tyrannies of Seventh Avenue or Paris. These shorts were worn by butch and femme alike, and for this reason were slow to be incorporated into many fashionable gay-girl wardrobes, to keep the signals clear. Clothes were often the most important way of broadcasting one's chosen sexual role.

Here and there throughout the room, the flash of brightly colored below-the-knee full skirts over low-necked tight bodices could be seen, along with tight sheath dresses and the shine of high thin heels next to bucks and sneakers and loafers.

Femmes wore their hair in tightly curled pageboy bobs, or piled high on their heads in sculptured bunches of curls, or in feather cuts framing their faces. That sweetly clean fragrance of beauty-parlor that hung over all black women's gatherings in the fifties was present here also, adding its identifiable smell of hot comb and hair pomade to the other aromas in the room.

Butches wore their hair cut shorter, in a D.A. shaped to a point in the back, or a short pageboy, or sometimes in a tightly curled poodle that predated the natural afro. But this was a rarity, and I can only remember one other black woman at that party besides me whose hair was not straightened, and she was an acquaintance of ours from the Lower East Side named Ida.

On a table behind the built-in bar stood opened bottles of gin, bourbon, scotch, soda and other various mixers. The bar itself was covered with little delicacies of all descriptions: chips and dips and little crackers and squares of bread laced with the usual dabs of egg-salad and sardine paste. There was also a platter of delicious fried chicken wings, and a pan of potato-and-egg salad dressed with vinegar. Bowls of olives and pickles surrounded the main dishes, with trays of red crab apples and little sweet onions on toothpicks.

But the centerpiece of the whole table was a huge platter of succulent and thinly sliced roast beef, set into an underpan of cracked ice. Upon the beige platter, each slice of rare meat had been lovingly laid out and individually folded up into a vulval pattern, with a tiny dab of mayonnaise at the crucial apex. The pink-brown folded meat around the pale cream-yellow dot formed suggestive sculptures that made a great hit with all the women present, and Pet, at whose house the party was being given and whose idea the meat sculptures were, smilingly acknowledged the many compliments on her platter with a long-necked graceful nod of her elegant dancer's head.

The room's particular mix of heat-smells and music gives way in my mind to the high-cheeked, dark young woman with the silky voice and appraising eyes (something about her mouth reminded me of Ann, the nurse I'd worked with when I'd first left home).

Perching on the edge of the low bench where I was sitting, Kitty absently wiped specks of lipstick from each corner of her mouth with the downward flick of a delicate forefinger.

"Audre . . . that's a nice name. What's it short for?"

My damp arm hairs bristled in the Ruth Brown music, and the heat. I could not stand anybody messing around with my name, not even with nicknames.

"Nothing. It's just Audre. What's Kitty short for?"

"Afrekete," she said, snapping her fingers in time to the rhythm of it and giving a long laugh. "That's me. The black pussycat."

She laughed again. "I like your hairdo. Are you a singer?"

"No." She continued to stare at me with her large direct eyes.

I was suddenly too embarrassed at not knowing what else to say to meet her calmly erotic gaze, so I stood up abruptly and said, in my best Laurel's-terse tone, "Let's dance."

Her face was broad and smooth under too-light make-up, but as we danced a fox-trot she started to sweat, and her skin took on a deep shiny richness. Kitty closed her eyes part way when she danced, and her one gold-rimmed front tooth flashed as she smiled and occasionally caught her lower lip in time to the music.

Her yellow poplin shirt, cut in the style of an Eisenhower jacket, had a zipper that was half open in the summer heat, showing collarbones that stood out like brown wings from her long neck. Garments with zippers were highly prized among the more liberal set of gay-girls, because these could be worn by butch or femme alike on certain occasions, without causing any adverse or troublesome comments. Kitty's narrow, well-pressed khaki skirt was topped by a black belt that matched my own except in its newness, and her natty trimness made me feel almost shabby in my well-worn riding pants.

I thought she was very pretty, and I wished I could dance with as much ease as she did, and as effortlessly. Her hair had been straightened into short feathery curls, and in that room of well-set marcels and D.A.'s and pageboys, it was the closest cut to my own.

Kitty smelled of soap and Jean Naté, and I kept thinking she was bigger than she actually was, because there was a comfortable smell about her that I always associated with large women. I caught another spicy herb-like odor, that I later identified as a combination of coconut oil and Yardley's lavender hair pomade. Her mouth was full, and her lipstick was dark and shiny, a new Max Factor shade called "WARPAINT."

The next dance was a slow fish that suited me fine. I never knew whether to lead or to follow in most other dances, and even the effort to decide which was as difficult for me as having to decide all the time the difference between left and right. Somehow that simple distinction had never become automatic for me, and all that deciding usually left me very little energy with which to enjoy the movement and the music.

But "fishing" was different. A forerunner of the later one-step, it was, in reality, your basic slow bump and grind. The low red lamp and the crowded St. Alban's parlor floor left us just enough room to hold each other frankly, arms around neck and waist, and the slow intimate music moved our bodies much more than our feet.

That had been in St. Alban's, Queens, nearly two years before, when Muriel had seemed to be the certainty in my life. Now in the spring of this new year I had my own apartment all to myself again, but I was mourning. I avoided visiting pairs of friends, or inviting even numbers of people over to my house, because the happiness of couples, or their mere togetherness, hurt me too much in its absence from my own life, whose blankest hole was named Muriel. I had not been back to Queens, nor to any party, since Muriel and I had broken up, and the only people I saw outside of work and school were those friends who lived in the Village and who sought me out or whom I ran into at the bars. Most of them were white.

"Hey, girl, long time no see." Kitty spotted me first. We shook hands. The bar was not crowded, which means it probably was the Page Three, which didn't fill up until after midnight. "Where's your girlfriend?"

I told her that Muriel and I weren't together any more. "Yeah? That's too bad. You-all were kinda cute together. But that's the way it goes. How long you been in the 'life'?"

I stared at Kitty without answering, trying to think of how to explain to her, that for me there was only one life — my own —

however I chose to live it. But she seemed to take the words right out of my mouth.

"Not that it matters," she said speculatively, finishing the beer she had carried over to the end of the bar where I was sitting. "We don't have but one, anyway. At least this time around." She took my arm. "Come on, let's dance."

Kitty was still trim and fast-lined, but with an easier looseness about her smile and a lot less make-up. Without its camouflage, her chocolate skin and deep, sculptured mouth reminded me of a Benin bronze. Her hair was still straightened, but shorter, and her black Bermuda shorts and knee socks matched her astonishingly shiny black loafers. A black turtleneck pullover completed her sleek costume. Somehow, this time, my jeans did not feel shabby beside hers, only a variation upon some similar dress. Maybe it was because our belts still matched — broad, black, and brass-buckled.

We moved to the back room and danced to Frankie Lymon's "Goody, Goody," and then to a Belafonte calypso. Dancing with her this time, I felt who I was and where my body was going, and that feeling was more important to me than any lead or follow.

The room felt very warm even though it was only just spring, and Kitty and I smiled at each other as the number ended. We stood waiting for the next record to drop and the next dance to begin. It was a slow Sinatra. Our belt buckles kept getting in the way as we moved in close to the oiled music, and we slid them around to the side of our waists when no one was looking.

For the last few months since Muriel had moved out, my skin had felt cold and hard and essential, like thin frozen leather that was keeping the shape expected. That night on the dance floor of the Page Three as Kitty and I touched our bodies together in dancing, I could feel my carapace soften slowly and then finally melt, until I felt myself covered in a warm, almost forgotten, slip of anticipation, that ebbed and flowed at each contact of our moving bodies.

I could feel something slowly shift in her also, as if a taut string was becoming undone, and finally we didn't start back to the bar at all between dances, but just stood on the floor waiting for the next record, dancing only with each other. A little after midnight, in a silent and mutual decision, we split the Page together, walking blocks through the West Village to Hudson Street where her car was parked. She had invited me up to her house for a drink.

The sweat beneath my breasts from our dancing was turning cold in the sharpness of the night air as we crossed Sheridan Square. I paused to wave to the steadies through the plate glass windows of Jim Atkins's on the corner of Christopher Street.

In her car, I tried not to think about what I was doing as we rode uptown almost in silence. There was an ache in the well beneath my stomach, spreading out and down between my legs like mercury. The smell of her warm body, mixed with the smell of feathery cologne and lavender pomade, anointed the car. My eyes rested on the sight of her coconut-spicy hands on the steering wheel, and the curve of her lashes as she attended the roadway. They made it easy for me to coast beneath her sporadic bursts of conversation with only an occasional friendly grunt.

"I haven't been downtown to the bars in a while, you know? It's funny, I don't know why I don't go downtown more often. But every once in a while, something tells me go and I go. I guess it must be different when you live around there all the time." She turned her gold-flecked smile upon me.

Crossing 59th Street, I had an acute moment of panic. Who was this woman? Suppose she really intended only to give me the drink which she had offered me as we left the Page? Suppose I had totally misunderstood the impact of her invitation, and would soon find myself stranded uptown at 3:00 A.M. on a Sunday morning, and did I even have enough change left in my jeans for carfare home? Had I put out enough food for the kittens? Was Flee coming over with her camera tomorrow morning, and would she feed the cats if I wasn't there? If I wasn't there. If I wasn't there.

If I wasn't there. The implication of that thought was so shaking it almost threw me out of the car.

I had only enough money for one beer that night, so I knew I wasn't high, and reefer was only for special occasions. Part of me felt like a raging lioness, inflamed in desire. Even the words in my head seemed borrowed from a dime-store novel. But that part of me was drunk on the thighed nearness of this exciting unknown dark woman, who calmly moved us through upper Manhattan, with her patent-leather loafers and her camel's-hair swing coat and her easy talk, from time to time her gloved hand touching my denimed leg for emphasis.

Another piece of me felt bumbling, inept, and about four years old. I was the idiot playing at being a lover, who was going to be found out shortly and laughed at for my pretensions, as well as rejected out of hand.

Would it be possible — was it ever possible — for two women to share the fire we felt that night without entrapping or smothering each other? I longed for that as I longed for her body, doubting both, eager for both.

And how was it possible, that I should be dreaming the roll of this woman's sea into and around mine, when only a few short hours ago, and for so many months before, I had been mourning the loss of Muriel, so sure that I would continue being brokenhearted forever? And what then if I had been mistaken?

We came out of the Park Drive at Seventh Avenue and 110th Street, and as quickly as the light changed on the now deserted avenue, Afrekete turned her broad-lipped beautiful face to me, with no smile at all. Her great lidded luminescent eyes looked directly and startlingly into mine. It was as if she had suddenly become another person, as if the wall of glass formed by my spectacles, and behind which I had become so used to hiding, had suddenly dissolved.

In an uninflected, almost formal voice that perfectly matched and thereby obliterated all my question marks, she asked,

"Can you spend the night?"

And then it occurred to me that perhaps she might have been having the same questions about me that I had been having about her. I was left almost without breath by the combination of her delicacy and her directness — a combination which is still rare and precious.

For beyond the assurance that her question offered me — a declaration that this singing of my flesh, this attraction, was not all within my own head — beyond that assurance was a batch of delicate assumptions built into that simple phrase that reverberated in my poet's brain. It offered us both an out if necessary. If the answer to the question might, by any chance, have been no, then its very syntax allowed for a reason of impossibility, rather than of choice — "I can't," rather than "I won't." The demands of another commitment, an early job, a sick cat, etc., could be lived with more easily than an out-and-out rejection.

Even the phrase "spending the night" was less a euphemism for making love than it was an allowable space provided, in which one could move back or forth. If, perhaps, I were to change my mind before the traffic light and decide that no, I wasn't gay, after all, then a simpler companionship was still available.

I steadied myself enough to say, in my very best Lower East Side Casual voice, "I'd really like to," cursing myself for the banal words, and wondering if she could smell my nervousness and my desperate desire to be suave and debonair, drowning in sheer desire.

We parked half-in and half-out of a bus stop on Manhattan Avenue and 113th Street, in Gennie's old neighborhood.

Something about Kitty made me feel like a roller coaster, rocketing from idiot to goddess. By the time we had collected her mail from the broken mailbox and then climbed six flights of stairs to her front door, I felt that there had never been anything else my body had intended to do more, than to reach inside of her coat and take Afrekete into my arms, fitting her body into the curves of mine tightly, her beige camel's-hair coat billowing around us both, and her gloved hand still holding the door key.

In the faint light of the hallway, her lips moved like surf upon the water's edge.

It was a 1½ room kitchenette apartment with tall narrow windows in the narrow, high-ceilinged front room. Across each window, there were built-in shelves at different levels. From these shelves tossed and frothed, hung and leaned and stood, pot after clay pot of green and tousled large and small-leaved plants of all shapes and conditions.

Later, I came to love the way in which the plants filtered the southern exposure sun through the room. Light hit the opposite wall at a point about six inches above the thirty-gallon fish tank that murmured softly, like a quiet jewel, standing on the wrought-iron legs, glowing and mysterious.

Leisurely and swiftly, translucent rainbowed fish darted back and forth through the lit water, perusing the glass sides of the tank for morsels of food, and swimming in and out of the marvelous world created by colored gravels and stone tunnels and bridges that lined the floor of the tank. Astride one of the bridges, her bent head observing the little fish that swam in and out between her legs, stood a little jointed brown doll, her smooth naked body washed by the bubbles rising up from the air unit located behind her.

Between the green plants and the glowing magical tank of exotic fish, lay a room the contents of which I can no longer separate in my mind. Except for a plaid-covered couch that opened up into the double bed which we set rocking as we loved that night into a bright Sunday morning, dappled with green sunlight from the plants in Afrekete's high windows.

I woke to her house suffused in that light, the sky half-seen through the windows of the top-floor kitchenette apartment, and Afrekete, known, asleep against my side.

Little hairs under her navel lay down before my advancing tongue like the beckoned pages of a well-touched book.

How many times into summer had I turned into that block from Eighth Avenue, the saloon on the corner spilling a smell of sawdust and liquor onto the street, a shifting indeterminate number of young and old black men taking turns sitting on two upturned milk-crates, playing checkers? I would turn the corner into 113th Street toward the park, my steps quickening and my fingertips tingling to play in her earth.

And I remember Afrekete, who came out of a dream to me always being hard and real as the fine hairs along the underedge of my navel. She brought me live things from the bush, and from her farm set out in cocoyams and cassava — those magical fruit which Kitty bought in the West Indian markets along Lenox Avenue in the 140s or in the Puerto Rican *bodegas* within the bustling market over on Park Avenue and 116th Street under the Central Railroad structures.

"I got this under the bridge" was a saying from time immemorial, giving an adequate explanation that whatever it was had come from as far back and as close to home — that is to say, was as authentic — as was possible.

We bought red delicious pippins, the size of French cashew apples. There were green plantains, which we half-peeled and then planted, fruit-deep, in each other's bodies until the petals of skin lay like tendrils of broad green fire upon the curly darkness between our upspread thighs. *There were ripe red finger bananas, stubby and sweet, with which I parted your lips gently, to insert the peeled fruit into your grape-purple flower.*

I held you, lay between your brown legs, slowly playing my tongue through your familiar forests, slowly licking and swallowing as the deep undulations and tidal motions of your strong body slowly mashed ripe banana into a beige cream that mixed with the juices of your electric flesh. Our bodies met again, each surface touched with each other's flame, from the tips of our curled toes to our tongues, and locked into our own wild rhythms, we rode each other across the thundering space, dripped like light from the peak of each other's tongue.

We were each of us both together. Then we were apart, and sweat sheened our bodies like sweet oil.

Sometimes Afrekete sang in a small club further uptown on Sugar Hill. Sometimes she clerked in the Gristede's Market on 97th Street and Amsterdam, and sometimes with no warning at all she appeared at the Pony Stable or Page Three on Saturday night. Once, I came home to Seventh Street late one night to find her sitting on my stoop at 3:00 A.M., with a bottle of beer in her hand and a piece of bright African cloth wrapped around her head, and we sped uptown through the dawn-empty city with a summer thunder squall crackling above us, and the wet city streets singing beneath the wheels of her little Nash Rambler.

There are certain verities which are always with us, which we come to depend on. That the sun moves north in summer, that melted ice contracts, that the curved banana is sweeter. Afrekete taught me roots, new definitions of our women's bodies — definitions for which I had only been in training to learn before.

By the beginning of summer the walls of Afrekete's apartment were always warm to the touch from the heat beating down on the roof, and chance breezes through her windows rustled her plants in the window and brushed over our sweat-smooth bodies, at rest after loving.

We talked sometimes about what it meant to love women, and what a relief it was in the eye of the storm, no matter how often we had to bite our tongues and stay silent. Afrekete had a seven-year-old daughter whom she had left with her mama down in Georgia, and we shared a lot of our dreams.

"She's going to be able to love anybody she wants to love," Afrekete said, fiercely, lighting a Lucky Strike. "Same way she's going to be able to work any place she damn well pleases. Her mama's going to see to that."

Once we talked about how black women had been committed without choice to waging our campaigns in the enemies' strongholds, too much and too often, and how our psychic landscapes had been plundered and wearied by those repeated battles and campaigns.

"And don't I have the scars to prove it," she sighed. "Makes you tough though, babe, if you don't go under. And that's what I like about you; you're like me. We're both going to make it because we're both too tough and crazy not to!" And we held each other and laughed and cried about what we had paid for that toughness, and how hard it was to explain to anyone who didn't already know it that soft and tough had to be one and the same for either to work at all, like our joy and the tears mingling on the one pillow beneath our heads.

And the sun filtered down upon us through the dusty windows, through the mass of green plants that Afrekete tended religiously.

I took a ripe avocado and rolled it beneath my hands until the skin became a green case for the soft mashed fruit inside, hard pit at the core. *I rose from a kiss in your mouth to nibble a hole in the fruit skin near the navel stalk, squeezed the pale yellow-green fruit juice in thin ritual lines back and forth over and around your coconut-brown belly.*

The oil and sweat from our bodies kept the fruit liquid, and I massaged it over your thighs and between your breasts until your brownness shone like a light through a veil of the palest green avocado, a mantle of goddess pear that I slowly licked from your skin.

Then we would have to get up to gather the pits and fruit skins and bag them to put out later for the garbagemen, because if we left them near the bed for any length of time, they would call out the hordes of cockroaches that always waited on the sidelines within the walls of Harlem tenements, particularly in the smaller older ones under the hill of Morningside Heights.

Afrekete lived not far from Genevieve's grandmother's house.

Sometimes she reminded me of Ella, Gennie's stepmother, who shuffled about with an apron on and a broom outside the room where Gennie and I lay on the studio couch. She would be singing her non-stop tuneless little song over and over and over:

Momma kilt me
Poppa et me
Po' lil' brudder
suck ma bones...

And one day Gennie turned her head on my lap to say uneasily, "You know, sometimes I don't know whether Ella's crazy, or stupid, or divine."

And now I think the goddess was speaking through Ella also, but Ella was too beaten down and anesthetized by Phillip's brutality for her to believe in her own mouth, and we, Gennie and I, were too arrogant and childish — not without right or reason, for we were scarcely more than children — to see that our survival might very well lay in listening to the sweeping woman's tuneless song.

I lost my sister, Gennie, to my silence and her pain and despair, to both our angers and to a world's cruelty that destroys its own young in passing — not even as a rebel gesture or sacrifice or hope for another living of the spirit, but out of not noticing or caring about the destruction. I have never been able to blind myself to that cruelty, which according to one popular definition of mental health, makes me mentally unhealthy.

Afrekete's house was the tallest one near the corner, before the high rocks of Morningside Park began on the other side of the avenue, and one night on the Midsummer Eve's Moon we took a blanket up to the roof. She lived on the top floor, and in an unspoken agreement, the roof belonged mostly to those who had to live under its heat. The roof was the chief resort territory of tenement-dwellers, and was known as Tar Beach.

We jammed the roof door shut with our sneakers, and spread our blanket in the lee of the chimney, between its warm brick wall and the high parapet of the building's face. This was before the blaze of sulphur lamps had stripped the streets of New York of trees and shadow, and the incandescence from the lights below faded this far up. From inside the parapet wall we could see the dark shapes of the basalt and granite outcroppings looming over us from the park across the street, outlined, curiously close and suggestive.

We slipped off the cotton shirts we had worn and moved against each other's damp breasts in the shadow of the roof's chimney, making moon, honor, love, while the ghostly vague light drifting upward from the street competed with the silver hard sweetness of the full moon, reflected in the shiny mirrors of our sweat-slippery dark bodies, sacred as the ocean at high tide.

I remember the moon rising against the tilted planes of her upthrust thighs, and my tongue caught the streak of silver reflected in the curly bush of her dappled-dark maiden hair. *I remember the full moon like white pupils in the center of your wide irises.*

The moons went out, and your eyes grew dark as you rolled over me, and I felt the moon's silver light mix with the wet of your tongue on my eyelids.

Afrekete Afrekete ride me to the cross-roads where we shall sleep, coated in the woman's prayer. The sound of our bodies meeting is the prayer of all strangers and sisters, that the discarded evils, abandoned at all crossroads, will not follow us upon our journeys.

When we came down from the roof later, it was into the sweltering midnight of a west Harlem summer, with canned music in the streets and the disagreeable whines of over-tired and overheated children. Nearby, mothers and fathers sat on stoops or milk crates and striped camp chairs, fanning themselves absently and talking or thinking about work as usual tomorrow and not enough sleep.

It was not onto the pale sands of Whydah, nor the beaches of Winneba or Annambu, with cocopalms softly applauding and crickets keeping time with the pounding of a tar-laden, treacherous, beautiful sea. It was onto 113th Street that we descended after our meeting under the Midsummer Eve's Moon, but the mothers and fathers smiled at us in greeting as we strolled down to Eighth Avenue, hand in hand.

I had not seen Afrekete for a few weeks in July, so I went uptown to her house one evening since she didn't have a phone. The door was locked, and there was no one on the roof when I called up the stairwell.

Another week later, Midge, the bartender at the Pony Stable, gave me a note from Afrekete, saying that she had gotten a gig in Atlanta for September, and was splitting to visit her mama and daughter for a while.

We had come together like elements erupting into an electric storm, exchanging energy, sharing charge, brief and drenching. Then we parted, passed, reformed, reshaping ourselves the better for the exchange.

I never saw Afrekete again, but her print remains upon my life with the resonance and power of an emotional tattoo.

◆

AT LEAST ME AND RAFAEL TRIED
Paul Butler

Sometimes I write about handsome young princes trapped in towers and other handsome princes that come to save them. I guess those stories are not very real. I make believe, or lie. This story don't have too many lies, only little fibs I had to say to make things seem even. This story is about me, and it's about Rafael. My teacher for the High School Equivalency Test says write, write, write, class we *must* learn to *write*. She says if you can do it good, you can make anything beautiful, even something that is ugly. I don't believe her, but the thought warms me up, know what I mean? And so I write. Usually at night, if my arms ain't too tired from work. I guess it's better than what I used to do at night — I mean, in the men's rooms. Anyway, it fills up the same kind of space inside me.

Before writing, but after the men's rooms, there was Rafael. He was beautiful.

Not just in the humpy way that a lot of Puerto Ricans are beautiful, but in a way maybe only I could see. The first time I saw him was in the men's room of the Belmont and Clark subway station. I'm just off work and cruisin'. I used to do that all the time cause I never felt like going straight home. I don't have no people, or anyone to live with. My granny raised me, and she passed on when I was sixteen. Don't go talking and feeling all sorry for me. I like it this way; I feel kind of free. A lot of young dudes down at El Ranchero, they say they can't come out, least not while their parents are alive. Come to think of it, I guess I would have tried to hide it from Granny too. Sometimes people loving you kind of puts a fence around you and you don't stray. Well, I didn't have no fence and I could cruise all night if I so pleased. And a lot of times I

Paul Butler, *At Least Me and Rafael Tried, in* AURORA: A FEMINIST JOURNAL, Spring 1982, at 17.

did. Which brings me back to the subway station.

I liked cruising Belmont and Clark cause that's the subway a lot of businessmen take home from work. The Brooks Brothers, that's what I call them. They really get me off. I picture them, hopping their three piece suits up the stairs in the suburbs, with a briefcase in their hands. Petting the dog on the way in. I don't know, they really get me off, they are so ... so United States of America. More than a couple of them stop off in the men's room to see what's up. When we do it, I close my eyes, so I don't have to see the pukey little stall. I imagine. Like I'm doing it with the guy on *Father Knows Best*. The Brooks Brother closes his eyes like he's dreaming too. What about, I don't know. Something racial, I bet. I'm a big black stud rapping their insides out. But that's ok, it's cool for the time that we're doing it, everything's cool and me and the Brooks Brother are warm and safe and kind of lost. But it's a happy kind of lost. I felt lost like that all the time with Rafael. But it's taking me forever to tell you how we met. I had just walked into the men's room. All the stalls were taken but nobody was waiting to get in one. I stooped down on the floor to look at the shoes in the stalls. You can tell a lot looking at shoes. If I am in the mood for Puerto Ricans I look for crazy colored gym shoes, especially with bright shoe strings. But if I'm cruising for a Brooks Brother, I try to find something dark and shiny, maybe patent leather. Anything else, I'm careful about. Cowboy boots usually means suede trade which I don't go in for too much. And two tones, or boat shoes or anything else too fancy means what I call women. I hate women, they gross me out. They make people hate faggots. Me and my friends down at El Ranchero, if we are feeling rowdy, we chase 'em, and smear lipstick all over their face. Jesus, if you're gonna walk like that, and talk all breathy, why don't you just fucking go ahead and have an operation and be a real woman? That's the queers that are sick. Me and my friends are men. Anyway, I'm on

the floor and I hear a toilet flush and before I can stand all the way up, this beautiful Puerto Rican guy walks out of the stall. He was wearing a corduroy suit. Listen, "beautiful" is not a word I throw around, but I don't know so many big words and when I think of Rafael, it's the only one that does him up proper. I don't want to tell you what he looked like cause it wasn't so much what he looked like but how he made me feel. He made me feel like this: in High, my white boy creative arts teacher said he would die for the Mona Lisa. Said he would up and die to save it from a fire or something. Rafael made me feel like I could die for him. Just looking made me feel that way. He was like the first time you dig a new song on the box. The kind of song that tells your story to you. And you think this guy singing knows my story better than I do. And something connected to your insides explodes. That is how I felt, on the floor. Tuesday, October, during the rush hour, in the men's room at Belmont and Clark. Like God was doing me a favor, or something. The P.R.'s eyes lit up when he first looked. I was practically living in the weight room back then and working a real tough guy number. I was big, black, brawny, baaad as a motherfucker. But then the dude saw me getting up from the floor and he looked at me like I was a piece of shit, and then, even worse, like he didn't see me at all. He walked over to the basin and washed his hands. Only Rafael, forever Mr. Neat and Clean, would have washed his hands at that sink, it was so nasty looking. I was surprised the water didn't sting. Then the man left the room. I didn't know whether I should chase after him, or what. All I knew is I had seen something I was supposed to have. When I dropped out of high school, the only subject I dug was American History. Right before I left, we was learning about this thing called Manifest Destiny, about how the Americans felt God wanted them to have the whole damn continent, all the way to California. I swear on my grandmother's grave, that's how I felt about Rafael. God wanted him for me. I used to jack off a lot thinking about guys like him. Cross between a humpy Puerto Rican and a Brooks Brother. He would come and rescue me, like in one of my handsome prince stories. Rescue me from what I don't know — maybe from packing books into boxes all day long, maybe from being a fag, even though I don't know if I would want to be rescued from that. Anyway, I always had this idea of this dream man, and just looking at Rafael, he came mighty close. Now that it's over, it sounds like something that would happen in a corny, straight movie, maybe the late, late show. But I want you to understand how I felt, and sometimes you really feel like a movie. That good.

I left the men's room, and went out into the station. I didn't really expect to see him; Belmont and Clark is really busy during rush hour. I wasn't too worried. You gotta understand, I was really believing that Manifest Destiny stuff. I would just go back to the station the next day at the same time and he'd be there.

I did and he was. He didn't look too surprised to see me, neither. I just stared at him, did not take my eyes off him from the time he entered the stall till the time he came back out, washed his hands and left. This happened every day for about a week. I never said nothing. If it's one thing you can't teach me nothing about, it's how to cruise a guy. You do it slowly, like catching a butterfly. After the second day, I was not worried that he wouldn't want me. If he didn't, he would not have kept coming back. The Tuesday after the Tuesday I first saw him, he looked at the mirror above the sink where he washed his hands. He saw me watching him. He asked, still washing his hands, "What you want?" He had a real bad accent, he did not speak English so good, I could tell right off. That was okay, according to my high school equivalency test teacher, I do not speak English so good either.

"You know what I want?" I said, real cool. Some of the rules for cruisin' are kind of stupid. The more you want it, the less you

should act like you want it. But dig it, you follow the rules if you want the prize.

"You come with me," he said. It was kind of a question.

I was looking at his eyes in the mirror. Some people's eyes you can drown in. "Yes," I answered the question.

We left the men's room and walked to a turnstyle in the subway station. He handed me a token. "Where are we going?" I asked, like it made a difference. Friggin' white boys ask that sometime, then don't go with you when they hear where you live.

"I have a place. Not far." I guess he thought that was all I needed to know. In English, Rafael never said anymore than what he needed to say. Sometimes I would be in his apartment late at night and the phone would ring. His sister in Puerto Rico. Then, he would go on and on in long Spanish sentences. To me, Spanish is like a poem, everything rhyming and music. I would feel him, and try to guess what he was saying, but those times, he acted like I wasn't even in the room.

We went North on the subway, then walked a few blocks. He lived in a mixed neighborhood; it wasn't too bad. I guess they paid him alright wherever he wore those corduroy suits. Finally, we turned into a building that had a bank on the ground floor. Lake View Savings and Loan.

"This is where I live." Up, up, up to the fifth floor, into one of the brown doors in a long hallway of brown doors, then...

Well, I don't want to write what we did. Putting it in words makes it sound dirty, or something and it wasn't. It was very clean.

It was October, and Rafael and I started going together. Maybe it was the best October I ever seen. I thought Rafael was just what I always knew he was like, even before I met him. My humpy Brooks Brother. My rescuer. He said I reminded him of the boys he played soccer with when he was a little *niño*. He never knew a guy who looked like me could be a fag. I didn't look like one at all and especially around him I was working the macho trip to the max cause I knew that was what he liked. I would look at the football games on the tube after we did it. That was bullshit. I don't go for sports that much. But he got so turned on watching me. Me, sitting on the edge of the bed in my shorts trying to act like I was really into the game. I know we shoulda been straight with each other from the start. But everything was so mellow. So sweet.

Friday nights, sometimes Saturday night too, I would take him down to El Ranchero. My friends said to me they liked him but they would keep their distance. I think he was too much Brooks Brothers for them, always with a suit coat on, and a tie. For a while he was real stiff, couldn't get used to guys dancin' and making out all around us. Then he cooled out, and come to find out, he could dance as good as any of us. And dancing is one thing where me and my friends get down. When Mario played a salsa, *man oh man, we wore out the floor*. The suede trade and the women would sit down because they knew that was a dance for us alone. The hot and sweaty little room. The raunchy music. Sirens and flashing lights. The sounds we made to the beat: *"Gittee gee, gittee gee, gitteegeegittee-geegitteegee"* and *"boy oh boy to the bang bang boogie to the rhythm of the boogie to be."* And I think God made drums for black and P.R. faggots. That, and Rafael was maybe all I needed to live. Don't you know I've done poppers and angel dust and once, when I went with a rich guy, cocaine, but ain't nothin' comes close to that October, Rafael high. I could have stopped time, I swear that's how good he made me feel. I could have stopped time and I should have too. October and November and December at El Ranchero, just stompin' to the beat of the band.

Okay, okay, okay. Well, I told you I would be lying sometime to make things seem even. Maybe it was not all that magic. Cause even then there were some clues. How he would take off his jacket and tie soon as he came home from work, even though the way I had it pic-tured, he should always be wearing them. How I would always have to be the one to say something if some straights were bothering us if we were maybe walking too close together on the street. And some things I don't want to say, some in bed things that I liked, but he didn't. Cause he wanted me to be like the dude all the time and him like the woman. He hadn't made the scene long enough to know that's not how it works. I don't feel whole if I'm trapped into being the dude all the time which is the same as being the heavy all the time. If I wanted that trip, I'd be straight. And honest, I did not give a shit about the Super Bowl or the NCAA playoffs but he always wanted me watching them. I never said nothing, I couldn't. I knew he liked to think of me that way and like I told you, at the beginning I kind of led him on, just to keep him. Now, when we did it, we both closed our eyes and sometimes I don't even think he knew I was there, I was just a body to mean whatever was in his dreams. But I could still *look* at him and if I saw him with only my eyes he was still what I wanted him to be. And it was good to have a place to come to nights. In my city, December is cold.

In the summer, when I was little, I loved to catch lightning bugs. I would snatch them out the air and put them in a mayonnaise jar with holes punched in the top. At first, they lit up every few minutes, and then less and less. I could watch for a whole hour without them lighting up. I can't let go too easy the things I like, especially being a fag, cause the things I like don't come along too often. But on Christmas Day, it was like time to trash the jar.

See we were supposed to get each other things we thought we could both enjoy. I bought him a blue jean jacket, but that was only half. Down at El Ranchero, everybody was starting to wear patches that said things like "State Police" and "Hell's Angels." I bought one that said "Highway Safety Patrol" and sewed it onto the arm of the jacket. That was one of my things — there I am stuck in the middle of a super highway. It's pitch black outside and below zero. Right before I pass out, Rafael zips up in something like a tank. He tells me come on, don't worry, everything's cool. We drink some warm soup and he starts rubbing our hands together so I won't get frostbite. The rest is personal. But it was just the kind of jacket I imagined him in. Christmas morning he opens the package and I can see he wants to laugh. "What is this?"

"You can see what it is."

"No, this I mean," he points at the patch.

"Nothing. Just...kind of a joke, that's all."

"Highway Safety Patrol. This is something I should be giving you." His eyes were mixed-up, sad, like a little boy whose bag got snatched on Halloween.

"How come it's something that you should get me?"

"Highway Safety Patrol. Man, that's your job."

"Rafael, I work in a book store. That's my job."

"Come on man. You know what I mean."

I know what he means all right. I feel like crying but if I do, that will flip him out completely. I just look at him.

"*Vaya, hombre,* open what I got you."

He bought me a striped soccer uniform, the kind the Chicago Sting wear. Just what I frigging wanted. He wants me to put it on, so I do. He loves it, and we make out under the tree, he in his jacket, me in my uniform. The sex isn't that hot. My fault.

After that, I can't see him with just my eyes anymore, even though he wore the jacket sometimes. I stop watching sports. He wants me to go to the doctor. He thinks I'm sick cause I don't get excited about nothing no more. Then day by day he gets fed up with me, especially since I just completely stop working the butch trip. I'm just plain old me, whole, man and woman, boy and girl and I get an attitude like take it or leave it alone. Only reason I don't split first is cause I feel like its my fault to begin with. I'm the one who fooled him. He deserves the kind of happy, punch drunk feeling you get when you can think, Well, at least *I* left the son of a bitch. And maybe I hope he'll

stay, that he can love the whole me. Doesn't happen. Middle of January, we have a big blow-up about a little thing. He leaves and I come home from work the next day and find all my stuff laid out on the table. A note is propped up against my gym shoes. *"Es la hora."* It's time. I kind of make myself laugh. I think well at least I learned a bit of Spanish. It's the last laugh I get for a long time. Rafael never calls, not to say how are you doing or nothing. Kind of cold, I think. You get involved with somebody, you should wonder how they're doing every now and then. I guess the whole me kind of threw him for a loop. Maybe he found a real soccer player, if any of them be faggots. Rafael could work them.

I don't have no comment on the whole thing. I'm just telling what happened. I don't cruise no more, but I still imagine things. Don't want people imagining no more things about me.

So sometimes in my class that gets you ready to take the high school equivalency test, we do this one exercise that I hate. After we read a story, we have to find out what is the main idea and what is the best title. I ain't showing this to nobody, this is my personal business, but I know what my friends would say. Faggots wasn't intended to have affairs the same way straights do; it's two different worlds. Their best title would be something like, "Another Example of a Faggot Romance." Sometimes those dudes get my blood up and I know they are wrong. They are so wrong. I ain't sure what the main idea of all this is. But days when I am not horny and not lonely and am thinking clear headed, there are a lot of main ideas, a lot of morals. Just cause I didn't make it with Rafael don't mean that none of us can't never make it. Do it? That's what I think on good days like today and that's why I named the story what I did. Days when I am tired of not having nobody, but feel like I can't be a *whole* person if I want somebody to want me, I think my friends might be right.

II. MARRIAGE

A. The Constitutional Status of Marriage

Marriage is fundamentally a matter of state law. Nevertheless, "as creating the most important relation in life, as having more to do with the morals and civilization of a people than any other institution,"[1] marriage holds a special place in constitutional law. As long ago as 1923, the Supreme Court stated that the liberty guaranteed by the due process clause includes the right to marry.[2]

LOVING v. VIRGINIA

388 U.S. 1 (1967)

MR. CHIEF JUSTICE WARREN delivered the opinion of the Court.

This case presents a Constitutional question never addressed by this Court: whether a statutory scheme adopted by the State of Virginia to prevent marriages between persons solely on the basis of racial classifications violates the equal protection and due process clauses of the Fourteenth Amendment. For reasons which seem to us to reflect the central meaning of those Constitutional commands, we conclude that these statutes cannot stand consistently with the Fourteenth Amendment.

In June 1958, two residents of Virginia, Mildred Jeter, a Negro woman, and Richard Loving, a white man, were married in the District of Columbia pursuant to its laws. Shortly after their marriage, the Lovings re-turned to Virginia and established their marital abode in Caroline County. At the October Term, 1958, of the Circuit Court of Caroline County, a grand jury issued an indictment charging the Lovings with violating Virginia's ban on interracial marriages. On January 6, 1959, the Lovings pleaded guilty to the charge and were sentenced to one year in jail; however, the trial judge suspended the sentence for a period of 25 years on the condition that the Lovings leave the State and not return to Virginia together for 25 years. He stated in an opinion that:

> "Almighty God created the races white, black, yellow, malay and red, and He placed them on separate continents. And but for the interference with His arrangement there would be no cause for such marriages. The fact that

---

1. *Maynard v. Hill*, 125 U.S. 190, 205 (1888).
2. *Meyer v. Nebraska*, 262 U.S. 390 (1923).

He separated the races shows that He did not intend for the races to mix."

After their convictions, the Lovings took up residence in the District of Columbia. On November 6, 1963, they filed a motion in the state trial court to vacate the judgment and set aside the sentence on the ground that the statutes which they had violated were repugnant to the Fourteenth Amendment . . . On January 22, 1965, the state trial judge denied the motion to vacate the sentences, and the Lovings perfected an appeal to the Supreme Court of Appeals of Virginia. . . .

The Supreme Court of Appeals upheld the constitutionality of the antimiscegenation statutes and, after modifying the sentence, affirmed the convictions.

The two statutes under which appellants were convicted and sentenced are part of a comprehensive statutory scheme aimed at prohibiting and punishing interracial marriages. The Lovings were convicted of violating § 20-58 of the Virginia Code:

> *"Leaving State to evade law.* If any white person and colored person shall go out of this State, for the purpose of being married, and with the intention of returning, and be married out of it,

and afterwards return to and reside in it, cohabiting as man and wife, they shall be punished as provided in § 20-59, and the marriage shall be governed by the same law as if it had been solemnized in this State. The fact of their cohabitation here as man and wife shall be evidence of their marriage."

Section 20-59, which defines the penalty for miscegenation, provides:

> *"Punishment for marriage.* If any white person intermarry with a colored person, or any colored person intermarry with a white person, he shall be guilty of a felony and shall be punished by confinement in the penitentiary for not less than one nor more than five years."

Other central provisions in the Virginia statutory scheme are § 20-57, which automatically voids all marriages between "a white person and a colored person" without any judicial proceeding,[3] and §§ 20-54 and 1-14 which, respectively, define "white persons" and "colored persons and Indians" for purposes of the statutory prohibitions.[4] The Lovings have never disputed in the course

---

3. Section 20-57 of the Virginia Code provides:

    "Marriages void without decree. All marriages between a white person and a colored person shall be absolutely void without any decree of divorce or other legal process." *Va. Code Ann.*, § 20-57 (1960 Repl. Vol.).

4. Section 20-54 of the Virginia Code provides:

    "Intermarriage prohibited; meaning of term 'white persons.' It shall hereafter be unlawful for any white person in this State to marry any save a white person, or a person with no other admixture of blood than white and American Indian. For the purpose of this chapter, the term 'white person' shall apply only to such person as has no trace whatever of any blood other than Caucasian; but persons who have one-sixteenth or less of the blood of the American Indian and have no other non-Caucasic blood shall be deemed to be white persons. All laws heretofore passed and now in effect regarding the intermarriage of white and colored persons shall apply to marriages prohibited by this chapter." *Va. Code Ann.*, § 20-54 (1960 Repl. Vol.).

    The exception for persons with less than one-sixteenth "of the blood of the American Indian" is apparently accounted for, in the words of a tract issued by the Registrar of the State Bureau of Vital Statistics, by "the desire of all to recognize as an integral and honored part of the white race the descendants of John Rolfe and Pocahontas . . . ." Plecker, The New Family and Race Improvement, 17 Va. Health Bull., Extra No. 12, at 25-26 (New Family Series No. 5, 1925), cited in Wadlington, *The* Loving *Case: Virginia's Anti-Miscegenation Statute in Historical Perspective,* 52 VA. L. REV. 1189, 1202, n. 93 (1966).

    Section 1-14 of the Virginia Code provides:

of this litigation that Mrs. Loving is a "colored person" or that Mr. Loving is a "white person" within the meanings given those terms by the Virginia statutes.

Virginia is now one of 16 States which prohibit and punish marriages on the basis of racial classifications.[5] Penalties for miscegenation arose as an incident to slavery and have been common in Virginia since the colonial period. The present statutory scheme dates from the adoption of the Racial Integrity Act of 1924, passed during the period of extreme nativism which followed the end of the First World War. The central features of this Act, and current Virginia law, are the absolute prohibition of a "white person" marrying other than another "white person," a prohibition against issuing marriage licenses until the issuing official is satisfied that the applicants' statements as to their race are correct, certificates of "racial composition" to be kept by both local and state registrars, and the carrying forward of earlier prohibitions against racial intermarriage.

I

In upholding the constitutionality of these provisions in the decision below, the Supreme Court of Appeals of Virginia referred to its 1955 decision in *Naim v. Naim*, 87 S. E. 2d 749 (Va. 1955), as stating the reasons supporting the validity of these laws. In *Naim*, the state court concluded that the State's legitimate purposes were "to preserve the racial integrity of its citizens," and to prevent "the corruption of blood," "a mongrel breed of citizens," and "the obliteration of racial pride," obviously an endorsement of the doctrine of White Supremacy. The court also reasoned that marriage has traditionally been subject to state regulation without federal intervention, and, consequently, the regulation of marriage should be left to exclusive state control by the Tenth Amendment.

While the state court is no doubt correct in asserting that marriage is a social relation subject to the State's police power, *Maynard v. Hill*, 125 U.S. 190 (1888), the State does not contend in its argument before this Court that its powers to regulate marriage are unlimited notwithstanding the commands of the Fourteenth Amendment. Nor could it do so in light of *Meyer v. Nebraska*, 262 U.S. 390 (1923), and *Skinner v. Oklahoma*, 316 U.S. 535 (1942). Instead, the State argues that the meaning of the Equal Protection Clause, as illuminated by the statements of the Framers, is only that state penal laws containing an interracial element as part of the definition of the offense must apply equally to whites and Negroes in the sense that members of each race are punished to the same degree. Thus, the State contends that, because its miscegenation statutes pun-

---

"*Colored persons and Indians defined.* Every person in whom there is ascertainable any Negro blood shall be deemed and taken to be a colored person, and every person not a colored person having one fourth or more of American Indian blood shall be deemed an American Indian; except that members of Indian tribes existing in this Commonwealth having one fourth or more of Indian blood and less than one sixteenth of Negro blood shall be deemed tribal Indians." *Va. Code Ann.* § 1-14 (1960 Repl. Vol.).

5. After the initiation of this litigation, Maryland repealed its prohibitions against interracial marriage, *Md. Laws* 1967, c. 6, leaving Virginia and 15 other States [Alabama; Arkansas; Delaware; Florida; Georgia; Kentucky; Louisiana; Mississippi; Missouri; North Carolina; Oklahoma; South Carolina; Tennessee; Texas; West Virginia] with statutes outlawing interracial marriage.

Over the past 15 years, 14 states have repealed laws outlawing interracial marriages: Arizona, California, Colorado, Idaho, Indiana, Maryland, Montana, Nebraska, Nevada, North Dakota, Oregon, South Dakota, Utah, and Wyoming.

The first state court to recognize that miscegenation statutes violate the Equal Protection Clause was the Supreme Court of California. *Perez v. Sharp*, 198 P. 2d 17 (Cal. 1948).

ish equally both the white and the Negro participants in an interracial marriage, these statutes, despite their reliance on racial classifications, do not constitute an invidious discrimination based upon race. The second argument advanced by the State assumes the validity of its equal application theory. The argument is that, if the Equal Protection Clause does not outlaw miscegenation statutes because of their reliance on racial classifications, the question of constitutionality would thus become whether there was any rational basis for a State to treat interracial marriages differently from other marriages. On this question, the State argues, the scientific evidence is substantially in doubt and, consequently, this Court should defer to the wisdom of the state legislature in adopting its policy of discouraging interracial marriages.

Because we reject the notion that the mere "equal application" of a statute containing racial classifications is enough to remove the classifications from the Fourteenth Amendment's proscription of all invidious racial discriminations, we do not accept the State's contention that these statutes should be upheld if there is any possible basis for concluding that they serve a rational purpose. The mere fact of equal application does not mean that our analysis of these statutes should follow the approach we have taken in cases involving no racial discrimination where the Equal Protection Clause has been arrayed against a statute discriminating between the kinds of advertising which may be displayed on trucks in New York City, *Railway Express Agency, Inc. v. New York*, 336 U.S. 106 (1949), or an exemption in Ohio's ad valorem tax for merchandise owned by a nonresident in a storage warehouse, *Allied Stores of Ohio, Inc. v. Bowers*, 358 U.S. 522 (1959). In these cases, involving distinctions not drawn according to race, the Court has merely asked whether there is any rational foundation for the discriminations, and has deferred to the wisdom of the state legislatures. In the case at bar, however, we deal with statutes con-

taining racial classifications, and the fact of equal application does not immunize the statute from the very heavy burden of justification which the Fourteenth Amendment has traditionally required of state statutes drawn according to race.

The State argues that statements in the Thirty-ninth Congress about the time of the passage of the Fourteenth Amendment indicate that the Framers did not intend the Amendment to make unconstitutional state miscegenation laws. Many of the statements alluded to by the State concern the debates over the Freedmen's Bureau Bill, which President Johnson vetoed, and the Civil Rights Act of 1866, enacted over his veto. While these statements have some relevance to the intention of Congress in submitting the Fourteenth Amendment, it must be understood that they pertained to the passage of specific statutes and not to the broader, organic purpose of a constitutional amendment. As for the various statements directly concerning the Fourteenth Amendment, we have said in connection with a related problem, that although these historical sources "cast some light" they are not sufficient to resolve the problem; "[a]t best, they are inconclusive. The most avid proponents of the post-War Amendments undoubtedly intended them to remove all legal distinctions among 'all persons born or naturalized in the United States.' Their opponents, just as certainly, were antagonistic to both the letter and the spirit of the Amendments and wished them to have the most limited effect." *Brown v. Board of Education*, 347 U.S. 483, 489 (1954). *See also Strauder v. West Virginia*, 100 U.S. 303, 310 (1880). We have rejected the proposition that the debates in the Thirty-ninth Congress or in the state legislatures which ratified the Fourteenth Amendment supported the theory advanced by the State, that the requirement of equal protection of the laws is satisfied by penal laws defining offenses based on racial classifications so long as white and Negro participants in the offense were similarly punished. *McLaughlin v. Florida*, 379 U.S. 184 (1964).

The State finds support for its "equal application" theory in the decision of the Court in *Pace v. Alabama*, 106 U.S. 583 (1883). In that case, the Court upheld a conviction under an Alabama statute forbidding adultery or fornication between a white person and a Negro which imposed a greater penalty than that of a statute proscribing similar conduct by members of the same race. The Court reasoned that the statute could not be said to discriminate against Negroes because the punishment for each participant in the offense was the same. However, as recently as the 1964 Term, in rejecting the reasoning of that case, we stated "*Pace* represents a limited view of the equal protection clause which has not withstood analysis in the subsequent decisions of this Court." *McLaughlin v. Florida*, 379 U.S. at 188. As we there demonstrated, the Equal Protection Clause requires the consideration of whether the classifications drawn by any statute constitute an arbitrary and invidious discrimination. The clear and central purpose of the Fourteenth Amendment was to eliminate all official state sources of invidious racial discrimination in the States. *Slaughter-House Cases*, 16 Wall. 36, 71 (1873); *Strauder v. West Virginia*, 100 U.S. 303, 307-308 (1880); *Ex parte Virginia*, 100 U.S. 339, 344-345 (1880); *Shelley v. Kraemer*, 334 U.S. 1 (1948); *Burton v. Wilmington Parking Authority*, 365 U.S. 715 (1961).

There can be no question but that Virginia's miscegenation statutes rest solely upon distinctions drawn according to race. The statutes proscribe generally accepted conduct if engaged in by members of different races. Over the years, this Court has consistently repudiated "[d]istinctions between citizens solely because of their ancestry" as being "odious to a free people whose institutions are founded upon the doctrine of equality." *Hirabayashi v. United States*, 320 U.S. 81, 100 (1943). At the very least, the Equal Protection Clause demands that racial classifications, especially suspect in criminal statutes, be subjected to the "most rigid scrutiny," *Korematsu v. United States*, 323 U.S. 214, 216 (1944), and, if they are ever to be upheld, they must be shown to be necessary to the accomplishment of some permissible state objective, independent of the racial discrimination which it was the object of the Fourteenth Amendment to eliminate. Indeed, two members of this Court have already stated that they "cannot conceive of a valid legislative purpose . . . which makes the color of a person's skin the test of whether his conduct is a criminal offense." *McLaughlin v. Florida*, 379 U.S. at 198 (Stewart, J., joined by Douglas, J., concurring).

There is patently no legitimate overriding purpose independent of invidious racial discrimination which justifies this classification. The fact that Virginia prohibits only interracial marriages involving white persons demonstrates that the racial classifications must stand on their own justification, as measures designed to maintain White Supremacy.[11] We have consistently denied the constitutionality of measures which restrict the rights of citizens on account of race. There can be no doubt that restricting the freedom to marry solely because of racial classifications violates the central meaning of the Equal Protection Clause.

---

11. Appellants point out that the State's concern in these statutes, as expressed in the words of the 1924 Act's title, "An Act to Preserve Racial Integrity," extends only to the integrity of the white race. While Virginia prohibits whites from marrying any nonwhite (subject to the exception for the descendants of Pocahontas), Negroes, Orientals, and any other racial class may intermarry without statutory interference. Appellants contend that this distinction renders Virginia's miscegenation statutes arbitrary and unreasonable even assuming the constitutional validity of an official purpose to preserve "racial integrity." We need not reach this contention because we find the racial classifications in these statutes repugnant to the Fourteenth Amendment, even assuming an even-handed state purpose to protect the "integrity" of all races.

II

These statutes also deprive the Lovings of liberty without due process of law in violation of the Due Process Clause of the Fourteenth Amendment. The freedom to marry has long been recognized as one of the vital personal rights essential to the orderly pursuit of happiness by free men.

Marriage is one of the "basic civil rights of man," fundamental to our very existence and survival. *Skinner v. Oklahoma*, 316 U.S. 535, 541 (1942). *See also Maynard v. Hill*, 125 U.S. 190 (1888). To deny this fundamental freedom on so unsupportable a basis as the racial classifications embodied in these statutes, classifications so directly subversive of the principle of equality at the heart of the Fourteenth Amendment, is surely to deprive all the State's citizens of liberty without due process of law. The Fourteenth Amendment requires that the freedom of choice to marry not be restricted by invidious racial discriminations. Under our Constitution, the freedom to marry, or not marry, a person of another race resides with the individual and cannot be infringed by the State.

These convictions must be reversed.

It is so ordered.

MR. JUSTICE STEWART, concurring.

I have previously expressed the belief that "it is simply not possible for a state law to be valid under our Constitution which makes the criminality of an act depend upon the race of the actor." *McLaughlin v. Florida*, 379 U.S. 184, 198 (concurring opinion). Because I adhere to that belief, I concur in the judgment of the Court.

Notes

1. Since *Loving*, the Supreme Court has struck down a state statute that burdened the marriage rights of those who have outstanding child support obligations, *Zablocki v. Redhail*, 434 U.S. 374 (1978), and a state regulation that burdened the marriage rights of prisoners, *Turner v. Safley*, 482 U.S. 78 (1987).

2. The right to marry established in *Loving* is closely related to the right of (marital) privacy established in *Griswold v. Connecticut*, 381 U.S. 479 (1965) (striking ban on contraceptive use by married couples), where the Court observed that marriage "is an association that promotes a way of life, not causes; a harmony in living, not political faiths; a bilateral loyalty, not commercial or social projects" and "for as noble a purpose as any involved in our prior decisions." *Id.* at 486.

    In *Bowers v. Hardwick*, 478 U.S. 186 (1986), see pages 132-148, *supra*, the Supreme Court refused to extend the right of privacy to homosexual sodomy. Justice Blackmun, dissenting in *Bowers v. Hardwick*, observed that "[t]he parallel between *Loving* and this case is almost uncanny." *Id.* at 210 n.5 (1986). Indeed, in defending the constitutionality of its sodomy statute, the state of Georgia conceded at oral argument that sexual behavior within the statute's definition could not be prosecuted if it occurred between spouses. *See id.* at 218 n.10 (1986) (Blackmun, J., dissenting). In a subsequent case, the sodomy law upheld in *Hardwick* as applied to homosexual partners was struck down as unconstitutional as applied to married partners because "[g]overnment has no business with a married couple's private consensual sexual practices." *Moseley v. Esposito*, No. 89-6897-1 (Ga. Super. Ct. Sept. 6, 1989), *cited in* Arthur Leonard, *Georgia Court Says Married Folks Can Do Sodomy*, 1989

LESBIAN/GAY L. NOTES 52. It is clear that "a fascinating legal anomaly would result if a state relied on *Hardwick* to prosecute a married lesbian or gay couple." Nan Hunter, *Marriage, Law, and Gender: A Feminist Inquiry*, 1 LAW & SEXUALITY 9, 10 n.2 (1991).

3. It has been argued that bans on gay sexual relations violate the right of privacy established in *Griswold*, not because they intrude on sexual intimacy as Justice Blackmun argued in his *Hardwick* dissent, but rather because:

> childrearing, marriage, and the assumption of a specific sexual identity are undertakings that go on for years, define roles, direct activities, operate on or even create intense emotional relations, enlist the body, inform values, and in sum substantially shape the totality of a person's daily life and consciousness. Laws that force such undertakings on individuals may properly be called "totalitarian," and the right to privacy exists to protect against them.

Jed Rubenfeld, *The Right to Privacy*, 102 HARV. L. REV. 737, 801-02 (1989).

4. Although this chapter is concerned primarily with same-sex relationships, it should be noted that lesbians and gay men sometimes find themselves in opposite-sex marriages. Moreover, opposite-sex marriages also include many bisexual men and women. *See generally* BRENDA MADDOX, MARRIED AND GAY (1982). Same-sex relations *before* marriage are not generally considered grounds for divorce or annulment of marriages. *See, e.g., Woy v. Woy*, 737 S.W.2d 769 (Mo. Ct. App. 1987) (holding that wife's lesbian activities before marriage did not justify annulment on basis of fraud); *Freitag v. Freitag*, 242 N.Y.S.2d 643 (Sup. Ct.1963) (holding that the husband's concealment of prior homosexual tendencies did not justify annulment because the court was unable to conclude that there was a "true case of homosexuality" or that the husband's "condition" was "incurable"). In some states, sexual relations with members of the same sex *during* marriage may constitute grounds for divorce even where not specifically enumerated as grounds for divorce, *see, e.g., Bales v. Hack*, 509 N.E.2d 95 (Ohio Ct. App. 1986), but the move toward "no-fault" divorce in almost every state has diminished the need to establish grounds. Nevertheless, factors such as same-sex relations may play a significant role in determining alimony and custody of children. *See, e.g., R.G.M. v. D.E.M.*, 410 S.E.2d 564 (S.C. 1991) (finding that wife's extra-marital lesbian relationship constitutes adultery and therefore bars an alimony award under state statute); *see also* Chapter Six, *infra*.

B. The Community's Debate Over Marriage

The following exchange between Thomas Stoddard and Paula Ettelbrick, two gay and lesbian rights advocates, appeared under the heading *Gay Marriage: A Must or a Bust?* in OUT/LOOK magazine in (1989).

◆

WHY GAY PEOPLE SHOULD SEEK
THE RIGHT TO MARRY

Thomas Stoddard

Even though, these days, few lesbians and gay men enter into marriages recognized by law, absolutely every gay person has an opinion on marriage as an "institution." (The word "institution" brings to mind, perhaps appropriately, museums.) After all, we all know quite a bit about the subject. Most of us grew up in marital households. Virtually all of us, regardless of race, creed, gender, and culture, have received lectures on the propriety, if not the sanctity, of marriage — which usually suggests that those who choose not to marry are both unhappy and unhealthy. We all have been witnesses, willing or not, to a lifelong parade of other people's marriages, from Uncle Harry and Aunt Bernice to the Prince and Princess of Wales. And at one point or another, some nosy relative has inevitably inquired of every gay person when he or she will finally "tie the knot" (an intriguing and probably apt cliché).

I must confess at the outset that I am no fan of the "institution" of marriage as currently constructed and practiced. I may simply be unlucky, but I have seen preciously few marriages over the course of my forty years that invite admiration and emulation. All too often, marriage appears to petrify rather than satisfy and enrich, even for couples in their twenties and thirties who have had a chance to learn the lessons of feminism. Almost inevitably, the partners seem to fall into a "husband" role and a "wife" role, with such latter-day modifications as the wife who works in addition to raising the children and managing the household.

Let me be blunt: in its traditional form, marriage has been oppressive, especially (although not entirely) to women. Indeed, until the middle of the last century, marriage was, at its legal and social essence, an extension of the husband and his paternal family. Under the English common law, wives were among the husband's "chattel" — personal property — and could not, among other things, hold property in their own names. The common law crime of adultery demonstrates the unequal treatment accorded to husbands and wives: while a woman who slept with a man who wasn't her husband committed adultery, a man who slept with a woman not his wife committed fornication. A man was legally incapable of committing adultery, except as an accomplice to an errant wife. The underlying offense of adultery was not the sexual betrayal of one partner by the other, but the wife's engaging in conduct capable of tainting the husband's bloodlines. (I swear on my *Black's Law Dictionary* that I have not made this up!)

Nevertheless, despite the oppressive nature of marriage historically, and in spite of the general absence of edifying examples of modern heterosexual marriage, I believe very strongly that every lesbian and gay man should have the right to marry the same-sex partner of his or her choice, and that the gay rights movement should aggressively seek full legal recognition for same-sex marriages. To those who might not agree, I respectfully offer three explanations, one practical, one political and one philosophical.

Thomas Stoddard, *Why Gay People Should Seek The Right To Marry*, OUT/LOOK, Fall 1989, at 9.

THE PRACTICAL EXPLANATION

The legal status of marriage rewards the two individuals who travel to the altar (or its secular equivalent) with substantial economic and practical advantages. Married couples may reduce their tax liability by filing a joint return. They are entitled to special government benefits, such as those given surviving spouses and dependents through the Social Security program. They can inherit from one another even when there is no will. They are immune from subpoenas requiring testimony against the other spouse. And marriage to an American citizen gives a foreigner a right to residency in the United States.

Other advantages have arisen not by law but by custom. Most employers offer health insurance to their employees, and many will include an employee's spouse in the benefits package, usually at the employer's expense. Virtually no employer will include a partner who is not married to an employee, whether of the same sex or not. Indeed, very few insurance companies even offer the possibility of a group health plan covering "domestic partners" who are not married to one another. Two years ago, I tried to find such a policy for Lambda, and discovered that not one insurance company authorized to do business in New York — the second-largest state in the country with more than 17 million residents — would accommodate us. (Lambda has tried to make do by paying for individual insurance policies for the same-sex partners of its employees who otherwise would go uninsured but these individual policies are usually narrower in scope than group policies, often require applicants to furnish individual medical information not required under most group plans, and are typically much more expensive per person).

In short, the law generally presumes in favor of every marital relationship, and acts to preserve and foster it, and to enhance the rights of the individuals who enter into it. It is usually possible, with enough money and the right advice, to replicate some of the benefits conferred by the legal status of marriage through the use of documents like wills and power of attorney forms, but that protection will inevitably, under current circumstances, be incomplete.

The law (as I suspect will come as no surprise to the readers of this journal) still looks upon lesbians and gay men with suspicion, and this suspicion casts a shadow over the documents they execute in recognition of a same-sex relationship. If a lesbian leaves property to her lover, her will may be invalidated on the grounds that it was executed under the "undue influence" of the would-be beneficiary. A property agreement may be denied validity because the underlying relationship is "meretricious" — akin to prostitution. (Astonishingly, until the mid-seventies, the law throughout the United States deemed "meretricious" virtually *any* formal economic arrangement between two people not married to one another, on the theory that an exchange of property between them was presumably payment for sexual services; the Supreme Court of California helped unravel this quaint legal fantasy in its 1976 ruling in the first famous "alimony" case, *Marvin v. Marvin*.) The law has progressed considerably beyond the uniformly oppressive state of affairs before 1969, but it is still far from enthusiastic about gay people and their relationships — to put it mildly.

Moreover, there are some barriers one simply cannot transcend outside of a formal marriage. When the Internal Revenue Code or the Immigration and Naturalization Act say "married," they mean "married" by definition of state statute. When the employer's group health plan says "spouse," it means "spouse" in the eyes of the law, not the eyes of the loving couple.

But there is another drawback. Couples seeking to protect their relationship through wills and other documents need knowledge, determination and — most importantly — money. No money, no lawyer. And no lawyer, no protection. Those who lack the sophistication or the wherewithal to retain a lawyer are simply stuck in most circumstances. Extending the right to marry to gay couples would assure that those at the bottom of the economic ladder have a chance to secure their relationship rights, too.

THE POLITICAL EXPLANATION

The claim that gay couples ought to be able to marry is not a new one. In the seventies, same-sex couples in three states — Minnesota, Kentucky and Washington — brought constitutional challenges to the marriage statutes, and in all three instances they failed. In each of the three, the court offered two basic justifications for limiting marriage to male-female couples: history and procreation. Witness this passage from the Supreme Court of Minnesota's 1971 opinion in *Baker v. Nelson*: "The institution of marriage as a union of man and woman, uniquely involving the procreating and rearing of children within a family, is as old as the book of Genesis.... This historic institution manifestly is more deeply founded than the asserted contemporary concept of marriage and societal interests for which petitioners contend."

Today no American jurisdiction recognizes the right of two women or two men to marry one another, although several nations in Northern Europe do. Even more telling, until earlier this year, there was little discussion within the gay rights movement about whether such a right should exist. As far as I can tell, no gay organization of any size, local or national, has yet declared the right to marry as one of its goals.

With all due respect to my colleagues and friends who take a different view, I believe it is time to renew the effort to overturn the existing marriage laws, and to do so in earnest, with a commitment of money and energy, through both the courts and the state legislatures. I am not naive about the likelihood of imminent victory. There is none. Nonetheless — and here I will not mince words — I would like to see the issue rise to the top of the agenda of every gay organiza-

tion, including my own (although the judgment is hardly mine alone).

Why give it such prominence? Why devote resources to such a distant goal? Because marriage is, I believe, the political issue that most fully tests the dedication of people who are *not* gay to full equality for gay people, and also the issue most likely to lead ultimately to a world free from discrimination against lesbians and gay men.

Marriage is much more than a relationship sanctioned by law. It is the centerpiece of our entire social structure, the core of the traditional notion of "family." Even in its present tarnished state, the marital relationship inspires sentiments suggesting that it is something almost suprahuman. The Supreme Court, in striking down an anti-contraception statute in 1965, called marriage "noble" and "intimate to the degree of being sacred." The Roman Catholic Church and the Moral Majority would go — and have gone — considerably further.

Lesbians and gay men are now denied entry to this "noble" and "sacred" institution. The implicit message is this: two men or two women are incapable of achieving such an exalted domestic state. Gay relationships are somehow less significant, less valuable. Such relationships may, from time to time and from couple to couple, give the appearance of a marriage, but they can never be of the same quality or importance.

I resent — indeed, I loathe — that conception of same-sex relationships. And I am convinced that ultimately the only way to overturn it is to remove the barrier to marriage that now limits the freedom of every gay man and lesbian.

That is not to deny the value of "domestic partnership" ordinances, statutes that prohibit discrimination based on "marital status," and other legal advances that can enhance the rights (as well as the dignity) of gay couples. Without question, such advances move us further along the path to equality. But their value can only be partial. (The recently enacted San Francisco "domestic partnership" ordinance, for example, will have practical value only for gay people who happen to be employed by the City of San Francisco and want to include their non-marital spouses in part of the city's fringe benefit package; the vast majority of gay San Franciscans — those employed by someone other than the city — have only a symbolic victory to savor.) Measures of this kind can never assure full equality. Gay relationships will continue to be accorded a subsidiary status until the day that gay couples have *exactly* the same rights as their heterosexual counterparts. To my mind, that means either that the right to marry be extended to us, or that marriage be abolished in its present form for all gay couples, presumably to be replaced by some new legal entity — an unlikely alternative.

THE PHILOSOPHICAL EXPLANATION

I confessed at the outset that I personally found marriage in its present avatar rather, well, unattractive. Nonetheless, even from a philosophical perspective, I believe the right to marry should become a stated goal of the gay rights movement.

First, and most basically, the issue is not the desirability of marriage, but rather the desirability of the *right* to marry. That I think two lesbians or two gay men should be entitled to a marriage license does not mean that I think all gay people should find appropriate partners

and exercise the right, should it eventually exist. I actually rather doubt that I, myself, would want to marry, even though I share a household with another man who is exceedingly dear to me. There are others who feel differently, for economic, symbolic, or romantic reasons. They should, to my mind, unquestionably have the opportunity to marry if they wish and otherwise meet the requirements of the state (like being old enough).

Furthermore, marriage may be unattractive and even oppressive as it is currently structured and practiced, but enlarging the concept to embrace same-sex couples would necessarily transform it into something new. If two women can marry, or two men, marriage — even for heterosexuals — need not be a union of a "husband" and a "wife." Extending the right to marry to gay people — that is, abolishing the traditional gender requirements of marriage — can be one of the means, perhaps the principal one, through which the institution divests itself of the sexist trappings of the past.

Some of my colleagues disagree with me. I welcome their thoughts and the debates and discussions our different perspectives will trigger. The movement for equality for lesbians and gay men can only be enriched through this collective exploration of the question of marriage. But I do believe many thousands of gay people want the right to marry. And I think, too, they will earn that right for themselves sooner than most of us imagine.

◆

SINCE WHEN IS MARRIAGE A PATH TO LIBERATION?
Paula Ettelbrick

"Marriage is a great institution, if you like living in institutions," according to a bit of T-shirt philosophy I saw recently. Certainly, marriage is an institution. It is one of the most venerable, impenetrable institutions in modern society. Marriage provides the ultimate form of acceptance for personal intimate relationships in our society, and gives

Paula Ettelbrick, *Since When Is Marriage a Path To Liberation?*, OUT/LOOK, Fall 1989, at 9.

those who marry an insider status of the most powerful kind.

Steeped in a patriarchal system that looks to ownership, property, and dominance of men over women as its basis, the institution of marriage long has been the focus of radical feminist revulsion. Marriage defines certain relationships as more valid than all others. Lesbian and gay relationships, being neither legally sanctioned or commingled by blood, are always at the bottom of the heap of social acceptance and importance.

Given the imprimatur of social and personal approval which marriage provides, it is not surprising that some lesbians and gay men among us would look to legal marriage for self-affirmation. After all, those who marry can be instantaneously transformed from "outsiders" to "insiders," and we have a desperate need to become insiders.

It could make us feel OK about ourselves, perhaps even relieve some of the internalized homophobia that we all know so well. Society will then celebrate the birth of our children and mourn the death of our spouses. It would be easier to get health insurance for our spouses, family memberships to the local museum, and a right to inherit our spouse's cherished collection of lesbian mystery novels even if she failed to draft a will. Never again would she have to go to a family reunion and debate about the correct term for introducing our lover/partner/significant other to Aunt Flora. Everything would be quite easy and very nice.

So why does this unlikely event so deeply disturb me? For two major reasons. First, marriage will not liberate us as lesbians and gay men. In fact, it will constrain us, make us more invisible, force our assimilation into the mainstream, and undermine the goals of gay liberation. Second, attaining the right to marry will not transform our society from one that makes narrow, but dramatic, distinctions between those who are married and those who are not married to one that respects and encourages choice of relationships and family diversity. Marriage runs counter to two of the primary goals of the lesbian and gay movement: the affirmation of gay identity and culture; and the validation of many forms of relationships.

When analyzed from the standpoint of civil rights, certainly lesbians and gay men should have a right to marry. But obtaining a right does not always result in justice. White male firefighters in Birmingham, Alabama have been fighting for their "rights" to retain their jobs by overturning the city's affirmative action guidelines. If their "rights" prevail, the courts will have failed in rendering justice. The "right" fought for by the white male firefighters, as well as those who advocate strongly for the "rights" to legal marriage for gay people, will result, at best, in limited or narrowed "justice" for those closest to power at the expense of those who have been historically marginalized.

The fight for justice has as its goal the realignment of power imbalances among individuals and classes of people in society. A pure "rights" analysis often fails to incorporate a broader understanding of the underlying inequities that operate to deny justice to a fuller range of people and groups. In setting our priorities as a community, we must combine the concept of both rights and justice. At this point in time, making legal marriage for lesbian and gay couples a priority would set an agenda of gaining rights for a few, but would do nothing to correct the power imbalances between those who are married (whether gay or straight) and those who are not. Thus, justice would not be gained.

Justice for gay men and lesbians will be achieved only when we are accepted and supported in this society *despite* our differences from the dominant culture and the choices we make regarding our relationships. Being queer is more than setting up house, sleeping with a person of the same gender, and seeking state approval for doing so. It is an identity, a culture with many variations. It is a way of dealing with the world by diminishing the constraints of gender roles which have for so long kept women and gay people oppressed and invisible. Being queer means pushing the parameters of sex, sexuality, and family, and in the process transforming the very fabric of society. Gay liberation is inexorably linked to women's liberation. Each is essential to the other.

The moment we argue, as some among us insist on doing, that we should be treated as equals because we are really just like married couples and hold the same values to be true, we undermine the very purpose of our movement and begin the dangerous process of silencing our different voices. As a lesbian, I am fundamentally different from non-lesbian women. That's the point. Marriage, as it exists today, is antithetical to my liberation as a lesbian and as a woman because it mainstreams my life and voice. I do not want to be known as "Mrs. Attached-To-Somebody-Else." Nor do I want to give the state the power to regulate my primary relationship.

Yet, the concept of equality in our legal system does not support differences, it only supports sameness. The very standard for equal protection is that people who are similarly situated must be treated equally. To make an argument for equal protection, we will be required to claim that gay and lesbian relationships are the same as straight relationships. To gain the right, we must compare ourselves to married couples. The law looks to the insiders as the norm, regardless of how flawed or unjust their institutions, and requires that those seeking the law's equal protection situate themselves in a similar posture to those who are already protected. In arguing for the right to legal marriage, lesbians and gay men would be forced to claim that we are just like heterosexual couples, have the same goals and purposes, and vow to structure our lives similarly. The law provides no room to argue that we are different, but are nonetheless entitled to equal protection.

The thought of emphasizing our sameness to married heterosexuals in order to obtain this "right" terrifies me. It rips away the very heart and soul of what I believe it is to be a lesbian in this world. It robs me of the opportunity to make a difference. We end up mimicking all that is bad about the institution of marriage in our effort to appear to be the same as straight couples.

By looking to our sameness and de-emphasizing our differences, we don't even place ourselves in a position of power that would allow us to transform marriage from an institution that emphasizes property and state regulation of relationships to an institution which recognizes one of many types of valid and respected relationships. Until the constitution is interpreted to respect and encourage differences, pursuing the legalization of same-sex marriage would be leading our movement into a trap; we would be demanding access to the very institution which, in its current form, would undermine *our* movement to recognize many different kinds of relationships. We would be perpetuating the elevation of married relationships and of "couples" in general, and further eclipsing other relationships of choice.

Ironically, gay marriage, instead of liberating gay sex and sexuality, would further outlaw all gay and lesbian sex which is not performed in a marital context. Just as sexually active non-married women face stigma and double standards around sex and sexual activity, so too would non-married gay people. The only legitimate gay sex would be that which is cloaked in and regulated by marriage. Its legitimacy would stem not from an acceptance of gay sexuality, but because the Supreme Court and society in general fiercely protect the privacy of marital relationships. Lesbians and gay men who did not seek the state's stamp of approval would clearly face increased sexual oppression.

Undoubtedly, whether we admit it or not, we all need to be accepted by the broader society. That motivation fuels our work to eliminate discrimination in the workplace and elsewhere, fight for custody of our children, create our own families, and so on. The growing discussion about the right to marry may be explained in part by this need for acceptance. Those closer to the norm or to power in this country are more likely to see marriage as a principle of freedom and equality. Those who are more acceptable to the mainstream because of race, gender, and economic status are more likely to want the right to marry. It is the final acceptance, the ultimate affirmation of identity.

On the other hand, more marginal members of the lesbian and gay community (women, people of color, working class and poor) are less likely to see marriage as having relevance to our struggles for survival. After all, what good is the affirmation of our relationships (that is, marital relationships) if we are rejected as women, black, or working class?

The path to acceptance is much more complicated for many of us. For instance, if we choose legal marriage, we may enjoy the right to add our spouse to our health insurance policy at work, since most employment policies are defined by one's marital status, not family relationship. However, that choice assumes that we have a job *and* that our employer provides us with health benefits. For women, particularly women of color who tend to occupy the low-paying jobs that do not provide healthcare benefits at all, it will not matter one bit if they are able to marry their women partners. The opportunity to marry will neither get them the health benefits nor transform them from outsider to insider.

Of course, a white man who marries another white man who has a full-time job with benefits will certainly be able to share in those benefits and overcome the only obstacle left to full societal assimilation — the goal of many in his class. In other words, gay marriage will not topple the system that allows only the privileged few to obtain decent health care. Nor will it close the privilege gap between those who are married and those who are not.

Marriage creates a two-tier system that allows the state to regulate relationships. It has become a facile mechanism for employers to dole out benefits, for businesses to provide special deals and incentives, and for the law to make distinctions in distributing meager public funds. None of these entities bothers to consider the relationship among people; the love, respect, and need to protect that exists among all kinds of family members. Rather, a simple certificate of the state, regardless of whether the spouses love, respect, or even see each other on a regular basis, dominates and is supported. None of this dynamic will change if gay men and lesbians are given the option of marriage.

Gay marriage will not help us address the systemic abuses inherent in a society that does not provide decent health care to all of its citizens, a right that should not depend on whether the individual (1) has sufficient resources to afford health care or health insurance, (2) is working and receives health insurance as part of compensation, or (3) is married to a partner who is working and has health coverage which is extended to spouses. It will not address the underlying unfairness that allows businesses to provide discounted services or goods to families and couples — who are defined to include straight, married people and their children, but not domestic partners.

Nor will it address the pain and anguish of an unmarried lesbian who receives word of her partner's accident, rushes to the hospital and is prohibited from entering the intensive ward or obtaining information about her condition solely because she is not a spouse or family member. Likewise, marriage will not help the gay victim of domestic violence who, because he chose not to marry, finds no protection under the law to keep his violent lover away.

If the laws change tomorrow and lesbians and gay men were allowed to marry, where would we find the incentive to continue the progressive movement we have started that is pushing for societal and legal recognition of all kinds of family relationships? To create other options and alternatives? To find a place in the law for the elderly couple who, for companionship and economic reasons, live together but do not marry? To recognize the right of a long-time, but unmarried, gay partner to stay in his rent-controlled apartment after the death of his lover, the only named tenant on the lease? To recognize the family relationship of the lesbian couple and the two gay men who are jointly sharing child-raising responsibilities? To get the law to acknowledge that we may have more than one relationship worthy of legal protection?

Marriage for lesbians and gay men still will not provide a real choice unless we continue the work our community has begun to spread the privilege around to other relationships. We must first break the tradition of piling benefits and privileges on to those who are married, while ignoring the real life needs of those who are not. Only when we de-institutionalize marriage and bridge the economic and privilege gap between the married and the unmarried will each of us have a true choice. Otherwise, our choice not to marry will continue to lack legal protection and societal respect.

The lesbian and gay community has laid the groundwork for revolutionizing society's views of family. The domestic partnership movement has been an important part of this progress insofar as it validates non-marital relationships. Because it is not limited to sexual or romantic relationships, domestic partnership provides an important opportunity for many who are not related by blood or marriage to claim certain minimal protections.

It is crucial, though, that we avoid the pitfall of framing the push for legal recognition of domestic partners (those who share a primary residence and financial responsibilities for each other) as a stepping stone to marriage. We must keep our eyes on the goals of providing true alternatives to marriage and of radically reordering society's views of family.

The goals of lesbian and gay liberation must simply be broader than the right to marry. Gay and lesbian marriages may minimally transform the institution of marriage by diluting its traditional patriarchal dynamic, but they will not transform society. They will not demolish the two-tier system of the "haves" and the "have-nots." We must not fool ourselves into believing that marriage will make it acceptable to be gay or lesbian. We will be liberated only when we are respected and accepted for our differences and the diversity we provide to this society. Marriage is not a path to that liberation.

Notes

1. In arguing that lesbians and gay men should not want to enter the institution of marriage, Ettelbrick "essentializes" marriage. *See* Nan Hunter, *Marriage, Law, and Gender: A Feminist Inquiry*, 1 LAW & SEXUALITY 9, 17 (1991). By contrast, some commentators have expanded Stoddard's point that "[m]arriage between men or between women could . . . destabilize the cultural meaning of marriage," with positive implications for the institution. *Id*. They feel that, because "[h]omosexual couples by necessity throw into question the allocation of specific functions — whether professional, personal, or emotional — between the sexes," Jed Rubenfeld, *The Right of Privacy*, 102 HARV. L. REV. 737, 800 (1989), "[l]egalization of lesbian and gay marriage poses a threat to gender systems, not simply to antilesbian and antigay bigotry." Hunter, *supra*, at 18. In fact, say some, "it might do something amazing to the entire institution of marriage to recognize the unity of two 'persons' between whom no superiority or inferiority could be presumed on the basis of gender." CATHARINE MACKINNON, FEMINISM UNMODIFIED: DISCOURSES ON LIFE AND LAW 27 (1987).

2. Others, like Ettelbrick, have argued that this debate can be seen as one over who will be helped and who will be hurt by the legalization of same-sex marriage. *See* Harlon Dalton, *Reflections on the Lesbian and Gay Marriage Debate*, 1 LAW & SEXUALITY 1, 5 (1991). Some believe that, because "legal marriage is going to help some and hurt some roughly according to existing ranking of social power," lesbians and gay men should "be wary of package deals"

and instead adopt a strategy that allows "them to select the benefits from the burdens and to discard those aspects of marriage and divorce law that are not in their various interests." *See* Nitya Duclos, *Some Complicating Thoughts on Same-Sex Marriage*, 1 LAW & SEXUALITY 31, 59-61 (1991). Others, like Stoddard, emphasize that the costs of "picking and choosing" are often prohibitive for poorer couples.

3. Still others see in the achievement of marriage rights for gay people the weakening of efforts to redefine "couplehood" or "family" for those who arrange their lives outside the standard nuclear model because of cultural beliefs, sexual orientation, disability, or financial situation. Some lesbians have expressed the concern that gay marriage will cause society's lack of respect for "choice of relationships and family diversity" to be shared by other lesbians:

    > The specter of lesbian marriage and lesbian quasi-marriage . . . poses the danger of demarcating acceptable lesbians (married couples) from unacceptable lesbians (unmarried), as well as threatens to hetero-relationize and erase lesbianism. Marriage is an attempt to limit the multiplicity of relationships and the complexities of coupling in the lesbian experience.

    Ruthann Robson & S.E. Valentine, *Lov(h)ers: Lesbians as Intimate Partners and Lesbian Legal Theory*, 63 TEMP. L. Q. 511, 540 (1990).

4. Similarly, the legalization of same-sex marriage threatens to leave out those people who arrange their lives around two or more primary relationships. *See, e.g.,* Donna Minkowitz, *Patricia Ireland Takes the Reins*, ADVOCATE, Dec. 17, 1991, at 38, 40 (interviewing the president of the National Organization of Women, who has a male husband and a female companion); ARNO KARLEN, THREESOMES: STUDIES IN SEX, POWER, AND INTIMACY 148-78 (1988) (describing a three-way marriage).

C. The Prohibition of Same-Sex Marriage

BAKER v. NELSON

191 N.W.2d 185 (Minn. 1971),
appeal dismissed, 409 U.S. 810 (1972)

■ ■ ■

PETERSON, J.

■ ■ ■

Petitioners, Richard John Baker and James Michael McConnell, both adult male persons, made application to respondent, Gerald R. Nelson, clerk of Hennepin County District Court, for a marriage license. Re-spondent declined to issue the license on the sole ground that petitioners were of the same sex, it being undisputed that there were otherwise no statutory impediments to a heterosexual marriage by either petitioner.

■ ■ ■

1. Petitioners contend, first, that the absence of an express statutory prohibition against same-sex marriages evinces a legislative intent to authorize such marriages. We think, however, that a sensible reading of the statute discloses a contrary intent.

Minn.St.C. 517, which governs "marriage," employs that term as one of common usage, meaning the state of union between persons of the opposite sex.[1] It is unrealistic to think that the original draftsmen of our marriage statutes, which date from territorial days, would have used the term in any different sense. The term is of contemporary significance as well, for the present statute is replete with words of heterosexual import such as "husband and wife" and "bride and groom."

We hold, therefore, that Minn. St. c. 517 does not authorize marriage between persons of the same sex and that such marriages are accordingly prohibited.

2. Petitioners contend, second, that Minn. St. c. 517, so interpreted, is unconstitutional. There is a dual aspect to this contention: The prohibition of a same-sex marriage denies petitioners a fundamental right guaranteed by the Ninth Amendment to the United States Constitution, arguably made applicable to the states by the Fourteenth Amendment, and petitioners are deprived of liberty and property without due process and are denied the equal protection of the laws, both guaranteed by the Fourteenth Amendment.[2]

These constitutional challenges have in common the assertion that the right to marry without regard to the sex of the parties is a fundamental right of all persons and that restricting marriage to only couples of the opposite sex is irrational and invidiously discriminatory. We are not independently

persuaded by these contentions and do not find support for them in any decisions of the United States Supreme Court.

The institution of marriage as a union of man and woman, uniquely involving the procreation and rearing of children within a family, is as old as the book of Genesis. *Skinner v. Oklahoma* ex rel. *Williamson*, 316 U.S. 535, 541 (1942), which invalidated Oklahoma's Habitual Criminal Sterilization Act on equal protection grounds, stated in part: "Marriage and procreation are fundamental to the very existence and survival of the race." This historic institution manifestly is more deeply founded than the asserted contemporary concept of marriage and societal interests for which petitioners contend. The due process clause of the Fourteenth Amendment is not a charter for restructuring it by judicial legislation.

Griswold v. Connecticut, 381 U.S. 479 (1965), upon which petitioners rely, does not support a contrary conclusion. A Connecticut criminal statute prohibiting the use of contraceptives by married couples was held invalid, as violating the due process clause of the Fourteenth Amendment. The basic premise of that decision, however, was that the state, having authorized marriage, was without power to intrude upon the right of privacy inherent in the marital relationship. Mr. Justice Douglas, author of the majority opinion, wrote that this criminal statute "operates directly on an intimate relation of husband and wife," and that the very idea of its enforcement by police search of "the sacred precincts of marital bedrooms for telltale signs of the use of contraceptives . . . is repulsive to the notions of privacy surrounding the marriage relationship." In a separate opinion for three justices, Mr. Justice

---

1. Webster's Third New International Dictionary (1966) p. 1384 gives this primary meaning to marriage: "1 a: the state of being united to a person of the opposite sex as husband or wife."

   Black, Law Dictionary (4 ed.) p. 1123 states this definition: "Marriage . . . is the civil status, condition, or relation of one man and one woman united in law for life, for the discharge to each other and the community of the duties legally incumbent on those whose association is founded on the distinction of sex."

2. We dismiss without discussion petitioners' additional contentions that the statute contravenes the First Amendment and Eighth Amendment of the United States Constitution.

Goldberg similarly abhorred this state disruption of "the traditional relation of the family — a relation as old and as fundamental as our entire civilization."

The equal protection clause of the Fourteenth Amendment, like the due process clause, is not offended by the state's classification of persons authorized to marry. There is no irrational or invidious discrimination. Petitioners note that the state does not impose upon heterosexual married couples a condition that they have a proved capacity or declared willingness to procreate, posing a rhetorical demand that this court must read such condition into the statute if same-sex marriages are to be prohibited. Even assuming that such a condition would be neither unrealistic nor offensive under the *Griswold* rationale, the classification is no more than theoretically imperfect. We are reminded, however, that "abstract symmetry" is not demanded by the Fourteenth Amendment.

Loving v. Virginia, 388 U.S. 1 (1967), upon which petitioners additionally rely, does not militate against this conclusion. Virginia's antimiscegenation statute, prohibiting interracial marriages, was invalidated solely on the grounds of its patent racial discrimination. As Mr. Chief Justice Warren wrote for the court:

> "Marriage is one of the 'basic civil rights of man,' fundamental to our very existence and survival. To deny this fundamental freedom on so unsupportable a basis as the racial classifications embodied in these statutes, classifications so directly subversive of the principle of equality at the heart of the Fourteenth Amendment, is surely to deprive all the State's citizens of liberty without due process of law. The Fourteenth Amendment requires that the freedom of choice to marry not be restricted by invidious racial discriminations."[5]

Loving does indicate that not all state restrictions upon the right to marry are beyond reach of the Fourteenth Amendment. But in common sense and in a Constitutional sense, there is a clear distinction between a marital restriction based merely upon race and one based upon the fundamental difference in sex.

We hold, therefore, that Minn. St. c. 517 does not offend the First, Eighth, Ninth, or Fourteenth Amendments to the United States Constitution.

MCCONNELL v. ANDERSON

451 F.2d 193 (8th Cir. 1971),
cert. denied, 405 U.S. 1046 (1972)

STEPHENSON, Circuit Judge.

This case has its origin in a July 9, 1970 resolution of the University of Minnesota Board of Regents not to approve the application of James Michael McConnell to head, at the rank of Instructor, the cataloging division of the University's St. Paul campus library on the

---

5. *See also McLaughlin v. Florida*, 379 U.S. 184 (1964), in which the United States Supreme Court, for precisely the same reason of classification based only upon race, struck down a Florida criminal statute which proscribed and punished habitual cohabitation only if one of an unmarried couple was white and the other black.

ground that his "personal conduct, as represented in the public and University news media, is not consistent with the best interest of the University." McConnell's complaint alleged that he was offered the division head appointment in April 1970; that he accepted the offer in May 1970, but that the offer was withdrawn, pursuant to the foregoing resolution, after he and another male publicly applied for a marriage license at the Hennepin County, Minnesota Clerk's office.

On July 22, 1970, McConnell brought suit for injunctive relief in the United States District Court for the District of Minnesota . . . . [H]is complaint asserted that he was a homosexual and that the Board's resolution not to approve his employment application was premised on the fact of his homosexuality and upon his desire, as exemplified by the marriage license incident, specifically to publicly profess his "earnest" belief that homosexuals are entitled to privileges equal to those afforded heterosexuals. In further detail he alleged that the Board . . . subjected him to arbitrary, unreasonable and discriminatory action working a deprivation of his Fourteenth Amendment rights to equal protection of the laws and due process of law. . . . [The District Court] after conducting an oral hearing at which evidence was taken, entered judgment for McConnell and enjoined the Board from refusing to employ him "solely because, and on the grounds that he is a homosexual and that thereby 'his personal conduct, as presented in the public and University news media, is not consistent with the best interest of the University.'" 316 F.Supp. 809 (D. Minn. 1970). . . . We . . . reverse.

. . . McConnell apparently is well-educated and otherwise able, possessing both an academic degree and a master's degree; that he formerly was employed as Acquisitions Librarian at Park College in Missouri; that he is a member of the organization known as FREE (Fight Repression of Erotic Expression); that on May 18, 1970, McConnell and a friend referred to in the record as "Jack Baker" encountered Dr. Hopp and informed him of their intention to obtain a license to marry; that during this conversation Dr. Hopp expressed concern that such an occurrence might well jeopardize favorable consideration of McConnell's employment application; that about three hours later on the same day, McConnell and Jack Baker appeared at the Hennepin County Clerk's office and made formal application for the license; that this event received the attention of the local news and television media; that the Board's Faculty, Staff and Student Affairs Committee, on June 24, 1970, convened to initially consider the matter of McConnell's proposed appointment and voted that it be not approved; that McConnell promptly was so advised and given notice that he could request a hearing at the Committee's next scheduled meeting on July 9; that McConnell requested a hearing; that he and his counsel appeared at the meeting and were furnished copies of the resolution in its proposed form; that McConnell and his counsel took advantage of this opportunity to present information they deemed supportive of his application, and that at the conclusion of the presentation on McConnell's behalf, the Committee adopted the resolution. It perhaps is well at this point to note that McConnell makes no claim that the Board denied him procedural due process.

■ ■ ■

It is McConnell's position that the Board's decision not to approve his employment application reflects "a clear example of the unreasoning prejudice and revulsion some people feel when confronted by a homosexual." That being so, he argues that the Board's action was arbitrary and capricious and thus violative of his constitutional rights. We do not agree.

It is our conclusion that the Board possessed ample specific factual information on the basis of which it reasonably could conclude that the appointment would not be consistent with the best interests of the University. We need only to observe that the Board was given the unenviable task and duty of passing upon and judging McConnell's application against the background of his actual conduct. So postured, it is at once apparent that this is not a case involving mere homosexual propensities on the part of a prospective employee. Neither is it a case in which an applicant is excluded from employment because of a desire clandestinely to pursue homosexual conduct. It is, instead, a case in which something more than remunerative employment is sought; a case in which the applicant seeks employment on his own terms; a case in which the prospective employee demands, as shown both by the allegations of the complaint and by the marriage license incident as well, the right to pursue an activist role in *implementing* his unconventional ideas concerning the

societal status to be accorded homosexuals and, thereby, to foist tacit approval of this socially repugnant concept upon his employer, who is, in this instance, an institution of higher learning.[7] We know of no constitutional fiat or binding principle of decisional law which requires an employer to accede to such extravagant demands. We are therefore unable fairly to categorize the Board's action here as arbitrary, unreasonable or capricious.

■ ■ ■

Reversed, with directions to dissolve the injunction and to dismiss the action on the merits.

---

7. In the District Court McConnell apparently argued that he has the right to apply for a marriage license and that such is "symbolic speech" within the protection of the Free Speech and Due Process clauses of the First and Fourteenth Amendments. He relies largely on *Tinker v. Des Moines Ind. School Dist.*, 393 U.S. 503 (1969), a case from this circuit. Although this contention is not pressed here, we feel constrained to observe that we do not believe that *Tinker*, when read in light of its distinctive facts, can afford McConnell any comfort in this regard.

SINGER v. HARA

522 P.2d 1187 (Ct. App. Wash. 1974), *review denied,*
84 Wash. 2d 1008 (1974)

SWANSON, Chief Judge.

. . . [A]ppellants applied for a marriage license on September 20, 1971, and after respondent Hara refused to grant such a license, the motion to show cause was filed on April 27, 1972. In an order dated August 9, 1972, the trial court denied the motion . . . .

Appellants argue three basic assignments of error, namely, (1) the trial court

erred in concluding that the Washington marriage statutes, RCW 26.04.010 et seq., prohibit same-sex marriages; (2) the trial court's order violates the Equal Rights Amendment (ERA) to the Washington State Constitution, Const. art. 31, § 1; and (3) the trial court's order violates the eighth, ninth and fourteenth amendments to the United States Constitution.[1]

Directing our attention to appellants' first assignment of error, it is apparent from

---

1. Appellants also list as an "assignment of error" the assertion that the trial court's order "was based on the erroneous and fallacious conclusion that same-sex marriages are destructive to society." In support of this assertion, appellants

a plain reading of our marriage statutes that the legislature has not authorized same-sex marriages. Appellants argue that RCW 26.04.010 which authorizes marriages by "persons of the age of eighteen years, who are otherwise capable" includes no requirement that marriage partners be limited to one male and one female and that the phrase "who are otherwise capable" refers to the prohibitions of RCW 26.04.020-26.04.040 against certain marriages involving persons who are habitual criminals, diseased, insane, etc., but there is no prohibition against same-sex marriages. Appellants argue that the legislature has not defined the competency of marriage but only the competency of individuals seeking to marry; inasmuch as the appellants are both legally "capable" of marriage, they argue state law permits them to marry each other. As the state points out, however, the statutory language of RCW 26.04.010 relied upon by the appellants merely reflects a 1970 amendment which substituted the word "persons" for the prior references to "males" and "females" to implement the legislature's elimination of differing age requirements for marriage by the respective sexes. Further, RCW 26.04.210, relating to the affidavits required for the issuance of a marriage license, makes reference to "the male" and "the female" which clearly dispels any suggestion that the legislature intended to authorize same-sex marriages.[3] The trial court correctly concluded that the applicable marriage statutes do not permit same-sex marriage.

Appellants next argue that if, as we have held, our state marriage laws must be construed to prohibit same-sex marriages, such laws are unconstitutional when so applied. In this context, we consider appellants' second assignment of error which is directed to the proposition that the state prohibition of same-sex marriages violates the ERA which recently became part of our state constitution. The question thus presented is a matter of first impression in this state and, to our knowledge, no court in the nation has ruled upon the legality of same-sex marriage in light of an equal rights amendment. The ERA provides, in relevant part:

> Equality of rights and responsibility under the law shall not be denied or abridged on account of sex.

In seeking the protection of the ERA, appellants argue that the language of the

---

devote nearly 40 pages of their brief to what they characterize as a discussion of "the concept of homosexuality and same-sex marriages through the eyes of other important disciplines — that of the sociologists, theologians, scientists, and doctors." Appellants state that "a basic understanding of homosexuals and society is a precondition to an enlightened discussion of the legal grounds raised . . . " Although we do not quarrel with that proposition, we deem it appropriate to observe that appellants' discussion in that regard does not present a legal argument, nor is there any evidence in the record to suggest that the trial court in fact based its order on the "erroneous and fallacious conclusion" to which appellants take exception. Therefore, while we recognize that appellants have presented a valuable context for the discussion of their legal points, we have endeavored to confine this opinion to discussion of the legal issues presented without attempting to present our views on matters of sociology, theology, science and medicine.

3. Similarly, in the 1970 version of RCW 26.04.010 which was the statute in effect when appellants applied for their license, the proviso made reference to "the female," thus implying that a male was contemplated as the other marriage partner; if same-sex marriages had been contemplated, the legislature probably would have used the plural and referred to "females." The 1973 amendment to the proviso merely eliminated the provision that the statutory age requirement could only be waived by a superior court judge of the county in which the female resides and provided that such a waiver could be granted by a superior court judge of a county in which either party resides.

It is also noteworthy that the 1972 amendments to our state community property laws (RCW 26.16), by which the legislature sought to establish sexual equality in the management of community property, retain references to "husband" and "wife." Again, it is apparent that the legislature did not contemplate that sexual equality included provision for same-sex marriage.

amendment itself leaves no question of interpretation and that the essential thrust of the
ERA is to make sex an impermissible legal
classification. Therefore, they argue, to construe state law to permit a man to marry a
woman but at the same time to deny him the
right to marry another man is to construct an
unconstitutional classification "on account
of sex." In response to appellants' contention, the state points out that all same-sex
marriages are deemed illegal by the state,
and therefore argues that there is no violation
of the ERA so long as marriage licenses are
denied equally to both male and female
pairs. In other words, the state suggests that
appellants are not entitled to relief under the
ERA because they have failed to make a
showing that they are somehow being treated
differently by the state than they would be if
they were females. Appellants suggest, however, that the holdings in *Loving v. Virginia*,
388 U.S. 1 (1967); *Perez v. Lippold*, 198
P.2d 17 (Cal. 1948) [striking down
California's miscegnation statute]; and
J.S.K. Enterprises, Inc. v. Lacey, 492 P.2d
600 (Wash. 1971), are contrary to the position taken by the state. We disagree.

■ ■ ■

Although appellants suggest an analogy between the racial classification involved in
Loving and *Perez* and the alleged sexual
classification involved in the case at bar, we
do not find such an analogy. The operative
distinction lies in the relationship which is
described by the term "marriage" itself, and
that relationship is the legal union of one
man and one woman. Washington statutes,
specifically those relating to marriage
(RCW 26.04) and marital (community)
property (RCW 26.16), are clearly founded
upon the presumption that marriage, as a
legal relationship, may exist only between
one man and one woman who are otherwise
qualified to enter that relationship.[6] Similarly although it appears that the appellate
courts of this state until now have not been
required to define specifically what constitutes a marriage, it is apparent from a review
of cases dealing with legal questions arising
out of the marital relationship that the definition of marriage as the legal union of one
man and one woman who are otherwise
qualified to enter into the relationship not
only is clearly implied from such cases, but
also was deemed by the court in each case
to be so obvious as not to require recitation.[7]
Finally, the courts known by us to have
considered the question have all concluded
that same-sex relationships are outside of
the proper definition of marriage. *Jones v.
Hallahan*, 501 S.W.2d 588 (Ky.Ct.App.
1973); *Baker v. Nelson*, 191 N.W.2d 185
(Minn. 1971); *Anonymous v. Anonymous*,
325 N.Y.S.2d 499 (Sup.Ct. 1971). Appellants have cited no authority to the contrary.

Given the definition of marriage which
we have enunciated, the distinction between
the case presented by appellants and those
presented in *Loving* and *Perez* is apparent.
In *Loving* and *Perez*, the parties were barred
from entering into the marriage relationship

---

6. In this regard, we are aided by the rule of statutory construction that words of a statute must be understood in their
   usual and ordinary sense in the absence of a statutory definition to the contrary. We need not resort to the quotation of
   dictionary definitions to establish that "marriage" in the usual and ordinary sense refers to the legal union of one man
   and one woman.

7. Of course, many other cases could be cited and, in the context of the definition of marriage, it is significant that courts
   considering questions involving that legal relationship frequently utilize gender-related terms such as "husband" and
   "wife." For example, in divorce cases, which may be characterized as cases involving the dissolution of marriage, a
   commonly cited rule is that the amount of alimony to be awarded, if any, "depends upon the needs of the wife and the
   ability of the husband to pay . . . " Although, in appropriate circumstances, alimony may be awarded to "the husband"
   rather than to "the wife," it is clear that all marriages have one "husband" and one "wife." In the relationship proposed
   by appellants, there is no "wife" and therefore there can be no marriage.

because of an impermissible racial classification. There is no analogous sexual classification involved in the instant case because
appellants are not being denied entry into the
marriage relationship because of their sex;
rather, they are being denied entry into the
marriage relationship because of the recognized definition of that relationship as one
which may be entered into only by two persons who are members of the opposite sex.[8]
As the court observed in *Jones v. Hallahan*:
"In substance, the relationship proposed by
the appellants does not authorize the issuance of a marriage license because what they
propose is not a marriage." *Loving* and *Perez*
are inapposite.

J.S.K. Enterprises, Inc. v. Lacey, supra,
is also factually and legally dissimilar to the
case at bar. In that case, this court held that
a city ordinance which permitted massagists
to administer massages only to customers of
their own sex constituted discrimination on
the basis of sex, prohibited by the equal
protection clause of the fourteenth amendment to the United States Constitution, and
also violated RCW 49.12.200, relating to the
right of women to pursue any employment.
We see no analogy between the right of
women to administer massages to men and
the question of whether the prohibition

against same-sex marriages is unconstitutional. The right recognized in *J.S.K. Enterprises, Inc.*, on the basis of principles
applicable to employment discrimination
has nothing to do with the question presented
by appellants.

Appellants apparently argue, however,
that notwithstanding the fact that the equal
protection analysis applied in *Loving*, *Perez*
and *J.S.K. Enterprises, Inc.*, may render
those cases distinguishable from the case at
bar, the absolute language of the ERA requires the conclusion that the prohibition
against same-sex marriages is unconstitutional. In this context, appellants suggest that
definition of marriage, as the legal union of
one man and one woman, in and of itself,
when applied to appellants, constitutes a violation of the ERA. Therefore, appellants
contend, persons of the same sex must be
presumed to have the constitutional right to
marry one another in the absence of a countervailing interest or clear exception to the
ERA.

Appellants cite no case law in support of
their position, but direct our attention to the
analysis set forth in Note, *The Legality of
Homosexual Marriage*, 82 YALE L.J. 573
(1973), and in Brown, Emerson, Falk &
Freedman, *The Equal Rights Amendment: A*

---

8. Appellants argue that *Loving* and *Perez* are analogous to the case at bar notwithstanding what might be the "definition"
of marriage. They argue that at the time *Loving* and *Perez* were decided, marriage *by definition* barred interracial
marriages and that the *Loving* and *Perez* courts changed that definition through their interpretation of the Fourteenth
Amendment. Appellants suggest that the ERA operates in a manner analogous to the Fourteenth Amendment to require
us to change the definition of marriage to include same-sex marriages. We disagree. The *Loving* and *Perez* courts did
not change the basic definition of marriage as the legal union of one man and one woman; rather, they merely held that
the race of the man or woman desiring to enter that relationship could not be considered by the state in granting a
marriage license. In other words, contrary to appellants' contention, the Fourteenth Amendment did not require any
change in the definition of marriage and, as we hold today, neither does the ERA.

   To further illustrate our view, we suggest two examples of a situation which, contrary to the situation presented
in the case at bar, would raise questions of possible sexual discrimination prohibited by the ERA. First, if the
anti-miscegenation statutes involved in *Loving* and *Perez* had permitted white males to marry black females but
prohibited white females from marrying black males, then it is arguable that the statutes would be invalid not only
because of an impermissible racial classification under the Fourteenth Amendment but also because of an impermissible
sexual classification under the ERA. Second, if the state legislature were to change the definition of marriage to include
the legal union of members of the same sex but also provide that marriage licenses and the accompanying protections
of the marriage laws could only be extended to male couples, then it is likely that the state marriage laws would be in
conflict with the ERA for failure to provide equal benefits to female couples.

Constitutional Basis for Equal Rights for Women, 80 YALE L.J. 871 (1971). The latter article, however, is clearly written in the context of the impact of the ERA upon the rights of women and men as individuals and the authors make no suggestion that the ERA requires a change in the definition of marriage to include same-sex relationships. The authors suggest that the ERA prohibition of sex discrimination is "absolute," meaning that one person may not be favored over another where sex is the only distinguishing factor between the two. In that context, the authors state at 892:

> From this analysis it follows that the constitutional mandate must be absolute. The issue under the Equal Rights Amendment cannot be different but equal, reasonable or unreasonable classification, suspect classification, fundamental interest, or the demands of administrative expediency. Equality of rights means that sex is not a factor. This at least is the premise of the Equal Rights Amendment.

The author of the note, *The Legality of Homosexual Marriage*, *supra*, applies the aforementioned analysis of the ERA in the totally different context of same-sex relationships and thus concludes that the ERA requires that such relationships be accommodated by state marriage laws. We are not persuaded by such reasoning. We do not believe that approval of the ERA by the people of this state reflects any intention upon their part to offer couples involved in same-sex relationships the protection of our marriage laws. A consideration of the basic purpose of the ERA makes it apparent why that amendment does not support appellants' claim of discrimination. The primary purpose of the ERA is to overcome discriminatory legal treatment as between men and women "on account of sex." The popular slogan, "Equal pay for equal work," particularly expresses the rejection of the notion that merely because a person is a woman, rather than a man, she is to be treated differently than a man with qualifications equal to her own.

Prior to adoption of the ERA, the proposition that women were to be accorded a position in the law inferior to that of men had a long history.[10] Thus, in that context, the purpose of the ERA is to provide the legal protection, as between men and women, that apparently is missing from the state and federal Bills of Rights, and it is in light of that purpose that the language of the ERA must be construed. To accept the appellants' contention that the ERA must be interpreted to prohibit statutes which refuse to permit same-sex marriages would be to subvert the purpose for which the ERA was enacted by expanding its scope beyond that which was undoubtedly intended by the majority of the citizens of this state who voted for the amendment.

---

10. For example, Mr. Justice Bradley, in his concurring opinion upholding the refusal of a state court to license a woman to practice law in *Bradwell v. Illinois*, 83 U.S. (16 Wall.) 130, 141 (1872) stated in part:

> [The] civil law, as well as nature herself, has always recognized a wide difference in the respective spheres and destinies of man and woman. Man is, or should be, woman's protector and defender. The natural and proper timidity and delicacy which belongs to the female sex evidently unfits it for many of the occupations of civil life. The constitution of the family organization, which is founded in the divine ordinance, as well as in the nature of things, indicates the domestic sphere as that which properly belongs to the domain and functions of womanhood. The harmony, not to say identity, of interests and views which belong, or should belong, to the family institution is repugnant to the idea of a woman adopting a distinct and independent career from that of her husband. . . .
> . . . The paramount destiny and mission of woman are to fulfil the noble and benign offices of wife and mother. This is the law of the Creator.

We are of the opinion that a common-sense reading of the language of the ERA indicates that an individual is afforded no protection under the ERA unless he or she first demonstrates that a right or responsibility has been denied solely because of that individual's sex. Appellants are unable to make such a showing because the right or responsibility they seek does not exist. The ERA does not create any new rights or responsibilities, such as the conceivable right of persons of the same sex to marry one another; rather, it merely insures that existing rights and responsibilities, or such rights and responsibilities as may be created in the future, which previously might have been wholly or partially denied to one sex or to the other, will be equally available to members of either sex. The form of discrimination or difference in legal treatment which comes within the prohibition of the ERA necessarily is of an invidious character because it is discrimination based upon the fortuitous circumstance of one's membership in a particular sex per se. This is not to say, however, that the ERA prohibits all legal differentiations which might be made among males and females. A generally recognized "corollary" or exception to even an "absolute" interpretation of the ERA is the proposition that laws which differentiate between the sexes are permissible so long as they are based upon the unique physical characteristics of a particular sex, rather than upon a person's membership in a particular sex per se. *See* Brown, Emerson, Falk & Freedman, *The Equal Rights Amendment: A Constitutional Basis for Equal Rights for Women, supra* at 893-96.

In the instant case, it is apparent that the state's refusal to grant a license allowing the appellants to marry one another is not based upon appellants' status as males, but rather it is based upon the state's recognition that our society as a whole views marriage as the appropriate and desirable forum for procreation and the rearing of children. This is true even though married couples are not required to become parents and even though some couples are incapable of becoming parents and even though not all couples who produce children are married. These, however, are exceptional situations. The fact remains that marriage exists as a protected legal institution primarily because of societal values associated with the propagation of the human race. Further, it is apparent that no same-sex couple offers the possibility of the birth of children by their union. Thus the refusal of the state to authorize same-sex marriages results from such impossibility of reproduction rather than from an invidious discrimination "on account of sex." Therefore, the definition of marriage as the legal union of one man and one woman is permissible as applied to appellants, notwithstanding the prohibition contained in the ERA, because it is founded upon the unique physical characteristics of the sexes and appellants are not being discriminated against because of their status as males per se. In short, we hold the ERA does not require the state to authorize same-sex marriage.

Appellants' final assignment of error is based primarily upon the proposition that the state's failure to grant them a marriage license violates the equal protection clause of the Fourteenth Amendment to the United States Constitution.[11] The threshold question presented involves the standard by which to measure appellants' constitutional argument. We have held that the effect of our state marriage statutes is to prohibit same-sex marriages, and as a general proposition

---

11. Appellants also claim that their rights under the Eighth and Ninth Amendments, and under the Due Process Clause of the Fourteenth Amendment have been violated. In view of the conclusion we have reached with reference to appellants' claim under the Equal Protection Clause of the Fourteenth Amendment, we deem it unnecessary to discuss appellants' contentions with regard to the right to privacy under the Ninth Amendment and the right to due process under the Fourteenth Amendment. Further, we have determined that appellants' argument that denial of a marriage license to them constitutes cruel and unusual punishment prohibited by the Eighth Amendment is without merit.

such statutes must be presumed constitutional. The operative effect of such a presumption is that the statutory classification in question — the exclusion of same-sex relationships from the definition of marriage — does not offend the Equal Protection Clause if it rests upon some reasonable basis.

Appellants contend, however, that a standard stricter than such a "reasonable basis" test must be applied to the operation of our state marriage laws. Appellants point out that a fundamental right — the right to marry — is at stake in the instant litigation, directing our attention to *Loving v. Virginia, supra; Skinner v. Oklahoma*, 316 U.S. 535 (1942); and *Meyer v. Nebraska*, 262 U.S. 390 (1923). Moreover, appellants, reasoning primarily by analogy from *Loving* and related cases, argue that the statutory prohibition against same-sex marriages constitutes a classification based upon sex. Therefore, appellants urge that the applicable standard under the Equal Protection Clause requires that the classification be deemed "inherently suspect" and one which may not be sustained unless the state demonstrates that a "compelling state interest" so requires.

We do not take exception to the proposition that the Equal Protection Clause of the Fourteenth Amendment requires strict judicial scrutiny of legislative attempts at sexual discrimination. Our state Supreme Court has held that a legislative classification based upon sex is inherently suspect, *Hanson v. Hutt*, 517 P.2d 599 (Wash. 1973), as has a plurality of the United States Supreme

Court, *Frontiero v. Richardson*, 411 U.S. 677 (1973). As we have already held in connection with our discussion of the ERA, however, appellants do not present a case of sexual discrimination. Appellants were not denied a marriage license because of their sex; rather, they were denied a marriage license because of the nature of marriage itself.

Appellants appear to recognize the distinction we make because they also argue that the definition of marriage as it is reflected in our marriage statutes constitutes an inherently suspect classification because it discriminates against homosexuals as a group. In other words, appellants appear to present the alternative argument that although they are not being discriminated against because they are males, they are being discriminated against because they happen to be homosexual.

Although appellants present argument to the contrary,[12] we agree with the state's contention that to define marriage to exclude homosexual or any other same-sex relationships is not to create an inherently suspect legislative classification requiring strict judicial scrutiny to determine a compelling state interest. *Baker v. Nelson*, 191 N.W.2d 185 (Minn. 1971); *see Jones v. Hallahan, supra; Anonymous v. Anonymous, supra; see generally*, Note, *The Legality of Homosexual Marriage, supra* at 574-83. The state contends that the exclusion of same-sex relationships from our marriage statutes may be upheld under the traditional "reasonable

---

12. Appellants argue, in part, that homosexuals constitute a class having characteristics making any legislative classification applicable to them one having common denominators of suspectability. Thus, they argue homosexuals constitute "a politically voiceless and invisible minority," that being homosexual, generally speaking, is an immutable characteristic, *see Korematsu v. United States*, 323 U.S. 214 (1944); and that homosexuals are a group with a long history of discrimination subject to myths and stereotypes. *See generally*, Note, *The Legality of Homosexual Marriage, supra* at 575-78.

We are not unmindful of the fact that public attitude toward homosexuals is undergoing substantial, albeit gradual, change. *See generally*, Comment, *Homosexuality and the Law — A Right to be Different?*, 38 ALBANY L. REV. 84 (1973). Notwithstanding these considerations, we express no opinion upon the desirability of revising our marriage laws to accommodate homosexuals and include same-sex relationships within the definition of marriage. That is a question for the people to answer through the legislative process. We merely hold such a legislative change is not constitutionally required.

basis" or "rational relationship" test to which we have previously made reference. We agree.[13]

There can be no doubt that there exists a rational basis for the state to limit the definition of marriage to exclude same-sex relationships. Although, as appellants contend, other cultures may have fostered differing definitions of marriage, marriage in this state, as elsewhere in the nation, has been deemed a private relationship of a man and a woman (husband and wife) which involves "interests of basic importance in our society." *See Boddie v. Connecticut*, 401 U.S. 371, 376 (1971). Accordingly, subject to constitutional limitations, the state has exclusive dominion over the legal institution of marriage and the state alone has the "prerogative of creating and overseeing this important institution." *Coleman v. Coleman*, 291 N.E.2d 530 (Ohio 1972). *See also O'Neill v. Dent*, 364 F.Supp. 565 (E.D.N.Y. 1973).

We do not seek to define in detail the "interests of basic importance" which are served by retaining the present definition of marriage as the legal union of one man and one woman. The societal values which are involved in this area must be left to the examination of the legislature. For constitutional purposes, it is enough to recognize that marriage as now defined is deeply rooted in our society. Although, as appellants hasten to point out, married persons are not required to have children or even to engage in sexual relations, marriage is so clearly related to the public interest in af-

fording a favorable environment for the growth of children that we are unable to say that there is not a rational basis upon which the state may limit the protection of its marriage laws to the legal union of one man and one woman. Under such circumstances, although the legislature may change the definition of marriage within constitutional limits, the constitution does not require the change sought by appellants. As the court observed in *Baker v. Nelson, supra* at 186:

> The institution of marriage as a union of man and woman, uniquely involving the procreation and rearing of children within a family, is as old as the book of Genesis.... This historic institution manifestly is more deeply founded than the asserted contemporary concept of marriage and societal interests for which petitioners contend. The due process clause of the Fourteenth Amendment is not a charter for restructuring it by judicial legislation....
>
> The equal protection clause of the Fourteenth Amendment, like the due process clause, is not offended by the state's classification of persons authorized to marry.

Thus, for the reasons stated in this opinion, we hold that the trial court correctly concluded that the state's denial of a marriage license to appellants is required by our state statutes and permitted by both the state and federal constitutions.

The judgment is affirmed.

---

13. Appellants suggest that there is an intermediate "balancing" test applicable to equal protection analysis which allows no presumption in favor of the interests of either the individual or the state. Such an intermediate test, which some commentators have argued represents a merger of or departure from the "two tier" analysis involved in the application of the "strict scrutiny" and "rational basis" tests, may well be implied by recent opinions of the United States Supreme Court. *See, e.g., Frontiero v. Richardson, supra; Reed v. Reed*, 404 U.S. 71 (1971). Whatever the merits of such academic analysis, it is our view that the so-called traditional "rational relationship" test necessarily involves a balancing of the nature of a particular legislative classification, the interests of the individual affected by such classification, and the interests of the state (presumption of constitutionality) applicable to such legislative classification. Therefore, we shall continue to refer to the alternative tests of "strict scrutiny" and "rational basis" because there appears to be no need to define an intermediate test.

Notes

1. In addition to the courts in *Baker* and *Singer*, a Kentucky appellate court also rejected a challenge to its marriage statute in the early 1970s. *Jones v. Hallahan*, 501 S.W.2d 588 (Ky. Ct. App. 1973). Since those cases, three other challenges have also failed: *Dean v. District of Columbia*, No. 90-13892, (D.C. Super. Ct. Dec. 30, 1991) (gay men) (on appeal); *Baehr v. Lewin*, No. 91-1394-05, (Haw. Cir. Ct. 1st Cir. Sept. 3, 1991) (lesbians and gay men) (on appeal); *DeSanto v. Barnsley*, 476 A.2d 952 (Pa. Super. Ct. 1984) (gay men).

2. Unlike the other cases, *DeSanto* did not arise as a challenge to state officials' refusal to approve a marriage license. Instead, John DeSanto filed for divorce (with its concomitant benefits of alimony and equitable division of property) from William Barnsley, his lover of ten years. The appellate court affirmed the trial court's dismissal of the case, refusing to recognize common law marriages between persons of the same sex. The *Dean* decision also stated, in *dicta*, that common law marriages "require[] a male and a female participant." *Dean*, slip op. at 21.

3. Other courts have ruled against same-sex marriage in different contexts. An intermediate appellate court in New York, faced with a case in which a man had married another man who he thought was a woman, relied on dictionary definitions of marriage in ruling that "[t]he marriage ceremony itself was a nullity." *Anonymous v. Anonymous*, 325 N.Y.S.2d 499, 501 (Sup. Ct. 1971). In 1988, a circuit judge in Indiana denied two gay prisoners a license to marry and fined them $2,800 because "[t]heir claims about Indiana law and constitutional rights are wacky and sanctionably so." *See* Arthur Leonard, *Judge Denies Marriage License to Gay Male Prisoners*, 1988 LESBIAN/GAY L. NOTES 63. And in October 1991 an Ohio probate judge denied a marriage license to a gay couple, asserting that state law prohibits same-sex marriage. *See* Arthur Leonard, *Gay Washingtonians Sue for Marriage License*, 1991 LESBIAN/GAY L. NOTES 3.

4. In addition, the attorneys-general of six states have issued opinions that same-sex marriage is prohibited in their states despite statutory silence: Alabama (Mar. 1, 1983); Colorado (Apr. 24, 1975); Kansas (Aug. 4, 1977); Mississippi (July 10, 1978); South Carolina (Aug. 12, 1976); and Tennessee (Feb. 29, 1988). According to the South Carolina opinion, same-sex common law marriage is also prohibited. Furthermore, adopting the reasoning of *Singer*, the Maine Attorney General issued a formal opinion (Oct. 30, 1984) that adoption of the Equal Rights Amendment in Maine would not require the licensing of same-sex marriages.

5. While many of the cases rely on religion as the basis for not recognizing gay marriage, theologians have in fact debated issues of sexual orientation for several decades. *See generally* THE SAME SEX (Rev. Ralph W. Weltge ed., 1969); John Gallagher, *Rights Issues Split Protestant Churches: More Battles Expected*, ADVOCATE, June 10, 1991, at 14. Today, several Protestant denominations in the United States — notably the Unitarian Universalist Church and many Quaker congregations — recognize same-sex unions. *See* Plaintiffs' Memorandum on the History of Same-Sex Marriage, apps. 21 & 22, *Dean v. District of Columbia*, No. 90-13892 (D.C. Super. Ct. Dec. 30, 1991). Interestingly, there is strong evidence that the Catholic Church consecrated same-sex marriages from the fifth through at least the thirteenth century. *See id.* at John Boswell, *Homosexuality and Religious Life: A Historical Approach*, in HOMOSEXUALITY IN THE PRIESTHOOD AND RELIGIOUS LIFE 3, 11 (Jeanne Gramick ed., 1989). *See generally* John Boswell, CHRISTIANITY, SOCIAL TOLERANCE, AND HOMOSEXUALITY (1980).

   Same-sex marriages have also been recognized by many cultures outside the Judeo-Christian tradition. *See id.* at 26, 54 (1980) (arguing that same-sex marriages existed in ancient Greece, Boeotia, and Crete); CLELLAN FORD & FRANK BEACH, PATTERNS OF SEXUAL BEHAVIOR 130-31

(1951) (stating that many tribal cultures had same-sex marriages); JONATHAN KATZ, GAY AMERICAN HISTORY 281-334, 439-89 (1976) (describing same-sex marriages among Native American tribes); James McGough, *Deviant Marriage Patterns In Chinese Society, in* NORMAL AND ABNORMAL BEHAVIOR IN CHINESE CULTURE 171, 171-201 (Arthur Kleinman & Tsung-Yi Lin eds., 1981) (describing same-sex marriages in Imperial China). It has been argued that prohibitions on same-sex marriage violate freedom of religion. *See* Sherryl Michaelson, Note, *Religion and Morality Legislation: A Reexamination of Establishment Clause Analysis*, 59 N.Y.U. L. REV. 301, 307-11, 388-97 (1984).

6. A number of cases discuss procreation and child-rearing as a fundamental purpose of marriage, although no states actually require couples to procreate — or to be capable of procreation — as a condition precedent to receiving a marriage license. Moreover, *Griswold v. Connecticut* could be read as establishing the proposition that the state must recognize marriages even if procreation is actively avoided. The refusal to recognize same-sex marriages because they do not lead to procreation has been criticized as violative of religious freedom. *See* Sherryl Michaelson, Note, *Religion and Morality Legislation: A Reexamination of Establishment Clause Analysis*, 59 N.Y.U. L. REV., 301, 309-10, 393 (1984). Interestingly, some scholars believe that biblical prohibitions against same-sex sexual acts are less a condemnation of homosexuality than a result of the emphasis on procreation for perpetuation of the species. *See* MAURY JOHNSTON, GAYS UNDER GRACE: A GAY CHRISTIAN'S RESPONSE TO THE MORAL MAJORITY 57 (1983).

7. Like James McConnell, who had his job offer withdrawn by the University of Minnesota after he challenged that state's marriage laws — *see supra* at 408; *see also* KAY TOBIN & RANDY WICKER, THE GAY CRUSADERS 135-55 (1972) — others who have challenged the same-sex marriage bans have often done so at great personal cost. John Singer, the plaintiff in *Singer v. Hara*, was fired by his employer (ironically, the federal Equal Employment Opportunity Commission) partially as a result of the publicity surrounding his attempt to marry Paul Barwick. Singer challenged his discharge but lost. *See supra* at 285, discussing *Singer v. United States Civil Serv. Comm'n*, 530 F.2d 247 (1976), *vacated*, 429 U.S. 1034 (1977).

Even those who do not seek legal recognition of their same-sex marriages may risk employers' retaliations. Georgia Attorney General Michael Bowers (the defendant and petitioner in *Bowers v. Hardwick*) withdrew a job offer to Robin Shahar on learning that she planned to marry her lover in a religious ceremony. Shahar has challenged Bowers' action primarily as a violation of her religious freedom. *Shahar v. Bowers*, 58 Fair Empl. Prac. Cas. (BNA) 668 (N.D. Ga. 1992) (denying motion to dismiss).

Furthermore, the military's ban on lesbians and gay men provides as a basis for separation a finding that "[t]he member has married or attempted to marry a person known to be of the same biological sex . . . ." U.S. Army Reg. 135-175 § 2-39(c).

8. In the context of some gay rights statutes, political expediency has led proponents to disavow that their legislation would confer marriage rights on lesbians and gay men. Thus, for instance, Massachusetts' gay rights law states unequivocally, " Nothing in this act shall be construed so as to legitimize or validate a 'homosexual marriage,' so-called, or to provide health insurance or related employee benefits to a 'homosexual spouse', so-called." MASS. ANN. LAWS ch. 151B § 4 (notes) (Law. Co-op 1992). *See* Peter Cicchino, Bruce Deming & Katherine Nicholson, Note, *Sex, Lies, and Civil Rights: A Critical History of the Massachusetts Gay Civil Rights Bill*, 26 HARV. C.R.-C.L. L. REV. 549, 612 (1991).

Regardless of their legislative history, laws that prohibit discrimination on the basis of sexual orientation have not proved useful in challenges to same-sex marriage bans. The first such decision, by the Illinois Human Relations Commission, found that Chicago's anti-discrimination ordinance was not intended to overturn the state's marriage laws. *See* Arthur Leonard, *Gay Jounalists Can't Marry (Each Other)*, 1990 LESBIAN/GAY L. NOTES 9.

The *Dean* decision considered the legislative history of the District of Columbia Human Rights Act, one of the broadest in the country, which requires that lesbians and gay men be accorded "equal opportunity to participate in all aspects of life." D.C. CODE ANN. § 1-2511 (1987). Nevertheless, the court relied instead on inferences from the contemporaneous enactment of the District of Columbia's marriage law. The court went so far as to say that even if the Human Rights Act were applicable, "it simply is inaccurate to say that plaintiffs were denied a marriage license due to their 'sexual orientation'. Two heterosexuals of the same sex who, for *whatever* reason, had sought such a license, would have been similarly treated." *See Dean*, slip op. at 25-26 (emphasis in original).

Although Hawaii has a gay rights law, the plaintiffs in *Baehr v. Lewin* did not rely on it. The court cited the law, though, for the ironic proposition that gay men and lesbians in the state are not politically powerless and therefore are not entitled to special solicitousness from the courts as a suspect class such as Blacks, foreigners, or naturalized U.S. citizens. *See Baehr*, slip op. at 5.

9. No nation legally recognizes same-sex marriages. Nevertheless, Sweden, Denmark, and several municipalities in the Netherlands do afford lesbian and gay couples the traditional property rights of marriage, although none allows for adoption or joint custody of children by gay couples. While the Swedish law recognizes "co-habitees," thereby equating gay couples with unmarried heterosexual couples, the Danish law recognizes gay couples who enter into "registered partnerships" that are more like marriage. Over 400 Danish gay couples registered within twenty days of this law's taking effect in October 1989. The Netherlands also has a national law that gives all couples, straight or gay, married or unmarried, equal tax treatment. *See News In Brief*, ADVOCATE, July 16, 1991, at 35 (discussing marriage law in the Netherlands); Sheila Rule, *Rights for Gay Couples in Denmark*, N. Y. TIMES, Oct. 2, 1989, at 8; Arthur Leonard, *Denmark Approves Lesbian and Gay Marriage*, 1989 LESBIAN/GAY L. NOTES 39; Eva Ahlberg, *Live-In Lovers in Sweden, Including Gays, Given Same Rights as Married Couples*, L. A. TIMES, Mar. 27, 1988, at 15.

The Danish law requires that at least one partner be a Danish citizen, raising some interesting immigration law issues. Six countries (Australia, Denmark, the Netherlands, New Zealand, Norway, and Sweden) recognize gay partners of several years' duration for immigration and residency purposes. *See* Arthur Leonard, *More Countries Recognize Gay Partners Immigration*, 1991 LESBIAN/GAY L. NOTES 82. The United States, which only recently rescinded its outright ban on immigration of lesbians and gay men, *see* Arthur Leonard, *Congress Repeals Anti-Gay Immigration Policies*, 1990 LESBIAN/GAY L. NOTES 77, does not recognize gay partners for immigration purposes. *See Adams v. Howerton*, 673 F.2d 1036 (9th Cir.), *cert. denied*, 458 U.S. 1111 (1982).

10. Regardless of their legal rights, many lesbian and gay couples choose to "marry" in a social or religious sense. The 1988 Partners National Survey of Lesbian and Gay Couples (cited in Elizabeth Rhodes, *New Ties That Bind*, SEATTLE TIMES, July 21, 1991, at K1) showed that gay couples observe the following relationship rituals: 57 percent of women and 36 percent of men wear rings; 19 percent of women and 11 percent of men hold a ceremony; and 12 percent of women and 9 percent of men participate in some other ritual.

Some newspapers now run announcements of lesbian and gay ceremonies on their wedding pages. *See* Arthur Leonard, *Private Sector Recognition for Domestic Partners*, 1991 LESBIAN/GAY L. NOTES 4; Al Patrick, *Wedding Notes Go Gay at Inquirer,* PHILADELPHIA GAY NEWS, Mar. 13-19, 1992, at 1. An attempt has been made by at least one state legislator to include a lesbian couple in resolutions honoring anniversaries of state citizens. *See* Arthur Leonard, *Honoring Lesbian Couple Not Routine*, 1991 LESBIAN/GAY L. NOTES 41 (describing efforts in the Texas House of Representatives to pass a resolution honoring a lesbian couple's twentieth anniversary).

◆

MY MARRIAGE TO VENGEANCE
David Leavitt

When I got the invitation to Diana's wedding — elegantly embossed, archaically formal (the ceremony, it stated, would take place at "twelve-thirty o'clock")—the first thing I did was the TV Guide crossword puzzle. I was not so much surprised by Diana getting married as I was by her inviting me. What, I wondered, would motivate a person like Diana to ask her former lover, a woman she had lived with for a year and a month and whose heart she had suddenly and callously broken, to a celebration of her union with a man? It seems to me that that is asking for trouble.

I decided to call Leonore, who had been a close friend of Diana's and mine during the days when we were together, and who always seemed to have answers. "Leonore, Diana's getting married," I said when she picked up the phone.

"If you ask me," Leonore said, "she's wanted a man since day one. Remember that gay guy she tried to make it with? He said he wanted to change, have kids and all?" She paused ominously, "It's not him, is it?"

I looked at the invitation. "Mark Charles Cadwallader," I said.

"Well, for his sake," Leonore said, "I only hope he knows what he's getting into. As for Miss Diana, her doings are of no interest to me."

"But, Leonore," I said, "the question is: Should I go to the wedding?" imagining myself, suddenly, in my red T-shirt that said BABY BUTCH (a present from Diana), reintroducing myself to her thin, severe, long-necked mother, Marjorie Winters.

"I think that would depend on the food," Leonore said.

After I hung up, I poured myself some coffee and propped the invitation in front of me to look at. For the first few seconds it hadn't even clicked who was getting married. I had read: "Mr. and Mrs. Humphrey Winters cordially invite you to celebrate the wedding of their daughter, Diana Helaine," and thought: Who is Diana Helaine? Then it hit me, because for the whole year and a month, Diana had refused to tell me what her middle initial stood for — positively refused, she said, out of embarrassment, while I tried to imagine what horrors could lie behind that "H" — Hildegarde? Hester? Hulga? She was coyly, irritatingly insistent about not letting the secret out, like certain girls who would have nothing to do with me in eighth grade. Now she was making public to the world what she insisted on hiding from me, and it made perfect sense. Diana Helaine, not a different person, is getting married, I thought, and it was true, the fact in and of itself didn't surprise me. During the year and a month, combing the ghost of her once knee-length hair, I couldn't count how many times she'd said, very off-the-cuff, "You know, Ellen, sometimes I think this lesbian life is for the birds. Maybe I should just give it up, get married and have two point four babies." I'd smile and say, "If you do that, Diana, you can count on my coming to the wedding with a shotgun and shooting myself there in front of everybody." To which, still strumming her hair like a guitar and staring into the mirror, she would respond only with a faint smile, as if she could think of nothing in the world she would enjoy more.

First things first: We were lovers, and I don't mean schoolgirls touching each other in exploratory ways in dormitories after dark. I

DAVID LEAVITT, *My Marriage To Vengeance, in* A PLACE I'VE NEVER BEEN 35 (1990).

mean, we lived together, shared tampons and toothpaste, had one bed to sleep on, and for all the world (and ourselves) to see. Diana was in law school in San Francisco, and I had a job at Milpitas State hospital (I still do). Each day I'd drive an hour and a half there and an hour and a half back, and when I got home Diana would be waiting for me in bed, a fat textbook propped on her lap. We had couple friends, Lenore and Callie, for instance, and were always invited to things together, and when she left me, we were even thinking about getting power of attorney over each other. I was Diana's first woman lover, though she had had plenty of boyfriends. I had never slept with a boy, but had been making love with girls since early in high school. Which meant that for me, being a lesbian was just how things were. But for Diana — well, from day one it was adventure, event and episode. For a while we just had long blushing talks over pizza, during which she confessed she was "curious." It's ridiculous how many supposedly straight girls come on to you that way — plopping themselves down on your lap and fully expecting you to go through all the hard work of initiating them into Sapphic love out of sheer lust for recruitment. No way, I said. The last thing I need is to play guinea pig, testing ground, only to be left when the fun's over and a new boyfriend shows up on the horizon. But no, Diana said. I mean, yes, I think I *do*. I mean, I think I *am*. At which point she would always have just missed the last bus home and have to spend the night in my bed, where it was only a matter of time before I had no more defenses.

After we became lovers, Diana cut her hair off, and bought me the BABY BUTCH T-shirt. She joined all sorts of groups and organizations, dragged me to unsavory bars, insisted, fiercely, on telling her parents everything. (They did not respond well.) Only in private did she muse over her other options. I think she thought she was rich enough not to have to take any vow or promise all that seriously. Rich people are like that, I have noticed. They think a love affair is like a shared real estate venture they can just buy out of when they get tired of it.

Diana had always said the one reason she definitely wanted to get married was for the presents, so the day before the wedding I took my credit card and went to Nordstrom's, where I found her name in the bridal registry and was handed a computer printout with her china pattern, silver, stainless and other assorted requirements. I was already over my spending limit, so I bought her the ultimate — a Cuisinart — which I had wrapped to carry in white crepe paper with a huge yellow bow. Next came the equally important matter of buying myself a dress for the wedding. It had been maybe five, six years since I'd owned a dress. But buying clothes is like riding a bicycle — it comes back — and soon, remembering age-old advice from my mother on hems and necklines, I had picked out a pretty yellow sundress with a spattering of daisies, and a big, wide-brimmed hat.

The invitation had been addressed to Miss Ellen Britchkey and guest, and afterwards, in the parking lot, that made me think about my life — how there was no one in it. And then, as I was driving home from Nordstrom's, for the first time in years I had a seizure of accident panic. I couldn't believe I was traveling sixty miles an hour, part of a herd of speeding cars which passed and raced each other, coming within five or six inches of collision and death every ten seconds. It astonished me to realize that I drove every day of my life, that every day of my life I risked ending my life, that all I had to do was swerve the wrong way, or look only in the front and not the side mirror, and I might hit another car, or hit a child on the way to a wedding, and have to live for the rest of my life with the guilt, or die. Horrified, I headed right, into the slow lane. The slow lane was full of scared women, crawling home alone. It was no surprise to me. I was one with the scared women crawling home alone. After Diana left me, I moved down the peninsula to a miniature house —

that is the only way to describe it — two rooms with a roof, and shingles, and big pretty windows. It was my solitude house, my self-indulgence house, my remorse-and-secret-pleasure house. There I ate take-out Chinese food, read and reread *Little House on the Prairie*, stayed up late watching reruns of *Star Trek* and *The Honeymooners*. I lived by my wits, by survival measures. The television was one of those tiny ones, the screen smaller than a human face.

Diana — I only have one picture of her, and it is not a good likeness. In it she wears glasses and has long, long hair, sweeping below the white fringe of the picture, to her behind. She cut all her hair off as an offering to me the day after the first night we made love, and presented it that evening in a box — two neat braids, clipped easily as toenail parings, offered like a dozen roses. I stared at them, the hair still braided, still fresh with the smell of shampoo, and joked that I had bought her a comb, like in "The Gift of the Magi." "Don't you see?" she said. "I did it for you — I changed myself for you, as an act of love." I looked at her, her new boyish bangs, her face suddenly so thin-seeming without its frame of yellow hair. She was used to big gestures, to gifts that made an impact.

"Diana," I lied (for I had loved her long hair), "it's the most generous thing anyone's ever done for me." To say she'd done it for me — well, it was a little bit like a mean trick my sister pulled on me one Christmas when we were kids. She had this thing about getting a little tiny tree to put on top of the piano. And I, of course, wanted a great big one, like the Wagner family down the block. And then, about ten days before Christmas, she said, "Ellen, I have an early Christmas present for you," and she handed me a box, inside which were about a hundred miniature Christmas-tree ornaments.

I can recognize a present with its own motive.

If I've learned one thing from Diana, it's that there's more to a gift than just giving.

The next day was the day of the wedding, and somehow, without hitting any children, I drove to the hotel in Hillsborough where the ceremony and reception were taking place. A doorman escorted me to a private drawing room where, nervous about being recognized, I kept the Cuisinart in front of my face as long as I could, until finally an older woman with a carnation over her breast, apparently an aunt or something, said, "May I take that, dear?" and I had to surrender the Cuisinart to a table full of presents, some of which were hugely and awkwardly wrapped and looked like human heads. I thanked her, suddenly naked in my shame, and sturdied myself to brave the drawing room, where the guests milled. I recognized two or three faces from college, all part of Diana's set — rich, straight, preppy, not the sort I had hung around with at all. And in the distance I saw her very prepared parents, her mother thin and severe-looking as ever in a sleeveless black dress, her streaked hair cut short, like Diana's, her neck and throat nakedly displaying a brilliant jade necklace, while her father, in his tuxedo, talked with some other men and puffed at a cigar. Turning to avoid them, I almost walked right into Walter Bevins, who was Diana's gay best friend, or "hag fag," in college, and we were so relieved to see each other we grabbed a couple of whiskey sours and headed to as secluded a corner as we could find. "Boy, am I glad to see a familiar face," Walter said. "Can you believe this? Though I must say, I never doubted Diana would get married in anything less than splendor."

"Me neither," I admitted. "I was just a little surprised that Diana was getting married at all."

"Weren't we all!" Walter said. "But he seems like a nice guy. A lawyer, of course. *Very* cute, a real shame that he's heterosexual, if you ask me. But apparently she loves him and he loves her, and that's just fine. Look, there he is."

Walter pointed to a tall, dark man with a mustache and beard who stood in the middle of a circle of elderly women. To my horror, his eye caught ours, and he disentangled himself from the old women and walked over to where we were sitting. "Walter," he said. Then he looked at me and said, "Ellen?"

I nodded and smiled.

"Ellen, Ellen," he said, and reached out a hand which, when I took it, lifted me from the safety of my sofa onto my feet. "It is such a pleasure to meet you," he said. "Come with me for a second. I've wanted a chance to talk with you for so long, and once the wedding takes place — who knows?"

I smiled nervously at Walter, who raised a hand in comradeship, and was led by the groom through a door to an antechamber, empty except for a card table piled high, with bridesmaids' bouquets. "I just want you to know," he said, "how happy Diana and I are that you could make it. She speaks so warmly of you. And I also want you to know, just so there's no tension, Diana's told me everything and I'm fully accepting of her past."

"Thank you, Mark," I said, horrified that at my age I could already be part of someone's "past." It sounded fake to me, as if lesbianism was just a stage Diana had passed through, and I was some sort of perpetual adolescent, never seeing the adult light of heterosexuality.

"Charlie," Mark said. "I'm called Charlie."

He opened the door, and as we were heading back out into the drawing room, he said, "Oh, by the way, we've seated you next to the schizophrenic girl. Your being a social worker and all, we figured you wouldn't mind."

"Me?" I said. "Mind? Not at all."

"Thanks. Boy, is Diana going to be thrilled to see you."

Then he was gone into the crowd.

Once back in the drawing room I searched for Walter, but couldn't seem to find him. I was surrounded on all sides by elderly women with elaborate, peroxided hairdos. Their purses fascinated me. Some were hard as shell and shaped like kidneys, others made out of punctured leather that reminded me of birth control pill dispensers.

Suddenly I found myself face to nose with Marjorie Winters, whose eyes visibly bulged upon recognizing me. We had met once, when Diana had brought me home for a weekend, but that was before she had told her mother the nature of our relationship. After Diana came out — well, I believe the exact words were, "I never want that woman in my house again."

"Ellen," Marjorie said now, just as I had imagined she might. "What a surprise." She smiled, whether with contempt or triumph I couldn't tell.

"Well, you know I wouldn't miss Diana's wedding, Mrs. Winters," I said, smiling. "And this certainly is a lovely hotel."

She smiled. "Yes, isn't it? Red, look who's here," she said, and motioned over her husband, who for no particular reason except that his name was Humphrey was called Red. He was an amiable, absent-minded man, and he stared at me in earnest, trying to figure out who I was.

"You remember Diana's friend Ellen, from college, don't you?"

"Oh yes," he said. "Of course." Clearly he knew nothing. I believe his wife liked to keep him in a perpetual dark like that, so that he wouldn't be distracted from earning money.

"Ellen's a social worker," Marjorie said, "at the state hospital at Milpitas. So Diana and I thought it would be a good idea to seat her next to the schizophrenic girl, don't you think?"

"Oh yes," Red said. "Definitely. I imagine they'll have a lot of things to talk about."

A little tinkling bell rang, and Marjorie said, "Oh goodness, that's my cue. Be a dear, and do take care of Natalie." Squeezing my hand, she was gone. She had won, and she was glorying in her victory. And not for the first time that day, I wondered. Why is it that the people who always win always win?

The guests were beginning to move outdoors, to the garden, where the ceremony was taking place. Lost in the crowd, I spied Walter and maneuvered my way next to him. "How's it going, little one?" he said.

"I feel like a piece of shit," I said. I wasn't in the mood to make small talk.

"That's what weddings are for," he said cheerfully. We headed through a pair of french doors into a small, beautiful garden, full of blooming roses and wreaths and huge baskets of wisteria and lilies. Handsome, uniformed men — mostly brothers of the groom, I presumed — were helping everyone to their seats. Thinking we were a couple, one of them escorted Walter and me to one of the back rows, along with several other young couples, who had brought their babies and might have to run out to change a diaper or something in the middle of the ceremony.

As soon as everyone was seated the string quartet in the corner began to play something sweet and Chopin-like, and then the procession started — first Diana's sister, who was matron of honor, then the bridesmaids, each arm in arm with an usher, each dressed in a different pastel dress which was coordinated perfectly with her bouquet; and then, finally, Diana herself, looking resplendent in her white dress. Everyone gave out little oohs and aahs as she entered, locked tight between her parents. It had been two years since we'd seen each other, and looking at her, I thought I'd cry. I felt like such a piece of nothing, such a worthless piece of garbage without her — she was really that beautiful. Her hair was growing back, which was the worst thing. She had it braided and piled on her head and woven with wildflowers. Her skin was flawless, smooth — skin I'd touched hundreds, thousands of times — and there was an astonishing brightness about her eyes, as if she could see right through everything to its very heart. From the altar, the groom looked on, grinning like an idiot, a proud possessor who seemed to be saying, with his teary grin, see, look what I've got, look what chose me. And Diana too, approaching him at the altar, was all bright smiles, no doubt, no regret or hesitation registering in her face, and I wondered what she was thinking now; if she was thinking about her other life,

her long committed days and nights as a lesbian.

The music stopped. They stood, backs to us, the audience, before the reverent reverend. He began to lecture them solemnly. And then I saw it. I saw myself stand up, run to the front of the garden, and before anyone could say anything, do anything, pull out the gun and consummate, all over the grass, my own splendid marriage to vengeance.

But of course I didn't do anything like that. Instead I just sat there with Walter and listened as Diana, love of my life, my lover, my life, repeated the marriage vows, her voice a little trembly, as if to suggest she was just barely holding in her tears. They said their "I do"s. They exchanged rings. They kissed, and everyone cheered.

At my table in the dining room were seated Walter; the Winterses' maid, Juanita; her son; the schizophrenic girl; and the schizophrenic girl's mother. It was in the darkest, most invisible corner of the room, and I could see it was no accident that Marjorie Winters had gathered us all here — all the misfits and minorities, the kooks and oddities of the wedding. For a minute, sitting down and gazing out at the other tables, which were full of beautiful women and men in tuxedos, I was so mad at Diana I wanted to run back to the presents table and reclaim my Cuisinart, which I really couldn't afford to be giving her anyway, and which she certainly didn't deserve. But then I realized that people would probably think I was a thief and call the hotel detective or the police, and I decided not to.

The food, Leonore would have been pleased to know, was mediocre. Next to me, the schizophrenic girl stabbed with her knife at a pathetic-looking little bowl of melon balls and greenish strawberries, while her mother looked out exhaustedly, impatiently, at the expanse of the hotel dining room. Seeing that the schizophrenic girl had started, Juanita's son, who must have been seven feet tall, began eating as well, but she slapped his hand. Not wanting to embarrass him by staring, I looked at the schizophrenic girl. I knew she was the schizophrenic girl by her glasses — big, ugly, red ones from the seventies, the kind where the temples start at the bottom of the frames — and the way she slumped over her fruit salad, as if she was afraid someone might steal it.

"Hello," I said to her.

She didn't say anything. Her mother, dragged back into focus, looked down at her and said, "Oh now, Natalie."

"Hello," Natalie said.

The mother smiled. "Are you with the bride or the groom?" she asked.

"The bride."

"Relation?"

"Friend from college."

"How nice," the mother said. "We're with the groom. Old neighbors. Natalie and Charlie were born the same day in the same hospital, isn't that right, Nat?"

"Yes," Natalie said.

"She's very shy," the mother said to me, and winked.

Across the table Walter was asking Juanita's son if he played basketball. Shyly, in a Jamaican accent, he admitted that he did. His face was as arch and stern as that of his mother, a fat brown woman with the eyes of a prison guard. She smelled very clean, almost antiseptic.

"Natalie, are you in school?" I asked.

She continued to stab at her fruit salad, not really eating it as much as trying to decimate the pieces of melon.

"Tell the lady, Natalie," said her mother.

"Yes."

"Natalie's in a very special school," the mother said.

"I'm a social worker," I said. "I understand about Natalie."

"Oh really, you are?" the mother said, and relief flushed her face. "I'm so glad. It's so painful, having to explain — you know — "

Walter was trying to get Juanita to reveal the secret location of the honeymoon. "I'm not saying," Juanita said. "Not one word."

"Come on," said Walter. "I won't tell a soul, I swear."

"I'm on TV," Natalie said.

"Oh now," said her mother.

"I am. I'm on *The Facts of Life*. I'm Tuti."

"Now, Natalie, you know you're not."

"And I'm also on *All My Children* during the day. It's a tough life, but I manage."

"Natalie, you know you're not to tell these stories."

"Did someone mention *All My Children*?" asked Juanita's son.

Walter, too, looked interested.

"My lips are forever sealed," Juanita said to no one in particular. "There's no chance no way no one's going to get me to say one word."

Diana and Ellen, Ellen and Diana. When we were together, everything about us seethed. We lived from seizure to seizure. Our fights were glorious, manic, our need to fight like an allergy, something that reddens and irritates the edges of everything and demands release. Once Diana broke the air conditioner and I wouldn't forgive her. "Leave me alone," I screamed.

"No," she said. "I want to talk about it. Now."

"Well, I don't."

"Why are you punishing me?" Diana said. "It's not my fault."

"I'm not punishing you."

"You are. You're shutting me up when I have something I want to say."

"Damn it, won't you just leave me alone? Can't you leave anything alone?"

"Let me say what I have to say, damn it!"

"What?"

"I didn't break it on purpose! I broke it by accident!"

"Damn it, Diana, leave me the fuck alone! Why don't you just go away?"

"You are so hard!" Diana said, tears in her eyes, and slammed out the door into the bedroom.

After we fought, consumed, crazed, we made love like animals, then crawled about the house for days, cats in a cage, lost in a torpor of lazy carnality. It helped that the air conditioner was broken. It kept us slick. There was always, between us, heat and itch.

Once, in those most desperate, most re-morse-filled days after Diana left, before I moved down the peninsula to my escape-hatch dream house, I made a list which was titled "Reasons I love her."

1. Her hair.
2. Her eyes.
3. Her skin. (Actually, most of her body except maybe her elbows.)
4. The way she does voices for the plants when she waters them, saying things like "Boy, was I thirsty, thanks for the drink." (This one was a lie. That habit actually infuriated me.)
5. Her advantages: smart and nice.
6. Her devotion to me, to us as a couple.
7. How much she loved me.
8. Her love for me.
9. How she loves me.

There was less to that list than met the eye. When Diana left me — and it must be stated, here and now, she did so cruelly, callously, and suddenly — she said that the one thing she wanted me to know was that she still considered herself a lesbian. It was only me she was leaving. "Don't think I'm just another straight girl who used you," she insisted, as she gathered all her things into monogrammed suitcases. "I just don't feel we're right for each other. You're a social worker. I'm not good enough for you. Our lives, our ideas about the world — they're just never going to mesh."

Outside, I knew, her mother's station wagon waited in ambush. Still I pleaded. "Diana," I said, "you got me into this thing. You lured me in, pulled me in against my will. You can't leave just like that."

But she was already at the door. "I want you to know," she said, "because of you, I'll be able to say, loud and clear, for the rest of my life, I am a lesbian," and kissed me on the cheek.

In tears I stared at her, astonished that this late in the game she still thought my misery at her departure might be quelled by abstract gestures to sisterhood. Also that she could think me that stupid. I saw through her quaking, frightened face, her little-boy locks.

"You're a liar," I said, and, grateful for the anger, she crumpled up her face, screamed, "Damn you, Ellen," and ran out the door.

As I said, our fights were glorious.

All she left behind were her braids.

Across the dining room, Diana stood with Charlie, holding a big knife over the wed-ding cake. Everyone was cheering. The knife sank into the soft white flesh of the cake, came out again clung with silken frosting and crumbs. Diana cut two pieces. Their arms intertwined, she and Charlie fed each other.

Then they danced. A high-hipped young woman in sequins got up on the bandstand and sang, "Graduation's almost here, my love, teach me tonight."

After the bride and groom had been given their five minutes of single glory on the dance floor, and the parents and grand-parents had joined them, I felt a tap on my shoulder. "Care to tango *avec* me, my dear?" Walter said.

"Walter," I said, "I'd be delighted."

We got up from the table and moved out onto the floor. I was extremely nervous, sweating through my dress. I hadn't actually spoken to Diana yet, doubting she'd even seen me. Now, not three feet away, she stood, dancing and laughing, Mrs. Mark Charles Cadwallader.

I kept my eyes on Walter's lapel. The song ended. The couples broke up. And then, there she was, approaching me, all smiles, all bright eyes. "Ellen," she said, embracing me, and her mother shot us a wrathful glance. "Ellen. Let me look at you."

She looked at me. I looked at her. Close up, she looked slightly unraveled, her makeup smeared, her eyes red and a little tense. "Come with me to the ladies' room," she said. "My contacts are killing me."

She took my hand and swept me out of the ballroom into the main hotel lobby. Everyone in the lobby stared at us frankly, presuming, I suppose, that she was a runaway bride, and I her maid. But we were only running away to the ladies' room.

"These contacts!" she said once we got there, and opening one eye wide peeled off a small sheath of plastic. "I'm glad you came," she said, placing the lens on the end of her tongue and licking it. "I was worried that you wouldn't. I've felt so bad about you, Ellen, worried about you so much, since — well, since things ended between us. I was hoping this wedding could be a reconciliation for us. That now we could start again. As friends."

She turned away from the lamplit mirror and flashed me a big smile. I just looked up at her.

"Yes," I said. "I'd like that."

Diana removed the other lens and licked it. It seemed to me a highly unorthodox method of cleaning. Then, nervously, she replaced the lens and looked at herself in the mirror. She had let down her guard. Her face looked haggard, and red blush was streaming off her cheeks.

"I didn't invite Leonore for a reason," she said. "I knew she'd do something to embarrass me, come all dyked out or something. I'm not trying to deny my past, you know. Charlie knows everything. Have you met him?"

"Yes," I said.

"And isn't he a wonderful guy?"

"Yes."

"I have nothing against Leonore. I just believe in subtlety these days. You, I knew I could count on you for subtlety, some class. Leonore definitely lacks class."

It astonished me, all that wasn't being said. I wanted to mention it all — her promise on the doorstep, the gun, the schizophrenic girl. But there was so much. Too much. Nowhere to begin.

When she'd finished with her ablutions, we sat down in parallel toilets. "It is nearly impossible to pee in this damned dress," she said to me through the divider. "I can't wait to get out of it."

"I can imagine," I said.

Then there was a loud spilling noise, and Diana gave out a little sigh of relief. "I've got a terrible bladder infection," she said. "Remember in college how it was such a big status symbol to have a bladder infection because it meant you were having sex? Girls used to come into the dining hall clutching big jars of cranberry juice and moaning, and the rest of us would look at them a little jealously." She faltered. "Or some of us did," she added. "I guess not you, huh, Ellen?"

"No, I was a lesbian," I said, "and still am, and will be until the day I die." I don't know why I said that, but it shut her up.

For about thirty seconds there was not a sound from the other side of the divider, and then I heard Diana sniffling. I didn't know what to say.

"Christ," Diana said, after a few seconds, and blew her nose. "Christ. Why'd I get married?"

I hesitated. "I'm not sure I'm the person to ask," I said. "Did your mother have anything to do with it?"

"Oh, Ellen," Diana said, "please!" I heard her spinning the toilet paper roll. "Look," she said, "you probably resent me incredibly. You probably think I'm a sellout and a fool and that I was a royal bitch to you. You probably think when Charlie does it to me I lie there and pretend I'm feeling something when I'm not. Well, it's not true. Not in the least." She paused. "I was just not prepared to go through my life as a social freak, Ellen. I want a normal life, just like everybody. I want to go to parties and not have to die inside trying to explain who it is I'm with. Charlie's very good for me in that way, he's very understanding and generous." She blew her nose again. "I'm not denying you were part of my life, that our relationship was a big thing for me. I'm just saying it's finished. That part's finished."

Defiantly she flushed.

We stood up, pulled up our underpants and stepped out of the toilet booths to face each other. I looked Diana right in the eye, and I noticed her weaken. I saw it. I could have kissed her or something, I knew, and made her even more unhappy. But I didn't really see the point.

Afterwards, we walked together out of the ladies' room, back into the ballroom, where we were accosted by huge crowds of elderly women with purses that looked to me like the shellacked sushi in certain Japanese restaurant windows.

"Was it okay?" Walter asked me, taking my arm and leading me back to our table for cake.

"Yes," I said. "Okay." But he could see from my face how utterly miserable I was.

"Don't even try," Juanita said, giggling hysterically to herself as we got back to the table. "You're not getting a word out of me, so don't even begin to ask me questions."

Once I knew a schizophrenic girl. Her name was Holly Reardon and she was my best friend from age five to eight. We played house a lot, and sometimes we played spaceship, crawling together in to a cubbyhole behind my parents' sofa bed, then turning off the lights and pretending the living room was some fantastic planet. We did well with our limited resources. But then money started disappearing, and my mother sat me down one day and asked me if I had noticed the money always disappeared when Holly came to visit. I shook my head vigorously no, refusing to believe her. And then one day my favorite stuffed animal, a dog called Rufus, disappeared, and I didn't tell my mother, and didn't tell my mother, until one day she said to me, "Ellen, what happened to Rufus?" and I started to cry. We never found Rufus. Holly had done something with him. And it wasn't because of me that she went away, my parents assured me, it wasn't because of me that her parents closed up the house and had to move into an apartment. Holly was not well. Years later, when I went to work at the state hospital, I think somewhere, secretly, I hoped Holly would be there,

a patient there, that we might play house and spaceship in the linen closets. But of course she wasn't. Who knows where she is now?

After the wedding I felt so depressed I had ice cream for dinner. I did several acrostic puzzles. I watched *The Honeymooners* and I watched *Star Trek*. I watched Sally Jesse Raphael. I watched *The Twilight Zone*. Fortunately, it was not one of the boring Western ones, but an episode I like particularly, about a little girl with a doll that says things like, "My name is Talking Tina and I'm going to kill you." I wished I'd had a doll like that when I was growing up. Next was *Night Gallery*. I almost never watch *Night Gallery*, but when I do, it seems I always see the same episode, the one about two people who meet on a road and are filled with a mysterious sense of deja vu, of having met before. It turns out they live in the mind of a writer who has been rewriting the same scene a thousand times. Near the end they rail at their creator to stop tormenting them by summoning them into existence over and over, to suffer over and over. At the risk of mysticism, it seems to me significant that every time I have tuned into *Night Gallery* in my life it is this episode I have seen.

Then there was nothing more good to watch.

I got up, paced around the house, tried not to think about any of it: Holly Reardon, or Natalie, or Diana, or those poor people living in the mind of a writer and getting rewritten over and over again. I tried not to think about all the Chinese dinners I wasn't going to be able to have because I'd spent so much money on that Cuisinart for Diana, who probably could afford to buy herself a hundred Cuisinarts if she wanted. I tried not to think about their honeymoon, about what secret, glorious place they were bound for. It was too late for it to still make me mad that the whole world, fired up to stop me and Diana, was in a conspiracy to protect the privacy of the angelic married couple she had leapt into to save herself, to make sure their perfect honeymoon wasn't invaded by crazy lesbian ex-lovers with shotguns and a whole lot of unfinished business on their minds. Unfortunately, any anger I felt, which might have saved me, was counteracted by how incredibly sorry I felt for Diana, how sad she had seemed, weeping in the ladies' room on her wedding day.

I went to the closet and took out Diana's braids. God knows I hadn't opened the box for ages. There they were, the braids, only a little faded, a little tangled, and of course, no longer smelling of shampoo. I lifted one up. I was surprised at how silky the hair felt, even this old. Carefully, to protect myself, I rubbed just a little of it against my face. I shuddered. It could have been her.

I went to the bed, carrying the braids with me. I laid them along my chest. I have never had long hair. Now I tried to imagine what it felt like, tried to imagine I was Diana imagining me, a woman she had loved, a woman she had given her hair, a woman who now lay on a bed somewhere, crying, using all the strength she could muster just to not force the braids down her throat. But I knew Diana was on a plane somewhere in the sky, or in a car, or more likely than that, lying in a heart-shaped bed while a man hovered over her, his hands running through her new hair, and that probably all she was thinking was how much better off she was than me, how much richer, and how lucky to have escaped before she was sucked so far in, like me, that it would be too late to ever get out. Was I so pathetic? Possibly. And possibly Diana was going to be happier for the choice she had made. But I think, more likely, lying on that mysterious bed, she was contemplating a whole life of mistakes spinning out from one act of compromise, and realizing she preferred a life of easy mistakes to one that was harder but better. Who was I to criticize? Diana had her tricks, and so did Juanita, and so, for that matter, did that schizophrenic girl stabbing at her melon balls. We all had our little tricks.

I took the braids off myself. I stood up. A few hairs broke loose from the gathered ropes, fell lightly to the floor. They didn't even look like anything; they might have been pieces of straw.

III. NON-MARITAL FORMS OF RECOGNITION

Regardless of whether they support the legal recognition of same-sex marriage or would want to marry, lesbians and gay men have taken on the responsibilities of coupling; not surprisingly, gay people have also endeavored to create or receive some of the rights and benefits that are automatically enjoyed by married couples. These include: rights to spousal shares of marital property upon death of one partner; tax benefits (including joint income tax returns, dependency deductions, gift tax exemptions, and exemptions for alimony and property settlements); rights in tort law (including emotional distress, wrongful death actions, and loss of consortium); rights in criminal law (including immunity from compelled testimony and the marital communication privilege); non-exclusion under zoning laws; visitation privileges in hospitals and other institutions; authority to make decisions for an ill spouse; employee benefits for spouses (including health insurance, medical leave, and bereavement leave); government benefits (including Social

Security and veterans payments to spouses, workers compensation for those whose spouses move for job-related reasons); lower fees for married couples (including automobile and life insurance, family travel rates, and family memberships); immigration benefits; and draft exemptions.

These efforts often place same-sex couples in alliances with unmarried opposite-sex couples and other "non-traditional" families that face similar obstacles to legal recognition and benefits. A recent poll found some public support for such recognition, although 69% of respondents opposed the extension of married couples' rights to same-sex couples and 61% opposed their extension to unmarried couples.[1] Nevertheless, these couples have achieved significant successes in some contexts in some jurisdictions.

This portion of the chapter considers three methods lesbians and gay men employ to seek legal recognition for their relationships. First, gay couples often execute traditional legal instruments such as contracts and wills. Second, gay couples attempt to establish themselves in legally-recognized relationships — for example through domestic partnership or adoption — that provide them with packages of rights and benefits. And third, lesbians and gay men prod — through negotiation and litigation — government agencies and private businesses to recognize their relationships by granting rights and benefits, such as health care coverage for their partners, typically extended to married couples.

A. Legal Instruments

Some of the legal benefits of a marital relationship can be created by executing legal instruments such as wills, contracts, trusts, and powers of attorney. With such instruments, a gay partner (of either gender) may be able to ensure that her property passes to her partner after death, that she can make medical and financial decisions for her incapacitated partner (including the decision to terminate life-support systems), that she and her partner will financially support each other if one loses her source of income, that she will be supported by her partner after a break-up, and that she will receive a share of the common property after a break-up. The following cases examine the enforceability of such contracts.

JONES v. DALY

176 Cal. Rptr. 130 (Ct. App. 1981)

LILLIE, Associate Justice.

■ ■ ■

Defendants are the executors of the estate of James Daly, who died in July 1978. The complaint contains seven causes of action. The first cause of action (for declaratory relief) alleges: Plaintiff, Randal Jones, first met James Daly in December 1975. Between that time and March 1976, they "met

---

1. *For Better or Worse?*, NEWSWEEK, Winter/Spring 1990, at 18 (special issue).

on frequent occasions, dated, engaged in sexual activities and, in general, acted toward one another as two people do who have discovered a love, one for the other." In March 1976 plaintiff and Daly orally agreed that plaintiff would move into Daly's condominium with Daly, quit his job, go travelling with Daly and "cohabit with him [Daly] as if [they] were, in fact, married." They also entered into an oral agreement (referred to hereinafter, in the language of the complaint, as "cohabitors agreement") whereby each agreed: during the time "they lived and cohabited together," they would combine their efforts and earnings and would share equally any and all property accumulated as a result of their efforts, whether individual or combined, except that Daly would give plaintiff a monthly allowance for his personal use, and they "would hold themselves out to the public at large as cohabiting mates, and [plaintiff] would render his services as a *lover*, companion, homemaker, traveling companion, housekeeper and cook to Daly (emphasis added)"; and "in order that [plaintiff] would be able to devote a substantial portion of his time to Daly's benefit as his lover, companion, homemaker, traveling companion, housekeeper and cook," plaintiff would abandon "a material portion" of his potential career as a model, and in return Daly would furnish financial support to plaintiff for the rest of his life. Pursuant to and in reliance on the "cohabitors agreement," plaintiff and Daly "cohabited and lived together continuously" from March 1976 until Daly's death, and plaintiff allowed himself to be known to the general public "as the lover and cohabitation mate of Daly." Plaintiff performed all of the terms and conditions required to be performed by him under the "cohabitors agreement." During the time that plaintiff and Daly "lived and cohabited together" they acquired, as a result of their efforts and earnings, substantial real and personal property (hereinafter, in the language of the complaint, "cohabitors' equitable property"). Plaintiff does not know

the exact nature and extent of such property, but he believes it has a value in excess of $2 million and will amend the complaint to reflect the true value when it is ascertained. Under the "cohabitors agreement," all of the "cohabitors' equitable property" was to be shared and divided equally between plaintiff and Daly. All of such property is in the possession of defendant executors and under their control. Plaintiff has demanded that defendants recognize his interest in the "cohabitors' equitable property," but defendants refuse to do so. On November 1, 1978, plaintiff filed in the proceeding for probate of Daly's estate a creditor's claim, wherein he claimed one-half of the estate; defendants denied the claim. An actual controversy has arisen and now exists between plaintiff and defendants in that plaintiff contends, and defendants deny, that as a result of the "cohabitors agreement" plaintiff is entitled to one-half of all of the "cohabitors' equitable property" as a tenant in common with the estate of Daly and that defendants are under a duty to pay to plaintiff, on behalf of the estate, a reasonable sum for his support. Plaintiff desires a judicial determination of the validity of the "cohabitors agreement" and the respective rights, duties and obligations of plaintiff and defendants under that agreement.

The terms of the "cohabitors agreement" alleged in the first cause of action are incorporated into each of the subsequent causes of action other than the sixth and seventh causes of action. The second and third causes of action seek payment of plaintiff's creditor's claim rejected by defendants. The fourth cause of action seeks half of the "cohabitors' equitable property" on the theory of a constructive trust. The fifth cause of action alleges an implied in fact agreement between plaintiff and Daly for the equal division of all assets standing in Daly's name. The sixth and seventh causes of action are common counts which seek $300,000 as the reasonable value of plaintiff's services to Daly.

. . . One of the arguments advanced by defendants in support of their demurrer was that under *Marvin v. Marvin*, 557 P.2d 106 (Cal. 1976), the "cohabitors agreement" is unenforceable because the complaint shows on its face that plaintiff's rendition of sexual services to Daly was an express and inseparable part of the consideration for the agreement.

In *Marvin v. Marvin*, a woman sued a man with whom she had lived for approximately six years without marriage alleging: that she and defendant entered into an oral agreement that while the parties lived together they would combine their efforts and earnings and would share equally in any and all property accumulated as a result of their efforts, whether individual or combined, that they would hold themselves out to the general public as husband and wife and that plaintiff would give up her career as an entertainer and singer in order to devote her full time to defendant as his companion, homemaker, housekeeper and cook; in return defendant agreed to provide for all of plaintiff's financial support and needs for the rest of her life. Plaintiff further alleged that after she had lived with defendant for almost six years, he forced her to leave his household and refused to recognize her rights under the contract. Plaintiff prayed for declaratory relief, asking the court to determine her contractual and property rights, and also to impose a constructive trust on half of the property acquired during the course of the relationship. The trial court granted defendant's motion for judgment on the pleadings. The Supreme Court reversed the judgment, stating: "In summary, we base our opinion on the principle that adults who voluntarily live together and engage in sexual relations are nonetheless as competent as any other persons to contract respecting their earnings and property rights. Of course, they cannot lawfully contract to pay for the performance of sexual services, for such a contract is, in essence, an agreement for prostitution and unlawful for that reason. But they may agree to pool their earnings and to hold all property acquired during the relationship in accord with the law governing

community property; conversely they may agree that each partner's earnings and the property acquired from those earnings remains the separate property of the earning partner. *So long as the agreement does not rest upon illicit meretricious consideration*, the parties may order their economic affairs as they choose, and no policy precludes the courts from enforcing such agreements."

In determining whether the "cohabitors agreement" rests upon illicit meretricious consideration, we are guided by the following principles [from *Marvin*]: "[A] contract between nonmarital partners, even if expressly made in contemplation of a common living arrangement, is invalid only if sexual acts form an inseparable part of the consideration for the agreement. In sum, a court will not enforce a contract for the pooling of property and earnings if it is explicitly and inseparably based upon services as a paramour." The complaint herein alleges: Following their initial meeting, plaintiff and Daly "dated, engaged in sexual activities and, in general, acted towards one another as two people do who have discovered a love, one for the other"; plaintiff orally agreed "to cohabit with [Daly] as if [they] were, in fact, married"; at the same time they entered into the "cohabitors agreement" whereby they agreed that during the time "they lived and cohabited together" they would hold themselves out to the public at large as "cohabiting mates" and plaintiff would render his services to Daly as "a *lover,* companion, homemaker, traveling companion, housekeeper and cook" (emphasis added); in order that plaintiff would be able to devote his time to Daly's benefit "as his lover, companion, homemaker, traveling companion, housekeeper and cook," he would abandon his career; plaintiff and Daly "cohabited and lived together" and pursuant to and in reliance on the "cohabitors agreement," plaintiff allowed himself to be known to the general public as the "lover and cohabitation mate" of Daly. These allegations clearly show that plaintiff's rendition of sexual services to Daly was an inseparable part of the consideration for the "cohabitors agreement," and indeed was the predominant consideration.

Plaintiff argues that the complaint is not subject to the foregoing interpretation because the "accepted California concept of cohabitation is the mutual assumption of those marital rights, duties and obligations which are usually manifested by married people, including but *not necessarily dependent upon sexual relations*"; and while one meaning of the word "lover" is paramour, it also may mean a person in love or an affectionate or benevolent friend. (Webster's Third New Internat. Dict. (1966) p. 1340.) Pleadings must be reasonably interpreted; they must be read as a whole and each part must be given the meaning that it derives from the context wherein it appears. The complaint alleges that plaintiff and Daly engaged in sexual activities, agreed to cohabit and to hold themselves out to the public as cohabiting mates, and entered into the "cohabitors agreement" whereby plaintiff was to render services to Daly as a lover. Viewed in the context of the complaint as a whole, the words "cohabiting" and "lover" do not have the innocuous meanings which plaintiff ascribes to them. These terms can pertain only to plaintiff's rendition of sexual services to Daly.

Marvin states that "even if sexual services are part of the contractual consideration, any *severable* portion of the contract supported by independent consideration will still be enforced." That principle is inapplicable in the present case. There is no severable portion of the "cohabitors agreement" supported by independent consideration. According to the allegations of the complaint, the agreement provided that the parties would share equally the earnings and property accumulated as a result of their efforts while they lived together and that Daly would support plaintiff for the rest of his life. Neither the property sharing nor the support provision of the agreement rests upon plaintiff's acting as Daly's traveling companion, housekeeper or cook as distinguished from acting as his lover. The latter

service forms an inseparable part of the consideration for the agreement and renders it unenforceable in its entirety.

Since plaintiff's right to relief under the second through the fifth causes of action depends upon the validity of the "cohabitors agreement," the trial court properly sustained the demurrer thereto.

Appellant argues that the sixth and seventh causes of action (labelled, respectively, common counts in quantum meruit and for labor and services rendered) incorporated therein neither the "cohabitors agreement" nor any of the other allegations of the first cause of action relating to sexual services rendered by plaintiff to Daly, thus they are not subject to general demurrer. However, the common counts which are here sufficiently pleaded are so permeated with the same reason for the rendition of the "services rendered" by plaintiff, i.e., the sexual cohabitation of the parties, that it cannot be said that the agreement by Daly to pay for those services does not also rest upon illegal meretricious consideration.

We note that the period covered by the services rendered by plaintiff alleged in the common counts — March 1976 through July 1978 — is the same time span covered by the "cohabitors agreement" alleged in the first cause of action; that the $ 300,000 prayed for in the common counts as the reasonable value of such services is alleged to be "equivalent approximately to one-half of the total estate of Daly," and that it is a one-half interest in the "cohabitors' equitable property" acquired during the cohabitation of the parties that is prayed for under the "cohabitors agreement" in the other causes of action; and that incorporated into the common counts are allegations of the first cause of action relating to plaintiff's presentation of his creditor's claim to Daly's estate (a copy of which is attached to the complaint and incorporated therein by reference) which expressly rests on an "oral agreement" entered into "[a]bout March, 1976 through in or about July 1978," which "oral agreement" is obviously the precise "cohabitors agreement" described in the first cause of action.

While the simple pleading of the common counts standing alone would appear to be innocuous enough to withstand defendants' challenge, a common sense reading of the entire complaint promptly dispels any notion that the same element of illegal meretricious consideration that so infects the "cohabitors agreement" as to render it unenforceable does not as well dominate the common counts; and the reality of the situation dictates the conclusion that the recovery under the sixth and seventh causes of action is based on the exact set of circumstances specifically pleaded in the first cause of action. . . .

■ ■ ■

The judgment is affirmed.

WHORTON v. DILLINGHAM

248 Cal. Rptr. 405 (Ct. App.1988)

WORK, J.

I

■ ■ ■

The alleged facts include the following. At the time the parties began dating and entered into a homosexual relationship, Whorton was studying to obtain his Associate in Arts degree, intending to enroll in a four-year college and obtain a Bachelor of Arts degree. When the parties began living together in 1977, they orally agreed that Whorton's exclusive, full-time occupation was to be Dillingham's chauffeur, bodyguard, social and business secretary, partner and counselor in real estate investments, and to appear on his behalf when requested. Whorton was to render labor, skills, and personal services for the benefit of Dillingham's business and investment endeavors. Additionally, Whorton was to be Dillingham's constant companion, confidant, traveling and social companion, and lover, to terminate his schooling upon obtaining his Associate in Arts degree, and to make no investment without first consulting Dillingham.

In consideration of Whorton's promises, Dillingham was to give him a one-half equity interest in all real estate acquired in their joint names, and in all property thereafter acquired by Dillingham. Dillingham agreed to financially support Whorton for life, and to open bank accounts, maintain a positive balance in those accounts, grant Whorton invasionary powers to savings accounts held in Dillingham's name, and permit Whorton to charge on Dillingham's personal accounts. Dillingham was also to engage in a homosexual relationship with Whorton. Importantly, for the purpose of our analysis, the parties specifically agreed that any portion of the agreement found to be legally unenforceable was severable and the balance of the provisions would remain in full force and effect.

Whorton allegedly complied with all terms of the oral agreement until 1984 when Dillingham barred him from his premises. Dillingham now refuses to perform his part of the contract by giving Whorton the promised consideration for the business services rendered.

II

Adults who voluntarily live together and engage in sexual relations are competent to contract respecting their earnings and property rights. Such contracts will be enforced "unless expressly and inseparably based upon an illicit consideration of sexual services . . . ." (*Marvin v. Marvin*, 557 P.2d 106 (Cal. 1976).) One cannot lawfully contract to pay for the performance of sexual services since such an agreement is in essence a bargain for prostitution.

A standard which inquires whether an agreement involves or contemplates a sexual relationship is vague and unworkable because virtually all agreements between nonmarital (and certainly, marital) cohabiters involve or contemplate a mutual sexual relationship. Further, a compact is not totally invalid merely because the parties may have contemplated creating or continuing a sexual relationship, but is invalid only to the extent it rests upon a consideration of sexual services. Thus, "even if sexual services are part of the contractual consideration, any *severable* portion of the contract supported by independent consideration will still be enforced." For instance, contracting parties may make a variety of arrangements regarding their property rights — i.e., agree to pool their earnings and to hold all property in accord with the law governing community property, or to treat monetary earnings and property as separate property of the earning partner, or to keep property separate but compensate one party for services which benefit the other, or to pool only a part of their earnings and property, etc. "So long as the agreement does not rest upon illicit meretricious consideration, the parties may order their economic affairs as they choose, and no policy precludes the courts from enforcing such agreements."

Regarding the issue of what constitutes adequate consideration, *Marvin* notes "[a] promise to perform homemaking services is, of course, a lawful and adequate consider-ation for a contract . . . ." *Marvin* expressly rejects the argument that the partner seeking to enforce the contract must have contributed either property or services additional to ordinary homemaking services.

In *Marvin*, the plaintiff alleged the parties orally agreed that while they lived together they would combine their efforts and earnings and would share equally all property accumulated as a result of their efforts, that they would hold themselves out to the general public as husband and wife, that plaintiff would render services as companion, homemaker, housekeeper and cook, that plaintiff would give up her career in order to provide these services full time, and that in return defendant would provide for all of plaintiff's financial support for the rest of her life. The court stated:

> ". . . plaintiff alleges that the parties agreed to pool their earnings, that they contracted to share equally in all property acquired, and that defendant agreed to support plaintiff. The terms of the contract as alleged do not rest upon any unlawful consideration."

The holding in *Marvin* suggests the court determined that the contract before it did not *expressly* include sexual services as part of the consideration, and thus, it did not need to reach the issue of whether there were severable portions of the contract supported by independent consideration. The only reference to sexual services in *Marvin*'s alleged facts was that the parties agreed to hold themselves out to the public as husband and wife, which apparently the court did not interpret as expressly indicating sexual services were part of the consideration.

III

Unlike the facts of *Marvin*, here the parties' sexual relationship was an express, rather than implied, part of the consideration for their contract. The contract cannot be enforced to the extent it is dependent on sexual services for consideration, and the complaint does not state a cause of action to the extent it asks for damages from the termination of the sexual relationship.

The issue here is whether the sexual component of the consideration is severable from the remaining portions of the contract.[1] We reiterate the guiding language of *Marvin*: "[E]ven if sexual services are part of the contractual consideration, any *severable* portion of the contract supported by independent consideration will still be enforced." One test for determining the enforceability of a contract having both lawful and unlawful factors for consideration is stated in the Restatement Second of Contracts, section 183, "If the parties' performances can be apportioned into corresponding pairs of part performances so that the parts of each pair are properly regarded as agreed equivalents and one pair is not offensive to public policy, that portion of the agreement is enforceable by a party who did not engage in serious misconduct." (See also Civ. Code, § 1599: "Where a contract has several distinct objects, of which one at least is lawful, and one at least is unlawful, in whole or in part, the contract is void as to the latter and valid as to the rest.")

Tyranski v. Piggins, 205 N.W.2d 595, 596-597 (Mich. Ct. App. 1973), evaluates the issue of severability as follows:

"Professor Corbin and the drafters of the Restatement of Contracts both write that while bargains in whole or in part in consideration of an illicit relationship are unenforceable, agreements between parties to such a relationship with respect to money or property will be enforced if the agreement is independent of the illicit relationship.

"Neither these authorities nor the large body of case law in other jurisdictions . . . articulate a guideline for de-termining when the consideration will be regarded as 'independent', and when it is so coupled with the meretricious acts that the agreement will not be enforced. A pattern does, however, emerge upon reading the cases.

"Neither party to a meretricious relationship acquires, by reason of cohabitation alone, rights in the property accumulations of the other during the period of the relationship. But where there is an express agreement to accumulate or transfer property following a relationship of some permanence and *an additional consideration in the form of either money or of services, the courts tend to find an independent consideration.*

"Thus, a plaintiff who can show an actual contribution of money, pursuant to an agreement to pool assets and share accumulations, will usually prevail. Services, such as cooking meals, laundering clothes, 'caring' for the decedent through sickness, have been found to be adequate and independent considerations in cases where there was an express agreement."

Of particular significance is the decision in *Latham v. Latham*, 547 P.2d 144 (Or. 1976). In *Latham*, the court overruled a demurrer where complainant pleaded an agreement to live with defendant, to care for, and to furnish him with all the amenities of married life. The court recognized the alleged agreement specifically included the sexual services implicit in cohabitation. Thus, as here, the sexual aspect of the agreement appeared on the face of the complaint. In overruling a demurrer based on public policy, the court stated it was not validating an agreement in which sexual intercourse was the only or primary consideration, but only one of the factors incident to the burdens and amenities of married life.

---

1. Dillingham does not assert *Marvin* is inapplicable to same-sex partners, and we see no legal basis to make a distinction.

Thus, the crux of our analysis is whether Whorton's complaint negates as a matter of law, a trier of fact finding he made contributions, apart from sexual services, which provided independent consideration for Dillingham's alleged promises pertaining to financial support and property rights. The services which plaintiff alleges he agreed to and did provide included being a chauffeur, bodyguard, secretary, and partner and counselor in real estate investments. If provided, these services are of monetary value, and the type for which one would expect to be compensated unless there is evidence of a contrary intent. Thus, they are properly characterized as consideration independent of the sexual aspect of the relationship. By way of comparison, such services as being a constant companion and confidant are not the type which are usually monetarily compensated nor considered to have a "value" for purposes of contract consideration, and, absent peculiar circumstances, would likely be considered so intertwined with the sexual relationship as to be inseparable.

We hold that Whorton — based on allegations he provided Dillingham with services of a chauffeur, bodyguard, secretary, and business partner — has stated a cause of action arising from a contract supported by consideration independent of sexual services. Further, by itemizing the mutual promises to engage in sexual activity, Whorton has not precluded the trier of fact from finding those promises are the consideration for each other and independent of the bargained for consideration for Whorton's employment.

We believe our holding does not conflict with that in *Jones v. Daly*, 176 Cal. Rptr. 130 (Ct. App. 1981), where services provided by the complaining homosexual partner were limited to "lover, companion, homemaker, traveling companion, housekeeper and cook . . . ." The court there found the pleadings unequivocally established that plaintiff's rendition of sex and other services naturally flowing from sexual cohabitation was an inseparable part of the consideration for the so-called cohabitor's agreement. The court stated:

> "According to the allegations of the complaint, the agreement provided that the parties would share equally the earnings and property accumulated as a result of their efforts while they lived together and that Daly would support plaintiff for the rest of his life. *Neither the property sharing nor the support provision of the agreement rests upon plaintiff's acting as Daly's traveling companion, housekeeper or cook as distinguished from acting as his lover.* The latter service forms an inseparable part of the consideration for the agreement and renders it unenforceable in its entirety."

Jones is factually different in that the complaining party did not allege contracting to provide services apart from those normally incident to the state of cohabitation itself. Further, Jones's complaint stated the agreement was premised on that they "would hold themselves out to the public at large as cohabiting mates . . . ." In contrast, Whorton's complaint separately itemizes services contracted for as companion, chauffeur, bodyguard, secretary, partner and business counselor. These, except for companion, are significantly different than those household duties normally attendant to non-business cohabitation and are those for which monetary compensation ordinarily would be anticipated. Accepting Whorton's allegations as true, we cannot say as a matter of law any illegal portion of the contract is not severable so as to leave the balance valid and enforceable, especially where it is alleged the parties contemplated such a result when entering into their agreement.

■ ■ ■

The judgment is reversed.

Notes

1. Overturning two lower court decisions, Georgia's Supreme Court ruled that a contract between two lesbian partners is enforceable. *Crooke v. Gilden*, 414 S.E.2d 645 (Ga. 1992). Crooke and Gilden were lesbian partners who formalized their joint financial affairs through a contract that never mentioned any sexual relationship. After they split up, one of the women reneged on the contractual obligations. The other went into court to enforce the contract. The lower Georgia courts refused to enforce the contract, each reading a sexual component into the contract and thus finding the document void. In reversing the lower courts, the Georgia Supreme Court found the document to contain sufficient consideration on its face and — invoking the parol evidence rule — refused to look beyond the promises contained in the contract.

2. If a partner in a gay couple dies without a will, the surviving partner will not be entitled to any portion of the deceased's estate. *See, e.g., Re Estate of Cooper*, 564 N.Y.S.2d 684 (Sur. Ct. 1990).

3. Even written wills between gay partners are often contested by the deceased person's family, which may have been unaware or disapproving of his or her relationship or sexual orientation. *See* Jeffrey Sherman, *Undue Influence and the Homosexual Testator*, 42 PITT. L. REV. 225, 267 (1981).

B. Domestic Partnership and Adoption

Although they assist a gay couple in managing financial affairs and planning for the future, legal instruments do not provide them with external validation of the part of their relationship that goes beyond that of contracting parties. The law generally treats them as unrelated for all purposes outside the legal instruments. Two types of legal relationships available to some lesbians and gay men — domestic partnership and adoption — provide some external validation as well as packages of rights, benefits, and responsibilities that some gay couples find attractive.

1. DOMESTIC PARTNERSHIP

SAN FRANCISCO DOMESTIC PARTNERSHIP ORDINANCE

(Jan. 15, 1991)

The People amend The San Francisco Administrative Code by adding a new Chapter, to read:

RECOGNITION OF DOMESTIC PARTNERSHIPS
Sec. 1.   PURPOSE

The purpose of this ordinance is to create a way to recognize intimate committed relationships, including those of lesbians and gay men who otherwise are denied the right to identify the partners with whom they share their lives. All costs of registration must be covered by fees to be established by ordinance.

Sec. 2.   DEFINITIONS

(**a**) *Domestic Partnership.* Domestic Partners are two adults who have chosen to share one another's lives in an intimate and committed relationship of mutual caring, who live together, and who have agreed to be jointly responsible for basic living expenses incurred during the Domestic Partnership. They must sign a Declaration of Domestic Partnership, and establish the partnership under section 3 of this chapter.

(**b**) *"Live Together."* "Live together" means that two people share the same living quarters. It is not necessary that the legal right to possess the quarters be in both of their names. Two people may live together even if one or both have additional living quarters. Domestic Partners do not cease to live together if one leaves the shared quarters but intends to return.

(**c**) *"Basic Living Expenses."* "Basic living expenses" means the cost of basic food and shelter. It also includes the expenses which are paid at least in part by a program or benefit for which the partner qualified because of the domestic partnership. The individuals need not contribute equally or jointly to the cost of these expenses as long as they agree that both are responsible for the costs.

(**d**) *"Declaration of Domestic Partnership."* A "Declaration of Domestic Partnership" is a form provided by the county clerk. By signing it, two people agree to be jointly responsible for basic living expenses which they incur during the domestic partnership and that this agreement can be enforced by anyone to whom those expenses are owed. They also state under penalty of perjury that they met the definition of domestic partnership when they signed the statement, that neither is married, that they are not related to each other in a way which

would bar marriage in California, and that neither had a different domestic partner less than six months before they signed. This last condition does not apply if the previous domestic partner died. The form will also require each partner to provide a mailing address.

Sec. 3.   ESTABLISHING A DOMESTIC PARTNERSHIP

(**a**) *Methods.* Two persons may establish a Domestic Partnership by either:

1. presenting a signed Declaration of Domestic Partnership to the County Clerk, who will file it and give the partners a certificate showing that the Declaration was filed; or
2. having a Declaration of Domestic Partnership notarized and giving a copy to the person who witnessed the signing (who may or may not be the notary)

(**b**) *Time Limitation.* A person can not become a member of a Domestic Partnership until at least six months after any other Domestic Partnership of which he or she was a member ended. This does not apply if the earlier domestic partnership ended because one of the members died.

(**c**) *Residence Limitation.* The county clerk will only file Declarations of Domestic Partnership if:

1. the partners have a residence in San Francisco; or

2. at least one of the partners works in San Francisco.

Sec. 4.   ENDING DOMESTIC PARTNERSHIPS

(**a**) *When the Partnership Ends.* A Domestic Partnership ends when:

1. one partner sends the other a written notice that he or she has ended the partnership; or
2. one of the partners dies; or
3. one of the partners marries or the partners no longer live together.

(**b**) *Notice the Partnership has ended.*

(1) *To Domestic Partners.* When a Domestic Partnership ends, at least one of the partners must sign a notice saying that the partnership has ended. The notice must be dated and signed under penalty of perjury. If the Declaration of Domestic Partnership was filed with the county clerk, the notice must be filed with the clerk; otherwise, the notice must be notarized. The partner who signs the notice must send a copy to the other partner.

(2) *To Third Parties.* When a Domestic Partnership ends, a Domestic Partner who has given a copy of a Declaration of Domestic Partnership to any third party, (or, if that partner has died, the surviving member of the domestic partnership) must give that third party a notice signed under penalty of perjury stating that the partnership has ended. The notice must be sent within 60 days of the end of the Domestic Partnership.

(3) *Failure to Give Notice.* Failure to give either of the notices required by this subsection will neither prevent nor delay termination of the Domestic Partnership. Anyone who suffers any loss as a result of failure to send either of these notices may sue the partner who was obliged to send it for actual losses.

Sec. 5 COUNTY CLERK'S RECORDS

(**a**) *Amendments to Declarations.* A Partner may amend a Declaration of Do-

mestic Partnership filed with the County Clerk at any time to show a change in his or her mailing address.

(**b**) *New Declarations of Domestic Partnerships.* No person who has filed a Declaration of Domestic Partnership with the county clerk may file another Declaration of Domestic Partnership until six months after a notice the partnership has ended has been filed. However, if the Domestic Partnership ended because one of the partners died, a new Declaration may be filed anytime after the notice the partnership ended.

(**c**) *Maintenance of County Clerk's Records.* The County Clerk will keep a record of all Declarations of Domestic Partnership, Amendments to Declarations of Domestic Partnership and all notices that a partnership has ended. The records will be maintained so that Amendments and notices a partnership has ended are filed with the Declaration of Domestic Partnership to which they apply.

(**d**) *Filing Fees.* The Board of Supervisors will set the filing fee for Declarations of Domestic Partnership and Amendments. No fee will be charged for notices that a partnership has ended. The fees charged must cover the city's cost of administering this ordinance.

Sec. 6. LEGAL EFFECT OF DECLARATION OF DOMESTIC PARTNERSHIP

(**a**) *Obligations.* The obligations of domestic partners to each other are those described in the definition.

(**b**) *Duration of Rights and Duties.* If a domestic partnership ends, the partners incur no further obligations to each other.

Notes

1. In the last decade, over two dozen municipalities in the United States and Canada —
   including Los Angeles, San Francisco, Seattle, Vancouver, Minneapolis, Toronto, and New
   York City — have begun to offer lesbian and gay couples the new legal structure of domestic
   partnership. NAN HUNTER, SHERYL MICHAELSON & THOMAS STODDARD, THE RIGHTS OF
   LESBIANS AND GAY MEN 80 (3d ed. 1992). Domestic partnership ordinances vary tremen-
   dously, particularly in three critical areas: (1) the definition of domestic partners; (2) the
   benefits that accrue to partners; and (3) the responsibilities of partners to each other.
2. An ordinance similar to that printed above was enacted by San Francisco's Board of Supervisors
   but then repealed by voters in a ballot referendum in 1989. The current version was approved by
   voters on November 6, 1990, and signed by Mayor Art Agnos on January 15, 1991, becoming
   effective on February 13, 1991. On Valentine's Day, over 250 couples registered. *See* Christopher
   Elliott, *Gay, Lesbian Couples Get "Partnered" in San Francisco*, L.A. TIMES, Feb. 15, 1991, at
   A3. Previous versions had been vetoed by Mayor Dianne Feinstein and delayed by Mayor Agnos
   because of concerns about their costs. *See* Arthur Leonard, *San Francisco Enacts Domestic
   Partnership Law*, 1989 LESBIAN/GAY L. NOTES 31-32. Today, San Francisco extends the full
   panoply of benefits, including health insurance, to domestic partners of city employees. *See* SAN
   FRANCISCO, CAL. ADMIN. CODE ch. 62.
3. San Francisco's provisions that the partners are jointly and legally responsible for the basic
   living expenses they incur were "included as a mechanism of balancing the rights and duties
   aspects of the legislation." *See* Nan Hunter, *Marriage, Law, and Gender: A Feminist Inquiry*,
   1 LAW & SEXUALITY 9, 24 n.69 (1991). In the California municipalities of Berkeley, Santa
   Cruz, and West Hollywood, partners must certify that they are "responsible for [each other's]
   welfare." *See id.*
4. Madison, Wisconsin anticipated that its "alternative family" ordinance would cost $42,000
   per year, mostly for expanded health insurance, but the report accompanying the proposed
   ordinance "stressed that the [Equal Opportunity Commission] does not believe that the
   monetary cost of this proposed ordinance should be an overriding factor. The [Commission]
   believes that one cannot put a price tag on civil rights."
5. Cost is not the only concern of those who oppose domestic partnership ordinances. In
   Washington, D.C., a bill to give medical benefits to registered domestic partners of city
   employees and to encourage private employers to do likewise has been opposed by some
   religious leaders on grounds that it sanctions both gay relationships and unmarried straight
   relationships. *See* Rene Sanchez, *D.C. Council Rethinks Live-In Partners Bill*, WASH. POST,
   Apr. 4, 1992, at A1. In addition, on similar grounds a married couple in Ann Arbor, Michigan,
   challenged a city ordinance that recognizes same-sex relationships, but a Washtenaw County
   circuit court judge ruled that they did not have standing to bring the challenge. *See* ADVOCATE,
   March 24, 1992, at 33.
6. Offering benefits to domestic partners has raised a number of novel tax issues for employers
   and employees. Although domestic partnerships have no effect on a taxpayer's marital status
   (since this is determined by state law), benefits for domestic partners who do not qualify as
   "dependents" under the tax code (see discussion of tax issues below) must be included in the
   employee's income to the extent their fair market value exceeds what the employee contributed to their cost. *See* IRS Priv. Ltr. Rul. 91-09-060 (Mar. 4, 1991); Arthur Leonard, *IRS
   Rules on Tax Effects of Domestic Partner Benefits*, 1991 LESBIAN/GAY L. NOTES 33.
7. No domestic partnership law has been enacted on a state-wide basis. In some states, however,
   non-traditional families can register as private, non-profit associations. *See* Tamar Lewin,

California Lets Nontraditional Families Register, N.Y. TIMES, Dec. 17, 1990, at A15. Such laws are primarily symbolic, but registration may assist same-sex couples in receiving benefits from employers and other organizations.

2. ADOPTION

IN RE THE ADOPTION OF ROBERT PAUL P.

471 N.E.2d 424 (N.Y. 1984)

JASEN, J.

We are asked to decide whether it was error for Family Court to deny the petition of a 57-year-old male to adopt a 50-year-old male with whom he shares a homosexual relationship.

Appellants are two adult males who have resided together continuously for more than 25 years. The older of the two, who was 57 years of age when this proceeding was commenced, submitted a petition to adopt the younger, aged 50 at the time. The two share a homosexual relationship and desire an adoption for social, financial and emotional reasons.[1] Following a hearing at which both parties to the prospective adoption testified, and upon receipt of a probation investigation that was favorable to the parties, Family Court denied the petition. That court con-

cluded that the parties were attempting to utilize an adoption for the purposes properly served by marriage, wills and business contracts and that the parties lacked any semblance of a parent-child relationship.

The Appellate Division unanimously affirmed, without opinion, and granted leave to appeal to this court. We now affirm for the reasons that follow.

Our adoption statute embodies the fundamental social concept that the relationship of parent and child may be established by operation of law. Despite the absence of any blood ties, in the eyes of the law an adopted child becomes "the natural child of the adoptive parent" with all the attendant personal and proprietary incidents to that relationship. Indeed, the adoption laws of New York, as well as those of most of the States, reflect the general acceptance of the ancient principle

---

1. The parties' affidavit, attached to the petition, states the following reasons for the proposed adoption:

"2. The two of us have lived together for a period of over 25 years. We consider ourselves to be a family, though this might not be true in the traditional sense. Though not the only reason for our petition, our present living arrangements, in a leased apartment, are not formalized and we fear the possibility of eviction; our financial and personal lives are entwined together and though it is not expected, we are concerned about the disposition of our estates upon death and lastly, though not least, we expect to live out our lives together and are concerned about the ability and right under the law for each of us to take care of the other should unexpected events occur.

"3. Though the above reasons indicate financial, economic and practical considerations for our petition, not of any lesser extent and perhaps of more importance, are the many personal, emotional and sentimental reasons for which we present our petition. Simply stated we are a family and seek to formalize such."

of *adoptio naturam imitatur* — i.e., adoption imitates nature, which originated in Roman jurisprudence, which, in turn, served as a guide for the development of adoption statutes in this country.

In imitating nature, adoption in New York, as explicitly defined in section 110 of the Domestic Relations Law, is "the legal proceeding whereby a person takes another person into the *relation of child* and thereby acquires the rights and incurs the responsibilities of *parent*." It is plainly not a quasi-matrimonial vehicle to provide nonmarried partners with a legal imprimatur for their sexual relationship, be it heterosexual or homosexual. Moreover, any such sexual intimacy is utterly repugnant to the relationship between child and parent in our society, and only a patently incongruous application of our adoption laws — wholly inconsistent with the underlying public policy of providing a parent-child relationship for the welfare of the child — would permit the employment of adoption as the legal formalization of an adult relationship between sexual partners under the guise of parent and child.

While the adoption of an adult has long been permitted under the Domestic Relations Law, there is no exception made in such adoptions to the expressed purpose of legally formalizing a parent-child relationship. Adoption laws in this State, first enacted in 1873, initially only provided for the "adoption of minor children by adult persons." As early as 1915, however, the statute was amended to allow adoption of "a person of the age of twenty-one years and upwards" and presently the law simply provides that an unmarried adult or married adults together "may adopt another *person*" without any restriction on the age of the "adoptive child" or "adoptee". Despite these and other statutory changes since adoption came into existence in New York, the basic function of giving legal effect to a parent-child relationship has remained unaltered.

Indeed, although the statutory prerequisites may be less compelling than in the case of the adoption of a minor, an adult adoption must still be "in the best interests of the [adoptive] child" and "the familial, social, religious, emotional and financial circumstances of the adoptive parents which may be relevant" must still be investigated. Neither the explicit statutory purpose nor criteria have been diluted for adult adoptions, and this court has no basis for undoing what the Legislature has left intact.

Moreover, deference to the narrow legislative purpose is especially warranted with adoption, a legal relationship unknown at common law. It exists only by virtue of the legislative acts that authorize it. Although adoption was widely practiced by the Egyptians, Greeks and Romans, it was unknown in England until the Adoption of Children Act of 1926, more than 50 years subsequent to the enactment of adoption laws in New York. Adoption in this State is "solely the creature of, and regulated by, statute law" and "'[t]he Legislature has supreme control of the subject'." Consequently, because adoption is entirely statutory and is in derogation of common law, the legislative purposes and mandates must be strictly observed.

Here, where the appellants are living together in a homosexual relationship and where no incidents of a parent-child relationship are evidenced or even remotely within the parties' intentions, no fair interpretation of our adoption laws can permit a granting of the petition. Adoption is not a means of obtaining a legal status for a nonmarital sexual relationship — whether homosexual or heterosexual. Such would be a "cynical distortion of the function of adoption." Nor is it a procedure by which to legitimize an emotional attachment, however sincere, but wholly devoid of the filial relationship that is fundamental to the concept of adoption.

While there are no special restrictions on adult adoptions under the provisions of the Domestic Relations Law, the Legislature could not have intended that the statute be employed "to arrive at an unreasonable or absurd result." Such would be the result if the Domestic Relations Law were interpreted to permit one lover, homosexual or heterosexual, to adopt the other and enjoy the sanction of the law on their feigned union as parent and child.

There are many reasons why one adult might wish to adopt another that would be entirely consistent with the basic nature of adoption, including the following: a childless individual might wish to perpetuate a family name; two individuals might develop a strong *filial* affection for one another; a stepparent might wish to adopt the spouse's adult children; or adoption may have been forgone, for whatever reason, at an earlier date. But where the relationship between the adult parties is utterly incompatible with the creation of a parent-child relationship between them, the adoption process is certainly not the proper vehicle by which to formalize their partnership in the eyes of the law. Indeed, it would be unreasonable and disingenuous for us to attribute a contrary intent to the Legislature.[3]

If the adoption laws are to be changed so as to permit sexual lovers, homosexual or heterosexual, to adopt one another for the purpose of giving a nonmatrimonial legal status to their relationship, or if a separate institution is to be established for the same purpose, it is for the Legislature, as a matter of State public policy, to do so. Absent any such recognition of that relationship coming from the Legislature, however, the courts ought not to create the same under the rubric of adoption.

Accordingly, the order of the Appellate Division should be affirmed, with costs.

MEYER, J. (dissenting).

Having concluded in *People v. Onofre* that government interference with a private consensual homosexual relationship was unconstitutional because it would not "do anything other than restrict individual conduct and impose a concept of private morality chosen by the State", the court now inconsistently refuses to "permit the employment of adoption as the legal formalization of an adult relationship between sexual partners under the guise of parent and child."

. . . I write . . . to emphasize the extent to which, in my view, the majority misconceives the meaning and purpose of article 7 of the Domestic Relations Law.

Under that article the relationship of parent and child is not a *condition* precedent to adoption; it is rather the *result* of the adoption proceeding. This is clear from the provisions of sections 110 and 117. The second unnumbered paragraph of section 110 defines "adoption" as "the legal proceeding whereby a person *takes another* person *into the relation of child* and *thereby acquires the rights* and incurs the responsibilities *of parent* in respect of such other person," and section 117, which spells out the "effect of adoption," provides in the third unnumbered paragraph of subdivision 1 that, "The adoptive parents or parent and the adoptive child *shall sustain toward each other the legal relation of parent and child* and shall have all the rights and be subject to all the duties of that relation including the rights of inheritance from and through each other and the natural and adopted kindred of the adoptive parents or parent." From those

---

3. The dissent's reliance on *People v. Onofre* [the New York sodomy case] is misplaced. The issue in this case is not whether private consensual homosexual conduct is legally proscribable — this court has already answered that question in the negative and the decision today in no way affects or conflicts with that holding. The sole issue addressed today is whether adoption under the Domestic Relations Law is an appropriate means to legally formalize an indisputedly and entirely nonfilial relationship between sexual partners — regardless of whether their relationship is homosexual or heterosexual. The decision today in no way imposes or chooses a "concept of private morality" nor in any way judges the propriety or morality of the parties' "individual conduct."

provisions and the statement in the opening sentence of section 110 that, "An adult unmarried person . . . may adopt another person", no other conclusion is possible than that the Legislature has not conditioned adult adoption upon there being a parent-child relationship, but rather has stated that relationship to be the result of adoption. Indeed, had it intended to impose limitations of age, consent of others, sexual orientation, or other such condition upon adult adoption, it could easily have done so.

Nor will it do to argue . . . that because the Legislature that provided for adoption of adults continued the proscription against homosexuality, it did not envision adoption as a means of formalizing a homosexual relationship. The wording of section 110 being sufficiently broad to permit such formalization once the prior criminal proscription has been declared unconstitutional, to deny it that effect is to ignore the rule that a court is "not at liberty to restrict by conjecture, or under the guise or pretext of interpretation, the meaning of" the language chosen by the Legislature. It is "incumbent upon the courts to give effect to legislation as it is written, and not as they or others might think it should be written."

Contrary to the suggestion of the majority that the adoption statute must be strictly construed, it "has been most liberally and beneficently applied." True, *Stevens v. Halstead* held its use for the purpose of passing property from a 70-year-old physically infirm man to a married 47-year-old woman with whom he was living in an adulterous relationship to be improper. But that holding was predicated on the conception that it was "against public policy to admit a couple living in adultery to the relation of parent and child" and because "[t]his meretricious relationship, and the undue influence which imposed the will of defendant on decedent, condemn the adoption." Here, however, there is no suggestion of undue influence and the relationship, which by the present decision is excised from the adoption statute's broad wording, has, since the *Onofre* decision, been subject to no legal impediment. That it remains morally offensive to many cannot justify imposing upon the statute a limitation not imposed by the Legislature.

What leads to the majority's conclusion that the relationship of the parties "is utterly incompatible with the creation of a parent-child relationship between them" is that it involves a "nonmarital sexual relationship." But nothing in the statute requires an inquiry into or evaluation of the sexual habits of the parties to an adult adoption or the nature of the current relationship between them. It is enough that they are two adults who freely desire the legal status of parent and child. The more particularly is this so in light of the absence from the statute of any requirement that the adoptor be older than the adoptee, for that, if nothing else, belies the majority's concept that adoption under New York statute imitates nature, inexorably and in every last detail.

Under the statute "the relationship of parent and child, with all the personal and property rights incident to it, may be established, independently of blood ties, by operation of law;" existence of a parent-child relationship is not a condition of, but a result of, adoption. The motives which prompt the present application are in no way contrary to public policy; in the words of Mr. Justice Holmes, they are "perfectly proper." Absent any contravention of public policy, we should be "concerned only with the clear, unqualified statutory authorization of adoption" and should, therefore, reverse the Appellate Division's order.

Notes

1. Despite *Robert Paul P.*, courts in New York have apparently continued to grant adoption petitions between gay and lesbian lovers. For instance, a more recent decision of an intermediate appellate court in New York involving the adoption of one adult woman by another, *East 53rd Street Associates v. Mann*, 503 N.Y.S.2d 752 (App. Div. 1986), "suggests that as long as the adoption petition appears on its face to indicate a filial relationship or a wish to secure property rights, the court will not delve deeper to discover the 'true' motives propelling the adoption." *Developments in the Law — Sexual Orientation and the Law*, 102 HARV. L. REV. 1508, 1628 (1989). Moreover, because adoption is irrevocable (unless someone else adopts the "child"), there are still many gay couples in adoptive relationships although their relationships have ended.

2. Adult adoption is permitted and relatively unrestricted in all but two states (Arizona and Nebraska). In four states (California, Connecticut, Massachusetts and Nevada), the adoptor simply must be older than the adoptee. In New Jersey, the age difference must be ten years older than the adoptee; in Puerto Rico it must be sixteen years. In the two states that ban lesbians or gay men from adopting children (Florida and New Hampshire) these bans would also seem to apply to the adoption of adults. And in some other states (Hawaii, Idaho, Ohio and Virginia), certain restrictions on adult adoption are likely to have the practical effect of preventing one partner in a couple from adopting the other. *See* Jeffrey Sherman, *Undue Influence and the Homosexual Testator*," 42 U. PITT. L. REV. 225, 254-56 (1981).

3. After James McConnell and Jack Baker were denied the right to marry in *Baker v. Nelson*, *supra* at 406, McConnell adopted Baker in order to establish a legal relationship. *See* KAY TOBIN & ROBIN WICKER, THE GAY CRUSADERS 150 (1972).

4. The legal effects of adoption vary from state to state, but in no state does adoption confer any power on the adoptor over the adoptee. In all states adoption automatically disinherits the parents and siblings (but not any children) of both the adoptor and the adoptee, if either should die intestate. *See* Jeffrey Sherman, *Undue Influence and the Homosexual Testator*, 42 U. PITT. L. REV. 221, 253 (1981). This has the added effect of denying parents and siblings standing to contest the will of the adoptor or (in most states) of the adoptee, since standing is conferred only on those who would gain if the probate court throws out the will and distributes the estate as if no will had existed. *See id.* at 254, 256. Still, the adoption itself may be contested after death, suggesting that adoption "will not appreciably reduce the risk that [the decedent's] testamentary design will be overturned by disappointed relatives." *Id.* at 260; *see* SEXUAL ORIENTATION AND THE LAW § 1.05[2][a] (Roberta Achtenberg ed., 1985 & Release #3, Oct. 1990).

5. For many couples, though, adoption has its drawbacks. As noted above, it is irrevocable, meaning that a former lover who had been adopted may challenge a later will. *See, e.g., Succession of Bacot*, 502 So.2d 1118 (La. Ct. App. 1987), *cert. denied*, 503 So.2d 466 (La. 1987). Furthermore, in most states an adoptee loses the right to inherit from her natural parents, if they die without wills, or to contest these wills. *See* Jeffrey Sherman, *Undue Influence and the Homosexual Testator*, 42 U. PITT. L. REV. 221, 257 (1981). Finally, inheritance rights are usually determined by the law in force at the time of death, not at the time of adoption, making adoption a "somewhat speculative estate planning technique." *Id.* at 256 n.147.

   In some states, adoption may create an additional complication for same-sex partners: incest. Although "the prohibition against incest will probably not be a bar to the adoption of a homosexual lover" under present state statutes, *id.* at 259, a minor amendment could outlaw (or, in those states with sodomy laws, doubly outlaw) any sexual relations within an adoptive lesbian or gay relationship.

C. Recognition for Specific Purposes

Because legal instruments, domestic partnership, and adoption do not provide gay couples with all of the legal rights, benefits, and responsibilities that they choose for their relationships, many have made efforts to have courts, government agencies, employers and businesses accord them legal recognition in specific contexts, from rent control protection to spousal insurance benefits to legal guardianship of an incapacitated lover. Many jurisdictions ban discrimination in some contexts on the basis of marital status[1] or sexual orientation. Plaintiffs' efforts have invoked these laws as well as more general laws whose definitions of "family," "spouse," or similar terms are susceptible to broader interpretations.

1. BENEFITS AND PROTECTIONS IN LIVING ARRANGEMENTS

BRASCHI v. STAHL ASSOCS. CO.

543 N.E.2d 49 (N.Y. 1989)

TITONE, J.   *I*

In this dispute over occupancy rights to a rent-controlled apartment, the central question to be resolved on this request for preliminary injunctive relief is whether appellant has demonstrated a likelihood of success on the merits by showing that, as a matter of law, he is entitled to seek protection from eviction under New York City Rent and Eviction Regulations 9 NYCRR 2204.6 (d) (formerly New York City Rent and Eviction Regulations § 56 [d]). That regulation provides that upon the death of a rent-control tenant, the landlord may not dispossess "either the surviving spouse of the deceased tenant or some other member of the deceased tenant's *family* who has been living with the tenant." Resolution of this question requires this court to determine the meaning of the term "family" as it is used in this context.

Appellant, Miguel Braschi, was living with Leslie Blanchard in a rent-controlled apartment located at 405 East 54th Street from the summer of 1975 until Blanchard's death in September of 1986. In November of 1986, respondent, Stahl Associates Company, the owner of the apartment building, [began processes of eviction against] appellant contending that he was a mere licensee with no right to occupy the apartment since only Blanchard was the tenant of record. In December of 1986 respondent served appellant with a notice to terminate informing appellant that he had one month to vacate the apartment and that, if the apartment was not vacated, respondent would commence summary proceedings to evict him.

---

1. *See* John Beattie, Note, *Prohibiting Marital Status Discrimination: A Proposal for the Protection of Unmarried Couples*, 42 HASTINGS L. J. 1415, 1417–19 (1991).

Appellant then initiated an action seeking a permanent injunction and a declaration of entitlement to occupy the apartment. By order to show cause appellant then moved for a preliminary injunction, pendente lite, enjoining respondent from evicting him until a court could determine whether he was a member of Blanchard's family within the meaning of 9 NYCRR 2204.6 (d). After examining the nature of the relationship between the two men, Supreme Court concluded that appellant was a "family member" within the meaning of the regulation and, accordingly, that a preliminary injunction should be issued. The court based this decision on its finding that the long-term interdependent nature of the 10-year relationship between appellant and Blanchard "fulfills any definitional criteria of the term 'family.' "

The Appellate Division reversed, concluding that section 2204.6 (d) provides noneviction protection only to "family members within traditional, legally recognized familial relationships." Since appellant's and Blanchard's relationship was not one given formal recognition by the law, the court held that appellant could not seek the protection of the noneviction ordinance. After denying the motion for preliminary injunctive relief, the Appellate Division granted leave to appeal to this court. . . . We now reverse.

II

. . .

It is fundamental that in construing the words of a statute "[t]he legislative intent is the great and controlling principle." Indeed, "the general purpose is a more important aid to the meaning than any rule which grammar or formal logic may lay down." Statutes are ordinarily interpreted so as to avoid objectionable consequences and to prevent hardship or injustice. Hence, where doubt exists as to the meaning of a term, and a choice between two constructions is afforded, the consequences that may result from the different interpretations should be considered. In addition, since rent-control laws are remedial in nature and designed to promote the public good, their provisions should be interpreted broadly to effectuate their purposes. Finally, where a problem as to the meaning of a given term arises, a court's role is not to delve into the minds of legislators, but rather to effectuate the statute by carrying out the purpose of the statute as it is embodied in the words chosen by the Legislature.

The present dispute arises because the term "family" is not defined in the rent-control code and the legislative history is devoid of any specific reference to the noneviction provision. All that is known is the legislative purpose underlying the enactment of the rent-control laws as a whole.

Rent control was enacted to address a "serious public emergency" created by "an acute shortage in dwellings," which resulted in "speculative, unwarranted and abnormal increases in rents." These measures were designed to regulate and control the housing market so as to "prevent exactions of unjust, unreasonable and oppressive rents and rental agreements and to forestall profiteering, speculation and other disruptive practices tending to produce threats to the public health . . . [and] to prevent uncertainty, hardship and dislocation." Although initially designed as an emergency measure to alleviate the housing shortage attributable to the end of World War II, "a serious public emergency continues to exist in the housing of a considerable number of persons." Consequently, the Legislature has found it necessary to continually reenact the rent-control laws, thereby providing continued protection to tenants.

To accomplish its goals, the Legislature recognized that not only would rents have to be controlled, but that evictions would have to be regulated and controlled as well.

Hence, section 2204.6 of the New York City Rent and Eviction Regulations, which authorizes the issuance of a certificate for the eviction of persons occupying a rent-controlled apartment after the death of the named tenant, provides, in subdivision (d), noneviction protection to those occupants who are either the "surviving spouse of the deceased tenant or *some other member of the deceased tenant's family* who has been living with the tenant [of record]." The manifest intent of this section is to restrict the landowners' ability to evict a narrow class of occupants other than the tenant of record. The question presented here concerns the scope of the protections provided. Juxtaposed against this intent favoring the protection of tenants, is the over-all objective of a gradual "transition from regulation to a normal market of free bargaining between landlord and tenant" (*see, e.g.*, ADMINISTRATIVE CODE OF CITY OF NEW YORK, § 26- 401). One way in which this goal is to be achieved is "vacancy decontrol," which automatically makes rent-control units subject to the less rigorous provisions of rent stabilization upon the termination of the rent-control tenancy.

Emphasizing the latter objective, respondent argues that the term "family member" as used in 9 NYCRR 2204.6 (d) should be construed, consistent with this State's intestacy laws, to mean relationships of blood, consanguinity and adoption in order to effectuate the over-all goal of orderly succession to real property. Under this interpretation, only those entitled to inherit under the laws of intestacy would be afforded noneviction protection. Further, as did the Appellate Division, respondent relies on our decision in *Matter of Robert Paul P.*, arguing that since the relationship between appellant and Blanchard has not been accorded legal status by the Legislature, it is not entitled to the protections of section 2204.6 (d), which, according to the Appellate Division, applies only to "family members within traditional, legally recognized familial relationships".

Finally, respondent contends that our construction of the term "family member" should be guided by the recently enacted noneviction provision of the Rent Stabilization Code (9 NYCRR 2523.5[a], [b][1], [2]), which was passed in response to our decision in *Sullivan* v *Brevard Assocs.,* 488 N.E.2d 1208 (N.Y.1985), and specifically enumerates the individuals who are entitled to noneviction protection under the listed circumstances (9 NYCRR 2520.6 [o]).

However, as we have continually noted, the rent-stabilization system is different from the rent-control system in that the former is a less onerous burden on the property owner, and thus the provisions of one cannot simply be imported into the other. Respondent's reliance on *Matter of Robert Paul P.* is also misplaced, since that case, which held that one adult cannot adopt another where none of the incidents of a filial relationship is evidenced or even remotely intended, was based solely on the purposes of the adoption laws (*see*, DOMESTIC RELATIONS LAW, § 110) and has no bearing on the proper interpretation of a provision in the rent-control laws.

We also reject respondent's argument that the purpose of the noneviction provision of the rent-control laws is to control the orderly succession to real property in a manner similar to that which occurs under our State's intestacy laws. The noneviction provision does not concern succession to real property but rather is a means of protecting a certain class of occupants from the sudden loss of their homes. The regulation does not create an alienable property right that could be sold, assigned or otherwise disposed of and, hence, need not be construed as coextensive with the intestacy laws. Moreover, such a construction would be inconsistent with the purposes of the rent-control system as a whole, since it would afford protection to distant blood relatives who actually had but a superficial relationship with the deceased tenant while denying that protection to unmarried lifetime partners.

Finally, the dissent's reliance on *Hudson View Props. v. Weiss*, 450 N.E.2d 234 (N.Y. 1983) is misplaced. In that case we permitted the eviction of an unrelated occupant from a rent-controlled apartment under a lease explicitly restricting occupancy to "immediate family". However, the tenant in *Hudson View* conceded "that an individual not part of her immediate family" occupied the apartment, and, thus, the sole question before us was whether enforcement of the lease provision was violative of the State or City Human Rights Law. Whether respondent tenant was, in fact, an "immediate family" member was neither specifically addressed nor implicitly answered.

Contrary to all of these arguments, we conclude that the term family, as used in 9 NYCRR 2204.6(d), should not be rigidly restricted to those people who have formalized their relationship by obtaining, for instance, a marriage certificate or an adoption order. The intended protection against sudden eviction should not rest on fictitious legal distinctions or genetic history, but instead should find its foundation in the reality of family life. In the context of eviction, a more realistic, and certainly equally valid, view of a family includes two adult lifetime partners whose relationship is long term and characterized by an emotional and financial commitment and interdependence. This view comports both with our society's traditional concept of "family" and with the expectations of individuals who live in such nuclear units.[1] In fact, Webster's Dictionary defines "family" *first* as "a group of people united by certain convictions or common affiliation" (WEBSTER'S NINTH NEW COLLEGIATE DICTIONARY 448 (1984); *see* BALLANTINE'S LAW DICTIONARY 456 (3d ed. 1969) ("family" defined as "(p)rimarily, the collective body of persons who live in one house and under one head or management"); BLACK'S LAW DICTIONARY 543 (Special Deluxe 5th ed. 1979). Hence, it is reasonable to conclude that, in using the term "family," the Legislature intended to extend protection to those who reside in households having all of the normal familial characteristics. Appellant Braschi should therefore be afforded the opportunity to prove that he and Blanchard had such a household.

This definition of "family" is consistent with both of the competing purposes of the rent-control laws: the protection of individuals from sudden dislocation and the gradual transition to a free market system. Family members, whether or not related by blood, or law who have always treated the apartment as their family home will be protected against the hardship of eviction following the death of the named tenant, thereby furthering the Legislature's goals of preventing dislocation and preserving family units which might otherwise be broken apart upon eviction.[3] This approach will foster the transition from rent control to rent stabilization by drawing a distinction between those individuals who are, in fact, genuine family members, and those who are mere roommates or newly discovered relatives hoping

---

1. Although the dissent suggests that our interpretation of "family" indefinitely expands the protections provided by section 2204.6(d), its own proposed standard — legally recognized relationships based on blood, marriage or adoption — may cast an even wider net, since the number of blood relations an individual has will usually exceed the number of people who would qualify by our standard.

3. We note, however, that the definition of family that we adopt here for purposes of the noneviction protection of the rent-control laws is completely unrelated to the concept of "functional family," as that term has developed under this court's decisions in the context of zoning ordinances (*see Baer v. Town of Brookhaven*, 537 N.E.2d 619 (N.Y. 1989); *McMinn v. Town of Oyster Bay*, 66 N.Y. 2d 544; *Group House v. Board of Zoning & Appeals*, 380 N.E.2d 207 (N.Y.1978). Those decisions focus on a locality's power to use its zoning powers in such a way as to impinge upon an individual's ability to live under the same roof with another individual. They have absolutely no bearing on the scope of noneviction protection provided by section 2204.6(d).

to inherit the rent-controlled apartment after the existing tenant's death.[4]

The determination as to whether an individual is entitled to noneviction protection should be based upon an objective examination of the relationship of the parties. In making this assessment, the lower courts of this State have looked to a number of factors, including the exclusivity and longevity of the relationship, the level of emotional and financial commitment, the manner in which the parties have conducted their everyday lives and held themselves out to society, and the reliance placed upon one another for daily family services (*see, e.g., Athineos v. Thayer*, N.Y.L.J., Mar. 25, 1987, at 14, col. 4 [Civ. Ct., Kings County], *affd.* N.Y.L.J., Feb. 9, 1988, at 15, col. 4 [App. Term, 2d Dept.] [orphan never formally adopted but lived in family home for 34 years]; *2-4 Realty Assocs. v. Pittman*, 523 N.Y.S.2d 7 (Civ.Ct.1887) [two men living in a "father-son" relationship for 25 years]; *Zimmerman v. Burton*, 434 N.Y.S.2d 127 (Civ.Ct. 1980) and *Rutar Co. v. Yoshito*, No. 53042/79 [Civ. Ct., NY. County] [unmarried heterosexual life partners]; *Gelman v. Castaneda*, N.Y.L.J., Oct. 22, 1986, at 13, col. 1 [Civ. Ct., NY County] [male life partners]). These factors are most helpful, although it should be emphasized that the presence or absence of one or more of them is not dispositive since it is the totality of the relationship as evidenced by the dedication, caring and self-sacrifice of the parties which should, in the final analysis, control. Appellant's situation provides an example of how the rule should be applied.

Appellant and Blanchard lived together as permanent life partners for more than 10 years. They regarded one another, and were regarded by friends and family, as spouses. The two men's families were aware of the nature of the relationship, and they regularly visited each other's families and attended family functions together, as a couple. Even today, appellant continues to maintain a relationship with Blanchard's niece, who considers him an uncle.

In addition to their interwoven social lives, appellant clearly considered the apartment his home. He lists the apartment as his address on his driver's license and passport, and receives all his mail at the apartment address. Moreover, appellant's tenancy was known to the building's superintendent and doormen, who viewed the two men as a couple.

Financially, the two men shared all obligations including a household budget. The two were authorized signatories of three safe-deposit boxes, they maintained joint checking and savings accounts, and joint credit cards. In fact, rent was often paid with a check from their joint checking account. Additionally, Blanchard executed a power of attorney in appellant's favor so that appellant could make necessary decisions — financial, medical and personal — for him during his illness. Finally, appellant was the named beneficiary of Blanchard's life insurance policy, as well as the primary legatee and coexecutor of Blanchard's estate. Hence, a court examining these facts could reasonably conclude that these men were much more than mere roommates.

Inasmuch as this case is before us on a certified question, we conclude only that appellant has demonstrated a likelihood of success on the merits, in that he is not excluded,

---

4. Also unpersuasive is the dissent's interpretation of the "roommate" law which was passed in response to our decision in *Hudson View Props. v. Weiss*, 450 N.E.2d 234 (N.Y.1983). That statute allows roommates to live with the named tenant by making lease provisions to the contrary void as against public policy (REAL PROPERTY LAW, § 235-f[2]). The law also provides that "occupant's" (roommates) do not automatically acquire "any right to continued occupancy in the event that the tenant vacates the premises" (§ 235-f[6]). Occupant is defined as "a person, other than a tenant or a member of a tenant's immediate family" (§ 235-f[1][b]). However, contrary to the dissent's assumption that this law contemplates a distinction between related and unrelated individuals, no such distinction is apparent from the Legislature's unexplained use of the term "immediate family."

as a matter of law, from seeking noneviction protection. Since all remaining issues are beyond this court's scope of review, we remit this case to the Appellate Division so that it may exercise its discretionary powers in accordance with this decision.

■ ■ ■

BELLACOSA, J., concurring.

My vote to reverse and remit rests on a narrower view of what must be decided in this case than the plurality and dissenting opinions deem necessary.

The issue is solely whether petitioner qualifies as a member of a "family", as that generic and broadly embracive word is used in the anti-eviction regulation of the rent-control apparatus. The particular anti-eviction public policy enactment is fulfilled by affording the remedial protection to this petitioner on the facts advanced on this record at this preliminary injunction stage. The competing public policy of eventually restoring rent-controlled apartments to decontrol, to stabilization and even to arm's length market relationships is eclipsed in this instance, in my view, by the more pertinently expressed and clearly applicable anti-eviction policy.

Courts, in circumstances as are presented here where legislative intent is completely indecipherable (Division of Housing and Community Renewal, the agency charged with administering the policy, is equally silent in this case and on this issue), are not empowered or expected to expand or to constrict the meaning of the legislatively chosen word "family," which could have been and still can be qualified or defined by the duly constituted enacting body in satisfying its separate branch responsibility and prerogative. Construing a regulation does not allow substitution of judicial views or preferences for those of the enacting body when the latter either fails or is unable or deliberately refuses to

specify criteria or definitional limits for its selected umbrella word, "family", especially where the societal, governmental, policy and fiscal implications are so sweeping. For then, "the judicial function expands beyond the molecular movements, in Holmes' figure, into the molar."

The plurality opinion favors the petitioner's side by invoking the nomenclature of "nuclear"/ "normal"/ "genuine" family versus the "traditional"/ "legally recognizable" family selected by the dissenting opinion in favor of the landlord. I eschew both polar camps because I see no valid reason for deciding so broadly; indeed, there are cogent reasons not to yaw towards either end of the spectrum.

The application of the governing word and statute to reach a decision in this case can be accomplished on a narrow and legitimate jurisprudential track. The enacting body has selected an unqualified word for a socially remedial statute, intended as a protection against one of the harshest decrees known to the law — eviction from one's home. Traditionally, in such circumstances, generous construction is favored. Petitioner has made his shared home in the affected apartment for 10 years. The only other occupant of that rent-controlled apartment over that same extended period of time was the tenant-in-law who has now died, precipitating this battle for the apartment. The best guidance available to the regulatory agency for correctly applying the rule in such circumstances is that it would be irrational not to include this petitioner and it is a more reasonable reflection of the intention behind the regulation to protect a person such as petitioner as within the regulation's class of "family". In that respect, he qualifies as a tenant in fact for purposes of the interlocking provisions and policies of the rent-control law. Therefore . . . there would unquestionably be irreparable harm by not upholding the preliminary relief Supreme Court has decreed; the likelihood of success seems quite good since four Judges of this court, albeit by different rationales, agree at least that petitioner fits under the beneficial umbrella of the regulation; and the balance of equities would appear to favor petitioner.

The reasons for my position in this case are as plain as the inappropriate criticism of the dissent that I have engaged in ipse dixit decision-making. It should not be that difficult to appreciate my view that no more need be decided or said in this case under the traditional discipline of the judicial process. Interstitial adjudication, when a court cannot institutionally fashion a majoritarian rule of law either because it is fragmented or because it is not omnipotent, is quite respectable jurisprudence. We just do not know the answers or implications for an exponential number of varied fact situations, so we should do what courts are in the business of doing — deciding cases as best they fallibly can. Applying the unvarnished regulatory word, "family", as written, to the facts so far presented falls within a well-respected and long-accepted judicial method.

SIMONS, J., dissenting

I would affirm. The plurality has adopted a definition of family which extends the language of the regulation well beyond the implication of the words used in it. In doing so, it has expanded the class indefinitely to include anyone who can satisfy an administrator that he or she had an emotional and financial "commitment" to the statutory tenant. Its interpretation is inconsistent with the legislative scheme underlying rent regulation, goes well beyond the intended purposes of 9 NYCRR 2204.6(d), and produces an unworkable test that is subject to abuse. The concurring opinion fails to address the problem. It merely decides, ipse dixit, that plaintiff should win.

■ ■ ■

Central to any interpretation of the regulatory language is a determination of its purpose. There can be little doubt that the purpose of section 2204.6(d) was to create succession rights to a possessory interest in real property where the tenant of record has died or vacated the apartment. It creates a new tenancy for every surviving family member living with decedent at the time of death who then becomes a new statutory tenant until death or until he or she vacates the apartment. The State concerns underlying this provision include the orderly and just succession of property interests (which includes protecting a deceased's spouse and family from loss of their longtime home) and the professed State objective that there be a gradual transition from government regulation to a normal market of free bargaining between landlord and tenant. Those objectives require a weighing of the interests of certain individuals living with the tenant of record at his or her death and the interests of the landlord in regaining possession of its property and rerenting it under the less onerous rent-stabilization laws. The interests are properly balanced if the regulation's exception is applied by using objectively verifiable relationships based on blood, marriage and adoption, as the State has historically done in the estate succession laws, family court acts and similar legislation. The distinction is warranted because members of families, so defined, assume certain legal obligations to each other and to third persons, such as creditors, which are not imposed on unrelated individuals and this legal interdependency is worthy of consideration in determining which individuals are entitled to succeed to the interest of the statutory tenant in rent-controlled premises. Moreover, such an interpretation promotes certainty and consistency in the law and obviates the need for drawn out hearings and litigation focusing on such intangibles as the strength and duration of the relationship and the extent of the emotional and financial interdependency. So limited, the regulation may be viewed as a tempered response, balancing the rights of landlords with those of the tenant. To come within that protected class, individuals must comply with State laws relating to marriage or adoption. Plaintiff cannot avail himself of these institutions, of course, but that only points up the need for a legislative solution, not a judicial one.

Aside from these general considerations, the language itself suggests the regulation should be construed along traditional lines. Significantly, although the problem of unrelated persons living with tenants in rent-controlled apartments has existed for as long as rent control, there has been no effort by the State Legislature, the New York City Council or the agency charged with enforcing the statutes to define the word "family" contained in 9 NYCRR 2204.6(d) and its predecessors and we have no direct evidence of the term's intended scope. The plurality's response to this problem is to turn to the dictionary and select one definition, from the several found there, which gives the regulation the desired expansive construction.[*] I would search for the intended meaning of the words by looking at what the Legislature and the Division of Housing and Community Renewal (DHCR), the agency charged with implementing rent control, have done in related areas. These sources produce persuasive evidence that both bodies intend the word family to be interpreted in the traditional sense.

The legislative view may be found in the "roommate" law enacted in 1983 (REAL PROPERTY LAW, § 235-f, L. 1983, ch. 403). That statute granted rights to persons living with, but unrelated to, the tenant of record. The statute was a response to our unanimous decision in *Hudson View Props. v. Weiss*. In *Hudson View* the landlord, by a provision in the lease, limited occupancy to the tenant of record and the tenant's "immediate family." When the landlord tried to evict the unmarried heterosexual partner of the named tenant of record, she defended the proceeding by claiming that the restrictive covenant in the lease violated provisions of the State and City Human Rights Laws prohibiting discrimination on the basis of marital status. We held that the exclusion had nothing to do with the tenants' unmarried status but depended on the lease's restriction of occupancy to the tenant and the tenant's "immediate family." Implicitly, we decided that the term "immediate family" did not include individuals who were unrelated by blood, marriage or adoption, notwithstanding "the close and loving relationship" of the parties.

The Legislature's response to *Weiss* was measured. It enacted REAL PROPERTY LAW, § 235-f(3), (4) which provides that occupants of rent-controlled accommodations, whether related to the tenant of record or not, can continue living in rent-controlled and rent-stabilized apartments *as long as the tenant of record continues to reside there.* Lease provisions to the contrary are rendered void as against public policy (subd. [2]). Significantly, the statute provides that no unrelated occupant "shall . . . acquire any right to continued occupancy in the event the tenant vacates the premises or acquire any other rights of tenancy" (subd.[6]). Read against this background, the statute is evidence the Legislature does not contemplate that individuals unrelated to the tenant of record by blood, marriage or adoption should enjoy a right to remain in rent-con-

---

[*] For example, the definitions found in BLACK'S LAW DICTIONARY 543 (Special Deluxe 5th ed.) are: "Family. The meaning of word 'family' necessarily depends on field of law in which word is used, purpose intended to be accomplished by its use, and facts and circumstances of each case . . . Most commonly refers to group of persons consisting of parents and children; father, mother and their children; immediate kindred, constituting fundamental social unit in civilized society . . . A collective body of persons who live in one house and under one head or management. A group of blood-relatives; all the relations who descend from a common ancestor, or who spring from a common root. A group of kindred persons . . . Husband and wife and their children, wherever they may reside and whether they dwell together or not" (citations omitted). The term is similarly defined in the other dictionaries cited in the plurality opinion.

trolled apartments after the death of the tenant.

There is similar evidence of how DHCR intends the section to operate. Manifestly, rent stabilization and rent control are closely related in purpose. Both recognize that, because of the serious ongoing public emergency with respect to housing in the City of New York, restrictions must be placed on residential housing. The DHCR promulgates the regulations for both rent-regulation systems, and the eviction regulations in rent control and the exceptions to them share a common purpose with the renewal requirements contained in the Rent Stabilization Code (*compare* 9 NYCRR 2204.6[d] *with* 9 NYCRR 2523.5[b]). In the Rent Stabilization Code, the Division of Housing and Community Renewal has made it unmistakably clear that the definition of family includes only persons related by blood, marriage or adoption. Since the two statutes and the two regulations share a common purpose, it is appropriate to conclude that the definition of family in the rent-control regulations should be of similar scope.

Specifically, the rent-stabilization regulations provide under similar circumstances that the landlord must offer a renewal lease to "any member of such tenant's family . . . who has resided in the housing accommodation as a primary resident from the inception of the tenancy or commencement of the relationship." Family for purposes of these two provisions is defined in section 2520.6(o) as: "A husband, wife, son, daughter, stepson, stepdaughter, father, mother, stepfather, stepmother, brother, sister, nephew, niece, uncle, aunt, grandfather, grandmother, grandson, granddaughter, father-in-law, mother-in-law, son-in-law, or daughter-in-law of the tenant or permanent tenant."

All the enumerated relationships are traditional, legally recognized relationships based on blood, marriage or adoption. That being so, it would be anomalous, to say the least, were we to hold that the agency, hav-

ing intentionally limited succession rights in rent-stabilized accommodations to those related by blood, marriage or adoption, intended a different result for rent-controlled accommodations; especially so when it is recognized that rent control was intended to give way to rent stabilization and that the broader the definition of family adopted, the longer rent-controlled tenancies will be perpetuated by sequentially created family members entitled to new tenancies. These expressions by the Legislature and the DHCR are far more probative of the regulation's intended meaning than the majority's selective use of a favored dictionary definition.

Finally, there are serious practical problems in adopting the plurality's interpretation of the statute. Any determination of rights under it would require first a determination of whether protection should be accorded the relationship (i.e., unmarrieds, nonadopted occupants, etc.) and then a subjective determination in each case of whether the relationship was genuine, and entitled to the protection of the law, or expedient, and an attempt to take advantage of the law. Plaintiff maintains that the machinery for such decisions is in place and that appropriate guidelines can be constructed. He refers particularly to a formulation outlined by the court in *2-4 Realty Assocs.* v *Pittman*, 523 N.Y.S.2d 7 (Cir.Ct. 1987), which sets forth six different factors to be weighed. The plurality has essentially adopted his formulation. The enumeration of such factors, and the determination that they are controlling, is a matter best left to Legislatures because it involves the type of policymaking the courts should avoid, but even if these considerations are appropriate and exclusive, the application of them cannot be made objectively and creates serious difficulties in determining who is entitled to the statutory benefit. Anyone is potentially eligible to succeed to the tenant's premises and thus, in each case, the agency will be required to make a determination of eligibility based solely on subjective factors such as the "level of emotional and financial commitment" and "the manner in which the parties have conducted their everyday lives and held themselves out to society."

By way of contrast, a construction of the regulation limited to those related to the tenant by blood, marriage or adoption provides an objective basis for determining who is entitled to succeed to the premises. That definition is not, contrary to the claim of the plurality, "inconsistent with the purposes of the rent-control system" and it would not confer the benefit of the exception on "distant blood relatives" with only superficial relationships to the deceased. Certainly it does not "cast an even wider net" than does the plurality's definition. To qualify, occupants must not only be related to the tenant but must also "[have] been living with the tenant." We applied the "living with" requirement in *829 Seventh Ave. Co. v. Reider*, 493 N.E. 2d 939 (N.Y. 1986), when construing the predecessor to section 2204.6(d), and refused to extend the exception to a woman who occupied an apartment for the five months before the death of her grandmother, the statutory tenant, because she was not "living with" her grandmother. We held that the granddaughter, to be entitled to the prem-

ises under the exception, was required to prove more than blood relationship and co-occupancy; she also had to prove an intention to make the premises her permanent home. Since she had failed to establish that intention, she was not entitled to succeed to her grandmother's tenancy. That ruling precludes the danger the plurality foresees that distant relatives will be enabled to take advantage of the exception contained in section 2204.6(d).

Rent control generally and section 2204.6, in particular, are in substantial derogation of property owners' rights. The court should not reach out and devise an expansive definition in this policy-laden area based upon limited experience and knowledge of the problems. The evidence available suggests that such a definition was not intended and that the ordinary and popular meaning of family in the traditional sense should be applied. If that construction is not favored, the Legislature or the agency can alter it as they did after our decisions in *Hudson View Props. v. Weiss* and *Sullivan v. Brevard Assocs.*

Accordingly, I would affirm the order of the Appellate Division.

WACHTLER, C.J., taking no part.

Notes

1. For further commentary on the *Braschi* case, see James Esseks, *Redefining the Family*, 25 HARV. C.R.-C.L. L. REV. 183, 186-87 (1990).
2. The dissent argues that legislatures, not courts, should define "family," and other commentators have agreed. *See* Hubert Barnhardt, III, *Let the Legislatures Define the Family: Why Default Statutes Should be Used to Eliminate Potential Confusion*, 40 EMORY L.J. 571 (1991); Andrew Sullivan, *Here Comes the Groom: A (Conservative) Case for Gay Marriage*, NEW REPUBLIC, Aug. 28, 1989, at 20. In fact, a New York State legislator proposed leglislation to overrule *Braschi* and revert to a more traditional definition of family. *See* Arthur Leonard, *NY Legislator Proposes Overruling of Braschi*, 1991 LESBIAN/GAY L. NOTES 19; Alexander Grannis, *Apartment Rules Will Stop Landlords from Heartless Evictions; Legislative Inaction*, N. Y. TIMES, Jan. 10, 1990, at A26 (letter to the editor). Other New York State legislators have introduced a domestic partnership bill in response to *Braschi*. *See* Franz Leichter & William Passannante, *To Free NonMarried Couples from Legal Limbo*, N. Y. TIMES, Dec.

27, 1989, at A22 (letter to the editor). Another criticism of the decision states that it will turn landlords into spies. *See What's A Family: Turning Landlords Into Spies*, N. Y. TIMES, July 11, 1989, at A18.

3. *Braschi* technically applied only to rent-controlled apartments, of which there are about 100,000 in New York. Rent stabilized apartments, on the other hand, number more than a million. The New York State Division of Housing and Community Renewal has adopted regulations codifying *Braschi* and applying its test to rent stabilized apartments as well, N.Y. COMP. CODES R. & REGS. tit. 9, § 2204.6(d)(3)(i) (Supp. 1992), and this move has been upheld against a challenge from landlords. *See Rent Stabilization Ass'n of N.Y. v. Higgins*, 562 N.Y.S.2d 962 (App. Div. 1990).

4. Since *Braschi*, lower courts in New York have consistently applied the plurality opinion's test to protect surviving family members, although in the process of doing so, they have uncovered other issues. In *Lerad Realty Co. v. Reynolds*, *cited in* Arthur Leonard, *NY Courts Develop New "Family" Principles After* Braschi,1990 LESBIAN/GAY LAW NOTES 63 (Civ. Ct. N.Y. Co. 1990), the court ruled that a surviving gay life partner could succeed to his deceased lover's rent controlled tenancy notwithstanding the fact that neither had "come out" to their blood relations. And in *Picon v. O.D.C. Assocs.*, No. 22894/86, (Sup. Ct. Jan. 28, 1991), the court ruled that the surviving life partner's "affair" with another man did not invalidate his claim to the rent controlled apartment of his deceased lover.

5. *Braschi* arose after Blanchard and Braschi had lived together for a number of years. Under other circumstances, the couple's very living together might have been illegal or subjected either or both of them to eviction. *See generally Developments in the Law — Sexual Orientation and the Law*, 102 HARV. L. REV. 1610-16 (1989). Zoning restrictions that prohibit occupancy by individuals who are not related by blood, marriage, or adoption have generally been upheld as constitutional. *Compare Moore v. City of East Cleveland*, 431 U.S. 494 (1977) (striking a restriction on related individuals' cohabitation) *with Village of Belle Terre v. Boraas*, 416 U.S. 1 (1974) (upholding a restriction on unrelated individuals' cohabitation).

6. Landlords and housing cooperatives also sometimes insist on lease provisions that restrict occupancy to legally-related individuals. *See, e.g., Maryland Comm'n on Human Relations v. Greenbelt Homes*, 475 A.2d 1192 (Md. 1984) (finding that restrictions are not discrimination on the basis of marital status); *Hudson View Properties v. Weiss*, 450 N.E.2d 234 (N.Y. 1983) (finding that restrictions are not discrimination on the basis of marital status); *Evangelista Assocs. v.* Bland, 458 N.Y.S.2d 996 (Civ. Ct. 1983) (finding that restrictions are not discrimination on the basis of sexual orientation).

7. Public housing rules are set by the federal Department of Housing and Urban Development (HUD), subject to approval by local housing authorities. In 1977, HUD opened public housing to families defined as "two or more persons, sharing residency whose income and resources are available to meet the family's needs and who are related by blood, marriage or operation of law, or have evidenced a stable family relationship," 24 C.F.R. § 812.2(d)(1) (1977), the last clause pertaining to same-sex and unmarried couples. Within a month, the regulation was nullified by an act of Congress, primarily to deny eligibility to same-sex couples. *See* 123 Cong. Rec. 19,076 (1977) (statement of Rep. Boland). Several courts have required local housing authorities to open their doors to unmarried straight couples, *see Hann v. Hous. Auth. of City of Easton*, 709 F. Supp. 605 (E.D. Pa. 1989); *James v.* New York City Hous. Auth., 622 F. Supp. 135 (S.D.N.Y. 1985); *Atkisson v. Kern County Hous. Auth.*, 130 Cal. Rptr. 375 (Cal. Ct. App. 1976), but prohibitions on same-sex couples have not been challenged.

8. Under the Food Stamp Program, any "household" that satisfies the financial criteria may qualify. Although the original statute restricted recipient households to those in which everyone was related by blood or marriage, this restriction was struck down as unrelated to

the overall purpose of the statute. *See United States Dep't of Agric. v.* Moreno, 413 U.S. 528 (1973). *See generally* NAN HUNTER ET AL., THE RIGHTS OF LESBIANS AND GAY MEN 97-98 (3d ed. 1992).

STATE v. HADINGER

573 N.E.2d 1191 (Ohio Ct. App. 1991)

STRAUSBAUGH, Judge.

This is an appeal by plaintiff, state of Ohio, from a judgment of the Franklin County Municipal Court dismissing the charge of domestic violence against defendant on the basis that under Ohio law two women cannot be married and therefore could not be living in a spousal relationship. The record indicates that on August 6, 1990, defendant, Carol Hadinger, was charged with domestic violence in violation of R.C. 2919.25. The complaint provides in pertinent part:

"Complainant being duly sworn states that Carol Hadinger at Franklin County Ohio, on or about the 6th day of August 1990 did knowing [*sic*] cause physical harm to a household member, to wit, Ellensara Evans, person living as spouse, by means of biting said other person on the right hand. . . ."

■ ■ ■

. . .[P]laintiff argues that the trial court construed R.C. 2919.25 too narrowly so as to preclude its application to the facts in the present case. R.C. 2919.25 provides in pertinent part:

"(A) No person shall knowingly cause or attempt to cause physical harm to a family or household member.

". . .

"(D) As used in this section and section 2919.26 of the Revised Code:

"(1) 'Family or household member' means any of the following, who is residing or has resided with the offender:

"(a) A spouse, a person living as a spouse, or a former spouse of the offender;

". . .

"(2) 'Person living as a spouse' means a person who is living or has lived with the offender in a common law marital relationship, who otherwise is cohabiting with the offender, or who otherwise has cohabited with the offender within one year prior to the date of the alleged commission of the act in question."

R.C. 2919.25 specifically includes in its definition of a "person living as a spouse" a person who is otherwise cohabiting with the offender. No cases have been cited nor have we discovered any case law which defines the term "cohabit" as used in R.C. 2919.25(E)(2). However, for reference purposes we note that "cohabitation" has been defined in various other domestic relations cases. While these cases are limited by law and by their facts to persons of opposite sex, they do provide an appropriate starting point for our decision in the present case. In *Sindel v. Sindel*, 7 O.O.3d 223 (1975), this court held:

". . : The ordinary meaning of cohabitation is, of course, the act of living together. What constitutes living together is a question of fact in each particular case. . . . Ordinarily, isolated acts of sexual intercourse during the two-year period, unaccompanied by other aspects of living together, would not constitute cohabitation. Conversely, cohabitation can be based entirely on acts of living together without sexual relations. . . ." *Id.* at 226.

In *Lester v. Lester*, Franklin App. No. 81AP-84, unreported, 1981 WL 3186 (May 14, 1981), this court quoted from the *Sindel* decision and reiterated that "cohabitation means the act of living together."

While involving the termination of sustenance alimony, this court held in paragraph two of its syllabus in *Fuller v. Fuller*, 461 N.E.2d 1348 (Ohio App. 1983):

"Cohabitation *usually* will be manifested by a man and woman living together in the same household and behaving as would a husband and wife, although there need not be an actual assertion of marriage."

In *Taylor v. Taylor*, 465 N.E.2d 476, 478 (Ohio App. 1983), the court held:

". . . Sexual intercourse, in short, is not the *sine qua non* of the 'cohabitation' intended . . . . It may be a persuasive indicium of cohabitation, but it is not everything.

". . . [W]e conclude that the cause should be remanded to the trial court for a determination of the issue of cohabitation absent reliance on the *conclusive* nature of a sexual relationship between the parties."

The one factor common among each of the foregoing cases was that the parties were living together. This is also common to the definition of "cohabit" set forth by Random House Dictionary: "to live together as husband and wife, usually without legal or religious sanction . . . to live together in an intimate relationship. . . ."

Again, none of the cases cited involved two persons of the same sex and we are therefore in the present case faced with a unique factual situation. While the trial court apparently imposed the requirement that persons to be charged pursuant to R.C. 2919.25 have the ability to marry, such does not appear to be the case given the broad language of the statute. Given the language of R.C. 2919.25, this court concludes that the legislature intended that the domestic violence statute provide protection to persons who are cohabiting regardless of their sex. We believe that to read the domestic violence statute otherwise would eviscerate the efforts of the legislature to safeguard, regardless of gender, the rights of victims of domestic violence. We decline to adopt such a restrictive position and therefore conclude that R.C. 2919.25(E)(2) defining a "person living as a spouse" as a person "who otherwise is cohabiting with the offender" does not in and of itself exclude two persons of the same sex. Accordingly, plaintiff's second assignment of error is well-taken and is sustained.

■ ■ ■

Notes

1. As is evident from the *Hadinger* case, lesbian and gay families experience domestic violence. *See* Elizabeth Rhodes, *Closeted Violence*, SEATTLE TIMES, May 23, 1991, at F1; Martha Mahoney, *Legal Images of Battered Women: Redefining the Issue of Separation*, 90 MICH. L. REV. 1, 32-34, 49-53 (1991).

2. Although the "battered woman syndrome" has usually been applied only to women whose abusers are men, two recent trials have applied it in the context of lesbian relationships. In the first, in Los Angeles, the defendant was convicted of battering despite her lover's having recanted the charges. *See* Angela West, *Prosecutorial Activism: Confronting Heterosexism in a Lesbian Battering Case*, 15 HARV. WOMEN'S L.J. 249 (Spring 1992); *Lesbian Convicted of Beating Her Lover*, L.A. TIMES, Oct. 30, 1990, at B2. In the second, in Boise, Idaho, the defendant was acquitted of stabbing her lover based on a claim of self-defense against her lover's abuse. *See* Arthur Leonard, *Lesbian Defendant Prevails on Battered-Spouse Syndrome*, 1991 LESBIAN/GAY L. NOTES 25.

2. BENEFITS AND PROTECTIONS IN THE WORKPLACE

PHILLIPS v. WISCONSIN PERSONNEL COMMISSION

482 N.W.2d 121 (Wisc. App. 1992)

EICH, C.J.

■ ■ ■

The commission found the following facts, and they do not appear to be in dispute. Phillips has a committed lesbian relationship with Tommerup which is recognized by their families, friends, neighbors and co-workers. They share their incomes, rent a home and own an automobile together. They carry joint renters and auto insurance and take their vacations together. Tommerup has been financially dependent on Phillips since 1986, when she returned to school to seek a graduate degree. If the option were legally available to them in Wisconsin, they would marry.

Phillips applied to her employing agency, DHSS [Department of Health and Social Services], to change her health insurance from individual to family coverage so as to provide insurance for Tommerup as her "dependent." DHSS forwarded the application to the Department of Employee Trust Funds (DETF), the administrator of the state health insurance plan. Because sec. 40.02(20), Stats., and applicable DETF rules define "dependents" eligible for insurance coverage in terms of the employee's "spouse" or children,[2] her application was denied.

---

2. Section 40.02(20), Stats., defines "dependent" for purposes of the employee trust fund:

"Dependent" means the spouse, minor child, including stepchildren of the current marriage dependent on the employee for support and maintenance, or child of any age, including stepchildren of the current marriage, if handicapped.... For group insurance purposes only, the department may promulgate rules with a different definition of "dependent" than the one otherwise provided in this subsection for each group insurance plan.

Exercising the rulemaking authority delegated to it . . . the department adopted a rule defining "dependent" for health insurance purposes as: "[A]n employee's spouse and an employee's unmarried child who is dependent upon the employee or the employee's former spouse for at least 50% of support and maintenance...."

Phillips then filed a discrimination complaint with the personnel commission. The commission dismissed the complaint for failure to state a claim upon which relief could be granted and the circuit court affirmed.

I. CLAIMS UNDER THE FAIR EMPLOYMENT ACT

■ ■ ■

Marital Status Discrimination

"[T]he broad purpose of the WFEA [Wisconsin Fair Employment Act] is to eliminate practices that have a discriminatory impact as well as practices which on their face amount to invidious discrimination." Among other things, the act prohibits employers from discriminating against individuals on the basis of their marital status.

The legislature has established a standard health insurance plan which provides a "family coverage option" for "eligible dependents" of state employees and a "single coverage option" for other employees. As indicated above, the legislature and DETF have defined "dependent" in terms of the employee's spouse and certain of his or her children. Thus, to the degree it allows married employees to include their spouses and dependent children in their health insurance coverage, the state may be said to offer greater health insurance benefits to its married employees than to its single employees. The issue is whether the law and administrative rules implementing that dual coverage system conflict with the Fair Employment Act. We agree with the personnel commission and the trial court that they do not.

A basic rule of statutory construction is that the intent of the legislature should control the interpretation. This is especially true when two laws are claimed to be inconsistent: "Whenever a court is confronted with apparently inconsistent legislation, its goal is to ascertain the intent of the legislative body and construe the law accordingly." In such a situation, the aim is to reconcile the two laws, if at all possible; not to nullify one or the other.

Although single and married employees are treated differently under the current benefits scheme in that dependent coverage is available to a married worker's spouse, we agree with the commission that "the legislature did not intend this kind of differentiation on the basis of marital status to be violative of the WFEA." As the commission points out, nothing in the legislative history of the act suggests that it was intended to prevent the state from providing dependent health insurance benefits to an employee's spouse without extending them to an unmarried companion.

We note that the legislature added "marital status discrimination" as a form of discrimination prohibited by the WFEA at the same time it amended sec. 40.02(20) to adopt the current definition of "dependent." And "[w]hen the legislature enacts a statute, it is presumed to act with full knowledge of the existing laws, including statutes." We agree with the trial court that the commission could reasonably conclude from the timing of these amendments that the legislature did not intend that one would nullify the other.

We also note in this regard that while there is, admittedly, disparate treatment in this case, not all disparate treatment is discriminatory. It is only where similarly situated persons are treated differently that discrimination is an issue.

Here, the legislature has declared that eligibility for family health insurance coverage is determined by marriage or the presence of dependent children. We have no doubt that Phillips and Tommerup have a committed relationship that partakes of many of the attributes of marriage in the traditional sense. Despite this, however, the fact that Phillips regards Tommerup as her "spouse equivalent" does not make her "similarly situated" to a married employee in the context of a discrimination analysis. For good or ill, the fact is that under current Wisconsin law Phillips, unlike a spouse, has no legal relationship to Tommerup. The law imposes no mutual duty of general support, and no responsibility for provision of medical care, on unmarried couples of any gender, as it does on married persons. *See*, for example, sec. 49.90(1)(m), Stats., which declares that "each spouse has an equal obligation to support the other spouse," an obligation that may be compelled by the state and enforced in the courts. Thus, Phillips's legal status is not similar to that of a married employee,[6] and, for the reasons discussed, we conclude that the trial court and the commission properly rejected her claim of marital status discrimination under the Fair Employment Act.

Sexual Orientation Discrimination

Phillips argues that the rule's use of the term "spouse" to determine eligibility for dependent health insurance coverage has the effect of discriminating against her on the basis of her sexual orientation. Her position on this issue is substantially the same as that argued in support of her claim of marital status discrimination; it, too, emphasizes her inability to enter into a legal marriage with Tommerup. Again, we sustain the commission's ruling as reasonable.

In *Hinman v. Dept. of Personnel Admin.*, 213 *Cal. Rptr.* 410, 419 (Cal. App. 1985), the court upheld the denial of dental benefit coverage to unmarried partners of homosexual state employees against a challenge that to

do so discriminated on the basis of sexual orientation. In that case, as here, eligibility for dependent coverage was limited to the employee's "spouse" or unmarried dependent child, and the court rejected the appellant's claim that the provision distinguished between heterosexual and homosexual employees, concluding that it distinguished only between married and unmarried employees and that such a distinction was not improper.

In this case, the personnel commission ruled that Phillips's complaint failed to state a claim for discrimination based on sexual orientation because the challenged DETF rule distinguishes between married and unmarried employees, not between homosexual and heterosexual employees. Family coverage for Tommerup would be denied to Phillips if she were an unmarried *hetero*sexual — male or female — just as it is to her as a lesbian female.

And while she complains that she is not married to Tommerup only because she may not legally marry another woman, that is not a claim of sexual orientation discrimination in employment; it is, as we have noted earlier, a claim that the marriage laws are unfair because of their failure to recognize same-sex marriages. It is a result of *that* restriction, not the insurance eligibility limitations in the statute and the DETF rule, that Phillips is unable to extend her state employee health insurance benefits to Tommerup. And, as we said at the outset of this opinion, any change in that policy is for the legislature, not the courts.[8]

---

6. Phillips correctly points out that the rule includes "stepchild" in its definition of "dependent" and thus reaches beyond the bounds of legal dependency — at least as far as children are concerned. But, as we note elsewhere in this opinion, her claims in this case are grounded on the provisions of the rule limiting insurance coverage to the employee's "spouse." The provisions allowing coverage for an employee's children are not at issue.

8. [The court here refers to its n. 1 which appears at the outset of the decision as follows:]

Understandably, most of Phillips's arguments on gender and sexual orientation discrimination/classification are grounded on the fact that Wisconsin does not recognize same-sex marriages. Because dependent insurance coverage is not available to companions of unmarried state employees, and because she may not legally marry her female companion, Phillips claims she is being discriminated against because of her sexual orientation. She also contends that the rule discriminates on the basis of gender because male employees with female companions may legally marry their companions and secure the extended insurance benefits.

Gender Discrimination

Phillips next contends that the rule's use of the term "spouse" to define eligible dependents discriminates against her on the basis of gender. She argues that "as a female, she was being treated differently from all other *similarly situated males* [because] she could never qualify [Tommerup] . . . as a 'dependent' . . . by . . . marrying her." Thus, she maintains, "because only the opposite gender (males), can marry [Tommerup] . . . and qualify her as a 'dependent,' " the law and rule discriminate against her and all other female state employees.

Here, too, we agree with the court and commission that they do not — and for essentially the same reasons. As the commission noted, Phillips is not being treated differently from "similarly situated males." The only males whose situations are similar to hers are those with male "spousal equivalents"; and they, like Phillips, may not secure dependent health insurance coverage for their companions. Since the rule affects unmarried males and unmarried females equally, the personnel commission could reasonably conclude that Phillips has not stated a claim of gender discrimination.

II. CONSTITUTIONAL (EQUAL PROTECTION) CLAIMS

Phillips next argues that the DETF rule violates the equal protection guarantees of art. I, sec. 1 of the Wisconsin Constitution, in that it creates a classification of people who are denied certain employment benefits on the basis of marital status, sexual orientation and gender.

■ ■ ■

There are varying levels of analysis in equal protection cases. Generally, a government regulation will be presumed to be consonant with equal protection requirements as long as the classification drawn by the regulation has a "rational basis"; that is, if it "rationally furthers some legitimate, articulated state purpose." *Ben-Shalom v. Marsh*, 881 F.2d 454, 463 (7th Cir. 1989), *cert. denied*, 494 U.S. 1004 (1990). The United States Supreme Court has said, however, that when a statute or rule classifies by race, alienage, or national origin, "these laws are subjected to strict scrutiny and will be sustained only if they are suitably tailored to serve a compelling state interest." *City of Cleburne v. Cleburne Living Center*, 473 U.S. 432, 440 (1985).

Phillips first contends that sexual orientation and marital status are suspect classifications deserving the highest level of scrutiny. The trial court rejected that contention, relying on *Ben-Shalom*, 881 F.2d at 464 n.8, where the court stated that increased scrutiny — anything over and above the "rational basis" test — "is presently reserved for classifications by race, alienage, national origin, gender and illegitimacy." Specifically, *Ben-Shalom* re-

---

Phillips's inability to marry Tommerup is thus the key to her argument. But whether to allow or disallow same-sex marriages — or even whether to allow extension of state employee health insurance benefits to companions of unmarried state employees of whatever gender or sexual orientation — is a legislative decision, not one for the courts. Indeed, the point is well made in the briefs of the American Civil Liberties Union Foundation and the American Civil Liberties Union of Wisconsin Foundation, as *amici curiae*, when, urging us to rule that state insurance coverage be extended to employees' companions, they suggest that we can ensure responsible administration of such a program by "creat[ing] a scheme" to ensure that benefits are extended only to same-sex couples with adequate "indicia of commitment" to each other — or a "registration scheme" that "is enforceable and guards against fraud."

"Creation" of verification and registration systems designed to facilitate the extension of state employee benefits to the employees' unmarried companions — and an enforcement mechanism to ensure that only stable and committed same-sex couples are eligible for such benefits — is precisely the type of action committed to the legislature, as the policymaking branch of government. It is beyond all powers of this or any other court.

versed a district court decision directing the United States Army to reenlist a lesbian soldier, stating that "homosexuals do not constitute a suspect or quasi-suspect class entitled to greater than rational basis scrutiny for equal protection purposes." *Accord Woodward v. United States*, 871 F.2d 1068, 1076 (Fed. Cir. 1989), *cert. denied*, 494 U.S. 1003 (1990); *High Tech Gays v. Defense Indus. Sec. Clearance Office*, 895 F.2d 563 (9th Cir. 1990).

Phillips disagrees with that conclusion and counters with two citations. First, she points to a passage in Professor Tribe's text, AMERICAN CONSTITUTIONAL LAW, 2d ed. 1988, discussing the history of discrimination against homosexuals and concluding that "homosexuality should . . . be added . . . to the list of classifications that trigger increased judicial solicitude." *See also Watkins v. United States Army*, 837 F.2d 1428, 1444-48 (9th Cir. 1988) (analysis of relevant factors under U.S. Supreme Court decisions "ineluctably leads us to the conclusion that homosexuals constitute . . . a suspect class"). She also suggests that the fact that WFEA prohibits sexual orientation and marital status discrimination should, by itself, lead to higher scrutiny of such classifications in an equal protection analysis with respect to this claim.

We deem it unnecessary to reach the precise question, however. Because the law and rule challenged by Phillips in this case do not classify by sexual orientation, we do not even reach the threshold of an equal protection analysis.

As we noted above, Phillips's insurance application was denied not because of her sexual orientation, but because the person to whom she wished dependent coverage extended was not her spouse. She is thus in the same position as all unmarried heterosexual males and females; and because the rule does not classify on the basis of sexual orientation, the trial court correctly held that Phillips's complaint failed to state an equal protection claim on that basis.

Phillips's claim of improper classification based on gender meets a similar fate. While, as we have indicated, classifications based on gender are subject to an elevated level of scrutiny, her claim must fail at the very outset because, again, dependent insurance coverage is unavailable to unmarried companions of both male *and* female employees. A statute is only subject to a challenge for gender discrimination under the equal protection clause when it discriminates on its face, or in effect, between males and females. Because the rule does not classify by gender, that ends our inquiry.

■ ■ ■

Notes

1. As noted in *Phillips*, in *Hinman v. Department of Personnel Admin.*, 213 Cal. Rptr. 410 (Ct. App. 1985), a California appellate court had rejected a similar case brought by a gay man seeking dental benefits for his partner. Hinman alleged that the state's denial of partner benefits to lesbian and gay employees violated protections forbidding discrimination on the basis of sexual orientation and marital status. As in *Phillips*, the court disagreed with both arguments.

2. An appellate court in New York affirmed a lower court decision denying the city's motion to dismiss in a pending case challenging the failure of the city to provide health insurance benefits to the partners of lesbian and gay teachers. *Gay Teachers Assoc. v. Board of Educ. of N.Y.*, 585 N.Y.S. 2d. 1016 (App. Div. 1992).

3. In some instances, local ordinances require private employers to provide certain benefits to lesbian and gay couples, among others. In Washington, D.C., businesses with over fifty employees must

provide unpaid leave to those who need to care for ill family members, defined as "those with whom the employee shares or has shared within the last year a mutual residence and with whom the employee maintains an intimate relationship." *See* Arthur Leonard, *Ithaca, NY, Passes Domestic Partnership Ordinance*, 1988 LESBIAN/GAY L. NOTES 45; 1990 LESBIAN/GAY L. NOTES 55.

4. In *Rovira v. A.T. & T.*, Sandra Rovira and her sons are suing the employer of her now deceased partner of twelve years for the $55,000 in death benefits due to the employee's "spouse," "dependent children under the age of 23," and other dependent "relatives" on grounds that denial of benefits to them constitutes discrimination on the basis of sexual orientation and marital status. Although the state law claims were dismissed, the federal ERISA claims remain. *See Rovira v. A.T. & T.*, 760 F. Supp. 376 (S.D.N.Y. 1991).

5. As a result of a 1982 labor settlement, the *Village Voice*, a New York City newspaper, became the first private employer to offer partnership benefits to its lesbian and gay employees. *See* Joanne Wojcik, *Newspaper First to Offer Domestic Partnership Plan*, BUS. INS., Mar. 11, 1991, at 30. When employers agree to provide benefits, they are most often given to unmarried straight and gay couples on equal terms. *See, e.g.,* David Tuller & Marc Sandalow, *Next Step for Partners' Benefits*, S. F. CHRON., May 14, 1991, at A1 (Levi-Strauss and Morrison & Foerster); Claudia Deutsch, *Managing; Insurance for Domestic Partners*, N. Y. TIMES, July 28, 1991, § 3, at 3 (Ben & Jerry's Homemade, Inc., American Friends Service Committee, Greenpeace, National Organization for Women, and Planned Parenthood). Still, some employers have extended benefits only to gay couples and not to unmarried straight couples on the ground that straight couples are not precluded from marrying. *See* James Barron, *Bronx Hospital Gives Gay Couples Spouse Benefits*, N.Y. TIMES, Mar. 27, 1991, at A1 (Montefiore Hospital); Arthur Leonard, *Domestic Partnership Cause Advances*, 1991 LESBIAN/GAY L. NOTES 67 (Lotus Development Corporation).

6. The Internal Revenue Code does not recognize same-sex couples, which has led to mixed results for gay and lesbian taxpayers. *See generally* Patricia Cain, *Same-Sex Couples and the Federal Tax Laws*, 1 LAW & SEXUALITY 97 (1991). On the one hand, lesbian and gay partners whose incomes are similiar and below the top tax bracket avoid the "marriage penalty" that pushes married couples (even those filing separately) into a higher tax bracket, and they are not jointly and severally liable on each other's tax returns. On the other hand, unlike married spouses, lesbian and gay partners with disparate incomes cannot file jointly to avoid overly progressive rates on the higher earning partner. They cannot transfer property to each other free of income, estate, and gift taxes. Similarly, if they break up they cannot divide property or make support payments without paying taxes. *See, e.g.,* Douglas Kahn, *Taxing Question: Break Point for Navratilova*, N.J.L.J., December 9, 1991, at 57; SEXUAL ORIENTATION AND THE LAW, § 3.06 (Roberta Achtenberg, ed., 1985 & Release #4, Dec. 1991). And, as noted below, they must include in income any benefits their employers provide to their partners.

Furthermore, it is often difficult for a lesbian or a gay man to claim a partner as a dependent for income tax purposes. Although the partner may be a member of the same household and may be truly financially dependent, the exemption is specifically unavailable if the relationship is "in violation of local law." 26 U.S.C. § 152(b)(5)(1986). Unmarried straight couples in such circumstances need to be aware of laws against "cohabitation," *see Peacock v. Commissioner*, 37 Tax Ct. Mem. Dec. (CCH) 177 (1978), which are on the books in many states, but may be unconstitutional. *See Doe v. Duling*, 603 F. Supp. 960, 966-69 (E.D. Va. 1985) (holding law against cohabitation unconstitutional), *vacated on other grounds*, 782 F.2d 1202 (4th Cir. 1986). Likewise, lesbian and gay couples may need to be aware of sodomy statutes, although no court has applied them in this context.

Perhaps the most important tax question for lesbian and gay couples who pool their incomes is whether the transfers of wealth between them are taxable. Such transfers would generally meet the income tax definition of "gifts" and may also be considered "support payments," both of which are excludable as income to the transferee. *See* Cain, *supra*, at 114-16. Since the definition of "gift" differs for income tax and gift tax purposes, such transfers also might not have to be counted toward the annual $10,000 exemption from gift taxes, which otherwise would be exceeded for couples with disparate incomes, subjecting their personal living expenses to high taxes. The argument is that these transfers are not made to evade income taxes or to deplete the estate that will eventually be subject to inheritance taxes. Furthermore, they are often made pursuant to a legally enforceable agreement, much as interspousal support payments are considered non-gift-taxable because they are made pursuant to state marriage law. *See id.* at 123-29. Nevertheless, no rulings or court decisions have been made specifically on these points.

7. As in the tax context, marriage can also work to one's detriment in the Social Security context, where disability benefits are reduced for anyone who is married, even if the spouse is also receiving benefits, on the reasoning that two can live as cheaply as one. Furthermore, "a man and a woman" holding themselves out as "husband and wife" to the community in which they reside are considered married for purposes of this program. *See* 42 U.S.C. § 1382c(d)(2)(1992); *see also Smith v. Sullivan*, 767 F. Supp. 186 (C.D. Ill. 1991) (upholding constitutionality of the scheme). Nevertheless, the gendered phrasing of the statute would seem to preclude its application to same-sex couples.

8. In the context of unemployment compensation, courts have split on the eligibility of unmarried heterosexual partners for benefits if their partners move for job-related reasons. *Compare Norman v. Unemployment Ins. Appeals Bd.*, 663 P.2d 904 (Cal. 1983) (upholding denial of benefits), *with Reep v. Commissioner of Dep't of Employment and Training*, 593 N.E. 2d 1297 (Mass. 1992) (reversing denial of benefits). There are no recorded decisions dealing with same-sex couples, but the analysis would likely be similar.

9. In the context of workers' compensation benefits for "dependents" of covered employees, courts have generally not recognized the claims of an unmarried or unrelated cohabitant. *See Developments in the Law — Sexual Orientation and the Law*, 102 HARV. L. REV. 1508, 1618 (1989). The California Workers' Compensation Appeals Board, however, in *Donovan v. Workers' Compensation Appeals Bd.*, 187 Cal. Rptr. 869 (Ct. App. 1982), did recognize the death benefits claim of a same-sex partner if he could show he had been a "good faith member" of the deceased person's household.

10. Gay and lesbian couples have successfully obtained a variety of other spousal benefits, including discount privileges for spouses employed by department stores, *see* Arthur Leonard, *Partnership Benefits Spreading at D.C. Stores*, 1990 LESBIAN/GAY L. NOTES 25, and challenged bars on taking same-sex companions on vacations won under company incentive programs, *see* Arthur Leonard, 1989 LESBIAN/GAY L. NOTES 68. In addition, lesbian and gay couples — after legal challenges — have received "family" rates from some organizations and been allowed to use their frequent flier miles for travel with life partners. *See, e.g.,* Arthur Leonard, *Gays Take on Discriminatory Frequent Flyer Programs*, 1989 LESBIAN/GAY L. NOTES 33.

11. Universities provide a variety of benefits to married students and their spouses, and several extend these to same-sex partners. According to a 1990 Survey, 13 schools recognize same-sex partners of students for the purposes of housing; 4 for access to health services; and 6 for discounts on facility entrance fees. *See* NATIONAL GAY AND LESBIAN TASK FORCE POLICY INSTITUTE, DOMESTIC PARTNERS/NON-TRADITIONAL FAMILY RECOGNITION IN CAMPUS BENEFIT POLICIES (1990). Universities are often major local employers, and the survey found that 10

offer bereavement leave for same-sex partners of faculty and staff; 7 offer sick leave; 7 offer parenting leave; and 1 offers tuition reduction. *See id.* Many of these also recognize other unmarried couples and require an affidavit, evidence of a joint bank account, or other proof of relationship.

12. Insurance companies also provide special rates and coverages for married couples. For instance, auto insurance rates for single people are 25 to 40 percent more than for married couples. Even in states that prohibit discrimination on the basis of sexual orientation or marital status, insurers merely have to show some actuarial basis for the differential, in which gay life partners can be lumped with single teenagers. *See* NAN HUNTER ET AL., THE RIGHTS OF LESBIANS AND GAY MEN 94 (3d.ed.1992). Nevertheless, the American Automobile Association of Southern California now offers married rates to gay couples, as a result of a legal settlement. *See* Arthur Leonard, LESBIAN/GAY L. NOTES, June 1985, at 23.

    Further complications result when claims are filed on behalf of gay life partners under individual policies that cover "spouses," "family members," or "dependents." Although there are no reported cases involving same-sex couples in this situation, courts have generally been reluctant to cover household members not related by blood, adoption, or marriage, *see generally* 36 A.L.R. 4th 588, and have refused coverage to a gay man under a casualty insurance policy covering his life partner's "resident relatives." *Eisner v. Aetna Casualty & Surety Co.*, N.Y.L.J., Nov. 16, 1988, at 22 (Sup. Ct. Nov. 3, 1988).

    For a discussion of the special issues life insurance sometimes poses for gay couples, see HUNTER ET AL., *supra*, at 92-94.

3. GUARDIANSHIP

IN RE GUARDIANSHIP OF KOWALSKI

478 N.W.2d 790 (Minn. Ct. App. 1991)

DAVIES, Judge.

■ ■ ■

FACTS

Sharon Kowalski is 35 years old. On November 13, 1983, she suffered severe brain injuries in an automobile accident which left her in a wheelchair, impaired her ability to speak, and caused severe loss of short-term memory.

At the time of the accident, Sharon was sharing a home in St. Cloud with her lesbian partner, appellant Karen Thompson. They had exchanged rings, named each other as insurance beneficiaries, and had been living together as a couple for four years. Sharon's parents were not aware of the lesbian relationship at the time of the accident. Sharon's parents and siblings live on the Iron Range, where Sharon was raised.

In March of 1984, both Thompson and Sharon's father, Donald Kowalski, cross-petitioned for guardianship. Thompson, expecting that she would have certain visitation rights and input into medical decisions, agreed to the appointment of Mr. Kowalski as Sharon's guardian. The guardianship order, however, gave complete control of visitation to Kowalski, who subsequently received court approval to terminate Thompson's visitation rights on July 25, 1985. Kowalski immediately relocated Sharon from a nursing home in Duluth to one in Hibbing.

In May of 1988, Judge Robert Campbell ordered specialists at Miller-Dwan Medical Center to examine Sharon to determine her level of functioning and whether Sharon could express her wishes on visitation. The doctors concluded that Sharon wished to see Thompson, and the court permitted Thompson to reestablish visitation in January of 1989. The doctors also recommended in 1989 that Sharon be relocated to Trevilla at Robbinsdale, where she currently resides. After Sharon's move, Thompson was permitted to bring Sharon to her St. Cloud home for semi-monthly weekend visits.

In late 1988, Kowalski notified the court that, due to his own medical problems, he wished to be removed as Sharon's guardian. The court granted his request effective May 1990. After being notified of Kowalski's request to relinquish guardianship, Thompson, on August 7, 1989, filed a petition for appointment as successor guardian of Sharon's person and estate. No competing petition was filed.

The court held a hearing on Thompson's petition on August 2, 1990. The court wished to conduct further evidentiary hearings, and evidence was taken in both Duluth and Minneapolis over the next several months.

Karen Tomberlin is a friend of the Kowalski family. She did not file a petition for guardianship. Rather, she contacted Sharon's attorney indicating that she wished to testify in opposition to Thompson's petition and submitted a letter to the court suggesting that she be considered as an alternative guardian. Sharon's attorney, in a letter to the trial court prior to the initial August 2, 1990, hearing on Thompson's petition, also included Tomberlin's name as a possibility for guardianship.

The evidentiary hearings in Minneapolis and Duluth were directed toward evaluating Thompson's petition. Thompson called approximately 16 medical witnesses, all of whom had treated Sharon and had firsthand knowledge of her condition and care. Thompson thus exercised little choice as to which medical witnesses were called from Miller-Dwan and Trevilla. The trial court appointed the Miller-Dwan evaluation team, and it was that team which recommended Sharon's transfer to Trevilla. The court also appointed the social worker who testified at the hearing. These witnesses testified about Thompson's interaction with Sharon and the medical staff, Sharon's recovery progress, and Sharon's ability reliably to express her preference in this matter.

The court also heard testimony from three witnesses in opposition to Thompson's petition: Debra Kowalski, Sharon's sister; Kathy Schroeder, a friend of Sharon and the Kowalskis; and Tomberlin. These witnesses had no medical training, each had visited Sharon infrequently in recent years, and none had accompanied Sharon on any outings from the institution. Sharon's parents chose not to attend the hearing.

On April 23, 1991, the trial court denied Thompson's petition for guardianship and simultaneously appointed Tomberlin as guardian without conducting a separate hearing into her qualifications. Thompson appeals to this court.

ISSUE

Did the trial court abuse its discretion in denying appellant's petition for guardianship of Sharon Kowalski?

ANALYSIS

■ ■ ■

I.

Guardianship proceedings are governed by Minn.Stat. §§ 525.539-525.6198 (1990).

Minn.Stat. § 525.551, subd. 5, provides that after a hearing on a petition for guardianship,

> [t]he court shall make a finding that appointment of the person chosen as guardian or conservator is in the best interests of the ward.

The statute defines the "best interests of the ward" to be:

> [A]ll relevant factors to be considered or evaluated by the court in nominating a guardian or conservator, including but not limited to:
>
> (1) the reasonable preference of the ward or conservatee, if the court determines the ward or conservatee has sufficient capacity to express a preference;
>
> (2) the interaction between the proposed guardian or conservator and the ward or conservatee; and
>
> (3) the interest and commitment of the proposed guardian or conservator in promoting the welfare of the ward or conservatee and the proposed guardian's or conservator's ability to maintain a current understanding of the ward's or conservatee's physical and mental status and needs. In the case of a ward or conservatorship of the person, welfare includes:
>
> > (i) food, clothing, shelter, and appropriate medical care;
> >
> > (ii) social, emotional, religious, and recreational requirements; and
> >
> > (iii) training, education, and rehabilitation.

Kinship is not a conclusive factor in determining the best interests of the ward or conservatee but should be considered to the extent that it is relevant to the other factors contained in this subdivision.

There is no language in the statute specifically directing that a guardian be a neutral, detached party. To the contrary, when taken as a whole, the statute's enumerated factors direct that a guardian be someone who is preferred by the ward if possible, has a positive interaction with the ward, and has high involvement with, and commitment to, promoting the ward's welfare. This necessarily entails a guardian with demonstrated understanding and knowledge of the ward's physical and emotional needs.

1. The Ward's Expressed Preference

The court heard testimony from its appointed evaluation team at Miller-Dwan about Sharon's ability to express a reliable preference as to where and with whom she wanted to be. After a four-month evaluation, the doctor overseeing the evaluation submitted the following recommendation to the court:

> We believe Sharon Kowalski has shown areas of potential and ability to make rational choices in many areas of her life and she has consistently indicated a desire to return home. And by that, she means to St. Cloud to live with Karen Thompson again. Whether that is possible is still uncertain as her care will be difficult and burdensome. We think she deserves the opportunity to try.

All the professional witnesses concurred in this conclusion, including Sharon's current treating physician. No contradictory evidence was provided from any professionals who worked with Sharon.

The three lay witnesses who opposed Thompson's petition were skeptical that Sharon could reliably express her wishes, saying that Sharon changed her mind too often to believe what she said, given her impaired short-term memory.

Despite the uncontradicted medical testimony about Sharon's capability to make choices in her life, the trial court concluded that Sharon could not express a reliable preference for guardianship. This court finds that, in the absence of contradictory evidence about Sharon's decision-making capacity from a professional or anyone in daily contact with her, the trial court's conclusion was clearly erroneous.

A ward with sufficient capacity may express a wish as to a guardian under Minn.Stat., § 525.539, subd. 7, and may also nominate a successor guardian under Minn.Stat. § 525.59. If the ward has sufficient capacity, the ward's choices may only be denied by the court if found not to be in the ward's best interests. *Id.* It is clear that Sharon's expressed preference to live with Thompson and to return home to St. Cloud is a significant factor that must be considered in the guardianship proceeding.

2. Petitioner's Qualifications

The medical professionals were all asked about Thompson's qualifications with respect to the statutory criteria. The testimony was consistent that Thompson: (1) achieves outstanding interaction with Sharon; (2) has extreme interest and commitment in promoting Sharon's welfare; (3) has an exceptional current understanding of Sharon's physical and mental status and needs, including appropriate rehabilitation; and (4) is strongly equipped to attend to Sharon's social and emotional needs.

Sharon's caretakers described how Thompson has been with Sharon three or more days per week, actively working with her in therapy and daily care. They described Thompson's detailed knowledge of Sharon's condition, changes, and needs.

The doctors unanimously testified that their long-term goal for Sharon's recovery is to assist her in returning to life outside an institution. It is undisputed that Thompson is the only person willing or able to care for Sharon outside an institution. In fact, Thompson has built a fully handicap-accessible home near St. Cloud in the hope that Sharon will be able to live there. On the other hand, Sharon's sister testified that none of her relatives is able to care for Sharon at home, and that her parents can no longer take Sharon for overnight visits. Tomberlin testified that she is not willing or

able to care for Sharon at home and is in a position only to supervise Sharon's needs in an institution.

Sharon's doctors and therapists testified that care for Sharon on an outing and in a home setting could be provided by a person acting alone. While Thompson would certainly need assistance for bathing, therapy, and medical care, the doctors testified that this can be accomplished with the assistance of a home health care organization.

The medical witnesses also testified about Thompson's effectiveness with Sharon's rehabilitation. They all agreed that Sharon can be stubborn and will often refuse to cooperate in therapy. They testified, however, that Thompson is best able to get Sharon motivated to work through the sometimes painful therapy. Moreover, Thompson is oftentimes the only one who can clean Sharon's mouth and teeth, since Sharon is apparently highly sensitive to invasion of her mouth. Oral hygiene is crucial to prevent recurrence of a mouth fungus which can contribute to pain and tooth loss, further inhibiting Sharon's communication skills and her ability to eat solid foods.

Finally, the medical witnesses were asked how Thompson interacted with the staff and whether she was troublesome or overbearing in her demands for Sharon. No witness responded that Thompson caused trouble, but rather each said she is highly cooperative and exceptionally attentive to what treatments and activities are in Sharon's best interests. The court-appointed social worker also testified that Thompson was attentive to Sharon's needs, and would be a forceful advocate for Sharon's rehabilitation.

The trial court concluded that "[c]onstant, *long-term* medical supervision in a neutral setting, such as a nursing home . . . is the ideal for Sharon's long-term care," and that "Ms. Thompson is incapable of providing, as a single caretaker, the necessary health care to Sharon at Thompson's home in St. Cloud." (Emphasis in original.) These conclusions are without evidentiary support and clearly erroneous as they are directly contradicted by the testimony of Sharon's doctors and other care providers. The court is not in a position to make independent medical determinations without support in the record.

3. The Court's Choice of a "Neutral" Guardian

The trial court recognized Thompson and Sharon as a "family of affinity" and acknowledged that Thompson's continued presence in Sharon's life was important. In its guardianship decision, however, the court responded to the Kowalski family's steadfast opposition to Thompson being named guardian. Debra Kowalski testified that her parents would refuse ever to visit Sharon if Thompson is named guardian. The trial court likened the situation to a "family torn asunder into opposing camps," and concluded that a neutral third party was needed as guardian.

The record does not support the trial court's conclusion that choosing a "neutral" third party is now necessary. Thompson testified that she is committed to reaching an accommodation with the Kowalskis whereby they could visit with Sharon in a neutral setting or in their own home. While acknowledging Thompson's demonstrated willingness to facilitate all parties' involvement with Sharon, the trial court failed to address any alternative visitation arrangements for the Kowalskis such as Thompson's suggestion that Tomberlin be a neutral driver for Sharon on regular visits to the Iron Range.

Thompson's appointment as guardian would not, of itself, result in the family ceasing to visit Sharon. The Kowalskis are free to visit their daughter if they wish. It is not the court's role to accommodate one side's threatened intransigence, where to do so would deprive the ward of an otherwise suitable and preferred guardian.

The court seized upon Tomberlin as a neutral party in this case. This decision, however, is not supported by sufficient evidence in the record as to either Tomberlin's suitability for guardianship or her neutrality. The record is clear that at all times, the focus of the evidentiary hearing was to evaluate Thompson's qualifications to be guardian, not to evaluate the qualifications of Tomberlin. The medical and therapy staff were not questioned about Tomberlin's interaction with Sharon, her knowledge and current understanding of Sharon's medical and physical needs, or her ability to attend to Sharon's other social and emotional needs. Sharon's current treating physician testified that she had had no interaction with Tomberlin, and she was not asked to evaluate Tomberlin's knowledge of, or interaction with, Sharon. In fact, given that Tomberlin rarely visited Sharon, it is unlikely that these witnesses would have been able to comment knowledgeably on Tomberlin's qualifications.

The trial court's written findings on Tomberlin's qualifications are merely a recitation of the statutory criteria without reference to any evidence presented in court. Given that none of the witnesses except Debra Kowalski and Schroeder were questioned about Tomberlin, there was no substantive basis on which the court could make a reasoned determination that she is superior to Thompson.

There was equally little evidence establishing Tomberlin's neutrality in this case. Tomberlin testified that all her information about Sharon's situation has come directly from the Kowalskis and that she talks with them weekly. Tomberlin lives near the Kowalskis and helped facilitate the appearance at the hearing of Schroeder and Debra Kowalski in opposition to Thompson. Both in her deposition and at the hearing, Tomberlin testified that her first and primary goal as guardian was to relocate Sharon to the Iron Range, close to her family. This testimony undermines the one "qualification" relied on by the trial court in appointing Tomberlin—her role as an impartial mediator.

4. Court-Identified Deficiencies in Appellant's Petition

Part of the court's attempt to find a third party to act as Sharon's guardian apparently stemmed from certain past decisions and actions of the parties. The court found fault with Thompson on several issues the court viewed as contrary to Sharon's best interest.

Specifically, the court suggested that Thompson's statement to the family and to the media that she and Sharon are lesbians was an invasion of privacy, perhaps rising to the level of an actionable tort. The court also took issue with Thompson taking Sharon to public events, including some gay and lesbian-oriented gatherings and other community events where Thompson and Sharon were featured guests. Finally, the court concluded that Thompson's solicitation of legal defense funds and her testimony that she had been involved in other relationships since Sharon's accident raised questions of conflicts of interest with Sharon's welfare.

The record does not support the trial court's concern on any of these issues. First, while the extent to which Sharon had publicly acknowledged her sexual preference at the time of the accident is unclear, this is no longer relevant. Since the accident, Sharon's doctors and therapists testified that Sharon has voluntarily told them of her relationship with Thompson. Moreover, Sharon's doctor testified that it was in Sharon's best interest for Thompson to reveal the nature of their relationship promptly after the accident because it is crucial for doctors to understand who their patient was prior to the accident, including that patient's sexuality.

Second, there was no evidence offered at the hearing to suggest that Sharon is harmed or exploited by her attendance at public events. In fact, the court authorized Sharon to travel with Thompson to receive an award at the National Organization for Women's annual convention. A staff person who accompanied Sharon to one of these events testified that Sharon "had a great time" and interacted well with other people.

A doctor who observed Sharon at two different events testified that Sharon enjoyed herself and was happy to be in attendance. The only negative testimony about these outings consisted of speculation from Schroeder and Debra Kowalski that they did not think Sharon would enjoy the events, particularly those that were gay and lesbian-oriented in nature. They were, however, never in attendance and had no opportunity to evaluate Sharon's reaction firsthand.

Finally, there is no evidence in the record about a conflict of interest over Thompson's collection of defense funds or her other personal relationships. The evidence showed the money was raised in Thompson's own name to help defray the cost of years of litigation and that none of it was used for her personal expenses. Thompson testified that whatever extra money raised was used to purchase special equipment for Sharon, such as her voice machine, motorized wheelchair, hospital bed, and a special lift for transfers.

Only one doctor was questioned about the issue of Thompson's social life. The doctor routinely deals with families of brain-injured patients, and testified that each family deals with such a crisis in its own way. She said it is not uncommon for spouses to make changes in their personal lives while maintaining their commitment to the injured person. Thompson testified that anyone who is involved in her life understands that she and Sharon are "a package deal," and that nothing would interfere with her commitment to Sharon's well-being. The other witnesses who testified about Thompson's interaction with Sharon over the past seven years could find no reason to question Thompson's commitment to Sharon's best interests.

■ ■ ■

CONCLUSION

While the trial court has wide discretion in guardianship matters, this discretion is not boundless. The Minnesota guardianship statutes are specific in their requirement that factual findings be made on a guardian's qualifications. The statutes also consistently require the input of the ward where possible. Upon review of the record, it appears the trial court clearly abused its discretion in denying Thompson's petition and naming Tomberlin guardian instead.

All the medical testimony established that Sharon has the capacity reliably to express a preference in this case, and she has clearly chosen to return home with Thompson if possible. This choice is further supported by the fact that Thompson and Sharon are a family of affinity, which ought to be accorded respect.

Thompson's suitability for guardianship was overwhelmingly clear from the testimony of Sharon's doctors and caretakers. At the same time, evidence of Tomberlin's qualifications was not in the record. More-over, Tomberlin's status as a neutral party was undermined by evidence of her close ties to the Kowalskis and her expressed intention to relocate Sharon, contrary to the doctors' recommendations that Sharon have a less-restrictive environment near Thompson.

We reverse the trial court and grant Thompson's petition. While under Minn. Stat. § 525.56, subd. 1, a guardian always remains subject to court control, it should be made clear that this court is also reversing specific restrictions on the guardian's decision-making power that might be read into the trial court order. She is free to make whatever decisions she and the doctors feel are necessary to achieve Sharon's best interests, including decisions regarding Sharon's location. Thompson is, however, directed to continue efforts at accommodating visitation between Sharon and the Kowalskis, without unreasonable restrictions.

■ ■ ■

Notes

1. For commenatary on the *Kowalski* case see Nan Hunter, *Sexual Dissent and the Family*, 253 NATION 406, 408-410 (Oct. 7, 1991); Anne B. Goldstein, *Representing Lesbians*, 1 TEXAS J. OF WOMEN AND L. 301 (1992).

2. Hospitals and other public institutions often deny visitation rights to people, such as lesbian and gay partners, who do not have a tie of kinship. One court ruled that, in the context of non-contact visits to prison inmates, such rules are so arbitrary as to be unconstitutional. *See Doe v. Sparks*, 733 F. Supp. 227 (W.D. Pa. 1990). Still, prohibitions on overnight visitation with legally unrelated persons have been upheld. *See In Re Cummings*, 640 P.2d 1101 (Cal. 1982).

3. In *Coon v. Joseph*, 237 Cal. Rptr. 873 (Ct. App. 1987), a California appellate court refused to recognize a gay relationship to be a sufficiently "close relationship" so as to allow a gay man to recover emotional distress damages after witnessing an assault against his lover.

4. In *Rowe v. Bennett*, 514 A.2d 802 (Me. 1986), a Maine court allowed an emotional distress action by a lesbian against the female psychotherapist who provided relationship counseling to her and her lover and then began dating her lover.

SIX

Lesbian and Gay Parenting

No connection between family, marriage, or procreation on the one hand and homosexual activity on the other has been demonstrated. . . .
Bowers v. *Hardwick*, 478 U.S. 186, 191 (1986)

[W]e protect the family because it contributes so powerfully to the happiness of individuals, not because of a preference for stereotypical households. . . . The fact that individuals define themselves in a significant way through their intimate sexual relationships with others suggests, in a Nation as diverse as ours, that there may be many "right" ways of conducting those relationships.
Id. at 204–05 (Blackmun, J., dissenting)

I. INTRODUCTION

In 1987 it was estimated that approximately three million gay men and lesbians in the United States were parents, and between eight and ten million children were raised in gay or lesbian households.[1] The law first encountered lesbian and gay parents in the context of the dissolution of heterosexual marriages. Increasingly, however, due in part to the availability of reproductive technologies, same-sex couples are bearing and raising children within gay or lesbian family units.[2] Alternative fertilization, *in vitro fertilization*, and surrogate motherhood give lesbians and gay men the opportunity to bring children into their relationships.

---

1. *ABA Annual Meeting Provides Forum for Family Law Experts*, 13 Fam. L. Rep. (BNA) 1512, 1513 (1987).

2. Nancy Polikoff, *This Child Does Have Two Mothers: Redefining Parenthood to Meet the Needs of Children in Lesbian-Mother and Other Nontraditional Families*, 78 GEO. L.J. 459, 459 n.2, n.15 (1990); *The Lesbian Baby Boom*, NEWSDAY, July 13, 1989, at 8; *Gay Couples Begin a Baby Boom*, BOSTON GLOBE, Feb. 6, 1989, at 2.

In addition to using reproductive technology, lesbians and gay men use existing legal mechanisms such as adoption and foster care to become parents.

The first section of this chapter considers how courts have used homosexuality as a basis for denying lesbian and gay parents custody and visitation rights. These cases examine common conceptions about gay and lesbian parenting. The second section considers the legal issues that are raised when lesbian and gay families are formed by adoption, foster care, alternative insemination, and surrogacy. After this overview of the formation of same-sex families, the chapter concludes with a section examining the legal consequences of the dissolution of lesbian and gay families.

◆

MAN CHILD: A BLACK LESBIAN FEMINIST'S RESPONSE
Audre Lorde

This article is not a theoretical discussion of Lesbian Mothers and their sons, nor a how-to article. It is an attempt to scrutinize and share some pieces of that common history belonging to my son and to me. I have two children: a fifteen-and-a-half-year-old daughter Beth, and a fourteen-year-old son Jonathan. This is the way it was/is with me and Jonathan, and I leave the theory to another time and person. This is one woman's telling.

I have no golden message about the raising of sons for other lesbian mothers, no secret to transpose your questions into certain light. I have my own ways of rewording those same questions, hoping we will all come to speak those questions and pieces of our lives we need to share. We are women making contact within ourselves and with each other across the restrictions of a printed page, bent upon the use of our own/one another's knowledges.

The truest direction comes from inside. I give the most strength to my children by being willing to look within myself, and by being honest with them about what I find there, without expecting a response beyond their years. In this way they begin to learn to look beyond their own fears.

All our children are outriders for a queendom not yet assured.

My adolescent son's growing sexuality is a conscious dynamic between Jonathan and me. It would be presumptuous of me to discuss Jonathan's sexuality here, except to state my belief that whomever he chooses to explore this area with, his choices will be nonoppressive, joyful, and deeply felt from within, places of growth.

One of the difficulties in writing this piece has been temporal; this is the summer when Jonathan is becoming a man, physically. And our sons must become men — such men as we hope our daughters, born

AUDRE LORDE, *Man Child: A Black Lesbian Feminist's Response, in* SISTER OUTSIDER: ESSAY AND SPEECHES 72 (1984).

and unborn, will be pleased to live among. Our sons will not grow into women. Their way is more difficult than that of our daughters, for they must move away from us, without us. Hopefully, our sons have what they have learned from us, and a howness to forge it into their own image.

Our daughters have us, for measure or rebellion or outline or dream; but the sons of lesbians have to make their own definitions of self as men. This is both power and vulnerability. The sons of lesbians have the advantage of our blueprints for survival, but they must take what we know and transpose it into their own maleness. May the goddess be kind to my son, Jonathan.

Recently I have met young Black men about whom I am pleased to say that their future and their visions, as well as their concerns within the present, intersect more closely with Jonathan's than do my own. I have shared vision with these men as well as temporal strategies for our survivals and I appreciate the spaces in which we could sit down together. Some of these men I met at the First Annual Conference of Third World Lesbians and Gays held in Washington D.C. in October 1979. I have met others in different places and do not know how they identify themselves sexually. Some of these men are raising families alone. Some have adopted sons. They are Black men who dream and who act and who own their feelings, questioning. It is heartening to know our sons do not step out alone.

When Jonathan makes me angriest, I always say he is bringing out the testosterone in me. What I mean is that he is representing some piece of myself as a woman that I am reluctant to acknowledge or explore. For instance, what does "acting like a man" mean? For me, what I reject? For Jonathan, what he is trying to redefine?

Raising Black children — female and male — in the mouth of a racist, sexist, suicidal dragon is perilous and chancy. If they cannot love and resist at the same time, they will probably not survive. And in order to survive they must let go. This is what mothers teach — love, survival — that is, self-definition and letting go. For each of these, the ability to feel strongly and to recognize those feelings is central: how to feel love, how to neither discount fear nor be overwhelmed by it, how to enjoy feeling deeply.

I wish to raise a Black man who will not be destroyed by, nor settle for, those corruptions called **power** by the white fathers who mean his destruction as surely as they mean mine. I wish to raise a Black man who will recognize that the legitimate objects of his hostility are not women, but the particulars of a structure that programs him to fear and despise women as well as his own Black self.

For me, this task begins with teaching my son that I do not exist to do his feeling for him.

Men who are afraid to feel must keep women around to do their feeling for them while dismissing us for the same supposedly "inferior" capacity to feel deeply. But in this way also, men deny themselves their own essential humanity, becoming trapped in dependency and fear.

As a Black woman committed to a liveable future, and as a mother loving and raising a boy who will become a man, I must examine all my possibilities of being within such a destructive system.

Jonathan was three-and-one-half when Frances, my lover, and I met; he was seven when we all began to live together permanently. From the start, Frances' and my insistence that there be no secrets in our household about the fact that we were lesbians has been the source of problems and strengths for both children. In the beginning, this insistence grew out of the knowledge, on both our parts, that whatever was hidden out of fear could always be used either against the children or ourselves — one imperfect but useful argument for honesty. The knowledge of fear can help make us free.

for the embattled
there is no place
that cannot be
home
*nor is.**

For survival, Black children in America must be raised to be warriors. For survival, they must also be raised to recognize the enemy's many faces. Black children of lesbian couples have an advantage because they learn, very early, that oppression comes in many different forms, none of which have anything to do with their own worth.

To help give me perspective, I remember that for years, in the name calling at school, boys shouted at Jonathan not — "your mother's a lesbian" — but rather — "your mother's a nigger."

When Jonathan was eight years old and in the third grade we moved, and he went to a new school where his life was hellish as a new boy on the block. He did not like to play rough games. He did not like to fight. He did not like to stone dogs. And all this marked him early on as an easy target.

When he came in crying one afternoon, I heard from Beth how the corner bullies were making Jonathan wipe their shoes on the way home whenever Beth wasn't there to fight them off. And when I heard that the ringleader was a little boy in Jonathan's class his own size, an interesting and very disturbing thing happened to me.

My fury at my own long-ago impotence, and my present pain at his suffering, made me start to forget all that I knew about violence and fear, and blaming the victim, I started to hiss at the weeping child, "The next time you come in here crying...," and I suddenly caught myself in horror.

This is the way we allow the destruction of our sons to begin — in the name of protection and to ease our own pain. My son get beaten up? I was about to demand that he buy that first lesson in the corruption of power, that might makes right. I could hear myself beginning to perpetuate the age-old distortions about what strength and bravery really are.

And no, Jonathan didn't have to fight if he didn't want to, but somehow he did have to feel better about not fighting. An old horror rolled over me of being the fat kid who ran away, terrified of getting her glasses broken.

About that time a very wise woman said to me, "Have you ever told Jonathan that once you used to be afraid, too?"

The idea seemed far-out to me at the time, but the next time he came in crying and sweaty from having run away again, I could see that he felt shamed at having failed me, or some image he and I had created in his head of mother/woman. This image of women being able to handle it all was bolstered by the fact that he lived in a household with three strong women, his lesbian parents and his forthright older sister. At home, for Jonathan, power was clearly female.

And because our society teaches us to think in an either/or mode — kill or be killed, dominate or be dominated — this meant that he must either surpass or be lacking. I could see the implications of this line of thought. Consider the two Western classic myth/models of mother/son relationships: Jocasta/Oedipus, the son who fucks his mother, and Clytemnestra/Orestes, the son who kills his mother.

It all felt connected to me.

I sat down on the hallway steps and took Jonathan on my lap and wiped his tears. "Did I ever tell you about how I used to be afraid when I was your age."

---

*   From "School Note" in *The Black Unicorn* (W.W. Norton & Company: New York, 1978), p. 55.

I will never forget the look on that little boy's face as I told him the tale of my glasses and my after-school fights. It was a look of relief and total disbelief, all rolled into one.

It is as hard for our children to believe that we are not omnipotent as it is for us to know it, as parents. But that knowledge is necessary as the first step in the reassessment of power as something other than might, age, privilege, or the lack of fear. It is an important step for a boy, whose societal destruction begins when he is forced to believe that he can only be strong if he doesn't feel, or if he wins.

I thought about all this one year later when Beth and Jonathan, ten and nine, were asked by an interviewer how they thought they had been affected by being children of a feminist.

Jonathan said that he didn't think there was too much in feminism for boys, although it certainly was good to be able to cry if he felt like it and not to have to play football if he didn't want to. I think of this sometimes now when I see him practicing for his Brown Belt in Tae Kwon Do.

The strongest lesson I can teach my son is the same lesson I teach my daughter: how to be who he wishes to be for himself. And the best way I can do this is to be who I am and hope that he will learn from this not how to be me, which is not possible, but how to be himself. And this means how to move to that voice from within himself, rather than to those raucous, persuasive, or threatening voices from outside, pressuring him to be what the world wants him to be.

And that is hard enough.

Jonathan is learning to find within himself some of the different faces of courage and strength, whatever he chooses to call them. Two years ago, when Jonathan was twelve and in the seventh grade, one of his friends at school who had been to the house persisted in calling Frances "the maid." When Jonathan corrected him, the boy then referred to her as "the cleaning woman."

Finally Jonathan said, simply, "Frances is not the cleaning woman, she's my mother's lover." Interestingly enough, it is the teachers at this school who still have not recovered from his openness.

Frances and I were considering attending a lesbian/feminist conference this summer, when we were notified that no boys over ten were allowed. This presented logistic as well as philosophical problems for us, and we sent the following letter:

Sisters:

Ten years as an interracial lesbian couple has taught us both the dangers of an oversimplified approach to the nature and solutions of any oppression, as well as the danger inherent in an incomplete vision.

Our thirteen-year-old son represents as much hope for our future world as does our fifteen-year-old daughter, and we are not willing to abandon him to the killing streets of New York City while we journey west to help form a Lesbian-Feminist vision of the future world in which we can all survive and flourish. I hope we can continue this dialogue in the near future, as I feel it is important to our vision and our survival.

The question of separatism is by no means simple. I am thankful that one of my children is male, since that helps to keep me honest. Every line I write shrieks there are no easy solutions.

I grew up in largely female environments, and I know how crucial that has been to my own development. I feel the want and need often for the society of women, exclusively. I recognize that our own spaces are essential for developing and recharging.

As a Black woman, I find it necessary to withdraw into all-Black groups at times for exactly the same reasons — difference in stages of development and differences in levels of interaction. Frequently, when speaking with men and white women, I am reminded of how difficult and time-consuming it is to have to reinvent the pencil every time you want to send a message.

But this does not mean that my responsibility for my son's education stops at age ten, any more than it does for my daughter's. However, for each of them, that responsibility does grow less and less as they become more woman and man.

Both Beth and Jonathan need to know what they can share and what they cannot, how they are joined and how they are not. And Frances and I, as grown women and lesbians coming more and more into our power, need to relearn the experience that difference does not have to be threatening.

When I envision the future, I think of the world I crave for my daughters and my sons. It is thinking for survival of the species — thinking for life.

Most likely there will always be women who move with women, women who live with men, men who choose men. I work for a time when women with women, women with men, men with men, all share the work of a world that does not barter bread or self for obedience, nor beauty, nor love. And in that world we will raise our children free to choose how best to fulfill themselves. For we are jointly responsible for the care and raising of the young, since *that* they be raised is a function ultimately, of the species.

Within that tripartite pattern of relating/existence, the raising of the young will be the joint responsibility of all adults who choose to be associated with children. Obviously, the children raised within each of these three relationships will be different, lending a special savor to that eternal inquiry into how best can we live our lives.

Jonathan was three-and-a-half when Frances and I met. He is now fourteen years old. I feel the living perspective that having lesbian parents has brought to Jonathan is a valuable addition to his human sensitivity.

Jonathan has had the advantage of growing up within a nonsexist relationship, one in which this society's pseudo-natural assumptions of ruler/ruled are being challenged. And this is not only because Frances and I are lesbians, for unfortunately there are some lesbians who are still locked into patriarchal patterns of unequal power relationships.

These assumptions of power relationships are being questioned because Frances and I, often painfully and with varying degrees of success, attempt to evaluate and measure over and over again our feelings concerning power, our own and others'. And we explore with care those areas concerning how it is used and expressed between us and between us and the children, openly and otherwise. A good part of our biweekly family meetings is devoted to this exploration.

As parents, Frances and I have given Jonathan our love, our openness, and our dreams to help form his visions. Most importantly, as the son of lesbians, he has had an invaluable model — not only of a relationship — but of relating.

Jonathan is fourteen now. In talking over this paper with him and asking his permission to share some pieces of his life, I asked Jonathan what he felt were the strongest negative and the strongest positive aspects for him in having grown up with lesbian parents.

He said the strongest benefit he felt he had gained was that he knew a lot more about people than most other kids his age that he knew, and that he did not have a lot of the hang-ups that some other boys did about men and women.

And the most negative aspect he felt, Jonathan said, was the ridicule he got from some kids with straight parents.

"You mean, from your peers?" I said.

"Oh no," he answered promptly. "My peers know better. I mean other kids."

II. PARENTING DISPUTES ARISING FROM HETEROSEXUAL MARRIAGES

A. Two Approaches

♦

LEROY'S BIRTHDAY

Raymina Mays

LeRoy was sitting in the easy chair, next to the stereo and not paying much attention to the rise and fall of Nina Simone's voice. When he was a boy he'd pound a closed hand on the arm of a chair to keep time. He knew the words to "Here Comes the Sun," but he did not sing. Knew how to weave in and out of the song, harmonize, meet Nina with his own melodious movements, but he did not. He just sat there, in the chair, fire in his eyes. Shaken. The impact of the I-don't-love-you-anymore of his voice still hanging over the silence.

April couldn't believe she was sitting on the couch across from him. Couldn't believe she was chain-smoking Nuella's cigarettes, blowing smoke rings but thinking fire. Couldn't remember if that room had ever been that hot.

LeRoy was ten when he last visited her and Nuella. It was after his daddy got custody though there had been no divorce or custody case. His daddy decided by himself that he'd keep LeRoy with him. He'd spend his weekends, Thanksgivings, and one month of his summer vacation with his momma. If she wanted to buy LeRoy's clothes and toys and pay for all or some of his education, she could. But, if she had any thoughts about trying to keep LeRoy for

good she could forget them because a judge would have to settle the problem, making known officially that she was an unfit mother, a dyke, and no woman besides. Then, she would in fact, never see LeRoy. Never live on the south side of town where she was living or never be able to live in the town of Busheville for that matter. And Roy, LeRoy's daddy, was sure she'd back away from a scandal like that.

Roy had his way about the arrangements, even though word got around town that she was in love with Nuella and had been seen in the bar on Forty-second Street, where Nuella and women in love hung out. Somebody in the neighborhood found out, threw bricks through their garage windows and spray-painted DYKE on one its doors and BULLDAGGER on the other, and she and Nuella had to move. They moved to South Bend, close to the bar of which Nuella had part ownership.

Every Saturday she and Nuella would drive to Busheville, pick up LeRoy at his daddy's house and give him what they thought was a week's worth of love in two days.

One Sunday morning while LeRoy was visiting, he walked in on April and Nuella while they were in bed to tell them that if

Raymina Mays, *LeRoy's Birthday, in* HOME GIRLS: A BLACK FEMINIST ANTHOLOGY 168 (Barbara Smith ed., 1983).

they planned to catch any fish that day they'd better get to it. Fish biting and them laying up in bed.

That was LeRoy's last weekend with them because as far as she could tell LeRoy had gone back and told his daddy that he liked being around April and Nuella because they loved each other, slept together, held each other.

Hell broke loose with Roy in Busheville because that was exactly what he wanted to hear. He had no witnesses before, to prove that April was actually sleeping with Nuella. Where speculation only lent itself to name calling and partial custody, a witness, her son, sent Roy to a lawyer and a judge and it became legal that she couldn't see LeRoy any more.

During the first few years she'd ride past his school or where he lived and look for him, then she gave him up entirely and she and Nuella tried to learn how to live without him. On his birthdays they'd buy wine and bad-mouth all the blues and the bitterness that the loss had caused.

April wanted badly to know how LeRoy remembered things and how long it had taken him to hate her. She was thinking those thoughts before he rang her doorbell because it was his birthday. Nuella had gone out to buy wine and she had been sitting in the easy chair, next to the stereo feeling good about

being thirty-seven and looking forward to thirty-eight. Having considerably warm feelings about Nuella and their years together. When the bell rang April ran to answer it because she thought that it was Nuella. LeRoy stood six feet tall in front of her. His bowed-legs gave him away. April reached for him, but he stepped to the side and brushed past her into the living room. He seemed to be looking for Nuella, so April told him about the store and the wine, but before she could tell him the reasons for it, he said he couldn't stay long and he had just three things to say. One, he hated her because she was a lesbian. Two, he'd never forgive her. Three, she was not his mother and she was no woman besides.

For what seemed like days he had been sitting in the easy chair, his words still echoing in April's ears, and her own words echoing in her own ears. Her words that she loved Nuella. And, when he asked if that was all she had to say for herself, the words "yes," that her life with Nuella was not open for debate with him at that moment and ever, because circumstances put ten years between that kind of sharing. Not open for discussion right then. That if he wanted apologies, she was only sorry that he had to grow up around such stupidity and intolerance. That it was his birthday, his birthday and he could stay if he wanted to.

CHICOINE v. CHICOINE

479 N.W.2d 891 (S.D. 1992)

MILLER, Chief Justice.

■ ■ ■

FACTS

Michael and Lisa Chicoine were married on March 5, 1983, in Jefferson, South Dakota.

The couple had two children, James, who was born on January 30, 1986, and Tyler, who was born October 23, 1987. Sometime during her pregnancy with Tyler, Lisa began the first of a series of admitted lesbian affairs which put a great strain on Chicoines' marriage. This was an open and notorious affair, and Lisa's lover even demanded that she be present for Tyler's delivery.

In February 1989, Lisa and her lover broke up; thereafter, Lisa entered a treatment program for anorexia nervosa. After Lisa left treatment, she returned to the marital home and openly began a series of homosexual affairs.

In August of 1989, Lisa and the children moved out of the Chicoines' home and into the home of one of her lovers. During this time, Lisa and her lover made plans for Lisa to divorce Michael and obtain custody of the children for them to raise after she and her lesbian lover were "married." Shortly thereafter, Michael obtained a temporary custody order and brought the children home.

In late August 1989, Michael filed for divorce on the grounds of extreme cruelty. After a trial on the merits, the court granted Michael a divorce and awarded him custody of the children. Lisa, who was undergoing treatment for various psychological problems, did not contest the custody award.

On the issue of visitation, the trial court found that while "Lisa had been less than discrete about her sexual preference" in the past and while she admitted her behavior in front of the children was inappropriate, it was in the children's best interest for Lisa to have restricted visitation rights. Lisa was awarded visitation every other weekend from 7:00 P.M. on Friday to 7:00 P.M. on Sunday; three weeks in the summer; and, alternating holidays as follows: New Years Day, Easter, Memorial Day, 4th of July, Labor Day, Veteran's Day, Thanksgiving Day, Christmas Eve; and Mother's Day. *The only restrictions were that no unrelated female or homosexual male could be present during the children's visits.*

The trial court also divided Chicoines' property. Michael received all of the farmland and all of the farm machinery, livestock and crops. Lisa received a car, cash she had already withdrawn ($19,000), and a cash award of $41,912.

DECISION

I

WHETHER THE TRIAL COURT ABUSED ITS DISCRETION IN GRANTING UNSUPERVISED OVERNIGHT VISITATION.

Michael argues the trial court abused its discretion in allowing unsupervised overnight visitations to Lisa. The trial court has broad discretion in awarding custody of minor children and likewise visitation rights; therefore, the trial court's decision can only be reversed upon a clear showing of an abuse of that discretion.

In cases such as this, the court's primary consideration is the best interests of the children. Michael contends the children's development will be harmed by the continued exposure to Lisa's homosexual lifestyle; therefore, it is not in their "best interests" to have unsupervised overnight visits with their mother.

■ ■ ■

The record in this case reveals:

1. Lisa has experienced myriad psychological problems including an eating disorder, depression, suicidal threats, sexual abuse as a child and active homosexual relationships with several female partners.

2. In the last two years of the marriage, Lisa was absent from the home frequently.

3. Lisa openly admits that she is an active homosexual and that she had many sexual encounters with female partners *during* the marriage to Michael.

4. Lisa and the children moved out of the marital home and into Lisa's lover's home.

5. Lisa and her lover were affectionate toward each other in front of the chil-

dren, caressing, kissing and saying "I love you."

6. The oldest son reacted by saying "Mommy don't touch," or "Don't!" when Lisa and her lover held hands.

7. Lisa and her lover were in an intimate position in bed when the oldest son entered the room. Lisa told her son to go back to bed and when questioned by her son as to why she was lying on top of the other woman, Lisa told him she was telling secrets. Lisa did not stop the sexual act to comfort her son.

8. On at least two occasions, Lisa took the children to gay bars in Sioux City when she was out looking for her lover.

9. On some occasions when the children were not present, Lisa publicly danced with females, kissing and caressing them on the dance floor.

10. On some occasions, James and Tyler were allowed to get in bed to sleep with Lisa and her lover. Sometimes, Lisa would be unclothed.

11. Lisa and her lover discussed getting married and raising the children in a homosexual marriage.

12. Lisa admits that it is inappropriate to hold hands, kiss and show affection to her lesbian partners in front of her children.

13. Lisa has openly exposed her homosexual feelings in front of her sons on more than one occasion.

14. Dr. Arbis testified that "unless Lisa blatantly and consciously encourages them [the children] to engage in sexual behavior, or *blatantly exhibits her sexual behavior in front of them*, they will not receive any adverse developmental messages in terms of their own sexual preferences."

Although the trial court tried to protect the children through the visitation restrictions, "we are troubled by the order's incomplete response to the uncontroverted evidence concerning the harm threatened to the children" by its granting extensive, unsupervised, overnight visitation. The trial court has a duty to ensure the children are protected at every turn . . . . "[a]t the very least, trial courts have the authority, and at times the obligation, to require a homestudy. . . . so it can be assured that the children are not placed, or do not remain, in surroundings seriously detrimental to their well-being."

[T]his is one of those situations where the trial court had the obligation to do more. Judges in these cases have the awesome responsibility to protect children and '[t]he parents' personal wishes and desires must yield to what the court in the discharge of its duty regards as the children's best interest.

Lisa and her psychologist have indicated that they believe she is now prepared and capable of providing a suitable environment for the children. At this juncture, this conclusion appears to us to be both speculative and premature. We are not reassured, given Lisa's past actions, that she will put the needs of her children first.

The trial court must have shared these doubts, since it placed restrictions on the visitation rights. However, these restrictions, especially considering the liberal visitation rights granted, are difficult, if not impossible, to enforce. Before granting such liberal visitation rights, the trial court must avail itself of other means, including a home study, to be assured that the children are not placed in an unsafe or unstable environment. Similarly, the trial court must provide adequate enforcement measures to assure compliance with any restrictions imposed should it persist in granting overnight visitation.

We reverse and remand with the direction that the trial court reconsider this issue in light of this holding.

■ ■ ■

HENDERSON, Justice (specially concurring in part; dissenting in part)

I join the writing of the Chief Justice concerning the reversal of the trial court on the liberal grant of visitation unto the lesbian mother. For years, she has followed a life of perversion and openly flaunted it before these children. At the hour of judicial atonement, she now pretends to have changed. This present façade is of transitory mood and a cunning plan, by employing a psychologist, to wrest away good judgment from the judicial officers hereunto attending this case.

Lesbian mother has harmed these children forever. To give her rights of reasonable visitation so that she can teach them to be homosexuals, would be the zenith of poor judgment for the judiciary of this state. Until such time that she can establish, after years of therapy and demonstrated conduct, that she is no longer a lesbian living a life of abomination (see Leviticus 18:22), she should be totally stopped from contaminating these children.[1]

After years of treatment, she could then petition for rights of visitation. My point is: she is not fit for visitation at this time. Her conduct is presently harmful to these children. Thus, she should have no visitation. *L. v. D.*, 630 S.W.2d 240 (Mo. App. 1982). *See also S.E.G.* v. *R.A.G.*, 735 S.W.2d 164 (Mo. Ct. App. 1987). Therein, the court ordered restricted visitation. Said case supports the Chief Justice of this state. In *Kallas* v. *Kallas*, 614 P.2d 641 (Utah 1980), the court approved of restrictions to prevent harmful effects upon children. Some courts have taken a position, under "sodomy statutes" that a homosexual partner (parent) is a criminal and therefore not a fit parent. *See* 102 HARVARD L.REV. 620-621 (January 1989). Note SDCL 22-22-2 setting forth acts constituting sodomy in this state. SDCL 22-22-1 defines rape as a felony. It appears that homosexuals, such as Lisa Chicoine, are committing felonies, by their acts against nature and God. *Actus naturae, actus Deus.* This is an old Latin phrase, which became a legal maxim.[2] Literally, it means an act against nature is an act against God. As of four years ago, twenty-four states and the District of Columbia imposed criminal sanctions on consenting adults who engage in private homosexual intercourse. *See*, Note, *Constitutional Challenges To Sodomy Statutes In the Context of Homosexual Activity After Bowers* v. *Hardwick*, S.D.L.REV. 323 (1987). In the case of *In Re B.*, 380 N.Y.S.2d 848 (1976), mother lost custody to father, after she admitted to being a homosexual. In said case, various experts testified to the emotional problems suffered by children being exposed to such a life style. In the case before this Court, the record reflects, by expert testimony, that there existed harmful effects to these children by their continued exposure to Lisa Chicoine's homosexual behavior and life style.

There appears to be a transitory phenomenon on the American scene that homosexuality is okay. Not so. The Bible decries it. Even the pagan "Egyptian Book of the Dead" bespoke against it. Kings could not become heavenly beings if they had lain

---

1. Every judicial decision of consequence, in my opinion, reflects a moral judgment.

2. For those who advocate that exercising a moral judgment is a violation of separation of "church and state," may I express: Those advocates would turn the First Amendment on its head proposing, in effect, that any belief can be fully exercised except religious belief. Judges have values, or should have. We need not be value-neutral. Why must I, or any judge, *e.g.*, follow Freud or Marx?

with men. In other words, even the pagans, centuries ago, before the birth of Jesus Christ, looked upon it as total defilement.[3] This case is in a divorce setting. If it were under the juvenile code of this state, rights to a child could be *totally terminated*, through a petition, by reason of "environment ... injurious to the child's welfare" imposed by parents upon a child. If petition is sustained, after a dispositional hearing, rights may be terminated by the court.

In *J.L.P.(H.)* v. *D.J.P.*, 643 S.W.2d 865 (Mo. Ct. App.1982) that court held that the trial court did not err in restricting visitation of a homosexual father. At page 870 thereof, it quotes a New York Supreme Court case and a New Jersey Superior Court case, both jurisdictions severely curtailing visitation rights. *In Re Jane B.*, 380 N.Y.S.2d 848 (1976); *In Re J.S. & C.*, 324 A.2d 90 (N.J. 1974), *aff'd per curiam*, 362 A.2d 54 (N.J. App. 1976).

Here, Lisa Chicoine's conduct is so aggravated and her mental dementia is so apparent, that until she has years of treatment, she should not have any visitation at all. She can order to show cause to have visitation when it is established she will not harm these children further.

■ ■ ■

[Justice Henderson further noted that the property division made by the trial court] compounded and perpetuated an existing wrong for it rewards a rejection of the good things in the sacrament of marriage. I would pray that God help the decent hard-working young farmers and ranchers of this state.

They have a tough road to hoe and they are rapidly becoming extinct. They are the vanishing Americans of this era, not the Mohicans. May the fires of matrimonial hell prevail against them not. In the property award, she has received far more than she deserved considering her minimal contributions to the marriage (indeed, she destroyed it) and her slight efforts to the accumulation of marital property. I would reverse the trial court on the property distribution; it is unfair and an abuse of discretion. . . .

CAVEAT

A caption in an article from the *Arizona Republic* dated December 27, 1991, taken from the *San Francisco Examiner*: "Radical Gay Group Dead After Infighting." Extracted portions are quoted: "The radical gay group Queer Nation is dead—a victim of its success in offending not only mainstream culture but its own membership as well." "It was an incredible free-for-all" at the end, member Alan Carson said. "People, mostly women, began to feel alienated," he said. "Some people were grabbing all the opportunities and the spotlight, drowning out a more diverse array of voices." "Disputes reportedly were resolved through screaming matches."

There is hope for our Nation. We have witnessed an upheaval in the churches over sexual ethics. This was recently epitomized in the Presbyterian Church (USA) which, essentially, knocked down efforts to condone sex relations of homosexuals.

---

3. Article VI of the United States Constitution provides that, *inter alia*, "no religious test shall ever be required as a conviction to any office or public trust of the United States." Notice the word "ever." Too many constitutional scholars engage in careless theory concerning church-state conflict; this thought process, often, is an effort to impose a religious gag upon judges of our country.

◆

MY LIFE YOU ARE TALKING ABOUT
Minnie Bruce Pratt

The ugliness, the stupid repetition
when I mention my children, or these poems,
or myself as mother. My anger when someone
tries to make my life into a copy of
an idea in her head, flat, paper thin.

How can I make any of this into a poem?
What do I mean by *this*? For instance:

Me standing by the xerox machine, clack, slide, whish. Another
teacher, I've known her five years, asks what I've been writing,
lately,

and I say: *These poems about my children,*

holding up the pages. Her face blanks. I'd never seen that
happen, the expression, a blank face—vacant, emptied.

She says: *I didn't know you had children.*

So I say: *That's what these are about. Not many people know*
             I have children. They were taken from me.

She says: *You're kidding.*

I say: *No, I'm not kidding. I lost my children because I'm*
             a lesbian.

She says: *But how could that happen to someone with a Ph.D.?*

I lean against a desk. I want to slap her with anger.

Instead,
I answer: *I'm a pervert, a deviant, low as someone on the street,*
             as a prostitute, a whore. I'm unnatural, queer. I'm a
             lesbian. I'm not fit to have children.

I didn't
explain: A woman who's loose with men is trash; a woman
             with a woman is to be punished.

Because this woman was supposed to be a feminist and
understand something.

Minnie Bruce Pratt, *My Life You Are Talking About, in* Crime Against Nature 67 (1990).

I walk away, carrying off the poems,
useless words, black tracks on flimsy paper.
So much for the carry-over of metaphor
and the cunning indirection of the poet (me)

who lures the listener (her) deeper and deeper
with bright images, through thorns, a thicket,
into a hidden openness (the place beyond the self:
see any of the preceding or following poems).

So much for the imagination. I don't say:
You've known for years who I am. Have you
never imagined what happened to me day
in and out, out in your damned straight world?

Why give her a poem to use to follow me
as I gather up the torn bits, a path made
of my own body, a trail to find
what has been lost, what has been taken,

when, if I stand in the room, breathing,
sweating a little, with a shaky voice,
blood-and-bones who tells what happened,
I get her disbelief? Or worse:

A baby-faced lesbian, her new baby snug in her closed arms,
smiles, matronizing, smug, and asks had I ever thought of
having children?

Have you ever thought of having children?

What I thought as the pay-phone
doctor's voice pronounced jovial
stunning pregnancy, advised philosophy
(why he had five, this one's only my
second) was: Where would my life be
in this concept *mother-of-two?*
There was no one around to see.
I could cry all I wanted while
I sat down and got used to the idea.

At a friend's house for dinner, we talk about my boys, her
girl, the love affairs of others, how I like morning bed with
my lover. She complains how sex is hard to get with a three-
year-old around, glances at me as if to say: You have it so
easy. Does say:

Well, if you had children.

In his crib the first baby bangs
his head on the side, little worm
wailing lost earth. He burrows,
pushes through, in, out my vagina,
while in another room, I cringe
at the push of his father's penis.

Other side of the door, the two boys
half-grown, rest gangly in their sleep.
In bed, her hand slides, cold, doubtful
from my breast. She frets: *What are they
thinking?* While I whisper, hot, heat
in my breath, how I lost them for touch,
dangerous touch, and we would not believe
the mean knifing voice that says we lose
every love if we touch. We pull close,
belly to belly, kiss, push, push,
no thought in writhe against ache,
our sweaty skin like muddy ground
when we come back to being there in bed,
and to the sleeping presence of children.

In a classroom, we wind through ideas about women, power,
the loss of children, men and ownership, the loss of self,
the lesbian mother. They have heard me tell how it has been
for me. The woman to my left, within hand's reach, never
turns her face toward me. But speaks about me:

It's just not good for children to be in that kind of home.

I am stripped, naked, whipped.
Splintered by anger, wordless.
I want to break her, slash her.
My edged eyes avoid her face.

I say: *Why do you think this?*

I do not say: What have you lost? What have you ever
                    lost?

Later I say: *This is my life you are talking about.*

She says: *I didn't mean it personally.*

Over the phone, someone I've known for years asks what am I
writing now?

I say: *I'm working hard on some poems about my
                    children.*

She says: Oh, how sweet. How sweet.

S.N.E. v. R.L.B.

699 P.2d 875 (Alaska 1985)

COMPTON, Justice.

■ ■ ■

I. FACTUAL AND PROCEDURAL BACKGROUND

Father is 34 years old. After a prior marriage ended in a divorce, Father met and then began living with Mother. After one and a half years, they married, but three months later they divorced. Mother was pregnant at the time of the marriage and divorce. Following this divorce, Father again remarried. Mother gave birth to the child four months after the divorce.

Mother is 33 years old. She, too, had been married before she met Father. She is presently a graduate student on leave from her regular employment. She is a lesbian, now living in Washington with a female companion. Father knew of Mother's sexual ambivalence when they married.

Mother and Father entered a child custody agreement at the time of the divorce, naming Mother primary custodian and granting Father reasonable visitation rights. The question of the best interests of the child was not litigated at that time, since the child was still *in utero*.

Three years after signing the custody agreement, Father moved for a change of legal custody in the best interests of the child, contending that Mother was a lesbian with radical political views, that she was emotionally unstable, and that he was in fact the child's pri-

mary parent and custodian. The superior court awarded custody to Father.

II. CUSTODY AWARD STANDARD

The best interests of the child control the outcome of all child custody disputes.

■ ■ ■

III. THE NEXUS REQUIREMENT

■ ■ ■

When a court determines the best interests of the child under the changed circumstances doctrine, the scope of judicial inquiry is limited to facts directly affecting the child's well-being. We have often endorsed the requirement that there be a nexus between the conduct of the parent relied on by the court and the parent-child relationship.

For example, that a mother is living with another man in an adulterous relationship does not justify denying her custody absent any indication of adverse effects on the child. Nor does bearing children out of wedlock or instability in relationships warrant a custody change where the parent's conduct does not adversely affect the child or the mother's parenting abilities. Even the mental health of the custodial parent is "relevant only insofar as it has or can be expected to negatively affect the child."

Father maintained in the superior court and on appeal that this case does not involve sexual preference discrimination issues. This is not supported by the record, which is replete with evidence that Mother is a lesbian.[4]

The trial court found that there had been substantial changes in circumstances justifying a custody modification. Specifically, the court entered Finding of Fact 51, which states:

> There has been a change of circumstances in the parties' lives since the original decree sufficient to warrant a review and change of custody to plaintiff as follows:
>
> (a) At the time of the earlier decree [the child] was unborn and custody in plaintiff was physically impossible;
>
> (b) A child has an overriding need to be with its mother during the first days and months of its life, if possible, and that phase of [the child's] life has passed;
>
> (c) Plaintiff and [his current wife] have become at least equal caretakers of [the child] and defendant has relinquished that authority in [the child's] life to them;
>
> (d) Defendant has since the original decree significantly changed personally including a choice to live a homosexual lifestyle;
>
> (e) Defendant has moved her residence to Seattle, Washington, and has left her profession, perhaps permanently, so that [the child's] household, community and contact with his father and most appropriate male role model will be significantly altered unless custody is changed to plaintiff;
>
> (f) Defendant has demonstrated an inability at times to cope with child rearing without significant support from plaintiff or others;
>
> (g) Defendant has actively interfered with the development of an open, frequent and loving relationship between plaintiff and their son....

Finding of Fact 51(d) reflects the taint apparent throughout the record.

In marked contrast to the wealth of testimony that Mother is a lesbian, there is no suggestion that this has or is likely to affect the child adversely.[6] The record contains evidence showing that the child's development to date has been excellent, that Mother has not neglected him, and that there is no increased likelihood that a male child raised by a lesbian would be homosexual. Simply put, it is impermissible to rely on any real or imagined social stigma attaching to Mother's status as a lesbian. *Cf. Palmore* v. *Sidoti*, 466 U.S. 429 (1984).

---

4. Sixteen of the 22 witnesses who testified discussed homosexuality. Sixteen of the 51 Findings of Fact and 2 of the 13 Conclusions of Law refer to Mother's lesbianism.

6. The only nexus found by the superior court between Mother's sexual preference and a possible adverse effect on the child related to the likely duration of Mother's current relationship. The superior court found that this relationship might be less stable and longlasting than Father's most recent marriage. However, this was essentially conjecture by the court, since there was no evidence Mother's relationship was not committed. Instead, the court relied on its own unsupported opinion that homosexual relationships are unstable and usually of short duration.

Since the lower court's findings were impermissibly tainted by reliance in part on the fact that Mother is a lesbian, we remand this case to the superior court to consider whether there has been a substantial change in circumstances justifying a custody modification. Consideration of a parent's conduct is appropriate only when the evidence supports a finding that a parent's conduct has or reasonably will have an adverse impact on the child and his best interests.

■ ■ ■

Notes

1. While *Chicoine* did not explicitly hold that it could never be in the best interests of a child to be in the custody of a gay or lesbian parent, the case is typical of the so-called *per se* approach, which presumes that the homosexuality of a parent, by itself, is sufficient to bar an award of custody or visitation. Regardless of the gay or lesbian parent's childrearing skills or relation to the child, it is presumed that the child will be harmed by such custody because of the very nature of homosexuality and likely adverse reaction of the community. *See* e.g., *Thigpen v. Carpenter*, 730 S.W.2d 510 (Ark. Ct. App. 1987); *Jacobson v. Jacobson*, 314 N.W.2d 78 (N.D. 1981); *S v. S*, 608 S.W.2d 64 (Ky. Ct. App. 1980); *Dailey v. Dailey*, 635 S.W.2d 391 (Tenn. Ct. App. 1981); *Roe v. Roe*, 324 S.E.2d 691 (Va. 1985); *M.J.P. v. J.G.P.*, 640 P.2d 966 (Okla. 1982); *S.E.G. v. R.A.G.*, 735 S.W.2d 164 (Mo. Ct. App. 1987).

2. In *Roe v. Roe*, 324 S.E.2d 691 (Va. 1985), the Virginia Supreme Court explicitly stated the *per se* approach to custody and visitation. Though there was no evidence before the court to indicate that the child was being harmed by the father's homosexuality, the Virginia Supreme Court found that the award of restricted custody to the gay father constituted an abuse of discretion by the trial court. "The father's continuous exposure of the child to his immoral and illicit relationship renders him an unfit and improper custodian as a matter of law." *Id.* at 694. The court concluded "that the best interests of the child will only be served by protecting her from the burdens imposed by such behavior, insofar as practicable." *Id.* at 694.

3. *S.N.E.* exemplifies the nexus test that has been adopted by a majority of jurisdictions in the United States. The test attempts to promote the best interests of the child by considering only those factors that can be shown to have an identifiable connection with the welfare of the child. Moral beliefs, stereotypes, and social biases that cannot be shown to have a substantial connection to the best interest of the child are not considered by the court. *See, e.g., In Re Marriage of Birdsall*, 243 Cal. Rptr. 287 (Ct. App. 1988) (holding that a parent is not unfit, as a matter of law, merely because he or she is homosexual); *D.H. v. J.H.*, 418 N.E.2d 286 (Ind. Ct. App. 1981) (holding that homosexuality standing alone without evidence of any adverse effect upon the welfare of the child does not render the homosexual parent unfit as a matter of law to have custody of the child); *Bezio v. Patenaude*, 410 N.E.2d 1207 (Mass. 1980) (holding that in the absence of evidence suggesting a correlation between the mother's homosexuality and her fitness as a parent, a court cannot presume that a lesbian household would adversely affect the children); *DiStefano v. DiStefano*, 401 N.Y.S.2d 636 (App. Div. 1978) (holding that while the sexual life style of a parent may be considered in custody cases, such consideration must be limited to its effect upon the welfare of the children).

B. Common Fears and Rationales Expressed By Courts

PALMORE v. SIDOTI

466 U.S. 429 (1984)

CHIEF JUSTICE BURGER delivered the opinion of the Court.

We granted certiorari to review a judgment of a state court divesting a natural mother of the custody of her infant child because of her remarriage to a person of a different race.

I

When petitioner Linda Sidoti Palmore and respondent Anthony J. Sidoti, both Caucasians, were divorced in May 1980 in Florida, the mother was awarded custody of their 3-year-old daughter.

In September 1981 the father sought custody of the child by filing a petition to modify the prior judgment because of changed conditions. The change was that the child's mother was then cohabiting with a Negro, Clarence Palmore, Jr., whom she married two months later. Additionally, the father made several allegations of instances in which the mother had not properly cared for the child.

. . . the court made a finding that "there is no issue as to either party's devotion to the child, adequacy of housing facilities, or respectability of the new spouse of either parent."

■ ■ ■

The court then concluded that the best interests of the child would be served by awarding custody to the father. The court's rationale is contained in the following:

"The father's evident resentment of the mother's choice of a black partner is not sufficient to wrest custody from the mother. It is of some significance, however, that the mother did see fit to bring a man into her home and carry on a sexual relationship with him without being married to him. Such action tended to place gratification of her own desires ahead of her concern for the child's future welfare. *This Court feels that despite the strides that have been made in bettering relations between the races in this country, it is inevitable that Melanie will, if allowed to remain in her present situation and attains school age and thus more vulnerable to peer pressures, suffer from the social stigmatization that is sure to come.*"

■ ■ ■

II

The judgment of a state court determining or reviewing a child custody decision is not ordinarily a likely candidate for review by this Court. However, the court's opinion, after stating that the "father's evident resentment of the mother's choice of a black partner is not sufficient" to deprive her of custody, then turns to what it regarded as the damaging impact on the child from remaining in a racially mixed household. This raises important federal concerns arising from the

Constitution's commitment to eradicating discrimination based on race.

The Florida court did not focus directly on the parental qualifications of the natural mother or her present husband, or indeed on the father's qualifications to have custody of the child. The court found that "there is no issue as to either party's devotion to the child, adequacy of housing facilities, or respectability of the new spouse of either parent." This, taken with the absence of any negative finding as to the quality of the care provided by the mother, constitutes a rejection of any claim of petitioner's unfitness to continue the custody of her child.

The court correctly stated that the child's welfare was the controlling factor. But that court was entirely candid and made no effort to place its holding on any ground other than race. Taking the court's findings and rationale at face value, it is clear that the outcome would have been different had petitioner married a Caucasian male of similar respectability.

A core purpose of the Fourteenth Amendment was to do away with all governmentally imposed discrimination based on race. Classifying persons according to their race is more likely to reflect racial prejudice than legitimate public concerns; the race, not the person, dictates the category. Such classifications are subject to the most exacting scrutiny; to pass constitutional muster, they must be justified by a compelling governmental interest and must be "necessary . . . . to the accomplishment" of their legitimate purpose, *McLaughlin* v. *Florida*, 379 U.S. 184, 196 (1964). *See Loving* v. *Virginia*, 388 U.S. 1, 11 (1967).

The State, of course, has a duty of the highest order to protect the interests of minor children, particularly those of tender years. In common with most states, Florida law mandates that custody determinations be made in the best interests of the children involved. The goal of granting custody based on the best interests of the child is indisputably a substantial governmental interest for purposes of the Equal Protection Clause.

It would ignore reality to suggest that racial and ethnic prejudices do not exist or that all manifestations of those prejudices have been eliminated. There is a risk that a child living with a stepparent of a different race may be subject to a variety of pressures and stresses not present if the child were living with parents of the same racial or ethnic origin.

The question, however, is whether the reality of private biases and the possible injury they might inflict are permissible considerations for removal of an infant child from the custody of its natural mother. We have little difficulty concluding that they are not. The Constitution cannot control such prejudices but neither can it tolerate them. Private biases may be outside the reach of the law, but the law cannot, directly or indirectly, give them effect. "Public officials sworn to uphold the Constitution may not avoid a constitutional duty by bowing to the hypothetical effects of private racial prejudice that they assume to be both widely and deeply held." *Palmer* v. *Thompson*, 403 U.S. 217, 260-261 (1971) (White, J., dissenting).

This is by no means the first time that acknowledged racial prejudice has been invoked to justify racial classifications. In *Buchanan* v. *Warley*, 245 U.S. 60 (1917), for example, this Court invalidated a Kentucky law forbidding Negroes to buy homes in white neighborhoods.

> "It is urged that this proposed segregation will promote the public peace by preventing race conflicts. Desirable as this is, and important as is the preservation of the public peace, this aim cannot be accomplished by laws or ordinances which deny rights created or protected by the Federal Constitution."

Whatever problems racially mixed households may pose for children in 1984 can no more support a denial of constitutional rights than could the stresses that residential integration was thought to entail in 1917. The effects of racial prejudice, however real, cannot justify a racial classification removing an infant child from the custody of its natural mother found to be an appropriate person to have such custody.

The judgment of the District Court of Appeal is reversed.

S.E.G. v. R.A.G.

735 S.W.2d 164 (Mo. Ct. App. 1987)

■ ■ ■

. . . [T]he facts of this case are as follows: Husband and Wife were married in 1973 when Wife was 16 and Husband was 20. They had four children, Sam, born August 4, 1973, Amy, born December 11, 1975, Hannah, born March 2, 1979, and Ruth, born November 19, 1982. Respondent (Husband) is a case worker (no formal degree) with Missouri Division of Family Services. Appellant (Wife) teaches natural child birth classes and baby-sits out of the family home in Union, Missouri. The parties separated in June, 1984. Both continue to reside in Union. On April 19, 1985, a decree of dissolution was entered granting custody of the four minor children, family home, maintenance and support to Wife. Ten days thereafter, on May 3, 1985, Husband filed motion for a new trial or amended judgment upon learning of his wife's homosexual relationship. On July 18, 1985, the order was amended granting primary custody of the minor children to Husband. We affirm.

■ ■ ■

In November, 1984, Wife met Kitty Ann Shelby (a/k/a "Airrow") at an Adult Children of Alcoholics meeting. In February, 1985, the two women became sexually involved. Both women define themselves as lesbians. Airrow resides in St. Louis but several times a week drives into Union to spend the night with Wife. Airrow and Wife sleep in the same bed at the family home in Union and evidence indicates that the youngest child has on occasion slept with them. Airrow and Wife are open about their relationship with the children and the community.

Both sides presented evidence as to the effects of the parent's homosexuality on the minor children in their custody. Wife, as well as the American Civil Liberties Union (A.C.L.U.), cite articles that indicate there are no significant differences among heterosexual parents and homosexual divorced parents and their children.[1] Of course, the trial court has the authority to find the evidence presented not credible. Since it is our duty to protect the moral growth and the best interests of the minor children, we find Wife's arguments lacking. Union, Missouri is a small, conservative community with a population of about 5,500. Homosexuality

---

1. *See* Herrington, *Children of Lesbians, Developmentally Typical*, PSYCHIATRIC NEWS, Oct. 19, 1979, at 23; Green, R., *The Best Interests of the Child With a Lesbian Mother*, BULLETIN of AA PL, vol. 10, no. 1, 1982, at 7-15.

is not openly accepted or widespread. We wish to protect the children from peer pressure, teasing, and possible ostracizing they may encounter as a result of the "alternative life style" their mother has chosen. In the face of this argument, Wife cites *Palmore* v. *Sidoti*, 466 U.S. 429, 433 (1984), where it was held "the Constitution cannot control such prejudices but neither can it tolerate them." *Palmore* involved an interracial marriage where the mother was seeking custody of her child in her own interracial home. We do not agree that *Palmore* applies to the situation at hand. Homosexuals are not offered the constitutional protection that race, national origin, and alienage have been afforded. *Bowers* v. *Hardwick*, 478 U.S. 186 (1986). *See also State* v. *Walsh*, 713 S.W.2d 508, 511 (Mo. banc 1986).

Wife contends that homosexuals have parental rights as well as heterosexuals, and that those rights cannot be denied solely on the basis of Wife's lesbian relationship. There must be a nexus between harm to the child and the parent's homosexuality. It has been held, however, that "these rights will fail in the face of evidence that their exercise will result in emotional harm to a child or will be detrimental to the child's welfare." *N.K.M.* v. *L.E.M.*, 606 S.W.2d 179, 186 (Mo.App., W.D.1980). Wife and lover show affection toward one another in front of the children. They sleep together in the same bed at the family home in Union. When Wife and four children travel to St. Louis to see Airrow, they also sleep together there. All of these factors present an unhealthy environment for minor children. Such conduct can never be kept private enough to be a neutral factor in the development of a child's values and character. We will not ignore such conduct by a parent which may have an effect on the children's moral development.

This analysis is sufficient to answer the aspects of Wife's and A.C.L.U.'s constitutional arguments. We find no persuasion in Wife's citation of cases from other states favoring homosexual parental custody or un-

restricted visiting privileges. Custody shall remain with the father. This point is denied.

In her second point, Wife contends that the trial court erred in finding that Husband was not an alcoholic and did not sexually abuse his children. It can be gleaned from the record that Wife, upon threat of divorce, encouraged Husband to admit himself to a treatment center. Husband entered White Deer Alcoholic Treatment Center where he was treated for about a month. However, Dr. Beach, who does the alcoholic intake evaluations at Jefferson Barracks Hospital, testified there were no objective or medical indicia of alcoholism in Husband's records at White Deer Center. Dr. Beach testified that Husband was not an alcoholic. Husband admitted at trial that he was an alcoholic but has not had a drink since May 1984. We defer to the trial court to determine the credibility of the witnesses and to draw conclusions where there is conflicting testimony.

Upon review, we find no evidence of child molestation by Husband. Wife's allegations are clearly unsubstantiated. None of the testifying experts could identify these children as victims of sexual abuse. In child custody cases, the evidence is permitted to take a wide range, and the trial courts can presumably sort out the incompetent and the irrelevant. The trial court did not err in finding Husband was not an alcoholic or a child molester. These points are denied.

Thirdly, Wife and A.C.L.U. argue that the trial court erred in restricting her visitation on the grounds that she is a homosexual. In the few cases in our state dealing directly with the problem of a homosexual parent seeking primary custody, all courts have awarded custody to the non-homosexual parent, and restricted the homosexual parent's visitation rights, again relying on the impact upon the child. *J.L.P.(H.)* v. *D.J.P.*, 643 S.W.2d 865, 871 (Mo.App., W.D.1982). We are not presuming that Wife is an uncaring mother. The environment, however, that she would choose to rear her children in is unhealthy for their growth. She has chosen not to make her sexual preference private but invites acknowledgment and imposes her preference upon her children and her community. The purpose of restricting visitation is to prevent extreme exposure of the situation to the minor children. We are not forbidding Wife from being a homosexual, from having a lesbian relationship, or from attending gay activist or overt homosexual outings.

We are restricting her from exposing these elements of her "alternative life style" to her minor children. We fail to see how these restrictions impose or restrict her equal protection or privacy rights where these restrictions serve the best interest of the child. These limitations were properly imposed. This point is denied.

■ ■ ■

M.P. v. S.P.

404 A.2d 1256 (N.J. Super. Ct. App. Div. 1979)

ANTELL, J. A. D.

Defendant (former wife) was awarded a divorce for sexual cruelty by judgment dated September 11, 1969, after a six-year marriage from which two children were born, Franceen, (fictitious name) on June 8, 1964, and Joy (fictitious name) on July 15, 1968. She received custody of the daughters, and until the determination before us for review they have always resided with their mother, a period of about seven years after the divorce.

On May 20, 1975, the Chancery Division ordered defendant to show cause why custody of the children should not be transferred to plaintiff on the ground that defendant "is an unfit mother." . . . . After a number of hearings, the last of which was on January 22, 1976, the trial judge, by letter opinion dated August 30, 1976, awarded custody to the father . . . . Defendant appeals on the ground that the trial judge erred in modifying the judgment and divesting her of custody.

Central to this appeal is the fact that defendant is an admitted practicing homosexual. She argues that the action below was

taken because of this fact alone and is therefore not legally sustainable.

■ ■ ■

. . . at least from the time of their separation in 1967 plaintiff has been aware of defendant's homosexual propensities. As he knew when they separated, defendant was involved in an affair with another woman (Barbara), one which continued through and beyond the date of the divorce.

■ ■ ■

The trial judge apparently weighed against defendant the fact that she was caught up "in an attempt to find her own identity and to deal with the problems" arising from her sexual status. However, he did not explain what problems he had in mind or in what way her problems or her quest for identity were different from those of most ordinary people; more importantly, he made no attempt to articulate a relationship between any of this and the welfare of the children. The judge also noted that defendant's ongoing liaison with her lesbian companion had "materially upset the older child and will have a slight influence in all probability, from the credible evidence, on the younger child." On an earlier occasion the judge had ordered that defendant not share Joyce's company at any time when the children were present, and this order has not been violated. Furthermore, there is nothing in the record to show any nexus between defendant's sexual companionship and the older girl's reaction.

Nowhere do we find documented in the record any specific instances of sexual misconduct by defendant or evidence that she tried in any way to inculcate the girls with her sexual attitudes. To the contrary, the evidence is affirmatively to the effect that she never displayed any sexual behavior in the presence of her children, and that she refrains from any demonstration of affection toward other women when the girls are present. Moreover, she is not a member of any homosexual organization. . . .

It is well settled that the best interests of the child are of primary concern to the court in any matter involving the custody of minor children. Since the conditions which would satisfy the best interests of a child during all of its minority cannot be conclusively determined in a single decree, custody orders are always held to be modifiable upon a showing of changed circumstances that would affect the welfare of the child. The party seeking the modification bears the burden of showing sufficient changed circumstances so as to require modification.

In assessing a claim of changed circumstances deference is given to the length and stability of the existing custody relationship. The potential for damage which resides in removing a child from its psychological parent has been recognized in a number of cases. . . . So important is this factor . . . . that one seeking to change the child's custodial status quo . . .

. . . will have the burden of proving by a preponderance of the credible evi-

dence that the potentiality for serious psychological harm accompanying or resulting from such a move will not become a reality.

Not only did plaintiff offer no proof to meet this formidable burden, but, as we noted earlier, the trial judge made no findings which pointed to a change of circumstances. The only conclusion to be drawn is, as defendant claims, that the custody order was modified for the sole reason that she is a homosexual and without regard to the welfare of the children. This conclusion gains added support from our further analysis of the record and the determinations before us for review.

■ ■ ■

. . . [P]laintiff argues that a change of circumstance may . . . be found in the fact that defendant's variant sexual orientation now causes embarrassment to the girls in the eyes of their peers. . . .

It is first observed that the trial judge made no finding of fact which lends support to plaintiff's claim. All he said was that Franceen had been "upset" by Joyce, defendant's lesbian friend, a problem earlier resolved by banishing Joyce from the presence of the children. The only evidence of "embarrassment" is to be found in Franceen's testimony about conversations with her friends, in which she was asked why her mother dated other women. Nothing therein suggests that these were in any way traumatizing. We know of no finding by the trial judge that Franceen is "pressured by her peers," nor how such a finding could be supported by the proofs. In fact, we do not understand the sense in which this expression is used in the dissenting opinion or the weight which such a finding could be accorded within the context of this case.

Plaintiff's argument overlooks, too, the fact that the children's exposure to embarrassment is not dependent upon the identity of the parent with whom they happen to reside. Their discomfiture, if any, comes about not because of living with defendant, but because she is their mother, because she is a lesbian, and because the community will not accept her. Neither the prejudices of the small community in which they live nor the curiosity of their peers about defendant's sexual nature will be abated by a change of custody. Hard facts must be faced. These are matters which courts cannot control, and there is little to gain by creating an artificial world where the children may dream that life is different than it is.

Furthermore, the law governing grants of custody does not yield to such narrow considerations. Of overriding importance is that within the context of a loving and supportive relationship there is no reason to think that the girls will be unable to manage whatever anxieties may flow from the community's disapproval of their mother. In *Commonwealth ex rel. Lucas v. Kreischer*, 299 A.2d 243 (Pa. Sup.Ct.1973), the trial court awarded custody of the children, whose mother had entered into an interracial marriage, to their father because of the "almost universal prejudice and intolerance of interracial marriage." In reversing, the Supreme Court of Pennsylvania rested its determination upon the following observation, which we deem pertinent, made by the dissenting judge of the intermediate appellate court:

> "[I]n a multiracial society such as ours racial prejudice and tension are inevitable. If . . . children are raised in a happy and stable home, they will be able to cope with prejudice and hopefully learn that people are unique individuals who should be judged as such."

Mistaken also, in our view, is plaintiff's assumption that the welfare of the children cannot be served unless they are sheltered from all the adversities that are inherent to their basic life situation. Regrettably, the decision as to where custody shall lie must be made in terms of available alternatives, and in this case neither holds out the promise of a completely unguent environment. While one is troubled by the possible problems that may arise from defendant's homosexual bent, the evidence also strongly features a disturbed and abrasive personal relationship between Joy and plaintiff's present wife which has resulted in the administration of unduly harsh discipline to this child. She also dislikes and fears plaintiff.

Conceding that Franceen prefers to live with her father and his present wife, reservations as to the advisability of such a course are at least suggested by testimony describing talks between the wife and Franceen. In these the 11-year-old was told, with explanatory detail, how great a "stud" her father is. Also germane to the flavor of this "stable atmosphere" are certain nude pictures of the present wife, who posed in the family home for four "photographers," including one who also serves as the family dentist. Although the wife denied that to the "best of my knowledge" these were ever viewed by the children, they had been left under the pillows of a couch in the living room. And, if it is "the thinking of the vast majority of society" that concerns us, it should be noted that before marrying plaintiff the wife underwent an illegal abortion of an out-of-wedlock child fathered by another man.

Nor may we disregard the appalling character of the sexual onslaughts carried out during their marriage by plaintiff upon defendant for which the divorce was granted. Without detailing his singular conduct or the variety of foreign objects he introduced into her person, we acknowledge our willingness to understand how these could well have stifled forever her initial efforts to enjoy heterosexual love in a conventional relationship.

Although plaintiff's sexual behavior cannot, perhaps, be categorized in terms which are as emotionally charged as "homosexual" or "lesbian," it is so far out of the ordinary as to create the most acute anxieties about entrusting so troubled and deviant a personality with the responsibility of creating an environment for the upbringing of two young girls. Even if the rule of changed circumstances were not applicable and we were free to weigh anew the relative advantages of these two arrangements, taken with the considerations previously noted, plaintiff's conduct illuminates the completely speculative nature of any determination that because she is a lesbian, custody with defendant will be more destructive of the children's welfare than with plaintiff.

If defendant retains custody, it may be that because the community is intolerant of her differences these girls may sometimes have to bear themselves with greater than ordinary fortitude. But this does not necessarily portend that their moral welfare or safety will be jeopardized. It is just as reasonable to expect that they will emerge better equipped to search out their own standards of right and wrong, better able to perceive that the majority is not always correct in its moral judgments, and better able to understand the importance of conforming their beliefs to the requirements of reason and tested knowledge, not the constraints of currently popular sentiment or prejudice.

Taking the children from defendant can be done only at the cost of sacrificing those very qualities they will find most sustaining in meeting the challenges inevitably ahead. Instead of forbearance and feelings of protectiveness, it will foster in them a sense of shame for their mother. Instead of courage and the precept that people of integrity do not shrink from bigots, it counsels the easy option of shirking difficult problems and following the course of expedience. Lastly, it diminishes their regard for the rule of human behavior, everywhere accepted, that we do not forsake those to whom we are indebted for love and nurture merely because they are held in low esteem by others.

We conclude that the children's best interests will be disserved by undermining in this way their growth as mature and principled adults. Extensive evidence in the record upon which we have not commented amply confirms the trial judge's finding that defendant is a worthy mother. Nothing suggests that her homosexual preference in itself presents any threat of harm to her daughters or that in the ordinary course of their development they will be unable to deal with whatever vexation may be caused to their spirits by the community.

Careful attention has been given to the nature of the relief to be awarded. Although advantages are evident in remanding for further hearings by which the current status of the matter may be ascertained, after a thorough examination of the entire record we are satisfied that the welfare of the children will only be impaired without corresponding benefit by prolonging any further these already protracted proceedings. The order under review is therefore reversed and the custody provision contained in the judgment of divorce dated September 11, 1969 is reinstated.

■ ■ ■

Notes

1. *Peer and Community Harassment.* As in *S.E.G.*, in *Jacobson* v. *Jacobson*, 314 N.W.2d 78, 81 (N.D. 1981), the Supreme Court of North Dakota held that in light of society's mores toward homosexuality and the mother's involvement in a lesbian relationship, it was not in

the best interest of the children to be placed in the custody of their mother. The court reasoned:

> [W]e cannot lightly dismiss the fact that living in the same house with their mother and her lover may well cause the children to "suffer from the slings and arrows of a disapproving society" to a much greater extent than would an arrangement wherein the children were placed in the custody of their father with visitation rights in the mother. Although we agree with the trial court that the children will be required to deal with the problem regardless of which parent has custody, it is apparent to us that requiring the children to live, day-to-day, in the same residence with the mother and her lover means that the children will have to confront the problem to a significantly greater degree than they would if living with their father.

While there is no empirical evidence that conclusively supports or contradicts the fear of stigmatization and harassment, what evidence does exist indicates that the fear of harassment far exceeds the actual incidence of harassment. *See, e.g.*, Mary Hotvedt & Jane Mandel, *Children of Lesbian Mothers, in* HOMOSEXUALITY: SOCIAL, PSYCHOLOGICAL, AND BIOLOGICAL ISSUES 282 (W. Paul et al. eds., 1982); Susan Golombok et al., *Children in Lesbian and Single-Parent Households: Psychosexual and Psychiatric Appraisal*, 24 J. CHILD PSYCHOL. AND PSYCHIATRY 551-72 (1983); and Sharon Huggins, *A Comparative Study of Self-Esteem of Adolescent Children of Divorced Lesbian Mothers and Divorced Heterosexual Mothers, in* HOMOSEXUALITY AND THE FAMILY 123-35 (Frederick Bozett ed., 1989).

2. *Child Sexual Abuse.* Some courts make explicit allegations that lesbians and gay men are, generally speaking, child sexual abusers. For example, a Missouri judge who rejected expert testimony that 95% of sexual molestation of children is committed by heterosexuals stated, "Every trial judge . . . . knows that the molestation of minor boys by adult males is not as uncommon as the psychological experts' testimony indicated." *J.L.P.(H.)* v. *D.J.P.*, 643 S.W.2d 865, 869 (Mo. Ct. App. 1982).

While typically they are unwilling to accuse an individual gay or lesbian parent of sexual abuse without any evidence supporting such a charge, courts do often hint at the general fear of "homosexual seduction." In *In Re J.S.& C*, 324 A.2d 97 (N.J. Super. Ct. Ch. Div. 1974), *aff'd*, 362 A.2d 54 (N.J. Super. Ct. App. Div. 1976), the court denied child custody and awarded only limited visitation to a gay father in part because:

> [An expert witness testified that] "the total environment to which the father exposed the children could impede healthy sexual development in the future." Specifically, he contended that, "the father's milieu could engender homosexual fantasies causing confusion and anxiety which would in turn affect the children's sexual development." He asserted, "it is possible that these children upon reaching puberty would be subject to either overt of covert homosexual seduction which would detrimentally influence their sexual development."

In addition to raising the hypothetical possibility of molestation, courts often note, for no apparent reason, that the gay or lesbian person denies sexual involvement with children. *See, e.g., In re Jane B.*, 380 N.Y.S.2d 848, 854 (Sup.Ct.1976) (stating that "[the mother's lesbian lover] further testified that she has had no physical relationship with the infant, Jane B., or any other child and that any homosexual relationships have been with adult females").

The perceived risk of child molestation is unsupported by empirical studies. Indeed, the available research indicates that child molestation is committed primarily by heterosexual men. AMERICAN HUMANE ASSOCIATION, CHILDREN'S DIVISION, PROTECTING THE CHILD VICTIM OF SEX CRIMES COMMITTED BY ADULTS 216–17 (V. DeFrancis ed., 1969) (concluding that 97% of sex offenders against children are male and that 90% of the victims are female).

3. *"Interference With Normal Heterosexual Development."* In *S v. S*, 608 S.W.2d 64, 66 (Ky. Ct. App. 1980), which held that a custody award to a lesbian mother was not in the best interest of the child and potentially endangered the physical, mental, or emotional health of the child, the court stated:

> [T]here is excellent scientific research on the effects of parental modeling on children. Speculating from such data, it is reasonable to suggest that Shannon [the child] may have difficulties in achieving a fulfilling heterosexual identity of her own in the future [if she were to continue to live with her lesbian mother]. There would seem to me to be no rational reason for purposely submitting a child to these additional and potentially debilitating influences.

In fact, the fears that children raised by gay or lesbian parents will "learn" to be gay, or will otherwise suffer some form of psychological debilitation are not supported by empirical studies. *See, e.g.*, NATIONAL INSTITUTE OF MENTAL HEALTH TASK FORCE ON HOMOSEXUALITY, FINAL REPORT AND BACKGROUND PAPER 15 (1972); Mary B. Harris & Pauline Turner, *Gay and Lesbian Parents*, 12 J. HOMOSEXUALITY 101 (Winter 1985–86).

4. *Sodomy Laws.* Courts sometimes rely on the existence of a sodomy law within the state to bolster the denial of custody or visitation to a gay or lesbian parent. In *Thigpen* v. *Carpenter*, 730 S.W.2d 510 (Ark. Ct. App. 1987), the court applied a *per se* test to deny a lesbian mother custody of her child: "[I]t has never been necessary to prove that illicit sexual conduct on the part of the custodial parent is detrimental to the children. Arkansas courts have presumed that it is." *Id.* at 513. In a concurring opinion, Judge Cracraft relied on *Bowers* v. *Hardwick* to address the mother's due process claim:

> In her testimony, the appellant graphically described the sexual activities she engaged in with another female with whom she shared a bedroom in an Austin, Texas, house in which the children would also reside. The people of both Texas and Arkansas have declared the conduct she described to be so adverse to public morals and policy as to warrant criminal sanctions. Arkansas Statutes Annotated § 41-1813 (Repl.1977) defines her conduct as "sodomy," and Tex.Penal Code Ann. § 21.06 (Vernon 1974) labels that activity "homo-sexual conduct." The statutes of both states authorize the imposition of criminal penalties against those who engage in that conduct.
>
> In *Bowers* v. *Hardwick*, 478 U.S. 186 (1986), the Supreme Court of the United States held that Georgia's law imposing felony penalties for homosexual sodomy violated no constitutional guarantees. . . . Noting in its opinion the deep-rooted abhorrence with which homosexual sodomy has been historically viewed by the people of this country since before the adoption of the Constitution, the Court rejected due process arguments by simply stating that, if all laws based on moral choices were to be invalidated under the due process clause, the courts would indeed be very busy.
>
> The people of this state have declared, through legislative action, that sodomy is immoral, unacceptable, and criminal conduct. This clear declaration of public policy is certainly one that a chancellor may note and consider in child custody cases where, as here, the custodial contestant has declared her fixed determination to continue that course of illegal conduct for the rest of her life, in a home in which the children also reside, and to justify her conduct to the children if and when they find her out.

The Supreme Court of Virginia, in *Roe v. Roe*, 324 S.E.2d 691, 694 (Va 1985), also relied on the existence of the state's sodomy statute:

[A]s an illustration of the relative degree of abhorrence by which our society regards such conduct [homosexuality], adultery is a class four misdemeanor in Virginia (Code § 18.2–365) which is seldom prosecuted, while the conduct inherent in the father's relationship is punishable as a class six felony (Code § 18.2–361) which is prosecuted with considerable frequency and vigor, as evidenced by the decided cases annotated under those respective sections in the Code. However that may be, we have no hesitancy in saying that the conditions under which this child must live daily are not only unlawful but also impose an intolerable burden upon her by reason of the social condemnation attached to them, which will inevitably afflict her relationships with her peers and with the community at large.

5. *Lack of Legal Recognition of Same-Sex Couples*. In *Jacobson v. Jacobson*, 314 N.W.2d 78 (N.D. 1981), the Supreme Court of North Dakota reversed the judgment of a trial court which awarded a lesbian custody of her children. The court relied in part on the fact that the mother's relationship with another woman was not recognized by the law.

It is not inconceivable that one day our society will accept homosexuality as "normal." Certainly it is more accepted today than it was only a few years ago. We are not prepared to conclude, however, that it is not a significant factor to be considered in determining custody of children, at least in the context of the facts of this particular case. Because the trial court has determined that both parents are "fit, willing and able" to assume custody of the children we believe the homosexuality of Sandra is the overriding factor. Sandra admitted to a sexual relationship with Sue prior to the termination of the marriage. Although that relationship was adulterous as defined by Section 12.1-20-09, N.D.C.C., that fact alone does not influence us. Rather, it is the conceded fact that after the divorce Sandra and Sue would establish a relationship in which they would be living together which gives us concern. In paragraph 9 of its findings the trial court stated:

"The Plaintiff [Sandra] has admitted a relationship with an adult woman [who] is likewise a strong, intelligent person; they have been discreet about their relationship; it is not outwardly apparent; thus far the children do not appear to be aware of it; the women intend to continue this relationship permanently and live together in the future; the relationship is a positive one; several people are aware of the relationship and it is clear that at some point the children will become aware of it."

Our statutes do not prohibit sexual relations between adult persons who are not married to other persons. Although Section 12.1-20-10, N.D.C.C., makes it a crime for a person to live openly and notoriously with a person of the opposite sex as a married couple without being married to the other person, the statutes contain no such provision with regard to persons of the same sex. The reason is obvious—neither North Dakota nor any other State in this nation, insofar as we can determine, recognizes a legal sexual relationship between two persons of the same sex. Thus, despite the fact that the trial court determined the relationship between Sandra and Sue to be a "positive one," it is a relationship which, under the existing state of the law, never can be a legal relationship. Whether or not it will remain a stable relationship is yet to be determined. Sue is considerably younger than Sandra.

Id. at 80.

C. Restrictions on Lesbian and Gay Parents

IN RE J.S.& C.

324 A.2d 90 (N.J. Super. Ct. Ch. Div. 1974), *aff'd,* 362 A.2d 54
(N.J. App. Div. 1976)

■ ■ ■

Plaintiff mother seeks to limit visitation rights so as to exclude overnight stays with the father. The basis for her request is the belief that the homosexual environment to which the father exposes the children is deleterious and not in their best interest. The father contends the Constitution prohibits restriction of parental rights on the basis of homosexuality. In addition, he offered expert testimony to rebut allegations of the mother that exposure to a homosexual parent or the parent's homosexual friends and their way of life is detrimental to children generally and his children specifically.

More than six days of testimony was heard from expert and fact witnesses. I make the following findings of fact necessary to decide this case: The mother and father were married in 1960. Three minor children, two boys and a girl, were born of the marriage. The parents separated around the time of the *pendente lite* order in July of 1971. The father is an avowed and publicly known homosexual. He associates with other homosexuals and is presently living with a homosexual lover. During the visits with the father, the children associate with the father's homosexual lover and acquaintances.

■ ■ ■

The parental rights of a homosexual, like those of a heterosexual, are constitutionally protected. Fundamental rights of parents may not be denied, limited or restricted on the basis of sexual orientation, *per se.* The right of a parent, including a homosexual parent, to the companionship and care of his or her child, insofar as it is for the best interest of the child is a fundamental right protected by the First, Ninth and Fourteenth Amendments to the United States Constitution. That right may not be restricted without a showing that the parent's activities may tend to impair the emotional or physical health of the child.

■ ■ ■

Restriction of full contact between a father and child interferes with family relationships and impedes the father's right to participate in his children's rearing and education.

The courts of New Jersey have expressed a policy encouraging protection of family relationships by favoring full visitation rights in order "to insure that [the children] shall not only retain the love of both parents but shall at all times and constantly be 'deeply imbued with love and respect for both parents.' "

The court thus concludes that the fact that one of the parents is a homosexual does not *per se* provide sufficient basis for a deprivation of visitation rights.

Although a deprivation of the parent's visitation rights due solely to homosexuality would be unjustified discrimination, this fact does not prevent or relieve a court from the duty of closely examining any claim where it is alleged that exposure to a specific homosexual parent may have a detrimental effect on a child.

Three expert witnesses, Dr. John Money and Dr. Richard Green for defendant, and Dr. Richard Gardner for plaintiff, all recognized authorities in their fields, testified in the areas of child psychiatry, sexual development and homosexuality.

The first question broached by these experts was whether exposure to the father's homosexuality might be deleterious to the children. They all agreed that homosexuality was not *per se* a mental disorder and that a balanced exposure would not be harmful to the children. All concluded that the children have a close, loving and respectful relationship with their father. Dr. Gardner stated, "I am strongly advising that there be visitation. I feel that it would be very detrimental to both him and his children were there not to be visitation." They agreed that the father had been a good parent. Dr. Gardner stated, "The fact that they were so healthy indicated that he [the father] was providing a healthy atmosphere for them and had done so at least in the past to provide them with a stable personality."

In my interview with the children I found them to be well adjusted and anxious to continue their relationship with their father. I conclude that granting visitation rights to the father will serve the best interests of the children.

A second and more difficult problem concerns the court. Whether the defendant father's visitation rights should be restricted and if so to what extent.

■ ■ ■

Although parents possess various rights such as custody and visitation these rights will fall in the face of evidence that their exercise will result in emotional or physical harm to a child or will be detrimental to the child's welfare.

■ ■ ■

It is clear that the court may impose a limitation of defendant's visitation rights if it determines that it will serve the best interest of the children.

The mother's request for a severe limitation of defendant's visitation rights is based on her position that defendant's total involvement with and dedication to furthering homosexuality has created an environment exposure to which in anything more than a minimal amount would be harmful to the children.

The extent of defendant's involvement in homosexuality, homosexuals and with various movements furthering the cause of homosexuality is uncontradicted. He has been a leader of the Gay Activists Alliance and is currently employed as a Director of the National Gay Task Force at a net salary of $ 89.78 a week. In the past defendant has earned a substantial income which was utilized to help support the children. He has now decided to forego this income in favor of the gay rights movement.

Since his separation from plaintiff, defendant has had several homosexual lovers. He presently lives with a male lover in a building occupied almost entirely by homosexuals. A business undertaking in which he is currently involved is owned primarily by homosexuals.

Defendant has involved the children in his attempts to further homosexuality. They have accompanied him on protest marches, at rallies and were filmed with him for a television show which discussed homosexuality. They have been present with him at "The Firehouse", a meeting hall for homosexuals, where one witness has testified he observed men, "fondling each other, necking and petting." They have slept overnight at defendant's apartment while he slept with a male lover. The evidence and testimony also indicate that pornographic periodicals with a homosexual orientation are available to the children at defendant's residence. Both my interview with the children and the testimony at the hearing indicated that homosexuality and gay rights are a common if not the most common topic of conversation when the children are with defendant.

The extent of the influence of the father over S and C was made evident to the court by children's drawings offered by defendant as exhibits D12a and b and c. D12a portrays a figure holding two signs which say, "Gay is proud" and "Join us!!!" D12c portrays a dog dressed to resemble a policeman stating, "Hey you, get out of here," to figures holding signs which say, "We want equal rights !!" These pictures present themes which would not occur to children of this age without prodding and indoctrination by an adult.

My interview with S, an 11-year-old girl, and C, an 8-year-old boy, elicited no aversion on their part to visiting with defendant. Neither appeared disturbed by their father's activities; however, they expressed their wishes not to be involved in the gay movement. They did not have a grasp of what homosexuality or gay rights involved and were chiefly interested in continuing to enjoy their father's company. J, a 12-year-old boy, stated that he is unhappy when his father is with a male friend and he does not wish to stay overnight. He also indicated that he does not want to participate in gay activities.

Although the experts agreed there was very little chance that exposure to a homosexual environment would alter the children's sexual orientation and at the present time they are well adjusted, Dr. Gardner indicated that the milieu that produced three healthy children was the milieu that existed prior to the separation. He was convinced that defendant's involvement in the gay movement had become an obsessive preoccupation and that the children's exposure to the concentrated and unidirectional environment this produced should be limited.

Dr. Gardner stated: "I believe he [defendant] is different with regard to the amount of activity that he is involved in, that it goes beyond the bedroom, that his political activities appear to be a significant involvement in his life which go way above and beyond the actual homosexual involvement." Dr. Gardner did not feel that defendant's preoccupation was "realistically changeable" and that controls had to be structured, "so that in any area that you can physically and in a concrete way remove exposure to any potential homosexual experience, that will be good preventive psychiatry as I see it." He felt strongly that there should be visitation but that there should be a change in those things in the environment "that can lessen the exposure to homosexuality."

Additionally, Dr. Gardner stated, "the total environment to which the father exposed the children could impede healthy sexual development in the future." Specifically, he contended that, "the father's milieu could engender homosexual fantasies causing confusion and anxiety which would in turn affect the children's sexual development." He asserted, "it is possi-

ble that these children upon reaching puberty would be subject to either overt or covert homosexual seduction which would detrimentally influence their sexual development."

In response to a question concerning the limitations on visitation which should be imposed Dr. Gardner replied, "my recommendation would be that there not be any overnight visitation for any of the three children, both weekends and during summers."

Dr. Money and Dr. Green do not concur with Dr. Gardner's conclusion regarding the possible ill effects on the children which continued unlimited exposure to the homosexually oriented milieu in which defendant has submerged himself might cause. Nevertheless, it is clear to the court from the overall tenor of the testimony from all three experts that any pronouncements by them in this area must contain a relatively high percentage of speculation. As recently as December 1973, when the Board of Trustees of the American Psychiatric Association reclassified homosexuality from a mental disorder to a sexual disorientation, they were met with strong opposition from among the members. The inability of psychiatrists to reach any degree of unanimity even as to a basic definition or classification of homosexuality is strong evidence of the diverse and myriad analyses which would erupt were the controversy presently before this court presented to the Association.

The lack of understanding and controversy which surrounds homosexuality, together with the immutable effects which are engendered by the parent-child relationship, demands that the court be most hesitant in allowing any unnecessary exposure of a child to an environment which may be deleterious.

Defendant has asserted that addicts and people convicted of violent crimes do not lose their visitation rights unless there is a showing that the parent will physically harm the children or not provide for them. He requests that at least the same standards be applied to him. I agree that the same standards should be applied to defendant in determining the extent of visitation but the factors which enter into consideration must be more inclusive than the threat of mere physical harm. We are dealing in the present case with a most sensitive issue which holds the possibility of inflicting severe mental anguish and detriment on three innocent children. All the efforts of this court are directed toward preventing this from occurring.

Where a bank robber is allowed full visitation rights, as defendant has hypothesized, surely the exercise of these rights whether expressed or implicit is restricted to exclude his exposing the child to any aspects of this most unacceptable line of endeavor. Similarly, a homosexual who openly advocates violations of the New Jersey statutes forbidding sodomy, N.J.S.A. 2A:143-1 and related statutes, may also be restricted.

Based on the testimony given, the evidence received and my interviews with J, S and C, I conclude that allowing defendant to continue unrestricted visitation would not be in the best interest of the children and that a reasonable limitation will not in any way

hinder the continuance and furtherance of the sound parent-child relationships which exist between defendant and J, S and C.

In accordance with the above, I direct that defendant be afforded visitation with J, S and C on alternate Sundays from 10 A.M. to 7 P.M., on Christmas, Easter and Thanksgiving from 3 P.M. to 7 P.M., and three weeks during the summer at an address other than his present Spring Street residence.

During such periods of visitation the defendant shall:

1. not cohabit or sleep with any individual other than a lawful spouse,

2. not take the children or allow them to be taken to "The Firehouse," and

3. not involve the children in any homosexual related activities or publicity.

4. not be in the presence of his lover.

BIRDSALL v. BIRDSALL

243 Cal. Rptr. 287 (Ct. App. 1988)

SONENSHINE, Associate Justice.

A homosexual father challenges a court order prohibiting him from exercising overnight visitation with his minor son in the presence of any third person known to be homosexual.

I

In March 1985, after eight and one-half years of marriage, Greg and Linda Birdsall separated. Greg's petition to dissolve the marriage requested, among other things, primary physical custody of their son, Shaun, born April 20,

1979, joint legal custody, and visitation rights reserved to Linda. In her response, Linda requested sole legal and physical custody, with reasonable visitation to Greg.

At the hearing on Linda's initial order to show cause, the parties stipulated to joint legal custody with physical custody to Linda. Greg was allowed specific visitation of one weekend each month, from 6 P.M. Friday to 6 P.M. Sunday, Monday afternoons after school until 7 P.M., and alternating legal holidays. Because Greg is homosexual, Linda requested a restraining order precluding him from exercising his overnight visitation rights at his residence. Greg stipulated to this request, and the parties also agreed to have psychological examinations for themselves and the minor child.

At trial, the parties again agreed Linda would have physical custody of Shaun. The visitation issue, however, was submitted to the court for determination, with the following result: Greg was awarded reasonable visitation consisting of one weekend per month, Mondays after school, alternate legal holidays, and two weeks during the summer. In addition, Greg was prohibited from exercising his overnight visitation in the presence of anyone known to be homosexual.

Greg alleges the trial court erred in directing him not to exercise his overnight visitation "in the presence of any friend, acquaintance or associate who is known to be homosexual." He argues the evidence was insufficient to support the court's conclusion this restriction is in Shaun's best interests.

At the time of trial, Greg was leasing a three-bedroom townhouse which he shared with two other homosexual men. He had never engaged in sexual relations with either of these men. He was dating a man who visited his residence approximately twice a month. One of his roommates had a relationship with someone who visited once or twice a week, occasionally staying overnight. Greg testified he had no intention of raising Shaun as a homosexual. Linda testified she did not believe Greg would engage in homosexual acts in front of Shaun.

Linda, a practicing Jehovah's Witness, had been raising Shaun in accordance with this religion. Greg had previously been a Jehovah's Witness but was excommunicated for homosexuality.[2] He had mixed feelings about this faith but believed it was Linda's choice as to whether Shaun would be raised as a Jehovah's Witness. Shaun was then receiving five hours of religious training each week.

Linda testified Shaun's behavior, after visitations with Greg, was hyper, rude, inso-

lent, and unaffectionate. She also said the child would come home depressed and do poorly in school for a few days thereafter.

II.

[The court noted, first, that California law requires that unless] it is shown that parental visitation would be detrimental to the best interests of the child, reasonable visitation rights must be awarded.

■ ■ ■

[And second, that the] court may not . . . determine custody on the basis of sexual preference alone. Indeed, a parent is not unfit, as a matter of law, merely because he or she is homosexual. But the court may consider a parent's homosexuality as a factor *along with* the other evidence presented.

. . . *Nadler* [v. *Superior Court*, 63 Cal. Rptr. 352 (Ct. App. 1967)] determined a parent's homosexuality does not, without more, allow a court to deprive him or her of primary custody. It follows that unrestricted time spent with a homosexual parent is not presumed to be detrimental to the child.

■ ■ ■

In his memorandum of decision, the trial judge here indicated his belief a parent has no constitutional right to unrestricted visitation with his or her child. He further acknowledged his understanding the majority of American jurisdictions allow reasonable restrictions if they are found to be in the best interests of the child. The court also believed Shaun's exposure to "completely opposite life styles," i.e., his father's homosexuality and his mother's religion, "could impair the child's emotional development."

But an affirmative showing of harm or likely harm to the child is necessary in order to restrict parental custody or visitation.[4] After reviewing this record, we conclude the evi-

---

2. Jehovah's Witnesses believe homosexuality is immoral and scripturally prohibited.

dence of detriment to the child is insufficient to support restricted visitation with the father.

The lower court's memorandum of decision contains premises and conclusions which have no support in the record. To conclude Greg's "sexual practices have hardly been discreet" from the fact "his church membership was terminated due to it" is meritless. There is no evidence of any indiscretion attendant upon Greg's acknowledgment of his homosexuality or of his leaving the church.

Following a similar line of reasoning, the trial court stated Greg "obviously recognizes some possibility of harm to the child from his life style." This statement is partly based upon an inference drawn from Greg's original agreement to restricted visitation. However, the stipulated restraining order was only intended to be a temporary measure until the court could resolve the dispute. " '[T]here is no showing that [Greg], by agreeing to that judgment, acknowledged that [the restraining order] was in the best interest of [the] child.' " The trial court's observation that Greg has not attempted to interfere with Shaun's religious training is similarly devoid of any obvious indication of Greg ascribing a detrimental value to his life style.

In addition, the court misstates Greg's testimony, saying "he indicated that he does not want his son to become a homosexual." Greg only said he would not raise his son as a homosexual. A denial of any intention to attempt to indoctrinate Shaun into a homosexual lifestyle is not the equivalent of the trial court's statement and cannot support an inference that Greg believes his life style would be detrimental to his child.

No evidence was presented to show the circumstances of this case require a restraining order be placed on Greg's visitation. No current harm to the child can be attributed to Greg's sexual orientation. And there is no evidence of future detriment. The unconventional life style of one parent, or the opposing moral positions of the parties, or the outright condemnation of one parent's beliefs by the other parent's religion, which may result in confusion for the child, do not provide an adequate basis for restricting visitation rights. Evidence of one parent's homosexuality, without a link to detriment to the child, is insufficient to constitute harm. In the absence of any indication of harm, the restraining order is unreasonable and must be vacated.

III.

That portion of the judgment designated "3(a)," which reads: "Petitioner shall not exercise overnight visitation with the minor child of the parties, namely, SHAUN GREGORY BIRDSALL, in the presence of any friend, acquaintance or associate who is known to be homosexual" is vacated. . . .

Note

Other cases imposing restrictions on the custody and visitation rights of lesbian and gay parents include *S.E.G.* v. *R.A.G.*, 735 S.W.2d 164 (Mo. Ct. App. 1987); and *In Re Jane B.*, 380 N.Y.S.2d 848 (Sup. Ct. 1976).

---

4. Linda urges us to follow the example of some of our sister states that have imposed restraining orders solely to limit the child's exposure to a parent's homosexuality, without evidence of harm justifying such limitations. This position is clearly contrary to California law which does not find homosexual parents to be *per se* unfit for primary custody. Implicitly, we have rejected the contention that, as a matter of law, a homosexual parent's visitation must be subject to restraining orders.

III. THE FORMATION OF GAY AND LESBIAN FAMILIES

A. Adoption

When children are adopted, the law establishes a permanent and exclusive parental relationship between the adoptive parents and the children. The rights and responsibilities of both biological parents are terminated and transferred to the adoptive parents. The adoption establishes the children's right to inherit from the adoptive parents and to sue the adoptive parents for child support.

There are a number of different ways children may become eligible for adoption. First, the biological parents may consent to the adoption, thereby transferring all parental rights and responsibilities to an adoptive parent. Second, the biological parents' rights and responsibilities may be terminated by the state upon a judicial finding that the parents have abandoned, neglected, or abused a child. The state may place the child in foster care or permit the child to be adopted depending on the circumstances. Finally, in reaction to an increasing number of step-families, second parent adoptions have been approved recently by some state courts. Unlike traditional adoptions, second parent adoptions do not extinguish the parental rights of both biological parents. An adoptive co-parent — a stepmother, stepfather, or same-sex partner — becomes a legal parent of a child, but the parental rights and responsibilities of the biological parent are not extinguished.

New Hampshire and Florida are the only two jurisdictions with statutory bans on lesbian and gay adoption and foster parenting; cases considering these laws follow in part (1). Other states in practice prohibit lesbians and gay men from adopting; these practices are considered in part (2) below. Part (3) looks at second parent adoptions.

1. STATUTORY RESTRICTIONS

IN RE OPINION OF THE JUSTICES

530 A.2d 21 (N.H. 1987)

[During consideration of a law "prohibiting homosexuals from adopting, being foster parents or running day care centers" the New Hampshire House of Representatives requested that the state's Supreme Court give its opinion as to the constitutionality of the act. The Court initially declined to issue an opinion on the act, instead asking the House of Representatives to provide a definition of "homosexuality" and a statement of factual findings about the nexus between homosexuality as the legislature would define it and the unfitness of homosexuals as declared by the bill. After the House responded the court issued the following decision.]

■ ■ ■

[The House resolved,] "That for the purposes of HB 70, a homosexual is defined as any person who performs or submits to any sexual act involving the sex organs of one person and the mouth or anus of another person of the same gender; and

"That the general court has chosen over the years to enact statutes relative to adopting children, providing foster care, and licensing day care centers in order to further the best interests of our state's children. These statutory enactments of the state do not involve intrusion into the private lives of consenting adults, but rather further the public and governmental interest in providing for the health, safety, and proper training for children who will be the subject of governmentally approved or licensed activities relating to such children. The general court finds that, as a matter of public policy, the provision of a healthy environment and a role model for our children should exclude homosexuals, as defined by this act, from participating in governmentally sanctioned programs of adoption, foster care, and day care. Additionally, the general court finds that being a child in such programs is difficult enough without the added social and psychological complexities that a homosexual life style could produce. The general court makes this statement in a deliberative and balanced manner both recognizing the rights of consenting adults, as limited by the

Supreme Court of the United States in *Bowers* v. *Hardwick*, and the rights of the children of this state, who are intimately affected by the policies of this state in the above governmentally sanctioned programs, to positive nurturing and a healthy environment for their formative years. . . .

■ ■ ■

The undersigned justices of the Supreme Court submit the following answers to the questions contained in your resolutions submitted to this court on March 4 and April 3, 1987. . . .

House Bill 70, if enacted, would prohibit homosexual persons from being foster parents, adoptive parents, or child care agency operators. It would accomplish this objective by amending the relevant statutes: RSA 170-B:4 would be amended to preclude homosexual persons from adopting any individual. RSA 170-F:6, I (Supp.1986) would be amended to exclude from the category of appropriate adoptive families those foster families "in which one or more of the adults is a homosexual." In like manner, RSA 161:2, IV (Supp.1986) would be amended to prohibit the Department of Health and Human Services from granting a license to any foster family home which contains one or more adult homosexual persons. The last substantive section of the bill would amend RSA 170-E:4 (Supp.1986) by adding a new paragraph mandating denial of any application for a license to operate a child-care facility "if the department determines that the applicant is unfit for licensure by reason of being a homosexual." We read this provision of the bill as requiring denial in any case where the applicant is found to be a homosexual within the meaning of the proposed definition. While our reading of this last section of the bill is only one possible reading, as its language is ambiguous regarding whether the department would have discretion to determine that a particular applicant's homosexuality would not render him or her unfit to operate a child-care agency, this more restrictive reading comports most closely with the bill's announced purpose to "*prohibit[] any person who is homosexual* from adopting any person, from being licensed as a member of a foster family, and *from running day care centers*."

Before expressing our opinion on the questions posed by the house of representatives, two preliminary observations regarding the definition of homosexuality contained in House Resolution 32 are in order. The resolution would define a homosexual for purposes of House Bill 70 as "any person who performs or submits to any sexual act involving the sex organs of one person and the mouth or anus of another person of the same gender." This very narrow definition of homosexual behavior contains no requirement that the acts or submission thereto be uncoerced, nor does there appear to be any temporal limitation regarding when the acts are to have occurred. Therefore, we assume for purposes of our analysis, first, that one who performs or submits to the acts described in the definition does so both voluntarily and knowingly; by doing so, we are able to avoid the patently absurd result of the inclusion of a victim of homosexual rape within the scope of the definition and his or her consequent preclusion from adopting, from becoming a foster parent, and from operating a child care agency. Second, we interpret the definition's present tense usage to mean that the acts bringing an individual within the definition's ambit must be or have been committed or submitted to on a current basis reasonably close in time to the filing of an application for licensure or a petition for adoption. This interpretation thus excludes from the definition of homosexual those persons who, for example, had one homosexual experience during adolescence, but who now engage in exclusively heterosexual behavior.

In addition, we note that we shall consider in this opinion only prospective application of the exclusions contained in the bill. We therefore express no opinion on the constitutionally of applications which would result in the interruption or termination of any existing arrangements.

Finally, we caution that this opinion makes no attempt to anticipate particular issues that may arise only as the statutory amendments are in fact applied, assuming enactment of the bill. There is no practical opportunity to deal with the range of such possible issues in advance.

The first question we have been asked to answer is whether the bill, if enacted into law, would violate the equal protection clauses of either the State or Federal Constitution.

For purposes of federal equal protection analysis, homosexuals do not constitute a suspect class, nor are they within the ambit of the so-called "middle tier" level of heightened scrutiny, as sexual preference is not a matter necessarily tied to gender, but rather to inclination, whatever the source thereof. Nor is there a fundamental right to engage in homosexual sodomy. *See Bowers* v. *Hardwick*. There is, further, no such right to adopt, to be a foster parent, or to be a child care agency operator, as these relationships are legal creations governed by statute. Therefore, since no suspect or quasi-suspect class or fundamental right is involved, the proper test to apply in determining the bill's constitutionality for federal equal protection purposes is whether the legislation is "rationally related to a legitimate governmental purpose." *Cleburne* v. *Cleburne Living Center, Inc.*, 473 U.S. 432, 446 (1985).

The purpose of the bill, as stated in House Resolution 32, is to promote "the provisions of a healthy environment[,] . . . role model[s] . . . [and] positive nurturing" to children affected by State-approved or -licensed activities and to eliminate the "social and psychological complexities" which living in a homosexual environment could produce in such children. In general, we accept the assertion that the provision of appropriate role models is a legitimate government purpose. The question, then, is whether a blanket exclusion of homosexuals from adoption, foster parentage, and child-care agency licensure is rationally related to the achievement of this purpose. It is not our business to inquire into the wisdom or desirability of the legislature's choice. It may, however, be preferable to deal with the present issue as the State may now do, as one of a number of relevant factors on a case-by-case basis. The question before us is nonetheless the narrow one, whether the proposed choice may constitutionally be made.

It is our opinion that the exclusion of homosexuals, as narrowly defined by your [the House's] resolution, from foster parentage and adoption can be found to be rationally related to the bill's purpose, expressed in House Resolution 32, to provide appropriate role models for children, but we are unable to conclude that such an exclusion vis-a-vis operators of all types of child-care agencies is so related. The rationale underlying the role model theory is that persons in the position of parents are the primary role models after whom children consciously or unconsciously pattern themselves. Although opponents of the bill have cited a number of studies that find no correlation between a homosexual orientation of parents and the sexual orientation of their children, the source of sexual orientation is still inadequately understood and is thought to be a combination of genetic and environmental influences. Given the reasonable possibility of environmental influences, we believe that the legislature can rationally act on the theory that a role model can influence the child's developing sexual identity. Obviously, this theory most likely holds true in the parent-child or other familial context. We are not satisfied, however, that it would hold true outside such a context (nor, of course, are we dealing with the termination of parental rights, or others otherwise affecting existing familial relationships). Thus, we are unable to accept the role model theory as

providing a rational basis on which to exclude homosexuals as a class from operating all of the types of facilities defined in RSA chapter 170-E (Supp.1986). To extend it to all such facilities would, we believe, paint with too broad a brush and extend the theory beyond the point of its rational application. This is especially evident in light of the bill's use of the term "applicant" as the entity whose sexuality is at issue. It would often be the case that the applicant would not be a human being at all, but rather a corporation, for example. In addition, even if the applicant were a human being, he or she might have little or no contact with the children for whom services were to be provided, in which case the applicant's sexual preference would be irrelevant.

Moreover, any analysis of rational basis must take into account the State's especially great responsibility in the foster care and adoption contexts to provide for the welfare of the children affected by placement decisions. In foster care and adoption cases the State by law has either the exclusive, or a highly significant, responsibility to choose what is best for the child. In the day care context, however, parental responsibility for choice supplements the State's obligations.

Our analysis must also consider the fact that foster care and adoption involve giving one or two individuals custody of an control over children so placed, and that, as a result, the choice of the child's care provider becomes especially important. In contrast, the non-continuous nature of the provision of many day care services, like the non-continuous nature of the supervision of children involved in teaching, for example, weakens the role model rationale to the point that we are unable to say that the bill is constitutional as to child-care agencies other than foster family homes.

To reiterate the point, it is in those living situations approximating a familial or parent-child arrangement that the role model theory provides a rational basis on which to exclude homosexuals as defined by the resolution from participation therein, because it is in the familial context that the theory of learned sexual preference is most likely to be true. We are not satisfied that the theory would provide a rational basis for a blanket exclusion of all homosexuals from being day care center operators or other non-full time child caretakers. Such cases must be the subject of specific determinations by licensing authorities.

The question of whether the bill violates the equal protection guarantee of the New Hampshire Constitution involves a similar inquiry. As under the Federal Constitution, no suspect class is involved, nor is heightened scrutiny requiring application of the fair and substantial relation test appropriate. The proper test under the State Constitution is, again, the rational relationship test. We have determined above that the proposed legislation is rationally related to a legitimate governmental purpose insofar as it applies to adoption and foster care. Therefore, no right of equal protection of the laws under the State Constitution would be violated by the proposed legislation except, possibly, as we have noted, as to child-care agencies other than foster family homes. For that reason, there is no need to give further consideration to the issue of the constitutionality of the exclusion of homosexuals from operating child-care agencies other than foster family homes, and we will treat the bill as though that provision had been excised.

The second question we have been asked to render an opinion on is whether House Bill 70 would violate the due process clause of either the Federal or State Constitution. We answer that it would not. First and foremost, there is no cognizable liberty or property interest in becoming a foster parent or in adopting a child, and thus no entitlement thereto. Mere desire or expectation does not rise to the level of an interest requiring procedural due process protections. If the question is intended to raise an issue of substantive due process, the answer is again in the negative, because the exclu-

sion of homosexuals from these activities bears a rational relationship to the government's legitimate objective of providing adopted and foster children with appropriate parental role models.

Second, with regard to the related notion that the classification created by the bill would function as an irrebuttable presumption at constitutional odds with due process, we note that the bill does not speak of a presumption, although the request for opinion does employ the term. We answer that the classification so created is not one of the sort struck down by the United States Supreme Court in *Stanley* v. *Illinois*, 405 U.S. 645 (1972) or in *Vlandis* v. *Kline*, 412 U.S. 441 (1973). *Vlandis* involved a presumption of non-residency that could have been presumption at issue. *Stanley* similarly involved a presumption that unwed fathers were unfit parents. *Stanley* thus was concerned both with an immediately disprovable presumed fact and a *legally cognizable* interest not at issue here, namely, that of a parent in the custody of his own children, and a risk of harm from parental unfitness that could readily be remedied when and if it actually occurred.

In contrast, the classification created here embodies a prediction of a risk not immediately disprovable by contrary evidence and one that does not implicate any fundamental interest, and it addresses a risk of harm that would not be readily reversible in those cases in which it could be expected to occur. Thus, *Stanley* and *Vlandis* are inapposite . . . .

Therefore, the proposed bill does not unconstitutionally deprive homosexuals as defined of due process of the laws under either the State or Federal Constitution.

The third question posed by the legislature is whether the proposed bill would violate any substantive right to privacy under either the State or Federal Constitution. We answer that it would not, resting our determination upon the United States Supreme Court's decision in *Bowers* v. *Hardwick*, wherein the Court stated that the substantive due process line of cases exemplified by *Griswold* v. *Connecticut* did not confer a fundamental right to engage in consensual homosexual sodomy because "[n]o connection between family, marriage, or procreation on the one hand and homosexual activity on the other has been demonstrated. . . . Moreover, any claim that these cases nevertheless stand for the proposition that any kind of private sexual conduct is constitutionally insulated from state proscription is unsupportable." In addition, we note that no intrusion by the State in this context is possible unless and until an individual invites it by voluntarily seeking to adopt or to be licensed as a foster parent. Only then would the State pose questions about the individual's private life, as the agent responsible for preserving and furthering the welfare of its children. We should add that this opinion is not meant to suggest that the State might have a similar authority to delve into the privacy of existing marital or custodial relationships. The same result would hold true under the State Constitution.

Likewise, there is no infringement upon any right of freedom of association under either the Federal or State Constitution, as the existence of any such right in this context must necessarily depend upon the assertion and recognition of rights to privacy or to engage in adoption or foster care, which we have explicitly rejected. Because, moreover, there is no privacy-grounded right to engage in consensual homosexual sodomy, *see Bowers supra*, there is no corresponding right to freedom of association for such a purpose. Because we find no right to privacy or association which would be infringed by this bill if enacted into law, we answer questions three and four in the negative, as we do also question five.

The remaining question posed for our consideration is that contained in House Resolution 32: "whether the legislature can properly classify children in the care of the state as a class for purposes of excluding homosexuals from adopting them or serving as foster parents or day care operators." We respectfully decline to answer the question posed because it is not germane to the constitutional issues raised. The pertinent classification is that of the group subject to the bill, to wit: homosexuals, as narrowly defined by the resolution, and not the group intended to be protected, namely, children in the care of the State. Therefore, we respectfully decline to answer the supplemental question posed by House Resolution 32.

In conclusion, therefore, we answer that, as to the first question posed in House Resolution 23, the bill, if embodying the assumptions expressed in this opinion, would be constitutional as applied to adoption and the licensing of foster parents, but we do not accept the role model theory as establishing the required rational relationship in the day care context. We answer the remaining four questions, with application only to adoption and foster care, in the negative, and we respectfully decline to answer the additional question posed by House Resolution 32.

BATCHELDER, J. dissenting.

The resolution which we review today avows that the purpose of House Bill 70 is to protect children rather than to punish homosexual conduct. Ironically, homosexual conduct as defined in the resolution, is not a crime in our State, yet heterosexual adultery is. The State is never more humanitarian than when it acts to protect the health of its children. The State is never less humanitarian than when it denies public benefits to a group of its citizens because of ancient prejudices against that group.

The bill presumes that every homosexual is unfit to be an adoptive parent or to provide foster or day care. It thus precludes every homosexual from demonstrating his or her skills as a parent. Financial stability is irrelevant; the strength to discipline a child firmly yet patiently is irrelevant; and the courage and love to be generous and loyal, the intelligence to provide proper education, and similar attributes are all irrelevant. Yet the legislature has no rational basis for concluding that homosexuals will be deficient in these characteristics "in the run of cases." The legislature received no meaningful evidence to show that homosexual parents endanger their children's development of sexual preference, gender role identity, or general physical and psychological health any more than heterosexual parents. The legislature received no such evidence because apparently the overwhelming weight of professional study on the subject concludes that no difference in psychological and psychosexual development can be discerned between children raised by heterosexual parents and children raised by homosexual parents. This, of course, is the conclusion reached by the large majority of the House Judiciary Committee in reply to this court's request for factual findings.

. . . While parenting an adopted or foster child is not a fundamental right, as parenting one's own biological child is, *Stanley* v. *Illinois*, 405 U.S. 645, 651-52 (1972), parenting is so ingrained in our culture that to deny the opportunity to adopt or provide foster care is a deprivation of liberty only in a lesser degree. In *Vlandis* v. *Kline*, 412 U.S. 441 (1973), the United States Supreme Court held that an irrebuttable presumption touching on a statutory benefit violated due process "when the State has reasonable alternative means of making the crucial determination."

Reasonable alternative methods exist to evaluate the qualifications of homosexuals who apply to adopt or offer foster care. [The adoption laws], as currently framed, allow ample scope for the investigating agency to deny a homosexual's application to adopt or to offer foster or day care when its investigation reveals that the applicant cannot provide a healthy, caring, nurturing environment for a child. The present division of children and youth services standards state:

"Foster parent applicants shall be free from physical, mental or emotional illness which, as evidenced in the documentation obtained and the observations made by DCYS, would impair his or her ability to assume and carry out the responsibilities of foster care." [and] "The physical and mental health of all foster home applicant household members shall not adversely affect the health of the child in care."

Although neither regulation mentions homosexuality, they are broad enough to permit the division to consider any applicant's sexual conduct in determining the applicant's fitness.

In *Vlandis*, the State established its presumption by stipulating one criterion as the sole relevant inquiry regarding present and future residency. Applicants were not denied an opportunity to submit evidence relevant to that criterion, but could not submit evidence on any other point which would in fact be relevant. House Bill 70 has an identical operation. Concedely, the indicia of residency are more objective than are the indicia of parental fitness, but that is no ore than a matter of the weight of the evidence in individual determinations. In this view, the presumed fact that homosexual parents are unfit is no less disprovable than the fact presumed in *Stanley supra* that unwed parents are unfit.

The applicant may be heard, in the first instant, only on the issue of homosexuality, and not on the larger issue of his or her ability to be a good parent, in the best interest of the child. It is this preclusive effect of the bill's irrebuttable presumption that leads me to conclude it would violate both federal and New Hampshire constitutional due process. Therefore, I agree that the bill is unconstitutional as to the day care provisions, but would also hold the bill unconstitutional as to its adoptive and foster parent provisions.

SEEBOL v. FARIE

No. 90-923-CA-18 (16th Judicial Circuit, Monroe County, Florida,
Mar. 15, 1991)

LESTER, J.

Plaintiff, EDWARD SEEBOL, challenges the unconstitutionality of §63.042(3), *Fla. Stat.* (1990), which prohibits homosexuals from adopting. After review of the pleadings and law, the court finds that section 63.042(3) violates Plaintiff's right to privacy under the Florida Constitution, and his rights to equal protection and due process of law under the Florida and Federal Constitutions.

I. FACTUAL BACKGROUND

A. The Florida Adoption Statute

Adoption is defined as a personal relationship created by one capable of adopting and one capable of being adopted. Adoption, unknown at common law, is statutory in nature and can be decreed only in accordance with statute. In adoption proceedings, as in child custody proceedings, the court's primary duty is to serve the best interests of the child. The legislative intent of the Florida adoption statute is to:

> protect and promote the well-being of persons being adopted and their natural and adoptive parents and to provide to all children who can benefit by it a permanent family life.

Courts are directed to enter orders as deemed necessary and suitable to promote and protect the best interest of the person to be adopted. Suitability to adopt has rarely been challenged in Florida; advanced age and modest income of prospective adoptive parents have been rejected as grounds to deny adoption. . . .

The Florida adoption statute, approved by the legislature in 1977, §63.042(3) holds, "No person eligible to adopt under this statute may adopt if that person is a homosexual." Since the enactment of the statute, unforeseen circumstances have occurred. The state of Florida amended its constitution to provide for a right to privacy. Society has become increasingly knowledgeable of homosexual behavior and more tolerant of this sexual orientation. Births of substance abused newborns and HIV infected newborns has sharply increased in the state. The Department of Health and Rehabilitative Services has experienced a corresponding crisis in the adoption placement of these impaired children.

B. The Children's Best Interests

In child custody proceedings, several jurisdictions have recently determined that the homosexuality of parents should not be a bar to either custody or visitation, *Matter of Marriage of Cabalquinto*, 669 P.2d 886 (Wash. 1983); *M.A.B.* v. *R.B.*, 510 N.Y.S.2d 960 (N.Y. App. Div. 1986)(impermissible as a matter of law to determine custody on basis of father's homosexual orientation): *S.N.E.* v. *R.L.B.*, 699 P.2d 875 (Alaska 1985) (consideration of mother's homosexual orientation appropriate only when shown to have adverse effect on child's health); *Benzio* v. *Patenaude*, 410 N.E.2d 1207 (Mass. 1980) (mother's homosexual orientation irrelevant to parenting skills). These courts, which have adopted the nexus approach to a parent's homosexuality, consider the parent's heterosexual or homosexual activity in custody determinations only if it is shown to adversely affect the child. Such decisions reflect the results of recent studies which have shown children raised by homosexual parents to exhibit normal behavior patterns.

Mental health experts have found the incidence of same-sex orientation among the children of homosexual parents as randomly and in the same proportion as found among children in the general population, Susoeff, *Assessing Children's Best Interests When a Parent Is Gay or Lesbian: Toward a Rational Custody Standard*, 32 UCLA L. Rev. 852, 882 (1985). Psychiatrists have found that children adopt sexual orientations independently of their parents, and that homosexual men and women do not learn sexual preference by watching the sexual preference of their parents.

Furthermore, experts agree that a child brought up in the tranquil home of a homosexual parent is better off than one growing up in a heterosexual home marked by domestic turmoil and lack of affection.

Although no appellate decision in Florida has addressed this issue, a circuit court recently adopted the nexus approach and awarded custody of a child to her deceased mother's homosexual partner, *In Re Pearlman*, No. 87-24926 DA (Fla. 17th Cir. Ct. 1989). The court found no evidence that the mother's partner's sexual preference had previously had, or would in the future have, any detrimental effect on the child. The court recognized the prevailing view in other jurisdictions that homosexuality should not in itself render a parent or custodian unfit for custody of, or visitation with, a minor child; *contra Roe* v. *Roe*, 324 S.E.2d 691 (Va. 1985)(father's homosexual relationship rendered him unfit custodian as a matter of law); *but cf. J.P.* v. *P.W.*, 772 S.W.2d 786 (Mo. Dist. Ct. App. 1989)(court cannot ignore effect parent's sexual conduct may have on child's future moral development and ordered supervised visitation with homosexual father).

The Supreme Court of Ohio recently approved the adoption of a special-needs child by his psychological counselor who is a homosexual, *In Re Adoption of Charles B.*, 552 N.E.2d 884 (Ohio 1990). The court's decision to allow the adoption relied heavily upon the absolute lack of evidence in the trial court that the adoption would not be in the child's best interest. Testimony showed, to the contrary, that the adoption would be in the child's best interest because his special needs required an adoptive parent with stability and flexibility, and the willingness to seek needed services. It was recognized that permanent placement in a judicially approved home environment was preferable to confining the child to an institution or to the life of transience from one foster home to another. Most importantly, Ohio recognized the advisability of permitting adoption on a case by case basis since the facts in each adoption case will vary. In deciding whether to approve an adoption, the court must consider all relevant factors before determining whether the child's best interest will be served.

C. Plaintiff Seebol

Plaintiff, Edward Seebol, resides in Key West and applied to the State of Florida to adopt a special-needs child. Mr. Seebol has been a well respected resident and businessman of this city for twenty years. He has been participating in the state guardianship and guardian ad litem programs, and since the mid-1980s he has worked relentlessly in AIDS education and assistance to affected individuals. He is presently executive director of AIDS Help, Inc. He was notified by the Department of Health and Rehabilitative Services that since his application response revealed that he was a homosexual, the Department was unable to approve his application.

II. CONCLUSIONS OF LAW

A. The Right to Privacy in Florida

The right to privacy in Florida ensures that individuals may be free from governmental interference with their sexual orientation,

Art. I, §23, Fla. Const. During the adoption application process, the Department of Health and Rehabilitative Services inquires as to the sexual orientation of applicants. If the prospective parent answers truthfully that he or she is homosexual, the prospective parent is deemed ineligible to adopt. Significantly, the statute disqualifies not only prospective parents who engage in private sexual conduct, but also those who express a mere orientation toward homosexuality, even if unaccompanied by homosexual behavior. As will be demonstrated below, the inquiry into sexual orientation and consideration thereof, without regard for the child's best interests, violates Florida's right to privacy.

The Florida right to privacy has been described as " 'the most comprehensive of rights and the right most valued by civilized man,' " *Rasmussen* v. *South Florida Blood Service*, 500 So.2d 533, 535(Fla. 1987)[quoting *Stanley* v. *Georgia*, 394 U.S. 557, 564 (1969)] and has been extended to include matters concerning procreation, contraception, family relationships, childrearing and education, *Roe* v. *Wade*, 410 U.S. 113, 152–153; *compare Bowers* v. *Hardwick*, 478 U.S. 186, (1986)(no federal constitutional right to engage in homosexual sodomy).[3]

The right to privacy was adopted in recognition of the state's, not the federal government's, responsibility for the protection of personal privacy, and was intended to encompass a broader realm of privacy rights than in the Federal Constitution. The right has been defined as an imbedded belief, rooted in constitutional traditions, that the individual has a fundamental right to be left alone so that he or she is free to lead a private life according his or her beliefs, free from unreasonable government intrusion. Privacy has been used interchangeably with the concept of liberty, both of which imply a fundamental right of self-determination subject only to the state's compelling and overriding interest. The right to privacy in Florida has been construed to limit public disclosure of personal matters, to extend to personal decision making, and to the right of a teenage woman to decide whether to end her pregnancy.

The Florida Supreme Court has never directly addressed whether Art. I, §23 encompasses sexual orientation. However, in 1978, two years before the ratification of Article I, §23, the Florida Supreme Court held that a bar candidate's mere preference for homosexuality did not threaten his fitness to practice law. *In Re: Florida Board of Bar Examiners*, 358 So.2d 7, 10 (Fla. 1978). The Florida Supreme Court recognized that "[g]overnmental regulation in the area of private morality is generally considered anachronistic in the absence of *a clear and convincing showing that there is a substantial connection* between the private acts regulated and public interests and welfare." In so holding, the Court relied on the due process and equal protection clauses, which are among the underpinnings of the right to privacy under the Federal Constitution. The strong message from *In Re: Florida Board of Bar Examiners* is that sexual orientation was entitled, in 1978, to at least some measure of constitutional protection.

The fact that two years later the people chose to expand constitutional protection for privacy strongly supports the position that they felt existing constitutional projections were inadequate and that the Florida right to privacy should encompass a broader realm of privacy rights than that in the Federal Constitution. That broader realm certainly must include protection for an individual's sexual orientation, which is a "decision[] vitally affecting his private life according to his own conscience," and pro-

---

3. Retired Supreme Court Justice Lewis F. Powell, Jr., recently announced that he recognized his mistake in not voting for an extension of the constitutional right to privacy in *Bowers* v. *Hardwick*. Justice Powell now found the 5-4 majority opinion "'inconsistent in a general way'" with the precedent established by *Roe* v. *Wade*. *When Second Thoughts In Case Come Too Late*, N. Y. TIMES, Nov. 5, 1990, §A, at 9.

tection against penalization of sexual orientation.

By inquiring into sexual orientation, and then penalizing an applicant based on his truthful response to that inquiry, the challenged statute unconstitutionally punishes the exercise of the right to privacy of prospective adoptive parents, *cf. Harris* v. *McRae*, 448 U.S. 297 (1980). In *Harris,* the United States Supreme Court, while upholding restrictions on federal funding for abortions, recognized a distinction between not subsidizing the exercise of constitutional rights and penalizing the exercise of those rights:

> A substantial constitutional question would arise if Congress had attempted to withhold all medicaid benefits from an otherwise eligible candidate simply because that candidate had exercised her constitutionally protected freedom to terminate her pregnancy by abortion. This would be analogous to *Sherbert* v. *Verner*, 374 U.S. 398, where this Court held that a State may not, consistent with the First and Fourteenth Amendments, withhold all unemployment compensation benefits from a claimant who would otherwise be eligible for such benefits but for the fact that she is unwilling to work one day per week on her Sabbath.

The statute challenged here attempts to withhold the benefits of adoption to an otherwise qualified candidate because of that person's sexual orientation, and thus penalizes the exercise of that right.

The question, then, becomes whether the state has a compelling interest in inquiring into sexual orientation and, if so, whether its interest is advanced by this statutory scheme through the least intrusive means. In this case, the state has asserted no compelling interest, or, for that matter, any substantial or even rational interest.

Even if it had, the government interest involved is protecting the best interests of children to be adopted, and providing all children who can benefit from it a permanent family life, §63.022. Moreover, the statute specifically recognizes that adoption can and does benefit adoptive parents. While the state's interest in protecting the best interests of children is admittedly compelling, that interest is not advanced by this statutory exclusion. Further, the state's interest in advancing the best interests of adoptive parents is totally frustrated by excluding an entire class of parents based upon their sexual orientation.

The statute suffers from the trite notions of homosexuals' unsuitability as fit parents and evidences discrimination through archaic stereotypes associated with homosexuals. Homosexuals have been proven to be capable, loving parents whose sexual orientation is not necessarily adopted by their children. Determining parents' suitability to adopt on a case by case basis, *In Re Adoption of Charles B.*, would be a less intrusive means to accomplish the important state interest at stake. The sexual orientation of the adoptive parent should be considered as a factor in determining the adoption only if shown to directly and adversely affect the child. The statutory exclusion of one class of persons to become adoptive parents based upon their sexual orientation unconstitutionally, thus, interferes with their right to privacy under the Florida Constitution.

B. Equal Protection of Law

The equal protection clauses of the State and Federal Constitutions guarantee that all citizens similarly situated be treated alike, U.S. Const. amend. XIV, §1.; Art. I, §2, Fla. Const., *City of Cleburne* v.*Cleburne Living Center*, 473 U.S. 432, 439 (1985). Government regulations challenged as violative of the equal protection clause are subjected to three standards of review; strict scrutiny, heightened scrutiny, and rational basis review, depending upon the nature of the class claiming discrimination. Governmental regulations are presumed valid under the equal protection clause as long as the classification drawn by the regulation "rationally furthers some legitimate, articulated state purpose." However, governmental regulations that infringe upon the rights of a suspect class or violate a fundamental right will be subjected to strict scrutiny and sustained only if found suitably tailored to serve a compelling state interest.

Homosexuals clearly constitute a suspect class under equal protection analysis, *Watkins* v. *United States Army*, 875 F.2d 699, 711–724 (9th Cir. 1989) (Norris, J. concurring), *vacating* 847 F.2d 1329 (9th Cir. 1989) (extending suspect class status to homosexuals), *cert. denied*, No. 89–1806, Nov. 5, 1990.[4]

To warrant suspect class inquiry, it must first be determined whether the class at issue has been subjected to purposeful discrimination. It has been recognized that "'homosexuals have historically been the object of pernicious and sustained hostility,'" *id., quoting Rowland* v. *Mad River Local School Dist.*, 470 U.S. 1009, 1014 (1985) (Brennan J., dissenting from denial of cert.); *see* Note, *The Constitutional Status of Sexual Orientation: Homosexuality As A Suspect Classification*, 98 HARV.L.REV. 1285, 1299–1305 1985); Note, *An Argument for the Application of Equal Protection Heightened Scrutiny to Classifications Based on Homosexuality*, 57 S.CAL.L.REV. 797, 799–807(1984).

The second factor to determine is whether the class is defined by a trait that bears no relationship to its ability to perform or function in society, *Frontiero* v. *Richardson*, 411 U.S. 677, 686, (1973). It has been conclusively proven that homosexuals are fit parents and that their children do not learn sexual orientation from them. Most stereotypes previously associated with homosexuals have been proven incorrect; homosexuality is no longer considered a mental or emotional illness; nor have homosexuals been proven more likely than heterosexuals to be child molesters. Furthermore, the argument that children should not be parented by homosexuals because they will be subjected to community and peer harassment is constitutionally unsound, *see Palmore* v. *Sidoti*, 466 U.S. 429 (1984). Discrimination against homosexuals, thus, bears deep-seated prejudice rather than reality, *Watkins*, 875 F.2d at 725.

A third factor to be considered is the political powerlessness of the minority group, *Cleburne*, 473 U.S. at 441. Because of past stigmatization associated with homosexuality, many homosexuals conceal their sexual orientation and fail to participate in organizations seeking gay rights advances. The homosexuals who do advocate their rights are not openly received, nor endorsed, by legislators. The continued existence of laws discriminating against homosexuals, the judiciary's approval of such laws, and the legislators' unwillingness to repeal them, all prove homosexuals' political powerlessness.

Lastly, the suspect class must be defined by traits which are immutable. "[S]cientific research indicates that we have little control over our sexual orientation and that once acquired, our sexual orientation is largely impervious to change," *Watkins*, at 726.

Since homosexuals should constitute a suspect class, the statutory exclusion at issue must be upheld only if necessary to a compelling government interest, accomplished by the least restrictive means. Although the government interest, the best interests of children, is absolutely compelling, it is defi-

---

4. Because there is no fundamental right to engage in homosexual conduct, *Bowers* v. *Hardwick*, 478 U.S. 186, several federal courts have denied suspect class status to homosexuals, *High Tech Gays* v. *Defense Industrial Security Clearance Office*, 895 F.2d 563 (9th Cir. 1990), *Ben-Shalom* v. *Marsh*, 881 F.2d 454 (7th Cir. 1989)(not addressing suspect class status), reversing 703 F.Supp. 1372, 1380 (E.D.Wis. 1989)(extending suspect class status to homosexuals), cert. denied, 110 S.Ct. 1296 (1990); *Woodward v. United States*, 871 F.2d 1068 (D.C.Cir. 1989), cert. denied, 110 S.Ct. 1295 (1990);*Padula v. Webster*, 822 F.2d 97 (D.C.Cir.1987).

nitely not accomplished by the least restrictive means. The Florida adoption statute which denies eligibility to prospectively fit parents defeats its very purpose of providing to all children who can benefit by adoption a permanent family life. The statute is poorly tailored to achieve its compelling interest and must be stricken.

Even were this court to deny suspect class status to homosexuals, the regulation at issue is also not rationally related to a legitimate, articulated state purpose. The best interests of children are not supported by the regulation which is clearly irrelevant to the promotion of any legitimate state goal. A governmental regulation which spites its own articulated goals, cannot sustain any level of constitutional analysis. The Florida adoption statute, thus, is blatantly unconstitutional and must be stricken.

■ ■ ■

ORDERED AND ADJUDGED that § 63.042, Fla. Stat. (1990) is declared void because it violates Plaintiff's right to privacy under the Florida Constitution, and his rights to equal protection of law and due process of law under the Florida and Federal Constitutions, as stated in the opinion filed herewith which is incorporated into this final judgment.

Notes

1. U.S. Supreme Court Justice David H. Souter was a member of the New Hampshire Supreme Court at the time of the *Opinion of the Justices* decision and joined the majority's decision.
2. The Attorney General of Florida did not appeal the *Seebol* decision to the Florida Supreme Court. As a result, the *Seebol* holding is binding only on Florida's 16th judicial circuit. The statute barring homosexuals from adoption remains valid in other jurisdictions within Florida. Challenges to the statute are currently pending in several other parts of Florida. *See* Bob Knotts, *Lawsuit Seeks to Overturn Ban on Adoption by Gays*, SUN SENTINEL, June 3, 1992, at 2B; Michael Young, *Legal Knots Snarl Adoptions By Gay Couples*, SUN SENTINEL, Feb. 25, 1992, at 6E.

2. RESTRICTIONS IN PRACTICE

APPEAL IN PIMA COUNTY JUVENILE ACTION B-10489

727 P.2d 830 (Ariz. Ct. App. 1986)

HATHAWAY, C.J.

This appeal follows the juvenile court's order certifying appellant as nonacceptable to adopt children.

■ ■ ■

II. FINDINGS AND CONCLUSIONS

In Arizona, no person may petition to adopt a particular child unless he has met certain statutory requirements. First, he must be certified by the court as acceptable to adopt children. Once a certification of acceptability is issued and the identity of the potential adoptive child is known, additional investigation and reporting are required to determine the suitability of that child's placement with the applicant. After the child's suitability for adoption by the applicant is determined, the petition to adopt is filed and may not be heard or disposed of for an additional six months to allow continued investigation.

When a petition for certification is filed pursuant to [Arizona statutory requirements], an investigation is conducted and a report to the court is filed. The investigation may be conducted by the division, as in this case. The statute requires that the investigative report consider all relevant facts regarding an applicant's fitness to adopt including, without limitation, the applicant's social history, financial condition, moral fitness, religious background, physical health, mental health, fingerprint records and any prior court actions involving children. The report also must contain a "definite recommendation for certifying the applicant as being acceptable or nonacceptable."

The juvenile court, upon receiving the precertification report, "shall certify the applicant as being acceptable or nonacceptable to adopt children based on the investigation report and recommendations of such report." The investigation report which was filed by the division in this case recommended that appellant be certified as acceptable to adopt children.

■ ■ ■

In this case, the court specified the following circumstances and concluded that appellant was not acceptable to adopt children: That appellant is bisexual, that he lives alone and is employed, that he has had eight employment positions in eleven years; that he has sought personal counseling and that his family support system is limited.

■ ■ ■

The primary issue the court should consider when deciding whether to certify an applicant as suitable to adopt children is the best interest and welfare of any child who might be adopted by that person. The situation is akin to the problem before courts when determining custody or visitation as between natural parents, where the controlling standard is the best interest of the child. A fortiori, this criterion must control when considering adoption inasmuch as custody and visitation determinations are subject to modification upon changing conditions, while single-parent adoptions are final with no subsequent available option of shifting custody between parents. Once an adoption is final, the sole means of reversal is by termination of parental rights — a remedy not lightly undertaken.

As the dissent correctly notes, the judge was concerned over a child's reaction in the future on learning of appellant's sexual orientation. Appellant testified that he would seek advice from professionals for guidance to deal with that issue. After the adoption has been completed, however, there is no method by which the court or any state agency could require that such guidance be sought by appellant.

■ ■ ■

. . . We share the trial judge's concern that seeking counseling *per se* will not resolve all the potential problems that may occur once a child is placed with appellant. We defer to the trial court.

The amicus brief centers its argument on the self-presumed fact that the trial court based its decision solely on appellant's sexual orientation. The dissent also maintains that appellant's bisexuality was the sole reason for the denial of his petition to be certified as acceptable to adopt children. We disagree. As we have stated, we find ample evidence to support the trial court without examining that issue.

However, we believe appellant's ambivalence in his sexual preference was very appropriately a concern of the court. As we have stated previously, the primary concern of the court, to the exclusion of all else, is the best interest and welfare of any child. Certainly the sexual orientation of one who petitions to be certified as acceptable to adopt a child is a factor to be reviewed and evaluated by the court. Certification of acceptability for adoption should not be lightly undertaken. While a second hearing is required before a child may be adopted, the judge before whom such hearing is held may be expected to place considerable reliance upon the certification hearing.

We note the case cited by the dissent wherein the sexual orientation of a parent was not a sufficient factor to change custody or alter visitation rights. There are an equal number of cases wherein the courts did change the custody of minor children or alter visitation because of a parent's sexual activity. [The court here lists fourteen such cases.]

The fact that appellant is bisexual is not unlawful nor, standing alone, does it render him unfit to be a parent. It is homosexual conduct which is proscribed. [citing to the Arizona sodomy statute]. Such statutes have been held constitutional. *Bowers* v. *Hardwick*.

Appellant testified that it was possible that he at some future time would have some type of homosexual relationship with another man even with placement of a child in his home. He also testified that he did not believe the possibility of continued homosexual activity would have an adverse affect on a child that he might adopt. It would be anomalous for the state on the one hand to declare homosexual conduct unlawful and on the other create a parent after that proscribed model, in effect approving that standard, inimical to the natural family, as head of a state-created family. The trial court may have been dissatisfied with the showing with reference to appellant's conduct as dis-

tinguished from his homosexual predisposition.

Considering the record in the light most favorable to the trial court's ruling, we affirm.

HOWARD, Presiding Judge, dissenting.

The majority cloaks its opinion with "due regard" for the trial court's findings of fact and with the "norm of appellate review." Like the trial court, the majority gives credence to unsupported findings, and refused to acknowledge the sole reason for its ruling: the fact of appellant's bisexuality. The majority states that it is unnecessary to examine that issue and simultaneously holds that the state may not "create" a family with a homosexual parent. Considering the record in the light most favorable to the trial court's ruling, its conclusion is not supported by the findings and the findings are not supported by the testimony and evidence. I am accused by the majority of weighing the evidence. That is not true because there is nothing to weigh. All the evidence was in favor of the appellant. It is clear from the record that both the trial judge and the majority of this department have no intention of ever letting a bisexual adopt a child. I refuse to participate in such a decision. I, therefore, set forth the facts which merit a reversal of the trial court's order.

■ ■ ■

The court found that appellant "is a bisexual individual who has had, and may have in the future, sexual relationships with members of both sexes." The court's comments at the review hearing and the questions which the judge directed to appellant and the other witnesses focuses mainly on appellant's sexual orientation. The judge expressed concern with three main topics: whether appellant would "proselytize" homosexuality to a child and whether he is involved in gay rights organizations; whether an appropriate parent-child bond could be created with a bisexual or homosexual adoptive parent; and whether appellant's interest in children includes an unnatural or abnormal sexual interest or intent.

The witnesses testified that appellant is not overtly sexual, is not promiscuously or flamboyantly homosexual, does not frequent any bars, and is not active in gay rights groups. Appellant testified that he believes it is inappropriate to display sexual activities in front of children or to influence a child's sexual orientation in the manner suggested by the court. The division caseworker pointed out that published studies conclude that children have established their own sexual preference by the age of three years. The court's concerns regarding activism or proselytizing were not borne out by the evidence in this case.

At one point during the review hearing, the judge stated: "I'm more concerned with the bonding or whatever you want to call it, relationship that might ultimately exist or not exist because of the sexual situation." Many of the questions asked by the judge showed a concern for a child's future reaction to discovering or realizing that his adoptive parent is bisexual. Appellant testified that once a particular child has been placed with him, he intends to seek the advice of skilled professionals for guidance to deal properly with that particular issue. The division caseworker testified that appellant is capable of providing a proper approach to the issue and is a good role model for learning how to handle sexual issues in general in a responsible manner. She also testified that, depending on the individual child's age, prior experience and personality, a discussion of the matter with the child prior to adoption would be possible.

A socialworker and director of specialized mental health services at La Frontera with 26 years of counseling experience, who is a personal friend of appellant, testified that she has given opinions in a professional capacity as to the propriety of adoptive placement. In response to the court's questioning about a child's reaction to appellant's bisexuality, she testified that a child's future reaction to discovering appellant's sexual orientation would depend on the parent-child relationship which was established from the original time of placement and that the ultimate answers to the court's questions could be made only after appellant was matched with a particular potential adoptive child. She and the caseworker both emphasized the process of matching parent and child, that being "the beauty of adoption, the adult and child both have an opportunity to make the very best match."

The court also inquired of appellant whether his "relationship with any adoptive child would be essentially or totally asexual," and further asked, "Do you feel that you have any unusual urge or any unusual sexual attraction to younger boys? Do you feel the absence of any urge toward younger boys? Have you ever had any psychological tests that were intended to assess that relationship between you and younger boys?" Finally, the court requested of the socialworker who testified that there are no such tests:

> THE COURT: So I'd ask you to get back to me on — after you specifically contact psychologists, with whatever information you have, about whether there's any tests that they think would be helpful in assessing any abnormal tendencies toward children.

There is no evidence to support the court's comments regarding sexual interest in children or the conclusion that a bisexual or homosexual person is more likely to harbor such abnormal intent than a heterosexual. In fact, as the caseworker testified, there is no correlation between pedophiles and either heterosexuality or homosexuality. In addition, the majority of crimes committed by adults upon children are heterosexual and the vast majority of sexual acts committed upon children are committed by adult heterosexual males. *See Baker* v. *Wade*, 553

F. Supp. 1121, 1130 (N.D.Tex. 1982), *rev'd on other grounds*, 769 F.2d 289 (5th Cir.1985) (citing Sam Houston State University Criminal Justice Center, *Responding to Child Sexual Abuse*; *A Report to the 67th Session of the Texas Legislature* (1980)).[3] There is nothing in the record to support a concern in this area. Appellant's past experience in a foster child situation was investigated by the division caseworker and revealed no unusual or abnormal sexual attraction. As noted above, a friend of appellant's for more than 20 years who is the father of two young boys testified that appellant regularly babysits his children and that he and his wife have chosen to designate appellant as the legal guardian of their sons in the event such appointment by will would become necessary. Appellant has been accepted by and participates in the Big Brothers of Tucson organization and has had a "little brother" assigned to him since early 1985.

■ ■ ■

The majority opinion states that sexual orientation is a factor to be reviewed and evaluated in preadoption certification proceedings. The division caseworker who conducted the investigation testified that as to unmarried applicants, the division does determine sexual preference but that there is no policy to recommend or not recommend an applicant solely because he or she has been identified as a bisexual or homosexual. She testified that the division looks generally to whether an applicant's behavior, lifestyle and character would impact adversely on a particular child. In other words, an applicant will not be rejected solely on the basis of sexual orientation; rather, the inquiry focuses on style of living, honesty,

integrity, stability of living, strong employment and other general character considerations. The socialworker testified that such concerns would apply to any applicant, acknowledging as an example an unmarried heterosexual female applicant who "lives a fast life" and conducts relationships with many men. The inquiry as to sexuality focuses generally on promiscuity and flamboyancy in any situation, not merely in cases of identified homosexual or bisexual applicants. She noted that professionals in a multi-state training workshop concluded that homosexuality *per se* does not impact adversely on the success or failure of an adoptive parent. She also commended appellant's honesty and frankness in discussing his life and sexuality with her openly and without repeated questioning as is necessary with some applicants:

> [H]e struck me from the outset of our home interviews as being among the most candid candidate-applicant I've ever encountered, and . . . at the conclusion of the study, I felt that I had a stronger sense of this man's character, morality, and maturity than I do most of the clients.

She described appellant "as being a very mature individual who has resolved significant issues in his own life, has high standards in several areas of his life, and a strong commitment to become a parent to a child." She testified that she has had experience with a number of single-parent adoptions during her five years as a caseworker in the adoption unit and that appellant would be a good parent and role model for a child properly placed with him.

While there is no case law particularly applicable to the situation at hand, I believe the proper rule to be that homosexuality or

---

3. The brief of the amici curiae also cites American Humane Association, Children's Division, *Protecting the Child Victim of Sex Crimes Committed by Adults*, 216-17 (V. DeFrancis ed. 1969), which concluded that 97 percent of sex offenders against children are male and 90 percent of the victims are female.

bisexuality standing alone does not render an applicant unfit as a matter of law to adopt children. That is not to say, however, that every homosexual or bisexual is acceptable to adopt. The case-by-case approach to investigating adoptive applicants may reveal circumstances, as the division caseworker testified, which render an applicant nonacceptable.

The law governing child custody provides guidance. . .

■ ■ ■

The majority cites a recent United States Supreme Court decision [*Bowers* v. *Hardwick*] for the proposition that A.R.S. §§ 13-1411 and 13-1412 constitutionally proscribe homosexual conduct. It then concludes that the state may not "create" a family with a parent who has in the past, or may be in the future, engaged in such unlawful conduct. If an applicant's participation or potential participation in unlawful sexual practices may provide a valid basis for certifying an applicant as nonacceptable to adopt, then, in keeping with the majority's guidelines and the pronouncement of the Arizona Supreme Court,[6] it must be imperative that the juvenile court inquire into every applicant's conduct, past and future, with regard to the proscriptions of A.R.S. §§ 13-1408 (adultery) and 13-1409 (open and notorious cohabitation or adultery). Moreover, the inquiry must include extensive questioning of every applicant, regardless of marital status and sexual preference, to determine whether his or her sexual practices violate A.R.S. §§ 13-1411 and 13-1412.

There may be circumstances in the precertification investigation, such as flamboyance or promiscuity, which render an applicant nonacceptable to adopt children. However, the mere fact of appellant's bisexuality does not render him nonacceptable to adopt any children as a matter of law. Furthermore, based upon the division's investigation report, the testimony of the division caseworker, the other witnesses and the evidence, I believe that the juvenile court erred in concluding that appellant is nonacceptable for certification to adopt a child, because there was no evidence to support a finding of any negative circumstances relating to appellant's bisexuality in this case.

Absent traits of life style habits, such as overt sexuality or promiscuity, sexual preference alone should not be determinative of an application for preadoption certification. In appellant's case, as both experienced socialworkers testified, the inquiry must focus on an individual child to determine "the best match" and to determine whether his sexual orientation will or may adversely impact upon that particular child.

■ ■ ■

I would vacate the order of the juvenile court with directions to enter an order certifying appellant as acceptable to adopt children pursuant to A.R.S. § 8-105(A).

---

6. Without limitation to homosexual conduct, the Arizona Supreme Court has held that this state's statutory proscription of lewd and lascivious acts and sodomy constitutes proper legislative regulation of moral welfare and, therefore, does not violate the specific right of privacy guaranteed by our own constitution in Article 2, § 8. *State* v. *Bateman*, 547 P.2d 6, 10 (Ariz. 1976), *cert. denied*, 429 U.S. 864.

IN RE ADOPTION OF CHARLES B.

552 N.E.2d 884 (Ohio 1990)

PER CURIAM

■ ■ ■

The substantive issue before this court is whether Mr. B should be allowed to adopt Charles B. The court of appeals stated, in effect, that it could never be in a child's best interest to be adopted by a person such asMr. B. We do not agree and, therefore, reverse the judgment of the court of appeals and reinstate the judgment of the trial court.

■ ■ ■

Having established that Mr. B is not statutorily precluded from adopting Charles and that in Ohio the right to adopt is not absolute, we must now determine whether the trial court was correct in allowing the adoption of Charles to go forward or whether the court of appeals was correct in prohibiting the adoption. . . .

■ ■ ■

The record discloses that Charles, although still a young boy, already has endured many emotional as well as physical hardships. Charles has had a neglected and abused childhood. His natural parents signed a voluntary permanent surrender of him. He has been in the permanent custody of appellee since April 1985. Although appellee originally attempted to place Charles and his two sisters with one family, this plan was abandoned after appellee determined that individual placements would be better for Charles and his siblings.

The agency then developed a list of requirements for the family adopting Charles. These requirements were: a family of two parents with older siblings, at least one of which would be male; a family with a child-centered life style; a couple with definite parenting experience, preferably with adoption experience; parents with proven ability in dealing with behavior disorder issues; a family that is open to counseling; and a family that demonstrates an ability to deal with learning disabilities, speech problems and medical problems. A tall order, indeed.

In 1985, Charles was registered as an individual child available for adoption. In early 1987, Mr. B indicated to appellee his general interest in adopting a child, and Charles in particular. A supervisor of appellee's Family Services Unit indicated that if Mr. B had a home study completed, he would be given consideration to adopt Charles if no other final decision had been made prior to that time.

Several potential families were chosen by appellee for Charles. None of these potential adoptive families proved successful for Charles. In May 1987, appellee located a two-parent family for Charles. Appellee prepared both the family and Charles for eventual placement. Charles met the family in August 1987 but after several weeks, the family demonstrated, according to appellee, a "lack of commitment to adopting Charlie." Appellee, on October 1, 1987, decided not to place Charles with this family.

Throughout this time period, Mr. B's interest in adopting Charles never wavered. On December 18, 1987, Mr. B completed a pre-placement application wherein he expressed his desire to adopt Charles. On January 15, 1988, Mr. B filed a petition for the adoption of Charles in the Probate Division of the Court of Common Pleas of Licking County.

The record further discloses that Mr. B is aware of, and prepared to meet, Charles's physical and emotional problems. He has plans for Charles's medical care and education and has demonstrated an ability to discipline Charles when necessary. He also testified that he has accepted Charles as he is.

Witnesses called by Mr. B at the hearing testified that Mr. B has the necessary qualifications to be a good parent for Charles. The guardian stated that Mr. B and Charles have developed a close relationship and that Charles would like to make his home with Mr. B. The guardian further stated that Mr. B would have the support of his immediate family with sufficient female role models. The guardian concluded his report with a recommendation that the adoption be approved.

. . . While we have never addressed the precise issue now before us, we, and other Ohio courts, have dealt with a number of cases involving custody of children. We find a review of some of those cases to be helpful in our current deliberations.

This court in *In re Burrell*, 388 N.E.2d 738 (Ohio 1979), addressed whether two minor girls lacked proper parental care and supervision solely because their mother, with whom they lived, was also living with her boyfriend. We found that the evidence showed no conditions adverse to the normal development of the girls other than the fact that the mother lived with her boyfriend. We held:

". . .[S]uch conduct is only significant if it can be demonstrated to have an adverse impact upon the child sufficiently to warrant state intervention. That impact cannot be simply inferred in general, but must be specifically demonstrated in a clear and convincing manner. . . . "

The court of appeals in *Whaley* v. *Whaley*, 399 N.E. 2d 1270 (Ohio App. 1978), was called upon to decide whether a change in custody was warranted when the mother, who had custody of her daughter, was "romantically interested" in a married man whom she planned to marry after his divorce. The court discussed four possible responses available to a trial court when a parent was engaged in nonmarital sexual conduct. The court could find ". . . (1) it is conclusively presumed that the person is unfit to have custody or (2) it is rebuttably presumed that the person is unfit to have custody, or (3) it must be shown that such conduct has a direct adverse impact on the child, or (4) it is presumed that such conduct had a direct adverse impact on the child."

The court of appeals in *Whaley* adopted the third response:

"The third standard, that immoral conduct must be shown to have a direct or probable adverse impact on the welfare of the child in order to justify a change of custody, we believe to be the rule in Ohio. We believe it to be the better standard." The court found no evidence to support the trial court's decision to change custody of the girl. *See also Conkel* v. *Conkel*, 509 N.E. d 983 (Ohio App. 1987) (homosexual father could not be denied overnight visitation with his two sons on the basis of his homosexuality without evidence that the boys would be psychologically or physically harmed thereby). *But see, Roberts* v. *Roberts*, 489 N.E.2d 1067 (Ohio App. 1985) (where only evidence before trial court in a visitation modification hearing shows that minor children will be harmed by exposure to father's homosexual life style, the trial court abuses its discretion in failing to impose conditions to safeguard children's welfare and best interest).

While we readily concede that these cases can be easily distinguished from the case at bar, we have, nevertheless, considered their principles along with a number of other factors in reaching our conclusion. We do, therefore, think it proper to set forth these decisions in our opinion because they at least illustrate our point that the test to be used in *any* adoption is the "best interest of the child" standard. If there is information available that shows or indicates that adoption of a particular child would not be in the child's best interest, then that evidence should be presented at the adoption hearing.

What evidence was presented at the hearing? Appellee offered one witness. The witness, who is the Administrator of Social Services for appellee, testified that, except for a few classes in those areas, she had no formal education in either social work or psychology. She had met with Charles individually on only one occasion and for one hour. She had not observed Charles with Mr. B. The substance of her testimony concerned the fact that Mr. B did not meet appellee's "characteristic profile of preferred adoptive placement." Other than the information contained in the report on proposed adoption, appellee did not produce or introduce any other evidence. This was the entire case submitted on behalf of appellee's objection to the adoption. From appellee's standpoint, this is the record now before us.

In contrast, Mr. B himself testified and presented six other witnesses. These other witnesses were: (1) Dr. Joseph Shannon, who holds a Ph.D in psychology, (2) Dr. Victoria Blubaugh, who also holds a doctorate in psychology, (3) Mr. B's mother, (4) Mr. B's sister, (5) Carol Menge, vice president of Lutheran Social Services and herself an adoptive parent, and (6) Mr. K. Finally, the guardian ad litem gave an oral report recommending that the adoption be approved.

■ ■ ■

Given the state of the record before us, and accepting the proposition that in adoption proceedings the child's best interest is paramount, we now briefly review the law.

■ ■ ■

Thus, a trial court, when deciding whether to grant or deny a petition for adoption, must consider *all* relevant factors before determining what is in the child's best interest. Since the facts in each case will vary, and the advisability of permitting an adoption must be made on a case-by-case basis, the trial court must be allowed broad discretion in making the determination.

Upon review of the record now before us, we determine that the trial court did not abuse its discretion in granting the petition for adoption. . . . There is no evidence in this record that the trial court's attitude was unreasonable, arbitrary or unconscionable. Accordingly, we find that the trial court did not abuse its discretion when it placed Charles with Mr. B for adoption.

■ ■ ■

RESNICK, J., dissenting.

I respectfully dissent from the majority decision. However, I do not agree with the court of appeals wherein it found as a matter of law a homosexual is ineligible to adopt a minor. Existing Ohio law is very clear that a homosexual is not as a matter of law barred from adopting a child under R.C. 3107.03(B). When deciding whether to grant or deny a petition for adoption, a court must consider all relevant factors before determining what is in the child's best interest. The fact that the party seeking to become an adoptive parent is a homosexual should not, in and of itself, be determinative. However, neither can it be ignored. When a homosexual seeks to adopt a minor, a trial court must have before it sufficient evidence to show that the prospective parent's homosexuality will not have an adverse effect on the minor. The prospective parent must present evidence demonstrating that his or her homosexuality will not harm the child. Likewise, the party opposing the adoption by the homosexual must also submit evidence establishing not only that the homosexuality of the adopting parent had or will have an effect on the child, but also that the effect is or will be harmful.

The facts of each case must be considered, allowing the trial court broad discretion in determining whether there exists a nexus between the homosexuality of the prospective adoptive parent and the adoption which could have an adverse effect on the child. Other jurisdictions, when confronted with a parent's homosexuality in a child custody or visitation context, which is a similar situation to the one before us, have used a "nexus test" or an affirmative showing of harm to the child caused by the parent's sexual orientation. Based on the facts of this case there does exist a nexus between the homosexuality of Mr. B and the adoption of Charles B which could adversely affect the child and thus would not be in the best interest of the child.

Charlie is presently eight years of age. Due to his many problems he may not be as mature as an average eight year old. Charlie's natural mother and alleged father both signed voluntary permanent surrender papers. His family history evinces neglect and abuse. Charlie was tested by the Licking County Department of Human Services and the results indicate that he has a low functioning range I.Q., possible brain damage, and deficits in fine and gross motor skills. But, most importantly, Charlie has leukemia which presently is in remission. The treatment which Charlie received for leukemia has altered his immune system. To place Charlie in an environment with a homosexual who is engaged in a homosexual relationship is not in the best interest of the child.

While I agree that homosexuality is just one factor to be considered by the court in adoption proceedings, it should be weighed along with all other factors and the ultimate decision must be based upon the best interest of the child. I also agree that a nexus must be found to exist between the sexual preference of the father and the adoption which could have an adverse effect on the child. In this case that nexus was well established by Dr. Frederick B. Ruymann, M.D., Director, Hematology Division; Professor, Department of Pediatrics, Children's Hospital, the Ohio State University, wherein he stated in a letter to the court dated April 13, 1988 that adoption of Charlie by a homosexual ". . . would, with our present knowledge

place Charles at increased risk for exposure to HIV infection, i.e. infection with the AIDS virus. . . . Charles has an altered immune system. The AIDS virus attacks the immune system further destroying it."

Mr. B was aware of this problem and was tested, proving to be HIV negative. However, we must remember that adoption is not just for today but forever. Mr. B falls within a high-risk population for AIDS. Why place a child whose immune system has already been altered in such an environment? It was best stated by Kathleen Handley, Administrator of Social Services for the Licking County Department of Human Services, at the hearing that "[o]ur feeling is that professionally it would be an adoption risk . . . to place a child in a setting where there is no practiced precedent to give us support. We do not view this as a child that needs experimentation. He has too many other issues that he has to conquer in his life."

This case is distinguishable from . . . cases which hold that the lesbian or homosexual relationship standing alone is insufficient to adversely affect the welfare of the child. I am aware of research on this issue which shows that homosexuals can be effective parents. However, in this case not only do we have a homosexual relationship, but we also have a child who possesses mental and physical problems that could be exacerbated by this type of a life style.

In conclusion, Charlie thus far in his life has had many problems and there is nothing more that anyone would want for him than to be placed in a loving permanent home. But due to Charlie's many medical problems, a homosexual environment is not in his long-term best interest. I sincerely regret that the record in this case was not better developed by the appellee during trial. This was a difficult decision for the trial court to make and the manner in which it was tried on the part of the appellee made it even more difficult for the court. However, we are dealing with the life of an eight-year-old boy; therefore, the paramount concern is the well-being of this child. Because Charlie's immune system has been dramatically altered due to treatment for leukemia, in the long term, this adoption simply is not in his best interest. Therefore, I find that the trial court abused its discretion in granting the petition for adoption. I would affirm the court of appeals, however, not for reasons stated in its opinion but simply because Charlie is a very special little boy with unique and individual physical and mental problems. Thus, based upon those problems it is not in the best interest of Charlie to be adopted by Mr. B.

Note

1. At least one state has enacted regulations guaranteeing gay and lesbian people the same eligibility to become adoptive parents as heterosexual applicants. *See* 18 N.Y. COMP. CODES R. & REGS. tit. 18, § 421.16(h)(2)(1992)(stating that applicants for adoption shall not be rejected solely on the basis of homosexuality).

3. SECOND PARENT ADOPTIONS

Distinct from the traditional form of adoption, which extinguishes the parental rights and obligations of the biological or current legal parents, second parent adoption leaves the parental rights of one legally recognized parent intact and creates a second legally recognized parent for the child. Second parent adoptions have become fairly routine among children of heterosexual step-parents.

IN RE THE ADOPTION OF EVAN

583 N.Y.S.2d 997 (N.Y. Sur. 1992)

PREMINGER, Surrogate.

The petitioners in this adoption proceeding are two women: Valerie C., the biological mother of a six year old boy and her life partner, Diane F. They have raised the boy together since his birth and now seek legal recognition of their mutual status as parents. This appears to be the first such application in New York.

Because of the significant issues of first impression and the importance to the infant, the court appointed Professor Sylvia Law, distinguished professor of Family Law and Social Policy at New York University Law School, as guardian *ad litem* for the child. Professor Law was asked to investigate whether the proposed adoption is in the child's best interest. Her thoughtful and thorough report found that it was and recommends that the court grant the petition.

A home study by a licensed social worker retained by the Petitioners also found the adoption to be in the best interest of the child. The Court appointed a second licensed social worker to conduct an independent investigation. She agreed that the proposed adoption was in the boy's best interest.

The reports of Professor Law and the two socialworkers reveal the following facts:

The petitioners, Diane F. and Valerie C. have lived together in a committed, long term relationship, which they perceive as permanent, for the past fourteen years. Diane, age 39, is an Assistant Professor of Pediatrics and an attending physician at a respected teaching hospital. Valerie, age 40, holds a Ph. D. in developmental psychology and teaches at a highly regarded private school.

In 1985 Diane and Valerie decided to have a child together. Pursuant to their joint plan, Valerie was artificially inseminated with sperm obtained from a friend who formally relinquished any claim he might otherwise have had in relation to the child.

Evan was born in November of 1985 and has lived with the parties since his birth. Both home studies describe Diane as a warm, loving and nurturing woman who is committed to Evan and is an effective parent to him. Evan himself is evaluated as a bright, confident, and independent young boy with a strong parental bond with both women. He "seems to accept the fact that he has two mothers and seems to have an equal bond with both" and is a "charming, well-nourished, and articulate child who relates well to peers and adults." He has a strong parental relationship with Diane, whom he calls Mama D. and an equal relationship with his biological mother, Valerie, whom he refers to as Mama V."

It seems clear that the proposed adoption is in Evan's best interest. He is part of a family unit that has been functioning successfully for the past six years. The adoption would bring no change or trauma to his daily life; it would serve only to provide him with important legal rights which he does not presently possess. It would afford him additional economic security because Diane would become legally obligated to support

him. He would also be entitled to inherit from Diane and her family under the law of intestate succession and be eligible for social security benefits in the event of her disability or death. Of immediate practical import, he would be able to participate in the medical and educational benefits provided by her employment, which are more generous than those possessed by Valerie.

There is another potential benefit to Evan if he is adopted by Diane. Although today Evan enjoys the devotion and support of two parents who love him and each other, in the event of their separation, it would be beneficial for Evan to retain his filial ties to Diane. In such event, it is known to be better for a child to continue its relationship with both parents, and the law recognizes this by "presum[ing] that parental visitation is in the best interests of the child, absent proof that such visitation would be harmful." Yet if petitioners were to separate in the absence of adoption, under the law of New York (*Matter of Alison D. v. Virginia M.*, 572 N.E.2d 27 (N.Y. 1991) and some other jurisdictions (*Sporleders v. Hermes*, 471 N.W.2d 202 (Wis. 1991); *Nancy S. v. Michele G.*, 279 Cal. Rptr. 212 (Cal. App. 1991)) Diane would have no right to visitation even if it were demonstrated that denying visitation would be harmful to Evan. In *Alison D.* the Court of Appeals recognized that adoption would avoid this unfortunate result. The California court in *Nancy S.* recommended adoption as a solution, noting that "we see nothing in [our] statutory provisions [similar to those in New York] that would preclude a child from being jointly adopted by someone of the same sex as the natural parent."

Even if, as anticipated, the petitioners remain together, there is a significant emotional benefit to Evan from adoption which is perhaps even more crucial than the financial. Separate or together, the adoption brings Evan the additional security conferred by formal recognition in an organized society. As he matures, his connection with two involved, loving parents will not be a relationship seen as outside the law, but one sustained by the ongoing, legal recognition of an approved, court ordered adoption.

Having determined that adoption would, for all the above reasons, be in Evan's best interests, the issue remains whether there is anything in the law of this state which would prohibit it. The Court has scrutinized the relevant statutes and finds no obstacle.

Under New York law, "[a]n adult unmarried person or an adult husband and his adult wife together may adopt another person." As an unmarried adult, Diane is thus qualified to adopt. While the second phrase — requiring that husband and wife jointly agree to adopt a child — is not literally applicable here, the underlying policy also supports adoption in this case. The petitioners are a committed, time-tested life partnership. For Evan, they *are* a marital relationship at its nurturing supportive best and they seek second-parent adoption for the same reasons of stability and recognition as any couple might.

No provision of New York law requires that the adoptive parent be of any particular gender. Indeed, New York specifically prohibits discrimination against homosexuality in granting adoption. (18 NYCRR § 421.16 [h][2]).

New York law does require the consent of certain parties to an adoption. All of the consent requirements have been met in the instant case. Ordinarily a child over the age of 14 must consent to be adopted, but Evan is only six. The biological mother must consent and is one of the petitioners in this case. The biological father must consent if he has maintained "substantial and continuous or repeated contact with the child." Here the biological father has not met the standards that entitle him to object to adoption, and, in any event, he has explicitly waived any right to do so.

The only statutory provision which could be construed as impeding the instant adoption is DRL § 117(1), which provides that "the natural parents of the adoptive child shall be relieved of all parental duties toward and of all responsibilities for and shall have no rights over such adoptive child." If this provision were strictly enforced it would require termination of the parental rights of Valerie upon granting the adoption to Diane. This would be an absurd outcome which would nullify the advantage sought by the proposed adoption: the creation of a legal family unit identical to the actual family setup. The Court of Appeals has recognized, in another context, that

> "§ 117 itself does not pretend to discourage all contacts between an adoptive child and its natural relatives. Rather, the law contemplates that such contacts may exist and that the natural relatives may desire to perpetuate the sense of family. An adopted child may not . . . be isolated from his or her natural family."

Thus, particularly in situations in which the adoptive and biological relatives are known to one another and where the child has significant contacts with them, New York recognizes the value of continued relationship.

■ ■ ■

This Court has heretofore declined to apply the cut-off provisions of DRL § 117 when special circumstances exist. . . .

Thus where the adoptive and biological parents are in fact co-parents such as the instant case, New York law does not require a destructive choice between the two parents. Allowing continuation of the rights of both the natural and adoptive parent where compelled by the best interests of the child, is the only rational result and well within the equitable power of this court.

Other jurisdictions have taken a similar approach to cut-off provisions. *In Matter of the Petition of L.S. and V.L. for the Adoption of Minors (T) and (M)* (D.C. Super. Ct Fam Div. Nos. A269-90 and A270-90, Aug. 30,

1991, 17 FLR 1523 [Sept. 17, 1991]) the District of Columbia granted adoptions to two lesbian parents in a long-term committed relationship, who sought to adopt each other's biological child. After finding that adoptions would serve the children's best interests, the court considered the effect of a statute providing that upon adoption, "All rights and duties including those of inheritance and succession between the adoptee, his natural parents, their issue, collateral relatives, and so forth, are cut off, . . ." The court concluded that this should be read as directory rather than mandatory, citing the principle of statutory construction that

> "where no apparent actual or potential injury results to anyone from a failure to adhere to the provisions of a statute, a directory construction usually prevails in the absence of facts indicating that a mandatory construction was intended. . ."

The court observed that there, as here, to require a choice between the biological and adoptive parent

> "would be a particularly counterproductive and even ludicrous result, given the purpose underlying the filing of the petition and the court's finding that the petitioned adoptions would be in the best interests of each child." . . . [The provision] "is obviously not intended to apply to the situation presented by these cases. . .At bottom adoption cases are decided by application of the best interests of the child standard, and whenever possible other considerations give way to that standard if there is a conflict."

In another similar case, *In re Adoption of R.C.* (Vt. P. Ct, Addison Co. No. 9088, Dec. 9, 1991) a Vermont court also rejected a literal application of its cut-off provision, approving the statement that "it would be unfortunate if the court were compelled to conclude that adoptions so clearly in the best interests of the [child] could not be granted because of a literal reading of a statutory provision obviously not intended to apply to the situation presented. . . . This is particularly so where no party to these proceedings objects to the adoptions. . . ."

The fact that the petitioners here maintain an open lesbian relationship is not a reason to deny adoption.[1] New York law recognizes that a child's best interest is not predicated or controlled by parental sexual orientation. The law explicitly provides that agencies evaluating people who seek to adopt shall not reject applicants "solely on the basis of homosexuality." Rather decisions shall be made in relation to the best interests of adoptive children. 18 NYCRR § 421.16 [h] [2]. This is consistent with the more general principle that a parent's sexual orientation or sexual practices are presumptively irrelevant in resolving custody disputes and may be considered "only if they are shown to adversely affect the child's welfare." Consideration of sexual orientation or life style of a parent "must be limited to its present or reasonably predictable effect upon the children's welfare."

It is thus apparent that nothing in New York law prevents the granting of this adoption. Other jurisdictions have reached similar results. While there have been no appellate decisions, several trial courts have approved adoptions recognizing both partners in a lesbian couple as the legal parents of the children they are jointly raising. In some cases the non-biological mother has been permitted to adopt the child born to her lesbian partner, without terminating the par-

---

1. Concern that a child would be disadvantaged by growing up in a single-sex household is not borne out by the professional literature examined by this court. While the actual number of children being raised in households with a homosexual parent is unknown, estimates range from six million to eight to ten million. . . Research that has been done in recent years on the possible differences between children of gay and lesbian parents and children of heterosexual parents in otherwise comparable circumstances, reveals no disadvantages among the former in any significant respect.

ental rights of the biological mother.‡ Adoptions have been granted with the approval of the state agency or the guardian ad litem and over their objection. Lesbian couples have also been permitted to jointly adopt the children they are raising in cases where neither is the biological mother.

Finally, this is not a matter which arises in a vacuum. Social fragmentation and the myriad configurations of modern families have presented us with new problems and complexities that can not be solved by idealizing the past. Today a child who receives proper nutrition, adequate schooling and supportive sustaining shelter is among the fortunate, whatever the source. A child who also receives the love and nurture of even a single parent can be counted among the blessed. Here this Court finds a child who has all of the above benefits and two adults dedicated to his welfare, secure in their loving partnership, and determined to raise him to the very best of their considerable abilities. There is no reason in law, logic or social philosophy to obstruct such a favorable situation.

Petition granted.

Notes

1. In addition to *Adoption of Evan*, the first known second parent adoption to be granted to a same-sex couple in New York, second parent adoptions have been granted to same-sex couples in the states of Alaska, California, Minnesota, Oregon, Vermont, Washington, and in the District of Columbia.
2. Short of second parent adoption, which grants the co-parent full parental rights and responsibilities, lesbians and gay men have attempted to share parental rights and responsibilities with co-parents by using consent forms or the nomination of a guardian or conservator. Should assignments made through such documents be contested, however, it is never certain whether courts will respect them. *See In Re Estate of Susan Hamilton*, No. 24950, slip op. (Vt. P. Ct. 1989) (upholding the designation of a biological mother's lover as guardian in the face of a challenge brought by the child's grandparents).

B. Foster Care

The state has the obligation to protect the health and welfare of children. When a state becomes aware that parents have neglected, abused or abandoned their child, the state may remove the child from the harmful home environment. The child who is removed from his home is often placed in foster care while the state decides whether it is in the best interests of the child to be returned to his or her home. The foster care placement may be quite short

---

‡   At this point, the court cites the following cases: *In the Matter of the Petition of L.S. and V.L.*, *supra*; *In the Matter of the Adoption Petition of Nancy M.* [Cal. Super. Ct, San Francisco Co. No. 18744 (1990)]; *In re Child #1 and Child #2* [Wash. Super. Ct, Thurston Co. No. 89-5-0067-7, Nov. 16, 1989]; *In re E.B.G.* [Wash. Super. Ct, Thurston Co. No. 87-5-00137-5, March 29, 1989]; *In the Matter of the Adoption Petition of Carol* [Cal. Super. Ct, San Francisco Co. No. 18573 (1989)]; *In the Matter of Adoption Petition of Roberta Achtenberg* [Cal. Super. Ct, San Francisco Co No. AD 18490 (1989)]; *In re Adoption of a Minor Child* [Ala. Super Ct, Juneau No. 1Ju-86-73 P/A, Feb. 6, 1987]; *In re Adoption of A.O.L.* [Ala. Super. Ct, Juneau No. 154-85-25 P/A (1985).

if the child is able to return home within a few days, or it may last for several years if the state attempts to terminate the parental rights of the biological parent.

Foster care does not establish a legally recognized parent-child relationship regardless of the length of the placement. The foster parent is only a temporary guardian of the child and does not have the full rights and responsibilities of a true parent. The foster child may be removed from the foster home and returned to the biological parents or transferred to a different foster home at the discretion of the state. The foster child is a ward of the state and accordingly it is the state's obligation and right to determine her best interests.

◆

A TIME OF CHANGE
Neil Miller

BOSTON

I had first come upon the issue of gay and lesbian parenting in the spring of 1985 when "the foster-care case" emerged as front-page news in Boston. The Massachusetts Department of Social Services (DSS) had placed two brothers — aged twenty-two months and three and a half years — in the foster care of a gay male couple. When the *Boston Globe* published an article about the placement ("Some Oppose Foster Placement with Gay Couple"), the agency panicked. Within twenty-four hours, it ordered the two boys removed from the household.

Governor Michael Dukakis, until then viewed at least as a lukewarm supporter of gay rights and the gay community, strongly defended the removal of the boys. Indeed, many believed that the governor had ordered the removal himself, although his office denied this. Two weeks later, the state's Human Services secretary issued a new directive on foster-care placement. Previously, placements had been decided by social-workers on a case-by-case basis. Now, a hierarchy of desirable foster homes was es-

tablished. Under the new guidelines, only in "exceptional circumstances" would children be placed in nontraditional settings — that is, with single parents or unmarried couples. The latter placements could be made only with permission of the DSS commissioner. Although the new policy did not explicitly bar gays and lesbians from becoming foster parents, the Human Services secretary indicated that such a placement would be highly unlikely.

The result was a major controversy that galvanized Boston's gay community like no other event of the eighties except the AIDS epidemic. Gay and lesbian activists dogged the governor, picketing his appearances all over the state. The national gay press reported the story, tarnishing Dukakis's reputation as he tried to garner the support of gay and lesbian voters in the 1988 presidential primaries. Although the governor attempted to mollify the gay community by pushing hard for legislative approval of a gay-rights bill and by vetoing legislation that would have absolutely barred gays from becoming foster parents, the rift was deep.

NEIL MILLER, *A Time of Change, in* IN SEARCH OF GAY AMERICA: WOMEN AND MEN IN A TIME OF CHANGE 121-31 (1989).

The Dukakis foster-care policy was couched in relatively enlightened language about role models and the desirability of having two parents of the opposite sexes. Nonetheless, it seemed to inscribe as state policy the old canard that loving someone of your own sex meant you were somehow unfit to raise children, that you would molest them, "convert" them (to homosexuality), or at the very best provide a bad example. To many, it smacked of Anita Bryant's "Save Our Children" campaign of the seventies. And by telling gays they weren't fit to be parents (or at least not *as* fit as heterosexuals), the liberal governor found himself in collision with the evolution of gay self-acceptance and community, with the march of homosexual history.

At the time the foster-care case broke, I was a staff writer at the *Boston Phoenix*. Along with Scot Lehigh, the paper's state house reporter, I was assigned to cover the story. My task was to find out if the *Boston Globe* article about the neighborhood "controversy" that had triggered the removal of the two children was accurate; I was also supposed to gauge the reaction of the gay community. Scot's job was to see how high up in the Dukakis administration the order to remove the two boys had originated.

In my research, I found that two of the three individuals in the neighborhood whom the *Globe* had quoted as opposing the placement had clearly never even known about it until they were asked their opinion by the reporter writing the story. One even apologized to the foster parents after the article came out. The third person quoted was local activist who, according to our sources, had been attempting to stir up the neighbors on the issue for several days with little response. He and the *Globe* reporter had apparently created a dubious story of a neighborhood up in arms, and the Dukakis administration had fallen for it without bothering to do its own investigation.

As much as Scot tried, he could never quite prove that the decision to remove the children was made by Michael Dukakis himself. There were rumors of a lesbian "Deep Throat" who had overheard a telephone call to that effect, between the governor and Philip Johnston, the cabinet-level state Human Services secretary. But if this "Deep Throat" was a real person, we never found her. Scot did get Johnston to admit that the lower-ranking commissioner of the Department of Social Services had consulted with him throughout the decision-making process; he also gained an admission from someone close to the governor that Dukakis's office had been conferring with a Johnston aide, at least about media coverage of the issue.

In the end, it didn't much matter whether the *Globe* story had been concocted or whether it was Michael Dukakis himself or one of his subordinates who had broken up the foster family. The damage had been done. And it was not just gays and lesbians who were outraged. Scot, who is heterosexual, wrote in our article, "Through the incompetence and cowardice of the administration, the controversy exploded into a national news story in which the administrations's capitulation to homophobia ended up aiding and abetting the gay-baiting of Jerry Falwells and Jesse Helmses of the world."

The new state foster-care guidelines were in place, which required that applicants for a foster-parent license be asked about their sexual preference for the first time in the history of Massachusetts. Gay men, in particular, found their options for parenting restricted by the new state policy. They couldn't have children through artificial insemination, of course. Beyond co-parenting arrangements with lesbian friends, foster care and adoption had been the only ways gay men could become parents. Now, in view of the new state policy, adoption agencies were more reluctant than ever to approve gays as adoptive parents.

A couple of years after these events, I went to see Don Babets and David Jean, the two men who were at the center of the case. The couple lived in a modest home in the Fort Hill section of Boston, overlooking the Metropolitan Bay

Transit Authority yards where buses and trolleys were stored. It was a neighborhood of run-down, turn-of-the-century dwellings, of craters covered with vegetation where other houses had been burned down (Fort Hill had been the site of widespread arson). The area was predominantly black, but there were a number of white gay residents; in the seventies, a gay commune called the Fort Hill Faggots for Freedom had been established there. Although the commune had long since disbanded, some of former communards remained. Other white gays, like Don and David, gravitated to the decaying inner-city neighborhood where houses were still relatively affordable and some sense of community existed.

Don and David had been in the neighborhood for four years and together for eight when they applied to be foster parents. They hoped to establish a track record as parents and then apply to adopt a child. It was a try-out, designed to give them a "taste of parenting," as David put it, to see if they wanted to make a long-term commitment.

Don in particular had strong reasons for wishing to be a foster parent. His mother and father had both been adopted, and he had been legally adopted by his stepfather. A major influence in his life had been a Lutheran minister, who had seven adopted children of a variety of racial and national backgrounds. Don remembered going to the minister's house as a young man and being "really impressed." There were all the kids — black and brown and Asian — and pictures of Martin Luther King, Jr., and Malcolm X on the wall. "I thought, this is how it is supposed to be," said Don. And Don noted that "the other side of being adopted" was being abandoned. "When you have had that abandonment more or less healed through adoption," he said, "you have an obligation to pass that on."

At thirty-six, Don Babets was a tall, balding man who worked as an investigator for the Boston Fair Housing Agency. A sense of outrage smoldered just beneath his relaxed and friendly demeanor; he was someone, after all, who placed his trust in the promises and goodwill of the system and now felt betrayed. Don, who grew up in Cleveland, spent several years in the military in the seventies, during which time he was an active alcoholic. Eventually he got sober, left the military, and went to college. He worked as an alcoholism counsellor and later as a legislative aide to a Massachusetts state senator. While he was stationed at Fort Devens, just west of Boston, he met David Jean. David, thirty-two, was shy and unassuming. Unlike Don, who was a self-described "political type," David was an unlikely person to be at the center of a public flap and has never seemed comfortable in the role. Trained as a nutritionist, he had worked as a cook and dietitian; he was currently an administrator at a women's health center. The evening I visited, he made a shepherd's pie for dinner, using a recipe out of George Bernard Shaw's vegetarian cookbook.

David admitted that he never had a "burning desire" to have or adopt children. He had assumed that the possibility of becoming a parent was something he would forgo when he first accepted his gay identity. But, as time passed, he began to question why he couldn't be as capable a parent as any of his heterosexual counterparts. He, too, could provide "a stable home, a loving home. I did some thinking about what was important to a child," he said. "And I came to believe that what was important wasn't necessarily two parents of different sexes. What a child needs is love, understanding, acceptance. I can make brownies, too."

Don and David became the first openly gay couple to go through the Massachusetts Department of Social Services screening process to be licensed as foster parents. They attended the required six-week training program. They filled out an extensive forty-page questionnaire. A socialworker spent three half-days with them doing a "home study." "We were treated just as a straight couple would have been," said David. Finally, it was the associate DSS commissioner himself who approved their application.

They let friends, co-workers, and neighbors know what they were doing. Don, who is Catholic and was teaching Sunday school at his church, told the parents of his students. David informed the pastor at the neighborhood Unitarian-Universalist church that he attended regularly. They let their families know, too. Only Don's stepfather was critical. "You are just taking in someone else's trouble," he warned.

The couple were licensed as foster parents and prepared a child's bedroom for when the Department of Social Services called. But the DSS was hesitating. When the agency finally did contact them a full year later, Don and David were asked if they could take not one child but two. They agreed.

On the day they arrived, the two little boys, Michael and Paul, were hysterical, Don and David remembered. They were also bruised and battered. Michael, three and a half, had "a little imprint, a black-and-blue mark right in the middle of his backbone," said Don. "It was clear that he had been kicked. You could see the impression of the place between the sole and the upper shoe." Don and David had a rabbit that distracted the kids.

David did not exactly recall that first week with nostalgia. "I wasn't ready for it, I'll tell you," he said. "The kids would wake up every couple of hours. They kept throwing up in the night. And we were always washing clothes. The washer and dryer were going every night."

Don said that the first night the boys arrived, Michael threw a potato peeler at him. Don yelled at him. Then the boy threw a glass of water. Don took a step in his direction, and Michael immediately ducked. Don said it took a week to break him of that response. "I promised I would never hit him, and he pushed me a couple times to see if it was true," said Don. "I didn't hit him and trust started to be built."

After the first week, things began to calm down. The men took Michael and Paul for a haircut and then to a lumber yard to buy material to build a rabbit hutch. The following day, they took the kids to Mass and to the aquarium. The boys called them "Daddy Don" and "Daddy Dave." Meanwhile, David was learning new culinary approaches. "I always swore when I had my own kitchen I would never allow instant mashed potatoes," he said. "That was the first vow to go."

While Don and David were absorbed in washing clothes and building rabbit hutches, a neighbor named Ben Haith was making trouble. Haith was a black community activist who had been instrumental in organizing the neighborhood against arson. He had forged close links with the gay community, winning the endorsement of the Boston Lesbian and Gay Political Alliance in his unsuccessful race for a city council seat a couple of years before. Haith and Don Babets were also friends. Don had helped Haith gain the gay political group's support. According to Don, Haith had had dinner at his and David's home; Don had baby sat for Haith's kids.

It was unclear why Ben Haith was determined to make such a fuss over the new arrivals at the household down the street. Some people in the neighborhood suggested he felt his stature in the community was waning; he needed a cause to recapture his preeminent position. Others thought he was planning another city-council bid and was trying to use the issue to gain support among conservative black voters. When I interviewed him for the *Phoenix*, Haith seemed most upset that DSS officials had not consulted him first about the placement. He assailed the "dumping" of two children in the community as an extension of the abuse the neighborhood had taken on a host of other issues. "They expect us to go along with anything, and that angers the hell out of me," he said. "They are not looking at us as people but as some kind of guinea pigs."

Ironically, David first found out something was amiss after a conversation with Haith's wife, to whom he gave a ride home a couple of weeks after the kids arrived. As they drove, he related how the presence of two young children had completely altered their lives. "That's great," David recalled her saying. "But you have to be careful. There are some people who don't approve of this."

A few days later, the *Boston Globe* ran its story. That morning, Don received a call from the Department of Social Services. Agency officials told him that the boys' mother would have to sign a statement that she was aware that Don and David were gay and that she didn't object. Don met with her. "We took the boys to Mass for the first time in months on Sunday," he told her. She signed. But by then, Don said, the order to remove the kids had already been issued. The only reason that the DSS made the mother sign that document, Don said bitterly, was to protect the agency from a lawsuit.

And so late on a May afternoon, the socialworkers and the television cameras arrived on Don and David's front steps. David had already packed the kids' bags. Little Michael was asking, "Is Mommy all better now?" a reference to the mother's drinking problem. Don told him, "Mommy is still sick. But they are taking you to another place where there will be other boys and girls to play with." Don and David loaded the kids into the car. Paul, the youngest, screamed, "Where are we going?" and that was the last Don and David ever saw of them. The children had been in their household for just seventeen days.

For Don and David, the period after the boys' departure was difficult. They had to confront their own feelings about the loss of the kids — and their own guilt about what happened. For Don, the outspoken one who tended to see things in political terms, talking to the media provided an outlet; so did railing against the governor whom he increasingly saw as the villain of the piece; so did a suit to overturn the state's policy, which was filed by the Civil Liberties Union of Massachusetts and the Gay and Lesbian Advocates and Defenders (GLAD), the New England public-interest law firm. David, on the other hand, kept most of it inside. "I remember initially feeling like I had done something wrong by attempting to become a foster parent in the first place," he said. "It took a lot of working on myself to see that was ridiculous. But they were the first kids that we had. It was their first foster home and I wanted it to be good."

There were other problems to cope with. Rocks and bottles were thrown at their house. Teenagers drove by yelling epithets. Don and David appeared on national TV news a week before Don was to attend a family wedding in Cleveland. As a result, he felt compelled to call his aunts and uncles, all of whom would be at the ceremony, and tell them he was gay. Don and David's relationship went through some rough periods, as well. "It was a combination of trying to deal with our families, the media, the court case, mourning the losses, dealing with the guy down the street [Ben Haith]," said Don. "It was like taking a pair of glasses and suddenly seeing people in a new light."

■ ■ ■

Notes

1.   Don Babets and David Jean filed a lawsuit against the Department of Social Services alleging that the new regulations unlawfully discriminated against gay men and lesbians. *Babets v. Commonwealth*, Civil Action No. 81083 (Mass. Super Ct. filed Jan. 30, 1986). The lawsuit was settled in April 1990 when the Department of Social Services (D.S.S.) agreed to adopt regulations that would not bar the placement of children in the homes of gay and lesbian foster parents. The agreement provided that the new policy,

makes parenting experience the key factor. Individual socialworkers will still weigh all relevant factors, including marital status, race, sex, religion, sexual orientation, economic status, education, geographic location, and ethnic background, etc. However, a socialworker will not be able to place a child with a person or couple without parenting experience, unless it has been reviewed at a higher level.

Massachusetts Office of Human Services, *Agreement Reached in Foster Care Placement Lawsuit*, HUM. SERVICES NEWS (April 4, 1990) (accompanied by Proposed Department Regulation).

The proposed regulations provided that the D.S.S. shall consider, consistent with the best interest of the child, the following placement resources:

    a. placement in the child's own home;

    b. placement in family foster care with relative, with consideration given to extended family members and persons chosen by the parent(s) for substitute care;

    c. placement in family foster care with a married couple with parenting experience and with time available for parenting or with a person with parenting experience and with time available for parenting;

    d. placement in family foster care with a married couple without parenting experience and with time available for parenting or a person without parenting experience and with time available for parenting;

    e. placement in community residential care.

2. In 1989, the Massachusetts legislature became the second state in the nation to pass a statute prohibiting discrimination on the basis of sexual orientation in employment, housing, credit and public accommodations. 1989 Mass. Acts 516. The law, however, has no effect on discriminatory foster placements. In order to secure passage of the bill, supporters accepted an amendment that stated that nothing in the law should be construed to authorize or require the placement of children in the foster care of people whose sexual orientation may be injurious to the child. *See* Peter Cicchino, Bruce Deming & Katherine Nicholson, *Sex, Lies and Civil Rights: A Critical History of the Massachusetts Gay Civil Rights Bill*, 26 HARV. C.R.-C.L. L. REV. 549, 611 (1991).

3. In light of the potential difficulties faced by both parent and child when an openly gay or lesbian teenager is placed in the foster care of heterosexual foster parents, some state agencies actively recruit gay and lesbian foster parents for gay and lesbian teenagers. New York City, San Francisco, and Trenton, N.J., attempt to place gay teenagers with gay foster parents. HAYDEN CURRY & DENIS CLIFFORD, A LEGAL GUIDE FOR LESBIAN AND GAY COUPLES 7:25–28 (6th ed. 1991).

C. Reproductive Technology

1. ALTERNATIVE INSEMINATION

Alternative insemination, which requires virtually no medical expertise, can be performed at home without any involvement by state officials or medical professionals. To perform alternative insemination, a donor's sperm is collected and then injected with an instrument, such as a syringe or turkey baster, into a woman's uterus during her period of ovulation. Because of its simplicity, lesbians have increasingly used alternative insemination as a way of becoming mothers. As the following materials makes clear, however, alternative insemination is not without risk. The legal rights and obligations of the sperm donor, the birth mother, and the co-parent are difficult to define in advance of litigation.

◆

LESBIANS CHOOSING MOTHERHOOD: LEGAL IMPLICATIONS OF DONOR INSEMINATION AND CO-PARENTING

I. INTRODUCTION

Over the past decade, the lesbian community has experienced a baby boom. More and more lesbians are choosing to bring children into their lives, creating a diversity of alternative families. Because our lesbian-centered families are non-traditional, it remains unclear how the courts will interpret the laws that affect them. Because the courts are a part of — and reflect — our homophobic, racist, and sexist society, the potential for judicial hostility is always present.

II. ARTIFICIAL INSEMINATION BY DONOR

Though artificial insemination by donor has recently become popular among lesbians as the preferred method of conception, it is not a new procedure. A few doctors were already experimenting with donor insemination as long ago as the eighteenth century. By the turn of this century, this practice had become known as "ethereal conceptions." While all aspects of the early experiments in donor insemination were under the control of the doctors performing them, lesbians choosing donor insemination today are making their own decisions about selecting sperm donors and insemination methods, and are drafting parenting agreements that reflect their own needs and life situations.

There is no such thing as a "typical" lesbian family. A lesbian family might consist of a single lesbian raising her children on her own or with the help of an extended family she has developed in her community; two women in a monogamous relationship and their children; a lesbian mother and the donor sharing the joys and responsibilities of parenthood; or a group of life-long friends and their children who have chosen to live together as family. The possibilities are endless because each lesbian family is as unique as the individual lesbians who create it.

Throughout the 1970s and early 1980s, lesbians who became pregnant through donor insemination most often used an unknown donor who subsequently had no role in the child's life. This choice was one of the few means lesbians had to protect the integrity of their families and prevent interference from donors and the courts. In recent years, however, the choices lesbians are making about donor participation have begun to

NATIONAL CENTER FOR LESBIAN RIGHTS, LESBIANS CHOOSING MOTHERHOOD: LEGAL IMPLICATIONS OF DONOR INSEMINATION AND CO-PARENTING 1–7 (1991).

change. More lesbian mothers are now seeking some form of donor participation in their families. Donor participation can range from full parental rights and responsibilities to very limited visitation rights, or may merely reflect an understanding that the donor's identity will eventually be revealed to the child. While there are many valid reasons why some mothers may want some degree of donor participation in raising a child, this choice may also open them up to unexpected risks. Using an unknown donor is still the safest legal protection available, especially in states where no statutory or case law protections exist.

■ ■ ■

Is The Donor A Father?
A Statutory Analysis

One of the primary legal concerns among lesbians using donor insemination is whether the sperm donor will be recognized as the father of the child. The answers to this and other legal questions for women using donor insemination vary from state to state, depending on state laws and court decisions that determine the rights and responsibilities of the mother, donor, and the child conceived by donor insemination.

As donor insemination has gained in popularity, [33] states have responded by enacting legislation that establishes criteria for determining whether the child of donor insemination has a father and, if so, whether the donor is the father. About a third of these states have adopted language from a 1973 model law known as the Uniform Parentage Act ("U.P.A."), which reads:

(a) If, under the supervision of a licensed physician and with the consent of her husband, a wife is inseminated artificially with semen donated by a man not her husband, the husband is treated in law as if he were the natural father of a child thereby conceived.

The husband's consent must be in writing and signed by him and his wife. The physician shall certify their signatures and the date of the insemination, and file the husband's consent with the [State Department of Health], where it shall be kept confidential and in a sealed file. However, the physician's failure to do so does not affect the father and child relationship. All papers and records pertaining to the record of a court or of a file held by the supervising physician or elsewhere, are subject to inspection only upon an order of the court for good cause.

(b) *The donor of semen to a licensed physician for use in artificial insemination of a married woman other than the donor's wife is treated in law as if he were not the natural father of a child thereby conceived* (emphasis added).

For women who do not want a donor to be legally recognized as the father of a child born through donor insemination, statutes modeled after the U.P.A. provide protection against a paternity suit. But in order to invoke the protections of these laws, strict adherence to the statutory requirements must be maintained. In states where the U.P.A. language has been adopted verbatim, it is likely that only married women are protected, and then only with the consent of their husbands and under the supervision of a licensed physician. The explicit use of the word "married" in the statute seems to deny lesbians coverage under these statutes since lesbian relationships are not recognized as legal marriages in any state. It is possible, however, that a judge could interpret any one of these statutes more broadly to include coverage of unmarried women, including lesbians. Lesbians who live in these states and who do not want the donor to have parental rights should try to comply with all of the other requirements of these statues as a precaution. Since most of these statutes have not yet been tested in the courts, it is very important that you consult with an attorney who can tell you how the statue has been or is likely to be interpreted by judges in your state.

A growing number of states that have adopted the U.P.A. language have dropped the word "married" from their statutes, and they seem to apply to all women. In these states, then, lesbians who wish to establish that a sperm donor is not the legally-recognized father of a child conceived through donor insemination would theoretically not be barred from doing so — provided they complied with the requirements of the statute. Even in these states, however, it is very important to consult with an attorney about court interpretations of the statute in cases involving single women and lesbians. Many judges have strong inclinations to find a father for every child. When there is no husband to assume that role, some judges have been known to place a burden beyond the requirements of the statute on single women to demonstrate that the donor did not intend to be the father of the child (such as a written agreement by the donor to relinquish his parental rights).[7]

Four states [Conn., Idaho, Ohio, and Oregon] have adopted statutes that provide similar protections to those provided under the U.P.A.-based statutes, but are not modeled after the U.P.A.

Each statute contains provisions extinguishing the donor's rights, but each has different language and somewhat different requirements from any other donor insemination statute. While the language in the Idaho and Connecticut statutes appear to only apply to married women, the Ohio and Oregon statutes do not appear to have that restriction. . . .

Some donor insemination statutes only address the issue of whether a child conceived through donor insemination is legitimate. These "legitimacy" statutes are confined to marital situations and most focus only on the child's right to confirm the paternity of the mother's husband when the husband is not the donor. These statutes are of little or no use to a lesbian seeking to establish that a donor is not the father of her child, since they do not address the paternity status of an unrelated donor.

U.P.A. and "legitimacy" statutes that only address married women, and require the consent of the husband, are sometimes used to bar an unmarried woman from access to donor insemination. To our knowledge, the application of these "legitimacy" and U.P.A. statutes in this manner has not yet been challenged, but we believe that a strong argument can be made that denying single women legal access to donor insemination is unconstitutional.

It is also important to note that most donor insemination statutes involve physician performance or supervision of the insemination as a requirement to invoke the protections of the statute. In most cases it is a good idea to comply with this requirement, regardless of whether there is a state statute that provides protections to lesbians. In some states, civil or criminal penalties attach to those who perform donor insemination who are not licensed physicians. But even if there is no fear of civil or criminal prosecution, physician involvement serves to help establish in the eyes of most judges that conception occurred through donor insemination.

As of this writing, North Dakota is the only state to have adopted the 1988 model law known as the Uniform Status of Children of Assisted Conception Act ("U.S.C. A.C.A."). This model law was recently developed to address the rapid advances that are being made in reproductive technology, and is not limited to only donor insemination, but also addresses surrogacy and other modern reproductive methods. Because the

---

7. See *In re R.C.*, 775 P.2d 27 (Colo. 1989); *Jhordan C. v. Mary K.*, 224 Cal. Rptr. 530 (Ct. App. 1986); *see also, McIntyre v. Crouch*, 780 P.2d 239 (Ore.), *cert. denied*, 110 S.Ct. 1924 (1989), where the donor was granted the right to a court hearing in the absence of a written agreement establishing his intent to relinquish his parental rights.

U.S.C.A.C.A. was drafted much more recently than the U.P.A., its application is much more comprehensive in dealing with issues of parentage surrounding donor insemination. Concerning donor status, the language of this model statute reads unambiguously: "A donor is not a parent of a child conceived through assisted conception." Moreover, the published comments of the drafters of this model statute clearly state the intent to sever the donor's parental rights, even when the mother is not married:

> It should be noted...that under Section 4(a) nonparenthood is also provided for those donors who provide sperm for assisted conception by unmarried women. In that relatively rare situation, the child would have no legally recognized father.

While the U.S.C.A.C.A. appears to dispose of the problems for lesbians inherent in the U.P.A. statutes, its application has not yet been tested in the courts, and it may ultimately prove to be less protective of lesbian families than it appears. The interpretation of any statute rests, at least in part, on the personal values of the judge hearing the case, and is not always decided strictly by the letter of the law, particularly in cases involving a child's welfare. . . .

■ ■ ■

What Does It Mean If the Donor Is a Father?

If the donor is determined by the courts to be the father of a child, he can be granted legal recognition of certain rights and responsibilities regarding the child. The most significant of these are:

a. A right to seek sole or joint physical or legal custody of the child;

b. A right to regular visitation with the child when the child is in the mother's custody;

c. The right to seek decision-making authority regarding the child's education, health care and religion;

d. A right to custody of the child in the event of the mother's death or incapacity;

e. The right to seek to prevent a change in the child's geographic location of residence;

f. The right to prevent an adoption;

g. An obligation to provide child support; and

h. The right to have his name appear on the birth certificate as the father.

Some lesbians choosing donor insemination may want their children to know the donor as a father because they believe he will provide a positive male role model, because they want their children to have access to medical history and biological family members on the donor's side, or because of any number of other reasons. Other lesbians may not want the donor to be recognized as the father of their child because they want to avoid the possibility of harm to their families through legal and emotional conflict or because they do not want to involve men in their family circle. It is important, when making your decision, to remember that "donor" and "father" have very different legal meanings and implications.

While it is true there are many roles that a donor can assume that fall somewhere between being a donor in name alone, and being a full-fledged father, it is important to recognize that in our system of law there are only two options. Either the donor is merely a donor, with no parental rights or relationship with the child whatsoever, or he is the father, with all of his parental rights intact. There are no gray areas in the law here, and, when in doubt, the courts tend to grant donors full parental rights in cases involving single mothers. From the lesbian mother's perspective, unless she is prepared to fully co-parent her child with the donor under court order, she is much safer if the donor remains strictly a donor in the eyes of the law.

In states that have donor insemination statutes that cover single women, it is possible for lesbian mothers to safeguard against court intrusion by complying with the requirements of the statute. But even in states without these statutes it is a good idea to try establish the mother's and donor's intent of severing the donor's parental rights. The severance of the donor's rights does not necessarily prevent the child from gaining access to medical records or the identity of the donor, but it does permit the mother to define the parameters of the donor's involvement in her child's life, and may ultimately save the child from a traumatic custody battle.

The extent of the donor's involvement that you envision in your child's life will affect the donor method you choose, and should be carefully considered. If you choose to use a known donor, it is vital that you be very clear about your expectations, and that you thoroughly discuss his expectations as well.

You should understand that the more ongoing involvement a donor has in your child's life, the more likely it is that he will be successful in the future if he tries to assert his parental rights before a court of law, even in states that presumably have statutory protections from this. And behavior on your part that is inconsistent with a record that otherwise severs the parental rights of the donor may serve to negate all previous intent and allow the donor to assert his rights as the father. With no grey area, it does not take much to tip the scales from donor to father, and there virtually is no room for your ambivalence about the donor's legal role with your child.

■ ■ ■

JHORDAN C. v. MARY K.

224 Cal. Rptr. 530 (Ct. App. 1986)

■ ■ ■

By statute in California a "donor of semen *provided to a licensed physician* for use in artificial insemination of a woman other than the donor's wife is treated in law as if he were not the natural father of a child thereby conceived." (Civ. Code, § 7005 (b) . . . .)

■ ■ ■

In late 1978 Mary decided to bear a child by artificial insemination and to raise the child jointly with Victoria, a close friend who lived in a nearby town.[1] Mary sought a semen donor by talking to friends and acquaintances. This led to three or four potential donors with whom Mary spoke directly. She and Victoria ultimately chose Jhordan after he had one personal interview with Mary and one dinner at Mary's home.

---

1. As many as 20,000 women each year are artificially inseminated in the United States. Note, *Reproductive Technology and the Procreation Rights of the Unmarried*, 98 HARV.L.REV. 669, fn.1. (1985). By one estimate some 1,500 of these women are unmarried. Donovan, *The Uniform Parentage Act and Nonmarital Motherhood-by-Choice*, 11 N.Y.U.REV. OF LAW & SOC. CHANGE 193, 195 (1982-1983).

The parties' testimony was in conflict as to what agreement they had concerning the role, if any, Jhordan would play in the child's life. According to Mary, she told Jhordan she did not want a donor who desired ongoing involvement with the child, but she did agree to let him see the child to satisfy his curiosity as to how the child would look. Jhordan, in contrast, asserts they agreed he and Mary would have an ongoing friendship, he would have ongoing contact with the child, and he would care for the child as much as two or three times per week.

None of the parties sought legal advice until long after the child's birth. They were completely unaware of the existence of Civil Code section 7005. They did not attempt to draft a written agreement concerning Jhordan's status.

Jhordan provided semen to Mary on a number of occasions during a six-month period commencing in late January 1979. On each occasion he came to her home, spoke briefly with her, produced the semen, and then left. The record is unclear, but Mary, who is a nurse, apparently performed the insemination by herself or with Victoria.

Contact between Mary and Jhordan continued after she became pregnant. Mary attended a Christmas party at Jhordan's home. Jhordan visited Mary several times at the health center where she worked. He took photographs of her. When he informed Mary by telephone that he had collected a crib, playpen, and high chair for the child, she told him to keep those items at his home. At one point Jhordan told Mary he had started a trust fund for the child and wanted legal guardianship in case she died; Mary vetoed the guardianship idea but did not disapprove the trust fund.

Victoria maintained a close involvement with Mary during the pregnancy. She took Mary to medical appointments, attended birthing classes, and shared information with Mary regarding pregnancy, delivery, and child rearing.

Mary gave birth to Devin on March 30, 1980. Victoria assisted in the delivery. Jhordan was listed as the father on Devin's birth certificate.[2] Mary's roommate telephoned Jhordan that day to inform him of the birth. Jhordan visited Mary and Devin the next day and took photographs of the baby.

Five days later Jhordan telephoned Mary and said he wanted to visit Devin again. Mary initially resisted, but then allowed Jhordan to visit, although she told him she was angry. During the visit Jhordan claimed a right to see Devin, and Mary agreed to monthly visits.

Through August 1980 Jhordan visited Devin approximately five times. Mary then terminated the monthly visits. Jhordan said he would consult an attorney if Mary did not let him see Devin. Mary asked Jhordan to sign a contract indicating he would not seek to be Devin's father, but Jhordan refused.

■ ■ ■

We begin with a discussion of Civil Code section 7005, which provides in pertinent part:

"(a) If, under the supervision of a licensed physician and with the consent of her husband, a wife is inseminated artificially with semen donated by a man not her husband, the husband is treated in law as if he were the natural father of a child thereby conceived. . . .

"(b) The donor of semen provided to a licensed physician for use in artificial insemination of a woman other than the donor's wife is treated in law as if he were not the natural father of a child thereby conceived."

Civil Code section 7005 is part of the Uniform Parentage Act (UPA), which was approved in 1973 by the National Conference of Commissioners on Uniform State Laws. The UPA was adopted in California in 1975. Section 7005 is derived almost verbatim from the UPA as originally drafted, with

---

2. This occurred as a result of the filing of an amended birth certificate based upon a judgment against Jhordan in Sonoma County's action for reimbursement of public assistance benefits paid for the child.

one crucial exception. The original UPA restricts application of the nonpaternity provision of subdivision (b) to a "*married* woman other than the donor's wife." The word "married" is excluded from subdivision (b) of section 7005, so that in California, subdivision (b) applies to all women, married or not.

Thus the California Legislature has afforded unmarried as well as married women a statutory vehicle for obtaining semen for artificial insemination without fear that the donor may claim paternity, and has likewise provided men with a statutory vehicle for donating semen to married and unmarried women alike without fear of liability for child support. Subdivision (b) states only one limitation on its application: the semen must be "provided to a licensed physician." Otherwise, whether impregnation occurs through artificial insemination or sexual intercourse, there can be a determination of paternity with the rights, duties and obligations such a determination entails.

A. INTERPRETATION OF THE STATUTORY NONPATERNITY PROVISION

Mary and Victoria first contend that despite the requirement of physician involvement stated in Civil Code section 7005, subdivision (b), the Legislature did not intend to withhold application of the donor nonpaternity provision where semen used in artificial insemination was not provided to a licensed physician. They suggest that the element of physician involvement appears in the statute merely because the Legislature assumed (erroneously) that all artificial insemination would occur under the supervision of a physician. Alternatively, they argue the requirement of physician involvement is merely directive rather than mandatory.

We cannot presume, however, that the legislature simply assumed or wanted to recommend physician involvement, for two reasons.

First, the history of the UPA (the source of section 7005) indicates conscious adoption of the physician requirement. The initial "discussion draft" submitted to the drafters of the UPA in 1971 did not mention the involvement of a physician in artificial insemination; the draft stated no requirement as to how semen was to be obtained or how the insemination procedure was to be performed. The eventual inclusion of the physician requirement in the final version of the UPA suggests a conscious decision to require physician involvement.

Second, there are at least two sound justifications upon which the statutory requirement of physician involvement might have been based. One relates to health: a physician can obtain a complete medical history of the donor (which may be of crucial importance to the child during his or her lifetime) and screen the donor for any hereditary or communicable diseases. Indeed, the commissioners' comment to the section of the UPA on artificial insemination cites as a "useful reference" a law review article which argues that health considerations should require the involvement of a physician in statutorily authorized artificial insemination. This suggests that health considerations underlie the decision by the drafters of the UPA to include the physician requirement in the artificial insemination statute.

Another justification for physician involvement is that the presence of a professional third party such as a physician can serve to create a formal, documented structure for the donor-recipient relationship, without which, as this case illustrates, misunderstandings between the parties regarding the nature of their relationship and the donor's relationship to the child would be more likely to occur.

It is true that nothing inherent in artificial insemination requires the involvement of a physician. Artificial insemination is, as demonstrated here, a simple procedure easily performed by a woman in her own home. Also, despite the reasons outlined above in favor of physician involvement, there are countervailing considerations against requiring it. A requirement of physician involvement, as Mary argues, might offend a woman's sense of privacy and reproductive autonomy, might result in burdensome costs to some women, and might interfere with a woman's desire to conduct the procedure in a comfortable environment such as her own home or to choose the donor herself.[7]

However, because of the way section 7005 is phrased, a woman (married or unmarried) can perform home artificial insemination or choose her donor and still obtain the benefits of the statute. Subdivision (b) does not require that a physician independently obtain the semen and perform the insemination, but requires only that the semen be "provided" to a physician. Thus, a woman who prefers home artificial insemination or who wishes to choose her donor can still obtain statutory protection from a donor's paternity claim through the relatively simple expedient of obtaining the semen, whether for home insemination or from a chosen donor (or both), through a licensed physician.

Regardless of the various countervailing considerations for and against physician involvement, our legislature has embraced the apparently conscious decision by the drafters of the UPA to limit application of the donor nonpaternity provision to instances in which semen is provided to a licensed physician. The existence of sound justifications for physician involvement further supports a determination the legislature intended to require it. Accordingly, section 7005, subdivision (b), by its terms does not apply to the present case. The Legislature's apparent decision to require physician involvement in order to invoke the statute cannot be subject to judicial second-guessing and cannot be disturbed, absent constitutional infirmity.

B. CONSTITUTIONAL CONSIDERATIONS

Mary and Victoria next contend that even if section 7005, subdivision (b), by its terms does not apply where semen for artificial insemination has not been provided to a licensed physician, application of the statute to the present case is required by constitutional principles of equal protection and privacy (encompassing rights to family autonomy and procreative choice).

1. Equal protection

Mary and Victoria argue the failure to apply section 7005, subdivision (b), to unmarried women who conceive artificially with semen not provided to a licensed physician denies equal protection because the operation of other paternity statutes precludes a donor's assertion of paternity where a *married* woman undergoes artificial insemination with semen not provided to a physician.

This characterization of the effect of the paternity statutes as applied to married women is correct. In the case of the married woman her husband is the presumed father, and *any* outsider — including a semen donor, regardless of physician involvement — is precluded from maintaining a paternity action unless the mother "relinquishes for, consents to, or proposes to relinquish for or consent to, the adoption of the child." An action to establish paternity by blood test can be brought only by the husband or mother.

But the statutory provision at issue here — Civil Code section 7005, subdivision (b) — treats married and unmarried women equally. Both are denied application of the statute where semen has not been provided to a licensed physician.

---

7. One article on the subject of artificial insemination notes that many women prefer to choose a known donor because this "eliminates potential difficulties in gaining access to medical information, permits the prospective mother to make the choice of donor herself, and allows the child access to paternal roots." Kern & Ridolfi, *The Fourteenth Amendment's Protection of a Woman's Right to be a Single Parent through Artificial Insemination by Donor*, 7 WOMEN'S RIGHTS L.RPTR. 251, 256 (1982).

The true question presented is whether a completely different set of paternity statutes — affording protection to husband and wife from any claim of paternity by an outsider — denies equal protection by failing to provide similar protection to an unmarried woman. The simple answer is that, within the context of this question, a married woman and an unmarried woman are not similarly situated for purposes of equal protection analysis. In the case of a married woman, the marital relationship invokes a long-recognized social policy of preserving the integrity of the marriage. No such concerns arise where there is no marriage at all. Equal protection is not violated by providing that certain benefits or legal rights arise only out of the marital relationship. For example, spousal support may be awarded pursuant to Civil Code section 4801 upon the breakup of a marital relationship, but not upon the breakup of a nonmarital relationship.

2. Family autonomy

Mary and Victoria contend that they and Devin compose a family unit and that the trial court's ruling constitutes an infringement upon a right they have to family autonomy, encompassed by the constitutional right to privacy. But this argument begs the question of which persons comprise the family in this case for purposes of judicial intervention. Characterization of the family unit must precede consideration of whether family autonomy has been infringed.

The semen donor here was permitted to develop a social relationship with Mary and Devin as the child's father. During Mary's pregnancy Jhordan maintained contact with her. They visited each other several times, and Mary did not object to Jhordan's collection of baby equipment or the creation of a trust fund for the child. Mary permitted Jhordan to visit Devin on the day after the child's birth and allowed monthly visits thereafter. The record demonstrates no clear understanding that Jhordan's role would be limited to provision of semen and that he would have no parental relationship with

Devin; indeed, the parties' conduct indicates otherwise.

We do not purport to hold that an oral or written nonpaternity agreement between the parties would have been legally binding; that difficult question is not before us (and indeed is more appropriately addressed by the Legislature). We simply emphasize that for purposes of the family autonomy argument raised by Mary, Jhordan was not excluded as a member of Devin's family, either by anonymity, by agreement, or by the parties' conduct.

In short, the court's ruling did not infringe upon any right of Mary and Victoria to family autonomy, because under the peculiar facts of this case Jhordan was not excluded as a member of Devin's family for purposes of resolving this custody dispute.

3. Procreative Choice

Mary and Victoria argue that the physician requirement in Civil Code section 7005, subdivision (b), infringes a fundamental right to procreative choice, also encompassed by the constitutional right of privacy.

But the statute imposes no restriction on the right to bear a child. Unlike statutes in other jurisdictions proscribing artificial insemination other than by a physician, subdivision (b) of section 7005 does not forbid self-insemination; nor does the statute preclude personal selection of a donor or in any other way prevent women from artificially conceiving children under circumstances of their own choice. The statute simply addresses the perplexing question of the legal status of the semen donor, and provides a method of avoiding the legal consequences that might otherwise be dictated by traditional notions of paternity.

C. VICTORIA'S STATUS AS A DE FACTO PARENT

Finally, Mary and Victoria contend that even if the paternity judgment is affirmed Victoria should be declared a de facto parent, based on her day-to-day attention to Devin's needs, in order to guarantee her present visitation rights and ensure her parental status in any future custody or visitation proceedings. Present resolution of the de facto parenthood issue for these purposes would be premature and merely advisory. Victoria's visitation rights have been legally recognized and preserved by court order. If no further custody or visitation proceedings occur, the issue of Victoria's de facto parent status and its legal effect will never arise.[9]

CONCLUSION

We wish to stress that our opinion in this case is not intended to express any judicial preference toward traditional notions of family structure or toward providing a father where a single woman has chosen to bear a child. Public policy in these areas is best determined by the legislative branch of government, not the judicial. Our Legislature has already spoken and has afforded to unmarried women a statutory right to bear children by artificial insemination (as well as a right of men to donate semen) without fear of a paternity claim, through provision of the semen to a licensed physician. We simply hold that because Mary omitted to invoke Civil Code section 7005, subdivision (b), by obtaining Jhordan's semen through a licensed physician, and because the parties by all other conduct preserved Jhordan's status as a member of Devin's family, the trial court properly declared Jhordan to be Devin's legal father.

The judgment is affirmed.

Notes

1. *Use of an Unknown Sperm Donor*. Using an unknown donor is often considered the best way for a lesbian to guarantee that a donor will not assert parental rights at some later time. The anonymity of the woman and the donor may be maintained through the use of a sperm bank or a "go-between." Most sperm banks have procedures that permit a woman to be inseminated without the sperm donor learning of her identity. Sperm banks often screen donors for health problems and physical characteristics. Thus, although the mother does not know the donor's identity, she may still screen for certain physical traits and can more safely assume that her own health will not be jeopardized by the insemination. In addition, the woman's legal rights under the Uniform Parentage Act are preserved because the use of sperm bank generally qualifies as "physician supervision" under the U.P.A. *See* NATIONAL CENTER FOR LESBIAN RIGHTS, LESBIANS CHOOSING MOTHERHOOD: LEGAL IMPLICATIONS OF DONOR INSEMINATION AND

---

9. A person with whom a child does not reside full time usually cannot be considered a de facto parent. De facto parent status is, however, legally possible under such circumstances. One court observed, "Although psychological parenthood is said to result from 'day-to-day attention to [the child's] needs for physical care, nourishment, comfort, affection, and stimulation,' appellants fail to point to any authority or body of professional opinion that equates daily attention with full-time residency. To the contrary, the record contains uncontradicted expert testimony that while psychological parenthood usually will require residency on a '24-hour basis,' it is not an absolute requirement; further, that the frequency and quality of . . . visits . . . provided an adequate foundation to establish the crucial parent-child relationship." The court-appointed psychologist in the present case testified that Victoria had indeed become a psychological parent. The trial court rejected this testimony and made a contrary determination under the present facts. This determination, however, will not be binding in any subsequent litigation, since the facts inevitably will have changed (if for no other reason than the mere passage of time and its effect on the relationship between Victoria and Devin).

CO-PARENTING 12 (1991). Nevertheless, some sperm banks will provide sperm only to married heterosexual couples.

2. *Use of an Alternative Insemination Donor's Agreement.* In *Jhordan C.*, the sperm donor and the recipient mother had very different perceptions regarding what role the donor would play in raising the child. One can only speculate whether the court would have reached a different result if the donor and mother had clearly expressed their intentions in a written agreement. In a Colorado case, a sperm donor prevailed in his paternity suit even though his parental rights and responsibilities should have been extinguished under the terms of Colorado's U.P.A.-based statute. The judge based his decision on the fact that the woman was unmarried, that the donor was known, that the donor claimed to have provided emotional and financial support to the woman and the child, and that no written agreement to the contrary existed. *In re R.C.*, 775 P.2d 27 (Colo. 1989).

2. SURROGACY

Under a surrogacy arrangement, a woman — the surrogate mother — agrees to be artificially inseminated with a man's sperm and further agrees to relinquish all her parental rights to the child in favor of the father. Despite the widespread publicity and controversy surrounding surrogacy, the actual use of surrogate motherhood is uncommon. As of 1987, it was estimated that only 500 births had resulted from 'surrogate' motherhood.[1] By comparison, approximately 350,000 children were born through alternative insemination by 1987.[2]

In re Baby M.[3] involved an infertile married couple, the Sterns, who had entered a surrogacy contract with Mary Beth Whitehead, the surrogate mother, which provided that the surrogate would be impregnated with Mr. Stern's sperm, carry the baby to term, and then turn the child over to Sterns for adoption. Whitehead was to be paid $10,000 when she delivered a live child to the Sterns, $1,000 in the event of a still birth, and $1,000 if she had an abortion at the Sterns' request. The case arose when Whitehead refused to surrender the child to the Sterns in violation of the surrogacy contract. The New Jersey Supreme Court held that the surrogacy agreement was unenforceable because it conflicted with the law and public policy of the state: "While we recognize the depth of the yearning of infertile couple to have their own children, we find the payment of money to a 'surrogate' mother illegal, perhaps criminal, and potentially degrading to women." Several other state courts that have considered surrogacy contracts have reached the same conclusion.[4]

---

1. *See* Iver Peterson, *Surrogates Often Improvise Birth Pacts*, N. Y. TIMES, Feb. 25, 1987, at B2.

2. *See* J. LASKER & S. BORG, IN SEARCH OF PARENTHOOD 33 (1987).

3. 537 A.2d 1227 (N.J. 1988).

4. *See Miroff* v. *Surrogate Mother*, 13 Fam. L. Rep. (BNA) 1260 (Ind. Super. Ct. 1986) (declaring a surrogacy contract underlying an adoption contrary to public policy); *Yates* v. *Kean*, 14 Fam. L. Rep. (BNA) 1160 (Mich. Cir. Ct. 1987) (refusing to enforce a surrogacy contract). *But see In re Baby Girl L.J.*, 505 N.Y.S.2d 813 (N.Y. Sur. Ct. 1986) (concluding that surrogacy contracts do not violate New York law which prohibit monetary payments for adoption).

In addition to a smattering of courts, a few state legislatures have considered the legality of surrogacy contracts. As of 1990, six states — Indiana, Kentucky, Louisiana, Michigan, Nebraska, and North Dakota — had enacted legislation prohibiting the enforcement of surrogacy arrangements and one state — Iowa — permitted the enforcement of surrogacy contracts.

IV. Dissolution Of Lesbian And Gay Families

NANCY S. v. MICHELE G.

279 Cal. Rptr. 212 (Ct. App. 1991)

STEIN, Associate Justice

Appellant, Michele G., appeals from a judgment under the Uniform Parentage Act (*Civ. Code*, § 7000 et seq.) determining that respondent, Nancy S., is the only parent of the two minor children that respondent conceived by artificial insemination during her relationship with appellant. The judgment further provided that respondent, as the only legal parent of the two minor children, is entitled to sole legal and physical custody and that any further contact between appellant and the children shall only be by respondent's consent.

■ ■ ■

In August of 1969, appellant and respondent began living together, and in November of that year they had a private "marriage" ceremony. Eventually they decided to have children by artificially inseminating respondent. In June of 1980, respondent gave birth to a daughter, K. Appellant was listed on the birth certificate as the father, and K. was given appellant's family name. On June 13, 1984, respondent gave birth to a son, S. Again appellant was listed as the father on the birth certificate, and S. was given

appellant's family name. Both children refer to appellant and respondent as "Mom." Although the parties considered arranging for appellant to adopt the children, they never initiated formal adoption proceedings.

In January of 1985 appellant and respondent separated. They agreed that K. would live with appellant and that S. would live with respondent. They arranged visitation so that appellant would have K. five days a week and respondent would have S. five days a week, but the children would be together, either at appellant's or respondent's home for four days a week. After approximately three years, respondent wanted to change the custody arrangement so that each had custody of both children 50 percent of the time. Appellant opposed any change, and attempts to mediate the dispute failed.

■ ■ ■

Civil Code section 4600, subdivision (c) provides that, in any proceeding where there is at issue the custody of a minor child, "Before the court makes any order awarding custody to a person . . . other than a parent, without the consent of the parents, it shall make a finding that an award of custody to a parent would be detrimental to the child and the award to a nonparent is required to serve the best interests of the child." Appellant acknowledges that, regardless of the statutory basis of the underlying proceeding, i.e., whether it was brought under the Uniform Parentage Act, or as a guardianship, dependency, or dissolution proceeding, she is entitled to seek custody and visitation over the objections of the children's natural mother, based on the "best interests" of the children, only if she has alleged facts upon which the court could determine that she is a parent of the children.

The Uniform Parentage Act defines a parent as one who is the natural or adoptive parent of a child. The existence of the relationship of parent and child may be proved between a child and its natural mother by proof of her having given birth to the child, between a child and an adoptive parent by proof of adoption, and between a natural father and a child as provided in the act.

It is undisputed that appellant is not the natural mother of K. and S., and that she has not adopted either child. She does not contend that she and respondent had a legally recognized marriage when the children were born. Based on these undisputed facts, the court correctly determined that appellant could not establish the existence of a parent-child relationship under the Uniform Parentage Act.

Appellant nonetheless asserts that the Uniform Parentage Act does not provide the exclusive definition of a parent. She asserts that her allegations of a long-term relationship in which she has become a "psychological parent" of the children would, if proved,[4] entitle her to seek custody and visitation as if the dispute were between two legally recognized parents. She advances several legal theories to support her assertion that she has acquired "parental rights," i.e, the right to seek custody and visitation on an equal footing with the children's natural mother and over their natural mother's objections.

A. DE FACTO PARENTHOOD

A de facto parent is "that person who, on a day-to-day basis, assumes the role of parent, seeking to fulfill both the child's physical needs and his psychological need for affection and care." *In re B.G.*, 523 P.2d 244 (Cal. 1974). Appellant alleged that she helped facilitate the conception and birth of both children and immediately after their birth assumed all the responsibilities of a parent. K. lived with appellant until the underlying dispute arose, and S. also lived with appellant until appellant and respondent separated, and thereafter S. visited with appellant on a regular basis. These facts may well entitle appellant to the status of a "de facto" parent. It does not, however, follow that as a "de facto" parent appellant has the same rights as a parent to seek custody and visitation over the objection of the children's natural mother. . . .

No cases support appellant's contention that if she could prove her status as a de facto parent, she would be entitled to seek custody of respondent's children according to the same standards applied in a dispute between two parents. To the contrary, the cases establish that nonparents, even if they qualify as "de facto parents," may be recognized in guardianship or dependency proceedings and may even obtain custody over children with whom they have established a de facto parent-child relationship, but that custody can be awarded to a de facto parent *only* if it is established by clear and convincing evidence that parental custody is detrimental to the children.

---

4. Although appellant's allegations regarding her relationship to the two children have not been proved, the record strongly suggests that appellant could prove that since their birth she has, from the children's point of view, especially as to K., performed the role of a loving mother.

Appellant argues that, in this case, the "detriment" standard should not apply because appellant is not an "outsider" and does not seek to exclude the parent but wants to share custody. In *all* of the cases involving a "de facto" parent, the individual claiming such status necessarily is not an "outsider" and, like appellant, has undoubtedly developed deep psychological and emotional bonds with the child. Nonetheless, the courts and our Legislature have chosen to place paramount importance upon the relationship between the natural or adoptive parent and the child. Even the discretionary visitation provided nonparents by Civil Code section 4601 "must give way to the paramount right to parent if the visitation creates conflicts and problems. . . . The critical importance in California of the right to parent has been affirmed and reaffirmed. It only gives way upon a showing of parental unfitness, detrimental to the child's welfare." *In re Marriage of Jenkens*, 172 Cal.Rptr. 331 (Cal, App.1981).

B. IN LOCO PARENTIS

Appellant next advances the theory that the common law doctrine of "in loco parentis" could be applied to confer upon her the same rights as a parent to seek custody and visitation of S. and K. In the context of torts, the concept of in loco parentis has been used to impose upon persons standing "in loco parentis" the same rights and obligations imposed by statutory and common law upon parents. It has also been applied to confer certain benefits upon a child, such as more favorable inheritance tax treatment, or workers' compensation benefits. The concept of "in loco parentis," however, has never been applied in a custody dispute to give a nonparent the same rights as a parent, and we are unpersuaded that the concept should be so extended.

■ ■ ■

C. PARENTHOOD BY EQUITABLE ESTOPPEL

Appellant argues that the court could apply the doctrine of equitable estoppel to prevent respondent from denying the existence of a parent-child relationship that she allegedly encouraged and supported for many years and which she now denies for the sole purpose of obtaining unfettered control over the custody of the children.

In California, equitable estoppel has been invoked for the purpose of imposing support obligations on a husband who has represented to his wife's children that he is their natural father and subsequently seeks to deny paternity for the purpose of avoiding support obligations. Equitable estoppel has never been invoked in California against a natural parent for the purpose of awarding custody and visitation to a nonparent.

Other states, however, have begun to use the doctrine of equitable estoppel to prevent a wife from denying the paternity of her husband. For example, in *In re Paternity of D.L.H.*, 419 N.W.2d 283 (Wisc. Ct. App. 1987), the court held that a wife could be estopped to deny the paternity of her husband, even where human leukocyte antigen (HLA) tests had excluded the husband as the natural father. The husband knew, even before the child's birth, that he was not the biological father but promised to raise the child as his own. He had developed a strong relationship with the child and had paid support to the mother after the couple separated. The court held it was error to dismiss the husband from the paternity proceedings after the HLA tests excluded him as the natural father, and remanded to permit him to prove the elements of equitable estoppel. The court, however, specifically reserved the question whether, even if the wife were estopped to deny paternity, the husband would have the status of a parent in a custody dispute and could thereby invoke the standard of the best interests of the child. Even if the doctrine of equitable estoppel could be used against a wife and in favor of a husband to award custody as if the dispute were between two natural parents, we note that the use of the doctrine of equitable estoppel, in these out-of-state cases, is rooted in "[o]ne of the strongest presumptions in law [i.e.] that a child born to a married woman is the legitimate child of her husband." No similar presumption applies in this case.

It is important not to confuse appellant's argument regarding equitable estoppel with the concept of an "equitable parent." The concept of an "equitable parent" has been recognized by the Michigan Court of Appeals in a divorce proceeding to permit a husband, who is not the biological father of a child born during the marriage, to obtain the status of a parent in a custody dispute with the natural mother, and to have the custody dispute settled as if it were between two natural parents, according to the child's best interests. *Atkinson* v. *Atkinson*, 408 N.W.2d 516, 517-520 (Mich. Ct. App. 1987). The primary difference between the concept of an "equitable parent" and the equitable estoppel theory advanced by appellant is that the "equitable parent" theory is rooted in a statutory recognition of "equitable adoption" for purposes of inheritance and may require proof of an express or implied contract to adopt. At least one California court has already declined to adopt the concept of an "equitable parent" for the purpose of awarding joint custody to a stepfather over the objections of the child's natural mother despite the fact that California, like Michigan, recognizes the doctrine of "equitable adoption" for purposes of inheritance under Probate Code section 6408. *See In re Marriage of Lewis & Goetz*, 250 Cal.Rptr.30 (Cal. App. 1988). The court stressed that

given the "complex practical, social and constitutional ramifications" of expanding the class of persons entitled to assert parental rights, the decision was better left to the Legislature.

D. FUNCTIONAL DEFINITION OF PARENTHOOD

Finally, appellant urges us to adopt what she describes as a "functional" definition of parenthood in order to protect on-going relationships between children and those who function as their parents. In accordance with this new definition, the class of persons entitled to seek custody and visitation according to the same standards as a natural parent would include "anyone who maintains a functional parental relationship with a child when a legally recognized parent created that relationship with the intent that the relationship be parental in nature." *See* Polikoff, *This Child Does Have Two Mothers: Redefining Parenthood to Meet the Needs of Children in Lesbian-Mother and Other Nontraditional Families*, 78 GEO. L.J. 459, 464 (1990).

We agree with appellant that the absence of any legal formalization of her relationship to the children has resulted in a tragic situation. As is always the case, it is the children who will suffer the most as a result of the inability of the adults, who they love and need, to reach an agreement. We do not, however, agree that the only way to avoid such an unfortunate situation is for the courts to adopt appellant's novel theory by which a nonparent can acquire the rights of a parent, and then face years of unraveling the complex practical, social, and constitutional ramifications of this expansion of the definition of parent.[8]

---

8. Although the validity of an adoption in these circumstances is not before us, we note that Civil Code section 221 provides, in part, that "[a]ny unmarried minor child may be adopted by any adult person . . ." We see nothing in these provisions that would preclude a child from being jointly adopted by someone of the same sex as the natural parent. *Cf. Marshall* v. *Marshall*, 239 P. 36 (Cal. 1925).

E. CONCLUSION

Although the facts in this case are relatively straightforward regarding the intent of the natural mother to create a parental relationship between appellant and her children, expanding the definition of a "parent" in the manner advocated by appellant could expose other natural parents to litigation brought by child-care providers of long standing, relatives, successive sets of step-parents or other close friends of the family. No matter how narrowly we might attempt to draft the definition, the fact remains that the status of individuals claiming to be parents would have to be litigated and resolu-

tion of these claims would turn on elusive factual determinations of the intent of the natural mother, the perceptions of the children, and the course of conduct of the party claiming parental status. By deferring to the Legislature in matters involving complex social and policy ramifications far beyond the facts of the particular case, we are not telling the parties that the issues they raise are unworthy of legal recognition. To the contrary, we intend only to illustrate the limitations of the courts in fashioning a comprehensive solution to such a complex and socially significant issue.

The judgment is affirmed.

Notes

1. In addition to *Nancy S.*, courts in four other states have ruled on the visitation rights of a lesbian co-parent following separation from her child's biological mother. *See Kulla* v. *McNulty*, 472 N.W.2d 175 (Minn. Ct. App. 1991) (holding that a co-parent does not have standing to acquire custody or assert visitation rights); *In re Alison D.* v. *Virginia M.*, 572 N.E.2d 27, 28 (N.Y. 1991) (holding that co-parent did not have standing to bring visitation petition because she was not a "parent" as defined in visitation statute); *Sporleder* v. *Hermes* (*In re Z.J.H.*), 471 N.W.2d 202, 204 (Wis. 1991) (holding that a co-parent does not have standing to acquire custody or assert visitation rights); *A.C.* v. *C.B.*, 829 P.2d 660 (N.M. Ct. App. 1992) (granting standing to non-biological lesbian mother to seek continued relationship with child she co-parented).
2. In the New York case, *Alison D.* v. *Virginia M.*, 572 N.E.2d 27 (N.Y. 1991), a lesbian couple planned for the conception and birth of a child by artificial insemination and agreed to share jointly all rights and responsibilities for raising the child. The child was born in 1981, and as agreed the couple jointly cared for and made decisions regarding the child. By the time the couple ended their relationship in 1983, the child referred to both parents as "mommy." Pursuant to a separation agreement, the co-parent moved out of the family home, was required to continue to pay one-half of the home mortgage and major household expenses, and was granted visitation rights so that she could continue her relationship with the child. The agreement continued in effect without incident for three years. Beginning in 1986, the biological mother began to restrict the co-parent's visitation and in 1987, she terminated all contact between the co-parent and child. The co-parent then filed suit requesting an award of visitation rights.

The finding of the trial court that the co-parent was not a legal parent within the meaning of the domestic relations statute was affirmed on appeal by New York's highest court. The high court posited, "At issue in this case is whether petitioner [the co-parent], a biological stranger to a child who is properly in the custody of his biological mother, has standing to seek visitation. . . ." *Id.* at 28. The court reasoned,

> Although the Court is mindful of [the co-parent's] understandable concern for and interest in the child and of her expectation and desire that her contact with the child would continue, she has no right under Domestic Relations Law § 70 to seek visitation and, thereby, limit or diminish the right of the concededly fit biological parent to choose with whom her child associates. She is not a "parent" within the meaning of section 70.

Id. at 29.

Though the statute provides a mechanism for "either parent" to bring a habeas corpus proceeding to determine a child's custody and visitation, the court defined "parent" to include only biological or adoptive parents. The court considered this definition of parent necessary to protect the integrity of the natural family:

> To allow the courts to award visitation — a limited form of custody — to a third person would necessarily impair the parents' right to custody and control. Petitioner [co-parent] concedes that respondent [biological parent] is a fit parent. Therefore she has no right to petition the court to displace the choice made by this fit parent in deciding what is in the child's best interests.

Id.

3. In *Sporleder* v. *Hermes (In re Z.J.H.)*, 471 N.W.2d 202 (Wis. 1991), a lesbian couple of eight years adopted a child after an unsuccessful attempt to have a child through alternative insemination. One parent, Hermes, legally adopted the child. The co-parent, Sporleder, was the primary care taker of the adopted child because Hermes worked outside of the home. The couple entered a co-parenting contract which provided that if the couple separated they would use mediation to determine who received physical custody of the child, and that the non-custodial parent would have reasonable and liberal visitation rights. Several months after the child was placed in the home the couple separated. Hermes subsequently adopted the child and then prohibited Sporleder from visiting. Sporleder brought a lawsuit seeking, among other things, enforcement of the co-parenting contract. A majority of the Wisconsin Supreme Court held that the contract was unenforceable. Justice Callow analyzed enforceability of the co-parenting contract:

> We next conclude, as did the court of appeals, that rights to custody and visitation are controlled by statutory and case law, and cannot be contracted away. . . . Because we conclude that the legislative intent grants custody and visitation rights to non-parents only under the circumstances described above, the contract is void to the extent it purports to award custody or grant visitation rights to Sporleder.
>
> Additionally, in light of the societal and constitutional interests in maintaining the relationship between a natural or adoptive parent and that parent's child, public policy concerns militate against contractual provisions affecting this relationship.
>
> This court has recognized the public interest in protecting not only the rights of the natural or adoptive parent, but of the family unit as well. Hermes, as the legal parent, has all the rights and responsibilities which the law confers. She is legally responsible for the well-being of Z.J.H., and there is no indication that she has not fulfilled that responsibility. We have said that the court should not displace a fit and able parent for one who does not

have the legal status of a parent, even if such a person could do as good a job or even a better job of parenting. The co-parenting agreement, to the extent that it purports to award custody or grant visitation rights to Sporleder, is inconsistent with legislative intent behind the custody and visitation statutes, which prefer parents over third parties. It is also inconsistent with our conclusion that, unless circumstances compel a contrary conclusion, it is in Z.J.H.'s best interest to live in his legal parent's home.

■ ■ ■

We conclude that because of the public interest in maintaining a stable relationship between a child and his or her legal parent, the co-parenting agreement, to the extent that it purports to award custody or grant visitation rights to Sporleder, is unenforceable. While we recognize that Sporleder may have had a reasonable expectation that she would have continued contact with Z.J.H. under the agreement, enforcing the agreement would be contrary to legislative intent and the public interest.

Id. at 211-12.

Justice Bablitch filed a dissenting opinion that focused on the welfare of the child, Z.J.H.:

Everyone agrees that children of a dissolving traditional relationship deserve and need the protection of the courts. Yet the majority opinion holds that children of a dissolving non-traditional relationship are not entitled to the same protection. What logic compels that result? The legislature could not have intended such an absurd and cruel result, but that is what the majority of this court has determined.

Media accounts, and the majority opinion, focus solely on the rights of the adults in this non-traditional relationship that is dissolving. Lost in the media accounts, and in the majority opinion, are the interests of at least equal if not paramount concern: the interests of the child.

What about the child, Z.J.H.? Who speaks for him? What is in his interest? The majority denies him any legal significance. He is a nonentity in this battle between two parents. Because this is a non-traditional parental relationship, the result of the majority's decision is that the child's interests will not even be considered. It is as if he does not even exist.

But the child does exist. And thousands of others like him do exist. These children need, and deserve, the protection of the court as much as children of a dissolving traditional relationship. Their interests at least ought to be considered.

Id. at 214-15.

3. Though historically disfavored by courts, the functional definition of families is strongly advocated by some legal academics and by lesbian and gay rights litigants. *See, e.g.,* Nancy Polikoff, *This Child Does Have Two Mothers: Redefining Parenthood to Meet the Needs of Children in Lesbian-Mother and Other Nontraditional Families,* 78 Geo. l.j. 459 (1990).

4. The *Nancy S.* court noted that although the couple had considered arranging for second parent adoption of the children by the co-parent, they never initiated formal adoption proceedings. 279 Cal. Rptr. at 214. The court further noted that no provisions of the adoption statute would preclude a child from being jointly adopted by someone of the same sex as the natural parent. *Id.* at 219 n.8. The court attached some significance to the fact that the couple did not take advantage of a procedure — second parent adoption — that would have created a legally cognizable relationship between the co-parent and the children.

♦

OUR DAY IN COURT — AGAINST EACH OTHER: INTRA-COMMUNITY DISPUTES THREATEN ALL OF OUR RIGHTS

National Center for Lesbian Rights

Until recently, NCLR had a policy against participating in cases in which lesbians or gay men were suing each other. Today, that guideline is no longer appropriate. Increasingly, NCLR is becoming involved in intra-community conflicts because of our commitment to protect the broader rights of lesbians and gay men. Ironically, we are seeing that those rights are being threatened by court battles between individual members of the community. Take these examples:

• In Georgia, two women break up. They own a house and other property together and have a written agreement. This contract, prepared by their attorney, spelled out how they would divide these possessions should they ever break up. They are unable to negotiate a settlement, however, and one woman sues the other to enforce the agreement. In court, the other woman takes the position that the agreement is void because it is based on an illegal, lesbian relationship (remember Hardwick and the Georgia sodomy law?) The judge agrees with her and refuses to enforce the agreement.

• In Massachusetts, New York, and California, gay male donors have sued lesbians for visitation or custody of children they fathered. In some of these situations, there are written agreements about the rights of the donors, in others there are not, in all the cases, original understandings between the adults have become unclear, and the families have ended up in court.

• In California and New York, lesbian co-parents who have broken up have taken each other to court to fight over custody of their children. The birth mothers have asserted that the non-birth mothers are legal strangers to their children with no right to have any contact with them. So far, the courts have agreed with the birth mothers.

NCLR is involved in the Georgia case because it raises the question of lesbians' rights to enter into enforceable contracts. In the donor cases, NCLR is defending lesbian families against the legal system's attempts to impose heterosexual family models on us. The lesbian co-parent cases also present clear issues of recognizing our families and our right to define who is a parent outside of biological factors.

When we hear about these conflicts, though, many of us wonder why are we doing this to each other. What does this mean about our community? Is this internalized homophobia? Are these bad, politically incorrect, or sick people?

One reason lesbians and gay men are ending up in court against each other is that the legal system is the only forum available to most people to resolve disputes. We pay our taxes along with everyone else; we should have access to the legal system. Our community is not over-represented in the courts. If anything, we can be proud of how often we resolve conflicts outside of the legal system. In Los Angeles, San Francisco, New

National Center for Lesbian Rights, *Our Day In Court — Against Each Other: Intra-community Disputes Threaten All Of Our Rights*, NCLR NEWSLETTER 1 (Winter 1991–1992).

York and other places, we even are creating mediation panels and other alternative dispute-resolution options for ourselves.

The reasons we are taking such terrible positions against each other are twofold: because we can, and because we remain outside the legal system. If straight people could get out of contracts or eliminate a co-parent, they would. The legal system provides boundaries for the rest of society which it does not provide lesbians and gay men — boundaries to limit unconscionable acts, and boundaries to define and support families.

When straight people have children, they either know who the children's family is and have the support of the legal system in that definition, or they have the recourse to create a legally defined family, through step-parent adoption, for instance. Once these legal relationships are established, straight parents can predict what will happen in future situations. If they die or break-up, they have a legally recognized procedure for determining custody.

We do not have the ability to legitimate our families in these ways. Sometimes our family constellation matches the legal definition, but more often, it does not. Not only are we denied the legal protections and support our families need, we also can't rely on the predictability the law provides.

And so, when we're angry, we go to court and take sometimes extreme positions. We use the laws we hate against each other, or we are forced to distort our family to fit the limited legal definitions available to us.

It is unlikely that the woman in Georgia is a bad person, although her case could make bad law. Our picture of who she is distorted by the options available to her in our legal system, the same way her relationship and her intention in entering into the property agreement were distorted by the court's decision.

It is unproductive for us to analyze the facts of donor lawsuits or lesbian co-parent disputes, to try to decide who is right and who is wrong. There are always at least two valid positions in

family disputes. Donors sue for paternity because they can't sue just for visitation. Birth mothers deny the parenthood of their former partners because they honestly believe that is what the situation requires.

In many ways, our community has moved ahead of ourselves. We are becoming parents in greater numbers, but we don't have the legal framework to support our families. Nor do we have a broad understanding of family-law concepts and the balancing of interests essential to a resolution of disputes. This lack of familiarity often leads us to look at each case in isolation, rather than at the broader implications of a particular verdict. We are reduced to basing our opinions about these cases on the personalities involved rather than the principles.

What these cases do tell us is that a comprehensive examination of our laws is overdue. We must become more familiar with some of the concepts involved and step back and fashion what we need. As upsetting and disheartening (and painful for the parties involved) as these cases are, they should serve as an early warning of what issues we need to address and of some of the factors likely to arise in other cases.

What do we do when agreements and feelings change? How do we want to define who a parent is? What role should biology play? How do we consider the wishes of our children?

NCLR has been participating in roundtable discussions of these questions with other gay — and lesbian-rights advocates. And we will be sponsoring a series of public forums on some of the current issues arising in intra-community disputes. Without this dialogue and understanding, we will soon find lesbian and gay legal organizations arguing against each other in court, right along with the other members of our community.

We can heed the early warning these cases offer us and avoid increased polarization. These conflicts offer an opportunity to take great leaps in our understanding of who we are and what we want.

Conclusion

◆

WHOSE CONSTITUTION IS IT, ANYWAY?
Larry Kramer

I never knew what it felt like to be a nigger or a spic. Now I know. I'm a fag. Fags and niggers and spics aren't protected by the Constitution. Nor are junkies, whores, and broads.

Discrimination — consciously allowing some people to be treated as inferiors — is on the verge of totally bankrupting this country: financially, creatively, and morally.

This is not a good time in history to be a gay man or a lesbian, but particularly a gay man. I don't know if there ever was a completely good time to be gay, but for a little while there we were making some headway toward equality and acceptance. Until Ronald Reagan and AIDS came along, unfortunately at the same time.

I know you're celebrating the Constitution today. I don't feel very much like celebrating. The Constitution, as it is being administered today, doesn't protect me in the ways I need protection. In fact, I'm ashamed to be an American today — ashamed of how this precious document is being hypocritically misread and misapplied to suit those who would wish me and all like me dead. I personally think that conscious genocide is going on. This administration's determination — which has persisted for a very long seven years— not to do anything sufficient to fight the AIDS epidemic can only be construed as an attempt to see that minority populations

LARRY KRAMER, *Whose Constitution Is It, Anyway?*, in REPORTS FROM THE HOLOCAUST: THE MAKING OF AN AIDS ACTIVIST 177 (1987) (remarks made to a symposium sponsored by the New York Civil Liberties Union on Thursday, September 7, 1987, to celebrate the two-hundredth anniversary of the United States Constitution).

they do not favor will die. Seven year, 25,000 dead, over 50,000 cases, a quarter-million predicted in a few years' time, soon after that to be a million — and still there is no one in charge of combating AIDS, and still this city and this country do not provide adequate essential services, and still this government will not release the many life-saving drugs available in other countries, or educate the public so that a poor Florida family is not burned out of everything they have in this world.

I am going to tell you something you've never heard before. I am going to tell you the AIDS pandemic is the fault of the white, middle-class, male majority. AIDS is here because the straight world would not grant equal rights to gay people. If we had been allowed to get married, to have legal rights, there would be no AIDS cannonballing through America.

The concept of making a virtue out of sexual freedom, i.e., promiscuity, to use that loaded word, came about because gay men had nothing to call their own *but* their sexuality. The heterosexual majority has for centuries denied us every possible right of human dignity that the Constitution was framed to provide to all. The right to marry. The right to own property jointly without fear that the law will disinherit the surviving partner. The right to hold a job as an openly gay person. The right to have children. The right not to be discriminated against in just about every area and avenue and byway and nook and cranny that can be found in which hatred is stored. Indeed — the right to walk down the street holding hands, as you do when you are freely in love. Yes, the right to love. We are denied the right to love. Can you imagine being denied the right to love?

So, rightly or wrongly — wrongly as it turned out — we decided we would make a virtue of the only thing you didn't have control over: our sexuality. Had we possessed these rights you denied us, had we

been allowed to live respectably in a community as equals, there would never have been an AIDS. Had we been allowed to marry, we would not have felt the obligation to be promiscuous.

The poor, black, and Hispanic have also been forced into AIDS by your oppression. The awfulness of their destitution and deprivation, the absolutely zero chance they face to better their status in the world, forces them to seek peaceful respite and brief relief in the only oblivion available to them — the never-never land of drugs — which drugs, I might add, this country, for all the "Just Say No" mentality of an imbecilic First Lady, makes remarkably available through inept law enforcement and just plain looking the other way.

AIDS, having thus been caused to seed and sprout, is allowed to grow and fester and increase a millionfold. Yes, indeed, the white man made AIDS — the heterosexual white man. The heterosexual white man with money. The greedy heterosexual white man with money, who, two thousand years into the so-called Christian era, is still boss and master.

I am not going to speak in legalese, or cite the wretched decisions of the Supreme Court against us, or quote you lines from the Constitution or its Fourteenth Amendment or from the Bill of Rights. I am only going to say that some 25 million people constitute a sizable minority who are entitled to the same rights as everyone else. We do not practice behavior that can be changed, despite what that horrible monster, Robert Bork, or that equally horrible monster, the dogma of the Catholic Church, maintains as one reason for denying us these rights — that homosexuality can be changed. For decades, the psychiatric couches of the world sagged under the weight of gay people trying to change. At last, enlightened knowledge is finally beginning to concede the battle. We are born just as heterosexuals are born, just as people with blue eyes or people who are left-handed are born. Twenty-five million people cannot all be the result of any neurotic maladjustment or anything mothers or fathers do or don't do. Twenty-five million people are too many, too high a figure, to be anything but born, just as everyone else is born.

For our institutions — the Church, the Pope, the State, the Supreme Court — to pretend otherwise is, quite simply, immoral. How dare they presume to speak for God and for Everyman? Because of these immoral institutions and their immoral pronouncements, we have been estranged from our families, and we have been forced to create a ghetto. We have been forced to suffer. We were forced into AIDS.

Would that 25 million people were not so frightened and not so invisible and had more courage to say out loud, all and at once: We are equal, whether you like it or not.

But we are frightened of you, with good reason, because of what you have done to us and continue to do to us, which is yet another tragedy, this fear of ours. I do not think the Constitution had fear, as well as enforced suffering, in mind as a prerequisite for minorities living under it. But so it has turned out.

I have learned, during these past seven years, to hate. I hate everyone who is higher in the pecking order and in being so placed, like some incontinent pigeon, shits all over all of those below. And, sadly, tragically, as more and more of my friends die — the number is way over two hundred by now — I hate this country I once loved so much. And as each day Ronald Reagan and the Catholic Church and various self-styled spokespeople for God — the Right Wing, the Moral Ma-

jority, fundamentalists, Mormons, Southern Baptists, born-agains, Orthodox Jews, Hasidic Jews, La Rouchies, Jesse Helms, Representative Dannemeyer, Governor Duekmejian, Phyllis Schlafly, Jerry Falwell, enemies all — take the law into their own hands, a law that neither the framers of the Constitution nor Christ himself, if indeed there ever was a Christ, ever envisioned would be so used to cause the deaths of fellow men, I not only hate, but I know there will never be freedom, or peace on earth, or America the Beautiful, or Oh, Beautiful for Spacious Skies.

Oh, say can you see? our national anthem asks. Yes, I can see. I see a country more and more divided by hate. I see a country where the rich ignore the poor. I see a country where selfishness exceeds all other character traits. I see a country where education is no longer valued as the necessary force to give us strength and knowledge and compassion. I see a country where the media is controlled by and prepared for the privileged. I see a country where those less privileged have a voice that diminishes day by day until our cries are only heard as whispers. I see a country — and, I might add, a city — where crime and corruption and political chicanery and thefts of every conceivable sort are such a daily occurrence that we no longer protest and can no longer imagine a world otherwise. I see a country that the framers of the Constitution would be ashamed of. I know I am.

My country 'tis of thee? Oh, beautiful for spacious skies? God bless America? Oh, say, can you see by the dawn's early light? Our hymns have all turned into horseshit.

So go ahead and celebrate the anniversary of this once-precious document. I cannot do so.

◆

LET'S PUT OUR OWN HOUSE IN ORDER
Urvashi Vaid

We are here at the National Lesbian Conference because of the passion, love, excitement, and desire we feel for women. We are here because spectacular forces of evil prejudice threaten our very existence as lesbians.

It is this evil present in Judge Campbell's decision denying Karen Thompson guardianship of Sharon Kowalski. It is this evil that murdered Rebecca Wight, and wounded her lover, Claudia Brenner, as they were camping in the mountains of Pennsylvania. It is this evil found in the cowardly silence of all politicians who will not stand up to defend lesbians, will not pass laws to end the daily, massive, relentless mountain of prejudice we face.

Society identifies and defines us only through our relation (or lack thereof) to men — lesbians are masculine, man-haters, the sexual fantasies of straight men. Even social change movements, gay and lesbian organizations, civil rights and feminist organizations ghettoize the multiple issues of discrimination that we face. They still tokenize us or put our concerns and voices on the back burner. Until very recently we have had absolutely no images in mainstream culture of out, proud, powerful, strong, independent women.

We gather here at this conference in Atlanta in 1991: not 1981, not 1971, not 1961, but today. And the context of this time is ominous. The world in which we strive to live as openly lesbian has taken off its ugly white hood to show its sexist, anti-gay, racist, and capitalist face as never before.

When a Ku Klux Klansman can run for the U.S. Senate and get 44 percent of the vote — the hood is off. When the President of the United States is elected on the heels of an orchestrated racist campaign — the hood is off. Bush campaigned for Helms in North Carolina, vetoed the Civil Rights Act of 1990, introduced a Crime Bill that will strip our civil liberties. He speaks in strong support of the anti-choice, anti-woman, anti-abortion movement, and opposes equal rights for women. He has let our brothers and sisters with HIV and AIDS die from negligence, and he engineered a war to win re-election. The hood of evil is off.

A second piece of the context in which we gather is more hopeful. We meet at this lesbian conference at an historic moment in the lesbian and gay movement's history. At the workshops and caucuses I have attended it is clear that the 2,000 of us at this conference are deeply and intimately involved in our movement for freedom. Through our involvement, we are also changing the facts, the politics, and the content of our gay and lesbian organizations.

There is a revolution underway in the lesbian and gay liberation movement. The fact that organizations are developing multicultural plans and dealing with racism on their staffs and boards, and in their programs is a direct result of lesbian feminist organizing and politics. The fact that the gay and lesbian movement has begun to be multi-issue, that it is pro-choice, that it dares to speak out on the broad social issues of the day (like the war) — is a direct result of lesbian leadership. The fact that the feminist health agenda of the 1970s — disability rights, insurance reform, access to health care, welfare reform — is now on the central burner of the gay and lesbian movement

Urvashi Vaid, *Let's Put Our Own House In Order*, OUT/LOOK, Fall 1991 is in part a function of the painful experience of the AIDS crisis, and in part a result of lesbian-feminist analysis and organizing.

These parallel contexts of great danger and great change frame our meeting. As we have seen in this week together, the work we must do — our agenda for action — is large and quite specific! There are two big pieces to our national lesbian agenda: one is movement building, and another is public policy. Put another way, I believe that our lesbian agenda for the 1990s is about organizing and power; it is about taking and making, as Audre Lorde said, "Power out of hatred and destruction."

These are not easy agenda items to move.

MOVEMENT BUILDING

The experience of this conference suggests to me that we do not in fact have a national lesbian movement. We have a vital cultural movement, we have a huge amount of talent, we have a lot of grassroots leadership, we have lesbians active in a million projects. But the locus of lesbian community in our cities and towns today remains the same as it was in the 1950s. It remains The Bar, augmented by women's cultural events, the festival network, and local feminist and lesbian bookstores.

We have no national movement, no national newspaper, no national annual gathering place for lesbian activists to meet and talk politics, we have one annual state conference I am aware of — in Texas — and for all the talk of a national lesbian organization let me remind everyone that we have a national lesbian organization that struggles for its daily existence — the National Center for Lesbian Rights. How many of us support this ten-year-old pillar of lesbian advocacy?

The challenges to the re-creation of a lively, open, organized, and unafraid lesbian movement are manifest throughout this National Lesbian Conference. The NLC is a mirror of the current state of the movement. And the mirror shows us several harsh truth.

First truth: We are not one lesbian community, but a series of very splintered communities who have not, in fact, been working with each other at home or at this conference.

Second truth: At this conference, we have demonstrated that we do not trust each other at all; that we refuse to claim the cloak of leadership even when we have it — perhaps because we rightly fear the backlash or ostracism all lesbians who dare say the word leadership fear; that we do not understand that diversity politics is not about knee-jerk reactions or paying lip service but about action and internalizing the message, not about making sure that we have one of each — but learning and accepting that we have each in one.

Third truth: We will never feel entirely included — at this conference or anywhere — because the big social context excludes us completely. At this conference, I have met so many fierce powerful, seasoned, interesting lesbians, and it pains me that any of us might leave this place feeling dejected and hurt, angry and excluded. Let us not do that.

Fourth truth: Developing alternative decision-making processes is wonderful and radical, but all processes must be accountable and take responsibility for their actions.

Fifth truth: We can get so intense and focused on criticizing each other that we forget that we are in this together to change the fucked-up world outside.

We must begin in our own house to put it in order. We must begin by taking a deep collective breath and looking around at the fierce, powerful women that we are. Look at the skills we bring, and let go of perfectionism and purity politics based in fear. Instead enact a courageous and honest politics based in lesbian pride.

It is time for lesbians like me and you to bring our energies back home into our own movement and our own communities. It is time for us to mobilize on the grassroots level FIRST. Every state must have a lesbian conference to encourage involvement by lesbians. Every city and town should have lesbian activist networking breakfasts or potlucks to reconnect us to each other.

PUBLIC POLICY/POLITICS

On a political level, in the two years of planning for this conference, I sat through many discussions of the "lesbian political agenda." Lesbians have tried to define lesbian-specific issues. That is not my vision of my lesbian movement's political agenda.

My vision is to claim quite simply the fact that the lesbian agenda is (as it has always been) radical social change. It is the reconstruction of family; it is the reimagining and claiming of power; it is the reorganization of the economic system; it is the reinforcement of civil rights for all peoples; it is the enactment of laws and the creation of a society that affirms choice; it is the end to the oppression of women; the end to racism; the end to sexism, ableism, homophobia; the protection of our environment.

I have no problem claiming all these issues as the lesbian agenda for social change — because that is the truth. Lesbians have a radical social vision — we are the bearers of a truly new world order, not the stench of the same old world odor.

I am not suggesting that all of us drop the work we are doing to focus on this new exclusively lesbian thing called the lesbian agenda. I am suggesting that we continue to do what we are doing, but that we do it as OUT lesbians. That we claim our work as lesbian work, that we be out about who we are wherever we are.

I proudly claim our unique multi-issue perspective. I am proud of my lesbian community's politics of inclusion. I am engaged in my people's liberation. Let us just do it.

ACKNOWLEDGMENTS

Continued from page iv.

Crimes of Lesbian Sex, from LESBIAN (OUT)LAW, by Ruthann Robson. Copyright © 1992 by Ruthann Robson. Reprinted by permission of Firebrand Books, Ithaca, New York.

What Are You Doing In My Bedroom?, from THE COURAGE OF THEIR CONVICTIONS, by Peter Irons. Copyright © 1988 by Peter Irons. Reprinted with the permission of The Free Press, a Division of Macmillan, Inc.

Powell Changed Vote in Sodomy Case, by Al Kamen. Copyright © 1986 by THE WASHINGTON POST. Reprinted with permission.

Powell Regrets Backing Sodomy Law, by Ruth Marcus. Copyright © 1990 by The Washington Post. Reprinted with permission.

Moral Argument and Liberal Toleration: Abortion and Homosexuality, by Michael Sandel. Reprinted from 77 CALIFORNIA LAW REVIEW 521 (1989), copyright © 1989 by California Law Review, Inc., by permission of University of California Press and Michael Sandel.

CLOSE TO THE KNIVES: A MEMOIR OF DISINTEGRATION, by David Wojnarowicz. Copyright © 1991 by David Wojnarowicz. Published in the United States by Vintage Books, a division of Random House. Reprinted by permission of the Estate of David Wojnarowicz.

Gay Youth and the Right to Education, by Ruth Harlow and Donna Dennis. Reprinted from 4 YALE LAW AND POLICY REVIEW 446 (1986), copyright © 1991 by Yale Law and Policy Review, by permission of the Yale Law and Policy Review.

Cat, by Julie Carter. Copyright © 1983 by Julie Carter. Reprinted from HOME GIRLS: A BLACK FEMINIST ANTHOLOGY (Smith, ed.)., by permission of Kitchen Table: Women of Color Press, P.O. Box 908, Latham, NY 12110, and Julie Carter.

Sullivan Cold-Shoulders Suicide Report, by Susan Okie. Copyright © 1990 by THE WASHINGTON POST. Reprinted with permission.

One Life, One Prom, by Aaron Fricke. Reprinted from THE CHRISTOPHER STREET READER (Dennehy et al., eds.), copyright © 1983 by That New Magazine, Inc., by permission of Putnam Publishing Group.

The Campus Environment for Gay and Lesbian Life, by John D'Emilio. Reprinted from ACADEME MAGAZINE by permission of ACADEME and John D'Emilio.

ANOTHER MOTHER TONGUE, by Judith Grahn. Copyright © 1984 by Judith Grahn. Reprinted by permission of Beacon Press.

Selections from IN SEARCH OF GAY AMERICA: WOMEN AND MEN IN A TIME OF CHANGE, by Neil Miller, copyright © 1989 by Neil Miller. Used by permission of the Atlantic Monthly Press.

Undocumented Aliens in the Queer Nation, by Charles Fernandez, from OUT/LOOK: NATIONAL LESBIAN AND GAY QUARTERLY (Spring 1991). Copyright © 1991 by the OUT/LOOK Foundation. Reprinted by permission of OUT/LOOK.

AIDS Stories, by John Weir. Copyright © 1987 by HARPER'S MAGAZINE. All rights reserved. Reprinted from the September issue by special permission.

EMPLOYMENT DISCRIMINATION IN NEW YORK CITY: A SURVEY OF GAY MEN AND WOMEN, by the National Gay and Lesbian Task Force. Reprinted by permission of National Gay and Lesbian Task Force.

DANCER FROM THE DANCE, by Andrew Holleran. Copyright © 1978 by Andrew Holleran. Reprinted by permission of William Morrow and Company, Inc.

Work & Career: The Results (Survey), from OUT/LOOK: NATIONAL LESBIAN AND GAY QUARTERLY (Fall 1988). Copyright © 1988 by the OUT/LOOK Foundation. Reprinted by permission of OUT/LOOK.

Hands, from WINESBURG, OHIO, by Sherwood Anderson. Copyright © 1919 by B. W. Huebsch. Copyright © 1947 by Eleanor Copenhaver Anderson. Used by permission of Viking Penguin, a division of Penguin Books USA, Inc.

Statement of Perry Watkins, from MY COUNTY, MY RIGHT TO SERVE, by Mary Ann Humphrey. Copyright © 1990 by Mary Ann Humphrey. Reprinted by permission of HarperCollins Publishers.

Tar Beach, by Audre Lorde. Copyright © 1983 by Audre Lorde. Reprinted from HOME GIRLS: A BLACK FEMINIST ANTHOLOGY (Smith, ed.). by permission of Kitchen Table: Women of Color Press, P.O. Box 908, Latham, NY 12110, and the Estate of Audre Lorde.

At Least Me and Rafael Tried, by Paul Butler, from AURORA: A FEMINIST MAGAZINE (Winter 1982). Copyright © 1982 by Paul Butler. Reprinted by permission of Paul Butler.

Why Gay People Should Seek the Right to Marry, by Thomas Stoddard, from OUT/LOOK: NATIONAL LESBIAN AND GAY QUARTERLY (Fall 1989). Copyright © 1989 by the OUT/LOOK Foundation. Reprinted by permission of OUT/LOOK.

Since When Is Marriage a Path to Liberation?, by Paula Ettelbrick, from OUT/LOOK: NATIONAL LESBIAN AND GAY QUARTERLY (Fall 1989). Copyright © 1989 by the OUT/LOOK Foundation. Reprinted by permission of OUT/LOOK.

My Marriage to Vengeance, from A PLACE I'VE NEVER BEEN, by David Leavitt. Copyright © 1990 by David Leavitt. Used by permission of Viking Penguin, a division of Penguin Books USA, Inc.

Man Child: A Black Lesbian Feminist's Response, by Audre Lorde. Reprinted from SISTER OUTSIDER: ESSAY AND SPEECHES BY AUDRE LORDE, copyright © 1984 by Audre Lorde, by permission of Crossing Press.

Leroy's Birthday, by Raymina Mays. Copyright © 1983 by Raymina Mays. Reprinted from HOME GIRLS: A BLACK FEMINIST ANTHOLOGY (Smith, ed.), by permission of Kitchen Table: Women of Color Press, Inc., and Raymina Mays.

My Life You Are Talking About, from CRIME AGAINST NATURE, by Minnie Bruce Pratt. Copyright © 1990 by Minnie Bruce Pratt. Reprinted by permission of Firebrand Books, Ithaca, New York.

LESBIANS CHOOSING MOTHERHOOD: LEGAL IMPLICATIONS OF DONOR INSEMINATION AND CO-PARENTING, by the National Center for Lesbian Rights (1991). Reprinted by permission of the National Center for Lesbian Rights.

Our Day In Court — Against Each Other: Intra-Community Disputes Threaten All of Our Rights, by the National Center for Lesbian Rights, from NCLR NEWSLETTER (Winter 1991-1992). Reprinted by permission of the National Center for Lesbian Rights.

Whose Constitution Is It, Anyway?, from REPORTS FROM THE HOLOCAUST: THE MAKING OF AN AIDS ACTIVIST, by Larry Kramer. Copyright © 1989 by Larry Kramer. Reprinted by permission of St. Martin's Press, Inc., New York, NY.

Let's Put Our Own House in Order, by Urvashi Vaid, from OUT/LOOK: NATIONAL LESBIAN AND GAY QUARTERLY (Fall 1991). Copyright © 1991 by the OUT/LOOK Foundation. Reprinted by permission of OUT/LOOK.